Econometric Foundations

The text and accompanying CD ROM develop step by step a modern approach to econometric problems. They are aimed at talented upper-level undergraduates, graduate students, and professionals wishing to acquaint themselves with the principles and procedures for information processing and recovery from samples of economic data. In the real world such data are usually limited or incomplete, and the parameters sought are unobserved and not subject to direct observation or measurement. The text fully provides an operational understanding of a rich set of estimation and inference tools to master such data, including traditional likelihood based and non-traditional non-likelihood based procedures, that can be used in conjunction with the computer to address economic problems. The CD ROM contains reviews of probability theory and principles of classical estimation and inference in text-searchable electronic documents, an interactive Matrix Review Manual with GAUSS Light software, and an electronic Examples Manual. An instructor's guide with solution outlines for the questions and problems in each chapter, among other elements, can be downloaded by instructors from the internet at the online website www.econometricfoundations.com.

Ron C. Mittelhammer is a Professor at Washington State University. He is the author of *Mathematical Statistics for Economics and Business* (Springer-Verlag, 1996) as well as book chapters and numerous articles in refereed economics, statistics, and econometrics journals. Professor Mittelhammer's current research focus is on econometric theory for applications to a range of fields in economics. His skill as a teacher of statistics and econometrics has evolved over more than two decades of graduate-level teaching and is documented by teaching evaluations and awards.

George G. Judge is a Professor at the University of California, Berkeley. Professor Judge has also served on the faculty of the University of Illinois, University of Connecticut, and Oklahoma State University, and has been a visiting professor at several U.S. and European universities. He is the coauthor or editor of fourteen other books in econometrics and related fields, and author or coauthor of over 150 articles in referred journals. His research explores specification and evaluation of statistical decision rules, improved inference methods, parametric and semiparametric estimation and information recovery in the case of ill-posed inverse problems with noise. He is a Fellow of the Econometric Society, the *Journal of Econometrics*, and the American Agricultural Economics Association.

Douglas J. Miller is an Assistant Professor at Purdue University. Over the past five years, his primary teaching assignment has been graduate-level econometrics. He has delivered lectures on a range of econometric topics at several universities. He is coauthor of *Maximum Entropy Econometrics: Robust Estimation with Limited Data* (Wiley, 1996), and his research in theoretical and applied econometrics has been published in several book chapters and refereed journal articles.

Econometric Foundations

Ron C. Mittelhammer
Washington State University

George G. Judge
University of California, Berkeley

Douglas J. Miller
Purdue University

CAMBRIDGE
UNIVERSITY PRESS

PUBLISHED BY THE PRESS SYNDICATE OF THE UNIVERSITY OF CAMBRIDGE
The Pitt Building, Trumpington Street, Cambridge, United Kingdom

CAMBRIDGE UNIVERSITY PRESS
The Edinburgh Building, Cambridge CB2 2RU, UK http://www.cup.cam.ac.uk
40 West 20th Street, New York, NY 10011-4211, USA http://www.cup.org
10 Stamford Road, Oakleigh, Melbourne 3166, Australia
Ruiz de Alarcón 13, 28014 Madrid, Spain

First published 2000

Printed in the United States of America

Typeface Times Roman 10.5/13 pt. *System* LaTeX 2_ε [TB]

A catalog record for this book is available from the British Library.

Library of Congress Cataloging in Publication Data

Mittelhammer, Ron.

Econometric foundations / Ron C. Mittelhammer, George G. Judge, Douglas J. Miller.

p. cm.

ISBN 0-521-62394-4 hb

1. Econometrics. I. Judge, George G. II. Miller, Douglas. III. Title.
HB139.M575 2000
330′.01′5195 – dc21 99-40040
CIP

ISBN 0 521 62394 4 hardback

To

Linda and all of my students, past and future

Colleagues and students with whom I have shared a five-decade adventure

Katharine and Eric

Contents

CD-ROM

Preface

The focus of this book is on (1) developing a plausible basis for reasoning in situations involving incomplete–partial information and (2) developing principles and procedures for learning or recovering information from a sample of economic data. What makes this information recovery process interesting is that

- usually the conceptual model is incomplete or incorrectly specified;
- the data underlying an econometric analysis are limited, partial, or incomplete;
- the conceptual model contains parameters or components that are unknown and unobserved and, indeed, not subject to direct observation or measurement;
- the recovery of information on the unknown parameters or components requires the analyst to use indirect measurements based on observable data and then to solve the resulting inverse problem by mapping the indirect observations into information on the unknowns;
- the models may be ill-posed or, in the context of traditional procedures, may be underdetermined and the solution not amenable to being written in closed form;
- the procedures used for estimation may not be optimal, and their properties may not even be precisely discernible; and
- the inferences are subject to errors and distortions.

These problems, taken either individually or in some combination, represent the intellectual challenge of modern econometric analysis and research. Building on the productive efforts of our precursors in the areas of theoretical economics, inferential statistics, and econometrics, our objective in this book is to provide an operational understanding of a rich set of estimation and inference tools that may be used in theoretical and applied econometrics. In search of this goal, we present and interrelate an array of modern estimation and inference solutions for basic econometric models and data-sampling processes (DSPs). Expanding on this base, the reader should then be able to use this basic foundation to sort out the statistical implications of alternative estimation and inference procedures as they apply to a range of econometric inverse problems normally found in practice.

This book contains material appropriate for a sequence of courses in graduate econometrics. We recognize the importance of a good statistical foundation when studying econometrics. Because a semester that covers the statistical foundations of probability theory and the principles of estimation and inference is not always possible, we have provided two chapters on the accompanying CD that identify and interpret benchmark theorems and summarize the principal ideas involving the logic of probability and the principles of inference. The reader who does not understand all of the prerequisites should not be discouraged. Most of the book can be followed with a very basic knowledge of these areas. Moreover, we have tried to maintain a very deliberate pace in developing the proofs given throughout the book. In carrying through a range of fundamental economic DSPs, we first present details of the probability econometric model and then proceed to discuss estimation procedures, sampling properties, and a basis for inference.

The book is designed so the computer is a companion in each step of the teaching and learning process. By emphasizing the principles of estimation and inference for basic econometric models and then empirically demonstrating them on the computer, we hope to provide the reader with a deep understanding of the fundamental conceptual and empirical steps involved in econometric analyses. The hope is that students working their way through this book will acquire an operational understanding of a rich set of basic estimation and inference tools for use in applied econometric research. They should also develop a general framework for how information is integrated into a systematic approach for defining, structuring, estimating, and interpreting problems of estimation and inference.

Econometrics is a work in progress. Anyone who doubts this should review a sampling of econometric books starting in the mid-1930s and map the development of econometrics over time. Advances in econometric methodology have been substantial in both content and number, and they continue at a geometric rate. We have now reached a point in the development of econometrics at which no one book can possibly encompass even the majority of known procedures and results in the field. For example, we have not included a times series component. This was not an oversight but rather a realization that this area is a subject area all its own and that many fine books provide a foundation for this important area of econometrics.

Our strategy in this book is to provide the reader with a firm conceptual and empirical understanding of those basic econometric models and procedures that provide the roots or foundations for the large majority of variations found in specialized books and journal articles. We hope to equip the reader with the ability to read and better comprehend alternative and more advanced econometric methodologies in the literature as well as to understand new developments in the field. Using modern techniques to address some basic problem areas in econometrics, we have tried to remove some of the confusion, tune out the noise, and set the mind in order for a time.

Organization of the Book

General

By design the book starts with the specification and analysis of the simplest parametric and semiparametric probability models. Then, chapter by chapter, the specification and reasoning process is generalized. Our objective is to cover a sufficient scope of concepts and procedures to give the analyst an adequate conceptual foundation from which to choose, learn about, and implement methods of analysis that avoid assumptions he or she does not wish to make in the formulation, estimation, and inference of probability models consistent with economic sampling processes.

Learning goals include a rigorous basic understanding of

- the rationale used to specify an econometric model consistent with the underlying data-sampling process and available prior information;
- the corresponding rationale used to choose, design, and evaluate an appropriate estimation and inference procedure for a given information set;
- the programming of estimation and inference procedures on the computer based on commercial or custom-written (by the reader) software; and
- the interpretation of numerical results generated from each econometric procedure applied to a given information set and the types of legitimate inference statements one can and cannot make.

Specific

The book is organized into ten parts. In Part I, we discuss a general approach to searching for econometric knowledge and introduce an array of fundamental probability–econometric models that are used in practice to characterize economic data sampling processes (DSP). Part II is concerned with estimation and inference procedures for parametric and semiparametric variants of the linear regression models. Here we consider estimation and inference in the case of both parametric and semiparametric models. Part III introduces the concept of extremum estimators and examines nonlinear-in-the-parameters regression models and nonnormal formulations.

Part IV is concerned with stochastic right-hand-side variables, moment-based specifications of DSPs, empirical likelihood, and information theoretic procedures whose solutions cannot be written in closed form. In Part V the possibly restrictive independent and identically distributed noise component structure of the probability model is relaxed, and estimation and inference procedures for handling this more general error covariance model are developed.

Part VI examines instrumental variables, the general method of moments for overdetermined problems, and the simultaneous equations probability model. Part VII takes up the important problem of discovering or choosing the underlying probability model. Information recovery in discrete choice, and nonparametric models is discussed in Part VIII. Part IX deals with basic concepts of Bayesian inference and their application to the regression model in the face of friendly and unfriendly posterior distributions.

Part X ends the book with an assessment of the econometric road that has been traveled and the econometric challenges ahead. A discussion of Monte Carlo methods for simulation and moment approximation purposes is presented in an appendix to the book.

Foundation chapters dealing with probability theory and principles of estimation and inference along with a chapter on information recovery in ill-posed inverse problems, appear as fully text-searchable electronic documents on the CD at the back of the book. Also included on the CD is a computer interactive (ToolBook) Matrix Review manual, a GAUSS light software package and an electronic GAUSS tutorial manual. These will help you compute outcomes and simulate the behavior of the econometric estimation and inference procedures, and the manual also includes tips on how to run and program with the GAUSS programming language. Finally, an electronic interactive (Toolbook) Examples manual is included on the CD. It provides computer illustrations, written in the GAUSS language, of all of the principal econometric procedures developed in the text. An instructor's guide with solution outlines for the questions and problems in each chapter, among other elements, can be downloaded by instructors from the internet at the online website www.econometricfoundations.com.

We have made a valiant effort to get the chapter sequence right. In fact, we tinkered with it right up until publication. Although each student and instructor will follow the chapter sequence that best serves his or her teaching and learning goals, we ordered the chapters to ensure that the reader could enter each chapter with the tools necessary to understand it.

A Comment

Many view econometrics as a potpourri or bag of tricks, and the cookbook metaphor for econometrics textbooks has become commonplace. Unfortunately, this philosophy can produce analysts who know a list of econometric recipes but who have an insufficient understanding of which techniques to apply in a given situation or how to interpret the results of an application properly. As the inventory of econometric procedures has grown, the importance of understanding when it is appropriate to apply each econometric procedure, as well as knowing the appropriate interpretation of the results, has grown more than proportionately. The number of reference works that describe the growing inventory has expanded pari passu. These reference works will be accessible to the well-trained analyst who has mastered the basic philosophy and principles on which econometrics is founded. However, analysts who have done little more than memorize the recipes in a conceptual econometric cookbook will find the growing literature on new econometric methods impenetrable. Our goal is for you to be able to determine or create the econometric procedures that are applicable to your problem and then be able to apply them empirically and interpret the results appropriately. This is what this book is about, and this is what we think modern graduate econometrics instruction should be about.

Acknowledgments

This book represents the direct and indirect contributions of many individuals. A first step in the process involves finding an editor who understands the subject matter and shares your goals. In Scott Parris we found such a person, and he has been a full partner every step of the way, from getting informed reviews of our prospectus through the book production phase. To write this book we have had to stand on the shoulders of many of our predecessors in theoretical and applied statistics and econometrics. We hope we have acknowledged these persons appropriately in the many references throughout the book.

At a formative stage, the suggestions of William Barnett, Helmut Lütkepohl, and Scott Cardell were facilitative and enlightening regarding the scope of topics that should be covered, the depth of coverage, and the goals and overall focus of the book.

At a later stage, when the chapters were reaching a second rough form, Gene Savin, Tom Marsh, William Griffiths, Carter Hill, Arnold Zellner, Bruce McCullough, Tong Li, Rafic Fahs, Marco van Akkeren and Art Owen made major contributions in terms of scope and content. Marsh also contributed to the computer examples in Chapters 6 and 17. Special thanks to the "Econometric Applications" classes of 1997–1999 for enduring and providing real-time feedback relating to beta versions of the text and software as it was being developed.

We express our deep appreciation to the creators of GAUSS software – Aptech Systems. Inc., of Maple Valley, Washington, for granting us the right to use and distribute a version of their powerful programming package. In particular, expert consultations, support, and documentation with respect to software programming with GAUSS was generously provided by Ron Schoenberg, also of the University of Washington. Gordon Stone and Nathan Lohonen provided patient and knowledgeable technical assistance on implementing GAUSS and furnished helpful technical information at the computer-systems level. Gail Horecny and Dan Meine, our ever helpful liaisons to Aptech, paved the way for our intimate cooperation with Aptech-GAUSS and were always available to see to it that our questions would get answers. Special thanks also go to Ruud Koning for preparing the GAUSS tutorial manual and GAUSS technical archive file, and to T. C. Lee for checking the integrity of the CD Rom.

We are also deeply grateful to the Asymetrix Corporation of Bellevue, Washington, for generously allowing us to use their versatile and powerful multimedia authoring software package, ToolBook Instructor, to produce the electronic manuals that accompany the textbook. Special thanks to Scott Sherman for serving as liaison between Asymetrix and the authors, and to Jeff Rhodes and Chris Bell of Platte Canyon Multimedia Software Corporation for providing us with expert help on ToolBook software and GVI development.

Finally, we wish to acknowledge the support professionals that we worked with on an almost daily basis. Brenda Campbell was a word-processing and equation-rendering dynamo who also doubled as an expert multimedia consultant, layout advisor, and electronic document creator par excellence. Mary Graham, with intelligence and good humor, turned page after page of words and symbols written in red ink into beautiful copy. Working with Mary and Brenda, Dana Keil and Joel Adlen provided expert help in smoothing out computer-related word-processing problems, particularly the ticklish cross-platform challenges. It is hard to imagine that the project would have ever come to completion without the dedication and hard work of this fine team of professionals.

To these individuals, and all the others too numerous to mention, we wish to express our warm thanks and appreciation.

Ron Mittelhammer
George Judge
Douglas Miller

PART ONE

Information Processing and Recovery

The economic systems we invent lead to outcomes we label economic data. When viewing these outcomes as being interrelated by an underlying theory, we are naturally curious as to the existence, validity, and quantification of interrelationships between observable economic data outcomes. However, conceptual representations of these interrelationships can involve economic parameters that are unobservable. This then leads to the interesting question of how to go about using the indirect information on unobservables, represented by observable sample data, to recover information on the unobservables. Because the sample data information is usually partial and incomplete, we face the ultimate question, How do we go about learning from a sample of economic data or, on a more general level, how do we go about the search for quantitative economic knowledge? Chapters 1 and 2 frame a way to think about this inverse problem and begin the development of a plausible basis of reasoning in the face of partial–incomplete sample information. In particular, the knowledge search process suggested in Chapters 1 and 2 identifies the origin of the econometric model and the role it plays in information processing and recovery.

CHAPTER 1

The Process of Econometric Information Recovery

MOST econometric problems begin with several fundamental questions. One basic question is, How does one develop a plausible basis for reasoning in situations involving partial–incomplete information? Another basic question relates to how one goes about learning from a sample of data.

For the theoretical econometrician, questions tend to be of a nonempirical and hypothetical what-if type: What if a sample of data is described by a particular imagined sampling process? This leads to the question of how one characterizes the sampling process in terms of a probability model that properly identifies the stochastic characteristics of the sampling process as well as the data-restricting constraints, the knowns and unknowns of the problem, and the observable and unobservable components in the model. Given that the data-sampling process can be described by a probability model that expresses the state of knowledge about possible real-world outcomes, another question then arises relating to how one devises effective estimation and hypothesis-testing procedures that will allow the recovery of estimates of the unknowns and provide a basis for making inferences. The theoretical econometrician may, by a process of interpretation, ultimately associate the conceptualized sampling process with a set of *observable economic data*. At this point in the theoretical econometrician's investigation the probability model is interpretable as an econometric model having economic meaning with both real-world economic and statistical implications.

For the applied econometrician, the econometric problem begins with a real-world economic question, perhaps involving the implications of scarcity and choice or perhaps the allocative or distributive impacts, resulting from an action or decision. The next step involves restating the real-world question within a theoretical–conceptual economic model framework in which real-world components are identified to facilitate drawing logic-based conclusions about the question. This step exposes structure and defines the explicit economic model to be used in the empirical analysis of the economic question.

1.1. Introduction

Given a theoretical–conceptual economic playing field, a basis is needed for connecting the real-world data outcomes with their counterparts in the economic model. By visualizing some imagined sampling process by which the outcomes may have evolved and then characterizing this sampling process by a probability model, an econometric model is born. This model then acts as a vehicle for expressing knowledge about real-world outcomes and identifies knowns, unknowns, and observed and unobservable model components. If the applied econometrician is fortunate, the resulting econometric model may be consistent with a probability model that already exists in the literature and for which a well-defined basis for estimation and inference is already available. In this case the applied econometrician will use established statistical procedures to address research questions. On the other hand, the econometric model may not be consistent with a commonly specified and evaluated data-sampling process. Consequently, the applied econometrician must assume the role of the theoretical econometrician in first developing effective estimation and hypothesis-testing procedures and then carrying through the estimation and inference stages needed to answer research questions.

As one reads through this chapter and the chapters ahead, it will at times be necessary to assume the roles of both a theoretical and an applied econometrician to derive maximum benefit from the econometric venture. One goal of the exercises in each chapter is to lead and inspire the reader in this direction. Before going on to consider the question of how to specify a probability–econometric model to provide a basis for learning from a sample of observations, we focus some attention on the real-world component referred to as economic data.

1.2. The Nature of Economic Data

Why do we have books on econometrics? Why not just have books devoted to statistics for economists? What is it that makes economics unique relative to other fields of science?

One thing that tends to make economics and econometrics unique is the nature of economic data and the special characteristics of the sampling processes by which economic data are obtained. In providing an answer to the opening questions of this section, William Barnett, in private correspondence, points us to a classic article by Schumpter in *Econometrica*, Vol. 1, No. 1, 1933, "The Common Sense of Econometrics." In this article Schumpter wrote, "Econometrics is the most quantitative . . . of all sciences, physics not excluded. . . . Every economist is an econometrician whether he wants to be or not." His rationale is that the economy produces and inherently depends upon numbers. Indeed, the very act of transacting in markets depends explicitly upon the numerical values of such variables as quantities and prices. But in physics, for example, the physical world can and will operate without dependence upon numerical measurement of variables. Scientists have to construct devices to measure temperature, pressure, speed, weight, and the like because nature does not "quote" these numbers in

markets or even identify a need to know these numbers. So in this sense, as Schumpter observed, economics is inherently more quantitative than any other scientific field.

Economies and markets carry out experiments and produce numerical data through the very nature of their operation. However, they do so in a manner that is not usually in accordance with statistically designed experiments. Although physical scientists can be viewed, as they are in Schumpter's article, as being disadvantaged by the need to measure data, in comparison with economists, who need only record the numerical data that the economy produces, physical scientists have the advantage of being able to run controlled experiments and to generate their data in a manner consistent with established and understood experimental designs. Because the economy is not a statistically designed experiment, economists must in many cases utilize ill-conditioned data. This is a principal reason why econometrics requires special tools for probability model formulation, estimation, and inference and why econometrics is characterized as an experiment in nonexperimental model building. The uncertain nature of economic outcomes goes a long way to explaining why almost everyone, at one time or another, has felt comfortable assuming the role of an economist on certain issues (How often have you heard the phrase "I am not an economist, but... ?") and why all economists are in one way or another econometricians.

1.3. The Probability Approach to Economics

The probability theory that you encountered in your courses in theoretical statistics (and that is reviewed in an electronic document on the CD that accompanies this text) has important implications for how one should organize, incorporate, and utilize data and prior information in quantitative economic analyses. In economic problems characterized by incomplete knowledge and uncertainty, this theory, through a process of abstraction and interpretation by analysts, defines a reasoning process for expressing our knowledge about real-world outcomes, for recovering information from data, and for assessing its validity. The calculus of reasoning defined by probability theory facilitates learning and problem resolution and defines a logical basis for evaluating decisions and making choices.

Like Mozart's *Don Giovanni*, conceptual tools such as random variables and stochastic processes, as well as models of economic systems, have been invented or created by theoreticians and empirical analysts rather than discovered. The participants or players in a postulated economic system are presumed to define economic processes that result in measurable outcomes and, by a process of interpretation on the part of the econometrician, these outcomes are viewed in probabilistic form. In most econometric problems, at least a portion of the information available for analysis will be in the form of a sample of data that has been generated as an outcome of some real-world economic process. In addition, the analyst generally has some prior knowledge about the relevant economic processes and institutions that may have conditioned the sample outcomes. If one views the outcomes of the economic system as having come from an imagined sampling process, concepts such as random variables and probability distributions can be used as conceptual tools to characterize the full complement of existing knowledge about these economic observables. In particular, a probability model associated with the imagined sampling process can be defined that serves as a vehicle for describing our state of knowledge relating to how the observable economic data were obtained. Given this information repository, the fundamental econometric problem is concerned with transforming the conceptual probability model and the sample information associated with it into more specific knowledge about the unknown model components and parameters that represent characteristics of real-world economic processes.

1.4. The Process of Searching for Quantitative Economic Knowledge

In searching for quantitative economic knowledge contained in a sample of data, one must begin with some understanding of the economic process to which the data relate as well as some conception of the underlying sampling process by which the data were obtained. Otherwise, a sample of data is merely a collection of numbers with no contextual meaning or information value. Thus, to have a basis for interpreting the observed data, one needs a conceptual model of the process to which the data refer or some basis for specifying a *data-sampling process* (DSP) that links the sample of observations to our state of knowledge about how these observations were obtained.

The first step in this search for economic knowledge is for the analyst to identify an *economic process* that the analyst seeks to understand and about which there is incomplete knowledge and uncertainty (henceforth refer to Figure 1.1). By *process* we mean a particular method of doing something that generally involves several steps, operations, and interacting components and that leads to an observable outcome or result. For example, this might be the method by which, given prices and a budget constraint, consumers decide on market purchases (consumer decision process) or the method by which a commodity market leads to a product price (a market price equilibrium process).

The next step is a *process of abstraction* whereby *predata* theories, facts, assumptions, and an imagined sampling process whose outcomes are related to random variables are logically molded together into a *probability–econometric model* of the economic process. In a formal and often idealized way, the econometric model summarizes the analyst's state of knowledge about the mechanisms that are thought to underlie the workings of the economic process under study and the sampling process by which observed data are obtained. The model, which is an abstraction, may be expressed in a variety of ways such as mathematical equations, algorithms, behavioral rules, diagrams, or all of these.

1.4.1. Econometric Model Components

It may be useful to think of an econometric model as being composed of components that include an economic model, a sampling model, and a probability model (Figure 1.1). The *economic model* component distinguishes an *econometric* model from a biological, physical, psychometric, or sociometric model. Models in other disciplines are defined

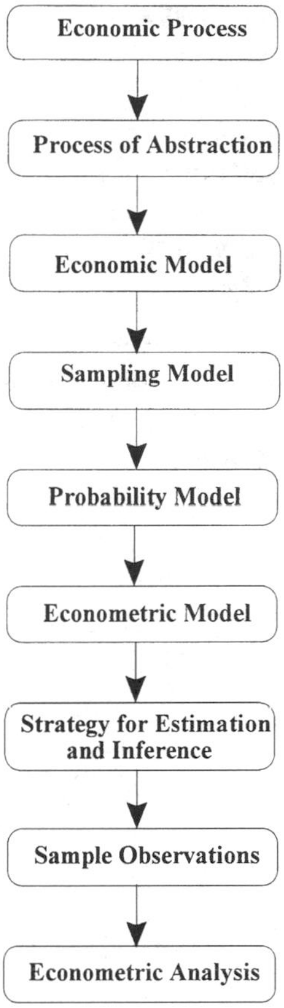

Figure 1.1: Process of Economic Information Recovery.

when appropriate discipline-specific theories, concepts, and knowledge are substituted in place of the economic model component. The economic model is based on a combination of the analyst's understanding of the institutions and mechanisms operating within the economic process being modeled and the economic theory thought to be relevant for explaining data outcomes produced by the economic process.

Once the economic model has been postulated, interpretations and questions relating to the workings of the economic process may be deduced from it. In this way the economic model provides a basis for defining relevant economic variables, forming tentative explanations, and suggesting hypotheses. However, this process of deduction tells us nothing per se about the actual truth or falsity of any explanations, hypotheses, or conclusions. It only ensures that conclusions *deductively* generated from the economic model are internally consistent with the definitions and postulates on which the model is based *provided that* the rules of logic have been applied correctly.

The *sampling model* characterizes a sampling process linkage between observable economic data and the postulated real-world components of the economic model. In particular, the sampling model identifies an imagined sampling process postulating that the observed data are the outcome of a collection of random variables

$\mathbf{Y} = \{Y_1, Y_2, \ldots, Y_n\}$. At this point, general assumptions regarding the sampling characteristics of the random variables enter the analysis. For example are the random variables independent and identically distributed (iid), independent or dependent.

Moving farther in the direction of a formal basis for stating specific stochastic characteristics of the random variables in the imagined sampling process, the *probability model* postulates that the economic data are the outcome of some random variable or vector $\mathbf{Y}$ having a joint probability distribution that belongs to some set of potential probability distributions, such as $\{F(\mathbf{y}; \boldsymbol{\theta}), \boldsymbol{\theta} \in \Omega\}$. If the elements in the set of probability distributions cannot be identified or indexed by a finite vector of parameter values $\boldsymbol{\theta}$, we may more generally denote the collection of probability distributions as $F(\mathbf{y}) \in \Psi$. By postulating such a probability model, the analyst effectively defines the range of possibilities for the joint probability distribution thought to characterize the behavior of potential sample outcomes. Unknown, uncontrolled, and unobservable components of the probability model are represented by parameters, random variables, or both. Together, the probability and sampling models identify both the candidates for the joint probability distribution of the observed data and the degree of interdependence, or lack thereof, among the individual data observations.

The combination of the probability, sampling, and economic models results in an *econometric model* that links a specified sampling process to the data. The adjective *econometric* arises from the realization, identification, and incorporation of an economic component into the formation and interpretation of the model. The econometric model represents our knowledge of the sampling of economic data in terms of a collection of random variables, $\mathbf{Y} = \{Y_1, Y_2, \ldots, Y_n\}$, that have a certain economic interpretation, a certain dependence structure, and a joint probability distribution that belongs to some set of probability distributions $\{F(\mathbf{y}; \boldsymbol{\theta}), \boldsymbol{\theta} \in \Omega\}$ or $F(\mathbf{y}) \in \Psi$. Having defined the econometric model, the analyst has effectively specified a complete model of the sampling of the economic data under investigation. This means that, if values for the unknown and unobservable components of the perceived econometric model were known or assumed, the analyst would expect, or hope, that data consistent with the economic process being analyzed could be simulated from the econometric model. To the extent that the econometric model represents an accurate depiction of the true data-sampling process, the simulated outcomes could be used to produce additional samples of economic data relating to the economic process under study.

1.4.2. Econometric Analysis

Given a fully specified econometric model, the analyst has created a complete probabilistic and economic description and interpretation of the imagined sampling process for the economic data being analyzed. The model thus provides a complete picture of the analyst's state of knowledge about a set of economic outcomes and identifies *what is assumed* and *what is left to be discovered in the research process.*

An analyst's econometric model of sample outcomes for the random variables $\mathbf{Y}$ is usually specified in terms of a *systematic* or *signal component* and an unobservable random *error*, *disturbance*, or *noise component* ε. The two components are assumed to combine in a way that determines the *exact* values of observed sample outcomes.

In particular, the extent to which the value of $\mathbf{Y}$ cannot be functionally represented in terms of the systematic component is accounted for by some function of ε, the content of which in some sense reflects the development of economics as a science. An example is the additive formulation $\mathbf{Y} = \mathbf{g}(\mathbf{X}, \boldsymbol{\theta}) + \varepsilon$ in which the sum of the systematic and noise components represents the sample outcome, where $\boldsymbol{\theta}$ is a vector of unknown and unobservable parameters and $\mathbf{X}$ is a set of conditioning variables. More specific examples of the characterization of $\mathbf{Y}$ in terms of systematic and noise components will be examined in Chapter 2.

Once the econometric model has been specified, the applied econometrician's objective is to proceed to the econometric analysis of the model. A necessary ingredient for such an analysis is the collection of *sample observations* of economic data relating to the economic process under study. The analyst must then also devise a *strategy for estimation and inference* in which appropriate statistical procedures for information discovery and recovery are identified within the context of the model being analyzed.

Given the sample observations and identified statistical procedures, the analyst then conducts an *econometric analysis* by applying the statistical procedures to the sample data and generating estimates and inferences. The analyst then provides a statistical and economic interpretation of the results obtained to complete the econometric analysis of the economic process.

1.5. The Inverse Problem

A challenge in econometric analyses is that unknown and uncontrolled components of the econometric model cannot generally be observed directly, and thus the analyst must use indirect observations based on observable data to recover information on these components. This challenge is associated with a concept in systems and information theory called the *inverse problem*, which is the problem of recovering information about unknown and uncontrolled components of a model from indirect observations on these components. The adjective *indirect* refers to the fact that, although the observed data are considered to be directly influenced by the values of model components, the observations are not themselves the direct values of these components but only indirectly reflect the influence of the components. Thus, the relationship characterizing the effect of unobservable components on the observed data must be somehow inverted to recover information about the unobservable model components from the data observations. Because econometric relations generally contain a systematic and a noise component, the problem of recovering information about unknowns and unobservables $(\boldsymbol{\theta}, \varepsilon)$ from sample observations $(\mathbf{y}, \mathbf{x})$ within the context of an econometric model $\mathbf{Y} = \eta(\mathbf{X}, \varepsilon, \boldsymbol{\theta})$ is referred to as an *inverse problem with noise*. A solution to this inverse problem is of the general form $(\mathbf{y}, \mathbf{x}) \Rightarrow (\boldsymbol{\theta}, \varepsilon)$.

Motivation for viewing a problem in econometric analysis as an inverse problem can be provided by a familiar illustration involving the theory of the firm. Firm managers need to make decisions concerning the profit-maximizing mix of inputs and levels of outputs under fixed prices. To make these optimizing decisions, information is needed on unknown components of the real-world production process such as the marginal products of inputs. The marginal products are not directly observable, but we can observe the levels of outputs that result when various levels of inputs are used. These observable outcomes of the production process are *indirect* observations on the marginal products that, although not equal to the values of the marginal products themselves, are influenced by their values. Thus, we are confronted with an inverse problem: How can we best use the observed levels of input and output to recover information about the unobservable marginal products? At this point, in the absence of effective methods of information recovery, it must be clear that few, if any, rational or informed bets could be devised relative to the values of unknown, unobserved, and unobservable components of our econometric models. The principal objective of this book is to provide a foundation for the development of effective information recovery methods for this and other inverse problems.

1.6. A Comment

We view an economic–probability–econometric model as a starting point that lets us state, for all to see, what we are maintaining, or willing to assume, is known and what we consider unknown and seek to discover relative to an economic process under investigation. One of our econometric friends once remarked that he would rather be asked by a curious 3-year-old where babies come from than to try to answer the question, Where do econometric models come from? Perhaps it is less important where they come from than what the models represent, which is a starting place – a postulational base that leads to questions, experimentation, data collection, estimation, and finally inference and conclusions. In other words, they are the basis for a research process in which the model, the data, and the method of information recovery are interdependent links in the knowledge search and recovery chain. In Chapter 2, we review some interesting econometric questions and begin to examine the process of progressing from an economic model to a probability–econometric model. Our intention is to start the reader thinking about the estimation and inference methods for solving inverse problems with noise.

1.7. Notation

Before moving to Chapter 2 to begin our conceptualization of some alternative econometric models, we review here some notational conventions that give meaning to Figure 1.1 and the formulations we use in this book. A scalar random variable is denoted by a capital letter such as X or Y. A multivariate random variable in the form of a vector or matrix is denoted by a bold capital letter such as **X** or **Y**. A subscripted index distinguishes between different random variables. For example, we will use Y_i to indicate one representative of a collection of random variables, $(\mathrm{Y}_1, \mathrm{Y}_2, \ldots, \mathrm{Y}_n)$. Random variables whose outcomes we seek to explain will be referred to as *dependent variables*. We will also be interested in *explanatory variables*, whose values are used to help explain the values of dependent variables.

It is most often the case that an econometric model will contain more than one explanatory variable. An index is then needed if we wish to distinguish the explanatory variables from one another for a given observation. Depending on the circumstances, explanatory variables may either be fixed or random. In either case we will use a double subscript, where the first subscripted index denotes the observation number and the second specifies the particular explanatory variable number. We normally use **X** or **x** for a matrix of random or fixed explanatory variables, respectively. We emphasize that in either the random or fixed case, boldface denotes a vector or a matrix, whereas a nonboldfaced symbol will denote a scalar. Thus, if the explanatory variables are random, then X_{ij} represents the ith potential observation on the jth random explanatory variable. If the explanatory variables are fixed, then x_{ij} is the ith value of the jth fixed explanatory variable. An alternative notation for indicating the (i, j)th element of the explanatory variable matrix will be the standard matrix element notation $X[i, j]$ or $x[i, j]$. We will also represent the ith row of the explanatory variable matrix by $\mathbf{X}_{i\cdot}$ or $\mathbf{x}_{i\cdot}$, or in standard matrix notation, by $\mathbf{X}[i, .]$ or $\mathbf{x}[i, .]$. The corresponding notation for designating the jth column of the explanatory variable matrix will be $\mathbf{X}_{\cdot j}$ or $\mathbf{x}_{\cdot j}$, and in standard matrix notation $\mathbf{X}[., j]$ or $\mathbf{x}[., j]$.

As an example of the preceding notation, we may develop a model of individual incomes Y_i using observations on explanatory variables representing scores on intelligence tests, years of schooling, highest degree obtained, grade point average (GPA), gender, race, and geographical region. In general functional notation we may then specify that $Y_i = g(\mathbf{X}_{i\cdot})$ or $Y_i = g(\mathbf{X}[i, .])$, for $i = 1, \ldots, n$.

In representing general functions of variables, we will on occasion need to distinguish between *scalar* and *vector* functions of variables. The general notation will be $g(\mathbf{x})$ and $\mathbf{g}(\mathbf{x})$, respectively, where again, boldface denotes a vector. Furthermore, it is often the case in representing the systematic part of econometric models that the same functional definition is applied to each data observation. In this case, we will use the notation $g(\mathbf{x}_{i\cdot})$ to denote the function applied to the observation $\mathbf{x}_{i\cdot}$ and then continue to use $\mathbf{g}(\mathbf{x})$ to denote the vector of all of the observations, that is, $\mathbf{g}(\mathbf{x}) = [g(\mathbf{x}_{1\cdot}), g(\mathbf{x}_{2\cdot}), \ldots, g(\mathbf{x}_{n\cdot})]'$.

In some circumstances, we will want to characterize the values of dependent variables over time. In cases where we want to emphasize the temporal nature of the observations we will use a t subscript to denote the time index. For example, one may be interested in the values of a dependent and associated explanatory variables at n distinct time periods. The dependent and explanatory variables at time t will be denoted by Y_t and $\mathbf{X}_{t\cdot}$ or $\mathbf{X}[t, .]$, respectively. A data set of n observations over time would then consist of y_t and $\mathbf{x}_{t\cdot}$ or $\mathbf{x}[t, .]$ for $t = 1, \ldots, n$, where y_t is the observed value of the random variable Y_t, and $\mathbf{x}_{t\cdot}$ or $\mathbf{x}[t, \cdot]$ is the observed value of $\mathbf{X}_{t\cdot}$ at time t.

Note that there will be a few exceptions to the conventions introduced above when precedent in the literature is so strong as to warrant an exception. An exception already encountered in the text is the use of ε to denote the *random* variable representing the noise component of an econometric model. Because we will later use **e** to denote an outcome of the noise component, as is very often done in the literature, we avoid confusion with the letter **E**, which is the conventional notation for mathematical expectation, and instead choose ε to be the random variable whose outcome is **e**. We will be careful to identify notational exceptions when they are first introduced in the text, and, regarding exceptions to the capital letter–random variable convention, we will endeavor to use Greek-letter alternatives.

Now that we have a context for discussing econometric models and the notation to represent them formally, in Chapter 2 we identify and classify a range of econometric models that will be of major interest as we work our way through the chapters to come.

1.8. Idea Checklist – Knowledge Guides

1. Assume you are a theoretical econometrician. Identify a general format that you might use in developing a research project or reporting a working paper or journal article.
2. Assume you are an applied econometrician. Identify a general format that you might use in developing a research project or reporting a working paper or journal article.
3. To use later as a basis of comparison for how much your understanding of econometric analysis has matured, write a short essay on the topic: Where do econometric models come from?
4. To use later as a basis of comparison for how much your understanding of econometric analysis has matured, write a short essay on the topic: Is econometrics necessary?
5. Test your ability to specify a simple linear statistical model that involves a set of data from which you want to recover information on a mean-location level and a variance-scale parameter.

CHAPTER 2

Probability–Econometric Models

IN this chapter, we examine the process by which one represents whatever knowledge is available or assumed about economic processes and systems in terms of a probability–econometric model. Our purpose is to identify a basis for recovering information about the system or process from a sample of data. Building on the information discovery process discussed in the Chapter 1, we examine, through the use of examples of data-sampling processes (DSPs), some of the basic issues involved in specifying probability models that, through a process of abstraction and interpretation, become the basis for econometric estimation and inference. The connection between a probability model and the economic data-sampling process (DSP) being analyzed is made via an analyst's interpretation of the probability model within the substantive context of economic theory and known institutional knowledge relating to the economic process under study. The end product of the analyst's interpretive efforts is an econometric model of the DSP that connects the theory to the data.

For each instance in which a probability model is defined, one must strive to be precise about the type of DSP assumed and the unknown and unobservable characteristics of the corresponding probability model. In pursuing estimation and inference goals, it is imperative that our state of knowledge about the known and unknown components of the probability model be clearly identified in both pre- and postdata senses. Conceptual tools such as probability distributions, random variables, stochastic noise, independence, and moment assumptions are used, within the logic provided by probability theory, to characterize the analyst's state of knowledge about the phenomenon the investigator hopes to understand or to make inferences about. The objectives of estimation and inference, as well as the procedures employed to accomplish these objectives, are determined by the known and unknown characteristics of the probability model used to characterize the DSP of an economic system or process. It follows that a poorly conceived probability model can lead to inappropriate choices of statistical procedures for obtaining information about unknown characteristics of the DSP and thus incorrect estimation and inference objectives and conclusions.

We now begin to consider some of the basic issues involved in defining probability models of data sampling processes.

2.1. Parametric, Semiparametric, and Nonparametric Models

There are many meaningful ways to categorize probability models and corresponding econometric models, and there is no way to examine all of the possibilities in this chapter or in this book. However, to foreshadow some of the possible data-sampling models discussed in the chapters ahead, we group models into those that have parametric, semiparametric, or nonparametric forms. In some sense this grouping reflects differences in the information the analyst has, or thinks he or she has, about the economic process that is being modeled.

2.1.1. Parametric Models

Historically the most common form of model used in econometrics, and one that receives considerable emphasis in this book, is the *parametric model.* The definition of this type of model involves a finite number of constants or *parameters* $\boldsymbol{\theta}$ whose values are an integral part of the specification of the model but whose values are unobserved and unspecified. The values of the unknown and unobserved parameters are designated to reside in a set of values called the *parameter space* Ω. Once all of the parameters of a parametric model are assigned specific numerical values, a unique DSP and probability model are identified based on a fully defined probability distribution. In effect, the potential data-sampling models, which form the basis for characterizing an econometric model, are fully indexed by the finite number of parameters whose values range over the values in the parameter space. In a problem of statistical inference based on a parametric model, the values of the parameters or functions of parameters represent the model characteristics of fundamental interest. Given the probability model and a corresponding set of sample observations, it is the values of the unknown parameters that we seek to recover.

To illustrate the idea of a parametric model, suppose the analyst visualizes a DSP that results in the outcome of a random vector **Y** together with observations on the values of various explanatory variables represented by the matrix **x**. A possible econometric model specification that characterizes the DSP underlying these data may be expressed as

Model 2.1.1

Y Characterization:	$Y_i = g(\mathbf{x}_{i\cdot}, \boldsymbol{\beta}) + \varepsilon_i,\ i = 1, \ldots, n$
Systematic component:	$g(\mathbf{x}_{i\cdot}, \boldsymbol{\beta}) = \mathbf{x}_{i\cdot}\boldsymbol{\beta},\ i = 1, \ldots, n$; $\mathbf{x}_{i\cdot}$'s are fixed and known
Noise component:	ε_i's $\sim$ iid $N(0, \sigma^2),\ i = 1, \ldots, n$
Parameters:	$\boldsymbol{\beta} \in R^k,\ \sigma^2 > 0$
Type:	Parametric

Given particular values for $\boldsymbol{\beta}$ and σ^2, a unique DSP for **Y** is identified. In this parametric model, $\boldsymbol{\beta}$ and σ^2 are, respectively, a vector and a scalar representing unknown and unobservable parameters, and the ε_i's are independent and identically distributed (iid) unknown and unobservable *normal* random variables representing the noise component of the model.

2.1.2. Nonparametric and Semiparametric Models

In contrast to parametric models, *nonparametric* and *semiparametric models* are sampling models that cannot be fully defined in terms of the values of a finite number of parameters. Note that *nonparametric* does not necessarily mean that the model is devoid of parameters, although such may be the case. The *non* in *nonparametric model* means that it is *not* a parametric model in the sense of defining probability models that are completely and uniquely identified once the values of a finite number of parameter values are known. A *semiparametric model* is a model whose DSP is defined in terms of two components; one is fully determined once the values of a finite number of parameters are known (this is the parametric component), whereas the other is not amenable to being fully defined by the values of any finite collection of parameters (the nonparametric component).

To illustrate the idea of nonparametric models, again suppose the analyst visualizes a DSP that results in the outcome of a random vector **Y** together with observations on the values of various explanatory variables represented by the matrix **x**. A possible nonparametric econometric model specification that characterizes the DSP underlying these data is given by

Model 2.1.2

Y Characterization:	$Y_i = g(\mathbf{x}_{i\cdot}) + \varepsilon_i,\ i = 1, \ldots, n$
Systematic component:	$g(\mathbf{x}_{i\cdot})$ left *unspecified*; $\mathbf{x}_{i\cdot}$'s are fixed and known
Noise component:	$E[\varepsilon_i] = 0$, and $\mathrm{var}(\varepsilon_i) = \sigma^2$ for $i = 1, \ldots, n$
Parameters:	$\sigma^2 > 0$
Type:	Nonparametric

We emphasize that $g(\mathbf{x}_{i\cdot})$ is used generically in the model to refer to some nondescript function that assigns a numerical value to $\mathbf{x}_{i\cdot}$ and does *not* refer to a specific algebraic function definition. In fact, in nonparametric regression, little else is usually assumed about the shape of the regression function beyond some degree of smoothness. Note that there is no finite number of parameters that can be used to index all of the possible probability distributions encompassed by the model. In particular, there is no probability distribution for **Y** that is fully or uniquely identified upon specification of a finite number of parameters. Note further that the model does contain a parameter σ^2 that represents the variance of both the ε_i's and the Y_i's.

One possible semiparametric econometric model for characterizing the DSP underlying a data sample is

Model 2.1.3

Y Characterization:	$Y_i = g(\mathbf{x}_{i\cdot}, \boldsymbol{\beta})\varepsilon_i,\ i = 1, \ldots, n$
Systematic component:	$g(\mathbf{x}_{i\cdot}, \boldsymbol{\beta}) = \prod_{j=1}^{k} x_{ij}^{\beta_j},\ i = 1, \ldots, n$; x_{ij}'s are fixed and known
Noise component:	$E[\varepsilon_i] = 0$, $\text{var}(\varepsilon_i) = \sigma^2$, ε_i's are independent for $i = 1, \ldots, n$
Parameters:	$\boldsymbol{\beta} \in R^k,\ \sigma^2 > 0$
Type:	semiparametric

Note that, given a value for $\boldsymbol{\beta}$, the "parametric component", $g(\mathbf{x}_{i\cdot}, \boldsymbol{\beta})$, of the model's representation of a DSP is completely and uniquely specified. However, a DSP is not fully and uniquely defined upon specifying the values of the parameters $\boldsymbol{\beta}$ and σ^2 because the form of the probability distribution underlying the ε_i's, and hence the probability distribution of **Y**, are unknown.

► **Example 2.1.1:** To demonstrate the concepts underlying the models discussed in this section, we provide the GAUSS program C2DSP.gss in the examples manual. The purpose of the program is to simulate input and output data consistent with one of two common production technologies. The square-root production function specifies output as a function of a single variable input (e.g., wheat produced from fertilizer) and takes the form of Model 2.1.2. The Cobb–Douglas production function specifies output as a function of two variable inputs (e.g., capital and labor) and takes the form of Model 2.1.3.

The GAUSS program begins by asking the reader to select the type and parameters for the production function (you may also allow GAUSS to select the model for you). Then, the variable inputs and noise elements are generated (refer to the book appendix chapter on Monte Carlo simulation for information about pseudorandom number generation) and combined to form output observations that are consistent with the stated model. GAUSS then provides a series of plots illustrating the signal component and the noisy observations.

Our focus in the chapters immediately ahead will be on parametric and semiparametric models. Consequently, in the next section we examine a collection of models that provides a basis for illustrating the connection between a visualized DSP and the parameters of a corresponding econometric model. The models also provide a basis for defining some interesting inverse problems with noise that will ultimately be the basis for developing a range of useful estimation and inference procedures. Nonparametric models will be examined in Chapter 21.

2.2. The Classical Linear Regression Model

We start our discussion of parametric and semiparametric probability models with the linear regression model in which the data are of the form $(\mathrm{y}_i, \mathbf{x}_{i.})$, $i = 1, 2, \ldots, n$, $\mathbf{x}_{i.}$ is a row vector of dimension $k \geq 1$, and y_i is a real number. It may be useful, in the context of Chapter 1, to think of these linear regression models as a basis for modeling such economic relations as demand relations, supply relations, and production functions. In this context, the vector $\mathbf{x}_{i.}$ would contain explanatory variable values for the ith observation in the form of such economic observables as prices, income, input levels, and the like. Correspondingly, the dependent variable outcome y_i would reflect such outcomes as the quantity consumed, the quantity supplied, and output.

In the linear econometric model, the observation y_i is considered, through an imagined DSP, to be the observed value of the random variable

$$\mathrm{Y}_i = \mathbf{X}_{i.}\boldsymbol{\beta} + \varepsilon_i \tag{2.2.1}$$

where $\boldsymbol{\beta} \in \mathrm{R}^k$ is a column vector and ε_i represents an unobservable random noise component. The entire column vector of dependent variable outcomes $[\mathrm{y}_1, \ldots, \mathrm{y}_n]'$ is considered to be the observed value of the $(n \times 1)$ random vector

$$\mathbf{Y} = \mathbf{X}\boldsymbol{\beta} + \boldsymbol{\varepsilon} \tag{2.2.2}$$

where $\mathbf{Y} = (\mathrm{Y}_1, \mathrm{Y}_2, \ldots, \mathrm{Y}_n)'$, $\mathbf{X}$ is a random $(n \times k)$ explanatory variable matrix, $\boldsymbol{\beta} = [\beta_1, \ldots, \beta_k]'$ is a $(k \times 1)$ vector of unknown parameters, and $\boldsymbol{\varepsilon}$ is an $(n \times 1)$ vector of random variables representing the unobservable noise elements of the model.

If the explanatory variables are *fixed* rather than random, such as in the case of a controlled experiment, then the outcome of the dependent variable vector is considered to be an outcome of the $(n \times 1)$ random vector

$$\mathbf{Y} = \mathbf{x}\boldsymbol{\beta} + \boldsymbol{\varepsilon}. \tag{2.2.3}$$

In this case, $\mathbf{x}$ is a $(n \times k)$ nonstochastic matrix of explanatory variables and in some cases is referred to as a design matrix when its entries have been controlled, and therefore *designed*, by the analyst. The remaining variables and parameters are defined as before.

2.2.1. Establishing a Linkage between Dependent and Explanatory Variables

Suppose we know our data are obtained from a sampling process that is in accordance with the linear model (2.2.2). What does this say about the distribution of the random vector $\mathbf{Y}$ and the relationship between outcomes of $\mathbf{X}$ and outcomes of $\mathbf{Y}$? The answer is that it tells us very little indeed because, at this point in the model specification and in the absence of more complete information about the sampling process, *any* probability distribution for $\mathbf{Y}$ is considered possible by the model. Thus, even if we knew the true value of $\boldsymbol{\beta}$, and thus had complete knowledge of the value of $\mathbf{x}\boldsymbol{\beta}$, we would know effectively *nothing* about what this implies for the outcome of $\mathbf{Y}$. To make the linear model at all useful in describing a DSP and operational in terms of estimation and inference, additional information, assumptions, or both are needed relating to the stochastic characteristics of model components. The additional information will be introduced as a set of maintained assumptions that represent whatever additional knowledge is available about the DSP. The resulting probability model used to characterize the DSP is then ultimately composed of some combination of facts, postulates, conjectures, and assumed conditions.

2.2.1.a. Mean of **Y**

Consider extending the linear model specification (2.2.2) by adding the assumption that the conditional expectation of **Y**, given **X**, is equal to $\mathbf{X}\boldsymbol{\beta}$; that is, we assume that

$$\textbf{Assumption 2.1} \quad \mathrm{E}[\mathbf{Y} \,|\, \mathbf{X}] = \mathbf{X}\boldsymbol{\beta}. \tag{2.2.4}$$

In other words, we are assuming that the *regression function* of **Y** on **X** is the linear function $\mathbf{X}\boldsymbol{\beta}$. This means that, regardless of the outcome of **X**, the expected or mean value of **Y**, given the outcome **x**, is then defined by the value of $\mathbf{x}\boldsymbol{\beta}$. We have thus established a stochastic linkage between outcomes of the explanatory variables and outcomes of **Y**. It follows from this linear regression assumption and the relationship

$$\mathrm{E}[\mathbf{Y} \,|\, \mathbf{X}] = \mathbf{X}\boldsymbol{\beta} + \mathrm{E}[\boldsymbol{\varepsilon} \,|\, \mathbf{X}] \tag{2.2.5}$$

that $\mathrm{E}[\boldsymbol{\varepsilon} \,|\, \mathbf{X}] = \mathbf{0}$. An application of the double expectation theorem then implies that $\mathrm{E}[\boldsymbol{\varepsilon}] = \mathrm{E}_{\mathbf{X}}[\mathrm{E}[\boldsymbol{\varepsilon} \,|\, \mathbf{X}]] = \mathbf{0}$.

The previous assumption subsumes the case of a fixed **x** as a special case. In particular, if **X** is degenerate on the value **x**, then conditional and unconditional expectations coincide. In this case Assumption 2.1 can be equivalently stated as $\mathrm{E}[\mathbf{Y}] = \mathbf{x}\boldsymbol{\beta}$, and it follows from (2.2.5) that $\mathrm{E}[\boldsymbol{\varepsilon}] = \mathbf{0}$.

2.2.1.b. Variability and Interdependence of **Y** Elements

Although by Assumption 2.1 we have indicated that the distribution of **Y** is centered on $\mathbf{x}\boldsymbol{\beta}$, given **x**, nothing has been stated regarding the relative variability of the outcomes of the Y_i's around their central values, the $\mathbf{x}_{i.}\boldsymbol{\beta}$'s. An assumption that is sometimes appended to the linear model is that dependent variable values are conditionally (on **x**) equally variable, or *homoscedastic* (i.e., equally spread), as indicated in Assumption 2.2.

We also have not yet indicated to what extent there exists a stochastic interrelationship between the elements of the dependent variable vector **Y**. An assumption that is sometimes made is that the elements Y_i, $i = 1, \ldots, n$ of the dependent variable vector are conditionally (on **x**) uncorrelated with one another, which is to say that the Y_i's exhibit *no autocorrelation* (i.e., no self-correlation). Conditional on **X**, the assumptions relating to homoscedasticity and no autocorrelation can be stated collectively as

$$\textbf{Assumption 2.2} \quad \mathbf{cov}(\mathbf{Y} \,|\, \mathbf{X}) = \sigma^2\mathbf{I}. \tag{2.2.6}$$

Given the linear relationship (2.2.2), Assumption 2.2 implies that the conditional covariance matrix of the noise component is given by $\mathbf{cov}(\boldsymbol{\varepsilon} \,|\, \mathbf{X}) = \sigma^2\mathbf{I}$, and thus by the double expectation theorem the unconditional covariance matrix of the noise component equals $\mathbf{cov}(\varepsilon) = \sigma^2\mathbf{I}$.

Note at this point that it does *not* follow from our assumptions that the unconditional covariance matrix of $\mathbf{Y}$ is given by $\mathbf{cov}(\mathbf{Y}) = \sigma^2\mathbf{I}$. Given (2.2.2), $\mathbf{cov}(\mathbf{Y})$ will depend on the covariance matrix of $\mathbf{X}$ and the covariances between the elements of $\mathbf{X}$ and ε, as well as the covariance matrix of ε. However, in the special case where the $\mathbf{X}$ matrix is degenerate on the value $\mathbf{x}$, Assumption 2.2 is equivalent to $\mathbf{cov}(\mathbf{Y}) = \sigma^2\mathbf{I}$, and it then follows as well that $\mathbf{cov}(\varepsilon) = \sigma^2\mathbf{I}$.

► **Example 2.2.2:** To check the validity of Assumptions 2.1 and 2.2, many authors recommend plotting the observed data. However, it is occasionally difficult to detect departures from these assumptions visually (i.e., autocorrelation or heteroscedasticity) for a given sample. To demonstrate the advantages and pitfalls of using simple graphical tools to check model assumptions, we provide the GAUSS program C2Noise.gss in the examples manual. Each time the reader runs the program, GAUSS selects one of five data-sampling processes and produces a random sample accordingly. The data are then plotted for the reader to observe, and the reader attempts to identify the (unknown) sampling process. How well can you do?

2.2.1.c. Joint Probability Distribution of $(\mathbf{X}, \varepsilon)$

We have not yet made any assumption regarding the joint probability distribution of $(\mathbf{X}, \varepsilon)$. Of course, if $\mathbf{X}$ is degenerate, one need only contemplate the distribution of the noise component ε because there is then effectively no *joint* distribution of $(\mathbf{X}, \varepsilon)$ to speak of. If the matrix of explanatory variables $\mathbf{X}$ is random, then a basic question to consider is whether, and to what extent, the random variables $\mathbf{X}$ and ε are interrelated. To appreciate the fundamental modeling issue involved in such an interrelationship, consider a conditional version of (2.2.2):

$$\mathbf{Y}\,|\,\mathbf{X} = \mathbf{X}\boldsymbol{\beta} + \varepsilon\,|\,\mathbf{X}. \tag{2.2.7}$$

We emphasize that (2.2.7) is interpreted as a linear relationship between $\mathbf{Y}$, $\mathbf{X}$, and ε conditional on the explanatory variable matrix $\mathbf{X}$. If the noise component is assumed to be independent of the explanatory variables, then the conditional and unconditional distributions of the noise component ε are identical. In this case, values of the explanatory variables indicate the location shift from the conditional distribution of $\varepsilon\,|\,\mathbf{x}$ (with $\mathrm{E}[\varepsilon\,|\,\mathbf{X}] = \mathbf{0}$) to the conditional distribution of $\mathbf{Y}\,|\,\mathbf{x}$ centered at $\mathbf{x}\boldsymbol{\beta}$. On the other hand, if $\mathbf{X}$ and ε are not independent, so that the distribution of $\varepsilon\,|\,\mathbf{x}$ changes as $\mathbf{x}$ changes, then changes in explanatory variable values alter not only the conditional mean of $\mathbf{Y}\,|\,\mathbf{x}$, but other characteristics of the distribution of $\mathbf{Y}\,|\,\mathbf{x}$ as well. Thus, the fundamental issue regarding the specification of the probability model is whether the explanatory variables serve solely to explain the mean level of the dependent variable's probability distribution or whether they explain other aspects of the distribution as well.

For the sake of illustration we adopt the assumption that the explanatory variables and the noise component are independent random variables:

$$\textbf{Assumption 2.3} \quad \mathbf{X} \text{ is distributed independently of } \varepsilon \tag{2.2.8}$$

The assumption implies that the joint probability distribution of $(\mathbf{X}, \varepsilon)$ is equal to the product of their respective marginal distributions and the outcomes of **X** and ε are drawn independently from these marginal distributions. The outcome of either random variable then has no effect on the outcome of the other. With Assumption 2.3 in place, we can be more definitive about the form of the unconditional covariance matrix of the dependent variable vector **Y**. In particular, the variance of Y_i is given by $\boldsymbol{\beta}'\mathbf{cov}(\mathbf{X}_{i.})\,\boldsymbol{\beta} + \sigma^2$ for $i = 1, \ldots, n$, where $\mathbf{cov}(\mathbf{X}_{i.})$ is the covariance matrix associated with the random variables in the ith row of **X**. The unconditional covariances of the elements in **Y** will depend on the nature of the stochastic interdependence among the rows of **X**. If the rows of **X** are independently distributed, the covariances will be zero. In the special case where the **X** matrix is fixed, being degenerate on the value **x**, then we are back to the case where $\mathbf{cov}(\mathbf{Y}) = \mathbf{cov}(\varepsilon) = \sigma^2\mathbf{I}$.

2.2.1.d. Summary: Conditional Moments

Collectively applying Assumptions 2.1 through 2.3 to the model $\mathbf{Y} = \mathbf{X}\boldsymbol{\beta} + \varepsilon$ is a conceptual device that can be viewed as a shorthand way of describing our state of knowledge about the DSP in the form of the moments of the conditional distribution of **Y** given **X**. The assumptions imply that the conditional expectation of **Y** given **X**, $\mathrm{E}[\mathbf{Y} \mid \mathbf{X}]$, is $\mathbf{X}\boldsymbol{\beta}$, and the conditional covariance matrix of **Y** given **X**, $\mathbf{cov}(\mathbf{Y} \mid \mathbf{X})$, is the covariance matrix of the distribution of ε, given **X**, assumed to be $\sigma^2\mathbf{I}$. Using the historical term *regression* to denote a conditional expectation, $\mathrm{E}[\mathbf{Y} \mid \mathbf{X}]$ is the regression of **Y** on **X**, and Assumption 2.1 then also describes an important functional property of this regression. In particular, when $\mathrm{E}[\mathbf{Y} \mid \mathbf{X}]$ is a linear function of **X**, as is presupposed in Assumption 2.1, the regression function is said to be *linear in the variables.* Note that if, for a given **X**, $\mathrm{E}[\mathbf{Y} \mid \mathbf{X}]$ is also a linear function of the parameters $\boldsymbol{\beta}$, then this property is referred to as the regression being *linear in the parameters.* In general, it is possible for an econometric model to depict regressions that are linear in both **X** and parameters, nonlinear in **X** but linear in the parameters, linear in **X** and nonlinear in parameters, and nonlinear in both **X** and parameters.

2.2.2. The Distribution of **Y** around the Systematic Component

Analysts sometimes postulate the types of probability distribution shapes that are thought to characterize the distribution of the noise component, which then defines the types of distributions that are possible for the dependent variable of the econometric model as well. These assumptions are enforced by specifying a particular family of probability distributions for the noise component or dependent variable either unconditionally or conditional on the explanatory variables. Of course, the conditional (on **X**) and unconditional distributions of ε will be identical if **X** is independent of ε, whereas the conditional and unconditional distributions of **Y** will generally differ. In the linear regression context, multivariate conditional normality of $\mathbf{Y}$ is often assumed, which is typically characterized in terms of an assumption on the noise component terms under the assumption of independence of $\mathbf{X}$ and $\boldsymbol{\varepsilon}$:

$$\textbf{Assumption 2.4} \quad \varepsilon_i\text{'s} \sim \text{iid}\,\text{N}(0, \sigma^2) \text{ or } \boldsymbol{\varepsilon} \sim \text{N}(\mathbf{0}, \sigma^2\mathbf{I}_n). \tag{2.2.9}$$

The cumulative information contained in all of the maintained assumptions to this point permits us to summarize the probability model of the DSP, in the case of random explanatory variables $\mathbf{X}$, compactly as

$$\mathbf{Y} \,|\, \mathbf{X} \sim \text{N}(\mathbf{X}\boldsymbol{\beta}, \sigma^2\mathbf{I}_n). \tag{2.2.10}$$

When the explanatory variable matrix is either fixed or is conditioned on the value $\mathbf{x}$, the probability model of the DSP, given this value of $\mathbf{x}$, can be specified as

$$\mathbf{Y} \,|\, \mathbf{x} \sim \text{N}(\mathbf{x}\boldsymbol{\beta}, \sigma^2\mathbf{I}_n). \tag{2.2.11}$$

Both probability model representations of the DSP imply that the random vector $\mathbf{Y}$, given the value of $\mathbf{x}$, is a multivariate normally distributed random vector with mean vector $\mathbf{x}\boldsymbol{\beta}$ and covariance $\sigma^2\mathbf{I}_n$. Thus, we have visualized the process of sampling data values of $\mathbf{Y}$ as one in which an outcome of Y_1 is randomly selected from a population of values having the univariate distribution $\text{N}(\mathbf{x}_{1\cdot}\boldsymbol{\beta}, \sigma^2)$, where the elements of $\mathbf{x}_{1\cdot} = (\text{x}_{11}, \ldots, \text{x}_{1k})$ are given, fixed numbers. Then, an outcome of Y_2 is selected from a population of values having the distribution $\text{N}(\mathbf{x}_{2\cdot}\,\boldsymbol{\beta}, \sigma^2)$, where $\mathbf{x}_{2\cdot} = (\text{x}_{21}, \ldots, \text{x}_{2\text{k}})$ are given, fixed numbers. The sampling process continues until the n observations on the n elements of $\mathbf{Y}$ are obtained.

Because we have assumed the random observation vector $\mathbf{Y}$ is distributed as multivariate normal with mean vector $\mathbf{x}\boldsymbol{\beta}$ and covariance $\sigma^2\mathbf{I}_n$, we can express the joint probability density function for the random vector $\mathbf{Y}$ analytically as

$$\text{f}(\mathbf{y}; \mathbf{x}, \boldsymbol{\beta}, \sigma^2) = (2\pi\sigma^2)^{-n/2} \exp\left[\frac{-(\mathbf{y} - \mathbf{x}\boldsymbol{\beta})'(\mathbf{y} - \mathbf{x}\boldsymbol{\beta})}{2\sigma^2}\right], \tag{2.2.12}$$

where $\boldsymbol{\beta}$ and σ^2 are unknown parameters of the distribution. This provides a complete characterization of the probability model for the sample data $\mathbf{Y}$, given $\mathbf{x}$, where the absence of any conditions on the parameter space implies that $\boldsymbol{\beta} \in \text{R}^k$ and $\sigma^2 > 0$. The probability model thus provides the basis for specifying an imagined sampling process underlying observed outcomes from an economic system or process. The illustrative model specification we have outlined above has formed the basis for a substantial amount of econometric analysis in the empirical literature.

2.2.3. Inverse Problems: Estimation, Inference, and Interpretation

The linear regression model implies a DSP based on a set of maintained assumptions about the underlying sampling process that is intended or assumed to be consistent with the observed sample data. The principal reason for specifying the model is to identify known and unknown components of the DSP and to establish a basis for choosing appropriate estimation and inference objectives and procedures for recovering information about the unknowns.

The linear regression models $\mathbf{Y} = \mathbf{X}\boldsymbol{\beta} + \varepsilon$ or $\mathbf{Y} = \mathbf{x}\boldsymbol{\beta} + \varepsilon$ and the associated probability models provide a useful context in which to begin discussion of the concept of an inverse problem with noise. Even though we can observe actual outcomes from a real-world economic system or process in the form $(\mathrm{y}_i, \mathbf{x}_i)$, $i = 1, \ldots, n$, the unknown parameters $\boldsymbol{\beta}$ and σ^2 and the noise component ε that are assumed in the regression–probability model to affect the values of these outcomes are unobservable. Consequently, the data $(\mathrm{y}_i, \mathbf{x}_{i\cdot})$, $i = 1, \ldots, n$ do not represent direct observations on $\boldsymbol{\beta}, \sigma^2$, or ε. In particular, there is no inverse function relationship that will allow us to solve for the values of $\boldsymbol{\beta}$, σ^2, or ε, in terms of $(\mathbf{y}, \mathbf{x})$. This situation frames the estimation and inference challenge: How can we use the information contained in $\mathbf{y}$ and $\mathbf{x}$ effectively to recover information, make inferences, or both, about the unknown and unobservable $\boldsymbol{\beta}$, σ^2, or ε? Answers to these types of information-recovery questions are the principal focus of the chapters ahead.

Given the probability specification of the linear regression model postulated through a process of abstraction, the conversion to an *econometric* model is completed through a process of interpretation. For example, within the context of the microeconomic theory of consumer choice, the regression model may be interpreted as a DSP for a demand relation. The dependent variable $\mathrm{Y}_{i\cdot}$ then represents per capita consumption; the explanatory variables $\mathbf{x}_{i\cdot}$ represent own price, prices of substitutes and complements, and per capita income; $\boldsymbol{\beta}$ represents the unknown consumer response coefficients; and ε_i represents all of the unspecified elements that may affect the level of consumption, including any inherent unexplainable component of human behavior. Alternatively, a variant of the regression model may be used to represent a production function, a supply function, an investment relationship, and so on. It may be useful at this point for the reader to examine several applied econometric studies that have been reported in working papers and journal articles to see how clearly the researcher has described the underlying DSP and developed the concomitant bridge to the corresponding econometric model. As the reader will come to realize, there must be a high degree of compatibility between the actual and assumed DSP if estimates and inferences relating to model parameters are to have substantive meaning.

2.2.4. Some Variants of the Linear Regression Model

Now that we have a template for specifying the probability model of a DSP relating to an economic system or process, we will examine how some alternative probability model specifications change the nature of the DSP characterization and the inverse problem and, concomitantly, change the nature of the estimation and inference problem. The specification changes we examine ahead take into account some special characteristics of the underlying DSP that can arise in empirical practice.

2.2.4.a. Linear Models with Nonspherical Noise

The case in which the noise component of the linear model is nonspherical refers to the situation involving the random variables $\mathbf{Y}$ and ε, where $\mathrm{var}(\varepsilon_i \mid \mathbf{X}) \neq \mathrm{var}(\varepsilon_j \mid \mathbf{X})$ for at least some values of $i \neq j$ (called *heteroscedasticity*), where $\mathrm{cov}(\varepsilon_i, \varepsilon_j) \neq 0$ for at least some values of $i \neq j$ (called *autocorrelation* or *autocovariance*), or both. Consequently, the assumption $\mathbf{cov}[\varepsilon \mid \mathbf{X}] = \sigma^2 \mathbf{I}_n$ or $\mathbf{cov}[\varepsilon] = \sigma^2 \mathbf{I}_n$ does not hold, and the random noise components have unequal variance or nonzero covariance values.

The nonspherical noise component specification is appropriate when the DSP is such that $\mathrm{E}[\mathbf{Y} \mid \mathbf{X}] = \mathbf{X}\boldsymbol{\beta}$ and $\mathbf{cov}(\mathbf{Y} \mid \mathbf{X}) = \sigma^2 \boldsymbol{\Psi}$, where $\boldsymbol{\Psi} \neq \mathbf{I}_n$. For example, in specifying an econometric model for a consumption function, the model may need to reflect the fact that the variability in consumption for persons with low income can be very different from those in a high-income bracket. This DSP characteristic can be represented in the model by introducing additional parameters for the different variances of the Y_i's. For another example, consider the specification of an econometric model of the quantity of a commodity supplied over time. It may be necessary to account for weather or other environmentally induced supply disruptions that persist over time and that create dependence among sequential observations on quantities supplied. This DSP characteristic can be modeled by introducing parameters that represent nonzero correlations (or covariances) between elements of the noise vector ε, which establishes associated correlations among the elements in $\mathbf{Y}$. The identity and number of elements in ε sharing nonzero correlation parameters depend on the nature of the persistence with which elements of the noise vector ε_i exert influence on the value of Y_{i+j}, $j = 1, \ldots, n$.

2.2.4.b. Interdependence of the Explanatory and Noise Components

Another interesting modeling situation occurs when the random variables $\mathbf{Y}$ and $\mathbf{X}$ are considered to be jointly determined and $\mathbf{X}$ is not distributed independently of ε. In other words, one or more of the explanatory variables are correlated with the noise component. In the context of economics, in which it is often claimed that "everything depends on everything else," this situation can occur in a variety of ways and has significant implications relating to how one should handle the problems of estimation and inference. We provide two illustrations of situations in which this type of underlying DSP is especially relevant.

Case 1: In many situations, economic data should be considered as having been generated from a system of economic relations that are stochastic and simultaneous. Simultaneity implies an instantaneous feedback or joint determination between the dependent variables and one or more explanatory random variables contained in a model, and thus a correlation between these variables and the noise component must exist. For example, consider the simple model of demand, supply, and price equilibrium given by

$$\begin{aligned} \text{Demand: } \mathbf{Q}_\mathrm{d} &= \mathrm{a}_1 + \mathrm{a}_2\mathbf{P} + \varepsilon_\mathrm{d} \\ \text{Supply: } \mathbf{Q}_\mathrm{S} &= \mathrm{b}_1 + \mathrm{b}_2\mathbf{P} + \varepsilon_\mathrm{S} \\ \text{Equilibrium: } \mathbf{Q}_\mathrm{d} &= \mathbf{Q}_\mathrm{S} \end{aligned} \tag{2.2.13}$$

Solving the model for $\mathbf{P}$ results in

$$\mathbf{P} = \left(\frac{\mathrm{b}_1 - \mathrm{a}_1}{\mathrm{a}_2 - \mathrm{b}_2}\right) + \left(\frac{\varepsilon_\mathrm{s} - \varepsilon_\mathrm{d}}{\mathrm{a}_2 - \mathrm{b}_2}\right), \tag{2.2.14}$$

and it is clear that one should suspect that the explanatory price variable **P** in either the supply or demand equation is *not* independent of the noise components of those equations because the equilibrium value of **P** depends on both ε_s and ε_d. In particular, even if ε_d is independent of ε_s, there will be nonzero correlation between **P** and both ε_s and ε_d. This DSP has significant implications for the procedures that can be used for estimation and inferences for this model, as we will see later in the text.

Case 2: In most cases, economic relationships are considered to be stochastic and to contain a noise component, and most economic data are also considered to be partial–incomplete and thus can contain measurement errors. In these cases observed values of an explanatory variable can be represented as $x_{ij}^* = x_{ij} + v_{ij}$, where v_{ij} is a measurement error outcome and now x_{ij} represents the true but *unobserved* value. Specifying the econometric model in terms of *observable* data then means that the noise component also contains a measurement error component that is correlated with one or more of the observable explanatory variables used in the econometric model. That is, if we specify the econometric model

$$\mathrm{Y}_i = \sum_{j=1}^{k} x_{ij}\beta_j + \varepsilon_i, \quad i = 1, \ldots, n \tag{2.2.15}$$

but x_{ij} is unobservable and is replaced by the observable x_{ij}^*, we then are dealing with the alternative econometric model

$$\begin{aligned} \mathrm{Y}_i &= \sum_{j=1}^{k} (\mathrm{X}_{ij}^* - \mathrm{V}_{ij})\beta_j + \varepsilon_i \\ &= \sum_{j=1}^{k} \mathrm{X}_{ij}^*\beta_j + \left(\varepsilon_i - \sum_{j=1}^{k} \mathrm{V}_{ij}\beta_j\right) \\ &= \sum_{j=1}^{k} \mathrm{X}_{ij}^*\beta_j + \mathrm{U}_i, \quad i = 1, \ldots, n. \end{aligned} \tag{2.2.16}$$

It follows that the explanatory variable $\mathrm{X}_{ij}^* = x_{ij} + \mathrm{V}_{ij}$ and noise vector element $\mathrm{U}_i = (\varepsilon_i - \sum_{j=1}^{k} \mathrm{V}_{ij}\beta_j)$ are expected to be dependent because they have the random variable V_{ij} in common. Again, this type of econometric model has implications for how the inverse problem can effectively be solved.

2.2.4.c. Nonlinear Regression Models

A regression model that is *linear* in the parameters $\boldsymbol{\beta}$ as well as *linear* in the explanatory variables **X** represents a restriction that may not be consistent with the underlying DSP of a real-world economic system or process. To mitigate this restriction, the econometric model may be expressed in the more general *nonlinear* form

$$\mathbf{Y} = \mathbf{g}(\mathbf{X}, \boldsymbol{\beta}) + \boldsymbol{\varepsilon} \tag{2.2.17}$$

where **g** is a nonlinear vector-valued function of **X** and $\boldsymbol{\beta}$. Within this nonlinear model context, variants of Assumptions 2.1 through 2.4 can be applied to achieve various types of relationships between values of **X**, values of $\mathbf{g}(\mathbf{X}, \boldsymbol{\beta})$, and ultimately values of **Y**. For example, if $E(\varepsilon \mid \mathbf{X}) = \mathbf{0}$ is assumed, then (2.2.17) becomes a nonlinear regression model, for then $E(\mathbf{Y} \mid \mathbf{X}) = \mathbf{g}(\mathbf{X}, \boldsymbol{\beta})$. This nonlinear regression model and inverse problems associated with it will be analyzed beginning in Chapter 8.

In some cases, it is possible to transform a nonlinear model into a model that is linear in the parameters, in which case a linear regression model might apply to the transformed model. For example, consider the nonlinear model (perhaps of a production function) $\mathbf{Y} = \beta_1 \mathbf{x}^{\beta_2} \mathbf{e}^{\varepsilon}$. The logarithmic transformation of this model results in a *linear* econometric model $\ln(\mathbf{Y}) = \ln(\beta_1) + \beta_2 \ln(\mathbf{x}) + \varepsilon$ that is linear in the parameters $\beta_1^* = \ln(\beta_1)$ and β_2 and that is also linear in the logarithms of the dependent and explanatory variables. Alternatively, the nonlinear model $\mathbf{Y} = \beta_1 \mathbf{x}^{\beta_2} + \varepsilon$ cannot be transformed into a form that is linear in the parameters and linear in some functions of $\mathbf{Y}$ and $\mathbf{X}$.

2.2.4.d. Discrete Choice and Limited Dependent Variable Models

In economic analysis many variables of interest are discrete rather than continuous. A consumer who makes a purchase chooses among a discrete set of brands, makes, models, and sizes. A person who travels from Berkeley to San Francisco chooses among the discrete alternatives of driving a car, going by bus, taking a ferry, or riding the subway (BART). Because economic theory is in reality a general theory of choice, a good basis exists for econometric modeling of these dichotomous–polychotomous choices. Nonlinear models of the general form

$$\mathbf{Y} = \eta(\mathbf{X}, \boldsymbol{\beta}, \varepsilon) \tag{2.2.18}$$

can be used for modeling these discrete-choice problems. For conventional binomial models, the ith element of η can be defined as

$$\eta_i(\mathbf{X}_{i\cdot}, \boldsymbol{\beta}, \varepsilon_i) = \begin{cases} 1 & \text{if } \quad \mathbf{X}_{i\cdot}\boldsymbol{\beta} + \varepsilon_i > 0 \\ 0 & \text{otherwise} \end{cases} \tag{2.2.19}$$

This type of model can be used to represent the outcome of a collection of dichotomous choices coded as 0 and 1.

Alternatively, censored dependent variable models may be defined as

$$\eta_i(\mathbf{X}_{i\cdot}, \boldsymbol{\beta}, \varepsilon_i) = \begin{cases} \mathbf{X}_{i\cdot}\boldsymbol{\beta} + \varepsilon_i & \text{if } \quad \mathbf{X}_{i\cdot}\boldsymbol{\beta} + \varepsilon_i > 0, \\ 0 & \text{otherwise.} \end{cases} \tag{2.2.20}$$

This type of model can be used to represent the outcome of a choice between 0 or some positive level of something such as a choice between not purchasing a good ($y_i = 0$) or purchasing some positive amount of the good.

Additional flexibility in the preceding models can be obtained by replacing the linear function $\mathbf{X}_{i\cdot}\boldsymbol{\beta}$ with a nonlinear function, say $h_i(\mathbf{X}_{i\cdot}, \boldsymbol{\beta})$. The preceding specifications yield parametric models once a parametric family of distributions for ε_i is specified. For example, if ε_i in (2.2.19) is logistically distributed, the model is a binomial logit, and the probability that $y_i = 0$ is $1/(1 + e^{\mathbf{X}_{i\cdot}\boldsymbol{\beta}})$. These and related statistical models pose many interesting inverse problems, and concomitant estimation and inference problems, as we will see in succeeding chapters.

2.3. A Class of Probability Models

All of the statistical models discussed in the preceding sections, as well as all of the statistical models discussed in the chapters ahead, are subsumed by the class of models characterized in Table 2.1. Specific probability models used in practice are defined through the specification of a subset of the specific characteristics identified in Table 2.1. For example, in defining a classical, single-equation, parametric linear regression model, one may specify that

- $\mathbf{Y}$ has an *unlimited range, moments* $\mathrm{E}(\mathbf{Y}\,|\,\mathbf{X}) = \mathbf{X}\boldsymbol{\beta}$ and $\mathbf{cov}(\mathbf{Y}\,|\,\mathbf{X}) = \sigma^2\mathbf{I}$, Y_i have *univariate dimension*, and $\mathbf{Y}$ is a *continuous* random vector;
- $\eta(\mathbf{x}, \boldsymbol{\beta}, \boldsymbol{\varepsilon})$ is *linear* in $\boldsymbol{\beta}$, and *additive* in $\boldsymbol{\varepsilon}$;
- $\mathbf{x}$ is *fixed* and *exogenous*;
- $\boldsymbol{\beta}$ is *fixed* and of *finite dimension*;
- $\boldsymbol{\varepsilon}$ has *moments* $\mathrm{E}[\boldsymbol{\varepsilon}\,|\,\mathbf{x}] = \mathbf{0}$ and $\mathbf{cov}(\boldsymbol{\varepsilon}\,|\,\mathbf{x}) = \sigma^2\mathbf{I}$;
- the parameter space Ω is *unconstrained*; and
- $\mathrm{f}(\mathbf{e}\,|\,\mathbf{x}, \boldsymbol{\varphi})$ is a member of the *normal* parametric family, so that $\boldsymbol{\varepsilon} \sim \mathrm{N}(\mathbf{0}, \sigma^2\mathbf{I})$.

Note that by assuming the foregoing model specification, one also has implicitly assumed other characteristics of the model, including (refer to Table 2.1)

- $\mathbf{h}(\mathbf{x}, \boldsymbol{\beta}, \boldsymbol{\varphi}) = \mathbf{x}\boldsymbol{\beta}$, and thus that the parameter vector $\boldsymbol{\varphi}$ is effectively suppressed in the expectation function for $\mathbf{Y}$;
- $\boldsymbol{\Sigma}_{\mathbf{Y}}(\mathbf{x}, \boldsymbol{\beta}, \boldsymbol{\varphi}) = \boldsymbol{\Sigma}_{\boldsymbol{\varepsilon}}(\mathbf{x}, \boldsymbol{\varphi}) = \sigma^2\mathbf{I}$, and thus that the covariance matrices of $\mathbf{Y}$ and $\boldsymbol{\varepsilon}$ are unaffected by the values of $\mathbf{x}$ and $\boldsymbol{\beta}$, and the variance parameter σ^2 is an element of the parameter vector $\boldsymbol{\varphi}$ associated with the probability density function (PDF) of $\boldsymbol{\varepsilon}$;
- $\eta(\mathbf{x}, \boldsymbol{\beta}, \boldsymbol{\varepsilon})$ can be linear or nonlinear in the explanatory variables $\mathbf{x}$; and
- the elements in $\boldsymbol{\varepsilon}$ are iid.

Unless otherwise noted, there is a common set of specific characteristics of probability model that will be tacitly assumed to apply to all of the models contained in the class portrayed by Table 2.1. These common model characteristics are given:

Common Set of Probability Model Characteristics

1. $\mathbf{x}$ has full-column rank (with probability 1 in the case of random $\mathbf{X}$), and its values are observable;
2. $\mathbf{Y}$ is an observable random variable;
3. $\boldsymbol{\beta}$ is an unknown and unobservable scalar or vector; and
4. $\boldsymbol{\varepsilon}$ is an unknown and unobservable random vector.

Table 2.1. *Class of Probability Models*

General Probability Model						
(Dependent $\mathbf{Y}$) =	Function η	(Explanatory $\mathbf{X}$,	Parameters $\boldsymbol{\beta}$,	Noise ε),	PDF $\varepsilon\|\mathbf{x} \sim \mathbf{f}(\mathbf{e}\|\mathbf{x};\varphi)$	Parameter Space $(\boldsymbol{\beta},\varphi) \in \Omega$,
Specific Model Characteristics						
$\mathbf{Y}$	$\eta(\mathbf{X},\boldsymbol{\beta},\varepsilon)$	$\mathbf{X}$	$\boldsymbol{\beta}$	ε	Ω	$\mathbf{f}(\mathbf{e}\|\mathbf{x},\varphi,)$
• **RV Type** • discrete • continuous • mixed • **Range** • unlimited • limited • **$\mathbf{Y}_i$ Dimension** • univariate • multivariate • **Moments** • $E[\mathbf{Y}\|\mathbf{X}] = \mathbf{h}(\mathbf{X},\boldsymbol{\beta},\varphi)$ • $\mathbf{cov}(\mathbf{Y}\|\mathbf{X}) = \Sigma_Y(\mathbf{X},\boldsymbol{\beta},\varphi)$	• **Functional Form** • in $\mathbf{X}$ • linear • linear transformable • nonlinear • in $\boldsymbol{\beta}$ • linear • linear transformable • nonlinear • in ε • additive • nonadditive	• **RV Type** • degenerate (fixed) • random • $\mathbf{X}$ and ε are independent • $\mathbf{X}$ and ε are uncorrelated • $\mathbf{X}$ and ε are dependent • **Genesis** • endogenous • simultaneous • predetermined • exogenous	• **RV Type** • degenerate (fixed) • random • subjectively • data-based • **Dimension** • finite • unspecified	• **RV Type** • iid • independent, non-indentical • dependent • **Moments** • $E[\varepsilon\|\mathbf{X}] = \mathbf{0}$ • $\mathbf{cov}(\varepsilon\|\mathbf{X}) = \Sigma_\varepsilon(\mathbf{X},\varphi)$	• **Prior Info** • unconstrained • equality constrained $\mathbf{c}(\boldsymbol{\beta}) = \mathbf{r}$ • inequality constrained $\mathbf{c}(\boldsymbol{\beta}) \leq \mathbf{r}$ • stochastic prior information $(\boldsymbol{\beta},\varphi) \sim p(\boldsymbol{\beta},\varphi)$	• **PDF Family** • normal • non-normal • unspecified

By *observable* we simply mean that specific numerical values can be attributed to the elements of a vector. In the case of a random vector, the vector is observable if outcomes of the random vector result in specific numerical values.

In applications it is imperative that the probability model be defined unambiguously and in as much detail as the analyst's information allows. In any econometric analysis, the probability model is the centerpiece that identifies the underlying assumed DSP and the unknowns of interest, frames the relationship between the inputs and outputs of the inverse problem, and determines which estimation and inference procedures are appropriate.

2.4. Class of Inverse Problems and Solutions

The class of probability models in Table 2.1 implies an associated class of inverse problems. At the most general level the inverse problem takes the form

$$(\mathbf{Y}, \mathbf{X}) \Rightarrow \{\boldsymbol{\beta}, \varphi, \varepsilon, \mathrm{f}(\mathbf{e}\,|\,\mathbf{x}; \varphi)\} \Rightarrow \mathrm{f}_{\mathbf{Y}}(\mathbf{y}\,|\,\mathbf{X}; \boldsymbol{\beta}, \varphi), \tag{2.4.1}$$

meaning that observations on $(\mathbf{Y}, \mathbf{X})$ are used to infer information about the values of any parameters $(\boldsymbol{\beta}, \varphi)$ and the probability distributions of ε and $\mathbf{Y}$. Note that because $\mathbf{Y}$ and ε are functionally related via the probability model (Table 2.1), the distribution of $(\mathbf{Y}\,|\,\mathbf{X}; \boldsymbol{\beta}, \varphi)$ will generally be *implied* by the distribution of ε. If the specific model characteristics are chosen so as to define a parametric model, then the inverse problem for the statistical model simplifies to

$$(\mathbf{Y}, \mathbf{X}) \Rightarrow \{\boldsymbol{\beta}, \varphi, \varepsilon\}. \tag{2.4.2}$$

In the case of the preceding classical parametric linear regression model, the inverse problem is defined by

$$(\mathbf{Y}, \mathbf{X}) \Rightarrow \{\boldsymbol{\beta}, \sigma^2, \varepsilon\}. \tag{2.4.3}$$

The types of inverse problem solutions that are generally pursued in econometric practice can be categorized into three basic forms. We list these below with a brief description of each in the context of expressing or inferring information about the value of a function of the parameters $\mathbf{q}(\boldsymbol{\beta}, \varphi)$ or, more generally, a function of the distribution of $\mathbf{Y}$, $\mathbf{q}(\mathrm{f}_{\mathbf{Y}})$. Detailed discussions of these topics, as they relate to specific probability models, can be found throughout the remainder of the book.

1. *Point Estimation.* The objective of point estimation is to reduce uncertainty about functions of parameters $\mathbf{q}(\boldsymbol{\beta}, \varphi)$ or, more generally, functions of the distribution of $\mathbf{Y}$, $\mathbf{q}(\mathrm{f}_{\mathbf{Y}})$. Information is expressed by choosing a specific value from the possibility space as the best representative of $\mathbf{q}(\cdot)$. The objective is pursued through the choice of a point-valued function that maps the range of $(\mathbf{Y}, \mathbf{X})$ to the possibility space for $\mathbf{q}(\cdot)$, say $\mathbf{t} : (\mathbf{y}, \mathbf{x}) \rightarrow \hat{\mathbf{q}}$. The point-valued mapping is chosen to achieve various criteria relating to the proximity of estimates $\hat{\mathbf{q}}$ to the unknown and unobservable value of $\mathbf{q}(\cdot)$. The criteria are either interpreted within a predata context that considers point estimates that would occur across all hypothetical sample outcomes of $(\mathbf{Y}, \mathbf{X})$ (classical) or else within a postdata context

that considers only the information contained in the particular sample outcome actually observed (Bayesian).

2. *Confidence (Classical) and Credible (Bayesian) Region Estimation.* The objective here is to reduce uncertainty about the value of $\mathbf{q}(\cdot)$ and express our state of knowledge by reducing the range of possibilities to only a subset of the possibility space. The objective is pursued through the choice of a *set-valued* function that maps the range of $(\mathbf{Y}, \mathbf{X})$ to the possibility space for $\mathbf{q}(\cdot)$, say as $\mathbf{t} : (\mathbf{y}, \mathbf{x}) \to \mathrm{C}(\mathbf{y}, \mathbf{x})$, where $\mathrm{C}(\mathbf{y}, \mathbf{x})$ is *a set* of possible values for $\mathbf{q}(\cdot)$. The set-valued mapping is chosen so that the true value of $\mathbf{q}(\cdot)$ is contained in the set $\mathrm{C}(\mathbf{y}, \mathbf{x})$ with a predata level of confidence, τ (classical), or a postdata level of posterior probability, τ (Bayesian).
3. *Hypothesis Testing.* The objective of hypothesis testing is to narrow uncertainty regarding the value of $\mathbf{q}(\boldsymbol{\beta}, \boldsymbol{\varphi})$ or $\mathbf{q}(f_{\mathbf{Y}})$ by generating an answer to the question of which of two hypothesized subsets of the possibility space, say H_0 or H_a, contains the unknown value of $\mathbf{q}(\cdot)$. The objective is pursued through the choice of a bivalued function that maps the range of $(\mathbf{Y}, \mathbf{X})$ into the decision H_0 or H_a. The function is chosen to achieve various criteria relating to the accuracy of decisions. The criteria are either interpreted within a predata context that considers decisions that would be made across all hypothetical sample outcomes of $(\mathbf{Y}, \mathbf{X})$ (classical) or else within a postdata context that considers only the information contained in the particular sample outcome actually observed (Bayesian).

A common unifying theme in the solutions for the class of models depicted in Table 2.1 will be the choice of a function of the sample data whose outcomes represent point estimates, confidence–credible regions, or hypothesis decisions that achieve established measures of accuracy in a predata (classical) or postdata (Bayesian) context.

2.5. Concluding Comments

In Chapter 1 we discussed the role of the econometric model in economic research, and in this chapter we have presented a sample of parametric and semiparametric econometric models that have been used in empirical work to represent characteristics of economic DSPs. Each type of economic data has its own peculiarities that often require the specification of a unique probability–econometric model to reflect its sampling characteristics. When one recognizes this fact, the futility of a philosophy that "one model fits all" types of economic data sets or DSPs is all too clear. Before beginning an econometric analysis, it is therefore important to be creative and flexible in specifying probability–econometric models and in subsequently addressing the estimation and inference questions associated with the inverse problems that the probability models imply. Probability models are conceptual tools that essentially permit the analyst to express his or her state of knowledge about an economic DSP as reflected in the eyes of the beholder. Traditional or existing probability-model specifications should not be used to supplant substantive knowledge in a particular subject area.

The purpose of this chapter has been to provide the reader with (1) a framework for thinking about the problem of modeling the sampling characteristics of economic data, (2) an idea of where probability–econometric models come from and the logical basis from which they evolve, and (3) a creative process for framing inverse problems that may form a basis for analyzing an observed sample of data. In other words this chapter, along with Chapter 1, is concerned with the question of how, in the context of nonexperimental modelbuilding, we may go about conceptualizing the process of recovering information from a sample of economic data. Consistent with the process described in Figure 1.1 in Chapter 1, we have focused attention on the probability–econometric model and the corresponding sampling process it describes. In this process we use conceptual properties such as random variables, stochastic noise process, and the like to convey our state of knowledge about real economic properties such as prices and quantities. These conceptual properties give us a way to express our partial–incomplete state of knowledge about the real economic properties that we seek to understand. Given the econometric model as a knowledge summarizing and organizing device, the next question we will address in the chapters ahead is how to devise solutions to various inverse problems with noise. For additional perspective on the range of econometric models, see Berndt (1990) and Dempster (1998). In terms of probability models, see Cox (1990) and Lehmann (1990).

2.6. Exercises

2.6.1. Idea Checklist – Knowledge Guides

---

1. Where do economic, probability, and econometric models come from, and what is their purpose?
2. Is it possible for the data to "speak for itself" in the absence of a probability, econometric, or other kind of model? Why or why not?
3. What are the primary differences among parametric, semiparametric, and nonparametric models?
4. What is the role of assumptions when defining a probability or econometric model?
5. Is the probability model "a mirror of the DSP"?
6. Where does the noise component of an econometric model come from? Why is it needed?
7. What are some implications for estimation and inference of the probability model being incorrectly specified?
8. Using a subject area with which you are familiar, describe the conceptual process of econometric model discovery.

2.6.2. Problems

2–1 Suppose you are willing to assume that $\mathbf{Y} \mid \mathbf{x} \sim \mathrm{N}(\mathbf{x}\boldsymbol{\beta}, \sigma^2\mathbf{I})$. Specify in vector–matrix form the statistical model that could be used in recovering the location and scale parameters if $\mathbf{x}$ is a vector of unit values.

2–2 Consider a product or commodity that you consume on a regular basis (e.g., coffee). In the context of consumer-choice theory, list the factors that influence your consumption such as your income or the price of the good. If y is the quantity consumed and $\mathbf{x}$ is the vector of explanatory factors, suppose $\mathbf{y}$ may be related to $\mathbf{x}$ as in Model 2.1.1. In this setting, how would you interpret the noise components, and what types of influences might they represent?

2–3 For the product or commodity used in Exercise 1, list the inputs used to produce this good. In the context of the microeconomic theory of production, suppose the quantity of the good supplied, y, is a function of the vector of inputs **x** through the general functional form given by Model 2.1.3. In this setting, how would you interpret the noise components and what types of influences might they represent? Would an additive error term (as in Model 2.1.1) be more suitable for a production model?

2–4 Suppose the manufacturer of the product in Exercise 3 would like an estimate of the function $\mathbf{g}(\mathbf{x}, \boldsymbol{\beta})$ for Model 2.1.3 to understand better the quantitative responsiveness of the production process to variations in input levels. Data consistent with the production process for different levels of the inputs are a basic ingredient if one is to estimate this function. Describe a controlled experiment that you could conduct to generate data that may be used to estimate $\mathbf{g}(\mathbf{x}, \boldsymbol{\beta})$. What are the potential errors that may appear in this data?

2–5 Now that you have considered the nature of the disturbances present in the supply and demand models above, do Assumptions 2.1 to 2.3 seem reasonable given what you know about the product of interest? If so, why, and if not, why not?

2–6 The supply and the demand for products are often jointly determined, and one such complete model of the joint determination process may be stated, as in (2.2.13). Suppose that the supply and demand of the commodity you identified in questions 1 through 4 above are in fact jointly determined. Given the factors you identified that may contribute to the model noise, could any of these factors influence both the supply and demand components of the model? If so, and you ignored the interdependency, how do you think this situation would affect your ability to estimate the unknown parameters and draw inferences?

2.7. References

Berndt, E. R. (1990), *The Practice of Econometrics*, Reading, MA: Addison–Wesley.

Cox, D. R. (1990), "Models in Statistical Analysis," *Statistical Science*, Vol. 5, pp. 169–74.

Dempster, A. P. (1998), "Logical Statistics I: Models and Modeling," *Statistical Science*, Vol. 13, pp. 248–78.

Lehmann, E. L. (1990), "Model Specification," *Statistical Science*, Vol. 5, pp. 160–68.

PART TWO

Regression Model – Estimation and Inference

In the next four chapters the focus is on specifying two alternative versions of the linear regression–probability model and developing an estimation and inference basis for the corresponding model parameters. In this context you will be introduced to the least-squares and maximum likelihood estimation rules that will be used throughout the remainder of the book. The least-squares rule dates back to Gauss and LeGendre around 1805, and the maximum likelihood rule was proposed by Fisher over three quarters of a century ago. Special attention is directed toward identifying the corresponding finite sample and asymptotic statistical-sampling properties of each estimator.

Given point estimates for the unknown and unobservable parameters, questions then turn to confidence region estimation and hypothesis testing and the interesting world of finite sample and asymptotic test statistics. Ultimately, discussions relating to the truth or falsity of designated hypotheses lead us to preliminary test estimation rules and a somewhat daunting list of associated conceptual issues. Not to worry – as someone once remarked, no one ever said inference is easy.

Computer-based examples are included to provide an operational understanding of each probability model and associated estimation and inference rules.

CHAPTER 3

The Multivariate Normal Linear Regression Model: ML Estimation

In this chapter we present our first detailed examination of a probability model for representing the data-sampling process (DSP) associated with some real-world economic process. Beginning with this chapter, we will include a table in the introduction that, through the definition of specific characteristics of various model components, identifies the form and scope of the probability model being studied. The details of the model specification delineated in these tables will effect the types of economic processes and associated DSPs that will be congruent with the model and also effect the types of estimation and inference procedures that can be used to recover information on the unknown and uncertain components of the model effectively. In terms of the general class of probability models portrayed in Table 2.1, this chapter deals with the special case delineated in Table 3.1.

The particular inverse problem associated with the probability model identified in Table 3.1 involves using observations on $(\mathbf{Y}, \mathbf{x})$ to recover information on the values or functions of the unknown and unobservable $\boldsymbol{\beta}$, σ^2, and ε. In this chapter we will focus most of our attention on establishing a basis for recovering information about the unknown explanatory variable coefficient vector $\boldsymbol{\beta}$ and the variance parameter σ^2. To solve this inverse problem, we will seek estimators that process sample data into estimates of the unknowns. The quality of the estimators and the associated estimates are judged by the statistical properties of the estimators, which we identify as well.

3.1. The Linear Regression Model

On the basis of specific model characteristics presented in Table 3.1, we have specified the following linear functional relationship as a fundamental component of our model of the DSP:

$$\mathbf{Y} = \mathbf{x}\boldsymbol{\beta} + \boldsymbol{\varepsilon} \tag{3.1.1}$$

where $\mathbf{Y} = (\mathrm{Y}_1, \mathrm{Y}_2, \ldots, \mathrm{Y}_n)'$ is a $(n \times 1)$ vector of observable random variables whose range is contained in R^n, $\mathbf{x}$ is an $(n \times k)$ matrix reflecting the numerical values taken on by

Table 3.1. *Normal Parametric Linear Regression Probability Model*

Model Component	Specific Characteristics	
$\mathbf{Y}$	RV Type:	continuous
	Range:	unlimited
	Y_i dimension:	univariate
	Moments:	$E[\mathbf{Y} \mid \mathbf{x}] = \mathbf{x}\boldsymbol{\beta}$, and $\mathbf{cov}(\mathbf{Y} \mid \mathbf{x}) = \sigma^2\mathbf{I}$
$\eta(\mathbf{x}, \boldsymbol{\beta}, \varepsilon)$	Functional Form:	linear in $\mathbf{x}$ and $\boldsymbol{\beta}$, additive in ε, as $\mathbf{x}\boldsymbol{\beta} + \varepsilon$
$\mathbf{x}$	RV Type:	degenerate (fixed), full-column rank
	Genesis:	exogenous to the model
$\boldsymbol{\beta}$	RV Type:	degenerate (fixed)
	Dimension:	finite (fixed)
ε	RV Type:	iid
	Moments:	$E[\varepsilon \mid \mathbf{x}] = \mathbf{0}$, and $\mathbf{cov}(\varepsilon \mid \mathbf{x}) = \sigma^2\mathbf{I}$
Ω	Prior info:	none
$f(\mathbf{e} \mid \mathbf{x}; \varphi)$	PDF family:	$N(\mathbf{e}; \mathbf{0}, \sigma^2\mathbf{I})$

n explanatory variables, $\boldsymbol{\beta}$ is a k-dimensional fixed vector of unknown and unobservable parameters representing coefficients multiplying the explanatory variables, and ε is a $(n \times 1)$ noise vector of unobserved and unobservable random variables. Note we are departing from our convention of using capital letters to denote random variables in the case of ε because of the widespread practice in the literature of reserving the letter epsilon, ε, for the random noise (or disturbance or error) vector of regression relationships.

3.1.1. The Linearity Assumption and the Inverse Problem

The linear specification (3.1.1), in the absence of any other assumptions, suggests an inverse problem; that is, the outcomes of the observable random variables $\mathbf{Y}$ and the value of $\mathbf{x}$ can be considered *indirect observations* on the unknown and unobservable $\boldsymbol{\beta}$ and ε. We hope to use these indirect observations in some manner to recover information about $\boldsymbol{\beta}$ and ε. By *indirect* observations we mean that the pair of observed values $(\mathbf{y}, \mathbf{x})$ are not direct observations on the values of $\boldsymbol{\beta}$ and ε. Rather, $(\mathbf{y}, \mathbf{x})$ *indirectly* convey information about $\boldsymbol{\beta}$ and ε through the relation $\mathbf{e} = \mathbf{y} - \mathbf{x}\boldsymbol{\beta}$ that is implied directly by (3.1.1), where $\mathbf{e}$ denotes an outcome of ε.

Note that the relation between $(\mathbf{y}, \mathbf{x})$ and $(\boldsymbol{\beta}, \mathbf{e})$ implied by (3.1.1) is not one-to-one. In particular, there are n equations in $(n + k)$ unknowns. Thus, observing $(\mathbf{y}, \mathbf{x})$ is not equivalent to observing $(\boldsymbol{\beta}, \mathbf{e})$. We cannot solve for unique values of $(\boldsymbol{\beta}, \mathbf{e})$ given the values $(\boldsymbol{y}, \boldsymbol{x})$ because the system of equations is undetermined for deriving specific values of $(\boldsymbol{\beta}, \mathbf{e})$. If only (3.1.1) is utilized in the conceptualization process, the information recovered about $(\boldsymbol{\beta}, \mathbf{e})$ from having observed $(\mathbf{y}, \mathbf{x})$ is that $(\boldsymbol{\beta}, \mathbf{e})$ is no longer free to assume any value in $R^k \times R^n$ space but rather must reside in the reduced k-dimensional space represented by the set $\Gamma = \{(\boldsymbol{\beta}, \mathbf{e}): \mathbf{e} = \mathbf{y} - \mathbf{x}\boldsymbol{\beta}, \mathbf{e} \in \mathbf{R}^n, \boldsymbol{\beta} \in \mathbf{R}^k\}$. Although information has been gained about the unknown $(\boldsymbol{\beta}, \mathbf{e})$, this is generally far less than would be considered useful in any practical sense. In particular, we have no basis for choosing a particular value in the set Γ as the best, or even as a good, estimate of $(\boldsymbol{\beta}, \mathbf{e})$. And we have yet to mention any information gained regarding the value of σ^2. Additional model structure is necessary before more precise solutions to the inverse problem can be obtained.

3.1.2. Linearity and Beyond: Sampling Implication of Model Assumptions

In order for the inverse problem to possess more informative solutions, we need to go beyond simply specifying the linear relationship (3.1.1) and be more specific regarding sampling characteristics of the random components of the model. Such specificity was presented in the Table 3.1 in which additional specific probability model characteristics were delineated. In this subsection, we discuss major implications of these assumed model characteristics as they relate to the behavior of the DSP. We take up the issue of what these additional model characteristics imply about the problem of estimating $\boldsymbol{\beta}$ and σ^2 in subsequent sections.

The assumption that $\mathbf{x}$ is fixed implies that repeated observations on $(\mathbf{Y}, \mathbf{x})$ consist of varying values for the sample outcome of the random vector $\mathbf{Y}$ paired with the same constant value of the matrix of explanatory variable values $\mathbf{x}$. In the context of the linear relationship $\mathbf{Y} = \mathbf{x}\boldsymbol{\beta} + \varepsilon$, only the outcomes of $\mathbf{Y}$ and ε change in repeated sampling, and the value of $\mathbf{x}\boldsymbol{\beta}$ remains exactly the same from sample to sample. In effect, our conceptual sampling model is one in which values of $\mathbf{Y}$ are sampled conditionally on the fixed values of the explanatory variables.

Because $\mathbf{x}$ is fixed, conditioning on $\mathbf{x}$ is redundant, and thus moment assumptions relating to ε and $\mathbf{Y}$ can be stated unconditionally. The first-order moment assumptions that $E[\varepsilon] = \mathbf{0}$ and $E[\mathbf{Y}] = \mathbf{x}\boldsymbol{\beta}$ are equivalent; either assumption implies the other. The practical implication of the fixed $\boldsymbol{x}$ and moment assumptions is that $\mathbf{x}\boldsymbol{\beta}$ represents the mean value of $\mathbf{Y}$ and that the outcome of the elements of ε denotes deviations in the respective outcomes of $\mathbf{Y}$ from their mean values.

The second-order moment assumptions $\mathbf{cov}(\varepsilon) = \sigma^2\mathbf{I}$ and $\mathbf{cov}(\mathbf{Y}) = \sigma^2\mathbf{I}$ are also equivalent given the fixed nature of $\boldsymbol{x\beta}$ in the linear relationship $\mathbf{Y} = \mathbf{x}\boldsymbol{\beta} + \varepsilon$. This assumption implies that both the ε_i's and the Y_i's are homoscedastic, meaning that all of the ε_i's and all of the Y_i's have precisely the same variability and that the common variance equals σ^2. The assumption also implies that the covariance between any two elements of ε or any two elements of $\mathbf{Y}$ is equal to zero and thus that there is no linear association of any degree between the elements in ε or $\mathbf{Y}$. This is referred to as the ε_i's (or the Y_i's) exhibiting no autocorrelation (or no autocovariance).

The assumption that $\eta(\mathbf{x}, \boldsymbol{\beta}, \varepsilon)$ is linear in $\boldsymbol{x}$ is not as restrictive as it might at first appear. The value of the matrix $\mathbf{x}$ can be a highly nonlinear function of more fundamental variables, say $\mathbf{z}$, allowing the current statistical model to be nonlinear in

$\mathbf{z}$ as $\boldsymbol{\eta}(\mathbf{x}(\mathbf{z}), \boldsymbol{\beta}, \varepsilon)$. For example,

$$Y_i = \beta_1 z_{i1}^2 + \beta_2(z_{i2}/z_{i3}) + \beta_3 \sin(z_{i4}) + \beta_4 \exp(z_{i5}) + \varepsilon_i \quad (3.1.2)$$

is consistent with the linear statistical model upon defining $x_{i1} = z_{i1}^2$, $x_{i2} = z_{i2}/z_{i3}$, $x_{i3} = \sin(z_{i4})$, and $x_{i4} = \exp(z_{i5})$. Linearity in both $\mathbf{x}$ and $\boldsymbol{\beta}$ and additivity in ε may also be achieved through transforming a model that in original form violates one or more of the assumptions. For example, the Cobb–Douglas production function

$$Q_i = \delta_1 \ell_i^{\delta_2} k_i^{\delta_3} \varepsilon_i^* \quad (3.1.3)$$

can be transformed into linear model form as

$$\ln(Q_i) = \ln(\delta_1) + \delta_2 \ln(\ell_i) + \delta_3 \ln(k_i) + \ln(\varepsilon_i^*)$$

or

$$Y_i = \beta_1 + \beta_2 x_{i1} + \beta_3 x_{i2} + \varepsilon_i \quad (3.1.4)$$

for appropriate definitions of the x_{ij}'s, β_i's, ε_i's, and Y_i's. Thus, the scope of the linear model includes models that are nonlinear in the explanatory variables and parameters or nonadditive in the noise component, or both, and that can be *transformed* into the linear model form delineated in Table 3.1. Models that are inherently nonlinear in the parameters and that cannot be transformed into linearity such as

$$Y_i = \beta_1 + \beta_2 x_{i1} + \beta_2 x_{i2}^{\beta_3} + \varepsilon_i \quad (3.1.5)$$

are explicitly ruled out of the current class of probability models.

The assumption that $\mathbf{Y}$ is a continuous random variable without a priori limits on its range implies that sample outcomes of $\mathbf{Y}$ can take any numerical value without restriction. In practice, this assumption is often adopted as an idealization. With respect to taking all values in a continuum, the abstraction is usually defended via the argument that smoothing between discrete observation points has no practical detrimental effects when probabilities are assigned to events of interest in a particular applied problem. Similarly, because the range of $\mathbf{Y}$ may in reality be restricted is often abstracted away from by arguing that, as a practical matter, one can utilize unrestricted random variables having PDFs whose tail probabilities (i.e., the probabilities of outcomes occurring outside of the restricted range) are negligible. Note the continuity of $\mathbf{Y}$ implies the continuity of ε in this model.

The assumption that there is no prior information on the parameter space Ω implies that there are no functional or inequality restrictions binding together admissible values of the parameters represented by $\boldsymbol{\beta}$ and σ^2. Note that certain economic models, such as in the theory of the consumer or the firm, imply neoclassical functional restrictions on the admissible values of parameters that would not be explicitly imposed in the current model.

If the PDF family for $\mathbf{Y}$ were to be left unspecified, then literally any probability distribution that does not violate the stated specific independence and moment conditions could be considered a potential probability distribution for ε. Any corresponding distribution for ε given by the distribution of $\mathbf{Y} - \mathbf{x}\boldsymbol{\beta}$ is then admissible as the PDF of ε. In this eventuality, the model would be clearly *semiparametric*. In the next subsection we consider the transition to a parametric model induced by the assumption of normality for the noise component, and we examine general issues relating to the problem of estimating the unknown parameters of the model.

3.1.3. The Parametric Model

Our focus in this chapter is on developing a basis for recovering information about the unknowns of the probability model of a DSP by using independent sample observations from a DSP in which the probability model is based on a fully specified parametric family of probability distributions. In particular, we focus on the maximum likelihood (ML) concept and a multivariate normal specification of the probability model component of the econometric model. Given this parametric model specification, the question naturally arises, How can one make use of all of the stated model information when solving the associated inverse problem?

In this parametric version of the linear regression model, one possibility is to make use of the likelihood function and the ML principle (Berger and Wolpert (1984)) introduced by R. A. Fisher. The basic idea in the ML approach is to find the value of the parameter vector, say $\boldsymbol{\theta}$, that maximizes the likelihood associated with the sample outcomes $\mathbf{y}$ that are actually observed. As a result of Fisher's idea, likelihood methods for parametric estimation and hypothesis testing have emerged that have good statistical properties in a wide range of applications, and, in particular, an elegant asymptotic theory underpins their use. In essence, the asymptotic ML theory applies if, in an open set of parameter values, the likelihood function, defined algebraically by the joint density function of the random sample $\mathbf{Y}$, is closely approximated in probability by a concave quadratic function whose maximum point converges appropriately to the true parameter vector $\boldsymbol{\theta}$ as the sample size increases. This is ensured if certain regularity conditions, as will be identified later, are fulfilled.

In this chapter we will concentrate our attention on the use of a normal distribution and linear regression models to develop ML theory as a basis for point estimation. Methods of inference for this parametric model will be developed in Chapter 4. However, we will also note some more general ML theory in the context of extremum estimators in parametric models. In addition, we will introduce the idea of biased estimation and, in a loss-risk context, investigate the admissibility of the ML estimator (in the chapter appendix). Further applicability of ML theory to a range of alternative models and probability distribution specifications will be demonstrated in subsequent chapters. We will see that the likelihood function $\mathrm{L}(\boldsymbol{\theta};\mathbf{y})$ provides a window to the data that is a fundamental component of many classical and Bayesian inference procedures.

3.2. Maximum Likelihood Estimation of β and σ^2

In this section we examine the use of maximum likelihood methods, in the context of the linear regression model, for solving the inverse problem of generating information on $\boldsymbol{\beta}$ and σ^2 when the noise component, and thus $\mathbf{Y}$ itself, has a probability distribution in the multivariate normal parametric family.

3.2.1. The Normal Linear Regression Model

Consider the probability model characteristics presented in Table 3.1 together with the linear regression model specification

$$\mathbf{Y} = \mathbf{x}\boldsymbol{\beta} + \boldsymbol{\varepsilon} \tag{3.2.1}$$

where $\mathbf{Y}$ is a $(n \times 1)$ random dependent variable vector, $\mathbf{x}$ is a $(n \times k)$ nonstochastic explanatory variable matrix, $\boldsymbol{\beta}$ is a $(k \times 1)$ vector of unknown parameters $\mathbf{Y} \sim \mathrm{N}(\mathbf{x}\boldsymbol{\beta}, \sigma^2\mathbf{I}_n)$ and $\boldsymbol{\varepsilon} \sim \mathrm{N}(\mathbf{0}, \sigma^2\mathbf{I}_n)$.

Given the normality assumption, we can define the joint probability density function for a sample of observations $\mathbf{y}$ as

$$\mathrm{f}(\mathbf{y}; \mathbf{x}, \boldsymbol{\beta}, \sigma^2) = (2\pi\sigma^2)^{-n/2} \exp\left[\frac{-(\mathbf{y} - \mathbf{x}\boldsymbol{\beta})'(\mathbf{y} - \mathbf{x}\boldsymbol{\beta})}{2\sigma^2}\right]. \tag{3.2.2}$$

If $\boldsymbol{\beta}$ and σ^2 were known, we could then make probability statements about outcomes of $\mathbf{Y}$. In this fully parameterized model formulation, a notable amount of information about the sampling process is available, but the parameters $\boldsymbol{\beta}$ and σ^2 nonetheless remain unknown and unobservable. We now examine a criterion that suggests how we might make use of the additional sample information to estimate and make inferences about $\boldsymbol{\beta}$ and σ^2.

3.2.2. The Maximum Likelihood (ML) Criterion

Considering the problem of how to make use of the information provided by the specification of an explicit parametric family of joint density functions such as (3.2.2), R. A. Fisher had the idea of choosing values for the unknowns $\boldsymbol{\beta}$ and σ^2 that would identify the particular PDF in the parametric family that assigned the maximum probability or probability density to the event of obtaining the sample outcome $\mathbf{y}$ actually observed. Thus, in essence, the ML principle chooses the probability density for which the actual observed data outcome is most probable or likely. More formally, in terms of (3.2.2), Fisher's idea was to find a set of parameter values $\boldsymbol{\beta}, \sigma^2$ that maximized the likelihood function, where the likelihood function is simply a reinterpretation of $\mathrm{f}(\mathbf{y}; \mathbf{x}, \boldsymbol{\beta}, \sigma^2)$ as a function of $\boldsymbol{\beta}$ and σ^2, given the values of $\mathbf{y}$ and $\mathbf{x}$, and is denoted by $\mathrm{L}(\boldsymbol{\beta}, \sigma^2; \mathbf{y}, \mathbf{x})$. That is, the algebraic expressions that define both the likelihood function and the joint PDF of the random sample are identical. Consequently, the likelihood function for the problem at hand is

$$\mathrm{L}(\boldsymbol{\beta}, \sigma^2; \mathbf{y}, \mathbf{x}) = \mathrm{f}(\mathbf{y}; \mathbf{x}, \boldsymbol{\beta}, \sigma^2) = (2\pi\sigma^2)^{-n/2} \exp\left[\frac{-(\mathbf{y} - \mathbf{x}\boldsymbol{\beta})'(\mathbf{y} - \mathbf{x}\boldsymbol{\beta})}{2\sigma^2}\right]. \tag{3.2.3}$$

Note that the likelihood function involves all of the unknown parameters of the probability model for the sample data $\mathbf{y}$.

In terms of a general formulation of the ML inverse problem, we denote all of the unknown parameters of the statistical model generically by the vector $\boldsymbol{\theta}$. The value of the likelihood function $\mathrm{L}(\boldsymbol{\theta}; \boldsymbol{y}, \boldsymbol{x})$ is the probability density or mass function of the random sample $\mathbf{Y}$ evaluated at $\mathbf{y}$ and indexed by $\boldsymbol{\theta} \in \Omega$. If each y_i depends on explanatory variables only through the values of $\mathbf{x}[i, .]$, the likelihood function for an iid data sample is given by $L(\boldsymbol{\theta}; \mathbf{y}, \mathbf{x}) = \prod_{i=1}^{n} L(\boldsymbol{\theta}; y_i, \mathbf{x}[i, .])$. Given the observed sample data $\mathbf{y}$, the ML estimate of $\boldsymbol{\theta}$ is the vector $\hat{\boldsymbol{\theta}}$ such that $L(\hat{\boldsymbol{\theta}};\ \mathbf{y},\ \mathbf{x}) \geq L(\boldsymbol{\theta};\ \mathbf{y}, \mathbf{x})$ for all $\boldsymbol{\theta} \in \Omega$, and the estimate is unique if the inequality is strict. In many applications, the ML estimate can be represented as the value of $\boldsymbol{\theta}$ that solves the set of first-order conditions $\frac{\partial L(\boldsymbol{\theta};\mathbf{y},\mathbf{x})}{\partial \boldsymbol{\theta}} = \mathbf{0}$. In any case, the choice of $\boldsymbol{\theta}$ that maximizes $L(\boldsymbol{\theta};\ \mathbf{y}, \mathbf{x})$ will be a function of the outcome $\mathbf{y}$ of $\mathbf{Y}$. The ML *estimator* is then the random variable $\hat{\boldsymbol{\theta}}(\mathbf{Y})$ that maps the observed outcome of $\mathbf{Y}$ to the ML estimate.

3.2.3. Maximum Likelihood Estimators for β and σ^2

To determine an ML estimator for $\boldsymbol{\beta}$ and σ^2, assume a sample of observations $\mathbf{y}$ has been obtained from the DSP based on the normal probability model. To simplify the maximum likelihood estimation problem, we rewrite the likelihood function (3.2.3) in the following logarithmic form:

$$\ln L(\boldsymbol{\beta}, \sigma^2; \mathbf{y}, \mathbf{x}) = -\frac{n}{2}\ln 2\pi - \frac{n}{2}\ln\sigma^2 - \frac{(\mathbf{y}-\mathbf{x}\boldsymbol{\beta})'(\mathbf{y}-\mathbf{x}\boldsymbol{\beta})}{2\sigma^2}. \tag{3.2.4}$$

Because the logarithmic transformation is monotonically increasing in L, the maxima of ln(L) and L occur at precisely the same value of $(\boldsymbol{\beta}, \sigma^2)$. The ML estimates for $\boldsymbol{\beta}$ and σ^2 can be obtained by solving the following optimality (first-order) conditions:

$$\frac{\partial \ln L(\boldsymbol{\beta}, \sigma^2; \mathbf{y}, \mathbf{x})}{\partial \boldsymbol{\beta}} = \frac{\mathbf{x}'\mathbf{y} - \mathbf{x}'\mathbf{x}\boldsymbol{\beta}}{\sigma^2} = \mathbf{0} \tag{3.2.5}$$

and

$$\frac{\partial \ln L(\boldsymbol{\beta}, \sigma^2; \mathbf{y}, \mathbf{x})}{\partial \sigma^2} = \frac{-n}{2\sigma^2} + \frac{1}{2\sigma^4}(\mathbf{y}-\mathbf{x}\boldsymbol{\beta})'(\mathbf{y}-\mathbf{x}\boldsymbol{\beta}) = 0 \tag{3.2.6}$$

The ML estimate of $\boldsymbol{\beta}$ is given by

$$\hat{\mathbf{b}} = (\mathbf{x}'\mathbf{x})^{-1}\mathbf{x}'\mathbf{y}, \tag{3.2.7}$$

and the ML estimate of σ^2 is given by

$$S^2_{\mathrm{ML}} = (\mathbf{y} - \mathbf{x}\hat{\mathbf{b}})'(\mathbf{y} - \mathbf{x}\hat{\mathbf{b}})/n. \tag{3.2.8}$$

► **Example 3.2.1:** To demonstrate the likelihood concepts, we consider a simple location model $\mathbf{Y} = \beta + \varepsilon$ for which $\varepsilon \sim N(\mathbf{0}, \mathbf{I})$. The GAUSS program requests a value for β and the sample size n from the user and then uses the procedure rndn() to generate a pseudorandom sample. For the given sample, GAUSS plots the associated likelihood function for a range of values for β. The reader should find that the maximum of the likelihood function coincides with the maximum likelihood estimate of β, the sample average of the observed $\mathbf{y}$.

3.2.4. Distribution, Moments, and Bias Properties of the ML Estimator

Because the ML estimator for $\boldsymbol{\beta}$ is a linear combination of the multivariate normally distributed vector $\mathbf{Y}$, and because we know that $\mathbf{cY} \sim \mathrm{N}(\mathbf{cx}\boldsymbol{\beta}, \sigma^2\mathbf{cIc}')$ if $\mathbf{Y} \sim \mathrm{N}(\mathbf{x}\boldsymbol{\beta}, \sigma^2\mathbf{I})$ (see Chapter E1; or Mittelhammer, p. 206), it follows that the ML estimator

$$\hat{\boldsymbol{\beta}} = (\mathbf{x}'\mathbf{x})^{-1}\mathbf{x}'\mathbf{Y} \tag{3.2.9}$$

has a normal distribution $\mathrm{N}(\boldsymbol{\beta}, \sigma^2(\mathbf{x}'\mathbf{x})^{-1})$. Therefore, the ML estimator $\hat{\boldsymbol{\beta}}$ has a mean vector $\boldsymbol{\beta}$, and thus the estimator is *unbiased* and its covariance matrix is equal to $\sigma^2(\mathbf{x}'\mathbf{x})^{-1}$.

A check of the sampling characteristics of the ML estimator for σ^2 reveals that it has mean

$$\begin{aligned} \mathrm{E}\left[\mathrm{S}^2_{\mathrm{ML}}\right] &= \mathrm{E}\left[\frac{(\mathbf{Y} - \mathbf{x}\hat{\boldsymbol{\beta}})'(\mathbf{Y} - \mathbf{x}\hat{\boldsymbol{\beta}})}{n}\right] \\ &= \mathrm{E}\left[\frac{\boldsymbol{\varepsilon}'(\mathbf{I}_n - \mathbf{x}(\mathbf{x}'\mathbf{x})^{-1}\mathbf{x}')\boldsymbol{\varepsilon}}{n}\right] = \mathrm{E}\left[\frac{\boldsymbol{\varepsilon}'\mathbf{m}\boldsymbol{\varepsilon}}{n}\right], \\ &= \mathrm{E}\left[\frac{\boldsymbol{\varepsilon}'\mathbf{m}\boldsymbol{\varepsilon}}{n-k}\right]\left(\frac{n-k}{n}\right) = \frac{\sigma^2(n-k)}{n} \end{aligned} \tag{3.2.10}$$

where we have used the substitution $\mathbf{Y} - \mathbf{x}\hat{\boldsymbol{\beta}} = [\mathbf{I}_n - \mathbf{x}(\mathbf{x}'\mathbf{x})^{-1}\mathbf{x}']\boldsymbol{\varepsilon} = \mathbf{m}\boldsymbol{\varepsilon}$, and that the matrix $\mathbf{m}$ is symmetric and idempotent. Consequently, $\mathrm{S}^2_{\mathrm{ML}}$ is a *biased* estimator of σ^2. However, for fixed k, the bias diminishes and converges to zero as the sample size n increases.

We can determine the variance and sampling distribution of $\mathrm{S}^2_{\mathrm{ML}}$ by first noting that because $\boldsymbol{\varepsilon} \sim \mathrm{N}(\mathbf{0}, \sigma^2\mathbf{I}_n)$, $\sigma^{-1}\boldsymbol{\varepsilon} \sim \mathrm{N}(\mathbf{0}, \mathbf{I}_n)$ and $\mathbf{m}$ is idempotent with rank $(n-k)$, then $\boldsymbol{\varepsilon}'\mathbf{m}\boldsymbol{\varepsilon}/\sigma^2 \sim \chi^2_{n-k}$, which is a general result concerning symmetric idempotent quadratic forms in iid standard normal random variables (see Section 4.2 in Chapter 4 for further results along these lines). It follows from moment properties of the Chi-square distribution that $\mathrm{E}[\boldsymbol{\varepsilon}'\mathbf{m}\boldsymbol{\varepsilon}/\sigma^2] = n-k$ and $\mathrm{var}(\boldsymbol{\varepsilon}'\mathbf{m}\boldsymbol{\varepsilon}/\sigma^2) = 2(n-k)$. Therefore,

$$\mathrm{var}\left(\mathrm{S}^2_{\mathrm{ML}}\right) = \mathrm{var}\left(\frac{\sigma^2}{n}\frac{\boldsymbol{\varepsilon}'\mathbf{m}\boldsymbol{\varepsilon}}{\sigma^2}\right) = \frac{2\sigma^4(n-k)}{n^2}, \tag{3.2.11}$$

and if either the change of variable or moment generating approach for deriving the distribution of $\mathrm{S}^2_{\mathrm{ML}}$ is used, it follows that

$$\mathrm{S}^2_{\mathrm{ML}} \sim \mathrm{Gamma}\left(\frac{n-k}{2}, \frac{2\sigma^2}{n}\right). \tag{3.2.12}$$

The bias-corrected MLE is most often used in practice to estimate σ^2 and is defined by

$$\mathrm{S}^2 = \frac{(\mathbf{Y} - \mathbf{x}\hat{\boldsymbol{\beta}})'(\mathbf{Y} - \mathbf{x}\hat{\boldsymbol{\beta}})}{n-k} = \left(\frac{n}{n-k}\right)\mathrm{S}^2_{\mathrm{ML}}, \tag{3.2.13}$$

so that

$$\mathrm{E}[\mathrm{S}^2] = \sigma^2, \quad \mathrm{var}(\mathrm{S}^2) = \frac{2\sigma^4}{n-k}, \quad \text{and} \quad \mathrm{S}^2 \sim \mathrm{Gamma}\left(\frac{n-k}{2}, \frac{2\sigma^2}{n-k}\right). \tag{3.2.14}$$

► **Example 3.2.2:** Although the reader should be able to verify the distributional properties presented in Section 3.2.4, we note that we can also use a Monte Carlo simulation exercise to demonstrate the results numerically. The GAUSS program provided in the examples manual generates pseudorandom draws for a normal linear regression model. For each replicated sample, GAUSS computes and stores the ML estimate of $\boldsymbol{\beta}$. The sample mean, covariance, and empirical distribution function (EDF) of the simulated estimates are computed and compared with the expected value, covariance, and cumulative distribution function (CDF) of the actual normal sampling distribution for the ML estimator.

3.3. Efficiency of the Bias-Adjusted ML Estimators of β and σ^2

Given that ε and $\mathbf{Y}$ are each multivariate normally distributed, we can show that $\hat{\boldsymbol{\beta}}$ and S^2 are efficient estimators of $\boldsymbol{\beta}$ and σ^2 within the class of unbiased estimators. That is, $(\hat{\boldsymbol{\beta}}, S^2)$ is the minimum variance unbiased estimator (MVUE) of $(\boldsymbol{\beta}, \sigma^2)$. Note in particular that this result implies that the MLE $\hat{\boldsymbol{\beta}}$ is the BLUE (best linear unbiased estimator) for $\boldsymbol{\beta}$ because the linear (in $\mathbf{Y}$) estimator $\hat{\boldsymbol{\beta}}$ is best in the class of *all* unbiased estimators, and thus it is surely the best within the restricted class of *linear* unbiased estimators of $\boldsymbol{\beta}$ as well.

Given that $\hat{\boldsymbol{\beta}}$ and S^2 are unbiased, the issue of efficiency can be addressed in a relatively straightforward way by invoking Lehmann–Scheffe's Completeness theorem (Chapter E2; Mittelhammer, p. 420). What is involved is showing that $\hat{\boldsymbol{\beta}}$ and S^2 are functions of complete sufficient statistics, which then implies immediately by the "unbiasedness" of these estimators that the estimator $(\hat{\boldsymbol{\beta}}, S^2)$ is MVUE. Regarding sufficiency, recall that sufficient statistics are a collection of functions of the random sample that summarizes all of the information in the data useful for estimating the unknown parameter vector (or functions of it). To show that $\hat{\boldsymbol{\beta}}$ and S^2 are functions of sufficient statistics, and indeed that they are sufficient statistics themselves, first rewrite the joint density of $\mathbf{Y}$ equivalently as

$$f(\mathbf{y}; \mathbf{x}, \boldsymbol{\beta}, \sigma^2) = (2\pi\sigma^2)^{-n/2} \exp\left\{-\frac{1}{2\sigma^2}[(n-k)S^2 + (\hat{\mathbf{b}} - \boldsymbol{\beta})'\mathbf{x}'\mathbf{x}(\hat{\mathbf{b}} - \boldsymbol{\beta})]\right\}. \quad (3.3.1)$$

Then by a direct application of the Neyman Factorization theorem (Chapter E2; Mittelhammer, p. 392), it is evident that because the joint PDF can be factored into a function of $(S^2, \hat{\mathbf{b}}, \boldsymbol{\beta}, \sigma)$(say (3.3.1) itself) and a function of $\mathbf{y}$ not involving the parameters (say the constant function $h(\mathbf{y}) \equiv 1$), $\hat{\boldsymbol{\beta}}$ and S^2 are sufficient statistics for the parameters. In addition to being sufficient statistics, it can be shown that $\hat{\boldsymbol{\beta}}$ and S^2 are also functions of *complete* sufficient statistics and are complete sufficient statistics themselves and thus that the MVUE property follows. The most direct way of demonstrating this result is by noting that (3.3.1) belongs to the exponential class of distributions and then using the close connection between this class of distributions and complete sufficient statistics (Chapter E2; Mittelhammer, pp. 462–3).

Another way to investigate the efficiency of $\hat{\boldsymbol{\beta}}$ and S^2 is through establishing the Cramer–Rao lower bound (CRLB) on the covariance matrix of unbiased estimators of

$(\hat{\boldsymbol{\beta}}, \sigma^2)$ (Chapter E2; Mittelhammer p. 412). The CRLB makes use of the so-called information matrix

$$\mathbf{I}(\boldsymbol{\theta}) = \mathrm{E}\left[\frac{\partial \ln \mathrm{L}(\boldsymbol{\theta}; \mathbf{Y}, \mathbf{x})}{\partial \boldsymbol{\theta}} \frac{\partial \ln \mathrm{L}(\boldsymbol{\theta}; \mathbf{Y}, \mathbf{x})}{\partial \boldsymbol{\theta}'}\right] = -\mathrm{E}\left[\frac{\partial^2 \ln \mathrm{L}(\boldsymbol{\theta}; \mathbf{Y}, \mathbf{x})}{\partial \boldsymbol{\theta} \partial \boldsymbol{\theta}'}\right], \tag{3.3.2}$$

which for the case at hand equals

$$\mathbf{I}(\boldsymbol{\beta}, \sigma^2) = \begin{bmatrix} \sigma^{-2}\mathbf{x}'\mathbf{x} & \mathbf{0} \\ \mathbf{0} & \dfrac{n}{2\sigma^4} \end{bmatrix}. \tag{3.3.3}$$

The inverse of $\mathbf{I}(\boldsymbol{\beta}, \sigma^2)$ is given by

$$\mathbf{I}(\boldsymbol{\beta}, \sigma^2)^{-1} = \begin{bmatrix} \sigma^2(\mathbf{x}'\mathbf{x})^{-1} & \mathbf{0} \\ \mathbf{0} & \dfrac{2\sigma^4}{n} \end{bmatrix} \tag{3.3.4}$$

and represents a lower bound (i.e., the CRLB) for the covariance matrix of any unbiased estimators of $\boldsymbol{\beta}$ and σ^2. Specifically, for any unbiased estimator $\hat{\boldsymbol{\theta}}$, $\mathbf{cov}(\hat{\boldsymbol{\theta}}) \succeq \mathbf{I}(\boldsymbol{\theta})^{-1}$, meaning that the resulting difference $\mathbf{cov}(\hat{\boldsymbol{\theta}}) - \mathbf{I}(\boldsymbol{\theta})^{-1}$ is positive semidefinite. The covariance matrix for the unbiased estimators $\hat{\boldsymbol{\beta}}$ and S^2 is

$$\mathbf{cov}(\hat{\boldsymbol{\beta}}, \mathrm{S}^2) = \begin{bmatrix} \sigma^2(\mathbf{x}'\mathbf{x})^{-1} & \mathbf{0} \\ \mathbf{0} & \dfrac{2\sigma^4}{n-k} \end{bmatrix}. \tag{3.3.5}$$

Thus, the CRLB is attained for the covariance matrix of $\hat{\boldsymbol{\beta}}$ but not for the variance of S^2. This proves that $\hat{\boldsymbol{\beta}}$ is the MVUE of $\boldsymbol{\beta}$ but leaves the MVUE property unsettled with regard to S^2. However, even though the variance of S^2 does not attain its CRLB, we know from our previous discussion based on complete sufficient statistics that an unbiased estimator of σ^2 with a variance smaller than $\mathrm{var}(S^2) = 2\sigma^4/(n-k)$ does *not* exist. Thus, although S^2 does not achieve the CRLB, it is nevertheless the MVUE of σ^2.

► **Example 3.3.1:** We include the GAUSS program C3MLE.gss in the examples manual to demonstrate the calculation of the numerical ML estimates of $\boldsymbol{\beta}$ and σ^2. Then we use two methods to compute estimates of information matrix and the covariance matrix of the ML estimator. The Newton–Raphson algorithm is used to compute the numerical ML estimates, and the reader can refer to Chapter 8 for more details regarding the algorithm.

3.4. Consistency, Asymptotic Normality, and Asymptotic Efficiency of ML Estimators of β and σ^2

3.4.1. Consistency

Consistency of the ML estimator of $\boldsymbol{\beta}$ can be demonstrated if two additional probability model assumptions are made relating to the limiting behavior of the $\boldsymbol{x}$ matrix. In particular, it is sufficient that the matrix $\mathbf{x}$ be such that $(\mathbf{x}'\mathbf{x})^{-1}$ exists for all n (so that the ML estimator exists), and $\mathrm{tr}(\mathbf{x}'\mathbf{x})^{-1} \to \mathbf{0}$ as $n \to \infty$. Furthermore, the fact that $\mathrm{E}[\hat{\boldsymbol{\beta}}] = \boldsymbol{\beta}$ and $\mathrm{var}(\hat{\beta}_j) \to 0$ as $n \to \infty\ \forall j$ (because $\sigma^2 \mathrm{tr}(\mathbf{x}'\mathbf{x})^{-1} = \sum_{j=1}^{k} \mathrm{var}(\beta_j)$) implies that $\hat{\boldsymbol{\beta}} \xrightarrow{p} \boldsymbol{\beta}$ via mean-square convergence of $\hat{\boldsymbol{\beta}}$ to $\boldsymbol{\beta}$. This is a mild restriction on $\mathbf{x}$ that should most often be achieved in practice. In effect, all that is required is that $\mathrm{tr}(\mathbf{x}'\mathbf{x}) = \sum_{i=1}^{n} \sum_{j=1}^{k} \mathrm{x}_{ij}^2 \to \infty$ as $n \to \infty$ and that the ratio of the largest to the smallest eigenvalues of $\mathbf{x}'\mathbf{x}$ (i.e., the *condition number* of $\boldsymbol{x}'\boldsymbol{x}$) is upper bounded. An upper bound on the condition number of $\boldsymbol{x}'\boldsymbol{x}$ implies that the columns in $\boldsymbol{x}$ are prevented from becoming too close to exhibiting linear dependence and concomitantly that the $\boldsymbol{x}'\boldsymbol{x}$ matrix is prevented from becoming too close to being singular. We formalize this result in the following theorem.

Theorem 3.4.1 (Consistency of the ML Estimator of $\boldsymbol{\beta}$): *Assume the conditions of the probability model in Table 3.1 and assume further that* $\mathrm{tr}(\mathbf{x}'\mathbf{x}) = \sum_{i=1}^{n} \sum_{j=1}^{k} \mathrm{x}_{ij}^2 \to \infty$ *as* $n \to \infty$ *and the ratio of the largest to the smallest eigenvalues of* $\mathbf{x}'\mathbf{x}$ *is upper-bounded as* $\frac{\lambda_L(\mathbf{x}'\mathbf{x})}{\lambda_s(\mathbf{x}'\mathbf{x})} \leq \delta$, *where* δ *is some finite positive constant. Then* $\hat{\boldsymbol{\beta}} \xrightarrow{p} \boldsymbol{\beta}$.

Thus, as the number of sample observations increases, all of the hypothetical outcomes of the ML estimator eventually cluster in a small neighborhood around the appropriate value of the unknown and unobservable $\boldsymbol{\beta}$, whatever its value, with probability converging to 1. We are thus assured that the ML estimator will recover the appropriate value of $\boldsymbol{\beta}$ for a large enough sample size.

► **Example 3.4.1:** In general, we cannot prove that an estimator is consistent by numerical simulation. However, we can demonstrate the consistency of the ML estimator of $\boldsymbol{\beta}$ given that we know the property holds for a particular model. In a GAUSS exercise, the reader selects up to four sample sizes (n) for a simple linear regression model as well as the number of Monte Carlo trials (m) to conduct for each version of the model. Then, the sampling distributions of the estimator are simulated for each sample size, and the accompanying box plots should indicate that the sampling distribution becomes more concentrated on the true parameter values as the sample size becomes large (see examples manual).

We can also show that the bias-adjusted ML estimator S^2 is a *consistent* estimator of σ^2. The proof of this result follows directly from the gamma distribution of S^2 and mean square convergence.

Theorem 3.4.2 (Consistency of S^2 for Estimating σ^2): *Under the assumptions of the probability model in Table 3.1,* $\mathrm{S}^2 \xrightarrow{p} \sigma^2$.

Thus, as the number of sample observations increases, all of the hypothetical outcomes of the bias-adjusted ML estimator S^2 eventually cluster in a small neighborhood around the appropriate value of the unknown and unobservable σ^2, whatever its value, with probability converging to 1. We are assured that the ML estimator will recover the appropriate value of σ^2 for a large enough sample size. The reader can extend Theorem 3.4.2 using the probability limit relationship

$$\text{plim}\left(\mathrm{S}^2_{\mathrm{ML}}\right) = \text{plim}\left(\frac{n-k}{n}S^2\right) = \text{plim}\left(\frac{n-k}{n}\right)\text{plim}(\mathrm{S}^2) = 1\cdot\text{plim}(S^2) \tag{3.4.1}$$

to show that the biased ML estimator $\mathrm{S}^2_{\mathrm{ML}}$ is also a consistent estimator of σ^2.

► **Example 3.4.2:** To assist the reader in computing the bias-adjusted ML estimator of σ^2, we provide the GAUSS procedure s2(). Then, we use a Monte Carlo simulation exercise to demonstrate the consistency of the bias-adjusted ML estimator. As in Example 3.4.1, the reader selects the size of the replicated samples (n) and the number of Monte Carlo trials (m). GAUSS presents box plots of the simulated sampling distributions for the bias-adjusted estimator, and the reader should find that these become more concentrated on the true value of σ^2 as n becomes large.

3.4.2. Asymptotic Normality

Regarding the asymptotic normality of $\hat{\boldsymbol{\beta}}$, first note that $\hat{\boldsymbol{\beta}}$ is in fact normally distributed for every n, that is, $\hat{\boldsymbol{\beta}} \sim N(\boldsymbol{\beta}, \sigma^2(\mathbf{x}'\mathbf{x})^{-1})$, as noted previously in Section 3.2.4. Therefore, the issue of asymptotic or approximate normality is somewhat moot. Nonetheless, for completeness, and as a precursor to more involved asymptotic arguments in later chapters, we provide a simple argument supporting the assertion that the ML estimator of $\boldsymbol{\beta}$ is *asymptotically* normally distributed.

Given the finite sample normality of $\hat{\boldsymbol{\beta}}$, it follows via standard results on the distribution of linear combinations of multivariate normally distributed random variables and properties of the symmetric square-root matrix ($\mathbf{m}^{1/2}\mathbf{m}^{-1}\mathbf{m}^{1/2} = \mathbf{I}$) that

$$(\mathbf{x}'\mathbf{x})^{1/2}(\hat{\boldsymbol{\beta}} - \boldsymbol{\beta}) \sim N(\mathbf{0}, \sigma^2\mathbf{I}), \forall n. \tag{3.4.2}$$

Regarding the definition and properties of the symmetric square-root matrix used in (3.4.2), note that, because ($\mathbf{x}'\mathbf{x}$) is a positive definite symmetric matrix, there always exists a symmetric square-root matrix for ($\mathbf{x}'\mathbf{x}$), which we denote by $(\mathbf{x}'\mathbf{x})^{1/2}$, such that $(\mathbf{x}'\mathbf{x})^{1/2}(\mathbf{x}'\mathbf{x})^{-1}(\mathbf{x}'\mathbf{x})^{1/2} = \mathbf{I}_k$. In particular this symmetric square-root matrix can be defined by $(\mathbf{x}'\mathbf{x})^{1/2} \equiv \mathbf{p}\boldsymbol{\Lambda}^{1/2}\mathbf{p}'$, where $\boldsymbol{\Lambda}$ is the diagonal matrix of eigenvalues of ($\mathbf{x}'\mathbf{x}$), $\boldsymbol{\Lambda}^{1/2}$ is the diagonal matrix obtained from $\boldsymbol{\Lambda}$ by replacing its diagonal with the square roots of the diagonal elements of $\boldsymbol{\Lambda}$, and $\mathbf{p}$ is the corresponding eigenvector matrix. It follows that

$$\begin{aligned}(\mathbf{x}'\mathbf{x})^{1/2}(\mathbf{x}'\mathbf{x})^{-1}(\mathbf{x}'\mathbf{x})^{1/2} &= (\mathbf{p}\boldsymbol{\Lambda}^{1/2}\mathbf{p}')(\mathbf{p}\boldsymbol{\Lambda}^{-1}\mathbf{p}')(\mathbf{p}\boldsymbol{\Lambda}^{1/2}\mathbf{p}') \\ &= \mathbf{p}\boldsymbol{\Lambda}^{1/2}\boldsymbol{\Lambda}^{-1}\boldsymbol{\Lambda}^{1/2}\mathbf{p}' = \mathbf{p}\mathbf{p}' = \mathbf{I}_k \end{aligned} \tag{3.4.3}$$

because $\mathbf{p}'\mathbf{p} = \mathbf{p}\mathbf{p}' = \mathbf{I}_n$ and $\mathbf{p}' = \mathbf{p}^{-1}$ for eigenvectors of symmetric positive definite matrices (see matrix review manual for more details and examples).

Associated with the sequence of random vectors

$$\{(\mathbf{x}'\mathbf{x})^{1/2}(\hat{\boldsymbol{\beta}} - \boldsymbol{\beta}), n = 1, 2, 3, \ldots\}, \tag{3.4.4}$$

it follows from (3.4.2) that there is the respective sequence of probability distributions given by

$$\{N(\mathbf{0}, \sigma^2\mathbf{I}), n = 1, 2, 3, \ldots\}. \tag{3.4.5}$$

It follows trivially that the limiting distribution of the sequence of identical $N(\mathbf{0}, \sigma^2\mathbf{I})$ distributions is the distribution $N(\mathbf{0}, \sigma^2\mathbf{I})$ itself. Therefore, we have that

$$(\mathbf{x}'\mathbf{x})^{1/2}(\hat{\boldsymbol{\beta}} - \boldsymbol{\beta}) \xrightarrow{d} N(\mathbf{0}, \sigma^2\mathbf{I}) \tag{3.4.6}$$

from which it follows directly that

$$\hat{\boldsymbol{\beta}} \overset{a}{\sim} \mathrm{N}(\boldsymbol{\beta}, \sigma^2(\mathbf{x}'\mathbf{x})^{-1}). \tag{3.4.7}$$

Regarding the asymptotic distribution of the bias-adjusted ML estimator S^2, it can be shown under the assumptions in Table 3.1 that S^2 is asymptotically normally distributed with mean σ^2 and asymptotic variance $2\sigma^4/n$ as

$$\mathrm{S}^2 \overset{a}{\sim} \mathrm{N}(\sigma^2, 2\sigma^4/n) \tag{3.4.8}$$

Theorem 3.4.3 (Asymptotic Normality of $\mathbf{S^2}$ for Estimating $\boldsymbol{\sigma^2}$): *Under the assumptions of the probability model in Table 3.1, it follows that* $(\frac{2\sigma^4}{n})^{-1/2}(S^2 - \sigma^2) \xrightarrow{d} N(0, 1)$ *and thus* $\mathrm{S}^2 \overset{a}{\sim} N(\sigma^2, (\frac{2\sigma^4}{n}))$.

(for proofs, see Appendix 3.10; Mittelhammer, p. 447). The reader can extend the reach of (3.4.8) to the case of the biased ML estimator $\mathrm{S}^2_{\mathrm{ML}}$ by arguing that the factor $n/(n-k)$ that separates S^2 from S^2_{ML} is asymptotically negligible. It follows that the limiting distribution and asymptotic distribution results for S^2 as stated in (3.4.8) apply equally well to the ML estimator S^2_{ML}.

► **Example 3.4.3:** The result stated in Theorem 3.4.3 is based on a first-order asymptotic approximation to the distribution of S^2 (refer to the chapter appendix for the proof). As discussed in the Monte Carlo appendix, the bootstrap procedure may be used to form a numerical approximation to the distribution. For this example, GAUSS generates a single pseudorandom sample for a normal linear regression model. On the basis of the observed sample, GAUSS uses the parametric and nonparametric bootstrap estimators of the noise distribution to simulate the DSP. The bootstrap samples are used to compute the replicated S^2 estimates, and the resulting bootstrap EDFs are compared with the limiting normal CDF.

3.4.3. Asymptotic Efficiency

The issue of asymptotic efficiency is also somewhat moot because we have shown in the preceding section that $\hat{\boldsymbol{\beta}}$ is efficient $\forall n$. For completeness, we provide an argument in support of the asymptotic efficiency of the ML estimator. Let $\boldsymbol{\theta} = \binom{\boldsymbol{\beta}}{\sigma^2}$, $\mathbf{q}(\boldsymbol{\theta}) \equiv \boldsymbol{\beta}$, and note that the CRLB for estimating $\mathbf{q}(\boldsymbol{\theta})$ is given by

$$\text{CRLB}(\mathbf{q}(\boldsymbol{\theta})) = \frac{\partial \mathbf{q}(\boldsymbol{\theta})}{\partial \boldsymbol{\theta}'}[\mathbf{I}(\boldsymbol{\theta})]^{-1}\frac{\partial \mathbf{q}(\boldsymbol{\theta})}{\partial \boldsymbol{\theta}}, \tag{3.4.9}$$

where $\mathbf{I}(\boldsymbol{\theta})$ is as defined in (3.3.2). Then, if we recall the definition of $\mathbf{I}(\boldsymbol{\theta})$ presented in (3.3.3) and note that in this case, $\underset{k\times(k+1)}{\frac{\partial \mathbf{q}(\boldsymbol{\theta})}{\partial \boldsymbol{\theta}'}} = [\mathbf{I}_k : \mathbf{0}]$, it follows that

$$\left(\frac{\partial \mathbf{q}(\boldsymbol{\theta})}{\partial \boldsymbol{\theta}'}[\mathbf{I}(\boldsymbol{\theta})]^{-1}\frac{\partial \mathbf{q}(\boldsymbol{\theta})}{\partial \boldsymbol{\theta}}\right)^{-1/2}(\hat{\boldsymbol{\beta}} - \boldsymbol{\beta}) = [\sigma^2(\mathbf{x}'\mathbf{x})^{-1}]^{-1/2}(\hat{\boldsymbol{\beta}} - \boldsymbol{\beta}) \sim \mathrm{N}(\mathbf{0}, \mathbf{I})\,\forall n \tag{3.4.10}$$

and thus that convergence in distribution of the left-hand side of (3.4.10) to N(**0, I**) applies trivially. It follows immediately from (3.4.10) that an approximate or asymptotic distribution of the ML estimator $\hat{\boldsymbol{\beta}}$ is given by

$$\hat{\boldsymbol{\beta}} \overset{a}{\sim} N\left(\boldsymbol{\beta}, \left[\frac{\partial \mathbf{q}(\boldsymbol{\theta})}{\partial \boldsymbol{\theta}'}[\mathbf{I}(\boldsymbol{\theta})]^{-1}\frac{\partial \mathbf{q}(\boldsymbol{\theta})}{\partial \boldsymbol{\theta}}\right]\right) = \mathrm{N}(\boldsymbol{\beta}, \sigma^2(\mathbf{x}'\mathbf{x})^{-1}). \tag{3.4.11}$$

We thus have an estimator that *asymptotically* achieves the CRLB for estimating $\boldsymbol{\beta}$, and we can conclude that $\hat{\boldsymbol{\beta}}$ is asymptotically efficient for estimating $\boldsymbol{\beta}$ (for additional discussion on the concept of asymptotic efficiency, see chapter E2; Mittelhammer, pp. 388, 419).

Regarding the asymptotic efficiency of the bias-adjusted ML estimator S^2, let $\boldsymbol{\theta} = [{}^{\boldsymbol{\beta}}_{\sigma^2}]$ and $\mathrm{q}(\boldsymbol{\theta}) \equiv \sigma^2$. Then, if one recalls the definition of $\mathbf{I}(\boldsymbol{\theta})$ presented in (3.3.3) and notes that in this case $\underset{1\times(k+1)}{\frac{\partial \mathrm{q}(\boldsymbol{\theta})}{\partial \boldsymbol{\theta}'}} = [\mathbf{0} \vdots 1]$, it follows from (3.4.8) that

$$\left[\frac{\partial \mathrm{q}(\boldsymbol{\theta})}{\partial \boldsymbol{\theta}'}\mathbf{I}(\boldsymbol{\theta})^{-1}\frac{\partial \mathrm{q}(\boldsymbol{\theta})}{\partial \boldsymbol{\theta}}\right]^{-1/2}(\mathrm{S}^2 - \sigma^2) = \left(\frac{2\sigma^4}{n}\right)^{-1/2}(\mathrm{S}^2 - \sigma^2) \overset{d}{\to} \mathrm{N}(0, 1) \tag{3.4.12}$$

and also that

$$\mathrm{S}^2 \overset{a}{\sim} N\left(\sigma^2, \left[\frac{\partial \mathrm{q}(\boldsymbol{\theta})}{\partial \boldsymbol{\theta}'}\mathbf{I}(\boldsymbol{\theta})^{-1}\frac{\partial \mathrm{q}(\boldsymbol{\theta})}{\partial \boldsymbol{\theta}}\right]\right) = N\left(\sigma^2, \left(\frac{2\sigma^4}{n}\right)\right). \tag{3.4.13}$$

We thus have an estimator that asymptotically achieves the CRLB for estimating σ^2, and we can conclude that S^2 is asymptotically efficient for estimating σ^2.

The reader can show that the asymptotic efficiency property also applies to the biased ML estimator $\mathrm{S}^2_{\mathrm{ML}}$. The demonstration can proceed by arguing that the factor $n/(n-k)$ that separates S^2 from S^2_{ML} is asymptotically negligible. It follows that the limiting distribution and asymptotic distribution results for S^2 stated in (3.4.12) and (3.4.13) apply equally well to the ML estimator S^2_{ML}.

3.5. Summary of the Finite Sample and Asymptotic Sampling Properties of the ML Estimator

In summary, under the current statistical model assumptions, the ML estimator $\hat{\boldsymbol{\beta}}$ of $\boldsymbol{\beta}$ is unbiased, BLUE, MVUE and efficient, normally distributed in finite samples, consistent, asymptotically normally distributed, and asymptotically efficient. We emphasize that it is the multivariate normality of $\mathbf{Y}$ and ε that allows us to deduce the properties of finite sample normality as well as finite sample and asymptotic efficiency of the ML estimator for $\boldsymbol{\beta}$ within the linear regression model framework. In the absence of a parametric model assumption, such as multivariate normality, it is generally not possible to deduce the efficiency properties of the estimator. Furthermore, the finite sample normal distribution of the estimator is a direct result of the multivariate normality assumption and will not hold in the absence of this assumption.

Regarding sampling properties of the bias-adjusted ML estimator S^2 of σ^2, the estimator is unbiased, MVUE and efficient, gamma-distributed in finite samples, consistent, asymptotically normally distributed, and asymptotically efficient. We again emphasize that it is the multivariate normality of $\mathbf{Y}$ and ε that allows us to deduce the properties of the bias-adjusted ML estimator S^2 being gamma-distributed in finite samples as well as the properties of finite sample and asymptotic efficiency of this bias-adjusted ML estimator within the linear regression model framework. In the absence of a parametric model assumption, such as multivariate normality, it is generally not possible to deduce the efficiency properties of the estimator. Furthermore, the finite sample gamma distribution of the estimator is a direct result of the multivariate normality assumption and will not hold in the absence of this assumption.

Finally, regarding the sampling properties of the biased ML estimator $\mathrm{S}^2_{\mathrm{ML}}$ of σ^2, the estimator is biased in finite samples, gamma-distributed in finite samples, consistent, asymptotically normally distributed, and asymptotically efficient. The provisos regarding the connection between the multivariate normality assumption and the efficiency and finite sample distribution properties noted when discussing the sampling properties of S^2 apply equally well here.

We emphasize that the classical approach to evaluating the statistical properties of a point estimator is done in an unconditional predata context. That is, we contemplate the properties of the estimator in the context of all of the hypothetical samples of data that *could have* occurred, not in the sense of what *actually did* occur. Because the estimator is a function of the random sample $\mathbf{Y}$, the estimator itself is evaluated in the context of all of the hypothetically possible estimator outcomes that could have occurred before the data's actually being observed. This idea is represented symbolically by the very expressions for the ML estimators themselves (e.g., (3.2.9) and (3.2.13)), which indicate that estimators are functions of the random vector $\mathbf{Y}$. Thus, the estimators can conceptually assume various values depending on what outcome occurs for $\mathbf{Y}$. Note that by basing our choice and evaluation of an estimator for $\boldsymbol{\theta}$ on the sampling distribution of $\mathbf{Y}$, the information obtained about $\boldsymbol{\beta}$ from point estimation not only depends on the observed data being analyzed but also on whatever data sets one might have observed, but did not.

3.6. Estimating ε and cov($\hat{\beta}$)

To make both the finite and the asymptotic covariance matrix of $\hat{\boldsymbol{\beta}}$ operational, we need a solution to the inverse problem of recovering the value of the unknown covariance matrix $\sigma^2(\mathbf{x}'\mathbf{x})^{-1}$. We remarked previously that one solution to this problem was to replace the unknown σ^2 by the estimator S^2. We may also be interested in recovering values for the unknown and unobservable noise component $\boldsymbol{\varepsilon}$ of the linear regression model. We examine both of these inverse problems in this section.

3.6.1. An Estimator for $\boldsymbol{\varepsilon}$

Because the random noise vector is unknown and unobservable, we must again utilize indirect observations on $\boldsymbol{\varepsilon}$ in developing an estimation procedure for $\boldsymbol{\varepsilon}$. Indirect observations on the random vector $\boldsymbol{\varepsilon}$ are given by outcomes of the estimator

$$\hat{\boldsymbol{\varepsilon}} = \mathbf{Y} - \mathbf{x}\hat{\boldsymbol{\beta}} = [\mathbf{I}_n - \mathbf{x}(\mathbf{x}'\mathbf{x})^{-1}\mathbf{x}']\mathbf{Y} = [\mathbf{I}_n - \mathbf{x}(\mathbf{x}'\mathbf{x})^{-1}\mathbf{x}']\boldsymbol{\varepsilon} = \mathbf{m}\boldsymbol{\varepsilon}. \tag{3.6.1}$$

Note that $\mathbf{m}$ is a $(n \times n)$ symmetric idempotent matrix and thus that $\mathbf{m} = \mathbf{mm} = \mathbf{mm}' = \mathbf{m}'\mathbf{m}$. Furthermore, $\mathbf{m}$ has rank $(n-k)$ because the rank of an idempotent matrix equals its trace, which is given by $\text{tr}(\mathbf{m}) = \text{tr}[\mathbf{I}_n - \mathbf{x}(\mathbf{x}'\mathbf{x})^{-1}\mathbf{x}'] = \text{tr}[\mathbf{I}_n - \mathbf{x}'\mathbf{x}(\mathbf{x}'\mathbf{x})^{-1}] = \text{tr}(\mathbf{I}_n - \mathbf{I}_k) = n - k$. Because $\mathbf{m}$ is singular, it is not possible to invert $\mathbf{m}$ and solve for the unknown value of $\boldsymbol{\varepsilon}$ in (3.6.1). It is interesting to note, however, that certain linear combinations of the noise vector are in fact *observable*, namely, any linear combination $\mathbf{c}'\boldsymbol{\varepsilon}$ for which $\mathbf{c}'\mathbf{x} = \mathbf{0}$, for then it follows from (3.6.1) that $\mathbf{c}'\hat{\boldsymbol{\varepsilon}} = \mathbf{c}'\boldsymbol{\varepsilon}$.

From results on the means and covariance matrices of linear combinations of random variables, it can be shown that the expectation of $\hat{\boldsymbol{\varepsilon}}$ is identical with the expectation of $\boldsymbol{\varepsilon}$, namely $\text{E}[\hat{\boldsymbol{\varepsilon}}] = \text{E}[\boldsymbol{\varepsilon}] = \mathbf{0}$, and the covariance matrix of $\hat{\boldsymbol{\varepsilon}}$ is equal to $\mathbf{cov}(\hat{\boldsymbol{\varepsilon}}) = \sigma^2[\mathbf{I}_n - \mathbf{x}(\mathbf{x}'\mathbf{x})^{-1}\mathbf{x}'] = \sigma^2\mathbf{m}$, which is a singular matrix. Using standard results on linear combinations of multivariate normally distributed random variables, it can also be argued that, because $\boldsymbol{\varepsilon} \sim \text{N}(\mathbf{0}, \sigma^2\mathbf{I})$, then $\hat{\boldsymbol{\varepsilon}} \sim \text{N}(\mathbf{0}, \sigma^2\mathbf{m})$. Note that this latter distribution is a *singular* or *degenerate* multivariate normal distribution because the $(n \times n)$ covariance matrix $\sigma^2\mathbf{m}$ has a rank of only $(n-k)$. Furthermore, within the class of estimators that are linear functions of $\mathbf{Y}$ and that have an expectation that agrees with the expectation of $\boldsymbol{\varepsilon}$ (i.e., an expectation of zero), it can be shown that the estimator $\hat{\boldsymbol{\varepsilon}}$ defined by (3.6.1) has the smallest possible covariance matrix. Thus, in this sense, $\hat{\boldsymbol{\varepsilon}}$ can be thought of as the *best linear unbiased estimator* of the noise component.

Regarding the large sample behavior of the estimator $\hat{\boldsymbol{\varepsilon}}$, if $\mathbf{x}(\mathbf{x}'\mathbf{x})^{-1}\mathbf{x}' \to \mathbf{0}$ as $n \to \infty$, then it is intuitively reasonable to conclude from (3.6.1) that the entries in $\hat{\boldsymbol{\varepsilon}}$ would converge in probability, and thus in distribution, to the corresponding elements in $\boldsymbol{\varepsilon}$. This result is proved in the appendix, Section 3.10. Then asymptotically, the elements of $\hat{\boldsymbol{\varepsilon}}$ and $\boldsymbol{\varepsilon}$ coincide, and thus in the limit the inverse problem of recovering point-value information about the $\boldsymbol{\varepsilon}$ outcomes $\mathbf{e}$ is amply solved because $\hat{\boldsymbol{\varepsilon}}$ fully recovers information about the sampling behavior of $\boldsymbol{\varepsilon}$. Note further that the asymptotic or limiting probability distribution of $\hat{\varepsilon}_i$ is the univariate normal distribution $\text{N}(0, \sigma^2)$ because the probability distribution of $\hat{\varepsilon}_i$ is coincident with whatever the distribution of ε_i happens to be in the limit as $n \to \infty$ and $\varepsilon_i \sim \text{N}(0, \sigma^2)$. Also note that for the consistency result to hold, it is *not* sufficient that $(\mathbf{x}'\mathbf{x})^{-1} \to \mathbf{0}$ because, for example, an $\mathbf{x}$ matrix consisting of the single column vector $\mathbf{x} = (2^1, 2^2, 2^3, \ldots)'$ satisfies $(\mathbf{x}'\mathbf{x})^{-1} \to \mathbf{0}$ but not $\mathbf{x}(\mathbf{x}'\mathbf{x})^{-1}\mathbf{x}' \to \mathbf{0}$. The convergence condition $(\mathbf{x}'\mathbf{x})^{-1} \to \mathbf{0}$ *is* sufficient for the convergence condition $\mathbf{x}(\mathbf{x}'\mathbf{x})^{-1}\mathbf{x}' \to \mathbf{0}$ if the entries in $\mathbf{x}$ are *bounded* in absolute value, which is a reasonable assumption in most applied problems.

3.6.2. An Estimator for $\mathbf{cov}(\hat{\boldsymbol{\beta}})$

Having recovered information on the point value of σ^2 through the use of the bias-adjusted ML estimator S^2, as discussed in Sections 3.2–3.4, we are now in a position to revisit the problem of generating an operational version of the finite sample and asymptotic covariance matrices of $\hat{\boldsymbol{\beta}}$, both of which are represented by $\mathbf{cov}(\hat{\boldsymbol{\beta}}) = \sigma^2(\mathbf{x}'\mathbf{x})^{-1}$. In particular, an estimator of the covariance matrix can be defined simply by replacing the unknown and unobservable σ^2 with the unbiased and consistent estimator S^2. We then obtain an estimator of the covariance matrix as follows:

$$\widehat{\mathbf{cov}}(\hat{\boldsymbol{\beta}}) = S^2(\mathbf{x}'\mathbf{x})^{-1}. \tag{3.6.2}$$

The estimator is *unbiased* because

$$E[\widehat{\mathbf{cov}}(\hat{\boldsymbol{\beta}})] = E[S^2(\mathbf{x}'\mathbf{x})^{-1}] = E[S^2](\mathbf{x}'\mathbf{x})^{-1} = \sigma^2(\mathbf{x}'\mathbf{x})^{-1}. \tag{3.6.3}$$

The estimator also represents the MVUE estimator of each of the $k(k+1)/2$ unique elements $\sigma^2(\mathbf{x}'\mathbf{x})^{-1}_{i,j}$ of the covariance matrix $\mathbf{cov}(\hat{\boldsymbol{\beta}})$, where $(\mathbf{x}'\mathbf{x})^{-1}_{i,j}$ denotes the (i, j)th element of $(\mathbf{x}'\mathbf{x})^{-1}$. This follows because linear combinations of MVUE estimators are MVUE for the corresponding linear combinations of the estimands, and each element of the estimator $\widehat{\mathbf{cov}}(\hat{\boldsymbol{\beta}}) = S^2(\mathbf{x}'\mathbf{x})^{-1}$ is a linear combination (scalar multiple) of the MVUE estimator S^2 of the form $(\mathbf{x}'\mathbf{x})^{-1}_{i,j}S^2$, the corresponding linear combination of the estimand σ^2 being $(\mathbf{x}'\mathbf{x})^{-1}_{i,j}\sigma^2$ (Chapter E2; Mittelhammer, pp. 406–7). Furthermore, the covariance estimator is *consistent* in the sense that $S^2 - \sigma^2 \xrightarrow{p} 0$ implies that $\widehat{\mathbf{cov}}(\hat{\boldsymbol{\beta}}) - \mathbf{cov}(\hat{\boldsymbol{\beta}}) = (S^2 - \sigma^2)(\mathbf{x}'\mathbf{x})^{-1} \xrightarrow{p} \mathbf{0}$ if $(\mathbf{x}'\mathbf{x})^{-1}$ is $\mathbf{o}(n^{1/2})$, which can be assumed to hold very generally (in fact it is typically assumed that $(\mathbf{x}'\mathbf{x})^{-1} \to \mathbf{0}$). Finally, using results on linear combinations of (asymptotically) normally distributed random variables, one can argue that the (i, j)th element of $\mathbf{cov}(\hat{\boldsymbol{\beta}})$ is *asymptotically normally distributed* (recall (3.4.8)) as

$$\widehat{\mathbf{cov}}_{i,j}(\hat{\boldsymbol{\beta}}) \overset{a}{\sim} N\left(\sigma^2(\mathbf{x}'\mathbf{x})^{-1}_{i,j},\ \frac{2\sigma^4}{n}\left[(\mathbf{x}'\mathbf{x})^{-1}_{i,j}\right]^2\right). \tag{3.6.4}$$

3.7. Concluding Remarks

In this chapter we have introduced a method of econometric analysis for obtaining information from a sample of data in the context of the multivariate normal linear regression model. At this point we review some of the ground that has been covered in this chapter.

If it is assumed that the parametric family of probability distributions encompassing the DSP can be specified, the likelihood approach makes explicit the natural conditional idea that only the observed data $\mathbf{y}$ are relevant regarding evidence or judgments about the parameters $\boldsymbol{\theta}$. Given the observed data $\mathbf{y}$, the likelihood function $L(\boldsymbol{\theta};\mathbf{y}) = f(\mathbf{y};\boldsymbol{\theta})$

is the key concept in the likelihood approach. As we have noted, $f(\mathbf{y};\boldsymbol{\theta})$ essentially measures the propensity for $\mathbf{y}$ to occur if $\boldsymbol{\theta}$ is the parameter value. Thus, the intuition underlying the name "likelihood function" is that a value of $\boldsymbol{\theta}$ for which the probability or probability density $f(\mathbf{y};\boldsymbol{\theta})$ is large is more "likely" to be true than a value of $\boldsymbol{\theta}$ for which $f(\mathbf{y};\boldsymbol{\theta})$ is small. The ML principle chooses $f(\mathbf{y};\boldsymbol{\theta})$, through the choice of $\boldsymbol{\theta}$, that has the highest propensity to have generated the value $\mathbf{y}$ actually observed. So as an estimation criterion, it seems natural to proceed by choosing the $\boldsymbol{\theta}$, given the observed data, that maximizes the likelihood function.

Furthermore, under the likelihood principle, when making inferences about $\boldsymbol{\theta}$ after $\mathbf{y}$ is observed, we assumed that all the relevant information about $\boldsymbol{\theta}$ is contained in the likelihood function for the observed $\mathbf{y}$. At this point it is important to emphasize that the likelihood approach assumes only that all *data* information is contained in $L(\boldsymbol{\theta};\mathbf{y})$. However, such things as nonsample prior and loss function information may also be relevant in an econometric analysis. Also at this point it is helpful to remind ourselves that there is actually a sharp contrast between the likelihood and the classical unconditional perspectives. The classical approach suggests that we develop predata measures of the precision of our estimation procedures in evaluating the effectiveness of procedures. In contrast, the likelihood function is a postdata concept based on the observed sample, and the likelihood function encourages a postdata conditional method of reasoning in the face of incomplete information.

Much has been written to provide a general rationale for the likelihood approach. Perhaps the most convincing rationale in its defense is the almost universally accepted sufficiency principle, leading to the concept of sufficient statistics that are functions of the data and that summarize all the available sample information concerning $\boldsymbol{\theta}$. In this regard, Dynkin (1951) showed that knowing less than the likelihood function results in the loss of some of the information in the data. The idea that all of the data information about model parameters is represented by the likelihood function is referred to as the *likelihood principle* (Berger and Wolpert (1984)). Estimators defined as solutions to the problem of maximizing likelihood can be shown to be functions of sufficient statistics. However, one of the most glaring limitations of the likelihood approach is that there is no loss context and thus no indication of how the likelihood function *should* be used in reaching decisions or making inferences concerning $\boldsymbol{\theta}$. A natural pitfall is to try to interpret the likelihood function as some kind of probability density for $\boldsymbol{\theta}$. The Bayesian approach to inference, developed later in Chapters 22 through 24, is one way of using the likelihood function to form a posterior distribution that may be used to draw probabilistic conclusions about $\boldsymbol{\theta}$.

We will show in Chapter 7 that the general (not necessarily based on normality) ML estimator is a member of a class of estimators called "Extremum Estimators," which subsume a large majority of the estimators used in econometric practice and for which a common unified asymptotic theory can be provided. Further, we will study the concept of estimating equations in Chapter 11, which provides a *finite* sample optimality justification for the *general* ML approach that is analogous to the best linear unbiased estimator (BLUE) property of least-squares estimators to be discussed in Chapter 5.

Finally, in Appendix Section 3.9 of this chapter, we examine the concept of admissibility of the ML estimator and in so doing introduce the concept of biased estimation and indicate how one can approach the problem of estimation within a decision–theoretic framework. Readers whose understanding of normal and Chi-square distribution theory is not current may wish to read Chapter 4 before studying Section 3.9.

3.8. Exercises

3.8.1. Idea Checklist – Knowledge Guides

---

1. What is a likelihood function, and why is the rule "maximize the likelihood function" an acceptable basis for estimation and inference?
2. What is the likelihood principle? What is its relevance to performing statistical inference?
3. What is the sufficiency principle, and what is its relevance to performing statistical inference?
4. What is the purpose of examining asymptotic properties of the ML estimator? Is there any purpose to doing so when finite sample properties can be established?
5. The ML estimator was shown in the chapter appendix to be *inadmissible* – should we then not use it?
6. What would be the main differences between the properties of $\hat{\boldsymbol{\beta}}$ in the semiparametric case (i.e., in the absence of the normal distribution assumption but with the remaining assumptions in place) and the multivariate normal case of the current chapter?

3.8.2. Problems

3–1 Prove that the ML estimators for $\boldsymbol{\beta}$ and σ^2 are sufficient statistics and interpret the meaning of sufficiency.

3–2 Use the change of variable technique or the moment generating approach to prove the result stated in (3.2.12). Also, prove the result stated in (3.2.14). Discuss the relevance of your findings for the distributional properties of the ML and bias-adjusted ML estimators of σ^2.

3–3 Is it possible to develop a minimum mean-squared error estimator of σ^2? If so, demonstrate its bias and variance and compare it with the other estimators of σ^2 that we have developed. If not, why not?

3–4 Demonstrate that $\boldsymbol{\varepsilon}'\mathbf{m}\boldsymbol{\varepsilon}/\sigma^2$ is distributed as $\chi^2_{(n-k)}$.

3–5 Define how and why the CRLB is useful in establishing the efficiency of an ML estimator. Show in what sense the CRLB approach is useful in establishing the efficiency of the ML estimator of the parameter vector $(\boldsymbol{\beta}, \sigma^2)$ in the multivariate normal linear regression model.

3–6 Show that in the class of unbiased estimators of $\boldsymbol{\beta}$, the ML estimator $\hat{\boldsymbol{\beta}}$ minimizes quadratic risk,

$$\rho(\boldsymbol{\beta}, \hat{\boldsymbol{\beta}}) = \mathrm{E}(\boldsymbol{\beta} - \hat{\boldsymbol{\beta}})'(\boldsymbol{\beta} - \hat{\boldsymbol{\beta}}).$$

3–7 Repeat the preceding problem showing that the ML estimator minimizes mean forecasting risk

$$\rho(\mathbf{x}\boldsymbol{\beta}, \mathbf{x}\hat{\boldsymbol{\beta}}) = (\boldsymbol{\beta} - \hat{\boldsymbol{\beta}})'\mathbf{x}'\mathbf{x}(\boldsymbol{\beta} - \hat{\boldsymbol{\beta}}).$$

3–8 Suppose that multivariate normality is assumed for the noise component, but in fact the noise component is *not* multivariate normally distributed. Is it possible that the MLE of $\boldsymbol{\beta}$ is still consistent? Asymptotically normal? Asymptotically efficient? Explain.

3.8.3. Computer Problems

3–1 Write a GAUSS program to simulate the empirical distributions and moment properties of S^2 and S^2_{ML}. (Hint: Use the GAUSS program provided for Example 3.2.2 as a guide.) In particular, compare the simulated statistical properties of S^2 and S^2_{ML} with the analytical properties stated in (3.2.12) and (3.2.14). Do the moments and EDFs appear to converge as n becomes large? Use the GAUSS procedure cdfgam() to print the analytical CDFs on the EDF plots.

3–2 The data set in the file C3Klein.dat contains the data used by Klein to fit an aggregate consumption function known as Model I. The annual data cover the sample period 1920–41, and the variables are real aggregate consumption (C), real corporate profits (P), and real private and government wages (W).

a. Compute the ML parameter estimates and the estimated covariance matrix for the regression of consumption on an intercept plus profits, lagged profits, and wages. What is the estimated marginal propensity to consume out of wage income?
b. Compute the James–Stein estimates of the model parameters and compare the estimates with the ML estimates. How do the marginal propensity estimates compare?
c. Although the James–Stein estimator is biased with unknown covariance, we can use the bootstrap procedure (refer to the Monte Carlo book appendix) to simulate the moments of this nonlinear estimator. A simple way to simulate Klein's Model I is to resample the ML residuals and compute the parameter estimates in repeated samples (other authors have proposed more sophisticated bootstrap procedures for shrinkage estimators). Compare the empirical moments and distribution functions for the ML and James–Stein estimators.

3–3 To compare the finite sample gamma and limiting normal distributions for S^2 (refer to Equation (3.2.14) and Theorem 3.4.3), plot the CDFs for given values of σ^2, n, and, k. How do the CDFs compare as the sample size increases?

3–4 Write a GAUSS program designed to simulate the mean and variance of the error estimator $\hat{\boldsymbol{\varepsilon}}$. As well, numerically demonstrate that $\hat{\boldsymbol{\varepsilon}}$ is a consistent estimator of the noise vector. (Hint: Use Example 3.4.1 or 3.4.2 as a guide.)

3.9. Appendix: Admissibility of ML Estimator – Introduction to Biased Estimation

The maximum likelihood approach, as developed in this chapter, is central to estimation and inference in parametric probability models. The great appeal of the likelihood-based methods in parametric estimation, as well as in hypothesis testing, is due to their wide range of applicability and an asymptotic theory that provides a common normal distribution-based foundation for evaluating the ML estimator's statistical behavior when certain general regularity conditions are fulfilled. If not enough information about the underlying data-sampling process is available to specify the functional form of the likelihood function, then nonlikelihood methods are used in general such as those presented in Chapter 5.

The resulting sampling properties that underlie classical estimation procedures are *not conditioned* on the observed data and are relevant only in a hypothetical 'pre-data' sense. This classical approach provides us with a basis for evaluating information recovery procedures *before* we have seen the data. However, the concept of a likelihood function is inherently based on making use of the observed data and, thus, has a conditional perspective. Also, although maximizing the likelihood function $L(\boldsymbol{\theta}; \mathbf{y}, \mathbf{x})$ through the choice of the parameter vector $\boldsymbol{\theta}$ has intuitive appeal, the estimation objective function is not defined directly on the basis of any consideration of loss functions relating to the choice of estimator for $\boldsymbol{\theta}$.

At this point, we revisit the problem of estimating $\boldsymbol{\beta}$ in the parametric (multivariate normal) linear regression probability model from a decision–theoretic perspective and adopt a quadratic loss function to measure the severity of potential losses encountered when attempting to estimate $\boldsymbol{\beta}$. This will provide us with one possible choice of decision–theoretic context in which we can evaluate the behavior of the ML estimator relative to other competitors within the classical view of predata statistical properties. We will then see whether the heuristic and conditional-on-data likelihood approach can be improved upon in a predata evaluative context. In the linear model, under the assumption of multivariate normality, we will see that the ML estimator is *inadmissible* under quadratic loss.

A decision–theoretic framework for estimator choice will generally involve (1) a set of "states of nature" that describes our state of knowledge about the DSP, (2) a set of actions or decisions $\{D_1, D_2, \ldots, D_p\}$, and (3) a loss function $\ell(\mathbf{d}_i, \boldsymbol{\theta}_j)$ that measures the loss associated with decision $\mathbf{d}_i$ if the true state of nature is $\boldsymbol{\theta}_j$. In the context of this chapter, the states of nature are the parameters $\boldsymbol{\theta} \in \Omega$ that index the family of probability distributions, and the possible decisions represent alternative estimation procedures. Given that the estimation strategies are random variables based on $\mathbf{Y}$, the loss assigned to each decision and state is also a random variable. From the classical perspective, the predata performance of the estimators may be compared by computing the expected loss or risk, $E_{\theta_j}[\ell(D_i, \boldsymbol{\theta}_j)]$, under state $\boldsymbol{\theta}_j$. For two estimators D_1 and D_2, we say that D_1 is inadmissible relative to D_2 if $E_{\theta_j}[\ell(D_2, \boldsymbol{\theta}_j)] \leq E_{\theta_j}[\ell(D_1, \boldsymbol{\theta}_j)]$ for all j and with strict inequality for some j.

Given these decision–theoretic concepts and the likelihood method of estimation presented in this chapter, we now extend our discussion of the statistical properties of the ML approach.

3.9.1. Is the ML Estimator Inadmissible?

To this point, we examined sampling properties that we felt might give estimation rules a useful normative context. We found that the ML rule for our normal linear statistical model was minimum-variance unbiased. This is a welcome result, but one may be wondering what was given up in terms of increased sampling variability in order to have the ML estimator produce estimates that achieve their target on average. In other words, one wonders whether there could be an inverse relationship between estimator bias and sampling variability. The mean-squared error (MSE) criterion or the squared-error loss function is one way of reflecting the possible trade-off between estimator bias and variability. Consequently, if one were willing to trade a bit of increased bias for decreased estimator variance, the MSE would be a measure that could be used to reflect the bias–variance trade-off. This suggests that we seek an estimator for our multivariate normal linear regression model that may be biased but that would yield a payoff in terms of decreased sampling variability.

Charles Stein, over four decades ago, began contemplating this problem and was able to prove, under conditions generally found in practice, as well as under the multivariate normality of the noise component of the linear regression model, that under a squared-error loss function *there existed* an estimator that everywhere in the parameter space had an associated risk equal to or less than the ML estimator developed in this chapter. In other words, when a squared-error loss is used to reflect a trade-off between bias and variance, the ML estimator is *inadmissible*. This set off a search for an estimator that would achieve this enticing dominance of the widely used ML estimator. Finally, James and Stein (1961) were able to demonstrate such a normative estimation rule. It turned out to be a nonlinear function of the ML estimator.

To motivate the rule that they came up with, we use the orthonormal linear statistical model

$$\mathbf{Y} = \mathbf{x}\boldsymbol{\beta} + \varepsilon \tag{3.9.1}$$

where $\mathbf{x}'\mathbf{x} = \mathbf{I}_k$, $\varepsilon \sim \mathrm{N}(\mathbf{0}, \mathbf{I}_n)$, and the ML estimator is $\hat{\boldsymbol{\beta}} = (\mathbf{x}'\mathbf{x})^{-1}\mathbf{x}'\mathbf{Y} = \mathbf{x}'\mathbf{Y}$. Their idea was to *shrink* the ML estimator (estimates) toward zero, thereby reducing variance while possibly producing bias. This led to an estimator of the form

$$\boldsymbol{\beta}^{\mathrm{S}} = (1 - \mathrm{c}/\hat{\boldsymbol{\beta}}'\hat{\boldsymbol{\beta}})\hat{\boldsymbol{\beta}} = \hat{\boldsymbol{\beta}} - (\mathrm{c}/\hat{\boldsymbol{\beta}}'\hat{\boldsymbol{\beta}})\hat{\boldsymbol{\beta}}, \tag{3.9.2}$$

where at this point the shrinking parameter c can be considered an unspecified scalar. Our suspicion, of course, is that this is a biased estimator, and this is confirmed because

$$\mathrm{E}[\boldsymbol{\beta}^{\mathrm{S}}] = \mathrm{E}[\hat{\boldsymbol{\beta}}] - \mathrm{E}[(\mathrm{c}/\hat{\boldsymbol{\beta}}'\hat{\boldsymbol{\beta}})\hat{\boldsymbol{\beta}}], \tag{3.9.3}$$

which is generally unequal to $\boldsymbol{\beta}$ unless $c = 0$.

To represent the possible trade-off between the bias and variance of $\boldsymbol{\beta}^{\mathrm{S}}$, James and Stein used the squared-error loss measure (SEL), which implies the risk function

$$\begin{aligned} \rho(\boldsymbol{\beta}, \boldsymbol{\beta}^{\mathrm{S}}) &= \mathrm{E}[(\boldsymbol{\beta}^{\mathrm{S}} - \boldsymbol{\beta})'(\boldsymbol{\beta}^{\mathrm{S}} - \boldsymbol{\beta})] \\ &= \mathrm{E}[(\hat{\boldsymbol{\beta}} - \boldsymbol{\beta})'(\hat{\boldsymbol{\beta}} - \boldsymbol{\beta})] - 2\mathrm{c} + 2\mathrm{c}\boldsymbol{\beta}'\mathrm{E}(\hat{\boldsymbol{\beta}}/\hat{\boldsymbol{\beta}}'\hat{\boldsymbol{\beta}}) + \mathrm{c}^2\mathrm{E}(1/\hat{\boldsymbol{\beta}}'\hat{\boldsymbol{\beta}}) \end{aligned} \tag{3.9.4}$$

What James and Stein then proceeded to find was the value of c that would make the risk function for $\boldsymbol{\beta}^{\mathrm{S}}$ a minimum. Note, under the assumed DSP, that $\hat{\boldsymbol{\beta}}'\hat{\boldsymbol{\beta}}$ has a noncentral Chi-square(k, λ) distribution with noncentrality parameter $\lambda = \boldsymbol{\beta}'\boldsymbol{\beta}/2$ because $\hat{\boldsymbol{\beta}} \sim \mathrm{N}(\boldsymbol{\beta}, \mathbf{I})$. Using theorems contained in Judge and Bock (1978, p. 171), one can demonstrate that $\rho(\boldsymbol{\beta}, \boldsymbol{\beta}^{\mathrm{S}}) = k - \mathrm{c}[2(k-2) - c]\mathrm{E}[1/\chi_k^2]$, where $\chi_k^2 \sim$ Chi-square(k, λ). Thus, $\rho(\boldsymbol{\beta}, \boldsymbol{\beta}^{\mathrm{S}}) \le \rho(\boldsymbol{\beta}, \hat{\boldsymbol{\beta}}) = k$ for all $\boldsymbol{\beta}$, if $0 \le c \le 2(k-2)$, and the value of c that minimizes the risk $\rho(\boldsymbol{\beta}, \boldsymbol{\beta}^{\mathrm{S}})$ is $c = k-2$. Consequently, under a squared-error measure,

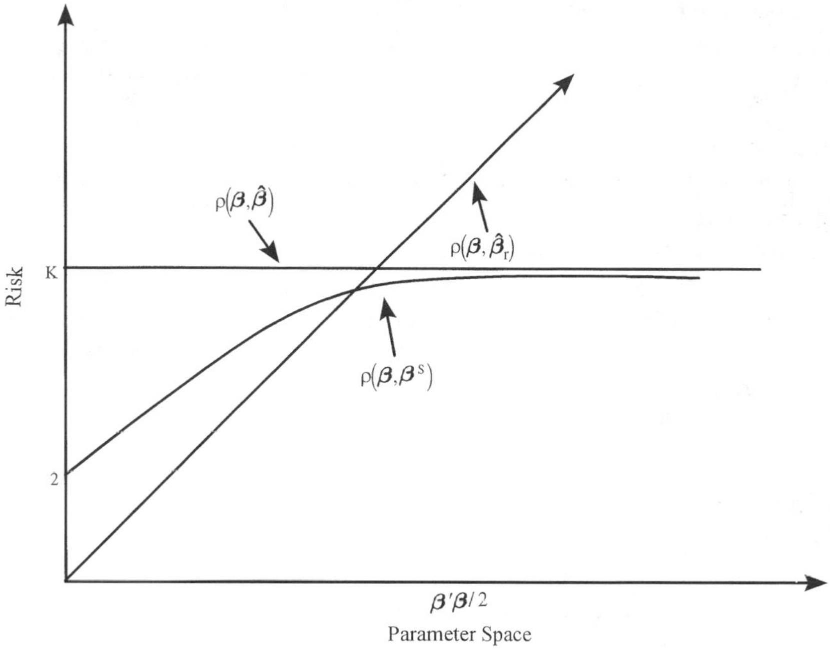

Figure 3.1: Risk Characteristics of the James and Stein, ML and Restricted ML Estimators.

the nonlinear James and Stein estimator

$$\boldsymbol{\beta}^{\mathrm{S}} = [1 - (\mathrm{K} - 2)/\hat{\boldsymbol{\beta}}'\hat{\boldsymbol{\beta}}]\hat{\boldsymbol{\beta}} \tag{3.9.5}$$

dominates the best unbiased ML estimator in terms of squared-error risk. When $\boldsymbol{\beta} = \mathbf{0}$, the risk of $\boldsymbol{\beta}^{\mathrm{S}}$ is equal to 2 and as $\boldsymbol{\beta}'\boldsymbol{\beta} \to \infty$ the risk of $\boldsymbol{\beta}^{\mathrm{S}}$ converges to k, which is the risk of the ML estimator. The risk characteristics of $\boldsymbol{\beta}^{\mathrm{S}}$ are given in Figure 3.1.

The James and Stein estimator will be discussed further in later chapters. For now, we hope that this introduction to biased estimation has provided some clarification of how one can approach the problem of estimation within a decision–theoretic context. Many alternatives exist for how to make the "best" use of the data to solve an inverse problem at hand. For the current probability model, one could insist on using the unbiased ML estimator. However, this section underscores that decisions regarding the class of estimators chosen have consequences in terms of the sampling properties of the estimators.

3.9.2. Risk Comparisons for Restricted and Unrestricted ML Estimator

Before closing this subsection, we introduce another risk function that will figure prominently in the interpretation of an estimator that we discuss in later chapters. Consider again the DSP used in demonstrating the sampling performance of the James–Stein estimator. Consider the use of a *restricted* ML estimator in which estimates are obtained by maximizing the likelihood function subject to restrictions on the parameter values. In particular, consider the restriction $\boldsymbol{\beta} = \mathbf{0}$. Under this restriction, the restricted ML estimator will of course satisfy $\hat{\boldsymbol{\beta}}_r = \mathbf{0}$, and there is no variability in $\hat{\boldsymbol{\beta}}_r$ from sample to sample. Consequently, under SEL the risk function for the restricted ML estimator is $\mathrm{E}[(\hat{\boldsymbol{\beta}}_r - \boldsymbol{\beta})'(\hat{\boldsymbol{\beta}}_r - \boldsymbol{\beta})] = \boldsymbol{\beta}'\boldsymbol{\beta}$. If, in terms of Figure 3.1, we graph the risk of this restricted ML estimator, we then have an estimator that has unbounded risk. It has a risk of zero at the origin, when $\boldsymbol{\beta} = \mathbf{0}$, and a risk of $\boldsymbol{\beta}'\boldsymbol{\beta}$ otherwise. Thus, the restricted ML estimator can be very good or very bad depending on the actual value of $\boldsymbol{\beta}$. If $\boldsymbol{\beta}'\boldsymbol{\beta} < k$, which means the risk of the *restricted* ML estimator is less than the risk of the *unrestricted* ML estimator, then clearly it makes sense to use the restriction $\boldsymbol{\beta} = \mathbf{0}$. However, $\boldsymbol{\beta}$ is an unknown parameter vector. In this context, how do we reach a decision as to whether or not to make use of the parameter restriction? We will return to this question when we discuss model specification issues in later chapters.

► **Example 3.9.1:** To demonstrate the quadratic risk properties of the ML and shrinkage estimators, we provide the GAUSS program C3Jstein.gss in the Examples Manual. For comparison purposes, we compute the ML and James–Stein estimates of $\boldsymbol{\beta}$ for an observed sample of data. Then, we use a Monte Carlo exercise to simulate the quadratic risk of four competing estimation rules: ML, restricted ML (subject to $\boldsymbol{\beta} = \mathbf{0}$), James–Stein, and an extension of the James–Stein estimator known as the positive-part Stein rule. The reader should find that the simulated risk functions are very similar to Figure 3.1 and that the James–Stein estimator is inadmissible relative to the positive-part estimator.

3.10. Appendix: Proofs

PROOF: THEOREM 3.4.1, CONSISTENCY OF THE ML ESTIMATOR: Because the trace of a square matrix is equal to the sum of the eigenvalues of the matrix, then $\mathrm{tr}(\mathbf{x}'\mathbf{x}) \to \infty$ as $n \to \infty$ implies that $\sum_{j=1}^{k} \lambda_j(\mathbf{x}'\mathbf{x}) \to \infty$ as $n \to \infty$. Given that $\lambda_L(\mathbf{x}'\mathbf{x}) \leq \delta\lambda_s(\mathbf{x}'\mathbf{x})$ with δ a finite positive constant, then the sum of the eigenvalues of $\mathbf{x}'\mathbf{x}$ can increase without bound only if $\lambda_s(\mathbf{x}'\mathbf{x}) \to \infty$ as $n \to \infty$. Because the eigenvalues of $(\mathbf{x}'\mathbf{x})^{-1}$ are the reciprocals of the eigenvalues of $\mathbf{x}'\mathbf{x}$, it follows that the *largest* eigenvalue of $(\mathbf{x}'\mathbf{x})^{-1}$ is such that $\lambda_L((\mathbf{x}'\mathbf{x})^{-1}) = \frac{1}{\lambda_s(\mathbf{x}'\mathbf{x})} \to 0$ as $n \to \infty$, implying that all k of the eigenvalues of $(\mathbf{x}'\mathbf{x})^{-1}$ converge to zero (recall that the eigenvalues of a positive semidefinite matrix are all nonnegative). Then $\mathrm{tr}(\mathbf{x}'\mathbf{x})^{-1} = \sum_{j=1}^{k} \lambda_j(\mathbf{x}'\mathbf{x})^{-1} \to \sum_{j=1}^{k} 0 = 0$ as $n \to \infty$, implying that $\mathrm{var}(\hat{\beta}_j) \to 0$ as $n \to \infty\ \forall j$ so that $\hat{\boldsymbol{\beta}} \to \boldsymbol{\beta}$ by mean-square convergence. ■

PROOF: THEOREM 3.4.2, CONSISTENCY OF S^2 FOR ESTIMATING σ^2: The estimator S^2 can be written as

$$S^2 = \frac{(\mathbf{Y} - \mathbf{x}\hat{\boldsymbol{\beta}})'(\mathbf{Y} - \mathbf{x}\hat{\boldsymbol{\beta}})}{n-k} = \frac{\mathbf{Y}'(\mathbf{I}_n - \mathbf{x}(\mathbf{x}'\mathbf{x})^{-1}\mathbf{x}')\mathbf{Y}}{n-k} \tag{3.10.1}$$

Upon substitution of $\mathbf{Y} = \mathbf{x}\boldsymbol{\beta} + \varepsilon$, it follows from (3.10.1) that

$$S^2 = \frac{\varepsilon'[\mathbf{I}_n - \mathbf{x}(\mathbf{x}'\mathbf{x})^{-1}\mathbf{x}']\varepsilon}{n-k} = \frac{\varepsilon'\varepsilon - \varepsilon'\mathbf{x}(\mathbf{x}'\mathbf{x})^{-1}\mathbf{x}'\varepsilon}{n-k}$$

$$= \frac{n}{n-k}\left(\frac{\varepsilon'\varepsilon}{n}\right) - \frac{\varepsilon'\mathbf{x}(\mathbf{x}'\mathbf{x})^{-1}\mathbf{x}'\varepsilon}{n-k}. \qquad (3.10.2)$$

The second expression following the last equality in (3.10.2) converges in probability to 0 by an application of Markov's inequality because the term is a nonnegative valued scalar random variable, and then $\forall\, a > 0$

$$\lim_{n\to\infty} P\left(\frac{\varepsilon'\mathbf{x}(\mathbf{x}'\mathbf{x})^{-1}\mathbf{x}'\varepsilon}{n-k} < a\right) \geq 1 - \lim_{n\to\infty} \frac{E\left(\frac{\varepsilon'\mathbf{x}(\mathbf{x}'\mathbf{x})^{-1}\mathbf{x}'\varepsilon}{n-k}\right)}{a}$$

$$= 1 - \lim_{n\to\infty}[\sigma^2 k/(n-k)] = 1, \qquad (3.10.3)$$

and thus $\text{p}\lim\left(\frac{\varepsilon'\mathbf{x}(\mathbf{x}'\mathbf{x})^{-1}\mathbf{x}'\varepsilon}{n-k}\right) = 0$. The first expression to the right of the equality in (3.10.2) converges to σ^2 by Slutsky's theorem and Khinchin's weak law of large numbers (WLLN) because $\frac{\varepsilon'\varepsilon}{n} = n^{-1}\sum_{i=1}^{n}\varepsilon_i^2$ is the mean of n iid random variables having expected value $E[\varepsilon_i^2] = \sigma^2$, and $n/(n-k) \to 1$ as $n \to \infty$, so that $\text{p}\lim(\frac{n}{n-k}(\frac{\varepsilon'\varepsilon}{n})) = 1 \cdot \sigma^2 = \sigma^2$. Thus, $\text{plim } S^2 = \sigma^2$. ■

PROOF: ASYMPTOTIC NORMALITY OF S^2 FOR ESTIMATING σ^2: Under the assumptions of the probability model in Table 3.1, it follows that

$$W = \frac{(n-k)S^2}{\sigma^2} \sim \text{Chi-square}(n-k, 0) \qquad (3.10.4)$$

in which case, by the standard additivity property of the central Chi-square distribution, one can view W as the sum of $n-k$ iid Chi-square(1, 0) random variables, each Chi-square(1, 0) random variable having a mean of 1 and a variance of 2. Then it follows directly from the Lindeberg–Levy Central Limit theorem that, as $n \to \infty$,

$$\frac{(n-k)^{-1}W - 1}{[2/(n-k)]^{1/2}} = \frac{(S^2/\sigma^2) - 1}{[2/(n-k)]^{1/2}} \xrightarrow{d} N(0, 1). \qquad (3.10.5)$$

Multiplying the left-hand side of (3.10.5) by $[n/(n-k)]^{1/2} \to 1$ has no effect on the limiting distribution via Slutsky's theorem, and thus

$$\frac{(S^2/\sigma^2) - 1}{(2/n)^{1/2}} \xrightarrow{d} N(0, 1), \qquad (3.10.6)$$

from which it follows directly that

$$S^2 \overset{a}{\sim} N\left(\sigma^2, \left(\frac{2\sigma^4}{n}\right)\right). \qquad (3.10.7)$$

■

PROOF: CONSISTENCY OF THE ESTIMATOR $\hat{\varepsilon}_{\mathrm{i}}$ FOR ε_{i}: If $\boldsymbol{\iota}_{\mathrm{i}}$ represent an $(n \times 1)$ vector of zeros except for a value of 1 in the ith position, it follows that $(\varepsilon_{\mathrm{i}} - \hat{\varepsilon}_{\mathrm{i}}) = \boldsymbol{\iota}_{\mathrm{i}}'\mathbf{x}(\mathbf{x}'\mathbf{x})^{-1}\mathbf{x}'\boldsymbol{\varepsilon}$. Then, using results on the expectations of linear combinations of random variables, we have that $\mathrm{E}(\varepsilon_i - \hat{\varepsilon}_i) = 0$ and $\mathrm{var}(\varepsilon_i - \hat{\varepsilon}_i) = \sigma^2\boldsymbol{\iota}_i'\mathbf{x}(\mathbf{x}'\mathbf{x})^{-1}\mathbf{x}'\boldsymbol{\iota}_i$. Thus, if $\mathbf{x}(\mathbf{x}'\mathbf{x})^{-1}\mathbf{x}' \to \mathbf{0}$, then $\mathrm{var}(\varepsilon_i - \hat{\varepsilon}_i) \to 0$, and so

$$\hat{\varepsilon}_{\mathrm{i}} \xrightarrow{\mathrm{m}} \varepsilon_{\mathrm{i}}\ \forall \mathrm{i} \Rightarrow \hat{\varepsilon}_{\mathrm{i}} \xrightarrow{\mathrm{p}} \varepsilon_{\mathrm{i}}\ \forall \mathrm{i} \Rightarrow \hat{\varepsilon}_{\mathrm{i}} \xrightarrow{\mathrm{d}} \varepsilon_{\mathrm{i}} \forall \mathrm{i}. \qquad (3.10.8)$$

■

3.11. References

Berger, J., and R. Wolpert (1984), *The Likelihood Principle*, Vol. 6, IMS Monograph Series, Hayward, CA.

Dynkin, E. B. (1951), "Necessary and Sufficient Statistics for Families of Distributions," *Sel. Transl. Math. Stat. and Prob.*, Vol. 1, pp. 23–41.

Judge, G., and M. E. Bock (1978), *The Statistical Implications of Pre-Test and Stein Rule Estimators in Econometrics*, North-Holland, Amsterdam.

Judge, G., W. E. Griffiths, R. Carter Hill, H. Lütkepohl, and T. C. Lee (1985), *The Theory and Practice of Econometrics*, 2nd ed., New York: John Wiley and Sons.

James, W., and C. Stein (1961), "Estimation with Quadratic Loss," *Proceedings of the Fourth Berkeley Symposium*, pp. 361–79, Berkeley, California Press.

Mittelhammer, R. C. (1996), *Mathematical Statistics for Economics and Business*, New York: Springer–Verlag.

CHAPTER 4

The Multivariate Normal Linear Regression Model: Inference

4.1. Introduction

In Chapter 3, we considered a multivariate normal linear regression sampling model (Table 3.1) together with the maximum likelihood (ML) estimation principle and demonstrated that the ML estimator of $\boldsymbol{\beta}$,

$$\hat{\boldsymbol{\beta}} = (\mathbf{x}'\mathbf{x})^{-1}\mathbf{x}'\mathbf{Y} \sim \mathrm{N}(\boldsymbol{\beta}, \sigma^2(\mathbf{x}'\mathbf{x})^{-1}), \tag{4.1.1}$$

is the minimum-variance unbiased estimator as well as being consistent, asymptotically normal, and asymptotically efficient. In terms of the unknown and unobservable parameter σ^2, we demonstrated that the ML estimator

$$\mathrm{S}^2_{\mathrm{ML}} = (\mathbf{Y} - \mathbf{x}\hat{\boldsymbol{\beta}})'(\mathbf{Y} - \mathbf{x}\hat{\boldsymbol{\beta}})/n = \boldsymbol{\varepsilon}'\mathbf{m}\boldsymbol{\varepsilon}/n, \tag{4.1.2}$$

where $\mathbf{m} = \mathbf{I} - \mathbf{x}(\mathbf{x}'\mathbf{x})^{-1}\mathbf{x}'$, is a biased but consistent estimator. Also using the result $\boldsymbol{\varepsilon}'\mathbf{m}\boldsymbol{\varepsilon}/\sigma^2 \sim \text{Chi-square}(n-k, 0)$ (where $\text{Chi-square}(n-k, 0)$ denotes the Chi-square probability distribution with $n-k$ degrees of freedom and noncentrality parameter 0, i.e., a central Chi-square distribution), the distribution of $\mathrm{S}^2_{\mathrm{ML}}$ is

$$\mathrm{S}^2_{\mathrm{ML}} \sim \mathrm{Gamma}\left(\frac{n-k}{2}, \frac{2\sigma^2}{n}\right). \tag{4.1.3}$$

The bias-corrected ML estimator

$$\mathrm{S}^2 = \left(\frac{n}{n-k}\right)\mathrm{S}^2_{\mathrm{ML}} \sim \mathrm{Gamma}\left(\frac{n-k}{2}, \frac{2\sigma^2}{n-k}\right) \tag{4.1.4}$$

is the minimum variance unbiased estimator and is consistent, asymptotically normal, and asymptotically efficient for estimating σ^2.

We now exploit our knowledge of the multivariate normal probability model and of the finite and asymptotic sampling properties of the corresponding ML point estimators to define procedures for conducting statistical inference based on the information contained in a given sample of observations. In facing this issue, we will use the ideas of Neyman–Pearson to reduce a complicated inverse problem to solutions involving

Table 4.1. *Linear Semiparametric Regression Model*

Model Component	Specific Characteristics	
$\mathbf{Y}$	RV Type:	continuous
	Range:	unlimited
	Y_i dimension:	univariate
	Moments:	$E[\mathbf{Y} \mid \mathbf{x}] = \mathbf{x}\boldsymbol{\beta}$ and $\mathbf{cov}(\mathbf{Y} \mid \mathbf{x}) = \sigma^2\mathbf{I}$
$\eta(\mathbf{x}, \boldsymbol{\beta}, \varepsilon)$	Functional Form:	linear in $\mathbf{x}$ and $\boldsymbol{\beta}$, additive in ε, as $\mathbf{x}\boldsymbol{\beta} + \varepsilon$
$\mathbf{x}$	RV Type:	degenerate (fixed), full-column rank
	Genesis:	exogenous to the model
$\boldsymbol{\beta}$	RV Type:	degenerate (fixed)
	Dimension:	finite (fixed)
ε	RV Type:	iid
	Moments:	$E[\varepsilon \mid \mathbf{x}] = \mathbf{0}$, and $\mathbf{cov}(\varepsilon \mid \mathbf{x}) = \sigma^2\mathbf{I}$
Ω	Prior info:	none
$f(\mathbf{e} \mid \mathbf{x}, \varphi)$	PDF family:	$N(\mathbf{e}; \mathbf{0}, \sigma^2\mathbf{I})$

hypothesis testing and confidence intervals and regions. A review of the basic concepts in these areas is provided in Chapter E2, which deals with the principles of classical inference. (For more extensive coverage, see Mittelhammer, Chapters 9 and 10.)

The characteristics of the probability model assumed in this chapter are presented in Table 4.1.

4.2. Some Basic Sampling Distributions of Functions of $\hat{\beta}$ and S^2

In developing inference procedures for $\boldsymbol{\beta}$ and σ^2, it will be useful first to establish the sampling distributions of a few key functions of the estimators $\hat{\boldsymbol{\beta}}$ and S^2. Because the maximum likelihood estimator $\hat{\boldsymbol{\beta}}$ is a linear function of the normally distributed vector $\mathbf{Y} = \mathbf{x}\boldsymbol{\beta} + \varepsilon$, we can utilize the following representation of the estimator in developing hypothesis testing statistics:

$$\hat{\boldsymbol{\beta}} = \boldsymbol{\beta} + (\mathbf{x}'\mathbf{x})^{-1}\mathbf{x}'\varepsilon = \boldsymbol{\beta} + \mathbf{u}, \qquad \text{where } \mathbf{u} = (\mathbf{x}'\mathbf{x})^{-1}\mathbf{x}'\varepsilon \sim N(\mathbf{0}, \sigma^2(\mathbf{x}'\mathbf{x})^{-1}). \tag{4.2.1}$$

Therefore $(\hat{\boldsymbol{\beta}} - \boldsymbol{\beta}) \sim N[\mathbf{0}, \sigma^2(\mathbf{x}'\mathbf{x})^{-1}]$. Then, by standard properties of linear combinations of normally distributed random variables and properties of the symmetric square-root matrix $(\mathbf{x}'\mathbf{x})^{1/2}$ (recall that $(\mathbf{x}'\mathbf{x})^{1/2}(\mathbf{x}'\mathbf{x})^{-1}(\mathbf{x}'\mathbf{x})^{1/2} = \mathbf{I}_k$; see the discussion in Section 3.4.2, and consult the matrix review manual),

$$(\mathbf{x}'\mathbf{x})^{1/2}(\hat{\boldsymbol{\beta}} - \boldsymbol{\beta}) \sim N(\mathbf{0}, \sigma^2\mathbf{I}_k) \tag{4.2.2}$$

and $(\mathbf{x}'\mathbf{x})^{1/2}(\hat{\boldsymbol{\beta}} - \boldsymbol{\beta})/\sigma$ is a k-dimensional vector of standard normal random variables. Therefore, because $(\mathbf{x}'\mathbf{x})^{1/2}(\mathbf{x}'\mathbf{x})^{1/2} = (\mathbf{x}'\mathbf{x})$, we have the sum of squares of k iid N(0, 1) random variables represented by the quadratic form (recall (4.2.1))

$$[\sigma^{-1}(\hat{\boldsymbol{\beta}}-\boldsymbol{\beta})'(\mathbf{x}'\mathbf{x})^{1/2}][(\mathbf{x}'\mathbf{x})^{1/2}(\hat{\boldsymbol{\beta}}-\boldsymbol{\beta})\sigma^{-1}] = \frac{(\hat{\boldsymbol{\beta}}-\boldsymbol{\beta})'(\mathbf{x}'\mathbf{x})(\hat{\boldsymbol{\beta}}-\boldsymbol{\beta})}{\sigma^2} = \frac{\boldsymbol{\varepsilon}'\mathbf{x}(\mathbf{x}'\mathbf{x})^{-1}\mathbf{x}'\boldsymbol{\varepsilon}}{\sigma^2} \sim \text{Chi-square}(k,0) \qquad (4.2.3)$$

where Chi-square(k, 0) is a noncentral Chi-square distribution with k degrees of freedom and noncentrality parameter equal to 0. In other words (4.2.3) is a central Chi-square with k degrees of freedom, and $\mathbf{x}(\mathbf{x}'\mathbf{x})^{-1}\mathbf{x}'$ is a symmetric idempotent matrix having trace, and thus rank k.

Regarding the probability distribution of general linear combinations of the entries in the $\hat{\boldsymbol{\beta}}$ parameter vector, it follows from $\hat{\boldsymbol{\beta}} \sim \mathrm{N}(\boldsymbol{\beta}, \sigma^2(\mathbf{x}'\mathbf{x})^{-1})$ and standard results on linear combinations of multivariate normally distributed random variables that

$$\mathbf{c}\hat{\boldsymbol{\beta}} \sim \mathrm{N}(\mathbf{c}\boldsymbol{\beta}, \sigma^2\mathbf{c}(\mathbf{x}'\mathbf{x})^{-1}\mathbf{c}'), \qquad (4.2.4)$$

where $\mathbf{c}$ is a $(j \times k)$ matrix assumed to have rank $j \leq k$. Then $(\mathbf{c}\hat{\boldsymbol{\beta}} - \mathbf{c}\boldsymbol{\beta}) = \mathbf{c}(\hat{\boldsymbol{\beta}} - \boldsymbol{\beta}) \sim \mathrm{N}[\mathbf{0}, \sigma^2\mathbf{c}(\mathbf{x}'\mathbf{x})^{-1}\mathbf{c}']$. Furthermore, because $\mathbf{c}(\mathbf{x}'\mathbf{x})^{-1}\mathbf{c}'$ is symmetric and positive definite, we can use the symmetric square-root matrix for $[\mathbf{c}(\mathbf{x}'\mathbf{x})^{-1}\mathbf{c}']^{-1}$, say $\mathbf{q} \equiv [\mathbf{c}(\mathbf{x}'\mathbf{x})^{-1}\mathbf{c}']^{-1/2}$ such that $\mathbf{q}[\mathbf{c}(\mathbf{x}'\mathbf{x})^{-1}\mathbf{c}']\mathbf{q} = \mathbf{I}_j$, to obtain

$$\mathbf{qc}(\hat{\boldsymbol{\beta}} - \boldsymbol{\beta}) \sim \mathrm{N}(\mathbf{0}, \sigma^2\mathbf{I}_j). \qquad (4.2.5)$$

Therefore, because $\mathbf{qq} = [\mathbf{c}(\mathbf{x}'\mathbf{x})^{-1}\mathbf{c}']^{-1/2}[\mathbf{c}(\mathbf{x}'\mathbf{x})^{-1}\mathbf{c}']^{-1/2} = [\mathbf{c}(\mathbf{x}'\mathbf{x})^{-1}\mathbf{c}']^{-1}$, we have the sum of squares of j iid N(0, 1) random variables represented by the quadratic form (recall (4.2.1))

$$[\sigma^{-1}(\hat{\boldsymbol{\beta}}-\boldsymbol{\beta})'\mathbf{c}'\mathbf{q}][\mathbf{qc}(\hat{\boldsymbol{\beta}}-\boldsymbol{\beta})\sigma^{-1}] = \frac{(\hat{\boldsymbol{\beta}}-\boldsymbol{\beta})'\mathbf{c}'[\mathbf{c}(\mathbf{x}'\mathbf{x})^{-1}\mathbf{c}']^{-1}\mathbf{c}(\hat{\boldsymbol{\beta}}-\boldsymbol{\beta})}{\sigma^2} = \frac{\boldsymbol{\varepsilon}'\mathbf{x}(\mathbf{x}'\mathbf{x})^{-1}\mathbf{c}'[\mathbf{c}(\mathbf{x}'\mathbf{x})^{-1}\mathbf{c}']^{-1}\mathbf{c}(\mathbf{x}'\mathbf{x})^{-1}\mathbf{x}'\boldsymbol{\varepsilon}}{\sigma^2} \sim \text{Chi-square}(j,0), \qquad (4.2.6)$$

where $\mathbf{x}(\mathbf{x}'\mathbf{x})^{-1}\mathbf{c}'[\mathbf{c}(\mathbf{x}'\mathbf{x})^{-1}\mathbf{c}']^{-1}\mathbf{c}(\mathbf{x}'\mathbf{x})^{-1}\mathbf{x}'$ is a symmetric idempotent matrix having trace, and thus rank j.

Regarding the estimator S^2, recall from (4.1.4) that $\mathrm{S}^2 \sim \mathrm{Gamma}(\frac{n-k}{2}, \frac{2\sigma^2}{n-k})$. Then, via a change of variables or the moment-generating function approach, it can be shown (recall (3.2.14)) that

$$\frac{(n-k)\mathrm{S}^2}{\sigma^2} = \frac{\boldsymbol{\varepsilon}'(\mathbf{I} - \mathbf{x}(\mathbf{x}'\mathbf{x})^{-1}\mathbf{x}')\boldsymbol{\varepsilon}}{\sigma^2} \sim \text{Chi-square}(n-k, 0). \qquad (4.2.7)$$

We can use (4.2.7) directly to develop a hypothesis test for the value of σ^2, as will be seen later.

A final important distributional result to note is that the random variable (4.2.7) and either (4.2.3) or (4.2.6) are *independent*. This follows from a result concerning the independence of quadratic forms in multivariate, normally distributed random variables, which states that if $\mathbf{Z} \sim \mathrm{N}(\mathbf{0}, \sigma^2\mathbf{I})$, then $\mathbf{Z}'\mathbf{m}_1\mathbf{Z}$ and $\mathbf{Z}'\mathbf{m}_2\mathbf{Z}$ are independent random variables if $\mathbf{m}_1$ and $\mathbf{m}_2$ are symmetric idempotent matrices and $\mathbf{m}_1\mathbf{m}_2 = \mathbf{0}$. In the case at hand, note that the quadratic form involving the random vector $\sigma^{-1}\varepsilon \sim \mathrm{N}(\mathbf{0}, \mathbf{I}_n)$ in (4.2.3) is based on the matrix $\mathbf{x}(\mathbf{x}'\mathbf{x})^{-1}\mathbf{x}'$, and the quadratic form (4.2.7) is based on the matrix $[\mathbf{I} - \mathbf{x}(\mathbf{x}'\mathbf{x})^{-1}\mathbf{x}']$. Given that $\mathbf{x}(\mathbf{x}'\mathbf{x})^{-1}\mathbf{x}'[\mathbf{I} - \mathbf{x}(\mathbf{x}'\mathbf{x})^{-1}\mathbf{x}'] = \mathbf{0}$, it follows that the quadratic forms (4.2.3) and (4.2.7) are independent random variables. The independence of (4.2.6) and (4.2.7) can be proven analogously. As we will see later, one can then demonstrate that ratios involving (4.2.3) or (4.2.6) divided by (4.2.7), which are ratios of independent Chi-square random variables, can be used to construct test statistics based on F-distributions when each of the Chi-square random variables are divided by their respective degrees of freedom.

4.3. Hypothesis Testing

In the general usage of the term, a *hypothesis* is a statement of some unproven theory, proposition, or conjecture that is tentatively presented as an explanation for the origin or behavior of a certain set of observed facts or outcomes. When the unproven theories, propositions, or conjectures relate specifically to probability model characteristics within the context of a classical (and later also a Bayesian) inverse problem, the hypothesis is referred to as a *statistical hypothesis*. Statistical hypothesis testing is concerned with making decisions regarding the truth of hypotheses relating to characteristics of the probability model associated with the DSP underlying the observed sample data. These hypotheses can be statements regarding the true values of the parameters underlying the probability distribution of the random sample if the DSP characteristics of interest are representable as functions of parameters. Alternatively, interest may center on propositions regarding the true values of means, variances, modes, quantiles, gradients, or elasticities that may not be representable as functions of parameters. Our principal focus here will be on the case in which parameters are involved, and so hypotheses will generally be expressed in the form $\mathbf{c}(\boldsymbol{\theta}) \in \mathrm{A}$, where A is a set of hypothesized values for some vector function $\mathbf{c}(\boldsymbol{\theta})$ of the parameters $\boldsymbol{\theta}$. However, any arguments ahead that do not explicitly require parameter values can be applied to nonparametric cases as well. Henceforth, we will assume the context is always one of *statistical* hypothesis testing, and thus we will suppress the adjective *statistical.*

We emphasize that the classical approach to evaluating the statistical properties of hypothesis testing procedures is conducted in an unconditional predata context. We are thus contemplating or evaluating the behavior of the test procedure in the context of all of the hypothetical samples of data that *could* have occurred, not in the sense of what actually *did* occur. By basing our choice of hypothesis testing procedure on the sampling distribution of $\mathbf{Y}$, the information obtained about $\boldsymbol{\beta}$ and σ^2 from test decisions depends not only on the data being analyzed but also on whatever data sets one might have observed but did not.

Finally, we stress that in econometrics, conclusions and judgments are not reached purely through logical deductions from theoretical arguments but rather through amassing sufficient evidence from observed data for or against a proposition. The classical test procedures presented in this section are designed in a *predata* sense to reject false propositions and not reject true ones with known probabilities (represented by probabilities of Type-I and Type-II errors), and it is these test characteristics that define the weight of evidence leading to a classical test decision.

4.3.1. Test Statistics

All hypothesis-testing procedures used in empirical work will be based on the outcome of some function of the random sample $T = t(\mathbf{Y})$, and this function is referred to as a *test statistic*. A subset of the range of such a test statistic will be defined as the *rejection* region, say C^T, and whether or not a hypothesis is rejected will depend on whether or not an observed outcome of the statistic resides in the rejection region, that is, $t(\mathbf{y}) \in C^T \Leftrightarrow$ reject hypothesis. A test of a hypothesis is fully defined by the test statistic T and rejection region C^T. Note that the use of such a procedure for deciding whether to reject a hypothesis also implies a partition of the range of potential random-sample outcomes into rejection and nonrejection regions, the rejection region being defined as $C = \{\mathbf{y} : t(\mathbf{y}) \in C^T\}$. It follows that a hypothesis test can be conducted equivalently by rejecting the hypothesis if $\mathbf{y} \in C$, and so the test can be defined in terms of the sample outcome $\mathbf{y}$ and rejection region C. The use of the test statistic is convenient because decisions are based on the value of a scalar t as opposed to a multivariate value $\mathbf{y}$. Furthermore, the use of a test statistic facilitates the assessment of the statistical properties of a test because the distribution of the test statistic will be univariate as opposed to the generally high-dimensional multivariate distribution of the random sample.

The design of good classical hypothesis-testing procedures relies on the identification of appropriate test statistics concomitant with appropriate rejection and nonrejection regions that lead to correct decisions regarding the truth of the hypothesis with high probability. We will discuss later the basic concepts underlying the definition of good hypothesis-testing procedures. We note, as in point estimation, that in practice it is often the case that one must be satisfied with *good* as opposed to *optimal* procedures because optimality is often difficult to achieve, sometimes unattainable, and in any case often undefinable in any unique way. There is more consensus regarding what *good* procedures are and how they are defined. Thus, although we will discuss notions of optimality in hypothesis testing and will point out procedures that are considered optimal in certain testing situations, we will not devote substantial attention to the concept.

4.3.2. Generalized Likelihood Ratio (GLR) Test

In an attempt to establish a widely applicable method for defining hypothesis testing procedures with generally *good* properties even in complex cases, the so-called *generalized likelihood ratio test* procedure was suggested early on by Neyman and Pearson. They made this suggestion without regard to whether the procedure is ultimately optimal in any sense. The generic form of the generalized likelihood ratio test is presented below. The term *generalized* indicates that the likelihood ratio test is based on the ratio of two maxima (or suprema, if the maxima do not exist) of likelihood functions over subsets of the parameter space as opposed simply to the ratio of two likelihood functions evaluated at two specific parameter values.

Definition 4.3.1 (Generalized Likelihood Ratio (GLR) Test of level α): Let the joint PDF of the random sample $\mathbf{y}$ be $f(\mathbf{y};\boldsymbol{\theta})$ and the associated likelihood function be $L(\boldsymbol{\theta};\mathbf{y})$. The *generalized likelihood ratio* statistic associated with the null hypothesis H_0 and alternative hypothesis H_a is

$$\Lambda = \lambda(\mathbf{Y}) = \frac{\max_{\boldsymbol{\theta}\in H_0} L(\boldsymbol{\theta};\mathbf{Y})}{\max_{\boldsymbol{\theta}\in H_0\cup H_a} L(\boldsymbol{\theta};\mathbf{Y})}, \tag{4.3.1}$$

and the associated level α GLR test of H_0 versus H_a is given by $\{\Lambda, C^{\Lambda}\}$, where the critical region is defined as $C^{\Lambda} = [0, \tau]$ and τ is chosen such that $\max_{\boldsymbol{\theta}\in H_0} \pi(\boldsymbol{\theta}) = \max_{\boldsymbol{\theta}\in H_0} P_{\boldsymbol{\theta}}(\lambda(\mathbf{y}) \le \tau) = \alpha$.

Note in the definition that $\pi(\boldsymbol{\theta}) = P_{\boldsymbol{\theta}}[\lambda(\mathbf{y}) \le \tau]$ refers to the probability that $\lambda(\mathbf{y}) \le \tau$ when the probability is based on the PDF $f(\mathbf{y};\boldsymbol{\theta})$. The function $\pi(\boldsymbol{\theta})$ represents the power function of the test, that is, a function that indicates the probability that the test will reject H_0 given a value of the parameter vector $\boldsymbol{\theta}\in\Omega$ (Chapter E2; Mittelhammer, p. 530). The maxima can be replaced by the suprema in the definition if the former do not exist.

Regarding the intuitive rationale for the definition of the test, note the numerator of the GLR represents the largest value of the likelihood (or the smallest upper bound on all of the likelihood values if there is no largest value and the supremum is used in place of the maximum) that can be assigned to an observed value of $\mathbf{y}$ among all choices for the PDF of the random sample that are contained in the null hypothesis. Similarly, the denominator of the GLR represents the largest value of the likelihood (or smallest upper bound to this value) assignable to $\mathbf{y}$ among all choices for the PDF of the random sample available in the entire probability model. It is clear that, because the likelihood function is nonnegative valued, $\lambda \in [0, 1]$, and the smaller the value, the smaller the ratio of likelihood function maxima. If the likelihood ratio is small enough, so that in effect the value of $\mathbf{y}$ observed is sufficiently less likely to have occurred under H_0 than under H_a, then one rejects the null hypothesis. How small the GLR value needs to be to conclude that H_0 is false is determined by the level of protection against Type-I error (the probability of rejecting a true H_0) that is desired – the more protection, the lower the ratio needs to be before a rejection decision can be reached.

4.3.3. Properties of the GLR Test

Although the design of the GLR test seems intuitively reasonable, and the test can be applied to a large array of complicated hypotheses, no explicit optimality criteria are used in its definition, and this begs the question of how good the test properties actually are in practice. In terms of finite sample properties, little in the way of general results can be proved for the GLR tests. However, it can be shown that the test has the important property of being *invariant* with respect to (1) functional representation of the null hypothesis, (2) reparameterizations of model parameters (i.e., 1-to-1 transformations of the parameter space), and (3) units of measurement for model variables (i.e., 1-to-1 transformations of model variables). Other popular tests in econometric practice, including the Lagrangian multiplier and Wald tests (discussed in Chapter 6), do not necessarily possess these invariance properties. Furthermore, it is encouraging to note that in special cases where the classical Neyman–Pearson lemma (E-2), or its extension to one-sided alternatives, produce a uniformly most powerful (UMP) test, the GLR approach produces the same test (Mittelhammer, pp. 602–5). And when the monotone likelihood ratio (MLR) approach produces a UMP test of a composite null hypothesis versus a one-sided alternative, the GLR test will be this same test (Mittelhammer, p. 606).

More generally, considering the roughly 70-year history of the GLR test (beginning with Neyman and Pearson in the 1930s), we can say that the method has produced tests with good and sometimes optimal power properties across a wide range of empirical hypothesis-testing situations in classical statistics and econometrics. Within the context of parametric models, the GLR test may be the closest thing to a "Swiss army knife" in the analyst's hypothesis-testing tool kit. Indeed, the GLR approach leads to many of the T, Chi-square, and F tests used in econometric practice that are, in certain cases, uniformly most powerful unbiased (UMPU), uniformly most powerful invariant (UMPI), and sometimes even UMP. Nonetheless, it must be admitted that for all its successes, there is no a priori guarantee that the GLR test possesses any optimal properties in a given hypothesis-testing situation and, in relatively rare cases, the GLR test may not be a good test at all. In using the test, the researcher is obliged to pay attention to the power function of the test to determine if the power characteristics are acceptable in any given testing situation.

The situation regarding general properties of the GLR test is notably better when asymptotic properties are considered. The most definitive results relate to the case where the analyst is testing j functionally independent restrictions $\mathbf{c}(\boldsymbol{\theta}) = \mathbf{r}$ on the parameters of the joint PDF of the random sample, a case that arises frequently in econometric practice (Mittelhammer, pp. 608–13). Here $\mathbf{r}$ is a $(j \times 1)$ vector of constants. We will examine the case of linear restrictions in the next section and the case of nonlinear hypotheses in later chapters.

4.3.4. Testing Hypotheses Relating to Linear Restrictions on $\boldsymbol{\beta}$

Cases often arise in practice in which the analyst is interested in testing hypotheses that are in the form of linear restrictions on the entries in the $\boldsymbol{\beta}$ vector. Examples of such tests include hypotheses that an individual element of $\boldsymbol{\beta}$ is equal to zero, a subvector of the elements of $\boldsymbol{\beta}$ equals the zero vector, or the sum of a number of the β_i's equals some constant. For example, a hypothesis of constant returns to scale may be represented by the sum of the output elasticities in a Cobb–Douglas production function equaling 1. These types of hypotheses corresponding to linear restrictions on the elements of the $\boldsymbol{\beta}$ vector can be represented in the generic form $\mathbf{c}\boldsymbol{\beta} = \mathbf{r}$. Here, $\mathbf{c}$ is a $(j \times k)$ matrix of fixed constants representing the coefficients that define the linear combinations of the entries in $\boldsymbol{\beta}$ that are of interest, and $\mathbf{r}$ is a $(j \times 1)$ vector representing the corresponding hypothesized values of the individual linear combinations. It is henceforth assumed that the rank of the **c** matrix equals j because otherwise, either one or more restrictions on the $\boldsymbol{\beta}$ vector are redundant owing to the linear dependency in the rows of **c**, or worse, the restrictions are inconsistent. The latter condition will occur if the linear dependence among the rows of **c** characterized by $\mathbf{a}'\mathbf{c} = \mathbf{0}$ for an appropriate vector or matrix **a** is not also satisfied by the elements in **r**, that is, if $\mathbf{a}'\mathbf{r} \neq \mathbf{0}$.

4.3.4.a. The GLR Test Statistic

In developing a test procedure for the null hypothesis $H_0\colon \mathbf{c}\boldsymbol{\beta} = \mathbf{r}$ versus $H_a\colon \mathbf{c}\boldsymbol{\beta} \neq \mathbf{r}$, consider the use of the generalized likelihood ratio approach given in Definition 4.3.1. If we let $\boldsymbol{\theta} = (\boldsymbol{\beta}', \sigma^2)'$ the GLR is given by

$$\lambda(\mathbf{Y}) = \frac{\max_{\boldsymbol{\theta}\in H_0} L(\boldsymbol{\theta}; \mathbf{Y})}{\max_{\boldsymbol{\theta}} \mathbf{L}(\boldsymbol{\theta}; \mathbf{Y})} \tag{4.3.2}$$

The denominator is simply the likelihood function evaluated at the ML estimator $(\hat{\boldsymbol{\beta}}', S^2_{ML})$, that is,

$$\begin{aligned} \max_{\boldsymbol{\theta}} \mathbf{L}(\boldsymbol{\theta}; \mathbf{Y}) &= \left(2\pi S^2_{ML}\right)^{-n/2} \exp\left[-\frac{1}{2S^2_{ML}}(\mathbf{Y} - \mathbf{x}\hat{\boldsymbol{\beta}})'(\mathbf{Y} - \mathbf{x}\hat{\boldsymbol{\beta}})\right] \\ &= \left(2\pi S^2_{ML}\right)^{-n/2} \exp\left(-\frac{n}{2}\right) \end{aligned} \tag{4.3.3}$$

The numerator is the likelihood function evaluated at the *restricted* ML estimator $(\hat{\boldsymbol{\beta}}_r', S_r^2)$, the restrictions being $\mathbf{c}\boldsymbol{\beta} = \mathbf{r}$. The reader can demonstrate that the restricted MLE of $\boldsymbol{\beta}$ is given by

$$\hat{\boldsymbol{\beta}}_r = \hat{\boldsymbol{\beta}} + (\mathbf{x}'\mathbf{x})^{-1}\mathbf{c}'[\mathbf{c}(\mathbf{x}'\mathbf{x})^{-1}\mathbf{c}']^{-1}(\mathbf{r} - \mathbf{c}\hat{\boldsymbol{\beta}}) \tag{4.3.4}$$

(see Chapter 6 and the discussion of the Lagrange multiplier test). The maximum likelihood estimator S_r^2 will be subsequently defined as

$$S_r^2 = \frac{(\mathbf{Y} - \mathbf{x}\hat{\boldsymbol{\beta}}_r)'(\mathbf{Y} - \mathbf{x}\hat{\boldsymbol{\beta}}_r)}{n}. \tag{4.3.5}$$

Then

$$\max_{\boldsymbol{\theta}\in H_0} \mathbf{L}(\boldsymbol{\theta}; \mathbf{Y}) = \left(2\pi S_r^2\right)^{-n/2} \exp\left(-\frac{n}{2}\right). \tag{4.3.6}$$

The GLR test statistic can then be expressed as

$$\lambda(\mathbf{Y}) = \left(\frac{S_r^2}{S^2}\right)^{-n/2} = \left(\frac{\hat{\boldsymbol{\varepsilon}}_r'\,\hat{\boldsymbol{\varepsilon}}_r}{\hat{\boldsymbol{\varepsilon}}'\,\hat{\boldsymbol{\varepsilon}}}\right)^{-n/2} \tag{4.3.7}$$

where $\hat{\boldsymbol{\varepsilon}}_r \equiv \mathbf{Y} - \mathbf{x}\hat{\boldsymbol{\beta}}_r$.

4.3.4.b. The GLR Test: Distribution and F-Statistic Equivalent

To identify the sampling distribution of the GLR test statistic so that a critical region for the test can be defined, note that if H_0: $\mathbf{c}\boldsymbol{\beta} = \mathbf{r}$ is true

$$\begin{aligned}\hat{\varepsilon}_r &= \mathbf{Y} - \mathbf{x}\hat{\boldsymbol{\beta}}_r = \mathbf{Y} - \mathbf{x}[\hat{\boldsymbol{\beta}} + (\mathbf{x}'\mathbf{x})^{-1}\mathbf{c}'[\mathbf{c}(\mathbf{x}'\mathbf{x})^{-1}\mathbf{c}']^{-1}(\mathbf{r} - \mathbf{c}\hat{\boldsymbol{\beta}})] \\ &= (\mathbf{I}_n - \mathbf{x}(\mathbf{x}'\mathbf{x})^{-1}\mathbf{x}')\varepsilon - \mathbf{x}(\mathbf{x}'\mathbf{x})^{-1}\mathbf{c}'[\mathbf{c}(\mathbf{x}'\mathbf{x})^{-1}\mathbf{c}']^{-1}\mathbf{c}(\boldsymbol{\beta} - \hat{\boldsymbol{\beta}}) \\ &= (\mathbf{I}_n - \mathbf{x}(\mathbf{x}'\mathbf{x})^{-1}\mathbf{x}' + \mathbf{x}(\mathbf{x}'\mathbf{x})^{-1}\mathbf{c}'[\mathbf{c}(\mathbf{x}'\mathbf{x})^{-1}\mathbf{c}']^{-1}\mathbf{c}(\mathbf{x}'\mathbf{x})^{-1}\mathbf{x}')\varepsilon, \qquad (4.3.8)\end{aligned}$$

where the matrix in parentheses premultiplying ε is symmetric and idempotent with rank $(n - k + j)$. If one recalls (4.2.6) and the fact that $\hat{\varepsilon}'\hat{\varepsilon} = \varepsilon'[\mathbf{I}_n - \mathbf{x}(\mathbf{x}'\mathbf{x})^{-1}\mathbf{x}']\varepsilon$, it follows that

$$\begin{aligned}\hat{\varepsilon}_r'\hat{\varepsilon}_r &= \hat{\varepsilon}'\hat{\varepsilon} + \varepsilon'\mathbf{x}(\mathbf{x}'\mathbf{x})^{-1}\mathbf{c}'[\mathbf{c}(\mathbf{x}'\mathbf{x})^{-1}\mathbf{c}']^{-1}\mathbf{c}(\mathbf{x}'\mathbf{x})^{-1}\mathbf{x}'\varepsilon \\ &= \hat{\varepsilon}'\hat{\varepsilon} + (\hat{\boldsymbol{\beta}} - \boldsymbol{\beta})'\mathbf{c}'[\mathbf{c}(\mathbf{x}'\mathbf{x})^{-1}\mathbf{c}']^{-1}\mathbf{c}(\hat{\boldsymbol{\beta}} - \boldsymbol{\beta}). \qquad (4.3.9)\end{aligned}$$

The GLR statistic can then be written, if it is assumed H_0: $\mathbf{c}\boldsymbol{\beta} = \mathbf{r}$ is true, as

$$\lambda(\mathbf{Y}) = \left[1 + \frac{(\mathbf{c}\hat{\boldsymbol{\beta}} - \mathbf{r})'[\mathbf{c}(\mathbf{x}'\mathbf{x})^{-1}\mathbf{c}']^{-1}(\mathbf{c}\hat{\boldsymbol{\beta}} - \mathbf{r})}{\hat{\varepsilon}'\hat{\varepsilon}}\right]^{-n/2} \qquad (4.3.10)$$

The critical region for the outcome of $\lambda(\mathbf{Y})$ is of the form $[0, \tau]$ for $\tau < 1$, as indicated in Definition 4.3.1. Given (4.3.10), it follows after some algebraic manipulation that rejecting H_0 when $\lambda(\mathbf{Y}) \leq \tau$ is equivalent to rejecting H_0 when

$$F = \frac{(\mathbf{c}\hat{\boldsymbol{\beta}} - \mathbf{r})'[\mathbf{c}(\mathbf{x}'\mathbf{x})^{-1}\mathbf{c}']^{-1}(\mathbf{c}\hat{\boldsymbol{\beta}} - \mathbf{r})}{jS^2} \geq f_{1-\alpha} \qquad (4.3.11)$$

for an appropriate choice of the constant $f_{1-\alpha}$. In particular, note that $\lambda(\mathbf{Y}) = [1 + (\frac{j}{n-k})F]^{-n/2}$, and thus $\lambda(\mathbf{Y})$ and F are inversely monotonically related.

Under H_0 (i.e., on the assumption H_0 is true), the probability distribution of the F-statistic (on the left-hand side of the inequality in (4.3.11)) is the (central) Fdistribution with j numerator and $(n-k)$ denominator degrees of freedom. This follows because (1) from (4.2.6) where $(\mathbf{c}\hat{\boldsymbol{\beta}} - \mathbf{r})'[\sigma^2\mathbf{c}(\mathbf{x}'\mathbf{x})^{-1}\mathbf{c}']^{-1}(\mathbf{c}\hat{\boldsymbol{\beta}} - \mathbf{r})/j \sim \chi_j^2/j$, and $\chi_j^2 \sim$ Chi-square$(j, 0)$, (2) from (4.2.7) where $\frac{(n-k)S^2}{(n-k)\sigma^2} \sim \chi^2_{n-k}/(n-k)$, and $\chi^2_{n-k} \sim$ Chi-square$(n - k, 0)$, (3) the two χ^2-distributed random variables are independent (recall the discussion following (4.2.7)), and (4) the ratio of two independent χ^2 random variables, each divided by their respective degrees of freedom, has a central Fdistribution (Chapter E1; Mittelhammer, p. 345).

Given the preceding relationship between the GLR and F statistics, and given the known distributional characteristics of F, in practice the GLR test is generally conducted in terms of a critical region for the F statistic, the test being of the general form $\{F, C^F\}$. In particular, the test of H_0: $\mathbf{c}\boldsymbol{\beta} = \mathbf{r}$ versus H_a: $\mathbf{c}\boldsymbol{\beta} \neq \mathbf{r}$ is performed by choosing the $100(1 - \alpha)\%$ quantile of the F-distribution $f_{1-\alpha}$ so as to define an α-size test, that is, $f_{1-\alpha}$ is chosen to satisfy $\int_{f_{1-\alpha}}^{\infty} F(z; j, n-k, 0)\,dz = \alpha$, and the critical region for the test is defined by $C^F = [f_{1-\alpha}, \infty]$. Then H_0 is rejected if the outcome of F, say f, is such that $f \geq f_{1-\alpha}$. The value of $f_{1-\alpha}$ can be obtained using the GAUSS procedure cdffc() iteratively to find the value of $f_{1-\alpha}$ such that $\text{cdffc}(f_{1-\alpha}, j, n-k) = \alpha$.

Under H_0: $\mathbf{c}\boldsymbol{\beta} \neq \mathbf{r}$, the test statistic F in (4.3.11) has a *noncentral* F distribution with positive-valued noncentrality parameter

$$\lambda = \frac{1}{2}(\mathbf{c}\boldsymbol{\beta} - \mathbf{r})'[\sigma^2\mathbf{c}(\mathbf{x}'\mathbf{x})^{-1}\mathbf{c}']^{-1}(\mathbf{c}\boldsymbol{\beta} - \mathbf{r}). \tag{4.3.12}$$

The positive value of the noncentrality follows because, under H_a, the numerator noncentral χ^2 random variable of the F ratio is the sum of squares of j independent normal random variables having unit variances but nonzero means represented by the mean vector $\boldsymbol{\delta} = [\sigma^2\mathbf{c}(\mathbf{x}'\mathbf{x})^{-1}\mathbf{c}']^{-1/2}(\mathbf{c}\boldsymbol{\beta} - \mathbf{r}) \neq \mathbf{0}$. In general, the sum of squares of the elements of a multivariate normal random vector distributed as $N(\boldsymbol{\delta}, \mathbf{I})$ has a *noncentral* Chi-square distribution with noncentrality parameter $\lambda = \boldsymbol{\delta}'\boldsymbol{\delta}/2$ (Chapter E1; Mittelhammer, p. 666). Also the ratio of a noncentral Chi-square random variable to an independent central Chi-square random variable characterizes a noncentral F-distribution whose noncentrality parameter is equivalent to that of the numerator noncentral Chi-square random variable (Chapter E1; Mittelhammer, p. 667). The GAUSS procedure cdffnc() can be used to calculate the power function of the F-test, where

$$\pi(\lambda) = 1 - \text{cdffnc}(f_{1-\alpha}, j, n-k, \sqrt{2\lambda}) = \int_{f_{1-\alpha}}^{\infty} F(z; j, n-k, \lambda)\, dz, \tag{4.3.13}$$

and $F(z; j, n-k, \lambda)$ denotes a noncentral F-distribution with j numerator, $(n-k)$ denominator degrees of freedom, and noncentrality parameter λ (note the different parameterization of noncentrality that is implemented in the GAUSS procedure).

► **Example 4.3.1:** To demonstrate the F-test (4.3.11) of the linear restriction $\mathbf{c}\boldsymbol{\beta} = \mathbf{r}$, we provide the GAUSS program C4GLR_F.gss in the examples manual. The GAUSS procedure GLR_F() reports the observed test statistic and p-value for a given data sample. Then, the power function of the F-test is simulated by a Monte Carlo exercise and compared with the actual power function computed from the noncentral F distribution.

4.3.4.c. Sampling Properties of the GLR-F Test of $\mathbf{c}\boldsymbol{\beta} = \mathbf{r}$

The power function of the F-test of H_0: $\mathbf{c}\boldsymbol{\beta} = \mathbf{r}$, and thus of the GLR test as well, is monotonically increasing in the noncentrality parameter (4.3.12) (Chapter E1; Mittelhammer, p. 668). Therefore, the test is *unbiased*. Given the consistency of the bias-adjusted ML estimator $(\hat{\boldsymbol{\beta}}, S^2)$, the F-test (and GLR test) will also be a consistent test. The general motivation for consistency is provided by two basic observations. First of all, as $n \to \infty$, the critical region of the test will converge to a *fixed interval* with a finite positive lower bound because if $F \sim F(j, n-k, 0)$ then $jF \xrightarrow{d} \chi^2_j$ as $n \to \infty$, and so the lower bound of the critical region will converge to the quantile value $f^*_{1-\alpha}$ that satisfies

$$\int_{jf^*_{1-\alpha}}^{\infty} \text{Chi-square}(z; j, 0)\, dz = \alpha, \tag{4.3.14}$$

that is, $f^*_{1-\alpha} = \chi^2_{1-\alpha}/j$ in the limit as $n \to \infty$. Secondly, if $\boldsymbol{\xi} = \mathbf{c}\boldsymbol{\beta} - \mathbf{r} \neq \mathbf{0}$ and $\text{tr}(\mathbf{x}'\mathbf{x})^{-1} \to \mathbf{0}$, then the noncentrality parameter is such that

$$\lambda = \frac{1}{2}\boldsymbol{\xi}'[\sigma^2 \mathbf{c}(\mathbf{x}'\mathbf{x})^{-1}\mathbf{c}']^{-1}\boldsymbol{\xi} \to \infty \tag{4.3.15}$$

(see Mittelhammer, p. 627, for further details). Then, in the limit as $n \to \infty$ the probability of rejecting $H_0\colon \mathbf{c}\boldsymbol{\beta} = \mathbf{r}$ if $H_a\colon \mathbf{c}\boldsymbol{\beta} \neq \mathbf{r}$ is true is represented by

$$\lim_{\lambda \to \infty} \int_{jf^*_{1-\alpha}}^{\infty} \text{Chi-square}(z; j, \lambda)\, dz = 1 \tag{4.3.16}$$

for any fixed value of $jf^*_{1-\alpha}$, this is a standard property of the noncentral Chi-square distribution, and so the F-test is *consistent*.

If $\mathbf{c}$ contains two or more rows, then there *does not exist* a UMP, or even a UMPU test of $H_0\colon \mathbf{c}\boldsymbol{\beta} = \mathbf{r}$. However, if only *one* linear restriction is being tested, then the F-test (or GLR test) is UMPU, and in this case it is customary to use the square root of the F-statistic, which equals the T-statistic

$$T = \frac{\mathbf{c}\hat{\boldsymbol{\beta}} - r}{[S^2\, \mathbf{c}(\mathbf{x}'\mathbf{x})^{-1}\mathbf{c}']^{1/2}} \sim T(n-k, \delta) \tag{4.3.17}$$

in place of the F-statistic to perform the test. The T-statistic in (4.3.17) has a noncentral T-distribution with $(n-k)$ degrees of freedom and noncentrality parameter $\delta = \frac{\mathbf{c}\boldsymbol{\beta} - r}{(\sigma^2 \mathbf{c}(\mathbf{x}'\mathbf{x})^{-1}\mathbf{c}')^{1/2}}$ (Chapter E1; Mittelhammer, pp. 586–88). Under H_0, the T-statistic has the usual central (or Student's) T-distribution. The critical region of the T-test, $\{T, C^T\}$, is given by $C^T = (-\infty, -t_{1-\alpha/2}] \cup [t_{1-\alpha/2}, \infty)$, where

$$\int_{t_{1-\alpha/2}}^{\infty} T(z; n-k, 0)\, dz = \alpha/2. \tag{4.3.18}$$

The $100(1-\alpha/2)\%$ quantile of the central T-distribution, $t_{1-\alpha/2}$, can be found directly via the GAUSS procedure cdftci(), as $t_{1-\alpha/2} = \text{cdftci}(\alpha/2, n-k)$. Because $F = T^2$, note that the bounds on the critical regions for the F and T tests are related, for $f_{1-\alpha} = (t_{1-\alpha/2})^2$, and in this case of testing a scalar hypothesis $H_0\colon \mathbf{c}\boldsymbol{\beta} = r$, the T, F, and GLR tests are all equivalent.

Because the T-test is equivalent to the F-test (and the GLR test), we can conclude at once that the T-test is unbiased and consistent. Its power function can be inferred directly from its associated F-test equivalent, or else the power function can be calculated directly from the noncentral T-distribution as

$$\begin{aligned} \pi(\delta) &= \int_{-\infty}^{-t_{1-\alpha/2}} T(z; n-k, \delta)\, dz + \int_{t_{1-\alpha/2}}^{\infty} T(z; n-k, \delta)\, dz \\ &= \text{cdftnc}(-t_{1-\alpha/2}, n-k, \delta) + [1 - \text{cdftnc}(t_{1-\alpha/2}, n-k, \delta)], \end{aligned} \tag{4.3.19}$$

where the GAUSS procedure cdftnc(w, v, δ) is the cumulative distribution function of the noncentral T-distribution with v degrees of freedom and noncentrality parameter δ. The proof that the T-test and equivalent F and GLR tests are UMPU follows from $\mathbf{Y}$'s having an exponential class distribution. The demonstration of this fact is somewhat involved, and the reader can consult Mittelhammer, pp. 579–85, for an exposition of the approach leading to a proof. It can also be shown that the T-test and the equivalent F and GLR tests are UMPI tests, where the class of invariant tests in this case refers to invariance with respect to orthonormal transformations of the random sample **Y** (H. Bunke and O. Bunke, 1986, pp. 220–1).

► **Example 4.3.2:** To demonstrate the T-test (4.3.17) of the linear restriction $\mathbf{c}\boldsymbol{\beta} = \mathrm{r}$, we provide the GAUSS program C4GLR_T.gss in the examples manual. For a given sample, the GAUSS procedure GLR_T() reports the observed test statistic and p-value for the two-tailed test. Then, the power function of the T-test is simulated by a Monte Carlo exercise and compared with the actual power function computed from the noncentral T distribution.

4.3.5. Testing Linear Inequality Hypotheses

Cases sometimes arise in which the hypothesis of interest involves an inequality rather than an exact restriction on a linear combination of the elements in $\boldsymbol{\beta}$. A test of linear inequality hypotheses may be conducted using the T-statistic introduced in Section 4.3.4.c. Consider the null hypothesis $\mathrm{H}_0\colon \mathbf{c}\boldsymbol{\beta} \le \mathrm{r}$, where $\mathbf{c}$ is a row vector and r is some scalar constant. The test statistic is defined by

$$\mathrm{T} = \frac{\mathbf{c}\hat{\boldsymbol{\beta}} - \mathrm{r}}{[\mathrm{S}^2\, \mathbf{c}(\mathbf{x}'\mathbf{x})^{-1}\mathbf{c}']^{1/2}} \sim \mathrm{T}(n - k, \delta), \tag{4.3.20}$$

where the noncentrality parameter of the T-distribution equals $\delta = \frac{\mathbf{c}\boldsymbol{\beta} - \mathrm{r}}{[\sigma^2 \mathbf{c}(\mathbf{x}'\mathbf{x})^{-1}\mathbf{c}']^{1/2}}$. The test $\{\mathrm{T}, \mathrm{C}^{\mathrm{T}}\}$ has a critical region equal to $\mathrm{C}^{\mathrm{T}} = [\mathrm{t}_{1-\alpha}, \infty)$, and the test rule is

$$\text{reject } \mathrm{H}_0\colon \mathbf{c}\boldsymbol{\beta} \le \mathrm{r} \quad \text{iff} \quad t \ge t_{1-\alpha}, \tag{4.3.21}$$

where $t_{1-\alpha}$ is the $100(1-\alpha)\%$ quantile of the T-distribution; that is, $t_{1-\alpha}$ solves the integral equation

$$t_{1-\alpha} = \arg_{\mathrm{t}}\left[\int_{\mathrm{t}}^{\infty} \mathrm{T}(\mathrm{z}; n - k, 0)\, \mathrm{dz} = \alpha\right]. \tag{4.3.22}$$

The value of $t_{1-\alpha}$ can be found by the GAUSS command cdftci $(\alpha, n-k)$, which calculates the inverse of the *complement* of the cumulative central T-distribution, the upper tail probability being α and degrees of freedom being $(n-k)$. The power function of the test is given by

$$\pi(\delta) = \int_{t_{1-\alpha}}^{\infty} \mathrm{T}(\mathrm{z}; n-k, \delta)\, \mathrm{dz} = 1 - \mathrm{cdftnc}(t_{1-\alpha}, n-k, \delta), \tag{4.3.23}$$

where the GAUSS procedure cdftnc() calculates the value of the CDF of the noncentral T-distribution having $(n-k)$ degrees of freedom and noncentrality δ. Because $\pi(\delta)$ is monotonically increasing in δ, the test is *unbiased*. The test is also *consistent*, which can be motivated from two fundamental observations. First of all, as $n \to \infty$, and thus $\mathrm{v} = n - k \to \infty$,

$$\mathrm{T}(\mathrm{z}; \mathrm{v}, 0) \to \mathrm{N}(\mathrm{z}; 0, 1), \tag{4.3.24}$$

so that $t_{1-\alpha} \to z_{1-\alpha}$, where $z_{1-\alpha}$ is the $100(1-\alpha)\%$ quantile of the standard normal distribution that solves $\int_{z_{1-\alpha}}^{\infty} N(z; 0, 1)\, dz = \alpha$. Secondly, as $v \to \infty$, $T(z; v, \delta) \to N(\delta, 1)$, and if $\mathbf{c}(\mathbf{x}'\mathbf{x})^{-1}\mathbf{c}' \to 0$ so that $\mathbf{c}\hat{\boldsymbol{\beta}}$ is a consistent estimator of $\mathbf{c}\boldsymbol{\beta}$, and if H_0 is false so that $\mathbf{c}\boldsymbol{\beta} - r > 0$, then $\delta = \frac{\mathbf{c}\boldsymbol{\beta} - r}{[\sigma^2 \mathbf{c}(\mathbf{x}'\mathbf{x})^{-1}\mathbf{c}']} \to \infty$. Thus, in the limit as $n \to \infty$, the probability of rejecting H_0: $\mathbf{c}\boldsymbol{\beta} \leq r$ if H_a: $\mathbf{c}\boldsymbol{\beta} > r$ is true is coincident with

$$\lim_{\delta \to \infty} \int_{z_{1-\alpha}}^{\infty} N(z; \delta, 1)\, dz = 1, \tag{4.3.25}$$

and thus the test is consistent.

It can be shown that the T-test of H_0: $\mathbf{c}\boldsymbol{\beta} \leq r$ is UMPU. For the method of proof, the reader can consult Mittelhammer, pp. 579–85. It can also be shown that the T-test is UMPI in the class of tests invariant to orthonormal transformations of the random sample **Y** (H. Bunke and O. Bunke, pp. 220–1).

By appropriate inequality reversals in the preceding arguments, one can define a T-test of the null hypothesis H_0: $\mathbf{c}\boldsymbol{\beta} \geq r$. Precisely the same test statistic (4.3.19) is used to perform the test, but the critical region of the test is changed to $CR^T = (-\infty, -t_{1-\alpha}] = (-\infty, t_\alpha]$. All of the preceding discussion relating to test properties applies, mutatis mutandis, so that the test is unbiased, consistent, UMPU, and UMPI.

► **Example 4.3.3:** To demonstrate the T-test of a linear inequality restriction $\mathbf{c}\boldsymbol{\beta} \leq r$, we provide the GAUSS program C4T_INEQ.gss in the examples manual. For a given sample, the GAUSS procedure GLR_T() reports the observed test statistic and p-value for the one-tailed test. Then, the power function of the T-test is simulated by Monte Carlo exercise and compared with the actual power function computed from the noncentral T distribution.

4.3.6. Bonferroni Joint Tests of Inequality and Equality Hypotheses about $\boldsymbol{\beta}$

Situations arise in which the analyst is interested in testing more than one inequality restriction on the entries in the $\boldsymbol{\beta}$-vector. The tests can be performed by repeated applications of the T-test in the preceding section to the different inequality restrictions of interest. However, one must remember that the size of the joint test of all of the inequality restrictions is affected by the number of inequalities tested. A bound on the size of the joint test can be defined by using Bonferroni's probability inequality (Chapter E1; Mittelhammer, p. 17). In particular, letting A_i represent the event that the T-test of the ith inequality restriction does *not* reject the inequality hypothesis, it follows directly from Bonferroni's inequality that the probability of not rejecting *any* of the m inequalities is bounded by

$$P\left(\bigcap_{i=1}^{m} A_i\right) \geq 1 - \sum_{i=1}^{m} P(\overline{A_i}) \tag{4.3.26}$$

Because the *joint* hypothesis that *all* of the inequality restrictions are true is rejected when one or more of the inequality restrictions are rejected, the event $\overline{(\cap_{i=1}^{m} A_i)}$

represents the rejection of the joint hypothesis. Thus, the size of the joint test of m inequality restrictions, conducted as a set of m individual T-tests, is bounded as

$$\alpha = \mathrm{P}\left(\overline{\bigcap_{i=1}^{m} \mathrm{A_i}}\right) = 1 - \mathrm{P}\left(\bigcap_{i=1}^{m} \mathrm{A_i}\right) \le \sum_{i=1}^{m} \mathrm{P}(\overline{\mathrm{A}}_i) = \sum_{i=1}^{m} \alpha_i \qquad (4.3.27)$$

where α_i represents the size of the ith T-test. Thus, the *level* of the joint test, or a bound on the size of the joint test of m inequality restrictions based on m individual T-tests, can be stated as $\sum_{i=1}^{m} \alpha_i$, and if each individual T-test has the same size α_*, then the level of the joint test becomes $m\alpha_*$. The preceding test of m inequality restrictions is referred to as a *Bonferroni joint test*.

► **Example 4.3.4:** To demonstrate the joint test of m linear inequality restrictions $\mathbf{c}\boldsymbol{\beta} \le \mathrm{r}$, we provide the GAUSS program C4BJoint.gss in the examples manual. For a given sample, the GAUSS procedure GLR_T() reports the observed test statistic and p-value for the set of m one-tailed tests. Then, a Monte Carlo exercise is conducted to simulate the size of the Bonferroni joint test and compare it with the intended Type-I error rate.

A Bonferroni joint test of m *equality* restrictions can be defined as well, and the reader is asked to define such a test along with the appropriate bound on the level of Type-I error for the test. However, the aforementioned GLR or F tests provide exact control over the *size* of the joint test, whereas the Bonferroni approach only bounds the size of the test. Thus, the Bonferroni approach tends to be a less powerful test of the joint hypothesis for a given test level. Nonetheless, the Bonferroni approach is often used in conjunction with a GLR or other joint test to determine which of the equality restrictions is causing the rejection. The next example illustrates this idea.

► **Example 4.3.5:** The GAUSS program C4BTest.gss in the examples manual is designed to demonstrate the Bonferroni approach for testing linear equality hypotheses of the form $\mathbf{c}\boldsymbol{\beta} = \mathbf{r}$. For a given sample, the GAUSS procedure GLR_F() reports the observed test statistic and p-value for an exact size F-test, and the results are compared with the set of individual T-tests. Then, a Monte Carlo exercise is conducted to simulate the size of the Bonferroni joint test and compare it with the power of the associated F-test as well as the intended Type-I error rate.

As a final note, the Bonferroni approach to testing inequality and equality restrictions can be applied even when normality for $\mathbf{Y}$ is *not* assumed. In this case, one must rely on the asymptotic normal distribution of the T-statistic, and then all of the preceding results apply in an approximative asymptotic sense. See Chapter 6 for further details.

4.3.7. Testing Hypotheses about σ^2

The analyst is sometimes interested in testing hypotheses relating to the magnitude of the variance of $\mathbf{Y}$ or ε. The hypothesis is most often in the form of an inequality restriction such as $\mathrm{H_0}: \sigma^2 \le \sigma_0^2$ versus $\mathrm{H_a}: \sigma^2 > \sigma_0^2$, or similarly with the inequalities reversed. The GLR procedure can be applied to test $H_0: \sigma^2 \leq \sigma_0^2$ versus $H_a: \sigma^2 > \sigma_0^2$ by forming the likelihood ratio

$$\lambda(\mathbf{Y}) = \frac{\max_{\sigma^2 \leq \sigma_0^2, \boldsymbol{\beta}} L(\boldsymbol{\beta}, \sigma^2 \mid \mathbf{Y}, \mathbf{x})}{\max_{\sigma^2, \boldsymbol{\beta}} L(\boldsymbol{\beta}, \sigma^2 \mid \mathbf{Y}, \mathbf{x})}. \tag{4.3.28}$$

Algebraic manipulation of the expression $\lambda(\mathbf{Y})$ reveals that $\lambda(\mathbf{Y}) \leq c$ iff $\frac{(n-k)S^2}{\sigma_0^2} \geq \tau$ for an appropriate value of τ chosen so as to define a test with the desired size.

In the event that $\sigma^2 = \sigma_0^2$, we know that $\frac{(n-k)S^2}{\sigma_0^2} \sim$ Chi-square$(n-k, 0)$, and so choosing $\tau_{1-\alpha} \equiv \chi^2_{1-\alpha}$ to satisfy $\int_{\chi^2_{1-\alpha}}^{\infty}$ Chi-square$(z; n-k, 0)\, dz = \alpha$, and using the test rule

$$\text{reject } H_0: \sigma^2 \leq \sigma_0^2 \quad \text{iff} \quad \frac{(n-k)\, s^2}{\sigma_0^2} \geq \chi^2_{1-\alpha} \tag{4.3.29}$$

rejects H_0 with probability α, and thus the probability of Type-I error at this point in the parameter space is α. Now consider the power function of the test across all potential values of σ^2:

$$\begin{aligned}
\pi(\sigma^2) &= P\left[\frac{(n-k)\, s^2}{\sigma_0^2} \geq \chi^2_{1-\alpha} \middle| \sigma^2\right] \\
&= P\left[\frac{(n-k)\, s^2}{\sigma^2} \geq \frac{\sigma_0^2}{\sigma^2}\chi^2_{1-\alpha} \middle| \sigma^2\right] \\
&= \int_{\frac{\sigma_0^2 \chi^2_{1-\alpha}}{\sigma^2}}^{\infty} \text{Chi-square}(z; n-k, 0)\, dz.
\end{aligned} \tag{4.3.30}$$

It is evident that the power function is monotonically increasing in σ^2 with $\pi(\sigma^2) < \alpha\ \forall \sigma^2 < \sigma_0^2$ and $\pi(\sigma^2) > \alpha\ \forall \sigma^2 > \sigma_0^2$. Thus, the test (4.3.28) is an *unbiased* test having size α. The test is also consistent, for note that $\frac{S^2}{\sigma^2} \xrightarrow{p} 1$ and $\frac{\chi^2_{1-\alpha}}{n-k} \rightarrow 1$ as $n \rightarrow \infty$, and thus if $\sigma^2 > \sigma_0^2$, then $(\frac{S^2}{\sigma^2} - \frac{\sigma_0^2}{\sigma^2}\frac{\chi^2_{1-\alpha}}{n-k}) \xrightarrow{p} 1 - \frac{\sigma_0^2}{\sigma^2} > 0$, and thus the probability of the rejection event converges to 1.

For a demonstration that the Chi-square test of $H_0: \sigma^2 \leq \sigma_0^2$ is UMPU, see Mittelhammer, pp. 576–9. By appropriate inequality reversals, the preceding discussion can be used to define an unbiased, consistent, and UMPU test of $H_0: \sigma^2 \geq \sigma_0^2$.

► **Example 4.3.6:** To demonstrate the test of the inequality hypothesis $H_0: \sigma^2 \leq \sigma_0^2$, we provide the GAUSS program C4Chisq.gss in the examples manual. For a given sample, the GAUSS program reports the observed test statistic and p-value for the one-tailed test. Then, the power function of the test is approximated by Monte Carlo simulation and compared with the actual power function.

4.4. Confidence Interval and Region Estimation

In general terms within the context of a classical inverse problem, a *confidence region* refers to a subset (the *region*) of the range of possible values for unknown probability model characteristics that contains the true value of these characteristics with a predefined level of *confidence*. In the case in which some or all of the unknown characteristics can be expressed as functions of parameters, as $\mathbf{c}(\boldsymbol{\theta})$, then a confidence region will be in the form of a set of values, say A, for which there is a predefined level of confidence that $\mathbf{c}(\boldsymbol{\theta}_0) \in \mathrm{A}$, where $\boldsymbol{\theta}_0$ denotes the true value of the parameter vector. When $\mathbf{c}(\boldsymbol{\theta})$ is a scalar and the set A is in the form of an interval of real numbers, then the confidence region is referred to alternatively as a *confidence interval*. The case involving functions of parameters is the one most often encountered in applied work, and so in the discussion to follow the notation $\mathbf{c}(\boldsymbol{\theta})$ is used to indicate some scalar or vector-valued inverse problem characteristic of interest that depends on a finite dimensional parameter vector $\boldsymbol{\theta}$. One can suppress the dependence of the point value $\mathbf{c}(\boldsymbol{\theta})$ on parameters in any of the following arguments that do not explicitly require parameter values, making such arguments applicable to nonparametric contexts as well.

4.4.1. Meaning of "Confidence" Interval or Region

The preceding general description begs the question of what is meant by the term *confidence*. In classical confidence region estimation, one seeks a set-valued function of the random sample $\mathbf{Y}$, say $\mathbf{A}(\mathbf{Y})$, that maps sample outcomes $\mathbf{y}$ into sets of values, say $\mathrm{A}(\mathbf{y})$, such that that the event "$\mathbf{c}(\boldsymbol{\theta}_0)$ is contained in $\mathrm{A}(\mathbf{y})$" occurs with a predefined level of probability. The minimum (or infimum – recall that the infimum is the largest lower bound, or the minimum if it exists) value of the probability of the event that $\mathbf{c}(\boldsymbol{\theta}) \in \mathrm{A}(\mathbf{y})$ across all possibilities for $\boldsymbol{\theta}$ is what is called the *confidence coefficient*, or simply *confidence* for short. Regarding terminology, in classical confidence region estimation the set-valued function $\mathrm{A}(\mathbf{Y})$ is the confidence region (or confidence set) *estimator*, the set of values $\mathrm{A}(\mathbf{y})$ is the confidence region *estimate*, and the *confidence coefficient*, or simply *confidence*, associated with the confidence region is given by the value $\min_{\theta}[\mathrm{P}(\mathbf{c}(\boldsymbol{\theta}) \in \mathrm{A}(\mathbf{y}))] = \tau$ (use the infimum if the minimum does not exist). In calculating the probabilities underlying the minimization problem, we emphasize that the probability distributions indexed by the respective $\boldsymbol{\theta}$ values are used.

Note carefully that *confidence* is a *predata* concept – it refers to the minimum (or infimum) probability of the event that the confidence region estimator will generate an estimate that contains the true value $\mathbf{c}(\boldsymbol{\theta}_0)$ prior to any particular data or sample outcome of $\mathbf{Y}$ being observed. As such, *confidence* is a property of the estimator $\mathrm{A}(\mathbf{Y})$ and *not* the estimate $\mathrm{A}(\mathbf{y})$. In the *postdata* environment, the set $\mathrm{A}(\mathbf{y})$ either does or does not contain $\mathbf{c}(\boldsymbol{\theta}_0)$; there are no probabilities involved, and the analyst will generally not know which event in this dichotomy actually did occur. Thus, although users of classical confidence regions have predata *confidence* in the proposition that their confidence region estimators *will* produce sets of values that contain $\mathbf{c}(\boldsymbol{\theta}_0)$, postdata confidence region outcomes either may or may not accomplish this goal. In the long run, if one could observe repeated random sample outcomes of $\mathbf{Y}$ and generate associated confidence regions estimates for $\mathbf{c}(\boldsymbol{\theta}_0)$ ad infinitum, confidence region estimates would contain $\mathbf{c}(\boldsymbol{\theta}_0)$ at least $100\tau\%$ of the time if the confidence region had a confidence coefficient of τ.

4.4.2. Rationale for the Use of Confidence Regions

At this point, after having already examined principles for generating best-point estimates of the true value of $\mathbf{c}(\boldsymbol{\theta})$, the reader may question the utility of generating confidence regions for $\mathbf{c}(\boldsymbol{\theta}_0)$. After all, if we already have the best estimate of $\mathbf{c}(\boldsymbol{\theta}_0)$, why should we examine a range of estimates that will include estimates of $\mathbf{c}(\boldsymbol{\theta}_0)$ other than the best estimate? Perhaps the most compelling motivation for examining confidence regions is related to the sobering observation that point estimators, even optimal ones (e.g., MVUE, BLUE), will generate incorrect values for $\mathbf{c}(\boldsymbol{\theta}_0)$ with notable frequency, and in the case in which the estimator is a continuous random variable, the estimator is essentially certain (i.e., with probability 1) to generate an estimate of the value $\mathbf{c}(\boldsymbol{\theta}_0)$ that is literally *wrong*! The latter observation follows directly from the fact that the probability of the event $\mathbf{t}(\mathbf{y}) = \mathbf{c}(\boldsymbol{\theta}_0)$ is equal to *zero* if $\mathbf{T} = \mathbf{t}(\mathbf{Y})$ is a continuous random variable, and even when the estimator $\mathbf{T}$ is discrete, this probability is nevertheless generally far less than 1 in applications. The confidence region estimator allows one to generate estimates that are *correct*, in the sense of generating a *range* of values that contains the true $\mathbf{c}(\boldsymbol{\theta})$ with a *known* predefined minimum probability of occurrence. As will be seen later, confidence regions then provide a measure of the precision of point estimates. That is, if confidence regions are small and narrowly concentrated around point estimates, and if there is also a high degree of confidence that the region contains the true $\mathbf{c}(\boldsymbol{\theta})$, then it follows that the point estimates are close to $\mathbf{c}(\boldsymbol{\theta}_0)$ with high confidence and thus the point estimates of $\mathbf{c}(\boldsymbol{\theta}_0)$ are relatively precise.

4.4.3. Confidence Intervals, Regions, and Bounds for $\boldsymbol{\beta}$

In this section we examine specific procedures for generating confidence regions, intervals, and bounds for the elements of the parameter vector $\boldsymbol{\beta}$ in the multivariate normal linear regression model.

4.4.3.a. Confidence Regions and Intervals

Using the GLR (or equivalently, the F) tests of the hypothesis $\mathrm{H}_0\colon \mathbf{c}\boldsymbol{\beta} = \mathbf{r}$, confidence regions can be established for any set of $j \leq k$ functionally independent linear restrictions on $\boldsymbol{\beta}$ of interest. Using the F-statistic equivalent of the GLR test, a confidence region estimator with predata level of confidence $(1-\alpha)$ is defined via the duality principle (Chapter E2; Mittelhammer, p. 643) to be all of the potential $\mathbf{r}$-values in $\mathrm{H}_0\colon \mathbf{c}\boldsymbol{\beta} = \mathbf{r}$ that would *not* be rejected by a level-α F-test of the hypothesis. Thus, the confidence region estimator for $\mathbf{c}\boldsymbol{\beta}$ is given in general by

$$\mathrm{CR}^{\mathrm{GLR}} = \{\mathbf{r} : (\mathbf{c}\hat{\boldsymbol{\beta}} - \mathbf{r})'[\mathrm{S}^2\mathbf{c}(\mathbf{x}'\mathbf{x})^{-1}\mathbf{c}']^{-1}(\mathbf{c}\hat{\boldsymbol{\beta}} - \mathbf{r}) < \mathrm{j}\mathrm{f}_{1-\alpha}\} \tag{4.4.1}$$

and by

$$\mathrm{CR}^{\mathrm{GLR}} = (\mathbf{c}\hat{\boldsymbol{\beta}} - t_{1-\alpha/2}(S^2\mathbf{c}(\mathbf{x}'\mathbf{x})^{-1}\mathbf{c}')^{1/2},\ \ \mathbf{c}\hat{\boldsymbol{\beta}} + t_{1-\alpha/2}(S^2\mathbf{c}(\mathbf{x}'\mathbf{x})^{-1}\mathbf{c}')^{1/2}) \qquad (4.4.2)$$

in the special case where $\mathbf{c}\hat{\boldsymbol{\beta}}$ is a scalar (recall that in this latter case, $f_{1-\alpha} = (t_{1-\alpha/2})^2$). Because both the F and T statistics are continuous random variables, the strong inequalities in (4.4.1) and (4.4.2) can be changed to weak inequalities without having any effect on the confidence levels. Because the confidence regions are based on unbiased and consistent hypothesis-testing procedures, it follows from duality between testing and confidence region procedures (Chapter E2; Mittelhammer, pp. 643, 648) that the confidence region estimators are also unbiased and consistent. In the case of the confidence interval estimator (4.4.2), the property of uniformly most accurate unbiased (UMAU) (Chapter E2; Mittelhammer, p. 648) also applies, for the hypothesis test (recall (4.3.17) and the subsequent discussion) has the UMPU property.

► **Example 4.4.1:** To demonstrate the setup and application of a $100(1-\alpha)\%$ confidence region based on the F-test criterion, we provide the GAUSS program C4Region.gss in the examples manual. The GAUSS procedure FRegion() is used to compute the boundary of a confidence ellipse, which is plotted with the associated confidence intervals based on the T-test criterion under the Bonferroni size adjustment. Then, the coverage probabilities of the regions are approximated by Monte Carlo simulation and compared with the intended coverage probability.

4.4.3.b. One-Sided Confidence Bounds

One-sided confidence bounds for scalar $\mathbf{c}\boldsymbol{\beta}$ can be obtained by applying the duality principle to the T-tests of either H_0: $\mathbf{c}\boldsymbol{\beta} \leq r$ or H_0: $\mathbf{c}\boldsymbol{\beta} \geq r$. To define a *lower* confidence bound having confidence level $(1-\alpha)$, consider the level-α T-test of the null hypothesis H_0: $\mathbf{c}\boldsymbol{\beta} \leq r$. If the duality principle is used, the set of potential r-values that would *not* be rejected by the level-α test is characterized by

$$\begin{aligned}\mathrm{CR}^{\mathrm{T}} &= \left\{ r : \frac{\mathbf{c}\hat{\boldsymbol{\beta}} - r}{[S^2\mathbf{c}(\mathbf{x}'\mathbf{x})^{-1}\mathbf{c}']^{1/2}} < t_{1-\alpha} \right\} \\ &= (\mathbf{c}\hat{\boldsymbol{\beta}} - t_{1-\alpha}[S^2\mathbf{c}(\mathbf{x}'\mathbf{x})^{-1}\mathbf{c}']^{1/2}, \infty), \qquad (4.4.3)\end{aligned}$$

which defines the $(1-\alpha)$ level lower confidence bound estimator. The level $(1-\alpha)$ *upper* confidence bound estimator can be defined by applying the duality principle to the T-test of the hypothesis H_0: $\mathbf{c}\boldsymbol{\beta} \geq r$, yielding

$$\begin{aligned}\mathrm{CR}^{\mathrm{T}} &= \left\{ r : \frac{\mathbf{c}\hat{\boldsymbol{\beta}} - r}{[S^2\mathbf{c}(\mathbf{x}'\mathbf{x})^{-1}\mathbf{c}']^{1/2}} > -t_{1-\alpha} \right\} \\ &= (-\infty, \mathbf{c}\hat{\boldsymbol{\beta}} + t_{1-\alpha}[S^2\mathbf{c}(\mathbf{x}'\mathbf{x})^{-1}\mathbf{c}']^{1/2}) \qquad (4.4.4)\end{aligned}$$

As before, because the T-statistic is a continuous random variable, the strict inequalities in (4.4.3) and (4.4.4) can be changed to weak inequalities without having any effect on the confidence level of the confidence bound. Because the hypothesis tests on which the confidence bounds are based are unbiased and UMPU, the confidence intervals are unbiased and UMAU.

4.4.3.c. Bonferroni Joint Confidence Regions and Bounds

A joint confidence region or bound for more than one linear combination of the entries in $\boldsymbol{\beta}$ can be constructed by defining multiple confidence intervals or bounds of the type (4.4.2) through (4.4.4) and then bounding the level of their intersection based on Bonferroni's inequality. In particular, if $\mathrm{CR}_\mathrm{i}^\mathrm{Z}$ is a confidence interval or bound for $\mathbf{c}_\mathrm{i}\boldsymbol{\beta}$ having level $1-\alpha_i$ for $i=1,\ldots,m$, then using Bonferroni's inequality,

$$\mathrm{P}\big(\mathbf{c}_i\boldsymbol{\beta}\in \mathrm{CR}_\mathrm{i}^\mathrm{Z}, i=1,\ldots,m\big)\geq 1-\sum_{i=1}^{m}\mathrm{P}\big(\mathbf{c}_\mathrm{i}\boldsymbol{\beta}\notin \mathrm{CR}_\mathrm{i}^\mathrm{Z}\big)\geq 1-\sum_{i=1}^{m}\alpha_i. \quad (4.4.5)$$

Thus, the confidence level of the joint confidence region is $1-\sum_{i=1}^{m}\alpha_i$.

► **Example 4.4.2:** The GAUSS program C4Bounds.gss in the examples manual is designed to demonstrate the setup and application of joint one-sided confidence bounds based on the T-test criterion. The Bonferroni inequality is used to adjust the upper or lower bounds on individual components of the hypothesis to achieve the desired coverage. A Monte Carlo simulation exercise is conducted to compare the estimated coverage probability for upper- and lower-bounded regions with the intended coverage probability.

4.4.4. Confidence Bounds on σ^2

Confidence bounds on σ^2 can be defined by applying the duality principle of test-confidence region construction to the Chi-square tests of the hypotheses $\mathrm{H}_0\colon \sigma^2\leq\sigma_0^2$ given by (4.3.29). The set of σ_0^2 values that would *not* be rejected by the α-level Chi-square test,

$$\mathrm{CR}=\left\{\sigma_0^2:\frac{(n-k)\,\mathrm{S}^2}{\sigma_0^2}<\chi^2_{1-\alpha}\right\}=\left(\frac{(n-k)\,\mathrm{S}^2}{\chi^2_{1-\alpha}},\infty\right) \quad (4.4.6)$$

defines the level $(1-\alpha)$ lower-confidence bound on the value of σ^2. To define a $(1-\alpha)$ upper-confidence bound, the inequalities are reversed and the critical value of the test is changed to obtain

$$\mathrm{CR}=\left\{\sigma_0^2:\frac{(n-k)\,\mathrm{S}^2}{\sigma_0^2}>\chi^2_{\alpha}\right\}=\left[0,\frac{(n-k)\,\mathrm{S}^2}{\chi^2_{\alpha}}\right). \quad (4.4.7)$$

The confidence bounds are unbiased and UMAU because the hypothesis tests they are derived from are unbiased and UMPU. The strong inequalities in (4.4.6) through (4.4.7) can be changed to weak inequalities without affecting the confidence level of the confidence bounds.

► **Example 4.4.3:** To demonstrate the computation of a $100(1-\alpha)\%$ confidence region for the unbiased variance estimator S^2, we provide the GAUSS program C4S2CR.gss in the examples manual. For a given sample, GAUSS reports the upper and lower bounds stated in (4.4.6) and (4.4.7). Then, the coverage probability of the confidence interval is approximated by Monte Carlo simulation and compared with the intended coverage probability for several sample sizes (selected by the user).

4.5. Pretest Estimators Based on Hypothesis Tests: Introduction

We introduced in Section 3.9 the idea of a biased estimator and its corresponding risk function. In this context we also considered, under a squared-error loss (SEL) measure, the risk function for a restricted ML estimator $\hat{\boldsymbol{\beta}}_r$ subject to the restriction $\boldsymbol{\beta} = \mathbf{r} = \mathbf{0}$. This permitted us to compare the risk functions of the unrestricted and restricted ML estimators. Because the restricted and unrestricted ML risk functions, expressed as functions of $\boldsymbol{\beta}'\boldsymbol{\beta}$, crossed at points in the parameter space, we were left with the question of how to choose between the two alternative estimators. In regard to the problem of choosing between the restricted and unrestricted estimators, we now consider whether hypothesis testing can provide us with an answer to this decision problem.

In previous sections, we examined the process of using the available information to test statistical hypotheses. The hypothesis-testing framework provides, in both a pre- and postdata sense, a rule for choosing between an unrestricted estimator based on the data (sample) and a restricted estimator that reflects a particular hypothesis. Consequently, a choice between the estimators is suggested by the outcome of the associated hypothesis test. This choice or decision context leads to a two-stage estimation rule that is known as a preliminary test or *pretest estimator*, and such pretest rules are commonly used in applied research. Although many authors are silent on the issue of using pretest estimators, we believe it is important to indicate to the reader some of the statistical consequences of this decision rule.

4.5.1. The Pretest Estimator

To see the basis for, and the predata statistical consequences of this two-stage estimation procedure, we use for expository purposes a very simple linear regression model. Consider the statistical model $\mathbf{Y} = \mathbf{x}\beta + \varepsilon$, where $\mathbf{x}$ is an n-dimensional column vector scaled so that $\mathbf{x}'\mathbf{x} = 1$ and $\varepsilon \sim \mathrm{N}(\mathbf{0}, \sigma^2\mathbf{I}_n)$. As a test mechanism we use the GLR test statistic in its equivalent F-statistic form. In particular, to test the null hypothesis $\mathrm{H_0}$: $\beta = \mathrm{r}$ against the alternative hypothesis $\mathrm{H_a}$: $\beta \neq \mathrm{r}$, we use the test statistic

$$\mathrm{F} = \frac{(\hat{\beta} - \mathrm{r})^2}{\mathrm{S}^2}, \tag{4.5.1}$$

which, *if the null hypothesis is correct*, is distributed as a central F random variable with 1 and $(n - k)$ degrees of freedom. If the null hypothesis is incorrect and $\mathrm{E}[\hat{\beta} - \mathrm{r}] = (\beta - \mathrm{r}) = \delta \neq 0$, then F is distributed as a noncentral F-distribution with noncentrality parameter $(\beta - \mathrm{r})^2/2\sigma^2 = \delta'\delta/2\sigma^2$. In practice, when the critical region of the test is defined, the null hypothesis is temporarily *assumed* to be correct, and the central F distribution is used as the test statistic. The null hypothesis is rejected if $f \geq \tau = f_{1-\alpha}$, where in this case the critical value τ is determined for a given level of the test α by

$$\int_{\tau}^{\infty} \mathrm{F}(\mathrm{f}; 1, n - k, 0)\,\mathrm{df} = \mathrm{P}[\mathrm{f} \geq \tau] = \alpha. \tag{4.5.2}$$

If we accept the null hypothesis $\mathrm{H_0}$: $\beta = \mathrm{r}$, we use the restricted estimator (degenerate in this case) r as our estimator of β; if we reject the null hypothesis and thus accept the alternative that $\beta - r = \delta \neq 0$, we use the unrestricted maximum likelihood estimator $\hat{\beta}_{ML}$. Thus, the definition of the estimator depends on a preliminary test of the validity of restriction $\beta = r$, and the estimator is represented by

$$\hat{\hat{\beta}} = \begin{cases} r & \text{if } F < \tau \\ \hat{\beta}_{ML} & \text{if } F \geq \tau \end{cases} \tag{4.5.3}$$

Consequently, in a predata context, the estimator that results when a researcher uses the conventional accept–reject testing dichotomy to choose between the restricted and unrestricted estimator, can be written as

$$\begin{aligned} \hat{\hat{\beta}} &= I_{(0,\,\tau)}(F)r + I_{(\tau,\,\infty)}(F)\hat{\beta}_{ML} \\ &= I_{(0,\,\tau)}(F)r + \left[1 - I_{(0,\,\tau)}(F)\right]\hat{\beta}_{ML} \\ &= \hat{\boldsymbol{\beta}}_{ML} - I_{(0,\,\tau)}(F)(\hat{\beta}_{ML} - r), \end{aligned} \tag{4.5.4}$$

where $I_{(0,\,\tau)}(F)$ and $I_{[\tau,\,\infty)}(F)$ are indicator functions that take the values $I_{(0,\,\tau)}(F) = 1$ and $I_{[\tau,\,\infty)}(F) = 0$ if the outcome of F falls within the interval zero to τ and take the values $I_{(0,\,\tau)}(F) = 0$ and $I_{[\tau,\,\infty)}(F) = 1$ when the outcome of F is τ or greater. Therefore, in a repeated sampling context, the data, the hypothesized restriction, and the level of significance all determine the combination of the two estimators that is chosen.

If the level of significance α is equal to 1, then the pretest rule (4.5.4) always selects the ML estimator. Alternatively, the pretest estimator is equivalent to the restricted ML estimator if $\alpha = 0$. Therefore, the choice of α has a crucial role to play in determining the proportion of the time in repeated sampling that the restricted and unrestricted estimators are used and also determines the sampling performance of the pretest estimator. In terms of sampling properties, the mean of the pretest estimator (4.5.4) is

$$E[\hat{\hat{\beta}}] = \beta - E[I_{(0,\,\tau)}(F)(\hat{\beta}_{ML} - r)]. \tag{4.5.5}$$

If the null hypothesis is true and $\beta = r$, so that $\delta = \beta - r = 0$, the pretest estimator is unbiased. *For all $\delta \neq 0$, the pretest estimator is biased.*

4.5.2. The Pretest Estimator Risk Function

If, from a predata standpoint, we examine the performance of the pretest estimator under a squared-error risk measure, we may write the risk function as

$$\begin{aligned} \rho(\boldsymbol{\beta}, \hat{\hat{\boldsymbol{\beta}}}) &= E[(\hat{\hat{\boldsymbol{\beta}}} - \boldsymbol{\beta})'(\hat{\hat{\boldsymbol{\beta}}} - \boldsymbol{\beta})] \\ &= E[(\hat{\boldsymbol{\beta}}_{ML} - \boldsymbol{\beta} - I_{(0,\,\tau)}(F)(\hat{\boldsymbol{\beta}}_{ML} - \mathbf{r}))'(\hat{\boldsymbol{\beta}}_{ML} - \boldsymbol{\beta} - I_{(0,\,\tau)}(F)(\hat{\boldsymbol{\beta}}_{ML} - \mathbf{r}))] \\ &= E[(\hat{\boldsymbol{\beta}}_{ML} - \boldsymbol{\beta})'(\hat{\boldsymbol{\beta}}_{ML} - \boldsymbol{\beta})] - E[I_{(0,\,\tau)}(F)(\hat{\boldsymbol{\beta}}_{ML} - \boldsymbol{\beta})'(\hat{\boldsymbol{\beta}}_{ML} - \boldsymbol{\beta})] \\ &\quad + E[I_{(0,\,\tau)}(F)\boldsymbol{\delta}'\boldsymbol{\delta}] \\ &= \sigma^2 k - E[I_{(0,\,\tau)}(F)(\hat{\boldsymbol{\beta}}_{ML} - \boldsymbol{\beta})'(\hat{\boldsymbol{\beta}}_{ML} - \boldsymbol{\beta})] + \boldsymbol{\delta}'\boldsymbol{\delta}P[f < \tau] \end{aligned} \tag{4.5.6}$$

Judge and Bock (1978) and others have evaluated this risk function, and the sampling risk characteristics of (4.5.6) that emerge are presented in Figure 4.1. At the origin where $\boldsymbol{\delta} = \mathbf{0}$ and thus the hypothesis is correctly specified, and near the origin where the restrictions are "close" to being correct, the pretest estimator has lower risk than

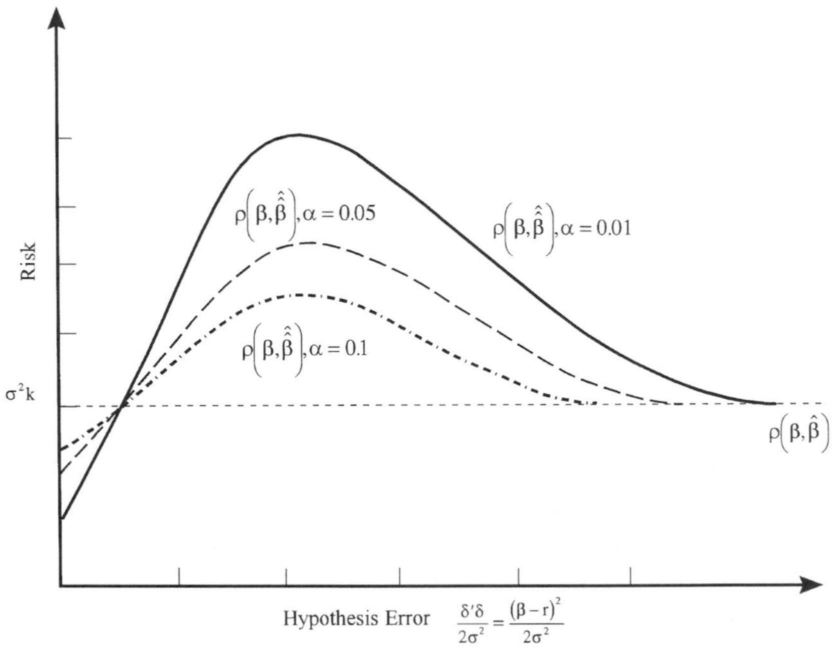

Figure 4.1: Characteristics of pretest estimator risk functions for different levels of α.

the unrestricted ML estimator. However, over a large range of the parameter space, the pretest estimator has a larger risk than the unrestricted ML estimator. As $\delta'\delta/2\sigma^2$ continues to increase, the risk of the pretest estimator eventually approaches the risk of the unrestricted ML estimator. The risk consequences of the choice of α, or equivalently of τ, which in practice is often chosen in a cavalier way, are also presented in Figure 4.1. This simple linear regression problem will be generalized in Chapter 15, and the corresponding risk and model specification implications will be reexamined.

► **Example 4.5.1:** The GAUSS program C4PTest.gss provided in the examples manual is designed to compare the quadratic risk properties of the restricted and unrestricted ML estimators with the pretest estimator. The risk functions presented in Figure 4.1 are estimated by Monte Carlo simulation and plotted for four different values of α.

4.6. Concluding Remarks

Given a probability model for the underlying DSP of some economic process, the emphasis then turns to how the evidence – the sample observations – changes our state of knowledge about aspects of the DSP and about the economic process for which our initial knowledge is partial or incomplete. In Chapter 3, point estimation rules were established that prescribe how sample observations are to be transformed into point estimates of unknown parameters. In a *predata* context, and in the context of the given parametric probability model, point estimators represent information about model parameters in terms of random variables whose probability distributions characterize the relative frequency with which various potential point estimates for unknown parameters will be generated in repeated sampling from the DSP. *Postdata*, a particular point estimate is produced that is either correct or not (the analyst will not know which is the case), and an incorrect estimate will be generated with positive probability (probability 1 in the case of a continuous random variable point estimator).

In this chapter we have used the ideas of Fisher, Neyman, and Pearson to extend the reach of point estimation and point estimates to region–interval estimation and hypothesis testing. Region–interval estimation rules have been established that prescribe how sample observations are to be transformed into *sets* of values whose purpose is to encompass the true value of unknown parameters with a predefined level of confidence. Hypothesis-testing procedures have been established that prescribe how sample observations are to be transformed into decisions regarding the validity of a hypothesis about values of parameters. In a *predata* context, and in the context of the given probability model, region–interval estimators represent information about model parameters in terms of random sets having known probability of generating set outcomes that contain true parameter values of interest. Also, in the same *predata* and probability model context, hypothesis testing rules represent information about model parameters in terms of random decision-making rules whose probability of making a correct decision regarding a proposition about model parameter values is fixed a priori. *Postdata*, region–interval estimators generate a set that either does or does not encompass the true parameters of interest, and hypothesis-testing procedures produce a decision about a hypothesis that is either right or wrong – the analyst will not know which is the case. The analyst needs to be aware that region–interval estimates and hypothesis testing decisions will be generated that are wrong with *positive* probability.

The main point to appreciate in the preceding comments is that there is a common postdata reality relating to the interpretation of the final output of the three classical information-generating procedures: point estimators, region–interval estimators, and testing procedures. In particular, their random nature and stochastic characteristics are all derived on the basis of logic applied in a predata context to characteristics of the probability model postulated for the DSP of the economic process, and the efficacy of the procedures are evaluated in this predata context. Postdata, these procedures produce results that are either right or wrong, with no equivocation. And predata, the logically derived stochastic characteristics of estimation and testing procedures are only as accurate as the probability model on which they are based.

As a final cautionary remark, note that regression models, and any statistical procedures applied to them, exist on a conceptual level and are related to any subject area knowledge and theories only through an analyst's interpretation of these models and procedures within such a subject area context. Tests of hypotheses apply directly to hypotheses about unknown components of probability models for DSPs and not to particular subject matter features of the data per se. Likewise, estimation procedures generate estimates of the values of unknown probability model components and not to particular features of an economic process per se. Consequently, statistical methodology, including hypothesis testing and confidence region estimation procedures, should not overshadow the theories and institutional knowledge about economic processes that were fundamental to connecting the data to a model at the outset.

The conclusion of a hypothesis test stating that a model parameter is or is not significantly different from the value zero rings hollow in the absence of relevant economic theories and institutional knowledge with which to interpret the context of the decision. Furthermore, there is no guarantee that a given hypothesis test is truly testing an economic theory, institutional behavior, or even the validity of a "model of a theory." Similarly, stating that the true value of a parameter is contained within a confidence interval with a predefined level of confidence makes little sense in the absence of relevant economic theories and institutional knowledge with which to interpret the context of a "true" value of a parameter. And so long as there exists the possibility that the model is incongruent with the underlying DSP of the economic process in some respects, the possibility remains that rejections or acceptances of hypotheses, as well as the actual confidence level of confidence interval or region, are affected or even determined by these incongruencies.

4.7. Exercises

4.7.1. Idea Checklist – Knowledge Guides

1. What is the Generalized Likelihood Ratio (GLR) test statistic, and why does it make sense as a test statistic? How do tests based on the GLR compare with tests based on F and T statistics?
2. Is there an optimum level of Type-I error of a hypothesis test? What approach would you follow to define and achieve such an optimal level?
3. What are the practical implications of the risk function for an equality-restricted pretest estimator under squared error loss?
4. What is your intuition regarding the behavior of the squared-error risk function of a pretest estimator based on *inequality* as opposed to equality restrictions?
5. What type of "confidence" does an analyst have in confidence regions generated by confidence region estimators? Why use confidence regions at all?
6. Why should one not simply design hypothesis tests that make *no* Type-I errors at all, that is, set $\alpha = 0$?
7. Why should one not simply design confidence regions that are *certain* to encompass the true value of the $\mathbf{q}(\theta)$ of interest, that is, set the confidence coefficient to 1?

4.7.2. Problems

4–1 Suppose you are conducting a test of a linear hypothesis and the test value of the T-statistic with 20 degrees of freedom is 2.20. Interpret this result and draft a conclusion–decision statement.

4–2 Assume the same test scenario as in Exercise 4.1. Within a confidence interval context, interpret the result in Exercise 1 and draft a conclusion statement.

4–3 Develop a procedure for generating a joint confidence region for β_1 and β_2 for the orthonormal linear model when $\mathbf{x}'\mathbf{x} = \mathbf{I}_k$ and give an interpretation of the result of using such a procedure. How would your result change if $\mathbf{x}'\mathbf{x}$ were just some positive, definite symmetric matrix?

4–4 In a testing context, what is the practical importance of the noncentrality parameters of the T or F distributions?

4–5 Given the risk characteristics of the pretest estimator displayed in Figure 4.1, discuss the decision problem of choosing an optimal α level of the test.

4–6 Derive the F statistic in (4.3.11) from (4.3.10).

4.7.3. Computer Exercises

---

1. Following Computer Exercise 2 from Chapter 3, please answer these questions about Klein's Model I:

a. Conduct a test to determine if the marginal propensity to consume is less than 1 (i.e., $H_0: \beta_4 \leq 1$). Also, compute a 90% confidence interval for β_4.

b. Plot the 90% joint confidence region (ellipse) for the coefficients on profit and lagged profit (β_2 and β_3). Also, plot the Bonferroni-adjusted individual confidence intervals for the coefficients such that the joint coverage probability is at least 90%.

c. Consider a pretest estimator based on the hypothesis $H_0: \beta_3 = 0$ (i.e., the coefficient on lagged profits is zero). Conduct a Monte Carlo exercise to simulate the quadratic risk function for the pretest estimator as well as the unrestricted and restricted ML estimators. Are your results similar to those reported by the GAUSS program C4PTest.gss?

d. Repeat the simulation exercise above (in c.), but draw bootstrap samples from the residuals instead of pseudorandom normal errors to simulate the DSP. How well do the simulated risk functions compare?

2. Throughout the chapter, we used the F-test and the T-test versions of the GLR test because critical values and p-values can easily be computed from the pivotal null distributions. For a given DSP of your choice, conduct a Monte Carlo exercise designed to simulate the sampling distribution of the GLR test statistic (4.3.10). How could you use the results of the exercise to conduct a simulation-based GLR test?

4.8. References

Bunke, H., and O. Bunke (1986), *Statistical Inference in Linear Models*, New York: John Wiley and Sons.

Judge, G., and M. E. Bock (1978), *The Statistical Implications of Pre-Test and Stein Rule Estimators in Econometrics*, Amsterdam: North-Holland.

Mittelhammer, R. C. (1996), *Mathematical Statistics for Economics and Business*, New York: Springer–Verlag.

CHAPTER 5

The Linear Semiparametric Regression Model: Least-Squares Estimation

IN this chapter we revisit the problem of point estimation in the linear regression probability model, which was first discussed in detail in Chapter 3. However, unlike the parametric model specification of Chapter 3 in which the probability distributions for **Y** and ε were specified explicitly to be in the multivariate normal family of distributions, this chapter examines a semiparametric model in which no explicit parametric density family assumption is made. The semiparametric model is potentially more encompassing of a variety of real-world economic processes because the model does not require the normality assumption, or any specific probability distribution assumption for that matter, and is hence less restrictive in this regard. We will see that much can still be accomplished in terms of defining useful solutions to the inverse problem of obtaining information about the unknown components of the probability model. However, it will also be seen that we will not be able to attribute the far-reaching optimality properties to inverse problem solutions that we were able to establish in the context of the parametric model context in Chapter 3. Such is the price paid for possessing less information about the DSP and probability model.

In terms of the general class of probability models portrayed in Table 2.1, this chapter deals with the special case delineated in Table 5.1.

The particular inverse problem associated with the probability model identified in Table 5.1 involves using observations on $(\mathbf{Y}, \mathbf{x})$ to recover information on the values or functions of the unknown and unobservable $\boldsymbol{\beta}$, σ^2, and ε. In this chapter our primary focus will be on establishing a basis for recovering information about the unknown explanatory variable coefficient vector $\boldsymbol{\beta}$ and the variance parameter σ^2. To solve this inverse problem, we will seek estimators that process sample data into estimates of the unknowns. The quality of the estimators and the associated estimates are judged by the statistical properties of the estimators, which we identify as well.

5.1. The Semiparametric Linear Regression Model

We remind the reader that in Section 3.1 we discussed the meaning and implications of the assumptions underlying the linear regression model. Apart from the remarks made

Table 5.1. *Linear Semiparametric Regression Model*

Probability Model Component	Specific Characteristics	
$\mathbf{Y}$	RV Type:	continuous
	Range:	unlimited
	Y_i dimension:	univariate
	Moments:	$E[\mathbf{Y} \mid \mathbf{x}] = \mathbf{x}\boldsymbol{\beta}$ and $\mathbf{cov}(\mathbf{Y} \mid \mathbf{x}) = \sigma^2\mathbf{I}$
$\eta(\mathbf{x}, \boldsymbol{\beta}, \varepsilon)$	Functional Form:	linear in $\mathbf{x}$ and $\boldsymbol{\beta}$, additive in ε, as $\mathbf{x}\boldsymbol{\beta} + \varepsilon$
$\mathbf{x}$	RV Type:	degenerate (fixed), full-column rank
	Genesis:	exogenous to the model
$\boldsymbol{\beta}$	RV Type:	degenerate (fixed)
	Dimension:	finite (fixed)
ε	RV Type:	iid or independent nonidentical
	Moments:	$E[\varepsilon \mid \mathbf{x}] = \mathbf{0}$ and $\mathbf{cov}(\varepsilon \mid \mathbf{x}) = \sigma^2\mathbf{I}$
Ω	Prior info:	none
$f(\mathbf{e} \mid \mathbf{x}, \varphi)$	PDF family:	unspecified

concerning the multivariate normal–parametric model assumption (Section 3.1.3), all of the rest of the discussion in Section 3.1 applies verbatim to the current semiparametric linear regression model, and so we will not repeat it here. The reader is encouraged to reread or review the discussion in Section 3.1 before proceeding.

On the basis of the specific model characteristics presented in Table 5.1, we have specified the following linear functional relationship as a fundamental component of our probability model of the data-sampling process:

$$\mathbf{Y} = \mathbf{x}\boldsymbol{\beta} + \varepsilon, \tag{5.1.1}$$

where $\mathbf{Y} = (Y_1, Y_2, \ldots, Y_n)'$ is a $(n \times 1)$ vector of observable random dependent variables whose range is contained in R^n, $\mathbf{x}$ is a $(n \times k)$ matrix reflecting the numerical values taken on by n fixed explanatory variables, $\boldsymbol{\beta}$ is a k-dimensional fixed vector of unknown and unobservable parameters, and ε is a $(n \times 1)$ noise component vector of unobserved and unobservable random variables. Furthermore, we have assumed that the mean of the noise component vector is the zero vector and thus that the value of $\mathbf{x}\boldsymbol{\beta}$ represents the mean of the dependent variable vector. We have also assumed that the covariance matrices of both the noise component and the dependent variable vector are identical and proportional to the identity matrix, the proportionality factor being represented by the common variance σ^2. Finally, we have assumed that the elements within the noise component and dependent variable vectors are independent random variables across observations. Note that we continue to depart from our convention of using capital letters to denote random variables in this instance owing to the widespread practice in the literature of reserving the letter epsilon, ε, for the random noise (or disturbance) vector of regression relationships. We continue to use $\mathbf{e}$ to denote an outcome of ε.

The linear regression model specification (5.1.1) suggests an inverse problem – the outcomes of the observable random variables $\mathbf{Y}$ and the value of $\mathbf{x}$ can be considered *indirect observations* on the unknown and unobservable $\boldsymbol{\beta}$ and ε. We hope to use these indirect observations in some manner to recover information about $\boldsymbol{\beta}$ and ε. By *indirect* observations we again mean that the pair of observed values $(\mathbf{y}, \mathbf{x})$ are not direct observations on the values of $\boldsymbol{\beta}$ and ε. Rather, $(\mathbf{y}, \mathbf{x})$ *indirectly* convey information about $\boldsymbol{\beta}$ and ε through the relation $\mathbf{e} = \mathbf{y} - \mathbf{x}\boldsymbol{\beta}$ that is implied directly by (5.1.1). Furthermore, the relation between $(\mathbf{y}, \mathbf{x})$ and $(\boldsymbol{\beta}, \mathbf{e})$ implied by (3.1.1) is not 1-to-1, and thus we cannot solve for unique values of $(\boldsymbol{\beta}, \mathbf{e})$ given the values $(\mathbf{y}, \mathbf{x})$ because the system of equations is undetermined for deriving specific values of $(\boldsymbol{\beta}, \mathbf{e})$.

At this point we have specified a probability model that is consistent with a particular type of DSP. We now move on to the estimation stage of the information recovery process.

5.2. The Problem of Estimating β

In this section we focus on solutions to the inverse problem of recovering information on the unknown and unobservable value of $\boldsymbol{\beta}$ from observations on the sample data $(\mathbf{Y}, \mathbf{x})$. The information we seek will be generated in the form of point estimates.

We have already noted that the linear relationship $\mathbf{y} = \mathbf{x}\boldsymbol{\beta} + \mathbf{e}$ cannot be solved for unique values of the unknown $\boldsymbol{\beta}$ and $\mathbf{e}$ in terms of the observables $\mathbf{y}$ and $\mathbf{x}$ because the relationship is a system of n equations in $(n + k)$ unknowns. And because neither $\boldsymbol{\beta}$ nor $\mathbf{e}$ is observable, there is no effective way of solving the equation system $\mathbf{y} = \mathbf{x}\boldsymbol{\beta} + \mathbf{e}$ for one of $\boldsymbol{\beta}$ or $\mathbf{e}$ in terms of values of the other. In effect, the inverse problem of solving for $(\boldsymbol{\beta}, \mathbf{e})$ in terms of $(\mathbf{y}, \mathbf{x})$ is underdetermined and ill posed. *What is a plausible basis for reasoning that might be used in choosing a unique value of $\boldsymbol{\beta}$ in this situation?*

The indeterminacy of $\boldsymbol{\beta}$ in the linear regression model caused by the ill-posed nature of the inverse problem is an instance of parameter indeterminacies that affect essentially all nontrivial probability models used in practice. By far the most widely adopted method for generating a unique inverse problem solution in such cases, and thus for obtaining a unique value of model parameters, is creatively to introduce a metric or estimation objective function representing some fundamental estimation criteria that are assumed to be appropriate or efficacious for the inverse problem at hand. Then the parameter value that optimizes the metric or objective function value is chosen as the solution to the inverse problem. Estimators that are defined by optimizing an estimation metric or estimation objective function are called *extremum estimators* because they are characterized by the "extreme" value of the chosen metric or objective function (the concept of extremum estimators will be discussed in detail in Chapter 7). The most popular metric for the case of the linear semiparametric regression model has been the squared error estimation metric leading to the least-squares principle, and we will examine this principle in detail ahead.

5.2.1. The Squared-Error Metric and the Least-Squares Principle

The most often used estimator for $\boldsymbol{\beta}$ in the linear semiparametric regression model is based on the least-squares principle dating back to Gauss, Laplace, and Legendre in the early nineteenth century. Readers should consult the article by Stigler (1981) for an interesting review of the origins of the least-squares principle. The least-squares estimator is defined through minimizing the squared-error metric

$$s(\boldsymbol{\beta}, \mathbf{Y}, \mathbf{x}) = \frac{1}{n}(\mathbf{Y} - \mathbf{x}\boldsymbol{\beta})'(\mathbf{Y} - \mathbf{x}\boldsymbol{\beta}) \tag{5.2.1}$$

with respect to the choice of $\boldsymbol{\beta}$. Before deriving the explicit form of the estimator, it is useful to consider the question of why this particular metric should be considered as an estimation objective function. Although the estimator derived from minimizing the squared-error metric will ultimately be shown to have several desirable statistical properties, are there any fundamental arguments that can be suggested at the outset in support of such an estimation metric? We will now see that some rationale in support of the metric can be provided, and this rationale can be extended later to nonlinear models as well.

One supporting argument for the metric is based on the following simple reasoning. Letting $\boldsymbol{\beta}_0$ denote the true value of the parameter vector, the linear semiparametric probability model characteristics in Table 5.1 imply that

$$\begin{aligned} \mathrm{E}[s(\boldsymbol{\beta}, \mathbf{Y}, \mathbf{x})] &= n^{-1}\mathrm{E}[(\mathbf{Y} - \mathbf{x}\boldsymbol{\beta}_0 + \mathbf{x}\boldsymbol{\beta}_0 - \mathbf{x}\boldsymbol{\beta})'(\mathbf{Y} - \mathbf{x}\boldsymbol{\beta}_0 + \mathbf{x}\boldsymbol{\beta}_0 - \mathbf{x}\boldsymbol{\beta})] \\ &= \sigma^2 + (\boldsymbol{\beta}_0 - \boldsymbol{\beta})'(n^{-1}\mathbf{x}'\mathbf{x})(\boldsymbol{\beta}_0 - \boldsymbol{\beta}). \end{aligned} \tag{5.2.2}$$

It is clear that because $(\mathbf{x}'\mathbf{x})$ is positive definite, the unique minimum of (5.2.2) is attained if $\boldsymbol{\beta} = \boldsymbol{\beta}_0$. Then, if the analyst could actually choose $\boldsymbol{\beta}$ so as to minimize $\mathrm{E}[s(\boldsymbol{\beta}, \mathbf{Y}, \mathbf{x})]$, the value of $\boldsymbol{\beta}_0$ would be recovered exactly. In practice, the distribution of $\mathbf{Y}$ is unknown, and the expectation in (5.2.2) cannot be calculated; thus, minimizing $\mathrm{E}[s(\boldsymbol{\beta}, \mathbf{Y}, \mathbf{x})]$ is not an operational objective. But a sample analog of (5.2.2) can be defined by eliminating the expectation operator, resulting in (5.2.1). Under an appropriate law of large numbers for independent random variables, (5.2.1) will converge to (5.2.2). Thus, one would expect that minimizing (5.2.1) through choice of $\boldsymbol{\beta}$ should result in an estimate close to $\boldsymbol{\beta}_0$ for large enough n. Minimizing (5.2.1) defines an (extremum) estimator based on minimizing the squared error metric $s(\boldsymbol{\beta}, \mathbf{Y}, \mathbf{x})$.

An alternative rationale for the squared error metric is based on an objective of predicting outcomes of the dependent variable. When searching for knowledge in the sciences it is customary to make use of an approach based on the objectives of understanding, predicting, and controlling the process under study. In the current problem context, if we understand the underlying DSP, then in choosing a point estimator for $\boldsymbol{\beta}$, say $\hat{\boldsymbol{\beta}}$, we may want to emphasize the quality of predictions of $\mathbf{Y}$ outcomes that are implied by the values of the random variable $\hat{\mathbf{Y}} = \mathbf{x}\hat{\boldsymbol{\beta}}$. But how do we operationalize this rather vague criterion focused on prediction quality?

If we want to choose $\hat{\boldsymbol{\beta}}$ in a way that avoids especially large prediction errors, we might want to choose a criterion for judging the quality of predictions that severely penalizes such errors. One such criterion is the minimization of the sum of squared prediction errors, or the quadratic loss criterion, which is based on the objective function

$$\mathrm{s}(\hat{\boldsymbol{\beta}}, \mathbf{Y}, \mathbf{x}) = n^{-1}(\mathbf{Y} - \hat{\mathbf{Y}})'(\mathbf{Y} - \hat{\mathbf{Y}}) = n^{-1}(\mathbf{Y} - \mathbf{x}\hat{\boldsymbol{\beta}})'(\mathbf{Y} - \mathbf{x}\hat{\boldsymbol{\beta}}). \tag{5.2.3}$$

Through the use of this criterion, the penalty associated with any individual prediction error outcome, $y_i - \hat{y}_i$, increases with the square of the error, and the total penalty is the sum of squared prediction errors. Note that the objective function (5.2.3) is stated in terms of the random vector $\mathbf{Y}$, and thus the value of the objective function is itself a random variable. Therefore, the possibility of various outcomes of $\mathbf{Y}$ is recognized by this prediction error metric. We emphasize that consideration of all of these possibilities is relevant in a *pre-data sense* only, which is the sense in which all classical estimation and inference procedures are conceived and evaluated.

The concept of *minimizing a random variable*, $\mathrm{s}(\hat{\boldsymbol{\beta}}, \mathbf{Y}, \mathbf{x})$, through the choice of $\hat{\boldsymbol{\beta}}$ is not a standard minimization problem. However we can minimize the *outcome* of $\mathrm{s}\left(\hat{\boldsymbol{\beta}}, \mathbf{Y}, \mathbf{x}\right)$ for every possible contingency for the outcome of $\mathbf{Y}$, which *is* a standard minimization problem, by allowing the choice of the value of $\hat{\boldsymbol{\beta}}$ to be a function of the *outcome* of $\mathbf{Y}$. In particular, given an *outcome* of $\mathbf{Y}$, the so-called *least-squares* (LS) criterion for choosing the *outcome* $\hat{\mathbf{b}}$ of $\hat{\boldsymbol{\beta}}$ is based on the solution to the standard unconstrained optimization problem

$$\mathbf{b} = \arg\min_{\beta}[\mathrm{s}(\boldsymbol{\beta}, \mathbf{y}, \mathbf{x})] = \arg\min_{\beta}[n^{-1}(\mathbf{y} - \mathbf{x}\boldsymbol{\beta})'(\mathbf{y} - \mathbf{x}\boldsymbol{\beta})]. \tag{5.2.4}$$

Because $\hat{\mathbf{b}}$ minimizes the sum of squared errors for each possible outcome $\mathbf{y}$,

$$\mathrm{s}(\hat{\mathbf{b}}, \mathbf{y}, \mathbf{x}) \leq \mathrm{s}(\tilde{\mathbf{b}}, \mathbf{y}, \mathbf{x})\,\forall\,\mathbf{y} \Rightarrow \mathrm{P}_{\mathbf{Y}}(\mathrm{s}(\hat{\mathbf{b}}, \mathbf{y}, \mathbf{x}) \leq \mathrm{s}(\tilde{\mathbf{b}}, \mathbf{y}, \mathbf{x})) = 1, \tag{5.2.5}$$

where $\tilde{\mathbf{b}}$ is any other choice of estimates. Thus, we can state that choosing such an estimator $\hat{\boldsymbol{\beta}}$ *minimizes* the *random* least-squares objective function $\mathrm{s}(\hat{\boldsymbol{\beta}}, \mathbf{Y}, \mathbf{x})$ in (5.2.3) and thus minimizes the sum of squared prediction errors *with probability 1*.

5.2.2. The Least-Squares Estimator

If we adopt the squared-error metric as the estimation objective function on which to base the estimator of $\boldsymbol{\beta}$ in the linear semiparametric regression model, the least-squares (LS) estimator is defined by

$$\hat{\boldsymbol{\beta}} = \arg\min_{\beta}\left[\frac{1}{n}(\mathbf{Y} - \mathbf{x}\boldsymbol{\beta})'(\mathbf{Y} - \mathbf{x}\boldsymbol{\beta})\right]. \tag{5.2.6}$$

Point estimates are given by

$$\mathbf{b} = \arg\min_{\beta}\left[\frac{1}{n}(\mathbf{y} - \mathbf{x}\boldsymbol{\beta})'(\mathbf{y} - \mathbf{x}\boldsymbol{\beta})\right]. \tag{5.2.7}$$

On the basis of the first-order conditions to the minimization problem in (5.2.7), the solution is given by the value of $\boldsymbol{\beta}$ that solves

$$2n^{-1}(\mathbf{x}'\mathbf{x}\boldsymbol{\beta} - \mathbf{x}'\mathbf{y}) = \mathbf{0}, \tag{5.2.8}$$

which leads to the *estimate*

$$\mathbf{b} = (\mathbf{x}'\mathbf{x})^{-1}\mathbf{x}'\mathbf{y}. \tag{5.2.9}$$

Note this estimation rule happens to be a linear function of the sample data $\mathbf{y}$. The LS *estimator* of $\boldsymbol{\beta}$ is then represented by (5.2.9) with the fixed outcome $\mathbf{y}$ replaced by the random variable $\mathbf{Y}$, which conceptually represents all of the possible values for the outcome $\mathbf{y}$ in a predata sense as

$$\hat{\boldsymbol{\beta}} = (\mathbf{x}'\mathbf{x})^{-1}\mathbf{x}'\mathbf{Y}. \tag{5.2.10}$$

Consequently, $\hat{\boldsymbol{\beta}}$ is a random vector, which raises interesting questions concerning its sampling characteristics. We examine the sampling properties of the LS estimator in the next section.

► **Example 5.2.1:** GAUSS provides three different commands for computing the ordinary LS estimate of $\boldsymbol{\beta}$, and the procedures differ in the amount of information required of, and provided to, the user. The most basic procedure is olsqr(), which requires the user to provide $\mathbf{y}$ and $\mathbf{x}$ and returns the LS parameter estimate. We also note that the estimate may be computed in GAUSS with the shorthand notation **y/x**. The procedures olsqr2() and ols() require more detailed input but also return more information about the fitted model. For our purposes here, we only require a subset of the information reported by these GAUSS procedures. To simplify matters, and to illustrate how a procedure can be written to generate the outcome of an estimator, we provide a GAUSS procedure named easyols() that is based on Equation (5.2.9) and is designed for use in the early chapters of the book. Although GAUSS employs a more robust algorithm for computing the LS estimates in olsqr(), the easyols() procedure should perform well in most situations (see the examples manual).

5.3. Statistical Properties of the LS Estimator

In this section we examine the statistical properties of the LS estimator defined in (5.2.9). As we emphasized in Chapter 3, the classical approach to evaluating the statistical properties of a point estimator is done in an unconditional predata context. Properties of estimator are considered in the context of all of the hypothetical samples of data that *could have* occurred, not in the sense of what *actually did* occur. Because estimators are functions of the random sample $\mathbf{Y}$, the estimators themselves are evaluated in the context of all of the hypothetically possible estimator outcomes that could have occurred before the data's actually being observed. In the case at hand, this idea is represented symbolically by the very expression for the LS estimator (5.2.10), which indicates that $\hat{\boldsymbol{\beta}}$ is a function of the random vector $\mathbf{Y}$. Thus, $\hat{\boldsymbol{\beta}}$ is a random vector that can conceptually assume various values, depending on what outcome occurs for $\mathbf{Y}$. Note that when our choice and evaluation of an estimator for $\boldsymbol{\beta}$ is based on the sampling distribution of $\mathbf{Y}$, the information obtained about $\boldsymbol{\beta}$ from point estimation not only depends on the observed data being analyzed but also on whatever data sets one may have observed but did not.

5.3.1. Mean, Covariance, and Unbiasedness

In terms of sampling properties, one important question concerns whether or not the LS estimator is unbiased. A direct demonstration of "unbiasedness" based on the definition of the LS estimator is reasonably straightforward. Note that

$$\begin{aligned} \mathrm{E}[\hat{\boldsymbol{\beta}}] &= \mathrm{E}[(\mathbf{x}'\mathbf{x})^{-1}\mathbf{x}'\mathbf{Y}] = \mathrm{E}[(\mathbf{x}'\mathbf{x})^{-1}\mathbf{x}'(\mathbf{x}\boldsymbol{\beta} + \boldsymbol{\varepsilon})] \\ &= \boldsymbol{\beta} + \mathrm{E}[(\mathbf{x}'\mathbf{x})^{-1}\mathbf{x}'\boldsymbol{\varepsilon}] = \boldsymbol{\beta}, \end{aligned} \tag{5.3.1}$$

which follows from the rules for taking expectations of linear combinations of random variables and because $\mathrm{E}[\boldsymbol{\varepsilon}] = \mathbf{0}$ is based on the assumptions of the probability model. Thus, from a classical predata perspective, the mean or average of all of the hypothetically possible outcomes of the LS estimator equals the target value $\boldsymbol{\beta}$, *no matter what its appropriate value*. Consequently, the LS estimator is *unbiased*. We emphasize that this and other estimator properties that we derive depend on the assumption that the probability model in Table 5.1 actually encompasses the true DSP. If not, and there is no appropriate $\boldsymbol{\beta} \in \Omega$ that defines an instance of the probability model for which $\mathrm{E}[\mathbf{Y}] = \mathbf{x}\boldsymbol{\beta}$; then $\mathrm{E}[\boldsymbol{\varepsilon}] \neq \mathbf{0}$, and (5.3.1) will not hold.

A direct derivation of the covariance matrix based on the definition of the LS estimator is also reasonably straightforward. The basic definition of the covariance matrix for a random vector $\hat{\boldsymbol{\beta}}$ having a mean vector $\mathrm{E}[\hat{\boldsymbol{\beta}}] = \boldsymbol{\beta}$ is given by

$$\mathbf{cov}(\hat{\boldsymbol{\beta}}) = \mathrm{E}[(\hat{\boldsymbol{\beta}} - \mathrm{E}[\hat{\boldsymbol{\beta}}])(\hat{\boldsymbol{\beta}} - \mathrm{E}[\hat{\boldsymbol{\beta}}])'] = \mathrm{E}[(\hat{\boldsymbol{\beta}} - \boldsymbol{\beta})(\hat{\boldsymbol{\beta}} - \boldsymbol{\beta})']. \tag{5.3.2}$$

In the specific case at hand, $\hat{\boldsymbol{\beta}} - \boldsymbol{\beta} = (\mathbf{x}'\mathbf{x})^{-1}\mathbf{x}'\boldsymbol{\varepsilon}$, so that

$$\begin{aligned} \mathbf{cov}(\hat{\boldsymbol{\beta}}) &= \mathrm{E}[(\mathbf{x}'\mathbf{x})^{-1}\mathbf{x}'\boldsymbol{\varepsilon}\boldsymbol{\varepsilon}'\mathbf{x}(\mathbf{x}'\mathbf{x})^{-1}] = [(\mathbf{x}'\mathbf{x})^{-1}\mathbf{x}'\,\mathrm{E}[\boldsymbol{\varepsilon}\boldsymbol{\varepsilon}']\mathbf{x}(\mathbf{x}'\mathbf{x})^{-1}] \\ &= \sigma^2(\mathbf{x}'\mathbf{x})^{-1}\mathbf{x}'\mathbf{x}(\mathbf{x}'\mathbf{x})^{-1} = \sigma^2(\mathbf{x}'\mathbf{x})^{-1}, \end{aligned} \tag{5.3.3}$$

which follows from the properties of the expectation operator and the assumption that $\mathrm{E}[\boldsymbol{\varepsilon}\boldsymbol{\varepsilon}'] = \mathbf{cov}(\boldsymbol{\varepsilon}) = \sigma^2\mathbf{I}$. This covariance matrix result provides predata information regarding the precision or variability of the LS estimator. The values of the diagonal elements in $\mathbf{cov}(\hat{\boldsymbol{\beta}})$ can be thought of as measuring the weighted-average squared deviations of the entries in $\hat{\boldsymbol{\beta}}$ from their means. The average is computed over all possible outcomes of $\hat{\boldsymbol{\beta}}$, and the weights in the average are based on the hypothetical propensities for the various estimator outcomes to occur. Similarly, the off-diagonal elements in $\mathbf{cov}(\hat{\boldsymbol{\beta}})$ measure the average cross-product deviations from their means of the various pairs of entries in $\hat{\boldsymbol{\beta}}$.

► **Example 5.3.1:** We can use the easyols() procedure to simulate the mean and variance of the least-squares estimator. In this exercise, the reader selects parameters for a simple linear regression model, and the mean and variance of the estimator are approximated by bootstrap simulation techniques and compared with the theoretical moments for the specified model (see the examples manual).

5.3.2. GAUSS Markov Theorem: $\hat{\boldsymbol{\beta}}$ Is BLUE, Not Necessarily MVUE

Now that we know the LS estimator is unbiased, we consider the problem of finding the best linear unbiased estimator (BLUE) of $\boldsymbol{\beta}$. We begin by writing any estimator of $\boldsymbol{\beta}$ that is linear in $\mathbf{Y}$ in the form $\mathbf{t}(\mathbf{Y}) = \mathbf{a}\,\mathbf{Y} + \mathbf{d}$, where $\mathbf{a}$ is a $(k \times n)$ matrix and $\mathbf{d}$ is a $(k \times 1)$ vector of real numbers. Under the current assumptions of the probability model, $\mathrm{E}[\mathbf{aY} + \mathbf{d}] = \mathbf{ax}\boldsymbol{\beta} + \mathbf{d}$, and if we desire the estimator to be unbiased, then it must be the case that $\mathbf{ax}\boldsymbol{\beta} + \mathbf{d} = \boldsymbol{\beta}$, *regardless* of the value of $\boldsymbol{\beta}$. This "unbiasedness" requirement implies the restrictions that $\mathbf{ax} = \mathbf{I}_k$ and $\mathbf{d} = \mathbf{0}$. Thus, the entire class of possible *linear unbiased* point estimators of $\boldsymbol{\beta}$ is represented by

$$\tilde{\boldsymbol{\beta}} = \mathbf{aY}, \text{ where } \mathbf{ax} = \mathbf{I}_k. \tag{5.3.4}$$

If the number of sample observations equals the number of unknown entries in $\boldsymbol{\beta}$ (i.e., if $k = n$), then the class of linear unbiased estimators of $\boldsymbol{\beta}$ is a singleton set because the only solution to $\mathbf{ax} = \mathbf{I}_k$ is then given by $\mathbf{a} = \mathbf{x}^{-1}$ (given that the *inverse of* $\mathbf{x}$ *exists* as assumed in Table 5.1). However, if the number of observations or data points exceeds the number of entries in $\boldsymbol{\beta}$, as is usually the case, then there are an infinite number of linear unbiased estimators of $\boldsymbol{\beta}$. We then face the task of identifying an "appropriate–best" unbiased way of summarizing and recovering the information contained in $\mathbf{y}$ to estimate $\boldsymbol{\beta}$.

Now consider the classical property of best linear unbiasedness, where *best* refers to the estimator with the minimum covariance matrix among all of the estimators in the linear unbiased class. Note that the covariance matrix of $\tilde{\boldsymbol{\beta}} = \mathbf{aY}$ is given by $\sigma^2\mathbf{aa}'$, and thus the BLUE for $\boldsymbol{\beta}$ is defined by

$$\hat{\boldsymbol{\beta}} = \mathbf{a}_*\mathbf{Y}, \text{ where } \mathbf{a}_* = \arg\min_{\mathrm{a}}[\sigma^2\mathbf{aa}' \text{ s.t. } \mathbf{ax} = \mathbf{I}_k]. \tag{5.3.5}$$

The reader will notice that this is *not* the usual case of constrained minimization of a *scalar* valued objective function. In this problem, we seek the minimum of a *positive definite matrix* subject to constraints. Note that a p.d. symmetric matrix $\mathbf{q}$ is minimized subject to constraints if $\mathbf{q}$ is such that $\mathbf{m} - \mathbf{q}$ is positive semidefinite for every other p.d. symmetric matrix $\mathbf{m}$ that satisfies the constraints (refer to the concept of magnitude comparisons of positive definite symmetric matrices given in the matrix review manual, as well as in Chapter E2).

The solution to the problem specified in (5.3.5) is the principal content of the famous Gauss–Markov theorem.

Theorem 5.3.1 (Gauss–Markov Theorem): *Given a DSP for which* $\mathbf{Y} = \mathbf{x}\boldsymbol{\beta} + \varepsilon$, $\mathrm{E}[\varepsilon] = \mathbf{0}$, $\mathbf{cov}(\varepsilon) = \sigma^2\mathbf{I}_n$, *and* $\mathbf{x}$ *has a full-column rank, the solution for the matrix* $\mathbf{a}_*$ *in* $\hat{\boldsymbol{\beta}} = \mathbf{a}_*\mathbf{Y}$ *that identifies the BLUE for* $\boldsymbol{\beta}$ *is given by* $\mathbf{a}_* = (\mathbf{x}'\mathbf{x})^{-1}\mathbf{x}'$, *which defines the least-squares estimator* $\hat{\boldsymbol{\beta}} = (\mathbf{x}'\mathbf{x})^{-1}\mathbf{x}'\mathbf{Y}$.

The point of this theorem is that we have now identified the solution to the inverse problem of obtaining the *best* point estimate of $\boldsymbol{\beta}$ under the conditions that we use linear unbiased functions of the sample data. We emphasize that the proof of the Gauss–Markov theorem does *not* rely on an assumption that the ε_i's are independent and identically distributed. The only conditions placed on the noise process are the assumptions regarding the first and second moments of ε. Our modest result illustrates the importance of the estimation objective function in developing estimation principles – a point that will become increasingly clear in the chapters ahead.

Note that we cannot claim that the LS estimator is the MVUE estimator of $\boldsymbol{\beta}$. In fact, in the absence of a parametric family of densities assumption, and concomitantly in the absence of the availability of such concepts as the Cramer–Rao Lower Bound, the information matrix, and (complete) sufficient statistics, the investigation of the MVUE property is essentially intractable. This means, in particular, that if we remove the restriction that the estimators we are examining must be in the linear class, we do *not* know that the LS estimator is best. The Gauss–Markov result applies only to linear estimators.

In the next subsection we take a short detour and examine the estimation problem in a decision theoretic context (Wald, 1950). We consider the "loss" incurred by using a sample estimate $\tilde{\boldsymbol{\beta}}(\mathbf{y})$ for the true value of $\boldsymbol{\beta}$ and the predata "risk" associated with such losses.

5.3.3. $\hat{\boldsymbol{\beta}}$ Is a Minimax Estimator of $\boldsymbol{\beta}$ under Quadratic Risk

A criterion that is often used to measure the performance of an estimator, say $\tilde{\boldsymbol{\beta}}$, is the squared-error loss or quadratic loss function

$$\ell(\boldsymbol{\beta}, \tilde{\boldsymbol{\beta}}) = (\tilde{\boldsymbol{\beta}} - \boldsymbol{\beta})'(\tilde{\boldsymbol{\beta}} - \boldsymbol{\beta}). \tag{5.3.6}$$

Using this criterion, the penalty associated with any individual estimation error outcome, $\tilde{\mathrm{b}}_{\mathrm{i}} - \beta_{\mathrm{i}}$, increases with the square of the error, and the total penalty is the sum of squared estimation errors. The quadratic risk function corresponding to (5.3.6) is

$$\rho(\boldsymbol{\beta}, \tilde{\boldsymbol{\beta}}) = \mathrm{E}[(\tilde{\boldsymbol{\beta}} - \boldsymbol{\beta})'(\tilde{\boldsymbol{\beta}} - \boldsymbol{\beta})]. \tag{5.3.7}$$

The risk is the predata expected loss and can be thought of as the average loss that an analyst will experience when using the estimator $\tilde{\boldsymbol{\beta}}(\mathbf{Y})$ to estimate the value $\boldsymbol{\beta}$, accounting for all hypothetically possible data outcomes of $\mathbf{Y}$. To use the quadratic risk criterion for deciding the best way to estimate $\tilde{\boldsymbol{\beta}}$, we will continue to consider linear functions of $\mathbf{Y}$, $\tilde{\boldsymbol{\beta}} = \mathbf{aY}$.

In an attempt to find the choice of the matrix $\mathbf{a}$ that minimizes the quadratic risk function, first note that the risk function for an estimator $\tilde{\beta}$ can be rewritten as

$$\begin{aligned} \mathrm{E}[(\tilde{\boldsymbol{\beta}} - \boldsymbol{\beta})'(\tilde{\boldsymbol{\beta}} - \boldsymbol{\beta})] &= \mathrm{E}[((\tilde{\boldsymbol{\beta}} - \mathrm{E}[\tilde{\boldsymbol{\beta}}]) + (\mathrm{E}[\tilde{\boldsymbol{\beta}}] - \boldsymbol{\beta}))'((\tilde{\boldsymbol{\beta}} - \mathrm{E}[\tilde{\boldsymbol{\beta}}]) + (\mathrm{E}[\tilde{\boldsymbol{\beta}}] - \boldsymbol{\beta}))] \\ &= \mathrm{E}[(\tilde{\boldsymbol{\beta}} - \mathrm{E}[\tilde{\boldsymbol{\beta}}])'(\tilde{\boldsymbol{\beta}} - \mathrm{E}[\tilde{\boldsymbol{\beta}}]) + (\mathrm{E}[\tilde{\boldsymbol{\beta}}] - \boldsymbol{\beta})'(\mathrm{E}[\tilde{\boldsymbol{\beta}}] - \boldsymbol{\beta})], \end{aligned} \tag{5.3.8}$$

which is the sum of the variances of the elements of $\tilde{\boldsymbol{\beta}}$ (the first inner product term on the right-hand side of the second equality in (5.3.8)) plus the sum of the squared biases of the elements in $\tilde{\boldsymbol{\beta}}$ for estimating the respective entries in $\boldsymbol{\beta}$. If $\tilde{\boldsymbol{\beta}} = \mathbf{aY}$ is substituted into (5.3.8), and then also substituted into $\mathbf{Y} = \mathbf{x}\boldsymbol{\beta} + \varepsilon$, the quadratic risk function becomes

$$\mathrm{E}[(\tilde{\boldsymbol{\beta}} - \boldsymbol{\beta})'(\tilde{\boldsymbol{\beta}} - \boldsymbol{\beta})] = \sigma^2 \operatorname{tr}(\mathbf{aa}') + \boldsymbol{\beta}'(\mathbf{ax} - \mathbf{I}_{\mathrm{k}})'(\mathbf{ax} - \mathbf{I}_{\mathrm{k}})\boldsymbol{\beta}, \tag{5.3.9}$$

where σ^2 tr($\mathbf{aa}'$) is the sum of the diagonal elements of the covariance matrix $\mathbf{cov}(\tilde{\boldsymbol{\beta}}) = \sigma^2(\mathbf{aa}')$, that is, the sum of the variances of the entries in $\tilde{\boldsymbol{\beta}}$. Note that for a given choice of $\mathbf{a}$, σ^2 tr($\mathbf{aa}'$) is a fixed number, but the second term in (5.3.9) is a function of $\boldsymbol{\beta}$ that exhibits no upper bound (as a function of $\boldsymbol{\beta}$) if the positive semidefinite matrix of the quadratic form, $(\mathbf{ax} - \mathbf{I}_k)'(\mathbf{ax} - \mathbf{I}_k)$, is not the zero matrix. Because $\boldsymbol{\beta}$ is unknown and unobservable, the only way to guard against the possibility of choosing an estimator that has arbitrarily large quadratic risk for some possible values of $\boldsymbol{\beta}$ is to choose the matrix $\mathbf{a}$ so that $(\mathbf{ax} - \mathbf{I}_k)'(\mathbf{ax} - \mathbf{I}_k) = \mathbf{0}$, which necessarily requires that $(\mathbf{ax} - \mathbf{I}_k) = \mathbf{0}$. One might think of this situation as one in which nature or some opponent is choosing the $\boldsymbol{\beta}$ vector, and we wish to choose $\mathbf{a}$ so that we can protect against a substantially "unfavorable" outcome resulting from nature's or the opponent's choice of $\boldsymbol{\beta}$. By choosing $(\mathbf{ax} - \mathbf{I}_k) = \mathbf{0}$, we remove the ability of nature or the opponent to inflict an arbitrarily large risk, and we maintain control over the level of risk that we are exposed to.

If we now seek to minimize (5.3.9), while constraining the choice of the matrix $\mathbf{a}$ so that it satisfies $(\mathbf{ax} - \mathbf{I}_k) = \mathbf{0}$, we are effectively choosing an estimator that minimizes the maximum risk possible, that is, we are defining the *linear minimax estimator* of $\boldsymbol{\beta}$. At this point, the solution to the inverse problem is a familiar one that we encountered in Section 5.3.2. Because the covariance matrix of our estimator, $\mathbf{cov}(\tilde{\boldsymbol{\beta}}) = \sigma^2(\mathbf{aa}')$, will be minimized subject to the constraints $(\mathbf{ax} - \mathbf{I}_k) = \mathbf{0}$ when $\mathbf{a} = (\mathbf{x}'\mathbf{x})^{-1}\mathbf{x}'$, so too will σ^2 tr ($\mathbf{aa}'$) be minimized. This leads to the BLUE and LS estimator $\hat{\boldsymbol{\beta}} = (\mathbf{x}'\mathbf{x})^{-1}\mathbf{x}'\mathbf{Y}$ presented in (5.2.10) with covariance matrix $\sigma^2(\mathbf{x}'\mathbf{x})^{-1}$ and quadratic risk $\mathrm{E}[(\hat{\boldsymbol{\beta}} - \boldsymbol{\beta})'(\hat{\boldsymbol{\beta}} - \boldsymbol{\beta})] = \sigma^2 \operatorname{tr}(\mathbf{x}'\mathbf{x})^{-1}$.

Given the preceding decision–theoretic detour, we now turn to an analysis of the asymptotic behavior of the least-squares estimator.

5.3.4. Consistency

Consistency of the LS estimator can be demonstrated if additional probability model assumptions are made relating to the limiting behavior of the $\mathbf{x}$ matrix. In particular, it is sufficient that the matrix $\mathbf{x}$ be such that $(\mathbf{x}'\mathbf{x})^{-1}$ exists for all n (so that the LS estimator exists) and $\operatorname{tr}(\mathbf{x}'\mathbf{x})^{-1} \to \mathbf{0}$ as $n \to \infty$ because then the fact that $\mathrm{E}[\hat{\boldsymbol{\beta}}] = \boldsymbol{\beta}$ and $\operatorname{var}(\hat{\beta}_j) \to 0$ as $n \to \infty\ \forall j$ (given that $\sigma^2 \operatorname{tr}(\mathbf{x}'\mathbf{x})^{-1} = \sum_{j=1}^{k} \operatorname{var}(\beta_j)$) implies that $\hat{\boldsymbol{\beta}} \xrightarrow{p} \boldsymbol{\beta}$ via mean-square convergence of $\hat{\boldsymbol{\beta}}$ to $\boldsymbol{\beta}$. This is a mild restriction on $\mathbf{x}$ that should most often be achieved in practice. In effect, all that is required is that $\operatorname{tr}(\mathbf{x}'\mathbf{x}) = \sum_{i=1}^{n} \sum_{j=1}^{k} \mathrm{x}_{ij}^2 \to \infty$ as $n \to \infty$ and the ratio of the largest to the smallest eigenvalues of $\mathbf{x}'\mathbf{x}$, that is, the *condition number* of $\mathbf{x}'\mathbf{x}$, be upper bounded. An upper bound on the condition number of $\mathbf{x}'\mathbf{x}$ implies that the columns in $\mathbf{x}$ are prevented from becoming too close to exhibiting linear dependence and concomitantly that the $\mathbf{x}'\mathbf{x}$ matrix is prevented from becoming too close to being singular. We will formalize this result in Theorem 5.3.2.

Theorem 5.3.2 (Consistency of the LS Estimator): *Assume the conditions of the probability model in Table 5.1 and assume further that* $\operatorname{tr}(\mathbf{x}'\mathbf{x}) = \sum_{i=1}^{n} \sum_{j=1}^{k}$

$\mathbf{x}_{ij}^2 \to \infty$ as $n \to \infty$ and the ratio of the largest to the smallest eigenvalues of $\mathbf{x}'\mathbf{x}$ is upper-bounded as $\frac{\lambda_L(\mathbf{x}'\mathbf{x})}{\lambda_s(\mathbf{x}'\mathbf{x})} \leq \delta$, where δ is some finite positive constant. Then $\hat{\boldsymbol{\beta}} \xrightarrow{p} \boldsymbol{\beta}$.

PROOF: See the proof of Theorem 3.4.1 in Section 3.10.

Thus, as the number of sample observations increases, all of the hypothetical outcomes of the LS estimator eventually cluster in a small neighborhood around the appropriate value of the unknown and unobservable $\boldsymbol{\beta}$, whatever its value, with probability converging to 1. We are thus assured that the LS estimator will recover the appropriate value of $\boldsymbol{\beta}$ for a large enough sample size.

► **Example 5.3.2:** In general, we cannot prove that an estimator is consistent by numerical simulation. However, we can demonstrate the consistency of the LS estimator given that we know the property holds for a particular model. In a GAUSS exercise, the reader selects up to four sample sizes (n) for a simple linear regression model as well as the number of bootstrap samples (m) to generate for each version of the model. Then, the sampling distributions of the estimator are simulated for each sample size, and the accompanying box plots should indicate that the sampling distribution becomes more concentrated on the true parameter values as the n becomes large (see the examples manual).

5.3.5. Asymptotic Normality

An analysis of whether or not the LS estimator is asymptotically normally distributed is somewhat more involved than the issue of consistency. Noting that $\hat{\boldsymbol{\beta}} = (\mathbf{x}'\mathbf{x})^{-1}\mathbf{x}'(\mathbf{x}\boldsymbol{\beta} + \varepsilon) = \boldsymbol{\beta} + (\mathbf{x}'\mathbf{x})^{-1}\mathbf{x}'\varepsilon$, we proceed by considering the limiting distribution of the random vector

$$n^{1/2}(\hat{\boldsymbol{\beta}} - \boldsymbol{\beta}) = n^{1/2}(\mathbf{x}'\mathbf{x})^{-1}\mathbf{x}'\varepsilon = (n^{-1}\mathbf{x}'\mathbf{x})^{-1}n^{-1/2}\,\mathbf{x}'\varepsilon. \tag{5.3.10}$$

Slutsky's theorem, the Cramer–Wold Device, and the Triangular Array Central Limit theorem (Chapter E1; Mittelhammer, Chapter 5) can be used to demonstrate asymptotic normality if additional assumptions are adopted concerning the behavior of $\mathbf{x}'\mathbf{x}$ as $n \to \infty$ together with a slightly stronger moment assumption on the noise component of the linear statistical model.

Theorem 5.3.3 (Asymptotic Normality of the LS Estimator): *Assume the conditions of the probability model in Table 5.1 and assume further that $n^{-1}\mathbf{x}'\mathbf{x} \to \Xi$, where Ξ is a finite positive definite symmetric matrix, the elements in $\mathbf{x}$ are bounded in absolute value, and $\mathrm{E}[|\varepsilon_i|^{2+\delta}] \leq \xi$ for some choice of positive finite constants δ and ξ. Then $n^{1/2}(\hat{\boldsymbol{\beta}} - \boldsymbol{\beta}) \xrightarrow{d} \mathrm{N}(\mathbf{0}, \sigma^2\Xi^{-1})$.*

The basic rationale for the asymptotic normality of $\hat{\boldsymbol{\beta}}$ is that, in the limit as $n \to \infty$, the LS estimator is a linear combination of multivariate normally distributed random variables and so is itself normally distributed. This realization is based on the limiting behavior of (5.3.10) in which $n^{-1/2}\mathbf{x}'\boldsymbol{\varepsilon} \xrightarrow{d} \mathrm{N}(\mathbf{0}, \boldsymbol{\Xi})$ and $(n^{-1}\mathbf{x}'\mathbf{x})^{-1} \rightarrow \boldsymbol{\Xi}^{-1}$.

From the preceding theorem, we know that $\hat{\boldsymbol{\beta}} \overset{a}{\sim} \mathrm{N}(\boldsymbol{\beta}, \sigma^2 n^{-1}\boldsymbol{\Xi}^{-1})$, but this asymptotic result involves the two unknowns σ^2 and $\boldsymbol{\Xi}$. We can provide an operational alternative to the use of the unobservable limit matrix $\boldsymbol{\Xi}$ via an appeal to Slutsky's theorem (which states that if $\mathbf{W}_n \xrightarrow{p} \mathbf{w}_0$ and $\mathbf{V}_n \xrightarrow{d} \mathbf{V}$, then $\mathbf{W}_n\mathbf{V}_n \xrightarrow{d} \mathbf{w}_0\mathbf{V}$). Let $\boldsymbol{\Xi}^{1/2}$ be the nonsingular symmetric square-root matrix for the positive definite symmetric matrix $\boldsymbol{\Xi}$, meaning that $\boldsymbol{\Xi} = \boldsymbol{\Xi}^{1/2}\boldsymbol{\Xi}^{1/2}$. Let $(\boldsymbol{\Xi}^{1/2})^{-1} = \boldsymbol{\Xi}^{-1/2}$, and note that $\mathbf{I}_n = \boldsymbol{\Xi}^{-1/2}\boldsymbol{\Xi}^{1/2} = \boldsymbol{\Xi}^{1/2}\boldsymbol{\Xi}^{-1/2}$. Because the matrices $\boldsymbol{\Xi}^{1/2}$ and $\boldsymbol{\Xi}^{-1/2}$ are continuous functions of their elements, and because $n^{-1}\mathbf{x}'\mathbf{x} \rightarrow \boldsymbol{\Xi}$, it follows that $(n^{-1}\mathbf{x}'\mathbf{x})^{1/2} \rightarrow \boldsymbol{\Xi}^{1/2}$ and $(\mathbf{x}'\mathbf{x})^{-1/2}\boldsymbol{\Xi}^{1/2} \rightarrow \mathbf{I}_n$. Then by Slutsky's theorem, the limiting distributions of $n^{1/2}(\hat{\boldsymbol{\beta}} - \boldsymbol{\beta})$ and $(\mathbf{x}'\mathbf{x})^{-1/2}\boldsymbol{\Xi}^{1/2}n^{1/2}(\hat{\boldsymbol{\beta}} - \boldsymbol{\beta})$ are identical, and by utilizing properties of linear combinations of multivariate normally distributed random variables, it follows that an asymptotic distribution for $\hat{\boldsymbol{\beta}}$ is given by

$$\hat{\boldsymbol{\beta}} \overset{a}{\sim} \mathrm{N}(\boldsymbol{\beta}, \sigma^2(\mathbf{x}'\mathbf{x})^{-1/2}\boldsymbol{\Xi}^{1/2}\boldsymbol{\Xi}^{-1}\boldsymbol{\Xi}^{1/2}(\mathbf{x}'\mathbf{x})^{-1/2}) = \mathrm{N}(\boldsymbol{\beta}, \sigma^2(\mathbf{x}'\mathbf{x})^{-1/2}(\mathbf{x}'\mathbf{x})^{-1/2})$$
$$= \mathrm{N}(\boldsymbol{\beta}, \sigma^2(\mathbf{x}'\mathbf{x})^{-1}). \qquad (5.3.11)$$

Thus, the asymptotic covariance matrix of $\hat{\boldsymbol{\beta}}$ is in precisely the same form as the finite covariance matrix of $\hat{\boldsymbol{\beta}}$.

The unknown and unobservable σ^2 remains in the expressions for the finite and asymptotic covariance matrices for the LS estimator. We will identify later a useful solution to the inverse problem of generating a consistent point estimate of the unknown σ^2. We will then revisit the problem of providing an observable representation of both the finite sample and asymptotic covariance matrices of the LS estimator.

► **Example 5.3.3:** Using the same simulation framework employed at the end of Section 5.3.4, we provide a GAUSS program in the examples manual to illustrate the asymptotic normality of the least-squares estimator. As before, the reader selects the sample size (n) and the number of samples (m) used in the bootstrap simulation exercise. The simulated distribution functions for the estimator and the normal distributions derived by the Central Limit theorem are presented for comparison purposes. As the sample size increases, the reader should observe that the empirical distribution functions converge to the normal distribution functions.

5.4. Estimating ε, σ^2, and cov($\hat{\beta}$)

To make both the finite and the asymptotic covariance matrix of $\hat{\boldsymbol{\beta}}$ operational empirically, we need a solution to the inverse problem of recovering the value of the unknown covariance matrix $\sigma^2(\mathbf{x}'\mathbf{x})^{-1}$. We may also be interested in recovering values for the unknown and unobservable noise component ε of the linear regression model. We examine both of these inverse problems in this section.

5.4.1. An Estimator for ε

Because the random noise vector is unknown and unobservable, we must again utilize indirect observations on ε in developing an estimation procedure for ε. Indirect observations on the random vector ε are given by outcomes of the estimator

$$\hat{\varepsilon} = \mathbf{Y} - \mathbf{x}\hat{\boldsymbol{\beta}} = [\mathbf{I}_n - \mathbf{x}(\mathbf{x}'\mathbf{x})^{-1}\mathbf{x}']\mathbf{Y} = [\mathbf{I}_n - \mathbf{x}(\mathbf{x}'\mathbf{x})^{-1}\mathbf{x}']\varepsilon = \mathbf{m}\varepsilon, \qquad (5.4.1)$$

as we noted previously in Equation (3.6.1). The properties of $\hat{\varepsilon}$ were also noted previously in Section 3.6.1, but we repeat them here for convenience. The matrix $\mathbf{m}$ is a $(n \times n)$ symmetric idempotent matrix for which $\mathbf{m} = \mathbf{mm} = \mathbf{mm}' = \mathbf{m}'\mathbf{m}$. Furthermore, $\mathbf{m}$ has rank $(n - k)$ because the rank of an idempotent matrix equals its trace, which is given by $\text{tr}(\mathbf{m}) = \text{tr}(\mathbf{I}_n - \mathbf{x}(\mathbf{x}'\mathbf{x})^{-1}\mathbf{x}') = \text{tr}(\mathbf{I}_n - \mathbf{x}'\mathbf{x}(\mathbf{x}'\mathbf{x})^{-1}) = \text{tr}(\mathbf{I}_n - \mathbf{I}_k) = n - k$. Because $\mathbf{m}$ is singular, it is not possible to invert $\mathbf{m}$ and solve for the unknown value of ε in (5.4.1). However certain linear combinations of the noise vector are in fact observable; namely, any linear combination $\mathbf{c}'\varepsilon$ for which $\mathbf{c}'\mathbf{x} = \mathbf{0}$, for then it follows from (5.4.1) that $\mathbf{c}'\hat{\varepsilon} = \mathbf{c}'\varepsilon$.

From the results on the means and covariance matrices of linear combinations of random variables, it can be shown that the expectation of $\hat{\varepsilon}$ is identical to the expectation of ε, namely $\text{E}[\hat{\varepsilon}] = \text{E}[\varepsilon] = \mathbf{0}$, and the covariance matrix of $\hat{\varepsilon}$ is equal to $\mathbf{cov}(\hat{\varepsilon}) = \sigma^2(\mathbf{I}_n - \mathbf{x}(\mathbf{x}'\mathbf{x})^{-1}\mathbf{x}')$, which is a singular matrix. It can also be shown, following an analog to the proof of the Gauss–Markov theorem, that within the class of estimators that are linear functions of $\mathbf{Y}$ and that have an expectation that agrees with the expectation of ε (i.e., an expectation of zero), the estimator $\hat{\varepsilon}$ defined by (5.4.1) has the smallest possible covariance matrix. Thus, in this sense, $\hat{\varepsilon}$ can be thought of as the *best linear unbiased estimator* of the noise component.

Regarding the large sample behavior of the estimator $\hat{\varepsilon}$, if $\mathbf{x}(\mathbf{x}'\mathbf{x})^{-1}\mathbf{x}' \rightarrow \mathbf{0}$ as $n \rightarrow \infty$, it is intuitively reasonable to conclude from (5.4.1) that the entries in $\hat{\varepsilon}$ would converge in probability, and thus in distribution, to the corresponding elements in ε. This is the content of Theorem 5.4.1.

Theorem 5.4.1 (Consistency of the Estimator $\hat{\varepsilon}_i$ for ε_i): *Under the conditions of the probability model in Table 5.1, and on the additional assumption, that* $\mathbf{x}(\mathbf{x}'\mathbf{x})^{-1}\mathbf{x}' \rightarrow \mathbf{0}$ *as* $n \rightarrow \infty$, *it follows that* $\hat{\varepsilon}_i \xrightarrow{p} \varepsilon_i \; \forall i$, *and thus* $\hat{\varepsilon}_i \xrightarrow{d} \varepsilon_i \forall i$.

PROOF: See the proof of Theorem 3.6.1 in Section 3.10.

The theorem makes clear that, asymptotically, the elements of $\hat{\varepsilon}$ and ε coincide, and thus that in the limit, the inverse problem of recovering point value information about the ε outcomes, $\mathbf{e}$, is effectively solved because $\hat{\varepsilon}$ fully recovers information about the behavior of ε. Note that the asymptotic probability distribution of $\hat{\varepsilon}_i$ clearly does not need to be a normal distribution; the distribution of $\hat{\varepsilon}_i$ is coincident with whatever the distribution of ε_i happens to be.

5.4.2. An Estimator for σ^2 and $\mathbf{cov}(\hat{\boldsymbol{\beta}})$

Turning our attention to the inverse problem of recovering information about the point value of σ^2, we note that it follows from (5.4.1) and the idempotency of $\mathbf{m}$ that

$$\hat{\varepsilon}'\hat{\varepsilon} = \varepsilon'(\mathbf{I}_n - \mathbf{x}(\mathbf{x}'\mathbf{x})^{-1}\mathbf{x}')\varepsilon. \tag{5.4.2}$$

Because $\hat{\varepsilon}'\hat{\varepsilon}$ is a scalar and the trace of a scalar is the scalar itself, we can use properties of the trace of a matrix to evaluate (5.4.2). Consequently,

$$\begin{aligned} \mathrm{E}[\hat{\varepsilon}'\hat{\varepsilon}] &= \mathrm{E}[\varepsilon'(\mathbf{I}_n - \mathbf{x}(\mathbf{x}'\mathbf{x})^{-1}\mathbf{x}')\varepsilon] = \mathrm{E}[\varepsilon'\mathbf{m}\varepsilon] \\ &= \mathrm{E}[\mathrm{tr}\,\varepsilon'\mathbf{m}\varepsilon] = \mathrm{E}[\mathrm{tr}\,\mathbf{m}\varepsilon\varepsilon'] = \mathrm{tr}\,\mathrm{E}[\mathbf{m}\varepsilon\varepsilon'] \\ &= \sigma^2\mathrm{tr}[\mathbf{I}_n - \mathbf{x}(\mathbf{x}'\mathbf{x})^{-1}\mathbf{x}'] = \sigma^2\mathrm{tr}(\mathbf{I}_n - \mathbf{I}_k) = \sigma^2(n-k). \end{aligned} \tag{5.4.3}$$

Therefore,

$$\mathrm{E}\left[\frac{\hat{\varepsilon}'\hat{\varepsilon}}{(n-k)}\right] = \sigma^2, \tag{5.4.4}$$

and the estimation rule

$$\mathrm{S}^2 = \frac{(\mathbf{Y} - \mathbf{x}\hat{\boldsymbol{\beta}})'(\mathbf{Y} - \mathbf{x}\hat{\boldsymbol{\beta}})}{n-k} = \frac{\mathbf{Y}'(\mathbf{I}_n - \mathbf{x}(\mathbf{x}'\mathbf{x})^{-1}\mathbf{x}')\mathbf{Y}}{n-k} \tag{5.4.5}$$

represents an *unbiased* estimator for σ^2.

We can also show that the estimator in (5.4.5) is a *consistent* estimator of σ^2. The proof of this result is based on Markov's probability inequality. In comparing the statements of Theorems 3.4.2 and 5.4.2, one should note the additional explicit assumption that the ε_i's are iid below.

Theorem 5.4.2 (Consistency of S^2 for Estimating σ^2): *Under the assumptions of the probability model in Table 5.1 and that the ε_i's are iid,* $\mathrm{S}^2 \xrightarrow{p} \sigma^2$.

PROOF: See the proof of Theorem 3.4.2 in Section 3.10.

It can be shown, under the additional assumption of finiteness of the fourth-order absolute moments of the ε_i's, that S^2 is asymptotically normally distributed with mean σ^2 and asymptotic covariance matrix $(\mu_4' - \sigma^4)/n$, where μ_4' is the fourth moment of the ε_i's (Mittelhammer, p. 447). Furthermore, S^2 would then be consistent for σ^2 within the current probability model even if the ε_i's were not iid so long as they still shared a common variance σ^2. Unlike the parametric case of Chapter 3, we cannot establish the finite sample distribution of this estimator, and we cannot claim that S^2 is the MVUE estimator of σ^2.

Having recovered information on the point value of σ^2, we are now in a position to revisit the problem of generating an operational version of the finite sample and asymptotic covariance matrices of $\hat{\boldsymbol{\beta}}$, both of which are represented by $\mathbf{cov}(\hat{\boldsymbol{\beta}}) = \sigma^2(\mathbf{x}'\mathbf{x})^{-1}$. In particular, an estimator of the covariance matrix can be defined by simply replacing the unknown and unobservable σ^2 with the unbiased and consistent estimator of σ^2

represented by S^2 of (5.4.5). We then obtain an estimator of the covariance matrix

$$\mathbf{c\hat{o}v}(\hat{\boldsymbol{\beta}}) = S^2(\mathbf{x}'\mathbf{x})^{-1}. \tag{5.4.6}$$

The estimator is *unbiased* because

$$E[\mathbf{c\hat{o}v}(\hat{\boldsymbol{\beta}})] = E[S^2(\mathbf{x}'\mathbf{x})^{-1}] = E[S^2](\mathbf{x}'\mathbf{x})^{-1} = \sigma^2(\mathbf{x}'\mathbf{x})^{-1}. \tag{5.4.7}$$

Furthermore, the covariance estimator is *consistent* in the sense that $S^2 - \sigma^2 \xrightarrow{p} 0$ implies that $\mathbf{c\hat{o}v}(\hat{\boldsymbol{\beta}}) - \mathbf{cov}(\hat{\boldsymbol{\beta}}) = (S^2 - \sigma^2)(\mathbf{x}'\mathbf{x})^{-1} \xrightarrow{p} \mathbf{0}$ if $(\mathbf{x}'\mathbf{x})^{-1}$ is $o(n^{1/2})$, which can be assumed to hold very generally. Using results on linear combinations of (asymptotically) normally distributed random variables, one can also argue that the (i, j)th element of $\mathbf{cov}(\hat{\boldsymbol{\beta}})$ is *asymptotically normally distributed* as

$$\text{c\hat{o}v}_{i,j}(\hat{\boldsymbol{\beta}}) \overset{a}{\sim} N\left(\sigma^2(\mathbf{x}'\mathbf{x})^{-1}_{i,j}, n^{-1}(\mu_4' - \sigma^4)\left[(\mathbf{x}'\mathbf{x})^{-1}_{i,j}\right]^2\right) \tag{5.4.8}$$

if it is assumed that S^2 has the aforementioned asymptotic normal distribution. Finally, unlike the parametric model examined in Chapter 3, we cannot claim that the covariance matrix estimator is the MVUE estimator of the elements of $\mathbf{cov}(\hat{\boldsymbol{\beta}})$.

► **Example 5.4.1:** To assist the reader in computing the unbiased estimator of σ^2, we provide a GAUSS procedure named s2() that uses the least-squares residuals to form the estimate. We then use the procedure to conduct a bootstrap simulation exercise designed to demonstrate the unbiasedness and consistency properties of the estimator (see the examples manual).

At this point we have succeeded in deriving estimation rules for recovering information concerning the unknowns in the linear regression model and have discussed their finite and large sample properties.

5.5. Critique

If we return to the class of probability models enumerated in Table 2.1, you will note that in this chapter we have chosen, relative to the possible array of probability model components, a very basic set of assumptions. Nonetheless, the resulting estimation problems are far from simple. However, the important thing is that in searching for an inverse problem solution for this DSP, we are led to general estimation procedures that will serve us well not only in this chapter but also in chapters ahead. In particular, we will see that the extremum estimation procedure, of which the least-squares procedure is an example, will serve as a unifying basis throughout the book for developing estimation rules and demonstrating corresponding sampling properties. Likewise, once we have defined an estimation rule, we now have a well-defined approach for evaluating its sampling properties and answering questions regarding such properties as unbiasedness, consistency, and asymptotic normality.

As we leave this chapter, we remind the reader of the classical sampling theory, pre-data context that forms the basis for evaluating the estimation rules we have examined.

Understanding the sampling theory basis for reasoning, as we have applied it to the semiparametric linear regression probability model in this chapter, is essential if we are to understand the meaning and limitations of what can be learned from a sample of data in more complicated DSPs normally found in practice.

5.6. Exercises

5.6.1. Idea Checklist – Knowledge Guides

---

1. What is the role of the metric or estimation objective function in developing an estimation procedure?
2. What is the role of statistical sampling properties in evaluating estimation procedures?
3. Why are asymptotic statistical properties important? When are they useful?
4. What is the relevance of the term *predata* in the discussion of the statistical properties of the least-squares estimator in this chapter?
5. What is the importance of the computer in
  a. teaching and learning econometrics;
  b. applying econometrics?

5.6.2. Problems

5–1 Consider the location and scale statistical model $\mathbf{Y} = \mathbf{x}\beta + \varepsilon = \mathbf{1}\beta + \varepsilon$, where $\mathbf{1}$ is a $(n \times 1)$ vector of 1's, $\varepsilon \sim (\mathbf{0}, \sigma^2 \mathrm{I}_n)$, and σ^2 is *known*. Here, β is the location parameter and σ^2 is the scale parameter. Develop a BLUE of the location parameter β and an unbiased estimator of its sampling variability. Discuss what happens to the sampling variability of the estimator of β as the sample size n increases.

5–2 Assume the regression model is of the form $\mathbf{Y} = \mathbf{x}_1\beta_1 + \mathbf{x}_2\beta_2 + \varepsilon$ and the researcher omits the second set of explanatory variables $\mathbf{x}_2$ and uses the least-squares estimation rule on the model $\mathbf{Y} = \mathbf{x}_1\beta_1 + \varepsilon_0$. Discuss the sampling properties of the corresponding estimator of β_1 and compare it with the sampling properties of the estimator applied to the correctly specified model. Is it possible for the estimator of β_1 in the restricted model to be better than the estimator of β_1 in the correctly specified model? How?

5–3 The condition number of a square matrix, $\mathbf{x}'\mathbf{x}$, is the ratio of its largest to its smallest eigenvalue (see Belsley, 1991). A large value of the condition number is indicative of a high degree of linear association between one or more columns of the matrix. Develop the sampling implications for the least-squares estimator associated with an $\mathbf{x}'\mathbf{x}$ matrix having a condition number of 1 versus an $\mathbf{x}'\mathbf{x}$ matrix with a high condition number in which two or more of the explanatory variables are highly linearly related and one of the characteristic roots of the $\mathbf{x}'\mathbf{x}$ matrix approaches zero.

5–4 Within the linear model context, determine a solution to the extremum problem arg $\max_{\boldsymbol{\beta}}[-(\mathbf{y} - \mathbf{x}\boldsymbol{\beta})'(\mathbf{y} - \mathbf{x}\boldsymbol{\beta})]$ subject to the linear restrictions $\mathbf{c}\boldsymbol{\beta} = \mathbf{r}$. Note this is a preview to the concept of restricted LS–extremum estimation that we will develop in a chapter 6.

5–5 For the location and scale statistical model formulated in Exercise 1, and a realized sample of data, suppose you want to ensure for the estimate of β that the zero moment condition

$\sum_{i=1}^{n} \mathrm{w}_i(\mathrm{y}_i - \beta) = 0$ is satisfied. This means that you would be seeking a set of weights w_i that would satisfy the sample moment condition. As it stands, there is an infinite set of solutions for the weights that will satisfy the moment condition. To obtain a unique solution for these unknown weights, consider the solution to the following optimization problem:

$$\arg\max_{\mathbf{w}} \left[n^{-1} \sum_i \ln \mathrm{w}_i \right]$$

subject to

$$\sum_i \mathrm{w}_i(\mathrm{y}_i - \beta) = 0$$
$$\sum_i \mathrm{w}_i = 1$$
$$\mathrm{w}_i \geq 0$$

Attempt to develop a solution to this problem. If you are able to solve the problem, you will find the optimal solution is $\hat{\mathrm{w}}_i = 1/n \, \forall i$. Discuss what this means for how to weight the sample observations and relate these weights to the least-squares solution for the problem. Note, this is a preview to the concepts of *extremum, maximum entropy, and empirical likelihood estimation* that we will develop in later chapters.

5–6 Equation (5.3.9) is a special case of the more general result that $\mathrm{E}[\mathbf{Z}'\mathbf{a}\mathbf{Z}] = \boldsymbol{\mu}'\mathbf{a}\boldsymbol{\mu} + \mathrm{tr}(\mathbf{a}\boldsymbol{\Sigma})$, where $\boldsymbol{\mu}$ and $\boldsymbol{\Sigma}$ are the mean and covariance matrix of $\mathbf{Z}$. Prove this more general result and demonstrate that Equation (5.3.9) is indeed a special case.

5–7 On the basis of logic similar to that used in the discussion and proof of the Gauss–Markov theorem, state and prove a theorem that determines the BLUE estimator of a linear combination of the elements in the parameter vector $\boldsymbol{\beta}$. That is, determine the BLUE of $\mathbf{c}\boldsymbol{\beta}$, where $\mathbf{c}$ is some $(1 \times k)$ row vector. (Hint: The estimator will be in the form $\mathbf{caY}$ for an appropriate definition of the $(k \times n)$ matrix $\mathbf{a}$.)

5.6.3. Computer Exercises

1. Write a GAUSS program to simulate a DSP characterized by $\mathbf{Y} = \mathbf{x}\boldsymbol{\beta} + \boldsymbol{\varepsilon}$, where $\boldsymbol{\varepsilon} \sim \mathrm{N}(\mathbf{0}_{25}, \sigma^2\mathbf{I}_{25})$. The fixed $\mathbf{x}$ matrix will be (25×2), where the first column will simply be a column of 1's, and the second column will be 25 iid outcomes from a uniform distribution on the internal [0,10]. The $\boldsymbol{\beta}$ vector will equal $\boldsymbol{\beta} = [{}^{1}_{2}]$. All experiments will be conducted conditional on the $\mathbf{x}$-matrix you generated in the previous step.

- **a.** Let $\sigma^2 = 1$; generate 500 outcomes of the LS estimator of $\boldsymbol{\beta}$. Calculate the empirical distribution function for $\hat{\beta}[2]$. Report the exercise for $\sigma^2 = 1$ and $\sigma^2 = 10$. Discuss the relationship between σ^2 and the LS estimator of $\beta[2]$.
- **b.** Repeat the preceding simulation exercise, calculating EDFs for the estimator S^2 of σ^2 given by (5.4.5). Discuss the relationship between σ^2 and the estimator S^2 of σ^2.
- **c.** Repeat the simulation exercise in a. above for the LS-based estimate of $\mathrm{E}[\mathrm{Y}_1 \mid \mathbf{x}[1,2]] = \beta_1 + \beta_2\mathbf{x}[1,2]$ defined by $\hat{\beta}_1 + \hat{\beta}_2\mathbf{x}[1,2]$.

2. Consider the DSP described in Problem 1, except now let $\boldsymbol{\varepsilon} \sim \mathrm{N}(\mathbf{0}_n, \sigma^2\mathbf{I}_n)$ and $\mathbf{x}$ be a $(n \times 2)$ matrix whose second column is obtained from n iid uniform [0,10] outcomes.

- **a.** Calculate $(\mathbf{x}'\mathbf{x})^{-1}$ for $n = 10$, 100, and 1000. Does it appear that $(\mathbf{x}'\mathbf{x})^{-1} \to \mathbf{0}$? Should it?

b. Calculate EDFs for $\hat{\beta}[2]$ based on 500 outcomes of LS estimator for $n = 10$, 100, and 1000. Discuss the relationship between n and the LS estimator of $\hat{\beta}[2]$.

c. Repeat the preceding exercise for the LS-based estimate of $\mathrm{E}[\mathrm{Y}_1 \mid \mathbf{x}[1, 2]] = \beta_1 + \beta_2\mathbf{x}[1, 2]$ defined by $\hat{\beta}_1 + \hat{\beta}_2\mathbf{x}[1, 2]$.

5.7. References

Belsley, D. A. (1991), *Conditioning Diagnostics*, New York: John Wiley and Sons.

Mittelhammer, R. C. (1996), *Mathematical Statistics for Economics and Business*, New York: Springer–Verlag.

Stigler, S. M. (1981), "Gauss and the Invention of Least Squares," *Annals of Statistics*, Vol. 9, pp. 465–74.

Wald, A. (1950), *Statistical Decision Functions*, New York: John Wiley and Sons.

5.8. Appendix: Proofs

THEOREM PROOF 5.3.1 GAUSS–MARKOV THEOREM: The entire class of point estimators that are *linear* in **Y**, as $\tilde{\beta} = \mathbf{aY}$, can be written equivalently as

$$\tilde{\boldsymbol{\beta}} = [(\mathbf{x}'\mathbf{x})^{-1}\mathbf{x}' + \mathbf{c}]\mathbf{Y} = \boldsymbol{\beta} + \mathbf{cx}\boldsymbol{\beta} + (\mathbf{x}'\mathbf{x})^{-1}\mathbf{x}'\varepsilon + \mathbf{c}\varepsilon, \tag{5.8.1}$$

where $\mathbf{c} = \mathbf{a} - (\mathbf{x}'\mathbf{x})^{-1}\mathbf{x}'$. In order for $\tilde{\boldsymbol{\beta}}$ in (5.8.1) to be unbiased, the condition $\mathrm{E}[\tilde{\boldsymbol{\beta}}] = \boldsymbol{\beta} + \mathbf{cx}\boldsymbol{\beta} = \boldsymbol{\beta}$ must hold *regardless* of the value of $\boldsymbol{\beta}$. This implies necessarily that $\mathbf{cx}\boldsymbol{\beta} = \mathbf{0}$. Using this unbiasedness condition, the covariance matrix for $\tilde{\boldsymbol{\beta}}$ is

$$\mathbf{cov}(\tilde{\boldsymbol{\beta}}) = \sigma^2(\mathbf{x}'\mathbf{x})^{-1} + \sigma^2\mathbf{cc}' = \mathbf{cov}(\hat{\boldsymbol{\beta}}) + \sigma^2\mathbf{cc}' \tag{5.8.2}$$

or

$$\mathbf{cov}(\tilde{\boldsymbol{\beta}}) - \mathbf{cov}(\hat{\boldsymbol{\beta}}) = \sigma^2\mathbf{cc}'. \tag{5.8.3}$$

Because $\mathbf{cc}'$ is positive semidefinite no matter what the entries in the matrix $\mathbf{c}$, it follows that $\mathbf{cov}(\tilde{\boldsymbol{\beta}}) - \mathbf{cov}(\hat{\boldsymbol{\beta}})$ is also positive semidefinite. Thus, we can conclude that within the class of linear unbiased estimators, the BLUE of $\boldsymbol{\beta}$ (i.e., the estimator with the minimum covariance matrix) is obtained by choosing $\mathbf{c} = \mathbf{0}$, yielding the estimator $\tilde{\boldsymbol{\beta}} = (\mathbf{x}'\mathbf{x})^{-1}\mathbf{x}'\mathbf{Y} = \hat{\boldsymbol{\beta}}$. ■

THEOREM PROOF 5.3.3 ASYMPTOTIC NORMALITY OF THE LS ESTIMATOR: Examine the $(k \times 1)$ random vectors $\mathbf{Z}_i = \mathbf{x}[i, .]'\varepsilon_i$ and note that $\mathrm{E}[\mathbf{Z}_i] = \mathbf{0}$ and $\mathbf{cov}(\mathbf{Z}_i) = \sigma^2\, \mathbf{x}[i,.]'\, \mathbf{x}[i,.]$. If $\boldsymbol{\tau}$ is any finite real vector for which $\boldsymbol{\tau}'\boldsymbol{\tau} = 1$, it follows that the random scalar $\mathrm{V}_i = \boldsymbol{\tau}'\mathbf{Z}_i$ is such that $\mathrm{E}[\mathrm{V}_i] = 0$ and $\mathrm{var}(\mathrm{V}_i) = \sigma^2\boldsymbol{\tau}'\mathbf{x}[i, .]'\, \mathbf{x}[i, .]\boldsymbol{\tau}$. It follows from Slutsky's theorem and $n^{-1}\mathbf{x}'\mathbf{x} \to \boldsymbol{\Xi}$ that the limiting distribution of $n^{1/2}\boldsymbol{\tau}'(\hat{\boldsymbol{\beta}} - \boldsymbol{\beta})$ is equivalent to the limiting distribution of the random vector

$$\boldsymbol{\Xi}^{-1}(n^{-1/2}\boldsymbol{\tau}'\mathbf{x}'\boldsymbol{\varepsilon}) = \boldsymbol{\Xi}^{-1}n^{-1/2}\left(\sum_{i=1}^{n}(\boldsymbol{\tau}'\mathbf{x}[i,.]')\varepsilon_i\right) = \boldsymbol{\Xi}^{-1}\left(n^{-1/2}\sum_{i=1}^{n}\mathrm{V}_i\right). \tag{5.8.4}$$

We now apply the Triangular Array CLT to demonstrate that the trailing parenthetical term in (5.8.4) is in fact asymptotically normally distributed. With regard to the denominator expression in the limit condition for the validity of the Triangular Array CLT, note that

$$\left[\sum_{i=1}^{n}\mathrm{var}(\mathrm{V_i})\right]^{1+\delta/2} = \left[\sigma^2\sum_{i=1}^{n}\boldsymbol{\tau}'\mathbf{x}[i,.]'\mathbf{x}[i,.]\boldsymbol{\tau}\right]^{1+\delta/2} = [\sigma^2\boldsymbol{\tau}'\mathbf{x}'\mathbf{x}\boldsymbol{\tau}]^{1+\delta/2}. \tag{5.8.5}$$

Regarding the numerator of the limit condition, note that

$$\sum_{i=1}^{n}\mathrm{E}|\mathrm{V_i}|^{2+\delta} \le \sum_{i=1}^{n}|\boldsymbol{\tau}'\mathbf{x}[i,.]'|^{2+\delta}\mathrm{E}|\varepsilon_i|^{2+\delta} \le \xi\sum_{i=1}^{n}|\boldsymbol{\tau}'\mathbf{x}[i,.]'|^{2+\delta} \le n\xi\zeta, \tag{5.8.6}$$

where ζ is a finite positive constant representing the upper bound on $|\tau'\mathbf{x}[i,.]'|^{2+\delta}$ implied by the boundedness of the elements in $\mathbf{x}$. It follows that

$$\lim_{n\to\infty}\frac{\sum_{i=1}^{n}\mathrm{E}|\mathrm{V}_i|^{2+\delta}}{\left(\sum_{i=1}^{n}\mathrm{var}(\mathrm{V}_i)\right)^{1+\delta/2}}$$
$$\le \lim_{n\to\infty}\frac{n\xi\zeta}{(\sigma^2\boldsymbol{\tau}'\mathbf{x}'\mathbf{x}\boldsymbol{\tau})^{1+\delta/2}} = \lim_{n\to\infty}\frac{n^{-\delta/2}\xi\zeta}{(\sigma^2\boldsymbol{\tau}'(n^{-1}\mathbf{x}'\mathbf{x})\boldsymbol{\tau})^{1+\delta/2}} = \frac{0}{(\sigma^2\boldsymbol{\tau}'\boldsymbol{\Xi}\boldsymbol{\tau})^{1+\delta/2}} = 0 \tag{5.8.7}$$

and thus that the limit condition of the Triangular Array CLT holds. It follows that

$$n^{-1/2}\boldsymbol{\tau}'\mathbf{x}'\boldsymbol{\varepsilon}/[\sigma^2\boldsymbol{\tau}'(n^{-1}\mathbf{x}'\mathbf{x})\boldsymbol{\tau}] \xrightarrow{d} \mathrm{N}(0,1), \tag{5.8.8}$$

and, because $\sigma^2\boldsymbol{\tau}'(n^{-1}\mathbf{x}'\mathbf{x})\boldsymbol{\tau} \to \sigma^2\boldsymbol{\tau}'\boldsymbol{\Xi}\boldsymbol{\tau}$, it follows from Slutsky's theorem that

$$n^{-1/2}\boldsymbol{\tau}'\mathbf{x}'\boldsymbol{\varepsilon} \xrightarrow{d} \mathrm{N}(\mathbf{0}, \sigma^2\boldsymbol{\tau}'\boldsymbol{\Xi}\boldsymbol{\tau}). \tag{5.8.9}$$

Then, by the Cramer–Wold device, $n^{-1/2}\mathbf{x}'\boldsymbol{\varepsilon}\xrightarrow{d}\mathrm{N}(\mathbf{0}, \sigma^2\boldsymbol{\Xi})$, and another application of Slutsky's theorem finally results in

$$n^{1/2}(\hat{\boldsymbol{\beta}} - \boldsymbol{\beta}) = (n^{-1}\mathbf{x}'\mathbf{x})^{-1}n^{-1/2}\mathbf{x}'\boldsymbol{\varepsilon} \xrightarrow{d} \boldsymbol{\Xi}^{-1}n^{-1/2}\mathbf{x}'\boldsymbol{\varepsilon} \xrightarrow{d} \mathrm{N}(\mathbf{0}, \sigma^2\boldsymbol{\Xi}^{-1}). \tag{5.8.10}$$

■

CHAPTER 6

The Linear Semiparametric Regression Model: Inference

IN this chapter we broaden the scope of hypothesis-testing and confidence-region estimation procedures to encompass the case of the linear *semiparametric* probability model. Unlike inference procedures for the case of a normal parametric probability model discussed in Chapter 4, the semiparametric nature of the current model does not make normal distribution theory available for use in characterizing the finite-sample probability distributions of our test statistics and confidence interval-region estimators. As such, inference in the semiparametric linear probability model will rely much more heavily on asymptotic results, which enables normal distribution theory to be used as a large sample approximation in establishing the sampling distributions of hypothesis testing and confidence region estimation procedures. In Chapters 12 and 13 we will demonstrate empirical likelihood procedures that can be used to obtain tests and confidence intervals in ways analogous to those used in parametric models.

The specific characteristics of the semiparametric linear probability model that will apply in the current chapter are indicated in Table 6.1.

On the basis of specific model characteristics in Table 6.1, the following linear functional relationship emerges as a fundamental component of the data-sampling process:

$$\mathbf{Y} = \mathbf{x}\boldsymbol{\beta} + \varepsilon,$$

where $\mathbf{Y} = (\mathrm{Y}_1, \mathrm{Y}_2, \ldots, \mathrm{Y}_n)'$ is a $(n \times 1)$ vector of observable random variables whose range is contained in R^n, $\mathbf{x}$ is a $(n \times k)$ matrix reflecting the numerical values taken by k explanatory variables, $\boldsymbol{\beta}$ is a k-dimensional fixed vector of unknown and unobservable parameters, and ε is a $(n \times 1)$ noise vector of unobserved and unobservable random variables. To recover information about the unknown parameter vector $\boldsymbol{\beta}$ in Chapter 5, we used the least-squares (LS) criterion to derive the LS estimator

$$\hat{\boldsymbol{\beta}} = (\mathbf{x}'\mathbf{x})^{-1}\mathbf{x}'\mathbf{Y},$$

which is BLUE and, under a squared-error loss measure, is a minimax estimator. Furthermore, $\hat{\boldsymbol{\beta}} \xrightarrow{\mathrm{p}} \boldsymbol{\beta}$ and $n^{1/2}(\hat{\boldsymbol{\beta}} - \boldsymbol{\beta}) \xrightarrow{\mathrm{d}} \mathrm{N}(\boldsymbol{\beta}, \sigma^2\boldsymbol{\Xi}^{-1})$ as $n \to \infty$, indicating the consistency and asymptotic normality properties of $\hat{\boldsymbol{\beta}}$. Furthermore, for the noise variance parameter,

Table 6.1. *Linear Semiparametric Probability Model*

Model Component	**Specific Characteristics**	
Y	RV Type:	continuous
	Range:	unlimited
	Y_i dimension:	univariate
	Moments:	$E[\mathbf{Y} \mid \mathbf{x}] = \mathbf{x}\boldsymbol{\beta}$ and $\mathbf{cov}(\mathbf{Y} \mid \mathbf{x}) = \sigma^2\mathbf{I}$
$\eta(\mathbf{x}, \boldsymbol{\beta}, \varepsilon)$	Functional Form:	linear in **x** and $\boldsymbol{\beta}$, additive in ε, as $\mathbf{x}\boldsymbol{\beta} + \varepsilon$
x	RV Type:	degenerate (fixed), full-column rank
	Genesis:	exogenous to the model
$\boldsymbol{\beta}$	RV Type:	degenerate (fixed)
	Dimension:	finite
ε	RV Type:	iid or independent nonidentical
	Moments:	$E[\varepsilon \mid \mathbf{x}] = \mathbf{0}$, and $\mathbf{cov}(\varepsilon \mid \mathbf{x}) = \sigma^2\mathbf{I}$
Ω	Prior info:	none
$f(\mathbf{e} \mid \mathbf{x}, \varphi)$	PDF family:	unspecified

it was demonstrated that

$$S^2 = (\mathbf{Y} - \mathbf{x}\hat{\boldsymbol{\beta}})'(\mathbf{Y} - \mathbf{x}\hat{\boldsymbol{\beta}})/(n-k)$$

is an unbiased estimator of σ^2 and, under an iid noise assumption, $S^2 \xrightarrow{p} \sigma^2$ so that S^2 is a consistent estimator. Under higher-order moment assumptions relating to the ε_i's, S^2 is asymptotically normally distributed with mean σ^2 and asymptotic covariance matrix $(\mu_4' - \sigma^4)/n$, where μ_4' is the fourth moment of the ε_i's.

We now examine how to solve the problem of inference for semiparametric linear regression models. We will see that the same random variables used in Chapter 5 to define estimation procedures, as well as the asymptotic properties attributed to them, figure prominently in the definition of hypothesis-testing and confidence-region estimation procedures. In the sections ahead we define a formal basis for making judgments about the truth or falsity of various propositions based on the evidence at hand in a semiparametric model context. We also define methods for generating sets that encompass unknown parameters with known (asymptotically valid) confidence.

We emphasize that the classical approach to evaluating the statistical properties of hypothesis testing and confidence region estimation procedures is in an unconditional predata context. We are thus contemplating or evaluating the behavior of test and confidence region procedures in the context of all of the hypothetical samples of data that could have occurred, not in the sense of what actually did occur. By basing our evaluation and choice of procedures on the sampling distribution of **Y**, the information we obtain about parameters from test decisions or confidence regions depends not only on the data being analyzed but also on whatever data sets one might have observed but did not.

As a final introductory remark we stress that in econometric analysis, conclusions and judgments are not reached purely through logical deductions from theoretical arguments but rather through the amassment of sufficient empirical evidence from observed data for or against a proposition. The classical test procedures presented in this chapter are defined in a predata sense to reject false propositions and not reject true ones with known predata probabilities, and it is these test characteristics that are used to define the weight of evidence that a classical test decision *will* make the correct decision. The classical confidence region procedures are defined in a predata sense to generate sets that cover true values of parameters with known predata probabilities, and it is these predata probability characteristics that are used to define the confidence one has that a stated confidence region *will* cover the true parameters. Once the data have been observed and the procedures implemented, the test decision is either right or wrong, the confidence region either does or does not contain the true parameters, and there are no probabilities to speak of in this frequentist type of postdata context.

6.1. Asymptotics: Why, What Kind, and How Useful?

6.1.1. Why?

We reemphasize that we make *no* specific distributional assumptions (e.g., normality) relating to ε or $\mathbf{Y}$ in the current semiparametric probability model, and it should come as no surprise under the least-squares estimation objective function that hypothesis testing and confidence region estimation procedures must be based on approximate or *asymptotic* distributions of statistics. There is simply no other basis for establishing the sampling distributions of general functions $\mathbf{t}(\mathbf{Y})$ of the sample data $\mathbf{Y}$ used in the definitions of tests and confidence sets that we will examine. In particular, the standard approaches for determining the distribution of $\mathbf{t}(\mathbf{Y})$ from the distribution of $\mathbf{Y}$ (e.g., change of variables, MGF, CDF approach) do not apply because a fundamental ingredient in such approaches, the PDF of $\mathbf{Y}$, is unknown. Nonetheless, it is often the case that a large-sample approximate (i.e., asymptotic) distribution for $\mathbf{t}(\mathbf{Y})$ can be established on the basis of moment assumptions and assumptions that limit the degree to which the elements of $\mathbf{Y}$ can exhibit interdependence. Such is the realm of central limit theorems (CLTs), which, when applicable, can result in well-known and tractable PDF families of distributions being available for characterizing the approximate distribution of test and confidence region statistics.

The approximate or asymptotic distributions become an ever more accurate representation of the true distribution of $\mathbf{t}(\mathbf{Y})$ as the sample size increases. Thus, asymptotic approximations provide us with a (approximate) distributional basis for implementing the classical predata paradigm of evaluating and specifying test and confidence region procedures in the context of their sampling behavior over all hypothetical sample outcomes that could be observed. In this context, the asymptotic distributions provide a characterization of the approximate relative frequencies with which the various hypothetical outcomes of $\mathbf{t}(\mathbf{Y})$ would occur.

6.1.2. What Kind?

All of the tests that we will consider rely, in one way or another, on the asymptotic normality of the LS estimator $\hat{\boldsymbol{\beta}}$ of $\boldsymbol{\beta}$, where $n^{1/2}(\hat{\boldsymbol{\beta}} - \boldsymbol{\beta}) \xrightarrow{d} \text{N}(\mathbf{0}, \sigma^2\Xi^{-1})$, $\hat{\boldsymbol{\beta}} \overset{a}{\sim} \text{N}(\boldsymbol{\beta}, \sigma^2(\mathbf{x}'\mathbf{x})^{-1})$, and $(n^{-1}\mathbf{x}'\mathbf{x}) \to \Xi$. One pair of tests that we will examine, the *Wald* (W) and the *Lagrange multiplier* (LM) tests, are used for testing hypotheses about the values of linear combinations of the elements in $\boldsymbol{\beta}$, as H_0: $\mathbf{c}\boldsymbol{\beta} = \mathbf{r}$ versus H_a: $\mathbf{c}\boldsymbol{\beta} \neq \mathbf{r}$. We will see that the W and LM statistics have asymptotic chi-square distributions derived from the asymptotic normality of $\hat{\boldsymbol{\beta}}$. We will also see that the tests are asymptotically equivalent, meaning that their asymptotic distributions are identical, and thus a choice between them cannot be made on the basis of their asymptotic behavior. Instead, a choice is sometimes based on computational convenience. The Wald test is based on the *unrestricted* (by H_0) LS estimator, whereas the Lagrange multiplier test is based on the *restricted* (by H_0) LS estimator. Thus, if either the restricted or unrestricted estimation of $\boldsymbol{\beta}$ is more straightforward to calculate, one of the tests might be preferable based on computational considerations, although in the current linear model context, neither calculation problem is burdensome. On the basis of the duality between hypothesis tests and confidence region estimation, Wald and Lagrange multiplier-based confidence regions can be defined that have predefined asymptotic levels of confidence for covering the true value of $\mathbf{c}\boldsymbol{\beta}$. The asymptotic coverage levels are derived from the asymptotic Chi-square distributions of the W and LM statistics, which in turn are derived from the asymptotic normality of $\hat{\boldsymbol{\beta}}$, as indicated previously.

We will also examine procedures for testing inequality hypotheses relating to the value of linear combinations $\mathbf{c}\boldsymbol{\beta}$ of the elements of the $\boldsymbol{\beta}$ vector. These tests will be based on Z-statistics whose asymptotic normal distribution is derived directly from the asymptotic normality of $\hat{\boldsymbol{\beta}}$. Thus, Z-tests will utilize asymptotic normal distributions in their definition and evaluation. Duality will again be used to define confidence bounds for the true value of $\mathbf{c}\boldsymbol{\beta}$ based on Z-statistics, from which the asymptotic level of confidence will be derived from the asymptotic normality of the Z-statistics.

In summary, central limit theory used to establish the asymptotic normality of the LS estimator of $\boldsymbol{\beta}$ will be extended to establish the asymptotic distributions and properties of Wald, Lagrange multiplier, and Z-test and confidence-region procedures relating to linear combinations of the elements in $\boldsymbol{\beta}$. We provide some brief remarks relating to the asymptotic inference procedure for the parameter σ^2 in Section 6.5.

6.1.3. How Useful?

The size, power, and other properties of hypothesis tests, as well as the confidence level and other properties of confidence sets based on asymptotic distribution theory are all approximate, for they are only valid asymptotically. A logical question to consider is, How accurate are the approximations?, the answer to which is directly related to how accurate the hypothesis tests and confidence region procedures are that are derived from the approximations. One might also ask, How large does n have to be to obtain an accurate approximation? Because the accuracy of asymptotic approximations, and the test and confidence procedures based on them, will generally improve as the sample size increases, one would expect that for large enough n accuracy would be achieved.

The preceding questions are of the utmost importance if one wishes to utilize asymptotic theory as a guide when performing and evaluating approximative inference based on asymptotic distributions of test- and confidence-region procedures. Unfortunately, there are no general answers to the questions. The rate at which the accuracy of an asymptotic approximation improves depends on many things that can change from problem to problem. These include what the true distribution of the sample data happens to be, the degree of interdependence among sample observations, and the form of the function used to define the statistic on which the test or confidence region procedure is based. In general, one must rely on previous experience, bootstrap simulations, or Monte Carlo experiments to provide an indication of how useful asymptotic approximations are in any given problem situation. We provide the reader with some experience in the context of bootstrap simulations and Monte Carlo experiments in several of the examples in this chapter. Practitioners sometimes take a more pragmatic view to the questions posed at the outset of this section: Given that there is no alternative to asymptotic approximations in a given problem situation, the asymptotic approach must be used if any inference is to be performed at all. The prudent pragmatist will explicitly acknowledge that any properties claimed for hypothesis tests and confidence-region estimators based on asymptotic distributions are only approximative.

It must also be recognized that the type of asymptotic approximation used in establishing the asymptotic distribution of a statistic can determine the accuracy of the approximation. We will deal primarily with *first-order approximations* derived from Taylor series expansions of various functions of random variables. The accuracy of these types of approximations is generally of order of magnitude $O(n^{-1/2})$, meaning that deviations between the asymptotic and actual distributions of a statistic converge to zero at the rate $n^{-1/2}$. The accuracy of asymptotic approximations can often be improved by using higher-order terms in a Taylor series expansion or else by using other types of asymptotic expansions such as Edgeworth or Cornish–Fisher expansions. In these cases, it is possible to achieve higher orders of approximation, where a kth order of approximation would refer to an accuracy of approximation having magnitude $O(n^{-k/2})$. The theory of higher-order approximations is an advanced topic that is beyond the scope of our study. The interested reader can consult Zaman (1996, Chapter 14) for an introductory treatment of the subject. Additional, more advanced readings and references can be found in Hall (1992). Finally, note that bootstrap estimates of the distributions and standard errors of statistics can provide approximations that are often more accurate than first-order asymptotic approximations (see Hall, 1992, and Navidi, 1989).

6.2. Hypothesis Testing: Linear Equality Restrictions on β

In this section we examine solutions to the inverse problem of recovering information relating to the validity of hypotheses about linear combinations of the unknown and unobservable parameter vector $\boldsymbol{\beta}$. As we noted in Chapter 4, cases often arise in practice in which the analyst is interested in testing hypotheses that are in the form of linear restrictions on the entries in the $\boldsymbol{\beta}$ vector. Examples of such tests include whether an individual element of $\boldsymbol{\beta}$ is equal to zero, whether a subvector of the elements of $\boldsymbol{\beta}$ equals the zero vector, or whether a linear combination of the β_i's equals some constant. For example, a hypothesis of constant returns to scale in a Cobb–Douglas production function may be represented as a restriction that the sum of the β_i's that correspond to the output elasticities of the function equals 1.

The hypotheses corresponding to linear restrictions on the elements of the $\boldsymbol{\beta}$ vector can be represented in the generic form $\mathbf{c}\boldsymbol{\beta} = \mathbf{r}$. Here, $\mathbf{c}$ is a $(j \times k)$ matrix of fixed constants representing the coefficients that define the linear combinations of the entries in $\boldsymbol{\beta}$ that are of interest, and $\mathbf{r}$ is a $(j \times 1)$ vector representing the corresponding hypothesized values of the individual linear combinations. As in Chapter 4, it is henceforth assumed that the rank of the $\mathbf{c}$ matrix equals j, for otherwise, either one or more restrictions on the $\boldsymbol{\beta}$ vector are redundant because of the linear dependency in the rows of $\mathbf{c}$, or worse, the restrictions are inconsistent. The latter condition will occur if the linear dependence among the rows of $\mathbf{c}$ characterized by $\mathbf{a}'\mathbf{c} = \mathbf{0}$, for an appropriate vector or matrix $\mathbf{a}$ is not also satisfied by the elements in $\mathbf{r}$, that is, if $\mathbf{a}'\mathbf{r} \neq \mathbf{0}$.

6.2.1. Wald (W) Tests

Adopting the asymptotic normal approximation for $\hat{\boldsymbol{\beta}}$, it follows from results on the distribution of linear combinations of normally distributed random variables (the result being $\mathbf{Z} \sim \mathrm{N}(\boldsymbol{\mu}, \boldsymbol{\Psi}) \Rightarrow \mathbf{aZ} + \mathbf{b} \sim \mathrm{N}(\mathbf{a}\boldsymbol{\mu} + \mathbf{b}, \mathbf{a}\boldsymbol{\Psi}\mathbf{a}')$) that $\mathbf{c}\hat{\boldsymbol{\beta}} - \mathbf{r} \overset{a}{\sim} \mathrm{N}(\mathbf{c}\boldsymbol{\beta} - \mathbf{r}, \sigma^2\mathbf{c}(\mathbf{x}'\mathbf{x})^{-1}\mathbf{c}')$. Consequently *if the null hypothesis* H_0: $\mathbf{c}\boldsymbol{\beta} = \mathbf{r}$ *is true*, then $\mathbf{c}\hat{\boldsymbol{\beta}} - \mathbf{r} \overset{a}{\sim} \mathrm{N}(\mathbf{0}, \sigma^2\mathbf{c}(\mathbf{x}'\mathbf{x})^{-1}\mathbf{c}')$. Again, on the basis of results relating to the distribution of linear combinations of normally distributed random variables and on properties of the symmetric square-root matrix (the result being $\mathbf{m}^{-1/2}\mathbf{m}\mathbf{m}^{-1/2} = \mathbf{I}$), it follows that $[\sigma^2\mathbf{c}(\mathbf{x}'\mathbf{x})^{-1}\mathbf{c}']^{-1/2}(\mathbf{c}\hat{\boldsymbol{\beta}} - \mathbf{r}) \overset{a}{\sim} \mathrm{N}(\mathbf{0}, \mathbf{I}_j)$.

Now because the sum of the squares of j independent standard normal random variables has a central Chi-square distribution with j degrees of freedom, we have that

$$(\mathbf{c}\hat{\boldsymbol{\beta}} - \mathbf{r}')[\sigma^2\mathbf{c}(\mathbf{x}'\mathbf{x})^{-1}\mathbf{c}']^{-1}(\mathbf{c}\hat{\boldsymbol{\beta}} - \mathbf{r}) \overset{a}{\sim} \text{Chi-square}(j, 0) \text{ under } \mathrm{H}_0, \tag{6.2.1}$$

where we remind the reader that Chi-square$(j, 0)$ denotes a noncentral Chi-square distribution with j degrees of freedom and noncentrality of 0, that is, a central Chi-square distribution with j degrees of freedom. Note that the phrase "under H_0" in (6.2.1) means "on the assumption the null hypothesis is true." Finally, because $\frac{\sigma^2}{S^2} \overset{p}{\to} 1$, where S^2 is the unbiased and consistent estimator of σ^2 defined by $S^2 = (\mathbf{Y} - \mathbf{x}\hat{\boldsymbol{\beta}})'(\mathbf{Y} - \mathbf{x}\hat{\boldsymbol{\beta}})/(n - k)$, it can be argued via Slutsky's theorem (which implies that if $\mathbf{W}_n \overset{p}{\to} \mathbf{w}_0$ and $\mathbf{V}_n \overset{d}{\to} \mathbf{V}$, then $\mathbf{W}_n\mathbf{V}_n \overset{d}{\to} \mathbf{w}_0\mathbf{V}$) that premultiplying the random variable in (6.2.1) by $\frac{\sigma^2}{S^2}$ will have no effect on the asymptotic distribution and thus that

$$\mathrm{W} = (\mathbf{c}\hat{\boldsymbol{\beta}} - \mathbf{r})'[S^2\mathbf{c}(\mathbf{x}'\mathbf{x})^{-1}\mathbf{c}']^{-1}(\mathbf{c}\hat{\boldsymbol{\beta}} - \mathbf{r}) \overset{a}{\sim} \text{Chi-square}(j, 0) \text{ under } \mathrm{H}_0. \tag{6.2.2}$$

The statistic W is referred to in the literature as the Wald statistic, which is named after Abraham Wald, who first derived its general form in 1943. The intuition underlying this test is that the more distant the outcomes of $\mathbf{c}\hat{\boldsymbol{\beta}}$ are from the hypothesized value of $\mathbf{c}\boldsymbol{\beta}$ represented by $\mathbf{r}$, the less plausible is H_0. The distance between $\mathbf{c}\hat{\boldsymbol{\beta}}$ outcomes and $\mathbf{r}$ is adjusted for the inherent variability in the estimator $\mathbf{c}\hat{\boldsymbol{\beta}}$ of $\mathbf{c}\boldsymbol{\beta}$ by measuring distance in the inverse asymptotic covariance metric $[\mathbf{c\hat{o}v}(\mathbf{c}\hat{\boldsymbol{\beta}})]^{-1} = [S^2\mathbf{c}(\mathbf{x}'\mathbf{x})^{-1}\mathbf{c}']^{-1}$. This results in distance being measured in standardized units that are free of units of measurement differences.

6.2.1.a. Distribution When H_0 Is False

If H_0 is not true, we consider alternative hypotheses of the form H_a: $\mathbf{c}\boldsymbol{\beta} = \mathbf{r} + n^{-1/2}\boldsymbol{\delta}$ for some choice of the finite vector of constants $\boldsymbol{\delta}$. The reasons for specifying the null hypothesis error in the particular form $n^{-1/2}\boldsymbol{\delta}$ may not be clear to the reader at this point. We simply note here that this form facilitates the definition of the asymptotic distribution of W under H_0 and we postpone a more detailed discussion of the importance and meaning of such alternatives to Section 6.2.1.c. Under alternative hypotheses of the form H_0, the statistic W has a *noncentral Chi-square distribution*, and the noncentrality parameter is a function of $\boldsymbol{\delta}$ as follows:

$$W \overset{a}{\sim} \text{Chi-square}(j, \lambda) \quad \text{with} \quad \lambda = \frac{1}{2}\boldsymbol{\delta}'(\sigma^2\mathbf{c}\boldsymbol{\Xi}^{-1}\mathbf{c}')^{-1}\boldsymbol{\delta}. \tag{6.2.3}$$

To motivate (6.2.3), return to the limiting distribution result for the LS estimator and note that Slutsky's theorem implies that $n^{1/2}(\mathbf{c}\hat{\boldsymbol{\beta}} - \mathbf{c}\boldsymbol{\beta}) \xrightarrow{d} N(\mathbf{0}, \sigma^2\mathbf{c}\boldsymbol{\Xi}^{-1}\mathbf{c}')$. Now proceed under the assumption that H_a: $\mathbf{c}\boldsymbol{\beta} = \mathbf{r} + n^{-1/2}\boldsymbol{\delta}$ is true, in which case it follows again from Slutsky's theorem that $\mathbf{Z} = n^{1/2}(\mathbf{c}\hat{\boldsymbol{\beta}} - \mathbf{r}) \xrightarrow{d} N(\boldsymbol{\delta}, \sigma^2\mathbf{c}\boldsymbol{\Xi}^{-1}\mathbf{c}')$. Then, from the standard characterization of the noncentral Chi-square distribution as the sums of squares of independent random variables of the form $V_i \sim N(\delta_i, 1)$ (Chapter E1; Mittelhammer, p. 666),

$$\mathbf{Z}'[\sigma^2(\mathbf{c}\boldsymbol{\Xi}^{-1}\mathbf{c}')]^{-1}\mathbf{Z} = n(\mathbf{c}\hat{\boldsymbol{\beta}} - \mathbf{r})'[\sigma^2\mathbf{c}\boldsymbol{\Xi}^{-1}\mathbf{c}']^{-1}(\mathbf{c}\hat{\boldsymbol{\beta}} - \mathbf{r}) \overset{a}{\sim} \text{Chi-square}(j, \lambda) \tag{6.2.4}$$

with the noncentrality parameter λ being defined as in (6.2.3). Finally, as we argued previously, $\sigma^2\boldsymbol{\Xi}^{-1}$ can be replaced by the consistent estimator $S^2(n^{-1}\mathbf{x}'\mathbf{x})^{-1}$ to obtain an operational and asymptotically equivalent version of the random variable in (6.2.4), leading to the definition of W in (6.2.2).

For purposes of relating asymptotic power function calculations to the values of $\boldsymbol{\delta}$ and σ^2, an operational version of the noncentrality parameter can be defined by replacing the limit matrix $\boldsymbol{\Xi}^{-1}$ by $n(\mathbf{x}'\mathbf{x})^{-1}$ as

$$\hat{\lambda} = \frac{1}{2}\boldsymbol{\delta}'[\sigma^2\mathbf{c}(n^{-1}\mathbf{x}'\mathbf{x})^{-1}\mathbf{c}']^{-1}\boldsymbol{\delta}. \tag{6.2.5}$$

The Wald test is asymptotically locally UMP invariant for testing H_0, where *locally* here means for the sequence of alternative hypotheses of the form H_a stated above, and the *invariance* refers to orthonormal linear transformations of the sample data. The test is also asymptotically UMP unbiased when only a scalar hypothesis is being tested (see Bunke and Bunke, 1986, pp. 229–35 van der Vaart, 1998, Chapter 15, and Mittelhammer, 1996, pp. 571–86).

6.2.1.b. Power Function Characteristics and Consistency

To conduct a Wald test of H_0: $\mathbf{c}\boldsymbol{\beta} = \mathbf{r}$, one must first decide on an acceptable asymptotic size of the test concomitant with acceptable power function characteristics. For a given choice of size, say α, the Wald test will be defined by solving an integral equation for a critical value τ, and then τ will be used to define a critical region C^W for the test as follows:

$$\tau = \arg_\tau \left[\int_\tau^\infty \text{Chi-square}(z; j, 0)\, dz = \alpha \right] \quad \text{and} \quad C^W = [\tau, \infty). \tag{6.2.6}$$

The test is then characterized by the pair $\{W, C^W\}$, and the test rule is "reject H_0 if $w \in C^W$." The specific value of τ in any application can be found directly using the GAUSS command cdfchii() as $\tau = \text{cdfchii}(1 - \alpha, j)$. The *asymptotic power function* can be defined by plotting the probability of rejecting H_0 as a function of λ, or if desired, as a function of δ and σ^2 if the approximation (6.2.5) is used. The power function, and its calculation using GAUSS, is defined by

$$\pi(\lambda) = \int_\tau^\infty \text{Chi-square}(z; j, \lambda)\, dz = 1 - \text{cdfchinc}[\tau, \text{j}, (2\lambda)^{1/2}]. \tag{6.2.7}$$

Regarding the solution of the integral via the GAUSS procedure cdfchinc(), note that the parameterization of the noncentrality parameter of the Chi-square distribution is *not* standardized in the literature, and other parameterizations include the one used in GAUSS, $(2\lambda)^{1/2}$ as well as the one used in SHAZAM software 2λ. Our parameterization of λ, as defined in (6.2.3), is more common in the econometrics literature.

The operational version of the Wald test used in practice, (6.2.2), is a consistent test of H_0: $\mathbf{c}\boldsymbol{\beta} = \mathbf{r}$. To see this, first note that if $\mathbf{c}\boldsymbol{\beta} = \mathbf{r} + \mathbf{v}$, where $\mathbf{v} \neq \mathbf{0}$, then $\mathbf{c}\hat{\boldsymbol{\beta}} - \mathbf{r} \xrightarrow{p} \mathbf{v}$ owing to the consistency of the least-squares estimator $\hat{\boldsymbol{\beta}}$ for estimating $\boldsymbol{\beta}$. If it is recalled that $n^{-1}\mathbf{x}'\mathbf{x} \rightarrow \boldsymbol{\Xi}$, it follows that

$$\begin{aligned} n^{-1}W &= (\mathbf{c}\hat{\boldsymbol{\beta}} - \mathbf{r})'[S^2\mathbf{c}(n^{-1}\mathbf{x}'\mathbf{x})^{-1}\mathbf{c}']^{-1}(\mathbf{c}\hat{\boldsymbol{\beta}} - \mathbf{r}) \\ &\xrightarrow{p} \mathbf{v}'[\sigma^2\mathbf{c}\boldsymbol{\Xi}^{-1}\mathbf{c}']^{-1}\mathbf{v} = \xi > 0. \end{aligned} \tag{6.2.8}$$

Then for any fixed value of $\tau > 0$ and small enough $\kappa > 0$ such that $\xi - \kappa > 0$,

$$\begin{aligned} \lim_{n\to\infty} P(w \geq \tau) &= \lim_{n\to\infty} P(n^{-1}w \geq n^{-1}\tau) \\ &\geq \lim_{n\to\infty} P(n^{-1}w > \xi - \kappa) \\ &\geq \lim_{n\to\infty} P(|n^{-1}w - \xi| < \kappa) = 1. \end{aligned} \tag{6.2.9}$$

Note the inequalities follow because, for n large enough, $n^{-1}w > \xi - \kappa \Rightarrow n^{-1}w \geq n^{-1}\tau$, and $|n^{-1}w - \xi| < \kappa \Rightarrow n^{-1}w > \xi - \kappa$. Thus, the outcome of W will reside in the critical region $C^W = [\tau, \infty)$ with probability $\rightarrow$ 1as $n \rightarrow \infty$ whenever H_0 is false; therefore, the Wald test is consistent.

6.2.1.c. Pitman Drift

Given the preceding discussion of test power and consistency, we can now explain why the sequence of hypotheses errors specified in H_a were chosen to be in the form $n^{-1/2}\boldsymbol{\delta}$. In the statistics literature, local alternatives to the null (restricted) model of the form $\mathbf{c}\boldsymbol{\beta} = \mathbf{r} + n^{-1/2}\boldsymbol{\delta}$ are said to take the *Pitman drift* form. The hypothesis error $n^{-1/2}\boldsymbol{\delta}$ is a mathematical device named after E. Pitman, who first used the local alternative concept in a 1949 article (some authors credit J. Neyman with the original use of the device in 1937). To motivate our need for *local* alternatives to H_0, consider the asymptotic power function for a consistent test. From (6.2.9), we know that the probability of rejection converges to 1 as $n \to \infty$, and thus the asymptotic power function is constant and equals 1 for all points in the alternate hypothesis space $\mathbf{c}\boldsymbol{\beta} \neq \mathbf{r}$. Therefore, the asymptotic power function for alternative hypotheses of the form H_a: $\mathbf{c}\boldsymbol{\beta} = \mathbf{r} + \mathbf{v}$ is not very useful for approximating the rejection rates of tests in finite samples because it is the constant function taking the value 1 for all $\mathbf{c}\boldsymbol{\beta} \neq \mathbf{r}$. Furthermore, because all consistent tests will have the same unit-valued asymptotic power function for alternative hypotheses H_a: $\mathbf{c}\boldsymbol{\beta} = \mathbf{r} + \mathbf{v}$, power comparisons among consistent tests based on these power functions are completely uninformative as to the relative power of the tests being compared.

The Pitman drift mechanism provides a convenient means to form useful asymptotic power functions by restricting our attention to a close neighborhood of H_0 (i.e., *local alternatives*) as the sample size increases. Although it is not necessary for errors in the restrictions $\mathbf{c}\boldsymbol{\beta} = \mathbf{r}$ actually to be functions of n, the power function calculations based on hypothesis errors of the form $n^{-1/2}\boldsymbol{\delta}$ can be thought of as a function of the direction vector $\boldsymbol{\delta}$, and the approximation of the power function becomes increasingly more accurate as $n^{-1/2}\boldsymbol{\delta} \to \mathbf{0}$. The rate of convergence is selected to coincide with the root-n convergence of the estimator under the central limit theorem. If the hypothesis error converges more rapidly (i.e., $n^{-1/2-\gamma}\boldsymbol{\delta}$ for $\boldsymbol{\delta} = O_p(1)$ and some $\gamma > 0$), the neighborhood shrinks too quickly and $\lambda = 0$ in the limit regardless of the value of $\boldsymbol{\delta}$. If the hypothesis error converges too slowly (i.e., $n^{-1/2+\gamma}\boldsymbol{\delta}$ for some $\gamma > 0$), then the mean of the limiting distribution for Z above would be $n^{\gamma}\boldsymbol{\delta}$, and the variable in fact does not converge in distribution.

In summary, the local alternative hypotheses defined by the Pitman drift form are conceptual mechanisms that facilitate derivation of useful power functions and define the meaning of *local* for locally UMP, UMP unbiased, or UMP invariant hypothesis tests. We add that it is generally for points in H_a within a local neighborhood of H_0 for which test power is the smallest of all points in H_a, and so it is highly relevant to examine the behavior of tests in this critical subset of H_a.

► **Example 6.2.1 (Wald Test of H_0: $\mathbf{c}\boldsymbol{\beta} = \mathbf{r}$ Calculation and Power):** The purpose of this GAUSS example program provided in the examples manual is to demonstrate the asymptotic power of the Wald test for the linear hypothesis H_0: $\mathbf{c}\boldsymbol{\beta} = \mathbf{r}$. First, we provide a GAUSS procedure mlr_wald() that computes the W statistic and the asymptotic p-value for the observed value of the test statistic. Then, we conduct a bootstrap simulation experiment to estimate the power function of the test and compare the estimate with the actual power function. The reader should observe that the estimated power function converges to the asymptotic power function as the number of bootstrap samples (m) and the sample size (n) become large.

6.2.2. Lagrange Multiplier (LM) Tests

The Lagrange Multiplier (LM) test is based on the statistical behavior of the Lagrange multipliers in the Lagrangian form of the *constrained* (by H_0) least-squares problem defining the *restricted* LS estimate

$$\mathbf{b}_r = \arg\min_{\boldsymbol{\beta}}[(\mathbf{y} - \mathbf{x}\boldsymbol{\beta})'(\mathbf{y} - \mathbf{x}\boldsymbol{\beta}) \text{ subject to } \mathbf{c}\boldsymbol{\beta} = \mathbf{r}]. \tag{6.2.10}$$

The Lagrange expression for the constrained least-squares minimization problem is

$$L(\boldsymbol{\beta}, \gamma) = (\mathbf{y} - \mathbf{x}\boldsymbol{\beta})'(\mathbf{y} - \mathbf{x}\boldsymbol{\beta}) - \gamma'(\mathbf{c}\boldsymbol{\beta} - \mathbf{r}), \tag{6.2.11}$$

where γ is a $(j \times 1)$ vector of Lagrange multipliers corresponding to the j constraints $\mathbf{c}\boldsymbol{\beta} = \mathbf{r}$. The first-order conditions for the stationary point of (6.2.11) are given by

$$\begin{aligned} \frac{\partial L}{\partial \boldsymbol{\beta}} &= -2\mathbf{x}'\mathbf{y} + 2\mathbf{x}'\mathbf{x}\boldsymbol{\beta} - \mathbf{c}'\gamma = \mathbf{0} \\ \frac{\partial L}{\partial \gamma} &= \mathbf{r} - \mathbf{c}\boldsymbol{\beta} = \mathbf{0}, \end{aligned} \tag{6.2.12}$$

which have solutions for $\boldsymbol{\beta}$ and γ given by

$$\begin{aligned} \mathbf{b}_r &= (\mathbf{x}'\mathbf{x})^{-1}\mathbf{x}'\mathbf{y} + \frac{1}{2}(\mathbf{x}'\mathbf{x})^{-1}\mathbf{c}'\gamma \\ &= \hat{\mathbf{b}} + (\mathbf{x}'\mathbf{x})^{-1}\mathbf{c}'[\mathbf{c}(\mathbf{x}'\mathbf{x})^{-1}\mathbf{c}']^{-1}(\mathbf{r} - \mathbf{c}\hat{\mathbf{b}}) \\ \gamma_r &= 2[\mathbf{c}(\mathbf{x}'\mathbf{x})^{-1}\mathbf{c}']^{-1}(\mathbf{r} - \mathbf{c}\hat{\mathbf{b}}), \end{aligned} \tag{6.2.13}$$

where $\mathbf{b}_r$ is the *restricted least-squares estimate* of $\boldsymbol{\beta}$ and $\mathbf{b} = (\mathbf{x}'\mathbf{x})^{-1}\mathbf{x}'\mathbf{y}$ is the unrestricted least-squares estimate. Substituting the random (unrestricted) least-squares estimator $\hat{\boldsymbol{\beta}} = (\mathbf{x}'\mathbf{x})^{-1}\mathbf{x}'\mathbf{Y}$ for $\mathbf{b}$ in (6.2.13), we know the Lagrange multiplier

$$\boldsymbol{\Gamma}_r = 2[\mathbf{c}(\mathbf{x}'\mathbf{x})^{-1}\mathbf{c}']^{-1}(\mathbf{r} - \mathbf{c}\hat{\boldsymbol{\beta}}) \tag{6.2.14}$$

is a random vector representing all of the hypothetically possible outcomes of the optimal Lagrange multiplier relating to all of the hypothetically possible $\hat{\boldsymbol{\beta}}$ outcomes in a classical predata context.

6.2.2.a. Classical Form of LM Tests

On the basis of the asymptotic normal approximation to the probability distribution of $\hat{\boldsymbol{\beta}}$, and under the null hypothesis H_0: $\mathbf{c}\boldsymbol{\beta} = \mathbf{r}$, it follows that $\mathbf{r} - \mathbf{c}\hat{\boldsymbol{\beta}} \overset{a}{\sim} N[\mathbf{0}, \sigma^2\mathbf{c}(\mathbf{x}'\mathbf{x})^{-1}\mathbf{c}']$. Then, from the properties of linear combinations of normally distributed random variables, $\frac{1}{2}\boldsymbol{\Gamma}_r \overset{a}{\sim} N(\mathbf{0}, \sigma^2[\mathbf{c}(\mathbf{x}'\mathbf{x})^{-1}\mathbf{c}']^{-1})$. The sum of the squares of j independent standard normal random variables has a central Chi-square distribution with j degrees of freedom, and we have that

$$\frac{\boldsymbol{\Gamma}_r'[\mathbf{c}(\mathbf{x}'\mathbf{x})^{-1}\mathbf{c}']\boldsymbol{\Gamma}_r}{4\sigma^2} \overset{a}{\sim} \text{Chi-square}(j, 0) \text{ under } H_0. \tag{6.2.15}$$

To define an observable version of the random variable in (6.2.15), we let S_r^2 represent the *restricted* estimator of σ^2, that is,

$$S_r^2 = \frac{(\mathbf{Y} - \mathbf{x}\hat{\boldsymbol{\beta}}_r)'(\mathbf{Y} - \mathbf{x}\hat{\boldsymbol{\beta}}_r)}{n - k + j}, \tag{6.2.16}$$

where $\hat{\boldsymbol{\beta}}_r$ denotes the restricted least-squares *estimator* whose outcomes are $\hat{\mathbf{b}}_r$. Under H_0, S_r^2 is an unbiased and consistent estimator of σ^2. Finally, because $\frac{\sigma^2}{S_r^2} \xrightarrow{p} 1$ under H_0, it can be argued via Slutsky's theorem that premultiplying the preceding random variable by $\frac{\sigma^2}{S_r^2}$ will have no effect on the asymptotic distribution, and thus

$$\text{LM} = \frac{\boldsymbol{\Gamma}_r'[\mathbf{c}(\mathbf{x}'\mathbf{x})^{-1}\mathbf{c}']\boldsymbol{\Gamma}_r}{4S_r^2} \overset{a}{\sim} \text{Chi-square}(j, 0) \text{ under } H_0. \tag{6.2.17}$$

The statistic LM was referred to in the literature as the Lagrange Multiplier statistic by J. Aitchison and S.D. Silvey (1958) in recognition of the fact that the statistic is a function of the Lagrange multiplier vector $\boldsymbol{\Gamma}_r$. The intuition underlying this test is that the farther the outcomes of $\boldsymbol{\Gamma}_r$ are from the zero vector, the less plausible is H_0 because the Lagrange multipliers are measuring the rate at which the LS objective function can be decreased as the restriction $\mathbf{c}\boldsymbol{\beta} = \mathbf{r}$ is relaxed. If the restrictions were in fact true, one would expect that there would, in general, be less opportunity to decrease the objective function by removing the constraints than when the restrictions are false, and, in fact, in this case $E[\boldsymbol{\Gamma}_r] = \mathbf{0}$. The distance between $\boldsymbol{\Gamma}_r$ outcomes and $\mathbf{0}$ is adjusted for the inherent variability in the estimator $\boldsymbol{\Gamma}_r$ by measuring distance in the inverse asymptotic covariance metric $[\widehat{\mathbf{cov}}(\boldsymbol{\Gamma}_r)]^{-1} = [\mathbf{c}(\mathbf{x}'\mathbf{x})^{-1}\mathbf{c}']/S_r^2$.

6.2.2.b. Score Form of LM Test

There is an alternative form of the LM statistic called the *score form of the LM statistic*, which was suggested by Rao (1948), that is algebraically equivalent to (6.2.17). To derive this form of the LM test, let $s(\boldsymbol{\beta}) = (\mathbf{y} - \mathbf{x}\boldsymbol{\beta})'(\mathbf{y} - \mathbf{x}\boldsymbol{\beta})$ and define the Lagrangian function for minimizing the sum of squares $s(\boldsymbol{\beta})$ subject to $\mathbf{H}_0\colon \mathbf{c}\boldsymbol{\beta} = \mathbf{r}$ as

$$L(\boldsymbol{\beta}, \gamma) = s(\boldsymbol{\beta}) - \gamma'(\mathbf{c}\boldsymbol{\beta} - \mathbf{r}). \tag{6.2.18}$$

The necessary conditions for the stationary point of (6.2.18) are given by

$$\begin{aligned} \frac{\partial L}{\partial \boldsymbol{\beta}} &= \frac{\partial s(\boldsymbol{\beta})}{\partial \boldsymbol{\beta}} - \mathbf{c}'\gamma = (-2\mathbf{x}'\mathbf{y} + 2\mathbf{x}'\mathbf{x}\boldsymbol{\beta}) - \mathbf{c}'\gamma = \mathbf{0} \\ \frac{\partial L}{\partial \gamma} &= \mathbf{r} - \mathbf{c}\boldsymbol{\beta} = \mathbf{0}. \end{aligned} \tag{6.2.19}$$

The Hessian matrix of the function $s(\boldsymbol{\beta})$ with respect to $\boldsymbol{\beta}$ is given by

$$\frac{\partial^2 s(\boldsymbol{\beta})}{\partial \boldsymbol{\beta} \partial \boldsymbol{\beta}'} = 2(\mathbf{x}'\mathbf{x}). \tag{6.2.20}$$

It follows from the necessary conditions evaluated at the estimators $\hat{\boldsymbol{\beta}}_r$ and $\boldsymbol{\Gamma}_r$ of $\boldsymbol{\beta}$ and γ that correspond to (6.2.18) through (6.2.19) that

$$\left.\frac{\partial s(\boldsymbol{\beta})}{\partial \boldsymbol{\beta}}\right|_{\hat{\boldsymbol{\beta}}_r} = \mathbf{c}'\boldsymbol{\Gamma}_r. \tag{6.2.21}$$

Then, upon substitution of (6.2.20) and (6.2.21) into the quadratic form (6.2.17), an equivalent representation of the LM statistic is defined as follows:

$$\mathrm{LM} = \frac{1}{2}\left.\frac{\partial s(\boldsymbol{\beta})}{\partial \boldsymbol{\beta}'}\right|_{\hat{\boldsymbol{\beta}}_r}\left[S_r^2\frac{\partial^2 s(\boldsymbol{\beta})}{\partial \boldsymbol{\beta}\partial \boldsymbol{\beta}'}\right]^{-1}\left.\frac{\partial s(\boldsymbol{\beta})}{\partial \boldsymbol{\beta}}\right|_{\hat{\boldsymbol{\beta}}_r}. \tag{6.2.22}$$

An advantage of the score form of the LM test is that calculation of the Lagrange multiplier is not needed to generate a value of the test statistic – all one needs for calculating (6.2.22) is the restricted least-squares estimate. To see this, note from (6.2.19) that

$$\left.\frac{\partial s(\boldsymbol{\beta})}{\partial \boldsymbol{\beta}}\right|_{\hat{\boldsymbol{\beta}}_r} = -2\mathbf{x}'\mathbf{y} + 2\mathbf{x}'\mathbf{x}\hat{\boldsymbol{\beta}}_r \tag{6.2.23}$$

is a function of the restricted least-squares estimator. Because S_r^2 in (6.2.16) is also a function of the restricted least-squares estimator and $\frac{\partial^2 s(\boldsymbol{\beta})}{\partial \boldsymbol{\beta}\partial \boldsymbol{\beta}'} = 2\mathbf{x}'\mathbf{x}$ is a fixed matrix independent of the value of $\hat{\boldsymbol{\beta}}_r$, it follows that the outcome of the LM statistic in (6.2.22) can be calculated once the outcome, $\hat{\mathbf{b}}_r$, of $\hat{\boldsymbol{\beta}}_r$ is observed.

6.2.2.c. Distribution When H_0 is False

Under *local alternatives* to H_0 of the form H_a: $\mathbf{c}\boldsymbol{\beta} = \mathbf{r} + n^{-1/2}\boldsymbol{\delta}$ for a choice of the finite vector of constants $\boldsymbol{\delta}$, the statistic LM has a noncentral Chi-square distribution, and the noncentrality parameter is a function of $\boldsymbol{\delta}$ as defined by

$$\mathrm{LM} \overset{a}{\sim} \text{Chi-square}(j, \lambda) \quad \text{with} \quad \lambda = \frac{1}{2}\boldsymbol{\delta}'(\sigma^2\mathbf{c}\boldsymbol{\Xi}^{-1}\mathbf{c}')^{-1}\boldsymbol{\delta}. \tag{6.2.24}$$

To motivate (6.2.24), return to the limiting distribution result for the LS estimator and note that Slutsky's theorem implies that $n^{1/2}(\mathbf{c}\hat{\boldsymbol{\beta}} - \mathbf{c}\boldsymbol{\beta}) \xrightarrow{d} N(\mathbf{0}, \sigma^2\mathbf{c}\boldsymbol{\Xi}^{-1}\mathbf{c}')$. Now proceed under the assumption that H_a: $\mathbf{c}\boldsymbol{\beta} = \mathbf{r} + n^{-1/2}\boldsymbol{\delta}$ is true, in which case it follows again from Slutsky's theorem that $\mathbf{Z} = n^{1/2}(\mathbf{c}\hat{\boldsymbol{\beta}} - \mathbf{r}) \xrightarrow{d} N(\boldsymbol{\delta}, \sigma^2\mathbf{c}\boldsymbol{\Xi}^{-1}\mathbf{c}')$. On the basis of (6.2.14),

$$-\frac{n^{1/2}}{2}[\mathbf{c}(\mathbf{x}'\mathbf{x})^{-1}\mathbf{c}']\boldsymbol{\Gamma}_r = n^{1/2}(\mathbf{c}\hat{\boldsymbol{\beta}} - \mathbf{r}) \xrightarrow{d} N(\boldsymbol{\delta}, \sigma^2\mathbf{c}\boldsymbol{\Xi}^{-1}\mathbf{c}'), \tag{6.2.25}$$

and because $(n^{-1}\mathbf{x}'\mathbf{x})^{-1} \to \boldsymbol{\Xi}^{-1}$, it follows from still another application of Slutsky's theorem and properties of the symmetric square root matrix that

$$-\frac{n^{-1/2}}{2}[\mathbf{c}\boldsymbol{\Xi}^{-1}\mathbf{c}']\boldsymbol{\Gamma}_r \xrightarrow{d} N(\boldsymbol{\delta}, \sigma^2\mathbf{c}\boldsymbol{\Xi}^{-1}\mathbf{c}') \quad \text{and} \quad -\frac{n^{-1/2}}{2\sigma}[\mathbf{c}\boldsymbol{\Xi}^{-1}\mathbf{c}']^{1/2}\boldsymbol{\Gamma}_r \xrightarrow{d} N(\boldsymbol{\delta}, \mathbf{I}_j). \tag{6.2.26}$$

Therefore, on the basis of the standard characterization of the noncentral Chi-square distribution (recall the discussion preceding (6.2.4)) it follows that

$$\frac{\boldsymbol{\Gamma}_r'[\mathbf{c}(n^{-1}\boldsymbol{\Xi}^{-1})\mathbf{c}']\boldsymbol{\Gamma}_r}{4\sigma^2} \overset{a}{\sim} \text{Chi-square}(j, \lambda) \tag{6.2.27}$$

with λ defined as in (6.2.24). As we argued in the case of the Wald statistic, an observable asymptotically equivalent version of (6.2.27) can be defined under H_0 by replacing σ^2 with S_r^2 and $n^{-1}\boldsymbol{\Xi}^{-1}$ with $(\mathbf{x}'\mathbf{x})^{-1}$, leading to the expression in (6.2.17).

6.2.2.d. Power Function Characteristics and Consistency

For purposes of relating asymptotic power function calculations to the values of $\boldsymbol{\delta}$ and σ^2, an asymptotically equivalent version of the noncentrality parameter can be utilized in the form

$$\hat{\lambda} = \frac{1}{2}\boldsymbol{\delta}'[\sigma^2\mathbf{c}(n^{-1}\mathbf{x}'\mathbf{x})^{-1}\mathbf{c}']^{-1}\boldsymbol{\delta}. \tag{6.2.28}$$

The LM test is asymptotically equivalent to the Wald test and so shares all of the Wald test's asymptotic properties. As in the case of the Wald test, an application of the LM test will begin with an appropriate choice of asymptotic size and power function $\pi(\lambda)$. The critical region of an asymptotic size α test will be defined by solving for the critical value τ and forming the critical region $C^{LM} = [\tau, \infty)$ in precisely the same way as (6.2.6). The asymptotic power function of the test can be defined using (6.2.7). The test $\{LM, C^{LM}\}$ is then "reject H_0 if $lm \in C^{LM}$".

The operational version of the LM test used in practice, (6.2.17) or (6.2.22), is a consistent test of H_0: $\mathbf{c}\boldsymbol{\beta} = \mathbf{r}$. The motivation for this result is analogous to the rationale provided for the consistency of the Wald test (recall (6.2.8) and (6.2.9)). The analogy begins by using (6.2.13) to represent the LM statistics as

$$LM = (\mathbf{c}\hat{\boldsymbol{\beta}} - \mathbf{r})'\left[S_r^2\mathbf{c}(\mathbf{x}'\mathbf{x})^{-1}\mathbf{c}'\right]^{-1}(\mathbf{c}\hat{\boldsymbol{\beta}} - \mathbf{r}) \tag{6.2.29}$$

and noting that S_r^2 converges in probability to a constant (not necessarily σ^2) whether or not H_0 is true. The reader is asked to complete the analogy, motivating the consistency of the LM test.

► **Example 6.2.2 (LM Test of H_0: $\mathbf{c}\boldsymbol{\beta} = \mathbf{r}$):** The GAUSS program included in the examples manual for this example demonstrates the steps involved in building a procedure mlr_lm() used to compute the score form of the LM test. To demonstrate the relationship between the distributions of the W and LM test statistics and associated power functions, GAUSS plots are provided for a series of hypothesis errors. The reader should use this procedure to conduct a bootstrap or Monte Carlo simulation of the asymptotic power function for the LM test (as in Example 6.2.1).

6.2.3. The W and LM Tests under Normality

In the preceding sections, we examined both Wald and Lagrange multiplier tests of H_0: $\mathbf{c}\boldsymbol{\beta} = \mathbf{r}$ versus H_a: $\mathbf{c}\boldsymbol{\beta} \neq \mathbf{r}$. In this section we reexamine these tests upon making the additional assumption that $\mathbf{Y}$ is multivariate normally distributed.

First of all, note that all of the asymptotic properties claimed previously for the Wald and Lagrange multiplier tests still apply in the current statistical model context. This is because all of the previous conditions assumed to exist in the derivation of the asymptotic properties can still be applied in the current context. The added assumption of normality allows us to establish the sampling distributions of the test statistics for finite sample sizes.

Beginning with the Wald test (6.2.2), we can now claim that under H_0

$$W = (\mathbf{c}\hat{\boldsymbol{\beta}} - \mathbf{r}')[S^2\mathbf{c}(\mathbf{x}'\mathbf{x})^{-1}\mathbf{c}']^{-1}(\mathbf{c}\hat{\boldsymbol{\beta}} - \mathbf{r}) \sim jF, \tag{6.2.30}$$

where the F statistic has the F-distribution with j and $(n - k)$ degrees of freedom and the same noncentrality parameter λ as the F-statistic identified in Chapter 4. It is apparent that the Wald test, $\{W, C^W\}$, will be *identical* to the F-test and GLR test presented in Chapter 4 because the critical region for W outcomes would be defined by $C^W = [jf_{1-\alpha}, \infty)$ with $f_{1-\alpha}$ being the $100(1-\alpha)\%$ quantile of the central F distribution having j and $(n - k)$ degrees of freedom. Thus, all of the properties claimed for the F and GLR tests apply to the Wald test as well, and all three tests are in fact identical.

Regarding the Lagrange multiplier test, begin with the Lagrange form of the constrained ML problem:

$$\ln L(\boldsymbol{\beta}, \sigma^2; \mathbf{Y}, \mathbf{x}) - \boldsymbol{\gamma}'(\mathbf{c}\boldsymbol{\beta} - \mathbf{r}). \tag{6.2.31}$$

The first-order conditions are

$$\begin{aligned} \frac{\partial \ln L(\boldsymbol{\beta}, \sigma^2; \mathbf{Y}, \mathbf{x})}{\partial \boldsymbol{\beta}} &= \mathbf{c}'\boldsymbol{\gamma} \\ \frac{\partial \ln L(\boldsymbol{\beta}, \sigma^2; \mathbf{Y}, \mathbf{x})}{\partial \sigma^2} &= \mathbf{0} \\ \mathbf{c}\boldsymbol{\beta} &= \mathbf{r}, \end{aligned} \tag{6.2.32}$$

which, given the log of the normal–distribution-based likelihood function, can be written as

$$\begin{aligned} \frac{-1}{2\sigma^2}(-2\mathbf{x}'\mathbf{Y} + 2\mathbf{x}'\mathbf{x}\boldsymbol{\beta}) &= \mathbf{c}'\boldsymbol{\gamma} \\ -\frac{n}{2\sigma^2} + \frac{(\mathbf{Y} - \mathbf{x}\boldsymbol{\beta})'(\mathbf{Y} - \mathbf{x}\boldsymbol{\beta})}{2\sigma^4} &= \mathbf{0} \\ \mathbf{c}\boldsymbol{\beta} &= \mathbf{r}. \end{aligned} \tag{6.2.33}$$

The restricted ML solution is given by

$$\begin{aligned} \hat{\boldsymbol{\beta}}_r &= \hat{\boldsymbol{\beta}} + (\mathbf{x}'\mathbf{x})^{-1}\mathbf{c}'[\mathbf{c}(\mathbf{x}'\mathbf{x})^{-1}\mathbf{c}']^{-1}(\mathbf{r} - \mathbf{c}\hat{\boldsymbol{\beta}}) \\ S^2_{ML_r} &= (\mathbf{Y} - \mathbf{x}\hat{\boldsymbol{\beta}}_r)'(\mathbf{Y} - \mathbf{x}\hat{\boldsymbol{\beta}}_r)/n \\ \boldsymbol{\Gamma}_r &= \frac{-1}{S^2_{ML_r}}([\mathbf{c}(\mathbf{x}'\mathbf{x})^{-1}\mathbf{c}']^{-1}[\mathbf{r} - \mathbf{c}\hat{\boldsymbol{\beta}}]). \end{aligned} \tag{6.2.34}$$

Now note that because $\hat{\boldsymbol{\beta}} \sim \mathrm{N}(\boldsymbol{\beta}, \sigma^2(\mathbf{x}'\mathbf{x})^{-1})$ it follows from results on the distribution of linear combinations of normally distributed random variables (Chapter E1) that if $\mathrm{H}_0\colon \mathbf{c}\boldsymbol{\beta} = \mathbf{r}$ is true, $-\mathrm{S}^2_{\mathrm{ML_r}}\boldsymbol{\Gamma}_\mathrm{r} \sim \mathrm{N}(\mathbf{0}, \sigma^2[\mathbf{c}(\mathbf{x}'\mathbf{x})^{-1}\mathbf{c}']^{-1})$, so that

$$\frac{\mathrm{S}^4_{\mathrm{ML_r}}\boldsymbol{\Gamma}'_\mathrm{r}\mathbf{c}(\mathbf{x}'\mathbf{x})^{-1}\mathbf{c}'\boldsymbol{\Gamma}_\mathrm{r}}{\sigma^2} \sim \text{Chi-square}(j, 0) \text{ under } \mathrm{H}_0. \tag{6.2.35}$$

The LM statistic can be defined by replacing the unknown and unobservable σ^2 in (6.2.35) by the bias-adjusted restricted MLE of σ^2 represented by $\mathrm{S}^2_\mathrm{r} = (n - k + j)^{-1} (\mathbf{Y} - \mathbf{x}\hat{\boldsymbol{\beta}}_\mathrm{r})'(\mathbf{Y} - \mathbf{x}\hat{\boldsymbol{\beta}}_\mathrm{r})$ resulting in

$$\mathrm{LM} = \frac{\mathrm{S}^4_{\mathrm{ML_r}}\boldsymbol{\Gamma}'_\mathrm{r}\mathbf{c}(\mathbf{x}'\mathbf{x})^{-1}\mathbf{c}'\boldsymbol{\Gamma}_\mathrm{r}}{\mathrm{S}^2_\mathrm{r}} = (\mathbf{c}\hat{\boldsymbol{\beta}} - \mathbf{r})'\left[\mathrm{S}^2_\mathrm{r}\mathbf{c}(\mathbf{x}'\mathbf{x})^{-1}\mathbf{c}'\right]^{-1}(\mathbf{c}\hat{\boldsymbol{\beta}} - \mathbf{r}). \tag{6.2.36}$$

The probability distribution of the LM statistic is quite complicated. We can characterize the distribution of LM in terms of either the W or F statistic. The key to this characterization lies in the algebraic identity

$$(\mathbf{c}\hat{\boldsymbol{\beta}} - \mathbf{r})'[\mathbf{c}(\mathbf{x}'\mathbf{x})^{-1}\mathbf{c}']^{-1}(\mathbf{c}\hat{\boldsymbol{\beta}} - \mathbf{r}) = \hat{\varepsilon}'_\mathrm{r}\hat{\varepsilon}_\mathrm{r} - \hat{\varepsilon}'\hat{\varepsilon}, \tag{6.2.37}$$

where $\hat{\varepsilon}_\mathrm{r} \equiv \mathbf{Y} - \mathbf{x}\hat{\boldsymbol{\beta}}_\mathrm{r}$ and $\hat{\varepsilon} \equiv \mathbf{Y} - \mathbf{x}\hat{\boldsymbol{\beta}}$, as the reader can demonstrate (or see P. Schmidt, 1976, p. 26). Then

$$\mathrm{LM} = \frac{\hat{\varepsilon}'_\mathrm{r}\hat{\varepsilon}_\mathrm{r} - \hat{\varepsilon}'\hat{\varepsilon}}{\hat{\varepsilon}'_\mathrm{r}\hat{\varepsilon}_\mathrm{r}/(n - k + j)}, \tag{6.2.38}$$

$$\mathrm{W} = \frac{\hat{\varepsilon}'_\mathrm{r}\hat{\varepsilon}_\mathrm{r} - \hat{\varepsilon}'\hat{\varepsilon}}{\hat{\varepsilon}'\hat{\varepsilon}/(n - k)} \tag{6.2.39}$$

and thus

$$\mathrm{LM} = \mathrm{W}\left(1 + \frac{\mathrm{W}}{n - k}\right)^{-1}\left(\frac{n - k + j}{n - k}\right). \tag{6.2.40}$$

Furthermore, because $\mathrm{W} = j\mathrm{F}$, the LM statistic can also be expressed as

$$\mathrm{LM} = j\mathrm{F}\left(1 + \frac{j\mathrm{F}}{n - k}\right)^{-1}\left(\frac{n - k + j}{n - k}\right) \tag{6.2.41}$$

It follows from (6.2.40) or (6.2.41) that the F, W, and GLR tests of $\mathrm{H}_0\colon \mathbf{c}\boldsymbol{\beta} = \mathbf{r}$ are identical to the LM test upon using the appropriate critical values for each test. In particular,

$$\mathrm{LM} \geq \tau \quad \text{iff} \quad \mathrm{W} \geq \frac{\tau(n - k)}{n - k + j - \tau} \quad \text{and} \quad \mathrm{F} \geq \frac{\tau(n - k)}{j(n - k + j - \tau)}. \tag{6.2.42}$$

As well, the power function of the LM test is *identical* to the power functions of the corresponding W, F, and thus GLR tests. Indeed, the power functions of all of the tests can be derived from the power function of the F test. The critical region of the LM test is given by $\mathrm{C}^{\mathrm{LM}} = [\tau, \infty)$, where (6.2.42) can be used to solve for a τ, which defines an α-level test with

$$\mathrm{F} \geq \mathrm{f}_{1-\alpha} = \frac{\tau(n - k)}{j(n - k + j - \tau)} \Rightarrow \tau = \frac{j\mathrm{f}_{1-\alpha}(n - k + j)}{n - k + j\mathrm{f}_{1-\alpha}}. \tag{6.2.43}$$

Power function calculations corresponding to the LM test can be calculated using the approach described for the Wald or F tests previously.

6.2.4. W and LM Tests: Interrelationships and Extensions

We emphasize that although asymptotically the W and LM tests are equivalent, they are generally not identical in finite samples in the absence of the normality assumption. Thus in this case it is quite possible that one test would reject H_0, whereas the other would not, and this is simply a reflection of the fact that the test statistics are based on different functions of **Y** with different small sample distributions that are unknown when the distribution of **Y** is unknown. If we were to introduce an explicit distributional specification for the noise component as we did in Chapter 4 and in the preceding subsection, we would have a third alternative testing procedure based on the value of *likelihood ratios*, which as we have already seen requires the estimation of *both* the unrestricted and restricted (by H_0) estimates of $\boldsymbol{\beta}$. The likelihood ratio test will have the same asymptotic distribution as the Wald and Lagrange Multiplier tests but can have small-sample behavior different than either of the other two types of tests.

There is an inequality relationship between the Wald and LM statistics noted in the literature that, if applicable, would imply that the asymptotic Wald test has a greater tendency for rejecting the null hypothesis than the asymptotic LM test in a predata sense. The genesis of this inequality relationship claim can be seen easily once we compare (6.2.29) with (6.2.2), from which it follows that $W \geq LM$ iff $S_r^2 \geq S^2$. Note that the latter inequality is *not* necessarily true in our context, where we utilize *unbiased* estimators of σ^2 when defining both S_r^2 and S^2 for use in the definition of the LM and Wald tests, respectively. In particular, we can see from Equation (6.2.40) that $1 + \frac{W}{n-k} > 1$ and $\frac{n-k+j}{n-k} > 1$; thus, the inequality $W \geq LM$ cannot be formed, and this result does not depend on the normality of $\boldsymbol{\varepsilon}$. The inequality *is* true if a denominator equal to n is used instead of $n-k+j$ or $n-k$ in the calculations of S_r^2 (6.2.16) and S^2 (6.2.5), respectively, in which case the analyst is using consistent but biased estimators of σ^2. The inequality $S_r^2 \geq S^2$, and thus $W \geq LM$, is then a simple consequence of the fact that the restricted minimum sum of squares on which S_r^2 is based can be no smaller than the unrestricted minimum sum of squares on which S^2 is based. The interested reader can consult the work of Berndt and Savin (1977) and the references therein for an additional relevant detailed discussion of this issue.

It is possible to test nonlinear restrictions, $\mathbf{c}(\boldsymbol{\beta}) = \mathbf{r}$, on the elements of the $\boldsymbol{\beta}$ vector using both Wald and LM type tests. We will defer an examination of nonlinear hypothesis tests until we have examined the nonlinear statistical model in Chapter 8. The results we present there for testing nonlinear restrictions on $\boldsymbol{\beta}$ will then also apply to the linear statistical model as a special case. It is also possible to test linear inequality hypotheses about $\boldsymbol{\beta}$. We examine procedures for doing so in Section 6.3.

6.3. Confidence Region Estimation

In this section we examine confidence–region-based solutions to the inverse problem of recovering information about the unknown and unobservable $\boldsymbol{\beta}$. We again must rely on asymptotic distributions when defining confidence-region estimators because, in the semiparametric model, we have made no specific distributional assumptions about either ε or $\mathbf{Y}$.

We can define a confidence region for any linear combination of the entries in $\boldsymbol{\beta}$, that is, $\mathbf{c}\boldsymbol{\beta}$, by exploiting the duality between confidence regions and the Wald and LM hypothesis-testing procedures examined previously. Recall that the duality principle implies that a confidence region for $\mathbf{c}\boldsymbol{\beta}$ having a $100(1-\alpha)\%$ confidence level can be defined by the set of $\mathbf{c}\boldsymbol{\beta}$ values that would *not* be rejected by an α-level test of the hypothesis H_0: $\mathbf{c}\boldsymbol{\beta} = \mathbf{r}$.

We again emphasize that the classical approach to evaluating statistical properties of inference procedures, this time relating to the confidence level of confidence regions, is in an unconditional predata context. We are thus evaluating the behavior of the confidence region estimator in the context of all of the hypothetical samples of data that *could have* occurred, not in the sense of what *actually did* occur. By basing our design of a confidence region estimator on the sampling distribution of $\mathbf{Y}$, the information obtained about $\boldsymbol{\beta}$ from confidence regions depends not only on the data being analyzed but also on whatever data sets one *could have* observed.

6.3.1. Wald-Based Confidence Regions

When examining a confidence region based on the Wald test, $\{\mathrm{W}, \mathrm{C}^{\mathrm{W}}\}$, with $\mathrm{C}^{\mathrm{W}} = [\tau, \infty)$, one should note that the test of H_0: $\mathbf{c}\boldsymbol{\beta} = \mathbf{r}$ is based on the test rule

$$\text{if } \mathrm{w} = \frac{(\mathbf{c}\hat{\mathbf{b}} - \mathbf{r})'[\mathbf{c}(\mathbf{x}'\mathbf{x})^{-1}\mathbf{c}']^{-1}(\mathbf{c}\hat{\mathbf{b}} - \mathbf{r})}{\mathrm{s}^2} \geq \tau, \quad \text{reject } \mathrm{H}_0, \tag{6.3.1}$$

where τ is the $100(1-\alpha)\%$ quantile of the central Chi-square distribution with j degrees of freedom, j being the row rank of $\mathbf{c}$. It follows that the set of hypotheses of the form H_0: $\mathbf{c}\boldsymbol{\beta} = \mathbf{r}$ that would *not* be rejected by the Wald test, and thus by the duality principle an asymptotic $100(1-\alpha)\%$ level confidence region for the value of $\mathbf{c}\boldsymbol{\beta}$ is given by

$$\mathrm{CR}^{\mathrm{W}} = \left\{\mathbf{r}: \frac{(\mathbf{c}\hat{\mathbf{b}} - \mathbf{r})'[\mathbf{c}(\mathbf{x}'\mathbf{x})^{-1}\mathbf{c}']^{-1}(\mathbf{c}\hat{\mathbf{b}} - \mathbf{r})}{\mathrm{s}^2} < \tau\right\}. \tag{6.3.2}$$

This confidence region will be an interval if $\mathbf{c}\boldsymbol{\beta}$ is a scalar, an ellipse if $\mathbf{c}\boldsymbol{\beta}$ is two-dimensional, and a hyperellipse otherwise, all of which will be centered at the value of $\mathbf{c}\hat{\mathbf{b}}$. This confidence region is asymptotically locally UMA invariant, which is inherited from the asymptotically locally UMP invariance property of the Wald test on which the confidence region is based. Note that one can use a weak inequality in (6.3.2), and thereby define a closed instead of an open confidence region, having the same asymptotic level of confidence, $100(1-\alpha)\%$, because the W statistic is a continuous random variable under the Chi-square approximation and the additional boundary points have zero probability.

► **Example 6.3.1 (Wald Confidence Region for $\mathbf{c}\boldsymbol{\beta}$):** The GAUSS procedure cregion() utilized in this example (contained in the examples manual) plots the joint confidence region for two parameters under the Wald criterion in Equation (6.3.2). The reader provides $\hat{\mathbf{b}}$, $\hat{\mathbf{cov}}(\hat{\boldsymbol{\beta}})$, and the desired coverage probability, and the associated joint confidence region is plotted by the GAUSS xy() procedure. To compare the empirical coverage probability of the joint region with the intended coverage level, the program conducts a bootstrap resampling exercise for a linear regression model specified by the reader.

At this point, we briefly discuss the procedure used in this example to compute the ellipsoidal boundary for the joint Wald confidence region. Given the confidence region described in Equation (6.3.2), we must choose the set of vectors $\mathbf{r} \in \mathrm{R}^{\mathrm{j}}$ such that the stated set-defining condition holds. For example, if $k = 4$ and $\mathbf{c}$ takes the form $\mathbf{c} = \begin{bmatrix} 0 & 1 & 0 & 0 \\ 0 & 0 & 1 & 0 \end{bmatrix}$, then the joint confidence region relates to a pair of parameters β_2 and β_3. We may plot the Wald joint confidence region in two dimensions by solving the associated quadratic equation for the pairs of parameter values (i.e., the $\mathbf{r}$'s) that define the boundary of the ellipse. Owing to the covariance terms, the process of directly solving for these parameter values is difficult. The problem can be greatly simplified by solving the problem under an orthogonal transformation. In particular, note that the inverse covariance matrix may be written as $[\mathrm{s}^2\mathbf{c}(\mathbf{x}'\mathbf{x})^{-1}\mathbf{c}']^{-1} = \mathbf{p}\boldsymbol{\Lambda}\mathbf{p}'$ where $\mathbf{p}$ is the $(j \times j)$ matrix of eigenvectors and $\boldsymbol{\Lambda} = \begin{bmatrix} \lambda_1 & 0 \\ 0 & \lambda_2 \end{bmatrix}$ is the diagonal matrix of eigenvalues for the inverse of the covariance matrix $\mathrm{s}^2\mathbf{c}(\mathbf{x}'\mathbf{x})^{-1}\mathbf{c}'$. Then, let $\mathbf{z} = \mathbf{p}'(\mathbf{c}\hat{\boldsymbol{\beta}} - \mathbf{r})$, and transform the quadratic expression in the Wald confidence set to $\lambda_1 \mathrm{z}_1^2 + \lambda_2 \mathrm{z}_2^2 = \tau$, which is an ellipse centered about the origin in z-space. We may then identify the plausible range of values for z_1 as $z_1 \in [-\sqrt{\tau/\lambda_1}, \sqrt{\tau/\lambda_1}]$ (given $z_2 = 0$) and can compute the associated values of z_2 that fall on the ellipsoidal boundary of the joint confidence region. Finally, we can convert the paired values of $\mathbf{z}$ to values of $\mathbf{r}$ by the transformation $\mathbf{r} = \mathbf{c}\hat{\boldsymbol{\beta}} - \mathbf{pz}$.

6.3.2. LM-Based Confidence Regions

A confidence region based on the duality principle applied to the LM test of H_0: $\mathbf{c}\boldsymbol{\beta} = \mathbf{r}$ can be defined by the set

$$\mathrm{CR}^{\mathrm{LM}} = \left\{ \mathbf{r} : \frac{[\gamma_{\mathrm{r}}(\mathbf{r})'\mathbf{c}(\mathbf{x}'\mathbf{x})^{-1}\mathbf{c}'\gamma_{\mathrm{r}}(\mathbf{r})]}{4\mathrm{S}_{\mathrm{r}}^2} < \tau \right\}, \tag{6.3.3}$$

where the optimal value of the Lagrange multiplier γ_{r} is a function of the value of $\mathbf{r}$ used in the restriction $\mathbf{c}\boldsymbol{\beta} = \mathbf{r}$. However, this direct application of the duality principle is not computationally straightforward because the values of $\mathbf{r}$ are not explicit in the formulation but rather are implicit in the value of γ_{r}. An alternative formulation of the confidence region in (6.3.3) that explicitly includes $\mathbf{r}$ can be derived from the score form of the LM test (6.2.29)

$$\mathrm{CR}^{\mathrm{LM}} = \left\{ \mathbf{r} : \frac{(\mathbf{c}\hat{\mathbf{b}} - \mathbf{r})'[\mathbf{c}(\mathbf{x}'\mathbf{x})^{-1}\mathbf{c}']^{-1}(\mathbf{c}\hat{\mathbf{b}} - \mathbf{r})}{\mathrm{S}_{\mathrm{r}}^2} < \tau \right\}. \tag{6.3.4}$$

Note the benefit of having **r** entering explicitly into the set-defining condition comes at the modest cost of requiring both the unrestricted and restricted estimates of $\boldsymbol{\beta}$ when defining $\mathrm{CR}^{\mathrm{LM}}$. In comparing this confidence region with (6.3.2), the reader will notice that $\mathrm{CR}^{\mathrm{LM}}$ will have larger or smaller length, area, or volume than CR^{W}, depending on whether $\mathrm{s}_{\mathrm{r}}^2$ is $>$ or $<$ s^2. As we discussed previously, if $\mathrm{W} \geq \mathrm{LM}$, which is the case when both $\mathrm{S}_{\mathrm{r}}^2$ and S^2 are defined with denominators of n instead of $(n-k+j)$ and $(n-k)$, producing biased but consistent estimators of σ^2, then the length, area, or volume of CR^{W} will be smaller than that of $\mathrm{CR}^{\mathrm{LM}}$.

As in the case of the Wald test, the LM confidence region will be an interval if $\mathbf{c}\boldsymbol{\beta}$ is a scalar, an ellipse if $\mathbf{c}\boldsymbol{\beta}$ is two-dimensional, and a hyperellipse otherwise, all of which will be centered at the value of $\mathbf{c}\hat{\mathbf{b}}$. This confidence region is asymptotically locally UMA invariant, which is inherited from the asymptotically locally UMP invariant property of the LM test on which the confidence regions is based. As in the Wald procedure, one can use a weak inequality in (6.3.4) while still maintaining the asymptotic confidence level at $100(1-\alpha)\%$ because LM is a continuous random variable under the Chi-square approximation and the added boundary points have probability zero.

It is also possible to define confidence regions for nonlinear functions of the elements of the $\boldsymbol{\beta}$ vector using duality applied to both Wald- and LM-type tests. We will defer an examination of confidence regions for nonlinear functions until we have examined the nonlinear statistical model in Chapter 8. The results we present there for defining confidence regions on nonlinear functions of $\boldsymbol{\beta}$ will then also apply to the linear statistical model as a special case.

► **Example 6.3.2 (LM Confidence Region for $\mathbf{c}\boldsymbol{\beta}$):** The GAUSS procedure cregion() is used in this example to form Wald and LM joint confidence regions for a pair of regression parameters. GAUSS plots both elliptical regions in the same graphics window for thc uscr to compare. Then GAUSS conducts a bootstrap resampling exercise to simulate the coverage probabilities for the W and LM-based regions. The user should find that the estimated coverage probabilities for both regions approach the intended .90 rate as n becomes large.

6.4. Testing Linear Inequality Hypotheses and Generating Confidence Bounds on β

Situations arise in practice in which the analyst is interested in testing hypotheses that are in the form of linear inequality restrictions on the elements of the $\boldsymbol{\beta}$-vector. For example, one might test a Cobb–Douglas production function for constant or decreasing returns to scalc, in which case one wishes to test whether the sum of the output elasticities, say $\sum_{i=1}^{m} \beta_i$, is less than or equal to 1. All hypotheses of this type can be expressed in the generic form H_0: $\mathbf{c}\boldsymbol{\beta} \leq \mathrm{r}$, or H_0: $\mathbf{c}\boldsymbol{\beta} \geq \mathrm{r}$, or perhaps with the weak inequalities replaced with strong inequalities. Here $\mathbf{c}$ is a $(1 \times k)$ row vector and r is a scalar. The analyst may also be interested in generating a lower or upper bound to the value of a scalar $\mathbf{c}\boldsymbol{\beta}$ that bounds the true value of $\mathbf{c}\boldsymbol{\beta}$ with a known predata level of confidence. We address these procedures in the subsections ahead.

6.4.1. Linear Inequality Hypotheses

The tests that we will consider rely on the asymptotic normality of the LS estimator of $\hat{\boldsymbol{\beta}}$ of $\boldsymbol{\beta}$, where $n^{1/2}(\hat{\boldsymbol{\beta}}-\boldsymbol{\beta}) \xrightarrow{d} \mathrm{N}(\mathbf{0}, \sigma^2\Xi^{-1})$ and $\hat{\boldsymbol{\beta}} \overset{a}{\sim} \mathrm{N}(\boldsymbol{\beta}, \sigma^2(\mathbf{x}'\mathbf{x})^{-1})$. On the basis of Slutsky's theorem, it follows that $n^{1/2}\mathbf{c}(\hat{\boldsymbol{\beta}}-\boldsymbol{\beta}) \xrightarrow{d} \mathrm{N}(\mathbf{0}, \sigma^2\mathbf{c}\Xi^{-1}\mathbf{c}')$; therefore, an asymptotically valid pivotal quantity for $\mathbf{c}\boldsymbol{\beta}$ is given by

$$\frac{\mathbf{c}\hat{\boldsymbol{\beta}}-\mathbf{c}\boldsymbol{\beta}}{[\sigma^2\mathbf{c}(\mathrm{n}\Xi)^{-1}\mathbf{c}']^{1/2}} \overset{a}{\sim} \mathrm{N}(0, 1) \tag{6.4.1}$$

if σ^2 and Ξ are known, which we temporarily assume.

Now consider testing the hypothesis H_0: $\mathbf{c}\boldsymbol{\beta} \leq \mathrm{r}$. Examine the test statistic

$$\mathrm{Z} = \frac{\mathbf{c}\hat{\boldsymbol{\beta}}-\mathrm{r}}{[\sigma^2\mathbf{c}(\mathrm{n}\Xi)^{-1}\mathbf{c}']^{1/2}}. \tag{6.4.2}$$

If $\mathbf{c}\boldsymbol{\beta}=\mathrm{r}$, then $\mathrm{Z} \overset{a}{\sim} \mathrm{N}(0,1)$, whereas if $\mathbf{c}\boldsymbol{\beta}=\mathrm{r}+n^{-1/2}\delta$, then $\mathrm{Z} \overset{a}{\sim} \mathrm{N}(\delta/[\sigma^2\mathbf{c}(\Xi^{-1})\mathbf{c}']^{1/2}, 1)$. Letting $\mathrm{z}_{1-\alpha}$ be the $100(1-\alpha)\%$ quantile of the standard normal distribution, it then follows from the power function of the test that the test rule

$$\text{reject } \mathrm{H}_0\text{: } \mathbf{c}\boldsymbol{\beta} \leq \mathrm{r} \quad \text{iff} \quad \mathrm{z} \geq \mathrm{z}_{1-\alpha} \tag{6.4.3}$$

defines an asymptotic level α and unbiased test of H_0. In particular, the power function is defined by

$$\pi(\delta) = \mathrm{P}(\mathrm{z} \geq \mathrm{z}_{1-\alpha}) \begin{bmatrix} < \\ = \\ > \end{bmatrix} \alpha \quad \text{if} \quad \delta \begin{bmatrix} < \\ = \\ > \end{bmatrix} 0. \tag{6.4.4}$$

The test is consistent. To see this, note that if $\mathbf{c}\boldsymbol{\beta}=\mathrm{r}+\mathrm{v}$, where $\mathrm{v}>0$, then

$$n^{-1/2}\mathrm{Z} = \frac{\mathbf{c}\hat{\boldsymbol{\beta}}-\mathrm{r}}{(\sigma^2\mathbf{c}\Xi^{-1}\mathbf{c}')^{1/2}} \xrightarrow{p} \frac{\mathrm{v}}{(\sigma^2\mathbf{c}\Xi^{-1}\mathbf{c}')^{1/2}} = \xi > 0. \tag{6.4.5}$$

Then, for any fixed value of $\mathrm{z}_{1-\alpha}$ and small enough $\kappa>0$ such that $\xi-\kappa>0$,

$$\begin{aligned}
\lim_{n\to\infty} \mathrm{P}(\mathrm{z} \geq \mathrm{z}_{1-\alpha}) &= \lim_{n\to\infty} \mathrm{P}(n^{-1/2}\mathrm{z} \geq n^{-1/2}\mathrm{z}_{1-\alpha}) \\
&\geq \lim_{n\to\infty} \mathrm{P}(n^{-1/2}\mathrm{z} > \xi-\kappa) \\
&\geq \lim_{n\to\infty} \mathrm{P}(|n^{-1/2}\mathrm{z}-\xi| < \kappa) = 1.
\end{aligned} \tag{6.4.6}$$

Note the inequalities follow because for n large enough, $n^{-1/2}\mathrm{z} > \xi-\kappa \Rightarrow n^{-1/2}\mathrm{z} \geq n^{-1/2}\mathrm{z}_{1-\alpha}$, and $|n^{-1/2}\mathrm{z}-\xi| < \kappa \Rightarrow n^{-1/2}\mathrm{z} > \xi-\kappa$. Thus, the outcome of z will reside in the critical region $\mathrm{C}^{\mathrm{Z}} = [\mathrm{z}_{1-\alpha}, \infty]$ with probability $\to 1$ as $n\to\infty$ whenever H_0 is false, and thus the Z-test is consistent.

Finally, on the basis of the asymptotic normality of $\hat{\boldsymbol{\beta}}$, one can utilize Neyman–Pearson theory to conclude that the test is an asymptotically uniformly most powerful unbiased test of H_0: $\mathbf{c}\boldsymbol{\beta} \leq \mathrm{r}$. Precisely the same test rule will define an asymptotically valid test of the strong inequality hypothesis H_0: $\mathbf{c}\boldsymbol{\beta} < \mathrm{r}$; that is, given the continuous nature of the normal approximation, the boundary point is irrelevant and all of the test properties remain in force.

To test the hypothesis $H_0: \mathbf{c}\boldsymbol{\beta} \geq r$ (or $H_0: \mathbf{c}\boldsymbol{\beta} > r$), the test statistic (6.4.2) can again be utilized. The test rule becomes (compare with (6.4.3))

$$\text{reject } H_0: \mathbf{c}\boldsymbol{\beta} \geq r \quad \text{iff} \quad z \leq z_\alpha, \tag{6.4.7}$$

where z_α is the $100\alpha\%$ quantile of the standard normal distribution. All of the previous test properties continue to hold, and thus in an asymptotic approximation sense, the test is unbiased, consistent, and UMPU.

Because σ^2 and Ξ are generally unknown and unobservable, they must be replaced in (6.4.2) by observables to make the test rule operational. With the application of the consistent estimator S^2 for σ^2 and $n^{-1}\mathbf{x}'\mathbf{x}$ for Ξ, the tests (6.4.3) and (6.4.7) can be conducted using the test statistic

$$\hat{Z} = \frac{\mathbf{c}\hat{\boldsymbol{\beta}} - r}{[S^2\mathbf{c}(\mathbf{x}'\mathbf{x})^{-1}\mathbf{c}']^{1/2}}. \tag{6.4.8}$$

The test is then characterized by $\{\hat{Z}, C^z\}$, with the critical region being $C^Z = [z_{1-\alpha}, \infty)$ or $C^Z = (-\infty, z_\alpha]$, depending on whether one is testing $H_0: \mathbf{c}\boldsymbol{\beta} \leq r$ or $H_0: \mathbf{c}\boldsymbol{\beta} \geq r$, respectively. Slutsky's theorem can be used to justify that all of the previous asymptotic properties of the test procedure apply when $\hat{Z}$ is used in place of Z.

A joint test of a collection of linear inequality hypotheses can be conducted on the basis of Bonferroni's probability inequality. In particular, one can conduct m individual tests of inequality hypotheses of the type discussed above and then interpret the collective outcome of the collection of tests as a joint test of $H_0: \mathbf{c}_i\boldsymbol{\beta} \leq r_i, i = 1, \ldots, m$. The size of the joint test is bounded by Bonferroni's inequality, for letting A_i represent the event that the ith test does not reject a true H_0 by mistake, the size of the joint test is bounded as $1 - P(\bigcap_{i=1}^m A_i) \leq \sum_{i=1}^m P(\bar{A}_i)$. The right-hand side bound equals the sum of the sizes of the m individual tests. For example, if two individual tests were conducted at the .05 level, one could then conclude that the joint test is conducted at the .10 level, with the size of the joint test being $\leq .10$.

► **Example 6.4.1 (Z-Test of $H_0: \mathbf{c}\boldsymbol{\beta} \geq \mathbf{r}$ Calculation and Power):** To demonstrate the one-sided Z-test for linear inequality hypotheses of the form $H_0: \mathbf{c}\boldsymbol{\beta} \geq \mathbf{r}$, we provide this example in the examples manual. The Z-test computations are conducted by the GAUSS procedure mlr_z(), which returns the observed test statistic and the asymptotic p-value if the row dimension of $\mathbf{c}$ is $j = 1$. If more than one linear inequality hypothesis is specified, the procedure returns the observed test statistic and the p-value for each of the separate hypotheses. The program conducts a bootstrap resampling exercise to compare the estimated and asymptotic power functions for the one-sided test.

6.4.2. Confidence Bounds for $\mathbf{c}\boldsymbol{\beta}$

Asymptotically valid upper or lower confidence bounds for $\mathbf{c}\boldsymbol{\beta}$ can be defined using the duality principle applied to the tests of inequality restrictions presented in Section 6.4.1. Using the operational version of the asymptotically valid test (6.4.3), an asymptotic level

$100(1-\alpha)\%$ *lower* confidence bound for $\mathbf{c}\boldsymbol{\beta}$ is given by the set of $\mathbf{c}\boldsymbol{\beta}$ values *not* rejected by the asymptotic α-level test as

$$\begin{aligned} \mathrm{CR}^{z} &= \left\{ \mathrm{r} : \frac{\mathbf{c}\hat{\mathbf{b}} - \mathrm{r}}{[\mathrm{s}^2 \mathbf{c}(\mathbf{x}'\mathbf{x})^{-1}\mathbf{c}']^{1/2}} < \mathrm{z}_{1-\alpha} \right\} \\ &= \{\mathrm{r} : \mathrm{r} > \mathbf{c}\hat{\mathbf{b}} - \mathrm{z}_{1-\alpha}[\mathrm{s}^2\mathbf{c}(\mathbf{x}'\mathbf{x})^{-1}\mathbf{c}']^{1/2}\}. \end{aligned} \tag{6.4.9}$$

Similarly, to define an asymptotic level $100(1-\alpha)\%$ *upper* confidence bound for $\mathbf{c}\boldsymbol{\beta}$, one can define the set of $\mathbf{c}\boldsymbol{\beta}$ values *not* rejected by the asymptotic α-level test (6.4.7) and yielding (note that $\mathrm{z}_{\alpha} = -\mathrm{z}_{1-\alpha}$)

$$\begin{aligned} \mathrm{CR}^{z} &= \left\{ \mathrm{r} : \frac{\mathbf{c}\hat{\mathbf{b}} - \mathrm{r}}{[\mathrm{s}^2 \mathbf{c}(\mathbf{x}'\mathbf{x})^{-1}\mathbf{c}']^{1/2}} > \mathrm{z}_{\alpha} \right\} \\ &= \{\mathrm{r} : \mathrm{r} < \mathbf{c}\hat{\mathbf{b}} + \mathrm{z}_{1-\alpha}[\mathrm{s}^2\mathbf{c}(\mathbf{x}'\mathbf{x})^{-1}\mathbf{c}']^{1/2}\}. \end{aligned} \tag{6.4.10}$$

A joint confidence bound for more than one linear combination of the entries in $\boldsymbol{\beta}$ can be specified by defining multiple confidence intervals of the type (6.4.9) and (6.4.10) and then bounding the level of their intersection based on Bonferroni's inequality. In particular, if $\mathrm{CR}_{\mathrm{i}}^{z}$ is a confidence region for $\mathbf{c}_{\mathrm{i}}\boldsymbol{\beta}$ having asymptotic level $1-\alpha_{\mathrm{i}}$ for $i = 1, \ldots, m$, then, on the basis of Bonferroni's inequality,

$$\mathrm{P}\big(\mathbf{c}_{\mathrm{i}}\boldsymbol{\beta} \in \mathrm{CR}_{\mathrm{i}}^{z},\ i = 1, \ldots, m\big) \geq 1 - \sum_{i=1}^{m} \mathrm{P}\big(\mathbf{c}_{\mathrm{i}}\boldsymbol{\beta} \notin \mathrm{CR}_{\mathrm{i}}^{z}\big) \geq 1 - \sum_{i=1}^{m} \alpha_{\mathrm{i}}. \tag{6.4.11}$$

Thus, the asymptotic confidence level of the joint confidence region is $1 - \sum_{i=1}^{m} \alpha_{\mathrm{i}}$.

► **Example 6.4.2 (Joint Confidence Bounds):** To compute the joint confidence bounds associated with linear inequality hypotheses, we can use the Bonferroni inequality to control the overall size of the individual components. We provide the GAUSS procedure cr_joint() used by this example in the examples manual to compute the confidence bounds for each element of $\mathbf{c}\boldsymbol{\beta}$ according to the overall coverage probability specified by the reader.

6.5. Critique

In searching for an inference solution in the context of a DSP for the semiparametric linear regression model, we are led under the least-squares estimation objective function to general estimation and inference procedures applicable not only to the probability model in this chapter but also in subsequent chapters in which we will have to rely on asymptotic results for inference purposes. For example, when distributional information is of an asymptotic kind, the Wald and Lagrange multiplier-type test statistics introduced in this chapter can be extended to provide a useful basis for inference not only in the linear-regression model context but in more general nonlinear model contexts as well.

Given this estimation and inference base, in Chapters 7 and 8 we take a large step toward more general probability models and focus on the estimation and inference problem within a general extremum estimation context as well as in a nonlinear regression model context. In the latter context we do not assume a specification that is linear in the parameters or one that can be transformed to be linear in the parameters. In this case, when only asymptotic results are generally possible, we have an example where the Wald and Lagrange multiplier test concepts developed in this chapter immediately apply.

The general availability of the Wald and Lagrange multiplier tests means that a two-stage procedure is also generally available that provides a basis for choosing between estimators based on the outcome of a hypothesis test. The estimator defined by such a two-stage decision procedure is often used in practice and is known as a preliminary test estimator. In Chapter 4 we illustrated some of its statistical properties. In the current context of the semiparametric linear model, the statistical properties of the pretest estimator in finite samples is generally unavailable, and thus investigating such properties must generally rely on asymptotic approximations, bootstrap resampling, or Monte Carlo simulation.

We note that it is possible to define asymptotically valid procedures for testing hypotheses and generating confidence intervals for the parameter σ^2. A statistic that could be used to satisfy both testing and confidence interval objectives can be based on the fact that under the additional assumption of finiteness of the fourth-order absolute moments of iid ε_i's, S^2 is asymptotically normally distributed with mean σ^2 and asymptotic covariance matrix $(\mu_4' - \sigma^4)/n$, where μ_4' is the fourth moment of the ε_i's. Thus, a Z-statistic having an asymptotic normal distribution can be formed as $Z = \frac{n^{1/2}(S^2 - \sigma^2)}{(\hat{\mu}_4' - \hat{\sigma}^4)^{1/2}}$, where $\hat{\mu}_4'$ and $\hat{\sigma}^4$ are consistent estimators of μ_4' and σ^4, to test hypotheses and generate confidence intervals and bounds for the true value of σ^2. Details are left to the reader.

As we leave this chapter, we remind the reader of the sampling theory, predata context that forms the basis for evaluating the estimation and testing rules we have developed and the inferences we draw from them. Understanding the sampling theory basis for reasoning in the basic probability models examined in Chapters 3–6 is essential if one expects to deal successfully with econometric problems of decision making under uncertainty and achieve our objective of learning from a sample of data in more complicated DSPs often found in practice. Also, the remarks in the concluding section of Chapter 4 relating to hypothesis tests are equally relevant to the discussion in this chapter.

6.6. Comprehensive Computer Application

We conclude our discussion of estimation and inference for the linear semiparametric regression model with a comprehensive GAUSS exercise written by Thomas Marsh and available in the examples manual. Using data gathered from federal sources, Marsh constructs a double-log model of the demand for manufactured housing as a function of the real housing price, interest rates, consumer credit terms, the proportion of consumer debt attributable to housing, and shipments of new manufactured homes. After reporting the estimation results, Marsh states a series of hypotheses regarding the model parameters and conducts the associated Wald and LM tests. Then, Marsh conducts a bootstrap simulation exercise designed to approximate the statistical properties of the least-squares estimator and the hypothesis tests for this model. For each of $m = 100$ bootstrap trials, the replicated data are formed by residual resampling, and the associated least-square estimates and test statistics are computed and stored. The results of the simulation exercise are graphically reported through the sample averages, empirical distribution functions, and box plots of the bootstrap estimates.

6.7. Exercises

6.7.1. Idea Checklist – Knowledge Guides

1. Why is statistical inference necessary?
2. What is the difference between asymptotic and finite sample inference?
3. Why is Chapter 6 restricted to asymptotic inference, and what are the statistical implications of this restriction?
4. What is the difference between hypothesis testing and confidence region estimation?
5. Discuss the implications of the predata, unconditional (on observed data) context of the inference procedures presented in this chapter and Chapter 4. Does it make sense to evaluate the performance of inference procedures on the basis of data that could occur but do not?

6.7.2. Problems

6–1 Under a squared-error loss measure, develop and compare, over the range of the parameter space, the characteristics of the risk of estimator $\hat{\boldsymbol{\beta}} = (\mathbf{x}'\mathbf{x})^{-1}\mathbf{x}'\mathbf{Y}$ in the linear statistical model to the risk of the estimator $\bar{\boldsymbol{\beta}} = \mathbf{0}$. Does this have any statistical implications relative to the problem of choosing a test of the null hypothesis $\boldsymbol{\beta} = \mathbf{0}$?

6–2 From a realized sample of 25 observations, suppose you obtain a point estimate of scalar β. (1) Suppose you want to test the hypothesis that $\beta = 0$ and under the Wald test suppose you obtained a test value of 2.3. State the inference that you would draw from this result. (2) Develop a corresponding statement regarding a confidence interval [.3, .9] for β.

6–3 Given the asymptotic power function of either the Wald or LM test of the hypothesis $\mathrm{H}_0\colon \mathbf{c}\boldsymbol{\beta} = \mathbf{r}$, explain why a nonrejection of the hypothesis by the test rule should not necessarily be interpreted as *literal acceptance* of H_0.

6–4 For large enough sample sizes, either the Wald or LM tests will be essentially certain to reject $\mathrm{H}_0\colon \mathbf{c}\boldsymbol{\beta} = \mathbf{r}$ if H_0 is false – true or false, and why?

6–5 Because the Wald and LM tests are asymptotically equivalent, it makes no difference which one is used in practice – true or false, and why?

6–6 What is a Pitman drift alternative to H_0, and why are these alternatives useful, relevant, or both?

6–7 Define the form of an asymptotic Wald-based confidence region for which we are 100% confident that $\mathbf{c}\boldsymbol{\beta}$ will be covered. Is such a region useful or informative?

6–8 Is there any practical problem in defining a joint test of hypothesis or joint confidence region based on a *large* collection of univariate tests or confidence intervals and Bonferroni's inequality?

6–9 Will the upper bound on $\mathbf{c}\boldsymbol{\beta}$ generated by a Wald-type upper confidence bound estimator ultimately converge to the true value of $\mathbf{c}\boldsymbol{\beta}$? Why or why not?

6.7.3. Computer Exercises

---

1. Use the housing model and data provided by Thomas Marsh to answer the following questions:
   a. Use the GAUSS procedure cr_joint() to plot the joint 90% confidence region (ellipse) for β_2 and β_4 (the coefficients for the own-price elasticity and the interest elasticity).
   b. Plot the joint one-sided 90% confidence region for $\beta_2 \leq 0$ and $\beta_4 \leq 0$. Do the upper bounds on these elasticities seem economically reasonable to you?
   c. Conduct joint Wald and LM tests of the hypothesis H_0: $\beta_5 = 0$ and $\beta_6 = 1$ (the coefficients for the installment credit and home shipment elasticities).
2. Use Theil's consumption data (C6Theil.dat) to answer the following questions:
   a. Compute LS estimates of a log–log textile demand equation. Use the GAUSS procedure restrict() to compute the restricted LS estimates under the null hypothesis that demand is homogeneous of degree zero. How do the estimates compare?
   b. Compute 90% confidence intervals for each of the estimated model parameters under both the Wald and LM criteria. In words, explain the meaning of the intervals. Do the interval estimates seem economically reasonable to you?
   c. Conduct Wald and LM tests of the null hypothesis that textile demand is homogeneous of degree zero. What do you conclude from the test results?
   d. Conduct a joint one-sided test of the hypothesis H_0: $0 \geq \beta_2 \geq -1$ and $0 \leq \beta_3 \leq 1$ at the 10% level (i.e., textile demand is own-price inelastic and income inelastic). Do your findings conform to your understanding of consumption economics?
3. Write a GAUSS program that conducts bootstrap or Monte Carlo simulations of both the Wald and the LM tests of a linear hypothesis $\mathbf{c}\boldsymbol{\beta} = \mathbf{r}$. (Hint: Use a copy of C6MLR_W.gss or C6MLR_LM.gss to get started.) In repeated samples, how often do the test decisions agree? How often do the test decisions disagree? How do your findings change as n increases?

6.8. References

Atchinson, J., and S. D. Silvey (1958), "Maximum Likelihood Estimation of Parameters Subject to Restraints," *Annals of Mathematical Statistics*, Vol. 29, pp. 313–828.

Berndt, R. B., and N. E. Savin (1977), "Conflict Among Criteria for Testing Hypotheses in the Multivariate Linear Regression Model," *Econometrica*, Vol. 45, pp. 1263–77.

Bunke, H., and O. Bunke (1986), *Statistical Inference in Linear Models*, New York: John Wiley and Sons.

Hall, P. (1992), *The Bootstrap and Edgeworth Expansion*, Springer Series in Statistics, New York: Springer–Verlag.

Mittelhammer, R. C. (1996), *Mathematical Statistics for Economics and Business*, New York: Springer–Verlag.

Navidi, W. (1989), "Edgeworth Expansions for Bootstrapping Regression Models," *American Statistician*, Vol. 14, pp. 1472–8.

Neyman, J. (1937), "Smooth Test for Goodness of Fit," *Skandinavisk Actuarietiskrift*, Vol. 20, pp. 144–99.

Pitman, E. (1949), "Notes on Nonparametric Statistical Inference," New York: Columbia University, mimeo.

Rao, C. R. (1948), "Large Sample Tests of Statistical Hypotheses." *Proceedings of the Cambridge Philosophical Society*, Vol. 44, pp. 50–7.

Schmidt, P. (1976), *Econometrics*, New York: Marcel Dekker.

van der Vaart, A. W. (1998), *Asymptotic Statistics*, Cambridge, UK: Cambridge University Press.

Wald, A. (1943), "Tests of Statistical Hypotheses Concerning Several Parameters When the Number of Observations is Large," *Transactions of the American Mathematical Society*, Vol. 54, pp. 426–82.

Zaman, A. (1996), *Statistical Foundations for Econometric Techniques*, San Diego: Academic Press.

PART THREE

Extremum Estimators and Nonlinear and Nonnormal Regression Models

In Chapter 7 the focus is on the large class of extremum estimators. The estimators in this class are defined through optimization of estimation objective functions, which include the least-squares and likelihood objective functions examined in Chapters 3–6. The extremum class encompasses most of the econometric estimators used in practice, and it provides a basis for a unified approach to the asymptotic theory of estimation and inference. In Chapter 8, in search of a more flexible probability model for characterizing the interrelationships between explanatory and dependent variable outcomes, we examine a nonlinear regression model of the form $\mathbf{Y} = \mathbf{g}(\mathbf{x}, \boldsymbol{\beta}) + \boldsymbol{\varepsilon}$ and identify a corresponding nonlinear least-squares estimator. Two classes of numerical algorithms are suggested for use in computing solutions to nonlinear least-squares estimation problems, and corresponding asymptotic estimator properties and test statistics are demonstrated. In Chapter 9 the nonlinear parametric *normal* regression model, where $\mathbf{g}(\mathbf{x}, \boldsymbol{\beta})$ is some vector function differentiable in $\boldsymbol{\beta}$, is considered along with maximum likelihood procedures for estimation and inference. The results are then extended to nonnormal specifications.

CHAPTER 7

Extremum Estimation and Inference

7.1. Introduction

We noted in Chapters 3 and 5 that the ML and LS estimators are members of a large class of estimators called "extremum (E) estimators." In fact, the E estimators represent a class of estimators that encompass most of the estimators used in econometric practice. In addition to the ML and LS estimators, the class includes the nonlinear least squares, generalized method of moments, empirical likelihood, information–theoretic, and minimum distance estimators that we take up in the chapters ahead. In addition the concept of E estimation provides a basis for a unified asymptotic theory applicable to a wide range of econometric estimators. To introduce the class of E estimators consider the inverse problems associated with the probability models identified in Table 7.1. The probability models imply inverse problems in which the observations $(\mathbf{Y}, \mathbf{x})$ are used to recover information on the values or functions of the unknown and unobservable $\boldsymbol{\beta}$, σ^2, and ε.

The ML and LS estimators introduced in Chapters 3 and 5 to provide point estimation solutions to inverse problems are special cases in which the estimator can be written in explicit closed form and the solution for $\hat{\boldsymbol{\beta}}$ outcomes is usually easily obtained. More generally, extremum estimators encompass any estimator that can be defined by optimizing an estimation metric or estimation objective function, depending on parameters $\boldsymbol{\theta}$ and data $(\mathbf{Y}, \mathbf{X})$. Specifically, these estimators can be defined as

$$\hat{\boldsymbol{\Theta}} = \arg \max_{\boldsymbol{\theta} \in \Omega} [\mathrm{m}(\boldsymbol{\theta}, \mathbf{Y}, \mathbf{X})], \qquad (7.1.1)$$

where we explicitly assume maximization is the objective. Of course, we can minimize an objective function by maximizing the negative of the same objective function. Note, we use random $\mathbf{X}$ here for future reference to cases where the explanatory variables are considered random. The fixed $\mathbf{x}$ case is subsumed by interpreting $\mathbf{X}$ as a degenerate random variable that assumes the value $\mathbf{x}$ with probability 1.

The properties of an extremum estimator depend on the properties of the estimation metric or estimation objective function being optimized. For the metrics commonly

Table 7.1. *Normal Parametric and Semiparametric Linear Regression Probability Models*

Model Component	Specific Characteristics	
$\mathbf{Y}$	RV Type:	continuous
	Range:	unlimited
	Y_i dimension:	univariate
	Moments:	$E[\mathbf{Y} \mid \mathbf{x}] = \mathbf{x}\boldsymbol{\beta}$, and $\mathbf{cov}(\mathbf{Y} \mid \mathbf{x}) = \sigma^2\mathbf{I}$
$\eta(\mathbf{x}, \boldsymbol{\beta}, \varepsilon)$	Functional Form:	linear in $\mathbf{x}$ and $\boldsymbol{\beta}$, additive in ε, as $\mathbf{x}\boldsymbol{\beta} + \varepsilon$
$\mathbf{x}$	RV Type:	degenerate (fixed), full-column rank
	Genesis:	exogenous to the model
$\boldsymbol{\beta}$	RV Type:	degenerate (fixed)
	Dimension:	finite (fixed)
ε	RV Type:	iid or independent nonidentical
	Moments:	$E[\varepsilon \mid \mathbf{x}] = \mathbf{0}$, and $\mathbf{cov}(\varepsilon \mid \mathbf{x}) = \sigma^2\mathbf{I}$
Ω	Prior info:	none
$f(\mathbf{e} \mid \mathbf{x}, \varphi)$	PDF family:	$N(\mathbf{e}; \mathbf{0}, \sigma^2\mathbf{I})$ or unspecified

used in econometric practice, the properties of consistency and asymptotic normality are achieved under general regularity conditions (where "regularity conditions" is just another term for "assumptions") relating to the probability model. Given the wide variety of different choices that are possible for the estimation objective function component of the extremum estimation problem, there are no broad finite sample property generalizations that can be made for extremum estimators, and so our focus vis-à-vis general sampling properties will be restricted to asymptotic properties.

When an extremum estimator can be defined as an *explicit* function of the data $(\mathbf{Y}, \mathbf{X})$, it is often possible, and often more straightforward, to analyze the estimator function directly to establish statistical properties of the estimator. Such was the case for the ML estimator of $\boldsymbol{\beta}$ and σ^2 in the context of the multivariate normal linear regression model as well as the LS estimator of $\boldsymbol{\beta}$ in the context of the semiparametric linear regression model. However, an extremum estimator may, as in chapters ahead, be defined only as an *implicit* function of the data that cannot be written in closed form, or else the estimator function may be too complicated to analyze directly. For example, this is often the case in applications of nonlinear least squares (Chapter 8), as well as the case of maximum likelihood procedures applied to nonlinear models or nonnormal probability distributions (Chapter 9). In these latter cases, general theorems on asymptotic properties of extremum estimators can be helpful in providing at least large sample results when small sample properties cannot be established.

We emphasize that the general extremum estimation context that we examine in sections ahead both subsume and transcend the probability models characterized in Table 7.1. We refer, both explicitly and implicitly, to the results of Chapters 3–6 as examples of the application of extremum estimation and inference, as well as note that examples of extremum estimation will abound in the chapters ahead. In this chapter, we also consider a series of examples based on the minimum absolute deviation (MAD) or least absolute error (LAE) criterion. For the linear regression model, the MAD estimator is

$$\hat{\boldsymbol{\beta}}_{\text{mad}} = \arg\min_{\boldsymbol{\beta}} \sum_{i=1}^{n} |\mathrm{y}_i - \mathbf{x}[i,.]\boldsymbol{\beta}| \tag{7.1.2}$$

In contrast to the LS estimator, the MAD estimator is selected by minimizing the sum of the *absolute* (rather than squared) residuals. Koenker and Bassett (1978) show that the estimator is robust to outliers among the observations.

► **Example 7.1.1:** The GAUSS program C7MAD.gss outlines the computational steps used to compose the GAUSS procedure mad() (both programs are provided in the examples manual). MAD estimates were originally computed by solving linear programming problems (see Wagner, 1959, or Koenker and Bassett, 1978), but a much simpler solution may be computed by a variant of the least-squares estimator. The algorithm used in the mad() procedure is adapted from original GAUSS code written by Ronald Schoenberg. GAUSS also generates a pseudorandom sample of observations and uses the procedure to compute the MAD parameter estimates.

The MAD objective function in (7.1.2) may be written as

$$\mathrm{m}(\boldsymbol{\beta}, \mathbf{y}, \mathbf{x}) = \sum_{i=1}^{n} |\mathrm{y}_i - \mathbf{x}[i,.]\boldsymbol{\beta}| = \sum_{i=1}^{n} (\mathrm{y}_i - \mathbf{x}[i,.]\boldsymbol{\beta})\,\mathrm{sgn}(\mathrm{y}_i - \mathbf{x}[i,.]\boldsymbol{\beta}), \tag{7.1.3}$$

where $\mathrm{sgn(z)} = -1$ if $\mathrm{z} < 0$ and $\mathrm{sgn(z)} = 1$ if $\mathrm{z} > 0$. By further noting that $\mathrm{sgn(z)} = \mathrm{z/abs(z)}$, we can rewrite (7.1.3) as a *weighted* least-squares objective function

$$\mathrm{m}(\boldsymbol{\beta}, \mathbf{y}, \mathbf{x}) = \sum_{i=1}^{n} \frac{(\mathrm{y}_i - \mathbf{x}[i,.]\boldsymbol{\beta})^2}{|\mathrm{y}_i - \mathbf{x}[i,.]\boldsymbol{\beta}|} \tag{7.1.4}$$

The weights for each observation are simply the reciprocals of the absolute deviations. If $\mathbf{q}(\boldsymbol{\beta})$ is a diagonal matrix with elements $\mathbf{q}_{\text{ii}}(\boldsymbol{\beta}) = |\mathrm{y}_i - \mathbf{x}[i,.]\boldsymbol{\beta}|^{-1}$, the weighted least-squares objective function may be stated in matrix form as $\mathrm{m}(\boldsymbol{\beta}, \mathbf{y}, \mathbf{x}) = (\mathbf{y} - \mathbf{x}\boldsymbol{\beta})'\mathbf{q}(\boldsymbol{\beta})(\mathbf{y} - \mathbf{x}\boldsymbol{\beta})$.

Although a direct solution to the problem is difficult to achieve because $\boldsymbol{\beta}$ appears in the numerator and denominator of (7.1.4), we can solve the problem by a procedure known as iterative weighted least squares. For some starting value $\boldsymbol{\beta}_0$ (perhaps the least-squares estimate of $\boldsymbol{\beta}$), we form an $(n \times k)$ matrix $\mathbf{w}$ and compute the subsequent estimate as $\boldsymbol{\beta}_1 = (\mathbf{w}'\mathbf{x})^{-1}\mathbf{w}'\mathbf{y}$. The weights in the denominator of (7.1.4) are included as $\mathbf{w} = \mathbf{qx}$, which has elements $\mathrm{w}_{ik} = \mathrm{x}_{ik}/|\mathrm{y}_i - \mathbf{x}[i,.]\boldsymbol{\beta}_0|$. The resulting estimate is used to compute new weights $\mathbf{q}(\boldsymbol{\beta}_1)$, and the process is repeated until the sequence of estimates converge such that $\boldsymbol{\beta}_{\mathrm{t}} \approx \boldsymbol{\beta}_{\mathrm{t}-1}$. The iterative estimation procedure is a special case of generalized least squares, which will be discussed in greater detail in Chapters 14 and 15.

7.2. ML and LS Estimators Expressed in Extremum Estimator Form

Using the concept of extremum estimation, one can formulate the general maximum likelihood estimator as the extremum estimator

$$\hat{\Theta} = \arg\max_{\theta \in \Omega}[\mathrm{m}(\boldsymbol{\theta}, \mathbf{Y}, \mathbf{x})], \tag{7.2.1}$$

where the estimation objective function is defined as

$$\mathrm{m}(\boldsymbol{\theta}, \mathbf{Y}, \mathbf{x}) \equiv \mathrm{L}(\boldsymbol{\theta}; \mathbf{Y}, \mathbf{x}). \tag{7.2.2}$$

Specific estimators are defined when $\mathrm{L}(\boldsymbol{\theta}; \mathbf{Y}, \mathbf{x})$ is given a specific functional form, such as the case in Chapter 3 in which $\mathrm{L}(\boldsymbol{\theta}; \mathbf{Y}, \mathbf{x})$ was based on the normal distribution.

In similar fashion, the least-square estimator can be characterized in standard extremum estimator form as the value of $\boldsymbol{\beta}$ that *maximizes* the metric or objective function

$$\mathrm{m}(\boldsymbol{\beta}, \mathbf{Y}, \mathbf{x}) = -\mathrm{s}(\boldsymbol{\beta}, \mathbf{Y}, \mathbf{x}) = -\frac{1}{n}(\mathbf{Y} - \mathbf{x}\boldsymbol{\beta})'(\mathbf{Y} - \mathbf{x}\boldsymbol{\beta}). \tag{7.2.3}$$

For this objective function, we have already seen in Chapter 5 that the LS-extremum estimator

$$\hat{\boldsymbol{\beta}} = \arg\max_{\boldsymbol{\beta}}[\mathrm{m}(\boldsymbol{\beta}, \mathbf{Y}, \mathbf{x})] = \arg\max_{\boldsymbol{\beta}}\left[-\frac{1}{n}(\mathbf{Y} - \mathbf{x}\boldsymbol{\beta})'(\mathbf{Y} - \mathbf{x}\boldsymbol{\beta})\right] \tag{7.2.4}$$

is characterized by the explicit estimator function $\hat{\boldsymbol{\beta}} = (\mathbf{x}'\mathbf{x})^{-1}\mathbf{x}'\mathbf{Y}$. Recognizing that the LS and ML estimators are in the class of extremum estimators permits us to use these cases for illustrating the general asymptotic results developed in the next section.

7.3. Asymptotic Properties of Extremum Estimators

We present two theorems relating to the consistency of extremum estimators and a theorem relating to asymptotic normality that cover a large number of applications. One of the consistency theorems relies on the compactness of the parameter space Ω and on the concept of *uniform convergence in probability* of random variables. Recall that a *compact* parameter space is one that is closed and bounded. Regarding the concept of *uniform* convergence in probability, note that a random variable $\mathrm{Z}(\boldsymbol{\theta})$ depending on the parameter vector $\boldsymbol{\theta}$ and on the size of the random sample n converges to a constant $\mathrm{c}(\boldsymbol{\theta})$ *uniformly* in probability on the parameter space Ω if

$$\lim_{n\to\infty} \mathrm{P}\left(\sup_{\theta\in\Omega} |\mathrm{z}(\boldsymbol{\theta}) - \mathrm{c}(\boldsymbol{\theta})| < \xi\right) = 1, \quad \forall \xi > 0. \tag{7.3.1}$$

The supremum can (always) be replaced by the maximum if the latter exists.

7.3.1. Consistency of Extremum Estimators

Our first consistency theorem for extremum estimators follows.

Theorem 7.3.1 (Consistency of Extremum Estimators): *The estimator* $\hat{\Theta} = \arg\max_{\theta\in\Omega}[\mathrm{m}(\boldsymbol{\theta}, \mathbf{Y}, \mathbf{X})]$ *converges in probability to the true value* $\boldsymbol{\theta}_0$ *of the parameter*

$\boldsymbol{\theta}$ *if*

a. $\mathrm{m}(\boldsymbol{\theta}, \mathbf{Y}, \mathbf{X})$ *converges uniformly in probability to a function of* $\boldsymbol{\theta}$, *say* $\mathrm{m}_0(\boldsymbol{\theta})$;

b. $\mathrm{m}_0(\boldsymbol{\theta})$ *is continuous in* $\boldsymbol{\theta}$;

c. $\mathrm{m}_0(\boldsymbol{\theta})$ *is uniquely maximized at* $\boldsymbol{\theta}_0$; *and*

d. Ω *is compact.*

PROOF: Newey and McFadden (1994), pp. 2121–2.

We emphasize that here, and henceforth, the phrase "true value, $\boldsymbol{\theta}_0$" is shorthand terminology for the idea that there exists an instance of the probability model that is congruent with the true data-sampling process, and this instance is indexed and identified by the parameter value $\boldsymbol{\theta}_0$.

Theorem 7.3.2 relaxes the requirements of compactness of the parameter space and of uniform convergence in probability of the estimation metric. The conditions are replaced by the requirements that the estimation metric $m(\boldsymbol{\theta}, \mathbf{Y}, \mathbf{X})$ be concave in $\boldsymbol{\theta}$ and exhibit ordinary convergence in probability and that the parameter space be convex.

Theorem 7.3.2 (Consistency of Extremum Estimators): *The estimator* $\hat{\boldsymbol{\Theta}} = \arg\max_{\boldsymbol{\theta}\in\Omega}[\mathrm{m}(\boldsymbol{\theta}, \mathbf{Y}, \mathbf{x})]$ *converges in probability to the true value* $\boldsymbol{\theta}_0$ *of the parameter* $\boldsymbol{\theta}$ *if*

a. $\mathrm{m}(\boldsymbol{\theta}, \mathbf{Y}, \mathbf{X}) \xrightarrow{p} \mathrm{m}_0(\boldsymbol{\theta})$, $\forall \boldsymbol{\theta} \in \Omega$, *where* $\mathrm{m}_0(\boldsymbol{\theta})$ *denotes a function of* $\boldsymbol{\theta}$;

b. $\mathrm{m}_0(\boldsymbol{\theta})$ *is concave in* $\boldsymbol{\theta}$;

c. $\mathrm{m}_0(\boldsymbol{\theta})$ *is uniquely maximized at* $\boldsymbol{\theta}_0$; *and*

d. Ω *is a convex set, with* $\boldsymbol{\theta}_0$ *in the interior of* Ω.

PROOF: Newey and McFadden (1994), pp. 2133–34.

The intuitive rationale underlying the consistency theorems is the same. In each case, the criterion function being optimized converges to a nonstochastic function of $\boldsymbol{\theta}$ that is maximized uniquely at the true value of $\boldsymbol{\theta}$. If the limit of the maximum of $\mathrm{m}(\boldsymbol{\theta}, \mathbf{Y}, \mathbf{X})$ is equal to maximum of the limit of $\mathrm{m}(\boldsymbol{\theta}, \mathbf{Y}, \mathbf{X})$, the arg max $\hat{\boldsymbol{\Theta}}$ of the estimation objective function will converge to the arg max of $\mathrm{m}_0(\boldsymbol{\theta})$, which is $\boldsymbol{\theta}_0$. The conditions a–d in each theorem are technical conditions ensuring that the limit of the maximum indeed is equal to the maximum of the limit and that the maximum occurs at $\boldsymbol{\theta}_0$. Newey and McFadden briefly discuss a few examples in which the distinction between the compactness and concavity conditions is important. Note that neither of the consistency theorems present *necessary* conditions for consistency.

► **Example 7.3.1:** As a member of the class of extremum estimators, the MAD estimator is consistent under suitable regularity conditions (Koenker and Bassett (1978)). Amemiya (1985, pp. 152–3), proves consistency under the conditions of Theorem 7.3.1. The GAUSS program C7Plim.gss provided in the example manual is designed to illustrate the consistency of the MAD estimator. For a sequence of sample sizes (selected by the user), GAUSS plots the extremum objective function for a special case of the estimator, $\mathrm{m}(\mu, \mathbf{y}) = \sum_{i=1}^{n} |y_i - \mu|$. The user should find that the characteristics of the function that may lead to multiple solutions in small samples diminish as n increases. Then, GAUSS conducts a nonparametric bootstrap simulation exercise to examine the consistency property for a linear regression model (selected by the user). The replicated parameter estimates are used to form box and whisker plots, and the user should find that the empirical distributions become more concentrated about the true parameter values (selected by the user) as n becomes larger.

7.3.2. Asymptotic Normality of Extremum Estimators

A general asymptotic normality result for extremum estimators is available if the estimation objective function is twice continuously differentiable in $\boldsymbol{\theta}$.

Theorem 7.3.3 (Asymptotic Normality of Extremum Estimators): *Let* $\hat{\boldsymbol{\Theta}} = \arg\max_{\boldsymbol{\theta}\in\Omega}[\mathrm{m}(\boldsymbol{\theta}, \mathbf{Y}, \mathbf{X})]$, *where*

a. $\hat{\boldsymbol{\Theta}} \xrightarrow{p} \boldsymbol{\theta}_0$, *and* $\boldsymbol{\theta}_0$ *denotes the true value of* $\boldsymbol{\theta}$;

b. $\boldsymbol{\theta}_0$ *is in the interior of* Ω;

c. $\mathrm{m}(\boldsymbol{\theta}, \mathbf{Y}, \mathbf{X})$ *is twice continuously differentiable in* $\boldsymbol{\theta}$, *at least in a neighborhood,* $\kappa(\boldsymbol{\theta}_0)$, *of* $\boldsymbol{\theta}_0$;

d. $n^{1/2}\frac{\partial \mathrm{m}(\boldsymbol{\theta},\mathbf{Y},\mathbf{X})}{\partial \boldsymbol{\theta}}\Big|_{\boldsymbol{\theta}_0} \xrightarrow{d} \mathrm{N}(\mathbf{0}, \boldsymbol{\Sigma})$;

e. $\lim_{n\to\infty} \mathrm{P}\left(\sup_{\boldsymbol{\theta}\in\kappa(\boldsymbol{\theta}_0)} \left\| \frac{\partial^2 \mathrm{m}(\boldsymbol{\theta},\mathbf{Y},\mathbf{X})}{\partial\boldsymbol{\theta}\partial\boldsymbol{\theta}'} - \mathbf{h}(\boldsymbol{\theta})\right\| < \xi\right) = 1, \forall \xi > 0$, *where* $\mathbf{h}(\boldsymbol{\theta})$ *is a function of* $\boldsymbol{\theta}$;

f. $\mathbf{h}(\boldsymbol{\theta})$ *is continuous and nonsingular at* $\boldsymbol{\theta}_0$.

Then $n^{1/2}(\hat{\boldsymbol{\Theta}} - \boldsymbol{\theta}_0) \xrightarrow{d} \mathrm{N}(\mathbf{0}, \mathbf{h}(\boldsymbol{\theta}_0)^{-1}\boldsymbol{\Sigma}\mathbf{h}(\boldsymbol{\theta}_0)^{-1})$.

PROOF: Newey and McFadden (1994), p. 2143.

Note that in the preceding theorem, $\|\mathbf{c}\|$ refers to the Euclidean distance from zero of the elements in the matrix $\mathbf{c}$, that is, $\|\mathbf{c}\| = [\mathrm{vec}(\mathbf{c})'\mathrm{vec}(\mathbf{c})]^{1/2}$, where $\mathrm{vec}(\cdot)$ denotes the columnwise vectorization (or vertical concatenation) of the elements in a matrix.

The basic rationale underlying the proof of Theorem 7.3.3 is that the extremum estimator is an asymptotically linear function of multivariate normally distributed random variables and thus that the estimator is itself asymptotically normally distributed. This is shown by first expanding the first-order conditions defining the extremum estimator in a Taylor series around $\boldsymbol{\theta}_0$, resulting in

$$\frac{\partial \mathrm{m}(\boldsymbol{\theta}, \mathbf{Y}, \mathbf{X})}{\partial \boldsymbol{\theta}} = \frac{\partial \mathrm{m}(\boldsymbol{\theta}, \mathbf{Y}, \mathbf{X})}{\partial \boldsymbol{\theta}}\bigg|_{\boldsymbol{\theta}_0} + \hat{\mathbf{h}}(\boldsymbol{\theta}_*)(\boldsymbol{\theta} - \boldsymbol{\theta}_0), \qquad (7.3.2)$$

where the value of $\boldsymbol{\theta}_*$ lies between $\boldsymbol{\theta}$ and $\boldsymbol{\theta}_0$, and may be different for each row of $\hat{\mathbf{h}}(\boldsymbol{\theta}_*)$. We emphasize that (7.3.2) is an equality, and not an approximation, which follows from the mean value theorem of calculus. Note that $\hat{\mathbf{h}}(\boldsymbol{\theta}_*)$ denotes the Hessian of the estimation objective function evaluated at $\boldsymbol{\theta}_*$. Evaluating (7.3.2) at $\boldsymbol{\theta}=\hat{\boldsymbol{\Theta}}$ results in a left-hand side value of $\mathbf{0}$ because $\hat{\boldsymbol{\Theta}}$ satisfies the first-order conditions. Then after multiplying (7.3.2) by $n^{1/2}$, the conditions of the theorem ensure that the first term on the right-hand side converges in distribution to $\mathrm{N}(\mathbf{0}, \Sigma)$, and $\hat{\mathbf{h}}(\boldsymbol{\theta}_*) \xrightarrow{p} \mathbf{h}(\boldsymbol{\theta}_0)$, and thus that solving for $n^{1/2}(\hat{\boldsymbol{\Theta}} - \boldsymbol{\theta}_0)$ yields

$$n^{1/2}(\hat{\boldsymbol{\Theta}} - \boldsymbol{\theta}_0) \xrightarrow{d} \mathbf{h}(\boldsymbol{\theta}_0)^{-1} n^{1/2} \left.\frac{\partial \mathrm{m}(\boldsymbol{\theta}, \mathbf{Y}, \mathbf{X})}{\partial \boldsymbol{\theta}}\right|_{\boldsymbol{\theta}_0}. \tag{7.3.3}$$

It follows that $n^{1/2}(\hat{\boldsymbol{\Theta}} - \boldsymbol{\theta}_0)$ has the limiting distribution stated in the theorem based on Slutsky's theorem (which states that if $\mathbf{W}_n \xrightarrow{p} \mathbf{w}_0$ and $\mathrm{V}_n \xrightarrow{d} \mathbf{V}$, then $\mathbf{W}_n\mathbf{V}_n \xrightarrow{d} \mathbf{w}_0\mathbf{V}$) and the fact that linear combinations of multivariate normally distributed random variables are normally distributed.

Theorem 7.3.3 provides only sufficient conditions for asymptotic normality of extremum estimators, and these conditions can be notably weakened in special cases. We will return to this issue when we discuss such concepts as generalized method of moments (GMM) estimators (Chapter 16), empirical likelihood estimators (Chapter 12), and maximum entropy estimators (Chapter 13). Given these general results, we return in the next section to the problem of estimating $\boldsymbol{\beta}$ and σ^2 in the multivariate normal linear regression model and see how we can investigate the asymptotic properties of ML estimators within the context of extremum estimation.

► **Example 7.3.2:** As a member of the class of extremum estimators, the MAD estimator is also asymptotically normal under suitable regularity conditions (Koenker and Bassett (1978), Amemiya (1985, p. 154)). The GAUSS program C7CLT.gss provided in the example manual is designed to demonstrate the limiting normal distribution of the MAD estimator. GAUSS conducts a nonparametric bootstrap simulation exercise to examine the asymptotic normality of the estimator for a linear regression model (selected by the user). The replicated parameter estimates are used to form EDFs for a sequence of sample sizes, and the user should find that the EDFs approach the limiting normal distribution as n becomes large.

7.4. Asymptotic Properties of Maximum Likelihood Estimators in an Extremum Estimator Context

We noted in Section 7.1 that the ML criterion for estimating $\boldsymbol{\theta}$ is subsumed under the extremum estimation concept. We also noted in Section 7.2 that the maximum likelihood estimator can be represented in extremum estimator form as

$$\hat{\boldsymbol{\Theta}} = \arg\max_{\boldsymbol{\theta}\in\Omega}[\mathrm{m}(\boldsymbol{\theta}, \mathbf{Y}, \mathbf{x})], \tag{7.4.1}$$

where the estimation objective function is defined specifically as

$$\mathrm{m}(\boldsymbol{\theta}, \mathbf{Y}, \mathbf{x}) \equiv \mathrm{L}(\boldsymbol{\theta}; \mathbf{Y}, \mathbf{x}). \tag{7.4.2}$$

Recognizing that the maximum likelihood estimator is in the class of extremum estimators allows us to transfer the general asymptotic results for extremum estimation discussed in Section 7.3 to the case of ML estimation. Of course the previous discussion in Section 3.4 settled the issue of the consistency and asymptotic normality of the ML or bias-adjusted ML estimator of $\boldsymbol{\beta}$ and σ^2 in the context of the multivariate normal linear regression model. However, we revisit the issue in the context of extremum estimation to establish and motivate more general results that can be applied to ML estimation problems in other parametric probability models.

7.4.1. Consistency of the ML-Extremum Estimator

The specialization of Theorem 7.3.1 to the case in which the extremum estimation objective function is expressed in terms of the likelihood function leads to a general theorem on the consistency of the ML estimator. For the purpose of establishing asymptotic results, we represent the estimation objective function in terms of the scaled (by the sample size) logarithmic transformation of the likelihood function, $\mathrm{m}(\boldsymbol{\theta}, \mathbf{Y}, \mathbf{x}) \equiv n^{-1} \ln \mathrm{L}(\boldsymbol{\theta}; \mathbf{Y}, \mathbf{x})$, and the extremum-ML estimator is then defined by

$$\hat{\boldsymbol{\Theta}} = \arg \max_{\boldsymbol{\theta} \in \Omega} [n^{-1} \ln \mathrm{L}(\boldsymbol{\theta}; \mathbf{Y}, \mathbf{x})]. \tag{7.4.3}$$

The restatement of Theorem 7.3.1 for the special case of consistency of the ML-extremum estimator follows, and the proof is analogous to that of Theorem 7.3.1.

Theorem 7.4.1 (Consistency of the ML-Extremum Estimator): *The ML-extremum estimator* $\hat{\boldsymbol{\Theta}}$ *in* (7.4.3) *converges in probability to the true value* $\boldsymbol{\theta}_0$ *of the parameter* $\boldsymbol{\theta}$ *if*

a. $n^{-1} \ln \mathrm{L}(\boldsymbol{\theta}; \mathbf{Y}, \mathbf{x})$ *converges uniformly in probability to a function of* $\boldsymbol{\theta}$, $\mathrm{L}_0(\boldsymbol{\theta})$*;*

b. $\mathrm{L}_0(\boldsymbol{\theta})$ *is continuous in* $\boldsymbol{\theta}$*;*

c. $\mathrm{L}_0(\boldsymbol{\theta})$ *is uniquely maximized at* $\boldsymbol{\theta}_0$*;*

d. Ω *is compact.*

Regarding the implications of conditions a–d in the theorem, our discussion following Theorems 7.3.1 and 7.3.2 remains relevant. In addition, the basic rationale underlying the theorem remains the same as before. If $n^{-1}\ln \mathrm{L}(\boldsymbol{\theta}; \mathbf{Y}, \mathbf{x})$ converges uniformly in probability to $\mathrm{L}_0(\boldsymbol{\theta})$, the latter being continuous and uniquely maximized by $\boldsymbol{\theta}_0$ over the compact set Ω, then the limit of the maximum is the maximum of the limit, and thus $\hat{\boldsymbol{\Theta}}$ converges to the value that maximizes $\mathrm{L}_0(\boldsymbol{\theta})$, namely, $\boldsymbol{\theta}_0$. Theorem 7.3.2 could also be specialized to provide a statement of the consistency of the ML estimator in the absence of compactness of the parameter space. We leave it to the reader to restate Theorem 7.3.2 for the likelihood function case. In general, a variety of different types of regularity conditions are available to achieve consistency of the ML-extremum estimator in addition to those stated above. The possibilities are considered broad enough that the property of consistency is assumed to hold quite generally in practice for the ML estimator.

7.4.2. Asymptotic Normality of the ML-Extremum Estimator

Theorem 7.3.3 on the asymptotic normality of extremum estimators can be restated for the special case of the ML-extremum estimator as follows. Again, the proof of the theorem is analogous to the proof of Theorem 7.3.3.

Theorem 7.4.2 (Asymptotic Normality of the ML-Extremum Estimator): *The ML-Extremum estimator* $\hat{\boldsymbol{\Theta}}$ *in* (7.4.3) *is asymptotically normally distributed as*

$$n^{1/2}(\hat{\boldsymbol{\Theta}} - \boldsymbol{\theta}_0) \xrightarrow{d} \mathrm{N}[\mathbf{0}, \mathbf{h}(\boldsymbol{\theta}_0)^{-1}\boldsymbol{\Sigma}\mathbf{h}(\boldsymbol{\theta}_0)^{-1}]$$

if

a. $\hat{\boldsymbol{\Theta}} \xrightarrow{p} \boldsymbol{\theta}_0$ *where* $\boldsymbol{\theta}_0$ *is the true value of* $\boldsymbol{\theta}$,

b. $\boldsymbol{\theta}_0$ *is in the interior of* Ω,

c. $n^{-1} \ln \mathrm{L}(\boldsymbol{\theta}; \mathbf{Y}, \mathbf{x})$ *is twice continuously differentiable in* $\boldsymbol{\theta}$, *at least in a neighbourhood,* $\kappa(\boldsymbol{\theta}_0)$, *of* $\boldsymbol{\theta}_0$,

d. $n^{-1/2} \frac{\partial \ln \mathrm{L}(\boldsymbol{\theta}; \mathbf{Y}, \mathbf{x})}{\partial \boldsymbol{\theta}}\Big|_{\boldsymbol{\theta}_0} \xrightarrow{d} \mathrm{N}(\mathbf{0}, \boldsymbol{\Sigma})$,

e. $n^{-1} \frac{\partial^2 \ln \mathrm{L}(\boldsymbol{\theta}; \mathbf{Y}, \mathbf{x})}{\partial \boldsymbol{\theta} \partial \boldsymbol{\theta}'}$ *converges uniformly in probability to the matrix function* $\mathbf{h}(\boldsymbol{\theta})\ \forall \boldsymbol{\theta} \in \kappa\ (\boldsymbol{\theta}_0)$, *and*

f. $\mathbf{h}(\boldsymbol{\theta})$ *is continuous and nonsingular at* $\boldsymbol{\theta} = \boldsymbol{\theta}_0$.

The implications of the assumptions and the rationale underlying the theorem parallel those presented following Theorem 7.3.3. In short, the conditions of the theorem ensure that the Taylor series expansion (let $\mathrm{L}(\boldsymbol{\theta}) \equiv \mathrm{L}(\boldsymbol{\theta}; \mathbf{Y}, \mathbf{x})$ and recall (7.3.3))

$$n^{-1/2}\frac{\partial \ln \mathrm{L}(\boldsymbol{\theta})}{\partial \boldsymbol{\theta}} = n^{-1/2}\frac{\partial \ln \mathrm{L}(\boldsymbol{\theta})}{\partial \boldsymbol{\theta}}\bigg|_{\boldsymbol{\theta}_0} + n^{-1}\frac{\partial^2 \ln \mathrm{L}(\boldsymbol{\theta})}{\partial \boldsymbol{\theta}\partial \boldsymbol{\theta}'}\bigg|_{\boldsymbol{\theta}_0} n^{1/2}(\boldsymbol{\theta} - \boldsymbol{\theta}_0) + \mathbf{o}_p(1), \tag{7.4.4}$$

when evaluated at $\boldsymbol{\theta} = \hat{\boldsymbol{\Theta}}$, can be solved for $n^{1/2}(\hat{\boldsymbol{\Theta}} - \boldsymbol{\theta}_0)$, yielding

$$n^{1/2}(\hat{\boldsymbol{\Theta}} - \boldsymbol{\theta}_0) = -\left[n^{-1}\frac{\partial^2 \ln \mathrm{L}(\boldsymbol{\theta})}{\partial \boldsymbol{\theta}\partial \boldsymbol{\theta}'}\bigg|_{\boldsymbol{\theta}_0}\right]^{-1} n^{-1/2}\frac{\partial \ln \mathrm{L}(\boldsymbol{\theta})}{\partial \boldsymbol{\theta}}\bigg|_{\boldsymbol{\theta}_0} + \mathbf{o}_p(1), \tag{7.4.5}$$

in which case conditions d and e in the theorem and Slutsky's theorem (which states that if $\mathbf{W}_n \xrightarrow{p} \mathbf{w}_0$ and $\mathbf{V}_n \xrightarrow{d} \mathbf{V}$, then $\mathbf{W}_n\mathbf{V}_n \xrightarrow{d} \mathbf{w}_0\mathbf{V}$) lead to the final statement of the theorem.

In the special case of the multivariate normal linear regression model, where $\boldsymbol{\theta} = \binom{\boldsymbol{\beta}}{\sigma^2}$, it can be shown that $\mathbf{h}(\boldsymbol{\theta}_0)^{-1}\boldsymbol{\Sigma}\mathbf{h}(\boldsymbol{\theta}_0)^{-1} = \left[\begin{array}{c|c} \sigma^2\Xi^{-1} & \mathbf{0} \\ \hline \mathbf{0} & 2\sigma^4 \end{array}\right]$ under the conditions in Table 7.1, Theorem 7.4.1, and Theorem 7.4.2, where $\lim_{n\to\infty} n^{-1}\mathbf{x}'\mathbf{x} = \Xi$. In applications, Ξ^{-1} is replaced by $n(\mathbf{x}'\mathbf{x})^{-1}$ and σ^4 is replaced by the estimator S^4 to achieve an operational version of the asymptotic covariance matrix of the limiting distribution. Thus, by applying Theorem 7.4.2 to the case of the multivariate normal regression model, we are led to the limiting distribution result

$$n^{1/2}(\hat{\Theta} - \boldsymbol{\theta}_0) \xrightarrow{d} \mathrm{N}\left(\mathbf{0}, \begin{bmatrix} \sigma^2\boldsymbol{\Xi}^{-1} & \mathbf{0} \\ \mathbf{0} & 2\sigma^4 \end{bmatrix}\right), \tag{7.4.6}$$

which is in agreement with the results stated previously in Section 3.4.2.

As in the case of consistency, various types of regularity conditions can be invoked for the MLE to exhibit asymptotic normality in addition to those discussed here. The possibilities are considered broad enough that the property of asymptotic normality is assumed to hold quite generally in practice for the ML estimator. Thus, a basis for asymptotic inference is established.

7.5. Asymptotic Properties of the Least-Squares Estimator in an Extremum Estimator Context

We noted in Section 7.1 that the LS criterion for estimating $\boldsymbol{\theta}$ is subsumed under the extremum estimation concept. We also noted in Section 7.2 that the LS estimator can be represented in extremum estimator form as

$$\hat{\boldsymbol{\beta}} = \arg\max_{\boldsymbol{\beta}}[\mathrm{m}(\boldsymbol{\beta}, \mathbf{Y}, \mathbf{x})] = \arg\max_{\boldsymbol{\beta}}\left[-\frac{1}{n}(\mathbf{Y} - \mathbf{x}\boldsymbol{\beta})'(\mathbf{Y} - \mathbf{x}\boldsymbol{\beta})\right] = (\mathbf{x}'\mathbf{x})^{-1}\mathbf{x}'\mathbf{Y}, \tag{7.5.1}$$

where the estimation objective function is defined specifically as

$$\mathrm{m}(\boldsymbol{\beta}, \mathbf{Y}, \mathbf{x}) = -\mathrm{s}(\boldsymbol{\beta}, \mathbf{Y}, \mathbf{x}) = -\frac{1}{n}(\mathbf{Y} - \mathbf{x}\boldsymbol{\beta})'(\mathbf{Y} - \mathbf{x}\boldsymbol{\beta}). \tag{7.5.2}$$

In this section we demonstrate how the general theorems in Section 7.3 on extremum estimator asymptotics, originally presented by Newey and McFadden (1994), can be applied to establish asymptotic properties of the LS estimator. The demonstrations serve as alternatives to Theorems 5.3.2 and 5.3.3 for establishing asymptotic properties of $\hat{\boldsymbol{\beta}}$. The demonstrations illustrate a method of establishing asymptotic properties that can also be applied to estimators in cases where more direct derivations of asymptotic properties are intractable.

7.5.1. Consistency of the LS–Extremum Estimator

A demonstration that the corresponding extremum estimator is consistent can be based on an application of Theorem 7.3.2. First of all, note that for the estimation objective function (7.5.2),

$$\begin{aligned}\mathrm{m}(\boldsymbol{\beta}, \mathbf{Y}, \mathbf{x}) &= -n^{-1}[(\mathbf{Y} - \mathbf{x}\boldsymbol{\beta}_0) + (\mathbf{x}\boldsymbol{\beta}_0 - \mathbf{x}\boldsymbol{\beta})]'[(\mathbf{Y} - \mathbf{x}\boldsymbol{\beta}_0) + (\mathbf{x}\boldsymbol{\beta}_0 - \mathbf{x}\boldsymbol{\beta})] \\ &= -n^{-1}\boldsymbol{\varepsilon}'\boldsymbol{\varepsilon} + 2n^{-1}(\boldsymbol{\beta} - \boldsymbol{\beta}_0)'\mathbf{x}'\boldsymbol{\varepsilon} - n^{-1}(\boldsymbol{\beta} - \boldsymbol{\beta}_0)'\mathbf{x}'\mathbf{x}(\boldsymbol{\beta} - \boldsymbol{\beta}_0),\end{aligned} \tag{7.5.3}$$

where $\boldsymbol{\beta}_0$ denotes the true value of $\boldsymbol{\beta}$ and thus $\boldsymbol{\varepsilon} = \mathbf{Y} - \mathbf{x}\boldsymbol{\beta}_0$. Now assume in addition to the probability model characteristics in Table 7.1 that either $\mathrm{E}\varepsilon_i^4 \leq \xi < \infty \, \forall i$, that is, the fourth-order moments of the ε_i's are bounded, or else the ε_i's are iid. Then, by a WLLN, or else by Khinchin's WLLN in the iid case, $-n^{-1}\boldsymbol{\varepsilon}'\boldsymbol{\varepsilon} \xrightarrow{p} -\sigma^2$ (see Chapter E1, or Mittelhammer (1996), Section 5.2).

Furthermore, assume that $n^{-1}\mathbf{x}'\mathbf{x} \to \boldsymbol{\Xi}$, a finite positive definite symmetric matrix. Then, because $\mathrm{E}[2n^{-1}(\boldsymbol{\beta} - \boldsymbol{\beta}_0)'\mathbf{x}'\boldsymbol{\varepsilon}] = \mathbf{0}$ and $\mathrm{var}(2n^{-1}(\boldsymbol{\beta} - \boldsymbol{\beta}_0)'\mathbf{x}'\boldsymbol{\varepsilon}) = 4\sigma^2 n^{-2}(\boldsymbol{\beta} - \boldsymbol{\beta}_0)'(n^{-1}\mathbf{x}'\mathbf{x})(\boldsymbol{\beta} - \boldsymbol{\beta}_0) \to 0$ as $n \to \infty$, it follows that $2n^{-1}(\boldsymbol{\beta} - \boldsymbol{\beta}_0)'\mathbf{x}'\boldsymbol{\varepsilon} \xrightarrow{p} 0$ by mean-square convergence. Then

$$\mathrm{m}(\boldsymbol{\beta}, \mathbf{Y}, \mathbf{x}) \xrightarrow{p} \mathrm{m}_0(\boldsymbol{\beta}) = -\sigma^2 - (\boldsymbol{\beta} - \boldsymbol{\beta}_0)'\boldsymbol{\Xi}(\boldsymbol{\beta} - \boldsymbol{\beta}_0), \ \forall \boldsymbol{\beta}, \tag{7.5.4}$$

which is concave in $\boldsymbol{\beta}$ because $\frac{\partial^2 \mathrm{m}_0(\boldsymbol{\beta})}{\partial \boldsymbol{\beta} \partial \boldsymbol{\beta}'} = -2\boldsymbol{\Xi}$ is negative definite. The unique maximum of $\mathrm{m}_0(\boldsymbol{\beta})$ occurs when $\boldsymbol{\beta} = \boldsymbol{\beta}_0$. Furthermore, because $\Omega = \mathrm{R}^k$ in the current statistical model, it follows that Ω is convex and $\boldsymbol{\beta}_0$ is clearly interior to Ω. Thus, all of the conditions of Theorem 7.3.2 are verified, and we can conclude that the LS–extremum estimator is consistent. If Ω were alternatively assumed to be compact, which is often an admissible assumption in practice, Theorem 7.3.1 could be invoked to provide an alternative demonstration of the consistency of the LS–extremum estimator.

7.5.2. Asymptotic Normality of the LS–Extremum Estimator

Regarding asymptotic normality of $\hat{\boldsymbol{\beta}}$, consider the application of Theorem 7.3.3. On the basis of the preceding consistency demonstration, we can claim that conditions a and b of Theorem 7.3.3 apply. We also know that $\mathrm{m}(\boldsymbol{\beta}, \mathbf{Y}, \mathbf{x})$ is twice continuously differentiable because $\frac{\partial^2 \mathrm{m}(\boldsymbol{\beta}, \mathbf{Y}, \mathbf{x})}{\partial \boldsymbol{\beta} \partial \boldsymbol{\beta}'} = -2n^{-1}\mathbf{x}'\mathbf{x}$, thus satisfying condition c. To establish condition d, note that

$$n^{1/2} \frac{\partial \mathrm{m}(\boldsymbol{\beta}, \mathbf{Y}, \mathbf{x})}{\partial \boldsymbol{\beta}}\bigg|_{\boldsymbol{\beta}_0} = 2n^{-1/2}[\mathbf{x}'(\mathbf{Y} - \mathbf{x}\boldsymbol{\beta}_0)] = 2n^{-1/2}\mathbf{x}'\boldsymbol{\varepsilon} \xrightarrow{d} \mathrm{N}(\mathbf{0}, 4\sigma^2\boldsymbol{\Xi}), \tag{7.5.5}$$

which follows from the same CLT arguments used in the proof of Theorem 5.3.3, and thus $\boldsymbol{\Sigma} = 4\sigma^2\boldsymbol{\Xi}$ in Theorem 7.3.3. Condition e can be established by noting that $\frac{\partial^2 \mathrm{m}(\boldsymbol{\beta}, \mathbf{Y}, \mathbf{x})}{\partial \boldsymbol{\beta} \partial \boldsymbol{\beta}'} = -2n^{-1}\mathbf{x}'\mathbf{x}$ does not depend on the value of $\boldsymbol{\beta}$, and thus condition e can be written as

$$\lim_{n\to\infty} \mathrm{P}\left(\sup_{\boldsymbol{\beta} \in \kappa(\boldsymbol{\beta}_0)} \| -2n^{-1}\mathbf{x}'\mathbf{x} - \mathbf{h}(\boldsymbol{\beta}) \| < \xi \right)$$
$$\equiv \lim_{n\to\infty} \mathrm{P}(\| -2n^{-1}\mathbf{x}'\mathbf{x} - \mathbf{h}_0 \| < \xi) = 1, \ \forall \xi > 0. \tag{7.5.6}$$

Thus, $\mathbf{h}(\boldsymbol{\beta}) \equiv \mathbf{h}_0 = -2\boldsymbol{\Xi}$, which as a constant function in $\boldsymbol{\beta}$ is certainly continuous in $\boldsymbol{\beta}$ and nonsingular at $\boldsymbol{\beta}_0$ because $\boldsymbol{\Xi}$ is nonsingular, establishing condition f. Having established all of the conditions of Theorem 7.3.3, it follows that

$$n^{1/2}(\hat{\boldsymbol{\beta}} - \boldsymbol{\beta}_0) \xrightarrow{d} \mathrm{N}[\mathbf{0}, (-2\boldsymbol{\Xi})^{-1}(4\sigma^2\boldsymbol{\Xi})(-2\boldsymbol{\Xi})^{-1}] = \mathrm{N}(\mathbf{0}, \sigma^2\boldsymbol{\Xi}^{-1}), \tag{7.5.7}$$

which is precisely the conclusion of Theorem 5.3.3. Thus, the LS–extremum estimator is asymptotically normally distributed. As we noted previously, the asymptotic distribution is estimated by replacing Ξ with $n^{-1}\mathbf{x}'\mathbf{x}$ and σ^2 with the consistent estimate s^2.

The preceding demonstrations of the asymptotic properties of the extremum estimator $\hat{\boldsymbol{\beta}}$ illustrate how the theorems in Section 7.3 can be applied. In the current linear regression model context we had the distinct advantage of also being able to establish these properties via a direct analysis of the explicit estimator function itself, as in Theorems 5.3.2 and 5.3.3. In more complicated estimation problems, we must often rely on indirect methods of deriving asymptotic properties based on results such as Theorems 7.3.1–7.3.3.

7.6. Inference Based on Extremum Estimation

Asymptotically valid hypotheses-testing and confidence-region procedures for the entire class of extremum estimators can be based on the asymptotic properties of the estimators in the class. This provides at least an approximate method of testing hypotheses and generating confidence regions about linear combinations of the elements in the parameter vector when finite sample distributions of test and confidence-region procedures cannot be established (we address nonlinear functions of the parameters in the next chapter). Utilizing the consistency and asymptotic normality of extremum estimators, asymptotically valid Wald, Lagrange multiplier, and pseudo-likelihood ratio tests (the latter also called quasi-likelihood, distance metric, or likelihood ratio [in the parametric case] tests) for the general hypothesis H_0: $\mathbf{c}\boldsymbol{\theta} = \mathbf{r}$ can readily be defined. Asymptotically valid tests of inequality hypotheses can be based on an asymptotically normally distributed Z-statistic. Confidence region estimators can be defined in the usual way based on duality with hypothesis testing procedures.

7.6.1. Lagrange Multiplier Tests and Confidence Regions

The Lagrange multiplier (LM) test is based on the statistical behavior of the Lagrange multipliers in the Lagrangian form of the *constrained* (by H_0) extremum estimation problem defining the *restricted* extremum estimate

$$\hat{\boldsymbol{\theta}}_r = \arg\max_{\boldsymbol{\theta}}[\mathrm{m}(\boldsymbol{\theta}, \mathbf{Y}, \mathbf{X}) \text{ subject to } \mathbf{c}\boldsymbol{\theta} = \mathbf{r}]. \tag{7.6.1}$$

The Lagrange form of the estimation objective function associated with constrained least-squares minimization problem can be defined as

$$\mathrm{L}(\boldsymbol{\theta}, \gamma) = [\mathrm{m}(\boldsymbol{\theta}, \mathbf{Y}, \mathbf{X}) - \gamma'(\mathbf{c}\boldsymbol{\theta} - \mathbf{r})], \tag{7.6.2}$$

where γ is a $(j \times 1)$ vector of Lagrange multipliers corresponding to the j constraints $\mathbf{c}\boldsymbol{\theta} = \mathbf{r}$.

The first-order conditions corresponding to (7.6.2) are given by

$$\frac{\partial \mathrm{L}}{\partial \boldsymbol{\theta}} = \frac{\partial \mathrm{m}(\boldsymbol{\theta}, \mathbf{Y}, \mathbf{X})}{\partial \boldsymbol{\theta}} - \mathbf{c}'\gamma = \mathbf{0} \tag{7.6.3}$$

and

$$\frac{\partial \mathrm{L}}{\partial \boldsymbol{\gamma}} = \mathbf{r} - \mathbf{c}\boldsymbol{\theta} = \mathbf{0}. \tag{7.6.4}$$

Let $\hat{\boldsymbol{\Theta}}_\mathrm{r}$ and $\boldsymbol{\Gamma}_\mathrm{r}$ denote the solutions to the restricted extremum estimation problem. Evaluate the first-order conditions at $(\hat{\boldsymbol{\Theta}}_\mathrm{r}, \boldsymbol{\Gamma}_\mathrm{r})$ and then expand $\frac{\partial \mathrm{m}(\boldsymbol{\theta}, \mathbf{Y}, \mathbf{X})}{\partial \boldsymbol{\theta}}\big|_{\hat{\boldsymbol{\Theta}}_\mathrm{r}}$ in (7.6.3) in a first-order Taylor series around the true value of $\boldsymbol{\theta}$, say $\boldsymbol{\theta}_0$. Assuming H_0: $\mathbf{c}\boldsymbol{\theta} = \mathbf{r}$ is *true*, it follows from (7.6.3) and (7.6.4) that

$$\left.\frac{\partial \mathrm{m}(\boldsymbol{\theta}, \mathbf{Y}, \mathbf{X})}{\partial \boldsymbol{\theta}}\right|_{\boldsymbol{\theta}_0} + \left.\frac{\partial^2 \mathrm{m}(\boldsymbol{\theta}, \mathbf{Y}, \mathbf{X})}{\partial \boldsymbol{\theta}\partial \boldsymbol{\theta}'}\right|_{\boldsymbol{\theta}_*} (\hat{\boldsymbol{\Theta}}_\mathrm{r} - \boldsymbol{\theta}_0) - \mathbf{c}'\boldsymbol{\Gamma}_\mathrm{r} = \mathbf{0}. \tag{7.6.5}$$

and

$$\mathbf{c}(\hat{\boldsymbol{\Theta}}_\mathrm{r} - \boldsymbol{\theta}_0) = \mathbf{0}. \tag{7.6.6}$$

Note that $\boldsymbol{\theta}_*$ in (7.6.5) is a convex combination of $\hat{\boldsymbol{\Theta}}_\mathrm{r}$ and $\boldsymbol{\theta}_0$. Furthermore, we have notationally suppressed the fact that different values of the $\boldsymbol{\theta}_*$ vector will generally be required for each row of $\frac{\partial^2 \mathrm{m}(\boldsymbol{\theta}, \mathbf{Y}, \mathbf{X})}{\partial \boldsymbol{\theta}\partial \boldsymbol{\theta}'}$. Multiplying (7.6.5) and (7.6.6) by $n^{1/2}$, and then rearranging terms leads to the partitioned matrix expression

$$\begin{bmatrix} -\left.\frac{\partial^2 \mathrm{m}(\boldsymbol{\theta}, \mathbf{Y}, \mathbf{X})}{\partial \boldsymbol{\theta}\partial \boldsymbol{\theta}'}\right|_{\boldsymbol{\theta}_*} & \mathbf{c}' \\ \mathbf{c} & \mathbf{0} \end{bmatrix} \begin{bmatrix} n^{1/2}(\hat{\boldsymbol{\Theta}}_\mathrm{r} - \boldsymbol{\theta}_0) \\ n^{1/2}\boldsymbol{\Gamma}_\mathrm{r} \end{bmatrix} = \begin{bmatrix} n^{1/2}\left.\frac{\partial \mathrm{m}(\boldsymbol{\theta}, \mathbf{Y}, \mathbf{X})}{\partial \boldsymbol{\theta}}\right|_{\boldsymbol{\theta}_0} \\ \mathbf{0} \end{bmatrix} \tag{7.6.7}$$

Given the conditions in Theorem 7.3.3 that ensure the consistency and asymptotic normality of the (unconstrained) extremum estimator we know that on the right side of (7.6.7), $n^{1/2}\frac{\partial \mathrm{m}(\boldsymbol{\theta}, \mathbf{Y}, \mathbf{X})}{\partial \boldsymbol{\theta}}\big|_{\boldsymbol{\theta}_0} \xrightarrow{d} \mathrm{N}(\mathbf{0}, \boldsymbol{\Sigma})$. Regarding the left-most partitioned matrix in (7.6.7), the upper left block is composed of derivatives evaluated at $\boldsymbol{\theta}_*$. However, in the limit, under H_0, $\hat{\boldsymbol{\Theta}}_\mathrm{r} \xrightarrow{p} \boldsymbol{\theta}_0$, and because $\boldsymbol{\theta}_*$ is a convex combinations of $\hat{\boldsymbol{\Theta}}_\mathrm{r}$ and $\boldsymbol{\theta}_0$, it follows that $\boldsymbol{\theta}_* \xrightarrow{p} \boldsymbol{\theta}_0$ as well. Then, from Slutsky's theorem (i.e., if $\mathbf{W}_n \xrightarrow{p} \mathbf{w}_0$ and $\mathbf{V}_n \xrightarrow{d} \mathbf{V}$, then $\mathbf{W}_n\mathbf{V}_n \xrightarrow{d} \mathbf{w}_0\mathbf{V}$) and given that $\frac{\partial^2 \mathrm{m}(\boldsymbol{\theta}, \mathbf{Y}, \mathbf{X})}{\partial \boldsymbol{\theta}\partial \boldsymbol{\theta}'}\big|_{\boldsymbol{\theta}_*} \xrightarrow{p} \mathbf{h}(\boldsymbol{\theta}_0)$ (see Theorem 7.3.3), the information content of (7.6.7) relating to the limiting distributions of $n^{1/2}(\hat{\boldsymbol{\Theta}}_\mathrm{r} - \boldsymbol{\theta}_0)$ and $n^{1/2}\boldsymbol{\Gamma}_\mathrm{r}$ is equivalent to that of

$$\begin{bmatrix} -\mathbf{h}(\boldsymbol{\theta}_0) & \mathbf{c}' \\ \mathbf{c} & \mathbf{0} \end{bmatrix} \begin{bmatrix} n^{1/2}(\hat{\boldsymbol{\Theta}}_\mathrm{r} - \boldsymbol{\theta}_0) \\ n^{1/2}\boldsymbol{\Gamma}_\mathrm{r} \end{bmatrix} = \begin{bmatrix} \mathbf{Z} \\ \mathbf{0} \end{bmatrix}, \tag{7.6.8}$$

where $\mathbf{Z} \sim \mathrm{N}(\mathbf{0}, \boldsymbol{\Sigma})$. Partitioned inversion of the left-most matrix leads to

$$n^{1/2}\boldsymbol{\Gamma}_\mathrm{r} = [\mathbf{c}(\mathbf{h}(\boldsymbol{\theta}_0)^{-1})\mathbf{c}']^{-1}\mathbf{c}\mathbf{h}(\boldsymbol{\theta}_0)^{-1}\mathbf{Z}. \tag{7.6.9}$$

Finally, by the properties of linear combinations of multivariate normally distributed random variables $\mathbf{Z}$, it follows from (7.6.9) that

$$n^{1/2}\boldsymbol{\Gamma}_\mathrm{r} \overset{a}{\sim} \mathrm{N}(\mathbf{0}, [\mathbf{c}(\mathbf{h}(\boldsymbol{\theta}_0)^{-1})\mathbf{c}']^{-1}(\mathbf{c}\mathbf{h}(\boldsymbol{\theta}_0)^{-1}\boldsymbol{\Sigma}\mathbf{h}(\boldsymbol{\theta}_0)^{-1}\mathbf{c}')[\mathbf{c}(\mathbf{h}(\boldsymbol{\theta}_0)^{-1})\mathbf{c}']^{-1}). \tag{7.6.10}$$

Note that for some estimation objective functions, and under the conditions of Theorem 7.3.3, the asymptotic covariance matrix in (7.6.10) can be substantially simplified to

$$n^{1/2}\boldsymbol{\Gamma}_{\mathrm{r}} \overset{\mathrm{a}}{\sim} \mathrm{N}(\mathbf{0}, (\mathbf{c}\boldsymbol{\Sigma}^{-1}\mathbf{c}')^{-1}) \tag{7.6.11}$$

because $\boldsymbol{\Sigma} = \tau\mathbf{h}(\boldsymbol{\theta}_0)$ for some scalar τ. Such is the case for both the ML and LS estimation objective functions examined in Chapters 3–6. For example, in the LS case with estimation objective function (7.5.2), $\boldsymbol{\Sigma} = 4\sigma^2\boldsymbol{\Xi}$ and $\mathbf{h}(\boldsymbol{\beta}_0) = -2\boldsymbol{\Xi}$, where $\boldsymbol{\Xi} = \lim_{n\to\infty}(n^{-1}\mathbf{x}'\mathbf{x})$, which is consistent with the asymptotic results for $\hat{\boldsymbol{\Gamma}}_{\mathrm{r}}$ obtained in Section 6.2.2.a.

7.6.1.a. Classical Form of LM Tests and Confidence Regions

On the basis of asymptotic normal approximation to the probability distribution of $\hat{\boldsymbol{\Gamma}}_{\mathrm{r}}$ in (7.6.10), and *on the assumption that* H_0 *is true*, we have that

$$[[\mathbf{c}(\mathbf{h}(\boldsymbol{\theta}_0)^{-1})\mathbf{c}']^{-1}(\mathbf{c}\mathbf{h}(\boldsymbol{\theta}_0)^{-1}\boldsymbol{\Sigma}\mathbf{h}(\boldsymbol{\theta}_0)^{-1}\mathbf{c}')[\mathbf{c}(\mathbf{h}(\boldsymbol{\theta}_0)^{-1})\mathbf{c}']^{-1}]^{-1/2}n^{1/2}\boldsymbol{\Gamma}_{\mathrm{r}} \overset{\mathrm{a}}{\sim} \mathrm{N}(\mathbf{0}, \mathbf{I}_j). \tag{7.6.12}$$

It follows immediately that, under H_0, the sum of the squares of the elements in the $(j \times 1)$ random vector in (7.6.12) has a central Chi-square distribution as

$$n\boldsymbol{\Gamma}_{\mathrm{r}}'[\mathbf{c}(\mathbf{h}(\boldsymbol{\theta}_0)^{-1})\mathbf{c}'](\mathbf{c}\mathbf{h}(\boldsymbol{\theta}_0)^{-1}\boldsymbol{\Sigma}\mathbf{h}(\boldsymbol{\theta}_0)^{-1}\mathbf{c}')^{-1}[\mathbf{c}(\mathbf{h}(\boldsymbol{\theta}_0)^{-1})\mathbf{c}']\boldsymbol{\Gamma}_{\mathrm{r}} \sim \text{Chi-square}(j, 0), \tag{7.6.13}$$

which can be simplified to

$$n\boldsymbol{\Gamma}_{\mathrm{r}}'(\mathbf{c}\boldsymbol{\Sigma}^{-1}\mathbf{c}')\boldsymbol{\Gamma}_{\mathrm{r}} \sim \text{Chi-square}(j, 0) \tag{7.6.14}$$

in the special case where $\boldsymbol{\Sigma} = \tau\mathbf{h}(\boldsymbol{\theta}_0)$.

To define an operational test of H_0 based on (7.6.13) or (7.6.14), the matrices $\boldsymbol{\Sigma}$ and $\mathbf{h}(\boldsymbol{\theta}_0)$ are replaced by consistent estimators, yielding

$$\mathrm{LM} = \mathrm{n}\boldsymbol{\Gamma}_{\mathrm{r}}'[\mathbf{c}(\hat{\mathbf{H}}(\boldsymbol{\theta}_0)^{-1})\mathbf{c}'](\mathbf{c}\hat{\mathbf{H}}(\boldsymbol{\theta}_0)^{-1}\hat{\boldsymbol{\Sigma}}\hat{\mathbf{H}}(\boldsymbol{\theta}_0)^{-1}\mathbf{c}')^{-1}[\mathbf{c}(\hat{\mathbf{H}}(\boldsymbol{\theta}_0)^{-1})\mathbf{c}']\boldsymbol{\Gamma}_{\mathrm{r}} \tag{7.6.15}$$

or the special case

$$\mathrm{LM} = \mathrm{n}\boldsymbol{\Gamma}_{\mathrm{r}}'(\mathbf{c}\hat{\boldsymbol{\Sigma}}^{-1}\mathbf{c}')\boldsymbol{\Gamma}_{\mathrm{r}}. \tag{7.6.16}$$

The LM test is conducted by rejecting H_0 when $\mathrm{lm} \geq \chi^2_{1-\alpha}$, where $\chi^2_{1-\alpha}$ is the $100(1-\alpha)\%$ quantile of the Chi-square $(j, 0)$ distribution. For example, in the LS case of Section 7.5, $\boldsymbol{\Sigma} = 4\sigma^2\boldsymbol{\Xi}$ is replaced by $4\mathrm{S}_r^2(n^{-1}\mathbf{x}'\mathbf{x})$, where S_r^2 is the restricted (under H_0) estimator of σ^2 (recall (6.2.16)) and $\mathbf{h}(\boldsymbol{\beta}_0) = -2\boldsymbol{\Xi}$ is replaced by $-2(n^{-1}\mathbf{x}'\mathbf{x})$. The resulting test statistic is precisely (6.2.17).

As we noted previously in Section 6.2.2.a, the intuition underlying this test is that the farther the outcomes of $\boldsymbol{\Gamma}_{\mathrm{r}}$ are from the zero vector, the less plausible is H_0 because the Lagrange multipliers are measuring the rate at which the extremum estimation objective function can be increased as the restriction $\mathbf{c}\boldsymbol{\theta} = \mathbf{r}$ is relaxed. If the restrictions were in fact true, one would expect that there would, in general, be less opportunity to increase the objective function by removing the constraints than when the restrictions are false, and, in fact, when the restrictions are true, $\mathrm{E}[\boldsymbol{\Gamma}_{\mathrm{r}}] = \mathbf{0}$. The distance between $\boldsymbol{\Gamma}_{\mathrm{r}}$ outcomes and $\mathbf{0}$ are adjusted for the inherent variability in the estimator $\boldsymbol{\Gamma}_r$ by measuring distance in the inverse asymptotic covariance metric $[\hat{\mathbf{cov}}(\boldsymbol{\Gamma}_r)]^{-1}$.

On the basis of an argument analogous to that presented in Section 6.2.2.c, it follows that the distribution of the LM statistic under Pitman drift alternatives $H_a: \mathbf{c}\boldsymbol{\theta} = \mathbf{r} + n^{-1/2}\boldsymbol{\delta}$ is given by

$$\mathrm{LM} \overset{a}{\sim} \text{Chi-square}(j, \lambda)$$

with

$$\lambda = \frac{1}{2}\boldsymbol{\delta}'[\mathbf{c}(\mathbf{h}(\boldsymbol{\theta}_0)^{-1})\mathbf{c}'](\mathbf{c}\mathbf{h}(\boldsymbol{\theta}_0)^{-1}\boldsymbol{\Sigma}\mathbf{h}(\boldsymbol{\theta}_0)^{-1}\mathbf{c}')^{-1}[\mathbf{c}(\mathbf{h}(\boldsymbol{\theta}_0)^{-1})\mathbf{c}']\boldsymbol{\delta}. \quad (7.6.17)$$

Estimates of power as a function of only $\boldsymbol{\delta}$ can be defined by replacing the unknown matrices $\boldsymbol{\Sigma}$ and $\mathbf{h}(\boldsymbol{\theta}_0)$ by consistent estimates. Under the condition $\boldsymbol{\Sigma} = \tau\mathbf{h}(\theta_0)$, the matrix of the quadratic form in (7.6.17) simplifies substantially, as noted previously. The LM test is asymptotically unbiased and consistent (see section 6.2.2.d for a method of proof). It is also asymptotically locally UMP invariant for testing H_0, where *locally* here means for the sequence of alternative hypotheses of the Pitman drift form and *invariance* is with respect to orthonormal transformations of the regression model, and it is asymptotically locally UMP unbiased (UMPU) when $\mathbf{c}\boldsymbol{\beta}$ is a scalar (see van der Vaart 1998, Chapter 15), and Bunke and Bunke (1986, pp. 224–35)).

Confidence regions based on the LM statistic in (7.6.15) and (7.6.16) can be formed in the usual way owing to the duality between confidence regions and hypothesis tests. So, all of the values of $\mathbf{r}$ that would *not* be rejected by the LM test at an α-level collectively represent a $100(1-\alpha)\%$ confidence region for $\mathbf{c}\boldsymbol{\theta}$. However, confidence regions based on the preceding LM statistics are often difficult to compute because the Lagrange multiplier $\boldsymbol{\Gamma}_r$ is generally only an implicit function of $\mathbf{r}$ (recall the related discussion surrounding (6.3.3)). It is sometimes possible to redefine the LM statistic explicitly in terms of the value of $\mathbf{r}$, as in the LS case of Section 6.3.2, which facilitates the calculation of the confidence region. No matter how it is calculated, the LM-based confidence region is asymptotically locally UMA invariant, which is inherited from the asymptotically locally UMP invariant property of the LM test on which the confidence region is based.

7.6.1.b. Score Form of LM Test and Confidence Regions

There is an asymptotically equivalent score form of the LM statistic suggested by Rao (1948) that can be defined and is similar to (6.2.22). To derive this form of the LM test, first note that from (7.6.3)

$$\mathbf{c}'\boldsymbol{\Gamma}_r = \left.\frac{\partial \mathrm{m}(\boldsymbol{\theta}, \mathbf{Y}, \mathbf{X})}{\partial \boldsymbol{\theta}}\right|_{\hat{\boldsymbol{\Theta}}_r}. \quad (7.6.18)$$

Furthermore, under H_0, so that $\hat{\boldsymbol{\Theta}}_r \xrightarrow{p} \boldsymbol{\theta}_0$, it follows from the conditions in Theorem 7.3.3 that

$$\hat{\mathbf{H}}(\boldsymbol{\theta}_0) = \left.\frac{\partial^2 \mathrm{m}(\boldsymbol{\theta}, \mathbf{Y}, \mathbf{X})}{\partial \boldsymbol{\theta}\partial \boldsymbol{\theta}'}\right|_{\hat{\boldsymbol{\Theta}}_r} \xrightarrow{p} \mathbf{h}(\boldsymbol{\theta}_0). \quad (7.6.19)$$

Then upon substitution of (7.6.18) and (7.6.19) into the quadratic form (7.6.15), an asymptotically equivalent representation of the LM statistic is defined as follows:

$$\mathrm{LM} = n\frac{\partial \mathrm{m}(\boldsymbol{\theta}, \mathbf{Y}, \mathbf{X})}{\partial \boldsymbol{\theta}'}\bigg|_{\hat{\Theta}_r} \hat{\mathbf{H}}(\boldsymbol{\theta}_0)^{-1}\mathbf{c}'[\mathbf{c}\hat{\mathbf{H}}(\boldsymbol{\theta}_0)^{-1}\hat{\boldsymbol{\Sigma}}\hat{\mathbf{H}}(\boldsymbol{\theta}_0)^{-1}\mathbf{c}']^{-1}\mathbf{c}\hat{\mathbf{H}}(\boldsymbol{\theta}_0)^{-1}\frac{\partial \mathrm{m}(\boldsymbol{\theta}, \mathbf{Y}, \mathbf{X})}{\partial \boldsymbol{\theta}}\bigg|_{\hat{\Theta}_r} \tag{7.6.20}$$

An advantage of the score form of the LM test is that calculation of the Lagrange multiplier is not needed to generate a value of the test statistic. The LM statistic in (6.2.2), defined within the LS context, is an example of such a case. In principle an asymptotic $100(1-\alpha)\%$ level confidence region could be defined via duality with the α-level LM test of hypothesis. However, as noted in the previous subsection, calculation of the boundary of the confidence region can be quite difficult and is not often done in practice.

7.6.2. Wald Tests and Confidence Regions

If the asymptotic normal approximation for the extremum estimator $\hat{\boldsymbol{\Theta}}$ implied by Theorem 7.3.3 is adopted, it follows from results on the distribution of linear combinations of normally distributed random variables $[\mathbf{Z} \sim \mathrm{N}(\boldsymbol{\mu}, \boldsymbol{\Psi}) \Rightarrow \mathbf{aZ} + \mathbf{b} \sim \mathrm{N}(\mathbf{a}\boldsymbol{\mu} + \mathbf{b}, \mathbf{a}\boldsymbol{\Psi}\mathbf{a}')]$ that $n^{1/2}(\mathbf{c}\hat{\boldsymbol{\Theta}} - \mathbf{r}) \stackrel{a}{\sim} \mathrm{N}(n^{1/2}(\mathbf{c}\boldsymbol{\theta} - \mathbf{r}), \mathbf{c}[\mathbf{h}(\boldsymbol{\theta})^{-1}\boldsymbol{\Sigma}\,\mathbf{h}(\boldsymbol{\theta})^{-1}]\mathbf{c}')$, where symbols are as defined previously. Consequently, *if the null hypothesis* $\mathrm{H}_0{:}\ \mathbf{c}\boldsymbol{\theta} = \mathbf{r}$ *is true*, then $n^{1/2}(\mathbf{c}\hat{\boldsymbol{\Theta}} - \mathbf{r}) \stackrel{a}{\sim} \mathrm{N}(\mathbf{0}, \mathbf{c}[\mathbf{h}(\boldsymbol{\theta})^{-1}\boldsymbol{\Sigma}\mathbf{h}(\boldsymbol{\theta})^{-1}]\mathbf{c}')$. Again based on results relating to the distribution of linear combinations of normally distributed random variables and on properties of the symmetric square-root matrix ($\mathbf{m}^{-1/2}\mathbf{m}\mathbf{m}^{-1/2} = \mathbf{I}$), it follows under H_0 that $[\mathbf{c}[\mathbf{h}(\boldsymbol{\theta})^{-1}\boldsymbol{\Sigma}\mathbf{h}(\boldsymbol{\theta})^{-1}]\mathbf{c}']^{-1/2} n^{1/2}(\mathbf{c}\hat{\boldsymbol{\Theta}} - \mathbf{r}) \stackrel{a}{\sim} \mathrm{N}(\mathbf{0}, \mathbf{I}_j)$.

Because the sum of the squares of j independent standard normal random variables has a central Chi-square distribution with j degrees of freedom, we have that

$$(\mathbf{c}\hat{\boldsymbol{\Theta}} - \mathbf{r})'[\mathbf{c}[\mathbf{h}(\boldsymbol{\theta})^{-1}(n^{-1}\boldsymbol{\Sigma})\mathbf{h}(\boldsymbol{\theta})^{-1}]\mathbf{c}']^{-1}(\mathbf{c}\hat{\boldsymbol{\Theta}} - \mathbf{r}) \stackrel{a}{\sim} \text{Chi-square}(j, 0) \ \text{ under } \mathrm{H}_0, \tag{7.6.21}$$

where we remind the reader that Chi-square$(j, 0)$ denotes a noncentral Chi-square distribution with j degrees of freedom and noncentrality of 0, that is, a central Chi-square distribution with j degrees of freedom. Recall that the phrase "under H_0" in (7.6.21) means "assuming the null hypothesis is true." Empirical implementation of the test of H_0 based on (7.6.21) requires that the asymptotic covariance matrix $[\mathbf{h}(\boldsymbol{\theta})^{-1}\boldsymbol{\Sigma}\mathbf{h}(\boldsymbol{\theta})^{-1}]$ utilized in (7.6.21) be replaced by a consistent estimator, and the form of this estimator will depend on the particular estimation objective function chosen. A consistent estimator can often be defined by consistently estimating each of the matrices in the covariance matrix expression, as $[\hat{\mathbf{H}}(\boldsymbol{\theta}_0)^{-1}\hat{\boldsymbol{\Sigma}}\hat{\mathbf{H}}(\boldsymbol{\theta}_0)^{-1}]$, where $\hat{\boldsymbol{\Sigma}}$ is some consistent estimator of $\boldsymbol{\Sigma}$. This leads to the operational version of the Wald statistic:

$$\mathrm{W} = (\mathbf{c}\hat{\boldsymbol{\Theta}} - \mathbf{r})'[\mathbf{c}[\hat{\mathbf{H}}(\boldsymbol{\theta}_0)^{-1}(n^{-1}\hat{\boldsymbol{\Sigma}})\hat{\mathbf{H}}(\boldsymbol{\theta}_0)^{-1}]\mathbf{c}']^{-1}(\mathbf{c}\hat{\boldsymbol{\Theta}} - \mathbf{r}) \stackrel{a}{\sim} \text{Chi-square}(j, 0) \ \text{ under } \mathrm{H}_0. \tag{7.6.22}$$

The test is conducted by rejecting H_0 when $\mathrm{w} \geq \chi^2_{1-\alpha}$, where $\chi^2_{1-\alpha}$ is the $100(1-\alpha)\%$ quantile of the Chi-square$(j, 0)$ distribution.

As we noted previously in Section 6.2.1, the intuition underlying this test is that the more distant the outcomes of $\mathbf{c}\hat{\boldsymbol{\theta}}$ are from the hypothesized value of $\mathbf{c}\boldsymbol{\theta}$ represented by $\mathbf{r}$, the less plausible is H_0. The distance between $\mathbf{c}\hat{\boldsymbol{\theta}}$ outcomes and $\mathbf{r}$ is adjusted for the inherent variability in the estimator $\mathbf{c}\hat{\boldsymbol{\theta}}$ of $\mathbf{c}\boldsymbol{\theta}$ by measuring distance in the inverse asymptotic covariance metric $[\mathbf{c}\hat{\mathbf{o}}\mathbf{v}(\mathbf{c}\hat{\boldsymbol{\theta}})]^{-1}$. This results in distance being measured in standardized units that are free of units of measurement differences.

Following an argument analogous to that presented in Section 6.2.1.a, it follows that the distribution of the Wald statistic under Pitman drift alternatives H_a: $\mathbf{c}\boldsymbol{\theta} = \mathbf{r} + \mathrm{n}^{-1/2}\boldsymbol{\delta}$ is given by

$$\mathrm{W} \overset{\mathrm{a}}{\sim} \text{Chi-square}(j, \lambda) \quad \text{with} \quad \lambda = \frac{1}{2}\boldsymbol{\delta}'[\mathbf{c}[\mathbf{h}(\boldsymbol{\theta})^{-1}\boldsymbol{\Sigma}\mathbf{h}(\boldsymbol{\theta})^{-1}]\mathbf{c}']^{-1}\boldsymbol{\delta}. \tag{7.6.23}$$

Estimates of power as a function of only $\boldsymbol{\delta}$ can be defined by replacing the asymptotic covariance matrix $[\mathbf{h}(\boldsymbol{\theta})^{-1}\boldsymbol{\Sigma}\mathbf{h}(\boldsymbol{\theta})^{-1}]$ in (7.6.23) with a consistent estimator, say $[\hat{\mathbf{H}}(\boldsymbol{\theta}_0)^{-1}\hat{\boldsymbol{\Sigma}}\hat{\mathbf{H}}(\boldsymbol{\theta}_0)^{-1}]$. Analogous to the case of the LM test, the Wald test is asymptotically locally UMP invariant for testing H_0 and asymptotically locally UMP unbiased when testing a scalar restriction. Furthermore, the approach of Section 6.2.1.b can be followed to conclude that the Wald test is a consistent test of H_0, and asymptotic "unbiasedness" is apparent from the asymptotic power function of the test.

When $\boldsymbol{\Sigma} = \tau\mathbf{h}(\boldsymbol{\theta}_0)$ for some scalar τ, as in the case of both ML and LS estimation, the Wald statistic can be simplified. For example, in the LS case with estimation objective function (7.5.2), $\boldsymbol{\Sigma} = 4\sigma^2\boldsymbol{\Xi}$ and $\mathbf{h}(\boldsymbol{\beta}_0) = -2\boldsymbol{\Xi}$, where $\boldsymbol{\Xi} = \lim_{n\to\infty}(n^{-1}\mathbf{x}'\mathbf{x})$. Making these substitutions in (7.6.21), and then following through on the implications for the test statistic (7.6.22) leads to a Wald statistic identical with that presented in (6.2.2) upon substitution of the consistent estimator S^2 for σ^2.

Confidence regions based on the Wald statistic can be defined in the usual way through duality with the Wald test of H_0: $\mathbf{c}\boldsymbol{\theta} = \mathbf{r}$. Specifically, an asymptotically valid $100(1-\alpha)\%$ confidence region estimate for $\mathbf{c}\boldsymbol{\theta}$ is defined by the set

$$\mathrm{CR}^{\mathrm{W}} = \{\mathbf{r}: (\mathbf{c}\hat{\boldsymbol{\theta}} - \mathbf{r})'[\mathbf{c}[\hat{\mathbf{H}}(\boldsymbol{\theta}_0)^{-1}(n^{-1}\hat{\boldsymbol{\Sigma}})\hat{\mathbf{H}}(\boldsymbol{\theta}_0)^{-1}]\mathbf{c}']^{-1}(\mathbf{c}\hat{\boldsymbol{\theta}} - \mathbf{r}) < \chi^2_{1-\alpha}\}. \tag{7.6.24}$$

This confidence region will be an interval if $\mathbf{c}\boldsymbol{\theta}$ is a scalar, an ellipse if $\mathbf{c}\boldsymbol{\theta}$ is two-dimensional, and a hyperellipse otherwise, all of which will be centered at the value of $\mathbf{c}\hat{\boldsymbol{\theta}}$. This confidence region is asymptotically locally UMA invariant, which is inherited from the asymptotically locally UMP invariant property of the Wald test on which the confidence region is based. The strong inequality can be changed to a weak inequality in (7.6.24), and thereby define a closed instead of an open confidence region, having the same asymptotic level of confidence, $100(1-\alpha)\%$, because the W statistic is a continuous random variable under the Chi-square approximation, and the additional boundary points have zero probability.

7.6.3. Pseudo-Likelihood Ratio Tests and Confidence Regions

The pseudo-likelihood ratio (PLR) test is based on the scaled difference between the constrained (by H_0) and unconstrained maximum values of the extremum estimation objective function. In particular, if the conditions of Theorem 7.3.3 are assumed and under H_0: $\mathbf{c}\boldsymbol{\theta} = \mathbf{r}$, it can be shown that the PLR statistic,

$$\text{PLR} = 2\tau^{-1}n[\text{m}(\hat{\boldsymbol{\Theta}}_\text{r}, \mathbf{Y}, \mathbf{X}) - \text{m}(\hat{\boldsymbol{\Theta}}, \mathbf{Y}, \mathbf{X})], \tag{7.6.25}$$

has a Chi-square(j,0) asymptotic distribution given that $\boldsymbol{\Sigma} = \tau\mathbf{h}(\boldsymbol{\theta}_0)$, where τ is some scalar value and both $\boldsymbol{\Sigma}$ and $\mathbf{h}(\boldsymbol{\theta}_0)$ retain their meanings from Sections 7.6.1 and 7.6.2. In (7.6.25), $\hat{\boldsymbol{\Theta}}$ is the unconstrained extremum estimator defined in (7.2.1), $\hat{\boldsymbol{\Theta}}_\text{r}$ is the restricted extremum estimator constrained by H_0: $\mathbf{c}\boldsymbol{\theta} = \mathbf{r}$ and defined in (7.6.1), and $j = \text{rank}(\mathbf{c})$. If the extremum estimation objective function is actually a scaled log-likelihood function, as in the ML-extremum estimator of (7.4.3), the modifier "pseudo" is dropped, and the statistic (7.6.25) is referred to as simply the likelihood ratio (LR) statistic, with the statistic identified by the notation LR. The reason these statistics are referred to as a "ratio" is in reference to the original LR statistic context in which one begins with the *ratio* of the constrained (by H_0) and unconstrained likelihood functions as a test statistic. In this context, the statistic (7.6.25) can then be thought of as a strictly monotonically increasing function of the likelihood ratio based on a logarithmic transformation, and so a test based on the statistic (7.6.25) is equivalent to a test based on the likelihood ratio. *Distance metric statistic* (DMS) is an alternative terminology for the statistic (7.6.25) that is currently gaining favor in the literature.

To motivate the asymptotic Chi-square distribution of the PLR, first represent the extremum estimation objective function for the constrained (by H_0) extremum estimator in a Taylor series expansion evaluated at the unconstrained extremum estimator as

$$\begin{aligned}\text{m}(\hat{\boldsymbol{\Theta}}_\text{r}, \mathbf{Y}, \mathbf{X}) &= \text{m}(\hat{\boldsymbol{\Theta}}, \mathbf{Y}, \mathbf{X}) + \left.\frac{\partial \text{m}(\boldsymbol{\theta}, \mathbf{Y}, \mathbf{X})}{\partial \boldsymbol{\theta}}\right|_{\hat{\boldsymbol{\Theta}}} (\hat{\boldsymbol{\Theta}}_\text{r} - \hat{\boldsymbol{\Theta}}) \\ &\quad + \frac{1}{2}(\hat{\boldsymbol{\Theta}}_\text{r} - \hat{\boldsymbol{\Theta}})' \left.\frac{\partial^2 \text{m}(\boldsymbol{\theta}, \mathbf{Y}, \mathbf{X})}{\partial \boldsymbol{\theta}\partial \boldsymbol{\theta}'}\right|_{\hat{\boldsymbol{\Theta}}_*} (\hat{\boldsymbol{\Theta}}_\text{r} - \hat{\boldsymbol{\Theta}}),\end{aligned} \tag{7.6.26}$$

where $\hat{\boldsymbol{\Theta}}_*$ is a convex combination of the restricted and unrestricted estimators $\hat{\boldsymbol{\Theta}}_\text{r}$ and $\hat{\boldsymbol{\Theta}}$, respectively. Because the unconstrained extremum estimator satisfies the first-order conditions for a maximum, it follows that $\frac{\partial \text{m}(\boldsymbol{\theta}, \mathbf{Y}, \mathbf{X})}{\partial \boldsymbol{\theta}}\big|_{\hat{\boldsymbol{\Theta}}.} = \mathbf{0}$ in (7.6.26). We can then subtract $\text{m}(\hat{\boldsymbol{\Theta}}, \mathbf{Y}, \mathbf{X})$ from both sides of (7.6.26) and multiply through by $2\tau^{-1}n$ to obtain

$$\begin{aligned}\text{PLR} &= 2\tau^{-1}n[\text{m}(\hat{\boldsymbol{\Theta}}_\text{r}, \mathbf{Y}, \mathbf{X}) - \text{m}(\hat{\boldsymbol{\Theta}}, \mathbf{Y}, \mathbf{X})] \\ &= \tau^{-1}n^{1/2}(\hat{\boldsymbol{\Theta}}_\text{r} - \hat{\boldsymbol{\Theta}})' \left.\frac{\partial^2 \text{m}(\boldsymbol{\theta}, \mathbf{Y}, \mathbf{X})}{\partial \boldsymbol{\theta}\partial \boldsymbol{\theta}'}\right|_{\hat{\boldsymbol{\Theta}}_*} (\hat{\boldsymbol{\Theta}}_\text{r} - \hat{\boldsymbol{\Theta}})n^{1/2}.\end{aligned} \tag{7.6.27}$$

Now note that under H_0, both $\hat{\boldsymbol{\Theta}}_\text{r} \xrightarrow{p} \boldsymbol{\theta}_0$ and $\hat{\boldsymbol{\Theta}} \xrightarrow{p} \boldsymbol{\theta}_0$, which then imply that $\hat{\boldsymbol{\Theta}}_* \xrightarrow{p} \boldsymbol{\theta}_0$. It follows from the conditions of Theorem 7.3.3 that $\frac{\partial^2 \text{m}(\boldsymbol{\theta}, \mathbf{Y}, \mathbf{X})}{\partial \boldsymbol{\theta}\partial \boldsymbol{\theta}'}\big|_{\hat{\boldsymbol{\Theta}}_*} \xrightarrow{p} \mathbf{h}(\boldsymbol{\theta}_0)$, and thus

$$\text{PLR} \stackrel{a}{=} \tau^{-1}n^{1/2}(\hat{\boldsymbol{\Theta}}_\text{r} - \hat{\boldsymbol{\Theta}})'\mathbf{h}(\boldsymbol{\theta}_0)(\hat{\boldsymbol{\Theta}}_\text{r} - \hat{\boldsymbol{\Theta}})n^{1/2} \tag{7.6.28}$$

where $\overset{a}{=}$ denotes "equivalent in asymptotic distribution to." Applying partitioned inversion to (7.6.8), it follows that

$$n^{1/2}(\hat{\Theta}_r - \theta_0) \overset{a}{=} -[\mathbf{h}(\boldsymbol{\theta}_0)^{-1} - \mathbf{h}(\boldsymbol{\theta}_0)^{-1}\mathbf{c}'[\mathbf{ch}(\boldsymbol{\theta}_0)^{-1}\mathbf{c}']^{-1}\mathbf{ch}(\boldsymbol{\theta}_0)^{-1}]\mathbf{Z} \qquad (7.6.29)$$

where $\mathbf{Z} \sim \mathrm{N}(\mathbf{0}, \boldsymbol{\Sigma})$. It also follows directly from Theorem 7.3.3 that

$$n^{1/2}(\hat{\Theta} - \boldsymbol{\theta}_0) \overset{a}{=} -\mathbf{h}(\boldsymbol{\theta}_0)^{-1}\mathbf{Z}. \qquad (7.6.30)$$

Then, subtracting (7.6.30) from (7.6.29) yields

$$n^{1/2}(\hat{\Theta}_r - \hat{\Theta}) \overset{a}{=} [\mathbf{h}(\boldsymbol{\theta}_0)^{-1}\mathbf{c}'[\mathbf{ch}(\boldsymbol{\theta}_0)^{-1}\mathbf{c}']^{-1}\mathbf{ch}(\boldsymbol{\theta}_0)^{-1}]\,\mathbf{Z}, \qquad (7.6.31)$$

and substituting (7.6.31) into (7.6.28) yields

$$\begin{aligned} \mathrm{PLR} &\overset{a}{=} \tau^{-1}\mathbf{Z}'[\mathbf{h}(\boldsymbol{\theta}_0)^{-1}\mathbf{c}'[\mathbf{ch}(\boldsymbol{\theta}_0)^{-1}\mathbf{c}']^{-1}\mathbf{ch}(\boldsymbol{\theta}_0)^{-1}]\,\mathbf{Z} \\ &\overset{a}{=} \mathbf{V}'[\tau^{-1}\boldsymbol{\Sigma}^{1/2}\mathbf{h}(\boldsymbol{\theta}_0)^{-1}\mathbf{c}'[\mathbf{ch}(\boldsymbol{\theta}_0)^{-1}\mathbf{c}']^{-1}\mathbf{ch}(\boldsymbol{\theta}_0)^{-1}\boldsymbol{\Sigma}^{1/2}]\,\mathbf{V}, \end{aligned} \qquad (7.6.32)$$

where $\mathbf{V} \sim \mathrm{N}(\mathbf{0}, \mathbf{I})$ and $\mathbf{Z} \equiv \boldsymbol{\Sigma}^{1/2}\,\mathbf{V}$.

If it is assumed that $\boldsymbol{\Sigma} = \tau\mathbf{h}(\boldsymbol{\theta}_0)$, the matrix of the quadratic form in the last line of (7.6.32) is symmetric, positive semidefinite, and idempotent with rank j. This can be demonstrated by straightforward multiplication of the matrix by itself and noting that τ will be negative. It follows that the quadratic form in (7.6.32) can be represented in eigenvalue–eigenvector form as

$$\mathrm{PLR} \overset{a}{=} \mathbf{V}'\mathbf{p}\boldsymbol{\Lambda}\mathbf{p}'\mathbf{V} = \mathbf{V}_*'\boldsymbol{\Lambda}\mathbf{V}_* = \sum_{i=1}^{j} \mathrm{V}_{i*}^2 \sim \text{Chi-square}(j, 0), \qquad (7.6.33)$$

where $\mathbf{V}_* \equiv \mathbf{p}'\mathbf{V} \sim \mathrm{N}(\mathbf{0}, \mathbf{I})$, $\mathbf{p}$ is the matrix of eigenvectors of the matrix of the quadratic form for which $\mathbf{p}'\mathbf{p} = \mathbf{I}$, and $\boldsymbol{\Lambda}$ is the diagonal matrix of eigenvalues, which consists of j values of 1 and the remaining values equal to 0 (recall that the eigenvalues of a symmetric idempotent matrix are all 0's and 1's, with the number of 1's equal to the rank of the matrix, which coincides with the trace of the matrix as well). We have assumed without loss of generality that the eigenvalues and eigenvectors have been ordered so that the unit eigenvalues occur in the first j diagonal positions of $\boldsymbol{\Lambda}$.

Therefore, the PLR statistic (7.6.25) is asymptotically Chi-square distributed with j degrees of freedom under the conditions stated. The test of $\mathrm{H}_0\colon \mathbf{c}\boldsymbol{\theta} = \mathbf{r}$ is conducted as usual by

$$\text{reject } \mathrm{H}_0\colon \mathbf{c}\boldsymbol{\theta} = \mathbf{r} \text{ iff plr} \geq \chi^2_{1-\alpha}, \qquad (7.6.34)$$

where $\chi^2_{1-\alpha}$ is the $100(1-\alpha)\%$ quantile of the Chi-square(j,0) distribution. In applications where τ, $\mathbf{h}(\boldsymbol{\theta}_0)$, or both are unknown, they are replaced by consistent estimators, in which case the asymptotic distribution of the test statistic is maintained. The test is consistent, asymptotically unbiased, and locally asymptotically uniformly most powerful invariant for alternative hypotheses of the Pitman drift form $\mathrm{H}_a\colon \mathbf{c}\boldsymbol{\theta} = \mathbf{r} + n^{-1/2}\boldsymbol{\delta}$. The asymptotic distribution of the PLR statistic under H_a is equivalent to the asymptotic distributions of both the Wald and LM statistics given that $\boldsymbol{\Sigma} = \tau\mathbf{h}(\boldsymbol{\theta}_0)$.

Regarding the special cases of ML and LS extremum estimation, the reader can demonstrate that the use of (7.6.25) in the normally distributed parametric linear regression model context yields precisely the same GLR test as discussed in Chapter 4. If the extremum estimator (7.5.1) is used based on the extremum estimation objective function (7.5.2), it can be shown that the PLR statistic is given by $(\frac{\hat{\varepsilon}_r'\hat{\varepsilon}_r - \hat{\varepsilon}'\hat{\varepsilon}}{\sigma^2})$, where $\hat{\varepsilon}_r$ and $\hat{\varepsilon}$ are, respectively, the restricted and unrestricted estimators of the noise component of the regression model and $\tau = -2\sigma^2$. In applications, σ^2 is replaced by the consistent estimate s^2, resulting in an asymptotically equivalent estimable version of the PLR statistic defined by $(\frac{\hat{\varepsilon}_r'\hat{\varepsilon}_r - \hat{\varepsilon}'\hat{\varepsilon}}{s^2})$. The reader will be asked to prove both of these claims in the problems.

In principle, confidence regions for $\mathbf{c}\boldsymbol{\theta}$ can be defined in the usual way based on duality with the PLR hypothesis test. Such a confidence region is defined by all of the potential hypothesized **r** values that would *not* be rejected by the test. However, the PLR form of the test is not the most computationally convenient form of test for computing the confidence-region boundaries. In applications, the Wald test is most often used to generate confidence regions.

7.6.4. Testing Linear Inequalities and Confidence Bounds

In a way analogous to the procedures examined in Section 6.4 for testing linear inequalities and generating confidence bounds based on the LS estimator in the linear regression model, it is possible to define such procedures more generally in the context of extremum estimation. A statistic that can be used to define these procedures is the Z-statistic which, for $\mathbf{c}\boldsymbol{\theta} = \mathrm{r} + n^{-1/2}\delta$, is given by

$$\mathbf{Z} = \frac{(\mathbf{c}\hat{\boldsymbol{\Theta}} - \mathrm{r})}{(\mathbf{c}[\hat{\mathbf{H}}(\boldsymbol{\theta}_0)^{-1}(n^{-1}\hat{\boldsymbol{\Sigma}})\hat{\mathbf{H}}(\boldsymbol{\theta}_0)^{-1}]\mathbf{c}')^{1/2}} \overset{a}{\sim} \mathrm{N}(\delta/[\sigma^2\mathbf{c}\mathbf{h}(\boldsymbol{\theta}_0)^{-1}\boldsymbol{\Sigma}\mathbf{h}(\boldsymbol{\theta}_0)^{-1}\mathbf{c}']^{1/2}, 1). \tag{7.6.35}$$

Letting $z_{1-\alpha}$ be the $100(1-\alpha)\%$ quantile of the standard normal distribution, it then follows from the power function of the test that the test rule

$$\text{reject } \mathrm{H}_0\colon \mathbf{c}\boldsymbol{\theta} \le \mathrm{r} \quad \text{iff} \quad \mathrm{z} \ge \mathrm{z}_{1-\alpha} \tag{7.6.36}$$

defines an asymptotic level α and unbiased test of H_0. In particular, the power function is defined by

$$\pi(\delta) = \mathrm{P}(\mathrm{z} \ge \mathrm{z}_{1-\alpha}) \begin{bmatrix} < \\ = \\ > \end{bmatrix} \alpha \quad \text{if} \quad \delta \begin{bmatrix} < \\ = \\ > \end{bmatrix} 0. \tag{7.6.37}$$

The test is also a consistent test of the null hypothesis (see the discussion surrounding (6.4.5) and (6.4.6) for motivation).

One can utilize Neyman–Pearson theory to conclude that the test is also an asymptotically uniformly most powerful unbiased test of $\mathrm{H}_0\colon \mathbf{c}\boldsymbol{\theta} \le \mathrm{r}$. Precisely the same test rule will define an asymptotically valid test of the strong inequality hypothesis $\mathrm{H}_0\colon \mathbf{c}\boldsymbol{\theta} < \mathrm{r}$ because, given the continuous nature of the normal approximation, the boundary point is irrelevant and all of the test properties remain in force.

To test the hypothesis $H_0: \mathbf{c}\boldsymbol{\theta} \geq r$ (or $H_0: \mathbf{c}\boldsymbol{\theta} > r$), the test statistic (7.6.35) can again be utilized. The test rule becomes

$$\text{reject } H_0: \mathbf{c}\boldsymbol{\theta} \geq r \quad \text{iff} \quad z \leq z_\alpha, \tag{7.6.38}$$

where z_α is the $100\alpha\%$ quantile of the standard normal distribution. All of the previous test properties continue to hold, and thus in an asymptotic approximation sense, the test is unbiased, consistent, and UMPU.

A set of inequality hypotheses can be tested based on the Bonferonni inequality approach, and the reader is directed to Example 6.4.1 and the discussion preceding the example for motivation. Confidence bounds for $\mathbf{c}\boldsymbol{\theta}$ can be defined in the usual way based on duality with tests of inequality hypotheses, and joint confidence bounds can again be based on Bonferonni's inequality. The reader is directed to Section 6.4.2 for the motivation underlying these procedures.

► **Example 7.6.1:** To demonstrate the application of the inferential concepts for the MAD estimator, we provide the GAUSS program C7Tests.gss in the examples manual. For a given sample generated from a linear regression model (selected by the user), GAUSS presents the results for a Wald test, a Z-test, and a joint confidence region for two of the model parameters. Then, the program conducts a nonparametric bootstrap resampling exercise designed to estimate the power function of the Wald test.

7.7. Critique

As the reader probably noted in Chapters 3 and 5, once the probability models were specified, the next question concerned the estimation criterion–objective to use in recovering the unknown parameters from the sample data. This suggests that a general method of defining estimators is through the definition of estimation metrics or estimation objective functions. This idea leads to a general class of extremum estimators that, for a wide range of probability models, serves as a basis for developing estimation rules and deriving sampling properties. In particular, once the estimation metric is chosen and the regularity conditions are specified, we have seen that the extremum concept provides a well-defined basis for deriving the corresponding estimator and answering questions regarding consistency and asymptotic normality. In addition, an asymptotic basis for inference is provided and, as we will see in the chapters ahead, the trinity of Wald, Lagrange multiplier and (pseudo or generalized) likelihood ratio test statistics from ML and LS estimation extends readily to this more general setting. Consequently, a unified framework for large sample theory of hypothesis-testing and confidence-region estimation emerges in the context of ML and LS methods as well as other traditional probability model formulations and inverse problem solutions.

We note that in many cases in practice we will not be able to solve the extremum estimation problem analytically, or even explicitly, for the value of the parameter vector that optimizes the estimation objective function. This is typical of cases in which the first-order conditions for the extremum estimation problem are highly nonlinear functions of the parameters. In these cases, one must resort to the computer and numerical procedures when solving for the extremum estimate of the parameter vector. Numerical procedures that can be used for optimizing extremum estimation objective functions will be discussed in the chapters ahead. In any case, if the reader has grasped the concept of extremum (E) estimation, he or she will be led inexorably to posing the correct estimation and inference questions when studying each new probability–econometric model ahead.

To place the concepts developed in this chapter in their proper context relative to the literature, it is important to note that what we call *extremum estimators*, Huber (1981) calls *M-estimators* (where the M denotes *ML-like*). In subsequent chapters, we will apply the extremum estimation concept to regression models that are inherently nonlinear and to models in which we relax the independent, identically distributed, or both random variable assumptions regarding the noise component of the model.

7.8. Exercises

7.8.1. Idea Checklist – Knowledge Guides

---

1. In what ways has this chapter given you a more general basis for thinking about the problem of estimation and inference?
2. How would you go about choosing an estimation metric or estimation objective function for a given probability model? In retrospect, do the ML and LS estimation metrics appear to be good choices within the class of extremum estimators for the respective probability models assumed in Chapters 3 and 5?
3. Why do you suppose the MAD estimator is more robust to outliers in the data than the LS estimator?
4. Discuss the functional form of the MAD estimator. Can you represent the estimator in closed form?

7.8.2. Problems

7–1 For the regression model with iid noise, prove that the MAD estimator (7.1.2) is consistent and asymptotically normal.

7–2 Develop a basis for inference for the estimator that you define in Problem 1.

7–3 For the location and scale model $Y_i = \beta + \varepsilon_i$, where the ε_i's are iid and have a bounded fourth moment, develop at least two different extremum estimators for this probability model and rank them in terms of sampling performance.

7–4 Show that the PLR test is equivalent to the GLR test of Chapter 4 in the case of the normally distributed parametric linear regression model.

7–5 Show that $\mathrm{PLR} = \left(\frac{\hat{\varepsilon}_r'\hat{\varepsilon}_r - \hat{\varepsilon}'\hat{\varepsilon}}{\sigma^2}\right)$ in the case of the semiparametric linear regression model of Chapter 6. Also argue that σ^2 can be replaced by s^2 without altering the asymptotic properties of the PLR test.

7.8.3. Computer Problems

7–1 Specify a regression model for a set of observations you collect that you believe may contain one or more outliers or that are generated by a DSP with thick (heavy) tails. For example, the DSPs for many financial data series are often described as having leptokurtic or heavy-tailed distributions. Compute the LS and MAD estimates of the model parameters and compare the results. Are there any economically important differences among the estimates?

7–2 Suppose we have a sample of n iid observations from the Uniform(0, θ) distribution.

a. What is the ML estimator of θ, $\hat{\theta}$, for this DSP? Do the conditions of Theorem 7.4.2 apply to this case?

b. Lehmann and Casella (1998, p. 485) claim that in large samples $n(\theta - \hat{\theta}) \xrightarrow{d} \text{Exp}(\theta)$ (note the nonstandard order of convergence). Write a GAUSS program designed to simulate the moments and sampling distribution of $\hat{\theta}$ for various n and θ. Do the results or your simulation exercise agree with the stated distributional claim?

c. The UMVU estimator of θ is $\tilde{\theta} = [(n+1)/n]\text{x}_{(n)}$, where $\text{x}_{(n)}$ is the largest observation in the sample. Extend the preceding simulation exercise to compare the statistical properties of the UMVUE with the MLE of θ.

7–3 Using the program provided for Example 7.6.1 (C7Tests.gss) as a guide, conduct a bootstrap or Monte Carlo simulation of the coverage probability for a Wald confidence region C^{W} based on the MAD and LS estimators. How do the estimated coverage probabilities compare, especially in samples of small size?

7–4 Koenker and Bassett (1978) consider a more general form of the MAD estimation criterion, $\text{m}(\boldsymbol{\beta}, \mathbf{y}, \mathbf{x}) = \theta \sum_{+} |\text{y}_i - \mathbf{x}[i, .]\boldsymbol{\beta}| + (1-\theta) \sum_{-} |\text{y}_i - \mathbf{x}[\text{i}, .]\boldsymbol{\beta}|$, where $\theta \in (0, 1)$. As such, the extremum estimation procedure can place relatively more or less emphasis on positive (+) or negative (−) deviations.

a. Rewrite the mad() procedure to allow the user to specify $\boldsymbol{\theta} \in (0, 1)$.

b. For various values of θ, repeat the simulation exercises conducted in Examples 7.3.1 and 7.3.2 and compare the results to the associated properties of the MAD ($\theta = 0.5$) and LS estimators.

7.9. References

Amemiya, T. (1985), *Advanced Econometrics*, Cambridge, MA: Harvard University Press.

Bunke, H., and O. Bunke (1986), *Statistical Inference in Linear Models*, New York: John Wiley and Sons.

Huber, P. J. (1981), *Robust Statistics*, New York: John Wiley and Sons.

Koenker, R., and G. Bassett, Jr. (1978), "Regression Quantiles," *Econometrica*, Vol. 46, pp. 33–50.

Lehmann, E., and G. Casella (1998), *Theory of Point Estimation*, New York, Springer–Verlag.

Mittelhammer, R. C. (1996), *Mathematical Statistics for Economics and Business*, New York: Springer–Verlag.

Newey, W. K., and D. McFadden (1994), "Large Sample Estimation and Hypothesis Testing," in *Handbook of Econometrics,* Vol. 4, Amsterdam: Elsevier, pp. 2111–45.

Rao, C. R. (1948), "Large Sample Tests of Statistical Hypotheses," *Proceedings of the Cambridge Philosophical Society*, Vol. 44, pp. 50–7.
van der Vaart, A.W. (1998), *Asymptotic Statistics*, Cambridge, UK: Cambridge University Press.
Wagner, H. (1959), "Linear Programming Techniques for Regression Analysis," *Journal of the American Statistical Association*, Vol. 54, pp. 206–12.

CHAPTER 8

The Nonlinear Semiparametric Regression Model: Estimation and Inference

OUR focus in Chapters 3–6 was on recovering information in the case of a probability model that is linear in the unknown parameters. In this chapter we examine a probability model that is more flexible than the linear model in representing the expectation of the dependent variable. In terms of the general class of probability models under consideration, we define the special case presented in Table 8.1.

Note in Table 8.1, and henceforth, that the notation $g(\mathbf{x}_{i\cdot}, \boldsymbol{\beta})$ indicates a *scalar* function value associated with the $(1 \times k)$ row vector of explanatory variable values $\mathbf{x}_{i\cdot}$ and the parameter vector $\boldsymbol{\beta}$, whereas $\mathbf{g}(\mathbf{x}, \boldsymbol{\beta})$ denotes an $(n \times 1)$ *vector* of function values associated with the $(n \times k)$ matrix of explanatory variable values $\mathbf{x}$ and the parameter vector $\boldsymbol{\beta}$ such as $\mathbf{g}(\mathbf{x}, \boldsymbol{\beta}) \equiv [g(\mathbf{x}_{1\cdot}, \boldsymbol{\beta}), \ldots, g(\mathbf{x}_{n\cdot}, \boldsymbol{\beta})]'$.

The particular inverse problem associated with the probability model delineated above concerns the recovery of information on the unknown and unobservable $\boldsymbol{\beta}$, σ^2, and $\boldsymbol{\varepsilon}$ from observations on sample outcomes of $(\mathbf{Y}, \mathbf{x})$. The procedures that we introduce in this chapter, and especially the methods for obtaining the optimal values of the estimation objective functions in the nonlinear model context, will prove very useful. In particular, the methods presented in the appendix to this chapter may be used to solve the extremum estimation problems discussed in Chapter 7 and throughout the remainder of the book.

8.1. The Nonlinear Regression Model

Building on the solution to the inverse problem of recovering information about unknowns and unobservables in the linear regression model, we now generalize our conceptualization of the data-sampling process underlying the sample data. Economic relationships and associated DSPs are often complex and, in many cases, are not well understood. In particular, we may have limited information on the form of the functional relationship between explanatory variables and the expected value of the dependent variable. We may only be able to postulate that the functional form belongs to some broad linear–nonlinear parametric family of functions. Consequently, restricting the

Table 8.1. *Nonlinear Semiparametric Regression Model*

Model Component	Specific Characteristics	
$\mathbf{Y}$	RV Type:	continuous
	Range:	unlimited
	Y_i dimension:	univariate
	Moments:	$E[\mathbf{Y}_i \mid \mathbf{x}_{i\cdot}] = g(\mathbf{x}_{i\cdot}, \boldsymbol{\beta}), \forall i$ $\mathbf{cov}(\mathbf{Y} \mid \mathbf{x}) = \sigma^2 \mathbf{I}$
$\eta(\mathbf{x}, \boldsymbol{\beta}, \varepsilon)$	Functional Form:	linear or nonlinear in $\mathbf{x}$ and $\boldsymbol{\beta}$, additive in ε, where $\eta(\mathbf{x}, \boldsymbol{\beta}, \varepsilon) = \mathbf{g}(\mathbf{x}, \boldsymbol{\beta}) + \varepsilon$, $\mathbf{g}(\mathbf{x}, \boldsymbol{\beta}) \equiv [g(\mathbf{x}_{1\cdot}, \boldsymbol{\beta}), \ldots, g(\mathbf{x}_{n\cdot}, \boldsymbol{\beta})]'$ and $\mathbf{g}$ is twice continuously differentiable in $\boldsymbol{\beta}$.
$\mathbf{x}$	RV Type:	degenerate (fixed)
	Genesis:	exogenous to the model
$\boldsymbol{\beta}$	RV Type:	degenerate (fixed)
	Dimension:	finite (fixed)
ε	RV Type:	iid or independent nonidentical
	Moments:	$E[\varepsilon \mid \mathbf{x}] = \mathbf{0}$, and $\mathbf{cov}(\varepsilon \mid \mathbf{x}) = \sigma^2 \mathbf{I}$
Ω	Prior info:	none
$f(\mathbf{e} \mid \mathbf{x}, \varphi)$	PDF family:	unspecified

functional relationship to linearity may have economic and statistical implications. To accommodate this desire for added generality, we need a basis for analyzing probability models that are nonlinear in the unknown parameters. To allow for more functional flexibility in the way explanatory variables $\mathbf{x}$ and parameters $\boldsymbol{\beta}$ can affect values of $E[\mathbf{Y} \mid \mathbf{x}]$ we examine the nonlinear regression model

$$\mathbf{Y} = \mathbf{g}(\mathbf{x}, \boldsymbol{\beta}) + \varepsilon. \tag{8.1.1}$$

In this specification, $\mathbf{Y} = (Y_1, Y_2, \ldots, Y_n)'$ is a $(n \times 1)$ vector of observable random variables whose range is contained in R^n, $\mathbf{x}$ is a $(n \times k)$ matrix representing n fixed values of k explanatory variables, $\boldsymbol{\beta}$ is a k-dimensional fixed vector of unknown and unobservable parameters, ε is a $(n \times 1)$ vector of unobservable random variables representing the elements of the noise component of the model, and $\mathbf{g}$ is a $(n \times 1)$ nonlinear vector-valued function of both $\mathbf{x}$ and $\boldsymbol{\beta}$ representing the systematic component of the model.

The nonlinear model specification (8.1.1) alone suggests an inverse problem of using the outcomes of the observable random vector $\mathbf{Y}$ and fixed observation matrix $\mathbf{x}$, which represent *indirect observations* on the unknown and unobservable $\boldsymbol{\beta}$ and ε, to recover information about $\boldsymbol{\beta}$ and ε. By *indirect* observations we again mean that the pair of observations $(\mathbf{y}, \mathbf{x})$ do not directly impart information on the values of $\boldsymbol{\beta}$ and ε themselves. Rather $(\mathbf{y}, \mathbf{x})$ *indirectly* conveys information about $\boldsymbol{\beta}$ and ε through the relation $\mathbf{e} = \mathbf{y} - \mathbf{g}(\mathbf{x}, \boldsymbol{\beta})$ implied by (8.1.1), where $\mathbf{e}$ denotes an outcome of ε. Note that the relation between $(\mathbf{y}, \mathbf{x})$ and $(\boldsymbol{\beta}, \mathbf{e})$ involves $(n+k)$ unknowns in n equations and thus is not 1-to-1. Therefore, we cannot solve for unique values of $(\boldsymbol{\beta}, \mathbf{e})$ given the values $(\mathbf{y}, \mathbf{x})$, and we cannot consider the observation $(\mathbf{y}, \mathbf{x})$ to be equivalent to observing $(\boldsymbol{\beta}, \mathbf{e})$. In particular, the system of equations is underdetermined for deriving unique values of $(\boldsymbol{\beta}, \mathbf{e})$. As in the case of the linear model, if no further mathematical or statistical structure is placed on the DSP model, then the information recovered about $(\boldsymbol{\beta}, \mathbf{e})$ from having observed $(\mathbf{y}, \mathbf{x})$ is only that $(\boldsymbol{\beta}, \mathbf{e})$ is no longer free to assume any value in $\mathrm{R}^k \times \mathrm{R}^n$ space but rather must reside in the reduced set $\Gamma = \{(\boldsymbol{\beta}, \mathbf{e}) : \mathbf{e} = \mathbf{y} - \mathbf{g}(\mathbf{x}, \boldsymbol{\beta}), \mathbf{e} \in \mathrm{R}^n, \boldsymbol{\beta} \in \mathrm{R}^k\}$. This is generally far less information about $(\boldsymbol{\beta}, \mathbf{e})$ than would be considered useful in any practical sense. And to this point we have said nothing about the unknown parameter σ^2.

As we go through the remainder of this chapter, we will follow a format similar to the one used in Chapters 3–6. First, we will discuss the implications of model assumptions. Then we will develop an estimation procedure for recovering the unknown parameters and discuss its sampling properties. Next, we will examine hypothesis-testing and confidence-region procedures and properties. Finally, computational problems in implementing nonlinear procedures will be addressed.

8.1.1. Assumed Probability Model Characteristics: Discussion

To derive meaningful solutions to the inverse problem, we must introduce more information regarding sampling characteristics and other components of the probability model than is conveyed by (8.1.1). The particular characteristics of the nonlinear semiparametric regression model and other added specificity are provided in Table 8.1. Recall that we introduced similar information in the context of the linear semiparametric regression model (5.1.1) in Table 5.1 of Chapter 5.

When we compare Tables 5.1 and 8.1, it is clear that the only essential difference between the two is the more general representation of the expected value of $\mathbf{Y}$ in the nonlinear regression model. A discussion of the implications of other model assumptions (other than nonlinearity) can be found in Section 3.1. Regarding the expectation of the dependent variable, it is assumed that $\mathrm{E}(\mathbf{Y} \mid \mathbf{x})$ can be represented as a twice continuously differentiable function of $\boldsymbol{\beta}$. Note that it is *not* assumed that this function is necessarily differentiable in the explanatory variable values. Note further that twice continuous differentiability is invoked to facilitate the derivation of asymptotic normality properties of the nonlinear least-squares–extremum estimator examined in this chapter but is not necessary for establishing consistency of this estimator.

As one might suspect, considerable flexibility is introduced into the regression model by allowing the conditional expectation function to be nonlinear in both $\mathbf{x}$ and $\boldsymbol{\beta}$. Furthermore, the linear model is completely subsumed by the nonlinear probability model because we can always define $\mathbf{g}(\mathbf{x}, \boldsymbol{\beta}) \equiv \mathbf{x}\boldsymbol{\beta}$. We present some examples of nonlinear regression models below.

► **Example 8.1.1:** Suppose a sample of data is obtained relating to the prices and levels of output and inputs for profit-maximizing firms operating in a competitive industry.

Owing to variations in transportation costs and local input market conditions, the firms do not face the same output and input prices. It is assumed that the firms utilize the same Cobb–Douglas production technology when producing their single output and that only labor and energy are variable inputs in the intermediate run. The dependent variable of interest is labor demand by the firms.

Let the production function of the firms be represented by

$$q = \beta_3 z_1^{\beta_1} z_2^{\beta_2} \tag{8.1.2}$$

so that the objective function of the profit maximizing firm is

$$\max_{z_1, z_2} \quad p\beta_3 z_1^{\beta_1} z_2^{\beta_2} - \sum_{i=1}^{2} r_i z_i, \tag{8.1.3}$$

where z_1 and z_2 are levels of labor and energy inputs, r_1 and r_2 are the corresponding input prices, and p is the output price. The solution to (8.1.3) yields the labor input demand function

$$z_1 = \left[r_1^{1-\beta_2}(\beta_1\beta_3 p)^{-1}\beta_2^{-\beta_2}(\beta_1 r_2)^{\beta_2}\right]^{\frac{1}{\beta_1+\beta_2-1}}. \tag{8.1.4}$$

In most cases it is implausible to assume that (8.1.4) should hold exactly. Instead it is appropriate to recognize that firms operate in an uncertain world in which machines break down, employee efficiency varies over time, scheduling problems arise, and environmental factors impact production. Discrepancies in (8.1.4) are accommodated in the model of labor demand by affixing a noise component to the equation, leading to a nonlinear model of the form (8.1.1),

$$y_i = g(\mathbf{x}_{i\cdot}, \boldsymbol{\beta}) + e_i, \tag{8.1.5}$$

where $y_i = z_i$ is labor demand of the ith firm, $\mathbf{x}_{i\cdot} = [r_{i1}, r_{i2}]$ is the vector of input prices facing the ith firm, $\boldsymbol{\beta} = (\beta_1, \beta_2, \beta_3)'$ are the production function parameters, $g(\mathbf{x}_{i\cdot}, \boldsymbol{\beta})$ is the conditional expectation function for the demand function defined specifically by the right-hand side of (8.1.4), and e_i is the outcome of the noise component for the ith firm.

► **Example 8.1.2:** Assume that a sample of data pertaining to the demand by consumers for two categories of goods is available. It is assumed that the consumers' utility functions have the constant elasticity of substitution (CES) form

$$u(z_1, z_2) = \left(z_1^{\beta_1} + z_2^{\beta_1}\right)^{1/\beta_1}, \tag{8.1.6}$$

where z_i is the consumption level of goods in category i. Letting p_i be the price level of good category i, the expenditure function associated with the CES utility function is

$$m = e(p_1, p_2, u) = \left(p_1^{\beta_1^*} + p_2^{\beta_1^*}\right)^{1/\beta_1^*} u, \tag{8.1.7}$$

where $\beta_1^* = \beta_1/(\beta_1 - 1)$.

Inverting the expenditure function to solve for u yields the indirect utility function, denoted by v, as follows:

$$\mathrm{v} = \left(\mathrm{p}_1^{\beta_1^*} + \mathrm{p}_2^{\beta_1^*}\right)^{-1/\beta_1^*} \mathrm{m}. \tag{8.1.8}$$

Then an application of Roy's identity yields the consumer's demand functions:

$$\mathrm{g_i}(\mathrm{p}_1, \mathrm{p}_2, \mathrm{m}) = \frac{-\partial \mathrm{v}/\partial \mathrm{p}_i}{\partial \mathrm{v}/\partial \mathrm{m}} = \frac{\mathrm{p}_i^{\beta_1^*-1}\mathrm{m}}{\mathrm{p}_1^{\beta_1^*} + \mathrm{p}_2^{\beta_1^*}}, \quad i = 1, 2. \tag{8.1.9}$$

To accommodate errors in judgment, optimization discrepancies, and random idiosyncratic consumer behavior, if we acknowledge a noise component in the sample outcomes, we have a nonlinear model in the form

$$\mathrm{y}_i = \mathrm{g}_i(\mathbf{x}_{i\cdot}, \boldsymbol{\beta}) + \mathrm{e}_i, \quad i = 1, 2, \tag{8.1.10}$$

where $\mathrm{y}_i = \mathrm{z}_i$ is the consumption of category i goods, $\mathbf{x}_{i\cdot} = [\mathrm{p}_{i1}, \mathrm{p}_{i2}, \mathrm{m}_i]$ is the vector of prices and expenditure levels, $\boldsymbol{\beta} = [\beta_1]$, and e_i is an outcome of the noise component. An additional subscript appended on y_i, x_i, and e_i can be used to denote observations on individual consumers.

8.1.2. The Inverse Problem

Given the functional relationship (8.1.1) and the attending assumptions that collectively describe the underlying probability model, we now require a solution to the inverse problem of using observations on $(\mathbf{Y}, \mathbf{x})$ to recover information about the unknowns and unobservables represented by $(\boldsymbol{\beta}, \sigma^2, \boldsymbol{\varepsilon})$. We will see that there are striking parallels to the inverse problem solutions presented previously for the linear model. We will utilize statistical estimation principles to seek functions of the observable $(\mathbf{Y}, \mathbf{x})$ that produce useful and defensible point estimates of the unknown and unobservable $\boldsymbol{\beta}$, $\boldsymbol{\varepsilon}$, and σ^2. We will also use asymptotic theory, together with hypothesis-testing and confidence-region estimating principles to provide additional types of inverse problem solutions. We emphasize that because the linear model is a special case of the nonlinear model (i.e., let $\mathbf{g}(\mathbf{x}, \boldsymbol{\beta}) \equiv \mathbf{x}\boldsymbol{\beta}$), *all* of the results that we present subsequently, including methods for testing hypotheses and generating confidence regions for *nonlinear functions of parameters*, apply to the linear model as well.

We emphasize that the nonlinear regression model is a conceptual abstraction used to express our state of knowledge about the DSP associated with the economic process under study. In providing inverse problem solutions, we are providing ways of generating information about the unknowns and unobservables of the probability model. Though more flexible in its representation of the conditional expectation function $\mathrm{E}[\mathbf{Y} \mid \mathbf{x}]$, inferences about nonlinear model components will provide useful information about components of the economic process under study only to the extent that the model is a useful approximation to, or is congruent with, the DSP underlying the observed data. Also, we remind the reader that the statistical properties of estimation and inference procedures are generally dependent on the probability model encompassing the DSP underlying the data. Relatedly, the very idea that there exists a "true value of $\boldsymbol{\theta}$" is predicated on the assumption that the probability model is congruent with the actual DSP for some $\boldsymbol{\theta}$ in the parameter space defined by the model.

8.2. The Problem of Estimating $\boldsymbol{\beta}$

In this section we examine solutions to the inverse problem of recovering information on the unknown and unobservable $\boldsymbol{\beta}$ from observations on the sample data $(\mathbf{Y}, \mathbf{x})$ when the probability model is based on the nonlinear functional relationship (8.1.1) and the specific probability model characteristics in Table 8.1. In this section, information will be generated in the form of point estimates of the unknowns.

8.2.1. The Nonlinear Least-Squares Estimator

We introduce the nonlinear least-squares (NLS) estimator in this section. The NLS estimator is an extremum estimator based on the estimation objective function

$$\mathrm{m}(\boldsymbol{\beta}, \mathbf{Y}, \mathbf{x}) = -\frac{1}{n}[\mathbf{Y} - \mathbf{g}(\mathbf{x}, \boldsymbol{\beta})]'[\mathbf{Y} - \mathbf{g}(\mathbf{x}, \boldsymbol{\beta})]. \tag{8.2.1}$$

The NLS-extremum estimator can be defined as

$$\hat{\boldsymbol{\beta}} = \arg\max_{\boldsymbol{\beta}}[\mathrm{m}(\boldsymbol{\beta}, \mathbf{Y}, \mathbf{x})] = \arg\min_{\boldsymbol{\beta}}\left[\frac{1}{n}[\mathbf{Y} - \mathbf{g}(\mathbf{x}, \boldsymbol{\beta})]'[\mathbf{Y} - \mathbf{g}(\mathbf{x}, \boldsymbol{\beta})]\right]. \tag{8.2.2}$$

A fundamental rationale in support of the choice of the squared-error metric for defining the extremum estimator can be provided in a way that is analogous to the arguments presented for the linear model in Chapter 5. It is instructive to revisit this rationale explicitly in the nonlinear model context because it highlights the importance of *parameter identification*, which we will discuss in more detail in the next subsection.

One supporting argument for the squared-error metric is based on the nonlinear analog to (5.2.2),

$$\begin{aligned}
-\,\mathrm{E}[\mathrm{m}(\boldsymbol{\beta}, \mathbf{Y}, \mathbf{x})] &= \frac{1}{n}\mathrm{E}[[\mathbf{Y} - \mathbf{g}(\mathbf{x}, \boldsymbol{\beta})]'[\mathbf{Y} - \mathbf{g}(\mathbf{x}, \boldsymbol{\beta})]] \\
&= \frac{1}{n}\mathrm{E}[[\mathbf{Y} - \mathbf{g}(\mathbf{x}, \boldsymbol{\beta}_0) + \mathbf{g}(\mathbf{x}, \boldsymbol{\beta}_0) - \mathbf{g}(\mathbf{x}, \boldsymbol{\beta})]'[\mathbf{Y} - \mathbf{g}(\mathbf{x}, \boldsymbol{\beta}_0) \\
&\quad + \mathbf{g}(\mathbf{x}, \boldsymbol{\beta}_0) - \mathbf{g}(\mathbf{x}, \boldsymbol{\beta})]] \\
&= \sigma^2 + \frac{1}{n}[\mathbf{g}(\mathbf{x}, \boldsymbol{\beta}_0) - \mathbf{g}(\mathbf{x}, \boldsymbol{\beta})]'[\mathbf{g}(\mathbf{x}, \boldsymbol{\beta}_0) - \mathbf{g}(\mathbf{x}, \boldsymbol{\beta})],
\end{aligned} \tag{8.2.3}$$

where $\boldsymbol{\beta}_0$ denotes the true value of the parameter vector in (8.2.3). If $\mathbf{g}(\mathbf{x}, \boldsymbol{\beta}_0) \neq \mathbf{g}(\mathbf{x}, \boldsymbol{\beta})\ \forall \boldsymbol{\beta} \neq \boldsymbol{\beta}_0$ (which we will see is a parameter identification condition), then it is clear that (8.2.3) is minimized uniquely at $\boldsymbol{\beta} = \boldsymbol{\beta}_0$. Thus, if the expectation in (8.2.3) could actually be calculated, minimizing (8.2.3) would recover $\boldsymbol{\beta}_0$ exactly. In practice, the probability distribution required to perform the expectations is unknown, and so the sample analog given by the negative of (8.2.1) is used instead. Under an appropriate law of large numbers, $-\mathrm{m}(\boldsymbol{\beta}, \mathbf{Y}, \mathbf{x})$ will converge to (8.2.3), and thus one would expect that minimizing (8.2.3), and thereby defining $\hat{\boldsymbol{\beta}}$ as in (8.2.2), should result in an estimate close to $\boldsymbol{\beta}_0$ for large enough n, justifying the choice of the squared-error metric.

An alternative rationale based on a prediction criterion is analogous to the rationale given relating to (5.2.3) in the linear model case. One need only replace $\hat{\mathbf{Y}} = \mathbf{x}\hat{\boldsymbol{\beta}}$ with $\hat{\mathbf{Y}} = \mathbf{g}(\mathbf{x}, \hat{\boldsymbol{\beta}})$, and the arguments are identical. So long as the squared-error metric $\mathrm{m}(\boldsymbol{\beta}, \mathbf{Y}, \mathbf{x})$ can be uniquely maximized, an NLS estimate can be calculated.

We now turn to the question of parameter identification, which relates to both whether $\mathbf{g}(\mathbf{x}, \boldsymbol{\beta}_0) \neq \mathbf{g}(\mathbf{x}, \boldsymbol{\beta})\ \forall \boldsymbol{\beta} \neq \boldsymbol{\beta}_0$ and whether a unique minimum to the sum of squares exists.

8.2.2. Parameter Identification Relative to a Probability Model

In order to be able to use sample data $(\mathbf{Y}, \mathbf{x})$ to recover point estimates of the unknown and unobservable parameters in any probability model specification, it is first necessary that the parameters be *identified relative to the probability model*. In general terms, this means that for each possible value of the parameter vector $(\boldsymbol{\beta}, \sigma^2)$, $(\mathbf{Y}, \mathbf{x})$ must reflect at least some characteristics of the probability model (e.g., means, variances, ranges, event probabilities) that are unique to that parameter value and that can be used to *identify* a unique value of the parameter vector. Intuitively, this makes sense because, if the behavior of the sample data is precisely the same in all measurable respects regardless of which of two vectors $(\boldsymbol{\beta}_0, \sigma_0^2)$ or $(\boldsymbol{\beta}_*, \sigma_*^2)$ is the true parameter vector, then there is no information contained in the outcomes of $(\mathbf{Y}, \mathbf{x})$ that can be used to distinguish between the two parameter vectors. In this case, $(\mathbf{y}, \mathbf{x})$ is effectively an indirect observation on *either* $(\boldsymbol{\beta}_0, \sigma_0^2)$ or $(\boldsymbol{\beta}_*, \sigma_*^2)$, and the parameter vector, $(\boldsymbol{\beta}, \sigma^2)$, is then *not identified* by *any* sample data from the DSP characterized by the probability model. Consequently, this means sample data do not contain sufficient information to discriminate among all of the unique values of $(\boldsymbol{\beta}, \sigma^2)$ that are possible within the probability model specified.

In the special case of the linear regression model, identification of the parameters relative to the probability model is assured if the $\mathrm{rank}(\mathbf{x}) = \mathrm{k}$ condition on the $(n \times k)$ matrix $\mathbf{x}$ holds. If the rank condition holds, then there are some characteristics of $(\mathbf{Y}, \mathbf{x})$ that are unique for every choice of $(\boldsymbol{\beta}, \sigma^2) \in \mathrm{R}^k \times \mathrm{R}^1_+$, where R^1_+ is the positive part of the real line, that is, $\mathrm{R}^1_+ = (0, \infty)$. To see this, first note that because the noise component is additive in the linear regression model, and because the elements of the noise component all have mean 0 and variance σ^2, it necessarily follows that the potential joint probability distributions for $\mathbf{Y}$ are distinguished in the probability model on the basis of the value of the mean vector of $\mathbf{Y}$, $\mathrm{E}[\mathbf{Y} \mid \mathbf{x}] = \mathbf{x}\boldsymbol{\beta}$, and the variance of the Y_i's, σ^2. In particular, by the additive nature of the noise component, the covariance matrix of $\mathbf{Y}$, $\mathbf{cov}(\mathbf{Y} \mid \mathbf{x}) = \sigma^2 \mathbf{I}_n$, is different for every choice of $\sigma^2 \in \mathrm{R}^1_+$. Furthermore, for each choice of $\boldsymbol{\beta} \in \mathrm{R}^k$, a unique value for the expected value of $\mathbf{Y}$, given by $\mathrm{E}[\mathbf{Y} \mid \mathbf{x}] = \mathbf{x}\boldsymbol{\beta}$, is defined. This latter result follows from the fact that if $\mathbf{x}\boldsymbol{\beta}_0 = \mathbf{x}\boldsymbol{\beta}_*$, so that the means and variances implied by $(\boldsymbol{\beta}_0, \sigma^2)$ and $(\boldsymbol{\beta}_*, \sigma^2)$ are indistinguishable, then $\boldsymbol{\beta}_0 \neq \boldsymbol{\beta}_*$ *cannot* be true because premultiplying $\mathbf{x}\boldsymbol{\beta}_0 = \mathbf{x}\boldsymbol{\beta}_*$ by $(\mathbf{x}'\mathbf{x})^{-1}\mathbf{x}'$ would imply that $\boldsymbol{\beta}_0 = (\mathbf{x}'\mathbf{x})^{-1}\mathbf{x}'\mathbf{x}\boldsymbol{\beta}_0 = (\mathbf{x}'\mathbf{x})^{-1}\mathbf{x}'\,\mathbf{x}\,\boldsymbol{\beta}_* = \boldsymbol{\beta}_*$. Thus, $\mathrm{rank}(\mathbf{x}) = \mathrm{k}$ implies the parameter identification condition $\mathbf{x}\boldsymbol{\beta}_0 \neq \mathbf{x}\boldsymbol{\beta}_*$ if $\boldsymbol{\beta}_0 \neq \boldsymbol{\beta}_*$, so that a unique probability distribution for **Y** given **x** is associated with every possible value of $(\boldsymbol{\beta}, \sigma^2)$. The parameter vector is identified relative to the probability model.

There are analog conditions for identifying the parameter vector in the nonlinear model. First of all, because it is still true that the noise component is additive in the nonlinear model, and because the elements of the noise component all have mean 0 and variance σ^2, it necessarily follows that the probability distributions for **Y** are distinguished in this probability model on the basis of the value of the mean vector of **Y**, $\mathrm{E}[\mathbf{Y} \mid \mathbf{x}] = \mathbf{g}(\mathbf{x}, \boldsymbol{\beta})$, and the variance of the Y_i's, σ^2. It is clear that the covariance matrix of **Y** is different for every choice of $\sigma^2 \in \mathrm{R}^1_+$, where $\mathbf{cov}(\mathbf{Y} \mid \mathbf{x}) = \sigma^2 \mathbf{I}_n$. However, the expected value of **Y** is given by $\mathrm{E}[\mathbf{Y} \mid \mathbf{x}] = \mathbf{g}(\mathbf{x}, \boldsymbol{\beta})$, and the condition $\mathrm{rank}(\mathbf{x}) = \mathrm{k}$ is now *not* sufficient to ensure that $\boldsymbol{\beta}_0 \neq \boldsymbol{\beta}_* \Rightarrow \mathbf{g}(\mathbf{x}, \boldsymbol{\beta}_0) \neq \mathbf{g}(\mathbf{x}, \boldsymbol{\beta}_*)$. There exist choices of $\mathbf{g}(\mathbf{x}, \boldsymbol{\beta})$ for which some, or even all, of the possible values of the parameter vector are not identifiable.

► **Example 8.2.1 (Values of a Parameter Vector That Are Not Identifiable):** Examine a nonlinear model of the form $\mathbf{Y} = \mathbf{g}(\mathbf{x}, \boldsymbol{\beta}) = \beta_1 \mathbf{1}_n + \beta_2 \mathbf{w} + \beta_3 \mathbf{w}^{\beta_4} + \boldsymbol{\varepsilon}$, where **Y** and **w** are two $(n \times 1)$ vectors, $\mathbf{1}_n$ is a $(n \times 1)$ vector of unit values, **w** is *not* a vector of identical constants so that $\mathbf{x} = [\mathbf{1}_n \ \mathbf{w}]$ has full column rank, $\mathrm{E}[\boldsymbol{\varepsilon} \mid \mathbf{x}] = \mathbf{0}$, and $\mathbf{cov}(\boldsymbol{\varepsilon} \mid \mathbf{x}) = \sigma^2 \mathbf{I}_n$. There are values of the (5×1) parameter vector $\boldsymbol{\theta} = [\beta_1, \beta_2, \beta_3, \beta_4, \sigma^2]' \in \mathrm{R}^4 \times \mathrm{R}^1_+$ that are *not* identifiable. This can be verified by inspection through the definition of nonsingleton sets of values for the parameter vector that all yield precisely the same value of the $\mathrm{E}[\mathbf{Y} \mid \mathbf{x}]$ vector and, indeed, precisely the same outcomes for **Y**. Two clear examples are the following:

Case 1: $\beta_4 = 0 \Rightarrow \mathrm{E}[\mathbf{Y} \mid \mathbf{x}] = \delta \mathbf{1}_n + \beta_2 \mathbf{w}$ and $\mathbf{y} = \delta \mathbf{1}_n + \beta_2 \mathbf{w} + \mathbf{e}$ for *every* value of $\boldsymbol{\theta}$ for which $\beta_1 + \beta_3 = \delta$, which is an infinite number of possible parameter vectors. Thus, any parameter vector value $\boldsymbol{\theta}$ for which $\beta_4 = 0$ is not identifiable.

Case 2: $\beta_4 = 1 \Rightarrow \mathrm{E}[\mathbf{Y} \mid \mathbf{x}] = \beta_1 \mathbf{1}_n + \delta \mathbf{w}$ and $\mathbf{y} = \beta_1 \mathbf{1}_n + \delta \mathbf{w} + \mathbf{e}$ for *every* value of $\boldsymbol{\theta}$ for which $\beta_2 + \beta_3 = \delta$, which is an infinite number of possible parameter vectors. Thus, any parameter vector value $\boldsymbol{\theta}$ for which $\beta_4 = 1$ is not identifiable.

As can be seen from the example, the problem of nonidentifiability of parameter vector values is related to the functional form of the nonlinear model as well as the set of potential parameter values, that is, the parameter space, specified in the probability model.

The concept of *parameter identification relative to a probability model* amounts to a global necessary condition for being able to distinguish between parameter values on the basis of the information contained in sample data. The condition thus also relates to whether it is possible to define *any* point estimation procedure whatsoever that can distinguish between all of the parameter values in the parameter space on the basis of information contained in the data. If the parameter values are not identifiable, then the answer is no.

We now formalize the preceding concept of parameter identification relative to a probability model.

Definition 8.2.1 (Parameter Identification Relative to a Probability Model): Let $P_F(\boldsymbol{\theta})$ be the set of all probability distribution for $\mathbf{Y} \mid \mathbf{x}$ that are consistent with a given probability model when the value of the parameter vector of interest is $\boldsymbol{\theta}$, and let Ω be the set of admissible values for the parameter vector.

a. The parameter value $\boldsymbol{\theta}_* \in \Omega$ is said to be *identifiable relative to the probability model*, or simply identifiable, if $P_F(\boldsymbol{\theta}) \cap P_F(\boldsymbol{\theta}_*) = \emptyset, \forall \boldsymbol{\theta} \in \Omega - \boldsymbol{\theta}_*$.

b. If the parameter values $\boldsymbol{\theta}_* \in \Omega$ and $\boldsymbol{\theta} \in \Omega$ are such that $P_F(\boldsymbol{\theta}) = P_F(\boldsymbol{\theta}_*)$, then the parameter values are said to be *observationally equivalent*.

c. If the value of the parameter vector $\boldsymbol{\theta}$ is identifiable for every value of $\boldsymbol{\theta} \in \Omega$, then the parameter vector is said to be *identified relative to the probability model*, or simply *identified*.

Thus, in formal terms, identifiability of a parameter vector value $\boldsymbol{\theta}_*$ hinges on whether $\boldsymbol{\theta}_*$ is associated with probability distributions for the random sample $\mathbf{Y}$ conditional on $\mathbf{x}$ that are distinct from probability distributions associated with other parameter values. In applications, the analyst must be sure to specify probability models whose parameter vectors are identified. Otherwise, it is clear that it will be impossible to discriminate, on the basis of sample data, between parameter values that are not identifiable or are observationally equivalent, or both. Identification involves appropriate choices of functional forms and may require restrictions on the admissible values of the parameters inherent in these functional forms, as is the case in Example 8.2.1.

Returning to the specific question of parameter identification in the nonlinear regression model, we see it follows from Definition 8.2.1, and the additive nature of the elements of the noise component, that the condition needed for the parameter vector to be identified is $\mathbf{g}(\mathbf{x}, \boldsymbol{\beta}_0) \neq \mathbf{g}(\mathbf{x}, \boldsymbol{\beta}_*)$ when $\boldsymbol{\beta}_0 \neq \boldsymbol{\beta}_*$. Observationally equivalent and unidentifiable parameter values $\boldsymbol{\beta}_0$ and $\boldsymbol{\beta}_*$, where $\boldsymbol{\beta}_0 \neq \boldsymbol{\beta}_*$, would be defined by the condition $\mathbf{g}(\mathbf{x}, \boldsymbol{\beta}_0) = \mathbf{g}(\mathbf{x}, \boldsymbol{\beta}_*)$.

8.2.3. Parameter Identification Relative to the Least-Squares Criterion and Given Data

The preceding discussion of parameter identification was concerned with whether it is conceptually possible to define *any* function of sample data capable of discriminating among all of the parameter values in the parameter space of a probability model. We now examine a narrower concept of parameter identification that relates to the possibility of distinguishing between the parameter values in a parameter space on the basis of a given sample of data and a particular estimation objective function, namely, the squared-error metric or the least-squares criterion (LSC). If not, then the probability model cannot be estimated using the NLS estimation procedure. In the discussion ahead, if the qualifier "relative to the LSC" is not explicitly stated, it will be taken as implicit.

Identification relative to the LSC and a given sample of data refers to whether the least-squares criterion will lead to a *unique* estimate of $\boldsymbol{\beta}$ for a given outcome $(\mathbf{y}, \mathbf{x})$ of

$(\mathbf{Y}, \mathbf{x})$. In Definition 8.2.2 we define

$$\mathrm{S}(\boldsymbol{\beta}) \equiv (\mathbf{Y} - \hat{\mathbf{y}})'(\mathbf{Y} - \hat{\mathbf{y}}) = [\mathbf{Y} - \mathbf{g}(\mathbf{x}, \boldsymbol{\beta})]'[\mathbf{Y} - \mathbf{g}(\mathbf{x}, \boldsymbol{\beta})] \tag{8.2.4}$$

so that *the nonlinear least-squares* (NLS) estimator can be defined by

$$\hat{\boldsymbol{\beta}} = \arg\min_{\boldsymbol{\beta}}[\mathrm{S}(\boldsymbol{\beta})] = \arg\max_{\boldsymbol{\beta}}[\mathrm{m}(\boldsymbol{\beta}, \mathbf{Y}, \mathbf{x})], \tag{8.2.5}$$

where $\mathrm{m}(\boldsymbol{\beta}, \mathbf{Y}, \mathbf{x}) \equiv -\frac{1}{n}\mathrm{S}(\boldsymbol{\beta})$.

Definition 8.2.2 (Identification Relative to the LSC and a Given Sample of Data): The parameter vector $\boldsymbol{\beta}$ in the nonlinear regression model is said to be *identified relative to the LSC and a given sample of data*, $(\mathbf{y}, \mathbf{x})$, if

$$\hat{\mathbf{b}} = \arg\min_{\boldsymbol{\beta}}[\mathrm{s}(\boldsymbol{\beta})] = \arg\min_{\boldsymbol{\beta}}[\mathbf{y} - \mathbf{g}(\mathbf{x}, \boldsymbol{\beta})]'[\mathbf{y} - \mathbf{g}(\mathbf{x}, \boldsymbol{\beta})] \tag{8.2.6}$$

is unique.

If one recalls that in the nonlinear probability model of Table 8.1, $\mathbf{g}(\mathbf{x}, \boldsymbol{\beta})$ is twice continuously differentiable with respect to the parameter vector $\boldsymbol{\beta}$, the first-order conditions for minimizing $\mathrm{s}(\boldsymbol{\beta})$ are given by

$$\frac{\partial \mathrm{s}(\boldsymbol{\beta})}{\partial \boldsymbol{\beta}} = -2\frac{\partial \mathbf{g}(\mathbf{x}, \boldsymbol{\beta})}{\partial \boldsymbol{\beta}}[\mathbf{y} - \mathbf{g}(\mathbf{x}, \boldsymbol{\beta})] = \mathbf{0}, \tag{8.2.7}$$

where the matrix $\frac{\partial \mathbf{g}(\mathbf{x}, \boldsymbol{\beta})}{\partial \boldsymbol{\beta}}$ is a $(k \times n)$ matrix whose (i, j)th entry is given by $\frac{\partial \mathrm{g}(\mathbf{x}_{j\cdot}, \boldsymbol{\beta})}{\partial \beta_i}$ with $\mathrm{g}(\mathbf{x}_{j\cdot}, \boldsymbol{\beta})$ being the jth element of the $(n \times 1)$ vector $\mathbf{g}(\mathbf{x}, \boldsymbol{\beta}) \equiv [\mathrm{g}(\mathbf{x}_{1\cdot}, \boldsymbol{\beta}), \ldots, \mathrm{g}(\mathbf{x}_{n\cdot}, \boldsymbol{\beta})]'$.

Note, as a point of reference, that in the special case in which $\mathbf{g}(\mathbf{x}, \boldsymbol{\beta}) \equiv \mathbf{x}\boldsymbol{\beta}$, these first-order conditions are precisely those for the linear model, Equation (5.2.8), apart from the scaling by n. The parameter vector $\boldsymbol{\beta}$ is identified, relative to the data $(\mathbf{y}, \mathbf{x})$, if there is one unique value $\hat{\mathbf{b}}$ that solves (8.2.7) and minimizes $\mathrm{s}(\boldsymbol{\beta})$ for the given outcome of $(\mathbf{Y}, \mathbf{x})$. A solution $\hat{\mathbf{b}}$ will be locally unique in the neighborhood of $\hat{\mathbf{b}}$ if the second-order conditions for the minimization problem are satisfied, that is, if the Hessian matrix $2\frac{\partial^2 \mathrm{s}(\boldsymbol{\beta})}{\partial \boldsymbol{\beta} \partial \boldsymbol{\beta}'}\big|_{\hat{\mathbf{b}}}$ is positive definite. If the Hessian is globally positive definite, then $\hat{\mathbf{b}}$ will be globally unique. More generally, if the function $\mathrm{s}(\boldsymbol{\beta})$ is strictly convex, then, if a minimum of $\mathrm{s}(\boldsymbol{\beta})$ exists at all, it will be unique. If we refer again to the special case of the linear model $\mathbf{g}(\mathbf{x}, \boldsymbol{\beta}) \equiv \mathbf{x}\boldsymbol{\beta}$, the second-order condition refers to the positive definiteness of the matrix $2\mathbf{x}'\mathbf{x}$, which follows if $\mathbf{x}$ has full-column rank, in which case the least-squares–extremum estimate is globally unique.

In practice, it is often the case that $\mathrm{s}(\boldsymbol{\beta})$ is not strictly convex, or the Hessian matrix of $\mathrm{s}(\boldsymbol{\beta})$ is not globally positive definite, or both. In cases in which multiple local minima exist, the question of identifiability with respect to the LSC and given data then refers to whether a unique minimum of all of the local minima exists. The challenge in practice is to identify the set of local minima so that the question of identification can be answered. This will involve finding all of the roots of the first-order conditions relating to the problem of minimizing $\mathrm{s}(\boldsymbol{\beta})$, using iterative search algorithms based on various starting values to identify the local minima, or both. The chapter appendix discusses minimization algorithms and will clarify what is meant by starting values. Examples of the application of NLS procedures will appear throughout the book, including the example that follows.

► **Example 8.2.3:** To demonstrate the identification concepts discussed in this section, we provide the GAUSS program C8Ident.gss in the examples manual. For a given sample generated from an overparameterized nonlinear regression model, GAUSS presents the surface and contour plots for the nonlinear least-squares objective function. The surface plots for the identified parameters are strictly convex, and nonstrict convexities appear in the surface and contour plots for the unidentified parameters.

8.3. Sampling Properties of the NLS Estimator

We provide an overview of sampling properties of the NLS estimator in this section. We assume throughout that the parameter vector is identified relative to the probability model. We begin immediately with a discussion of asymptotic properties simply because there is little that can be said about the NLS estimator with regard to generally applicable small-sample properties.

In the process of motivating asymptotic properties, we will note striking analogies to the linear-model case. The analogies are based on first-order approximations to the conditional expectation function of the model. We will provide more detail regarding asymptotic properties in Section 8.9.

Letting $\boldsymbol{\beta}_0$ denote the true value of $\boldsymbol{\beta}$, we can expand $\mathbf{g}(\mathbf{x}, \boldsymbol{\beta})$ in a first-order Taylor series around $\boldsymbol{\beta}_0$ as

$$\mathbf{g}(\mathbf{x}, \boldsymbol{\beta}) \approx \mathbf{g}(\mathbf{x}, \boldsymbol{\beta}_0) + \frac{\partial \mathbf{g}(\mathbf{x}, \boldsymbol{\beta}_0)}{\partial \boldsymbol{\beta}'}(\boldsymbol{\beta} - \boldsymbol{\beta}_0). \tag{8.3.1}$$

If we define $\mathbf{x}(\boldsymbol{\beta}_0) \equiv \frac{\partial \mathbf{g}(\mathbf{x}, \boldsymbol{\beta}_0)}{\partial \boldsymbol{\beta}'} \equiv \left.\frac{\partial \mathbf{g}(\mathbf{x}, \boldsymbol{\beta})}{\partial \boldsymbol{\beta}'}\right|_{\boldsymbol{\beta}_0}$ and substitute (8.3.1) into (8.2.4), the least-squares objective function can be represented as

$$\mathrm{S}(\boldsymbol{\theta}) \approx [\mathbf{Z} - \mathbf{x}(\boldsymbol{\beta}_0)\boldsymbol{\theta}]'[\mathbf{Z} - \mathbf{x}(\boldsymbol{\beta}_0)\boldsymbol{\theta}], \tag{8.3.2}$$

where $\mathbf{Z} \equiv \mathbf{Y} - \mathbf{g}(\mathbf{x}, \boldsymbol{\beta}_0) = \varepsilon$ and $\boldsymbol{\theta} = \boldsymbol{\beta} - \boldsymbol{\beta}_0$.

To the first-order of approximation, minimizing the right side of (8.3.2) is analogous to finding the least-squares estimator of $\boldsymbol{\theta}$ in the linear model $\mathbf{z} = \mathbf{x}(\boldsymbol{\beta}_0)\boldsymbol{\theta} + \mathbf{v}$, yielding

$$\hat{\boldsymbol{\theta}} = [\mathbf{x}(\boldsymbol{\beta}_0)'\mathbf{x}(\boldsymbol{\beta}_0)]^{-1}\mathbf{x}(\boldsymbol{\beta}_0)'\mathbf{z}. \tag{8.3.3}$$

It follows that the NLS estimator is given by

$$\hat{\boldsymbol{\beta}} \approx \boldsymbol{\beta}_0 + [\mathbf{x}(\boldsymbol{\beta}_0)'\mathbf{x}(\boldsymbol{\beta}_0)]^{-1}\mathbf{x}(\boldsymbol{\beta}_0)'\varepsilon. \tag{8.3.4}$$

Then *to the first-order of approximation*, the NLS estimator $\hat{\boldsymbol{\beta}}$ is unbiased, and its covariance matrix is $\sigma^2[\mathbf{x}(\boldsymbol{\beta}_0)'\mathbf{x}(\boldsymbol{\beta}_0)]^{-1}$, which follows directly from results on the means and covariance matrices of linear combinations of random variables. Furthermore, assuming regularity conditions on $\mathbf{x}(\boldsymbol{\beta}_0)$ and ε analogous to those applied to $\mathbf{x}$ and ε in the linear model case to achieve asymptotic results, we have that

$$n^{-1}\mathbf{x}(\boldsymbol{\beta}_0)'\mathbf{x}(\boldsymbol{\beta}_0) \to \Xi, \quad n^{-1}\mathbf{x}(\boldsymbol{\beta}_0)'\boldsymbol{\varepsilon} \xrightarrow{p} \mathbf{0}, \quad \text{and} \quad n^{-1/2}\mathbf{x}(\boldsymbol{\beta}_0)'\boldsymbol{\varepsilon} \xrightarrow{d} \mathrm{N}(\mathbf{0}, \sigma^2\Xi), \tag{8.3.5}$$

where Ξ is a finite, symmetric, positive definite matrix. Then to the first order of approximation,

$$n^{1/2}(\hat{\boldsymbol{\beta}} - \boldsymbol{\beta}_0) \xrightarrow{d} \mathrm{N}(\mathbf{0}, \sigma^2\Xi^{-1}) \quad \text{and} \quad \hat{\boldsymbol{\beta}} \overset{a}{\sim} \mathrm{N}(\boldsymbol{\beta}_0, \sigma^2[\mathbf{x}(\boldsymbol{\beta}_0)'\mathbf{x}(\boldsymbol{\beta}_0)]^{-1}), \tag{8.3.6}$$

which is analogous to the results for the linear model. Finally, given the limiting distribution result of (8.3.6), it follows that $n^{1/2}(\hat{\boldsymbol{\beta}} - \boldsymbol{\beta}_0)$ is $O_p(1)$, so that $(\hat{\boldsymbol{\beta}} - \boldsymbol{\beta}_0)$ is $o_p(1)$, $\hat{\boldsymbol{\beta}} - \boldsymbol{\beta}_0 \xrightarrow{p} \mathbf{0}$, and thus $\hat{\boldsymbol{\beta}}$ is a consistent estimator of $\boldsymbol{\beta}_0$.

All of the preceding approximations are accurate within small neighborhoods of the true parameter vector $\boldsymbol{\beta}_0$, which is derived from the accuracy of the first-order Taylor series in such neighborhoods. We will provide a more detailed motivation for the preceding asymptotic results in Section 8.9, where we will see that $\hat{\boldsymbol{\beta}}$ is almost certain to be in a neighborhood of $\boldsymbol{\beta}_0$ as $n \to \infty$ under general regularity conditions. As such, the analogy to the linear least-squares results is fully justified asymptotically. In practice, the asymptotic normality and asymptotic covariance results are used to provide a basis for hypothesis testing and confidence region estimation, as we will see in later sections of this chapter. An operational version of the asymptotic covariance matrix in (8.3.6) is obtained by replacing $\boldsymbol{\beta}_0$ and σ^2 with consistent NLS estimator outcomes.

► **Example 8.3.1:** To illustrate the consistency of the NLS estimator, we provide the GAUSS program C8Plim.gss in the examples manual. For a given nonlinear regression model, the bias and variance of the NLS estimator are estimated by Monte Carlo simulation for up to eight different sample sizes (selected by the user). The model satisfies the regularity conditions for consistency of the estimator, and the user should find that the estimated bias and variance decline to zero as the sample size increases. Thus, the NLS estimator converges in mean square and thus in probability to the true parameter values (also selected by the user).

As in the linear semiparametric models, we have not assumed knowledge of a particular probability model for the noise process in this chapter. To approximate the sampling distribution of the NLS estimator, we can use first-order asymptotic methods (see Section 8.9) or the bootstrap procedure (refer to the Monte Carlo appendix to the book). In the following example, we compare the performance of the bootstrap with results from a Monte Carlo simulation exercise in which the actual noise process is known.

► **Example 8.3.2:** To illustrate the asymptotic normality of the NLS estimator, we provide the GAUSS program C8CLT.gss in the examples manual. For a given nonlinear regression model, the NLS parameter estimates are replicated by nonparametric bootstrap and Monte Carlo simulation for up to four different sample sizes (selected by the user). GAUSS reports the empirical and asymptotic distribution functions for the NLS estimator, and the user should find that the bootstrap and Monte Carlo EDFs converge to the limiting normal distribution as the sample size increases. The box-and-whisker plots of the empirical distributions are also presented to demonstrate further the bias and variance properties of the NLS estimator.

8.4. The Problem of Estimating ε, σ^2, and cov($\hat{\beta}$)

8.4.1. An Estimator for ε

On the basis of an analogy to the linear model case and Equation (5.4.1), indirect observations on the random vector ε are given by outcomes of the estimator

$$\hat{\varepsilon} = \mathbf{Y} - \mathbf{g}(\mathbf{x}, \hat{\boldsymbol{\beta}}) = \varepsilon + [\mathbf{g}(\mathbf{x}, \boldsymbol{\beta}_0) - \mathbf{g}(\mathbf{x}, \hat{\boldsymbol{\beta}})], \tag{8.4.1}$$

where $\boldsymbol{\beta}_0$ is again being used to denote the true value of $\boldsymbol{\beta}$. As in the case of the linear model, it is not possible to invert the functional relationship and thereby solve for the value of ε – the noise component is indeed unobservable. The basic problem is that there are $(n + k)$ unknowns $(\varepsilon, \boldsymbol{\beta}_0)$ within the set of n equations given by (8.4.1), and thus the system is underdetermined.

Nothing in the way of general results can be stated regarding the finite sample expectation or covariance matrix of the estimator $\hat{\varepsilon}$. However, given the consistency of $\hat{\boldsymbol{\beta}}$ for $\boldsymbol{\beta}$, we can claim consistency of the estimator $\hat{\varepsilon}_i$ for ε_i, $\forall i$.

Theorem 8.4.1 (Consistency and Convergence in Distribution of the Estimator $\hat{\varepsilon}_i$ for ε_i): *Under the assumptions of the nonlinear regression model in Table 8.1 and the consistency of $\hat{\boldsymbol{\beta}}$ for $\boldsymbol{\beta}$, $\hat{\varepsilon}_i \xrightarrow{p} \varepsilon_i$, and thus, $\hat{\varepsilon}_i \xrightarrow{d} \varepsilon_i$, $\forall i$.*

Therefore, as n increases, the outcomes of $\hat{\varepsilon}_i$ eventually become indistinguishable from the outcomes of ε_i with probability converging to 1, and thus the distributions of $\hat{\varepsilon}_i$ and ε_i coincide as well.

Just as the NLS estimator $\hat{\boldsymbol{\beta}}$ is asymptotically linear in the noise component (8.3.4), we can also show that $\hat{\varepsilon}$ is asymptotically linear in ε, which emulates the relationship (5.4.1) in the linear model case. To see this, expand $\hat{\varepsilon}_i$ in a Taylor series around the point $\boldsymbol{\beta}_0$ based on the definition of $\hat{\varepsilon}_i$ implied by (8.4.1) to obtain

$$\hat{\varepsilon}_i = \mathrm{y}_i - \mathrm{g}(\mathbf{x}_{i\cdot}, \boldsymbol{\beta}_0) - \left.\frac{\partial \mathrm{g}(\mathbf{x}_{i\cdot}, \boldsymbol{\beta})}{\partial \boldsymbol{\beta}'}\right|_{\boldsymbol{\beta}_*} (\hat{\boldsymbol{\beta}} - \boldsymbol{\beta}_0), \tag{8.4.2}$$

where $\boldsymbol{\beta}_* = \lambda\hat{\boldsymbol{\beta}} + (1 - \lambda)\boldsymbol{\beta}_0$ for some $\lambda \in [0, 1]$ by the Mean Value theorem. Using the relationship $\hat{\boldsymbol{\beta}} = \boldsymbol{\beta}_0 + [\mathbf{x}(\boldsymbol{\beta}_0)'\mathbf{x}(\boldsymbol{\beta}_0)]^{-1}\mathbf{x}(\boldsymbol{\beta}_0)'\varepsilon + \mathbf{o}_p(n^{-1/2})$ from (8.3.4), substituting ε_i for $\mathrm{y}_i - \mathrm{g}(\mathbf{x}_{i\cdot}, \boldsymbol{\beta}_0)$, and letting $\mathbf{x}_i(\boldsymbol{\beta}_0) \equiv \left.\frac{\partial \mathrm{g}(\mathbf{x}_{i\cdot}, \boldsymbol{\beta})}{\partial \boldsymbol{\beta}'}\right|_{\boldsymbol{\beta}_0}$, one obtains

$$\hat{\varepsilon}_i = \varepsilon_i - \mathbf{x}_i(\boldsymbol{\beta}_*)[\mathbf{x}(\boldsymbol{\beta}_0)'\mathbf{x}(\boldsymbol{\beta}_0)]^{-1}\mathbf{x}(\boldsymbol{\beta}_0)'\varepsilon + \mathbf{o}_p(n^{-1/2}). \tag{8.4.3}$$

Given that $\mathrm{g}(\mathbf{x}_{i\cdot}, \boldsymbol{\beta})$ is continuously differentiable in $\boldsymbol{\beta}$, so that $\mathbf{x}_i(\boldsymbol{\beta})$ is a continuous function of $\boldsymbol{\beta}$, and given that $\hat{\boldsymbol{\beta}} \xrightarrow{p} \boldsymbol{\beta}_0$ so that $\boldsymbol{\beta}_* \xrightarrow{p} \boldsymbol{\beta}_0$, we have that $\mathbf{x}_i(\boldsymbol{\beta}_*) \xrightarrow{p} \mathbf{x}_i(\boldsymbol{\beta}_0)$. Substituting $\mathbf{x}_i(\boldsymbol{\beta}_0)$ for $\mathbf{x}_i(\boldsymbol{\beta}_*)$ in (8.4.3) and recognizing that an analogous argument holds $\forall i$, one finally obtains

$$\begin{aligned}\hat{\varepsilon} &= [\mathbf{I}_n - \mathbf{x}(\boldsymbol{\beta}_0)[\mathbf{x}(\boldsymbol{\beta}_0)'\mathbf{x}(\boldsymbol{\beta}_0)]^{-1}\mathbf{x}(\boldsymbol{\beta}_0)']\varepsilon + \mathbf{o}_p(n^{-1/2}) \\ &= \mathbf{m}(\boldsymbol{\beta}_0)\varepsilon + \mathbf{o}_p(n^{-1/2}),\end{aligned} \tag{8.4.4}$$

where now $\mathbf{o}_p(n^{-1/2})$ denotes an $(n \times 1)$ vector whose elements are each $o_p(n^{-1/2})$ and $\mathbf{m}(\boldsymbol{\beta}_0)$ denotes the outer-bracketed matrix in (8.4.4). Note that $\mathbf{m}(\boldsymbol{\beta}_0)$ is an $(n \times n)$ idempotent matrix of rank $(n - k)$. Comparing this result with Equation (5.4.1) establishes the asymptotically valid analogy between the linear and nonlinear cases.

One can also show that $\hat{\varepsilon}$ has the smallest limiting covariance matrix of all estimators that are asymptotically linear and consistent for ε (see Section 8.10.4 for an analogous argument relating to $\hat{\boldsymbol{\beta}}$). This is the asymptotic analog in the nonlinear model context to the argument preceding Theorem 5.4.1 indicating that $\hat{\varepsilon}$ is the BLUE of the noise component in the linear model.

8.4.2. An Estimator for σ^2 and $\mathbf{cov}(\hat{\boldsymbol{\beta}})$

Turning our attention to the inverse problem of recovering information about the value of σ^2, the representation of $\hat{\varepsilon}$ given in (8.4.4) is useful. As we did when considering the estimation of σ^2 in the linear model case (recall (5.4.2)–(5.4.5)), examine the inner product of the estimator $\hat{\varepsilon}$ and use (8.4.4) to conclude that

$$\hat{\varepsilon}'\hat{\varepsilon} = \varepsilon'\mathbf{m}(\boldsymbol{\beta}_0)\varepsilon + 2\varepsilon'\mathbf{m}(\boldsymbol{\beta}_0)\mathbf{o}_p(n^{-1/2}) + o_p(1), \tag{8.4.5}$$

where $\boldsymbol{\beta}_0$ denotes the true value for $\boldsymbol{\beta}$. Regarding the order of magnitude of the trailing term above, note that $\mathbf{o}_p(n^{-1/2})'\mathbf{o}_p(n^{-1/2})$ is the sum of n terms of order $o_p(n^{-1})$, which then is of order of magnitude $o_p(1) = n\, o_p(n^{-1})$. Dividing $\hat{\varepsilon}'\hat{\varepsilon}$ by $(n - k)$ then produces an estimator of σ^2 that is consistent.

> **Theorem 8.4.2 (Consistency of S^2 for Estimating σ^2):** *Under the assumption of the probability model in Table 8.1 and the consistency of $\hat{\boldsymbol{\beta}}$ for $\boldsymbol{\beta}$,* $S^2 = \frac{[\mathbf{Y}-\mathbf{g}(\mathbf{x},\hat{\boldsymbol{\beta}})]'[\mathbf{Y}-\mathbf{g}(\mathbf{x},\hat{\boldsymbol{\beta}})]}{n-k} = \frac{\hat{\varepsilon}'\hat{\varepsilon}}{n-k} \xrightarrow{p} \sigma^2$.

Note that had we divided $\hat{\varepsilon}'\hat{\varepsilon}$ by n instead of $(n - k)$, we would still have arrived at a consistent estimator of σ^2. Division by $(n - k)$ has the advantage that the resultant estimator is unbiased up to terms of order $o_p(n^{-1/2})$. That is, from the proof of Theorem 8.4.2 (see the proof appendix),

$$S^2 = \frac{\varepsilon'\mathbf{m}(\boldsymbol{\beta}_0)\varepsilon}{n-k} + o_p(n^{-1/2}), \tag{8.4.6}$$

and if we ignore the $o_p(n^{-1/2})$ terms, it is clear that $E[S^2] = \sigma^2$, which is the operative meaning of being *unbiased to order* $o_p(n^{-1/2})$. It can be shown that S^2 is asymptotically normally distributed under additional noise component moment and convergence assumptions. This and efficiency considerations will be deferred until more specific distributional assumptions are made regarding ε in the next chapter.

Having recovered information on the value of σ^2, we can now revisit the problem of generating an operational version of the asymptotic covariance matrix of the NLS estimator $\mathbf{cov}(\hat{\boldsymbol{\beta}}) = \sigma^2[\frac{\partial \mathbf{g}(\mathbf{x},\boldsymbol{\beta})}{\partial \boldsymbol{\beta}}|_{\boldsymbol{\beta}_0} \frac{\partial \mathbf{g}(\mathbf{x},\boldsymbol{\beta})}{\partial \boldsymbol{\beta}'}|_{\boldsymbol{\beta}_0}]^{-1}$, as defined in (8.3.6). Using the consistent estimator S^2 to replace σ^2 and replacing $\boldsymbol{\beta}_0$ with the consistent NLS estimator $\hat{\boldsymbol{\beta}}$ yields the estimator

$$\hat{\mathbf{cov}}(\hat{\boldsymbol{\beta}}) = S^2 \left[\frac{\partial \mathbf{g}(\mathbf{x},\boldsymbol{\beta})}{\partial \boldsymbol{\beta}}\bigg|_{\hat{\boldsymbol{\beta}}} \frac{\partial \mathbf{g}(\mathbf{x},\boldsymbol{\beta})}{\partial \boldsymbol{\beta}'}\bigg|_{\hat{\boldsymbol{\beta}}} \right]^{-1}. \tag{8.4.7}$$

Under the assumptions leading to the consistency, asymptotic normality, and asymptotic linearity of the NLS estimator, it can be shown that $n[\hat{\mathbf{cov}}(\hat{\boldsymbol{\beta}})]$ consistently estimates the covariance matrix of the limiting distribution of $n^{1/2}(\hat{\boldsymbol{\beta}} - \boldsymbol{\beta}_0)$ presented in (8.3.6).

8.5. Wald Statistics: Tests and Confidence Regions

We now examine solutions to the inverse problem of recovering information about hypothesized values of the unknown and unobservable parameter vector $\boldsymbol{\beta}$. We will discuss Wald tests and confidence regions in this section and Lagrange multiplier (LM) tests and confidence regions in Section 8.6. We will see that the Wald and LM tests and confidence regions are asymptotically equivalent. Analogous to our observations in Chapter 6, the Wald statistic will be based on the *unrestricted* (by H_0) set of NLS estimator parameter estimates, whereas the Lagrange multiplier statistic examined in Section 8.6 is based on *restricted* (by H_0) NLS estimates. We examine a third alternative – confidence-region test procedure based on the pseudo-likelihood ratio statistic in Section 8.7. All of the tests that we will consider rely in one way or another on the asymptotic normality of the NLS estimator, where $n^{1/2}(\hat{\boldsymbol{\beta}} - \boldsymbol{\beta}_0) \xrightarrow{d} N(\mathbf{0}, \sigma^2\Xi^{-1})$ and $\hat{\boldsymbol{\beta}} \overset{a}{\sim} N(\boldsymbol{\beta}_0, \sigma^2(\frac{\partial \mathbf{g}}{\partial \boldsymbol{\beta}}|_{\boldsymbol{\beta}_0} \frac{\partial \mathbf{g}}{\partial \boldsymbol{\beta}'}|_{\boldsymbol{\beta}_0})^{-1})$.

A generalized likelihood ratio test will be introduced in the next chapter, where a parametric model complete with a likelihood function specification will be defined. We will also defer an examination of hypotheses relating to σ^2 until the next chapter, and tests relating to $\boldsymbol{\varepsilon}$ will be deferred to Chapter 19, where we allow for the possibility that the noise component does not have a covariance matrix proportional to the identity matrix.

Because no specific distributional assumptions (e.g., normality) relating to $\boldsymbol{\varepsilon}$ or $\mathbf{Y}$ have been made in the current probability model, and inasmuch as the estimators on which test statistics will be based are nonlinear functions of the data, we rely on asymptotic theory to motivate size, power, and other properties of test procedures. Of course, we can also rely on bootstrap approximations to the sampling distributions of nonlinear estimators and the associated test statistics. As explained in the Monte Carlo appendix, the bootstrap procedure may provide a more refined approximation than the first-order asymptotic results.

8.5.1. Hypotheses Relating to Differentiable Functions of $\boldsymbol{\beta}$

We examined procedures for testing *linear* restrictions on $\boldsymbol{\beta}$ within the linear model context in Chapters 4 and 6. We now consider the more general problem of testing hypotheses relating to the values of nonlinear functions $\boldsymbol{\beta}$ of the form $\mathrm{H}_0: \mathbf{c}(\boldsymbol{\beta}) = \mathbf{r}$, where $\mathbf{c}(\boldsymbol{\beta})$ is some continuously differentiable vector function of $\boldsymbol{\beta}$, and $\mathbf{r}$ is a conformable vector of constants. Note that the case of linear restrictions can be considered a special case of the current discussion by defining $\mathbf{c}(\boldsymbol{\beta}) \equiv \mathbf{c}$, where $\mathbf{c}$ is a $(j \times k)$ matrix of fixed constants. Also note that the tests of *nonlinear* restrictions on $\boldsymbol{\beta}$ that are examined here apply to the *linear* model as a special case by setting $\mathbf{g}(\mathbf{x}, \boldsymbol{\beta}) \equiv \mathbf{x}\boldsymbol{\beta}$. Therefore, this section can also be considered a discussion of how one can test *nonlinear* restrictions on $\boldsymbol{\beta}$ in the context of a *linear* regression model. We will assume that the j coordinate functions in the $(j \times 1)$ vector function $\mathbf{c}(\boldsymbol{\beta})$ are functionally independent. Otherwise, either one or more restrictions on the $\boldsymbol{\beta}$ vector are redundant, or worse, the restrictions are inconsistent. The latter condition occurs if functional dependence among the rows of $\mathbf{c}$, say $\mathrm{h}(\mathbf{c}) = 0$, is not also satisfied by the elements of $\mathbf{r}$, that is, if $\mathrm{h}(\mathbf{r}) \neq 0$. A necessary condition for functional independence is that $j \leq k$, where k is the number of elements in $\boldsymbol{\beta}$. A sufficient condition is that the equation system $\mathbf{c}(\boldsymbol{\beta}) = \mathbf{r}$ can be solved for j of the elements of $\boldsymbol{\beta}$ in terms of $\mathbf{r}$ and the remaining $(k - j)$ elements of $\boldsymbol{\beta}$. The functional independence qualification parallels the full-row rank restriction on the matrix $\mathbf{c}$ that was assumed previously relating to the testing of linear restrictions in the linear model context.

8.5.2. Wald (W) Tests

In this subsection we derive the Wald test of the nonlinear hypothesis $\mathrm{H}_0: \mathbf{c}(\boldsymbol{\beta}) = \mathbf{r}$ (see Section 7.6.2 for a parallel discussion in the general context of extremum estimation and linear hypotheses). Given that $n^{1/2}(\hat{\boldsymbol{\beta}} - \boldsymbol{\beta}_0) \to \mathrm{N}(\mathbf{0}, \sigma^2 \boldsymbol{\Xi}^{-1})$, and on the assumption that $\mathbf{c}(\boldsymbol{\beta})$ is continuously differentiable, it follows directly from results on asymptotic distributions of differentiable functions of asymptotically normal random variables (Chapter E1; Mittelhammer, Section 5.6) that

$$n^{1/2}[\mathbf{c}(\hat{\boldsymbol{\beta}}) - \mathbf{c}(\boldsymbol{\beta}_0)] \xrightarrow{d} \mathrm{N}\left(\mathbf{0}, \sigma^2 \left[\left.\frac{\partial \mathbf{c}(\boldsymbol{\beta})}{\partial \boldsymbol{\beta}'}\right|_{\boldsymbol{\beta}_0} \boldsymbol{\Xi}^{-1} \left.\frac{\partial \mathbf{c}(\boldsymbol{\beta})}{\partial \boldsymbol{\beta}}\right|_{\boldsymbol{\beta}_0} \right]\right). \tag{8.5.1}$$

Under the null hypothesis, that is, *if the null hypothesis* $\mathrm{H}_0: \mathbf{c}(\boldsymbol{\beta}) = \mathbf{r}$ *is true*, it also follows that

$$\mathbf{c}(\hat{\boldsymbol{\beta}}) - \mathbf{r} \overset{a}{\sim} \mathrm{N}\left(\mathbf{0}, n^{-1}\sigma^2 \left[\left.\frac{\partial \mathbf{c}(\boldsymbol{\beta})}{\partial \boldsymbol{\beta}'}\right|_{\boldsymbol{\beta}_0} \boldsymbol{\Xi}^{-1} \left.\frac{\partial \mathbf{c}(\boldsymbol{\beta})}{\partial \boldsymbol{\beta}}\right|_{\boldsymbol{\beta}_0} \right]\right). \tag{8.5.2}$$

On the basis of properties of linear combinations of normally distributed random variables and on properties of the symmetric square-root matrix, a $(j \times 1)$ vector of asymptotically iid standard normal random variables can be defined as

$$\left(n^{-1}\sigma^2 \left[\left.\frac{\partial \mathbf{c}(\boldsymbol{\beta})}{\partial \boldsymbol{\beta}'}\right|_{\boldsymbol{\beta}_0} \boldsymbol{\Xi}^{-1} \left.\frac{\partial \mathbf{c}(\boldsymbol{\beta})}{\partial \boldsymbol{\beta}}\right|_{\boldsymbol{\beta}_0} \right]\right)^{-1/2} [\mathbf{c}(\hat{\boldsymbol{\beta}}) - \mathbf{r}] \overset{a}{\sim} \mathrm{N}(\mathbf{0}, \mathbf{I}_j). \tag{8.5.3}$$

Then, because the sum of squares of j iid standard normal random variables is a Chi-square random variable with j degrees of freedom,

$$[\mathbf{c}(\hat{\boldsymbol{\beta}}) - \mathbf{r}]' \left[n^{-1}\sigma^2 \left[\left.\frac{\partial \mathbf{c}(\boldsymbol{\beta})}{\partial \boldsymbol{\beta}'}\right|_{\boldsymbol{\beta}_0} \boldsymbol{\Xi}^{-1} \left.\frac{\partial \mathbf{c}(\boldsymbol{\beta})}{\partial \boldsymbol{\beta}}\right|_{\boldsymbol{\beta}_0} \right]\right]^{-1} \times [\mathbf{c}(\hat{\boldsymbol{\beta}}) - \mathbf{r}] \overset{a}{\sim} \text{Chi-square}(j, 0) \text{ under } \mathrm{H}_0. \tag{8.5.4}$$

To render (8.5.4) operational for testing hypotheses, σ^2 and $\boldsymbol{\Xi}$ are replaced by their respective consistent estimators S^2 and $[n^{-1}\frac{\partial \mathbf{g}(\mathbf{x},\boldsymbol{\beta})}{\partial \boldsymbol{\beta}}|_{\hat{\boldsymbol{\beta}}} \frac{\partial \mathbf{g}(\mathbf{x},\boldsymbol{\beta})}{\partial \boldsymbol{\beta}'}|_{\hat{\boldsymbol{\beta}}}]$. Because $\frac{\partial \mathbf{c}(\boldsymbol{\beta})}{\partial \boldsymbol{\beta}}$ is a continuous function of $\boldsymbol{\beta}$, and because $\hat{\boldsymbol{\beta}} \xrightarrow{p} \boldsymbol{\beta}_0$, a consistent estimator of this derivative is given by $\frac{\partial \mathbf{c}(\boldsymbol{\beta})}{\partial \boldsymbol{\beta}}|_{\hat{\boldsymbol{\beta}}}$. These substitutions do not alter the asymptotic distribution of the random variable (8.5.3) and (8.5.4), as can be justified via Slutsky's theorem, and so we are led to the Wald test statistic

$$\mathrm{W} = [\mathbf{c}(\hat{\boldsymbol{\beta}}) - \mathbf{r}]' \left[\mathrm{S}^2 \left.\frac{\partial \mathbf{c}(\boldsymbol{\beta})}{\partial \boldsymbol{\beta}'}\right|_{\hat{\boldsymbol{\beta}}} \left[\left.\frac{\partial \mathbf{g}(\mathbf{x},\boldsymbol{\beta})}{\partial \boldsymbol{\beta}}\right|_{\hat{\boldsymbol{\beta}}} \left.\frac{\partial \mathbf{g}(\mathbf{x},\boldsymbol{\beta})}{\partial \boldsymbol{\beta}'}\right|_{\hat{\boldsymbol{\beta}}} \right]^{-1} \left.\frac{\partial \mathbf{c}(\boldsymbol{\beta})}{\partial \boldsymbol{\beta}}\right|_{\hat{\boldsymbol{\beta}}} \right]^{-1} \times [\mathbf{c}(\hat{\boldsymbol{\beta}}) - \mathbf{r}] \overset{a}{\sim} \text{Chi-square}(j, 0) \text{ under } \mathrm{H}_0. \tag{8.5.5}$$

Note that if the restrictions are linear, so that $\mathbf{c}(\boldsymbol{\beta}) = \mathbf{c}\boldsymbol{\beta} = \mathbf{r}$, and if the probability model is a linear regression model, so that $\mathbf{g}(\mathbf{x}, \boldsymbol{\beta}) \equiv \mathbf{x}\boldsymbol{\beta}$, then (8.5.5) is identical to the Wald statistic discussed previously in Chapter 6 in the context of linear restrictions and linear models. Recall that the statistic W is referred to as the Wald statistic in honor of Abraham Wald, who first derived its general form (see the reference in Chapter 6). The intuition underlying the test is that the more distant the outcomes of the random vector $\mathbf{c}(\hat{\boldsymbol{\beta}})$ are from the hypothesized value of $\mathbf{c}(\boldsymbol{\beta})$ represented by $\mathbf{r}$, the less plausible is H_0. Distance is measured in the inverse asymptotic covariance metric, $[\mathbf{cov}(\mathbf{c}(\hat{\boldsymbol{\beta}}))]^{-1}$, estimated by the outermost inverse matrix in (8.5.5) to account for the inherent variability of $\mathbf{c}(\hat{\boldsymbol{\beta}})$ around its true value $\mathbf{c}(\boldsymbol{\beta}_0)$.

8.5.3. Wald Statistic Distribution under H_a

Under local alternatives to H_0 of the Pitman drift form, H_a: $\mathbf{c}(\boldsymbol{\beta}) = \mathbf{r} + n^{-1/2}\boldsymbol{\delta}$ for some finite vector $\boldsymbol{\delta}$, the Wald statistic has a noncentral Chi-square distribution with noncentrality parameter a function of $\boldsymbol{\delta}$ as follows:

$$\mathrm{W} \overset{a}{\sim} \text{Chi-square}(j, \lambda) \quad \text{with} \quad \lambda = \frac{1}{2}\boldsymbol{\delta}' \left[\sigma^2 \left.\frac{\partial \mathbf{c}(\boldsymbol{\beta})}{\partial \boldsymbol{\beta}'}\right|_{\boldsymbol{\beta}_0} \boldsymbol{\Xi}^{-1} \left.\frac{\partial \mathbf{c}(\boldsymbol{\beta})}{\partial \boldsymbol{\beta}}\right|_{\boldsymbol{\beta}_0} \right]^{-1} \boldsymbol{\delta} \tag{8.5.6}$$

(recall our discussion of Pitman drift in Chapter 6). This follows because, if H_a: $\mathbf{c}(\boldsymbol{\beta}) = \mathbf{r} + n^{-1/2}\boldsymbol{\delta}$ is true, then substitution for $\mathbf{c}(\boldsymbol{\beta}_0)$ into (8.5.1) and an application of Slutsky's theorem (which states that if $\mathbf{W}_n \xrightarrow{p} \mathbf{w}_0$ and $\mathbf{V}_n \xrightarrow{d} \mathbf{V}$, then $\mathbf{W}_n\mathbf{V}_n \xrightarrow{d} \mathbf{w}_0\mathbf{V}$) implies that

$$n^{1/2}[\mathbf{c}(\hat{\boldsymbol{\beta}}) - \mathbf{r}] \xrightarrow{d} \mathrm{N}\left(\boldsymbol{\delta}, \sigma^2 \left.\frac{\partial \mathbf{c}(\boldsymbol{\beta})}{\partial \boldsymbol{\beta}'}\right|_{\boldsymbol{\beta}_0} \boldsymbol{\Xi}^{-1} \left.\frac{\partial \mathbf{c}(\boldsymbol{\beta})}{\partial \boldsymbol{\beta}}\right|_{\boldsymbol{\beta}_0} \right), \tag{8.5.7}$$

and thus premultiplication by the inverse of the symmetric square root of the covariance matrix in (8.5.7) yields

$$\left[\sigma^2\left[\left.\frac{\partial \mathbf{c}(\boldsymbol{\beta})}{\partial \boldsymbol{\beta}'}\right|_{\boldsymbol{\beta}_0} \Xi^{-1} \left.\frac{\partial \mathbf{c}(\boldsymbol{\beta})}{\partial \boldsymbol{\beta}}\right|_{\boldsymbol{\beta}_0}\right]\right]^{-1/2} n^{1/2}[\mathbf{c}(\hat{\boldsymbol{\beta}}) - \mathbf{r}]$$

$$\overset{a}{\sim} \mathrm{N}\left(\left[\sigma^2\left[\left.\frac{\partial \mathbf{c}(\boldsymbol{\beta})}{\partial \boldsymbol{\beta}'}\right|_{\boldsymbol{\beta}_0} \Xi^{-1} \left.\frac{\partial \mathbf{c}(\boldsymbol{\beta})}{\partial \boldsymbol{\beta}}\right|_{\boldsymbol{\beta}_0}\right]\right]^{-1/2} \boldsymbol{\delta}, \mathbf{I}_j\right) \tag{8.5.8}$$

(compare with Equation 8.5.3 and note the difference in asymptotic means). Then the noncentral Chi-square distribution of W stated in (8.5.6) follows directly from the standard characterization of the noncentral χ^2 distribution as being the distribution of the sum of the squares of j independent $\mathrm{N}(\xi_i, 1)$ random variables, $i = 1, \ldots, j$, which has a noncentrality parameter $\lambda = \boldsymbol{\xi}'\boldsymbol{\xi}/2$ (Chapter E1; Mittelhammer, p. 666).

For purposes of relating asymptotic power function calculations to the values of $\boldsymbol{\delta}$ and σ^2, an operational estimated value of noncentrality can be defined by replacing Ξ by $n^{-1} \left.\frac{\partial \mathbf{g}(\mathbf{x}, \boldsymbol{\beta})}{\partial \boldsymbol{\beta}}\right|_{\hat{\boldsymbol{\beta}}} \left.\frac{\partial \mathbf{g}(\mathbf{x}, \boldsymbol{\beta})}{\partial \boldsymbol{\beta}'}\right|_{\hat{\boldsymbol{\beta}}}$, whereas $\left.\frac{\partial \mathbf{c}(\boldsymbol{\beta})}{\partial \boldsymbol{\beta}}\right|_{\boldsymbol{\beta}_0}$ can be replaced by $\left.\frac{\partial \mathbf{c}(\boldsymbol{\beta})}{\partial \boldsymbol{\beta}}\right|_{\hat{\boldsymbol{\beta}}}$ in the expression for λ given in (8.5.6). The Wald test is a consistent and asymptotically unbiased test, the latter property being evident from the monotonically increasing nature of the asymptotic power curve as a function of the noncentrality parameter. The test is also an asymptotically locally UMP invariant (UMPI) test of H_0, where *locally* here means for the sequence of alternative hypotheses of the Pitman drift form and *invariance* is with respect to orthonormal transformations of the regression model and is asymptotically locally UMP unbiased (UMPU) when $\mathrm{c}(\boldsymbol{\beta})$ is a scalar (see van der Vaart, 1998, Chapter 15, and Bunke and Bunke, 1986, pp. 224–235).

8.5.4. Test Application

To conduct a test of H_0: $\mathbf{c}(\boldsymbol{\beta}) = \mathbf{r}$, one chooses an asymptotic test size α that corresponds to acceptable asymptotic power function characteristics, leading to a critical value of the test statistic equal to $\chi^2_{1-\alpha}$ that represents the $100(1-\alpha)\%$ quantile of the Chi-square $(j, 0)$ distribution. The test is characterized by the pair $\{\mathrm{W}, \mathrm{C}^{\mathrm{W}}\}$, where the critical region is defined by $\mathrm{C}^{\mathrm{W}} = [\chi^2_{1-\alpha}, \infty)$, and the test rule is "reject H_0 if $\mathrm{W} \in \mathrm{C}^{\mathrm{W}}$." The GAUSS procedure cdfchii() can be used to define $\chi^2_{1-\alpha} = \text{cdfchii}(1-\alpha)$. Asymptotic power function values can be obtained by calculating

$$\begin{aligned} \pi(\lambda) &= \int_{\chi^2_{1-\alpha}}^{\infty} \text{Chi-square}(z; j, \lambda)\, dz \\ &= 1 - \text{cdfchinc}(\chi^2_{1-\alpha}, j, (2\lambda)^{1/2}), \end{aligned} \tag{8.5.9}$$

where cdfchinc() is a GAUSS procedure for calculating values of the noncentral Chi-square cumulative distribution function (CDF). Recall that our parameterization of the noncentral χ^2 distribution is based on λ, whereas the noncentrality parameterization in GAUSS is $(2\lambda)^{1/2}$. Approximate power calculations in terms of the value of $\boldsymbol{\delta}$ can be obtained by replacing σ^2 and Ξ in (8.5.6) by the aforementioned consistent estimators. It can be shown that the test is consistent following an argument similar to the one presented surrounding (6.2.8) and (6.2.9).

► **Example 8.5.1:** To demonstrate the statistical properties of the Wald test, we provide the GAUSS program C8WTest.gss in the examples manual. For a given sample, the GAUSS procedure NL_Wald() reports the observed Wald test statistic and p-value. Then, the power function for the Wald test is simulated by Monte Carlo exercise and compared with the limiting power function.

8.5.5. Confidence Region Estimation

In this section we examine Wald-type confidence region solutions to the inverse problem of recovering information about the unknown and unobservable $\boldsymbol{\beta}$. Because, to this point, we have made no specific distributional assumptions about either ε or $\mathbf{Y}$ in our specification of the probability model, we continue to rely on asymptotic distributions for defining confidence regions. However, as previously noted in this section, the bootstrap procedure may also be used to approximate the sampling distribution of the Wald test statistic and the associated confidence region.

We can define a confidence region for any continuously differentiable vector function of the entries in $\boldsymbol{\beta}$, say $\mathbf{c}(\boldsymbol{\beta})$, by exploiting the duality between confidence regions and the Wald hypothesis-testing procedure examined in the previous section. The duality principle implies that a confidence region for $\mathbf{c}(\boldsymbol{\beta})$ having $100(1-\alpha)\%$ confidence can be defined by the set of $\mathbf{c}(\boldsymbol{\beta})$ values that would *not* be rejected by an α-size test of the hypothesis H_0: $\mathbf{c}(\boldsymbol{\beta}) = \mathbf{r}$.

When examining a confidence region based on the Wald test, note that the test of H_0: $\mathbf{c}(\boldsymbol{\beta}) = \mathbf{r}$ rule of rejecting H_0 iff

$$\text{if } \mathrm{w} = \frac{[\mathbf{c}(\hat{\mathbf{b}}) - \mathbf{r}]' \left[\left.\frac{\partial \mathbf{c}(\boldsymbol{\beta})}{\partial \boldsymbol{\beta}'}\right|_{\hat{\mathbf{b}}} \left[\left.\frac{\partial \mathbf{g}(\mathbf{x},\boldsymbol{\beta})}{\partial \boldsymbol{\beta}}\right|_{\hat{\mathbf{b}}} \left.\frac{\partial \mathbf{g}(\mathbf{x},\boldsymbol{\beta})}{\partial \boldsymbol{\beta}'}\right|_{\hat{\mathbf{b}}} \right]^{-1} \left.\frac{\partial \mathbf{c}(\boldsymbol{\beta})}{\partial \boldsymbol{\beta}}\right|_{\hat{\mathbf{b}}} \right]^{-1} [\mathbf{c}(\hat{\mathbf{b}}) - \mathbf{r})]}{\mathrm{s}^2}$$

$$\geq \chi^2_{1-\alpha}, \tag{8.5.10}$$

where $\chi^2_{1-\alpha}$ is chosen so as to define an asymptotic size α test. It follows that the set of hypotheses of the form H_0: $\mathbf{c}(\boldsymbol{\beta}) = \mathbf{r}$ that would *not* be rejected by the Wald test, and thus, by the duality principle, a $100(1 - \alpha)\%$ confidence region for the value of $\mathbf{c}(\boldsymbol{\beta})$, is given by

$$\mathrm{CR}^{\mathrm{W}} = \left\{ \mathbf{r} : (\mathbf{c}(\hat{\mathbf{b}}) - \mathbf{r})' \left(\left.\frac{\partial \mathbf{c}(\boldsymbol{\beta})}{\partial \boldsymbol{\beta}'}\right|_{\hat{\mathbf{b}}} \left[\left.\frac{\partial \mathbf{g}(\mathbf{x}, \boldsymbol{\beta})}{\partial \boldsymbol{\beta}}\right|_{\hat{\mathbf{b}}} \left.\frac{\partial \mathbf{g}(\mathbf{x}, \boldsymbol{\beta})}{\partial \boldsymbol{\beta}'}\right|_{\hat{\mathbf{b}}} \right]^{-1} \left.\frac{\partial \mathbf{c}(\boldsymbol{\beta})}{\partial \boldsymbol{\beta}}\right|_{\hat{\mathbf{b}}} \right)^{-1} \right.$$

$$\left. \times (\mathbf{c}(\hat{\mathbf{b}}) - \mathbf{r}) < \chi^2_{1-\alpha} \mathrm{s}^2 \right\} \tag{8.5.11}$$

This confidence region will be an interval if $\mathbf{c}(\boldsymbol{\beta})$ is a scalar, an ellipse if $\mathbf{c}(\boldsymbol{\beta})$ is two-dimensional, and a hyperellipse otherwise, all of which will be centered at the value of $\mathbf{c}(\hat{\mathbf{b}})$. This confidence region estimator is asymptotically unbiased, consistent, asymptotically locally UMA invariant, and is asymptotically UMA unbiased when

$c(\boldsymbol{\beta})$ is a scalar, all of which are inherited from the corresponding asymptotic unbiasedness, consistency, UMPI, and UMPU properties of the Wald test on which the confidence region is based. Note that one can use a weak inequality in (8.5.11) and still define an asymptotic $100(1-\alpha)\%$ confidence region because, under the Chi-square approximation to the distribution of the Wald statistic, the boundary points have zero probability.

► **Example 8.5.2:** To demonstrate the setup and application of the Wald-based confidence region, we provide the GAUSS program C8CRWald.gss in the examples manual. For a given sample, the GAUSS procedure NL_WCR() is used to compute the boundary of the confidence ellipse for two of the model parameters. Then, the coverage probability for the Wald-based region is simulated by a Monte Carlo exercise and compared with the intended coverage probability.

8.6. LM Statistics: Tests and Confidence Regions

8.6.1. Lagrange Multiplier Distribution

The Lagrange multiplier (LM) test is based on the statistical behavior of the Lagrange multipliers in the Lagrangian form of the constrained (by H_0) nonlinear least-squares problem (see Section 7.6.1 for a parallel discussion in the general context of extremum estimation and linear hypotheses). The restricted NLS estimator is defined by

$$\hat{\boldsymbol{\beta}}_r = \arg\min_{\boldsymbol{\beta}}[S(\boldsymbol{\beta}) \text{ subject to } \mathbf{c}(\boldsymbol{\beta}) = \mathbf{r}], \tag{8.6.1}$$

where $S(\boldsymbol{\beta})$ is the error sum of squares function defined in (8.2.4). The Lagrangian form of the objective function for the restricted nonlinear least-squares minimization problem is given by

$$L(\boldsymbol{\beta}, \gamma) = S(\boldsymbol{\beta}) - \gamma'[\mathbf{c}(\boldsymbol{\beta}) - \mathbf{r}], \tag{8.6.2}$$

where γ is a $(j \times 1)$ vector of Lagrange multipliers. The first-order conditions for solving (8.6.2) are given by

$$\frac{\partial L}{\partial \boldsymbol{\beta}} = \frac{\partial S(\boldsymbol{\beta})}{\partial \boldsymbol{\beta}} - \frac{\partial \mathbf{c}(\boldsymbol{\beta})}{\partial \boldsymbol{\beta}}\gamma = \mathbf{0} \tag{8.6.3}$$

$$\frac{\partial L}{\partial \gamma} = \mathbf{r} - \mathbf{c}(\boldsymbol{\beta}) = \mathbf{0}. \tag{8.6.4}$$

Let $\hat{\boldsymbol{\beta}}_r$ and $\boldsymbol{\Gamma}_r$ denote the solutions to the restricted nonlinear least-squares minimization problem. Evaluate the first-order conditions at $(\hat{\boldsymbol{\beta}}_r, \boldsymbol{\Gamma}_r)$ and then expand $\frac{\partial S(\boldsymbol{\beta})}{\partial \boldsymbol{\beta}}\Big|_{\hat{\boldsymbol{\beta}}_r}$ in (8.6.3) and $\mathbf{c}(\boldsymbol{\beta})$ in (8.6.4) in a first-order Taylor series around the true value of $\boldsymbol{\beta}$, say $\boldsymbol{\beta}_0$. If it is assumed that H_0: $\mathbf{c}(\boldsymbol{\beta}) = \mathbf{r}$ is true,

$$\frac{\partial S(\boldsymbol{\beta})}{\partial \boldsymbol{\beta}}\bigg|_{\boldsymbol{\beta}_0} + \frac{\partial^2 S(\boldsymbol{\beta})}{\partial \boldsymbol{\beta} \partial \boldsymbol{\beta}'}\bigg|_{\boldsymbol{\beta}_*} (\hat{\boldsymbol{\beta}}_r - \boldsymbol{\beta}_0) - \frac{\partial \mathbf{c}(\boldsymbol{\beta})}{\partial \boldsymbol{\beta}}\bigg|_{\hat{\boldsymbol{\beta}}_r} \boldsymbol{\Gamma}_r = \mathbf{0} \tag{8.6.5}$$

and

$$\left.\frac{\partial \mathbf{c}(\boldsymbol{\beta})}{\partial \boldsymbol{\beta}'}\right|_{\boldsymbol{\beta}_+} (\hat{\boldsymbol{\beta}}_{\mathrm{r}} - \boldsymbol{\beta}_0) = \mathbf{0}. \tag{8.6.6}$$

Note that in (8.6.5) and (8.6.6), both $\boldsymbol{\beta}_*$ and $\boldsymbol{\beta}_+$ are convex combinations of $\hat{\boldsymbol{\beta}}_{\mathrm{r}}$ and $\boldsymbol{\beta}_0$. Furthermore, we have notationally suppressed the fact that different values of the $\boldsymbol{\beta}_*$ and $\boldsymbol{\beta}_+$ vectors will generally be required for each row of $\frac{\partial^2 \mathrm{S}(\boldsymbol{\beta})}{\partial \boldsymbol{\beta} \partial \boldsymbol{\beta}'}$ and $\frac{\partial \mathbf{c}(\boldsymbol{\beta})}{\partial \boldsymbol{\beta}'}$, respectively. Multiplying (8.6.5) by $n^{-1/2}$, multiplying (8.6.6) by $n^{1/2}$, and then rearranging terms leads to the partitioned matrix expression

$$\left[\begin{array}{c:c} -\frac{1}{n}\left.\frac{\partial^2 \mathrm{S}(\boldsymbol{\beta})}{\partial \boldsymbol{\beta}\,\partial \boldsymbol{\beta}'}\right|_{\boldsymbol{\beta}_*} & \left.\frac{\partial \mathbf{c}(\boldsymbol{\beta})}{\partial \boldsymbol{\beta}}\right|_{\hat{\boldsymbol{\beta}}_{\mathrm{r}}} \\ \hdashline \left.\frac{\partial \mathbf{c}(\boldsymbol{\beta})}{\partial \boldsymbol{\beta}'}\right|_{\boldsymbol{\beta}_+} & \mathbf{0} \end{array}\right] \left[\begin{array}{c} n^{1/2}(\hat{\boldsymbol{\beta}}_{\mathrm{r}} - \boldsymbol{\beta}_0) \\ \hdashline n^{-1/2}\boldsymbol{\Gamma}_{\mathrm{r}} \end{array}\right] = \left[\begin{array}{c} n^{-1/2}\left.\frac{\partial \mathrm{S}(\boldsymbol{\beta})}{\partial \boldsymbol{\beta}}\right|_{\boldsymbol{\beta}_0} \\ \hdashline \mathbf{0} \end{array}\right] \tag{8.6.7}$$

Assuming regularity conditions that ensure the consistency and asymptotic normality of the (unconstrained) NLS estimator (see Theorems 8.9.1 and 8.9.2 ahead), we know that on the right side of (8.6.7), $n^{-1/2}\left.\frac{\partial \mathrm{S}(\boldsymbol{\beta})}{\partial \boldsymbol{\beta}}\right|_{\boldsymbol{\beta}_0} \xrightarrow{d} \mathrm{N}(\mathbf{0}, 4\sigma^2\boldsymbol{\Xi})$. Regarding the left-most matrix in (8.6.7), the three nonzero matrix blocks are composed of derivatives evaluated at different values of $\boldsymbol{\beta}$. However, in the limit, these points coincide. In particular under H_0, $\hat{\boldsymbol{\beta}}_{\mathrm{r}} \xrightarrow{p} \boldsymbol{\beta}_0$, and since both $\boldsymbol{\beta}_*$ and $\boldsymbol{\beta}_+$ are convex combinations of $\hat{\boldsymbol{\beta}}_{\mathrm{r}}$ and $\boldsymbol{\beta}_0$, then $\boldsymbol{\beta}_* \xrightarrow{p} \boldsymbol{\beta}_0$ and $\boldsymbol{\beta}_+ \xrightarrow{p} \boldsymbol{\beta}_0$ as well. Then, from the continuity of $\frac{\partial \mathbf{c}(\boldsymbol{\beta})}{\partial \boldsymbol{\beta}}$, Slutsky's theorem, and on the assumption $n^{-1}\left.\frac{\partial^2 \mathrm{S}(\boldsymbol{\beta})}{\partial \boldsymbol{\beta}\partial \boldsymbol{\beta}'}\right|_{\boldsymbol{\beta}_*} \xrightarrow{p} 2\boldsymbol{\Xi}$ (see Theorem 8.9.2 and the discussion preceding (8.9.12)), the information content of (8.6.7) relating to the limiting distributions of $n^{1/2}(\hat{\boldsymbol{\beta}}_{\mathrm{r}} - \boldsymbol{\beta}_0)$ and $n^{-1/2}\boldsymbol{\Gamma}_{\mathrm{r}}$ is equivalent to that of

$$\left[\begin{array}{c:c} -2\boldsymbol{\Xi} & \left.\frac{\partial \mathbf{c}(\boldsymbol{\beta})}{\partial \boldsymbol{\beta}}\right|_{\boldsymbol{\beta}_0} \\ \hdashline \left.\frac{\partial \mathbf{c}(\boldsymbol{\beta})}{\partial \boldsymbol{\beta}'}\right|_{\boldsymbol{\beta}_0} & \mathbf{0} \end{array}\right] \left[\begin{array}{c} n^{1/2}(\hat{\boldsymbol{\beta}}_{\mathrm{r}} - \boldsymbol{\beta}_0) \\ \hdashline n^{-1/2}\boldsymbol{\Gamma}_{\mathrm{r}} \end{array}\right] = \left[\begin{array}{c} \mathbf{Z} \\ \hdashline \mathbf{0} \end{array}\right], \tag{8.6.8}$$

where $\mathbf{Z} \sim \mathrm{N}(\mathbf{0}, 4\sigma^2\boldsymbol{\Xi})$. Partitioned inversion of the left-most matrix leads to

$$n^{-1/2}\boldsymbol{\Gamma}_{\mathrm{r}} = \left[\left.\frac{\partial \mathbf{c}(\boldsymbol{\beta})}{\partial \boldsymbol{\beta}'}\right|_{\boldsymbol{\beta}_0} \boldsymbol{\Xi}^{-1} \left.\frac{\partial \mathbf{c}(\boldsymbol{\beta})}{\partial \boldsymbol{\beta}}\right|_{\boldsymbol{\beta}_0}\right]^{-1} \left.\frac{\partial \mathbf{c}(\boldsymbol{\beta})}{\partial \boldsymbol{\beta}'}\right|_{\boldsymbol{\beta}_0} \boldsymbol{\Xi}^{-1}\mathbf{Z}. \tag{8.6.9}$$

Because, by the properties of linear combinations of normally distributed random variables, we know that the right-hand side of (8.6.9) has the distribution

$$\mathrm{N}\left(\mathbf{0}, 4\sigma^2\left[\left.\frac{\partial \mathbf{c}(\boldsymbol{\beta})}{\partial \boldsymbol{\beta}'}\right|_{\boldsymbol{\beta}_0} \boldsymbol{\Xi}^{-1} \left.\frac{\partial \mathbf{c}(\boldsymbol{\beta})}{\partial \boldsymbol{\beta}}\right|_{\boldsymbol{\beta}_0}\right]^{-1}\right),$$

we can conclude that

$$\frac{1}{2}\boldsymbol{\Gamma}_{\mathrm{r}} \overset{a}{\sim} \mathrm{N}\left(\mathbf{0}, \sigma^2\left[\left.\frac{\partial \mathbf{c}(\boldsymbol{\beta})}{\partial \boldsymbol{\beta}'}\right|_{\boldsymbol{\beta}_0} (\mathrm{n}\boldsymbol{\Xi})^{-1} \left.\frac{\partial \mathbf{c}(\boldsymbol{\beta})}{\partial \boldsymbol{\beta}}\right|_{\boldsymbol{\beta}_0}\right]^{-1}\right). \tag{8.6.10}$$

8.6.2. Classical Form of LM Test

It follows from properties of the symmetric square-root matrix ($\mathbf{m}^{1/2}\mathbf{m}^{-1}\mathbf{m}^{1/2} = \mathbf{I}$) and linear combinations of normally distributed random variable that

$$\frac{1}{2\sigma}\left[\left.\frac{\partial \mathbf{c}(\boldsymbol{\beta})}{\partial \boldsymbol{\beta}'}\right|_{\boldsymbol{\beta}_0} (n\Xi)^{-1} \left.\frac{\partial \mathbf{c}(\boldsymbol{\beta})}{\partial \boldsymbol{\beta}}\right|_{\boldsymbol{\beta}_0}\right]^{1/2} \boldsymbol{\Gamma}_{\mathrm{r}} \overset{a}{\sim} \mathrm{N}(\mathbf{0}, \mathbf{I}_j). \tag{8.6.11}$$

Then, because the sum of the squares of j independent standard normal random variables has a Chi-square distribution with j degrees of freedom,

$$\frac{\boldsymbol{\Gamma}_{\mathrm{r}}'\left[\left.\frac{\partial \mathbf{c}(\boldsymbol{\beta})}{\partial \boldsymbol{\beta}'}\right|_{\boldsymbol{\beta}_0} (\mathrm{n}\Xi)^{-1} \left.\frac{\partial \mathbf{c}(\boldsymbol{\beta})}{\partial \boldsymbol{\beta}}\right|_{\boldsymbol{\beta}_0}\right]\boldsymbol{\Gamma}_{\mathrm{r}}}{4\sigma^2} \overset{a}{\sim} \text{Chi-square}(j, 0) \text{ under } \mathrm{H}_0. \tag{8.6.12}$$

An operational version of (8.6.12) is obtained by replacing σ^2 with

$$\mathrm{S}_{\mathrm{r}}^2 = \frac{[\mathbf{Y} - \mathbf{g}(\mathbf{x}, \hat{\boldsymbol{\beta}}_{\mathrm{r}})]'[\mathbf{Y} - \mathbf{g}(\mathbf{x}, \hat{\boldsymbol{\beta}}_{\mathrm{r}})]}{n - k + j}, \tag{8.6.13}$$

which is a consistent and unbiased-to-order $o_p(n^{-1/2})$ estimator of σ^2 assuming H_0 is true, substituting the consistent (under H_0) estimator $n^{-1}\left.\frac{\partial \mathbf{g}(\mathbf{x}, \boldsymbol{\beta})}{\partial \boldsymbol{\beta}}\right|_{\hat{\boldsymbol{\beta}}_{\mathrm{r}}} \left.\frac{\partial \mathbf{g}(\mathbf{x}, \boldsymbol{\beta})}{\partial \boldsymbol{\beta}'}\right|_{\hat{\boldsymbol{\beta}}_{\mathrm{r}}}$ for Ξ, and replacing $\left.\frac{\partial \mathbf{c}(\boldsymbol{\beta})}{\partial \boldsymbol{\beta}}\right|_{\boldsymbol{\beta}_0}$ with $\left.\frac{\partial \mathbf{c}(\boldsymbol{\beta})}{\partial \boldsymbol{\beta}}\right|_{\hat{\boldsymbol{\beta}}_{\mathrm{r}}}$ to yield

$$\mathrm{LM} = \frac{\boldsymbol{\Gamma}_{\mathrm{r}}'\left[\left.\frac{\partial \mathbf{c}(\boldsymbol{\beta})}{\partial \boldsymbol{\beta}'}\right|_{\hat{\boldsymbol{\beta}}_{\mathrm{r}}} \left[\left.\frac{\partial \mathbf{g}(\mathbf{x},\boldsymbol{\beta})}{\partial \boldsymbol{\beta}}\right|_{\hat{\boldsymbol{\beta}}_{\mathrm{r}}} \left.\frac{\partial \mathbf{g}(\mathbf{x},\boldsymbol{\beta})}{\partial \boldsymbol{\beta}'}\right|_{\hat{\boldsymbol{\beta}}_{\mathrm{r}}}\right]^{-1} \left.\frac{\partial \mathbf{c}(\boldsymbol{\beta})}{\partial \boldsymbol{\beta}}\right|_{\hat{\boldsymbol{\beta}}_{\mathrm{r}}}\right]\boldsymbol{\Gamma}_{\mathrm{r}}}{4\mathrm{S}_{\mathrm{r}}^2}$$

$$\overset{a}{\sim} \text{Chi-square}(j, 0) \text{ under } \mathrm{H}_0 \tag{8.6.14}$$

Note that if the restrictions are linear, so that $\mathbf{c}(\boldsymbol{\beta}) \equiv \mathbf{c}\boldsymbol{\beta} = \mathbf{r}$, and if the probability model is a linear regression model, so that $\mathbf{g}(\mathbf{x}, \boldsymbol{\beta}) \equiv \mathbf{x}\boldsymbol{\beta}$, then (8.6.14) is identical to the LM statistic (6.2.17) discussed previously in the context of linear restrictions and linear regression models. The intuition underlying the test is that the farther the outcomes of $\boldsymbol{\Gamma}_{\mathrm{r}}$ are from the zero vector, the less plausible is H_0 because the Lagrange multipliers are measuring the rate at which $\mathrm{S}(\boldsymbol{\beta})$ can be decreased as the restriction $\mathbf{c}(\boldsymbol{\beta}) = \mathbf{r}$ is relaxed. If the restrictions were true, one would expect there to be less opportunity in general to decrease $\mathrm{S}(\boldsymbol{\beta})$ when the constraints are relaxed. The distance between $\boldsymbol{\Gamma}_{\mathrm{r}}$ outcomes and $\mathbf{0}$ is measured in the inverse asymptotic covariance metric $[\mathbf{cov}(\boldsymbol{\Gamma}_{\mathrm{r}})]^{-1}$ to account for the inherent variability in the estimator $\boldsymbol{\Gamma}_{\mathrm{r}}$.

8.6.3. Score Form of LM Test

An alternative, numerically equivalent *score form of the LM statistic* (Rao, 1948) can be defined by first noting that

$$\left.\frac{\partial \mathbf{c}(\boldsymbol{\beta})}{\partial \boldsymbol{\beta}}\right|_{\hat{\boldsymbol{\beta}}_{\mathrm{r}}} \boldsymbol{\Gamma}_{\mathrm{r}} = \left.\frac{\partial \mathrm{S}(\boldsymbol{\beta})}{\partial \boldsymbol{\beta}}\right|_{\hat{\boldsymbol{\beta}}_{\mathrm{r}}} = -2\left.\frac{\partial \mathbf{g}(\mathbf{x}, \boldsymbol{\beta})}{\partial \boldsymbol{\beta}}\right|_{\hat{\boldsymbol{\beta}}_{\mathrm{r}}} \boldsymbol{\varepsilon}_{\mathrm{r}} \tag{8.6.15}$$

from (8.2.7) and (8.6.3). Then, substituting this into (8.6.14) yields

$$\mathrm{LM} = \varepsilon_{\mathrm{r}}' \frac{\left.\frac{\partial \mathbf{g}(\mathbf{x}, \boldsymbol{\beta})}{\partial \boldsymbol{\beta}'}\right|_{\hat{\boldsymbol{\beta}}_{\mathrm{r}}} \left[\left.\frac{\partial \mathbf{g}(\mathbf{x}, \boldsymbol{\beta})}{\partial \boldsymbol{\beta}}\right|_{\hat{\boldsymbol{\beta}}_{\mathrm{r}}} \left.\frac{\partial \mathbf{g}(\mathbf{x}, \boldsymbol{\beta})}{\partial \boldsymbol{\beta}'}\right|_{\hat{\boldsymbol{\beta}}_{\mathrm{r}}} \right]^{-1} \left.\frac{\partial \mathbf{g}(\mathbf{x}, \boldsymbol{\beta})}{\partial \boldsymbol{\beta}}\right|_{\hat{\boldsymbol{\beta}}_{\mathrm{r}}}}{\mathrm{S}_{\mathrm{r}}^2} \varepsilon_{\mathrm{r}}, \tag{8.6.16}$$

where $\varepsilon_{\mathrm{r}} = \mathbf{Y} - \mathbf{g}(\mathbf{x}, \hat{\boldsymbol{\beta}}_{\mathrm{r}})$. The advantage of the score form of the LM test is that the calculation of the Lagrange multipliers is not needed – all one needs is the outcome of the restricted least-squares estimate.

8.6.4. LM Statistic Distribution under $\mathrm{H_a}$

Under local alternatives to $\mathrm{H_0}$ of the Pitman drift form $\mathrm{H_a}$: $\mathbf{c}(\boldsymbol{\beta}) = \mathbf{r} + n^{-1/2}\boldsymbol{\delta}$ for some finite vector $\boldsymbol{\delta}$, the LM statistic has a noncentral Chi-square distribution with j degrees of freedom and noncentrality parameter a function of $\boldsymbol{\delta}$ as follows:

$$\mathrm{LM} \overset{\mathrm{a}}{\sim} \text{Chi-square}(j, \lambda) \quad \text{with} \quad \lambda = \frac{1}{2}\boldsymbol{\delta}' \left[\sigma^2 \left.\frac{\partial \mathbf{c}(\boldsymbol{\beta})}{\partial \boldsymbol{\beta}'}\right|_{\boldsymbol{\beta}_0} \Xi^{-1} \left.\frac{\partial \mathbf{c}(\boldsymbol{\beta})}{\partial \boldsymbol{\beta}}\right|_{\boldsymbol{\beta}_0} \right]^{-1} \boldsymbol{\delta}. \tag{8.6.17}$$

This result can be motivated by first noting that, under the assumption $\mathbf{c}(\boldsymbol{\beta}) = \mathbf{r} + n^{-1/2}\boldsymbol{\delta}$, Equation (8.6.6) changes such that the right-hand side $\mathbf{0}$ is replaced by $-n^{-1/2}\boldsymbol{\delta}$, so that the $\mathbf{0}$'s on the right-hand sides of (8.6.7) and (8.6.8) are replaced by $-\boldsymbol{\delta}$. It follows that (8.6.9) is changed by the addition of the term $-2[\left.\frac{\partial \mathbf{c}(\boldsymbol{\beta})}{\partial \boldsymbol{\beta}'}\right|_{\boldsymbol{\beta}_0} \Xi^{-1} \left.\frac{\partial \mathbf{c}(\boldsymbol{\beta})}{\partial \boldsymbol{\beta}}\right|_{\boldsymbol{\beta}_0}]^{-1}\boldsymbol{\delta}$ to the right-hand side, so that (8.6.10) then becomes

$$\frac{1}{2}\boldsymbol{\Gamma}_{\mathrm{r}} \overset{\mathrm{a}}{\sim} \mathrm{N}\left(-\left[\left.\frac{\partial \mathbf{c}(\boldsymbol{\beta})}{\partial \boldsymbol{\beta}'}\right|_{\boldsymbol{\beta}_0} \Xi^{-1} \left.\frac{\partial \mathbf{c}(\boldsymbol{\beta})}{\partial \boldsymbol{\beta}}\right|_{\boldsymbol{\beta}_0} \right]^{-1} n^{1/2}\boldsymbol{\delta},\ \sigma^2 \left[\left.\frac{\partial \mathbf{c}(\boldsymbol{\beta})}{\partial \boldsymbol{\beta}'}\right|_{\boldsymbol{\beta}_0} (\mathrm{n}\Xi)^{-1} \left.\frac{\partial \mathbf{c}(\boldsymbol{\beta})}{\partial \boldsymbol{\beta}}\right|_{\boldsymbol{\beta}_0} \right]^{-1} \right) \tag{8.6.18}$$

Then the noncentral Chi-square distribution of LM stated in (8.6.17) follows directly from the standard characterization of the noncentral χ^2 distribution as being the distribution of the sum of the squares of j independent $\mathrm{N}(\xi_i, 1)$ random variables, $i = 1, \ldots, j$, which has a noncentrality parameter $\lambda = \boldsymbol{\xi}'\boldsymbol{\xi}/2$ (Chapter E1; Mittelhammer, p. 666).

8.6.5. Test Application

As in the case of the Wald test, an application of the LM test will begin with an appropriate choice of asymptotic size α and asymptotic power function $\pi(\lambda)$. The test will be defined by the pair $\{\mathrm{LM}, \mathrm{C}^{\mathrm{LM}}\}$, where the critical region of the test $\mathrm{CR} = [\chi^2_{1-\alpha}, \infty)$, will be defined by choosing $\chi^2_{1-\alpha}$ so that $\int_{\chi^2_{1-\alpha}}^{\infty} \text{Chi-square}(z; j, 0)\, dz = \alpha$. The value of $\chi^2_{1-\alpha}$ can be found by using the GAUSS procedure cdfchii(), as $\chi^2_{1-\alpha} = \mathrm{cdfchii}(j, 1-\alpha)$. The test rule is "reject $\mathrm{H_0}$ iff $\mathrm{LM} \in \mathrm{C}^{\mathrm{LM}}$." The asymptotic power function calculations can be accomplished based on (8.5.9). The test has precisely the same asymptotic properties as the Wald test. However, the tests do not necessarily generate identical decisions in finite samples. For a given sample, we may also use the bootstrap procedure to approximate the critical value for the LM test.

► **Example 8.6.1:** To illustrate the statistical properties of the LM test, we provide the GAUSS program C8LMtest.gss in the examples manual. For a given sample, the GAUSS procedure NL_LM() reports the observed LM-statistic and the associated p-value. Then, the power function for the LM test is simulated by Monte Carlo exercise and compared to the limiting power function.

8.6.6. Confidence Region Estimation

A confidence region based on the duality principle applied to the LM test of H_0: $\mathbf{c}(\boldsymbol{\beta}) = \mathbf{r}$ can be defined by the set

$$\mathrm{CR}^{\mathrm{LM}} = \left\{ \mathbf{r} : \gamma(\mathbf{r})' \left(\left. \frac{\partial \mathbf{c}(\boldsymbol{\beta})}{\partial \boldsymbol{\beta}'} \right|_{\hat{\mathbf{b}}_r} \left[\left. \frac{\partial \mathbf{g}(\mathbf{x}, \boldsymbol{\beta})}{\partial \boldsymbol{\beta}} \right|_{\hat{\mathbf{b}}_r} \left. \frac{\partial \mathbf{g}(\mathbf{x}, \boldsymbol{\beta})}{\partial \boldsymbol{\beta}'} \right|_{\hat{\mathbf{b}}_r} \right]^{-1} \left. \frac{\partial \mathbf{c}(\boldsymbol{\beta})}{\partial \boldsymbol{\beta}} \right|_{\hat{\mathbf{b}}_r} \right) \right.$$
$$\left. \times\, \gamma(\mathbf{r}) < \chi^2_{1-\alpha} s^2_r \right\}, \tag{8.6.19}$$

where $\gamma(\mathbf{r})$ denotes that the optimal value of the Lagrange multiplier is a function of the value of $\mathbf{r}$ used in the restriction $\mathbf{c}(\boldsymbol{\beta}) = \mathbf{r}$. Note that the boundaries of this confidence region are considerably more difficult to compute than the Wald-based confidence region because the values of $\mathbf{r}$ are not explicit in the formulation but rather are implicit in the value of γ and s^2_r. Thus, this confidence region estimator is not often used in practice. The LM confidence region estimator has precisely the same asymptotic properties as the confidence region estimator based on the Wald test.

8.7. Pseudo-Likelihood Ratio Statistic: Tests and Confidence Regions

8.7.1. The Pseudo-Likelihood Ratio Statistic

The pseudo-likelihood ratio (PLR) test is based on the scaled difference between the constrained (by H_0) and unconstrained minimized values of the least-squares estimation objective function (see Section 7.6 for a parallel discussion in the general case of extremum estimation and linear constraints). In particular, if the conditions of Theorem 8.9.2 ahead are assumed and under H_0: $\mathbf{c}(\boldsymbol{\beta}) = \mathbf{r}$, it can be shown that the PLR statistic (recall (8.2.1) for the definition of $m(\boldsymbol{\beta}, \mathbf{Y}, \mathbf{x})$)

$$\mathrm{PLR} = 2\tau^{-1} n[m(\hat{\boldsymbol{\beta}}_r, \mathbf{Y}, \mathbf{X}) - m(\hat{\boldsymbol{\beta}}, \mathbf{Y}, \mathbf{X})] \tag{8.7.1}$$

has a Chi-square$(j, 0)$ asymptotic distribution when $\tau = 2\sigma^2$. In (8.7.1), $\hat{\boldsymbol{\beta}}$ is the unconstrained NLS estimator defined in (8.2.2), $\hat{\boldsymbol{\beta}}_r$ is the restricted NLS estimator constrained by H_0: $\mathbf{c}(\boldsymbol{\beta}) = \mathbf{r}$ and defined in (8.6.1), and it is assumed that $\mathbf{c}(\boldsymbol{\beta}) = \mathbf{r}$ represents j functionally independent restrictions on $\boldsymbol{\beta}$.

8.7.2. Distribution of PLR under H_0

To motivate the asymptotic Chi-square distribution of the PLR, we first represent the NLS estimation objective function for the constrained (by H_0) extremum estimator in a Taylor series expansion evaluated at the unconstrained extremum estimator as follows:

$$\mathrm{m}(\hat{\boldsymbol{\beta}}_{\mathbf{r}}, \mathbf{Y}, \mathbf{X}) = \mathrm{m}(\hat{\boldsymbol{\beta}}, \mathbf{Y}, \mathbf{x}) + \left.\frac{\partial \mathrm{m}(\boldsymbol{\beta}, \mathbf{Y}, \mathbf{x})}{\partial \boldsymbol{\beta}}\right|_{\hat{\boldsymbol{\beta}}} (\hat{\boldsymbol{\beta}}_{\mathbf{r}} - \hat{\boldsymbol{\beta}})$$
$$+ \frac{1}{2}(\hat{\boldsymbol{\beta}}_{\mathbf{r}} - \hat{\boldsymbol{\beta}})' \left.\frac{\partial^2 \mathrm{m}(\boldsymbol{\beta}, \mathbf{Y}, \mathbf{x})}{\partial \boldsymbol{\beta} \partial \boldsymbol{\beta}'}\right|_{\hat{\boldsymbol{\beta}}_*} (\hat{\boldsymbol{\beta}}_{\mathbf{r}} - \hat{\boldsymbol{\beta}}), \tag{8.7.2}$$

where $\hat{\boldsymbol{\beta}}_*$ is a convex combination of the restricted and unrestricted estimators $\hat{\boldsymbol{\beta}}_{\mathbf{r}}$ and $\hat{\boldsymbol{\beta}}$, respectively. Because the unconstrained extremum estimator satisfies the first-order conditions for a maximum, it follows that $\left.\frac{\partial \mathrm{m}(\boldsymbol{\beta}, \mathbf{Y}, \mathbf{x})}{\partial \boldsymbol{\beta}}\right|_{\hat{\boldsymbol{\beta}}} = \mathbf{0}$ in (8.7.2). We can then subtract $\mathrm{m}(\hat{\boldsymbol{\beta}}, \mathbf{Y}, \mathbf{x})$ from both sides of (8.7.2) and multiply through by $2\tau^{-1}n$ to obtain

$$\mathrm{PLR} = 2\tau^{-1}n[\mathrm{m}(\hat{\boldsymbol{\beta}}_{\mathbf{r}}, \mathbf{Y}, \mathbf{x}) - \mathrm{m}(\hat{\boldsymbol{\beta}}, \mathbf{Y}, \mathbf{x})]$$
$$= \tau^{-1}n^{1/2}(\hat{\boldsymbol{\beta}}_{\mathbf{r}} - \hat{\boldsymbol{\beta}})' \left.\frac{\partial^2 \mathrm{m}(\boldsymbol{\beta}, \mathbf{Y}, \mathbf{x})}{\partial \boldsymbol{\beta} \partial \boldsymbol{\beta}'}\right|_{\hat{\boldsymbol{\beta}}_*} (\hat{\boldsymbol{\beta}}_{\mathbf{r}} - \hat{\boldsymbol{\beta}})n^{1/2}. \tag{8.7.3}$$

Now note that under H_0, both $\hat{\boldsymbol{\beta}}_{\mathbf{r}} \xrightarrow{p} \boldsymbol{\beta}_0$ and $\hat{\boldsymbol{\beta}} \xrightarrow{p} \boldsymbol{\beta}_0$, which then implies that $\hat{\boldsymbol{\beta}}_* \xrightarrow{p} \boldsymbol{\beta}_0$. It follows from the conditions of Theorem 8.9.2 ahead that $\left.\frac{\partial^2 \mathrm{m}(\boldsymbol{\beta}, \mathbf{Y}, \mathbf{x})}{\partial \boldsymbol{\beta} \partial \boldsymbol{\beta}'}\right|_{\hat{\boldsymbol{\beta}}_*} \xrightarrow{p} \mathbf{h}(\boldsymbol{\beta}_0)$, and thus

$$\mathrm{PLR} \stackrel{a}{=} \tau^{-1}n^{1/2}(\hat{\boldsymbol{\beta}}_{\mathbf{r}} - \hat{\boldsymbol{\beta}})'\mathbf{h}(\boldsymbol{\beta}_0)(\hat{\boldsymbol{\beta}}_{\mathbf{r}} - \hat{\boldsymbol{\beta}})n^{1/2}, \tag{8.7.4}$$

where $\stackrel{a}{=}$ denotes "equivalent in asymptotic distribution to." Applying partitioned inversion to (8.6.8) yields

$$n^{1/2}(\hat{\boldsymbol{\beta}}_{\mathbf{r}} - \boldsymbol{\beta}_0) \stackrel{a}{=} \left\{\mathbf{h}(\boldsymbol{\beta}_0)^{-1} - \mathbf{h}(\boldsymbol{\beta}_0)^{-1}\frac{\partial \mathbf{c}}{\partial \boldsymbol{\beta}}\left[\frac{\partial \mathbf{c}}{\partial \boldsymbol{\beta}'}\mathbf{h}(\boldsymbol{\beta}_0)^{-1}\frac{\partial \mathbf{c}}{\partial \boldsymbol{\beta}}\right]^{-1}\frac{\partial \mathbf{c}}{\partial \boldsymbol{\beta}'}\mathbf{h}(\boldsymbol{\beta}_0)^{-1}\right\}\mathbf{Z}, \tag{8.7.5}$$

where $\mathbf{Z} \sim \mathrm{N}(\mathbf{0}, 4\sigma^2\boldsymbol{\Xi})$ and $\frac{\partial \mathbf{c}}{\partial \boldsymbol{\beta}} \equiv \left.\frac{\partial \mathbf{c}(\boldsymbol{\beta})}{\partial \boldsymbol{\beta}}\right|_{\boldsymbol{\beta}_*}$. It also follows directly from Theorem 8.9.2 ahead that

$$n^{1/2}(\hat{\boldsymbol{\beta}} - \boldsymbol{\beta}_0) \stackrel{a}{=} \mathbf{h}(\boldsymbol{\beta}_0)^{-1}\mathbf{Z}. \tag{8.7.6}$$

Then, subtracting (8.7.6) from (8.7.5) yields

$$n^{1/2}(\hat{\boldsymbol{\beta}}_{\mathbf{r}} - \hat{\boldsymbol{\beta}}) \stackrel{a}{=} -\left\{\mathbf{h}(\boldsymbol{\beta}_0)^{-1}\frac{\partial \mathbf{c}}{\partial \boldsymbol{\beta}}\left[\frac{\partial \mathbf{c}}{\partial \boldsymbol{\beta}'}\mathbf{h}(\boldsymbol{\beta}_0)^{-1}\frac{\partial \mathbf{c}}{\partial \boldsymbol{\beta}}\right]^{-1}\frac{\partial \mathbf{c}}{\partial \boldsymbol{\beta}'}\mathbf{h}(\boldsymbol{\beta}_0)^{-1}\right\}\mathbf{Z}, \tag{8.7.7}$$

and substituting (8.7.7) into (8.7.4) obtains

$$\mathrm{PLR} \overset{a}{=} \tau^{-1}\mathbf{Z}'\left[\mathbf{h}(\boldsymbol{\beta}_0)^{-1}\frac{\partial \mathbf{c}}{\partial \boldsymbol{\beta}}\left[\frac{\partial \mathbf{c}}{\partial \boldsymbol{\beta}'}\mathbf{h}(\boldsymbol{\beta}_0)^{-1}\frac{\partial \mathbf{c}}{\partial \boldsymbol{\beta}}\right]^{-1}\frac{\partial \mathbf{c}}{\partial \boldsymbol{\beta}'}\mathbf{h}(\boldsymbol{\beta}_0)^{-1}\right]\mathbf{Z}$$

$$\overset{a}{=} \mathbf{V}'\left[\tau^{-1}\boldsymbol{\Sigma}^{1/2}\mathbf{h}(\boldsymbol{\beta}_0)^{-1}\frac{\partial \mathbf{c}}{\partial \boldsymbol{\beta}}\left[\frac{\partial \mathbf{c}}{\partial \boldsymbol{\beta}'}\mathbf{h}(\boldsymbol{\beta}_0)^{-1}\frac{\partial \mathbf{c}}{\partial \boldsymbol{\beta}}\right]^{-1}\frac{\partial \mathbf{c}}{\partial \boldsymbol{\beta}'}\mathbf{h}(\boldsymbol{\beta}_0)^{-1}\boldsymbol{\Sigma}^{1/2}\right]\mathbf{V}, \qquad (8.7.8)$$

where $\boldsymbol{\Sigma}^{1/2} = (4\sigma^2\boldsymbol{\Xi})^{1/2}$ and $\mathbf{V} \sim \mathrm{N}(0, \mathbf{I})$.

If one assumes $-\frac{\partial^2 \mathrm{m}(\boldsymbol{\beta},\mathbf{Y},\mathbf{x})}{\partial\boldsymbol{\beta}\partial\boldsymbol{\beta}'}\Big|_{\boldsymbol{\beta}_0} = n^{-1}\frac{\partial^2 \mathrm{S}(\boldsymbol{\beta})}{\partial\boldsymbol{\beta}\partial\boldsymbol{\beta}'}\Big|_{\boldsymbol{\beta}_0} \overset{p}{\to} -\mathbf{h}(\boldsymbol{\beta}_0) = 2\boldsymbol{\Xi}$ (see Theorem 8.9.2 and the discussion preceding (8.9.12)), then, upon setting $\tau = -2\sigma^2$, the matrix of the quadratic form in the last line of (8.7.8) is symmetric and idempotent with rank j, as can be demonstrated by straightforward multiplication of the matrix by itself. It follows that the quadratic form in (8.7.8) can be represented in eigenvalue–eigenvector form as

$$\mathrm{PLR} \overset{a}{=} \mathbf{V}'\mathbf{p}\boldsymbol{\Lambda}\mathbf{p}'\mathbf{V} = \mathbf{V}_*'\boldsymbol{\Lambda}\mathbf{V}_* = \sum_{i=1}^{j} \mathrm{V}_{i*}^2 \sim \text{Chi-square}(j, 0), \qquad (8.7.9)$$

where $\mathbf{V}_* \equiv \mathbf{p}'\mathbf{V} \sim \mathrm{N}(\mathbf{0}, \mathbf{I})$, $\mathbf{p}$, is the matrix of eigenvectors of the matrix of the quadratic form for which $\mathbf{p}'\mathbf{p} = \mathbf{I}$, and $\boldsymbol{\Lambda}$ is the diagonal matrix of eigenvalues that consists of j values of 1 and the remaining values equal to 0 (recall that the eigenvalues of a symmetric idempotent matrix are all 0's and 1's and that the number of 1's equals rank of the matrix, which coincides with the trace of the matrix as well). We have assumed without loss of generality that the eigenvalues and eigenvectors have been ordered so that the unit eigenvalues occur in the first j diagonal positions of $\boldsymbol{\Lambda}$. Therefore, the PLR statistic (8.7.1) is asymptotically Chi-square distributed with j degrees of freedom under the conditions stated.

8.7.3. Test and Confidence Region Application and Properties

The test of H_0: $\mathbf{c}(\boldsymbol{\beta}) = \mathbf{r}$ is conducted by applying the decision rule

$$\text{reject } \mathrm{H}_0\text{: } \mathbf{c}(\boldsymbol{\beta}) = \mathbf{r} \quad \text{iff} \quad \mathrm{plr} \geq \chi^2_{1-\alpha} \qquad (8.7.10)$$

where $\chi^2_{1-\alpha}$ is the $100(1-\alpha)\%$ quantile of the Chi-square$(j, 0)$ distribution. In the typical case where $\tau = 2\sigma^2$ is unknown, it is replaced by a consistent estimator based on replacing σ^2 with s^2 (see Theorem 8.4.2), in which case the asymptotic distribution of the test statistic is maintained. The asymptotic distribution of the PLR statistic under $\mathrm{H_a}$ is identical to the asymptotic distributions of both the Wald and LM statistics given that $\boldsymbol{\Sigma} = \tau\mathbf{h}(\boldsymbol{\theta}_0)$. It follows that the asymptotic properties of the PLR test are precisely the same as for the Wald and LM tests.

Regarding the special cases of ML and LS extremum estimation, the reader can demonstrate that the use of (8.7.1) in the normally distributed parametric linear regression model context yields precisely the same GLR test discussed in Chapter 4. If the extremum estimator (7.5.1) is used based on the extremum estimation objective function (7.5.2), it can be shown that the PLR statistic is given by $(\frac{\hat{\varepsilon}_r'\hat{\varepsilon}_r - \hat{\varepsilon}'\hat{\varepsilon}}{\sigma^2})$, where $\hat{\varepsilon}_r$ and $\hat{\varepsilon}$ are, respectively, the restricted and unrestricted estimators of the noise component of the regression model and $\tau = -2\sigma^2$. In applications, σ^2 is again replaced by the consistent estimate s^2, resulting in an asymptotically equivalent estimable version of the PLR statistic defined by $(\frac{\hat{\varepsilon}_r'\hat{\varepsilon}_r - \hat{\varepsilon}'\hat{\varepsilon}}{s^2})$. The reader will be asked to prove both of these claims in the problems.

In principle, confidence regions for $\mathbf{c}(\boldsymbol{\beta})$ can be defined in the usual way based on duality with the PLR hypothesis test and are given by all of the potential hypothesized $\mathbf{r}$ values that would *not* be rejected by the test. The PLR confidence region estimator has the same asymptotic properties as the Wald or LM confidence region estimators. However, the PLR form of the test is not the most computationally convenient form of test for computing the confidence region boundaries. In applications, the Wald test is most often used for purposes of generating confidence regions via duality.

8.8. Nonlinear Inequality Hypotheses and Confidence Bounds

Situations arise in practice in which the analyst is interested in testing hypotheses that are in the form of inequalities relating to nonlinear functions of the elements of the $\boldsymbol{\beta}$-vector. For example, if a quadratic production function is being analyzed of the form

$$Y_i = \beta_1 x_{i1} + \beta_2 x_{i2} + \beta_3 x_{i1}^2 + \beta_4 x_{i1} x_{i2} + \beta_5 x_{i2}^2 + \varepsilon_i, \quad i = 1, \ldots, n, \tag{8.8.1}$$

the analyst may be interested in generating information regarding whether the function is concave. A necessary and sufficient condition for concavity is that the matrix of parameters $\begin{bmatrix} 2\beta_3 & \beta_4 \\ \beta_4 & 2\beta_5 \end{bmatrix}$ be negative semidefinite, which is the case iff $\beta_3 \le 0$, $\beta_4 \le 0$, and $4\beta_3\beta_5 - \beta_4^2 > 0$. The last inequality clearly involves a nonlinear function $\mathbf{c}(\beta) = 4\beta_3\beta_5 - \beta_4^2$ of the parameter vector. An analyst may also be interested in establishing confidence bounds for the value of $c(\boldsymbol{\beta})$.

8.8.1. Testing Nonlinear Inequalities: Z-Statistics

Nonlinear inequality hypotheses will be represented in the generic form H_0: $\mathbf{c}(\boldsymbol{\beta}) \le \mathbf{r}$ or H_0: $\mathbf{c}(\boldsymbol{\beta}) \ge r$ with the weak inequalities perhaps replaced with strong inequalities. The $c(\boldsymbol{\beta})$ function will be scalar valued and is assumed to be continuously differentiable. The tests we will consider depend on the asymptotic normality of the NLS estimator $\hat{\boldsymbol{\beta}}$, where $n^{1/2}(\hat{\boldsymbol{\beta}} - \boldsymbol{\beta}_0) \xrightarrow{d} N(\mathbf{0}, \sigma^2\Xi^{-1})$.

On the basis of Equation (8.5.1) and the fact that $c(\boldsymbol{\beta})$ is scalar valued, we have by Slutsky's theorem that

$$\frac{c(\hat{\boldsymbol{\beta}}) - c(\boldsymbol{\beta}_0)}{\left[\sigma^2 \left.\frac{\partial c(\boldsymbol{\beta})}{\partial \boldsymbol{\beta}'}\right|_{\boldsymbol{\beta}_0} (n\Xi)^{-1} \left.\frac{\partial c(\boldsymbol{\beta})}{\partial \boldsymbol{\beta}}\right|_{\boldsymbol{\beta}_0}\right]^{1/2}} \overset{a}{\sim} N(0, 1). \tag{8.8.2}$$

Assuming temporarily that Ξ and σ^2 are known, we can define the following test statistic for testing the null hypothesis H_0: $\mathbf{c}(\boldsymbol{\beta}) \le \mathbf{r}$:

$$Z = \frac{c(\hat{\boldsymbol{\beta}}) - r}{\left[\sigma^2 \left.\frac{\partial c(\boldsymbol{\beta})}{\partial \boldsymbol{\beta}'}\right|_{\boldsymbol{\beta}_0} (n\Xi)^{-1} \left.\frac{\partial c(\boldsymbol{\beta})}{\partial \boldsymbol{\beta}}\right|_{\boldsymbol{\beta}_0}\right]^{1/2}} \stackrel{a}{\sim} N\left(\frac{\delta}{\left[\sigma^2 \left.\frac{\partial c(\boldsymbol{\beta})}{\partial \boldsymbol{\beta}'}\right|_{\boldsymbol{\beta}_0} \Xi^{-1} \left.\frac{\partial c(\boldsymbol{\beta})}{\partial \boldsymbol{\beta}}\right|_{\boldsymbol{\beta}_0}\right]^{1/2}}, 1\right), \tag{8.8.3}$$

where $c(\boldsymbol{\beta}) = r + \delta/n^{1/2}$. Then, if one lets $z_{1-\alpha}$ be the $100(1-\alpha)\%$ quantile of the standard normal distribution, it follows from the power function that the test rule

$$\text{reject } H_0\colon c(\boldsymbol{\beta}) \le r \quad \text{iff} \quad z \ge z_{1-\alpha} \tag{8.8.4}$$

defines an asymptotic level α and asymptotically unbiased test of H_0. In particular, asymptotically,

$$P(z \ge z_{1-\alpha}) \begin{bmatrix} < \\ = \\ > \end{bmatrix} \alpha \quad \text{if} \quad \delta \begin{bmatrix} < \\ = \\ > \end{bmatrix} 0. \tag{8.8.5}$$

The test is also consistent, which can be demonstrated following an argument analogous to the one surrounding equations (6.4.5) and (6.4.6). Furthermore, Neyman–Pearson theory can be applied to show that the test is *asymptotically* uniformly most powerful. The preceding results apply equally well to the strong inequality hypothesis H_0: $c(\boldsymbol{\beta}) < r$ because the continuity of the normal approximation renders the boundary point irrelevant probabilistically.

To test H_0: $c(\boldsymbol{\beta}) \ge r$ (or H_0: $c(\boldsymbol{\beta}) > r$), the test statistic (8.8.3) can again be utilized. The test rule becomes (compare with (8.8.4))

$$\text{reject } H_0\colon c(\boldsymbol{\beta}) \ge r \quad \text{iff} \quad z \le z_\alpha, \tag{8.8.6}$$

where z_α is the $100\alpha\%$ quantile of the standard normal distribution. All of the previous test properties continue to hold, and thus in an asymptotic approximation sense, the test is unbiased, UMP, and consistent.

Because both σ^2 and Ξ are unobservable, they must be replaced by observables to render the test rules operational. In practice, because, $S^2 \xrightarrow{p} \sigma^2$, s^2 is used in place of σ^2, and because $n^{-1} \left.\frac{\partial \mathbf{g}(\mathbf{x}, \boldsymbol{\beta})}{\partial \boldsymbol{\beta}}\right|_{\hat{\boldsymbol{\beta}}} \left.\frac{\partial \mathbf{g}(\mathbf{x}, \boldsymbol{\beta})}{\partial \boldsymbol{\beta}'}\right|_{\hat{\boldsymbol{\beta}}} \to \Xi$, $n^{-1} \left.\frac{\partial \mathbf{g}(\mathbf{x}, \boldsymbol{\beta})}{\partial \boldsymbol{\beta}}\right|_{\mathbf{b}} \left.\frac{\partial \mathbf{g}(\mathbf{x}, \boldsymbol{\beta})}{\partial \boldsymbol{\beta}'}\right|_{\mathbf{b}}$ is used in place of Ξ. Also, because $\left.\frac{\partial c(\boldsymbol{\beta})}{\partial \boldsymbol{\beta}}\right|_{\hat{\boldsymbol{\beta}}} \xrightarrow{p} \left.\frac{\partial c(\boldsymbol{\beta})}{\partial \boldsymbol{\beta}}\right|_{\boldsymbol{\beta}_0}$ by the continuity of the derivative functions, $\left.\frac{\partial c(\boldsymbol{\beta})}{\partial \boldsymbol{\beta}}\right|_{\mathbf{b}}$ is used in place of $\left.\frac{\partial c(\boldsymbol{\beta})}{\partial \boldsymbol{\beta}}\right|_{\boldsymbol{\beta}_0}$. The operational version of the test statistic then becomes

$$\hat{Z} = \frac{c(\hat{\boldsymbol{\beta}}) - r}{\left[S^2 \left.\frac{\partial c(\boldsymbol{\beta})}{\partial \boldsymbol{\beta}'}\right|_{\hat{\boldsymbol{\beta}}} \left[\left.\frac{\partial \mathbf{g}(\mathbf{x}, \boldsymbol{\beta})}{\partial \boldsymbol{\beta}}\right|_{\hat{\boldsymbol{\beta}}} \left.\frac{\partial \mathbf{g}(\mathbf{x}, \boldsymbol{\beta})}{\partial \boldsymbol{\beta}'}\right|_{\hat{\boldsymbol{\beta}}}\right]^{-1} \left.\frac{\partial c(\boldsymbol{\beta})}{\partial \boldsymbol{\beta}}\right|_{\hat{\boldsymbol{\beta}}}\right]^{1/2}}, \tag{8.8.7}$$

and test decisions are based on the outcomes of $\hat{Z}$ in place of Z in (8.8.4) and (8.8.6).

To test a collection of nonlinear inequality hypotheses, Bonferroni's probability inequality can be used. See the discussion following (6.4.8) for details.

► **Example 8.8.1:** To illustrate the statistical properties of the Z-test for one-sided (inequality) hypotheses, we provide the GAUSS program C8Ztest.gss in the examples manual. For a given sample, the GAUSS procedure NL_Z() reports the observed test statistic and the associated p-value for the hypothesis H_0: $\beta_2 \leq 0$ and $\beta_3 \leq 0$. Then, the power function for the Z-test is simulated by Monte Carlo exercise and compared with the limiting power function.

8.8.2. Confidence Bounds

Asymptotically valid confidence bounds on $c(\boldsymbol{\beta})$ can be defined using the duality principle applied to the tests of inequality restrictions presented in Section 8.8.1. Using the operational version of the asymptotically valid test (8.8.4), a *lower*-bounded asymptotic level $(1-\alpha)$ confidence interval for $c(\boldsymbol{\beta})$ is given by the set of $c(\boldsymbol{\beta})$ values *not* rejected by the α-level test, that is,

$$CR^Z = \left\{ r : \frac{c(\hat{\mathbf{b}}) - r}{\left[s^2 \left.\frac{\partial c(\boldsymbol{\beta})}{\partial \boldsymbol{\beta}'}\right|_{\hat{\mathbf{b}}} \left[\left.\frac{\partial \mathbf{g}(\mathbf{x},\boldsymbol{\beta})}{\partial \boldsymbol{\beta}}\right|_{\hat{\mathbf{b}}} \left.\frac{\partial \mathbf{g}(\mathbf{x},\boldsymbol{\beta})}{\partial \boldsymbol{\beta}'}\right|_{\hat{\mathbf{b}}} \right]^{-1} \left.\frac{\partial c(\boldsymbol{\beta})}{\partial \boldsymbol{\beta}}\right|_{\hat{\mathbf{b}}} \right]^{1/2}} < z_{1-\alpha} \right\}$$

$$= \left\{ r : r > c(\hat{\mathbf{b}}) - z_{1-\alpha} \left[s^2 \left.\frac{\partial c(\boldsymbol{\beta})}{\partial \boldsymbol{\beta}'}\right|_{\hat{\mathbf{b}}} \left[\left.\frac{\partial \mathbf{g}(\mathbf{x},\boldsymbol{\beta})}{\partial \boldsymbol{\beta}}\right|_{\hat{\mathbf{b}}} \left.\frac{\partial \mathbf{g}(\mathbf{x},\boldsymbol{\beta})}{\partial \boldsymbol{\beta}'}\right|_{\hat{\mathbf{b}}} \right]^{-1} \left.\frac{\partial c(\boldsymbol{\beta})}{\partial \boldsymbol{\beta}}\right|_{\hat{\mathbf{b}}} \right]^{1/2} \right\}. \tag{8.8.8}$$

To define an *upper*-bounded asymptotic level $(1-\alpha)$ confidence interval for $c(\boldsymbol{\beta})$, one can define the set of $c(\boldsymbol{\beta})$ values *not* rejected by the asymptotic α-level test (8.8.6) yielding (note that $z_\alpha = -z_{1-\alpha}$)

$$CR^Z = \left\{ r : r < c(\hat{\mathbf{b}}) + z_{1-\alpha} \left[s^2 \left.\frac{\partial c(\boldsymbol{\beta})}{\partial \boldsymbol{\beta}'}\right|_{\hat{\mathbf{b}}} \left[\left.\frac{\partial \mathbf{g}(\mathbf{x},\boldsymbol{\beta})}{\partial \boldsymbol{\beta}}\right|_{\hat{\mathbf{b}}} \left.\frac{\partial \mathbf{g}(\mathbf{x},\boldsymbol{\beta})}{\partial \boldsymbol{\beta}'}\right|_{\hat{\mathbf{b}}} \right]^{-1} \left.\frac{\partial c(\boldsymbol{\beta})}{\partial \boldsymbol{\beta}}\right|_{\hat{\mathbf{b}}} \right]^{1/2} \right\} \tag{8.8.9}$$

These confidence bounds are asymptotically unbiased and in fact are asymptotically UMA.

A joint confidence bound for more than one nonlinear functional inequality can be defined based on Bonferroni's inequality. See the discussion following equation (6.4.10).

► **Example 8.8.2:** To illustrate the setup and application of the Z-based one-sided confidence intervals, we provide the GAUSS program C8CRZ.gss in the examples manual. For a given sample, GAUSS reports the 90% upper and lower bounded confidence intervals for the estimated parameters. Then the coverage probability for the Z-based intervals are simulated by a Monte Carlo exercise and compared with the intended coverage probability.

8.9. Asymptotic Properties of the NLS-Extremum Estimator

In this section we present additional details relating to the asymptotic properties of the NLS estimator, including consistency, asymptotic normality, asymptotic linearity, and the best asymptotically linear consistent property. The asymptotic properties are motivated within the context of extremum estimation, of which NLS is a special case, as noted in (8.2.1) and (8.2.2).

8.9.1. Consistency

A rigorous demonstration of consistency of the NLS estimator relies on technical arguments relating to the applicability of laws of large numbers to nonlinear functions of sample data. Unlike the linear model case, solutions for the estimator $\hat{\boldsymbol{\beta}}$ are most often in the form of implicit nonlinear functions instead of explicit linear functions of the random sample, which complicates the application of asymptotic theory. We will rely on the fact that the NLS estimator is an extremum estimator and use the theorems introduced in Section 7.3 to provide a formal motivation for the consistency of the estimator.

Theorem 7.3.1 on the consistency of extremum estimators is specialized for the case of the NLS estimator as follows in Theorem 8.9.1. The proof is analogous to the proof of Theorem 7.3.1.

Theorem 8.9.1 (Consistency of NLS Estimator): *The NLS estimator*

$$\hat{\boldsymbol{\beta}} = \arg\min_{\boldsymbol{\beta}}[n^{-1}\mathrm{S}(\boldsymbol{\beta})] = \arg\min_{\boldsymbol{\beta}}\left[\frac{1}{n}[\mathbf{Y}-\mathbf{g}(\mathbf{x},\boldsymbol{\beta})]'[\mathbf{Y}-\mathbf{g}(\mathbf{x},\boldsymbol{\beta})]\right]$$

converges in probability to the true value $\boldsymbol{\beta}_0$ of the parameter $\boldsymbol{\beta}$ if

a. *$n^{-1}\mathrm{S}(\boldsymbol{\beta})$ converges uniformly in probability to a function $\boldsymbol{\beta}$, say $\mathrm{s}_0(\boldsymbol{\beta})$;*

b. *$\mathrm{s}_0(\boldsymbol{\beta})$ is continuous in $\boldsymbol{\beta}$;*

c. *$\mathrm{s}_0(\boldsymbol{\beta})$ is uniquely minimized at $\boldsymbol{\beta}_0$; and*

d. *the parameter space for $\boldsymbol{\beta}$, $\boldsymbol{\Omega}$ is compact.*

Note that conditions a and c of the theorem together imply what is known as *asymptotic identification* of $\boldsymbol{\beta}$ based on the LSC criterion. That is, the limit of the average sum of squares function is uniquely minimized at whatever the true value of $\boldsymbol{\beta}$ happens to be. Condition d implies that the true value of $\boldsymbol{\beta}$ is contained in some closed and bounded set of values, which applies to a large number of applied problems. In effect, so long as one is certain that the absolute value of each of the elements of $\boldsymbol{\beta}$ is upper-bounded by some positive, perhaps very large, number, that is, $|\beta_i| \leq \xi_i < \infty, \forall i$, and a continuum of choices for the β_i's is possible, the assumption of compactness of the parameter space holds. The continuity of $\mathrm{s}_0(\boldsymbol{\beta})$ assumed in b is a weak condition that holds quite generally in practice. In fact, even if $n^{-1}\mathrm{S}(\boldsymbol{\beta})$ is discontinuous, it is quite possible that the limit function is still continuous.

Primitive conditions for both the continuity of $s_0(\boldsymbol{\beta})$ and the uniform convergence in probability of $n^{-1}S(\boldsymbol{\beta})$ to $s_0(\boldsymbol{\beta})$ can be found in Tauchen (1985, Lemma 1), Newey and McFadden (1994, Section 2.3), and White (1994, Appendix 2). The works of Andrews (1988), Pötscher and Prucha (1989), and Woolridge (1986) subsume a variety of conditions available as special cases or corollaries, and these articles can be examined for additional references as well. Consistency for unbounded parameter spaces follows from Theorem 7.3.2 applied to the least-squares estimation objective function, and a restatement of that theorem in the context of NLS estimation is left to the reader.

The intuitive rationale underlying the consistency of the NLS estimator, as well as the basic rationale underlying the proof of Theorem 8.9.1 and similar theorems, is as follows: The NLS estimator is defined by choosing $\boldsymbol{\beta}$ so as to minimize $n^{-1}S(\boldsymbol{\beta})$ for any given sample size n. The value of $S(\boldsymbol{\beta})$ is the sum of n random variables, and so one may hope that as n increases without bound a weak law of large numbers can be applied to this sum so that $n^{-1}S(\boldsymbol{\beta}) \xrightarrow{p} s_0(\boldsymbol{\beta})$. One would then anticipate that because $\hat{\boldsymbol{\beta}}$ minimizes $n^{-1}S(\boldsymbol{\beta})$ and because $n^{-1}S(\boldsymbol{\beta})$ converges to $s_0(\boldsymbol{\beta})$, $\hat{\boldsymbol{\beta}}$ should tend to the value, say $\boldsymbol{\beta}_*$, that minimizes $s_0(\boldsymbol{\beta})$. The logic to this point can be summarized as $\hat{\boldsymbol{\beta}} \Rightarrow \min_{\boldsymbol{\beta}} n^{-1}S(\boldsymbol{\beta}) \xrightarrow{p} \min_{\boldsymbol{\beta}} s_0(\boldsymbol{\beta}) \Rightarrow \boldsymbol{\beta}_*$, so $\hat{\boldsymbol{\beta}} \xrightarrow{p} \boldsymbol{\beta}_*$. Finally, if $s_0(\boldsymbol{\beta})$ is minimized at the true value of the parameter vector, that is, if $\boldsymbol{\beta}_* = \boldsymbol{\beta}_0$, then $\hat{\boldsymbol{\beta}} \xrightarrow{p} \boldsymbol{\beta}_*$ implies that $\hat{\boldsymbol{\beta}}$ converges to the true value of $\boldsymbol{\beta}$, that is, $\hat{\boldsymbol{\beta}} \xrightarrow{p} \boldsymbol{\beta}_0$ and the NLS estimator is consistent. However, this logic is subject to one potential flaw in that, without further conditions, it is not necessarily true that the probability limit of the minimum of $n^{-1}S(\boldsymbol{\beta})$ is equal to the minimum of the probability limit, $s_0(\boldsymbol{\beta})$. It is at this point that the continuity of $s_0(\boldsymbol{\beta})$ and uniform convergence in probability of $n^{-1}S(\boldsymbol{\beta})$ to $s_0(\boldsymbol{\beta})$ enter into the argument. The conditions ensure that the limit of the minimum is indeed the minimum of the limit so that $\hat{\boldsymbol{\beta}} \xrightarrow{p} \boldsymbol{\beta}_0$.

In general, the various types of regularity conditions needed for the NLS estimator to achieve consistency in the estimation of $\boldsymbol{\beta}$ are considered broad enough that the property of consistency is expected to hold quite generally in practice.

8.9.2. Asymptotic Normality

Demonstrating that the NLS estimator is asymptotically normally distributed relies on technical arguments relating to the applicability of central limit theory to nonlinear functions of the sample data. We examine standard results along these lines in this subsection. Theorem 7.3.3 on the asymptotic normality of extremum estimators is specialized to the case of the NLS estimator in Theorem 8.9.2. The proof is analogous to the proof of Theorem 7.3.3.

Theorem 8.9.2 (Asymptotic Normality of NLS Estimator): *The NLS estimator* $\hat{\boldsymbol{\beta}} = \arg\min_{\boldsymbol{\beta}}[n^{-1}S(\boldsymbol{\beta})] = \arg\min_{\boldsymbol{\beta}}[\frac{1}{n}[\mathbf{Y} - \mathbf{g}(\mathbf{x}, \boldsymbol{\beta})]'[\mathbf{Y} - \mathbf{g}(\mathbf{x}, \boldsymbol{\beta})]]$ *is asymptotically normally distributed as* $n^{1/2}(\hat{\boldsymbol{\beta}} - \boldsymbol{\beta}_0) \xrightarrow{d} N(\mathbf{0}, \mathbf{h}(\boldsymbol{\beta}_0)^{-1}\boldsymbol{\Sigma}\mathbf{h}(\boldsymbol{\beta}_0)^{-1})$ *if*

a. $\hat{\boldsymbol{\beta}} \xrightarrow{p} \boldsymbol{\beta}_0$, *where* $\boldsymbol{\beta}_0$ *is the true value of* $\boldsymbol{\beta}$*;*

b. *$\boldsymbol{\beta}_0$ is in the interior of Ω;*

c. *$n^{-1}\mathrm{S}(\boldsymbol{\beta})$ is twice continuously differentiable in $\boldsymbol{\beta}$, at least in the neighborhood, $\kappa(\boldsymbol{\beta}_0)$, of $\boldsymbol{\beta}_0$;*

d. $n^{-1/2}\frac{\partial \mathrm{S}(\boldsymbol{\beta})}{\partial \boldsymbol{\beta}}\Big|_{\boldsymbol{\beta}_0} \xrightarrow{d} \mathrm{N}(\mathbf{0}, \boldsymbol{\Sigma})$*;*

e. $-n^{-1}\frac{\partial^2 \mathrm{S}(\boldsymbol{\beta})}{\partial \boldsymbol{\beta}\partial \boldsymbol{\beta}'}$ *converges uniformly in probability to a matrix function* $\mathbf{h}(\boldsymbol{\beta})\ \forall \boldsymbol{\beta} \in \kappa(\boldsymbol{\beta}_0)$*; and*

f. *$\mathbf{h}(\boldsymbol{\beta})$ is continuous and nonsingular at $\boldsymbol{\beta} = \boldsymbol{\beta}_0$.*

Regarding the conditions of the theorem, note that condition b simply requires that the true value of $\boldsymbol{\beta}$ is not on the boundary of the parameter space. This holds automatically in the case where $\Omega = \mathrm{R}^k$, and if one can assume that $\boldsymbol{\beta}_0$ is contained in a given compact set, one can always enlarge the compact set to make $\boldsymbol{\beta}_0$ interior to the new enlarged compact set. Condition c will hold under the assumption that the conditional expected value function $\mathbf{g}(\mathbf{x}, \boldsymbol{\beta})$ is twice continuously differentiable for $\boldsymbol{\beta} \in \Omega$, as assumed in Table 8.1. Condition d assumes that a CLT can be applied to $n^{-1/2}\frac{\partial \mathrm{S}(\boldsymbol{\beta})}{\partial \boldsymbol{\beta}}\Big|_{\boldsymbol{\beta}_0} = -2n^{-1/2}\frac{\partial \mathbf{g}(\mathbf{x}, \boldsymbol{\beta})}{\partial \boldsymbol{\beta}}\Big|_{\boldsymbol{\beta}_0}\boldsymbol{\varepsilon}$. As a point of reference, note that in the linear regression model this specializes to applying a CLT to $-2n^{-1/2}\mathbf{x}'\boldsymbol{\varepsilon}$, which is precisely what was done in the proof of Theorem 5.3.3. A wide variety of CLTs can be applied to achieve condition d even when the ε_i's are neither independent nor identically distributed. For additional details and references on such CLTs, the reader can consult Mittelhammer (1996, Chapter 5), the books by White (1984, 1994), and electronic Chapter E1.

The uniform convergence condition e and the continuity and nonsingularity condition f together ensure that the scaled Hessian matrix converges to a nonsingular matrix whose elements are *functions* of the parameter vector $\boldsymbol{\beta}$ for all parameter values close to the true value, and these functions will be continuous at $\boldsymbol{\beta}_0$. Note in the special case of the linear regression model, this condition implies $-2n^{-1}\mathbf{x}'\mathbf{x} \rightarrow \mathbf{h}(\boldsymbol{\beta})$, a nonsingular matrix, $\forall \boldsymbol{\beta} \in \kappa(\boldsymbol{\beta}_0)$, which is precisely the condition used in the statement and proof of Theorem 5.3.3. Primitive conditions for uniform convergence in probability and continuity of the limit matrix can be found in the references presented in the discussion of conditions a and b of Theorem 8.9.1.

An overview of the rationale underlying the asymptotic normality of the NLS estimator, as well as the basic rationale underlying the proof of Theorem 8.9.2, is as follows: Outcomes of the NLS estimator can be characterized as solutions to the nonlinear first-order conditions (8.2.7), and these solutions are generally only implicit functions of $(\mathbf{y}, \mathbf{x})$. Therefore, we cannot isolate the algebraic expression for $\hat{\boldsymbol{\beta}}$ to which a CLT might be applied. An approach that allows us to isolate $\hat{\boldsymbol{\beta}}$ but that also introduces additional unknowns is the first-order Taylor series representation of the first-order conditions expanded about the true value of the parameter $\boldsymbol{\beta}$. Fortunately, because we have already established consistency of the NLS estimator, the additional unknowns introduced in this representation will vanish in the limit as $n \rightarrow \infty$.

The Taylor series expansion of the vector $n^{-1/2}\frac{\partial S(\boldsymbol{\beta})}{\partial \boldsymbol{\beta}}$ around the true and unknown value of β, β_0, can be represented as

$$n^{-1/2}\frac{\partial S(\boldsymbol{\beta})}{\partial \boldsymbol{\beta}} = n^{-1/2}\left.\frac{\partial S(\boldsymbol{\beta})}{\partial \boldsymbol{\beta}}\right|_{\boldsymbol{\beta}_0} + n^{-1}\left.\frac{\partial^2 S(\boldsymbol{\beta})}{\partial \boldsymbol{\beta}\partial \boldsymbol{\beta}'}\right|_{\boldsymbol{\beta}_*} n^{1/2}(\boldsymbol{\beta}-\boldsymbol{\beta}_0), \tag{8.9.1}$$

where $\boldsymbol{\beta}_*$ is a convex combination of $\boldsymbol{\beta}$ and $\boldsymbol{\beta}_0$ that may be different for every row of the gradient vector and represents the additional unknowns that we were alluding to in the previous paragraph. Note that in applying the Taylor series expansion to the vector, we suppress notationally the fact that the rows of $\frac{\partial^2 S(\boldsymbol{\beta})}{\partial \boldsymbol{\beta}\partial \boldsymbol{\beta}'}$ will generally be evaluated at different points lying between $\boldsymbol{\beta}$ and $\boldsymbol{\beta}_0$, as this will in any case not be an issue in the limit.

Setting $\boldsymbol{\beta}$ equal to $\hat{\boldsymbol{\beta}}$, we know that $\left.\frac{\partial S(\boldsymbol{\beta})}{\partial \boldsymbol{\beta}}\right|_{\hat{\boldsymbol{\beta}}} = \mathbf{0}$ because the NLS estimator will satisfy the first-order conditions for the minimization of $S(\boldsymbol{\beta})$. Then the left-hand side of (8.9.1) will be equal to a zero vector. Subtracting the $n^{-1/2}\left.\frac{\partial S(\boldsymbol{\beta})}{\partial \boldsymbol{\beta}}\right|_{\boldsymbol{\beta}_0}$ term from both sides of (8.9.1), and noting that the term has a $N(\mathbf{0}, \boldsymbol{\Sigma})$ limiting distribution by condition d, we can conclude that

$$\left[\frac{1}{n}\left.\frac{\partial^2 S(\boldsymbol{\beta})}{\partial \boldsymbol{\beta}\partial \boldsymbol{\beta}'}\right|_{\boldsymbol{\beta}_*}\right] n^{1/2}(\hat{\boldsymbol{\beta}}-\boldsymbol{\beta}_0) \xrightarrow{d} N(\mathbf{0}, \boldsymbol{\Sigma}). \tag{8.9.2}$$

Premultiplying (8.9.2) by $-\mathbf{h}(\boldsymbol{\beta}_0)^{-1}$, where the inverse exists by condition f, and invoking Slutsky's theorem leads to the result

$$-\mathbf{h}(\boldsymbol{\beta}_0)^{-1}\left[\frac{1}{n}\left.\frac{\partial^2 S(\boldsymbol{\beta})}{\partial \boldsymbol{\beta}\partial \boldsymbol{\beta}'}\right|_{\boldsymbol{\beta}_*}\right] n^{1/2}(\hat{\boldsymbol{\beta}}-\boldsymbol{\beta}_0) \xrightarrow{d} N(\mathbf{0}, \mathbf{h}(\boldsymbol{\beta}_0)^{-1}\boldsymbol{\Sigma}\mathbf{h}(\boldsymbol{\beta}_0)^{-1}) \tag{8.9.3}$$

based on results relating to linear combinations of multivariate normally distributed random variables and the inherent symmetry of $\mathbf{h}(\boldsymbol{\beta}_0)$ (via Young's theorem for twice continuously differentiable functions).

Finally, when $n \to \infty$, condition e ensures that the value of $n^{-1}\frac{\partial^2 S(\boldsymbol{\beta})}{\partial \boldsymbol{\beta}\partial \boldsymbol{\beta}'}$ is represented by the value of $-\mathbf{h}(\boldsymbol{\beta})$ for every $\boldsymbol{\beta}$ in a neighborhood of $\boldsymbol{\beta}_0$ with probability limiting to 1. And because $\boldsymbol{\beta}_*$ is a convex combination of $\hat{\boldsymbol{\beta}}$ and $\boldsymbol{\beta}_0$, the result $\hat{\boldsymbol{\beta}} \xrightarrow{p} \boldsymbol{\beta}_0$ stated in condition a implies that outcomes of $\boldsymbol{\beta}_*$ are in the neighborhood of $\boldsymbol{\beta}_0$ with probability limiting to 1 and, in fact, $\boldsymbol{\beta}_* \xrightarrow{p} \boldsymbol{\beta}_0$. Thus, when $n \to \infty$, $n^{-1}\left.\frac{\partial^2 S(\boldsymbol{\beta})}{\partial \boldsymbol{\beta}\partial \boldsymbol{\beta}'}\right|_{\boldsymbol{\beta}_*}$ is represented by $\mathbf{h}(\boldsymbol{\beta}_*)$, $\mathbf{h}(\boldsymbol{\beta}_*) \xrightarrow{p} \mathbf{h}(\boldsymbol{\beta}_0)$ because of the continuity of $\mathbf{h}(\boldsymbol{\beta})$ at $\boldsymbol{\beta} = \boldsymbol{\beta}_0$, and $n^{-1}\left.\frac{\partial^2 S(\boldsymbol{\beta})}{\partial \boldsymbol{\beta}\partial \boldsymbol{\beta}'}\right|_{\boldsymbol{\beta}_*} \xrightarrow{p} -\mathbf{h}(\boldsymbol{\beta}_0)$. Slutsky's theorem then implies that the left-hand-side of (8.9.3) converges in distribution to $n^{1/2}(\hat{\boldsymbol{\beta}}-\boldsymbol{\beta}_0)$, which leads to the limiting distribution statement in Theorem 8.9.2.

In general, the various types of regularity conditions needed for the NLS estimator to exhibit asymptotic normality are considered broad enough that asymptotic normality of $\hat{\boldsymbol{\beta}}$ is expected to hold quite generally in practice. The conditions stated in Theorem 8.9.2 are not the only conditions under which the NLS estimator achieves asymptotic normality. However, they are some of the more direct and more easily understood sets of conditions. Other approaches that can be used to generalize asymptotic normality results in various ways can be found in the works of Gordin (1969), Domowitz and White (1982), and Gallant and White (1988).

8.9.3. Asymptotic Linearity

We will now justify that the NLS estimator can be represented in the asymptotically linear (in ε) form

$$\hat{\boldsymbol{\beta}} = \boldsymbol{\beta}_0 + [\mathbf{x}(\boldsymbol{\beta}_0)'\mathbf{x}(\boldsymbol{\beta}_0)]^{-1}\mathbf{x}(\boldsymbol{\beta}_0)'\varepsilon + \mathbf{o}_p(n^{-1/2}), \qquad (8.9.4)$$

where $\mathbf{x}(\boldsymbol{\beta}_0) = \frac{\partial \mathbf{g}(\mathbf{x}, \boldsymbol{\beta})}{\partial \boldsymbol{\beta}'}\big|_{\boldsymbol{\beta}_0}$, and $\boldsymbol{\beta}_0$ is the true value of the parameter vector. Thus, as $n \to \infty$, the NLS estimator acts much the same as the least-squares estimator in the linear model, with $\mathbf{x}$ being replaced by $\mathbf{x}(\boldsymbol{\beta}_0)$, because in the linear model case upon substitution of $\mathbf{Y} = \mathbf{x}\boldsymbol{\beta}_0 + \varepsilon$,

$$\hat{\boldsymbol{\beta}} = (\mathbf{x}'\mathbf{x})^{-1}\mathbf{x}'\mathbf{Y} = \boldsymbol{\beta}_0 + (\mathbf{x}'\mathbf{x})^{-1}\mathbf{x}'\varepsilon. \qquad (8.9.5)$$

Recall (8.2.7) and note that

$$n^{-1/2} \frac{\partial \mathrm{S}(\boldsymbol{\beta})}{\partial \boldsymbol{\beta}}\bigg|_{\boldsymbol{\beta}_0} = -2n^{-1/2} \frac{\partial \mathbf{g}(\mathbf{x}, \boldsymbol{\beta})}{\partial \boldsymbol{\beta}}\bigg|_{\boldsymbol{\beta}_0} \varepsilon, \qquad (8.9.6)$$

$$n^{-1} \frac{\partial^2 \mathrm{S}(\boldsymbol{\beta})}{\partial \boldsymbol{\beta} \partial \boldsymbol{\beta}'}\bigg|_{\boldsymbol{\beta}_0} = 2n^{-1} \frac{\partial \mathbf{g}(\mathbf{x}, \boldsymbol{\beta})}{\partial \boldsymbol{\beta}}\bigg|_{\boldsymbol{\beta}_0} \frac{\partial \mathbf{g}(\mathbf{x}, \boldsymbol{\beta})}{\partial \boldsymbol{\beta}'}\bigg|_{\boldsymbol{\beta}_0} - 2n^{-1} \sum_{i=1}^{n} \varepsilon_i \frac{\partial^2 \mathbf{g}(\mathbf{x}_i, \boldsymbol{\beta})}{\partial \boldsymbol{\beta} \partial \boldsymbol{\beta}'}\bigg|_{\boldsymbol{\beta}_0}, \qquad (8.9.7)$$

and from condition e and f of Theorem 8.9.2,

$$n^{-1} \frac{\partial^2 \mathrm{S}(\boldsymbol{\beta})}{\partial \boldsymbol{\beta} \partial \boldsymbol{\beta}'}\bigg|_{\boldsymbol{\beta}_*} = n^{-1} \frac{\partial^2 \mathrm{S}(\boldsymbol{\beta})}{\partial \boldsymbol{\beta} \partial \boldsymbol{\beta}'}\bigg|_{\boldsymbol{\beta}_0} + \mathrm{o}_p(1). \qquad (8.9.8)$$

Also, because $n^{1/2}(\hat{\boldsymbol{\beta}} - \boldsymbol{\beta}_0)$ is $\mathrm{O}_p(1)$, (8.9.1) with $\hat{\boldsymbol{\beta}}$ in place of $\boldsymbol{\beta}$ can be rewritten as

$$\left[n^{-1} \frac{\partial^2 \mathrm{S}(\boldsymbol{\beta})}{\partial \boldsymbol{\beta} \partial \boldsymbol{\beta}'}\bigg|_{\boldsymbol{\beta}_0}\right] n^{1/2}(\hat{\boldsymbol{\beta}} - \boldsymbol{\beta}_0) = -n^{-1/2} \frac{\partial \mathrm{S}(\boldsymbol{\beta})}{\partial \boldsymbol{\beta}}\bigg|_{\boldsymbol{\beta}_0} + \mathbf{o}_p(n^{-1/2}). \qquad (8.9.9)$$

Finally, if the last term in (8.9.7) is $\mathrm{o}_p(1)$ and the gradient $\frac{\partial \mathbf{g}(\mathbf{x}, \boldsymbol{\beta})}{\partial \boldsymbol{\beta}}\big|_{\boldsymbol{\beta}_0}$ has full-row rank (the analog to $\mathbf{x}'$ having full-row rank in the linear model), then if one lets $\mathbf{x}(\boldsymbol{\beta}_0) \equiv \frac{\partial \mathbf{g}(\mathbf{x}, \boldsymbol{\beta})}{\partial \boldsymbol{\beta}'}\big|_{\boldsymbol{\beta}_0}$, (8.9.7)–(8.9.9) implies

$$n^{1/2}(\hat{\boldsymbol{\beta}} - \boldsymbol{\beta}_0) = n^{1/2}[\mathbf{x}(\boldsymbol{\beta}_0)'\mathbf{x}(\boldsymbol{\beta}_0)]^{-1}\mathbf{x}(\boldsymbol{\beta}_0)'\varepsilon + \mathrm{o}_p(1) \qquad (8.9.10)$$

or

$$\hat{\boldsymbol{\beta}} = \boldsymbol{\beta}_0 + [\mathbf{x}(\boldsymbol{\beta}_0)'\mathbf{x}(\boldsymbol{\beta}_0)]^{-1}\mathbf{x}(\boldsymbol{\beta}_0)'\varepsilon + \mathbf{o}_p(n^{-1/2}), \qquad (8.9.11)$$

as indicated in (8.9.4). Thus, the NLS estimator is in asymptotically linear form and is asymptotically analogous to the least-squares estimator in the linear model, as in (8.9.5).

The key to the result in (8.9.11) is clearly the vanishing of the last term in (8.9.7). A variety of weak laws of large numbers can be used to justify a probability limit of $\mathbf{0}$ for the term even if the ε_i's exhibit dependence. In the current probability model context delineated in Table 8.1 where the ε_i's are assumed to be independent with common variance σ^2, the trailing term in (8.9.7) has an expectation of $\mathbf{0}$, and the variance of the

(j, k)th entry in the matrix is given by

$$\text{var}\left(2n^{-1}\sum_{i=1}^{n}\varepsilon_i \left.\frac{\partial^2 g(\mathbf{x}_{i\cdot}, \boldsymbol{\beta})}{\partial\beta_j \partial\beta_k}\right|_{\boldsymbol{\beta}_0}\right) = \frac{4\sigma^2}{n^2}\sum_{i=1}^{n}\left[\left.\frac{\partial^2 g(\mathbf{x}_{i\cdot}, \boldsymbol{\beta})}{\partial\beta_j \partial\beta_k}\right|_{\boldsymbol{\beta}_0}\right]^2. \tag{8.9.12}$$

So long as this variance converges to zero as $n \to \infty$, the (j, k)th term converges in probability to zero. A sufficient condition for this to occur is that the second-order derivatives of $\mathbf{g}(\mathbf{x}, \boldsymbol{\beta})$ evaluated at $\boldsymbol{\beta} = \boldsymbol{\beta}_0$ are bounded. A necessary condition is that the sum of the squared second-order derivatives in the definition of the variance increases at a rate less than n^2, that is, the term should be $o(n^2)$ in magnitude. Note that in the linear model context, the summation term is identically zero.

In practice, the assumption that the trailing term in (8.9.7) vanishes and that (8.9.11) applies is made in virtually all of the regression model applications based on Table 8.1 assumptions. In practical terms, the assumption essentially amounts to an assertion that the average (across all data points) curvature in the conditional expectation function $\mathbf{g}(\mathbf{x}, \boldsymbol{\beta})$ moving in any direction in the parameter space from $\boldsymbol{\beta}_0$ does not become too extreme. This has important implications for the form of the asymptotic covariance matrix of the NLS estimator. In particular, it is evident that under asymptotic linearity, the result (8.9.11) implies that

$$\mathbf{asycov}(\hat{\boldsymbol{\beta}}) = \sigma^2[\mathbf{x}(\boldsymbol{\beta}_0)'\mathbf{x}(\boldsymbol{\beta}_0)]^{-1}, \tag{8.9.13}$$

which is directly analogous to the linear regression model result that asymptotically $\mathbf{cov}(\hat{\boldsymbol{\beta}}) = \sigma^2(\mathbf{x}'\mathbf{x})^{-1}$. In other words, under the condition that (8.9.12) converges to zero $\forall$j and k, the asymptotic covariance matrix of the NLS estimator stated in Theorem 8.9.2, $\mathbf{cov}(\hat{\boldsymbol{\beta}}) = \mathbf{h}(\boldsymbol{\beta}_0)^{-1}\Sigma\mathbf{h}(\boldsymbol{\beta}_0)^{-1}$, simplifies to (8.9.13). We assume, henceforth, that the NLS estimator exhibits asymptotic linearity and that (8.9.13) applies.

8.9.4. Best Asymptotically Linear Consistent Estimator (BALCE)

On the basis of the asymptotic results for the NLS estimator presented in the previous section we now examine the BALCE property of the estimator. The NLS estimator is of course not generally unbiased, nor is it a linear function of the sample information, and thus the issue of whether the NLS estimator is BLUE is moot. However, there is an asymptotically valid analog to the BLUE property that the NLS estimator possesses, namely, the estimator is a BALCE. In other words, the NLS estimator has the smallest limiting covariance matrix in the class of estimators that are consistent and asymptotically linear in the sample information up to a $o_p(n^{-1/2})$ discrepancy. In effect, what we are referring to is an asymptotic version of the Gauss–Markov theorem that applies to the NLS estimator. We make these ideas more precise in the following paragraphs.

Recall the characterization of the NLS estimator displayed in (8.9.4) and consider a class of estimators $\breve{\boldsymbol{\beta}}$ that have the following characterization:

$$\breve{\boldsymbol{\beta}} = \boldsymbol{\beta}_0 + \{[\mathbf{x}(\boldsymbol{\beta}_0)'\mathbf{x}(\boldsymbol{\beta}_0)]^{-1}\mathbf{x}(\boldsymbol{\beta}_0)' + n^{-1}\mathbf{w}'\}\varepsilon + \mathbf{o}_p(n^{-1/2}), \tag{8.9.14}$$

where $\mathbf{w}$ is any conformable $0(1)$ (bounded) matrix for which

$$n^{-1}\mathbf{w}'\varepsilon \xrightarrow{p} \mathbf{0}, \quad \text{plim}\, n^{-1}\mathbf{w}'\mathbf{x}(\boldsymbol{\beta}_0) \xrightarrow{p} \mathbf{0} \quad \text{and} \quad \text{plim}\, n^{-1}\mathbf{w}'\mathbf{w} \text{ exists}, \tag{8.9.15}$$

where $\boldsymbol{\beta}_0$ denotes the true value of $\boldsymbol{\beta}$. Under conditions guaranteeing the consistency of the NLS estimator, all of the estimators of the form (8.9.14) and (8.9.15) are also clearly consistent. Furthermore, $n^{1/2}(\breve{\boldsymbol{\beta}} - \boldsymbol{\beta}_0)$ is, up to a $o_p(1)$ term, a linear function of the noise component $\boldsymbol{\varepsilon}$ just as for the NLS estimator and for the least-squares estimator in the linear model case. Thus, we are in a class of estimators that are asymptotically linear in $\boldsymbol{\varepsilon}$ and consistent for estimating $\boldsymbol{\beta}$; that is, we are in the asymptotically linear consistent (ALC) class of estimators.

The NLS estimator is the most efficient estimator in the class; that is, it is the best ALC estimator. Best in this context refers to the smallest asymptotic covariance matrix of all estimators in the ALC class of estimators. The proof of this claim is patterned after the proof of the GAUSS–Markov theorem and can be found in the appendix of this chapter.

8.10. Concluding Comments

Introducing probability models that permit formulations that are both nonlinear in the variables and nonlinear in the parameters greatly enlarges the estimation and inference possibility space. The foundations laid in Chapters 3–7 provided a basis for many of the ways that we thought about this much richer problem. One new difficulty was that we had to be more concerned about the identification of the parameters in the problem. As in Chapters 5 and 6, we are restricted to asymptotic results in this chapter. Fortunately, the NLS estimator is consistent and asymptotically normal under regularity conditions typically fulfilled in practice. This means that the Wald, Lagrange multiplier, and pseudo-likelihood ratio tests can be used as a basis for hypothesis-testing and confidence-region estimation. The computer is, given a sample of data, critical to carrying through the estimations and inference stages in the case of nonlinear problems because it is often the case that estimators, and thus inference procedures based on them, do not exist in closed form. The understanding of nonlinear formulations achieved in this chapter, and the methods of solving for the NLS estimates discussed in the chapter appendix, will be useful in the next and later chapters in which we will encounter additional nonlinear inverse problems with noise.

8.11. Exercises

8.11.1. Idea Checklist – Knowledge Guides

---

1. Why do we need to consider *nonlinear* probability models?
2. What is *nonlinear* in a nonlinear model?
3. In what sense is a nonlinear LS estimator analogous to a linear LS estimator?
4. Why would an analyst want to test nonlinear hypotheses in linear models and linear hypotheses in nonlinear models?
5. Why does Chapter 8 concentrate on asymptotic properties of estimators and tests and not on finite sample properties?

6. In testing H_0: $\mathbf{c}(\boldsymbol{\beta}) = \mathbf{r}$, when should you use a Wald test, when should you use an LM test, and when should you use a pseudo-likelihood ratio test?
7. What is the role of the computer in analyzing nonlinear regression models?

8.11.2. Problems

8–1 Which of the following regression models can be transformed into linear models and which cannot?

a. $y_i = \beta_1 \left[\beta_2 x_{i1}^{-\beta_3} + (1 - \beta_2) x_{i2}^{-\beta_3}\right]^{-\beta_4/\beta_3} \exp(\varepsilon_i)$

b. $y_i = \beta_1 + \beta_2 \left[\frac{x_i^{\beta_3} - 1}{\beta_3}\right] + \varepsilon_i$

c. $y_i = \beta_1 x_i^{\beta_2} + \varepsilon_i$

d. $y_i = \beta_1 x_i^{\beta_2} \exp(\varepsilon_i)$

e. $y_i = [1 + \exp(\boldsymbol{\beta} x_i + \varepsilon_i)]^{-1}$

8–2 Refer to the constant elasticity of substitution (CES) production function in 1a and describe how you would test the hypothesis that:

a. $\beta_2 = .5$ ($\Rightarrow$ equal output share to the two inputs);

b. $\beta_4 < 1$ ($\Rightarrow$ decreasing returns to scale);

c. $\beta_3 = 0$ ($\Rightarrow$ Cobb–Douglas special case of CES production function);

d. $\beta_2 = .5$ and $\beta_4 = 1$.

8–3 Refer to the Box–Cox transform in 1b and describe how you would generate:

a. a confidence interval for β_3;

b. a confidence region for β_2 and β_3;

c. an upper confidence bound on β_3.

8–4 Show that the PLR test is equivalent to the GLR test of Chapter 4 in the case of the normally distributed parametric linear regression model.

8–5 Show that $\text{PLR} = \left(\frac{\hat{\varepsilon}_r'\hat{\varepsilon}_r - \hat{\varepsilon}'\hat{\varepsilon}}{\sigma^2}\right)$ in the case of the semiparametric nonlinear regression model of Chapter 8. Also argue that σ^2 can be replaced by the consistent estimator S^2 without altering the asymptotic properties of the PLR test.

8.11.3. Computer Exercises

---

1. Assume that $\beta_1 = 5$ and $\beta_2 = .5$ in model 1c. Generate 50 iid noise element outcomes as $\varepsilon_i \sim$ iid N (0, 2), set the accompanying 50 values contained in the (50×1) vector $\mathbf{x}$ to an equally spaced grid of values beginning with 1 and ending with 5.9, and simulate the outcomes of the 50 y_i's. Use the simulated data to

   a. Calculate the NLS estimator of β_1 and β_2 . How close are the estimates to the true values?

   b. Test the hypothesis that the probability model is linear in the x_i's.

   c. Generate a confidence interval for β_2.

   d. Repeat exercises 1b and 1c using the nonparametric bootstrap procedure to conduct the hypothesis test and generate the confidence interval. Do the bootstrap results differ from the results based on the first-order asymptotic approximation?

2. The data C8CES.dat contained in the directory "Exercises" of the CD contains 60 observations on (y_i, x_{i1}, x_{i2}) for model 1a. Use these data to

a. Estimate the parameters of Model 1a.

b. Calculate an estimate of the asymptotic covariance matrix of the NLS estimator.

c. Test all of the hypotheses referred to in Question 8.11.2.2.

3. As noted in Section 8.5.1, the problem of imposing nonlinear restrictions $\mathbf{c}(\boldsymbol{\beta}) = \mathbf{r}$ on the linear regression model is a special case of the methods discussed in this chapter.

a. State the problem and the associated first-order necessary conditions.

b. Following the developments of the Gauss–Newton and Newton–Raphson algorithms, how could you form an iterative rule useful for computing the restricted LS estimator? As a guide, you may consider the approach taken in the GAUSS program C8NL_RLS.gss provided in the examples manual.

c. Use Model 1d above to generate a sample of observations from a DSP characterized by $\beta_1 = \beta_2$. Then, estimate the linear version of the model subject to the nonlinear constraint associated with this restriction.

8.12. References

Andrews, D. W. K. (1988), "Laws of Large Numbers for Dependent Non-Identically Distributed Random Variables," *Econometric Theory*, Vol. 4, pp. 458–67.

Bunke, H., and O. Bunke (1986), *Statistical Inference in Linear Models*, New York: John Wiley and Sons.

Broyden, C. G. (1969), "A New Double-Rank Minimization Algorithm," *Notices of the American Mathematical Society*, Vol. 16, p. 670.

Davidon, W. C. (1959), "Variable Metric Methods for Minimization," AEC Research and Development Report ANL-5990, Argonne, IL: Argonne National Laboratory.

Dennis, J. E., Jr., and R. B. Schnabel (1983), *Numerical Methods for Unconstrained Optimization and Nonlinear Equations*, Englewood Cliffs, NJ: Prentice-Hall.

Domowitz, I., and H. White (1982), "Misspecified Models with Dependent Observations," *Journal of Econometrics*, Vol. 20, pp. 35–58.

Fletcher, R. (1970), "A New Approach to Variable Metric Algorithms," *Computer Journal*, Vol. 13, pp. 317–22.

Fletcher, R., and M. J. D. Powell (1963), "A Rapidly Convergent Descent Method for Minimization," *Computer Journal*, Vol. 6, pp. 163–68.

Gallant, R., and H. White (1988), *A Unified Theory of Estimation and Inference for Nonlinear Dynamic Models*, Oxford, UK: Basil Blackwell.

Goldfarb, D. (1970), "A Family of Variable Metric Methods Derived by Variational Means," *Mathematics of Computation*, Vol. 24, pp. 23–26.

Gordin, M. I. (1969), "The Central Limit Theorem for Stationary Processes," *Soviet Mathematics Doklady*, Vol. 10, pp. 1174–6.

Mittelhammer, R. C. (1996), *Mathematical Statistics for Economics and Business*, New York: Springer–Verlag.

Newey, W. K., and D. McFadden (1994), "Large Sample Estimation and Hypothesis Testing," in *Handbook of Econometrics*, Amsterdam: North–Holland, pp. 2111–245.

Pötscher, B., and I. Prucha (1989), "A Uniform Law of Large Numbers for Dependent and Heterogeneous Data Processes," *Econometrica*, Vol. 57, pp. 675–84.

Shanno, D. (1970), "Conditioning of Quasi-Newton Methods for Function Minimization," *Mathematics of Computation*, Vol. 24, pp. 647–54.
van der Vaart, A. W. (1998), *Asymptotic Statistics*, Cambridge, UK: Cambridge University Press.
White, H. (1994), *Estimation, Inference, and Specification Analysis*, Cambridge University Press.
Wooldridge, J. (1986), "Asymptotic Properties of Econometric Estimators," Doctoral Dissertation, Department of Economics, University of California, San Diego.

8.13. Appendixes

8.13.1. Appendix A: Computation of NLS Estimates (with Ronald Schoenberg)

Several methods are commonly used to solve nonlinear least-squares problems. The purpose of this appendix is to review three classes of numerical algorithms known as the Newton–Raphson, Gauss–Newton, and quasi-Newton methods. The techniques use approximations of the nonlinear regression function to solve the extremum problem iteratively from some starting value or initial estimate of the parameter vector. The Newton–Raphson and Gauss–Newton methods are relatively quick and easy to use if the gradient vectors or Hessian matrices of $S(\boldsymbol{\beta})$ can be analytically determined. In this section, we consider two simple GAUSS procedures designed to solve NLS problems by the Newton methods.

For many extremum estimation problems, the Hessian matrix may not be globally positive (or negative) definite or may be difficult to compute, and the Newton–Raphson and Gauss–Newton algorithms are not guaranteed to work. In such cases, we may use an extended class of algorithms known as quasi-Newton methods that build approximations to the Hessian matrix. A quasi-Newton estimation procedure named qnewton() is included in the GAUSS distribution provided with the book, and the procedure is based on the algorithm devised by Broyden, Fletcher, Goldfarb, and Shanno (BFGS).

8.13.2. Newton–Raphson Method

For optimization of general nonlinear functions, the computational tools used today are based on an idea developed by Sir Isaac Newton. To find the extremum of the nonlinear function, Newton located the extremum of a local approximation to the nonlinear function taken at some point on the surface of the function. Using this approach, we can find the extremum of the local approximation, generate a new local approximation at the extremum, find the extremum of the second approximation, and so on. Owing to the convenience of optimizing quadratic functions, we use a second-order Taylor series expansion for the local approximation.

More formally, consider a general nonlinear objective function $S(\boldsymbol{\beta})$ with choice parameters $\boldsymbol{\beta} \in \Omega$, and $S(\boldsymbol{\beta})$ may include the linear and nonlinear least-squares objective functions as special cases. To derive an iterative solution algorithm, consider a second-order (quadratic) Taylor series expansion of the objective function about an initial estimate of the unknown parameter vector $\boldsymbol{\beta}_0$:

$$\mathrm{S}(\boldsymbol{\beta}) \cong \mathrm{S}(\boldsymbol{\beta}_0) + \left.\frac{\partial \mathrm{S}(\boldsymbol{\beta})}{\partial \boldsymbol{\beta}'}\right|_{\beta_0} (\boldsymbol{\beta} - \boldsymbol{\beta}_0) + \frac{1}{2}(\boldsymbol{\beta} - \boldsymbol{\beta}_0)' \left[\left.\frac{\partial^2 \mathrm{S}(\boldsymbol{\beta})}{\partial \boldsymbol{\beta} \partial \boldsymbol{\beta}'}\right|_{\beta_0} \right] (\boldsymbol{\beta} - \boldsymbol{\beta}_0) \qquad (8.13.1)$$

The approximation on the right-hand side is a linear–quadratic function of $\boldsymbol{\beta}$ and is strictly convex if the Hessian matrix is positive definite. In the same manner as the ordinary least-squares problem, we calculate the derivatives of the quadratic approximation, set to zero, and solve for the extremum. Conditional on the initial estimate $\boldsymbol{\beta}_0$, the next iterate is

$$\boldsymbol{\beta}_1 = \boldsymbol{\beta}_0 - \left[\left.\frac{\partial^2 \mathrm{S}(\boldsymbol{\beta})}{\partial \boldsymbol{\beta} \partial \boldsymbol{\beta}'}\right|_{\beta_0} \right]^{-1} \left[\left.\frac{\partial \mathrm{S}(\boldsymbol{\beta})}{\partial \boldsymbol{\beta}}\right|_{\beta_0} \right]. \qquad (8.13.2)$$

By repeating the process, we solve a sequence of conditional linear-quadratic problems in which the current solution $\boldsymbol{\beta}_t$ is derived from the previous solution $\boldsymbol{\beta}_{t-1}$. Under the Newton–Raphson algorithm, the step taken during iteration t, $\delta_{t-1} = \boldsymbol{\beta}_t - \boldsymbol{\beta}_{t-1}$, is called the *direction*. The direction is a vector describing a segment of a path from the starting point to the next step in the iterative solution. The inverse of the Hessian matrix determines the *angle* of the direction, and the gradient determines the *size* of the direction.

If the objective function is quadratic, the extremum is identified in a single step, and $\boldsymbol{\beta}_1$ is the solution. If the function is locally convex, we can show that an iterative step improves on the previous value and decreases the value of the nonlinear least-squares objective function. To see this, evaluate the expansion (8.13.1) at the subsequent point in the iteration

$$\begin{aligned} \mathrm{S}(\boldsymbol{\beta}_t) \cong \mathrm{S}(\boldsymbol{\beta}_{t-1}) &+ \left.\frac{\partial \mathrm{S}(\boldsymbol{\beta})}{\partial \boldsymbol{\beta}'}\right|_{\beta_{t-1}} (\boldsymbol{\beta}_t - \boldsymbol{\beta}_{t-1}) \\ &+ \frac{1}{2}(\boldsymbol{\beta}_t - \boldsymbol{\beta}_{t-1})' \left[\left.\frac{\partial^2 \mathrm{S}(\boldsymbol{\beta})}{\partial \boldsymbol{\beta} \partial \boldsymbol{\beta}'}\right|_{\beta_{t-1}} \right] (\boldsymbol{\beta}_t - \boldsymbol{\beta}_{t-1}) \end{aligned} \qquad (8.13.3)$$

By substitution of the definition of $\boldsymbol{\beta}_t$, we find that

$$\mathrm{S}(\boldsymbol{\beta}_t) - \mathrm{S}(\boldsymbol{\beta}_{t-1}) \cong -\frac{1}{2}(\boldsymbol{\beta}_t - \boldsymbol{\beta}_{t-1})' \left[\left.\frac{\partial^2 \mathrm{S}(\boldsymbol{\beta})}{\partial \boldsymbol{\beta} \partial \boldsymbol{\beta}'}\right|_{\beta_{t-1}} \right] (\boldsymbol{\beta}_t - \boldsymbol{\beta}_{t-1}) < 0 \qquad (8.13.4)$$

The strict inequality holds if the Hessian matrix is positive definite at $\boldsymbol{\beta}_{t-1}$. As well, note that the approximation is only appropriate if $\boldsymbol{\beta}_t$ resides in a neighborhood of $\boldsymbol{\beta}_{t-1}$. The Newton–Raphson steps are not guaranteed to improve on the previous iteration if the Hessian is indefinite or if the vector $(\boldsymbol{\beta}_t - \boldsymbol{\beta}_{t-1})$ is relatively large under the Hessian matrix metric. Consequently, the presence of inflection points and local minima will complicate the search for a global minima. When the approximation is relatively accurate, the Hessian matrix has full rank and the algorithm exhibits quadratic convergence (Dennis and Schnabel, Theorem 2.1.1). Roughly speaking, quadratic convergence means that the number of accurate decimal placing in $\boldsymbol{\beta}_t$ doubles at each step.

If we are certain the problem has a unique solution, we can use a simplified version of the Newton–Raphson iteration known as the method of steepest descent. In this case, the Hessian matrix is replaced with an identity matrix

$$\boldsymbol{\beta}_t = \boldsymbol{\beta}_{t-1} - \left.\frac{\partial \mathrm{S}(\boldsymbol{\beta})}{\partial \boldsymbol{\beta}}\right|_{\boldsymbol{\beta}_{t-1}} \tag{8.13.5}$$

As the term "steepest descent" implies, the updating of $\boldsymbol{\beta}_{t-1}$ in the algorithm is solely determined by the slope of $\mathrm{S}(\boldsymbol{\beta}_{t-1})$. In general, the method of steepest descent converges to the solution more slowly than the Newton–Raphson method, but the total computing time may be reduced if the Hessian matrix is especially costly to compute.

► **Example 8.13.1:** To demonstrate the Newton–Raphson algorithm, we provide the GAUSS program C8NRalg.gss in the examples manual. The solution to NLS estimation problems is computed by the nraphson() procedure, and the program outlines the steps involved in applying the procedure to a simple nonlinear regression problem. Then, an NLS problem is solved with four different variants on the Newton–Raphson procedure (steepest descent versus Newton–Raphson using analytical and numerical derivatives).

8.13.3. Gauss–Newton Method

For nonlinear least-squares estimation problems, the Newton–Raphson approach may be modified to derive a simpler iterative algorithm. Consider the first-order Taylor series approximation of the nonlinear regression function $\mathrm{g}(\mathbf{x}_{i\cdot}, \boldsymbol{\beta})$ about the starting value $\boldsymbol{\beta}_0$

$$\mathrm{g}(\mathbf{x}_{i\cdot}, \boldsymbol{\beta}) \cong \mathrm{g}(\mathbf{x}_{i\cdot}, \boldsymbol{\beta}_0) + \left.\frac{\partial \mathrm{g}(\mathbf{x}_{i\cdot}, \boldsymbol{\beta})}{\partial \boldsymbol{\beta}'}\right|_{\boldsymbol{\beta}_0} (\boldsymbol{\beta} - \boldsymbol{\beta}_0). \tag{8.13.6}$$

Then, substitute the first-order approximation (8.13.6) in the nonlinear model (8.1.1) and rearrange to derive

$$\mathrm{u}_{0i} = \mathrm{Y}_i - \mathrm{g}(\mathbf{x}_{i\cdot}, \boldsymbol{\beta}_0) = \left.\frac{\partial \mathrm{g}(\mathbf{x}_{i\cdot}, \boldsymbol{\beta})}{\partial \boldsymbol{\beta}'}\right|_{\boldsymbol{\beta}_0} (\boldsymbol{\beta} - \boldsymbol{\beta}_0). \tag{8.13.7}$$

The left-hand side of the equation is simply the approximation error associated with the starting value $\boldsymbol{\beta}_0$, and the right-hand side is now a linear function of the unknown model parameters.

Consequently, the problem of estimating $\boldsymbol{\beta}$ in a neighborhood of $\boldsymbol{\beta}_0$ is a linear least-squares problem. Conditional on the starting value $\boldsymbol{\beta}_0$, the solution to the linear least-squares problem is

$$\boldsymbol{\beta}_1 = \boldsymbol{\beta}_0 - \left[\left.\frac{\partial \mathbf{g}(\mathbf{x}, \boldsymbol{\beta})}{\partial \boldsymbol{\beta}}\right|_{\boldsymbol{\beta}_0} \left.\frac{\partial \mathbf{g}(\mathbf{x}, \boldsymbol{\beta})}{\partial \boldsymbol{\beta}'}\right|_{\boldsymbol{\beta}_0}\right]^{-1} \left.\frac{\partial \mathbf{g}(\mathbf{x}, \boldsymbol{\beta})}{\partial \boldsymbol{\beta}}\right|_{\boldsymbol{\beta}_0} \mathbf{u}_0. \tag{8.13.8}$$

Here, $\mathbf{u}_0$ is the n-vector of approximation errors from (8.13.7), and the gradient vectors for each observation are stacked to form an $(n \times k)$ Jacobian matrix. Following our discussion of the Newton–Raphson algorithm, we can repeat the Gauss–Newton iterations until $\boldsymbol{\beta}_t \cong \boldsymbol{\beta}_{t-1}$. Criteria for evaluating the convergence of the iterative solution are discussed at the end of this section.

The principal advantage of the Gauss–Newton algorithm is convenience. First, note that the step taken to compute $\boldsymbol{\beta}_t$ from $\boldsymbol{\beta}_{t-1}$ is simply the linear regression of the approximation errors on the columns of the Jacobian matrix (evaluated at $\boldsymbol{\beta}_{t-1}$). Second, the method only requires the user to evaluate the nonlinear regression function and to compute the Jacobian matrix for each step. The Newton–Raphson method requires the gradient vector and Hessian matrix of $S(\boldsymbol{\beta})$, which are typically more costly to evaluate. Finally, the reader should note that the Gauss–Newton method is only applicable to extremum estimation problems that may be equivalently solved by minimizing the nonlinear least-squares objective function. As noted in the preceding section, the Newton–Raphson algorithm may be applied to a larger class of extremum objective functions.

► **Example 8.13.2:** To demonstrate the Gauss–Newton algorithm, we provide the GAUSS program C8GNewt.gss in the examples manual. The solution to NLS estimation problems is computed by the gausnewt() procedure, and the program outlines the steps involved in applying the procedure to a simple nonlinear estimation problem. Then, an NLS problem is solved with two different variants on the Gauss–Newton procedure (analytical versus numerical derivatives).

8.13.4. Quasi–Newton Methods

In many cases, the Hessian matrix used to compute the direction in the Newton–Raphson algorithm is difficult to state or computationally expensive to form. Consequently, researchers have sought ways to produce an inexpensive estimate of the Hessian matrix. The current quasi–Newton methods are based on the critical insight of Broyden (1969), who suggested using information from the current iteration to compute the new Hessian matrix. Let $\mathbf{s}_t = \boldsymbol{\beta}_{t+1} - \boldsymbol{\beta}_t = \boldsymbol{\delta}_t$ be the change in the parameters in the current iteration and $\boldsymbol{\eta}_t = \mathbf{g}_{t+1} - \mathbf{g}_t$ be the change in the gradient vector. Then, a natural estimate of the Hessian matrix at the next iteration, $\mathbf{h}_{t+1}$, would be the solution of the system of linear equations

$$\mathbf{h}_{t+1}\mathbf{s}_t = \boldsymbol{\eta}_t \tag{8.13.9}$$

That is, $\mathbf{h}_{t+1}$ is effectively the ratio of the change in gradient to the change in the parameters. This is called the quasi–Newton condition. There are many solutions to this set of linear equations, and Broyden suggested a solution in the form of a secant update:

$$\mathbf{h}_{t+1} = \mathbf{h}_t + \mathbf{u}\mathbf{v}' \tag{8.13.10}$$

Further work has developed other types of secant updates, the most important of which are the DFP (for Davidon, 1959, and Fletcher and Powell 1963) and the BFGS (for Broyden, 1969, Fletcher, 1970, Goldfarb, 1970, and Shanno, 1970).

The BFGS algorithm is generally regarded as the best-performing method, and the iterative steps used to update the Hessian matrix estimate take the form

$$\mathbf{h}_{t+1} = \mathbf{h}_t + \frac{\boldsymbol{\eta}_t \boldsymbol{\eta}_t'}{\boldsymbol{\eta}_t' \mathbf{s}_t} - \frac{\mathbf{h}_t \mathbf{s}_t \mathbf{s}_t' \mathbf{h}_t}{\mathbf{s}_t' \mathbf{h}_t \mathbf{s}_t} = \mathbf{h}_t + \frac{\boldsymbol{\eta}_t \boldsymbol{\eta}_t'}{\boldsymbol{\eta}_t' \mathbf{s}_t} - \frac{\mathbf{g}_t \mathbf{g}_t'}{\mathbf{g}_t' \mathbf{g}_t} \tag{8.13.11}$$

Note that we can take advantage of the fact that $\mathbf{h}_t \mathbf{s}_t = \mathbf{h}_t \boldsymbol{\delta}_t = \mathbf{g}_t$. The BFGS method is used in the GAUSS procedure qnewton(), but the update is made to the Cholesky factorization of the Hessian matrix (that is, to the matrix $\mathbf{r}_t$ where $\mathbf{h}_t = \mathbf{r}_t' \mathbf{r}_t$) rather than to $\mathbf{h}_t$ itself. In fact, the qnewton() procedure does not compute $\mathbf{h}_t$ anywhere in the iterations. The direction $\boldsymbol{\delta}_t$ is computed as a solution to

$$\mathbf{r}_t' \mathbf{r}_t \boldsymbol{\delta}_t = \mathbf{g}_t \tag{8.13.12}$$

using the GAUSS procedure cholsol() with arguments $\mathbf{r}_t$ and $\mathbf{g}_t$. Then, the subsequent Cholesky factorization $\mathbf{r}_{t+1}$ is computed as an update and a downdate to $\mathbf{r}_t$ through use of the GAUSS procedures cholup() and choldn(). In particular, the factorization $\mathbf{r}_{t+1}$ is generated by first adding the "observation"

$$\boldsymbol{\eta}_t / \sqrt{\boldsymbol{\eta}_t' \mathbf{s}_t} \tag{8.13.13}$$

and then removing the "observation"

$$\mathbf{g}_t / \sqrt{\boldsymbol{\delta}_t' \mathbf{g}_t} \tag{8.13.14}$$

► **Example 8.13.3:** To compare the performance of the nonlinear estimation algorithms, we provide the GAUSS program C8Newton.gss on the CD. For a given sample, GAUSS computes the NLS parameter estimates by the Gauss–Newton, Newton– Raphson, and steepest descent methods. GAUSS reports the solution values as well as the number of iterations required for convergence of each method. Then, the iterative paths taken by the algorithms to reach the solution values are plotted for the user.

8.13.5. Computational Issues

One of the first questions posed by users of the iterative solution algorithms is, How do I select the starting values? In some cases, we can use our subjective knowledge or nonsample information about the economic model to identify a range of values for each element of $\boldsymbol{\beta}$. If we lack any information about the plausible values of $\boldsymbol{\beta}$ and do not know much about the behavior of the nonlinear regression function, we can evaluate $S(\boldsymbol{\beta})$ at several starting values. By specifying a grid of values in the parameter space, we can use a grid-search approach to identify the approximate location of an extremum in the parameter space. As well, we may want or need to use more than one starting value in an attempt to verify that a solution identified by the algorithm is the global solution.

Given a set of starting values, we may then consider the important question of when to stop the iteration process. In practice, we choose some $\tau > 0$ such that $d_*(\boldsymbol{\beta}_t, \boldsymbol{\beta}_{t-1}) < \tau$ under some distance or tolerance measure d_* on the parameter space. By selecting an appropriate tolerance criterion, we can derive an estimate that is arbitrarily close to the actual solution for the nonlinear least-squares estimator $\hat{\boldsymbol{\beta}}$. One plausible convergence criteria is to stop iterating when the squared Euclidean norm of the Newton–Raphson step for iteration t is such that $\boldsymbol{\delta}'_{t-1}\boldsymbol{\delta}_{t-1} = (\boldsymbol{\beta}_t - \boldsymbol{\beta}_{t-1})'(\boldsymbol{\beta}_t - \boldsymbol{\beta}_{t-1}) < \tau$. We can also measure the norm of the gradient for the nonlinear least-squares objective function, which should be identically equal to a null vector where evaluated at the NLS estimator, and thus the stopping rule is $\mathbf{g}'_{t-1}\mathbf{g}_{t-1} < \tau$. Note that these criteria are equivalent if we consider convergence in the parameter space under the weighted Euclidean norm

$$\boldsymbol{\delta}'_{t-1}\mathbf{h}_{t-1}\boldsymbol{\delta}_{t-1} = (\boldsymbol{\beta}_t - \boldsymbol{\beta}_{t-1})' \left(\left. \frac{\partial \mathrm{S}(\boldsymbol{\beta})}{\partial \boldsymbol{\beta} \partial \boldsymbol{\beta}'} \right|_{\boldsymbol{\beta}_{t-1}} \right) (\boldsymbol{\beta}_t - \boldsymbol{\beta}_{t-1}) < \tau. \quad (8.13.15)$$

Finally, a more sensitive criterion can be established by measuring changes in each dimension of the parameter space such that $|\beta_t[\mathrm{k}] - \beta_{t-1}[\mathrm{k}]| < \tau_\mathrm{k}$ for each k. The elementwise convergence criteria may be useful if we are especially concerned about particular elements of $\boldsymbol{\beta}$. These convergence criteria may also be applied to the Gauss–Newton algorithm and to other iterative numerical procedures.

In some cases, these convergence criteria may be unable to distinguish actual convergence in extremum problems that are poorly scaled. A problem is said to be poorly scaled if the elements of the Hessian matrix and gradient vector have much different relative magnitudes, even at the solution. To avoid convergence problems due to scaling, the qnewton() procedure in GAUSS stops iterating when the following condition is satisfied

$$\max_\mathrm{k} |\mathrm{S}(\boldsymbol{\beta}_t)\mathbf{g}_{t,k}/\beta_{t,k}| < \tau. \quad (8.13.16)$$

The kth element of the gradient vector $\mathbf{g}_{t,k}$ is divided by the associated element of $\mathbf{b}$, and the algorithm continues until the largest of the scaled gradient elements is less than the convergence criterion.

The iterative steps in the parameter space provided by Equations (8.13.2), (8.13.5), and (8.13.8) are commonly referred to as “full” steps. As noted above, the full step is not guaranteed to improve on the previous iterate if the magnitude of the step $(\boldsymbol{\beta}_t - \boldsymbol{\beta}_{t-1})$ is large or if the function is locally indefinite. In this case, the algorithm may actually “step over” the solution value or $\mathrm{S}(\boldsymbol{\beta}_t) > \mathrm{S}(\boldsymbol{\beta}_{t-1})$. To avoid these problems and to reduce computation time, the algorithms may be modified to allow for smaller steps in the parameter space. As well, the iterative process may be hastened by using increments larger than the full Newton steps in relatively flat areas of the surface of the nonlinear least-squares objective function. Consider the modified Newton–Raphson algorithm

$$\boldsymbol{\beta}_t = \boldsymbol{\beta}_{t-1} - \lambda_t \left[\left. \frac{\partial^2 \mathrm{S}(\boldsymbol{\beta})}{\partial \boldsymbol{\beta} \partial \boldsymbol{\beta}'} \right|_{\boldsymbol{\beta}_{t-1}} \right]^{-1} \left[\left. \frac{\partial \mathrm{S}(\boldsymbol{\beta})}{\partial \boldsymbol{\beta}} \right|_{\boldsymbol{\beta}_{t-1}} \right]. \quad (8.13.17)$$

Here, the size of the Newton step is controlled with the parameter λ_t, which is equal to one in the standard Newton–Raphson algorithm. Sophisticated line search methods are designed to identify a value of λ_t such that $\mathrm{S}(\boldsymbol{\beta}_t - \lambda_t \boldsymbol{\delta}_t) < \mathrm{S}(\boldsymbol{\beta}_{t-1})$ before proceeding to the next iteration. One simple approach known as step-halving involves multiplying

λ_t by 0.5 until the step-size problem is resolved, and other methods include golden section search and polynomial and random fit. For example, the GAUSS procedure qnewton() is based on the polynomial search method developed by Dennis and Schnabel. If GAUSS cannot locate an acceptable step length in 40 attempts, qnewton() tries a random search.

Finally, we note that users should use analytical derivatives to solve numerical optimization problems whenever possible. Computer arithmetic is fundamentally flawed by the fact that computer numbers have a fixed number of decimal places. The standard double precision number in a personal computer carries about 16 significant places. However, a simple operation can destroy the accuracy of nearly all of those decimal places. For example, consider the Box–Cox transformation $(x^\lambda - 1)/\lambda$ when $x = 2$:

2^λ	$2^\lambda - 1$	λ	$(2^\lambda - 1)/\lambda$
1.000006931495828	6.931495828199630e-006	1.0e-005	0.69314958281
1.000000693147421	6.931474207938493e-007	1.0e-006	0.69314742079
1.000000069314720	6.931472040783149e-008	1.0e-007	0.69314720407
1.000000006931472	6.931471840943004e-009	1.0e-008	0.69314718409
1.000000000693147	6.931470952764585e-010	1.0e-009	0.69314709527
1.000000000069315	6.931477614102732e-011	1.0e-010	0.69314776141
1.000000000006932	6.931566431944702e-012	1.0e-011	0.69315664319
1.000000000000693	6.932232565759477e-013	1.0e-012	0.69322325657
1.000000000000069	6.927791673660977e-014	1.0e-013	0.69277916736
1.000000000000007	6.883382752675971e-015	1.0e-014	0.68833827526
1.000000000000001	6.661338147750939e-016	1.0e-015	0.66613381477

In theory, as λ approaches zero, $(2^\lambda - 1)/\lambda$ approaches $\ln(2) = 0.693147180559945$. In practice, a problem arises as λ approaches zero. Note that as λ gets smaller, the number of informative decimal places in 2^λ declines until, when $\lambda = 1.\text{e-}015$, none remain. The convergence of $(2^\lambda - 1)/\lambda$ itself falls apart around $\lambda = 1.\text{e-}011$.

The problem is due to the finite nature of the computer number, not to the implementation of the operators. The calculation of 2^λ is equivalent to adding a progressively smaller number to 1. Suppose we have a very small number known to 15 places of precision, 0.999999999999999e-15. If we add 1 to the number, we get 1.000000000000001 and 14 of the 15 decimal places in the smaller number are lost. The problem occurs in all computers and the apparent solution, adding more bits to the computer number, is only temporary because we can always find numbers so small that the problem occurs. For our purposes, we want to avoid numerical operations that combine relatively small numbers with relatively large numbers.

In the Newton methods, the calculation of the direction involves an inversion step and a matrix multiplication step, and numerical precision may be lost in either operation. Also, numerical precision may be lost in problems that are poorly scaled owing to the large differences in the relative magnitudes of elements in the gradient vector and Hessian matrix. To avoid scaling problems, the user should specify the problem so that the diagonal elements of the Hessian matrix are all of similar magnitudes. Further, numerical derivatives are computed by dividing a difference by a very small quantity, and the operation may result in a considerable loss in precision. In general, when using double precision with 16 places of accuracy, about 4 decimal places are lost in calculating a first derivative and another 4 with the second derivative. Thus, the quasi–Newton method and other algorithms based on numerical derivatives can lose up to 8 decimal places, and analytical derivatives should be used whenever possible. The qnewton() procedure provided with GAUSS employs the BFGS quasi–Newton algorithm that is designed to avoid these numerical difficulties.

8.13.6. Appendix B: Proofs

THEOREM PROOF 8.4.1 CONSISTENCY AND CONVERGENCE IN DISTRIBUTION OF THE ESTIMATOR ε_i FOR ε_i : This is a direct application of the result that the probability limit of a continuous function is the function of the probability limits. Applying the result to each of the elements in the vector equation (8.4.1) implies that

$$\begin{aligned} \text{p}\lim(\hat{\varepsilon}_i - \varepsilon_i) &= \text{p}\lim[\text{g}(\mathbf{x}_{i\cdot}, \boldsymbol{\beta}_0) - \text{g}(\mathbf{x}_{i\cdot}, \hat{\boldsymbol{\beta}})] \\ &= \text{g}(\mathbf{x}_{i\cdot}, \boldsymbol{\beta}_0) - \text{g}(\mathbf{x}_{i\cdot}, \boldsymbol{\beta}_0) = 0 \end{aligned} \tag{8.13.18}$$

because $\hat{\boldsymbol{\beta}} \xrightarrow{\text{p}} \boldsymbol{\beta}_0$. ■

THEOREM PROOF 8.4.2 CONSISTENCY OF S^2 FOR ESTIMATING $\boldsymbol{\sigma}^2$: Upon dividing (8.4.5) by $n-k$, the first term to the right of the equality, $\frac{\varepsilon'\mathbf{m}(\boldsymbol{\beta}_0)\varepsilon}{n-k}$, is precisely in the form to which the proof of Theorem 5.4.2 is applicable. Repeating that proof, with $\mathbf{x}$ replaced by $\mathbf{x}(\boldsymbol{\beta}_0)$, leads directly to the conclusion that p lim $\frac{\varepsilon'\mathbf{m}(\boldsymbol{\beta}_0)\varepsilon}{n-k} = \sigma^2$.

From the idempotency of $\text{m}(\boldsymbol{\beta}_0)$, and the algebraic form of the Cauchy–Schwarz inequality, the absolute value of the second term in the representation of (8.4.5) is such that

$$\left|\frac{\varepsilon'\mathbf{m}(\boldsymbol{\beta}_0)\mathbf{o}_\text{p}(n^{-1/2})}{n-k}\right| \le \left(\frac{\varepsilon'\mathbf{m}(\boldsymbol{\beta}_0)\varepsilon}{n-k}\right)^{1/2} \left(\frac{\mathbf{o}_\text{p}(n^{-1/2})'\mathbf{o}_\text{p}(n^{-1/2})}{n-k}\right)^{1/2}. \tag{8.13.19}$$

The first term to the right of the inequality has a probability limit equal to σ, and the second term is of order of magnitude $\text{o}_\text{p}(n^{-1/2})$; thus, the product of the terms converge in probability to zero. It follows that $\frac{\varepsilon'\mathbf{m}(\boldsymbol{\beta}_0)\mathbf{o}_\text{p}(n^{-1/2})}{n-k} \xrightarrow{\text{p}} 0$.

Finally, the last term in the representation of $\frac{\hat{\varepsilon}'\hat{\varepsilon}}{n-k}$ also converges to zero in probability because $\frac{\text{O}_\text{P}(1)}{n-k} = \text{o}_\text{p}(n^{-1}) \xrightarrow{\text{p}} 0$. Therefore, plim $\text{S}^2 = \sigma^2$. ■

PROOF THAT NLS ESTIMATOR IS BEST IN THE ASYMPTOTICALLY LINEAR CLASS (ALC) CLASS: For each of the estimators in the ALC class, the limiting behavior of $n^{1/2}(\breve{\beta} - \beta_0)$ is equivalent to the limiting behavior of

$$\{[n^{-1}\mathbf{x}(\boldsymbol{\beta}_0)'\mathbf{x}(\boldsymbol{\beta}_0)]^{-1}n^{-1/2}\mathbf{x}(\boldsymbol{\beta}_0)' + n^{-1/2}\mathbf{w}'\}\varepsilon, \tag{8.13.20}$$

the difference being $o_p(1)$. Given (8.9.15) and results on the covariance matrix of linear combinations of random variables, the limiting covariance matrix of (8.13.20) equals $\sigma^2(\Xi^{-1} + \text{plim}\, n^{-1}\mathbf{w}'\mathbf{w})$, which exceeds the limiting covariance matrix, $\sigma^2\Xi^{-1}$, of the NLS estimator by the positive semidefinite matrix $\sigma^2\text{plim}\, n^{-1}\mathbf{w}'\mathbf{w}$. Setting $\mathbf{w} = \mathbf{0}$ defines the estimator in the ALC class with the smallest limiting covariance matrix, indicating that the NLS estimator is best in the class. ■

CHAPTER 9

Nonlinear and Nonnormal Parametric Regression Models

In Chapters 3 and 4 we introduced the concept of a likelihood function and corresponding maximum likelihood (ML) estimators and inference procedures for the unknown parameters in the case of the multivariate normal linear regression model. In this chapter we extend this model by first considering estimation and inference in the context of multivariate normal nonlinear regression models, where $\mathbf{g}(\mathbf{x}, \boldsymbol{\beta})$ is some $(n \times 1)$ twice continuously differentiable vector function of $\boldsymbol{\beta}$. We then turn to the case where the random components of the model are *not* normally distributed but are still characterized by a parametric model. In this context, we examine models that have explicit nonnormal dependent variable specifications.

In terms of the general class of probability models discussed in this chapter, we will be concerned with the special cases delineated in Table 9.1.

The particular inverse problem associated with the probability models in Table 9.1 is one of recovering information on the unknown and unobservable $(\boldsymbol{\beta}, \sigma^2, \boldsymbol{\varepsilon})$ from sample outcomes of $(\mathbf{Y}, \mathbf{x})$.

9.1. The Normal Nonlinear Regression Model

In this section we reexamine estimation and inference procedures for the nonlinear regression model of Chapter 8 when we have the additional information that the noise component and thus the dependent variable are multivariate normally distributed. The probability model is based on the specific characteristics displayed in Table 9.1, where the characteristics labeled 1 in the table are used for model components in those cases in which there are two different choices of assumptions. In particular, the model is characterized by

$$\mathbf{Y} = \mathbf{g}(\mathbf{x}, \boldsymbol{\beta}) + \boldsymbol{\varepsilon}; \quad \boldsymbol{\varepsilon} \sim \mathrm{N}(\mathbf{0}, \sigma^2 \mathbf{I}_n), \tag{9.1.1}$$

where $\mathbf{g}(\mathbf{x}, \boldsymbol{\beta})$ is some twice continuously differentiable (in $\boldsymbol{\beta}$) $(n \times 1)$ vector function, and $\mathbf{x}$ is a fixed $(n \times k)$ matrix. The model is thus seen to be precisely as it was in Chapter 8 except for the addition of the multivariate normality assumption for the

Table 9.1. *Nonlinear Parametric and Semiparametric Regression Models*

Model Component	Specific Characteristics	
Y	RV Type:	continuous
	Range:	unlimited
	Y_i dimension:	univariate
	Moments:	1. $E[\mathbf{Y} \mid \mathbf{x}] = \mathbf{g}(\mathbf{x}, \boldsymbol{\beta})$, $\mathbf{cov}(\mathbf{Y} \mid \mathbf{x}) = \sigma^2 \mathbf{I}$, or 2. $E(\mathbf{Y} \mid \mathbf{x}) = \mathbf{g}(\mathbf{x}, \boldsymbol{\beta}, \sigma^2)$, $\mathbf{cov}(\mathbf{Y} \mid \mathbf{x}) = \Sigma_Y(\mathbf{x}, \boldsymbol{\beta}, \sigma^2)$
$\eta(\mathbf{x}, \boldsymbol{\beta}, \varepsilon)$	Functional Form:	linear or nonlinear in $\mathbf{x}$ and $\boldsymbol{\beta}$, and additive or nonadditive in ε, where 1. $\eta(\mathbf{x}, \boldsymbol{\beta}, \varepsilon) = \mathbf{g}(\mathbf{x}, \boldsymbol{\beta}) + \varepsilon$, $\mathbf{g}(\mathbf{x}, \boldsymbol{\beta}) \equiv [g(\mathbf{x}_{1\cdot}, \boldsymbol{\beta}), \ldots, g(\mathbf{x}_{n\cdot}, \boldsymbol{\beta})]'$. or 2. $\eta(\mathbf{x}, \boldsymbol{\beta}, \varepsilon) \equiv [\eta(\mathbf{x}_{1\cdot}, \boldsymbol{\beta}, \varepsilon_1), \ldots,$ $\eta(\mathbf{x}_{n\cdot}, \boldsymbol{\beta}, \varepsilon_n)]$, where $\mathbf{g}$ and η are twice continuously differentiable in $\boldsymbol{\beta}$.
x	RV Type:	degenerate (fixed)
	Genesis:	exogenous to the model
$\boldsymbol{\beta}$	RV Type:	degenerate (fixed)
	Dimension:	finite (fixed)
ε	RV Type:	iid, or independent nonidentical
	Moments:	$E[\varepsilon \mid \mathbf{x}] = 0$, and $\mathbf{cov}(\varepsilon \mid \mathbf{x}) = \sigma^2 \mathbf{I}$
Ω	Prior info:	none
$f(\mathbf{e} \mid \mathbf{x}, \varphi^2)$	PDF family:	1. multivariate normal 2. specified nonnormal parametric family

noise component. The discussion of the implications of model characteristics and the discussion of the inverse problem provided in Section 8.1 is completely relevant to the current probability model.

9.1.1. Maximum Likelihood–Extremum Estimation

The log likelihood function associated with (9.1.1) and the probability model in Table 9.1 can be expressed as

$$\ln L(\boldsymbol{\beta}, \sigma^2; \mathbf{y}, \mathbf{x}) = -\frac{n}{2}\ln(2\pi) - \frac{n}{2}\ln\sigma^2 - \frac{1}{2\sigma^2}[\mathbf{y} - \mathbf{g}(\mathbf{x}, \boldsymbol{\beta})]'[\mathbf{y} - \mathbf{g}(\mathbf{x}, \boldsymbol{\beta})]. \tag{9.1.2}$$

To maximize $L(\boldsymbol{\beta}, \sigma^2; \mathbf{y}, \mathbf{x})$ and thereby define the ML–extremum estimate $(\hat{\mathbf{b}}, s^2_{ML}) = \arg\max_{\beta,\sigma^2}[\ln L(\boldsymbol{\beta}, \sigma^2; \mathbf{y}, \mathbf{x})]$ of $\boldsymbol{\beta}$ and σ^2, a useful first step, both for computational and conceptual purposes, is to *concentrate* the likelihood function with respect to the parameter σ^2. In general, a likelihood function can be concentrated if the likelihood-maximizing optimal values of some of the parameters can be represented in terms of closed-form functions of the remaining parameters, these functions being referred to as *optimal value functions*. If so, the likelihood function is then *concentrated* down to a smaller set of unknown parameters by substitution of these optimal value functions into the likelihood function. A computational benefit of concentration is that the search for the maximum-likelihood estimate can then be conducted in a lower-dimensional space of unknowns. The maximum-likelihood estimates of any parameters concentrated out of the likelihood function can be recovered through use of the optimal value functions once the optimal values of the parameters in the concentrated likelihood function are determined.

We concentrate (9.1.2) by examining the first-order condition with respect to σ^2, which is given by

$$\frac{\partial \ln L(\boldsymbol{\beta}, \sigma^2; \mathbf{y}, \mathbf{x})}{\partial \sigma^2} = -\frac{n}{2\sigma^2} + \frac{1}{2(\sigma^2)^2}[\mathbf{y} - \mathbf{g}(\mathbf{x}, \boldsymbol{\beta})]'[\mathbf{y} - \mathbf{g}(\mathbf{x}, \boldsymbol{\beta})] = 0. \tag{9.1.3}$$

Solving this first-order condition for σ^2 yields

$$s^2_{ML}(\boldsymbol{\beta}) \equiv \sigma^2(\boldsymbol{\beta}) = \frac{1}{n}[\mathbf{y} - \mathbf{g}(\mathbf{x}, \boldsymbol{\beta})]'[\mathbf{y} - \mathbf{g}(\mathbf{x}, \boldsymbol{\beta})] \tag{9.1.4}$$

so that the ML estimate of σ^2 can be expressed as a *function of* $\boldsymbol{\beta}$. If we substitute the result (9.1.4) into (9.1.2), we have *concentrated* the log-likelihood function into a function of only $\boldsymbol{\beta}$ as follows:

$$\ln L_c(\boldsymbol{\beta}; \mathbf{y}, \mathbf{x}) = -\frac{n}{2}[\ln(2\pi) - \ln(n) + 1] - \frac{n}{2}\ln[\mathbf{y} - \mathbf{g}(\mathbf{x}, \boldsymbol{\beta})]'[\mathbf{y} - \mathbf{g}(\mathbf{x}, \boldsymbol{\beta})]. \tag{9.1.5}$$

Maximization of the concentrated likelihood function is then accomplished by minimizing $[\mathbf{y} - \mathbf{g}(\mathbf{x}, \boldsymbol{\beta})]'[\mathbf{y} - \mathbf{g}(\mathbf{x}, \boldsymbol{\beta})]$, which, of course, leads to the NLS-extremum estimates of Chapter 8. Thus, all of the previous sampling properties attributed to the NLS estimator apply to the ML estimator of $\boldsymbol{\beta}$ as well, because all of the conditions presupposed in Table 8.1 and Theorems 8.9.1 and 8.9.2 can be assumed to hold here. Thus, the ML estimator of $\boldsymbol{\beta}$ will be consistent, asymptotically normally distributed, and best in the class of asymptotically linear and consistent estimators. The ML estimator of σ^2 can be calculated based on (9.1.4) as $S^2_{ML} \equiv s^2_{ML}(\hat{\boldsymbol{\beta}})$.

The ML estimator is asymptotically efficient under general regularity conditions (see Mittelhammer, p. 482). In particular, the ML estimator, and thus also the NLS estimator of $\boldsymbol{\beta}$ will be asymptotically efficient under the current assumption that the noise elements are iid normally distributed. The asymptotic ML covariance matrix for $\hat{\boldsymbol{\beta}}$ is the same as the asymptotic covariance matrix of the nonlinear least-squares estimator developed in Chapter 8. To see this, note that the asymptotic covariance matrix of an efficient ML estimator is given in general by

$$\mathbf{cov}(\hat{\boldsymbol{\theta}}) = -\left[E\frac{\partial^2 \ln L(\boldsymbol{\theta}; \mathbf{Y}, \mathbf{x})}{\partial \boldsymbol{\theta} \partial \boldsymbol{\theta}'}\bigg|_{\boldsymbol{\theta}_0} \right]^{-1}, \tag{9.1.6}$$

where $\boldsymbol{\theta} = (\boldsymbol{\beta}, \sigma^2)$, and $\boldsymbol{\theta}_0$ denotes the true value of $\boldsymbol{\theta}$. Applying (9.1.6) to (9.1.2) yields

$$-\mathrm{E}\left[\left.\frac{\partial^2 \ln \mathrm{L}(\boldsymbol{\theta}; \mathbf{Y}, \mathbf{x})}{\partial\boldsymbol{\theta}\partial\boldsymbol{\theta}'}\right|_{\boldsymbol{\theta}_0}\right] = \left[\begin{array}{c|c} \frac{1}{\sigma_0^2}\left.\frac{\partial \mathbf{g}(\mathbf{x},\boldsymbol{\beta})}{\partial\boldsymbol{\beta}}\right|_{\boldsymbol{\beta}_0}\left.\frac{\partial \mathbf{g}(\mathbf{x},\boldsymbol{\beta})}{\partial\boldsymbol{\beta}'}\right|_{\boldsymbol{\beta}_0} & \mathbf{0} \\ \hline \mathbf{0} & \frac{n}{2\sigma_0^4} \end{array}\right]. \tag{9.1.7}$$

Therefore, the asymptotic covariance matrix of $\hat{\boldsymbol{\beta}}$ is given by

$$\mathbf{cov}(\hat{\boldsymbol{\beta}}) = \sigma_0^2\left[\left.\frac{\partial \mathbf{g}(\mathbf{x}, \boldsymbol{\beta})}{\partial\boldsymbol{\beta}}\right|_{\boldsymbol{\beta}_0}\left.\frac{\partial \mathbf{g}(\mathbf{x}, \boldsymbol{\beta})}{\partial\boldsymbol{\beta}'}\right|_{\boldsymbol{\beta}_0}\right]^{-1}, \tag{9.1.8}$$

which can be estimated by replacing $\boldsymbol{\beta}_0$ with the maximum likelihood (and equivalently nonlinear least-squares) estimate $\hat{\mathbf{b}}$ and replacing σ_0^2 with the maximum likelihood estimate

$$s_{\mathrm{ML}}^2 = \frac{[\mathbf{y} - \mathbf{g}(\mathbf{x}, \hat{\mathbf{b}})]'[\mathbf{y} - \mathbf{g}(\mathbf{x}, \hat{\mathbf{b}})]}{n}, \tag{9.1.9}$$

resulting in the estimate

$$\mathbf{c\hat{o}v}(\hat{\boldsymbol{\beta}}) = s_{\mathrm{ML}}^2\left[\left.\frac{\partial \mathbf{g}(\mathbf{x}, \boldsymbol{\beta})}{\partial\boldsymbol{\beta}}\right|_{\hat{\mathbf{b}}}\left.\frac{\partial \mathbf{g}(\mathbf{x}, \boldsymbol{\beta})}{\partial\boldsymbol{\beta}'}\right|_{\hat{\mathbf{b}}}\right]^{-1}. \tag{9.1.10}$$

We also know from (9.1.6) and (9.1.7) that the asymptotic variance of the maximum likelihood estimator of σ^2 is given by $2\sigma^4/n$, which can be consistently estimated by $2s_{\mathrm{ML}}^4/n$.

In summary, the added assumption of multivariate normality of the noise component results in the additional estimator property of asymptotic efficiency of the ML–NLS–extremum estimator $\hat{\boldsymbol{\beta}}$. The estimator S_{ML}^2 is asymptotically efficient as well.

9.1.2. Maximum Likelihood–Extremum Inference

On the basis of the asymptotic normality of the ML–extremum estimator and the inverse asymptotic covariance matrix result (9.1.7) it follows that $S_{\mathrm{ML}}^2 \overset{a}{\sim} \mathrm{N}(\sigma_0^2, 2\sigma_0^4/n)$. Then one-sided and two-sided hypotheses relating to σ_0^2 can be tested based on the Z-statistic

$$\mathrm{Z} = \frac{S_{\mathrm{ML}}^2 - \sigma_*^2}{\left(2S_{\mathrm{ML}}^4/n\right)^{1/2}} \overset{a}{\sim} \mathrm{N}\left(\frac{\sigma_0^2 - \sigma_*^2}{\left(2\sigma_0^4/n\right)^{1/2}}, 1\right) \tag{9.1.11}$$

for hypothesized values σ_*^2. In particular, we can define the following asymptotic level-α tests $\{Z, C^Z\}$:

H_0:	C^Z
$\sigma_0^2 \leq \sigma_*^2$	$[z_{1-\alpha}, \infty)$
$\sigma_0^2 \geq \sigma_*^2$	$(-\infty, z_\alpha]$
$\sigma_0^2 = \sigma_*^2$	$[z_{\alpha/2}, z_{1-\alpha/2}]$

, (9.1.12)

where z_τ is the $100\tau\%$ quantile of the standard normal distribution.

Because the ML– and NLS–extremum estimators of $\boldsymbol{\beta}$ are equivalent, all of the hypothesis testing and confidence region procedures developed in Chapter 8 for the NLS estimator based on Wald, Lagrange Multiplier, and Z-statistics can be applied directly to the ML estimator. In addition, it is now possible to utilize the generalized likelihood ratio (GLR) specialization of the pseudo-likelihood ratio test to test hypotheses of the form H_0: $\mathbf{c}(\boldsymbol{\beta}) = \mathbf{r}$, where $\mathbf{c}(\boldsymbol{\beta})$ is a nonlinear differentiable vector function of $\boldsymbol{\beta}$ (we are again assuming that the functions contained in the vector $\mathbf{c}(\boldsymbol{\beta})$ are functionally independent). On the basis of the GLR test statistic of Chapter 4, we obtain

$$\lambda(\mathbf{Y}) = \frac{\left(2\pi S_{\mathbf{r}}^2\right)^{-n/2} \exp(-n/2)}{\left(2\pi S_{\mathrm{ML}}^2\right)^{-n/2} \exp(-n/2)} = \left(\frac{S_{\mathbf{r}}^2}{S_{\mathrm{ML}}^2}\right)^{-n/2}, \tag{9.1.13}$$

where $S_{\mathbf{r}}^2 = [\mathbf{Y} - \mathbf{g}(\mathbf{x}, \hat{\boldsymbol{\beta}}_{\mathbf{r}})]'[\mathbf{Y} - \mathbf{g}(\mathbf{x}, \hat{\boldsymbol{\beta}}_{\mathbf{r}})]/n$ is the restricted (by H_0: $\mathbf{c}(\boldsymbol{\beta}) = \mathbf{r}$) maximum likelihood (or nonlinear least-squares) estimator of σ^2, with $\hat{\boldsymbol{\beta}}_{\mathbf{r}}$ being the restricted ML (or NLS) estimator of $\boldsymbol{\beta}$. Then, under the same regularity conditions that ensure the asymptotic normality of the ML estimator (also see sections 7.6.3 and 8.7.1), we have that

$$\mathrm{GLR} = -2 \ln \lambda(\mathbf{Y}) = n\left(\ln S_{\mathbf{r}}^2 - \ln S_{\mathrm{ML}}^2\right) \overset{a}{\sim} \text{Chi-square}(j, 0) \tag{9.1.14}$$

under H_0, where j is the row dimension of the vector function $\mathbf{c}(\boldsymbol{\beta}) = \mathbf{r}$.

The generalized likelihood ratio test, $\{\mathrm{GLR}, C^{\mathrm{GLR}}\}$ is conducted by applying the decision rule

$$\text{reject } H_0\text{: } \mathbf{c}(\boldsymbol{\beta}) = \mathbf{r} \quad \text{iff} \quad \mathrm{glr} \in C^{\mathrm{GLR}} \tag{9.1.15}$$

where $C^{\mathrm{GLR}} = [\chi^2_{1-\alpha,\infty}]$ and $\chi^2_{1-\alpha}$ is the $100(1-\alpha)\%$ quantile of the central Chi-square distribution with j degrees of freedom. It can be shown (Mittelhammer, pp. 613–4) that the asymptotic distribution of GLR under Pitman drift alternatives H_a: $\mathbf{c}(\boldsymbol{\beta}) = \mathbf{r} + n^{-1/2}\boldsymbol{\delta}$ is noncentral Chi-square, as Chi-square(glr; j, λ), with the noncentrality parameter equal to

$$\lambda = \frac{1}{2}\boldsymbol{\delta}' \left[\sigma^2 \left.\frac{\partial \mathbf{c}(\boldsymbol{\beta})}{\partial \boldsymbol{\beta}'}\right|_{\boldsymbol{\beta}_0} \boldsymbol{\Xi}^{-1} \left.\frac{\partial \mathbf{c}(\boldsymbol{\beta})}{\partial \boldsymbol{\beta}}\right|_{\boldsymbol{\beta}_0} \right]^{-1} \boldsymbol{\delta} \tag{9.1.16}$$

and $\Xi = \lim_{n\to\infty}[n^{-1}\frac{\partial \mathbf{g}(\mathbf{x},\boldsymbol{\beta})}{\partial \boldsymbol{\beta}}\big|_{\boldsymbol{\beta}_0}\frac{\partial \mathbf{g}(\mathbf{x},\boldsymbol{\beta})}{\partial \boldsymbol{\beta}'}\big|_{\boldsymbol{\beta}_0}]$. Thus, the asymptotic power characteristic of the GLR test are precisely the same as those of the Wald and LM tests presented in Chapters 7 and 8.

Confidence regions based on the GLR test can be constructed, in principle, based on the duality approach such as

$$\mathrm{CR}^{\mathrm{GLR}} = \left\{\mathrm{r}: n\left(\ln \mathrm{s}_{\mathrm{r}}^2 - \ln \mathrm{s}_{\mathrm{ML}}^2\right) < \chi^2_{1-\alpha}\right\} \tag{9.1.17}$$

for an asymptotic $100(1-\alpha)\%$ level of confidence. Computationally, the Wald test is more straightforward to use than the GLR test for confidence region purposes.

9.2. Nonnormality

In this section we examine cases involving ML–extremum estimation where the joint probability distribution of the dependent variable vector is not in the normal parametric family and the noise component has a distribution that may or may not be in the normal family. The possibilities in this context are endless, and there is no way that all of the variations on this theme can be addressed. We concentrate on two specific cases to illustrate the process of specifying the likelihood function and then implementing the ML–extremum procedure. The first case illustrates the issues and procedures involved in defining ML–extremum estimates of unknown parameters when nonnormality prevails for the distribution of $\mathbf{Y}$ but the noise component is still normally distributed. The second case illustrates issues and procedures when neither $\mathbf{Y}$ nor $\boldsymbol{\varepsilon}$ is normally distributed. We then engage in a general discussion of the basic approach that one follows when applying the ML–extremum estimation procedure to probability models that are not based on normal probability distributions, and we also examine the general issue of hypothesis-testing and confidence-region estimation in these cases. Other specific applications of ML–extremum estimation and inference procedures occur in later chapters.

9.2.1. A Nonnormal Dependent Variable, Normal Noise Component Case: The Box–Cox Transformation

If the sample observations on the dependent variable are not iid outcomes from a normal distribution, there may still exist a transformation such that the transformed observations are normally distributed. A particular example of such a situation, which is representative of probability models that arise in practice, is reflected by the specification

$$\mathrm{Y}_i = \exp(\mathbf{x}_{i\cdot}\boldsymbol{\beta} + \varepsilon_i), \quad i = 1, \ldots, n, \tag{9.2.1}$$

where $\varepsilon_i \sim$ iid Normal$(0, \sigma^2)$ and Y_i is log-normally distributed with mean $\exp(\mathbf{x}_{i\cdot}\boldsymbol{\beta} + .5\sigma^2)$ and variance $\exp(2\mathbf{x}_{i\cdot}\boldsymbol{\beta})[\mathrm{e}^{2\sigma^2} - \mathrm{e}^{\sigma^2}]$ (see Chapter E1; Mittelhammer, p. 358). This model is a special case of the general nonlinear model specification

$$\mathrm{Y}_i = \eta(\mathbf{x}_{i\cdot}, \boldsymbol{\beta}, \varepsilon_i), \quad \mathrm{E}[\mathrm{Y}_i] = \mathrm{g}(\mathbf{x}_{i\cdot}, \boldsymbol{\beta}, \sigma^2), \quad \mathrm{var}(\mathrm{Y}_i) = \sigma^2_{\mathrm{Y}_i}(\mathbf{x}_{i\cdot}, \boldsymbol{\beta}, \sigma^2), \tag{9.2.2}$$

which coincides with the characteristics labeled 2 in Table 9.1 (if two alternatives are listed). Applying a logarithmic transformation to (9.2.1) yields the linearized regression model

$$\mathrm{Y}_i^* = \ln(\mathrm{Y}_i) = \mathbf{x}_{i\cdot}\boldsymbol{\beta} + \varepsilon_i, \quad i = 1, \ldots, n, \tag{9.2.3}$$

which can be estimated by the traditional ML–LS extremum estimation procedures presented in Chapter 7. Hypothesis testing and confidence region estimation can be conducted using the results presented in Chapter 7.

In a more general context, Box and Cox (1964) consider the probability model

$$\mathrm{Y}_i(\lambda) \equiv \frac{\mathrm{Y}_i^\lambda - 1}{\lambda} = \mathbf{x}_{i\cdot}\boldsymbol{\beta} + \varepsilon_i \tag{9.2.4}$$

so that the dependent variable observations, the y_i's, are subject to a nonlinear power transformation that involves the unknown parameter λ. Note that this model can be cast in the form of (9.2.2) with the addition of the parameter λ. The value of λ is of course very important because a range of different DSPs emerge for the various choices of λ, including linear models ($\lambda = 1$), power transformation models ($\lambda \neq 0$ or 1), and semilogarithmic models (the limit of $(\mathrm{y}_i^\lambda - 1)/\lambda$ as $\lambda \to 0$ is $\ln(y_i)$). Note the Box–Cox model (9.2.4) subsumes (9.2.3) as a special case.

The original goal of Box and Cox was to identify a value of λ that would result in a DSP representation as close as possible to having an iid normal distribution for the noise component of (9.2.4). With this goal in mind, Box and Cox suggested that the parameters in (9.2.4) be estimated using the maximum likelihood procedure under the assumption that $\varepsilon_i \sim$ iid $\mathrm{N}(0, \sigma^2)$. On the basis of their suggestion, the log likelihood associated with the model (9.2.4) is given by

$$\begin{aligned}\ln \mathrm{L}(\boldsymbol{\beta}, \sigma^2, \lambda; \mathbf{y}, \mathbf{x}) = &-\frac{n}{2}\ln(2\pi) - \frac{n}{2}\ln(\sigma^2) - \frac{1}{2\sigma^2}[\mathbf{y}(\lambda) - \mathbf{x}\boldsymbol{\beta}]'[\mathbf{y}(\lambda) - \mathbf{x}\boldsymbol{\beta}] \\ &+ (\lambda - 1)\sum_i \ln(y_i),\end{aligned} \tag{9.2.5}$$

where $\mathbf{y}(\lambda) \equiv (\frac{\mathrm{y}_1^\lambda - 1}{\lambda}, \ldots, \frac{\mathrm{y}_n^\lambda - 1}{\lambda})'$. To determine the ML–extremum estimates of the parameters, the log likelihood function (9.2.5) can be directly maximized by a numerical optimization method such as the qnewton() procedure in GAUSS (see the appendix to Chapter 8).

An alternative method for calculating the ML–extremum estimates for (9.2.5) is first to obtain the concentrated likelihood function that depends only on λ and then search over λ for an optimum. This latter procedure is equivalent to solving a sequence of linear least-squares problems, one for each value of λ examined. Then for each value of λ examined, the associated optimal $\boldsymbol{\beta}$ and σ^2 would be found and substituted into ln(L); then the $(\lambda, \boldsymbol{\beta}, \sigma^2)$ value with the largest ln(L) would be chosen. More specifically, note that for a given value of λ, say λ_*, (9.2.5) is maximized by choosing

$$\hat{\mathbf{b}}(\lambda_*) = (\mathbf{x}'\mathbf{x})^{-1}\mathbf{x}'\mathbf{y}(\lambda_*) \quad \text{and} \quad \mathrm{s}_{\mathrm{ML}}^2(\lambda_*) = [\mathbf{y}(\lambda_*) - \mathbf{x}\hat{\mathbf{b}}(\lambda_*)]'[\mathbf{y}(\lambda_*) - \mathbf{x}\hat{\mathbf{b}}(\lambda_*)]/n \tag{9.2.6}$$

for $\boldsymbol{\beta}$ and σ^2 because, when λ_* is fixed, the log likelihood function is essentially characterizing a normal linear regression model (recall (3.2.4)) with a dependent variable $\mathbf{y}(\lambda_*)$ and explanatory variable values $\mathbf{x}$. The concentrated likelihood function is obtained by substituting $\hat{\mathbf{b}}(\lambda_*)$ and $s^2_{ML}(\lambda_*)$ for $\boldsymbol{\beta}$ and σ^2 in (9.2.5), resulting in

$$\ln L_c(\lambda_*; \mathbf{y}, \mathbf{x}) = -\frac{n}{2}[\ln(2\pi) - \ln(n) + 1] + (\lambda - 1)\sum_i \ln(y_i) - \frac{n}{2}\ln[[\mathbf{y}(\lambda_*) - \mathbf{x}\hat{\mathbf{b}}(\lambda_*)]'[\mathbf{y}(\lambda_*) - \mathbf{x}\hat{\mathbf{b}}(\lambda_*)]]. \tag{9.2.7}$$

The ML–extremum estimate for λ_* in (9.2.7) is found as $\hat{\lambda}_{ML} = \arg\max_{\lambda*}[\ln L_c(\lambda_*; \mathbf{y}, \mathbf{x})]$, and subsequently the ML–extremum estimates for $\boldsymbol{\beta}$ and σ^2 are defined using (9.2.6) as $\hat{\mathbf{b}} = \hat{\mathbf{b}}(\hat{\lambda}_{ML})$ and $s^2_{ML} = s^2_{ML}(\hat{\lambda}_{ML})$.

9.2.1.a. Extended Box–Cox Models

Additional flexibility can be introduced into the Box–Cox model by applying a transformation to the explanatory variables analogous to the transformation applied to the elements in $\mathbf{Y}$, leading to the functional form

$$Y_i(\lambda) = \beta_0 + \sum_{j=1}^{k} \beta_j x_{ij}(\lambda) + \varepsilon_i, \quad i = 1, \ldots, n, \tag{9.2.8}$$

where $x_{ij}(\lambda) \equiv \frac{x_{ij}^{\lambda} - 1}{\lambda}$. Still further flexibility can be obtained by allowing the value of the λ parameter to be different for each variable transformation as follows:

$$Y_i(\lambda_Y) = \beta_0 + \sum_{j-1}^{k} x_{ij}(\lambda_j) + \varepsilon_i, \quad i = 1, \ldots, n. \tag{9.2.9}$$

An estimation procedure analogous to the one described for the transformation (9.2.4) can be defined for either (9.2.8) or (9.2.9). It is important to note that there is a higher parameter dimensionality in the concentrated likelihood function associated with model (9.2.9) and that in applications convergence difficulties can occur quite often. To enhance understanding, it would be useful for the reader to work through the details of the ML–extremum estimation procedures in both cases.

9.2.1.b. The Normal Distribution: A Truncation Problem

Having described the application of the ML estimation procedure to the Box–Cox model in which the noise component is assumed to be multivariate normally distributed, we now must point out that the normality assumption *cannot* be strictly true! Because the transformation $y_i(\lambda)$ in (9.2.4) involves raising y_i to a power, the value of y_i cannot be negative if λ is a nonintegral value, and because $\lim_{\lambda\to 0} y_i(\lambda) = \ln(y_i)$, y_i cannot be zero. It follows that for $y_i > 0$, the range of the dependent variable in (9.2.4) is bounded as

$$Y_i(\lambda)\begin{bmatrix} > \\ < \end{bmatrix} - \lambda^{-1} \quad \text{if} \quad \lambda \begin{bmatrix} > \\ < \end{bmatrix} 0, \tag{9.2.10}$$

which in turn implies that the range of the noise component in (9.2.4) is bounded as

$$\varepsilon_i \begin{bmatrix} > \\ < \end{bmatrix} -(\mathbf{x}_{i.}\boldsymbol{\beta} + \lambda^{-1}) \quad \text{if} \quad \lambda \begin{bmatrix} > \\ < \end{bmatrix} 0. \tag{9.2.11}$$

Therefore, because the support of the normal distribution is the entire real line, ε_i cannot *literally* have a normal distribution in this nonlinear model specification.

There are several ways that the bounds on ε_i and $Y_i(\lambda)$ have been addressed in practice. The approach used most often has been simply to ignore the bound and proceed *as if* the normal distribution were an accurate *approximation* to the distribution of the noise component. This approach has merit if the truncation of the normal distribution implied by (9.2.11) is immaterial in practical terms, meaning that the probability that (9.2.11) is violated by $\varepsilon_i \sim N(0, \sigma^2)$ is very small. This will occur, for example, when $\mathbf{x}_{i.}\boldsymbol{\beta} + \lambda^{-1}$ is a relatively large positive number and the variance σ^2 is relatively small, for

$$P[e_i > -(\mathbf{x}_{i.}\boldsymbol{\beta} + \lambda^{-1})] = \int_{-[\mathbf{x}_{i.}\boldsymbol{\beta}+\lambda^{-1}]}^{\infty} N(z; 0, \sigma^2)\, dz \tag{9.2.12}$$

approaches 1 as $-[\mathbf{x}_{i.}\boldsymbol{\beta} + \lambda^{-1}]$ approaches negative infinity and σ^2 decreases.

It is interesting to note that the logarithmic model characterized by $\lambda \to 0_+$ (i.e., λ converges to 0 from positive values above 0) is such that (9.2.12) converges to 1, the truncation vanishes, and the assumption of normality is completely admissible, as expected. In practice, (9.2.12) will be close to 1 when $\lambda > 0$ and the conditional expectation of Y_i is high relative to the variation around the conditional mean, which is a scenario that is often encountered in practice. As a rough empirical guide to the severity of the truncation problem, one can calculate (9.2.12) using estimated values of unknown parameters and compare its proximity to the value 1.

An alternative method of estimating the Box–Cox model is to specify the truncation mechanism directly in the probability model. The limited dependent variable models discussed in Chapter 20 are an important class of such alternatives, and the research articles by Poirier (1978), Poirier and Ruud (1979), and Amemiya and Powell (1981) are important references in this regard. Authors have also proposed other means to overcome the practical difficulties associated with the Box–Cox model, and a key reference in this literature is Wooldridge (1992).

► **Example 9.2.1:** To demonstrate an application of the Box–Cox regression model, we provide the GAUSS program C9BoxCox.gss in the examples manual. The program outlines the steps involved in solving the concentrated ML problem. Then, GAUSS generates a random sample of size n for a nonlinear model (selected by the user) and computes the ML estimates. The asymptotic distribution of the estimator is approximated by Monte Carlo simulation, and the results are used to conduct a set of hypothesis tests regarding $\boldsymbol{\beta}$ and λ.

9.2.2. A Nonnormal Noise Component Case

There are many DSP models used in econometric practice for which a normally distributed noise component is not assumed. We will encounter additional models of this type in chapters ahead. In this section we simply examine the specification and estimation procedure for one such model based on the ML–extremum principle.

Suppose an analyst suspects that the noise component of a DSP model specification is symmetrically distributed around zero but that extreme outcomes for ε_i (i.e., large absolute values of ε_i) are relatively common. The analyst might then consider a distribution with considerably thicker tails than the normal distribution. One such distribution is the Cauchy distribution given by

$$\mathrm{f}(\mathrm{e}_i;\alpha) = \frac{1}{\pi\alpha[1+(\mathrm{e}_i/\alpha)^2]} \quad \text{for } \alpha > 0, \tag{9.2.13}$$

where α is a scale parameter governing the spread of the distribution. The standard Cauchy distribution, which is the distribution of the ratio of two independent standard normal random variables, is defined by setting $\alpha = 1$ in (9.2.13).

A probability model of the DSP having a linear systematic component could be specified as

$$\mathrm{Y}_i = \mathbf{x}_{i\cdot}\boldsymbol{\beta} + \varepsilon_i, \quad \varepsilon_i \sim \text{iid Cauchy}(\alpha), \quad i = 1, \ldots, n, \tag{9.2.14}$$

where $\boldsymbol{\beta}$ is a $(k \times 1)$ vector of parameters and $\alpha > 0$. Note that this is *not* in the form of the linear regression model discussed in Chapters 3–6 because $\mathrm{E}[\varepsilon_i]$ and $\mathrm{var}(\varepsilon_i)$ do not exist, and thus $\mathrm{E}[\mathrm{Y}_i]$ and $\mathrm{var}(\mathrm{Y}_i)$ do not exist as well. In fact, in this extreme case, we can say nothing about finite sample moments because *no moments of any order exist* for either ε_i or Y_i. What we can say is that the median of ε_i is 0, the median of Y_i is $\mathbf{x}_{i\cdot}\boldsymbol{\beta}$, and the scale of both ε_i and Y_i, referring to the scale parameter and thus spread of the Cauchy distribution, is equal to α. Estimation of the parameters of (9.2.14) via least squares would result in estimates that are neither consistent nor asymptotically normally distributed. With respect to Table 9.1, the specific model characteristics subsume this case *except* that moments of $\mathbf{Y}$ and $\boldsymbol{\varepsilon}$ are not defined.

To estimate the unknown parameters of (9.2.14) via ML–extremum estimation, we first need to define the likelihood function. This can be accomplished by using the change of variable approach for deriving the probability density of the $\mathbf{Y}_i$'s. Because $\varepsilon_i = \mathrm{y}_i - \mathbf{x}_{i\cdot}\boldsymbol{\beta}$ and thus $\frac{\partial \varepsilon_i}{\partial \mathrm{y}_i} = 1$, the distribution for y_i is

$$\mathrm{f}(\mathrm{y}_i;\alpha,\boldsymbol{\beta}) = \frac{1}{\pi\alpha\left[1+\left(\frac{\mathrm{y}_i-\mathbf{x}_{i\cdot}\boldsymbol{\beta}}{\alpha}\right)^2\right]} \quad \text{for } \alpha > 0. \tag{9.2.15}$$

Because the y_i's are independent, the joint distribution of $\mathbf{Y}$ is then represented by the product $\Pi_{i=1}^{n}\mathrm{f}(\mathrm{y}_i;\alpha)$, which leads to the log likelihood function

$$\ln \mathrm{L}(\alpha,\boldsymbol{\beta};\mathbf{y},\mathbf{x}) = -n\,\ln(\pi) - n\,\ln(\alpha) - \sum_{i=1}^{n}\ln\left[1+\left(\frac{\mathrm{y}_i-\mathbf{x}_{i\cdot}\boldsymbol{\beta}}{\alpha}\right)^2\right]. \tag{9.2.16}$$

The first-order conditions for solving the ML–extremum problem of maximizing (9.2.16) through choice of the parameters α and $\boldsymbol{\beta}$ are then

$$\frac{\partial \ln \mathrm{L}(\alpha, \boldsymbol{\beta}; \mathbf{y}, \mathbf{x})}{\partial \beta_j} = 2\alpha^{-2} \sum_{i=1}^{n} \left[1 + \left(\frac{\mathrm{y}_i - \mathbf{x}_{i\cdot}\boldsymbol{\beta}}{\alpha} \right)^2 \right]^{-1} (\mathrm{y}_i - \mathbf{x}_{i\cdot}\boldsymbol{\beta})\mathbf{x}_{ij} = 0 \quad \text{for } j = 1, \ldots, k \qquad (9.2.17)$$

and

$$\frac{\partial \ln \mathrm{L}(\alpha, \boldsymbol{\beta}; \mathbf{y}, \mathbf{x})}{\partial \alpha} = \frac{-n}{\alpha} + 2 \sum_{i=1}^{n} \left[1 + \left(\frac{\mathrm{y}_i - \mathbf{x}_{i\cdot}\boldsymbol{\beta}}{\alpha} \right)^2 \right]^{-1} \frac{(\mathrm{y}_i - \mathbf{x}_{i\cdot}\boldsymbol{\beta})^2}{\alpha^3} = 0. \qquad (9.2.18)$$

It is evident that the first-order conditions are highly nonlinear in the parameters and must be solved simultaneously (as opposed to sequentially in the linear regression model case with normally distributed errors) to obtain the parameter estimates. Iterative optimization algorithms, such as qnewton() in GAUSS, can be used in an attempt to maximize (9.2.16) with respect to choices of $\boldsymbol{\beta}$ and α. It should be noted, however, that it is common for multiple local optima to exist, and thus several different starting values for the algorithms should be used in an attempt to find the global maximum of the likelihood function.

The ML–extremum estimator in this case has all of the desirable asymptotic properties, including consistency, asymptotic normality, and asymptotic efficiency. The asymptotic distribution of the ML–extremum estimator is given by

$$\hat{\boldsymbol{\theta}} \overset{a}{\sim} \mathrm{N}\left(\boldsymbol{\theta}, \left[-\mathrm{E}\left[\left. \frac{\partial^2 \ln \mathrm{L}(\boldsymbol{\theta}; \mathbf{Y}, \mathbf{x})}{\partial \boldsymbol{\theta} \partial \boldsymbol{\theta}'} \right|_{\boldsymbol{\theta}_0} \right] \right]^{-1} \right), \qquad (9.2.19)$$

where $\boldsymbol{\theta}_0$ denotes the true value of the parameter vector. The asymptotic covariance matrix in (9.2.19) can be approximated by replacing $\boldsymbol{\theta}_0$ with the consistent ML estimator $\hat{\boldsymbol{\theta}}_{\mathrm{ML}}$, yielding

$$\hat{\boldsymbol{\theta}} \overset{a}{\sim} \mathrm{N}\left(\boldsymbol{\theta}, \left[- \left. \frac{\partial^2 \ln \mathrm{L}(\boldsymbol{\theta}; \mathbf{y}, \mathbf{x})}{\partial \boldsymbol{\theta} \partial \boldsymbol{\theta}'} \right|_{\hat{\boldsymbol{\theta}}_{\mathrm{ML}}} \right]^{-1} \right). \qquad (9.2.20)$$

► **Example 9.2.2:** To demonstrate the statistical properties of the Cauchy ML estimator, we provide the GAUSS program C9Cauchy.gss in the examples manual. The program outlines the steps involved in numerically solving the ML problem, and the ML estimates are computed for a given sample. Then, a Monte Carlo exercise is conducted to simulate the sampling properties of the MLE, and the sample moments and EDF of the replicated estimates are compared with the moments and PDF of the limiting normal distribution.

We conclude this section by noting that some ML–extremum problems based on nonnormal distributions may not have well-behaved solutions, and the conditions outlined in Theorems 7.4.1 and 7.4.2 relating to consistency and asymptotic normality may not apply. In some cases, the numerical optimization methods may identify a local solution, but other local maxima may exist. As noted in the appendix to Chapter 8, we may be able to use different starting values for the numerical algorithms to verify the robustness of the ML–extremum solution. Problems may also arise if the likelihood function is unbounded on the parameter space, and plots of the log likelihood or concentrated log likelihood function may provide useful information about the properties of the estimation objective.

► **Example 9.2.3:** We provide the GAUSS program C9LogNor.gss in the examples manual to illustrate one of the potential pitfalls in nonnormal ML estimation problems. The log likelihood and concentrated log likelihood functions for the three-parameter lognormal family are presented. For a given random sample outcome, the Newton–Raphson algorithm is used to compute the ML estimates of the model parameters. However, a plot of the concentrated log likelihood function indicates that the solution is only a local maximum.

9.3. General Considerations in Applying the ML–Extremum Criterion

In specifying a parametric probability model to which the principles of maximum likelihood are to be applied, the primary and essential ingredient is the definition of a likelihood function for the parameters of the model. Because the likelihood function is identical in algebraic form to the joint probability density function of the random sample $\mathbf{Y}$ conditioned on $\mathbf{x}$, the specification of an appropriate parametric family of PDFs for $\mathbf{Y}$ is essential as well. In the sense of extremum estimation, this step in an ML analysis is concerned with choosing an appropriate estimation objective function with which to define the extremum estimator.

In effect, an application of extremum estimation within the specific context of the maximum likelihood approach contains an inherent conceptual guide regarding the type of estimation objective function to be chosen. Namely, the analyst should use an estimation objective function expressed in terms of a parametric family of PDFs that contains a collection of probability distributions broad enough to encompass the correct distributional shape for $\mathbf{Y}$ outcomes. Characteristics such as symmetry or skewness, range of support, and thickness of distribution tails can all lead to the consideration of some parametric families and the elimination of others. In the final analysis, it is incumbent upon the analyst to choose a parametric family, and concomitantly a likelihood function, that is consistent with what is known about the stochastic behavior of the sample $\mathbf{Y}$ outcomes. In the absence of sufficient knowledge about the stochastic characteristics of the sample $\mathbf{Y}$, the analyst may be led to a pragmatic, but preferably flexible, choice of the family of functional forms for $\mathbf{Y}$'s joint distribution. However, one must keep in mind that the properties of ML estimators depend on the parametric family, or extremum estimation objective function, chosen, and *only* if the true data-sampling process is encompassed by the chosen parametric PDF family can one generally expect to achieve all of the properties commonly attributed to ML estimators, including asymptotic efficiency.

We emphasize that in the characterization of probability models such as those depicted in Table 9.1, the parametric PDF assumption can initially enter the model as a characterization of the stochastic behavior of the noise component as opposed to the stochastic behavior of the dependent variable. In principle, because the noise component ε is defined as the residual value that makes $\mathbf{Y} = \eta(\mathbf{x}, \boldsymbol{\beta}, \varepsilon)$ true, the probability distribution of $\mathbf{Y}$ can be derived from that of ε, and vice versa.

We next discuss general estimation and testing issues assuming that $f(\mathbf{y}; \mathbf{x}, \boldsymbol{\beta}, \varphi)$ is *properly specified*, which is to say, there exists an admissible choice of the parameter values $\boldsymbol{\beta}$ and φ that defines the true joint PDF of $\mathbf{Y}$ conditional on $\mathbf{x}$. In Chapter 11, we will introduce the notion of a *quasi-maximum likelihood estimator*, which relates to the important issue of the sampling behavior of the ML procedure when the likelihood function and PDF of $\mathbf{Y}$ are misspecified. The quasi-likelihood approach allows us to perform maximum–likelihood-like estimation when only lower-order conditional moments of the data are explicitly modeled.

9.3.1. Point Estimation

Once the joint parametric family of PDFs for $\mathbf{Y}$, conditional on $\mathbf{x}$, has been defined by the analyst's specification of a probability model, as in Section 9.2.1 and 9.2.2, the likelihood function, where $\boldsymbol{\theta} = [\boldsymbol{\beta}', \varphi']'$, is concomitantly defined as

$$L(\boldsymbol{\theta}; \mathbf{y}, \mathbf{x}) \equiv f(\mathbf{y}; \mathbf{x}, \boldsymbol{\theta}) \quad \text{for } \boldsymbol{\theta} \in \Omega. \tag{9.3.1}$$

At this point, the ML estimate is represented by the extremum estimator outcome

$$\hat{\boldsymbol{\theta}}_{\mathrm{ML}} = \arg\max_{\boldsymbol{\theta} \in \Omega}[L(\boldsymbol{\theta}; \mathbf{y}, \mathbf{x})]. \tag{9.3.2}$$

In simple probability models, such as the normal linear regression model, the solution to (9.3.2) can be found through an explicit closed-form solution to first-order conditions, as we saw in Chapter 3. In other cases, such as in Sections 9.2.1 and 9.2.2, explicit closed-form solutions to first-order conditions cannot be found, and computer-driven numerical iterative–optimization algorithms must be used to solve for $\hat{\boldsymbol{\theta}}_{\mathrm{ML}}$ in (9.3.2). No matter what approach is used to achieve the result, the ML–extremum *estimate* is the value of the parameter vector that maximizes the likelihood function (provided the objective function is well behaved so that the maximum is global and unique). The ML–extremum *estimator* is the random variable that results when the outcome $\mathbf{y}$ is replaced by the random variable $\mathbf{Y}$ in the likelihood function objective function of the extremum estimate definition (9.3.2), yielding

$$\hat{\boldsymbol{\Theta}}_{\mathrm{ML}} = \arg\max_{\theta \in \Omega}[L(\boldsymbol{\theta}; \mathbf{Y}, \mathbf{x})]. \tag{9.3.3}$$

Under a variety of general regularity conditions likely to hold in applications, such as those identified in Theorems 7.4.1 and 7.4.2, the ML–extremum estimator in (9.3.3) is consistent and asymptotically normally distributed. The asymptotic distribution can be estimated in practice as (recall Theorem 7.4.2)

$$\hat{\boldsymbol{\Theta}}_{\mathrm{ML}} \overset{a}{\sim} N[\boldsymbol{\theta}, n^{-1}\mathbf{h}(\hat{\boldsymbol{\theta}}_{\mathrm{ML}})^{-1}\hat{\boldsymbol{\Sigma}}\mathbf{h}(\hat{\boldsymbol{\theta}}_{\mathrm{ML}})^{-1}], \tag{9.3.4}$$

where

$$\mathbf{h}(\hat{\boldsymbol{\theta}}_{\mathrm{ML}}) = n^{-1} \left. \frac{\partial^2 \ln \mathrm{L}(\boldsymbol{\theta}; \mathbf{y}, \mathbf{x})}{\partial \boldsymbol{\theta} \partial \boldsymbol{\theta}'} \right|_{\hat{\boldsymbol{\theta}}_{\mathrm{ML}}} \tag{9.3.5}$$

and

$$\hat{\boldsymbol{\Sigma}} = n^{-1} \sum_{i=1}^{n} \left[\left. \frac{\partial \ln \mathrm{L}(\boldsymbol{\theta}; \mathrm{y}_i, \mathbf{x}_{i\cdot})}{\partial \boldsymbol{\theta}} \right|_{\hat{\boldsymbol{\theta}}_{\mathrm{ML}}} \left. \frac{\partial \ln \mathrm{L}(\boldsymbol{\theta}; \mathrm{y}_i, \mathbf{x}_{i\cdot})}{\partial \boldsymbol{\theta}'} \right|_{\hat{\boldsymbol{\theta}}_{\mathrm{ML}}} \right]. \tag{9.3.6}$$

The representation of the asymptotic distribution of the ML–extremum estimator can most often be simplified owing to the asymptotic efficiency of the ML estimator. In particular, the ML estimator will be asymptotically efficient when $\boldsymbol{\Sigma} = -\mathbf{h}(\boldsymbol{\theta}_0)$ in Theorem 7.4.2, which is generally the case in practice (Mittelhammer, pp. 480–2). It follows that the asymptotic distribution of the asymptotically efficient ML estimator can be represented as

$$\hat{\boldsymbol{\Theta}}_{\mathrm{ML}} \overset{a}{\sim} \mathrm{N}\left(\boldsymbol{\theta}, -\left[\left. \frac{\partial^2 \ln \mathrm{L}(\boldsymbol{\theta}; \mathbf{y}, \mathbf{x})}{\partial \boldsymbol{\theta} \partial \boldsymbol{\theta}'} \right|_{\hat{\boldsymbol{\theta}}_{\mathrm{ML}}} \right]^{-1} \right). \tag{9.3.7}$$

The asymptotic covariance matrices in either (9.3.4) or (9.3.7) may be difficult to express analytically, but numerical calculation of these matrices is relatively straightforward on the computer.

9.3.2. Testing and Confidence-Region Estimation

The Wald, LM, and GLR triad of asymptotically valid tests of $\mathrm{H}_0\colon \mathbf{c}(\boldsymbol{\theta}) = \mathbf{r}$ versus $\mathrm{H}_a\colon \mathbf{c}(\boldsymbol{\theta}) \neq \mathbf{r}$ can all be applied in the ML context based on the asymptotic normality of the ML estimator. Furthermore, asymptotically valid tests of inequality hypotheses of the general form $\mathrm{H}_0\colon \mathrm{c}(\boldsymbol{\theta}) \leq \mathrm{r}$ or $\mathrm{H}_0\colon \mathrm{c}(\boldsymbol{\theta}) \geq \mathrm{r}$ can be tested using the Z-test. In the case of the Wald and LM tests (as well as the Z-tests), the approach followed for the NLS context in Chapter 8 can be applied analogously to the ML context to motivate the definitions of test rules and their properties. Asymptotically valid confidence regions, intervals, and bounds can be defined in the usual way based on duality with hypothesis tests.

9.3.2.a. Wald Test

Consider the Wald test of $\mathrm{H}_0\colon \mathbf{c}(\boldsymbol{\theta}) = \mathbf{r}$, where it is assumed that $\mathbf{c}(\boldsymbol{\theta})$ is continuously differentiable. From the asymptotic normality of $\hat{\boldsymbol{\Theta}}_{\mathrm{ML}}$ defined in (9.3.7), it follows from results on the asymptotic distribution of differentiable functions of asymptotically normally distributed variables (Chapter E1; Mittelhammer, Section 5.6) that the asymptotic distribution of $\mathbf{c}(\hat{\boldsymbol{\Theta}}_{\mathrm{ML}})$ can be estimated as

$$\mathbf{c}(\hat{\boldsymbol{\Theta}}_{\mathrm{ML}}) \overset{a}{\sim} \mathrm{N}\left(\mathbf{c}(\boldsymbol{\theta}_0), -\left. \frac{\partial \mathbf{c}(\boldsymbol{\theta})}{\partial \boldsymbol{\theta}'} \right|_{\hat{\boldsymbol{\theta}}_{\mathrm{ML}}} \left[\left. \frac{\partial^2 \ln \mathrm{L}(\boldsymbol{\theta}; \mathbf{y}, \mathbf{x})}{\partial \boldsymbol{\theta} \partial \boldsymbol{\theta}'} \right|_{\hat{\boldsymbol{\theta}}_{\mathrm{ML}}} \right]^{-1} \left. \frac{\partial \mathbf{c}(\boldsymbol{\theta})}{\partial \boldsymbol{\theta}} \right|_{\hat{\boldsymbol{\theta}}_{\mathrm{ML}}} \right), \tag{9.3.8}$$

where $\boldsymbol{\theta}_0$ designates the true value of θ. Then the Wald statistic for testing H_0: $\mathbf{c}(\boldsymbol{\theta}) = \mathbf{r}$ is defined as

$$\mathrm{W} = [\mathbf{c}(\hat{\Theta}_{\mathrm{ML}}) - \mathbf{r}]' \left[-\left.\frac{\partial \mathbf{c}(\boldsymbol{\theta})}{\partial \boldsymbol{\theta}'}\right|_{\hat{\Theta}_{\mathrm{ML}}} \left[\left.\frac{\partial^2 \ln \mathrm{L}(\boldsymbol{\theta}; \mathbf{y}, \mathbf{x})}{\partial \boldsymbol{\theta} \partial \boldsymbol{\theta}'}\right|_{\hat{\Theta}_{\mathrm{ML}}} \right]^{-1} \left.\frac{\partial \mathbf{c}(\boldsymbol{\theta})}{\partial \boldsymbol{\theta}}\right|_{\hat{\Theta}_{\mathrm{ML}}} \right]^{-1} \times [\mathbf{c}(\hat{\Theta}_{\mathrm{ML}}) - \mathbf{r}], \tag{9.3.9}$$

which the reader can compare with (8.5.5).

Under H_0, W is asymptotically distributed as a central χ^2 random variable with j degrees of freedom, where j is the number of coordinate functions in $\mathbf{c}(\boldsymbol{\beta})$ assumed to be functionally independent. The rationale is analogous to (8.5.1)–(8.5.5). Under local alternatives of the Pitman drift form, H_a: $\mathbf{c}(\boldsymbol{\theta}) = \mathbf{r} + n^{-1/2}\boldsymbol{\delta}$, W has an asymptotic noncentral Chi-square distribution with noncentrality parameter

$$\lambda = \frac{1}{2}\boldsymbol{\delta}' \left[\left.\frac{\partial \mathbf{c}(\boldsymbol{\theta})}{\partial \boldsymbol{\theta}'}\right|_{\theta_0} \left[-\mathrm{plim}\left(n^{-1} \left.\frac{\partial^2 \ln \mathrm{L}(\boldsymbol{\theta}; \mathbf{Y}, \mathbf{x})}{\partial \boldsymbol{\theta} \partial \boldsymbol{\theta}'}\right|_{\theta_0} \right) \right]^{-1} \left.\frac{\partial \mathbf{c}(\boldsymbol{\theta})}{\partial \boldsymbol{\theta}}\right|_{\theta_0} \right] \boldsymbol{\delta}, \tag{9.3.10}$$

which the reader can compare with (8.5.6). The test $\{\mathrm{W}, \mathrm{C}^{\mathrm{W}}\}$ is applied in precisely the same way as described in Section 8.5.4, where the critical region is defined by $\mathrm{C}^{\mathrm{W}} = [\chi^2_{1-\alpha}, \infty)$ and the test rule is "reject H_0 if $\mathrm{w} \in \mathrm{C}^{\mathrm{W}}$." The appropriate method for calculating asymptotic power is also described in Section 8.5.4 and 8.6.5. Estimated power as a function of $\boldsymbol{\delta}$ can be obtained by replacing $\mathrm{p\,lim}[n^{-1} \frac{\partial^2 \ln \mathrm{L}(\boldsymbol{\theta};\mathbf{Y},\mathbf{x})}{\partial \boldsymbol{\theta} \partial \boldsymbol{\theta}'}|_{\theta_0}]$ by $n^{-1} \frac{\partial^2 \ln \mathrm{L}(\boldsymbol{\theta};\mathbf{Y},\mathbf{x})}{\partial \boldsymbol{\theta} \partial \boldsymbol{\theta}'}|_{\hat{\Theta}_{\mathrm{ML}}}$ here and ahead in the LM and GLR testing contexts as well.

9.3.2.b. Lagrange Multiplier Test

On the basis of the same approach used in the LM test discussion in Section 8.6, the LM statistic in *classical* form for testing H_0: $\mathbf{c}(\boldsymbol{\theta}) = \mathbf{r}$ is given by

$$\mathrm{LM} = \boldsymbol{\Gamma}_{\mathrm{r}}' \left[\left.\frac{\partial \mathbf{c}(\boldsymbol{\theta})}{\partial \boldsymbol{\theta}'}\right|_{\hat{\Theta}_{\mathrm{ML}}} \left(-\left.\frac{\partial^2 \ln \mathrm{L}(\boldsymbol{\theta}; \mathbf{y}, \mathbf{x})}{\partial \boldsymbol{\theta} \partial \boldsymbol{\theta}'}\right|_{\hat{\Theta}_{\mathrm{ML}}} \right)^{-1} \left.\frac{\partial \mathbf{c}(\boldsymbol{\theta})}{\partial \boldsymbol{\theta}}\right|_{\hat{\Theta}_{\mathrm{ML}}} \right] \boldsymbol{\Gamma}_{\mathrm{r}}, \tag{9.3.11}$$

where $\boldsymbol{\Gamma}_{\mathrm{r}}$ is the vector of Lagrange multipliers associated with constrained maximization of $\ln \mathrm{L}(\boldsymbol{\theta}; \mathbf{Y}, \mathbf{x})$ subject to the constraints $\mathbf{c}(\boldsymbol{\theta}) = \mathbf{r}$. The *score* form of the LM statistic is

$$\mathrm{LM} = \left.\frac{\partial \ln \mathrm{L}(\boldsymbol{\theta}; \mathbf{Y}, \mathbf{x})}{\partial \boldsymbol{\theta}'}\right|_{\hat{\Theta}_{\mathrm{ML}}} \left[-\left.\frac{\partial^2 \ln \mathrm{L}(\boldsymbol{\theta}; \mathbf{Y}, \mathbf{x})}{\partial \boldsymbol{\theta} \partial \boldsymbol{\theta}'}\right|_{\hat{\Theta}_{\mathrm{ML}}} \right]^{-1} \left.\frac{\partial \ln \mathrm{L}(\boldsymbol{\theta}; \mathbf{Y}, \mathbf{x})}{\partial \boldsymbol{\theta}}\right|_{\hat{\Theta}_{\mathrm{ML}}}. \tag{9.3.12}$$

The LM test has precisely the same asymptotic Chi-square distribution under H_0 and under local (Pitman drift) alternatives as the Wald test with the noncentrality parameter defined as in (9.3.10). The application of the test $\{\mathrm{LM}, \mathrm{C}^{\mathrm{LM}}\}$ involves defining the critical region as $\mathrm{C}^{\mathrm{LM}} = [\chi^2_{1-\alpha}, \infty)$, and the test rule is "reject H_0 if $\mathrm{lm} \in \mathrm{C}^{\mathrm{LM}}$." The power calculations are performed identically, as described in Sections 8.5.4 and 8.6.5 (see also Mittelhammer, pp. 616–22).

9.3.2.c. Generalized Likelihood Ratio Test

The GLR test of H_0: $\mathbf{c}(\boldsymbol{\theta}) = \mathbf{r}$ is based on the statistic (recall Definition 4.3.1)

$$\lambda(\mathbf{Y}) = \frac{\max_{\boldsymbol{\theta}\in H_0} L(\boldsymbol{\theta}; \mathbf{Y}, \mathbf{x})}{\max_{\boldsymbol{\theta}\in\Omega} L(\boldsymbol{\theta}; \mathbf{Y}, \mathbf{x})}. \tag{9.3.11}$$

Under the regularity conditions leading to the consistency and asymptotic normality of the ML estimator $\hat{\boldsymbol{\Theta}}$,

$$\text{GLR} = -2 \ln \lambda(\mathbf{Y}) \overset{a}{\sim} \text{Chi-square}(j, 0) \text{ under } H_0. \tag{9.3.12}$$

Under local Pitman drift alternatives, the asymptotic Chi-square distribution of $-2 \ln \lambda(\mathbf{Y})$ is precisely the same as for either the Wald or LM statistics with the noncentrality parameter again defined by (9.3.10). The GLR test $\{\text{GLR}, C^{\text{GLR}}\}$ uses the same critical region as the Wald and LM tests, and its asymptotic power calculations are performed in the same way as well (Mittelhammer, pp. 601–15).

9.3.2.d. Z-Test of Inequality Restrictions

Tests of scalar nonlinear inequality hypotheses of the form H_0: $c(\boldsymbol{\theta}) \leq r$ or H_0: $c(\boldsymbol{\theta}) \geq r$ can be based on the asymptotically normally distributed Z-statistic

$$Z = \frac{c(\hat{\boldsymbol{\Theta}}) - r}{\left[\left.\frac{\partial c(\boldsymbol{\theta})}{\partial \boldsymbol{\theta}'}\right|_{\hat{\boldsymbol{\Theta}}_{ML}} \left[- \left.\frac{\partial^2 \ln L(\boldsymbol{\theta}, \mathbf{y}, \mathbf{x})}{\partial\boldsymbol{\theta}\partial\boldsymbol{\theta}'}\right|_{\hat{\boldsymbol{\Theta}}_{ML}} \right]^{-1} \left.\frac{\partial c(\boldsymbol{\theta})}{\partial \boldsymbol{\theta}}\right|_{\hat{\boldsymbol{\Theta}}_{ML}} \right]^{1/2}} \tag{9.3.13}$$

(compare with 8.8.7). An asymptotic α-level test is defined by $\{Z, C^Z\}$, where the critical region is defined as $C^Z = [z_{1-\alpha}, \infty)$ or $(-\infty, z_\alpha]$ for testing H_0: $c(\boldsymbol{\theta}) \leq r$ or H_0: $c(\boldsymbol{\theta}) \geq r$, respectively, where z_τ is the $100\tau\%$ quantile of the standard normal distribution. The null hypothesis is rejected at the asymptotic α level if $z \in C^Z$. Power under Pitman drift alternatives $c(\boldsymbol{\theta}) = r + n^{-1/2}\delta$ can be calculated based on the asymptotic univariate normal distribution

$$Z \overset{a}{\sim} N\left(\left[\left.\frac{\partial c(\boldsymbol{\theta})}{\partial \boldsymbol{\theta}'}\right|_{\boldsymbol{\theta}_0} \left[-\text{p}\lim \left(n^{-1} \left.\frac{\partial^2 \ln L(\boldsymbol{\theta}, \mathbf{y}, \mathbf{x})}{\partial\boldsymbol{\theta}\partial\boldsymbol{\theta}'}\right|_{\boldsymbol{\theta}_0} \right) \right]^{-1} \left.\frac{\partial c(\boldsymbol{\theta})}{\partial \boldsymbol{\theta}}\right|_{\boldsymbol{\theta}_0} \right]^{-1/2} \delta, 1 \right), \tag{9.3.14}$$

where $\boldsymbol{\theta}_0$ can be replaced by $\hat{\boldsymbol{\theta}}_{ML}$ and the plim dropped from (9.3.14) to estimate power with respect to δ values. Further details of the Z-test, including the Bonferroni method of testing a set of inequality hypotheses based on the Z-test, are analogous to the NLS discussion in Section 8.8.1 and are left to the reader.

9.3.2.e. Confidence Regions

Confidence regions, intervals, and bounds can be generated in the usual way based on duality with hypothesis tests. In each case, the confidence region, interval, or bound represents the set of hypothesized values $\mathbf{r}$ for $\mathbf{c}(\boldsymbol{\theta})$ that would *not* be rejected by the respective hypothesis test on which the confidence region, interval, or bound is based. The procedures discussed in Sections 8.5.5, 8.6.6, 8.8.2, and 8.7.3 in the context of NLS estimation are all relevant here.

9.4. A Final Remark

Making use of the basic estimation and inference principles developed in Chapters 3–7, in this chapter we have indicated ways that an analysis of the traditional parametric regression model may be extended. In particular, we have examined cases in which maximum-likelihood procedures are applied to nonlinear probability models and models in which the noise component is not normally distributed. We have seen that the ML approach is a versatile method of generating estimates and conducting tests for a wide array of probability distributions in the context of both nonlinear and linear regression models. In Chapter 11 we apply the ML approach to misspecified likelihood functions, termed the quasi-likelihood approach and demonstrate how this still leads to estimators and test procedures with useful sampling properties. In particular, the quasi-likelihood approach will permit maximum likelihood-like estimation to be performed when only lower-order conditional moments of the data are explicitly modeled.

9.5. Exercises

9.5.1. Idea Checklist – Knowledge Guides

---

1. Are nonnormal PDFs needed in specifying econometric models? Should normality always be assumed?
2. What are the implications of the statement, "The solution for this estimation problem cannot be written in closed form"?
3. In practice, are ML estimators asymptotically efficient? Should ML estimators always be used in place of NLS estimators?
4. Where do likelihood function specifications come from?
5. Suppose an analyst assumes that the noise component of a linear regression model is multivariate normally distributed with a covariance matrix equal to $\sigma^2\mathbf{I}$ but he or she is not at all sure that the probability distribution of the noise component belongs to the normal parametric family. What are the properties of the estimator in this context?

9.5.2. Problems

9–1 A natural candidate for probability models of prices and other nonnegative variables is the two-parameter log-normal distribution ($\gamma = 0$ in the three-parameter model presented in the GAUSS program C9LogNor.gss on the CD). The distribution exhibits positive skewness and is related to the normal distribution through the natural log transformation. On the assumption that the noise elements in the linear regression model are log-normally distributed, state the log-normal likelihood function and derive the ML estimators of $\boldsymbol{\beta}$ and σ^2.

9–2 Assume random sampling from the logistic (μ, β) distribution. Please answer the following questions:

a. Compute the ML estimator of μ. Can you derive a closed-form MLE for β?
b. Is the ML estimator of μ consistent, asymptotically normal, and asymptotically efficient?
c. Use the ML estimator of μ to form the concentrated log-likelihood function. Can you derive a closed-form ML estimator of β from this objective function?

9–3 Define the likelihood function and then describe the procedure you would follow to calculate the ML–extremum estimates associated with the Box–Cox model (9.2.8).

9–4 Repeat the preceding question for the case of the Box–Cox model (9.2.9).

9.5.3. Computer Exercises

---

1. Although the local maxima identified in the GAUSS program C9LogNor.gss are not the ML estimator, some authors have suggested that this estimator exhibits favorable statistical properties. Conduct a Monte Carlo exercise to simulate the sampling properties of the local maxima. Does the estimator appear to be consistent and asymptotically normal?
2. Given the information in Problem 2 above, please answer the following questions about the logistic ML-estimation problem:
   a. For a given set of parameters μ and β and sample size n, generate a pseudorandom sample of observations for this distribution and compute the ML estimates of the parameters. Hint: Invert the logistic CDF, $F(x; \mu, \beta) = [1 + \exp[(x - \mu)/\beta]]^{-1}$, and use the probability integral transform to convert uniform (0, 1) random numbers to logistic random numbers. The reader may wish to refer to Example A.1.1 in the Monte Carlo Appendix for more details on this transformation.
   b. Conduct a Monte Carlo exercise to simulate the mean, variance, and sampling distribution of the ML estimators. Do the MLEs appear to be consistent and asymptotically normal?
3. Extend the GAUSS program provided for Example 9.2.1 (C9BoxCox.gss) by altering the DSP to be nonlinear in one of the explanatory variables (e.g., $\ln(x_2)$). Then, repeat the exercises in the program after including a separate Box–Cox transformation on this variable as well as the dependent variable (as in (9.2.9)).
4. Design a DSP for the Cobb–Douglas model with *additive* errors $Y_i = K_i^\alpha L_i^\beta + \varepsilon_i$ (note that the model cannot be transformed to be linear in the parameters). For a multivariate normal noise process $\varepsilon \sim N(\mathbf{0}, \sigma^2\mathbf{I})$ for some $\sigma^2 > 0$, generate a pseudorandom sample for this DSP and use the data to compute the ML estimates of α and β. How does the ML estimator perform in repeated Monte Carlo samples?

9.6. References

Amemiya, T., and J. L. Powell (1981), "A Comparison of the Box–Cox Maximum Likelihood Estimator and the Two-Stage Least Squares Estimator," *Journal of Econometrics*, Vol. 17, pp. 351–81.

Box, G. E. P., and D. R. Cox (1964), "An Analysis of Transformations," *Journal of Royal Statistical Society, Series* B, Vol. 26, pp. 211–43.

Mittelhammer, R. C. (1996), *Mathematical Statistics for Economics and Business*, New York: Springer–Verlag.

Poirier, D. (1978), "The Use of the Box–Cox Transformation in Limited Dependent Variable Models," *Journal of the American Statistical Association*, Vol. 73, pp. 284–7.

Poirier, D., and P. A. Ruud (1979), "The Use of the Box–Cox Transformation in Limited Dependent Variable Models," *Journal of the American Statistical Association*, Vol. 73, pp. 284–7.

Wooldridge, J. M. (1992), "Some Alternatives to the Box–Cox Regression Model," *International Economic Review*, Vol. 33, pp. 935–55.

PART FOUR

Avoiding the Parametric Likelihood

Although econometricians are a rather diverse group, they seem to share a general desire to *avoid* making strong distributional assumptions about the stochastic characteristics of probability models when a priori knowledge is insufficient to support such assumptions. One step in this direction, demonstrated in Chapter 10, is to use method of moments (MOM) estimation and inference procedures that were introduced over a century ago. Over the last two decades, in one way or another, generalizations of these procedures have found their way back into the econometric literature. Continuing in the direction of avoiding fully parametric likelihood-based techniques, in Chapter 11 we consider quasi-maximum likelihood (QML) alternatives in which only assumptions about means and second moments are made, and this information enters in the form of estimation functions or equations (EE). The QML approach also provides support for the use of maximum likelihood-type methods of analysis even when the family of probability distributions underlying the specification of the likelihood function is thought to be misspecified.

When there is insufficient information to specify the functional form of a parametric likelihood function, an empirical likelihood (EL) function based on a multinomial PDF supported on the sample of data is nonetheless still available under appropriate sampling conditions, and this is the subject of Chapter 12. The resulting EL estimator of model parameters has first-order asymptotic properties that are in many ways analogous to parametric methods. Furthermore, the empirical likelihood function behaves much the same as an ordinary likelihood function in terms of the usual likelihood ratio statistics that can be used for inference purposes.

Building on the MOM, QML, EE, and EL formulations noted above, in Chapter 13 we consider the Kullback–Leibler maximum entropy criterion or pseudodistance measure. Using this estimation criterion, we demonstrate how the resulting EL-like discrete sample probability weights derived from applying the maximum entropy principle define a class of extremum estimators and related test procedures for the parameters of regression and other models as well as lead to an alternative empirical likelihood function.

We note throughout the discussion that the asymptotics of all of the procedures examined in Chapters 11–13 are closely related. Many of the results presented in Part IV are new to, and have yet to appear in, the mainstream econometrics literature.

CHAPTER 10

Stochastic Regressors and Moment-Based Estimation

10.1. Introduction

In previous chapters we have analyzed methods of estimation and inference for the regression model

$$\mathbf{Y} = \mathbf{x}\boldsymbol{\beta} + \boldsymbol{\varepsilon}, \tag{10.1.1}$$

where the matrix of right-hand-side (RHS) explanatory variables is fixed or nonstochastic. In this chapter we generalize the regression model to include the case

$$\mathbf{Y} = \mathbf{X}\boldsymbol{\beta} + \boldsymbol{\varepsilon}, \tag{10.1.2}$$

where the matrix of RHS explanatory variables is random or a combination of fixed and random variables. Fixed or nonstochastic explanatory variables can, of course, be viewed as a special or limiting case in which the regressors are degenerate random variables. For present purposes, we consider $\mathbf{X}$ to be stochastic if any elements of $\mathbf{X}$ are nondegenerate random variables. Thus, if the first variable is a constant (i.e., $\mathrm{X}_{i1} \equiv 1, \forall i$) but one or more of the other variables are stochastic, we will use $\mathbf{X}$ rather than $\mathbf{x}$ to denote the explanatory variable matrix.

In many cases the economist must work with nonexperimental data in which outcomes of some of the explanatory variables are generated by some stochastic process and exhibit random behavior in repeated samples. Consequently, in this chapter we extend the probability model to accommodate a DSP in which a sample of size n is drawn from a multivariate population distribution that encompasses not only the dependent variable but also one or more of the explanatory variables. Under this model specification, our task will be to evaluate the sampling properties of alternative estimators and inference procedures when applied to the random dependent and explanatory variable data information.

In this chapter we also introduce the concept of moment-based estimation and inference. Moment-based estimation dates back over 100 years to Karl Pearson. His method of moments (MOM) procedure predates Fisher's 1925 maximum likelihood (ML) approach and is based on notably weaker assumptions. However the popularity of the method waned through most of the twentieth century owing to the development of competing methods like ML, which provide statistically optimal estimation and inference procedures by imposing greater restrictions on the DSP. Despite the relative lack of popularity, the MOM approach has occupied an important place in the historical development of statistics and econometrics.

Recently, the method of moments has been accorded renewed interest by econometricians for a variety of reasons. First of all, many contemporary researchers share a general desire to avoid making strong and often unsubstantiated distributional assumptions about the stochastic components of a probability model. In this vein, as we have come to realize, LS estimators can be represented as roots of first-order derivative equations characterizing the minimum of a sum-of-squares function that is not tied to any particular distributional assumption. Maximum likelihood estimators can also be defined as the roots of first-order derivative equations that characterize the maximum of a likelihood function. This raises the interesting question of whether the specification of equations from which estimators are derived should be the primary focus in defining estimators or whether attention should be focused on the particular (and often restrictive) distributional assumptions and estimation objective functions to which the equations refer.

Modern statistical theory has begun deemphasizing analysis of the roots or solutions of equations and is focusing more attention, as we do in Chapter 11, on analyzing the underlying equations from which the roots or solutions are derived. These equations are aptly called "estimating equations" (EEs). In this context, one considers directly the specification and sampling characteristics (e.g., bias and variance) of estimating functions underlying the specification of EEs rather than the sampling characteristics of the roots of the EEs (Godambe, 1997; Heyde (1997); McCullagh and Nelder (1989); see also Chapter 11 in this volume). The underlying rationale for the specification of such estimating equations can come from a myriad of sources and need not be first-order conditions relating to any optimization problem. Pearson's MOM approach can be interpreted within this context of defining estimating equations for estimating unknown parameters, and so, after 100 years have passed, the MOM approach, and extensions of it, are currently being vigorously reexamined within the context of modern statistical theory and practice.

Regarding additional rationale for the resurgence of interest in the MOM approach, many of the necessary first-order conditions (FOCs) reflecting stochastic optimal behavioral rules for economic decision makers can be interpreted as moment conditions, and moment-based estimators can often be applied directly to such cases. Also, even if we are willing to assume a particular probability model, with specific distributional assumptions, for the stochastic components of a model, the behavioral conditions may involve highly nonlinear functions of the random variables. In such cases, the moment-based approach often provides more tractable estimators of the unknown model parameters and can also provide useful starting values for numerical algorithms used to solve nonlinear ML and NLS estimation problems.

In terms of the general class of models portrayed in Table 2.1, we will be concerned with the special case in this chapter specified in Table 10.1.

Table 10.1. *Regression Models with Stochastic Regressors*

Model Component	Specific Characteristics	
$\mathbf{Y}$	RV Type:	continuous
	Range:	unlimited
	Y_i dimension:	univariate
	Moments:	$E[\mathbf{Y}] = E[\mathbf{X}]\boldsymbol{\beta}$ or $[\mathbf{g}(\mathbf{X}, \boldsymbol{\beta})]$, $E[\mathbf{Y} \mid \mathbf{X}] = \mathbf{X}\boldsymbol{\beta}$ or $\mathbf{g}(\mathbf{X}, \boldsymbol{\beta})$ and $\mathbf{cov}(\mathbf{Y} \mid \mathbf{X}) = \sigma^2 \mathbf{I}$
$\eta(\mathbf{X}, \boldsymbol{\beta}, \boldsymbol{\varepsilon})$	Functional Form:	linear or nonlinear in $\mathbf{X}$, $\boldsymbol{\beta}$, or both; additive in $\boldsymbol{\varepsilon}$
$\mathbf{X}$	RV Type:	stochastic, full-rank with probability 1
	Genesis:	exogenous to the model
$\boldsymbol{\beta}$	RV Type:	degenerate (fixed)
	Dimension:	finite
$\boldsymbol{\varepsilon}$	RV Type:	iid or non-iid
	Moments:	$E[\boldsymbol{\varepsilon} \mid \mathbf{X}] = \mathbf{0}$, and $\mathbf{cov}(\boldsymbol{\varepsilon} \mid \mathbf{X}) = \sigma^2\mathbf{I}$
Ω	Prior info:	none
$f(\mathbf{e} \mid \mathbf{x}, \varphi)$	PDF family:	unspecified or normal

If $Y_i, X_{i1}, X_{i2}, \ldots, X_{ik}$ are random variables with joint probability distribution $f(Y_i, X_{i1}, X_{i2}, \ldots, X_{ik})$, conditional distribution $f(Y_i \mid x_{i1}, x_{i2}, \ldots, x_{ik})$, and the expected value of Y_i conditional on $x[i, .] \equiv (x_{i1}, x_{i2}, \ldots, x_{ik})$ is $E[Y_i \mid \mathbf{x}[i, .]] = \mathbf{x}[i, .]\boldsymbol{\beta}$, then it is traditional to declare this linear conditional expectation relationship a *linear regression* of Y_i on $\mathbf{X}[i, .]$. In this context, the $\boldsymbol{\beta}$'s are unknown parameters, and the $\mathbf{x}[i, .]$'s are particular numerical outcomes of the random $\mathbf{X}[i, .]$ variables. If the conditional expectation is a nonlinear function such as $E[Y_i \mid \mathbf{x}[i, .]] = g(\mathbf{x}[i, .], \boldsymbol{\beta})$, then the relationship is referred to as a nonlinear regression of Y_i on $\mathbf{X}[i, .]$.

The particular inverse problem associated with the statistical model delineated above is represented by $(\mathbf{Y}, \mathbf{X}) \Rightarrow (\boldsymbol{\beta}, \sigma^2, \boldsymbol{\varepsilon})$. The analysis of stochastic regressors will be extended to encompass models with general noise covariance structure in Chapters 14 and 15 and extended further when we analyze the generalized method of moments (GMM) estimation and inference approach in Chapter 16.

10.2. Linear Model Assumptions, Estimation, and Inference Revisited

In terms of the underlying model assumptions when $\mathbf{X}$ is stochastic, suppose $\mathbf{X}$ and $\boldsymbol{\varepsilon}$ are statistically independent random variables. Adopting the additional assumptions that $E[\mathbf{X}]$ exists and $E[\boldsymbol{\varepsilon}] = \mathbf{0}$, we find that for (10.1.2)

$$E[\mathbf{Y}] = E[\mathbf{X}]\boldsymbol{\beta} + E[\boldsymbol{\varepsilon}] = E[\mathbf{X}]\boldsymbol{\beta}, \tag{10.2.1}$$

and thus the *expectation* of random variable $\mathbf{X}\boldsymbol{\beta}$ equals the mean of $\mathbf{Y}$. The independence assumption is reasonable if, for example, in a measurement error situation, the observation errors are sampled separately from, or are unrelated to, how the model noise component is sampled.

Now consider the case in which $\mathbf{X}$ and ε are only contemporaneously uncorrelated and not necessarily independent. Under the preceding assumptions that $\mathrm{E}[\varepsilon]=\mathbf{0}$, the zero contemporaneous correlation condition may be represented as $\mathrm{E}[\mathbf{X}'\varepsilon]=\mathbf{0}$, where the expectation is computed using the joint distribution of $\mathbf{X}$ and ε. This condition is sometimes referred to by stating that $\mathbf{X}$ and ε are *orthogonal in expectation*. Using the double expectation theorem, we can restate the zero correlation condition as

$$\mathrm{E}[\mathbf{X}'\varepsilon] = \mathrm{E}_{\mathbf{X}}[\mathrm{E}[\mathbf{X}'\varepsilon \mid \mathbf{X}]] = \mathrm{E}_{\mathbf{X}}[\mathbf{X}'\mathrm{E}[\varepsilon \mid \mathbf{X}]] = \mathbf{0}, \tag{10.2.2}$$

where $\mathrm{E}_{\mathbf{X}}[\cdot]$ denotes an expectation taken with respect to the marginal distribution of $\mathbf{X}$. Thus, a *sufficient condition* for the expectation (10.2.2) to hold is $\mathrm{E}[\varepsilon \mid \mathbf{X}] = \mathbf{0}$, which is a stronger assumption than orthogonality that is commonly maintained in practice. Note from (10.1.2) that the latter assumption is equivalent to the assumption that

$$\mathrm{E}[\mathbf{Y} \mid \mathbf{X}] = \mathbf{X}\boldsymbol{\beta} + \mathrm{E}[\varepsilon \mid \mathbf{X}] = \mathbf{X}\boldsymbol{\beta}, \tag{10.2.3}$$

that is, that the conditional expectation of $\mathbf{Y}$ is in fact a linear function of the explanatory variables $\mathbf{X}\boldsymbol{\beta}$. We henceforth assume the sufficient condition holds whenever we are referring to the case in which $\mathbf{X}$ and ε are not contemporaneously correlated. We emphasize that $\mathrm{E}[\varepsilon \mid \mathbf{X}]=\mathbf{0}$ also holds in the case in which $\mathbf{X}$ and ε are stochastically independent and $\mathrm{E}[\varepsilon]=\mathbf{0}$ because then conditional and unconditional expectations coincide. Thus (10.2.3) applies to the stochastically independent case as well.

Regarding second-order moments, it is possible to state the classical assumption about the conditional variance of ε as

$$\mathbf{cov}(\varepsilon \mid \mathbf{X}) = \mathrm{E}[\varepsilon\varepsilon' \mid \mathbf{X}] = \sigma^2\mathbf{I}_n \tag{10.2.4}$$

which is equivalent to $\mathrm{var}(\varepsilon_i \mid \mathbf{X})=\sigma^2$ for all i and $\mathbf{cov}(\varepsilon_i, \varepsilon_j \mid \mathbf{X})=0$ for all $i \neq j$. However, note from the degenerate nature of the random matrix $\mathbf{cov}[\varepsilon \mid \mathbf{X}]$ (note the conditional covariance matrix is a function of the random variable $\mathbf{X}$) indicated in (10.2.4) that $\mathbf{cov}[\varepsilon \mid \mathbf{x}]$ is a constant function that effectively does not depend on $\mathbf{x}$, with probability 1, and thus (10.2.4) is equivalent to $\mathbf{cov}(\varepsilon)=\mathrm{E}[\varepsilon\varepsilon']=\sigma^2\mathbf{I}_n$. The latter result also follows from the double expectation theorem, where one would take the expectation of (10.2.4) with respect to $\mathbf{X}$ to define the unconditional expectation $\mathrm{E}[\varepsilon\varepsilon']=\sigma^2\mathbf{I}_n$. These conditional moments for regression model (10.1.2) imply that

$$\mathrm{E}[\mathbf{Y} \mid \mathbf{x}] \equiv \mathbf{x}\boldsymbol{\beta} \quad \text{and} \quad \mathbf{cov}(\mathbf{Y} \mid \mathbf{x}) \equiv \sigma^2\mathbf{I}_n. \tag{10.2.5}$$

Therefore, the main practical consequence of stochastic explanatory variables in either the stochastically independent or contemporaneously uncorrelated case is the need to condition on outcomes of $\mathbf{X}$ in order for information linkages between the outcomes and expectation of $\mathbf{Y}$ and the observable values of $\mathbf{X}$ to be established. In more advanced econometric treatments of these models, one can also use the concepts of stationarity, ergodicity, and mixing processes to account for alternative stronger stochastic interrelationships between **X** and ε while still largely maintaining the standard statistical properties of LS estimators (see White, 1984, 1994).

When the $(n \times k)$ matrix **X** is random, the rank assumption rank $(\mathbf{x}) = k$ used in previous chapters can no longer be interpreted as a deterministic condition. To ensure that the LS estimator exists in the case at hand, the assumption is redefined to be $\mathrm{P}(\mathrm{rank}(\mathbf{x}) = k) = 1$, or equivalently $\mathrm{P}((\mathbf{x}'\mathbf{x})^{-1}\text{exists}) = 1$.

10.3. LS and ML Estimator Properties

In this section we review some of the implications of stochastic **X** for the inverse problem of point estimation. Specific topics will include the finite and asymptotic sampling properties of the LS and ML estimators.

10.3.1. LS Estimator Properties: Finite Samples

In this subsection we review some of the implications of stochastic **X** for the sampling properties of the LS estimator and the usual estimator of the noise variance based on the LS estimator. For regression model (10.1.2), if it is assumed that **X** and ε are either statistically independent or contemporaneously uncorrelated and if the other assumptions stated in the previous section are adopted, the least-squares estimator

$$\hat{\boldsymbol{\beta}} = (\mathbf{X}'\mathbf{X})^{-1}\mathbf{X}'\mathbf{Y} = \boldsymbol{\beta} + (\mathbf{X}'\mathbf{X})^{-1}\mathbf{X}'\varepsilon \tag{10.3.1}$$

exists with probability 1 and is also unbiased. The "unbiasedness" property follows from the condition $\mathrm{E}[\varepsilon \mid \mathbf{X}] = \mathbf{0}$ so that

$$\mathrm{E}[\hat{\boldsymbol{\beta}} \mid \mathbf{X}] = \boldsymbol{\beta} + \mathrm{E}[(\mathbf{X}'\mathbf{X})^{-1}\mathbf{X}'\varepsilon \mid \mathbf{X}] = \boldsymbol{\beta} + (\mathbf{X}'\mathbf{X})^{-1}\mathbf{X}'\mathrm{E}[\varepsilon \mid \mathbf{X}] = \boldsymbol{\beta} \tag{10.3.2}$$

so that $\mathrm{E}[\hat{\boldsymbol{\beta}}] = \mathrm{E}_{\mathbf{X}}[\hat{\boldsymbol{\beta}} \mid \mathbf{X}] = \mathrm{E}_{\mathbf{X}}[\boldsymbol{\beta}] = \boldsymbol{\beta}$.

In either the independent or contemporaneously uncorrelated cases, the conditional covariance matrix of the estimator follows from (10.2.4) as follows:

$$\begin{aligned} \mathbf{cov}(\hat{\boldsymbol{\beta}} \mid \mathbf{X}) &= \mathrm{E}[(\mathbf{X}'\mathbf{X})^{-1}\mathbf{X}'\varepsilon\varepsilon'\mathbf{X}(\mathbf{X}'\mathbf{X})^{-1} \mid \mathbf{X}] \\ &= (\mathbf{X}'\mathbf{X})^{-1}\mathbf{X}'\mathrm{E}[\varepsilon\varepsilon' \mid \mathbf{X}]\mathbf{X}(\mathbf{X}'\mathbf{X})^{-1} \\ &= \sigma^2(\mathbf{X}'\mathbf{X})^{-1}. \end{aligned} \tag{10.3.3}$$

We can then use the distribution of **X** and the double-expectation theorem to compute the unconditional covariance matrix of $\hat{\boldsymbol{\beta}}$ as

$$\mathbf{cov}(\hat{\boldsymbol{\beta}}) = \mathrm{E}_{\mathbf{X}}[\mathbf{cov}(\hat{\boldsymbol{\beta}} \mid \mathbf{X})] = \sigma^2\mathrm{E}[(\mathbf{X}'\mathbf{X})^{-1}] \tag{10.3.4}$$

given that $\mathrm{E}[(\mathbf{X}'\mathbf{X})^{-1}]$ exists.

Finally, we can compute the expected value of the usual unbiased variance estimator $\mathrm{S}^2 = (\mathbf{Y} - \mathbf{X}\hat{\boldsymbol{\beta}})'(\mathbf{Y} - \mathbf{X}\hat{\boldsymbol{\beta}})/(n-k)$. On the basis of an approach analogous to that used twice above, first note upon making the substitutions $\hat{\boldsymbol{\beta}} = (\mathbf{X}'\mathbf{X})^{-1}\mathbf{X}'\mathbf{Y}$, $\mathbf{Y} = \mathbf{X}\boldsymbol{\beta} + \varepsilon$, and $\mathrm{E}[\varepsilon\varepsilon' \mid \mathbf{X}] = \sigma^2 \mathbf{I}$ that

$$\begin{aligned}
\mathrm{E}[\mathrm{S}^2 \mid \mathbf{X}] &= \mathrm{E}[(\mathbf{Y} - \mathbf{X}\hat{\boldsymbol{\beta}})'(\mathbf{Y} - \mathbf{X}\hat{\boldsymbol{\beta}})/(n-k) \mid \mathbf{X}] \\
&= \mathrm{E}[\varepsilon'(\mathbf{I} - \mathbf{X}(\mathbf{X}'\mathbf{X})^{-1}\mathbf{X}')\varepsilon/(n-k) \mid \mathbf{X}] \\
&= \mathrm{tr}[(\mathbf{I} - \mathbf{X}(\mathbf{X}'\mathbf{X})^{-1}\mathbf{X}')\mathrm{E}(\varepsilon\varepsilon' \mid \mathbf{X})/(n-k)] \\
&= \sigma^2 \mathrm{tr}[(\mathbf{I} - \mathbf{X}(\mathbf{X}'\mathbf{X})^{-1}\mathbf{X}')/(n-k)] \\
&= \sigma^2[\mathrm{tr}(\mathbf{I}) - \mathrm{tr}((\mathbf{X}'\mathbf{X})^{-1}\mathbf{X}'\mathbf{X})]/(n-k) = \sigma^2. \qquad (10.3.5)
\end{aligned}$$

Then, applying the double expectation theorem, we have that

$$\mathrm{E}[\mathrm{S}^2] = \mathrm{E}_{\mathbf{X}}[\mathrm{E}[\mathrm{S}^2 \mid \mathbf{X}]] = \mathrm{E}_{\mathbf{X}}[\sigma^2] = \sigma^2. \qquad (10.3.6)$$

Therefore, the estimator S^2 is a conditionally and unconditionally unbiased estimator of σ^2.

We emphasize that even though $\hat{\boldsymbol{\beta}}$ is a linear function of $\mathbf{Y}$ that is now based on *stochastic* linear coefficients (i.e., *a stochastically linear function*), the estimators $\hat{\boldsymbol{\beta}}$ and S^2 are nonetheless *conditionally* and *unconditionally unbiased.*

10.3.2. LS Estimator Properties: Asymptotics

The asymptotic properties of the LS estimator when $\mathbf{X}$ is stochastic parallel those established in the case in which $\mathbf{x}$ is fixed. Regarding consistency of the LS estimator, we have the following consistency theorem, which relates to the asymptotic existence of $\hat{\boldsymbol{\beta}}$ as well.

Theorem 10.3.1 (Consistency of $\hat{\boldsymbol{\beta}}$ for Stochastic X): *Consider the linear statistical model* $\mathbf{Y} = \mathbf{X}\boldsymbol{\beta} + \varepsilon$ *delineated in* (10.2.1)–(10.2.5) *and suppose that*

1. $n^{-1}\mathbf{X}'\varepsilon \xrightarrow{p} \mathbf{0}$,

2. $n^{-1}\mathbf{X}'\mathbf{X} \xrightarrow{p} \Xi$, *a finite positive definite matrix.*

Then, $\hat{\boldsymbol{\beta}}$ *exists with probability converging to* 1 *and* $\hat{\boldsymbol{\beta}} \xrightarrow{p} \boldsymbol{\beta}$ *when* $n \to \infty$.

Condition 1 in Theorem 10.3.1 can be interpreted as an *asymptotic* orthogonality condition on $\mathbf{X}$ and ε. A sufficient condition for 1 to hold is that $\mathrm{E}[\varepsilon] = \mathbf{0}$, $\mathbf{X}$, and ε are independent random vectors, and $(\mathbf{X}[i, .], \varepsilon_i)$, $i = 1, \ldots, n$ are iid. Then, 1) follows immediately from Khinchin's weak law of large numbers (WLLN). More generally, condition 1 will hold if $\mathbf{X}$ and ε are only contemporaneously uncorrelated so long as the usual sample covariance estimator consistently estimates the (zero) covariance between the $\mathrm{X}[i, j]$'s and the ε_i's. This will occur if an appropriate WLLN for non-iid observations can be applied to the outcomes $(\mathrm{X}[i, j]\varepsilon_i)$, $i = 1, \ldots, n$, for every j, which will be possible if, roughly speaking, any dependence across the n sample outcomes $(\mathbf{X}[i, .]\varepsilon_i)$, $i = 1, \ldots, n$ is sufficiently weak and the variation in the $\mathrm{X}[i, j]$'s does not become excessively large (recall that the degree of variation in the ε_i's is currently assumed to be fixed at σ^2).

Condition 2 is the stochastic analog to the deterministic limit assumption invoked in Chapter 3 that $n^{-1}\mathbf{x}'\mathbf{x} \rightarrow \Xi$. In the current case, the probability limit will be rationalized by an appeal to a weak law of large numbers. For example, if the X[i, j]'s are iid random vectors having a finite mean and covariance matrix, then condition 2 follows immediately from Khinchin's WLLN. Such convergence can also occur when the **X**[i, .]'s are non-iid based on WLLNs applicable to such cases. Consistency of the LS estimator can even be proven using the weaker condition that $(n^{-1}\mathbf{X}'\mathbf{X})^{-1}$ is simply bounded in probability, that is, is $O_p(1)$ and does not require that $n^{-1}\mathbf{X}'\mathbf{X}$ have a probability limit. See White (1984), especially pages 20 and 25, for various alternatives along these lines.

We can also state that the estimator S^2 is consistent for σ^2. One such result is as follows:

Theorem 10.3.2 (Consistency of S^2 for Stochastic X): *Assume the conditions of Theorem* 10.3.1 *and also assume that either the* ε_i*'s are independent or else* $n^{-1}\varepsilon'\varepsilon \xrightarrow{p} \sigma^2$. *Then* $S^2 \xrightarrow{p} \sigma^2$.

As we remarked following Theorem 10.3.1, consistency of S^2 can be proven under weaker conditions. The most notable weakening concerns the relaxation of the existence of the probability limit of $n^{-1}\mathbf{X}'\mathbf{X}$. In fact, it is enough that $(n^{-1}\mathbf{X}'\mathbf{X})^{-1}$ be bounded in probability, that is, be $O_p(1)$, and then the consistency of S^2 follows even if $n^{-1}\mathbf{X}'\mathbf{X}$ does not converge in probability to anything. For enhanced understanding, it would be useful if the reader would examine the proof of Theorem 10.3.2 in the appendix and demonstrate that consistency is achieved under the weaker condition.

► **Example 10.3.1:** To demonstrate the consistency of the LS estimators $\hat{\boldsymbol{\beta}}$ and S^2 under stochastic **X**, we provide the GAUSS program C10LS1.gss in the examples manual. For a series of sample sizes selected by the user, GAUSS reports the sample moments and box and whisker plots of the replicated parameter estimates for a set of m Monte Carlo trials (m also selected by the user). Owing to the unbiasedness and consistency of the estimators, the user should find that the estimated bias is approximately zero and the variance of the estimators decline to zero as n increases.

Asymptotic normality of $\hat{\boldsymbol{\beta}}$ is analogous to the case in which **X** is fixed. As in Chapter 5, the result relies on the application of central limit theory to a properly scaled and centered $\hat{\boldsymbol{\beta}}$.

Theorem 10.3.3 (Asymptotic Normality of $\hat{\boldsymbol{\beta}}$): *Assume the conditions of Theorem* 10.3.1. *In addition, suppose that* $n^{-1/2}\mathbf{X}'\varepsilon \xrightarrow{d} N(\mathbf{0}, \sigma^2\Xi)$. *Then* $n^{1/2}(\hat{\boldsymbol{\beta}} - \boldsymbol{\beta}) \xrightarrow{d} N(\mathbf{0}, \sigma^2\Xi^{-1})$.

Various central limit theorems can be invoked to establish a normal limiting distribution for $n^{-1/2}\mathbf{X}'\varepsilon$. For example, the approach used in proving Theorem 5.3.3 could be adapted for this purpose. Regarding the estimation of the asymptotic covariance matrix

$\sigma^2\Xi^{-1}$, one can use the consistent estimator $S^2(n^{-1}\mathbf{X}'\mathbf{X})^{-1}$. The estimated asymptotic covariance matrix of $\hat{\boldsymbol{\beta}}$ is $s^2(\mathbf{x}'\mathbf{x})^{-1}$, which is identical to the case of nonstochastic **x**.

► **Example 10.3.2:** To demonstrate the asymptotic normality of the LS estimator $\hat{\boldsymbol{\beta}}$ under stochastic **X**, we provide the GAUSS program C10LS2.gss in the examples manual. In contrast to the Monte Carlo simulation exercise conducted in Example 10.3.1, this GAUSS program is based on an extension of the bootstrap resampling procedure that accommodates stochastic regressors. The procedure is often known as paired resampling because we jointly draw the bootstrap data from the dependent and explanatory variables $(y_i, \mathbf{x}_{i\cdot})$ to form the resampled data. For a series of sample sizes selected by the user, GAUSS reports the EDF of the replicated parameter estimates for a set of m bootstrap trials (m also selected by the user). The user should find that the EDF approaches the limiting normal CDF as n increases.

10.3.3. ML Estimation of $\boldsymbol{\beta}$ and σ^2 under Conditional Normality

When **X** is stochastic, it is clear that the PDF of $\mathbf{Y} = \mathbf{X}\boldsymbol{\beta} + \boldsymbol{\varepsilon}$ is no longer determined by a simple mean shifting of the distribution of $\boldsymbol{\varepsilon}$ because the probability distribution of **X** must now be accounted for as well. Furthermore, even the conditional distribution of $\mathbf{Y} \mid \mathbf{x}$ can be complicated because it is determined by a mean shifting (by $\mathbf{x}\boldsymbol{\beta}$) of the *conditional* distribution of $\boldsymbol{\varepsilon}$ given **x**, that is, $(\mathbf{Y} \mid \mathbf{x}) \sim \mathbf{x}\boldsymbol{\beta} + (\boldsymbol{\varepsilon} \mid \mathbf{x})$.

One inverse problem situation in which the familiar ML approach of Chapters 3 and 4 is directly applicable is the case in which $\boldsymbol{\varepsilon}$ and **X** are independent and the distribution of **X** does not depend on $\boldsymbol{\beta}$ or σ^2. In this case the distribution of $\mathbf{Y} \mid \mathbf{x}$ is in fact determined by a mean shifting of the distribution of $\boldsymbol{\varepsilon}$, that is, $(\mathbf{Y} \mid \mathbf{x}) \sim \mathbf{x}\boldsymbol{\beta} + \boldsymbol{\varepsilon}$. Thus, once the distribution of $\boldsymbol{\varepsilon}$ is specified, the distribution of $\mathbf{Y} \mid \mathbf{x}$ is defined directly via mean translation of the distribution of $\boldsymbol{\varepsilon}$. It follows in this case that the ML procedure for determining estimates of $\boldsymbol{\beta}$ and σ^2 and conducting testing and confidence region generation could proceed as in Chapters 3 and 4 if $\boldsymbol{\varepsilon} \sim N(\mathbf{0}, \sigma^2\mathbf{I})$, because then $(\mathbf{Y} \mid \mathbf{x}) \sim N(\mathbf{x}\boldsymbol{\beta}, \sigma^2\mathbf{I})$.

More generally, consider the following universal representation of the joint probability distribution of $(\mathbf{Y}, \mathbf{X})$,

$$(\mathbf{Y}, \mathbf{X}) \sim f(\mathbf{y}, \mathbf{x}; \boldsymbol{\beta}, \sigma^2, \boldsymbol{\xi}) = h\big(\mathbf{y}; \boldsymbol{\beta}, \sigma^2 \mid \mathbf{x}\big)g(\mathbf{x}; \boldsymbol{\xi}), \tag{10.3.7}$$

where $\boldsymbol{\xi}$ denotes the parameters of the marginal probability distribution of **X**, $g(\mathbf{x}; \boldsymbol{\xi})$. The log likelihood function for the parameters of the problem is then given by

$$\ln[L(\boldsymbol{\beta}, \sigma^2, \boldsymbol{\xi}; \mathbf{y}, \mathbf{x})] = \ln[h(\mathbf{y}; \boldsymbol{\beta}, \sigma^2 \mid \mathbf{x})] + \ln[g(\mathbf{x}; \boldsymbol{\xi})]. \tag{10.3.8}$$

It is clear that if the parameter vector $\boldsymbol{\xi}$ is unrelated to the parameters $(\boldsymbol{\beta}, \sigma^2)$, then the problem of finding the ML estimator of $(\boldsymbol{\beta}, \sigma^2)$ depends only on maximizing $\ln[h(\mathbf{y}; \boldsymbol{\beta}, \sigma^2 \mid \mathbf{x})]$, which is separable from the problem of finding the ML estimator of $\boldsymbol{\xi}$ via maximizing $\ln[g(\mathbf{x}; \boldsymbol{\xi})]$. The condition that $\boldsymbol{\xi}$ and $(\boldsymbol{\beta}, \sigma^2)$ are unrelated defines what Engle, Hendry, and Richard (1983) refer to as the *weak exogeneity* of **X**. In this case, once a specific parameteric family of distributions is specified for $h(\mathbf{y}; \boldsymbol{\beta}, \sigma^2 \mid \mathbf{x})$, ML analysis can proceed, conditional on $\mathbf{x}$, precisely as in Chapters 3 and 4.

Again consider the important special case $(\mathbf{Y} \mid \mathbf{x}) \sim N(\mathbf{x}\boldsymbol{\beta}, \sigma^2\mathbf{I})$. Then the joint distribution of $\mathbf{Y}$ and $\mathbf{X}$ (recall (10.3.7)) can be represented as

$$(\mathbf{Y}, \mathbf{X}) \sim \frac{1}{(2\pi)^{n/2}\sigma^n} \exp\left[-\frac{1}{2\sigma^2}(\mathbf{y} - \mathbf{x}\boldsymbol{\beta})'(\mathbf{y} - \mathbf{x}\boldsymbol{\beta})\right] g(\mathbf{x}; \boldsymbol{\xi}). \tag{10.3.9}$$

It follows that the ML estimators of $\boldsymbol{\beta}$ and σ^2 are given by the familiar equations $\hat{\boldsymbol{\beta}} = (\mathbf{X}'\mathbf{X})^{-1}\mathbf{X}'\mathbf{Y}$ and $S^2_{ML} = (\mathbf{Y} - \mathbf{X}\hat{\boldsymbol{\beta}})'(\mathbf{Y} - \mathbf{X}\hat{\boldsymbol{\beta}})/n$. Thus, given our results in Sections 10.3.1 and 10.3.2, the ML estimator of $\boldsymbol{\beta}$ is unbiased, whereas the ML estimator of σ^2 is biased, with a bias of $(-k/n)\sigma^2$, precisely as in the case of nonstochastic $\mathbf{x}$. The typical MLE asymptotics of consistency, asymptotic normality, and asymptotic efficiency also apply to these estimators. Furthermore, $\hat{\boldsymbol{\beta}}$ is conditionally normally distributed in finite samples, and $S^2 = (\frac{n}{n-k})S^2_{ML}$ is conditionally Chi-square $(n - k, 0)$ distributed. For enhanced understanding, it would be useful for the reader to complete the rationale for these results.

10.4. Hypothesis Testing and Confidence-Region Estimation

10.4.1. Semiparametric Case

Given the asymptotic normality of $\hat{\boldsymbol{\beta}}$, hypothesis tests in the semiparametric framework can be based on precisely the same Wald, Lagrange multiplier, pseudo-likelihood and Z-statistic procedures that were discussed in Chapters 6 and 8. The asymptotic distributions of the test statistics are again Chi-square (Wald, LM, and PLR statistics) and normal (Z-statistic). The key assumptions in making the transition from the nonstochastic to the stochastic $\mathbf{X}$ case are those listed in Theorems 10.3.1–10.3.3. As we remarked previously, these assumptions are sufficient conditions, but not necessary, and weaker conditions leading to the validity of the standard testing procedures can be found in White (1984, Section 4.2). Confidence regions can then be based on duality with the hypothesis-testing procedures precisely, again, as they were defined in Chapters 6 and 8.

10.4.2. Parametric Case

It is also true that the testing and confidence region procedures discussed in Chapters 4 and 9 relating to the parametric framework apply as well to the case where $\mathbf{X}$ is stochastic. However, the rationale for the transition from fixed to stochastic $\mathbf{X}$ is conceptually more involved in the parametric case when considering *finite* sample properties of test and confidence region procedures, and so we examine more of the details for this case here.

Consider the linear statistical model in the parametric case in which $(\mathbf{Y} \mid \mathbf{x}) \sim N(\mathbf{x}\boldsymbol{\beta}, \sigma^2\mathbf{I})$ and $(\varepsilon \mid \mathbf{x}) \sim N(\mathbf{0}, \sigma^2\mathbf{I})$. It follows immediately from the results in

Section 4.3, operating *conditionally* on **x**, that (recall (4.3.17))

$$(\mathrm{T}\,|\,\mathbf{x}) = \frac{\mathbf{c}\hat{\boldsymbol{\beta}} - \mathrm{r}}{[\mathrm{S}^2\mathbf{c}(\mathbf{x}'\mathbf{x})^{-1}\mathbf{c}']^{1/2}} \sim \mathrm{Tdist}(n-k, \delta) \tag{10.4.1}$$

and (recall (4.3.11))

$$(\mathrm{F}\,|\,\mathbf{x}) = \frac{(\mathbf{c}\hat{\boldsymbol{\beta}} - \mathbf{r})'[\mathbf{c}(\mathbf{x}'\mathbf{x})^{-1}\mathbf{c}']^{-1}(\mathbf{c}\hat{\boldsymbol{\beta}} - \mathbf{r})}{j\mathrm{S}^2} \sim \mathrm{Fdist}(j, n-k, \lambda). \tag{10.4.2}$$

Therefore, all of the finite sample properties relating to the T, F, Wald, LM, and GLR tests discussed in Section 4.3 apply, *conditionally* on **x**. Thus, all of the properties of confidence regions that are dual to these tests are identical to those described in Section 4.4 as well, also *conditionally* on **x**.

We now note that nothing changes to the distributions of T and F if we *do not condition* an **x**, and thus all of the finite sample test and confidence region procedures described in Sections 4.3 and 4.4 apply directly to the case of stochastic **X** *unconditionally*. To see this, consider the F (and concomitantly, the Wald, LM, and GLR) statistic (recall Sections 4.3 and 6.2.3). The joint PDF of F and **X** can be characterized by

$$\mathrm{h}(\mathrm{f}, \mathbf{x}; j, n-k, \lambda, \boldsymbol{\xi}) = \mathrm{h}_{\mathrm{F}|\mathbf{x}}(\mathrm{f}; j, n-k, \lambda\,|\,\mathbf{x})\mathrm{g}(\mathbf{x}; \boldsymbol{\xi}), \tag{10.4.3}$$

where $\mathrm{h}(\cdot)$, $\mathrm{h}_{\mathrm{F}|\mathbf{x}}(\cdot)$, and $\mathrm{g}(\cdot)$ are the probability distributions of $(\mathrm{F}, \mathbf{X})$, $\mathrm{F}\,|\,\mathbf{x}$, and **X**, respectively, and j, $n-k$, λ, and $\boldsymbol{\xi}$ are the parameters of the distributions.

The marginal probability distribution of F can be obtained in the usual way by integrating out **x** from the joint distribution of F and **X**. Recall from (10.4.2) that the distribution of $\mathrm{F}\,|\,\mathbf{x}$, which is the noncentral F-distribution, *does not depend on* **x**. Consequently,

$$\begin{aligned}
\mathrm{h}_{\mathrm{F}}(\mathrm{f}; j, n-k, \lambda) &= \int_{\mathrm{x}\in\mathrm{R}^{\mathrm{K}}} \mathrm{h}_{\mathrm{F}|\mathbf{x}}(\mathrm{f}; j, n-k, \lambda\,|\,\mathbf{x})\mathrm{g}(\mathbf{x}; \boldsymbol{\xi})\,\mathrm{d}\mathbf{x} \\
&= \mathrm{h}_{\mathrm{F}|\mathbf{x}}(\mathrm{f}; j, n-k, \lambda\,|\,\mathbf{x}) \underbrace{\int_{\mathrm{x}\in\mathrm{R}^{\mathrm{K}}} \mathrm{g}(\mathbf{x}; \boldsymbol{\xi})\,\mathrm{d}\mathbf{x}}_{=1} \\
&= \mathrm{Fdist}(\mathrm{f}; j, n-k, \lambda).
\end{aligned} \tag{10.4.4}$$

An analogous argument can be applied to the T-statistic to demonstrate that the conditional-on-**x** and unconditional distributions of T are the same noncentral *T*-distribution $\mathrm{Tdist}(t; n-k, \delta)$. Thus, the testing and confidence region procedures identified in Sections 4.3 and 4.4 apply to the stochastic **X** case as well.

► **Example 10.4.1:** To demonstrate the statistical properties of the T, F, and GLR test statistics under stochastic **X**, we provide the GAUSS program C10Tests.gss in the examples manual. For a given sample, the observed test statistics and p-values are reported for three separate hypotheses. Then, for one of the test procedures (selected by the user), the power function and sampling distribution of the statistic are estimated by Monte Carlo simulation. For comparison purposes, GAUSS compares the estimated power function and EDF (based on the replicated test statistics) to the limiting power function and CDF.

10.5. Summary: Statistical Implications of Stochastic X

We summarize the principal implications of $\mathbf{X}$ being stochastic as follows:

1. One needs to condition on the outcomes of $\mathbf{X}$ to establish information linkages between the outcomes and expectation of $\mathbf{Y}$ and the observable values of $\mathbf{X}$.
2. Under both independent and contemporaneously uncorrelated $\mathbf{X}$ and $\boldsymbol{\varepsilon}$, with $\mathrm{E}[\boldsymbol{\varepsilon} \mid \mathbf{X}] = \mathbf{0}$, the least-squares estimator is unconditionally unbiased, its unconditional covariance matrix is $\sigma^2\mathrm{E}[(\mathbf{X}'\mathbf{X})^{-1}]$, and $\mathrm{S}^2 = (\mathbf{Y} - \mathbf{X}\hat{\boldsymbol{\beta}})'(\mathbf{Y} - \mathbf{X}\hat{\boldsymbol{\beta}})/(n - k)$ is an unconditionally unbiased estimator of the noise component variance.
3. If $\boldsymbol{\varepsilon}$ is multivariate normally distributed and the distribution of $\mathbf{X}$ does not depend on $\boldsymbol{\beta}$ or σ^2, then $\hat{\boldsymbol{\beta}} = (\mathbf{X}'\mathbf{X})^{-1}\mathbf{X}'\mathbf{Y}$ and $\mathrm{S}^2_{\mathrm{ML}} = (\mathbf{Y} - \mathbf{X}\hat{\boldsymbol{\beta}})'(\mathbf{Y} - \mathbf{X}\hat{\boldsymbol{\beta}})/n$ are the ML estimators of $\boldsymbol{\beta}$ and σ^2.
4. The asymptotic properties of the LS estimators when $\mathbf{X}$ is stochastic, as well as properties for the ML estimator under conditional normality of $(\mathbf{Y} \mid \mathbf{x})$ and weak exogeneity of $\mathbf{X}$, follow those established for the case when the $\mathbf{x}$'s are fixed.
5. Given the asymptotic normality of the LS estimator, asymptotically valid hypothesis tests can be based on the Wald, Lagrange multiplier, pseudo-likelihood ratio, and Z-statistic procedures developed in Chapters 4 and 8.
6. Given the conditional normality of $(\mathbf{Y} \mid \mathbf{x})$ and the weak exogeneity of $\mathbf{X}$, standard T and F tests can be used to conduct hypothesis-testing and confidence-region estimation analogous to their use in Chapter 4.

10.6. Method of Moments Concept

Having generalized the regression model to include stochastic regressors and examined the corresponding statistical implications, now suppose we have a sample of iid observations from some unknown probability distribution and we want to estimate one or more parameters functionally related to the moments of the distribution. Under Pearson's method of moments (MOM), also referred to as the *ordinary* method of moments, the expected values of functions of a random variable having the unknown distribution are used to form moment functions that involve the unknown model parameters. *The values of the unknown parameters are estimated by finding the parameter values that solve a system of equations formed by equating unknown population moments with their sample moment counterparts* (the *generalized* method of moments is developed in Chapter 16).

For expository purposes, consider a simple special case of (10.1.1) for which we have a sample of n iid observations on outcomes of a scalar random variable Y having some unknown distribution with mean β and variance σ^2. That is, we consider a simple location and scale regression model for which the explanatory variables consist of a single column of 1's ($\mathbf{X} \equiv \mathbf{1}$). The first and second moments of Y about the origin, (i.e., around the point zero) are defined by $\mu_1' = \mathrm{E}[\mathrm{Y}] = \beta$ and $\mu_2' = \mathrm{E}[\mathrm{Y}^2] = \beta^2 + \sigma^2$, which we can view as a two-equation system defining two population moments in terms of two unknown parameters. The first equation directly identifies β as the first moment about the origin, and we can solve for the variance parameter because $\sigma^2 = \mathrm{E}[\mathrm{Y}^2] - (\mathrm{E}[\mathrm{Y}])^2$. Unless we know the population moments E[Y] and $\mathrm{E}(\mathrm{Y}^2)$ of Y, we cannot directly recover the values of the unknown parameters, β and σ^2. However, we can use the sample moments $\mathrm{m}_1' = n^{-1}\sum_i \mathrm{y}_i = \bar{\mathrm{y}}_n$ and $\mathrm{m}_2' = n^{-1}\sum_i \mathrm{y}_i^2$ as estimates of E[Y] and $\mathrm{E}(\mathrm{Y}^2)$. By substitution of the sample moments for the population moments, the MOM estimates of the model parameters β and σ^2 are defined, respectively, as

$$\hat{\mathrm{b}}_{\mathrm{mom}} = \mathrm{m}_1' = n^{-1}\sum_{i=1}^{n} \mathrm{y}_i = \bar{\mathrm{y}}_n \quad \text{and} \quad \mathrm{s}^2_{\mathrm{mom}} = \mathrm{m}_2' - (\mathrm{m}_1')^2 = n^{-1}\sum_{i=1}^{n} (\mathrm{y}_i - \bar{\mathrm{y}}_n)^2. \tag{10.6.1}$$

More generally, suppose we have a k-dimensional set of model parameters $\boldsymbol{\theta} \in \Omega$ and we can define a k-dimensional vector function of moment conditions

$$\mathrm{E}[\mathbf{h}(\mathrm{Y}, \boldsymbol{\theta})] = \mathbf{0} \tag{10.6.2}$$

that relates expectations of functions of $\mathbf{Y}$ with the parameter $\boldsymbol{\theta} \in \Omega$ that indexes the probability distribution of Y. For example, in our previous two-moment example, the two-dimensional vector function $\mathbf{h}(\mathrm{Y}, \boldsymbol{\theta})$ would be defined as

$$\mathrm{h}_1(\mathrm{Y}, \beta, \sigma) = \mathrm{Y} - \beta \quad \text{and} \quad \mathrm{h}_2(\mathrm{Y}, \beta, \sigma) = \mathrm{Y}^2 - \beta^2 - \sigma^2, \tag{10.6.3}$$

where β and σ^2 denote the mean and variance of Y. The MOM estimate $\hat{\boldsymbol{\theta}}$ is obtained by choosing the value of $\boldsymbol{\theta}$ that satisfies the sample moment counterpart to (10.6.2)

$$n^{-1}\sum_{i=1}^{n} \mathbf{h}(\mathrm{y}_i, \boldsymbol{\theta}) = \mathbf{0}, \tag{10.6.4}$$

where $\mathbf{y} = [\mathrm{y}_1, \mathrm{y}_2, \ldots \mathrm{y}_n]'$ is a sample outcome from a size n iid random sample from the distribution of Y. Given that the functional relationship between the moments and the model parameters may only be implicitly defined, we can rely on the implicit function theorem to ensure the existence of a unique solution to the MOM problem. Effectively, we require the Jacobian matrix $\frac{\partial \sum_{i=1}^{n} \mathbf{h}(\mathrm{y}_i, \boldsymbol{\theta})}{\partial \boldsymbol{\theta}}$ to have full rank of k (i.e., the dimension of $\boldsymbol{\theta}$) in a neighborhood of the solution.

10.6.1. Asymptotic Properties

There is some compelling intuition underlying the use of (10.6.4) to solve for $\boldsymbol{\theta}$ and thereby estimate the value of $\boldsymbol{\theta}$. First of all, if we could actually calculate the expectation on the left-hand side of (10.6.2) for any given $\boldsymbol{\theta}$ and then solve for the unique value of $\boldsymbol{\theta}$ that satisfies (10.6.2), we would have derived the *true* value, $\boldsymbol{\theta}_0$, of the unknown $\boldsymbol{\theta}$ and our estimate of $\boldsymbol{\theta}$ would of course be perfect. We emphasize that "true value" here means the value of $\boldsymbol{\theta}$ that indexes the probability distribution from which the Y values are actually sampled. Because the distribution underlying the expectation operation in (10.6.2) is generally not known, we approximate the expectation with the sample estimate of this expectation given by $n^{-1}\sum_{i=1}^{n} \mathbf{h}(\mathrm{y}_i, \boldsymbol{\theta})$. Because the Y_i's are iid, the $\mathbf{h}(\mathrm{Y}_i, \boldsymbol{\theta})$'s are also iid, and we will be able to utilize Khinchin's WLLN to claim that $n^{-1}\sum_{i=1}^{n}\mathbf{h}(\mathrm{Y}_i,\boldsymbol{\theta})\xrightarrow{\mathrm{p}}\mathrm{E}[\mathbf{h}(\mathrm{Y},\boldsymbol{\theta})]$. Then, we would anticipate that the value of $\boldsymbol{\theta}$ that solves $n^{-1}\sum_{i=1}^{n}\mathbf{h}(\mathrm{Y}_i,\boldsymbol{\theta})=\mathbf{0}$ should converge in probability to the value of $\boldsymbol{\theta}$ that solves $\mathrm{E}[\mathbf{h}(\mathrm{Y},\boldsymbol{\theta})]=\mathbf{0}$, which is to say that the MOM estimator should converge in probability to the true value, $\boldsymbol{\theta}_0$, of $\boldsymbol{\theta}$ and be a consistent estimator.

In fact, the preceding intuitive argument can be made rigorous if the convergence in probability of the sample moments to the population moments is *uniform*, $\mathrm{E}[\mathbf{h}(\mathrm{Y},\boldsymbol{\theta})]$ is continuous in $\boldsymbol{\theta}$, and the value of $\boldsymbol{\theta}$, say $\boldsymbol{\theta}_0$, that satisfies $\mathrm{E}[\mathbf{h}(\mathrm{Y},\boldsymbol{\theta})]=\mathbf{0}$ is unique. By uniform convergence in probability we mean that for all $n>m(\varepsilon,\delta)$, $\varepsilon>0$ and $\delta\in(0,1)$

$$\mathrm{P}\left[\sup_{\boldsymbol{\theta}}\left|n^{-1}\sum_{i=1}^{n}\mathbf{h}(\mathrm{y}_i,\boldsymbol{\theta})-\mathrm{E}[\mathbf{h}(\mathrm{Y},\boldsymbol{\theta}]\right|<\varepsilon\right]>1-\delta,\qquad(10.6.5)$$

where $|\cdot|$ denotes the Euclidean distance of the argument from the zero vector. An alternative and somewhat less informative way of writing the uniform convergence condition is given by $\lim_{n\to\infty}\mathrm{P}(\sup_{\boldsymbol{\theta}}|n^{-1}\sum_{i=1}^{n}\mathbf{h}(\mathrm{y}_i,\boldsymbol{\theta})-\mathrm{E}[\mathbf{h}(\mathrm{Y},\boldsymbol{\theta})]|<\varepsilon)=1,\forall\varepsilon>0$ (recall (7.3.1)). The condition (10.6.5) implies that there always exists a sample size for which $n^{-1}\sum_{i=1}^{n}\mathbf{h}(\mathrm{y}_i,\boldsymbol{\theta})$ and $\mathrm{E}[\mathbf{h}(\mathrm{Y},\boldsymbol{\theta})]$ are arbitrarily close in value with arbitrarily high probability *regardless* of the value of $\boldsymbol{\theta}$. It follows that if $\boldsymbol{\theta}_0$ is the unique value for which $\mathrm{E}[\mathbf{h}(\mathrm{Y},\boldsymbol{\theta}_0)]=\mathbf{0}$, then as $n\to\infty$, we are assured that for all $n>m(\varepsilon,\delta)$ and arbitrarily small ε and δ

$$\mathbf{P}\left[\left|n^{-1}\sum_{i=1}^{n}\mathbf{h}(\mathrm{y}_i,\boldsymbol{\theta}_0)\right|<\varepsilon\right]>1-\delta.\qquad(10.6.6)$$

Thus, $\mathrm{plim}(n^{-1}\sum_{i=1}^{n}\mathbf{h}(\mathrm{Y}_i,\boldsymbol{\theta}_0))=\mathbf{0}$, and by an analogous argument $\mathrm{plim}(n^{-1}\sum_{i=1}^{n}\mathbf{h}(\mathrm{Y}_i,\boldsymbol{\theta}_*))\neq\mathbf{0}$ for $\boldsymbol{\theta}_*\neq\boldsymbol{\theta}_0$, and thus

$$\hat{\boldsymbol{\theta}}=\arg_{\boldsymbol{\theta}}\left[n^{-1}\sum_{i=1}^{n}\mathbf{h}(\mathrm{Y}_i,\boldsymbol{\theta})=\mathbf{0}\right]\xrightarrow{\mathrm{p}}\boldsymbol{\theta}_0.\qquad(10.6.7)$$

A relatively straightforward proof of both consistency and asymptotic normality of the MOM estimator can be developed if the moment conditions can be stated as functions of sample moments about the origin as in (10.6.1). For the case of k moment conditions, suppose the sample moment condition in (10.6.4) may be written as

$$n^{-1}\sum_{i=1}^{n}\mathrm{h}_j(\mathrm{y}_i,\boldsymbol{\theta})=\mathrm{m}'_j-\mathrm{q}_j(\boldsymbol{\theta})=0,\quad j=1,2,\ldots,k,\qquad(10.6.8)$$

which is the sample analog of the k population moment conditions $\mathrm{E}[\mathbf{h}(\mathrm{Y},\boldsymbol{\theta})]=\boldsymbol{\mu}-\mathbf{q}(\boldsymbol{\theta})=\mathbf{0}$, where $\boldsymbol{\mu}=(\mu'_1,\mu'_2,\ldots,\mu'_k)'$. If the k-dimensional vector function $\mathbf{q}$ is continuous and satisfies the Jacobian rank condition in the neighborhood of the true parameter vector $\boldsymbol{\theta}_0$ so that the inverse vector function $\boldsymbol{\theta}_0=\mathbf{q}^{-1}(\mu'_1,\ldots,\mu'_k)$ exists at the point $\boldsymbol{\mu}=(\mu'_1,\mu'_2,\ldots,\mu'_k)'$ and is continuous in the neighborhood of $\boldsymbol{\mu}=(\mu'_1,\mu'_2,\ldots,\mu'_k)'$ based on the implicit function theorem, we can show that $\hat{\boldsymbol{\theta}}$ is a consistent estimator of $\boldsymbol{\theta}$. In particular, if the even ordered moments of Y about the origin exist up to order 2k (i.e., $\mu'_{2j}<\infty$ for all $j=1,\ldots,k$), then the sample moment statistics are unbiased with variances $n^{-1}[\mu'_{2j} - (\mu'_j)^2]$ (Mittelhammer, p. 316, Theorem 6.5). Thus, each M'_j converges in mean square and in probability to the associated population moment μ'_j. By the continuity and local uniqueness of the inverse mapping from the sample moments to the model parameters, Slutsky's theorem then implies that $\hat{\theta} = \mathbf{q}^{-1}(M'_1, \ldots, M'_k) \xrightarrow{p} \mathbf{q}^{-1}(\mu'_1, \ldots, \mu'_k) = \boldsymbol{\theta}_0$, and thus the MOM estimator is consistent. In addition, if the inverse mapping is continuously differentiable and the Jacobian matrix has full rank, it follows that

$$n^{1/2}(\hat{\boldsymbol{\Theta}} - \boldsymbol{\theta}_0) \overset{a}{\sim} \mathrm{N}[\mathbf{0}, \mathbf{G}\Sigma\mathbf{G}'], \tag{10.6.9}$$

where $\mathbf{G}$ is the $(k \times k)$ Jacobian matrix $\frac{\partial \mathbf{q}^{-1}(\mathbf{m})}{\partial \mathbf{m}'}$ evaluated at the value $\mathbf{m} = \boldsymbol{\mu}$ (Mittelhammer, p. 493, Theorem 8.24). The matrix Σ is the covariance matrix of the sample moments with the (j, k) element given by $\mu'_{j+k} - \mu'_j \mu'_k$.

► **Example 10.6.1:** To demonstrate the method of moments estimator, we provide the GAUSS program C10MOM.gss in the examples manual. To begin, the user selects the sample size n and parameters for a set of iid observations generated by a Beta($\alpha, \boldsymbol{\beta}$) DSP. GAUSS reports the MOM estimates of α and $\boldsymbol{\beta}$ as well as the approximate standard errors based on the large sample results presented in this section. Finally, GAUSS conducts a Wald test of the null hypothesis H_0: $\alpha = \boldsymbol{\beta}$ (i.e., the beta distribution is symmetric) and reports the test decision to the user.

As we have defined it to this point, the MOM procedure is restricted to iid outcomes from a population distribution. We will see in the section ahead that the MOM procedure applies directly to the classical linear regression model so long as the random variables $(\mathrm{Y}_i, \mathbf{X}_{i\cdot})$, $i = 1, \ldots, n$, are iid. We note, however, that a generalization of the MOM approach, aptly called the generalized method of moments (GMM), will be required to accommodate the case in which $\mathbf{X}$ is nonstochastic, or the case in which the $(\mathrm{Y}_i, \mathbf{X}_{i\cdot})$'s are not iid. The GMM approach that is presented in Chapter 16 can also accommodate cases in which there are more moment equations than unknown parameters and can be used to estimate parameters when $\mathrm{E}[\mathbf{X}'\boldsymbol{\varepsilon}] \neq \mathbf{0}$, $n^{-1}\mathbf{X}'\boldsymbol{\varepsilon} \neq \mathbf{0}$, or both, whereas the MOM application ahead relies on the population and empirical moment conditions $\mathrm{E}[\mathbf{X}'\boldsymbol{\varepsilon}] = \mathbf{0}$ and $n^{-1}\mathbf{X}'\boldsymbol{\varepsilon} = \mathbf{0}$, respectively.

10.6.2. A Linear Model Formulation

We can extend the MOM concept to the general case of the linear regression model (10.1.2) using the moment-based condition that the noise component elements and the explanatory variable values are contemporaneously uncorrelated. We assume the linear regression model with stochastic $\mathbf{X}$ given by (10.1.2) and that the n observations $\mathbf{z}_i = (\mathrm{y}_i, \mathbf{x}_{i\cdot})'$, $i = 1, \ldots, n$, are iid outcomes from some $(k+1) \times 1$ random variable $\mathbf{Z}$ having some population distribution. Consistent with the usual linear model assumptions, it is also assumed that $\mathbf{X}$ and $\boldsymbol{\varepsilon}$ satisfy the orthogonality or contemporaneous uncorrelatedness condition $\mathrm{E}[\mathbf{X}'\boldsymbol{\varepsilon}] = \mathbf{0}$. Because $\varepsilon_i \equiv \mathrm{Y}_i - \mathbf{X}_{i\cdot}\boldsymbol{\beta}\ \forall i$ and the $(\mathrm{Y}_i, \mathbf{X}_{i\cdot})$'s are iid, the orthogonality condition is equivalent to

$$\mathrm{E}[\mathbf{X}_{i\cdot}'(\mathrm{Y}_i - \mathbf{X}_{i\cdot}\boldsymbol{\beta})] = \mathbf{0}, \ \forall i\cdot \qquad (10.6.10)$$

The moment condition in (10.6.10) can be expressed in terms of the population random vector $\mathbf{Z}$ as

$$\mathrm{E}[\mathbf{h}(\mathbf{Z}, \boldsymbol{\beta})] = \mathrm{E}[\mathbf{Z}[2:\mathrm{k}](\mathbf{Z}[1] - \mathbf{Z}[2:\mathrm{k}]'\boldsymbol{\beta})] = \mathbf{0}, \qquad (10.6.11)$$

which then establishes population moment conditions that can be used in the MOM procedure for estimating $\boldsymbol{\beta}$. Given these population moment conditions, we follow the MOM format and use the corresponding sample moments to estimate the population moments. The sample analog of the population moment condition (10.6.11) is

$$n^{-1}\sum_{i=1}^{n} \mathbf{x}_{i\cdot}'(\mathrm{y}_i - \mathbf{x}_{i\cdot}\boldsymbol{\beta}) = n^{-1}[\mathbf{x}'(\mathbf{y} - \mathbf{x}\boldsymbol{\beta})] = \mathbf{0}, \qquad (10.6.12)$$

where $\mathbf{x}_{i\cdot}$ is the observed outcome for the ith row vector of $\mathbf{X}$, and to obtain the MOM estimate we choose a value for $\boldsymbol{\beta}$ that satisfies (10.6.12). Note that (10.6.12) is simply a scalar multiple of the first-order condition for the extremum problem

$$\hat{\mathbf{b}} = \arg\min_{\boldsymbol{\beta}}[(\mathbf{y} - \mathbf{x}\boldsymbol{\beta})'(\mathbf{y} - \mathbf{x}\boldsymbol{\beta})] = \arg\max_{\boldsymbol{\beta}}[-(\mathbf{y} - \mathbf{x}\boldsymbol{\beta})'(\mathbf{y} - \mathbf{x}\boldsymbol{\beta})]. \quad (10.6.13)$$

The resulting MOM estimate is therefore identical to the LS-extremum estimate. As is generally the case in MOM estimation problems, the MOM estimator $\hat{\boldsymbol{\beta}}$ is a consistent and asymptotically normal estimator under the regularity conditions stated in Chapter 5.

The MOM is a precursor to the modern so-called *estimating equations approach* that we will examine in Chapter 11 and beyond. In the MOM procedure, selected empirical moments are effectively equated to their expectations and then solved for parameters of interest. In Chapter 11 we revisit the practice of aggregating the data into sample moments as a basis for defining estimating equations and seek alternative weighting of the observations that lead to good or optimal estimates of parameters. For now, we emphasize that MOM estimators are consistent and asymptotically normal estimators of the model parameters under general conditions, and these estimators are based on only a few characteristics of the DSP and do not rely on strong assumptions regarding distributional form. At this point we can understand some of the underlying rationale for the heated discussions between Pearson and Fisher regarding the benefits (e.g., distributional robustness) and costs (e.g., *possible* nonoptimality) of choosing between the MOM and ML approach to estimation. For additional details on the ordinary method of moments, see Section 8.4 in Mittelhammer (1996).

10.6.3. Extensions to Nonlinear Models

The MOM approach can be extended to nonlinear regression models, $\mathbf{Y} = \mathbf{g}(\mathbf{X}, \boldsymbol{\beta}) + \boldsymbol{\varepsilon}$, under the iid assumption relating to the $(\mathbf{Y}_i, \mathbf{X}_{i\cdot})$'s. The extension also demonstrates that there is effectively no difference in how one applies NLS in the fixed or stochastic $\mathbf{X}$ case when $\mathbf{X}$ and $\boldsymbol{\varepsilon}$ are independent, or at least when the asymptotic orthogonality condition $n^{-1}\frac{\partial \mathbf{g}(\mathbf{X}, \boldsymbol{\beta})}{\partial \boldsymbol{\beta}}\boldsymbol{\varepsilon} \xrightarrow{p} \mathbf{0}$ for $n \to \infty$ holds.

The analog to the linear model moment conditions (10.6.10)–(10.6.12) can be based on the first-order conditions for minimizing the nonlinear least-squares objective function. In particular, the first-order conditions for minimizing $\sum_{i=1}^{n}[\mathrm{y}_i - \mathrm{g}(\mathbf{x}_{i\cdot}, \boldsymbol{\beta})]^2$ are given by

$$-2\sum_{i=1}^{n}\frac{\partial \mathrm{g}(\mathbf{x}_{i\cdot}, \boldsymbol{\beta})}{\partial \boldsymbol{\beta}}[\mathrm{y}_i - \mathrm{g}(\mathbf{x}_{i\cdot}, \boldsymbol{\beta})] = \mathbf{0}. \tag{10.6.14}$$

Note the analogy with (10.6.12), where the conditions would be identical if the superfluous scalar (-2) were replaced by n^{-1} and if $\mathrm{g}(\mathbf{x}_{i\cdot}, \boldsymbol{\beta}) \equiv \mathbf{x}_{i\cdot}\boldsymbol{\beta}$. If $\mathbf{Z}$ is the $(k+1)\times 1$ population random variable whose n iid outcomes are represented by $(\mathrm{y}_i, \mathbf{x}_{i\cdot})'$, $i = 1, \ldots, n$, the true population moment condition analogous to (10.6.11) is given by

$$\mathrm{E}\left[\frac{\partial \mathbf{g}(\mathbf{Z}[2:\mathrm{k}], \boldsymbol{\beta})}{\partial \boldsymbol{\beta}}[\mathbf{Z}[1] - \mathbf{g}(\mathbf{Z}[2:\mathrm{k}], \boldsymbol{\beta})]\right] = \mathbf{0}, \tag{10.6.15}$$

where the outer-bracketed term represents the population random variable whose n outcomes represent the n values in the summation term of (10.5.14). The sample moment analog to (10.6.14) then becomes (10.6.14) with (-2) replaced by n^{-1} as follows:

$$n^{-1}\sum_{i=1}^{n}\frac{\partial \mathrm{g}(\mathbf{x}_{i\cdot}, \boldsymbol{\beta})}{\partial \boldsymbol{\beta}}[\mathrm{y}_i - \mathrm{g}(\mathbf{x}_{i\cdot}, \boldsymbol{\beta})] = \mathbf{0}. \tag{10.6.16}$$

The MOM estimator for $\boldsymbol{\beta}$ is obtained by solving (10.6.16) for $\boldsymbol{\beta}$, which of course defines the NLS estimator for $\boldsymbol{\beta}$ as well. Under assumptions analogous to those contained in Theorems 10.3.1 and 10.3.3, namely

$$n^{-1}\frac{\partial \mathbf{g}(\mathbf{X}, \boldsymbol{\beta})}{\partial \boldsymbol{\beta}}\varepsilon \xrightarrow{\mathrm{p}} \mathbf{0} \tag{10.6.17}$$

$$n^{-1}\frac{\partial \mathbf{g}(\mathbf{X}, \boldsymbol{\beta})}{\partial \boldsymbol{\beta}}\frac{\partial \mathbf{g}(\mathbf{X}, \boldsymbol{\beta})}{\partial \boldsymbol{\beta}'} \xrightarrow{\mathrm{p}} \boldsymbol{\Xi}, \text{ a finite p.d. matrix,}$$

and

$$n^{-1/2}\frac{\partial \mathbf{g}(\mathbf{X}, \boldsymbol{\beta})}{\partial \boldsymbol{\beta}}\varepsilon \xrightarrow{\mathrm{d}} \mathrm{N}(0, \sigma^2\boldsymbol{\Xi}),$$

it follows that the MOM–NLS estimator of $\boldsymbol{\beta}$, when $\mathbf{X}$ is stochastic, is consistent and asymptotically normally distributed as

$$\hat{\boldsymbol{\beta}}_{\mathrm{NLS}} \overset{\mathrm{a}}{\sim} \mathrm{N}(\boldsymbol{\beta}, \sigma^2 n^{-1}\boldsymbol{\Xi}^{-1}). \tag{10.6.18}$$

The asymptotic covariance matrix can be estimated by

$$\mathrm{s}^2\left[\left.\frac{\partial \mathbf{g}(\mathbf{x}, \boldsymbol{\beta})}{\partial \boldsymbol{\beta}}\right|_{\hat{\mathbf{b}}_{\mathrm{NLS}}}\left.\frac{\partial \mathbf{g}(\mathbf{x}, \boldsymbol{\beta})}{\partial \boldsymbol{\beta}'}\right|_{\hat{\mathbf{b}}_{\mathrm{NLS}}}\right]^{-1}, \quad \text{where } \mathrm{s}^2 = [\mathbf{y} - \mathbf{g}(\mathbf{x}, \hat{\boldsymbol{\beta}}_{\mathrm{NLS}})]'[\mathbf{y} - \mathbf{g}(\mathbf{x}, \hat{\boldsymbol{\beta}}_{\mathrm{NLS}})]/n.$$

Because these results are identical to the results provided in Chapter 8 for the NLS estimator for fixed $\mathbf{x}$, it is apparent that estimation, testing, and confidence-region estimation proceed as developed in that chapter, regardless of whether $\mathbf{X}$ is fixed or stochastic.

► **Example 10.6.2:** To demonstrate the impact of stochastic **X** on the nonlinear least-squares estimator, we provide the GAUSS program C10NLS.gss in the examples manual. For a subset of the examples considered in Chapter 8, the program repeats the Monte Carlo simulation exercises with stochastic regressors and reports the statistical properties of the NLS estimator.

10.7. Concluding Comments

In this chapter we have enlarged the set of estimation and inference procedures to include stochastic–random explanatory variables. In particular, we considered the stochastic linear model $\mathbf{Y} = \mathbf{X}\boldsymbol{\beta} + \varepsilon$ under standard assumptions, including $\mathbf{cov}(\varepsilon) = \sigma^2\mathbf{I}$, and the marginal distribution of **X** does not depend on the parameters $\boldsymbol{\beta}$ and σ^2. In this case we found that if we express the joint distribution of the random variables **Y** and **X** in terms of the product of the marginal distribution of **X**, $g(\mathbf{x})$, and the conditional distribution of **Y** given **x**, $h(\mathbf{y} \mid \mathbf{x})$, then we could, as in the context of Chapters 3–6, treat this as a linear regression problem yielding the same estimators, inference procedures, and sampling properties as before. In Chapters 14 and 15 we will find that the results for the case of a general noise covariance matrix also apply as well as ML results in this case when the model is parametric in nature. Therefore, under regularity conditions relating to the independence, or at least contemporaneous uncorrelatedness of **X** and ε with $E[\varepsilon \mid \mathbf{X}] = \mathbf{0}$, effectively all of the previous results for estimation and inference in the linear regression model apply whether **X** is random or fixed.

In this chapter we have also enlarged the set of estimation and inference procedures to include moment estimators based on estimating functions that do not rely on strong distributional assumptions. In this context, we examined estimators under the conditions that the zero correlation or orthogonality assumption $E[\mathbf{X}'\varepsilon] = \mathbf{0}$ holds. In each case, the estimators were functions of the sample moments and had the desirable properties of consistency and asymptotic normality. Hypothesis-testing and confidence-region estimation followed the usual asymptotic approach based on the asymptotic normality of the estimators.

From an historical standpoint, Godambe and Heyde (1987) note that Gauss (in 1821–1823) developed the Gauss–Markov theorem using only the "first two moments" of the underlying distribution. Thus, it is important to note that the optimality, in finite samples, of least-squares estimators depends on assumptions concerning only the first two moments but is otherwise independent of the distributional form. On the other hand, maximum likelihood generally depends on the entire distributional form. Thus, as Godambe and Heyde note, the observation that the methods of maximum likelihood and least squares give identical results if the distribution is normal contains the germ of the modern theory of quasi-likelihood and leads to the concept of basing estimator definitions on a set of estimating equations. This is consistent with the method of moments approach that subsumes the least-squares procedure under appropriate moment conditions.

In the next chapter we introduce the closely related quasi-ML and estimating equations approaches to estimation and inference.

10.8. Exercises

10.8.1. Idea Checklist – Knowledge Guides

---

1. What are some of the reasons, in an economic context, why regressors may be stochastic as opposed to fixed?
2. What are the principal statistical implications of having stochastic, as opposed to fixed explanatory variables, if it is assumed they are independent of, or uncorrelated with, the noise component?
3. Given that the noise covariance matrix is $\sigma^2\mathbf{I}$, is the dependent variable $\mathbf{Y}$ more or less variable when $\mathbf{X}$ is random as opposed to fixed? Why?
4. Under the conditions of the preceding question, is the LS estimator of $\boldsymbol{\beta}$ more or less variable when $\mathbf{X}$ is random as opposed to fixed? Why?
5. What is meant by the statement that the case of a fixed explanatory variable matrix is a special case of a random explanatory variable matrix?
6. Discuss the claim that most estimators are functions of moment-based sample information.
7. What is the primary motivation for defining estimation and testing procedures in terms of solutions to moment-type equations?
8. Does the analyst lose information, or condition the type of information that can be recovered, when he or she transforms from the data to the moments and utilizes only moment information in the definition of estimators and testing procedures?
9. Is it possible to use the score function to give a finite sample justification for the ML estimator? For an answer to this question you may have to wait until Chapter 11.

10.8.2. Problems

10–1 Let $\mathbf{Y} = \mathbf{X}\boldsymbol{\beta} + \boldsymbol{\varepsilon}$ and $\hat{\boldsymbol{\varepsilon}} = \mathbf{Y} - \mathbf{X}\hat{\boldsymbol{\beta}} = \mathbf{Y} - \mathbf{X}(\mathbf{X}'\mathbf{X})^{-1}\mathbf{X}'\mathbf{Y}$. Assume that $n^{-1}\mathbf{X}'\boldsymbol{\varepsilon} \xrightarrow{p} \mathbf{0}$, $n^{-1}\mathbf{X}'\mathbf{Y} \xrightarrow{p} \boldsymbol{\Sigma}_{\mathbf{xy}}$, and $n^{-1}\mathbf{X}'\mathbf{X} \xrightarrow{p} \boldsymbol{\Sigma}_{\mathbf{xx}}$, where $\boldsymbol{\Sigma}_{\mathbf{xx}}$ is nonsingular. Show that $n^{-1}\hat{\boldsymbol{\varepsilon}}'\hat{\boldsymbol{\varepsilon}} \xrightarrow{p} \sigma^2$.

10–2 When $\mathbf{X}$ is random, it is generally not the case that $\mathbf{cov}(\mathbf{Y}) = \sigma^2\mathbf{I}$ when $\mathbf{cov}(\boldsymbol{\varepsilon}) = \sigma^2\mathbf{I}$. Why not? Define the unconditional covariance matrix of $\mathbf{Y}$ in this case.

10–3 When $\mathbf{cov}(\boldsymbol{\varepsilon}) = \sigma^2\mathbf{I}$, and under the other assumptions made in this chapter, one can show that $\mathrm{E}(\mathbf{Y} - \mathbf{X}\boldsymbol{\beta})(\mathbf{Y} - \mathbf{X}\boldsymbol{\beta})' = \sigma^2\mathbf{I}$. Does this contradict the condition in the preceding problem? Why not?

10–4 Regarding the ML procedure applied under conditional normality, as in Section 10.3.3, state and defend the asymptotic properties that can be attributed to the ML estimators of $\boldsymbol{\beta}$ and σ^2. Derive the form of the GLR test of the hypothesis $\mathbf{c}\boldsymbol{\beta} = \mathbf{r}$ and identify its finite and asymptotic properties.

10–5 For the two-parameter log-normal distribution, derive the MOM estimators of $\boldsymbol{\beta}$ and σ^2. How do the MOM estimators compare with the ML estimators of $\boldsymbol{\beta}$ and σ^2 derived in Problem 1 of section 9.5.2?

10.8.3. Computer Exercises

---

1. On the basis of results presented in this chapter, how do the statistical properties of confidence regions based on the T, F, or GLR tests compare with those of similar regions formed in the

nonstochastic case? Using the GAUSS program C10Tests.gss as a guide, conduct a Monte Carlo simulation of the coverage probabilities achieved by confidence regions based on the T, F, or GLR test statistics with stochastic **X**.

2. Use the GAUSS program C10LS2.gss from Example 10.3.2 as a guide and rewrite the programs used in Examples 10.3.1 and 10.4.1 to simulate the properties of the LS estimator by paired bootstrap procedure. How do the paired bootstrap resampling results compare with the Monte Carlo simulation results?
3. Construct a Monte Carlo experiment designed to simulate the properties of the LS estimator when the set of stochastic explanatory variables is correlated with the model disturbances. Hint: Consider a simple slope–intercept model in which the single explanatory variable is generated as $X = \alpha + \rho\varepsilon + \omega$ for some choice of α, ρ, and pseudorandom noise processes ε and ω such that $E[\varepsilon\omega] = 0$. If the variance of ε is σ^2, what is the covariance of ε and X?
4. Conduct a Monte Carlo exercise to simulate the sampling properties of the ML and MOM estimators for the log-normal model. How do the estimators compare as the sample size (n) increases?
5. Using the paired nonparametric bootstrap procedure for stochastic **X** from Example 10.3.2, repeat Computer Exercise 2 in Chapter 8. How does the bootstrap estimate of the covariance matrix for the NLS estimator compare with the estimated asymptotic covariance matrix under nonstochastic **X**?

10.9. References

Engle, R. F., D. F. Hendry, and J.-F. Richard (1983), "Exogeneity," *Econometrica*, Vol. 21, pp. 277–304.

Godambe, V. P. (1997), "Estimating Functions: A Synthesis of Least Squares and Maximum Likelihood Methods," in *Selected Proceedings of the Symposium on Estimation Functions*, I. V. Basawa, V. P. Godambe, and R. L. Taylor (Eds.), Vol. 32, Institute of Mathematical Statistics Lecture Notes–Monograph Series, Hayward, CA, pp. 5–16.

Godambe, V. B., and C. C. Heyde (1987), "Quasi-Likelihood and Optimal Estimators," *International Statistical Review*, Vol. 55, pp. 231–44.

Heyde, C. C. (1997), "Avoiding the Likelihood," in *Selected Proceedings of the Symposium on Estimation Functions*, I. V. Basawa, V. P. Godambe, and R. L. Taylor (Eds.), Vol. 32, Institute of Mathematical Statistics Lecture Notes-Monograph Series, Hayward, CA, pp. 35–42.

McCullagh, P., and J. A. Nelder (1989), *Generalized Linear Models*, 2nd ed., London: Chapman and Hall.

Mittelhammer, R. C. (1996), *Mathematical Statistics for Economics and Business*, New York: Springer–Verlag.

White, H. (1984), *Asymptotic Theory for Econometricians*, Orlando, FL: Academic Press.

White, H. (1994), *Estimation, Inference, and Specification Analysis*, New York: Cambridge University Press.

10.10. Appendix: Proofs

THEOREM PROOF 10.3.1: Because $n^{-1}\mathbf{X}'\mathbf{X} \xrightarrow{p} \Xi$ and the determinant is a continuous function of the elements of the matrix, it follows that $\det(n^{-1}\mathbf{X}'\mathbf{X}) \xrightarrow{p} \det(\Xi) > 0$, which is positive owing to the positive definite character of Ξ. Therefore, with probability converging to 1, the determinant of $n^{-1}\mathbf{X}'\mathbf{X}$ is positive and $\hat{\boldsymbol{\beta}} = (n^{-1}\mathbf{X}'\mathbf{X})^{-1}n^{-1}\mathbf{X}'\mathbf{Y}$ exists. Consistency follows from the fact that

$$\hat{\boldsymbol{\beta}} = \boldsymbol{\beta} + (n^{-1}\mathbf{X}'\mathbf{X})^{-1}n^{-1}\mathbf{X}'\varepsilon \xrightarrow{\text{p}} \boldsymbol{\beta} + \Xi^{-1}\mathbf{0} = \boldsymbol{\beta}. \tag{10.10.1}$$

■

THEOREM PROOF 10.3.2: We can express S^2 as

$$S^2 = (n-k)^{-1}(\mathbf{Y} - \mathbf{X}\hat{\boldsymbol{\beta}})'(\mathbf{Y} - \mathbf{X}\hat{\boldsymbol{\beta}})$$
$$= (n-k)^{-1}[\varepsilon'\varepsilon - \varepsilon'\mathbf{X}(\mathbf{X}'\mathbf{X})^{-1}\mathbf{X}'\varepsilon] \tag{10.10.2}$$

The right-hand side of (10.10.2) can be written as

$$\left(\frac{n}{n-k}\right)[(n^{-1}\varepsilon'\varepsilon) - (n^{-1}\varepsilon'\mathbf{X})(n^{-1}\mathbf{X}'\mathbf{X})^{-1}(n^{-1}\mathbf{X}'\varepsilon)]. \tag{10.10.3}$$

Then, because $n^{-1}\mathbf{X}'\varepsilon \xrightarrow{\text{p}} \mathbf{0}$, $[(n^{-1}(\mathbf{X}'\mathbf{X}))]^{-1} \xrightarrow{\text{p}} \Xi^{-1}$, $n^{-1}\varepsilon'\varepsilon \xrightarrow{\text{p}} \sigma^2$, and $(\frac{n}{n-k}) \to 1$, it follows immediately that $S^2 \xrightarrow{\text{p}} \sigma^2$. ■

THEOREM PROOF 10.3.3: The estimator $\hat{\boldsymbol{\beta}}$ can be expressed as $\hat{\boldsymbol{\beta}} = \boldsymbol{\beta} + (\mathbf{X}'\mathbf{X})^{-1}\mathbf{X}'\varepsilon$, and thus

$$n^{1/2}(\hat{\boldsymbol{\beta}} - \boldsymbol{\beta}) = (n^{-1}\mathbf{X}'\mathbf{X})^{-1}n^{-1/2}\mathbf{X}'\varepsilon. \tag{10.10.4}$$

Because $(n^{-1}\mathbf{X}'\mathbf{X})^{-1} \xrightarrow{\text{p}} \Xi^{-1}$ and $n^{-1/2}\mathbf{X}'\varepsilon \xrightarrow{\text{d}} \mathbf{Z} \sim \text{N}(\mathbf{0}, \sigma^2\Xi)$, it follows from Slutsky's theorem and results on linear combinations of normally distributed random variables that $n^{1/2}(\hat{\boldsymbol{\beta}} - \boldsymbol{\beta}) \xrightarrow{\text{d}} \Xi^{-1}\mathbf{Z} \sim (\mathbf{0}, \sigma^2\Xi^{-1})$. ■

CHAPTER 11

Quasi-Maximum Likelihood and Estimating Equations

In 1805 Legendre introduced the least-squares (LS) method, and around 1925 Fisher presented the concept of maximum likelihood. Both of these methods today play an important role in statistical–econometric methodology. These estimation and inference concepts also represent an important part of our discussion of estimations and inference procedures developed in Chapters 1–9. In this chapter, in recognition of the imperfect knowledge that surrounds most empirical analyses of data-sampling processes, we pursue the question of whether, and to what extent, likelihood-based techniques can be replaced, avoided, or generalized beyond the need for full parametric specifications of distributional assumptions. Furthermore, we consider whether, and in what sense, it is advantageous to make minimal assumptions on models, perhaps specifying only lower-order moments of the data such as means and covariance structure. Thus, we continue the theme begun in Chapter 10 of trying to avoid assumptions in the probability model specification that we do not wish to make.

Given the preceding areas of inquiry, in this chapter we generalize the concept of maximum likelihood by introducing two alternative yet closely related approaches to estimation and inference: the quasi-maximum likelihood (QML) and estimating equation (EE) approaches. In the process we bring about a synthesis of the least-squares and maximum likelihood estimation methodologies. There are two principal reasons for studying the QML approach that are prevalent in the statistical literature. For one, QML can be viewed as the study of the robustness of the ML approach to estimation and inference when the likelihood function is misspecified (e.g., see White, 1982, 1994). In this context, we will see that even if the PDF family is misspecified in the sense of the probability model's *not* encompassing the true DSP, it is still possible for an extremum estimator based on the likelihood function associated with the misspecified PDF family to possess good asymptotic properties. From this perspective the quasi(pseudo)-ML estimator can be viewed as a method to use in cases of potentially misspecified likelihood functions and parametric PDF families. Alternatively, the QML approach is seen as a method of weakening or minimizing probability distribution assumptions by explicitly specifying only the conditional mean or conditional variance functions, or both, associated with the data. The QML parameter estimators share certain key features and sampling properties

Table 11.1. *Semiparametric Regression Models*

Model Component	Specific Characteristics	
$\mathbf{Y}$	RV Type:	continuous
	Range:	unlimited
	Y_i dimension:	univariate
	Moments:	$E[\mathbf{Y} \mid \mathbf{x}] = \mathbf{g}(\mathbf{x}, \boldsymbol{\beta})$, $\mathbf{cov}(\mathbf{Y} \mid \mathbf{x}) = \sigma^2 I$
$\eta(\mathbf{x}, \boldsymbol{\beta}, \varepsilon)$	Functional Form:	linear or nonlinear in $\mathbf{x}$ and $\boldsymbol{\beta}$ and additive in ε, where $\eta(\mathbf{x}, \boldsymbol{\beta}, \varepsilon) = \mathbf{g}(\mathbf{x}, \boldsymbol{\beta}) + \varepsilon$, $\mathbf{g}(\mathbf{x}, \boldsymbol{\beta}) \equiv [g(\mathbf{x}_{1\cdot}, \boldsymbol{\beta}), \ldots, g(\mathbf{x}_{n\cdot}, \boldsymbol{\beta})]'$ where $\mathbf{g}$ is twice continuously differentiable in $\boldsymbol{\beta}$.
$\mathbf{x}$	RV Type:	degenerate (fixed)
	Genesis:	exogenous to the model
$\boldsymbol{\beta}$	RV Type:	degenerate (fixed)
	Dimension:	finite (fixed)
ε	RV Type:	iid, or independent nonidentical
	Moments:	$E[\varepsilon \mid \mathbf{x}] = \mathbf{0}$, and $\mathbf{cov}(\varepsilon \mid \mathbf{x}) = \sigma^2\mathbf{I}$
Ω	Prior info:	none
$f(\mathbf{e} \mid \mathbf{x}, \varphi^2)$	PDF family:	unspecified

with the ML estimators (e.g., see Wedderburn, 1974; Godambe, 1960; Heyde, 1997; and Desmond 1997), and at least to the first order of asymptotics, there is a sensible QML alternative to, or generalization of, virtually any likelihood methodology.

The estimating equation approach, in its most general form, can be interpreted as subsuming all of the parameter estimators currently used in practice. An elegant finite sample optimality theory has been developed for estimating equations that leads to, among other things, a general *finite* sample justification for the use of the ML approach in cases in which the form of the likelihood function is known. In recent years, the EE approach has also been used to *characterize* the class of QML estimators for a given probability model. In this context, the EE characterization leads to the finite sample optimality of the QML approach in the case in which the form of the likelihood function is not known (e.g., Godambe and Heyde, 1987; Heyde, 1994, 1997; Gourieroux, Monfort, and Trognon, 1984a and b). A main lesson of the estimation function theory is to deemphasize focusing primary attention on the form and properties of parameter estimators per se and to focus attention instead on the optimality of the estimating functions used to characterize estimators.

In terms of the general class of probability models discussed in this chapter, we will be concerned with the special cases delineated in Table 11.1.

The particular inverse problem associated with the probability models in Table 11.1 continues to be one of recovering information on the unknown and unobservable $(\boldsymbol{\beta}, \sigma^2, \varepsilon)$ from sample outcomes of $(\mathbf{Y}, \mathbf{x})$.

11.1. Quasi-Maximum Likelihood Estimation and Inference

Is it possible for an extremum estimator based on a likelihood function associated with a parametric PDF family to possess good asymptotic properties even if the PDF family is *misspecified* in the sense of not encompassing the true PDF of **Y**? Relatedly, is it possible for an analyst to specify only the conditional mean or conditional variance function, or both, relating to a DSP, and then perform a maximum likelihood-like estimation of the parameters in the absence of an explicitly defined likelihood function? These questions frame the problem area of *quasi-maximum likelihood* (QML) estimation (also sometimes referred to as pseudo-ML estimation), which is concerned with methods of generating consistent and asymptotically normal estimators for model parameters of potentially *misspecified* parametric likelihood functions or models for which only conditional moment functions have been specified.

For example, we have already seen that the assumption of normality in a linear or nonlinear regression model implies that the $\boldsymbol{\beta}$ vector of the model is estimated by linear or nonlinear least squares, respectively, when the ML procedure is employed. We have also seen that the LS or NLS estimators achieve consistency and asymptotic normality under general regularity conditions that *do not require normality*. Furthermore, the ML estimator for σ^2 under the normality assumption is based on the LS or NLS estimator of $\boldsymbol{\beta}$, and we know that this estimator of σ^2 is consistent and asymptotically normally distributed under general regularity conditions that also do not require the assumption of normality of the probability model distribution.

Thus, we have our first example of a *quasi*-ML estimator. In particular, we act *as if* the PDF of **Y** is in the normal parametric family, *even if we are not confident that it really is*, and we derive the ML estimates of the parameters from the normal-based likelihood function. *Within the regression model context, we achieve consistency and asymptotic normality under general conditions even if the likelihood function is misspecified. If the PDF specification happens to be correct, we generally gain the ML property of asymptotic efficiency*. As the reader might suspect, this observation grants the analyst wide latitude in invoking the normality assumption in regression-type models. Further, one sacrifices ML asymptotic efficiency only if one actually knows the correct parametric family of PDFs for **Y** but does not use this information in the ML estimation problem and instead uses a QML estimator. In the case where the analyst does not know the correct parametric family of PDFs for **Y**, then for all practical purposes the question of ML asymptotic efficiency is moot – one need not lament the loss of ML asymptotic efficiency when there is no basis for achieving it. We will see (in the discussion of the interrelationships between QML and EE estimation in Section 11.2) that the QML estimator achieves a restricted form of asymptotic efficiency within the class of QML estimators under consideration in a particular problem.

The QML–extremum (QML–E) approach achieves consistency and asymptotic normality for a wider array of problems than just regression models. The general rationale underlying the achievement of these asymptotic properties is rooted in the fact that QML estimators derived from maximizing some form of likelihood function are fundamentally extremum estimators. In this context, the quasi-likelihood function acts in some sense as a general estimation objective function that measures proximity of an estimated parameter value to the true parameter value. Under appropriate regularity conditions on the QML–E estimation objective function, such as those discussed in Chapter 7, the QML–E estimator will be consistent and asymptotically normally distributed whether or not the quasi-likelihood function happens to coincide with the true likelihood-joint PDF of the random sample underlying the observed data. So in QML–E estimation, the issue is not whether the likelihood is correctly specified vis-à-vis the true joint PDF of the underlying sampling process. Rather, the issue is whether the quasi-likelihood function is specified appropriately relative to extremum estimation regularity conditions that lead to useful estimators of parameters possessing at least the properties of consistency and asymptotic normality.

We now examine sampling properties of QML estimators and inference procedures. In our discussion of QML in the next section, we concentrate on QML estimators that are defined via maximizing (possibly incorrectly specified) likelihood functions, and we aptly refer to these estimators as QML–extremum (QML–E) estimators. Later, in our discussion of EE estimation in Section 11.3, we will return to the QML estimation context and examine the concept of QML estimators characterized by the solution of quasi-score functions defined in terms of estimating equations. It is in the EE context that optimality properties of the QML estimator will be established.

11.2. QML–E Estimation and Inference

The general results relating to achieving consistency and asymptotic normality based on a QML–E estimator parallel those discussed for the ML–extremum estimator, as presented in Section 7.4. We provide an overview of the basic arguments here and draw liberally on previous results for details. We also discuss the asymptotic properties of the QML–E estimator when consistency is not achieved and indicate that the QML estimator will still generally possess the useful property of representing the best approximation to the true PDF of the random sample in addition to retaining asymptotic normality.

11.2.1. Consistency and Asymptotic Normality

Let $\mathrm{L_Q}(\boldsymbol{\theta};\mathbf{y},\mathbf{x})$ denote a quasi-likelihood function based on a postulated joint PDF for the random sample $\mathbf{Y}\mid\mathbf{x}$ that may or may not coincide with the true PDF of $\mathbf{Y}\mid\mathbf{x}$. The QML–E estimator of $\boldsymbol{\theta}$ is defined in the typical way extremum estimators are defined as

$$\hat{\boldsymbol{\Theta}} = \arg\max_{\boldsymbol{\theta}\in\Omega}[\mathrm{m}(\boldsymbol{\theta},\mathbf{Y},\mathbf{x})] = \arg\max_{\boldsymbol{\theta}\in\Omega}[n^{-1}\ln \mathrm{L_Q}(\boldsymbol{\theta};\mathbf{Y},\mathbf{x})], \qquad (11.2.1)$$

where $\mathrm{m}(\boldsymbol{\theta},\mathbf{Y},\mathbf{x}) \equiv n^{-1}\ln \mathrm{L_Q}(\boldsymbol{\theta};\mathbf{Y},\mathbf{x})$.

A general theorem on the consistency of the QML–E estimator can be obtained by simply replacing $\mathrm{L}(\boldsymbol{\theta};\mathbf{Y},\mathbf{x})$ in Theorem 7.4.1 with the quasi-likelihood alternative given by $\mathrm{L_Q}(\boldsymbol{\theta};\mathbf{Y},\mathbf{x})$. A general consistency theorem for the QML–E that does not require that the parameter space be compact can be obtained from the general consistency result for extremum estimators by simply replacing $\mathrm{m}(\boldsymbol{\theta},\mathbf{Y},\mathbf{x})$ by $n^{-1}\mathrm{L_Q}(\boldsymbol{\theta};\mathbf{Y},\mathbf{x})$ in Theorem 7.3.2.

Asymptotic normality of the QML–E estimator follows directly by again replacing $L(\boldsymbol{\theta}; \mathbf{Y}, \mathbf{x})$ by the quasi-likelihood $L_Q(\boldsymbol{\theta}; \mathbf{Y}, \mathbf{x})$ in the statement of Theorem 7.4.2. The appropriate normal limiting distribution result is given by

$$n^{1/2}(\hat{\boldsymbol{\Theta}}_{QML} - \boldsymbol{\theta}_0) \xrightarrow{d} N(\mathbf{0}, \mathbf{h}(\boldsymbol{\theta}_0)^{-1}\boldsymbol{\Sigma}\mathbf{h}(\boldsymbol{\theta}_0)^{-1}), \tag{11.2.2}$$

where the symbols are as defined in Theorem 7.4.2 mutatis mutandis. We address the issue of consistent estimation of the asymptotic covariance matrix in Section 11.2.3.

Consider the special case in which the likelihood function is correctly specified in the sense that the PDF family on which the likelihood function is based contains the true PDF corresponding to the data-sampling process. Under general regularity conditions that ensure the asymptotic normality of the ML estimator (White, 1982) $\boldsymbol{\Sigma} = -\mathbf{h}(\boldsymbol{\theta}_0)$, and thus the familiar asymptotic normality result for ML estimation is obtained for the QML–E estimator as follows:

$$n^{1/2}(\hat{\boldsymbol{\Theta}}_{QML} - \boldsymbol{\theta}_0) \xrightarrow{d} N(\mathbf{0}, \boldsymbol{\Sigma}^{-1}) = N\left(\mathbf{0}, \operatorname*{plim}_{n\to\infty}\left(-\left[\frac{1}{n}\frac{\partial^2 \ln L_Q(\boldsymbol{\theta}; \mathbf{Y}, \mathbf{x})}{\partial\boldsymbol{\theta}\partial\boldsymbol{\theta}'}\bigg|_{\boldsymbol{\theta}_0}\right]^{-1}\right)\right). \tag{11.2.3}$$

However, unless the quasi-likelihood is in fact a correctly specified likelihood, the covariance matrix given in (11.2.3) is generally not the correct covariance matrix for the limiting distribution associated with the QML estimator. Thus, unless the analyst is confident of the functional specification of the likelihood function, the asymptotic covariance matrix defined in (11.2.2) should not be simplified to that in (11.2.3).

We now examine specific conditions on the quasi-likelihood specification that allow consistency and asymptotic normality to be achieved within the general regression model framework.

11.2.2. True PDF Approximation Property and Asymptotic Normality of Inconsistent QML–E Estimators

It is important to consider what, if any, useful properties can be attributed to the QML estimator in the case in which the estimator is based on a quasi-likelihood specification that does not possess sufficient regularity to allow consistency to be achieved. It turns out that even in this case, the QML estimator will generally produce estimates that narrow the analyst's ignorance regarding the true PDF underlying the data-sampling process in a meaningful way.

To provide an overview of the sense in which the QML estimator approximates the true PDF of the random sample, it is necessary to have a basic understanding of Kullback–Leibler discrepancy, which is a measure of the proximity of one probability distribution to another. It is sufficient for our current purposes to indicate only some of the basic properties of the measure, but the interested reader can consult Chapters 13 and electronic Chapter E3 for additional details. The concept will also be used again in Chapter 18 in the context of model discovery issues.

Let p($\mathbf{y}$) and $\pi(\mathbf{y})$ be two probability distributions for the random variable $\mathbf{Y}$. The Kullback–Leibler discrepancy of p($\mathbf{y}$) relative to $\pi(\mathbf{y})$ is defined by

$$\mathrm{KL}(\mathrm{p}, \pi) = \mathrm{E_p}\{\ln[\mathrm{p}(\mathbf{y})/\pi(\mathbf{y})]\}, \tag{11.2.4}$$

where $\mathrm{E_p}[]$ denotes an expectation taken with respect to the distribution p($\mathbf{y}$). For the discrepancy measure to be finite-valued, the support of p($\mathbf{y}$) must be a subset of the support of $\pi(\mathbf{y})$ (i.e., $\pi(\mathbf{y}) = 0$ for some y necessarily implies $\mathrm{p}(\mathbf{y}) = 0$). The KL discrepancy measure has several useful statistical properties (Kullback and Leibler, 1951 and Kullback, 1959). Of principal interest currently is the fact that $\mathrm{KL}(\mathrm{p}, \pi) \geq 0$, $\mathrm{KL}(\mathrm{p}, \pi)$ is a strictly convex function of $\mathrm{p} \geq 0$, and $\mathrm{KL}(\mathrm{p}, \pi) = 0$ iff $\mathrm{p}(\mathbf{y}) = \pi(\mathbf{y})$ for every $\mathbf{y}$. The closer $\mathrm{KL}(\mathrm{p}, \pi)$ is to zero, the more similar is the distribution p($\mathbf{y}$) relative to $\pi(\mathbf{y})$, and the distributions coincide only when $\mathrm{KL}(\mathrm{p}, \pi) = 0$. The greater the value of $\mathrm{KL}(\mathrm{p}, \pi)$, the greater the discrepancy between the distributions p($\mathbf{y}$) and $\pi(\mathbf{y})$.

Regarding the QML estimator, suppose that the true PDF underlying the data-sampling process is given by p($\mathbf{y}$) and the analyst bases the definition of the quasi-likelihood function on the PDF family $\pi(\mathbf{y}; \boldsymbol{\theta})$ for $\boldsymbol{\theta} \in \Omega_{\mathrm{Q}}$. Define $\boldsymbol{\theta}_*$ to be the value of θ that minimizes the Kullback–Leibler discrepancy of p($\mathbf{y}$) relative to $\pi(\mathbf{y}; \theta)$, that is,

$$\boldsymbol{\theta}_* = \arg\min_{\boldsymbol{\theta} \in \Omega_{\mathrm{Q}}}[\mathrm{KL}(\mathrm{p}, \pi; \boldsymbol{\theta})] = \arg\min_{\boldsymbol{\theta} \in \Omega_{\mathrm{Q}}}[\mathrm{E_p}[\ln(\mathrm{p}(\mathbf{y})/\pi(\mathbf{y}; \boldsymbol{\theta}))]]. \tag{11.2.5}$$

Thus, $\boldsymbol{\theta}_*$ is the parameter value associated with the quasi-likelihood specification that results in the least Kullback–Leibler discrepancy between the true PDF underlying the data-sampling process and the set of PDF candidates available from within the analyst's quasi-likelihood specification of the probability model. In effect, $\pi(\mathbf{y}; \boldsymbol{\theta}_*)$ is the best approximation of p($\mathbf{y}$) possible within the scope of the PDF candidates contained within the analyst's probability model. Under general regularity conditions no more restrictive than those required to achieve the usual asymptotic properties of ML estimators (White, 1982 and 1994, pp. 31–2), it follows that

$$\hat{\boldsymbol{\theta}}_{\mathrm{QML}} \xrightarrow{\mathrm{p}} \boldsymbol{\theta}_* \tag{11.2.6}$$

and thus the QML estimator consistently estimates $\boldsymbol{\theta}_*$. In other words, the QML estimator consistently estimates the particular value of the parameter $\boldsymbol{\theta}$ that provides the closest match possible (in terms of Kullback–Leibler discrepancy) between the analyst's probability model for $\mathbf{Y}$ and the true PDF for $\mathbf{Y}$. In the event that the PDF family $\pi(\mathbf{y}; \boldsymbol{\theta})$ for $\boldsymbol{\theta} \in \Omega_{\mathrm{Q}}$ contains p($\mathbf{y}$) for some $\boldsymbol{\theta}_0 \in \Omega_{\mathrm{Q}}$, so that $\pi(\mathbf{y}; \boldsymbol{\theta}_0) = \mathrm{p}(\mathbf{y})$, then $\boldsymbol{\theta}_* = \boldsymbol{\theta}_0$ and the QML estimator will consistently estimate the "true value" of $\boldsymbol{\theta}$ represented by $\boldsymbol{\theta}_0$.

It also follows, again under conditions no more restrictive than those required to achieve the usual asymptotic properties of ML estimators (White 1982, and 1994, Section 6.1) that the QML is asymptotically normally distributed as

$$n^{1/2}(\hat{\boldsymbol{\Theta}}_{\mathrm{QML}} - \boldsymbol{\theta}_*) \xrightarrow{\mathrm{d}} \mathrm{N}[\mathbf{0}, \mathbf{h}(\boldsymbol{\theta}_*)^{-1}\boldsymbol{\Sigma}_*\mathbf{h}(\boldsymbol{\theta}_*)^{-1}], \tag{11.2.7}$$

where symbols are as defined in Theorem 7.4.2 with $\boldsymbol{\theta}_*$ replacing $\boldsymbol{\theta}_0$, $\boldsymbol{\Sigma}_*$ defined by $n^{-1/2}\frac{\partial \ln \mathrm{L_Q}(\boldsymbol{\theta}; \mathbf{Y}, \mathbf{x})}{\partial \boldsymbol{\theta}}\Big|_{\boldsymbol{\theta}_*} \xrightarrow{\mathrm{d}} \mathrm{N}(\mathbf{0}, \boldsymbol{\Sigma}_*)$ and $\mathbf{h}(\boldsymbol{\theta}_*)$ defined by $n^{-1}\frac{\partial^2 \ln \mathrm{L_Q}(\boldsymbol{\theta}; \mathbf{Y}, \mathbf{x})}{\partial \boldsymbol{\theta}\partial \boldsymbol{\theta}'}\Big|_{\boldsymbol{\theta}_*} \xrightarrow{\mathrm{p}} \mathbf{h}(\boldsymbol{\theta}_*)$. Thus, although the asymptotic distribution of the QML estimator may not be centered on the true value of $\boldsymbol{\theta}$, the QML estimator is generally asymptotically normally distributed, and its distribution is centered on the value of $\boldsymbol{\theta}$ that provides the least Kullback–Leibler discrepancy between the analyst's probability model and the true PDF underlying the data-sampling process.

11.2.3. Consistent Estimation of the Asymptotic Covariance Matrix

On the assumption that the QML estimator converges to $\boldsymbol{\theta}_*$ or $\boldsymbol{\theta}_0$, the asymptotic covariance matrix given in (11.2.2) or (11.2.7) can be consistently estimated from sample observations. In particular, under the prevailing assumptions, the $\mathbf{h}(\boldsymbol{\theta}_*)$ or $\mathbf{h}(\boldsymbol{\theta}_0)$ matrix can be estimated by $\hat{\mathbf{h}}(\boldsymbol{\theta}_*)$ (or $\hat{\mathbf{h}}(\boldsymbol{\theta}_0)) = n^{-1}\frac{\partial^2 \ln \mathrm{L_Q}(\boldsymbol{\theta}; \mathbf{Y}, \mathbf{x})}{\partial\boldsymbol{\theta}\partial\boldsymbol{\theta}'}\Big|_{\hat{\boldsymbol{\theta}}_{\mathrm{QML}}}$. The $\boldsymbol{\Sigma}$ or $\boldsymbol{\Sigma}_*$ matrix can be estimated by $\hat{\boldsymbol{\Sigma}}$ (or $\hat{\boldsymbol{\Sigma}}_*) = n^{-1}\sum_{i=1}^{n}[\frac{\partial \ln \mathrm{L_Q}(\boldsymbol{\theta}; \mathrm{Y}_i, \mathbf{x}_{i\cdot})}{\partial\boldsymbol{\theta}}\Big|_{\hat{\boldsymbol{\theta}}_{\mathrm{QML}}} \frac{\partial \ln \mathrm{L_Q}(\boldsymbol{\theta}; \mathrm{Y}_i, \mathbf{x}_{i\cdot})}{\partial\boldsymbol{\theta}'}\Big|_{\hat{\boldsymbol{\theta}}_{\mathrm{QML}}}]$. Then, substituting these estimates into the asymptotic covariance matrices displayed in (11.2.2) or (11.2.7) provides consistent estimates of the covariance matrices. If the likelihood function is correctly specified and (11.2.3) applies, then $-[\hat{\mathbf{h}}(\boldsymbol{\theta}_0)]^{-1}$ can be used as the covariance matrix estimate.

11.2.4. Necessary and Sufficient Conditions for Consistency and Asymptotic Normality

Specific results regarding the types of quasi-likelihood specifications that will allow the QML estimator actually to achieve consistency and asymptotic normality in the estimation of $\boldsymbol{\theta}_0$ have been derived by Gourieroux et al. (1984a) for two very important cases. Note that Gourieroux et al. use the terminology pseudo-maximum likelihood in their work. The cases are distinguished by whether the analyst's probability model specifies the parametric representation of only the conditional mean $\mathrm{E}(\mathrm{Y}_i \mid \mathbf{x}_{i\cdot}) = \mathrm{g}(\mathbf{x}_{i\cdot}, \boldsymbol{\theta})$ (Case 1, or QML–E of Order 1) or whether the model *also* specifies the parametric representation of the conditional variance, $\mathrm{var}(\mathrm{Y}_i \mid \mathbf{x}_{i\cdot}) = \sigma^2(\mathbf{x}_{i\cdot}, \boldsymbol{\theta})$ (Case 2, or QML–E of Order 2). Note for future reference that these cases also apply to a *vector* $\mathbf{Y}_i$, in which case the analyst will specify parameterizations for the mean *vector* for Case 1 and also a *covariance matrix* for Case 2. Also note that in all of the probability models examined so far, with the exception of the Cauchy model in Section 9.2.2, we have $\sigma^2(\mathbf{x}_{i\cdot}, \boldsymbol{\theta}) \equiv \sigma^2\ \forall i$.

If the Y_i's are assumed to be independent, the QML–E of $\boldsymbol{\theta}$ for Case 1 is defined by the extremum estimator

$$\hat{\boldsymbol{\Theta}}_{\mathrm{QML}} = \arg\max_{\boldsymbol{\theta}\in\Omega_{\mathrm{Q}}}\left[\sum_{i=1}^{n} \ln \mathrm{f_Q}(\mathrm{Y}_i; \mathrm{g}(\mathbf{x}_{i\cdot}, \boldsymbol{\theta}))\right]$$
$$= \arg\max_{\boldsymbol{\theta}\in\Omega_{\mathrm{Q}}}[\mathrm{L_Q}(\boldsymbol{\theta}; \mathbf{Y}, \mathbf{x})], \qquad (11.2.8)$$

where the subscript Q denotes that the PDF $\mathrm{f_Q}[\mathrm{Y}_i; \mathrm{g}(\mathbf{x}_{i\cdot}, \boldsymbol{\theta})]$ is a quasi-specification of the PDF of Y_i. That is, the specified family of PDFs defined for $\boldsymbol{\theta} \in \Omega_{\mathrm{Q}}$ does not necessarily encompass the true PDF of Y_i, and thus $\mathrm{L_Q}$ again denotes a *quasi-likelihood*, being potentially a misspecified likelihood function.

For the QML–E of Order 2, and again on the assumption that the Y_i's are independent, the QML estimator of $\boldsymbol{\theta}$ is defined by the extremum estimator

$$\begin{aligned}\hat{\boldsymbol{\Theta}}_{QML} &= \arg\max_{\boldsymbol{\theta}\in\Omega_Q}\left[\sum_{i=1}^{n}\ln f_Q(Y_i; g(\mathbf{x}_{i\cdot}, \boldsymbol{\theta}), \sigma^2(\mathbf{x}_{i\cdot}, \boldsymbol{\theta}))\right]. \\ &= \arg\max_{\boldsymbol{\theta}\in\Omega_Q}[L_Q(\boldsymbol{\theta}; \mathbf{Y}, \mathbf{x})]. \qquad (11.2.9)\end{aligned}$$

11.2.4.a. QML–E Consistency

The fundamental consistency result for Case 1 models is stated in the following theorem:

Theorem 11.2.1 (Consistency of QML–E Estimator of Order 1): *Under general regularity conditions, including the assumption that* $E(Y_i \mid \mathbf{x}_{i\cdot}) = g(\mathbf{x}_{i\cdot}, \boldsymbol{\theta})\ \forall i$, *the QML–E estimator of Order 1 (11.2.8) is consistent iff the quasi-likelihood function is based on a PDF family in the linear exponential class*

$$f_Q(w; g) = \exp[c(g)w + d(g) + z(y)], \qquad (11.2.10)$$

where $c(\cdot)$, $d(\cdot)$, *and* $z(\cdot)$ *are real-valued functions.*

PROOF: Gouriéroux et al. (1984a).

Thus, so long as the analyst bases the quasi-likelihood function specification on a PDF family contained within the linear exponential class, consistency of the QML–E estimator can be expected. The class contains a large number of PDFs used in practice, including the Bernoulli, Binomial (for n given), negative binomial (for r given), Poisson, Gamma (for α given), and univariate normal (for σ^2 given). It can also be extended to include the multivariate normal (for $\boldsymbol{\Sigma}$ given), which allows us to apply the QML–E approach to systems of regression functions. The principal regularity condition for Theorem 11.2.1 to hold is that there exists a $\boldsymbol{\theta} \in \Omega_Q$, say $\boldsymbol{\theta}_0$, such that $g(\mathbf{x}_{i\cdot}, \boldsymbol{\theta}_0)$ is the true conditional expectation of Y_i, given $\mathbf{x}_{i\cdot}$. Thus, *although the likelihood function can be misspecified, the conditional mean function must be correctly specified.* The value $\boldsymbol{\theta}_0$ can then be interpreted as the "true value" of $\boldsymbol{\theta}$ in the sense that it indexes the true conditional mean function.

The fundamental consistency result for Case 2 is as follows.

Theorem 11.2.2 (Consistency of QML–E Estimator of Order 2): *Under general regularity conditions, including the assumptions that* $E(Y_i \mid \mathbf{x}_{i\cdot}) = g(\mathbf{x}_{i\cdot}, \boldsymbol{\theta})$ *and* $\mathrm{var}(Y_i \mid \mathbf{x}_{i\cdot}) = \sigma^2(\mathbf{x}_{i\cdot}, \boldsymbol{\theta})\ \forall i$, *the QML estimator of Order 2 (11.2.9) is consistent iff the quasi-likelihood function is based on a PDF family in the quadratic exponential class*

$$f_Q(w; g, \sigma^2) = \exp[c(g, \sigma^2)w + d(g, \sigma^2) + z(y) + h(g, \sigma^2)w^2], \qquad (11.2.11)$$

where $c(\cdot)$, $d(\cdot)$, $z(\cdot)$, *and* $h(\cdot)$ *are real-valued functions.*

PROOF: Gouriéroux et al. (1984a).

Thus, as long as the analyst bases his or her quasi-likelihood function on a PDF family contained within the quadratic exponential class for QML–E estimators of Order 2, consistency of the QML–E estimator can be expected. The primary example of a PDF family encompassed by the quadratic exponential family is the normal distribution with both μ and σ^2 unknown. The result can be extended to encompass applications of the QML–E approach to systems of equations, in which case the multivariate normal distribution with both $\boldsymbol{\mu}$ and $\boldsymbol{\Sigma}$ unknown applies. Note that using a quasi-likelihood function based on the normal distribution in a Case 2 regression model for which $\sigma^2(\mathbf{x}_{i\cdot}, \boldsymbol{\theta}) = \sigma^2 \; \forall i$ invokes a nonlinear (or possibly linear) least-squares estimator for $\boldsymbol{\beta}$ and the usual estimator for σ^2 derived from it. The principal regularity conditions for Theorem 11.2.2 to hold are that there exist some $\boldsymbol{\theta} \in \Omega_Q$, say $\boldsymbol{\theta}_0$, such that $g(\mathbf{x}_{i\cdot}, \boldsymbol{\theta}_0)$ is the true conditional expectation of Y_i, given $\mathbf{x}_{i\cdot}$, and $\sigma^2(\mathbf{x}_{i\cdot}, \boldsymbol{\theta}_0)$ is the true conditional variance of Y_i, given $\mathbf{x}_{i\cdot}$. Thus, *although the likelihood function can be misspecified, the conditional mean and variance functions must be correctly specified.* The value $\boldsymbol{\theta}_0$ can then be interpreted as the "true value" of $\boldsymbol{\theta}$ in the sense that it indexes the true conditional mean and conditional variance functions.

11.2.4.b. QML–E Asymptotic Normality

Asymptotic normality results for QML–E estimators of both Order 1 and Order 2 are the same, as indicated in Theorem 11.2.3.

Theorem 11.2.3 (Asymptotic Normality of QML–E Estimators): *Under general regularity conditions, including the conditions of either Theorems 11.2.1 or 11.2.2, a consistent QML estimator of Order 1 or Order 2 is asymptotically normally distributed as*

$$n^{1/2}(\hat{\boldsymbol{\Theta}}_{QML} - \boldsymbol{\theta}_0) \xrightarrow{d} N[\mathbf{0}, \mathbf{h}^{-1}(\boldsymbol{\theta}_0)\boldsymbol{\Sigma}(\boldsymbol{\theta}_0)\mathbf{h}^{-1}(\boldsymbol{\theta}_0)], \tag{11.2.12}$$

where

$$h(\boldsymbol{\theta}_0) = \underset{n\to\infty}{\text{plim}} \left[\frac{1}{n} \frac{\partial^2 \ln L_Q(\boldsymbol{\theta}; \mathbf{Y}, \mathbf{x})}{\partial \boldsymbol{\theta} \partial \boldsymbol{\theta}'} \bigg|_{\boldsymbol{\theta}_0} \right] \tag{11.2.13}$$

and

$$\boldsymbol{\Sigma}(\boldsymbol{\theta}_0) = \underset{n\to\infty}{\text{plim}} \left[n^{-1} \sum_{i=1}^{n} \left[\frac{\partial \ln L_Q(\boldsymbol{\theta}; Y_i, x_i)}{\partial \boldsymbol{\theta}} \bigg|_{\boldsymbol{\theta}_0} \frac{\partial \ln L_Q(\boldsymbol{\theta}; Y_i, x_i)}{\partial \boldsymbol{\theta}'} \bigg|_{\boldsymbol{\theta}_0} \right] \right] \tag{11.2.14}$$

PROOF: Gourièroux et al. (1984a).

As usual the "true" parameter vector value $\boldsymbol{\theta}_0$ can be replaced by the consistent estimator $\hat{\boldsymbol{\theta}}_{\mathrm{QML}}$, and then (11.2.13) can be consistently estimated by

$$\mathrm{h}(\hat{\boldsymbol{\theta}}_{\mathrm{QML}}) = n^{-1}\left[\left.\frac{\partial^2 \ln \mathrm{L_Q}(\boldsymbol{\theta}; \mathbf{Y}, \mathbf{x})}{\partial \boldsymbol{\theta} \partial \boldsymbol{\theta}'}\right|_{\hat{\boldsymbol{\theta}}_{\mathrm{QML}}}\right] \tag{11.2.15}$$

The term $\boldsymbol{\Sigma}(\boldsymbol{\theta}_0)$ in (11.2.14) can be consistently estimated by

$$\boldsymbol{\Sigma}(\hat{\boldsymbol{\theta}}_{\mathrm{QML}}) = n^{-1}\sum_{i=1}^{n}\left[\left.\frac{\partial \ln \mathrm{L_Q}(\boldsymbol{\theta}; \mathrm{y}_i, \mathrm{x}_{i\cdot})}{\partial \boldsymbol{\theta}}\right|_{\hat{\boldsymbol{\theta}}_{\mathrm{QML}}} \left.\frac{\partial \ln \mathrm{L_Q}(\boldsymbol{\theta}; \mathrm{y}_i, \mathrm{x}_{i\cdot})}{\partial \boldsymbol{\theta}'}\right|_{\hat{\boldsymbol{\theta}}_{\mathrm{QML}}}\right]. \tag{11.2.16}$$

Substituting (11.2.15) and (11.2.16) into (11.2.12) defines a consistent estimate of the asymptotic covariance matrix of $\hat{\boldsymbol{\Theta}}_{\mathrm{QML}}$.

11.2.5. QML Inference

Theorem 11.2.3 permits asymptotic tests and confidence-region procedures to be defined based on asymptotic normality. In fact, these procedures are precisely as described in Section 7.6 for the extremum estimation case upon making the substitution $\mathrm{m}(\boldsymbol{\theta}, \mathbf{Y}, \mathbf{x}) \equiv n^{-1}\mathrm{L_Q}(\boldsymbol{\theta}; \mathbf{Y}, \mathbf{x})$, replacing $\boldsymbol{\theta}_0$ with $\boldsymbol{\theta}_*$, and replacing $\hat{\boldsymbol{\Theta}}$ with $\hat{\boldsymbol{\Theta}}_{\mathrm{QML}}$; therefore, this discussion will not be repeated here. We caution the reader, however, that although the Wald and Lagrange multiplier tests and confidence regions apply generally to the QML case, the pseudo (or quasi-) likelihood ratio tests and confidence regions procedures do not. The reason for this caution is that *the condition* $\boldsymbol{\Sigma} = \tau\mathbf{h}(\boldsymbol{\theta}_0)$ *needed to establish the Chi-square distribution of the pseudo-likelihood ratio statistic will not hold in general unless the likelihood function is properly specified*, which is to say, not unless the quasi-likelihood function is in fact a genuine likelihood function and one is actually performing ML as opposed to QML estimation (see Wooldridge, 1994, pp. 2685–6 and 2691 and White, 1982, p. 8, for additional details). Relatedly, the asymptotic covariance matrix in (11.2.12) *cannot* generally be simplified as it was in (11.2.3), where ML, and not QML, was assumed. With this proviso regarding the form of the asymptotic covariance matrix, test and confidence region construction can proceed as generally prescribed in the extremum estimation context.

A deeper conceptual caution is required relating to the interpretation of hypotheses and confidence regions about the value of the parameter vector $\boldsymbol{\theta}_*$ in the QML–E context. Because $\boldsymbol{\theta}_*$ may not be the "true" value of the parameter vector, the analyst must be cognizant of this fact when interpreting the result of a hypothesis test in the context of QML–E estimation. In particular, in these cases the analyst will in effect be testing hypotheses about the value of a parameter vector that represents the best approximation to the true value of the parameter vector (in the sense described previously) and not the true value per se. Thus, rejection of a hypothesis such as $\mathrm{H_0}\colon \mathbf{c}(\boldsymbol{\theta}) = \mathbf{r}$ may be reflecting the fact that $\mathbf{c}(\boldsymbol{\theta}_*) \neq \mathbf{r}$ rather than $\mathbf{c}(\boldsymbol{\theta}_0) \neq \mathbf{r}$. Unfortunately, the rejection of a hypothesis remains an open question unless the analyst has substantial confidence that the conditional mean, conditional variance functions, or both are correctly specified. If a correctly specified linear or quadratic exponential class PDF was used in defining the quasi-likelihood function, in which case $\boldsymbol{\theta}_* = \boldsymbol{\theta}_0$, there is no ambiguity in interpreting the hypothesis. An analogous caution applies to the interpretation of confidence regions.

11.2.6. QML Generalizations

The necessary and sufficient conditions for the QML–E estimator to achieve consistency and asymptotic normality in the Case 1 situation has been extended by White (1994, Chapters 5 and 6) to the case in which the sample observations are serially correlated and are thus not independent. The results are essentially the same as those in Theorems 11.2.1 and 11.2.3, where the linear exponential class must again be the PDF on which the quasi-likelihood function is based.

It is beyond the scope of this book to engage in a more detailed analysis of various general forms of QML–E estimators and the conditions needed for them to achieve desirable asymptotic properties. The interested reader can consult White (1982, 1994), Phillips (1976), and Wooldridge (1994) for additional details and references along these lines. Instead, our primary focus in this book will be on the one QML–E estimator that has no doubt been the one most often used in practice – the QML–E estimator based on the likelihood function associated with a normal PDF specification for $\mathbf{Y}$. A QML–E estimator of Order 1 is then defined when σ^2 is set by the analyst to a fixed real number in the normal PDF definition and the mean can be defined as some parameterized function of $\mathbf{x}$, say as $\mathrm{E}[\mathrm{Y}_i \mid \mathbf{x}_{i\cdot}] = \mathrm{g}(\mathbf{x}_{i\cdot}, \boldsymbol{\theta})$. For example, setting $\sigma^2 = 1$ defines the QML–E–NLS estimator of $\boldsymbol{\beta}$ when the noise component elements, and thus the dependent variables of a regression model, are assumed to follow independent normal distributions. A QML–E estimator of Order 2 is defined when the σ^2 parameter is also expressed as a parametric function of $\mathbf{x}_{i\cdot}$. Setting $\mathrm{var}(\mathrm{Y}_i \mid \mathbf{x}_{i\cdot}) = \sigma^2(\mathbf{x}_{i\cdot}, \boldsymbol{\theta}) \equiv \sigma^2 \; \forall i$ defines the QML–E–NLS estimator for $\boldsymbol{\beta}$ and the usual associated ML-type estimator for σ^2. We will also examine in subsequent chapters some specific extensions of the QML–E procedure relating to cases where observations on $\mathbf{Y}$ are not independent, have unequal variances, or both.

► **Example 11.2.1:** To demonstrate the properties of the Case 1 QML–E estimator, we provide the GAUSS program C11QMLE1.gss in the examples manual. The exercise is based on an example provided in the article by Gourieroux, Monfort, and Trognon (1984b). For a sample of observations drawn from the Poisson distribution, three alternative versions of the QML–E objective function are considered: Poisson, gamma, and negative binomial. For comparison purposes, the log quasi-likelihood functions are plotted, and GAUSS reports the QML–E estimates under the three models. Then, the mean, variance, and distribution functions of the estimators are estimated by Monte Carlo simulation.

► **Example 11.2.2:** To demonstrate the properties of the Case 2 QML–E estimator, we provide the GAUSS program C11QMLE2.gss in the examples manual. Data samples are drawn from four distinct distributions (normal, Poisson, gamma, and beta), and the PDFs of the candidates are plotted for comparison purposes. Then, the normal quasi-likelihood function is used to estimate the unknown parameters of the underlying probability models. The mean, variance, and distribution functions of the estimators are estimated by Monte Carlo simulation and reported to the reader.

11.2.7. QML Summary Comments

Many professionals would argue that analysts work with misspecified likelihood functions a majority of the time. To specify a likelihood function, one must define a family of probability distributions that encompasses, for a collection of possible parameter values, the probabilities or density function values of all the potential samples of data that could have been observed based on the DSP being analyzed. For the specification of the likelihood to coincide with the true PDF underlying the DSP, the analyst must either have accurate and explicit knowledge of the probability mechanisms underlying the data sampling or have gained ample experience working with related data from previous experiments, or both. Unfortunately, it is often the case that the level of knowledge or experience required for specifying the correct functional form of the likelihood is insufficient. It is reassuring to know that the ML approach, even a misspecified (quasi) one, can lead to reasonable estimates of model parameters.

In practice, it is more likely the case that the analyst can at least specify a range of possible values for the dependent variable (e.g., nonnegative-valued, upper-bounded, lower-bounded, continuous, discrete, mixed continuous-discrete). Furthermore, previous research either by the analyst or others often provides adequate experience for specifying, at least qualitatively, some additional characteristics of the data-sampling process. These additional characteristics may include

1. which, and generally how, explanatory variables affect the expected value of the dependent variable;
2. which, and generally how, explanatory variables affect the variance of the dependent variable;
3. whether observations on the dependent variable can be considered statistically independent and, concomitantly, whether observations on dependent variable values can be considered to have zero covariances; and
4. whether the distribution of dependent variable values, given values for the explanatory variable values, can be considered symmetric or skewed either positively or negatively.

The QML approach allows one to proceed with a maximum likelihood-like analysis based on knowledge of only some of the functional characteristics of the DSP.

11.3. Estimating Equations: LS, ML, QML–E, and Extremum Estimators

Upon reviewing the LS–ML–QML–extremum estimation contexts it becomes apparent that the estimators we have examined heretofore can be recast in one way or another in terms of solving a vector of p-estimating equations

$$\mathbf{h}(\mathbf{Y}, \mathbf{x}, \boldsymbol{\theta}) = \mathbf{0} \tag{11.3.1}$$

for solutions in terms of the (p × 1) parameter vector $\boldsymbol{\theta}$. Estimators defined via solving estimating equations for the unknown parameters are characterized by

$$\hat{\boldsymbol{\Theta}}_{\mathrm{EE}} = \arg_{\theta}[\mathbf{h}(\mathbf{Y}, \mathbf{x}, \boldsymbol{\theta}) = \mathbf{0}], \tag{11.3.2}$$

where both $\boldsymbol{\theta}$ and $\mathbf{h}(\mathbf{Y}, \mathbf{x}, \boldsymbol{\theta})$ are (p × 1). Regarding the specific choice of (11.3.1) for defining LS, ML, QML–E, and general extremum estimation estimators in both the linear and nonlinear regression models, note that $\mathbf{h}(\mathbf{Y}, \mathbf{x}, \boldsymbol{\theta}) = \mathbf{0}$ can be specified to represent the first-order conditions to the respective extremum problems. The choice will be appropriate for all cases in which the first-order conditions characterize the global solution to the optimization problem, which occurs most of the time in practice. In particular, the choice of *estimating function* (EF) $\mathbf{h}(\mathbf{Y}, \mathbf{x}, \boldsymbol{\theta})$ for characterizing each of the estimators is represented in Table 11.2. Note that the scaling by n^{-1} used in the definitions of estimating functions in Table 11.2 is for purposes of examining asymptotic properties ahead and has no effect on the estimator solutions derived from the estimating equations. We emphasize that even in cases in which first-order conditions do not characterize solutions for estimators, the equations (11.3.1) and (11.3.2) still apply as an implicit representation of the estimator defined by the vector function of the data.

Recognizing the estimating equation (EE) approach as a common tie among all of the estimators in Table 11.2 suggests that there may be another level of specification, below the specification of estimation objective functions, that can serve as the primary focal point for defining estimators of unknown parameters for probability models. Indeed, this is the focus of the developing *estimating equations approach* to point estimation in the statistical literature. In this approach, it is recognized that *the sampling properties of estimators $\hat{\boldsymbol{\Theta}}_{\mathrm{EE}}$ defined via (11.3.2) are in fact derivable from the sampling properties of the estimating equations themselves, and so attention is directed towards the notion of specifying good, or if possible, optimal (in some sense) estimating equations.*

We note that when specifying estimating equations $\mathbf{h}(\mathbf{Y}, \mathbf{x}, \boldsymbol{\theta}) = \mathbf{0}$ directly (as opposed to being derived indirectly as first-order conditions to an extremum problem) to define estimators of parameters, it is possible that a QML–E approach is implied. By this we mean it may be the case that the system of partial differential equations

$$n^{-1}\frac{\partial \ln \mathrm{L_Q}(\boldsymbol{\theta}; \mathbf{y}, \mathbf{x})}{\partial \boldsymbol{\theta}} = \mathbf{h}(\mathbf{y}, \mathbf{x}, \boldsymbol{\theta}) \tag{11.3.3}$$

has a solution for $\ln \mathrm{L_Q}(\boldsymbol{\theta}; \mathbf{y}, \mathbf{x})$ that represents the logarithm of a genuine likelihood function associated with some parametric family of probability distributions. In this case the use of the estimating equation approach is clearly equivalent to a quasi-likelihood approach in which the QML estimator is solved for through first-order conditions. More

Table 11.2. *Estimating Equation Equivalencies of Common Estimating Principles*

$\boldsymbol{\theta}$ **Definition**	**Estimation Principle**	**Probability Model**	$\mathbf{h}(\mathbf{y}, \mathbf{x}, \boldsymbol{\theta})$
$\{\boldsymbol{\beta}, \sigma^2\}$	ML	Linear or Nonlinear Regression	$n^{-1}\frac{\partial \ln L(\boldsymbol{\theta};\mathbf{y},\mathbf{x})}{\partial \boldsymbol{\theta}}$
$\boldsymbol{\beta}$	LS	Linear Regression	$2n^{-1}(\mathbf{x}'\mathbf{x}\boldsymbol{\beta} - \mathbf{x}'\mathbf{y})$
$\boldsymbol{\beta}$	NLS	Nonlinear Regression	$2n^{-1}\frac{\partial \mathbf{g}(\mathbf{x},\boldsymbol{\beta})}{\partial \boldsymbol{\beta}}(\mathbf{g}(\mathbf{x}, \boldsymbol{\beta}) - \mathbf{y})$
$\boldsymbol{\beta}$ **or** $\{\boldsymbol{\beta}, \sigma^2\}$	Extremum Estimation	Linear or Nonlinear Regression	$\frac{\partial m(\boldsymbol{\theta},\mathbf{y},\mathbf{x})}{\partial \boldsymbol{\theta}}$
$\{\boldsymbol{\beta}, \sigma^2\}$	QML–E	Linear or Nonlinear Regression	$n^{-1}\frac{\partial \ln L_Q(\boldsymbol{\theta};\mathbf{y},\mathbf{x})}{\partial \boldsymbol{\theta}}$

generally, it may be the case that the system of partial differential equations

$$\frac{\partial m(\boldsymbol{\theta}; \mathbf{y}, \mathbf{x})}{\partial \boldsymbol{\theta}} = \mathbf{h}(\mathbf{y}, \mathbf{x}, \boldsymbol{\theta}) \tag{11.3.4}$$

has a solution for $m(\boldsymbol{\theta}; \mathbf{y}, \mathbf{x})$ that represents a genuine estimating objective function. In this case, the use of the estimating equation approach is equivalent to an extremum estimation approach in which the extremum estimator is solved for through first-order conditions. The point is that an estimator *initially* characterized as the solution to a set of estimating equations may have some equivalent QML–E or general extremum estimator characterization just as the estimators initially characterized as a QML–E or general extremum estimator will have an estimating equation characterization (recall Table 11.2).

It is useful to recognize that a necessary condition for an extremum estimator interpretation of an estimating equation characterization to exist is that the matrix of continuous derivatives $\frac{\partial \mathbf{h}(\mathbf{Y}, \mathbf{x}, \boldsymbol{\theta})}{\partial \boldsymbol{\theta}}$ be *symmetric*. This follows directly from Young's theorem regarding the symmetry of second-order partial derivatives of a twice continuously differentiable scalar function on open sets. In the current context, the scalar function is the objective function of the extremum estimation approach. A sufficient condition for the unique solution $\hat{\boldsymbol{\theta}} = \arg_{\boldsymbol{\theta}}[\mathbf{h}(\mathbf{y}, \mathbf{x}, \boldsymbol{\theta}) = \mathbf{0}]$ to represent the solution to the extremum problem $\hat{\boldsymbol{\theta}} = \arg\max_{\boldsymbol{\theta}}[\mathbf{m}(\mathbf{y}, \mathbf{x}, \boldsymbol{\theta})]$ is that $\frac{\partial \mathbf{h}(\mathbf{y}, \mathbf{x}, \boldsymbol{\theta})}{\partial \boldsymbol{\theta}}$ be continuous in $\boldsymbol{\theta}$, symmetric, and negative definite.

The estimating equation literature is large and growing, and we cannot enter into a global discussion of all of the issues involved in this estimation approach. Instead, we will focus on some basic principles here and then continue to develop the estimating equation idea in a number of specific estimation contexts throughout the remaining chapters. Interested readers wishing to delve more deeply into the use of estimating equations as a primary means of defining point estimators are advised to consult the works of Godambe and Kale (1991), Godambe (1991, 1997), Heyde (1989, 1994, 1997), Vinod (1997), Gallant and Tauchen (1996), and Desmond (1997) to begin additional readings and to obtain additional references on the subject.

11.3.1. Linear and Nonlinear Estimating Functions

To introduce some fundamental concepts relating to the use of estimating equations as a primary method of defining estimators of parameters, we first focus on identifying two basic functional forms for estimating functions, namely *linear* and *nonlinear* estimating functions. Linear in this context refers to the fact that the estimating function $\mathbf{h}(\mathbf{Y}, \mathbf{x}, \boldsymbol{\theta})$ is linear in the data $\mathbf{Y}$, conditional on $\mathbf{x}$. Linear estimating functions can be represented in the basic form

$$\mathbf{h}(\mathbf{Y}, \mathbf{x}, \boldsymbol{\theta}) = \boldsymbol{\eta}(\mathbf{x}, \boldsymbol{\theta})[\mathbf{y} - \mathbf{g}(\mathbf{x}, \boldsymbol{\theta})], \qquad (11.3.5)$$

where $\boldsymbol{\eta}(\mathbf{x}, \boldsymbol{\theta})$ is a $(\mathrm{p} \times n)$ matrix that may or may not depend on $\mathbf{x}$, the $(\mathrm{p} \times 1)$ parameter vector $\boldsymbol{\theta}$, or both, but the matrix does not depend on $\mathbf{Y}$. The linear estimating functions case is the most straightforward case in which to establish asymptotic distribution properties of the estimating function. In particular, if $\mathbf{g}(\mathbf{x}, \boldsymbol{\theta})$ represents the mean of $\mathbf{Y}$ conditional on $\mathbf{x}$, there is good reason to expect that a properly scaled estimating function will be asymptotically normally distributed for suitably chosen specifications of $\boldsymbol{\eta}(\mathbf{x}, \boldsymbol{\theta})$. In particular, when the Y_i's are independent, $\mathbf{h}(\mathbf{Y}, \mathbf{x}, \boldsymbol{\theta})$ can then be viewed as a weighted sum of independent random vectors as follows:

$$\mathbf{h}(\mathbf{Y}, \mathbf{x}, \boldsymbol{\theta}) = \sum_{i=1}^{n} \varepsilon_i \boldsymbol{\eta}_{i.}(\mathbf{x}, \boldsymbol{\theta})', \qquad (11.3.6)$$

where $\varepsilon_i = \mathrm{Y}_i - \mathrm{g}(\mathbf{x}_{i.}, \boldsymbol{\theta})$, $i = 1, \ldots, n$, are independent random variables so that central limit theory can generally be applied to establish asymptotic normality.

Two prominent examples of estimators that can be defined in the linear estimating equation framework using the combination of (11.3.2) and (11.3.5) are the least-squares estimators of $\boldsymbol{\beta}$ in the linear and nonlinear semiparametric regression models. In the linear regression case we would define the components of (11.3.5) as

$$\boldsymbol{\eta}(\mathbf{x}, \boldsymbol{\theta}) = \boldsymbol{\eta}(\mathbf{x}, \boldsymbol{\beta}) = -2n^{-1}\mathbf{x}' \quad \text{and} \quad \mathbf{g}(\mathbf{x}, \boldsymbol{\theta}) = \mathbf{g}(\mathbf{x}, \boldsymbol{\beta}) = \mathbf{x}\boldsymbol{\beta}. \qquad (11.3.7)$$

In the nonlinear regression case these components would be defined as

$$\boldsymbol{\eta}(\mathbf{x}, \boldsymbol{\theta}) = \boldsymbol{\eta}(\mathbf{x}, \boldsymbol{\beta}) = -2n^{-1}\frac{\partial \mathbf{g}(\mathbf{x}, \boldsymbol{\beta})}{\partial \boldsymbol{\beta}} \quad \text{and} \quad \mathbf{g}(\mathbf{x}, \boldsymbol{\theta}) = \mathbf{g}(\mathbf{x}, \boldsymbol{\beta}). \qquad (11.3.8)$$

Thus, we see that, although the estimating equations are linear in the data $\mathbf{Y}$, there is no reason why the parameters being estimated need to enter the probability model linearly. Additionally, the estimator defined via the solution to the estimating equations need not be linear in $\mathbf{Y}$.

Regarding the asymptotic distribution of the estimating function based on (11.3.7), note that under the regularity conditions used in Chapter 5 to establish the asymptotic normality of the linear least-squares estimator, it follows that

$$n^{1/2}\mathbf{h}(\mathbf{Y}, \mathbf{x}, \boldsymbol{\beta}) = 2n^{-1/2}(\mathbf{x}'\mathbf{x}\boldsymbol{\beta} - \mathbf{x}'\mathbf{Y}) = -2n^{-1/2}\mathbf{x}'\boldsymbol{\varepsilon} \xrightarrow{\mathrm{d}} \mathrm{N}(\mathbf{0}, 4\sigma^2\boldsymbol{\Xi}), \qquad (11.3.9)$$

where $n^{-1}\mathbf{x}'\mathbf{x} \rightarrow \boldsymbol{\Xi}$. Similarly, under the regularity conditions used in Chapter 8 to establish the asymptotic normality of the nonlinear least-squares estimator, it follows that

$$n^{1/2}\mathbf{h}(\mathbf{Y}, \mathbf{x}, \boldsymbol{\beta}) = 2n^{-1/2}\frac{\partial \mathbf{g}(\mathbf{x}, \boldsymbol{\beta})}{\partial \boldsymbol{\beta}}[\mathbf{g}(\mathbf{x}, \boldsymbol{\beta}) - \mathbf{Y}] = -2n^{-1/2}\frac{\partial \mathbf{g}(\mathbf{x}, \boldsymbol{\beta})}{\partial \boldsymbol{\beta}}\boldsymbol{\varepsilon} \xrightarrow{d} \mathrm{N}(\mathbf{0}, 4\sigma^2\Xi) \tag{11.3.10}$$

where $n^{-1}\frac{\partial \mathbf{g}(\mathbf{x}, \boldsymbol{\beta})}{\partial \boldsymbol{\beta}}\frac{\partial \mathbf{g}(\mathbf{x}, \boldsymbol{\beta})}{\partial \boldsymbol{\beta}'} \rightarrow \Xi$. As we noted above, it is generally the case that the scaled (generally by $n^{1/2}$) estimating function is asymptotically normally distributed for linear estimating functions used in practice.

Nonlinear estimating functions are nonlinear in the data $\mathbf{Y}$. A prominent example of this type of estimating function is either the linear or nonlinear regression model under multivariate normality when the objective is to estimate both $\boldsymbol{\beta}$ and σ^2. For example, in the linear regression case of Chapter 3, the estimating function could be specified as (compare with (3.2.5) and (3.2.6))

$$\mathbf{h}(\mathbf{Y}, \mathbf{x}, (\boldsymbol{\beta}, \sigma^2)) = \begin{bmatrix} n^{-1}(\mathbf{x}'\mathbf{Y} - \mathbf{x}'\mathbf{x}\boldsymbol{\beta}) \\ \dfrac{\mathbf{Y}'[\mathbf{I} - \mathbf{x}(\mathbf{x}'\mathbf{x})^{-1}\mathbf{x}']\mathbf{Y}}{\sqrt{2}(n-k)\sigma^2} - \dfrac{1}{\sqrt{2}} \end{bmatrix}, \tag{11.3.11}$$

which is clearly nonlinear in $\mathbf{Y}$, at least for the last element of the vector $\mathbf{h}(\mathbf{Y}, \mathbf{x}, (\boldsymbol{\beta}, \sigma^2))$. It is also clear that the estimator $\hat{\boldsymbol{\Theta}}_{\mathrm{EE}}$ obtained by solving the estimating equations based on (11.3.11) defines the bias-adjusted ML-type estimator of $\{\boldsymbol{\beta}, \sigma^2\}$, which is also the MVUE for the parameters in this case. Furthermore, regarding the asymptotic distribution of the estimating function (11.3.11), note that

$$n^{1/2}\mathbf{h}(\mathbf{Y}, \mathbf{x}, (\boldsymbol{\beta}, \sigma^2)) = \begin{bmatrix} n^{-1/2}\mathbf{x}'\boldsymbol{\varepsilon} \\ \dfrac{n^{1/2}\boldsymbol{\varepsilon}'[\mathbf{I} - \mathbf{x}(\mathbf{x}'\mathbf{x})^{-1}\mathbf{x}']\boldsymbol{\varepsilon}}{\sqrt{2}(n-k)\sigma^2} - \dfrac{n^{1/2}}{\sqrt{2}} \end{bmatrix} \xrightarrow{d} \mathrm{N}\left(\mathbf{0}, \begin{bmatrix} \sigma^2\Xi & \mathbf{0} \\ \mathbf{0} & 1 \end{bmatrix}\right), \tag{11.3.12}$$

on the assumption that $\{\boldsymbol{\beta}, \sigma^2\}$ in (11.3.11) are the true parameter values. Thus, it is *not* required that the estimating function be linear in the data for the scaled estimating function to have an asymptotic normal limiting distribution. It would be useful for the reader to verify (11.3.12) and to derive the finite sample distribution of the estimating function under the assumption of multivariate normality for the noise component of the regression model.

The preceding examples of linear and nonlinear estimating functions illustrate a number of properties in addition to asymptotic normality that will be important in our discussion ahead. First of all, note that the expectation and probability limit of each of the estimating functions equals the zero vector, that is, $\mathrm{E}_{\boldsymbol{\theta}}[\mathbf{h}(\mathbf{Y}, \mathbf{x}, \boldsymbol{\theta})] = \mathbf{0}$ and $\mathrm{plim}_{\boldsymbol{\theta}}[\mathbf{h}(\mathbf{Y}, \mathbf{x}, \boldsymbol{\theta})] = \mathbf{0}$, where $\mathrm{E}_{\boldsymbol{\theta}}[]$ and $\mathrm{p\,lim}_{\boldsymbol{\theta}}[]$ denote an expectation and a probability limit taken when the value of $\boldsymbol{\theta}$ is the true value of the parameter vector. Furthermore, on the assumption that the parameters are identified, both the expectation and probability limit are unequal to zero when $\boldsymbol{\theta}$ is not the true value, that is, $\mathrm{E}_{\boldsymbol{\theta}_0}[\mathbf{h}(\mathbf{Y}, \mathbf{x}, \boldsymbol{\theta})] \neq \mathbf{0}$ and $\mathrm{plim}_{\boldsymbol{\theta}_0}[\mathbf{h}(\mathbf{Y}, \mathbf{x}, \boldsymbol{\theta})] \neq \mathbf{0}$ when $\boldsymbol{\theta} \neq \boldsymbol{\theta}_0$. We will see ahead that these properties figure prominently in the evaluation of the efficacy of a set of estimating equations for parameter estimation and inference purposes.

Also note that estimating equations are not unique. Any one-to-one transformation of a set of estimating equations will result in the same estimator being defined by the equations. This allows for some flexibility in the specification of estimating functions but also suggests that some type of normalization of the estimating functions will be necessary if variances of competing sets of estimating functions are to be compared in a meaningful way.

11.3.2. Optimal Unbiased Estimating Functions: Finite Sample Optimality of ML

Much of the statistical literature relating to the evaluation of statistical properties in the EE estimation context is concerned with sampling properties of the estimating functions themselves rather than sampling properties of the estimators that the procedure produces. As one author remarked, "This is like admiring the pram rather than the baby." Although this may seem like an indirect way of evaluating the EE procedure, especially if the primary objective is to estimate the parameters of a probability model and not the estimating function per se, it turns out that choosing appropriate properties of the estimating function has important implications for the sampling properties of $\hat{\Theta}_{EE}$. At least at a general conceptual level, it is clear that there is a fundamental interrelationship between the sampling properties of $\mathbf{h}(\mathbf{Y}, \mathbf{x}, \boldsymbol{\theta})$ and the sampling properties of $\hat{\Theta}_{EE}$ because from (11.3.2), we have that $\hat{\Theta}_{EE} = \mathbf{h}^{-1}(\mathbf{Y}, \mathbf{x}, \mathbf{0})$, where $h^{-1}(\cdot)$ denotes the inverse function (or relation) of the estimating function evaluated at $\mathbf{h} = \mathbf{0}$. In effect, the EE estimator $\hat{\Theta}_{EE}$ inherits its sampling properties from the sampling properties of the estimating function via an inverse transformation, so the sampling properties of $\mathbf{h}(\mathbf{Y}, \mathbf{x}, \boldsymbol{\theta})$ are of fundamental importance.

11.3.2.a. Unbiasedness

One basic property of estimating functions that has been universally adopted in practice is that of *unbiasedness*. In the EE context, "unbiasedness" of an estimating function refers to the sampling characteristic

$$\mathrm{E}_{\theta}[\mathbf{h}(\mathbf{Y}, \mathbf{x}, \boldsymbol{\theta})] = \mathbf{0}, \qquad \forall \boldsymbol{\theta} \in \Omega, \tag{11.3.13}$$

where $\mathrm{E}_{\theta}[\,]$ denotes an expectation when $\boldsymbol{\theta}$ is true. What purpose does "unbiasedness" of an estimating function serve? On an intuitive level, "unbiasedness" is a natural requirement to ensure that the solution for $\boldsymbol{\theta}$ obtained from the estimating equations is close to the true value $\boldsymbol{\theta}_0$ in the case in which "little variation" in the estimating functions is present. In the polar case, where the variance is zero, a biased estimating equation would produce an incorrect value of $\boldsymbol{\theta}$ with probability 1 if the estimating equations could be solved uniquely for $\boldsymbol{\theta}$, which we will henceforth tacitly assume is always the case. Furthermore, note that the case of "little variation" in the estimating function is intuitively an ideal we seek, for it appears logical to expect that if $\mathbf{h}(\cdot)$ is highly variable, then the solution of the estimating equations for $\boldsymbol{\theta}$ would be highly variable as well because the value of $\boldsymbol{\theta}$ is effectively the "adjustment factor" that aligns a value of $\mathbf{h}(\mathbf{y}, \mathbf{x}, \boldsymbol{\theta})$ with zero when solving the estimating equations. An unbiased estimating function is then one way of guarding against the contradictory situation of having a good estimating equation (with little variation) produce a largely incorrect value of $\boldsymbol{\theta}$.

There are conceptually deeper reasons why unbiasedness is a desirable estimating function characteristic. First of all, under appropriate regularity conditions to be discussed further in the next section, solutions to unbiased estimating equations represent consistent estimators of the parameters of the estimating equations. Essentially, when the estimating equations are built up from a sum of the contributions of n individual data observations, as is most often the case in practice, laws of large numbers can be applied to ensure that a scaled version of the unbiased estimating equations converges to its zero expectation *if and only if* (with probability converging to 1) it is evaluated at the true parameter value $\boldsymbol{\theta}_0$. Thus, the solution value of $\boldsymbol{\theta}$ is drawn to $\boldsymbol{\theta}_0$ in the limit with probability limiting to 1. There is also mounting Monte Carlo evidence in finite sample contexts that suggests that unbiased estimating functions result in EE estimators with superior finite sampling properties than biased estimating functions (Breslow, 1990; Liang and Hanfelt, 1994; Liang and Zeger, 1995).

The unbiasedness criterion is also one component of a strong EE analogy with the classical theory of MVUE estimation in which one seeks an estimator within the unbiased class of estimators that has the smallest possible variance or covariance matrix. In the EE context, one seeks the estimating function from within the unbiased class of estimating functions that has the smallest possible variance, $\text{var(h)} = \text{E}_{\theta}[\text{h}(\mathbf{Y}, \mathbf{x}, \boldsymbol{\theta})^2]$ or covariance matrix, $\mathbf{cov(h)} = \text{E}_{\theta}[\mathbf{h}(\mathbf{Y}, \mathbf{x}, \boldsymbol{\theta})\,\mathbf{h}(\mathbf{Y}, \mathbf{x}, \boldsymbol{\theta})']$. The rationale for seeking such a MVUE in the EE context parallels our previous remarks presented at the beginning of this subsection – an unbiased estimating equation with little variation should provide a solution $\hat{\boldsymbol{\theta}}_{\text{EE}}$ that will be drawn more closely to $\boldsymbol{\theta}_0$ than a solution based on an estimating equation that is biased and has large variation. However, it is also important to note that estimators based on unbiased estimating functions are not necessarily unbiased. Rather, many EE estimators are defined in terms of nonlinear functions of the data and are biased in finite samples.

11.3.2.b. Optimal Estimating Functions: OptEF

An optimal estimating function, or OptEF, is an unbiased estimating function having the smallest variance or covariance matrix. A problem with implementing this concept of optimality is that the variance or covariance matrix of the estimating function $\mathbf{h}(\mathbf{Y}, \mathbf{x}, \boldsymbol{\theta})$ can be arbitrarily changed by applying scaling factors, full-rank $(\text{p} \times \text{p})$ linear transformations, or both, while not changing the implied EE estimator, or its sampling properties, at all. It is thus clear that some standardization of the estimating function is required for the OptEF concept to be meaningful operationally.

In the case of a scalar estimating function, Godambe (1960) was the first to suggest that the estimating function be standardized as

$$\text{h}_\text{s}(\mathbf{Y}, \mathbf{x}, \theta) = \frac{\text{h}(\mathbf{Y}, \mathbf{x}, \theta)}{\text{E}_{\theta}\left[\frac{\partial \text{h}(\mathbf{Y}, \mathbf{x}, \theta)}{\partial \theta}\right]} \tag{11.3.14}$$

so that the OptEF is then the unbiased estimating function that minimizes the variance of the *standardized* estimating function, the variance being defined as

$$\operatorname{var}(\mathrm{h_s}(\mathbf{Y}, \mathbf{x}, \theta)] = \frac{\mathrm{E}_\theta[\mathrm{h}(\mathbf{Y}, \mathbf{x}, \theta)^2]}{\left\{\mathrm{E}_\theta\left[\frac{\partial \mathrm{h}(\mathbf{Y},\mathbf{x},\theta)}{\partial\theta}\right]\right\}^2}. \tag{11.3.15}$$

It is clear that the variance of $\mathrm{h_s}(\mathbf{Y}, \mathbf{x}, \theta)$ is invariant to arbitrary scaling of $\mathrm{h}(\mathbf{Y}, \mathbf{x}, \theta)$ and leads to the same EE estimator, $\hat{\Theta}_{\mathrm{EE}}$, as $\mathrm{h}(\mathbf{Y}, \mathbf{x}, \theta)$.

In addition to the property of invariance to arbitrary scaling, the OptEF criterion of minimizing (11.3.15) has additional properties that make it a useful optimality criterion within the EE framework. First, note that the denominator expectation term in (11.3.15) is the average gradient of the estimating function and measures its average sensitivity to changes in the value of θ in the neighborhood of θ_0. In minimizing (11.3.15), there is an incentive to make the denominator as large as possible and the numerator as small as possible to make the ratio a minimum. Thus, by attempting to minimize (11.3.15), we are pursuing a dual objective of decreasing variance of the estimating function while increasing the expected sensitivity of its value to departures from the true value of θ, both of which should improve the tendency for the solved value of θ to reside close to θ_0. More concretely, it can be shown (see Section 11.3.4) that the right-hand side of (11.3.15) represents the asymptotic variance of the (generally) consistent EE estimator derived from $\mathrm{h}(\mathbf{Y}, \mathbf{x}, \theta)$, or equivalently from $\mathrm{h_s}(\mathbf{Y}, \mathbf{x}, \theta)$, and so the criterion has an asymptotic justification of seeking the unbiased estimating function that produces the consistent EE estimator of θ with the smallest asymptotic variance.

In the special case in which $\mathrm{h}(\mathbf{Y}, \mathbf{x}, \theta)$ is actually proportional to, or is a scaled version of the score or gradient function of a genuine log-likelihood function (recall Table 11.2), then under the standard regularity conditions applied to maximum likelihood estimation,

$$\begin{aligned} -\mathrm{E}_\theta\left[\frac{\partial \mathrm{h}(\mathbf{Y}, \mathbf{x}, \theta)}{\partial\theta}\right] &\propto \mathrm{E}_\theta\left[-\frac{\partial^2 \ln \mathrm{L}(\theta; \mathbf{Y}, \mathbf{x})}{\partial\theta^2}\right] \quad \text{and} \\ \mathrm{E}_\theta[\mathrm{h}(\mathbf{Y}, \mathbf{x}, \theta)^2] &\propto \mathrm{E}_\theta\left[\left(\frac{\partial \ln \mathrm{L}(\theta; \mathbf{Y}, \mathbf{x})}{\partial\theta}\right)^2\right], \end{aligned} \tag{11.3.16}$$

where the expectations on the right-hand sides of the proportionality operators in (11.3.16) *are equal*. In this case the OptEF criterion (11.3.15) becomes (note the proportionality factors ultimately cancel)

$$\operatorname{var}(\mathrm{h_s}(\mathbf{Y}, \mathbf{x}, \theta)) = \left[-\mathrm{E}_\theta\left[\frac{\partial^2 \ln \mathrm{L}(\theta; \mathbf{Y}, \mathbf{x})}{\partial\theta^2}\right]\right]^{-1}, \tag{11.3.17}$$

which is recognized as the ML variance and the Cramer–Rao lower bound (CRLB) for estimating the scalar θ. This provides an OptEF *finite* sample justification for ML estimation in the case of estimating a scalar parameter θ and is analogous to the Gauss–Markov theorem justification for LS estimation. This is discussed further in Section 11.3.2.c.

The OptEF criterion can be extended to the multivariate unbiased estimating equation framework in a natural way by replacing scalars with vectors and variances with covariance matrices. In particular, the multivariate OptEF criterion is stated in terms of the standardized vector estimating function

$$\mathbf{h}_s(\mathbf{Y}, \mathbf{x}, \boldsymbol{\theta}) = \left[\mathrm{E}_{\theta}\left[\frac{\partial \mathbf{h}(\mathbf{Y}, \mathbf{x}, \boldsymbol{\theta})}{\partial \boldsymbol{\theta}} \right] \right]^{-1} \mathbf{h}(\mathbf{Y}, \mathbf{x}, \boldsymbol{\theta}). \tag{11.3.18}$$

The covariance matrix of $\mathbf{h}_s(\mathbf{Y}, \mathbf{x}, \boldsymbol{\theta})$ is invariant to any arbitrary scaling or full-rank linear transformation of the rows of $\mathbf{h}(\mathbf{Y}, \mathbf{x}, \boldsymbol{\theta})$. The multivariate OptEF criterion is then to find the unbiased estimating function that minimizes, in the sense of symmetric positive definite matrix comparisons, the covariance matrix

$$\begin{aligned}\mathbf{cov}[\mathbf{h}_s(\mathbf{Y}, \mathbf{x}, \boldsymbol{\theta})] = &\left[\mathrm{E}_{\theta}\left[\frac{\partial \mathbf{h}(\mathbf{Y}, \mathbf{x}, \boldsymbol{\theta})}{\partial \boldsymbol{\theta}} \right] \right]^{-1} \mathrm{E}_{\theta}[\mathbf{h}(\mathbf{Y}, \mathbf{x}, \boldsymbol{\theta})\mathbf{h}(\mathbf{Y}, \mathbf{x}, \boldsymbol{\theta})'] \\ &\times \left[\mathrm{E}_{\theta}\left[\frac{\partial \mathbf{h}(\mathbf{Y}, \mathbf{x}, \boldsymbol{\theta})}{\partial \boldsymbol{\theta}'} \right] \right]^{-1}\end{aligned} \tag{11.3.19}$$

of the standardized estimating function (11.3.18). In addition to the invariance property of the OptEF measure, it can be shown, as in the scalar case (see Section 11.3.4 and Theorem 11.3.2), that the right-hand side of (11.3.19) represents the asymptotic covariance matrix of the (generally) consistent EE estimator derived from $\mathbf{h}(\mathbf{Y}, \mathbf{x}, \boldsymbol{\theta})$, or equivalently from $\mathbf{h}_s(\mathbf{Y}, \mathbf{x}, \boldsymbol{\theta})$, and thus the criterion has an asymptotic justification of seeking the unbiased estimating function that produces the consistent EE estimator of $\boldsymbol{\theta}$ with the smallest asymptotic covariance matrix. The multivariate OptEF criterion can also be interpreted as providing for minimizing the covariance matrix of $\mathbf{h}(\mathbf{Y}, \mathbf{x}, \boldsymbol{\theta})$ (the middle expected value in (11.3.19)) and maximizing expected sensitivity of the estimating function value to departures from $\boldsymbol{\theta}_0$ (the leading and trailing expected values in (11.3.19)). However, unlike the scalar case, the interpretation is complicated owing to the multiple directions from $\boldsymbol{\theta}_0$ in which the deviations can occur.

Analogous to the scalar case in the special case in which $\mathbf{h}(\mathbf{Y}, \mathbf{x}, \boldsymbol{\theta})$ is actually proportional to, or a scaled version of the score or gradient vector function corresponding to a genuine log-likelihood function (recall Table 11.2), it follows under the standard regularity conditions applied to maximum likelihood estimation that

$$-\mathrm{E}_{\theta}\left[\frac{\partial \mathbf{h}(\mathbf{Y}, \mathbf{x}, \boldsymbol{\theta})}{\partial \boldsymbol{\theta}} \right] \propto \mathrm{E}_{\theta}\left[-\frac{\partial^2 \ln \mathrm{L}(\boldsymbol{\theta}; \mathbf{Y}, \mathbf{x})}{\partial \boldsymbol{\theta} \partial \boldsymbol{\theta}'} \right] \tag{11.3.20}$$

and

$$\mathrm{E}_{\theta}[\mathbf{h}(\mathbf{Y}, \mathbf{x}, \boldsymbol{\theta})\mathbf{h}(\mathbf{Y}, \mathbf{x}, \boldsymbol{\theta})'] \propto \mathrm{E}_{\theta}\left[\frac{\partial \ln \mathrm{L}(\boldsymbol{\theta}; \mathbf{Y}, \mathbf{x})}{\partial \boldsymbol{\theta}} \frac{\partial \ln \mathrm{L}(\boldsymbol{\theta}; \mathbf{Y}, \mathbf{x})}{\partial \boldsymbol{\theta}'} \right], \tag{11.3.21}$$

where the expectations on the right-hand sides of (11.3.20) and (11.3.21) *are equal*. In this case the OptEF criterion (11.3.19) becomes (note that the proportionality factors ultimately cancel)

$$\mathbf{cov}(\mathbf{h}_s(\mathbf{Y}, \mathbf{x}, \boldsymbol{\theta})) = \left[-\mathrm{E}_{\theta}\left[\frac{\partial^2 \ln \mathrm{L}(\boldsymbol{\theta}; \mathbf{Y}, \mathbf{x})}{\partial \boldsymbol{\theta} \partial \boldsymbol{\theta}'} \right] \right]^{-1}, \tag{11.3.22}$$

which is recognized as the ML covariance matrix and the CRLB for estimating the parameter vector $\boldsymbol{\theta}$. This provides an OptEF *finite* sample justification for ML estimation in the case of estimating a vector parameter $\boldsymbol{\theta}$ and is analogous to the Gauss–Markov theorem justification for LS estimation. This is discussed further in Section 11.3.2.c.

► **Example 11.3.1:** Although the EE and LS estimators of $\boldsymbol{\beta}$ in the standard linear regression model are equivalent (see Table 11.2), the estimation procedures may be distinct under variations of the regression model. For a special case of the example presented by Heyde (1997, p. 5), we consider a heteroscedastic linear model in which $\text{var}(\varepsilon_i) = \sigma_i^2 = \sigma^2 \exp(\mathbf{x}[i,.]\boldsymbol{\beta})$. The unbiased estimating function for this problem $\mathbf{h}(\mathbf{y}, \boldsymbol{\beta}) = \sum_{i=1}^{n} \mathbf{x}[i,.]'\sigma_i^{-2}(y_i - \mathbf{x}[i,.]\boldsymbol{\beta})$ differs from the normal equations for the associated weighted least-squares problem (discussed at greater length in Chapters 14 and 15), which do not have null expected value. To compare the estimates based on the EE and WLS estimating functions, we provide the GAUSS program C11WLS.gss in the examples manual.

11.3.2.c. OptEF and ML: Finite Sample Optimality of the ML Estimator

The OptEF criterion provides a general finite sample optimality result and associated finite sample justification for the ML approach to estimation. In particular, Godambe (1960) showed that (11.3.17) is in fact the lower bound for the variance of *any* standardized unbiased scalar estimating function $h_s(\mathbf{Y}, \mathbf{x}, \theta)$ under the standard CRLB regularity conditions. Godambe's approach can be generalized to the vector-estimating function case $\mathbf{h}_s(\mathbf{Y}, \mathbf{x}, \boldsymbol{\theta})$, leading to the result that (11.3.22) is the lower bound for the covariance matrix of *any* standardized unbiased vector estimating function under the standard CRLB regularity conditions (see Kale, 1962, and Bhapkar, 1997).

It follows that an EE estimator based on an estimating function that is equal to the gradient of the log of the likelihood function is the OptEF estimator of $\boldsymbol{\theta}$. Therefore, the ML estimator (obtained via the solution to first-order conditions) is the OptEF estimator of $\boldsymbol{\theta}$. In practice, whenever the functional form of the likelihood function associated with a DSP can be properly specified, *the EE approach to estimation thus prescribes the ML estimator as the optimal (in finite samples) procedure for estimating the unknown parameter vector.*

11.3.3. Consistency of the EE Estimator

The consistency of an estimating equation (EE) estimator follows from both sampling and functional properties of the estimating functions themselves. In order to motivate the basic issues involved, first recall that the estimating function $\mathbf{h}(\mathbf{Y}, \mathbf{x}, \boldsymbol{\theta})$ is a scalar or multivariate random variable whose value depends on the outcomes of the random vector $\mathbf{Y}$ conditional on $\mathbf{x}$ and given a parameter value $\boldsymbol{\theta}$. The following theorem provides general regularity conditions leading to the consistency of the EE estimator.

Theorem 11.3.1 (Consistency of the EE Estimator): *The estimator* $\hat{\boldsymbol{\Theta}}_{\text{EE}} = \arg_{\boldsymbol{\theta}}[\mathbf{h}(\mathbf{Y}, \mathbf{x}, \boldsymbol{\theta}) = \mathbf{0}]$ *converges in probability to the true value* $\boldsymbol{\theta}_0$ *of the parameter*

$\boldsymbol{\theta}$ if

a. *$\mathbf{h}(\mathbf{Y}, \mathbf{x}, \boldsymbol{\theta})$ converges uniformly in probability to a function of $\boldsymbol{\theta}$, say $\mathbf{h}_*(\boldsymbol{\theta})$;*

b. *$\mathbf{h}_*(\boldsymbol{\theta})$ is continuous in $\boldsymbol{\theta}$,*

c. *$\mathbf{h}_*(\boldsymbol{\theta})$ equals $\mathbf{0}$ iff $\boldsymbol{\theta} = \boldsymbol{\theta}_0$, where $\boldsymbol{\theta}_0$ denotes the true value of $\boldsymbol{\theta}$, and*

d. *$\boldsymbol{\theta}_0$ resides in a compact parameter space Ω.*

The theorem indicates that the values for $\boldsymbol{\theta}$ that solve the estimating equations will converge to the value $\boldsymbol{\theta}_0$ that solves the "limiting" estimating equation $\mathbf{h}_*(\boldsymbol{\theta}) = \mathbf{0}$ with probability converging to 1 as $n \to \infty$, that is, $\hat{\boldsymbol{\Theta}}_{EE} \xrightarrow{p} \boldsymbol{\theta}_0$, and the EE estimator is therefore consistent. In effect the limit of the sequence of solutions to the estimating equations $\mathbf{h}(\mathbf{Y}, \mathbf{x}, \boldsymbol{\theta}) = \mathbf{0}$ is equal to the solution to the limiting estimating equation $\mathbf{h}_*(\boldsymbol{\theta}) = \mathbf{0}$ under the prevailing assumptions. Consistency can be achieved under weaker conditions than those listed in Theorem 11.3.1. For example, the parameter space need not be compact for consistency to be attained. See Crowder (1986) and Heyde (1997, Chapter 12) for alternative regularity conditions under which the EE estimator consistently estimates the parameter vector.

Note that in practice it is often more straightforward to verify consistency of an EE estimator through a direct application of a law of large numbers as opposed to verifying the general conditions of theorems relating to the consistency of EE estimators. Such is the case in Example 11.3.2, where the consistency of the EE–LS estimator is more easily demonstrated via an application of mean-square convergence, as in Chapter 5, than via verification of the general regularity conditions, which include verification of the uniform convergence in probability condition.

► **Example 11.3.2:** To illustrate the consistency of the EE estimator, examine the case of (11.3.7). Under the standard asymptotic regularity conditions for the semiparametric linear regression model (recall Chapter 5), where $n^{-1}\mathbf{x}'\mathbf{x} \to \boldsymbol{\Xi}$ is symmetric and positive definite and $n^{-1/2}\mathbf{x}'\boldsymbol{\varepsilon} \xrightarrow{d} \mathrm{N}(\mathbf{0}, \boldsymbol{\Xi})$, we have that

$$\operatorname{plim}[\mathbf{h}(\mathbf{Y}, \mathbf{x}, \boldsymbol{\beta})] = \operatorname{plim}[2n^{-1}(\mathbf{x}'\mathbf{x}\boldsymbol{\beta} - \mathbf{x}'\mathbf{Y})] = 2\boldsymbol{\Xi}(\boldsymbol{\beta} - \boldsymbol{\beta}_0) = \mathrm{h}_*(\boldsymbol{\beta}), \qquad (11.3.23)$$

where $\mathbf{h}_*(\boldsymbol{\beta})$ is clearly continuous in $\boldsymbol{\beta}$. Moreover, the convergence in probability of the estimating function to $\mathbf{h}_*(\boldsymbol{\beta})$ is uniform in $\boldsymbol{\beta} \in \Omega$. That is (recall 7.3.1),

$$\lim_{n\to\infty} \mathrm{P}(\sup_{\beta\in\Omega} |2n^{-1}(\mathbf{x}'\mathbf{x}\boldsymbol{\beta} - \mathbf{x}'\mathbf{Y}) - 2\boldsymbol{\Xi}(\boldsymbol{\beta} - \boldsymbol{\beta}_0)| < \xi)$$
$$= \lim_{n\to\infty} \mathrm{P}(\sup_{\beta\in\Omega} |2(n^{-1}\mathbf{x}'\mathbf{x} - \boldsymbol{\Xi})(\boldsymbol{\beta} - \boldsymbol{\beta}_0) - 2n^{-1}\mathbf{x}'\boldsymbol{\varepsilon})| < \xi) = 1, \quad \forall \xi > 0 \qquad (11.3.24)$$

because both $n^{-1}\mathbf{x}'\mathbf{x} - \boldsymbol{\Xi} \to \mathbf{0}$ and $n^{-1}\mathbf{x}'\boldsymbol{\varepsilon} \xrightarrow{p} \mathbf{0}$, and because $|\boldsymbol{\beta} - \boldsymbol{\beta}_0|$ is bounded by the compactness of Ω so that $2(n^{-1}\mathbf{x}'\mathbf{x} - \boldsymbol{\Xi})(\boldsymbol{\beta} - \boldsymbol{\beta}_0) \to \mathbf{0}$. Finally, because $\boldsymbol{\Xi}$ is nonsingular, it follows that $\mathbf{h}_*(\boldsymbol{\beta}) = 2\boldsymbol{\Xi}(\boldsymbol{\beta} - \boldsymbol{\beta}_0) = \mathbf{0}$ iff $\boldsymbol{\beta} = \boldsymbol{\beta}_0$. Therefore, $\hat{\boldsymbol{\beta}}_{EE} = \hat{\boldsymbol{\beta}}_{LS} \xrightarrow{p} \boldsymbol{\beta}_0$.

Recall that we are tacitly assuming that the estimating equations have a unique solution for the parameter vector. Consistency can be attained even when the estimating equations have multiple solutions. One method of choosing an EE solution that will produce a consistent estimator is to choose the root of the estimating equations closest (in Euclidean distance) to any other consistent estimator of the parameter vector (see Schervish, 1995, pp. 425–6).

11.3.4. Asymptotic Normality and Efficiency of EE Estimators

The EE estimator is asymptotically normally distributed under general regularity conditions similar to the conditions assumed to attain asymptotic normality for other estimators examined heretofore. To provide one set of conditions that ensure the asymptotic normality of the EE estimator, we will need to assume that the conditions of Theorem 11.3.1 hold, or in any case that the EE estimator is consistent for the parameter vector so that $\hat{\boldsymbol{\Theta}}_{\mathrm{EE}} \xrightarrow{p} \boldsymbol{\theta}_0$. Then, so long as (1) a scaled version of the estimating function is asymptotically normally distributed, (2) the estimating function is twice continuously differentiable so that it can be expanded in a Taylor series about the true value of the parameter vector, and (3) the Jacobian of the estimating function converges appropriately to an invertible matrix in the neighborhood of the true parameter value, asymptotic normality of the EE estimator of $\boldsymbol{\theta}$ will be attained.

Theorem 11.3.2 (Asymptotic Normality of the EE Estimator): *The estimator* $\hat{\boldsymbol{\Theta}}_{\mathrm{EE}} = \arg_{\boldsymbol{\theta}}[\mathbf{h}(\mathbf{Y}, \mathbf{x}, \boldsymbol{\theta}) = \mathbf{0}]$ *is such that* $\hat{\boldsymbol{\Theta}}_{\mathrm{EE}} \overset{a}{\sim} \mathrm{N}(\boldsymbol{\theta}_0, \boldsymbol{\Sigma}_{\mathrm{EE}})$*, where*

$$\boldsymbol{\Sigma}_{\mathrm{EE}} = \mathbf{cov}(\mathbf{h}_s(\mathbf{Y}, \mathbf{x}, \boldsymbol{\theta})) = \left(\mathrm{E}_{\boldsymbol{\theta}}\left[\frac{\partial \mathbf{h}(\mathbf{Y}, \mathbf{x}, \boldsymbol{\theta})}{\partial \boldsymbol{\theta}}\right]\right)^{-1} \mathrm{E}_{\boldsymbol{\theta}}[\mathbf{h}(\mathbf{Y}, \mathbf{x}, \boldsymbol{\theta})\mathbf{h}(\mathbf{Y}, \mathbf{x}, \boldsymbol{\theta})'] \times \left(\mathrm{E}_{\boldsymbol{\theta}}\left[\frac{\partial \mathbf{h}(\mathbf{Y}, \mathbf{x}, \boldsymbol{\theta})}{\partial \boldsymbol{\theta}'}\right]\right)^{-1}$$

if

a. $\hat{\boldsymbol{\Theta}}_{\mathrm{EE}} \xrightarrow{p} \boldsymbol{\theta}_0$,

b. $\mathbf{h}(\mathbf{Y}, \mathbf{x}, \boldsymbol{\theta})$ is twice continuously differentiable in a neighborhood of $\boldsymbol{\theta}_0$,

c. $\frac{\partial \mathbf{h}(\mathbf{Y}, \mathbf{x}, \boldsymbol{\theta})}{\partial \boldsymbol{\theta}}\Big|_{\boldsymbol{\theta}} \xrightarrow{p} \mathrm{E}\left[\frac{\partial \mathbf{h}(\mathbf{Y}, \mathbf{x}, \boldsymbol{\theta})}{\partial \boldsymbol{\theta}}\Big|_{\boldsymbol{\theta}_0}\right]$, *a nonsingular matrix, uniformly in* $\boldsymbol{\theta}$ *in a neighborhood of* $\boldsymbol{\theta}_0$,

d. $\boldsymbol{\Psi}^{-1/2}\mathbf{h}(\mathbf{Y}, \mathbf{x}, \boldsymbol{\theta}_0) \xrightarrow{d} \mathrm{N}(\mathbf{0}, \mathrm{I})$, *where* $\boldsymbol{\Psi} = \mathbf{cov}[\mathbf{h}(\mathbf{Y}, \mathbf{x}, \boldsymbol{\theta}_0)] = \mathrm{E}[\mathbf{h}(\mathbf{Y}, \mathbf{x}, \boldsymbol{\theta}_0)\mathbf{h}(\mathbf{Y}, \mathbf{x}, \boldsymbol{\theta}_0)']$.

A variety of alternative sufficient conditions can be stated that also lead to the asymptotic normality of $\hat{\boldsymbol{\Theta}}_{\mathrm{EE}}$. An informative source for additional details and references is the work of Heyde (1997, pp. 179–97).

The results of Theorem 11.3.2 confirm the statement made previously that the asymptotic covariance matrix of the EE estimator is the smallest covariance matrix attainable within whatever class of estimating functions was used in defining the EE estimator. This follows because minimizing this covariance matrix is in fact the EE estimation objective, as discussed in Section 11.3.2.b. Therefore, within the class of estimating functions examined, the EE estimator is also *asymptotically efficient*.

► **Example 11.3.3:** To demonstrate the large sample properties of an EE estimator, and also to demonstrate how simulation might be used to help identify consistent roots of estimating equations, we consider the problem of estimating θ from the estimating function $\mathrm{h}(\mathbf{Y},\theta) = \sum_{i=1}^{n}[\mathrm{a}(\mathrm{Y}_i - \theta) + \mathrm{b}[(\mathrm{Y}_i - \theta)^2 - \sigma^2]]$ (see Problem 4 at the end of the chapter for details). As indicated in the statement of the problem, there may be two solutions to the estimating function. To compare the sampling properties of the two EE estimators, the GAUSS program computes both roots for replicated Monte Carlo samples and compares the sample moments and EDFs as the sample size increases. As noted in Problem 4, the other parameters in the estimating function (a, b, and σ^2) are assumed known constants and are given in the GAUSS program.

11.3.5. Inference in the Context of EE Estimation

The asymptotic normality of the EE estimator leads to the usual types of test and confidence region procedures being available for testing hypotheses and generating confidence regions about the value of a nonlinear (or linear) differentiable $(j \times 1)$ vector function, $\mathbf{c}(\boldsymbol{\theta})$, of the parameter vector.

11.3.5.a. Wald and Z Tests and Confidence Regions

The asymptotic normality of the EE estimator allows the Wald statistic

$$\mathrm{W} = [\mathbf{c}(\hat{\boldsymbol{\Theta}}_{\mathrm{EE}}) - \mathbf{r}]' \left[\left.\frac{\partial \mathbf{c}(\boldsymbol{\theta})}{\partial \boldsymbol{\theta}'}\right|_{\hat{\boldsymbol{\Theta}}_{\mathrm{EE}}} \hat{\boldsymbol{\Sigma}}_{\mathrm{EE}} \left.\frac{\partial \mathbf{c}(\boldsymbol{\theta})}{\partial \boldsymbol{\theta}}\right|_{\hat{\boldsymbol{\Theta}}_{\mathrm{EE}}} \right]^{-1} [\mathbf{c}(\hat{\boldsymbol{\Theta}}_{\mathrm{EE}}) - \mathbf{r}]$$

$$\overset{a}{\sim} \text{Chi-square}(j, 0) \text{ under } \mathrm{H}_0 \tag{11.3.25}$$

to be used in the usual way to define asymptotically valid Chi-square tests of hypotheses of the form $\mathrm{H}_0\colon \mathbf{c}(\boldsymbol{\theta}) = \mathbf{r}$, where $\hat{\boldsymbol{\Sigma}}_{\mathrm{EE}}$ denotes a consistent estimator of the covariance matrix $\boldsymbol{\Sigma}_{\mathrm{EE}}$ of the asymptotic distribution in Theorem 11.3.2. In general, within the current probability model context, a consistent estimator can be obtained using

$$\hat{\mathrm{E}}\left[\left.\frac{\partial \mathbf{h}(\mathbf{Y},\mathbf{x},\boldsymbol{\theta})}{\partial \boldsymbol{\theta}}\right|_{\boldsymbol{\theta}_0} \right] = \left.\frac{\partial \mathbf{h}(\mathbf{Y},\mathbf{x},\boldsymbol{\theta})}{\partial \boldsymbol{\theta}}\right|_{\hat{\boldsymbol{\theta}}_{\mathrm{EE}}} \tag{11.3.26}$$

and

$$\hat{\mathrm{E}}[\mathbf{h}(\mathbf{Y},\mathbf{x},\boldsymbol{\theta}_0)\,\mathbf{h}(\mathbf{Y},\mathbf{x},\boldsymbol{\theta}_0)'] = n^{-1}\sum_{i=1}^{n} \mathbf{h}_*(\mathrm{Y}_i,\mathbf{x}_{i\cdot},\hat{\boldsymbol{\theta}}_{\mathrm{EE}})\,\mathbf{h}_*(\mathrm{Y}_i,\mathbf{x}_{i\cdot},\hat{\boldsymbol{\theta}}_{\mathrm{EE}})' \tag{11.3.27}$$

in Theorem 11.3.2, if it is assumed for the validity of (11.3.27) that the estimating functions can be defined in terms of a sum of the contributions of n observations as $\mathbf{h}(\mathbf{Y},\mathbf{x},\theta) = n^{-1}\sum_{i=1}^{n}\mathbf{h}_*(\mathrm{Y}_i,\mathbf{x}_{i\cdot},\theta)$ and the sample observations are independent (but not necessarily identically distributed). The power function of the test under Pitman drift alternatives is based in the usual way on the noncentral Chi-square distribution, as discussed in Chapter 8.

The Z-statistic

$$Z = \frac{[c(\hat{\Theta}_{EE}) - r]}{\left[\frac{\partial c(\theta)}{\partial \theta'}\Big|_{\hat{\Theta}_{EE}} \hat{\Sigma}_{EE} \frac{\partial c(\theta)}{\partial \theta}\Big|_{\hat{\Theta}_{EE}}\right]^{1/2}} \overset{a}{\sim} N(\delta, 1) \qquad (11.3.28)$$

could also be used in the usual way to define tests of scalar inequality hypotheses of the form H_0: $c(\theta) \leq r$ or H_0: $c(\theta) \geq r$, where critical values would be based on quantiles of the standard normal distribution (analogous to our discussion of the use of Z-tests in nonlinear regression model contexts in Chapter 8). Asymptotically valid confidence regions and confidence bounds based on either the W or Z tests can be constructed via duality with the hypothesis-testing procedure.

11.3.5.b. Generalized Score (Lagrange Multiplier-type) Tests and Confidence Regions

In the context of EE estimation there are alternatives to the Wald statistics that can be used to test hypotheses of the form H_0: $\mathbf{c}(\theta) = \mathbf{r}$ when the estimating equations can be interpreted as defining first-order conditions whose solution solves some extremum estimation problem. In these cases, the *generalized score statistic*, which is analogous to the score form of the usual Lagrange multiplier statistic, is given by (Qin and Lawless, 1994, p. 147; Gallant, 1987, Section 3.5)

$$GS = n\mathbf{h}(\mathbf{Y}, \mathbf{x}, \hat{\Theta}_{E_r})' \left[\frac{\partial \mathbf{h}}{\partial \theta}\Big|_{\hat{\Theta}_{E_r}}\right]^{-1} \frac{\partial \mathbf{c}}{\partial \theta}\Big|_{\hat{\Theta}_{E_r}} \hat{\mathbf{\Phi}}^{-1} \frac{\partial \mathbf{c}}{\partial \theta'}\Big|_{\hat{\Theta}_{E_r}} \left[\frac{\partial \mathbf{h}}{\partial \theta}\Big|_{\hat{\Theta}_{E_r}}\right]^{-1} \mathbf{h}(\mathbf{Y}, \mathbf{x}, \hat{\Theta}_{E_r})$$

$$\overset{a}{\sim} \text{Chi-square}(j, 0) \text{ under } H_0, \qquad (11.3.29)$$

where $\hat{\mathbf{\Phi}} = \frac{\partial \mathbf{c}}{\partial \theta'}\big|_{\hat{\Theta}_{E_r}} [\frac{\partial \mathbf{h}}{\partial \theta}\big|_{\hat{\Theta}_{E_r}}]^{-1} [n^{-1} \sum_{i=1}^{n} \mathbf{h}_*(Y_i, \mathbf{x}_{i\cdot}, \hat{\theta}_{E_r})\, \mathbf{h}_*(Y_i, \mathbf{x}_{i\cdot}, \hat{\theta}_{E_r})'][\frac{\partial \mathbf{h}}{\partial \theta'}\big|_{\hat{\Theta}_{E_r}}]^{-1} \frac{\partial \mathbf{c}}{\partial \theta}\big|_{\hat{\Theta}_{E_r}}$. Note that $\hat{\Theta}_{E_r}$ refers to the *restricted* extremum (E) estimator defined by constrained optimization under the restriction H_0: $\mathbf{c}(\theta) = \mathbf{r}$, where the extremum objective function $m(\mathbf{y}, \mathbf{x}, \theta)$ is implied by the partial differential equations $\mathbf{h}(\mathbf{y}, \mathbf{x}, \theta) = \frac{\partial m(\mathbf{y}, \mathbf{x}, \theta)}{\partial \theta}$. Again, the validity of the estimator $\hat{\mathbf{\Phi}}$ in (11.3.29) assumes that the sample observations are independent and the estimating functions can be defined in terms of a sum of n contributions as $\mathbf{h}(\mathbf{Y}, \mathbf{x}, \theta) = n^{-1} \sum_{i=1}^{n} \mathbf{h}_*(Y_i, \mathbf{x}_{i\cdot}, \theta)$. Tests are conducted in the usual way based on the critical regions constructed from the central Chi-square distribution with degrees of freedom j, which equals the number of functionally independent restrictions on θ being tested. Confidence regions follow from duality with the hypothesis test.

We note that the generalized score test can be applied even in cases in which an extremum objective function cannot be recovered from the partial differential equations $\mathbf{h}(\mathbf{y}, \mathbf{x}, \theta) = \frac{\partial m(\mathbf{y}, \mathbf{x}, \theta)}{\partial \theta}$. Details of this generalization can be found in Heyde and Morton (1993) and Heyde (1997, Section 7.2 and Chapter 9).

11.3.5.c. Pseudo-likelihood Ratio Tests and Confidence Regions

If it is assumed that a scalar function $m(\mathbf{Y}, \mathbf{x}, \boldsymbol{\theta})$ exists such that $\boldsymbol{\Psi}^{-1/2}\mathbf{h}(\mathbf{Y}, \mathbf{x}, \boldsymbol{\theta}) = \boldsymbol{\Psi}^{-1/2} \frac{\partial m(\mathbf{Y}, \mathbf{x}, \boldsymbol{\theta})}{\partial \boldsymbol{\theta}} \xrightarrow{d} N(\mathbf{0}, \mathbf{I})$, where $\boldsymbol{\Psi} = \mathbf{cov}(\mathbf{h}(\mathbf{Y}, \mathbf{x}, \boldsymbol{\theta}_0)) = E[\mathbf{h}(\mathbf{Y}, \mathbf{x}, \boldsymbol{\theta}_0)\mathbf{h}(\mathbf{Y}, \mathbf{x}, \boldsymbol{\theta}_0)']$, and $m(\mathbf{Y}, \mathbf{x}, \boldsymbol{\theta})$ is maximized at $\hat{\boldsymbol{\Theta}}_{EE}$, then there exists an analog to the pseudo-likelihood ratio statistic of the form

$$PLR = 2n\tau^{-1}[m(\mathbf{Y}, \mathbf{x}, \hat{\boldsymbol{\Theta}}_{EE_r}) - m(\mathbf{Y}, \mathbf{x}, \hat{\boldsymbol{\Theta}}_{EE})] \overset{a}{\sim} \text{Chi-square}(j, 0) \text{ under } H_0, \quad (11.3.30)$$

where again $\hat{\boldsymbol{\Theta}}_{E_r}$ denotes the *restricted* extremum estimator calculated under the restriction $H_0\colon \mathbf{c}(\boldsymbol{\theta}) = \mathbf{r}$, as described in Section 11.3.5.b. That is, in this context the EE estimator is effectively equivalent to an extremum estimator that maximizes the estimation objective function $m(\mathbf{Y}, \mathbf{x}, \boldsymbol{\theta})$, and so the results on pseudo-likelihood ratio tests presented in Section 7.6.3 apply here. Tests and confidence regions are again conducted in the usual way based on the asymptotic central Chi-square distribution of PLR under H_0. Additional details relating to the derivation and use of these and other test statistics for testing functional restrictions on the parameter vector, including discussion of the noncentral Chi-square distributions of these statistics under H_a, can be found in Heyde (1997, pp. 142–5) and Gallant (1987, Section 3.5).

► **Example 11.3.4:** To demonstrate the formation of inferences based on estimating equations, we provide the GAUSS program C11Tests.gss in the examples manual. The program considers the EE estimator of θ described in Example 11.3.3. For an observed sample, GAUSS conducts Wald, Z, and generalized score tests of separate hypotheses. GAUSS also uses the EE estimate to form a Wald-based confidence interval for θ. The user may wish to extend this example by constructing a Monte Carlo experiment designed to simulate the power of the tests or the coverage probability of the confidence interval.

11.4. Unifying-Linking OptEF and QML: QML–EE Estimation and Inference

In cases in which the likelihood function is unknown, the OptEF–ML estimator is unattainable. It then becomes relevant to consider whether the gradient of a quasi-likelihood function can be used to define a useful EE estimator of the parameters of a probability model. It turns out that a QML estimator defined by solving first-order conditions for the maximum of a particular type of quasi-likelihood function is an OptEF estimator in the class of linear unbiased estimating functions, which provides an analog to the Gauss–Markov result of linear least-squares theory.

In a more general setting, the current trend in the literature in both the EE and QML contexts is to define QML more broadly to encompass any estimator that can be solved through the use of estimating equations that exhibit certain basic properties analogous to typical properties exhibited by the gradients of log-likelihood functions (see Section 11.4.2). In these cases, the estimating equation is referred to as a *quasi-score* equation, and the existence of the quasi-likelihood function being implicitly maximized by solving the quasi-score equation is a secondary issue. We will refer to

QML estimators defined via the solution of EE and quasi-score equations by the notation QML–EE. Note that there will be a substantial nonnull intersection between QML–E and QML–EE-type estimators. In particular, this intersection consists of all cases in which an estimator is obtained by maximizing a quasi-likelihood and the maximum can be characterized by first-order conditions.

In order to appreciate the principal issues and results relating to the QML–EE approach, first note that when the appropriate likelihood function is not known, and so the true gradient or score function relating to the likelihood function is also not known, it would seem reasonable to search for an estimating equation that is in some sense "closest" to the optimal but unattainable estimating function $\mathbf{h}_{\text{opt}}(\mathbf{Y}, \mathbf{x}, \boldsymbol{\theta}) = n^{-1}\frac{\partial \ln L(\boldsymbol{\theta}; \mathbf{Y}, \mathbf{x})}{\partial \boldsymbol{\theta}}$ within the class of estimating functions being investigated. A possible criterion to judge closeness is the usual MSE criterion given in this context by

$$\text{mse}(\mathbf{h}, \mathbf{h}_{\text{opt}}) = \text{E}_{\text{F}}[[\mathbf{h}(\mathbf{Y}, \mathbf{x}, \boldsymbol{\theta}) - \mathbf{h}_{\text{opt}}(\mathbf{Y}, \mathbf{x}, \boldsymbol{\theta})]'[\mathbf{h}(\mathbf{Y}, \mathbf{x}, \boldsymbol{\theta}) - \mathbf{h}_{\text{opt}}(\mathbf{Y}, \mathbf{x}, \boldsymbol{\theta})]]. \quad (11.4.1)$$

Note we are using $\text{E}_{\text{F}}[]$ to denote an expectation taken with respect to the distribution F, and we are using this more general notion of expectation and not indicating an expectation as being taken for given values of parameter as $\text{E}_{\boldsymbol{\theta}}[]$, in recognition of the generally semiparametric nature of the current problem. Godambe and Heyde (1987) show that the minimization of $\text{mse}(\mathbf{h}, \mathbf{h}_{\text{opt}})$ through choice of the estimating equation $\mathbf{h}$ is implied by the minimization of (11.3.15) or (11.3.19) with respect to $\mathbf{h}$ (they also present a third equivalent criterion in terms of the generalized correlation between $\mathbf{h}$ and $\mathbf{h}_{\text{opt}}$).

Given the foregoing result, an OptEF, say $\mathbf{h}_{\text{opt}}^{\vartheta}$, within some class ϑ of unbiased estimating functions under investigation minimizes $\text{mse}(\mathbf{h}, \mathbf{h}_{\text{opt}})$ within the class of estimators. This is the principal reason the estimating equation $\mathbf{h}_{\text{opt}}^{\vartheta}$ is then referred to as a *quasi-score function*: It can be viewed as representing the closest (in terms of MSE) approximation to the true score function within the class of estimating functions represented by ϑ. Furthermore, it is conceptually possible to conceive of a quasi-likelihood function being defined from the quasi-score function via integration, treating $\mathbf{h}_{\text{opt}}^{\vartheta}(\mathbf{Y}, \mathbf{x}, \boldsymbol{\theta})$ as a vector of partial derivatives of this quasi-likelihood function. These analogues with maximum likelihood estimation lead to the interpretation of the EE estimator

$$\hat{\boldsymbol{\Theta}}_{\text{EE}}^{\vartheta} = \arg_{\boldsymbol{\theta}}[\mathbf{h}_{\text{opt}}^{\vartheta}(\mathbf{Y}, \mathbf{x}, \boldsymbol{\theta}) = \mathbf{0}] \quad (11.4.2)$$

as a QML estimator of $\boldsymbol{\theta}$. In fact, even when $\mathbf{h}_{\text{opt}}^{\vartheta}(\mathbf{Y}, \mathbf{x}, \boldsymbol{\theta})$ cannot be used to recover a proper likelihood function of some sort, it is now common to refer to the EE estimator defined via (11.4.2) as a QML estimator.

When a QML is defined via (11.4.2), the resulting QML–EE estimator is then, by definition, an OptEF estimator within the class of EE estimators implied by the set of estimating functions ϑ. In this case, all of the properties previously ascribed to the OptEF apply to the QML–EE estimator within the context of the restricted class of estimators represented by ϑ. Thus, the EE framework provides a definitive context in which the QML–EE estimator is optimal, and the ML–EE estimator is optimal when ϑ is broad enough to encompass the true score function.

11.4.1. The Best Linear-Unbiased QML–EE

A definitive and explicit result regarding the optimality of the QML–EE in the linear model context was first obtained by Wedderburn (1974) and extended by McCullagh and Nelder (1989), Godambe and Thompson (1989), and Godambe and Kale (1991). Wedderburn recognized that from an empirical point of view, the only assumptions necessary for calculating parameter estimates in a linear model are a specification of the conditional mean of **Y**, given **x**, and a specification of the relationship between the conditional mean and the conditional variance of **Y**. A fully specified likelihood function is not necessary. So instead of making assumptions about the form of the likelihood function, Wedderburn suggested consideration of the following general relationship between the conditional mean and covariance matrix of **Y** that shares key general characteristics of log-likelihood derivatives:

$$\mathbf{h}_W(\mathbf{Y}, \mathbf{x}, \boldsymbol{\beta}) = \frac{\partial \mathbf{g}(\mathbf{x}, \boldsymbol{\beta})}{\partial \boldsymbol{\beta}} \Sigma^{-1}[\mathbf{Y} - \mathbf{g}(\mathbf{x}, \boldsymbol{\beta})], \tag{11.4.3}$$

where $\boldsymbol{\beta}$ and Σ refer to the conditional mean and covariance matrix parameters of the standard nonlinear regression model. The subscript W is used to denote the Wedderburn form of the specification. Regarding the characteristics in common between (11.4.3) and typical derivatives of log-likelihood functions, note under the usual moment assumptions that $\mathrm{E}[\mathbf{Y} \mid \mathbf{x}] = \mathbf{g}(\mathbf{x}, \boldsymbol{\beta})$ and $\mathbf{cov}(\mathbf{Y} \mid \mathbf{x}) = \Sigma$, and, if it is assumed that Σ is independent of the parameter vector $\boldsymbol{\beta}$,

$$\begin{aligned}
\mathrm{E}[\mathbf{h}_W(\mathbf{Y}, \mathbf{x}, \boldsymbol{\beta})] &= \mathbf{0} \\
\mathbf{cov}(\mathbf{h}_W(\mathbf{Y}, \mathbf{x}, \boldsymbol{\beta})) &= \mathrm{E}[\mathbf{h}_W(\mathbf{Y}, \mathbf{x}, \boldsymbol{\beta})\, \mathbf{h}_W(\mathbf{Y}, \mathbf{x}, \boldsymbol{\beta})'] \\
&= \frac{\partial \mathbf{g}(\mathbf{x}, \boldsymbol{\beta})}{\partial \boldsymbol{\beta}} \Sigma^{-1} \frac{\partial \mathbf{g}(\mathbf{x}, \boldsymbol{\beta})}{\partial \boldsymbol{\beta}'} \\
-\mathrm{E}\left[\frac{\partial \mathbf{h}_W(\mathbf{Y}, \mathbf{x}, \boldsymbol{\beta})}{\partial \boldsymbol{\beta}}\right] &= \frac{\partial \mathbf{g}(\mathbf{x}, \boldsymbol{\beta})}{\partial \boldsymbol{\beta}} \Sigma^{-1} \frac{\partial \mathbf{g}(\mathbf{x}, \boldsymbol{\beta})}{\partial \boldsymbol{\beta}'} = \mathbf{cov}(\mathbf{h}_W(\mathbf{Y}, \mathbf{x}, \boldsymbol{\beta})).
\end{aligned} \tag{11.4.4}$$

These are analogous to the regular characteristics of a log-likelihood function, where

$$\begin{aligned}
\mathrm{E}\left[\frac{\partial \ln \mathrm{L}(\boldsymbol{\beta}; \mathbf{Y}, \mathbf{x})}{\partial \boldsymbol{\beta}}\right] &= \mathbf{0} \\
\mathbf{cov}\left(\left[\frac{\partial \ln \mathrm{L}(\boldsymbol{\beta}; \mathbf{Y}, \mathbf{x})}{\partial \boldsymbol{\beta}}\right]\right) &= \mathrm{E}\left[\frac{\partial \ln \mathrm{L}(\boldsymbol{\beta}; \mathbf{Y}, \mathbf{x})}{\partial \boldsymbol{\beta}} \frac{\partial \ln \mathrm{L}(\boldsymbol{\beta}; \mathbf{Y}, \mathbf{x})}{\partial \boldsymbol{\beta}'}\right] = \boldsymbol{\Psi} \\
-\mathrm{E}\left[\left[\frac{\partial^2 \ln \mathrm{L}(\boldsymbol{\beta}; \mathbf{Y}, \mathbf{x})}{\partial \boldsymbol{\beta} \partial \boldsymbol{\beta}'}\right]\right] &= \boldsymbol{\Psi} = \mathbf{cov}\left(\left[\frac{\partial \ln \mathrm{L}(\boldsymbol{\beta}; \mathbf{Y}, \mathbf{x})}{\partial \boldsymbol{\beta}}\right]\right).
\end{aligned} \tag{11.4.5}$$

Therefore, one might conjecture that $\mathbf{h}_W(\mathbf{Y}, \mathbf{x}, \boldsymbol{\beta})$ deserves consideration as a potential quasi-score specification for estimating the parameter vector $\boldsymbol{\beta}$. One might conjecture further that the system of partial differential equations represented by the estimating functions $\frac{\partial \ln \mathrm{L}_Q}{\partial \boldsymbol{\beta}} = \mathbf{h}_W(\mathbf{Y}, \mathbf{x}, \boldsymbol{\beta})$ would imply some form of proper quasi-likelihood function $\mathrm{L}_Q(\boldsymbol{\beta}; \mathbf{Y}, \mathbf{x})$ given that (11.4.4) holds and also that $\frac{\partial \mathbf{h}_W(\mathbf{Y}, \mathbf{x}, \boldsymbol{\beta})}{\partial \boldsymbol{\beta}}$ is a $(k \times k)$ symmetric matrix of continuous functions of $\boldsymbol{\beta}$ (assuming $\mathbf{g}(\mathbf{x}, \boldsymbol{\beta})$ is twice continuously differentiable).

In fact, both of the preceding conjectures have merit. Treating $\mathbf{h}_W(\mathbf{Y}, \mathbf{x}, \boldsymbol{\beta})$ in (11.4.3) as the partial derivatives of some quasi-likelihood function L_Q leads to the multivariate normal quasi-likelihood function

$$L_Q(\boldsymbol{\beta}; \mathbf{y}, \mathbf{x}) \propto \exp\left\{-\frac{1}{2}[(\mathbf{y} - \mathbf{g}(\mathbf{x}, \boldsymbol{\beta}))]'\boldsymbol{\Sigma}^{-1}[(\mathbf{y} - \mathbf{g}(\mathbf{x}, \boldsymbol{\beta}))]\right\}. \tag{11.4.6}$$

(where $\propto$ denotes "proportional to"). That (11.4.6) implies (11.4.3) can be verified directly by partially differentiating the logarithm of (11.4.6) with respect to the parameter vector $\boldsymbol{\beta}$. Therefore, the use of the estimating function (11.4.3) is equivalent to performing quasi-maximum likelihood estimation based on the multivariate normal distribution with a prespecified covariance matrix $\boldsymbol{\Sigma}$. In the case where $\boldsymbol{\Sigma} = \sigma^2\mathbf{I}$, with σ^2 not necessarily known, the QML estimator is equivalent to nonlinear ML–NLS estimation of $\boldsymbol{\beta}$ for the regression model $\mathbf{Y} = \mathbf{g}(\mathbf{x}, \boldsymbol{\beta}) + \varepsilon$.

Furthermore, $\mathbf{h}_W(\mathbf{Y}, \mathbf{x}, \boldsymbol{\beta})$ in (11.4.3) is the OptEF in the class of linear unbiased estimating functions, ϑ_u, for $\boldsymbol{\beta}$. To see this, first recall that the linear unbiased estimating functions for $\boldsymbol{\beta}$ are of the form $\mathbf{h}(\mathbf{Y}, \mathbf{x}, \boldsymbol{\beta}) = \boldsymbol{\eta}(\mathbf{x}, \boldsymbol{\beta})[\mathbf{y} - \mathbf{g}(\mathbf{x}, \boldsymbol{\beta})]$ (recall (11.3.5)) with $E[\mathbf{h}(\mathbf{Y}, \mathbf{x}, \boldsymbol{\beta})] = \mathbf{0}$. Unbiasedness is implied by the assumption that $\mathbf{g}(\mathbf{x}, \boldsymbol{\beta}) = E[\mathbf{Y} \mid \mathbf{x}]$. The OptEF criterion is then to choose the $(k \times n)$ matrix function $\boldsymbol{\eta}(\mathbf{x}, \boldsymbol{\beta})$ so as to minimize the covariance matrix of the standardized estimating function $\mathbf{h}_s(\mathbf{Y}, \mathbf{x}, \boldsymbol{\beta})$ (recall (11.3.19))

$$\mathbf{cov}(\mathbf{h}_s(\mathbf{Y}, \mathbf{x}, \boldsymbol{\beta})) = \left[\frac{\partial \mathbf{g}(\mathbf{x}, \boldsymbol{\beta})}{\partial \boldsymbol{\beta}}\boldsymbol{\eta}(\mathbf{x}, \boldsymbol{\beta})'\right]^{-1}[\boldsymbol{\eta}(\mathbf{x}, \boldsymbol{\beta})\boldsymbol{\Sigma}\boldsymbol{\eta}(\mathbf{x}, \boldsymbol{\beta})']\left[\boldsymbol{\eta}(\mathbf{x}, \boldsymbol{\beta})\frac{\partial \mathbf{g}(\mathbf{x}, \boldsymbol{\beta})}{\partial \boldsymbol{\beta}'}\right]^{-1}. \tag{11.4.7}$$

The choice $\boldsymbol{\eta}_{\text{opt}}(\mathbf{x}, \boldsymbol{\beta}) = \frac{\partial \mathbf{g}(\mathbf{x}, \boldsymbol{\beta})}{\partial \boldsymbol{\beta}}\boldsymbol{\Sigma}^{-1}$, leading to the estimating equation $\mathbf{h}_W(\mathbf{Y}, \mathbf{x}, \boldsymbol{\beta})$ defined in (11.4.3), minimizes the covariance matrix (11.4.7) of the standardized estimating function and defines the OptEF in the class ϑ_u of linear unbiased estimating functions for $\boldsymbol{\beta}$, resulting in the covariance matrix

$$\mathbf{cov}[\mathbf{h}_{\text{sopt}}(\mathbf{Y}, \mathbf{x}, \boldsymbol{\beta})] = \left[\frac{\partial \mathbf{g}(\mathbf{x}, \boldsymbol{\beta})}{\partial \boldsymbol{\beta}}\boldsymbol{\Sigma}^{-1}\frac{\partial \mathbf{g}(\mathbf{x}, \boldsymbol{\beta})}{\partial \boldsymbol{\beta}'}\right]^{-1}. \tag{11.4.8}$$

For proof, examine the matrix difference

$$\begin{aligned}
&[\mathbf{cov}(\mathbf{h}_{\text{sopt}}(\mathbf{Y}, \mathbf{x}, \boldsymbol{\beta}))]^{-1} - [\mathbf{cov}(\mathbf{h}_s(\mathbf{Y}, \mathbf{x}, \boldsymbol{\beta}))]^{-1} \\
&= \left[\frac{\partial \mathbf{g}(\mathbf{x}, \boldsymbol{\beta})}{\partial \boldsymbol{\beta}}\boldsymbol{\Sigma}^{-1}\frac{\partial \mathbf{g}(\mathbf{x}, \boldsymbol{\beta})}{\partial \boldsymbol{\beta}'}\right] - \left[\frac{\partial \mathbf{g}(\mathbf{x}, \boldsymbol{\beta})}{\partial \boldsymbol{\beta}}\boldsymbol{\eta}(\mathbf{x}, \boldsymbol{\beta})'\right] \\
&\quad \times [\boldsymbol{\eta}(\mathbf{x}, \boldsymbol{\beta})\boldsymbol{\Sigma}\boldsymbol{\eta}(\mathbf{x}, \boldsymbol{\beta})']^{-1}\left[\boldsymbol{\eta}(\mathbf{x}, \boldsymbol{\beta})\frac{\partial \mathbf{g}(\mathbf{x}, \boldsymbol{\beta})}{\partial \boldsymbol{\beta}'}\right] \\
&= \frac{\partial \mathbf{g}(\mathbf{x}, \boldsymbol{\beta})}{\partial \boldsymbol{\beta}}\boldsymbol{\Sigma}^{-1/2}[\mathbf{I} - \boldsymbol{\Sigma}^{1/2}\boldsymbol{\eta}(\mathbf{x}, \boldsymbol{\beta})'[\boldsymbol{\eta}(\mathbf{x}, \boldsymbol{\beta})\boldsymbol{\Sigma} \\
&\quad \times \boldsymbol{\eta}(\mathbf{x}, \boldsymbol{\beta})']^{-1}\boldsymbol{\eta}(\mathbf{x}, \boldsymbol{\beta})\boldsymbol{\Sigma}^{1/2}]\boldsymbol{\Sigma}^{-1/2}\frac{\partial \mathbf{g}(\mathbf{x}, \boldsymbol{\beta})}{\partial \boldsymbol{\beta}'}.
\end{aligned} \tag{11.4.9}$$

Note that the matrix in the outer-most brackets in the last line of (11.4.9) is idempotent for any choice of rank k matrix $\boldsymbol{\eta}(\mathbf{x}, \boldsymbol{\beta})$ and therefore the matrix is positive semidefinite, implying immediately that the matrix difference $[\mathbf{cov}(\mathbf{h}_s(\mathbf{Y}, \mathbf{x}, \boldsymbol{\beta}))] - [\mathbf{cov}(\mathbf{h}_{sopt}(\mathbf{Y}, \mathbf{x}, \boldsymbol{\beta}))]$ is also positive semidefinite (because if $\mathbf{c}$ and $\mathbf{d}$ are two positive definite symmetric matrices, then $\mathbf{c} - \mathbf{d}$ is psd $\Leftrightarrow \mathbf{d}^{-1} - \mathbf{c}^{-1}$ is psd). The matrix difference is the zero matrix iff $\boldsymbol{\eta}(\mathbf{x}, \boldsymbol{\beta}) = \boldsymbol{\eta}_{opt}(\mathbf{x}, \boldsymbol{\beta}) = \frac{\partial \mathbf{g}(\mathbf{x}, \boldsymbol{\beta})}{\partial \boldsymbol{\beta}} \boldsymbol{\Sigma}^{-1}$. It follows that $\mathbf{h}_{sopt}(\mathbf{Y}, \mathbf{x}, \boldsymbol{\beta}) \Leftrightarrow \mathbf{h}_W(\mathbf{Y}, \mathbf{x}, \boldsymbol{\beta})$ is the OptEF for $\boldsymbol{\beta}$ in the linear unbiased class of estimating functions and leads to the LS estimator when $\boldsymbol{\Sigma} = \sigma^2 \mathbf{I}$.

11.4.2. General QML–EE Estimation and Inference

In general, an EE estimator whose estimating function $\mathbf{h}(\mathbf{Y}, \mathbf{x}, \boldsymbol{\theta})$ adheres to the typical log-likelihood gradient properties (recall (11.4.4))

$$
\begin{aligned}
\mathrm{E}[\mathbf{h}(\mathbf{Y}, \mathbf{x}, \boldsymbol{\theta})] &= \mathbf{0} \\
\mathbf{cov}(\mathbf{h}(\mathbf{Y}, \mathbf{x}, \boldsymbol{\theta})) &= \mathrm{E}[\mathbf{h}(\mathbf{Y}, \mathbf{x}, \boldsymbol{\theta})\, \mathbf{h}(\mathbf{Y}, \mathbf{x}, \boldsymbol{\theta})'] \\
-\mathrm{E}\left[\frac{\partial \mathbf{h}(\mathbf{Y}, \mathbf{x}, \boldsymbol{\theta})}{\partial \boldsymbol{\theta}}\right] &= \mathbf{cov}(\mathbf{h}(\mathbf{Y}, \mathbf{x}, \boldsymbol{\theta}))
\end{aligned}
\tag{11.4.10}
$$

will be equivalently referred to as a QML–EE estimator, and the estimating function will be called a *quasi-score*, when $\mathbf{h}$ is the OptEF within the class ϑ of estimating functions under consideration. Two previous examples of such QML–EE estimators are the ML–EE estimator in the class of all unbiased estimating functions and the LS–EE estimator in the class of linear unbiased estimating functions. The intuitive rationale for calling such estimators *quasi-maximum likelihood* estimators is again that these estimators are generated via the solutions of *quasi-score functions*, which are functions closest in expected squared distance (MSE) to the optimal true score function underlying the DSP, as noted previously (recall the discussion following (11.4.1)). Thus, there is a strong analogy between solving *true-score functions* to define *true-maximum likelihood* estimators and solving *quasi-score functions* to define *quasi-maximum likelihood estimators*.

The computational analogy between QML–EE estimators and ML estimators is complete if the OptEF-based estimating equations $\mathbf{h}^{\vartheta}_{opt}(\mathbf{y}, \mathbf{x}, \boldsymbol{\theta}) = \mathbf{0}$ can be viewed as first-order conditions characterizing the maximum of the log of some quasi-likelihood function $\ln \mathrm{L_Q}(\boldsymbol{\theta}; \mathbf{y}, \mathbf{x})$. The question is equivalent to whether the OptEF, acting as first-order partial derivatives, can be integrated back to some $\ln \mathrm{L_Q}(\boldsymbol{\theta}; \mathbf{y}, \mathbf{x})$ function that exhibits a maximum at the EE solution point. The answer is yes, at least locally in the neighborhood of the solution point, if the matrix of derivatives $\frac{\partial \mathbf{h}^{\vartheta}_{opt}(\mathbf{y}, \mathbf{x}, \boldsymbol{\theta})}{\partial \boldsymbol{\theta}}$ is symmetric, continuous, and negative definite. We emphasize that in QML–EE estimation there is no particular reason why it is necessary actually to recover any quasi-likelihood function implied by the OptEF. However, if one wishes to use the pseudo-likelihood ratio statistic for testing hypotheses or generating confidence regions, the value of the quasi-likelihood function will be required (recall 11.3.30).

Besides the computational analogy, there is also a strong analogy in terms of statistical properties between ML and QML–EE estimators. In particular, *within their respective estimating function classes*, both estimators are associated with OptEFs, and they are consistent, asymptotically normally distributed, and asymptotically efficient.

11.5. Final Remarks

Referring to the basic estimation and inference principles developed in Chapters 3–9, and the QML principle of Section 11.2, in this chapter we have indicated ways in which ML, LS, NLS, QML, and general extremum estimation procedures can be unified under a single estimating equations (EE) framework. In addition, we have shown how the traditional ML estimation context can be extended through the concept of quasi-maximum likelihood (QML) within both the QML-extremum (QML–E) and QML–estimating equations (QML–EE) frameworks. In particular, we have noted QML–E cases in which the likelihood function used in the maximum likelihood procedure is misspecified in the sense that the true probability distribution of **Y** does not belong to the parametric family of distributions associated with the likelihood function. We have also noted QML–EE cases in which specifying only lower-order conditional moments of the sample data, such as means, variances, or both is sufficient for a quasi-maximum likelihood approach to estimation and inference to proceed. We have noted regularity conditions, encompassing both types of cases, that allow consistency, asymptotic normality, and restricted (to a class of estimators) asymptotic efficiency to remain intact in the QML context. And we have demonstrated a finite-sample optimality of both ML and QML procedures within the context of the theory of optimal estimating functions.

The overall general lesson from our introduction to QML and EE estimation–inference procedures is twofold. First of all, we have seen that applying the ML approach even to misspecified likelihood functions via the QML approach can still lead to estimators and inference procedures with useful sampling properties. Furthermore, an ML-like approach, with ML-like sampling properties, is available within the QML context even when only low-order conditional moments of the data are explicitly modeled.

Second, the EE approach provides a means of unifying and linking all of the estimation and inference procedures discussed heretofore under one paradigm, which will serve as a template for unification of additional estimation and inference procedures ahead. The EE approach achieves this unification by deemphasizing the amount of attention paid to analyzing the form and properties of the specific and varied parameter estimators themselves and increasing attention paid to the form and properties of the estimating functions from which the estimators are derived.

In the next chapter, we will attempt to avoid the explicit functional specification of likelihood functions entirely by introducing the nonparametric empirical likelihood (EL) concept. In this process, we will link the EL and the EE concepts to broaden the estimation and inference possibility space further.

11.6. Exercises

11.6.1. Idea Checklist – Knowledge Guides

---

1. QMLE is often referred to as a robust estimation procedure. Is it? Why?
2. Many respected econometricians would argue that applied analysts are working with, and estimate,

incorrectly specified models most of the time. Given the existence of QML estimators, does misspecification matter?

3. In practice, should one routinely use QML estimators in place of ML estimators to guard against misspecification of the likelihood function?

4. Suppose an analyst assumes that the noise component of a linear regression model is multivariate normally distributed with a covariance matrix equal to $\sigma^2\mathbf{I}$, but he or she is not at all sure that the probability distribution of the noise component belongs to the normal parametric family. Discuss the properties of the estimator in this context, being sure to note any role that the concept of quasi-likelihood has to play.

5. Is there a sensible QML alternative to any likelihood methodology, at least to the first-order of asymptotics?

6. What are some of the advantages of making minimal assumptions relative to probability models?

7. How does EE help to avoid specification of the likelihood?

8. What are the statistical benefits derived from deemphasizing the estimates (roots) and focusing on the underlying estimating equations?

9. How has estimating functions brought about a synthesis of the least-squares and maximum likelihood methodologies?

11.6.2. Problems

11–1 Suppose we know the conditional moments of a random variable match those of the two-parameter log-normal family (see Problem 1, Section 9.5.2) but are unsure of the particular form of the probability distribution. State and solve the associated QML estimation problem based on the normal quasi-likelihood function.

11–2 Consider a sample of n observations generated as $\mathrm{y}_i = \mu + \varepsilon_i$ for unknown μ where $\mathrm{var}(\varepsilon_i \mid \mathrm{y}_{i-1}) = \sigma^2 \mathrm{y}_{i-1}$.

a. On the assumption the variance σ^2 is known, state the normal quasi-likelihood function for an individual observation $\mathrm{f_Q}(\mathrm{y}_i; \mathrm{y}_{i-1}, \mu)$ and for the full sample. What is the QMLE–E estimator of μ?

b. Alternatively, consider the estimating function $\mathrm{h}(\mathbf{y}, \mu) = \sum_{i=1}^{n} (\mathrm{y}_i - \mu)$. Write the standardized estimating function $\mathrm{h_s}$ and derive the QMLE–EE estimator of μ. How does this approach differ from the QMLE–E estimation procedure?

11–3 Following Gong and Samaniego (1981), suppose you observe a sample of n iid observations $(\mathrm{y}_1, \ldots, \mathrm{y}_n)$ formed as the sum of a Poisson(λ) signal with Binomial (n, p) noise (i.e., discrete Poisson observations with discrete measurement errors) where n is known.

a. Show that the MOM estimators based on the first two moments are $\hat{\lambda} = \bar{\mathrm{y}} - \mathrm{n}\hat{\mathrm{p}}$ and $\hat{\mathrm{p}} = \sqrt{(\bar{\mathrm{y}} - \mathrm{s}^2)/\mathrm{n}}$ (assuming $\bar{\mathrm{y}} > \mathrm{s}^2$), where $\bar{\mathrm{y}}$ and s^2 are the sample mean and variance of the observations.

b. Use the moment equations as estimation functions to derive the standardized estimating equations for this problem. Are the EE estimators of λ and p based on the standardized functions identical to the MOM estimators?

c. State the normal quasi-likelihood function based on the mean and variance of the observations (QMLE–E of Order 2) and derive the associated necessary conditions for the QMLE–E estimators of λ and p.

d. Derive the large-sample covariance matrix for the QMLE–E estimators.

e. Can you derive the actual likelihood function for this data-sampling process?

11–4 On the basis of Heyde (1997, p. 182), consider the problem of estimating θ from the estimating function

$$h(\mathbf{Y}, \theta) = \sum_{i=1}^{n} \{a(Y_i - \theta) + b[(Y_i - \theta)^2 - \sigma^2]\}$$

The random variables Y_i are iid with mean θ and variance σ^2 (a, b, and σ^2 are known).

a. Show that there are two roots to the estimating function. Are there any conditions on the existence of the roots? What can we say about the existence of the solution as n becomes large?

b. Derive the probability limits of the two EE estimators based on these roots. Is one of the roots a consistent estimator of θ?

11.6.3. Computer Problems

11–1 Given the information in Problem 1 in the preceding section, simulate the moments and distribution of the normal QML estimator for this problem. How do the sampling properties of the QML estimator compare with the ML estimator?

11–2 To compare the original and standardized estimating functions in Problem 2, write a GAUSS program that simulates the expected value and variance of h and h_s. How do the sample mean and variance of the two functions behave as n increases? Are these unbiased estimating functions? Note that the pseudorandom sample may be recursively generated by choosing some starting value (i.e., $y_0 = 1$) and drawing $y_1 = \mu + \varepsilon_1 \sigma \sqrt{y_0}$, where ε_1 is a pseudorandom disturbance with mean zero and unit variance.

11–3 Write a GAUSS program that generates pseudorandom sample for the DSP described in Problem 3 in the preceding section. To generate the Poisson(λ) draws, you can use the rndp() procedure in GAUSS. To produce the Binomial (n, p) draws, you can generate n pseudorandom Uniform(0,1) numbers U_i and compute the sum of $Z_i - \mathbf{I}_{[0,\,p]}(U_i)$.

a. Conduct a Monte Carlo exercise designed to simulate the sampling properties of the MOM estimators for various n, p, and λ.

b. Repeat the simulation exercise for the QMLE–E estimators. Note that you may have to write a GAUSS procedure that numerically maximizes the quasi-likelihood function.

c. Compare the simulated sampling properties of the QMLE–E estimator with the large-sample approximation derived in Problem 3 in the preceding section.

11–4 Extend the GAUSS program provided for Example 11.3.1 (C11WLS.gss) to simulate the statistical properties of the EE and WLS estimators of β. Can you use analytical arguments to show that the estimators are unbiased, consistent, or asymptotically normal? Do your simulation results support any of the analytical findings? On the basis of the simulation results, what can you say about the comparative statistical properties of the two estimators?

11.7. References

Bhapkar, V. P. (1997), "Estimating Functions, Partial Sufficiency and Q-Sufficiency in the Presence of Nuisance Parameters," in *Selected Proceedings of the Symposium on Estimation*

Functions, I. V. Basawa, V. P. Godambe, and R. L. Taylor (Eds.), Vol. 32, Institute of Mathematical Statistics Lecture Notes – Monograph Series, Hayward, CA, pp. 83–104.

Breslow, N. (1990), "Tests of Hypotheses in Overdispersed Poisson Regression and Other Quasi-Likelihood Models," *Journal of the American Statistical Association*, Vol. 88, pp. 565–71.

Crowder, M. (1986), "On Consistency and Inconsistency of Estimating Equations," *Econometric Theory*, Vol. 2, pp. 305–30.

Desmond, A. F. (1997), "Prediction Functions and Geostatistics," in *Selected Proceedings of the Symposium on Estimation Functions*, I. V. Basawa, V. P. Godambe, and R. L. Taylor (Eds.), Vol. 32, Institute of Mathematical Statistics Lecture Notes – Monograph Series, Hayward, CA, pp. 353–68.

Gallant, R. (1987), *Nonlinear Statistical Models*, New York: John Wiley and Sons.

Gallant, A. R., and G. Tauchen (1996), "Which Moments to Match?", *Econometric Theory*, Vol. 12, pp. 657–81.

Godambe, V. P. (1960), "An Optimum Property of Regular Maximum Likelihood Estimation," *Annals of Mathematics and Statistics*, Vol. 31, pp. 1208–12.

Godambe, V. P. (1991), "Orthogonality of Estimating Functions and Nuisance Parameters," *Biometrika*, Vol. 78, pp. 143–51.

Godambe, V. P. (1997), "Estimating Functions: A Synthesis of Least Squares and Maximum Likelihood Methods," in *Selected Proceedings of the Symposium on Estimation Functions*, I. V. Basawa, V. P. Godambe, and R. L. Taylor (Eds.), Vol. 32, Institute of Mathematical Statistics Lecture Notes – Monograph Series, Hayward, CA, pp. 5–16.

Godambe, V. P., and C. C. Heyde (1987), "Quasi-likelihood and Optimal Estimation," *International Statistical Review*, Vol. 55, pp. 321–44.

Godambe, V. P., and B. K. Kale (1991), "Estimating Functions: An Overview," In V. P. Godambe (Ed.), *Estimating Functions*, Oxford, UK: Oxford University Press, pp. 3–20.

Godambe, V. P., and M. E. Thompson (1989), "An Extension of Quasi-likelihood Estimation (with discussion)," *Journal of Statistical Planning and Inference*, Vol. 22, pp. 137–72.

Gong, G., and F. J. Samaniego (1981), "Pseudo-Maximum Likelihood Estimation: Theory and Applications," *Annals of Statistics*, Vol. 9, pp. 861–69.

Gourieroux, C., A. Monfort, and A. Trognon (1984a), "Pseudo-Maximum Likelihood Methods: Theory," *Econometrica*, Vol. 52, pp. 681–700.

Gourieroux, C., A. Monfort, and A. Trognon (1984b), "Pseudo-Maximum Likelihood Methods: Applications to Poisson Models," *Econometrica*, Vol. 52, pp. 701–20.

Heyde, C. C. (1989), "Quasi-likelihood and Optimality for Estimating Functions: Some Current Unifying Themes," *Bulletin of the International Statistical Institute*, Vol. 53, Book 1, pp. 19–29.

Heyde, C. C. (1994), "A Quasi-likelihood Approach to the REML Estimating Equations," *Statistics and Probability Letters*, Vol. 21, pp. 381–4.

Heyde, C. C. (1997), *Quasi-likelihood and Its Application: A General Approach to Optimal Parameter Estimation*, New York: Springer–Verlag.

Heyde, C. C., and R. Morton (1993), "On Constrained Quasi-Likelihood Estimation," *Biometrika*, Vol. 80, pp. 755–61.

Kale, B. K. (1962), "An Extension of Cramér–Rao Inequality for Statistical Estimation Functions," *Skandinavisk Aktuarietidsk rift*, Vol. 45, pp. 60–89.

Kullback, S. (1959), *Information Theory and Statistics*, New York: John Wiley and Sons.

Kullback, S., and R. A. Liebler (1951), "On Information and Sufficiency," *Annals of Mathematical Statistics*, Vol. 22, pp. 79–86.

Liang, K. Y., and J. Hanfelt (1994), "On the Use of the Quasi-likelihood Method in Teratological Experiments," *Biometrics*, Vol. 50, pp. 872–80.
Liang, K. Y., and S. L. Zeger (1995), "Inference Based on Estimating Functions in the Presence of Nuisance Parameters (with discussion)," *Statistical Science*, Vol. 10, pp. 158–99.
McCullagh, P., and J. Nelder (1989), *Generalized Linear Models*, 2nd ed., London: Chapman and Hall.
Phillips, P. (1976), "On the Iterated Distance Estimator and the Quasi-Maximum Likelihood Estimator," *Econometrica*, Vol. 44, pp. 449–60.
Qin, J., and J. Lawless (1994), "Empirical Likelihood and General Estimating Equations," *The Annals of Statistics*, Vol. 22, pp. 300–25.
Schervish, M. J. (1995), *Theory of Statistics*, New York: Springer–Verlag.
Vinod, H. D. (1997), "Using Godambe–Durbin Estimating Functions in Econometrics," in *Selected Proceedings of the Symposium on Estimation Functions*, I. V. Basawa, V. P. Godambe, and R. L. Taylor (Eds.), Vol. 32, Institute of Mathematical Statistics Lecture Notes – Monograph Series, Hayward, CA, pp. 215–38.
Wedderburn, R. W. M. (1974), "Quasi-likelihood Functions, Generalized Linear Models, and the Gauss–Newton Method," *Biometrika*, Vol. 69, pp. 439–47.
White, H. (1982), "Maximum Likelihood Estimation of Misspecified Models," *Econometrica*, Vol. 50, pp. 1–16.
White, H. (1994), *Estimation, Inference, and Specification Analysis*, New York: Cambridge University Press.
Wooldridge, J. M. (1994), "Estimation and Inference for Dependent Processes" in *Handbook of Econometrics*, Vol. 4, R. F. Engle, and D. L. McFadden (Eds.), Amsterdam: Elsevier.

11.8. Appendix: Proofs

THEOREM PROOF 11.3.1. CONSISTENCY OF THE EE ESTIMATOR: The result stated in Theorem 11.5.1 follows from Theorem 7.3.1. Let $\|\mathbf{w}\| = (\mathbf{w}'\mathbf{w})^{1/2}$ be the standard measure of Euclidean distance of $\mathbf{w}$ from $\mathbf{0}$ and note that $\hat{\boldsymbol{\Theta}}_{\text{EE}} = \arg_{\boldsymbol{\theta}\in\Omega}[\mathbf{h}(\mathbf{Y}, \mathbf{x}, \boldsymbol{\theta}) = \mathbf{0}] = \arg\max_{\boldsymbol{\theta}\in\Omega}[-\|\mathbf{h}(\mathbf{Y}, \mathbf{x}, \boldsymbol{\theta})\|]$. Note further that because $\mathbf{h}_*(\boldsymbol{\theta})$ is continuous in $\boldsymbol{\theta}$ and equals zero iff $\boldsymbol{\theta} = \boldsymbol{\theta}_0$, $-\|\mathbf{h}_*(\boldsymbol{\theta})\|$ is continuous in $\boldsymbol{\theta}$ and is uniquely maximized at $\boldsymbol{\theta}_0$. Finally, $-\|\mathbf{h}(\mathbf{Y}, \mathbf{x}, \boldsymbol{\theta})\|$ converges uniformly in probability to $-\|\mathbf{h}_*(\boldsymbol{\theta})\|$ because $\mathbf{h}(\mathbf{Y}, \mathbf{x}, \boldsymbol{\theta})$ converges uniformly in probability to $\mathbf{h}_*(\boldsymbol{\theta})$. Then all of the assumptions of Theorem 7.3.1 hold, in which case $\hat{\boldsymbol{\Theta}}_{\text{EE}} \xrightarrow{p} \boldsymbol{\theta}_0$. ■

THEOREM PROOF 11.3.2. ASYMPTOTIC NORMALITY OF THE EE ESTIMATOR: Because the estimating function is twice continuously differentiable, the estimating equation can be expanded in a Taylor series about the true value of the parameter vector as

$$\mathbf{h}(\mathbf{Y}, \mathbf{x}, \hat{\boldsymbol{\Theta}}_{\text{EE}}) = \mathbf{h}(\mathbf{Y}, \mathbf{x}, \boldsymbol{\theta}_0) + \left.\frac{\partial \mathbf{h}(\mathbf{Y}, \mathbf{x}, \boldsymbol{\theta})}{\partial \boldsymbol{\theta}}\right|_{\boldsymbol{\Theta}_*} (\hat{\boldsymbol{\Theta}}_{\text{EE}} - \boldsymbol{\theta}_0) = \mathbf{0}, \quad (11.8.1)$$

where $\boldsymbol{\Theta}_*$ is some convex combination of $\hat{\boldsymbol{\Theta}}_{\text{EE}}$ and $\boldsymbol{\theta}_0$ that will in general be different for each of the rows in $\mathbf{h}(\mathbf{Y}, \mathbf{x}, \boldsymbol{\theta})$. Note that (11.8.1) equals $\mathbf{0}$ because the EE estimator $\hat{\boldsymbol{\Theta}}_{\text{EE}}$ solves the estimating equations by definition. If it is assumed that the gradient vector in (11.8.1) has full rank in the neighborhood of $\boldsymbol{\theta}_0$, then if $\boldsymbol{\Theta}_*$ resides in this neighborhood, it follows that

$$(\hat{\boldsymbol{\Theta}}_{\mathrm{EE}} - \boldsymbol{\theta}_0) = -\left[\left.\frac{\partial \mathbf{h}(\mathbf{Y}, \mathbf{x}, \boldsymbol{\theta})}{\partial \boldsymbol{\theta}}\right|_{\boldsymbol{\Theta}_*}\right]^{-1} \mathbf{h}(\mathbf{Y}, \mathbf{x}, \boldsymbol{\theta}_0). \tag{11.8.2}$$

Furthermore, if $\left.\frac{\partial \mathbf{h}(\mathbf{Y}, \mathbf{x}, \boldsymbol{\theta})}{\partial \boldsymbol{\theta}}\right|_{\boldsymbol{\theta}} \xrightarrow{p} \mathrm{E}[\left.\frac{\partial \mathbf{h}(\mathbf{Y}, \mathbf{x}, \boldsymbol{\theta})}{\partial \boldsymbol{\theta}}\right|_{\boldsymbol{\theta}}]$ uniformly for all values of $\boldsymbol{\theta}$ in a neighborhood of $\boldsymbol{\theta}_0$, then

$$\hat{\boldsymbol{\Theta}}_{\mathrm{EE}} \xrightarrow{p} \boldsymbol{\theta}_0 \Rightarrow \boldsymbol{\Theta}_* \xrightarrow{p} \boldsymbol{\theta}_0 \Rightarrow \left.\frac{\partial \mathbf{h}(\mathbf{Y}, \mathbf{x}, \boldsymbol{\theta})}{\partial \boldsymbol{\theta}}\right|_{\boldsymbol{\Theta}_*} \xrightarrow{p} \mathrm{E}\left[\left.\frac{\partial \mathbf{h}(\mathbf{Y}, \mathbf{x}, \boldsymbol{\theta})}{\partial \boldsymbol{\theta}}\right|_{\boldsymbol{\theta}_0}\right]. \tag{11.8.3}$$

Finally, if $\boldsymbol{\Psi}^{-1/2}\mathbf{h}(\mathbf{Y}, \mathbf{x}, \boldsymbol{\theta}_0) \xrightarrow{d} \mathrm{N}(\mathbf{0}, \mathbf{I})$, where $\boldsymbol{\Psi} = \mathrm{E}[\mathbf{h}(\mathbf{Y}, \mathbf{x}, \boldsymbol{\theta}_0)\,\mathbf{h}(\mathbf{Y}, \mathbf{x}, \boldsymbol{\theta}_0)']$, then it follows by Slutsky's theorem that $\boldsymbol{\Psi}^{-1/2}\mathrm{E}[\left.\frac{\partial \mathbf{h}(\mathbf{Y}, \mathbf{x}, \boldsymbol{\theta})}{\partial \boldsymbol{\theta}'}\right|_{\boldsymbol{\theta}_0}](\hat{\boldsymbol{\Theta}}_{\mathrm{EE}} - \boldsymbol{\theta}_0) \xrightarrow{d} \mathrm{N}(\mathbf{0}, \mathbf{I})$, and thus $\hat{\boldsymbol{\Theta}}_{\mathrm{EE}}$ has the asymptotic normal distribution, as stated in the theorem. ■

CHAPTER 12

Empirical Likelihood Estimation and Inference

IN contrast to the ML procedures developed in Chapters 3, 4, and 9, in this chapter we continue in the spirit of Chapter 11 to address the fact that in practice there is often insufficient information to specify the parametric form of the likelihood function underlying the DSP. Given this situation, it is possible to utilize the concept of unbiased estimating functions (EFs), as presented in Chapter 11, combined with the concept of *empirical likelihood* (EL) to define a (empirical) likelihood function for the parameter vector based on a nonparametric representation of the sample's PDF. This leads to the concept of maximum empirical likelihood (MEL) estimation and inference, which is in many ways analogous to parametric maximum likelihood methods. Specifically, MEL estimates are obtained by maximizing the (empirical) likelihood function, and the MEL estimator has first-order asymptotic sampling properties that are analogous to ML properties. The definition of a likelihood ratio based on the EL function, and its asymptotic probability distribution, are also analogous to the parametric generalized likelihood ratio.

Of particular importance is the fact that MEL estimation achieves, within the class of estimators derived from linear combinations of the available unbiased estimating functions, the same (optimal) asymptotic efficiency as the OptEF optimal estimator of Chapter 11. Therefore, the EL approach provides an operational way to utilize unbiased estimating function information in an asymptotically efficient way and thus effectively solves the problem of optimally (linearly) combining estimating equations into an OptEF (optimal estimating function) estimator. However, as in the nonlinear ML, QML, EE, and extremum estimation problems, the solutions to empirical likelihood problems often cannot be written in closed form and must be numerically computed.

In terms of the general class of statistical models portrayed in Table 2.1, we consider the cases delineated in Table 12.1.

The particular inverse problem associated with the statistical models in Table 12.1 is represented by

$$(\mathbf{Y}, \mathbf{X}) \Rightarrow (\boldsymbol{\beta}, \sigma^2, \varepsilon).$$

Table 12.1. *Semiparametric Regression Models*

Model Component	Specific Characteristics	
$\mathbf{Y}$	RV Type:	continuous
	Range:	unlimited
	Y_i dimension:	univariate
	Moments:	$E[\mathbf{Y} \mid \mathbf{x}] = \mathbf{g}(\mathbf{x}, \boldsymbol{\beta})$, $\mathbf{cov}(\mathbf{Y} \mid \mathbf{x}) = \sigma^2\mathbf{I}$
$\eta(\mathbf{X}, \boldsymbol{\beta}, \varepsilon)$	Functional Form:	linear or nonlinear in $\mathbf{x}$ and $\boldsymbol{\beta}$ and additive in ε, where $\eta(\mathbf{x}, \boldsymbol{\beta}, \varepsilon) = \mathbf{g}(\mathbf{x}, \boldsymbol{\beta}) + \varepsilon$, $\mathbf{g}(\mathbf{x}, \boldsymbol{\beta}) = [\mathbf{g}(\mathbf{x}_{1\cdot}, \boldsymbol{\beta}), \ldots, \mathrm{g}(\mathbf{x}_{n\cdot}, \boldsymbol{\beta})]'$ and $\mathbf{g}$ is twice continuously differentiable in $\boldsymbol{\beta}$.
$\mathbf{X}$	RV Type:	degenerate (fixed) or stochastic
	Genesis:	exogenous to the model
$\boldsymbol{\beta}$	RV Type:	degenerate(fixed)
	Dimension:	finite
ε	RV Type:	iid, or non-iid
	Moments:	$E[\varepsilon \mid \mathbf{X}] = \mathbf{0}$, and $\mathbf{cov}(\varepsilon \mid \mathbf{x}) = \sigma^2\mathbf{I}$
Ω	Prior info:	none
$f(\mathbf{e} \mid \mathbf{x}, \varphi^2)$	PDF family:	unspecified

12.1. Empirical Likelihood: iid Case

In contrast to the ML procedures presented in Chapters 3, 4, and 9, suppose we do not have enough information about the underlying to specify the parametric functional form of the likelihood function. In Chapter 11 the concepts of quasi-likelihood and estimating equations greatly expanded the scope of models for which a unified method of optimal parameter estimation and inference is available. For the estimation of parameters in the regression model in particular, as well as more general stochastic systems, we noted in Chapter 11 that it is possible to replace likelihood-based techniques by quasi-likelihood alternatives in which only assumptions about means and variances are made. The resulting quasi-maximum likelihood (QML) estimators were consistent, asymptotically normal, and had optimal efficiency properties within certain broad classes of estimators.

In this chapter, we continue to pursue estimators that are relatively free of specific distributional assumptions. We follow Owen (1988, 1990, 1991) and Qin and Lawless (1994), who demonstrate how the empirical likelihood (EL) procedure can be used in the case of independent or iid data, to define profile-likelihood functions based on a particular multinomial probability distribution that is supported on the sample data. The term *profile likelihood function* refers to a likelihood function that has been partially maximized with respect to a subset of its parameters conditional on given values of the remaining parameters. In previous chapters, we also refer to the profile likelihood function as a *concentrated likelihood function*.

12.1.1. The EL Concept

The general concept of empirical likelihood in the case of iid data begins with the conceptualization of a joint empirical probability mass function of the form $\Pi_{i=1}^{n} p_i$ that is supported on the random sample outcomes $y_1, \ldots, y_n$. The parameter p_i denotes the probability assigned to the ith sample outcome, y_i, and the outcome could be a vector as well as a scalar. To define the value of the empirical likelihood function for $\boldsymbol{\theta}$, the p_i's are selected to maximize $\Pi_{i=1}^{n} p_i$, subject to constraints defined in terms of moment equations, $E[\mathbf{h}(\mathbf{Y}, \boldsymbol{\theta})] = \mathbf{0}$, which can be interpreted as representing the expectation of an unbiased estimating equation $\mathbf{h}(\mathbf{Y}, \boldsymbol{\theta})$. The moment equations are represented empirically by $E_p[\mathbf{h}(\mathbf{Y}, \boldsymbol{\theta})] = \sum_{i=1}^{n} p_i \mathbf{h}(y_i, \boldsymbol{\theta}) = \mathbf{0}$, where $\boldsymbol{\theta}$ represents the parameters of interest, $\mathbf{Y}$ is interpreted to have the empirical distribution $p_i = P(y = y_i)$, $i = 1, \ldots, n$, and $E_p[\cdot]$ denotes an expectation taken with respect to the empirical distribution. The maximization step chooses the joint probability distribution $\Pi_{i=1}^{n} p_i$ for $\mathbf{Y}$ that assigns the maximum probability possible to the sample outcome $\mathbf{y}$ actually observed, subject to the information, or equivalently the constraints, represented by the empirical moment equations. In effect this maximization can be interpreted in the context of *constrained maximum likelihood* applied to the estimation of the parameters $\mathbf{p}$ of a multinomial distribution for the n different "types" of data outcomes represented by $y_1, y_2, \ldots, y_n$. The constraints in this ML problem are provided by the empirical moment equations, which serve to introduce $\boldsymbol{\theta}$, the remaining parameters other than $\mathbf{p}$, into the ML estimation problem. The profile or empirical likelihood function for $\boldsymbol{\theta}$ is then defined by substituting the constrained maximum value for each p_i, say $\hat{p}_i(\boldsymbol{\theta}; \mathbf{y})$, into $\Pi_{i=1}^{n} p_i$, yielding a function of $\boldsymbol{\theta}$ as $L_{EL}(\boldsymbol{\theta}; \mathbf{y}) = \Pi_{i=1}^{n} \hat{p}_i(\boldsymbol{\theta}; \mathbf{y})$.

The EL approach has an advantage over some parametric methods of inference for the regression model in that the analyst is only required to make mild assumptions on the existence of certain zero-valued moments associated with functions of the random sample and the parameters of interest. In particular, information relating to the PDF of the data-sampling process is assumed to be available in the form of functionally independent unbiased estimating functions involving the population random variable Y and the parameter vector of interest $\boldsymbol{\theta}$ (recall Chapter 11). The analyst is free to specify as many of these estimating functions as possible based on the information available, and these estimating functions can refer to whatever parameters the analyst has information about. This permits the analyst to deal with multiple pieces of information about an unknown distribution and the parameters of interest as well as deal with only those pieces of information that the analyst feels confident about.

As will become evident ahead, the EL function operates remarkably like an ordinary parametric likelihood function for estimation and inference purposes. In principle, the EL approach can produce estimates and confidence regions based on almost any reasonable set of estimating functions. By *reasonable* we mean that the estimating functions are unbiased and thus have zero expectations, have finite variances, and are based on independent or weakly dependent data observations.

We begin our discussion of the EL procedure by examining the details of the method in the iid case, which will further motivate the general concepts involved and define notation. In subsequent sections we provide details regarding how one utilizes the EL concept to perform maximum empirical likelihood (MEL) estimation of parameters for various probability models, including estimation of parameters of population distributions and parameters of regression functions. We also discuss how to test hypotheses and generate confidence regions and bounds based on the EL, including the use of the generalized empirical likelihood ratio (GELR) for inference purposes. Finally, we also indicate how the EL principle can be extended to data that are independent but not identically distributed, as well as to data that are weakly dependent.

12.1.2. Nonparametric Maximum Likelihood Estimate of a Population Distribution

To motivate the basic EL concept, we begin with the case of a simple iid random sample $\mathbf{Y} = (Y_1, Y_2, \ldots, Y_n)'$ from some common population PDF $f(y; \boldsymbol{\theta})$, where $\boldsymbol{\theta} \in \Omega$ (we emphasize that y denotes a scalar population variable value here as opposed to (bold) $\mathbf{y}$ representing the entire random sample vector). For simplicity we assume that the Y_i's are random scalars, but the argument applies, with minor adjustments, to iid random *vectors* as well. Under the current assumptions, the true likelihood function for the parameter vector $\boldsymbol{\theta}$ can be stated as $L(\boldsymbol{\theta}; \mathbf{y}) \equiv \Pi_{i=1}^{n} f(y_i; \boldsymbol{\theta})$.

12.1.2.a. A Nonparametric Likelihood Function

At the outset, assume that we have no parametric functional form specified for $f(y; \boldsymbol{\theta})$ in our probability model, and this means we do not make any assumption about the functional form of the common parametric family of PDFs for the distribution of the data observations. In this context, consider the inverse problem of using a random sample outcome $\mathbf{y} = (y_1, y_2, \ldots, y_n)$ to recover an estimate of the PDF of $\mathbf{Y}$. For this *nonparametric* problem setting, we can define a nonparametric likelihood function whose arguments are not parameters but entire probability density or mass functions as

$$L(f; \mathbf{y}) = \prod_{i=1}^{n} f(y_i). \tag{12.1.1}$$

Given a choice of *function* f(y) in (12.1.1), the nonparametric likelihood function $L(f; \mathbf{y})$ indicates the likelihood that f(y) is the true population distribution underlying the random sample outcome, $\mathbf{y}$. The nonparametric maximum likelihood (NPML) estimate of f(y) is defined by

$$\hat{f}(y) = \arg\max_{f}[L(f; \mathbf{y})] = \arg\max_{f}\left[\prod_{i=1}^{n} f(y_i)\right]. \tag{12.1.2}$$

Note this is mathematically different from extremum problems we have examined previously because we are asking for the choice of *function* f and *not* the choice of a parameter vector $\boldsymbol{\theta}$ that maximizes the likelihood function (12.1.1). Note that the feasible space for this maximization problem consists of all possible functions satisfying the properties of probability density or mass functions.

We can transform the maximization problem in (12.1.2) into a simpler parametric form by first observing that it is only the unknown parameter values $p_i = f(y_i)$, $i = 1, \ldots, n$ that matter in solving the maximum likelihood problem in (12.1.2). We can then define an *empirical* probability mass function of the multinomial type that represents discrete probability masses assigned to each of the finite number of observed sample outcomes. In this context, all of the probability weights must be positive because $p_i > 0\,\forall i$ or the joint likelihood for the observed sample is $\Pi_{i=1}^{n} f(y_i) = 0$, which is a minimum as opposed to a maximum value of $L(f; \mathbf{y})$. Thus, the preceding maximum likelihood problem (12.1.1) and (12.1.2) can be represented as a parametric maximum likelihood problem of finding the optimal choice of p_i's in a multinomial-type likelihood function in which each "type" of outcome occurs only once, leading to the solution

$$(\hat{p}_1, \ldots, \hat{p}_n) = \arg\max_{\mathbf{p}} \left[\prod_{i=1}^{n} p_i \right] = \arg\max_{\mathbf{p}} \left[n^{-1} \sum_{i=1}^{n} \ln(p_i) \right] \tag{12.1.3}$$

subject to $p_i > 0$, $\forall i$. Note the use of the logarithmic transformation in (12.1.3) does not alter the optimal solution for the p_i's because the log transform is a strictly monotonically increasing function of its argument. Likewise, scaling the objective function by n^{-1} has no effect on the optimal p_i's. We introduce the scaling factor to scale the value of the Lagrange multipliers in the Lagrange form of the constrained optimization problem that will define the EL function ahead. The scaling is *not* necessary for obtaining the statistical properties of EL estimation and testing procedures but maintains consistency with the literature on the EL approach and facilitates analysis of asymptotic properties.

Transforming the problem into the parametric form (12.1.3) makes it readily apparent that the objective function of the maximization problem is unbounded because the p_i's are unrestricted in value. Thus (12.1.2) or (12.1.3) has no solution unless a normalization condition on the p_i's is imposed. That some type of normalization is necessary is of course not surprising because the p_i's represent values of a PDF, which are necessarily normalized as $\sum_i f(y_i) = 1$ in the discrete case, $\int_{-\infty}^{\infty} f(y)\,dy$ in the continuous case, and in general $\int_{-\infty}^{\infty} dF(y) = 1$. Furthermore, in the case at hand, it is natural and completely general to use the normalization $\sum_{i=1}^{n} p_i = 1$ because values of $f(y_i)$ for arguments outside of the values contained in the sample outcome $\mathbf{y} = (y_1, y_2, \ldots, y_n)$ are irrelevant to the maximum likelihood problem (12.1.2) or (12.1.3). Also note that the normalization $\sum_{i=1}^{n} p_i = 1$ can be used even if the underlying population distribution refers to a continuous random variable because in practice likelihood functions need only be proportional to the underlying sampling distribution and not necessarily equal to it.

12.1.2.b. A Nonparametric ML Solution

Imposing the normalization condition on the p_i's, the solution to the problem of finding the NPML estimate of $f(y)$ can be defined in terms of the choice of p_i's that maximize $n^{-1} \sum_{i=1}^{n} \ln(p_i)$ subject to the constraint $\sum_{i=1}^{n} p_i = 1$. The Lagrange function associated with this constrained optimization problem is given by

$$L(\mathbf{p}, \eta) \equiv n^{-1} \sum_{i=1}^{n} \ln(p_i) - \eta \left(\sum_{i=1}^{n} p_i - 1 \right), \tag{12.1.4}$$

where the additional constraint $p_i > 0\,\forall i$ is implicitly imposed by the structure of the problem (i.e., setting any $p_i = 0$, such that $L(\cdot) = -\infty$, is never optimal in (12.1.4)). The first-order conditions derived from (12.1.4) are given by

$$\begin{aligned} \frac{\partial L(\mathbf{p}, \eta)}{\partial p_i} &= \frac{1}{np_i} - \eta = 0, \quad \forall i \\ \frac{\partial L(\mathbf{p}, \eta)}{\partial \eta} &= 1 - \sum_{i=1}^{n} p_i = 0, \end{aligned} \tag{12.1.5}$$

and thus the optimal p_i's are given by $\hat{p}_i = n^{-1}\,\forall i$, and the optimal value of the Lagrange multiplier is $\hat{\eta} = 1$. We emphasize that it is perfectly acceptable for some of the numerical values of the y_i's to be the same, that is, $y_i = y_j$ for $i \neq j$. Setting $\hat{p}_i = n^{-1}\,\forall y_i$ implies that the NPML estimate of the population probability distribution is

$$\hat{f}(y) = n^{-1} \sum_{i=1}^{n} I_{\{y_i\}}(y), \tag{12.1.6}$$

where $I_{\{y_i\}}(y) = 1$ if $y = y_i$ and $I_{\{y_i\}}(y) = 0$ otherwise; that is, $\hat{f}(y)$ equals the number of y_i's equal to y divided by n.

The NPML estimate of the *cumulative* probability distribution function associated with the PDF estimate (12.1.6) is given by

$$\hat{F}(y) = n^{-1} \sum_{i=1}^{n} I_{(-\infty, y_i]}(y), \tag{12.1.7}$$

where $I_{(-\infty,y_i]}(y) = 1$ if $y \leq y_i$ and $= 0$ otherwise; that is, $\hat{F}(y)$ is equal to the proportion of the sample outcomes whose values are $\leq$ y. The reader will recognize (12.1.7) as the classical *empirical distribution function* (EDF) based on the sample outcomes. Kiefer and Wolfowitz (1956) were the first to recognize that the EDF is the NPML estimate of the population distribution of a random sample. We know by the Glivenko–Cantelli theorem that the EDF converges in probability pointwise, and in fact uniformly, to the true population CDF as $n \to \infty$. Thus, the EDF is a useful estimate of F(y), and we have achieved this estimate of the CDF without any assumptions regarding a parametric family of PDFs to which F(y) belongs.

12.1.3. Empirical Likelihood Function for $\boldsymbol{\theta}$

Although the NPML estimation approach leads to a useful estimate of the population cumulative distribution function F(y), we clearly have no basis at this point for defining either a likelihood function or an estimator for $\boldsymbol{\theta}$. It is perhaps obvious that because the likelihood (12.1.1) is devoid of parameters, it cannot be used to distinguish likely from unlikely values of a parameter vector $\boldsymbol{\theta}$. To do so, we must introduce some linkage between the data, $(y_1, y_2, \ldots, y_n)$, the population distribution F(y), and the parameter vector of interest, $\boldsymbol{\theta}$. *This linkage is accomplished through the use of unbiased estimating functions to define estimating equation constraints on the NPML problem.* In effect, these constraints apply structure to the data and extract informational content when profiling the nonparametric likelihood.

12.1.3.a. Linking $\boldsymbol{\theta}$ and the EDF: Estimating Functions

In the EL approach, unbiased *estimating functions* (recall Section 11.3) are used to link the data, the population distribution, and the parameters. In particular, expectations of functions of the population random variable $Y \sim F(y)$ and $\boldsymbol{\theta}$, $E[\mathbf{h}(Y, \boldsymbol{\theta})]$, which equal zero iff θ is the true value of the parameter, is the basic form in which estimating function information is used. The vector function $\mathbf{h}(Y, \boldsymbol{\theta})$ itself can then be interpreted as an unbiased *estimating function*, as defined in Section 11.3. The basic rationale for utilizing such constraints is as follows: For arbitrary choices of the parameter vector value $\boldsymbol{\theta}$, the expected value of an estimating function will be some function of the chosen $\boldsymbol{\theta}$, say as $\mathbf{q}(\boldsymbol{\theta}) = E[\mathbf{h}(\mathbf{Y}, \boldsymbol{\theta})]$. Because the estimating function is unbiased, its expectation will by definition equal zero when $\boldsymbol{\theta}$ equals the true value of the parameter. By setting the expected value of the estimating function to zero, one is then stating a valid functional constraint, $\mathbf{q}(\boldsymbol{\theta}) = E[\mathbf{h}(\mathbf{Y}, \boldsymbol{\theta})] = \mathbf{0}$, that can be used to help identify the true parameter vector so long as the estimating function is truly unbiased. In fact, if the number of functionally independent estimating functions in the vector $\mathbf{h}(\mathbf{Y}, \boldsymbol{\theta})$ equals the number of parameters in the parameter vector $\boldsymbol{\theta}$, $\mathbf{q}(\boldsymbol{\theta}) = E[\mathbf{h}(\mathbf{Y}, \boldsymbol{\theta})] = \mathbf{0}$ can be solved for the true value of $\boldsymbol{\theta}$.

For example, suppose the parameter θ is used to represent the unknown value μ of the mean of a population distribution F. Then, the estimating function $h(Y, \theta) = Y - \theta$ is unbiased because if it were actually true that the value of $\theta = \mu$, so that θ is the true value of the parameter, then $E[h(Y, \theta)] = E[Y - \theta] = [\mu - \mu] = 0$. This information implies that we can form a valid constraint on the value of the parameter θ by specifying the moment equation $E[h(Y, \theta)] = E[Y - \theta] = [\mu - \theta] = 0$, which implies the valid constraint $\theta = \mu$. In this case, the moment constraint exactly identifies the "true value" of θ.

For another example, if $Y \sim F$ with mean μ and variance σ^2, and the vector estimating function $\mathbf{h}(Y, \boldsymbol{\theta}) = \begin{bmatrix} Y - \theta_1 \\ (Y - \theta_1)^2 - \theta_2 \end{bmatrix}$ is unbiased, one has a basis for defining valid constraints on the parameters θ_1 and θ_2 of the form

$$E[\mathbf{h}(Y, \boldsymbol{\theta})] = E\begin{bmatrix} Y - \theta_1 \\ (Y - \theta_1)^2 - \theta_2 \end{bmatrix} = \mathbf{0}. \tag{12.1.8}$$

The moment equation system (12.1.8) identifies θ_1 as the mean, $\mu = E[Y]$, and θ_2 as the variance, $\sigma^2 = \text{var}(Y) = E[(Y - E[Y])^2]$ of the population distribution F. If the expectations could actually be calculated in (12.1.8), and the system is solved for θ_1 and θ_2, the solved values would precisely equal the mean and variance of the population distribution, respectively.

At this point in our discussion, the use of unbiased estimating functions has succeeded in establishing a method for conceptually linking the parameters of interest $\boldsymbol{\theta}$ to the underlying population distribution. However, there are two fundamental and related problems still left unresolved in our conceptualization of an empirical likelihood function. First, the constraints $\mathbf{q}(\boldsymbol{\theta}) = E[\mathbf{h}(\mathbf{Y}, \boldsymbol{\theta})] = \mathbf{0}$ derived from the unbiased estimating functions make no reference to the empirical probability weights $\mathbf{p}$ and so do not represent any effective information or constraints on the choice of $\mathbf{p}$ in the NPML estimation problem. Furthermore, the expectations of the estimating functions cannot be calculated because F(y) is unknown, and thus solving a system of expected value or moment equations for parameter values that is based on the expectation of estimating functions is not possible in practice. We will see ahead that both problems are resolved by representing expectations in terms of empirical probability weights applied to the n iid observations, $\mathbf{h}(y_i, \boldsymbol{\theta})$, $i = 1, \ldots, n$, on the estimating functions.

To incorporate the moment equation information implied by unbiased estimating functions into empirical methods for estimating and testing hypotheses about $\boldsymbol{\theta}$, as well as for estimating the population distribution itself, the EL approach treats $E[\mathbf{h}(Y, \boldsymbol{\theta})] = \mathbf{0}$ as a valid structural constraint on the problem of maximizing the nonparametric likelihood (12.1.4). But because F(y) is unknown, one uses a set of empirically estimated probability weights, say $\hat{p}_i$'s, in place of F(y) as the probability distribution underlying the expectations that define the moment equations. For example, the *empirical* representation of the expectation of the estimating functions (12.1.8) under the EL approach leads to the parametric constraints

$$E_{\mathbf{p}}[\mathbf{h}(Y, \boldsymbol{\theta})] = \begin{bmatrix} \sum_{i=1}^{n} p_i y_i - \theta_1 \\ \sum_{i=1} p_i (y_i - \theta_1)^2 - \theta_2 \end{bmatrix} = \begin{bmatrix} 0 \\ 0 \end{bmatrix}, \tag{12.1.9}$$

where the notation $E_{\mathbf{p}}$ is again used to emphasize that expectations are being taken with respect to the empirical probability distribution $\mathbf{p} = (p_1, p_2, \ldots, p_n)'$ supported on the sample outcomes $(y_1, y_2, \ldots, y_n)$. More generally, the empirical representation of the moment constraints takes the form of the $(m \times 1)$ vector equation

$$E_{\mathbf{p}}[\mathbf{h}(Y, \boldsymbol{\theta})] = \sum_{i=1}^{n} p_i \mathbf{h}(y_i, \boldsymbol{\theta}) = \mathbf{0}. \tag{12.1.10}$$

Note that the *empirical* moment constraints derived from the concept of unbiased estimating functions *do* involve the empirical probabilities $\mathbf{p}$ explicitly and represent constraints on the choice of $\mathbf{p}$ in the NPML estimation of the empirical distribution function representation of the population distribution. This set of equations is appended as a set of structural constraints on the constrained maximization problem represented by (12.1.4), and a *scaled* (by n) *log-empirical likelihood function* for $\boldsymbol{\theta}$ is then defined as

$$n^{-1} \ln(L_{EL}(\boldsymbol{\theta}; \mathbf{y})) \equiv \max_{\mathbf{p}} \left[n^{-1} \sum_{i=1}^{n} \ln(p_i) \text{ s.t. } \sum_{i=1}^{n} p_i \mathbf{h}(y_i, \boldsymbol{\theta}) = \mathbf{0} \text{ and } \sum_{i=1}^{n} p_i = 1 \right]. \tag{12.1.11}$$

As we noted earlier, the constraints $p_i > 0 \, \forall i$ are imposed implicitly by the structure of the optimization problem. The Lagrange function associated with the constrained maximization problem can be represented as

$$L(\mathbf{p}, \eta, \boldsymbol{\lambda}) \equiv \left[n^{-1} \sum_{i=1}^{n} \ln(p_i) - \eta \left(\sum_{i=1}^{n} p_i - 1 \right) - \boldsymbol{\lambda}' \sum_{i=1}^{n} p_i \mathbf{h}(y_i, \boldsymbol{\theta}) \right]. \tag{12.1.12}$$

12.1.3.b. Comparing the Use of Estimating Functions in EE and EL Contexts

It is instructive at this point to highlight similarities and differences in the way estimating function information is used in the EL approach compared with the EE approach of Chapter 11. In the EL case, the estimating function $\mathbf{h}(\mathrm{Y}, \boldsymbol{\theta})$ relates to the population random variable Y, and information about $\boldsymbol{\theta}$ conveyed by the estimating function is expressed and used in *expectation* or moment form $\mathrm{E}[\mathbf{h}(\mathrm{Y}, \boldsymbol{\theta})] = \mathbf{0}$ to define constraints on the NPML problem that generates the empirical likelihood function. Given that the expectation is unknown because F(y) is unknown, an estimated empirical probability distribution is applied to observed sample outcomes of $\mathbf{h}(\mathrm{Y}, \boldsymbol{\theta})$, $\mathbf{h}(\mathrm{y}_i, \boldsymbol{\theta}), i = 1, \ldots, n$, to define an empirical expectation $\sum_{i=1}^n \mathrm{p}_i \mathbf{h}(\mathrm{y}_i, \boldsymbol{\theta})$ that approximates $\mathrm{E}[\mathbf{h}(\mathrm{Y}, \boldsymbol{\theta})]$ and that can be used in forming an empirical moment equation, as in (12.1.10). The empirical moment equation is ultimately the form in which sample information about the parameters of interest is represented and used in the definition of the empirical likelihood. Note that the empirical moment equation depends not only on the sample data $\mathbf{y}$ and parameter vector $\boldsymbol{\theta}$ but also on the empirical probabilities $\mathbf{p}$. When viewed in the context of estimating equations for $\boldsymbol{\theta}$, the system of m estimating equations $\mathbf{h}_{\mathrm{EL}}(\mathbf{y}, \boldsymbol{\theta}, \mathbf{p}) \equiv \sum_{i=1}^n \mathrm{p}_i \mathbf{h}(\mathrm{y}_i, \boldsymbol{\theta}) = \mathbf{0}$ is generally underdetermined for identifying the $(k \times 1)$ vector $\boldsymbol{\theta}$, because there are $(n + k)$ unknowns, $(\boldsymbol{\theta}, \mathbf{p})$, in the system. We will see ahead that such indeterminacy is solved by maximizing empirical likelihood with respect to both $\boldsymbol{\theta}$ and $\mathbf{p}$ to obtain *maximum empirical likelihood* estimates of the unknown parameters of interest.

In the EE context the estimating functions themselves, and *not* empirical expectations of them, are used directly to define a system of equations $\mathbf{h}(\mathbf{y}, \boldsymbol{\theta}) = \mathbf{0}$ involving the sample data vector $\mathbf{y}$ and parameter $\boldsymbol{\theta}$. Empirical probabilities $\mathbf{p}$ are not involved. The solution of the estimating equations for $\boldsymbol{\theta}$, $\hat{\boldsymbol{\theta}}_{\mathrm{EE}}(\mathbf{y})$, is the EE estimate of the parameter vector $\boldsymbol{\theta}$. The zero-expectation property of the estimating functions is useful in establishing the consistency of estimators derived from them. However, the expression and use of estimating equation information in empirical expectation form is not inherent to the EE procedure.

Despite the differing forms in which estimating function information is represented in the respective analyses, there is some notable degree of similarity in how estimating function information ultimately impacts an EE or EL analysis. To appreciate this similarity, first note that it is admissible to view each of the functions $\mathbf{h}(\mathrm{Y}_i, \boldsymbol{\theta}), i = 1, \ldots, n$ as an unbiased estimating function in its own right if $\mathbf{h}(\mathrm{Y}, \boldsymbol{\theta})$ is an unbiased estimating function. This, of course, follows because in the current context the Y_i's are iid with precisely the same probability distribution as the population random variable Y. Now note that the EL empirical moment constraints defined in terms of the conditional-on-$\boldsymbol{\theta}$ optimum empirical probability weights are given by

$$\mathbf{h}_*(\mathbf{Y}, \boldsymbol{\theta}) \equiv \mathrm{E}_{\hat{\mathbf{p}}}[\mathbf{h}(\mathrm{Y}, \boldsymbol{\theta})] \equiv \sum_{i=1}^{n} \hat{\mathrm{p}}_i(\boldsymbol{\theta}, \mathbf{y}) \mathbf{h}(\mathrm{y}_i, \boldsymbol{\theta}) = \mathbf{0}. \tag{12.1.13}$$

These empirical moment constraints can be interpreted as an $(m \times 1)$ vector of estimating equations in the sense of the EE estimation context of Section 11.3. In effect, EL provides a method for forming a convex combination of n $(m \times 1)$ estimating functions, $\mathbf{h}(y_i, \boldsymbol{\theta})$, $i = 1, \ldots, n$.

One might consider solving the estimating equation (12.1.13) for $\boldsymbol{\theta}$ in terms of $\mathbf{y}$ in a way analogous to the EE estimation approach. Values of $\boldsymbol{\theta}$ that satisfy the estimating equations (12.1.13) will surely exist because the value of $\mathbf{p}$ used in (12.1.13) and obtained by solving (12.1.11) necessarily satisfies the constraints $\sum_{i=1}^{n} p_i \mathbf{h}(y_i, \boldsymbol{\theta}) = \mathbf{0}$. However, (12.1.13) will generally not possess a unique solution for $\boldsymbol{\theta}$ but instead will be an identity in $\boldsymbol{\theta}$ for all values of $\boldsymbol{\theta}$ for which the empirical likelihood in (12.1.11) is defined. That is, $\mathbf{p}$ is not fixed in (12.1.13) but is rather itself a function of $\boldsymbol{\theta}$ that changes in value to accommodate whatever value of $\boldsymbol{\theta}$ is used in (12.1.11). We will see ahead that the maximum empirical likelihood estimate of $\boldsymbol{\theta}$, obtained by maximizing (12.1.11) with respect to $\boldsymbol{\theta}$, defines empirical probability weights for (12.1.13), say $\mathbf{p}^*$, that define the *optimal* convex combination of estimating functions, $\mathbf{h}_*(\mathbf{y}, \boldsymbol{\theta}) \equiv \sum_{i=1}^{n} p_i^* \mathbf{h}(y_i, \boldsymbol{\theta}) = \mathbf{0}$. The estimates of $\boldsymbol{\theta}$ that would be obtained by solving these latter estimating equations for $\boldsymbol{\theta}$, treating the optimal value $\mathbf{p}^*$ as *fixed*, are equal in efficiency to the OptEF (optimal estimating function) estimate for $\boldsymbol{\theta}$ within the class of estimators derived from linear combinations of the estimating functions $\mathbf{h}(Y_i, \boldsymbol{\theta})$, $i = 1, \ldots, n$. Thus, in the final analysis, the EL and OptEF approaches to estimating $\boldsymbol{\theta}$ are joined.

12.1.3.c. The Functional Form of the Empirical Likelihood Function

The value of the empirical likelihood function evaluated at $\boldsymbol{\theta}_*$, $L_{EL}(\boldsymbol{\theta}_*; \mathbf{y})$, is the maximal empirical probability $\Pi_{i=1}^{n} p_i$ that can be assigned to the random sample outcome $\mathbf{y}$ among all distributions of probability $\mathbf{p}$ supported on the y_i's and that satisfy the empirical moment equations $\sum_{i=1}^{n} p_i \mathbf{h}(y_i, \boldsymbol{\theta}_*) = \mathbf{0}$. In effect, the EL function assigns the most favorable likelihood weight possible to each value of $\boldsymbol{\theta}_*$ from within the family of multinomial distributions supported on the data and satisfying the moment equations. Note the comparison with an ordinary (parametric) likelihood function evaluated at $\boldsymbol{\theta}_*$, $L(\boldsymbol{\theta}_*; y)$, where the likelihood weight can be interpreted as the probability (or density value) $\Pi_{i=1}^{n} f(y_i; \boldsymbol{\theta}_*)$ assigned to the sample outcome $\mathbf{y}$ by the parametric family of PDFs, $f(y, \boldsymbol{\theta})$, $\boldsymbol{\theta} \in \Omega$, when $\boldsymbol{\theta} = \boldsymbol{\theta}_*$. In both the EL and parametric cases, the parameter vector $\boldsymbol{\theta}$ indexes a family of probability distributions that, given a sample of data $\mathbf{y}$, can then be interpreted as a likelihood function for $\boldsymbol{\theta}$ for which moment conditions $E_{\mathbf{p}}[\mathbf{h}(Y, \boldsymbol{\theta}_*)] = \mathbf{0}$ and $E[\mathbf{h}(Y, \boldsymbol{\theta}_*)] = \mathbf{0}$ hold, respectively (assuming the unbiasedness of $\mathbf{h}(Y, \boldsymbol{\theta})$).

We will now be considerably more precise about the functional form of the log-empirical likelihood function defined in (12.1.11). In particular, we will solve for the optimal $\mathbf{p}$, η, and $\boldsymbol{\lambda}$ in the Lagrange form of the problem (12.1.12) and then substitute optimal values for $\mathbf{p}$ back into the objective function of the maximization problem in (12.1.11) to recover a specific functional form for the EL function in terms of $\boldsymbol{\theta}$. The first-order conditions with respect to the p_i's are

$$\frac{\partial L(\mathbf{p}, \eta, \boldsymbol{\lambda})}{\partial p_i} = \frac{1}{n}\frac{1}{p_i} - \sum_{j=1}^{m} \lambda_j h_j(y_i, \boldsymbol{\theta}) - \eta = 0, \quad \forall i. \qquad (12.1.14)$$

From the implied equality $\sum_{i=1}^{n} p_i \frac{\partial L(\mathbf{p},\eta,\boldsymbol{\lambda})}{\partial p_i} = 0$ and (12.1.10) it follows that

$$\sum_{i=1}^{n} p_i \frac{\partial L(\mathbf{p}, \eta, \boldsymbol{\lambda})}{\partial p_i} = \frac{1}{n} n - \eta = 0, \tag{12.1.15}$$

and thus $\eta = 1$. The resulting unique optimal p_i weights implied by (12.1.14) can thus be expressed as a function of $\boldsymbol{\theta}$ and $\boldsymbol{\lambda}$ as

$$p_i(\boldsymbol{\theta}, \boldsymbol{\lambda}) = \left[n \left(\sum_{j=1}^{m} \lambda_j h_j(y_i, \boldsymbol{\theta}) + 1 \right) \right]^{-1}. \tag{12.1.16}$$

We can now use the solution for $\mathbf{p}$ given by (12.1.16) to solve for the Lagrange multipliers $\boldsymbol{\lambda}$ as a function of $\boldsymbol{\theta}$. Specifically, substituting (12.1.16) into the empirical moment equations (12.1.10) produces a system of equations that $\boldsymbol{\lambda}$ must satisfy as follows:

$$\sum_{i=1}^{n} p_i \mathbf{h}(y_i, \boldsymbol{\theta}) = \sum_{i=1}^{n} n^{-1} \left[\sum_{j=1}^{m} \lambda_j h_j(y_i, \boldsymbol{\theta}) + 1 \right]^{-1} \mathbf{h}(y_i, \boldsymbol{\theta}) = \mathbf{0}. \tag{12.1.17}$$

Under general regularity conditions that will normally hold in practice, Qin and Lawless (1994, pp. 304–5) show that a well-defined solution for $\boldsymbol{\lambda}$ in (12.1.17) exists. However, the solution $\boldsymbol{\lambda}(\boldsymbol{\theta})$ is an implicit function of $\boldsymbol{\theta}$, which we denote in general by

$$\boldsymbol{\lambda}(\boldsymbol{\theta}) = \arg_{\boldsymbol{\lambda}} \left[\frac{1}{n} \sum_{i=1}^{n} \left(\frac{1}{1 + \boldsymbol{\lambda}' \mathbf{h}(y_i, \boldsymbol{\theta})} \right) \mathbf{h}(y_i, \boldsymbol{\theta}) = \mathbf{0} \right]. \tag{12.1.18}$$

Furthermore, the solution $\boldsymbol{\lambda}(\boldsymbol{\theta})$ is continuous and differentiable in $\boldsymbol{\theta}$.

Substituting the optimal Lagrangian multiplier values $\boldsymbol{\lambda}(\boldsymbol{\theta})$ into the expression for the optimal $\mathbf{p}$ weights $p_i(\boldsymbol{\theta}, \boldsymbol{\lambda})$ in (12.1.16) allows the empirical probabilities to be represented in terms of $\boldsymbol{\theta}$ as $p_i(\boldsymbol{\theta}) \equiv p_i(\boldsymbol{\theta}, \lambda(\boldsymbol{\theta})) = [n(\sum_{j=1}^{m} \lambda_j(\boldsymbol{\theta}) h_j(y_i, \boldsymbol{\theta}) + 1)]^{-1}$. Then, substitution of the optimal $\mathbf{p}(\boldsymbol{\theta})$ values into the (unscaled) objective function $\sum_{i=1}^{n} \ln(p_i)$ in (12.1.11) yields the expression for the log-empirical likelihood function evaluated at $\boldsymbol{\theta}$

$$\ln[L_{EL}(\boldsymbol{\theta}; \mathbf{y})] = -\sum_{i=1}^{n} \ln(n[1 + \boldsymbol{\lambda}(\boldsymbol{\theta})' \mathbf{h}(y_i, \boldsymbol{\theta})]). \tag{12.1.19}$$

12.1.3.d. Summary of Empirical Likelihood Concept

The use of the empirical likelihood approach in the case of iid data may be summarized as follows: We assume that $Y_1, Y_2, \ldots, Y_n$ are iid random variables with a common probability distribution F. We are interested in the values of some or all of the parameters $\boldsymbol{\theta} \in R^k$ associated with F. Information relating to $\boldsymbol{\theta}$ and F is summarized by a set of estimating functions relating to the population random variable Y as $\mathbf{h}(Y, \boldsymbol{\theta}) = (h_1(Y, \boldsymbol{\theta}), \ldots, h_m(Y, \boldsymbol{\theta}))'$, where the expectation of the estimating functions $\mathbf{h}(Y, \boldsymbol{\theta})$ equals zero when evaluations occurs at the true value of $\boldsymbol{\theta}$, and thus

$E_\theta[\mathbf{h}(Y, \boldsymbol{\theta})] = \mathbf{0}$. The log-empirical likelihood function for $\boldsymbol{\theta}$ is then defined as

$$\ln[L_{EL}(\boldsymbol{\theta}; \mathbf{y})] \equiv \max_{\mathbf{p}} \left[\sum_{i=1}^{n} \ln(p_i) \text{ s.t. } \sum_{i=1}^{n} p_i \mathbf{h}(y_i, \boldsymbol{\theta}) = \mathbf{0} \text{ and } \sum_{i=1}^{n} p_i = 1 \right], \tag{12.1.20}$$

where the p_i's represent empirical probability weights assigned to the y_i observations, and $E_{\mathbf{p}}[\mathbf{h}(Y, \boldsymbol{\theta})] = \sum_{i=1}^{n} p_i \mathbf{h}(y_i, \boldsymbol{\theta}) = \mathbf{0}$ is the empirical representation of the moment equation $E[\mathbf{h}(Y, \boldsymbol{\theta})] = \mathbf{0}$ relating to the estimating functions.

We will provide some examples of the EL problem solution later in the chapter. We will also see that the log–EL function operates remarkably like an ordinary likelihood function for $\boldsymbol{\theta}$ when defining maximum (empirical) likelihood estimates of $\boldsymbol{\theta}$ and testing hypotheses about $\boldsymbol{\theta}$ based on (empirical) likelihood ratios. We also note ahead that the EL approach can be extended to the case in which the sample observations are independent but not iid as well as the case of weakly dependent sample observations.

12.2. Maximum Empirical Likelihood Estimation: iid Case

Given the characterization of the empirical likelihood function in (12.1.11) or (12.1.20), we now consider questions of estimation regarding the parameter vector $\boldsymbol{\theta}$.

12.2.1. Maximum Empirical Likelihood Estimator

Analogous to the case of ML estimation, we can define a maximum *empirical* likelihood (MEL) estimator of $\boldsymbol{\theta}$ by choosing the value of $\boldsymbol{\theta}$ that maximizes the empirical likelihood function (12.1.20), or maximizes the logarithm of the EL function, as follows:

$$\hat{\Theta}_{EL} = \arg\max_{\theta}[\ln(L_{EL}(\boldsymbol{\theta}; \mathbf{Y}))]. \tag{12.2.1}$$

The MEL estimator is thus an extremum estimator with the log–EL function being the estimation objective function. The solution for $\hat{\Theta}_{EL}$ is generally not obtainable in closed form because the $\boldsymbol{\lambda}(\boldsymbol{\theta})$ argument of the EL function is not a closed-form function of $\boldsymbol{\theta}$, and thus numerical optimization techniques are most often required to obtain outcomes of the MEL estimator. Qin and Lawless note two principal ways in which the empirical likelihood solution may be computed. First, the optimal Lagrange multipliers $\boldsymbol{\lambda}$ and the parameters $\boldsymbol{\theta}$ may be simultaneously selected to maximize the empirical likelihood function, where this problem would be defined by (12.1.12) after substituting (12.1.16) for the p_i's and setting $\eta = 1$. However, they note that the solution must satisfy the constraints $\hat{p}_i > 0$ so that $1 + \boldsymbol{\lambda}(\boldsymbol{\theta})' \mathbf{h}(y_i, \boldsymbol{\theta}) > n^{-1}\ \forall i$ and some of the saddle points for the problem may not satisfy this condition. Alternatively, we can use an initial starting value $\boldsymbol{\theta}_0$ for the parameter vector to compute an initial estimate of the Lagrange multipliers $\boldsymbol{\lambda}_1$. Then, we can sequentially iterate to the optimal values of $\boldsymbol{\theta}$ and $\boldsymbol{\lambda}$ that maximize the EL function based on a numerical gradient-search maximization algorithm.

Regarding the asymptotic properties of $\hat{\Theta}_{EL}$, Qin and Lawless (1994) show that the usual consistency and asymptotic normality properties of extremum estimators hold for the MEL estimator under general regularity conditions. They established these properties by invoking primitive conditions on the estimating equations rather than attempting to invoke theorems such as 7.3.1–7.3.3. Their regularity conditions relate to the twice continuous differentiability of $\mathbf{h}(\mathrm{Y}, \boldsymbol{\theta})$ with respect to $\boldsymbol{\theta}$ and the boundedness of $\mathbf{h}$ and its first and second derivatives, all in a neighborhood of the true parameter value $\boldsymbol{\theta}_0$. They also assume that the row rank of $\mathrm{E}[\frac{\partial \mathbf{h}(\mathrm{Y}, \boldsymbol{\theta})}{\partial \boldsymbol{\theta}}|_{\boldsymbol{\theta}_0}]$ equals the number of parameters in the vector $\boldsymbol{\theta}$ (Qin and Lawless, 1994, p. 305–6). These are relatively mild conditions that lead to the MEL estimator's being *consistent* and *asymptotically normal* with limiting distribution

$$n^{1/2}(\hat{\boldsymbol{\Theta}}_{\mathrm{EL}} - \boldsymbol{\theta}_0) \xrightarrow{\mathrm{d}} \mathrm{N}(\mathbf{0}, \boldsymbol{\Sigma}) \tag{12.2.2}$$

where

$$\boldsymbol{\Sigma} = \left[\mathrm{E}\left[\frac{\partial \mathbf{h}(\mathrm{Y}, \boldsymbol{\theta})}{\partial \boldsymbol{\theta}}\bigg|_{\boldsymbol{\theta}_0}\right][\mathrm{E}[\mathbf{h}(\mathrm{Y}, \boldsymbol{\theta})\,\mathbf{h}(\mathrm{Y}, \boldsymbol{\theta})'|_{\boldsymbol{\theta}_0}]]^{-1}\mathrm{E}\left[\frac{\partial \mathbf{h}(\mathrm{Y}, \boldsymbol{\theta})}{\partial \boldsymbol{\theta}'}\bigg|_{\boldsymbol{\theta}_0}\right]\right]^{-1}. \tag{12.2.3}$$

The covariance matrix $\boldsymbol{\Sigma}$ of the limiting normal distribution can be consistently estimated by

$$\hat{\Sigma} = \left[\left[\sum_{i=1}^{n} \hat{\mathrm{p}}_i \frac{\partial \mathbf{h}(\mathrm{y}_i, \boldsymbol{\theta})}{\partial \boldsymbol{\theta}}\bigg|_{\hat{\boldsymbol{\theta}}_{\mathrm{EL}}}\right]\left[\sum_{i=1}^{n} \hat{\mathrm{p}}_i \mathbf{h}(\mathrm{y}_i, \hat{\boldsymbol{\theta}}_{\mathrm{EL}})\mathbf{h}(\mathrm{y}_i, \hat{\boldsymbol{\theta}}_{\mathrm{EL}})'\right]^{-1} \times \left[\sum_{i=1}^{n} \hat{\mathrm{p}}_i \frac{\partial \mathbf{h}(\mathrm{y}_i, \boldsymbol{\theta})}{\partial \boldsymbol{\theta}'}\bigg|_{\hat{\boldsymbol{\theta}}_{\mathrm{EL}}}\right]\right]^{-1}, \tag{12.2.4}$$

where the $\hat{\mathrm{p}}_i$'s are the MEL estimates of the empirical probability distribution $\mathbf{p}$, which are characterized by (12.1.16) with $\boldsymbol{\theta}$ replaced by $\hat{\boldsymbol{\theta}}_{\mathrm{EL}}$ and $\boldsymbol{\lambda}$ replaced by $\hat{\boldsymbol{\lambda}}_{\mathrm{EL}} = \boldsymbol{\lambda}(\hat{\boldsymbol{\theta}}_{\mathrm{EL}})$. An alternative consistent estimate can also be defined by using (12.2.4) with all of the $\hat{\mathrm{p}}_i$'s replaced by n^{-1}, which amounts to applying probability weights based on the EDF instead of the empirical probability weights generated by the EL procedure. Because the latter incorporate the additional estimating function information, it would be expected that these probability weight estimates would be more efficient in finite samples if the estimating function information is accurate, where accurate in this context means that the estimating functions are unbiased. The limiting distribution of $\hat{\boldsymbol{\Theta}}_{\mathrm{EL}}$ allows asymptotic hypothesis tests and confidence regions to be constructed, as will be seen in sections ahead.

12.2.2. MEL Efficiency Property

The MEL estimator has an important efficiency property, and in motivating this property we will obtain further insights into the workings of the MEL method of parameter estimation. Upon reviewing the definition of the (scaled) log–EL function in (12.1.11), and in particular the constraint information utilized in the definition, it is apparent that the MEL estimate of $\boldsymbol{\theta}$ could be obtained as the solution $\hat{\boldsymbol{\theta}}_{\mathrm{EL}}$ to the system of equations

$$\mathbf{h_p}(\mathbf{y}, \boldsymbol{\theta}) \equiv \sum_{i=1}^{n} \hat{\mathrm{p}}_i \mathbf{h}(\mathrm{y}_i, \boldsymbol{\theta}) = \mathbf{0}, \tag{12.2.5}$$

where $\hat{\mathrm{p}}_i = \mathrm{p}_i[\hat{\boldsymbol{\theta}}_{\mathrm{EL}}, \boldsymbol{\lambda}(\hat{\boldsymbol{\theta}}_{\mathrm{EL}})]$ is the optimal value of p_i, for $i = 1, \ldots, n$. Therefore, the MEL method of estimation can be viewed as a procedure for combining the set of $n(m \times 1)$ estimating functions $\mathbf{h}(\mathrm{y}_i, \boldsymbol{\theta})$, $i = 1, \ldots, n$, into a vector-estimating equation $\mathbf{h}_{\mathrm{EL}}(\mathbf{y}, \boldsymbol{\theta}) = \mathbf{0}$ that can be solved for an estimate of $\boldsymbol{\theta}$.

A natural question to ask is whether the particular combination of the n estimating functions used in the MEL approach is in some sense the best combination. In fact, it is the best in an important sense, which we now clarify. Consider the class of estimation procedures that can be defined by a linear combination of the estimating equation information

$$\mathbf{h}_{\nu}(\mathbf{y}, \boldsymbol{\theta}) \equiv \sum_{i=1}^{n} \boldsymbol{\nu}(\boldsymbol{\theta})\, \mathbf{h}(\mathrm{y}_i, \boldsymbol{\theta}) = \mathbf{0}, \tag{12.2.6}$$

where $\boldsymbol{\nu}(\boldsymbol{\theta})$ is a $(k \times m)$ real-valued matrix function such that the $(k \times 1)$ vector equation $\mathbf{h}_{\nu}(\mathbf{y}, \boldsymbol{\theta}) = \mathbf{0}$ can be solved for the $(k \times 1)$ vector $\boldsymbol{\theta}$ as $\hat{\boldsymbol{\theta}}_{\nu}(\mathbf{y})$. McCullagh and Nelder (1989, p. 341) show that the optimal choice of $\boldsymbol{\nu}$, in the sense of defining a consistent estimator with minimum asymptotic covariance matrix, in the class of estimators for $\boldsymbol{\theta}$ defined as solutions to (12.2.6) is given by (also recall the discussion following (11.4.8))

$$\boldsymbol{\nu}(\boldsymbol{\theta}) = \mathrm{E}\left[\frac{\partial \mathbf{h}(\mathrm{Y}, \boldsymbol{\theta})}{\partial \boldsymbol{\theta}}\right] [\mathbf{cov}(\mathbf{h}(\mathrm{Y}, \boldsymbol{\theta}))]^{-1}, \tag{12.2.7}$$

where Y denotes the random variable whose probability distribution is the common population distribution of the Y_i's. Using the optimal definition of $\boldsymbol{\nu}$ in (12.2.7) defines an estimator for $\boldsymbol{\theta}$ that has precisely the same asymptotic covariance matrix as the MEL estimator (12.2.3) because, given the unbiased nature of the estimating equations, $\mathbf{cov}(\mathbf{h}(\mathrm{Y}, \boldsymbol{\theta})) = \mathrm{E}[\mathbf{h}(\mathrm{Y}, \boldsymbol{\theta})\, \mathbf{h}(\mathrm{Y}, \boldsymbol{\theta})']$ (McCullagh and Nelder, 1989, p. 341). Thus, the MEL estimator is equivalent in asymptotic distribution to the most efficient estimator in the class of estimators defined via the solution to estimating equations formed by linear combinations of the unbiased estimating functions, as in (12.2.6).

It is also useful to note that the asymptotic covariance matrix of the MEL estimator generally becomes smaller (by a positive semidefinite matrix) as the number of estimating equations on which it is based increases (Qin and Lawless, 1994, Corollary 1). In practice, this means that the greater the number of *correct* (i.e., unbiased) estimating functions used, the generally more accurate the MEL estimator becomes in estimating $\boldsymbol{\theta}$. Thus, one should utilize as much information as is available relating to valid estimating functions when using the MEL estimator to estimate $\boldsymbol{\theta}$. We examine a test of the validity of estimating equations in a later section.

12.2.3. MEL Estimation of a Population Mean

In this section we examine an extended illustrative example demonstrating the setup and properties of the MEL estimation approach for the case of estimating a population mean. We end this section with a numerical application in which a random sample of data from a population distribution is obtained and MEL estimates of the population mean, together with its estimated asymptotic variance, are computed.

We begin with a random sample $(Y_1, \ldots, Y_n)$ of scalars drawn from some population distribution F(y) assumed to have a finite mean. We introduce the scalar parameter θ to represent the unknown mean of F(y). To identify θ formally as the mean of F(y), we define the estimating function $h(Y, \theta) = Y - \theta$ and then state the moment equation

$$E[h(Y, \theta)] = E[Y - \theta] = 0, \tag{12.2.8}$$

so that $\theta = E[Y]$. We emphasize that it is possible for the number of estimating equations to exceed the dimension of the parameter vector of interest. In this case, the dimension is 1, and for the sake of clarity, we concentrate on the scalar case.

On the basis of (12.1.12), the Lagrange function associated with the constrained maximization problem that defines the scaled log-empirical likelihood function is given by

$$L(\mathbf{p}, \eta, \lambda) \equiv \left[n^{-1} \sum_{i=1}^{n} \ln(p_i) - \eta \left(\sum_{i=1}^{n} p_i - 1 \right) - \lambda \sum_{i=1}^{n} p_i (y_i - \theta) \right], \tag{12.2.9}$$

where $p_i > 0 \, \forall i$ is implicit in the structure of the problem. The first-order conditions with respect to the p_i's are

$$\frac{1}{n p_i} - \lambda(y_i - \theta) - \eta = 0, \quad i = 1, \ldots, n \tag{12.2.10}$$

where λ and η are Lagrange multipliers. The value of η can be solved for in precisely the same way as (12.1.15), implying that $\eta = 1$. Substituting $\eta = 1$ in (12.2.10) yields a solution for p_i given by

$$p_i(\theta, \lambda) = [n(1 + \lambda(y_i - \theta))]^{-1}, \tag{12.2.11}$$

which is the specific instance of (12.1.16) for the current problem. We can insert (12.2.11) and $\eta = 1$ into the Lagrange function of (12.2.9) to define a partially optimized function as follows:

$$n^{-1} \sum_{i=1}^{n} \ln(n^{-1}[1 + \lambda(y_i - \theta)]^{-1}) - \lambda \sum_{i=1}^{n} [n^{-1}[1 + \lambda(y_i - \theta)]^{-1}(y_i - \theta)]. \tag{12.2.12}$$

Optimization of (12.2.12) with respect to λ defines the Lagrange multiplier as a function of θ as

$$\lambda(\theta) = \arg_{\lambda} \left[\frac{1}{n} \sum_{i=1}^{n} \left[\frac{y_i - \theta}{1 + \lambda(y_i - \theta)} \right] = 0 \right], \tag{12.2.13}$$

where (12.2.13) is the implementation of the general equation (12.1.18) for the current problem. Note that $\lambda(\theta)$ is an *implicit* function of θ that cannot be expressed in closed form. Substituting this solution for λ into the expression

$\sum_{i=1}^{n} \ln(\mathrm{p}_i(\theta, \lambda)) = \sum_{i=1}^{n} \ln([n(1+\lambda(\mathrm{y}_i - \theta))]^{-1})$ (recall (12.2.11)) defines the log-EL function for θ as

$$\ln[\mathrm{L_{EL}}(\theta; \mathbf{y})] = -\sum_{i=1}^{n} \ln[n(1 + \lambda(\theta)(\mathrm{y}_i - \theta))], \qquad (12.2.14)$$

consistent with (12.1.19).

The MEL estimate of θ is then found by maximizing the log–EL function (12.2.14) with respect to θ. Regarding this maximization problem, first note that the log–EL function is continuous, differentiable, and concave in θ. Also, the feasible choices for θ must be in the interval $(\mathrm{y_s}, \mathrm{y_L})$, where $\mathrm{y_s}$ and $\mathrm{y_L}$ are the smallest and largest values in the set of sample outcomes $(\mathrm{y}_1, \mathrm{y}_2, \ldots, \mathrm{y}_n)$. In particular, given the estimating equation constraint $\sum_{i=1}^{n} \mathrm{p}_i \mathrm{y}_i = \theta$, together with $\sum_{i=1}^{n} \mathrm{p}_i = 1$ and $\mathrm{p}_i > 0\ \forall i$, we can see that the optimal value of θ must be a convex combination of the y_i's.

Further, we can show that the maximum of the EL or log–EL function is unique (in general, as well as in the current problem) by considering the contradictory claim that $\mathbf{p}^*$ *and* $\mathbf{p}^{**}$ are *both* maximum EL probability distributions. Then, the probability distribution $\mathbf{p}^0 = \alpha\mathbf{p}^* + (1-\alpha)\mathbf{p}^{**}$ also satisfies the moment equation constraints, as $\sum_{i=1}^{n} \mathrm{p}_i^0 \mathbf{h}(\mathrm{y}_i, \theta) = \mathbf{0}$, for any $\alpha \in (0, 1)$. Owing to the strict concavity of the natural logarithm, Jensen's inequality implies $\ln(\mathrm{p}_i^0) > \alpha \ln(\mathrm{p}_i^*) + (1-\alpha)\ln(\mathrm{p}_i^{**})\ \forall i$, and it follows that for the log–EL function of $\mathbf{p}^0$

$$\sum_{i=1}^{n} \ln\left(\mathrm{p}_i^0\right) > \alpha \sum_{i=1}^{n} \ln(\mathrm{p}_i^*) + (1-\alpha)\sum_{i=1}^{n} \ln(\mathrm{p}_i^{**}) = \sum_{i=1}^{n} \ln(\mathrm{p}_i^*) = \sum_{i=1}^{n} \ln(\mathrm{p}_i^{**}), \qquad (12.2.15)$$

which implies that the value of EL at $\mathbf{p}^0$ is larger than the common EL value at $\mathbf{p}^*$ *and* $\mathbf{p}^{**}$. Thus, we have a contradiction to the claim that $\mathbf{p}^*$ and $\mathbf{p}^{**}$ are both maximum EL probability distributions.

► **Example 12.2.1:** To demonstrate the numerical steps involved in computing MEL estimates, we provide the GAUSS program C12MEL1.gss in the examples manual. Following the preceding discussion, we consider the problem of estimating the population mean parameter θ. For a given sample of n iid observations, estimates of θ are based on the sample mean as well as the MEL estimator. For demonstration purposes, the MEL estimates are computed by joint numerical search for θ and λ and by iterative search based on appropriate starting values. The GAUSS program compares the number of iterations, the iterative paths to convergence, and computing times for the alternative MEL methods.

Numerical optimization algorithms such as suggested by Qin and Lawless (1994) can be used to maximize (12.2.14) and thereby solve for the MEL estimate of θ. The properties of the objective function noted above suggest that the solution is well defined and computable. Upon obtaining the solution for $\hat{\theta}_{\mathrm{EL}}$, an estimate of the asymptotic variance of the MEL estimator can be obtained based on (12.2.4) or else (12.2.4) with $\hat{\mathrm{p}}_i$'s replaced by n^{-1}. From the former approach, which is expected to be at least as efficient as the latter in finite samples when valid moment constraints are utilized, and by letting $\hat{p}_i = p_i(\hat{\theta}_{EL}, \lambda(\hat{\theta}_{EL})) = n^{-1}[1 + \lambda(\hat{\theta}_{EL})(y_i - \hat{\theta}_{EL})]^{-1}$ from (12.2.11), we have the following implementation of (12.2.4):

$$\hat{\Sigma} = \left[\left[\sum_{i=1}^{n} \hat{p}_i(-1)\right]\left[\sum_{i=1}^{n} \hat{p}_i(y_i - \hat{\theta}_{EL})^2\right]^{-1}\left[\sum_{i=1}^{n} \hat{p}_i(-1)\right]\right]^{-1} = \sum_{i=1}^{n} \hat{p}_i(y_i - \hat{\theta}_{EL})^2. \tag{12.2.16}$$

The variance estimate can be interpreted as the expectation of $(Y - E_{\hat{p}}Y)^2$ taken with respect to the empirical probability distribution $\hat{\mathbf{p}} = (\hat{p}_1, \ldots, \hat{p}_n)'$ and is thus a natural estimate of variance within the EL context. If, instead, $\hat{p}_i$'s are replaced by n^{-1}, then (12.2.16) defines the familiar ML-type estimate of the variance.

The purpose of the preceding discussion has been to illustrate and clarify issues relating to the general problem of maximizing the EL of θ, as well as estimating the asymptotic distribution of $\hat{\Theta}_{EL}$. We now note that in this simple case, the solution for the MEL estimate is readily apparent via inspection of (12.2.9). In particular recall from Section 12.1.1 that the *unconstrained* maximum of $n^{-1}\sum_{i=1}^{n}\ln(p_i)$ is obtained by $p_i = n^{-1}\ \forall i$, which corresponds to the standard EDF estimates of the probabilities of the y_i's. The same maximum objective function value is achievable in the current problem by setting $p_i = n^{-1}\ \forall i$, leading to the satisfaction of the estimating equation constraint at the solution $\hat{\theta}_{EL} = n^{-1}\sum_{i=1}^{n} y_i = \bar{y}$ for the MEL estimate. Note the asymptotic variance of the MEL estimator is then estimated via (12.2.16) to be $n^{-1}\sum_{i=1}^{n}(y_i - \bar{y})^2$, as one would expect. Thus, in this case the EL method coincides with using the sample mean for the estimator of the population mean and the ML-type estimator of the variance. Note for future reference that $\lambda(\hat{\theta}_{EL}) = \lambda(\bar{y}) = 0$ follows either from (12.2.13) or from the fundamental fact that the estimating equation constraint is not constraining at the optimal MEL solution.

► **Example 12.2.2:** To demonstrate the large sample properties of the MEL estimator, we provide the GAUSS program C12MEL2.gss in the examples manual. The program extends the problem of estimating the population mean parameter θ considered in Example 12.2.1. The user selects the number of Monte Carlo trials (m) and up to four sample sizes (n) used to conduct a simulation study of the statistical properties of the MEL estimator and the sample mean. The GAUSS program reports the sample moments, box and whisker plots, and EDFs for the replicated estimates to examine the consistency and asymptotic normality of the two estimators.

12.2.4. MEL Estimation Based on Two Moments

To provide some evidence regarding estimator performance, consider a sampling experiment reported by Qin and Lawless (1994). In this experiment, the sample outcomes $y_1, y_2, \ldots, y_n$ are consistent with a model with first and second moments satisfying $E[Y] = \theta$, $E[Y^2] = 2\theta^2 + 1$. One thousand samples of sizes 10, 20, 30, and 40 were generated from the population distribution $N(\theta, \theta^2 + 1)$ for two values of $\theta = 0, 1$. For each pair of sample sizes and θ values, the following three estimates of θ were obtained:

Table 12.2. *Estimated Mean and Variance of Three Estimators of* θ, *from* 1000 *Simulations*

	Sample Mean		MEL		MLE	
n	**Mean**	**Var**	**Mean**	**Var**	**Mean**	**Var**
			N(0, 1), true value of $\theta = 0$			
10	0.004484	0.067624	0.006848	0.061824	0.006482	0.058516
20	0.000956	0.049740	0.001945	0.048108	−0.002313	0.029835
30	−0.005714	0.031004	−0.005119	0.030921	−0.004360	0.029835
40	0.000956	0.024572	0.002931	0.024221	−0.000947	0.023431
			N(1, 2), true value of $\theta = 1$			
10	1.004317	0.128445	0.946416	0.086383	0.966406	0.083193
20	0.995677	0.106569	0.952668	0.062353	0.972931	0.059177
30	1.006338	0.068629	0.968523	0.035759	0.984540	0.034930
40	1.015897	0.044045	0.984512	0.021883	0.994275	0.020584

the sample mean (MEL using only first moment information), MEL based on both the first- and second-moment information, and ML based on the normal distribution. The results for the estimated mean and variance of the three estimators appear in Table 12.2. As might be expected, the empirical variance of the MEL estimator lies between the sample mean (only first-moment information) and the parametric ML estimator. The empirical bias of MEL appears to be somewhat inferior to the other two estimators. Note how the variance decreases in the case of all estimators as sample size increases, reflecting the consistency of all of the estimators.

► **Example 12.2.3:** To demonstrate the application of the EL concept to the two-moment case, we provide the GAUSS program C12MEL3.gss in the examples manual. The program replicates the results of the Monte Carlo experiment presented in Table 12.2. For a given sample drawn from the $N(\theta, \theta^2 + 1)$ model, the program outlines the steps used to compute the MEL estimate of θ. Then, the user selects the value of θ as well as the desired sample sizes for the DSP, and GAUSS reports the sample mean and variance of the alternative estimators.

12.3. Hypothesis Tests and Confidence Regions: iid Case

In this section we will establish the analogs in the EL context to the usual likelihood ratio, Wald, Lagrange multiplier, and Z-tests of hypotheses relating to the value of a continuously differentiable function $\mathbf{c}(\boldsymbol{\theta})$ of the parameter vector. Confidence regions can be constructed in the usual way through duality with the hypothesis tests. We will also examine a method for testing the validity of the moment equations used in the definition of the EL function.

12.3.1. Empirical Likelihood Ratio Tests and Confidence Regions for $\mathbf{c}(\boldsymbol{\theta})$

The empirical likelihood function $\mathrm{L_{EL}}(\boldsymbol{\theta}; \mathbf{y})$ bears a strong analogy to the ordinary likelihood function used in the ML procedure when constructing tests and confidence regions defined in terms of (empirical) likelihood ratios. Consider the test of the hypothesis $\mathrm{H_0}: \boldsymbol{\theta} = \boldsymbol{\theta}_0$ versus $\mathrm{H_0}: \boldsymbol{\theta} \neq \boldsymbol{\theta}_0$. The empirical likelihood ratio (ELR)

$$\mathrm{LR_{EL}}(\boldsymbol{\theta}_0; \mathbf{Y}) = \mathrm{L_{EL}}(\boldsymbol{\theta}_0; \mathbf{Y}) / \mathrm{L_{EL}}(\hat{\boldsymbol{\Theta}}_{\mathrm{EL}}; \mathbf{Y}) \tag{12.3.1}$$

is such that

$$-2\ln(\mathrm{LR_{EL}}(\boldsymbol{\theta}_0; \mathbf{Y})) \overset{a}{\sim} \text{Chi-square}(k, 0) \text{ under } \mathrm{H_0} \tag{12.3.2}$$

when there are $m \geq k$ functionally independent empirical moment restrictions used in the definition of the EL and the value of the $(k \times 1)$ parameter vector $\boldsymbol{\theta}$ is set equal to the true value $\boldsymbol{\theta}_0$ (Qin and Lawless, 1994, Theorem 2). Recall that Chi-square$(k, 0)$ denotes a Chi-square distribution with k degrees of freedom and a noncentrality parameter of zero, that is, a central Chi-square distribution with k degrees of freedom. An asymptotic level α test of $\mathrm{H_0}$ is then defined by the rule

$$\text{reject } \mathrm{H_0}: \boldsymbol{\theta} = \boldsymbol{\theta}_0 \quad \text{if} \quad -2\ \ln[\mathrm{LR_{EL}}(\boldsymbol{\theta}_0; \mathbf{y})] \geq \chi^2(1-\alpha, k, 0), \tag{12.3.3}$$

where $\chi^2(1-\alpha, k, 0)$ is the $100(1-\alpha)\%$ quantile of the central Chi-square distribution with k degrees of freedom. An asymptotic $100(1-\alpha)\%$ confidence region for $\boldsymbol{\theta}$ can be defined in the usual way applying the duality principle to the test procedure (12.3.3), resulting in the set of $\boldsymbol{\theta}_0$ values *not* rejected by the test.

The ELR can be used to construct other test and confidence regions for subsets of the $\boldsymbol{\theta}$ vector. There is again a direct analogy to the GLR test in the ML context. Partition the parameter vector into two subvectors as $\boldsymbol{\theta} = (\boldsymbol{\theta}_1' | \boldsymbol{\theta}_2')'$ where $\boldsymbol{\theta}_1$ is a $(\mathrm{q} \times 1)$ vector and $\boldsymbol{\theta}_2$ is then $(\mathrm{k} - \mathrm{q}) \times 1$. To test the hypothesis $\mathrm{H_0}: \boldsymbol{\theta}_1 = \boldsymbol{\theta}_1^0$ one defines the ELR

$$\mathrm{LR_{EL}}\left(\boldsymbol{\theta}_1^0; \mathbf{Y}\right) = \max_{\boldsymbol{\theta}_2} \left[\mathrm{L_{EL}}\left(\boldsymbol{\theta}_1^0, \boldsymbol{\theta}_2; \mathbf{Y}\right) / \mathrm{L_{EL}}(\hat{\boldsymbol{\Theta}}_{\mathrm{EL}}; \mathbf{Y})\right], \tag{12.3.4}$$

in which case (again assuming $m \geq k$)

$$-2\ln\left[\mathrm{LR_{EL}}\left(\boldsymbol{\theta}_1^0; \mathbf{Y}\right)\right] \overset{a}{\sim} \text{Chi-square}(\mathrm{q}, 0) \text{ under } \mathrm{H_0}, \tag{12.3.5}$$

and the test rule for $\mathrm{H_0}: \boldsymbol{\theta}_1 = \boldsymbol{\theta}_1^0$ is then

$$\text{reject } \mathrm{H_0} \quad \text{if} \quad -2\ln\left[\mathrm{LR_{EL}}\left(\boldsymbol{\theta}_1^0; \mathbf{y}\right)\right] \geq \chi^2(1-\alpha, \mathrm{q}, 0). \tag{12.3.6}$$

Among other things, this type of test can be used to examine whether certain parameters are irrelevant, that is, set $\boldsymbol{\theta}_1^0 = \mathbf{0}$ when conducting the test. Confidence regions for $\boldsymbol{\theta}_1$ can be constructed using the duality principle.

Extensions of the preceding tests and confidence region procedures to more general hypotheses of the form $\mathrm{H_0}: \mathbf{c}(\boldsymbol{\theta}) = \mathbf{r}$ are also possible, as indicated by Qin and Lawless (1995). In this case the maximization of the numerator of the empirical likelihood ratio is now constrained by the null hypothesis $\mathbf{c}(\boldsymbol{\theta}) = \mathbf{r}$, as

$$\mathrm{LR_{EL}}(\mathbf{Y}) = \max_{\boldsymbol{\theta}} [\mathrm{L_{EL}}(\boldsymbol{\theta}; \mathbf{Y}) / \mathrm{L_{EL}}(\hat{\boldsymbol{\Theta}}_{\mathrm{EL}}; \mathbf{Y}) \text{ subject to } \mathbf{c}(\boldsymbol{\theta}) = \mathbf{r}], \tag{12.3.7}$$

and the degrees of freedom in the asymptotic Chi-square distribution equals the number of functionally independent restrictions, say q, on the parameter vector that is implied by $\mathbf{c}(\boldsymbol{\theta}) = \mathbf{r}$. The test and confidence region procedures then proceed in the usual way based on the asymptotic Chi-square(q, 0) distribution of $-2\ln(\mathrm{LR_{EL}}(\mathbf{Y}))$ under H_0.

12.3.2. Wald Tests and Confidence Regions for $\mathbf{c}(\boldsymbol{\theta})$

It is possible to construct asymptotically valid tests and confidence regions based on Wald statistics in the usual way given the asymptotic normality of $\hat{\boldsymbol{\Theta}}_{\mathrm{EL}}$ indicated in (12.2.2)–(12.2.4). For example, to test the j functionally independent nonlinear equality restrictions $\mathbf{c}(\boldsymbol{\Theta}) = \mathbf{r}$, one could use the statistic

$$\mathrm{W} = [\mathbf{c}(\hat{\boldsymbol{\Theta}}_{\mathrm{EL}}) - \mathbf{r}]' \left[\left.\frac{\partial \mathbf{c}(\boldsymbol{\theta})}{\partial \boldsymbol{\theta}'}\right|_{\hat{\boldsymbol{\Theta}}_{\mathrm{EL}}} (n^{-1}\hat{\boldsymbol{\Sigma}}) \left.\frac{\partial \mathbf{c}(\boldsymbol{\theta})}{\partial \boldsymbol{\theta}}\right|_{\hat{\boldsymbol{\Theta}}_{\mathrm{EL}}} \right]^{-1}$$
$$\times [\mathbf{c}(\hat{\boldsymbol{\Theta}}_{\mathrm{EL}}) - \mathbf{r}] \overset{\mathrm{a}}{\sim} \text{Chi-square}(j, 0) \text{ under } \mathrm{H}_0, \tag{12.3.8}$$

where $\hat{\boldsymbol{\Sigma}}$ is defined in (12.2.4). The asymptotic level α test rule for is $\mathrm{H}_0\colon \mathbf{c}(\boldsymbol{\theta}) = \mathbf{r}$ is

$$\text{reject } \mathrm{H}_0 \quad \text{if} \quad \mathrm{w} \geq \chi^2(1-\alpha, j, 0). \tag{12.3.9}$$

A confidence region for $\mathbf{c}(\boldsymbol{\theta})$ with asymptotic level $100(1-\alpha)\%$ confidence can be defined based on duality with the Wald hypothesis test, where the confidence region would be the set of $\mathbf{r}$ vectors *not* rejected by the Wald test (12.3.9).

12.3.3. Lagrange Multiplier Tests and Confidence Regions for $\mathbf{c}(\boldsymbol{\theta})$

Lagrange multiplier (LM) tests of the hypothesis $\mathrm{H}_0\colon \mathbf{c}(\boldsymbol{\theta}) = \mathbf{r}$ can be defined in terms of the Lagrange multipliers $\boldsymbol{\xi}$ of the *constrained*, by H_0, maximum empirical likelihood problem expressed in Lagrange form by

$$n^{-1}\ln(\mathrm{L_{EL}}(\boldsymbol{\theta}; \mathbf{y})) + \boldsymbol{\xi}'[\mathbf{c}(\boldsymbol{\theta}) - \mathbf{r}]. \tag{12.3.10}$$

Qin and Lawless (1995) show that under H_0 (recall 12.2.3)

$$n^{1/2}\hat{\boldsymbol{\xi}} \overset{\mathrm{d}}{\to} \mathrm{N}\left(\mathbf{0}, \left[\left.\frac{\partial \mathbf{c}(\boldsymbol{\theta})}{\partial \boldsymbol{\theta}'}\right|_{\boldsymbol{\Theta}_0} \boldsymbol{\Sigma} \left.\frac{\partial \mathbf{c}(\boldsymbol{\theta})}{\partial \boldsymbol{\theta}}\right|_{\boldsymbol{\Theta}_0} \right]^{-1}\right), \tag{12.3.11}$$

in which case it follows that

$$n\hat{\boldsymbol{\xi}}' \left[\left.\frac{\partial \mathbf{c}(\boldsymbol{\theta})}{\partial \boldsymbol{\theta}'}\right|_{\boldsymbol{\Theta}_0} \boldsymbol{\Sigma} \left.\frac{\partial \mathbf{c}(\boldsymbol{\theta})}{\partial \boldsymbol{\theta}}\right|_{\boldsymbol{\Theta}_0} \right] \hat{\boldsymbol{\xi}} \overset{\mathrm{d}}{\to} \text{Chi-square}(j, 0) \text{ under } \mathrm{H}_0, \tag{12.3.12}$$

where as usual j is the number of functionally independent constraints on $\boldsymbol{\theta}$ implied by $\mathrm{H}_0\colon \mathbf{c}(\boldsymbol{\theta}) = \mathbf{r}$. An operational LM statistic is obtained from (12.3.12) by replacing $\boldsymbol{\theta}_0$ by the constrained EL estimate $\hat{\boldsymbol{\theta}}^{\mathrm{c}}_{\mathrm{EL}}$ and replacing $\boldsymbol{\Sigma}$ by $\hat{\boldsymbol{\Sigma}}$ based on the definition (12.2.4) with all estimates derived from the constrained EL procedure. The test is then conducted in the usual way based on critical values obtained from the Chi-square(j, 0) distribution. Confidence regions can (in principle) be derived from the hypothesis tests based on duality.

12.3.4. Z-Tests of Inequality Hypotheses for the Value of $\mathbf{c}(\boldsymbol{\theta})$

It is possible to construct asymptotically valid tests of scalar inequality hypotheses and define confidence bounds based on Z-statistics in the usual way given the asymptotic normality of $\hat{\Theta}_{EL}$ indicated in (12.2.2)–(12.2.4). For example, to test the nonlinear inequality restrictions $c(\Theta) \leq r$, one could use the statistic

$$Z = \frac{c(\hat{\Theta}) - r}{\left[\frac{\partial c(\boldsymbol{\theta})}{\partial \boldsymbol{\theta}'}\Big|_{\hat{\Theta}_{EL}} (n^{-1}\hat{\Sigma}) \frac{\partial c(\boldsymbol{\theta})}{\partial \boldsymbol{\theta}}\Big|_{\hat{\Theta}_{EL}}\right]^{1/2}} \overset{a}{\sim} N(\delta, 1), \tag{12.3.13}$$

where $\hat{\Sigma}$ is defined in (12.2.4) and

$$\delta = \frac{c(\boldsymbol{\theta}_0) - r}{\left[\frac{\partial c(\boldsymbol{\theta})}{\partial \boldsymbol{\theta}'}\Big|_{\Theta_0} \Sigma \frac{\partial c(\boldsymbol{\theta})}{\partial \boldsymbol{\theta}}\Big|_{\Theta_0}\right]^{1/2}}. \tag{12.3.14}$$

The asymptotic level-α test rule for H_0: $c(\boldsymbol{\theta}) \leq r$ is

$$\text{reject } H_0 \quad \text{if} \quad z \geq z_{(1-\alpha)}. \tag{12.3.15}$$

where $z(1-\alpha)$ is the $100(1-\alpha)\%$ quantile of the standard normal distribution. Reversing inequalities defines a test of the hypothesis H_0: $c(\boldsymbol{\theta}) \geq r$. Confidence bounds for $c(\boldsymbol{\theta})$ with asymptotic level $100(1-\alpha)\%$ confidence can be defined in the usual way based on duality with the Z tests, where the confidence region would be the set of r vectors *not* rejected by the Z test.

12.3.5. Testing the Validity of Moment Equations

Another test of interest in the EL context is the test of the validity of moment equations, H_0: $E[\mathbf{h}(Y, \boldsymbol{\theta})] = \mathbf{0}$. Note this is equivalent to testing the *unbiasedness* of the estimating functions used in the EL approach. Two natural ways of testing this hypothesis are through the use of the empirical likelihood ratio test and the Lagrange multiplier test.

The empirical likelihood ratio test of moment equation validity is defined in a natural way analogous to the way GLR tests of functional restrictions would be tested. First recall that if the estimating equation restrictions are removed from the optimization problem (12.1.11), then the EL is optimized at $\hat{p}_i = n^{-1}\ \forall i$, which is coincident with the classical empirical distribution function of the data. The value of the unrestricted empirical likelihood function is then $L_{EL}^* = n^{-n}$. Also note that $L_{EL}(\hat{\boldsymbol{\theta}}_{EL}; \mathbf{Y})$ is the maximum EL possible *subject to the estimating equation restrictions in* (12.1.10). Then, as one would anticipate, a test of the m estimating equation restrictions can be conducted based on the ELR statistic

$$LR_{EL}(\mathbf{Y}) = L_{EL}(\hat{\Theta}; \mathbf{Y})/L_{EL}^*, \tag{12.3.16}$$

which, if the moment constraints are correct, is such that

$$-2\ln[\mathrm{LR}_{\mathrm{EL}}(\mathbf{Y})] \overset{a}{\sim} \text{Chi-square}(m-k, 0). \tag{12.3.17}$$

The asymptotic α-level ELR test of the validity of the moment restrictions is then conducted as

$$\text{reject } \mathrm{H}_0\colon \mathrm{E}[\mathbf{h}(\mathrm{Y}, \boldsymbol{\theta})] = \mathbf{0} \quad \text{if} \quad -2\ln[\mathrm{LR}_{\mathrm{EL}}(\mathbf{y})] \geq \chi^2(1-\alpha, m-k, 0). \tag{12.3.18}$$

It is also possible to devise a Lagrange multiplier test of the validity of the estimating equation restrictions. This follows from the fact that the Lagrange multipliers associated with the moment constraints in the definition of the maximum empirical likelihood estimator are such that (Qin and Lawless, 1994, Theorem 1)

$$n^{1/2}\boldsymbol{\lambda}(\hat{\boldsymbol{\Theta}}_{\mathrm{EL}}) \overset{d}{\to} \mathrm{N}(\mathbf{0}, \boldsymbol{\Psi}) \tag{12.3.19}$$

where

$$\boldsymbol{\Psi} = [\mathrm{E}[\mathbf{h}\mathbf{h}'|_{\theta_0}]]^{-1}\left[\mathbf{I}_{\mathrm{m}} - \mathrm{E}\left[\left.\frac{\partial \mathbf{h}}{\partial \boldsymbol{\theta}}\right|_{\theta_0}\right]' \boldsymbol{\Sigma}\,\mathrm{E}\left[\left.\frac{\partial \mathbf{h}}{\partial \boldsymbol{\theta}}\right|_{\theta_0}\right][\mathrm{E}[\mathbf{h}\mathbf{h}'|_{\theta_0}]]^{-1}\right] \tag{12.3.20}$$

and $\boldsymbol{\Sigma}$ is as defined in (12.2.3). Note that $\boldsymbol{\Psi}$ is a $(m \times m)$ matrix of rank $(m-k)$, and so the limiting distribution in (12.3.19) is a *singular* normal distribution. The asymptotic covariance matrix $\boldsymbol{\Psi}$ can be estimated by replacing $\boldsymbol{\Sigma}$ with $\hat{\boldsymbol{\Sigma}}$ defined in (12.2.4) and making analogous substitutions in (12.3.20) to those made in (12.2.4) for the remaining unknown terms. The Lagrange multiplier test of the validity of the estimating equations is then based on the LM statistic

$$\mathrm{LM} = n\boldsymbol{\lambda}(\hat{\boldsymbol{\Theta}}_{\mathrm{EL}})'\hat{\boldsymbol{\Psi}}^{-}\boldsymbol{\lambda}(\hat{\boldsymbol{\Theta}}_{\mathrm{EL}}) \sim \text{Chi-square}(m-k, 0) \text{ under } \mathrm{H}_0, \tag{12.3.21}$$

where H_0 is the hypothesis that the restrictions are valid and $\hat{\boldsymbol{\Psi}}^{-}$ is the generalized inverse of $\hat{\boldsymbol{\Psi}}$. Note the degrees of freedom are $(m-k)$ because of the degree of singularity in the distribution of $\boldsymbol{\lambda}(\hat{\boldsymbol{\Theta}}_{\mathrm{EL}})$. The test rule is then based on the outcome lm of LM as follows:

$$\text{reject } \mathrm{H}_0\colon \mathrm{E}[\mathbf{h}(\mathrm{Y}, \boldsymbol{\theta})] = 0 \quad \text{if} \quad \mathrm{lm} \geq \chi^2(1-\alpha, m-k, 0). \tag{12.3.22}$$

12.3.6. MEL Testing and Confidence Intervals for Population Mean

In this section we continue the illustration begun in Section 12.2.3 and examine testing and confidence-interval generation within the MEL context. Suppose we were interested in testing the hypothesis that the population distribution has a zero mean so that $\mathrm{H}_0\colon \theta = 0$. The ELR in (12.3.1) could be used to test this hypothesis. The ELR test statistic can be specified as

$$-2\ln(\mathrm{LR}_{\mathrm{EL}}(0; \mathbf{y})) = 2\sum_{i=1}^{n} \ln[1 + \lambda(0)\mathrm{y}_i]. \tag{12.3.23}$$

To see this, note that (recall (12.2.14))

$$2\,\ln[\mathrm{L_{EL}}(\hat{\theta}_{\mathrm{EL}};\mathbf{y})] = -2\sum_{i=1}^{n}\ln[n(1+\lambda(\hat{\theta}_{\mathrm{EL}})(\mathrm{y}_i-\hat{\theta}_{\mathrm{EL}}))] = -2n\ln(n). \qquad (12.3.24)$$

because $\lambda(\hat{\theta}_{\mathrm{EL}}) = \lambda(\bar{\mathrm{y}}) = 0$, as we noted at the end of Section 12.2.3. Adding (12.3.24) to -2 times (12.2.14) evaluated at $\theta = 0$ leads immediately to (12.3.23). The test statistic can be calculated by first solving for λ in (12.2.13) with $\theta = 0$ and then substituting the solution value for $\lambda(0)$ into (12.3.23). The hypothesis $\mathrm{H_0}$: $\theta = 0$ could also be tested based on the familiar asymptotic result that $\hat{\Theta}_{\mathrm{EL}} = \bar{\mathrm{Y}} \overset{a}{\sim} \mathrm{N}(\mu, \sigma^2/n)$. The Wald test (12.3.8) and (12.3.9) for this problem is based on the statistic

$$\mathrm{W} = \bar{\mathrm{Y}}'[\mathrm{S}^2/n]^{-1}\bar{\mathrm{Y}} \overset{a}{\sim} \text{Chi-square}(1, 0) \text{ under } \mathrm{H_0} \qquad (12.3.25)$$

with the test rule being

$$\text{reject } \mathrm{H_0} \quad \text{if} \quad \mathrm{w} \geq \chi^2(1-\alpha, 1, 0), \qquad (12.3.26)$$

where $\mathrm{S}^2 = n^{-1}\sum_{i=1}^{n}(\mathrm{Y}_i - \bar{\mathrm{Y}})^2$. In either the ELR or Wald contexts, confidence regions for μ could be obtained in the usual way via duality.

For the problem of estimating and testing the population mean, the estimating equations (12.2.8) just identify the unknown parameters (i.e., $m = k$), and so the validity of the estimating equation (12.2.8) *cannot* be tested with either the ELR test (12.3.18) or the LM test (12.3.22). Note in particular that in the LM case, $\lambda(\bar{\mathrm{y}}) = 0$, for all outcomes in the sample space, and the Lagrange multiplier does not provide a meaningful basis for a test of (12.2.8). Likewise, it is straightforward to show that $\mathrm{LR_{EL}}(\mathbf{Y}) = 1$ in (12.3.17), and any test based on the ELR in this case would also be uninformative. However, we can conduct tests regarding hypothesized values of the location parameter $\theta = \theta_0$.

12.3.7. Illustrative MEL Confidence Interval Example

For the Qin and Lawless experiment discussed in Section 12.2.4 we now compare three methods of obtaining confidence intervals for θ. One method (ELR) obtains confidence intervals using the empirical likelihood ratio statistic (12.3.1) and the Chi-square approximation (12.3.2). The second method is based on a Z-statistic and the limiting normal distribution (12.2.2) and is referred to as NCI, denoting a normal confidence interval. The third method (GLR) uses the parametric generalized likelihood ratio statistic based on the normal distribution $\mathrm{N}(\theta, \theta^2 + 1)$. The average confidence interval length and empirical coverage probability for 1000 samples and sample sizes of 30 and 60 are given in Table 12.3.

In general the two EL methods yield coverage probability less than nominal coverages. As might be expected, the GLR approach based on the correct parametric likelihood yields intervals that are close to the nominal coverage probability. Also note that the average length of the EL confidence intervals compares favorably with the alternatives, being the shortest in half of the cases examined and always being shorter than GLR intervals.

Table 12.3. *Average Length (AVL) and Empirical Coverage (ECV) for Three Confidence Interval Methods, from 1000 Simulations*

		90%		95%	
		AVL	ECV	AVL	ECV
		$n = 30$			
$N(0, 1)$	ELR	0.55064	85.8%	0.65714	92.4%
	NCI	0.56965	86.0%	0.67889	92.0%
	GLR	0.60197	89.6%	0.72441	94.3%
$N(1, 2)$	ELR	0.56698	83.3%	0.67737	89.2%
	NCI	0.56863	84.3%	0.67767	90.1%
	GLR	0.61489	88.3%	0.73900	93.6%
		$n = 60$			
$N(0, 1)$	ELR	0.41535	89.5%	0.49611	95.4%
	NCI	0.41291	89.2%	0.49210	94.9%
	GLR	0.42549	90.8%	0.50950	96.1%
$N(1, 2)$	ELR	0.41200	88.6%	0.49267	94.1%
	NCI	0.40933	89.0%	0.48782	93.2%
	GLR	0.42845	91.3%	0.51265	96.1%

► **Example 12.3.1:** The GAUSS program C12MEL4.gss provided in the examples manual extends the preceding illustration. For a given sample, the program outlines the steps involved in the formation of confidence regions and the conduct of hypothesis tests. Then, for values of the parameter θ and the sample size n selected by the user, GAUSS replicates the results presented in Table 12.3.

12.4. MEL in the Linear Regression Model with Stochastic X

Owen (1991) and Kolaczyk (1994) have shown how the EL approach can be applied to the linear regression model. Whether or not the motivation for the regression application is completely analogous to the approach presented in Sections 12.1–12.3 depends on whether the explanatory variables are stochastic or not. When **X** is stochastic, our previous EL discussion directly applies to the regression case under the appropriate regularity conditions. We examine this case ahead. In Section 12.5, we examine the case where **x** is fixed, and we will see that more advanced (non-iid) asymptotic theory is then required to obtain useful asymptotic properties of the EL procedure.

12.4.1. MEL Regression Estimation for Stochastic X

Assume the explanatory variable matrix **X** is stochastic and non-nondegenerate (see Chapter 10 for a detailed discussion of the stochastic **X** case in the general regression context). We assume that **X** and ε are independent and furthermore that the conditional mean function for **Y** is given by $\mathrm{E}[\mathbf{Y} \mid \mathbf{x}] = \mathbf{x}\boldsymbol{\beta}$. We also assume that $(\mathrm{Y}_i, \mathbf{X}[i, .])$,

$i = 1, \ldots, n$ are iid random vectors. In this case, the application of the EL approach is analogous in motivation to the EL procedure given previously.

Regarding the form of the estimating functions to use in the EL procedure, Owen (1991) considers the $(k \times 1)$ vector function $\mathbf{h}((\mathrm{Y}_i, \mathbf{X}[i, .]), \boldsymbol{\beta}) = \mathbf{X}[i, .]'(\mathrm{Y}_i - \mathbf{X}[i, .]\boldsymbol{\beta})$ for any $i = 1, \ldots, n$. Note that under the prevailing assumptions we can deduce that

$$\mathrm{E}[\mathbf{h}((\mathrm{Y}_i, \mathbf{X}[i, .]), \boldsymbol{\beta})] = \mathrm{E}[\mathbf{X}[i, .]'(\mathrm{Y}_i - \mathbf{X}[i, .]\boldsymbol{\beta})] = \mathbf{0}, \quad \text{for } i = 1, \ldots, n, \tag{12.4.1}$$

when $\boldsymbol{\beta}$ is the true value of the parameter vector $\boldsymbol{\beta}$ in the linear regression model $\mathbf{Y} = \mathbf{X}\boldsymbol{\beta} + \varepsilon$, and thus the estimating functions are unbiased. In particular, (12.4.1) follows from the double expectation theorem upon first taking the expectation with respect to $\mathbf{Y}$ conditional on $\mathbf{x}$ and then taking the expectation with respect to $\mathbf{X}$. Furthermore, the random vectors $\mathbf{Z}[., i] \equiv \mathbf{X}[i, .]'(\mathrm{Y}_i - \mathbf{X}[i, .]\boldsymbol{\beta})$, $i = 1, \ldots, n$ are iid random vectors under the prevailing assumptions because $(\mathrm{Y}_i, \mathbf{X}[i, .])$, $i = 1, \ldots, n$ are iid.

The definition of the EL function for $\boldsymbol{\beta}$ can then follow the approach in (12.1.11). Specifically, the scaled (by n^{-1}) log-empirical likelihood is defined by solving a constrained maximization problem expressed in Lagrange form as

$$n^{-1} \sum_{i=1}^{n} \ln(\mathrm{p}_i) - \eta \left[\sum_{i=1}^{n} \mathrm{p}_i - 1 \right] - \boldsymbol{\lambda}' \sum_{i=1}^{n} \mathrm{p}_i \mathbf{x}[i, .]'(\mathrm{y}_i - \mathbf{x}[i, .]\boldsymbol{\beta}), \tag{12.4.2}$$

where $\mathrm{p}_i > 0\ \forall i$ is implicit in the structure of the problem. The development of the optimal solution to the maximization problem in (12.4.2) follows (12.1.12)–(12.1.18), leading to the functional form for the log–EL function given by

$$\ln[\mathrm{L}_{\mathrm{EL}}(\boldsymbol{\beta}; (\mathbf{y}, \mathbf{x}))] = -\sum_{i=1}^{n} \ln[n(1 + \boldsymbol{\lambda}(\boldsymbol{\beta})'[\mathbf{x}[i, .]'(\mathrm{y}_i - \mathbf{x}[i, .]\boldsymbol{\beta})])]. \tag{12.4.3}$$

The maximum empirical likelihood (MEL) estimator of $\boldsymbol{\beta}$ is then defined by

$$\hat{\boldsymbol{\beta}}_{\mathrm{EL}} = \arg\max_{\boldsymbol{\beta}}[\ln[\mathrm{L}_{\mathrm{EL}}(\boldsymbol{\beta}; (\mathbf{y}, \mathbf{x}))]]. \tag{12.4.4}$$

As indicated in (12.2.2)–(12.2.4), the MEL estimator $\hat{\boldsymbol{\beta}}_{\mathrm{EL}}$ is asymptotically normally distributed, where $n^{1/2}(\hat{\boldsymbol{\beta}}_{\mathrm{EL}} - \boldsymbol{\beta}_0) \xrightarrow{d} \mathrm{N}(\mathbf{0}, \boldsymbol{\Sigma})$, and the asymptotic covariance matrix can be estimated as

$$\hat{\boldsymbol{\Sigma}} = \left[\left[\sum_{i=1}^{n} \hat{\mathrm{p}}_i \mathbf{x}[i, .]'\mathbf{x}[i, .] \right] \left[\sum_{i=1}^{n} \hat{\mathrm{p}}_i (\mathrm{y}_i - \mathbf{x}[i, .]\hat{\mathbf{b}}_{\mathrm{EL}})^2 \mathbf{x}[i, .]'\mathbf{x}[i, .] \right]^{-1} \times \left[\sum_{i=1}^{n} \hat{\mathrm{p}}_i \mathbf{x}[i, .]'\mathbf{x}[i, .] \right]' \right]^{-1}. \tag{12.4.5}$$

Note that there is a close analogy between (12.4.5) and White's heteroscedasticity–robust estimate of the covariance matrix of $\hat{\boldsymbol{\beta}}_{\mathrm{LS}}$ discussed in Chapter 15 of this volume. In fact, this feature imparts a degree of robustness (to heteroscedasticity) to hypothesis-testing and confidence-region estimation based on the asymptotic normal distribution of the MEL estimator.

As in the case of applying the EL procedure to estimating the population mean, using the EL approach to estimate $\boldsymbol{\beta}$ in the linear regression model based on the unbiased estimating functions (12.4.1) leads to a familiar functional form for $\hat{\boldsymbol{\beta}}_{\text{EL}}$. In particular, note that $\hat{\mathbf{b}}_{\text{EL}} = \hat{\mathbf{b}}_{\text{LS}} = (\mathbf{x}'\mathbf{x})^{-1}\mathbf{x}'\mathbf{y}$ and $\text{p}_i = n^{-1}\ \forall i$ solve the estimating equation constraints in (12.4.2) and at the same time result in the maximum possible value of $n^{-1}\sum_{i=1}^{n}\ln(\text{p}_i)$ subject to the constraints $\sum_{i=1}^{n}\text{p}_i = 1$ and $\text{p}_i > 0\ \forall i$. That $n^{-1}\sum_{i=1}^{n}\ln(\text{p}_i)$ is maximized is apparent because $\text{p}_i = n^{-1}\ \forall i$ is in fact the solution for maximizing the EL *unconstrained* by estimating equations. To see that the estimating equation constraints are satisfied when $\text{p}_i = n^{-1}$ and $\boldsymbol{\beta} = \hat{\mathbf{b}}_{\text{LS}}$, note that

$$\sum_{i=1}^{n}\text{p}_i(\mathbf{x}[i,.]'(\text{y}_i - \mathbf{x}[i,.]\boldsymbol{\beta})) = n^{-1}\sum_{i=1}^{n}[\mathbf{x}[i,.]'(\text{y}_i - \mathbf{x}[i,.]\hat{\mathbf{b}})]$$
$$= n^{-1}(\mathbf{x}'\mathbf{y} - \mathbf{x}'\mathbf{x}\hat{\mathbf{b}}) = \mathbf{0} \qquad (12.4.6)$$

where the parenthetical expression to the right of the second equality in (12.4.6) is the set of normal equations that define the least-squares estimator.

Returning to the covariance matrix estimate in (12.4.5), and letting $\text{p}_i = n^{-1}$, $\hat{\mathbf{b}}_{\text{EL}} = \hat{\mathbf{b}}_{\text{LS}}$, and $\hat{\mathbf{e}} = \mathbf{Y} - \mathbf{x}\hat{\mathbf{b}}_{\text{LS}}$, we then have an exact representation of White's heteroscedastic robust (asymptotic) covariance matrix for the LS, and now MEL, estimator $\hat{\boldsymbol{\beta}}_{\text{EL}}$, as follows (see Chapter 15):

$$n^{-1}\hat{\boldsymbol{\Sigma}} = (\mathbf{x}'\mathbf{x})^{-1}\left[\sum_{i=1}^{n}\hat{\text{e}}_i^2\mathbf{x}[i,.]'\mathbf{x}[i,.]\right](\mathbf{x}'\mathbf{x})^{-1}. \qquad (12.4.7)$$

The asymptotic covariance matrix of estimator $\hat{\boldsymbol{\beta}}_{\text{EL}}$ is robust against heteroscedasticity and attains similar robustness in testing and in confidence region estimation. The derivation of the EL estimator and its asymptotic covariance matrix based on the unbiased estimating functions (12.4.1) represents alternative motivation for both the least-squares estimator for $\boldsymbol{\beta}$ and the heteroscedasticity–robust form of the covariance matrix estimator.

We also note for future reference (Chapter 16) that the EL approach can be extended to the case in which the estimating functions are based on weakly dependent observations rather than independent observations. This allows the EL approach to be applied to regression problems in which the data exhibit a convergent autocorrelation structure, for example (see Chapters 14 and 15). These extensions were provided by Kitamura (1997), who effectively applies the same EL procedure presented in previous sections to blocks of data observations as opposed to individual data observations. We will not investigate the details of this procedure here but rather will revisit this type of EL application in context when we investigate the case of weakly dependent data observations ahead.

12.4.2. EL-Based Testing and Confidence Regions When X Is Stochastic

Hypothesis-testing and confidence-region estimation proceeds analogously to the procedures identified in Section 12.3. In particular, upon replacing $\boldsymbol{\theta}$ with $\boldsymbol{\beta}$ in all of the previous discussions and formulas relating to hypothesis testing statistics and associated confidence regions procedures, all of the previous results apply identically. We emphasize that, as in the population mean example of Section 12.3.6, the ELR and LM specification tests of the estimating equations *cannot* be applied to the current problem. This is because the number of functionally independent estimating equations equals the number of unknown parameters, that is, $m = k$ in both (12.3.17) and (12.3.21).

12.4.3. Extensions to the Nonlinear Regression Model for Stochastic X

All of the preceding results for the linear regression model can be extended to the nonlinear regression model. The key to making the extensions is in the redefinition of the unbiased estimating functions used in the EL procedure. Specifically, the definition of the unbiased estimating functions now becomes

$$\mathbf{h}((Y_i, \mathbf{X}[i,.]), \boldsymbol{\beta}) = \frac{\partial g(\mathbf{X}[i,.], \boldsymbol{\beta})}{\partial \boldsymbol{\beta}}[Y_i - g(\mathbf{X}[i,.], \boldsymbol{\beta})]. \qquad (12.4.8)$$

Given this choice for $\mathbf{h}$, all of the preceding estimation, hypothesis-testing and confidence-region results in Sections 12.1–12.3 apply given that $\mathbf{h}$ adheres to the appropriate regularity conditions assumed to hold in previous sections. The reader will note that (12.4.8) represents the first-order conditions for solving the nonlinear least-squares estimation problem, and so it is no surprise that the EL and NLS estimators coincide in this case. The asymptotic covariance matrix of the EL estimator is a generalization of (12.4.7), where $\mathbf{x}[i,.]$ is replaced by $\frac{\partial g(\mathbf{X}[i,.],\boldsymbol{\beta})}{\partial \boldsymbol{\beta}'}$ for every i. The reader is asked to contemplate the details of the adjustments required in the formulas of Sections 12.1–12.3 to extend results to the nonlinear regression model.

12.5. MEL in the Linear Regression Model with Nonstochastic X: Extensions to the Non-iid Case

The case in which $\mathbf{x}$ is a fixed matrix of explanatory variables actually complicates rather than simplifies matters in applying the EL procedure to regression models. This is mainly because when $\mathbf{x}$ is degenerate, it is untenable to utilize laws of large numbers and central limit theorems based on the assumption of iid random variables to establish asymptotic properties of EL estimates and test procedures, as we will see ahead.

In the case where $\mathbf{x}$ is fixed, Owen (1991) uses the unbiased estimating functions $\mathbf{h}(Y_i, \boldsymbol{\beta}) = \mathbf{x}[i,.]'(Y_i - \mathbf{x}[i,.]\boldsymbol{\beta})$ for $i = 1, \ldots, n$, leading to the moment equations

$$E\mathbf{h}(Y_i, \boldsymbol{\beta}) = E[\mathbf{x}[i,.]'(Y_i - \mathbf{x}[i,.]\boldsymbol{\beta})] = \mathbf{0}, \qquad (12.5.1)$$

when $\boldsymbol{\beta}$ is the true value of the parameter vector $\boldsymbol{\beta}$. Note that (12.5.1) is analogous to (12.4.1) except that the fixed $\mathbf{x}$ replaces the stochastic $\mathbf{X}$. If we assume the conditions of the linear statistical model in Chapter 5 and include the assumption that ε_i's are iid in the linear model $\mathbf{Y} = \mathbf{x}\boldsymbol{\beta} + \boldsymbol{\varepsilon}$, then the random vectors $\mathbf{h}(Y_i, \boldsymbol{\beta}) = \mathbf{x}[i,.]'(Y_i - \mathbf{x}[i,.]\boldsymbol{\beta})$, $i = 1, \ldots, n$ are independent, but they are not iid because $\mathbf{cov}(\mathbf{h}(Y_i, \boldsymbol{\beta})) = \sigma^2\mathbf{x}[i,.]'\mathbf{x}[i,.]$, $\forall i$, which changes when the value of $\mathbf{x}[i,.]$ changes.

In this case, the intuition underlying the translation of the moment equations (12.5.1) into empirical expectations based on p_i weights is not directly supported. That is, there is no *common* distribution from which the $\mathbf{h}(y_i, \boldsymbol{\beta})$'s occur, and so the notion of specifying $E_{\mathbf{p}}[\mathbf{h}(Y, \boldsymbol{\beta})] = \sum_{i=1}^{n} p_i \mathbf{h}(y_i, \boldsymbol{\beta})$ as an expectation of a random vector taken with respect to an empirical representation, $(p_1, \ldots, p_n)$, of $\mathbf{h}(Y, \boldsymbol{\beta})$'s population distribution is not appropriate.

Owen (1991, Theorem 2) extended the notion of the EL procedure to cases in which the random sample $(Y_1, Y_2, \ldots, Y_n)$ being analyzed is a collection of independent but *not* necessarily identically distributed random variables. He utilized central limit theory based on the notion of triangular arrays (Electronic Chapter E1; Mittelhammer, p. 279), which is appropriate for cases in which the random variables involved are independent but not identically distributed. Kolaczyk (1994, Theorem 1 and trailing discussion) restated Owen's theorem in a way that can be applied directly to a wide array of different estimating equation specifications. We restate Owen's result in a way that is particularly, useful for our purposes.

Theorem 12.5.1 (EL for Independent, Nonidentically Distributed Random Variables): *Let* $\mathbf{h}(Y_i, \boldsymbol{\beta})$, $i = 1, \ldots, n$, *be a collection of independent random* $(k \times 1)$ *vectors for which* $E[\mathbf{h}(Y_i, \boldsymbol{\beta})] = \mathbf{0}$ *and* $\mathbf{cov}(\mathbf{h}(Y_i, \boldsymbol{\beta})) = \boldsymbol{\Psi}_i$, *where* $\boldsymbol{\beta}$ *is a* $(k \times 1)$ *parameter vector. Let* $\boldsymbol{\Psi}(n) = n^{-1} \sum_{i=1}^{n} \boldsymbol{\Psi}_i$, *and let* ξ_n^S *and* ξ_n^L *denote the smallest and largest eigenvalues of* $\boldsymbol{\Psi}(n)$, *respectively. Also assume*

1. $\lim_{n\to\infty} P(\mathbf{0} \in \mathrm{ch}\{\mathbf{h}(y_1, \boldsymbol{\beta}), \ldots, \mathbf{h}(y_n, \boldsymbol{\beta})\}) = 1$,
2. $n^{-2} \sum_{i=1}^{n} E[\|\mathbf{h}(Y_i, \boldsymbol{\beta})\|^4 / (\xi_n^L)^2] \to 0$ as $n \to \infty$, and
3. $\xi_n^S / \xi_n^L \geq c > 0 \; \forall n \geq k$,

where $\mathrm{ch}\{\cdot\}$ *denotes the convex hull of the set of vectors displayed in* $\{\cdot\}$. *Then the empirical likelihood ratio,* $LR_{EL}(\boldsymbol{\beta}) = L_{EL}(\boldsymbol{\beta})/L_{EL}(\hat{\boldsymbol{\beta}}_{EL})$, *where* $L_{EL}(\boldsymbol{\beta}) = \Pi_{i=1}^{n} p_i(\boldsymbol{\beta})$ *follows from the solution* $\mathbf{p}(\boldsymbol{\beta})$ *obtained from the constrained maximization problem (see (12.1.11))*

$$\max_{\mathbf{p}} \left[\sum_{i=1}^{n} \ln(p_i) \text{ s.t. } \sum_{i=1}^{n} p_i \mathbf{h}(y_i, \boldsymbol{\beta}) = \mathbf{0} \quad \text{and} \quad \sum_{i=1}^{n} p_i = 1 \right],$$

is such that

$$-2\ln(LR_{EL}(\mathbf{r})) \overset{a}{\sim} \text{Chi-square}(k, 0)$$

when $\boldsymbol{\beta} = \mathbf{r}$ *is true.*

PROOF: Owen (1991), Theorem 2.

Note that all of the regularity conditions, except 1, are typical of central limit theorems that are applied to collections of independent, nonidentically distributed random variables (for example, examine the Liapounov CLT, Electronic Chapter E1; Mittelhammer, pp. 276, 280), and can be considered mild restrictions on the inference problem. Regarding assumption 1, first recall that the convex hull of the vectors $\mathbf{v}_i, i = 1, \ldots, n$, consists of the set of all vectors that can be formed by convex combinations of the $\mathbf{v}_i$'s, as $\sum_{i=1}^{n} \mathrm{p}_i \mathbf{v}_i$, for $\sum_{i=1}^{n} \mathrm{p}_i = 1$ and $\mathrm{p}_i > 0\, \forall i$. Thus, assumption 1 simply states that the mean of the $\mathbf{h}(\mathrm{Y}_i, \boldsymbol{\beta})$'s, $\mathbf{0}$, is eventually contained within the convex hull of weighted averages of $\mathbf{h}(\mathrm{Y}_i, \boldsymbol{\beta})$'s sample outcomes with probability limiting to 1 as $n \to \infty$, which is also only a mild restriction in applications.

The importance of Theorem 12.5.1 is that, for the purposes of testing $\mathrm{H}_0\colon \boldsymbol{\beta} = \mathbf{0}$ or for generating confidence regions for the vector $\boldsymbol{\beta}$, one can proceed as usual within the EL context and use the methods analogous to Sections 12.2–12.4 to recover information about $\boldsymbol{\beta}$. The theorem extends to testing general hypotheses of the form $\mathrm{H}_0\colon \mathbf{c}(\boldsymbol{\beta}) = \mathbf{r}$ by replacing the empirical likelihood ratio statistic stated in the theorem with the statistic $\mathrm{LR}_{\mathrm{EL}}(\boldsymbol{\beta}) = \mathrm{L}_{\mathrm{EL}}(\hat{\boldsymbol{\beta}}^{c}_{\mathrm{EL}})/\mathrm{L}_{\mathrm{EL}}(\hat{\boldsymbol{\beta}}_{\mathrm{EL}})$, where $\hat{\boldsymbol{\beta}}^{c}_{\mathrm{EL}}$ is the MELE constrained by H_0. The empirical likelihood ratio is then asymptotically distributed as Chi-square$(j, 0)$ under H_0, where j is the number of functionally independent restrictions being tested. The work of Kitamura (1997) extends the work of Qin and Lawless (1994) to the non independent case and also extends Theorem 12.5.1 to encompass problem situations in which the number of estimating equations can exceed the number of unknown parameters. The same asymptotics apply as stated in the theorem and as well as from testing of the more general hypothesis $\mathrm{H}_0\colon \mathbf{c}(\boldsymbol{\beta}) = \mathbf{r}$.

Having reviewed Owen's general result on the application of the EL approach to non-iid random variables, we now note that the particular application to the linear regression model results in precisely the same estimator for $\boldsymbol{\beta}$, namely, $\hat{\boldsymbol{\beta}}_{\mathrm{LS}}$, precisely the same limiting distribution result, and precisely the same asymptotic covariance matrix estimate, $\hat{\boldsymbol{\Sigma}}$ in (12.4.7), whether or not $\mathbf{X}$ is stochastic. Hypothesis testing and dual-associated confidence region generation for hypotheses of the form $\mathrm{H}_0\colon \mathbf{c}(\boldsymbol{\beta}) = \mathbf{r}$ or $\mathrm{H}_0\colon \mathrm{c}(\boldsymbol{\beta}) \leq \mathrm{r}$ can proceed in effectively the same way whether $\mathbf{X}$ is stochastic or nonstochastic. These remarks apply to testing the validity of moment equations as well. Furthermore, extensions to the nonlinear regression model proceed as in the stochastic $\mathbf{X}$ case. The key to making all of these extensions is the use of laws of large numbers and central limit theorems that apply to independent, nonidentically distributed random variables.

▶ **Example 12.5.1:** To demonstrate the application of the EL concept to the linear regression model, we provide the GAUSS program C12MLREL.gss in the examples manual. For a given sample generated from a linear regression model, we show that the MEL and LS estimates of the location parameter $\boldsymbol{\beta}$ are identical. Then, the GAUSS program guides the user through an EL hypothesis test of a linear restriction on $\boldsymbol{\beta}$. The restricted MEL estimator is discussed by Qin and Lawless (1995).

12.6. Concluding Comments

In addition to the usual nonlinear and nonnormal regression model specifications and the quasi-maximum likelihood (QML) and estimating equation (EE) approaches to estimation and inference introduced in Chapter 11, we have introduced the method of maximum empirical likelihood (MEL) estimation and inference in this chapter. This significantly enlarges the scope of procedures available for solving inverse problems in cases in which full probability distribution specifications are not available. At this point, a few generalizations that emerge from the work of Owen (1991), Qin and Lawless (1994, 1995), and Kolaczyk (1994) are useful in terms of making comparisons among the alternative approaches to estimation and inference.

In terms of inference, QML uses either a normal approximation to the distribution of the maximum quasi-likelihood estimator or a Chi-square approximation to the distribution of the corresponding quasi-likelihood ratio statistic, when it exists. The EL and QML point estimates will be the same in linear regression models under classical assumptions, but the corresponding likelihood ratio curves and confidence regions need not be the same. The QML estimators developed in Sections 11.1 and 11.2 appear to rely on assumptions similar to the EL approach involving the first two moments and some weak conditions on the higher moments of the data. One important difference is that QML requires that the first two moments of the dependent variables be correctly specified if consistent estimates of the model parameters are to be obtained. Alternatively, EL only requires that the estimating functions have zero expectations, that is, the estimating function must only be unbiased, which imparts a degree of robustness to the EL approach. In the fully parametric case and through parametric methods of analysis, if the variance function (of parameters) is functionally misspecified, the normal approximation to estimators is still valid, but the Chi-square approximation and associated confidence limits of the usual test statistics are not valid. In general, under EL, if the variance is misspecified, there will be a loss of efficiency, but, over a large class of linear, nonlinear, and semiparametric models, test statistics and confidence regions will still be valid.

Finally, we note that EL shares the sampling properties of various nonparametric methods based on resampling of the data, such as the bootstrap. However, in contrast to the resampling methods, EL works by optimizing a continuously differentiable function, which makes it amenable to imposing side constraints on the parameters that add information to the data. Articles that provide additional details and extension of EL results include DiCiccio, Hall, and Romano (1989, 1991), DiCiccio and Romano (1990), and Hall (1990). In the next chapter we analyze the statistical implications of choosing an information theoretic–optimizing criterion as an alternative to EL.

12.7. Exercises

12.7.1. Idea Checklist – Knowledge Guides

---

1. Why should we be interested in making use of the ML concept if knowledge of the parametric family of probability distributions underlying the likelihood function is not available?
2. What is meant by the statement that the empirical likelihood function approach reweights the sample observations?

3. What are the statistical implications of the possibility of achieving first-order asymptotic results that are analogous to parametric methods when we cannot parametrically specify the likelihood function?
4. What is an appropriate characterization of EL that is akin to an extremum problem in which the unknowns exceed the data points and the solution cannot be written in closed form?
5. What is the link between the inference methods of QML, EE, and MEL?
6. What kinds of statistical hypotheses can be evaluated with the Lagrange multiplier estimator $\lambda(\hat{\theta}_{\mathrm{EL}})$?
7. What are the computational implications of using the EL approach?

12.7.2. Problems

12–1 Suppose we observe a sample of n iid observations with $\mathrm{E}[\mathrm{Y}]=\theta$ and $\mathrm{var}[\mathrm{Y}]=\theta$. Derive the EL weights for the observations and state the profile empirical likelihood function for θ.

12–2 Following Example 2 presented by Qin and Lawless, suppose we observe a bivariate sample of n iid observations $\{(\mathrm{x}_1, \mathrm{y}_1), \ldots, (\mathrm{x}_n, \mathrm{y}_n)\}$ with common mean θ.

a. Derive the empirical likelihood weights for each observed pair $(\mathrm{x}_i, \mathrm{y}_i)$.

b. Given the optimal Lagrange multiplier $\hat{\lambda}$ show that the EL estimator of θ is

$$\hat{\theta} = \sum_{i=1}^{n}\left[\frac{\mathrm{x}_i}{1+\hat{\lambda}(\mathrm{x}_i-\mathrm{y}_i)}\right] \bigg/ \sum_{i=1}^{n}\left[\frac{1}{1+\hat{\lambda}(\mathrm{x}_i-\mathrm{y}_i)}\right]$$

c. Suppose the random variables X and Y have variances σ_x^2 and σ_y^2 with covariance σ_{xy}. Using Equation (12.2.3), show that the asymptotic variance for $\hat{\theta}$ is $(\sigma_x^2\sigma_y^2 - \sigma_{xy}^2)/(\sigma_x^2+\sigma_y^2-2\sigma_{xy})$.

12–3 Consider an extension of the two-sample problem based on the estimating equations $[\mathrm{X}-\mu_X, \mathrm{Y}-\mu_Y, \mathrm{X}^2-\mu_X^2-\sigma_X^2, \mathrm{Y}^2-\mu_Y^2-\sigma_Y^2, (\mathrm{X}-\mu_X)(\mathrm{Y}-\mu_Y)-\rho\sigma_X\sigma_Y]$. Derive the EL weights and state the profile empirical likelihood function.

12–4 Suppose the sample data are not well behaved and severe outliers are present. How might this influence the specification of the moment constraints in the MEL problem, and what are the corresponding sampling property implications? In estimating a location parameter θ, can you suggest a way of combining the moment constraints for the mean and median to provide robustness against outliers?

12.7.3. Computer Exercises

---

1. Write a GAUSS program to generate a pseudorandom sample of $n=15$ Poisson(θ) observations for some $\theta>0$ of your choice. Then, plot the likelihood function based on the Poisson mass function and the profile empirical likelihood function based on the first moment of this sample. Are the likelihood functions comparable? What happens as you increase or decrease the sample size?
2. Design a Monte Carlo exercise to simulate the mean, variance, and sampling distribution of the EL estimator for the two-sample problem (i.e., Qin and Lawless, Example 2). Compare the simulated sampling properties with the limiting normal distribution for the EL estimator.

3. Write a GAUSS program to simulate the sampling properties of the Lagrange multiplier and the associated LM test statistic (see Equations (12.3.21) and (12.3.23)). To simplify matters, you may wish to use one of the computer examples presented in this chapter, or you may extend one of the programs you wrote to complete the preceding problems.

12.8. References

DiCiccio, T., P. Hall, and J. Romano (1991), "Empirical Likelihood is Bartlett-Correctable," *The Annals of Statistics*, Vol. 19, pp. 1053–61.

DiCiccio, T., and J. Romano (1990), "Nonparametric Confidence Limits by Resampling Methods and Least Favorable Families," *International Statistical Review*, Vol. 58, pp. 59–76.

DiCiccio, T. J., P. Hall, and J. Romano (1989), "Comparison of Parametric and Empirical Likelihood Functions," *Biometrika*, Vol. 76, pp. 465–76.

Hall, P. (1990), "Pseudo-Likelihood Theory for Empirical Likelihood," *The Annals of Statistics*, Vol. 18, pp. 121–40.

Kiefer and Wolfowitz (1956), "Consistency of the Maximum Likelihood Estimator in the Presence of Infinitely Many Incidental Parameters," *Annals of Mathematical Statistics*, Vol. 27, pp. 887–906.

Kitamura, Y. (1997), "Empirical Likelihood Methods with Weakly Dependent Processes," *Annals of Statistics*, Vol. 25, pp. 2084–2102.

Kolacyzk, E. (1994), "Empirical Likelihood for Generalized Linear Models," *Statistica Sinica*, Vol. 4, pp. 199–218.

McCullagh, P., and J. A. Nelder (1989), *Generalized Linear Models*, 2nd ed., London: Chapman and Hall.

Mittelhammer, R. C. (1996), *Mathematical Statistics for Economics and Business*, New York: Springer–Verlag.

Owen, A. (1988), "Empirical Likelihood Ratio Confidence Intervals for a Single Functional," *Biometrika*, Vol. 75, pp. 237–49.

Owen, A. (1990), "Empirical Likelihood Ratio Confidence Regions," *The Annals of Statistics*, Vol. 18, pp. 90–120.

Owen, A. (1991), "Empirical Likelihood for Linear Models," *The Annals of Statistics*, Vol. 19, pp. 1725–47.

Qin, J., and J. Lawless (1994), "Empirical Likelihood and General Estimating Equations," *The Annals of Statistics*, Vol. 22, pp. 300–25.

Qin, J., and J. Lawless (1995), "Estimating Equations, Empirical Likelihood, and Constraints on Parameters," *Canadian Journal of Statistics*, Vol. 23, pp. 145–59.

CHAPTER 13

Information Theoretic-Entropy Approaches to Estimation and Inference

BUILDING on the extremum (E) estimation, quasi maximum likelihood (QML) and estimating equations (EE) concepts introduced in Chapters 7 and 11, we demonstrated the empirical likelihood (EL) approach in Chapter 12 as a nonparametric method of inference. The EL approach yields an estimator that has sampling properties similar to resampling methods such as the bootstrap and an inference basis analogous to that used with parametric methods. However, instead of the resampling process underlying the bootstrap, the maximum empirical likelihood (MEL) method works by profiling a multinomial likelihood supported on the sample data.

In situations involving independent and identically distributed random variables, MEL has an advantage over some parametric methods in that it makes only mild assumptions about the existence of certain moments or estimating functions. By optimizing a continuous criterion function subject to a reasonable set of estimating equations, the MEL estimator has first order asymptotic sampling properties that are analogous to parametric MLE. Building on these results, in this chapter we specify an alternative information theoretic (IT) estimation objective function which is optimized subject to the same types of moment or estimating equation information as in the MEL case, and we develop its corresponding asymptotic sampling properties and associated inference procedures.

The types of statistical models we will be concerned with in this chapter are characterized in Table 13.1.

The inverse problem examined is of the form

$$(\mathbf{Y}, \mathbf{X}) \Rightarrow (\boldsymbol{\beta}, \sigma^2, \varepsilon).$$

13.1. Solutions to Systems of Estimating Equations and Kullback–Leibler Information

The procedures examined in the previous two chapters involved solutions of systems of estimating equations. In both the EL and EE contexts, the estimating equations

Table 13.1. *Semiparametric Regression Models*

Model Component	**Specific Characteristics**	
$\mathbf{Y}$	RV Type:	continuous
	Range:	unlimited
	Y_i dimension:	univariate
	Moments:	$E[\mathbf{Y} \mid \mathbf{X}] = \mathbf{g}(\mathbf{X}, \boldsymbol{\beta})$, $\mathbf{cov}(\mathbf{Y}) = \sigma^2\mathbf{I}$
$\eta(\mathbf{X}, \boldsymbol{\beta}, \varepsilon)$	Functional Form:	linear or nonlinear in $\mathbf{X}$ and $\boldsymbol{\beta}$ and additive in ε
$\mathbf{x}$	RV Type:	stochastic or degenerate (fixed)
	Genesis:	exogenous to the model
$\boldsymbol{\beta}$	RV Type:	degenerate (fixed)
	Dimension:	finite
ε	RV Type:	iid, or non-iid
	Moments:	$E[\varepsilon \mid \mathbf{X}] = \mathbf{0}$, and $\mathbf{cov}(\varepsilon \mid \mathbf{X}) = \sigma^2\mathbf{I}$
Ω	Prior info:	none
$f(\mathbf{e} \mid \mathbf{x}, \varphi^2)$	PDF family:	unspecified

were empirical analogs to expectation relations of the type $E[\mathbf{h}(\mathbf{Y}, \boldsymbol{\theta})] = \mathbf{0}$. We note that estimators for $\boldsymbol{\theta}$ defined as the solution to such moment equations subsume a large collection of familiar estimation procedures, including linear and nonlinear least squares. In fact, the idea of basing an estimator definition on the solution to estimating equations can be applied quite generally to extremum problems, as is especially evident when solutions (the extremum estimator) can be characterized by first-order conditions.

In the EL procedure, the focus was on a vector of estimating equations whose dimension m is at least as large as the dimension of the unknown parameter vector $\boldsymbol{\theta}$. The estimating equations were defined as empirical analogs to population moments $E[\mathbf{h}(Y, \boldsymbol{\theta})] = \mathbf{0}$. In the transition to empirical specifications of the moment conditions, a vector of n unknown nonnegative weights $\mathbf{p} = (p_1, p_2, \ldots, p_n)'$ was introduced, yielding the empirical moment equations $\sum_{i=1}^{n} p_i \mathbf{h}(y_i, \boldsymbol{\theta}) = \mathbf{0}$. This m-dimensional vector moment equation, coupled with the adding up restriction $\sum_{i=1}^{n} p_i = 1$, was sufficient to determine only $(m+1)$ of the $(n+k)$ unknowns $(\boldsymbol{\theta}, \mathbf{p})$, leaving $[n+k-(m+1)]$ of the unknowns undetermined. The underdetermined nature of the system of moment equations was resolved in Chapter 12 by the introduction of an estimation objective function $n^{-1}\sum_{i=1}^{n} \ln(p_i)$, which was maximized, subject to the moment equation constraints, to determine the $(n+k)$ unknowns $(\boldsymbol{\theta}, \mathbf{p})$. Relatedly, constrained estimation of $n^{-1}\sum_{i=1}^{n} \ln(p_i)$ for *given* values of $\boldsymbol{\theta}$ resulted in a maximum value function $\sum_{i=1}^{n} \ln[p_i(\boldsymbol{\theta})]$, which was interpreted as an *empirical log-likelihood function* for $\boldsymbol{\theta}$. The MEL estimator is defined by maximizing this empirical log-likelihood function with respect to $\boldsymbol{\theta}$. When the number of moment constraints m exceeds the number of unknown parameters k the MEL approach defines the optimal combination of the moment equations in the sense of duplicating the asymptotic efficiency of the most efficient estimating equations (EE) estimator. Recall that the efficient EE estimator is obtained from the most efficient set of k estimating equations that can be constructed from the information contained in linear combinations of the set of m moment equations.

To provide perspective on where we have been and where we are going with the concept of estimating equations and the general notion of an empirical representation of likelihood, return to the general inverse problem context, where we have the interesting and challenging task of recovering unobservables from observables. Indeed, progress in previous chapters has been measured by how and "how well" we solved such inverse problems. In many cases in economics we utilize unobservable probabilities to characterize information contained in observables (data). If we can *define a set of probability values that are consistent with the observables* of the problem, then the issue becomes how we can use these probabilities to provide a basis for estimation and inference for the remaining unknowns of direct interest. Note that in this inverse problem situation we have reversed the process of modeling data information via probabilities and have used the data information to recover values of the probabilities, which we then subsequently use in some fashion for further estimation and inference purposes. One can then view the recovered probability values as *inverse probabilities*, that is, the probability weight solutions to an inverse problem.

In Chapter 12, we considered the case of a finite and discrete (in terms of unknown probability weights) inverse problem with noise involving iid outcomes $y_1, \ldots, y_n$, which were observed along with certain empirical moment conditions. In that chapter we used an estimation objective function along with observed data to define a profile likelihood function and corresponding inverse probabilities; that is, we defined an empirical likelihood function associated with an empirical probability distribution. By choosing the criterion of maximizing the empirical likelihood function we identified a basis for recovering the unobservable inverse probabilities and also defined a solution to the estimation and inference problem relating to unknown parameters of the inverse problem.

The acts of maximizing the empirical likelihood function and producing the MEL estimator are but *one* way to define an empirical likelihood estimator that has good first-order asymptotic properties. In contrast to the traditional MEL formulation and solution, in this chapter we follow Golan and Judge (1996) and take a more general approach to examining an alternative estimation objective function for deriving solutions to sets of estimating equations called by various names, including *relative* entropy, *cross* entropy, *discriminant information*, and the *Kullback–Leibler information criterion* (KLIC). We will initially adopt the latter name in recognition of Kullback and Leibler (1951), whose seminal article stimulated the development and use of the criterion in the statistics literature. We will see that it subsumes the MEL approach as a special case and also encompasses an approach called the maximum entropy (ME) approach that we develop in detail. Axiomatic foundations of the entropy measure, used with the preceding optimizing criteria, exist and are discussed by Shore and Johnson (1980), Jaynes (1980), Skilling (1989), and Csiszar (1991). A more complete discussion of the ME principle as it applies to traditional types of ill-posed and ill-conditioned pure inverse problems, and inverse problems with noise, is presented in electronic Chapter E3.

13.1.1. Kullback–Leibler Information Criterion (KLIC)

We now provide some background on the Kullback–Leibler information concept. Kullback–Leibler (KL) information is a measure of the discrepancy between two probability distributions, say $p(\mathbf{y})$ and $\pi(\mathbf{y})$. The KL information in $p(\mathbf{y})$ relative to $\pi(\mathbf{y})$ (which is also referred to as the cross-entropy of p *relative to* π) is defined in the discrete case by

$$\mathrm{KL}(p, \pi) = \sum_{\mathbf{y}} p(\mathbf{y}) \ln[p(\mathbf{y})/\pi(\mathbf{y})] \tag{13.1.1}$$

and in the continuous case by

$$\mathrm{KL}(p, \pi) = \int_{\mathbf{y}} p(\mathbf{y}) \ln[p(\mathbf{y})/\pi(\mathbf{y})]\, d\mathbf{y}. \tag{13.1.2}$$

In the discrete case, we will alternatively denote the KL information as $\mathrm{KL}(\mathbf{p}, \boldsymbol{\pi}) = \sum_i p_i \ln(p_i/\pi_i)$, where $\mathbf{p}$ and $\boldsymbol{\pi}$ denote the finite or countable vectors of probability weights implied by the discrete distributions $p(\mathbf{y})$ and $\pi(\mathbf{y})$. The distribution in the second position of the argument list in $\mathrm{KL}(p, \pi)$, here π, is called the *reference distribution*. We refer to the first distribution in the argument list, here p, as the *subject distribution*.

The KL information in $\pi(\mathbf{y})$ relative to $p(\mathbf{y})$, $\mathrm{KL}(\pi, p)$, is obtained by reversing the roles of the reference and subject distributions, that is, p and π are reversed in (13.1.1) and (13.1.2). Note that the KL information metric is not symmetric in p and π, and thus in general $\mathrm{KL}(\pi, p) \neq \mathrm{KL}(p, \pi)$. Consequently, KL is not a true measure of the distance between p and π and is referred to instead as a *pseudodistance function*. For our purposes, this property is not particularly important because the reference distribution is taken to be fixed in estimation problems. We are only concerned about choosing the subject distribution p that solves the moment equations and that is as close as possible to the reference distribution π.

The KLIC has several useful statistical properties relating to sufficient statistics, information additivity, and hypothesis testing, and the interested reader is directed to Kullback and Leibler (1951), and Kullback (1959, 1983) for details. Our principal interest here is in the discrete case, and we henceforth focus our attention on this case. For our immediate purposes, it is useful to note that $\mathrm{KL}(\mathbf{p}, \boldsymbol{\pi}) \geq 0$ for every $\mathbf{p} \geq \mathbf{0}$, and $\mathrm{KL}(\mathbf{p}, \boldsymbol{\pi}) = 0$ iff $\mathbf{p} = \boldsymbol{\pi}$. Furthermore, $\mathrm{KL}(\mathbf{p}, \boldsymbol{\pi})$ is a strictly convex function of the elements of $\mathbf{p}$. The latter property follows directly from examining the second-order derivative matrix of $\mathrm{KL}(\mathbf{p}, \boldsymbol{\pi})$ with respect to $\mathbf{p}$ and recalling that $p_i \in [0, 1], \forall i$. Note that $w \ln(w)$ is *defined* to be 0 when $w = 0$. The closer $\mathrm{KL}(\mathbf{p}, \boldsymbol{\pi})$ is to zero, the more similar is the distribution $p(\mathbf{y})$ relative to $\pi(\mathbf{y})$, and the distributions coincide when $\mathrm{KL}(\mathbf{p}, \boldsymbol{\pi}) = 0$. The greater the value of $\mathrm{KL}(\mathbf{p}, \boldsymbol{\pi})$, the greater the discrepancy between the distributions $p(\mathbf{y})$ and $\pi(\mathbf{y})$.

Note that one can interpret the KL information value as the expectation of a log-likelihood ratio, and it is this context that Kullback (1959) and Gokhale and Kullback (1978) use it to discriminate between distributional hypotheses relating to the probability distributions of observed data. To illustrate, let $\boldsymbol{\theta}_1$ and $\boldsymbol{\theta}_2$ be two alternative values of the parameter vector leading to two alternative discrete probability distribution characterizations $f(\mathbf{y}; \boldsymbol{\theta}_1)$ and $f(\mathbf{y}; \boldsymbol{\theta}_2)$ for the distribution of $\mathbf{y}$. Consider the KL information in $f(\mathbf{y}; \boldsymbol{\theta}_1)$ relative to $f(\mathbf{y}; \boldsymbol{\theta}_2)$ given by

$$\begin{aligned} \mathrm{KL}(f(\mathbf{y};\boldsymbol{\theta}_1), f(\mathbf{y};\boldsymbol{\theta}_2)) &= \sum_{\mathbf{y}} [\ln(f(\mathbf{y};\boldsymbol{\theta}_1)/(f(\mathbf{y};\boldsymbol{\theta}_2))] f(\mathbf{y};\boldsymbol{\theta}_1) \\ &= \mathrm{E}_{\theta_1}[\ln(\mathrm{L}(\boldsymbol{\theta}_1;\mathbf{y})/\mathrm{L}(\boldsymbol{\theta}_2;\mathbf{y}))], \qquad (13.1.3) \end{aligned}$$

where $\mathrm{E}_{\theta_1}[\,]$ denotes an expectation taken with respect to the distribution $f(\mathbf{y}; \boldsymbol{\theta}_1)$. It is apparent that the KL information in (13.1.3) can be interpreted as a mean log-likelihood ratio, where averaging is done using weights provided by the subject distribution. Interpreting $\ln(f(\mathbf{y};\boldsymbol{\theta}_1)/f(\mathbf{y};\boldsymbol{\theta}_2)) = \ln(\mathrm{L}(\boldsymbol{\theta}_1;\mathbf{y})/\mathrm{L}(\boldsymbol{\theta}_2;\mathbf{y}))$ as the information in the data outcome $\mathbf{y}$ in favor of the hypothesis $\boldsymbol{\theta}_1$ relative to $\boldsymbol{\theta}_2$, Kullback then interprets (13.1.3) as the *mean information* provided by sample data in favor of $\boldsymbol{\theta}_1$ relative to $\boldsymbol{\theta}_2$ *under the assumption that $\boldsymbol{\theta}_1$ is actually true.*

13.1.2. Relationship Between the MEL Objective and KL Information

The KL information criterion can be defined in a way that subsumes the MEL estimation objective function as a special case. Establishing this relationship between the MEL approach and the KL information criterion provides us with an alternative rationale for the MEL estimation objective function $n^{-1}\sum_{i=1}^{n}\ln(p_i)$.

Consider the KL information criterion when the *reference* distribution is some discrete distribution $p(\mathbf{y})$ having discrete and finite support $\mathbf{y} \in \Gamma$, and the *subject* distribution is $\pi(\mathbf{y}) = n^{-1}\ \forall \mathbf{y} \in \Gamma$. In this context the KL information is given by

$$\mathrm{KL}(n^{-1}\mathbf{1}, \mathbf{p}) = \sum_{i=1}^{n} \frac{1}{n} \ln\left(\frac{1}{n} \Big/ p(\mathbf{y}_i)\right) = -n^{-1}\sum_{i=1}^{n}\ln(p_i) - \ln(n) \qquad (13.1.4)$$

where $\mathbf{1}$ represents a $(n \times 1)$ vector of ones so that $n^{-1}\mathbf{1} = [n^{-1}, \ldots, n^{-1}]'$ denotes a discrete uniform distribution, n is the number of elements in Γ, $\mathbf{p} = (p_1, p_2, \ldots, p_n)'$, and $p_i \equiv p(y_i)$. It is apparent that minimizing (13.1.4) is equivalent to maximizing the scaled (by n^{-1}) log-EL objective function $n^{-1}\sum_{i=1}^{n}\ln(p_i)$ because n is a constant in (13.1.4). Consequently, maximizing empirical likelihood is equivalent to minimizing KL information for the case at hand.

To see what additional rationale we have gained for solving systems of estimating equations via the EL principle, first recall the fundamental rationale for the EL objective function. The EL objective function was originally specified as $\prod_{i=1}^{n} p_i$ to provide an empirical representation of the joint PDF of a random sample of independent random variables. The function $\prod_{i=1}^{n} p_i$ thus has the natural interpretation of representing the joint PDF value of the independent random variables outcomes $y_1, y_2, \ldots, y_n$. Maximizing $\prod_{i=1}^{n} p_i$, or, equivalently, maximizing $n^{-1}\sum_{i=1}^{n}\ln(p_i)$, subject to m moment equations and the normalization restriction $\sum_{i=1}^{n} p_i = 1$, effectively chooses the p_i's so as to assign the *maximum joint probability* possible to the *observed* set of sample outcomes $(y_1, y_2, \ldots, y_n)$ from *among all possible probability assignments* that are consistent with the moment equations.

Now consider interpreting the objective of minimizing KL information as given by (13.1.4). In the absence of any constraints other than the normalization restriction $\sum_{i=1}^{n} p_i = 1$, we know by the previously discussed properties of KL information that $KL(n^{-1}\mathbf{1}, \mathbf{p})$ will be minimized when $p(y) = n^{-1}\ \forall\ y \in \Gamma$. Thus, the objective of minimizing $KL(n^{-1}\mathbf{1}, \mathbf{p})$ has the effect of drawing the p_i's toward the maximally uninformative distribution, that is, the uniform distribution on Γ. If minimizing $KL(n^{-1}\mathbf{1}, \mathbf{p})$ is constrained by m moment equations and the normalization restriction $\sum_{i=1}^{n} p_i = 1$, then the objective can be interpreted as choosing the p_i's to be as *maximally uninformative* as the estimating equation information will permit. In effect the objective is consistent with the goal of not wanting to assert more about the distribution of the Y_i's than is known from the moment equations. Regarding the set of distributions $\mathbf{p}$ that satisfy the moment equations, some distributions will assign probabilities to the sample outcomes that can be much different from the uniform distribution weights defined by the subject distribution. In effect, these distributions provide additional or extraneous information about the sample outcomes that is not justified by the available information (i.e., the information contained in the moment equations and subject distribution). By selecting $\mathbf{p}$ to minimize $KL(n^{-1}\mathbf{1}, \mathbf{p})$, we effectively remove extraneous information in the MEL–KL solution. Given the equivalence of the maximum EL and minimum KL information criteria, this "maximally uninformative p" interpretation of the KL principle can be used as a motivation for the EL principle as well.

We emphasize that the MEL–KL equivalence holds only when the uniform distribution is used as the subject distribution in defining the KL information function. From our previous discussion of the KLIC in Section 13.1.1, where we interpreted KL information as an expected log-likelihood ratio, we know that minimizing $KL(n^{-1}\mathbf{1}, \mathbf{p})$ can be interpreted as minimizing the mean information provided by sample data in favor of the uniform distribution relative to $p(\mathbf{y})$ *under the assumption that the uniform distribution is true*. In this case we are effectively calibrating our mean information measure in terms of the standard empirical distribution function weights n^{-1}, which is a reasonable thing to do – at least under iid sampling from a population distribution. *We are then choosing the reference distribution that minimizes mean information in favor of the empirical distribution weights.* This interpretation is of course consistent with the idea of drawing the reference distribution as closely as possible to the subject (uniform) distribution, which will concomitantly minimize the expected log-likelihood ratio. Further, we note that the lack of symmetry in the KL function is not a problem for MEL–KL estimation because we are holding the *subject* distribution fixed.

One may wonder what would happen if we reversed the roles of the subject and reference distributions in defining the KL information objective function to be used in solving the empirical moment equations. The result is a *maximum entropy* criterion (Jaynes 1957a,b, 1963, 1984), where the entropy metric provides a basis for determining the sample weights, or inverse probabilities in place of the EL criterion.

13.1.3. Relationship Between the Maximum Entropy (ME) Objective and KL Information

If we reverse the roles of the subject and reference distributions and minimize KL information subject to the empirical moment constraints $\sum_{i=1}^{n} \pi_i \mathbf{h}(\mathrm{y}_i, \boldsymbol{\theta}) = \mathbf{0}$ and normalization constraints $\sum_{i=1}^{n} \pi_i = 1$, then the KL information criterion is defined as

$$\mathrm{KL}(\boldsymbol{\pi}, n^{-1}\mathbf{1}) = \sum_{i=1}^{n} \pi_i \ln(n\pi_i) = \sum_{i=1}^{n} \pi_i \ln(\pi_i) + \ln(n), \tag{13.1.5}$$

and $\boldsymbol{\pi} = (\pi_1, \pi_2, \ldots, \pi_n)'$ denotes probability weights on the sample observations. Note that (13.1.5) simply has the subject and reference distributions reversed from what they were in Section 13.1.2. In particular, the standard empirical distribution function weights, n^{-1}, now represent the *reference* distribution. Minimizing KL information is clearly equivalent to maximizing $-\sum_{i=1}^{n} \pi_i \ln(\pi_i)$, which is precisely Shannon's (1948) *entropy* measure.

Shannon's entropy measure can be interpreted as a measure of the degree of uncertainty in a discrete probability distribution $\boldsymbol{\pi} = (\pi_1, \pi_2, \ldots, \pi_n)'$ representing the extent to which the distribution is concentrated on a few points as opposed to being dispersed over many points. Entropy takes its maximum value of $\log(n)$ when the distribution is maximally dispersed and thus uniformly distributed on the y_i's. Therefore, $-\sum_{i=1}^{n} \pi_i \ln(\pi_i)$ is maximized when $\boldsymbol{\pi}$ is maximally uninformative with regard to discriminating between likely and unlikely outcomes amongst $\mathrm{y}_1, \mathrm{y}_2, \ldots, \mathrm{y}_n$. Entropy takes on its minimum value 0 if the distribution is maximally informative in that $\boldsymbol{\pi}$ is degenerate on one particular y_i value, that is, $\pi_i = 1$ and $\pi_j = 0$, $\forall i \neq j$, where $0 \ln(0) \equiv 0$.

Now consider interpreting the objective of maximizing entropy or, equivalently, minimizing $\mathrm{KL}(\boldsymbol{\pi}, n^{-1}\mathbf{1})$ defined in (13.1.5). In the absence of any constraints other than the standard normalization $\sum_{i=1}^{n} \pi_i = 1$, it follows immediately from our preceding discussion regarding the maximal value of entropy that $\pi_i = n^{-1}$, $\forall i$, are the optimal choices of the π_i's. Therefore, as in the case of the MEL or minimum $\mathrm{KL}(n^{-1}\mathbf{1}, \mathbf{p})$ criterion, the choice of π_i's is drawn toward the maximally uninformative uniform distribution. If maximizing entropy or, equivalently, minimizing $\mathrm{KL}(\boldsymbol{\pi}, n^{-1}\mathbf{1})$ is constrained by m moment equations, then the objective can again be interpreted as choosing the π_i's to be as maximally uninformative as the moment equations will allow. Again, the objective is consistent with the goal of not wanting to assert more about the distribution of the Y_i's than is known via the moment equations. Extraneous information is "minimized out," just as it is for the MEL or $\mathrm{KL}(n^{-1}\mathbf{1}, \mathbf{p})$ criterion. In effect, one is making use of all of the information available for the problem (i.e., the moment constraints and uniform reference distribution), but one is also avoiding the unintentional introduction of assumptions about information that is not available.

What is the difference between MEL and maximum entropy empirical likelihood (MEEL) for obtaining empirical probability or likelihood weights, or equivalently, what is the difference between minimizing $\mathrm{KL}(n^{-1}\mathbf{1}, \mathbf{p})$ and $\mathrm{KL}(\boldsymbol{\pi}, n^{-1}\mathbf{1})$? The difference lies in the calibration of the mean information provided by sample data for and against the uniform and the $\boldsymbol{\pi}$ or $\mathbf{p}$ distribution of probabilities on the y_i's. In the former EL or $\text{KL}(n^{-1}\mathbf{1}, \mathbf{p})$ case, *averaging is performed with respect to the predata empirical distribution function weights,* n^{-1} for each Y_i. Then, assuming the uniform distribution to be true, the mean information is interpreted in the context of the expected information in favor of the uniform distribution relative to the postdata estimated probability distribution, $\mathbf{p}$. In the latter maximum entropy (ME) or $\text{KL}(\boldsymbol{\pi}, n^{-1}\mathbf{1})$ case, *averaging is performed with respect to the postdata probability distribution,* $\boldsymbol{\pi}$. Thus, if the $\boldsymbol{\pi}$ distribution is assumed to be true, the mean information is interpreted in the context of the expected information in favor of the $\boldsymbol{\pi}$-distribution relative to the predata EDF weights, n^{-1} for each Y_i.

► **Example 13.1.1:** The GAUSS program C13Comp.gss (provided in the example manual) demonstrates the properties and interpretation of the KLIC (cross-entropy) function. In particular, GAUSS graphically portrays the convexity and lack of symmetry of the pseudodistance function, and the KL measure is reported for a series of subject and reference distributions. Then, GAUSS examines the EL and Shannon entropy functions as special cases of KLIC, including the interpretation of Shannon entropy as a measure of the degree of uncertainty.

Heuristically, the ME or $\text{KL}(\boldsymbol{\pi}, n^{-1}\mathbf{1})$ criteria would seem the more appealing of the two approaches because it weights discrepancies between the uniform and $\boldsymbol{\pi}$ distributions using estimates of the probabilities of the y_i's that are based on observed data information rather than on a priori uniform weights. Assuming that the moment equation information is valid, one would then anticipate that the expected log-likelihood ratio, or mean sample information in favor or against the uniform distribution is estimated more efficiently in the ME approach because it is calculated with respect to probability weights inferred from a larger data-enriched information base. Consequently, the focus in this chapter is on the MEEL estimation objective function

$$\text{KL}(\boldsymbol{\pi}, n^{-1}\mathbf{1}) = \sum_{i=1}^{n} \pi_i \left[\ln(\pi_i) - \ln\left(\frac{1}{n}\right) \right] \tag{13.1.6}$$

instead of the MEL estimation objective function

$$\text{KL}(n^{-1}\mathbf{1}, \mathbf{p}) = \sum_{i=1}^{n} \frac{1}{n} \left[\ln\left(\frac{1}{n}\right) - \ln(\text{p}_i) \right], \tag{13.1.7}$$

which is, except for an additive constant, the negative of the traditional log–EL objective function.

► **Example 13.1.2:** To compare the MEEL and MEL estimation criteria, we consider a special case of the population mean problem presented in Example 12.2.1. The GAUSS program C13MEEL1.gss (provided in the examples manual) generates a pseudorandom sample of n iid observations (the sample size is selected by the user) with mean zero. If we know the actual mean is zero, the MEEL and MEL criteria are used to impose the population mean condition on the sample by reweighting the observations. The empirical distribution functions (EDFs) derived from the MEEL and MEL methods are compared with the actual CDF for the DSP.

13.2. The General MEEL Alternative Empirical Likelihood Formulation

If we use MEEL as a basis for estimating the π_i's of the multinomial likelihood function (and not MEL), the corresponding problem of estimating the unknown probability weights becomes

$$\underset{\pi}{\text{Max}}\ \mathrm{S}(\boldsymbol{\pi}) \equiv -\sum_{i=1}^{n} \pi_i \ln \pi_i \tag{13.2.1}$$

subject to

$$\sum_{i=1}^{n} \pi_i \mathrm{h}_j(\mathrm{y}_i, \boldsymbol{\theta}) = 0 \quad j = 1, 2, \ldots, m; \tag{13.2.2}$$

and

$$\sum_{i=1}^{n} \pi_i = 1 \quad \text{and} \quad \pi_i \geq 0\ \forall i. \tag{13.2.3}$$

Upon close examination of the problem formulation, it is evident that, except for the estimation objective function, the form of the problem and the basis for a solution within the maximum entropy context closely mirror the problem form and solution within the MEL context.

13.2.1. The MEEL Estimator and Likelihood

The Lagrangian form of the maximum entropy problem for a given value of θ, and first-order conditions with respect to π_i are

$$\mathrm{L}(\boldsymbol{\pi}, \boldsymbol{\lambda}, \eta) = -\sum_{i=1}^{n} \pi_i \ln \pi_i - \sum_{j=1}^{m} \lambda_j \left[\sum_{i=1}^{n} \pi_i \mathrm{h}_j(\mathrm{y}_i, \boldsymbol{\theta}) \right] + \eta \left(1 - \sum_{i=1}^{n} \pi_i \right) \tag{13.2.4}$$

$$\frac{\partial \mathrm{L}}{\partial \pi_i} = -\ln \pi_i - 1 - \sum_{j=1}^{m} \lambda_j \mathrm{h}_j(\mathrm{y}_i, \boldsymbol{\theta}) - \eta = 0. \tag{13.2.5}$$

The optimal MEEL π_i's, expressed as a function of $\boldsymbol{\theta}$, are

$$\pi_i(\boldsymbol{\theta}) = \frac{\exp\left[-\sum_{j=1}^{m} \lambda_j(\boldsymbol{\theta}) \mathrm{h}_j(\mathrm{y}_i, \boldsymbol{\theta})\right]}{\sum_{i=1}^{n} \exp\left[-\sum_{j=1}^{m} \lambda_j(\boldsymbol{\theta}) \mathrm{h}_j(\mathrm{y}_i, \boldsymbol{\theta})\right]}, \tag{13.2.6}$$

where the $\lambda_j(\boldsymbol{\theta})$'s are the m optimal Lagrange multipliers associated with the m moment constraints. Note that the constraints $\pi_i > 0\ \forall i$ are implicitly imposed by the structure of the optimization problem. This MEEL solution, with the π_i's expressed in an *exponential* form, should be compared with the MEL solution $\hat{\mathrm{p}}_i(\boldsymbol{\theta}) =$

$n^{-1}[\sum_{j=1}^{m}\lambda_j(\boldsymbol{\theta})\text{h}_j(\text{y}_i,\boldsymbol{\theta})+1]^{-1}$ for the p_i's developed in Equation (12.1.16). The MEEL objective function is strictly concave on linear constraints, the Hessian matrix with respect to π is negative definite, and the solution $\hat{\pi}$ is therefore unique and optimal (see Golan, Judge, and Miller, 1996, p. 24). The maximum entropy estimator for the parameter vector $\boldsymbol{\theta}$ is then defined as

$$\hat{\Theta}_{\text{MEEL}} = \arg\max_{\theta}[\text{L}_{\text{MEEL}}(\boldsymbol{\theta};\mathbf{Y})], \tag{13.2.7}$$

where

$$\text{L}_{\text{MEEL}}(\boldsymbol{\theta};\mathbf{Y}) \equiv \arg\max_{\theta}[\text{L}(\boldsymbol{\pi}(\boldsymbol{\theta}), \boldsymbol{\lambda}(\boldsymbol{\theta}), \eta(\boldsymbol{\theta}))]. \tag{13.2.8}$$

The MEEL-based alternative to MEL for representing an empirical likelihood for $\boldsymbol{\theta}$ is then given by the function $\text{L}_{\text{MEEL}}(\boldsymbol{\theta};\mathbf{y}) = \prod_{i=1}^{n}\pi_i(\boldsymbol{\theta})$.

► **Example 13.2.1:** To demonstrate the computation of the MEEL estimator, we repeat the population mean problem considered in Example 12.2.1. The GAUSS program C13MEEL2.gss (provided in the examples manual) is designed to solve the problem of estimating the population mean parameter θ. For a given sample of n iid observations, estimates of θ are based on the MEEL estimator as well as the sample mean. For demonstration purposes, the MEEL estimates are computed by joint numerical search for θ and λ and by iterative search based on appropriate starting values. The GAUSS program compares the number of iterations, the iterative paths to convergence, and computing times for the alternative MEL methods.

13.2.2. MEEL Asymptotics

Under general regularity conditions, including

1. the random sample outcome $(\text{y}_1, \text{y}_2, \ldots, \text{y}_n)$ represents n independent realizations of a random variable Y with probability distribution $\text{F}(\text{y};\boldsymbol{\theta})$;
2. there exists a unique value of the $(k \times 1)$ parameter vector $\boldsymbol{\theta}_0$ such that $\text{E}[\mathbf{h}(\text{Y},\boldsymbol{\theta}_0)] = \mathbf{0}$, and
3. $\mathbf{h}(\cdot)$ consists of $m \geq k$ functionally independent coordinate functions,

the MEEL estimator for $\boldsymbol{\theta}$ is consistent and asymptotically normally distributed. Consequently, asymptotic tests and confidence regions can be generated based on asymptotic normality of the estimator analogous to the MEL case in Chapter 12. In fact, Imbens (1997) demonstrates that under regularity conditions analogous to those assumed in the MEL context, the limiting distributions of the MEEL and MEL estimators for $\boldsymbol{\theta}$ are *identical*. The main regularity conditions, in addition to those listed above, are that $\mathbf{h}(\text{Y},\boldsymbol{\theta})$ must be twice continuous differentiable with respect to $\boldsymbol{\theta}$, $\mathbf{h}$, and its first and second derivatives must be bounded, all in a neighborhood of the true parameter value $\boldsymbol{\theta}_0$, and the row rank of the $(k \times m)$ matrix $\text{E}[\frac{\partial \mathbf{h}(\text{Y},\boldsymbol{\theta})}{\partial \boldsymbol{\theta}}|_{\boldsymbol{\theta}_0}]$ must equal the number of parameters in the $(k \times 1)$ vector $\boldsymbol{\theta}$. These are relatively mild conditions that lead to the

MEEL estimator being *consistent* and *asymptotically normal* with limiting distribution

$$n^{1/2}(\hat{\boldsymbol{\Theta}}_{\text{MEEL}} - \boldsymbol{\theta}_0) \xrightarrow{d} \text{N}(\mathbf{0}, \boldsymbol{\Sigma}), \tag{13.2.9}$$

where

$$\boldsymbol{\Sigma} = \left[\text{E}\left[\frac{\partial \mathbf{h}(\text{Y}, \boldsymbol{\theta})}{\partial \boldsymbol{\theta}} \bigg|_{\boldsymbol{\theta}_0} \right] (\text{E}[\mathbf{h}(\text{Y}, \boldsymbol{\theta})\mathbf{h}(\text{Y}, \boldsymbol{\theta})'|_{\boldsymbol{\theta}_0}])^{-1} \text{E}\left[\frac{\partial \mathbf{h}(\text{Y}, \boldsymbol{\theta})}{\partial \boldsymbol{\theta}'} \bigg|_{\boldsymbol{\theta}_0} \right] \right]^{-1} \tag{13.2.10}$$

(compare with (12.2.2 and (12.2.3)). The covariance matrix $\boldsymbol{\Sigma}$ of the limiting normal distribution can be consistently estimated by the estimator

$$\hat{\boldsymbol{\Sigma}} = \left[\left[\sum_{i=1}^{n} \hat{\pi}_i \frac{\partial \mathbf{h}(\text{y}_i, \boldsymbol{\theta})}{\partial \boldsymbol{\theta}} \bigg|_{\hat{\boldsymbol{\theta}}_{\text{MEEL}}} \right] \left[\sum_{i=1}^{n} \hat{\pi}_i \mathbf{h}(\text{y}_i, \hat{\boldsymbol{\theta}}_{\text{MEEL}}) \mathbf{h}(\text{y}_i, \hat{\boldsymbol{\theta}}_{\text{MEEL}})' \right]^{-1} \right.$$
$$\left. \times \left[\sum_{i=1}^{n} \hat{\pi}_i \frac{\partial \mathbf{h}(\text{y}_i, \boldsymbol{\theta})}{\partial \boldsymbol{\theta}'} \bigg|_{\hat{\boldsymbol{\theta}}_{\text{MEEL}}} \right] \right]^{-1}, \tag{13.2.11}$$

where the $\hat{\pi}_i$'s are the maximum entropy estimates of the empirical probability distribution $\boldsymbol{\pi}$, which are characterized by (13.2.6) with $\boldsymbol{\theta}$ replaced by $\hat{\boldsymbol{\theta}}_{\text{MEEL}}$ (compare with (12.2.4)). An alternative consistent estimate can also be defined by using (13.2.11) with all of the $\hat{\pi}_i$'s replaced by n^{-1}, which amounts to applying probability weights based on the EDF instead of the empirical probability weights generated by the ME procedure. Because the ME estimates incorporate the additional moment equation information, it would be expected that these probability weight estimates would be more efficient in finite samples. This assumes the moment equation information is accurate, or equivalently that the estimating functions on which the moment equations are based are unbiased.

Example 13.2.2: To demonstrate the large sample properties of the MEEL estimator, we provide the GAUSS program C13MEEL3.gss in the examples manual. The program extends the problem of estimating the population mean parameter θ considered in Example 13.2.1. The user selects the number of Monte Carlo trials (m) and up to four sample sizes (n) used to conduct a simulation study of the statistical properties of the MEEL estimator and the sample mean. The GAUSS program reports the sample moments, box and whisker plots, and EDFs of the replicated estimates to examine the consistency and asymptotic normality of the two estimators.

13.2.3. MEEL Inference

The asymptotic normal distribution of $\hat{\boldsymbol{\Theta}}_{\text{MEEL}}$ allows asymptotic hypothesis tests and confidence regions to be constructed. The asymptotic testing and confidence region procedures for the ME case are analogous to those developed for the MEL estimator based on its asymptotic normal distribution. The only essential differences in practice are that the MEL estimates of $\boldsymbol{\theta}$, $\boldsymbol{\pi}$, and $\boldsymbol{\lambda}$ are replaced by MEEL estimates in all test and confidence region formulas. We review the basic formulas in the following paragraphs (see Kitamura and Stutzer, 1997, and Imbens, 1997).

13.2.3.a. Testing H_0: $\mathbf{c}(\boldsymbol{\theta}) = \mathbf{r}$

The usual triad of asymptotically valid Wald, Lagrange Multiplier, and Pseudo-likelihood ratio test procedures are available to test the validity of functional restrictions on the parameters of the probability model. All of the test statistics will have the usual central Chi-square distribution, Chi-square$(j, 0)$, under the null hypothesis, where j denotes the number of functionally independent hypotheses represented by $\mathbf{c}(\boldsymbol{\theta}) = \mathbf{r}$. The tests are conducted by comparing the outcome of the test statistic with the $100(1-\alpha)\%$ quantile of the Chi-square$(j, 0)$ distribution, producing an asymptotic level-α test of the hypothesis. The Wald (W), Lagrange multiplier (LM), and pseudo-likelihood ratio (PLR) statistics are defined as follows:

$$W = [\mathbf{c}(\hat{\Theta}_{\mathrm{MEEL}}) - \mathbf{r}]' \left[\left.\frac{\partial \mathbf{c}}{\partial \boldsymbol{\theta}'}\right|_{\hat{\Theta}_{\mathrm{MEEL}}} (n^{-1}\hat{\boldsymbol{\Sigma}}) \left.\frac{\partial \mathbf{c}}{\partial \boldsymbol{\theta}}\right|_{\hat{\Theta}_{\mathrm{MEEL}}} \right]^{-1} [\mathbf{c}(\hat{\Theta}_{\mathrm{MEEL}}) - \mathbf{r}], \tag{13.2.12}$$

$$LM = \left[n^{-1} \sum_{i=1}^{n} \mathbf{h}\left(Y_i, \hat{\Theta}^{c}_{\mathrm{MEEL}}\right) \right]' [\hat{\boldsymbol{\Psi}}^{-1} (n^{-1}\hat{\boldsymbol{\Sigma}})^{-1} \hat{\boldsymbol{\Psi}}^{-1}] \left[n^{-1} \sum_{i=1}^{n} \mathbf{h}\left(Y_i, \hat{\Theta}^{c}_{\mathrm{MEEL}}\right) \right], \tag{13.2.13}$$

$$PLR = 2n\left[\ln(L_{\mathrm{MEEL}}(\hat{\Theta}_{\mathrm{MEEL}}; \mathbf{Y})) - \ln\left(L_{\mathrm{MEEL}}\left(\hat{\Theta}^{c}_{\mathrm{MEEL}}; \mathbf{Y}\right)\right) \right], \tag{13.2.14}$$

where

$$\hat{\boldsymbol{\Psi}} = \mathbf{c\hat{o}v}(\mathbf{h}(Y; \boldsymbol{\theta})) = n^{-1} \sum_{i=1}^{n} \mathbf{h}(Y_i; \hat{\Theta}_{\mathrm{MEEL}}) \mathbf{h}(Y_i; \hat{\Theta}_{\mathrm{MEEL}})' \tag{13.2.15}$$

and $\hat{\Theta}^{c}_{\mathrm{MEEL}}$ denotes the constrained MEEL estimator that satisfies the restriction H_0: $\mathbf{c}(\boldsymbol{\theta}) = \mathbf{r}$.

13.2.3.b. Testing H_0: $c(\boldsymbol{\theta}) \leq r$ or H_0: $c(\boldsymbol{\theta}) \geq r$

It is possible to construct asymptotically valid tests of scalar inequality hypotheses and define confidence bounds based on Z-statistics in the usual way given the asymptotic normality of $\hat{\Theta}_{\mathrm{MEEL}}$. For example, to test the nonlinear inequality restrictions $c(\boldsymbol{\theta}) \leq r$, one could use the statistic

$$Z = \frac{c(\hat{\Theta}_{\mathrm{MEEL}}) - r}{\left[\left.\frac{\partial c(\boldsymbol{\theta})}{\partial \boldsymbol{\theta}'}\right|_{\hat{\Theta}_{\mathrm{MEEL}}} (n^{-1}\hat{\boldsymbol{\Sigma}}) \left.\frac{\partial c(\boldsymbol{\theta})}{\partial \boldsymbol{\theta}}\right|_{\hat{\Theta}_{\mathrm{MEEL}}} \right]^{1/2}} \overset{a}{\sim} N(\delta, 1), \tag{13.2.16}$$

where

$$\delta = \frac{c(\boldsymbol{\theta}_0) - r}{\left[\left.\frac{\partial c(\boldsymbol{\theta})}{\partial \boldsymbol{\theta}'}\right|_{\boldsymbol{\theta}_0} \boldsymbol{\Sigma} \left.\frac{\partial c(\boldsymbol{\theta})}{\partial \boldsymbol{\theta}}\right|_{\boldsymbol{\theta}_0} \right]^{1/2}}. \tag{13.2.17}$$

The asymptotic level α test rule for H_0: $c(\boldsymbol{\theta}) \leq r$ is

$$\text{reject } H_0 \quad \text{if} \quad z \geq z(1-\alpha). \tag{13.2.18}$$

where $z_{(1-\alpha)}$ is the $100(1-\alpha)\%$ quantile of the standard normal distribution. Reversing inequalities defines a test of the hypothesis H_0: $c(\boldsymbol{\theta}) \geq r$.

13.2.3.c. Testing the Validity of Moment Equations

Another test of interest in the ME context is the test of the validity of moment equations H_0: $E[\mathbf{h}(Y, \boldsymbol{\theta})] = \mathbf{0}$. Note this is equivalent to testing the *unbiasedness* of the estimating functions used in the ME approach. Imbens et al. (1997) and Kitamura and Stutzer (1997) provide a variety of tests for the validity of moment equations. Two such tests parallel the likelihood ratio and Lagrange multiplier tests presented previously in the EL context and will be reviewed here. The reader can consult the references for additional variations.

A pseudo-likelihood ratio-type asymptotic Chi-square test of the moment equations can be based on a suitably scaled version of the KL information criterion as follows:

$$K = 2n[KL(\hat{\boldsymbol{\pi}}, n^{-1}\mathbf{1})] \overset{a}{\sim} \text{Chi-square}(m-k, 0) \text{ under } H_0. \tag{13.2.19}$$

The test is based on the KL information discrepancy between estimates of the probability weights satisfying the moment restrictions (the subject distribution) and the standard empirical distribution function probability weights n^{-1} $\forall i$ (the reference distribution). Here, m is the number of moment equations, and k is the dimension of the parameter vector. As in thc EL case, the test is only available if there are more moment equations than parameters to be estimated.

Regarding a Lagrange multiplier-type test of the moment equations, Imbens et al. (1997) examine three alternatives and find that in Monte Carlo simulations the following variant is superior:

$$LM = n\hat{\boldsymbol{\lambda}}'\mathbf{R}\hat{\boldsymbol{\lambda}} \overset{a}{\sim} \text{Chi-square}(m-k, 0) \text{ under } H_0 \tag{13.2.20}$$

where

$$\mathbf{R} = \left[\sum_{i=1}^{n} \hat{\pi}_i \mathbf{h}_i \mathbf{h}_i'\right]\left[\sum_{i=1}^{n} \hat{\pi}_i^2 \mathbf{h}_i \mathbf{h}_i'\right]^{-1}\left[\sum_{i=1}^{n} \hat{\pi}_i \mathbf{h}_i \mathbf{h}_i'\right], \tag{13.2.21}$$

$\mathbf{h}_i \equiv \mathbf{h}(Y_i, \hat{\boldsymbol{\Theta}})$, and $\mathbf{R}$ is a robust estimator of the covariance matrix of the moment functions (Imbens, Spady, and Johnson, 1998, p. 341). Again, the test is available only in the case in which the number of moment equations exceed the number of parameters being estimated. Through use of either the K or LM statistic, the test is conducted in the usual way by rejecting H_0 if the outcome of the statistic exceeds the $100(1-\alpha)\%$ quantile of the Chi-square$(m-k, 0)$ distribution.

13.2.3.d. Confidence Regions

Confidence regions and bounds for model parameters, as well as for the expectation of the moment functions in the case of the tests in Section 13.2.3.c, can be conducted in the usual way based on duality with hypotheses tests. In particular, the set of null hypotheses values *not* rejected by the respective α-level hypothesis test represent an asymptotic confidence region with asymptotic confidence level $(1 - \alpha)$.

► **Example 13.2.3:** We provide the GAUSS program C13MEEL4.gss in the examples manual to demonstrate the properties and application of hypothesis tests based on the MEEL estimator for the two-moment problem. For an observed sample, GAUSS conducts a series of hypothesis tests related to the two-moment problem and reports the results to the user. Then, GAUSS forms a joint confidence region for the moment parameters based on the Wald criterion. To examine the sampling properties of the test statistics and confidence regions based on the EE estimator, the user may wish to extend the GAUSS program for this example. For example, you may conduct a Monte Carlo simulation of the power and size of the test statistics or the coverage probability of the Wald-based region.

13.2.4. Contrasting the Use of Estimating Functions in EE and MEEL Contexts

It is instructive at this point to note similarities and differences in the way estimating function information is used in the MEEL approach compared with the EE approach of Chapter 12. In this regard, arguments analogous to those presented in Section 12.1.3.b relating to the MEL problem context apply here, and the reader is encouraged to reread that section with the MEEL estimator replacing the MEL estimator in the discussion context. We emphasize in that discussion that asymptotically, the MEEL approach provides an optimal method of combining estimating function information in the same way as the MEL procedure does. This view is supported by the fact that asymptotically, the MEEL and MEL estimators share precisely the same asymptotic distribution.

13.3. A Cross-Entropy Formalism and Solution

In the preceding section we applied the Kullback–Leibler information measure using a reference distribution with uniform probabilities n^{-1} in implementing the maximum entropy estimation objective. Now suppose that in addition to the m moment constraints there exists some additional a priori information relating to the unknown convexity weights or probabilities π stated in the form of a vector π°. Extending the entropy framework, the estimation objective function may be reformulated to minimize the *cross* entropy (CEEL – cross-entropy empirical likelihood) or Kullback–Leibler information discrepancy between π and the a priori value of π, π°. Thus, the problem is cast in terms of minimizing the constrained cross entropy (CE) between the probabilities π that are consistent with the information in the moment restrictions and the prior probabilities π° representing prior information on the sample probability weights π.

Returning to the MEL formulations of Chapter 12 in which restrictions are in the form of empirical moment equations, if we use the CEEL variant of the MEEL criterion, the extremum problem of recovering likelihood weights $\pi_i > 0$ can be expressed as

$$\min_{\pi} \mathrm{KL}(\boldsymbol{\pi}, \boldsymbol{\pi}^{\mathrm{o}}) \equiv \min_{\pi} \left[\sum_{i=1}^{n} \pi_i \ln\left(\pi_i / \pi_i^{\mathrm{o}}\right) \right] = \min_{\pi} \left[\sum_{i=1}^{n} \pi_i \ln \pi_i - \sum_{i=1}^{n} \pi_i \ln \pi_i^{\mathrm{o}} \right] \tag{13.3.1}$$

subject to the empirical moment conditions

$$\sum_{i=1}^{n} \pi_i \mathrm{h}_j(\mathrm{y}_i, \boldsymbol{\theta}) = 0, \quad j = 1, \ldots, m \tag{13.3.2}$$

and the adding-up constraint on the sum of the nonnegative empirical probability weights

$$\sum_{i=1}^{n} \pi_i = 1. \tag{13.3.3}$$

In this case, the discrepancy between the empirical and prior sample weights is measured by the empirical moment-constrained Kullback–Leibler information or cross-entropy criterion. Forming the Lagrangian function for the problem (13.3.1)–(13.3.3), the optimal solution to the cross-entropy problem is

$$\hat{\pi}_i = \frac{\pi_i^{\mathrm{o}} \exp\left[\sum_{j=1}^{m} \hat{\lambda}_j \mathrm{h}_j(\mathrm{y}_i, \boldsymbol{\theta})\right]}{\sum_{i=1}^{n} \pi_i^{\mathrm{o}} \exp\left[\sum_{j=1}^{m} \hat{\lambda}_j \mathrm{h}_j(\mathrm{y}_i, \boldsymbol{\theta})\right]}, \tag{13.3.4}$$

where the $\hat{\lambda}_j$'s are the optimal Lagrange multipliers associated with the moment constraints, and the $\hat{\pi}_i$'s are the optimal empirical weights used to form an empirical likelihood function for $\boldsymbol{\theta}$. Note that if the prior probability weights are uniform, that is, $\pi_i^{\mathrm{o}} = n^{-1}, \forall i$, then the CEEL solution (13.3.4) is identical to the MEEL solution (13.2.6) after accounting for the change in sign in the Lagrange multipliers (i.e., $\hat{\boldsymbol{\lambda}}_{\mathrm{CEEL}} = -\hat{\boldsymbol{\lambda}}_{\mathrm{MEEL}}$). In contrast to the traditional MEL or MEEL formulation, by using the CEEL formalism we can introduce prior information through the reference distribution $\boldsymbol{\pi}^{\mathrm{o}}$ that can have an impact on the likelihood weights. Note the inverse probabilities in (13.3.4) are a function of the data, the prior distribution, and a normalizing constant.

► **Example 13.3.1:** To demonstrate an application of the cross-entropy criterion with a nonuniform reference distribution, we provide the GAUSS program C13CEEL.gss in the examples manual. For a pseudorandom sample of n observations drawn from the $\mathrm{N}(\theta, 1)$ distribution, the CEEL estimates are computed for various sets of reference weights for the sample outcomes (selected by GAUSS or by the user). Then, GAUSS conducts a Monte Carlo simulation exercise to approximate the sampling properties of the CEEL estimator under each of the reference distributions. The number of simulation trials (m) and the set of sample sizes (n) are also selected by the user.

13.4. α-Entropy: Unifying the MEL, MEEL, and CEEL Estimation Objectives

The MEL, MEEL, and CEEL estimation objective functions can all be embedded in a more general entropy measure

$$\mathrm{H}(\mathbf{p}, \mathbf{q}, \alpha) = \frac{1}{\alpha(\alpha+1)} \sum_{i=1}^{n} \mathrm{p}_i \left[\left(\frac{\mathrm{p}_i}{\mathrm{q}_i} \right)^{\alpha} - 1 \right]. \tag{13.4.1}$$

In the entropy literature, the function is a special form of the more general α-entropy functional attributed to Renyi (1960). More recently, Cressie and Read (1984) have used $\mathrm{H}(\mathbf{p}, \mathbf{q}, \alpha)$ as a nonparametric measure of the discrepancy between distributions $\mathbf{p}$ and $\mathbf{q}$ and refer to the α-entropy function as a power divergence criterion.

It can be shown via a direct application of L'Hospital's rule that as $\alpha \to 0$, the limit of $\mathrm{H}(\mathbf{p}, \mathbf{q}, \alpha)$ is the cross-entropy function

$$\lim_{\alpha \to 0} \mathrm{H}(\mathbf{p}, \mathbf{q}, \alpha) = \mathrm{KL}(\mathbf{p}, \mathbf{q}) = \sum_{i=1}^{n} \mathrm{p}_i \ln \left(\frac{\mathrm{p}_i}{\mathrm{q}_i} \right). \tag{13.4.2}$$

In this case, the distribution $\mathbf{p}$ that minimizes α-entropy is identical to the distribution that minimizes KL information. If the reference distribution is uniform as $\mathrm{q}_i = n^{-1}\ \forall i$, then

$$\lim_{\alpha \to 0} \mathrm{H}(\mathbf{p}, n^{-1}\mathbf{1}, \alpha) = \mathrm{KL}(\mathbf{p}, n^{-1}\mathbf{1}) = \sum_{i=1}^{n} \mathrm{p}_i \ln(\mathrm{p}_i) + \ln(n) \tag{13.4.3}$$

so that minimizing α-entropy is then equivalent to the MEEL objective (recall (13.2.1)).

As $\alpha \to -1$, another application of L'Hospital's rule reveals that the limit of $\mathrm{H}(\mathbf{p}, \mathbf{q}, \alpha)$ is

$$\lim_{\alpha \to -1} \mathrm{H}(\mathbf{p}, \mathbf{q}, \alpha) = \mathrm{KL}(\mathbf{q}, \mathbf{p}) = -\sum_{i=1}^{n} \mathrm{q}_i \ln \left(\frac{\mathrm{p}_i}{\mathrm{q}_i} \right)$$

$$= -\sum_{i=1}^{n} \mathrm{q}_i \ln(\mathrm{p}_i) + \sum_{i=1}^{n} \mathrm{q}_i \ln(\mathrm{q}_i). \tag{13.4.4}$$

If the $\mathbf{q}$ distribution is uniform such that $\mathrm{q}_i = n^{-1}\ \forall i$, it follows that except for the added *constant* $\sum_{i=1}^{n} \mathrm{q}_i \ln(\mathrm{q}_i) = -\ln(n)$, $\lim_{\alpha \to -1} \mathrm{H}(\mathbf{p}, n^{-1}\mathbf{1}, \alpha)$ is equal to the negative of the scaled (by n^{-1}) log–MEL objective function for $\mathbf{p}$ (recall (12.1.3)). In this special case, the distribution $\mathbf{p}$ that minimizes α-entropy is equivalent to the maximum empirical likelihood distribution. Thus, the MEL and MEEL problems are nested within the minimum α-entropy framework, and this represents another basis for linking the estimation and inference principles.

13.5. Application of the Maximum Entropy Principle to the Regression Model

The application and interpretation of the maximum entropy principle within the regression model context is analogous to the MEL approach presented in Section 12.4 and differs only in terms of the specific functional form of the objective function. As in the case of MEL, whether or not the constraints $\sum_{i=1}^{n} \mathrm{p}_i \mathbf{h}(\mathrm{y}_i, \boldsymbol{\theta}) = \mathbf{0}$ on the objective of maximizing entropy can be interpreted in a straightforward manner as empirical moment constraints depends on whether the explanatory variable matrix $\mathbf{X}$ is stochastic or not. Notationally and conceptually, the pair $(\mathrm{y}_i, \mathbf{x}_{i.})$ now take the place of the scalar y_i in the estimating and moment equations of all preceding sections of this chapter. Also note that henceforth we use p_i's to denote the probability weights rather than distinguishing the MEEL solutions by the notation $\boldsymbol{\pi}$.

13.5.1. Stochastic X in the Linear Model

In the stochastic $\mathbf{X}$ case, where it is assumed that $\mathbf{X}$ and the noise component ε are uncorrelated and $(\mathrm{Y}_i, \mathbf{X}[i, .])$, for $i = 1, \ldots, n$ are iid random vectors, the $(k \times 1)$ vector estimating functions $\mathbf{h}((\mathrm{Y}_i, \mathbf{X}[i, .]), \boldsymbol{\beta}) = \mathbf{X}[i, .]'(\mathrm{Y}_i - \mathbf{X}[i, .]\boldsymbol{\beta})$ for $i = 1, \ldots, n$ are also iid. Furthermore, under the prevailing assumptions, we can deduce that

$$\mathbf{E}[\mathbf{h}((\mathrm{Y}_i, \mathbf{X}[i, .]), \boldsymbol{\beta})] = \mathbf{E}[\mathbf{X}[i, .]'(\mathrm{Y}_i - \mathbf{X}[i, .]\boldsymbol{\beta})] = \mathbf{0}, \qquad \text{for } i = 1, \ldots, n, \tag{13.5.1}$$

when $\boldsymbol{\beta}$ is the true value of the parameter vector $\boldsymbol{\beta}$ in the linear regression model $\mathbf{Y} = \mathbf{X}\boldsymbol{\beta} + \varepsilon$, and thus the estimating functions are unbiased, as in the MEL case of (12.4.1). It follows that $\sum_{i=1}^{n} \mathrm{p}_i \mathbf{h}(\mathrm{y}_i, \mathbf{x}_{i.}, \boldsymbol{\theta}) = \mathbf{0}$ represents an empirical characterization of the expectation of the unbiased estimating equation.

The Lagrangian form of the maximum entropy problem for a given value of $\boldsymbol{\beta}$, which bears a strong analogy to the definition of the constrained maximum empirical likelihood problem used to define the log-empirical likelihood for $\boldsymbol{\beta}$ in (12.4.2), is given by

$$\mathrm{L}(\mathbf{p}, \boldsymbol{\lambda}, \eta) = -\sum_{i=1}^{n} \mathrm{p}_i \ln(\mathrm{p}_i) - \boldsymbol{\lambda}' \sum_{i=1}^{n} \mathrm{p}_i (\mathbf{x}[i, .]'(\mathrm{y}_i - \mathbf{x}[i, .]\boldsymbol{\beta})) - \eta \left(\sum_{i=1}^{n} \mathrm{p}_i - 1 \right), \tag{13.5.2}$$

where $\mathrm{p}_i > 0 \ \forall i$ is implicitly imposed by the structure of the optimization problem (compare with (13.2.4)). The optimal solution for the p_i's in (13.5.2) is given by (recall (13.2.6))

$$\mathrm{p}_i(\boldsymbol{\beta}) = \frac{\exp\left(-\sum_{j=1}^{m} \lambda_j(\boldsymbol{\beta})[\mathbf{x}[i, j](\mathrm{y}_i - \mathbf{x}[i, .]\boldsymbol{\beta})]\right)}{\sum_{i=1}^{n} \exp\left(-\sum_{j=1}^{m} \lambda_j(\boldsymbol{\beta})[\mathbf{x}[i, j](\mathrm{y}_i - \mathbf{x}[i, .]\boldsymbol{\beta})]\right)}, \tag{13.5.3}$$

where $\boldsymbol{\lambda}(\boldsymbol{\beta})$ denotes the optimal value of the Lagrange multipliers associated with the moment constraints (note it is necessarily the case that $p_i > 0\ \forall i$). The optimal MEEL solution for the $\boldsymbol{\beta}$ parameter leads to the following definition for the MEEL estimator:

$$\boldsymbol{\beta}_{\text{MEEL}} = \arg\max_{\boldsymbol{\beta}}[\text{L}(\mathbf{p}(\boldsymbol{\beta}), \boldsymbol{\lambda}(\boldsymbol{\beta}), \eta(\boldsymbol{\beta}))]. \tag{13.5.4}$$

Under general regularity conditions, the MEEL estimator $\hat{\boldsymbol{\beta}}_{\text{MEEL}}$ is consistent and asymptotically normally distributed, completely analogous to the MEL estimator, where $n^{1/2}(\hat{\boldsymbol{\beta}}_{\text{MEEL}} - \boldsymbol{\beta}_0) \xrightarrow{d} \text{N}(\mathbf{0}, \boldsymbol{\Sigma})$. The covariance matrix of the limiting distribution can be estimated as

$$\hat{\boldsymbol{\Sigma}} = \left[\left[\sum_{i=1}^{n} \hat{p}_i \mathbf{x}[i,.]'\mathbf{x}[i,.]\right]\left[\sum_{i=1}^{n} \hat{p}_i (y_i - \mathbf{x}[i,.]\hat{\mathbf{b}}_{\text{MEEL}})^2 \mathbf{x}[i,.]'\mathbf{x}[i,.]\right]^{-1} \times \left[\sum_{i=1}^{n} \hat{p}_i \mathbf{x}[i,.]'\mathbf{x}[i,.]\right]'\right]^{-1} \tag{13.5.5}$$

(compare with (12.4.5)). As in the MEL case, there is a close analogy between (13.5.5) and White's heteroscedasticity-robust estimate of the covariance matrix of $\hat{\boldsymbol{\beta}}_{\text{LS}}$, as discussed further in Chapter 15. In fact, this feature imparts a degree of robustness (with respect to heteroscedasticity) to hypothesis-testing and confidence-region estimation based on the asymptotic normal distribution of the MEEL estimator.

As in the case of applying the MEL procedure to the linear regression model, using the MEEL approach to estimate $\boldsymbol{\beta}$ based on the empirical counterparts to the moment equations (13.5.1) leads to a familiar functional form for $\hat{\boldsymbol{\beta}}_{\text{MEEL}}$. In particular, note that $\hat{\mathbf{b}}_{\text{ME}} = \hat{\mathbf{b}}_{\text{LS}} = (\mathbf{x}'\mathbf{x})^{-1}\mathbf{x}'\mathbf{y}$ and $p_i = n^{-1}\ \forall i$ solve the empirical moment constraints in (13.5.2) and at the same time result in the maximum possible value of entropy $-\sum_{i=1}^{n} p_i \ln(p_i)$ subject to the constraints $\sum_{i=1}^{n} p_i = 1$ and $p_i > 0\ \forall i$. That $-\sum_{i=1}^{n} p_i \ln(p_i)$ is maximized is apparent because $p_i = n^{-1}\ \forall i$ is in fact the solution for maximizing the entropy *unconstrained*. To see that the empirical moment constraints are satisfied when $p_i = n^{-1}$ and $\boldsymbol{\beta} = \hat{\mathbf{b}}_{\text{LS}}$, note that

$$\sum_{i=1}^{n} p_i[\mathbf{x}[i,.]'(y_i - \mathbf{x}[i,.]\boldsymbol{\beta})] = n^{-1}\sum_{i=1}^{n}[\mathbf{x}[i,.]'(y_i - \mathbf{x}[i,.]\hat{\mathbf{b}})]$$
$$= n^{-1}(\mathbf{x}'\mathbf{y} - \mathbf{x}'\mathbf{x}\hat{\mathbf{b}}) = \mathbf{0} \tag{13.5.6}$$

where the parenthetical expression to the right of the second equality in (13.5.6) is the set of normal equations that define the least-squares estimator.

Returning to the covariance matrix estimate in (13.5.5) and letting $p_i = n^{-1}$, $\hat{\mathbf{b}}_{\text{MEEL}} = \hat{\mathbf{b}}_{\text{LS}}$, and $\hat{\mathbf{e}} = \mathbf{y} - \mathbf{x}\hat{\mathbf{b}}_{\text{MEEL}}$, we then have an exact representation of White's heteroscedastic robust (asymptotic) covariance matrix for the LS, and now MEEL, estimator $\hat{\boldsymbol{\beta}}_{\text{MEEL}}$, as (see Chapter 15) follows:

$$n^{-1}\hat{\boldsymbol{\Sigma}} = (\mathbf{x}'\mathbf{x})^{-1}\left[\sum_{i=1}^{n} \hat{e}_i^2 \mathbf{x}[i,.]'\mathbf{x}[i,.]\right](\mathbf{x}'\mathbf{x})^{-1}. \tag{13.5.7}$$

The asymptotic covariance matrix of estimator $\hat{\boldsymbol{\beta}}_{\text{MEEL}}$ is robust against heteroscedasticity and attains similar robustness in testing and in confidence-region estimation. The derivation of the MEEL estimator and its asymptotic covariance matrix represents alternative motivation for both the least-squares estimator for $\boldsymbol{\beta}$ and the heteroscedasticity-robust form of the covariance matrix estimator.

We also note for future reference that the MEEL approach can be extended to the case where the estimating functions are based on weakly dependent observations rather than independent observations. This allows the MEEL approach to be applied to regression problems in which the data exhibit a convergent autocorrelation structure as in Chapters 14 and 15. See Kitamura and Stutzer (1997) for additional details. We will not investigate the details of this procedure here but rather will revisit this type of MEEL application in context when we investigate the case of weakly dependent data observations in subsequent chapters.

13.5.2. Fixed x in the Linear Model

In the case where $\mathbf{x}$ is a fixed matrix of explanatory variables, the random vectors $\mathbf{h}((Y_i, \mathbf{x}[i,.]), \boldsymbol{\beta}) = \mathbf{x}[i,.]'(Y_i - \mathbf{x}[i,.]\boldsymbol{\beta})$ for $i = 1, \ldots, n$ will be independent, with zero mean when $\boldsymbol{\beta}$ is the true value of the parameter vector, but they are not generally iid. The translation of the unbiased moment equations into empirical expectations based on p_i weights is not directly supported. However, if the same basic asymptotic arguments as in Section 12.5 for the MEL case are followed, the application of ME to the regression model in the fixed $\mathbf{x}$ case results in precisely the same estimator for $\boldsymbol{\beta}$ as in the stochastic case. The same limiting distribution and asymptotic covariance matrix for the estimator are also applicable.

13.5.3. Extensions to Nonlinear Regression Models

All of the preceding results for the linear regression model can be extended to the nonlinear regression model. The key to making the extensions is in the redefinition of the unbiased estimating functions used in the MEEL procedure. Specifically, the definition of the unbiased estimating functions now becomes

$$\mathbf{h}((Y_i, \mathbf{X}[i,.]), \boldsymbol{\beta}) = \frac{\partial g(\mathbf{X}[i,.], \boldsymbol{\beta})}{\partial \boldsymbol{\beta}}[Y_i - g(\mathbf{X}[i,.], \boldsymbol{\beta})]. \tag{13.5.8}$$

The reader will note that setting (13.5.8) to zero represents the first-order conditions for solving the nonlinear least-squares estimation problem, and so it is no surprise that the MEEL and NLS estimators coincide in this case. The asymptotic covariance matrix of the MEEL estimator is a generalization of (13.5.5), where $\mathbf{x}[i,.]$ is replaced by $\frac{\partial g(\mathbf{X}[i,.], \boldsymbol{\beta})}{\partial \boldsymbol{\beta}'}$ for every i.

13.5.4. Inference in Regression Models

Hypothesis-testing and confidence-region estimation in the regression model can proceed using the methods outlined in Section 13.2.3, with $(y_i, \mathbf{x}_{i.})$ replacing y_i in the specification of the moment equations. The moment equations will be expressed in the form of (13.5.1) or (13.5.8).

13.6. Concluding Remarks – Which Criterion?

At this point we have examined two different estimation objective functions for solving empirical moment-type estimating equations for estimators of $\boldsymbol{\theta}$, MEL, and MEEL. In these two cases, we simultaneously obtain estimates of empirical probability or likelihood weights for the sample outcomes. We can define an empirical likelihood for $\boldsymbol{\theta}$ based on the value $L(\boldsymbol{\theta}) = \prod_{i=1}^{n} p_i(\boldsymbol{\theta})$, where $p_i(\boldsymbol{\theta})$ denotes the optimum empirical probability weights obtained from employing either the MEL or MEEL criteria, constrained by empirical moment constraints of the general form $\sum_{i=1}^{n} p_i(\boldsymbol{\theta})\mathbf{h}(y_i, \boldsymbol{\theta}) = \mathbf{0}$ and the normalization restriction $\sum_{i=1}^{n} p_i(\boldsymbol{\theta}) = 1$.

So, which criteria should be used in solving moment-type estimating equations for an estimate $\boldsymbol{\theta}$? The quick answer to this question is that the issue is not settled in the literature and no unequivocal answer can be given at this time. However, there are some considerations that should be noted in contemplating which approach to utilize in applications.

Under the standard regularity conditions used to establish the asymptotic properties of each of the estimators, the MEL and MEEL estimators are *asymptotically equivalent*. That is, they both lead to consistent estimators of $\boldsymbol{\theta}$ with the same asymptotic normal distributions (Imbens, 1997 and Imbens et al., 1998). Thus, a choice between the estimators cannot be based on their asymptotic distributions. Note that this asymptotic equivalence has the practical benefit that any test or confidence region procedure that applies to one of the estimation contexts based on the estimator's asymptotic normal distribution applies to both estimation contexts. In applications, one simply inserts the appropriate MEL or MEEL estimates into test or confidence region formulas to obtain operational asymptotically valid inference procedures. The asymptotic equivalence also implies that the MEL and MEEL estimators share the same asymptotic efficiency property (recall Section 12.2.2).

Furthermore, the MEL and MEEL procedures provide the means for directly estimating the population distribution of the $\mathbf{Y}_i$'s. In particular, an EDF-like estimate of the cumulative distribution function is given by

$$\hat{F}(y_0) = \sum_{i=1}^{n} \hat{p}_i \mathbf{I}_{(-\infty,\, y_i]}(y_0), \tag{13.6.1}$$

where $\hat{\mathbf{p}}$ is either the MEL or MEEL estimate of $\mathbf{p}$. By taking *correct* binding estimating equations into account, the MEL and MEEL estimators of the CDF of the population distribution are generally more efficient than the standard EDF estimator (Imbens, 1997, p. 365) and in any case are no less efficient. Moreover, the estimator (13.6.1) is in fact the *efficient* semiparametric estimator of the CDF based on the estimating equations $E[\mathbf{h}(Y, \boldsymbol{\theta})] = \mathbf{0}$ (Imbens, 1997, Theorem 2).

In addition, both the MEEL and MEL approaches can be viewed as being based on minimizing the weighted average discrepancies between the logs of the estimated probabilities π_i and empirical frequency weights n^{-1}, as noted in (13.1.6) and (13.1.7). However, to represent the expected discrepancy as accurately as possible, it would appear advisable to weight the discrepancies using an efficient p_i estimate based on the data, which the MEEL estimator represents, rather than using the inefficient n^{-1} estimates represented by the EDF weights. On this basis, the MEEL approach is favored over the MEL approach.

Finally, Imbens et al. (1998) show that the MEEL estimator is more robust against misspecification of the moment equations than is the MEL estimator. Thus, if there is considerable uncertainty regarding the validity of the moment equations, the use of the MEEL estimator may be preferred to the MEL estimator.

Given the current state of affairs, it would appear that the MEEL approach is to be recommended in cases characterized by independent data observations. The apparently less-robust MEL approach appears to be a viable competitor in cases in which there is substantial confidence in the validity of the moment restrictions and we are dealing with independent data observations.

In this chapter we have been able to demonstrate that MEL is not the only "nonparametric likelihood" approach. Like traditional empirical likelihood (Chapter 12), information theoretic–maximum entropy-based likelihood can be applied to any reasonable set of estimating functions and in some cases offers a superior alternative. It shares properties with various nonparametric methods based on resampling, such as the bootstrap, yet it offers a simple formulation based on an estimation objective function to be optimized subject to side constraints. Conceptually, the nonlinear inversion procedure is simple and generally tractable. And unlike the traditional empirical likelihood approach, MEEL allows the introduction of nonsample information concerning the unknown likelihood function weights and other unknown parameters through the cross-entropy principle. It would be useful at this stage for the reader to identify the linkages between the concepts developed in Chapters 7, 11, 12, and 13 and to contemplate the statistical implications of these ideas for the process of estimation and inference.

The inverse problems we have considered up to this point were well-posed and amenable to traditional estimation and inference procedures. In electronic Chapter E3, we introduce the problem of ill-posed, underdetermined pure inverse problems and ill-conditioned inverse problems with noise. As a solution basis for these types of problems, the entropy formalism is again examined.

Finally, we note that van Akkeren and Judge (1999) have extended the MEL and MEEL concepts and have suggested a data based information theoretic formulation for the linear model that uses a dual loss estimating criterion. The estimator has, relative to traditional estimators, excellent sampling properties and is especially effective in mitigating the sampling impacts of an ill-condition design matrix.

In the next two chapters we relax the homoscedastic, independent noise assumption and consider estimation and inference alternatives under a more general noise covariance specification.

13.7. Exercises

13.7.1. Idea Checklist – Knowledge Guides

1. In the context of the preceding chapters and extremum estimation, what is the importance of the distance measure in the analysis of probability models?
2. What is the fundamental idea underlying the Kullback–Leibler (KL) information measure and what is its importance and usefulness as a distance measure? What is the potential importance of KL information in providing a basis for comparing two competing statistical models?
3. What is the basic idea underlying Jayne's maximum entropy (ME) approach to information recovery in inverse problems?
4. What are the major differences in the MEL and MEEL approaches to estimation and inference? What are the similarities?
5. We believe that the last three chapters may have changed the way you think about the problem of estimation and inference. If so, what are the changes in your thinking and in the corresponding statistical implications. If not, why not?
6. What are the potential statistical implications of the differences in the likelihood weights obtained from the MEL and MEEL estimation objective functions?
7. What are inverse probabilities?

13.7.2. Problems

13–1 Prove the special cases of the α-entropy measure given by (13.4.2)–(13.4.4).

13–2 State the MEEL version of the two-moment problem described in Section 12.2.4. Derive the functional form of the probabilities assigned to the sample outcomes (as a function of θ and λ) and state the concentrated (profile) maximum entropy objective function.

13–3 Solve Problems 1–3 in Section 12.7.2. under the MEEL criterion.

13.7.3. Computer Problems

13–1 For various values of $\alpha \in (-1, 1)$, use the α-entropy objective function to solve the population mean problem. How do the properties of this more general MEEL estimator compare as you alter α?

13–2 Write a GAUSS program designed to replicate the sampling exercises summarized in Table 12.2 based on the MEEL estimator. How do the results for the MEEL estimator compare with the results presented in the table?

13–3 Write a GAUSS program designed to replicate the properties of the confidence regions based on the MEEL estimator (see Table 12.3). How do the properties of the MEEL-based regions compare with the characteristics of the confidence regions presented in the table?

13–4 Revise the GAUSS program provided for Example 12.5.1 (C12MEL5.gss) to examine the MEEL estimator for the linear regression model. Do your decisions based on the LR statistics for the MEEL estimator coincide with the associated decisions from the MEL case?

13.8. References

Cressie, N., and T. Read (1984), Multinomial Goodness of Fit Tests, *Journal of the Royal Statistical Society*, Series B, 46, pp. 440–64.

Golan, A., and G. Judge (1996), "A Maximum Entropy Approach to Empirical Likelihood Estimation and Inference," ARE Working Paper, p. 34, University of California.

Golan, A., G. G. Judge, and D. Miller (1996), *Maximum Entropy Econometrics: Robust Estimation with Limited Data*, New York: John Wiley and Sons.

Imbens, G. (1997), "One-Step Estimators for Over-Identified Generalized Method of Moment Models," *Review of Economic Studies*, Vol. 64, pp. 359–83.

Imbens, G., R. Spady, and P. Johnson (1998), "Information Theoretic Approaches to Inference in Moment Condition Models," *Econometrica*, Vol. 66, pp. 333–57.

Jaynes, E. T. (1957a), "Information Theory and Statistical Mechanics," *Physics Review*, Vol. 106, pp. 620–30.

Jaynes, E. T. (1957b), "Information Theory and Statistical Mechanics II," *Physics Review*, Vol. 108, pp. 171–90.

Kitamura, Y., and M. Stutzer (1997), "An Information-Theoretic Alternative to Generalized Method of Moments Estimation," *Econometrica*, Vol. 65, pp. 861–74.

Kullback, J. (1959), *Information Theory and Statistics*, New York: John Wiley and Sons.

Kullback, J., and R. A. Leibler (1951), "On Information and Sufficiency," *Annals of Mathematical Statistics*, Vol. 22, pp. 79–86.

Shore, J. E., and R. W. Johnson (1980), "Axiomatic Derivation of the Principle of Maximum Entropy and the Principle of Minimum Cross-Entropy," *IEEE Transactions on Information Theory*, Vol. IT-26, pp. 26–37.

van Akkeren and G. Judge (1999), "Extended Empirical likelihood estimation and inference" *Working paper*, University of California, Berkeley.

13.9. Supplemental References

Behara, M. (1990), *Additive and Nonadditive Measures of Entropy*, New York: John Wiley and Sons.

Brown, L. D. (1986), *Fundamentals of Statistical Exponential Families*, Hayward, CA: Institute of Mathematical Statistics.

Csiszar, I. (1991), "Why Least Squares and Maximum Entropy? An Axiomatic Approach to Inference for Linear Inverse Problems," *The Annals of Statistics*, Vol. 19, pp. 2032–66.

Gokhale, D. V., and S. Kullback (1978), *The Information in Contingency Tables*, New York: Marcel Dekker.

Good, I. J. (1963), "Maximum Entropy for Hypothesis Formulation, Especially for Multidimensional Contingency Tables," *Annals of Mathematical Statistics*, Vol. 34, pp. 911–34.

Jaynes, E. T. (1963), "Information Theory and Statistical Mechanics," In K. W. Ford (Ed.), *Statistical Physics*, (pp. 181–218), New York: W. A. Benjamin, Inc.

Jaynes, E. T. (1984), "Prior Information and Ambiguity in Inverse Problems," In D. W. McLaughlin (Ed.), *Inverse Problems*, (pp. 151–66), Providence, RI: American Mathematical Society.

Johansen, S. (1979), *An Introduction to the Theory of Regular Exponential Families*, Hayward, CA: Institute of Mathematical Statistics.

Kolacyzk, E. (1994), "Empirical Likelihood for Generalized Linear Models," *Statistica Sinica*, Vol. 4, pp. 199–218.

O'Sullivan, F. (1986), "A Statistical Perspective on Ill-Posed Inverse Problems," *Statistical Science*, Vol. 1, pp. 502–27.

Owen, A. (1990), "Empirical Likelihood Ratio Confidence Regions," *The Annals of Statistics*, Vol. 18, pp. 90–120.

Owen, A. (1991), "Empirical Likelihood for Linear Models," *The Annals of Statistics*, Vol. 19, pp. 1725–47.

Owen, A. B. (1988), "Empirical Likelihood Ratio Confidence Intervals for a Single Functional," *Biometrika*, Vol. 75, pp. 237–49.

Qin, J., and J. Lawless (1994), "Empirical Likelihood and General Estimating Equations," *The Annals of Statistics*, Vol. 22, pp. 300–25.

Renyi, A. (1960), "On Measures of Entropy and Information," *Proceeding of the Fourth Berkeley Symposium on Mathematics, Statistics, and Probability*, Vol. I, p. 547.

Shannon, C. E. (1948), "A Mathematical Theory of Communication," *Bell System Technical Journal*, Vol. 27, pp. 379–423.

Skilling, J. (1989), "The Axioms of Maximum Entropy," In J. Skilling (Ed.), *Maximum Entropy and Bayesian Methods in Science and Engineering*, (pp. 173–87), Dordrecht, The Netherlands: Kluwer Academic.

Zellner, A., and R. A. Highfield (1988), "Calculation of Maximum Entropy Distributions and Approximation of Marginal Posterior Distributions," *Journal of Econometrics*, Vol. 37, pp. 195–209.

PART FIVE

Generalized Regression Models

In Part V we focus on estimation and inference issues that arise when we *relax* the assumptions on the regression probability model that the noise component $\varepsilon = (\varepsilon_1, \varepsilon_2, \ldots, \varepsilon_n)'$ is a vector of identically distributed real-valued random variables with mean $E[\varepsilon_i] = 0$ and variance $\sigma^2 > 0$. In Chapter 14 we demonstrate the estimation and inference implications of a fixed and known noise covariance. Although this is not the situation that arises most often in practice, the context of a known noise covariance provides a focused and relatively straightforward way to establish notation as well as to identify fundamental estimation and inference concepts that can be extended to the more difficult case in which the noise covariance matrix is fixed and unknown, which is the case we examine in Chapter 15.

The focus of Chapter 15 is on how estimation and inference proceeds when one must recover information on unknown parameters affecting the conditional expectation of the dependent variable of the regression problem and information on the unknown covariance structure. We examine cases in which a parametric structure for the noise covariance matrix is known as well as cases in which such parametric structure is unavailable. In the latter case, robust methods of estimating covariance structure are identified. As in Part IV, the more general DSP assumptions often lead to the need for using asymptotics in the evaluation of the sampling properties of the estimators and test statistics.

CHAPTER 14

Regression Models with a Known General Noise Covariance Matrix

IN preceding chapters, we considered probability specifications of the regression model that assumed the elements of the noise component were iid, or at least independent with identical first- and second-order moments. Either assumption implies the special case of a noise component covariance matrix given by $\sigma^2\mathbf{\Psi} = \sigma^2\mathbf{I}_n$. By assuming the covariance matrix is proportional to the identity matrix, we reduced the number of unknowns in the covariance matrix from $n(n+1)/2$ to 1. Recognizing that this model specification will not be consistent with all DSPs normally found in practice, we now generalize the noise covariance specification and consider the inverse problem of recovering point values of $\boldsymbol{\beta}$ and σ^2 when the noise covariance is such that $\mathbf{\Psi} \neq \mathbf{I}_n$. The generalization allows the possibility that the errors are *autocorrelated* [$\text{cov}(\varepsilon_i\varepsilon_j) \neq 0$ for $i \neq j$], *heteroscedastic* [$\text{var}(\varepsilon_i) \neq \text{var}(\varepsilon_j)$ for $i \neq j$], or both and thereby broadens our modeling basis for expressing knowledge about the data-sampling processes underlying observed outcomes of economic processes.

In this chapter we consider the estimation and inference problem when $\mathbf{\Psi}$ is some *known* positive definite symmetric matrix. This chapter will serve to identify the central issues involved in specifying probability models that encompass general noise covariance structure. In Chapter 15, we consider how to cope with the case often found in practice in which the elements in $\mathbf{\Psi}$ are *unknown*. Later, in Chapter 19, we expand our analysis further and examine the difficult and elusive problem of attempting to identify and estimate the precise form of the general noise covariance structure via diagnostic testing.

The specific probability model characteristics that are assumed to hold in this chapter are presented in Table 14.1.

The particular inverse problem associated with the probability model delineated in Table 14.1 involves using observations on $(\mathbf{Y}, \mathbf{X})$ to recover information on the values or functions of the unknown n and unobservable $\boldsymbol{\beta}$, σ^2, and $\boldsymbol{\varepsilon}$.

The layout of the chapter is as follows: In Section 14.1, the statistical implications of ignoring the fact that $\mathbf{\Psi} \neq \mathbf{I}_n$ is considered, and the sampling properties of the corresponding estimators and inference procedures are reviewed. In Section 14.2, under the general noise specification where $\boldsymbol{\varepsilon} \sim \text{N}(\mathbf{0}, \sigma^2\mathbf{\Psi})$ and $\mathbf{\Psi}$ is known, the probability

Table 14.1. *Regression Models With Known General Noise Covariance Structure*

Model Component	Specific Characteristics	
$\mathbf{Y}$	RV Type:	continuous
	Range:	unlimited
	Y_i dimension:	univariate
	Moments:	$E[\mathbf{Y} \mid \mathbf{x}] = \mathbf{x}\boldsymbol{\beta}$ or $\mathbf{g}(\mathbf{x}, \boldsymbol{\beta})$ $\mathbf{cov}(\mathbf{Y} \mid \mathbf{x}) = \sigma^2\boldsymbol{\Psi}$, $\boldsymbol{\Psi}$ is a known positive definite symmetric matrix.
$\eta(\mathbf{x}, \boldsymbol{\beta}, \varepsilon)$	Functional Form:	linear or nonlinear in $\mathbf{x}$ and $\boldsymbol{\beta}$, additive in ε
$\mathbf{x}$	RV Type:	degenerate (fixed) or stochastic, with full-column rank
	Genesis:	exogenous to the model
$\boldsymbol{\beta}$	RV Type:	degenerate (fixed)
	Dimension:	finite
ε	RV Type:	non-iid
	Moments:	$E[\varepsilon \mid \mathbf{x}] = \mathbf{0}$, and $\mathbf{cov}(\varepsilon \mid \mathbf{x}) = \sigma^2\boldsymbol{\Psi}$, $\boldsymbol{\Psi}$ is a known positive definite symmetric matrix
Ω	Prior info:	none
$f(\mathbf{e} \mid \mathbf{x}, \varphi^2)$	PDF family:	normal or unspecified

model is transformed to be consistent with the DSP assumptions of the classical linear regression model (CLRM), and viable estimation and inference procedures are reviewed. In Section 14.3, the specification is generalized to a nonlinear regression model, for known $\boldsymbol{\Psi}$, and estimation and inference procedures are developed and their statistical implications are examined. In Section 14.4 we discuss how the noise covariance matrix can be parametrically modeled for a given autocorrelated or heteroscedastic noise process. Finally in Section 14.5, the model is generalized to include a set of regression equations in which the noise components across equations are contemporaneously correlated. Again, estimation and inference procedures for the array of unknowns are developed, and their corresponding sampling implications are examined.

14.1. Applying LS–ML to the Linear Model and Untransformed Data: Ignoring that $\boldsymbol{\Psi} \neq \mathbf{I}$

Some interesting practical questions to ask at this point are, What if we ignore the fact that $\boldsymbol{\Psi} \neq \mathbf{I}$ and proceed in the context of Chapters 3–6 to use the LS–ML (least squares–maximum likelihood) estimator $\hat{\boldsymbol{\beta}} = (\mathbf{x}'\mathbf{x})^{-1}\mathbf{x}'\mathbf{Y}$ to estimate $\boldsymbol{\beta}$? What are the sampling properties of $\hat{\boldsymbol{\beta}}$ under these circumstances? And how are testing and confidence region estimation procedures affected? We address these questions in this section. We will concentrate on the case in which **x** is fixed but note that the results can also be applied to the stochastic **X** case by proceeding *conditionally* on an outcome **x** of **X**. In the context of the ML approach discussed ahead, we may proceed by assuming conditional normality of $(\mathbf{Y} \mid \mathbf{x})$ (recall Section 10.3.3).

14.1.1. Point Estimation

First, note that the LS–ML estimator (henceforth it will be assumed that $(\mathbf{Y} \mid \mathbf{x})$ is multivariate normal in the case of ML) remains *unbiased* because $\mathrm{E}[\hat{\boldsymbol{\beta}}] = \mathrm{E}[(\mathbf{x}'\mathbf{x})^{-1}\mathbf{x}'\mathbf{Y}] = (\mathbf{x}'\mathbf{x})^{-1}\mathbf{x}'\mathrm{E}[\mathbf{Y}] = \boldsymbol{\beta}$, where $\mathrm{E}[\mathbf{Y}] = \mathbf{x}\boldsymbol{\beta}$. However, the covariance matrix of $\hat{\boldsymbol{\beta}}$ is no longer $\sigma^2(\mathbf{x}'\mathbf{x})^{-1}$. If one uses results relating to the moments of linear combinations of random variables and recalls that $\mathbf{cov}(\mathbf{Y}) = \mathbf{cov}(\boldsymbol{\varepsilon}) = \sigma^2\boldsymbol{\Psi}$, it follows that

$$\mathbf{cov}(\hat{\boldsymbol{\beta}}) = \sigma^2(\mathbf{x}'\mathbf{x})^{-1}\mathbf{x}'\boldsymbol{\Psi}\mathbf{x}(\mathbf{x}'\mathbf{x})^{-1}. \tag{14.1.1}$$

It is therefore apparent that $\sigma^2(\mathbf{x}'\mathbf{x})^{-1}$ represents the covariance matrix of the least-squares estimator *only if* $\boldsymbol{\Psi} = \mathbf{I}$.

The LS–ML estimator will remain *consistent* under general conditions. Because $\hat{\boldsymbol{\beta}}$ is unbiased, a sufficient condition for consistency is $\mathrm{tr}[\mathbf{cov}(\hat{\boldsymbol{\beta}})] \to 0$ as $n \to \infty$, so that $\hat{\boldsymbol{\beta}} \xrightarrow{m} \boldsymbol{\beta} \Rightarrow \hat{\boldsymbol{\beta}} \xrightarrow{p} \boldsymbol{\beta}$. Note that (see Mittelhammer, Lemma 8.4, p. 454)

$$\mathrm{tr}[\mathbf{cov}(\hat{\boldsymbol{\beta}})] = \mathrm{tr}[\boldsymbol{\Psi}\mathbf{x}(\mathbf{x}'\mathbf{x})^{-2}\mathbf{x}'] \leq \lambda_{\mathrm{L}}(\boldsymbol{\Psi})\mathrm{tr}(\mathbf{x}'\mathbf{x})^{-1}, \tag{14.1.2}$$

and thus if the largest eigenvalue of $\boldsymbol{\Psi}$, $\lambda_{\mathrm{L}}(\boldsymbol{\Psi})$, is bounded, then precisely the same condition as in Chapter 5, namely $\mathrm{tr}(\mathbf{x}'\mathbf{x})^{-1} \to 0$, is sufficient for consistency of $\hat{\boldsymbol{\beta}}$ when $\mathbf{cov}(\boldsymbol{\varepsilon}) = \sigma^2\boldsymbol{\Psi} \neq \sigma^2\mathbf{I}$. Even if $\lambda_{\mathrm{L}}(\boldsymbol{\Psi})$ is not bounded, all that is required for $\mathrm{tr}[\mathbf{cov}(\hat{\boldsymbol{\beta}})] \to 0$ is that $\lambda_{\mathrm{L}}(\boldsymbol{\Psi})$ does not increase towards infinity at a faster rate than $\mathrm{tr}(\mathbf{x}'\mathbf{x})^{-1}$ converges to zero, which is a presupposition that can reasonably be assumed to hold in most applications.

If $\mathbf{Y} \sim \mathrm{N}(\mathbf{x}\boldsymbol{\beta}, \sigma^2\boldsymbol{\Psi})$, then because $\hat{\boldsymbol{\beta}}$ is a linear combination of the entries in $\mathbf{Y}$, $\hat{\boldsymbol{\beta}} \sim \mathrm{N}[\boldsymbol{\beta}, \sigma^2(\mathbf{x}'\mathbf{x})^{-1}\mathbf{x}'\boldsymbol{\Psi}\mathbf{x}(\mathbf{x}'\mathbf{x})^{-1}]$ and the question of *asymptotic* normality is moot. Nevertheless, for completeness, note that

$$\begin{aligned} n^{1/2}(\hat{\boldsymbol{\beta}} - \boldsymbol{\beta}) &= n^{1/2}(\mathbf{x}'\mathbf{x})^{-1}\mathbf{x}'\boldsymbol{\varepsilon} = n^{1/2}(\mathbf{x}'\mathbf{x})^{-1}\mathbf{x}'\boldsymbol{\Psi}^{1/2}\boldsymbol{\Psi}^{-1/2}\boldsymbol{\varepsilon} \\ &= n^{1/2}(\mathbf{x}'\mathbf{x})^{-1}\mathbf{x}'\boldsymbol{\Psi}^{1/2}\boldsymbol{\varepsilon}_* = (n^{-1}\mathbf{x}'\mathbf{x})^{-1}n^{-1/2}\mathbf{w}'\boldsymbol{\varepsilon}_* \end{aligned} \tag{14.1.3}$$

is a linear combination of the iid elements of the random vector $\boldsymbol{\varepsilon}_* = \boldsymbol{\Psi}^{-1/2}\boldsymbol{\varepsilon} \sim \mathrm{N}(\mathbf{0}, \sigma^2\mathbf{I})$, where $\mathrm{E}[\varepsilon_*[i]] = 0$, $\mathrm{var}(\varepsilon_*[i]) = \sigma^2$, $\mathrm{E}\,|\,\varepsilon_*[i]\,|^{2+\delta} \leq \zeta < \infty$ for some $\delta > 0$ (because $\boldsymbol{\varepsilon}_*$ is normally distributed), and $\mathbf{w}' \equiv \mathbf{x}'\boldsymbol{\Psi}^{1/2}$. Then if $n^{-1}\mathbf{w}'\mathbf{w} = n^{-1}\mathbf{x}'\boldsymbol{\Psi}\mathbf{x} \to \mathbf{h}$, a finite positive definite symmetric matrix, the proof of Theorem 5.3.3 applies and yields $n^{-1/2}\mathbf{w}'\boldsymbol{\varepsilon}_* \xrightarrow{d} \mathrm{N}(\mathbf{0}, \sigma^2\mathbf{h})$. Then if $n^{-1}\mathbf{x}'\mathbf{x} \to \boldsymbol{\Xi}$, as we assumed previously in Chapter 5, it follows from Slutsky's theorem that

$$n^{1/2}(\hat{\boldsymbol{\beta}} - \boldsymbol{\beta}) = (n^{-1}\mathbf{x}'\mathbf{x})^{-1}n^{-1/2}\mathbf{w}'\boldsymbol{\varepsilon}_* \xrightarrow{d} \mathrm{N}(\mathbf{0}, \sigma^2\boldsymbol{\Xi}^{-1}\mathbf{h}\boldsymbol{\Xi}^{-1}). \tag{14.1.4}$$

Replacing $\boldsymbol{\Xi}$ and $\mathbf{h}$ by the consistent estimates $n^{-1}\mathbf{x}'\mathbf{x}$ and $n^{-1}\mathbf{x}'\boldsymbol{\Psi}\mathbf{x}$, respectively, we can define an asymptotic distribution for $\hat{\boldsymbol{\beta}}$ alternatively as

$$\hat{\boldsymbol{\beta}} \overset{a}{\sim} \mathrm{N}[\boldsymbol{\beta}, \sigma^2(\mathbf{x}'\mathbf{x})^{-1}\mathbf{x}'\boldsymbol{\Psi}\mathbf{x}(\mathbf{x}'\mathbf{x})^{-1}], \tag{14.1.5}$$

which is also the exact distribution of $\hat{\boldsymbol{\beta}}$ under the current normality assumption.

Even if normality does not hold, the asymptotic normality of $\hat{\boldsymbol{\beta}}$ indicated in (14.1.5) applies under general regularity conditions. The key requirement is that some central limit theorem can be applied to the sum of $(k \times 1)$ random vectors such as $n^{-1/2}\mathbf{w}'\boldsymbol{\varepsilon}_* = n^{-1/2}\sum_{i=1}^{n} \mathbf{w}[i, .]'\boldsymbol{\varepsilon}_*[i] \xrightarrow{d} \mathrm{N}(\mathbf{0}, \sigma^2\mathbf{h})$, in which case if $n^{-1}\mathbf{w}'\mathbf{w} = n^{-1}\mathbf{x}'\boldsymbol{\Psi}\mathbf{x} \rightarrow \mathbf{h}$ and $n^{-1}\mathbf{x}'\mathbf{x} \rightarrow \boldsymbol{\Xi}$ also apply, the asymptotic distribution in (14.1.5) follows directly.

In summary, the LS–ML estimator $\hat{\boldsymbol{\beta}}$ generally retains several of its attractive properties, including "unbiasedness," consistency, and finite (if normality is assumed for $\mathbf{Y}$) and asymptotic normality. We emphasize for future reference that these properties apply *whether or not* $\boldsymbol{\Psi}$ *is known*. We will see in Section 14.2 (see Equation (14.2.13), in particular) that $\hat{\boldsymbol{\beta}}$ is no longer either the BLUE or MVUE of $\boldsymbol{\beta}$, and thus estimator optimality is lost in this case. However, again for future reference, we note that foregoing optimality through the use of the LS–ML estimator is a real cost only in the current hypothetical and atypical case in which $\boldsymbol{\Psi}$ is known. We will come to see that when $\boldsymbol{\Psi}$ is unknown, the theoretically optimal estimator cannot be empirically implemented and is thus unavailable.

Regarding the use of S^2 to estimate σ^2, note that because

$$\mathrm{S}^2 = (n-k)^{-1}[\boldsymbol{\varepsilon}'\boldsymbol{\varepsilon} - \boldsymbol{\varepsilon}'\mathbf{x}(\mathbf{x}'\mathbf{x})^{-1}\mathbf{x}'\boldsymbol{\varepsilon}], \tag{14.1.6}$$

and because $\mathrm{E}[\boldsymbol{\varepsilon}\boldsymbol{\varepsilon}'] = \sigma^2\boldsymbol{\Psi}$,

$$\mathrm{E}[\mathrm{S}^2] = \sigma^2\, \mathrm{tr}[(\mathbf{I} - \mathbf{x}(\mathbf{x}'\mathbf{x})^{-1}\mathbf{x}')\boldsymbol{\Psi}]/(n-k). \tag{14.1.7}$$

Therefore, S^2 is a *biased* estimator of σ^2 except for the highly unlikely happenstance in which $\mathrm{tr}[(\mathbf{I} - \mathbf{x}(\mathbf{x}'\mathbf{x})^{-1}\mathbf{x}')\boldsymbol{\Psi}] = n - k$. Moreover, there is no inherent reason why the bias should dissipate as the sample size increases, and thus one cannot expect the estimator S^2 to be consistent.

Given that $\boldsymbol{\Psi}$ is known under the current assumptions, a *bias-corrected* estimator of σ^2 can be defined as $\mathrm{S}_*^2 = \xi(\boldsymbol{\Psi})\mathrm{S}^2$, where $\xi(\boldsymbol{\Psi}) \equiv (n-k)/\mathrm{tr}[(\mathbf{I} - \mathbf{x}(\mathbf{x}'\mathbf{x})^{-1}\mathbf{x}')\boldsymbol{\Psi}]$, so that $\mathrm{E}[\mathrm{S}_*^2] = \sigma^2$. If $\mathrm{tr}[(\mathbf{x}'\mathbf{x})^{-1}\mathbf{x}'\boldsymbol{\Psi}\mathbf{x}] \leq \tau < \infty$, which would be the case if $n^{-1}\mathbf{x}'\mathbf{x}$ and $n^{-1}\mathbf{x}'\boldsymbol{\Psi}\mathbf{x}$ each converge to a finite positive definite symmetric matrix (as was assumed earlier), and if it were also true that $\mathrm{tr}(\boldsymbol{\Psi}) \rightarrow \infty$ as $n \rightarrow \infty$, then S_*^2 would also be a *consistent* estimator of σ^2. This conclusion would follow directly from a proof analogous to that of Theorem 5.4.2 with S^2 premultiplied by the positive-valued $\xi(\boldsymbol{\Psi})$, as the reader can readily verify. Unless the elements of the noise vector ultimately converge to degenerate random variables having zero variances as $n \rightarrow \infty$, the condition $\mathrm{tr}(\boldsymbol{\Psi}) \rightarrow \infty$ as $n \rightarrow \infty$ is assured.

14.1.2. Testing and Confidence-Region Estimation

The preceding results relating to statistical properties of the estimators $\hat{\boldsymbol{\beta}}$ and S^2 have important implications for the construction of hypothesis testing and confidence region estimation procedures. Specifically, none of the GLR, Wald, LM, or Z-test and confidence region estimation procedures discussed in previous chapters apply in the current situation. The problem can be traced to the fact that the covariance matrix of $\hat{\boldsymbol{\beta}}$ is now *not* $\sigma^2(\mathbf{x}'\mathbf{x})^{-1}$ and the estimator S^2 of σ^2 is now generally biased and inconsistent. However, all of the previous inference procedures can be rehabilitated if (14.1.1) is used everywhere an expression for $\mathbf{cov}(\hat{\boldsymbol{\beta}})$ is required and if the bias-corrected S^2 (or its restricted counterpart in the case of LM tests and confidence regions) is used where estimates of σ^2 are required.

For example, under the normality assumption, the F-statistic for testing the null hypothesis $H_0\colon \mathbf{c}\boldsymbol{\beta} = \mathbf{r}$ would be defined as

$$F = \frac{(\mathbf{c}\hat{\boldsymbol{\beta}} - \mathbf{r})'[\mathbf{c}(\mathbf{x}'\mathbf{x})^{-1}\mathbf{x}'\boldsymbol{\Psi}\mathbf{x}(\mathbf{x}'\mathbf{x})^{-1}\mathbf{c}']^{-1}(\mathbf{c}\hat{\boldsymbol{\beta}} - \mathbf{r})}{\mathrm{j}S_*^2} \sim F(j, n-k, 0) \text{ under } H_0, \tag{14.1.8}$$

where $\mathbf{c}$ is $(j \times k)$ with rank j. An α-level test would be defined by

$$\text{reject } H_0\colon \mathbf{c}\boldsymbol{\beta} = \mathbf{r} \quad \text{if} \quad f \geq f_{1-\alpha}, \tag{14.1.9}$$

where $f_{1-\alpha}$ is the $100(1-\alpha)\%$ quantile of the central F-distribution with j numerator and $(n-k)$ denominator degrees of freedom. Similarly, to test the scalar inequality hypothesis $H_0\colon \mathbf{c}\boldsymbol{\beta} \leq \mathrm{r}$, one could use the T-statistic

$$T = \frac{\mathbf{c}\hat{\boldsymbol{\beta}} - \mathrm{r}}{[S_*^2\mathbf{c}(\mathbf{x}'\mathbf{x})^{-1}\mathbf{x}'\boldsymbol{\Psi}\mathbf{x}(\mathbf{x}'\mathbf{x})^{-1}\mathbf{c}']^{1/2}} \sim T(n-k, \delta), \tag{14.1.10}$$

where $\mathbf{c}$ is $(1 \times k)$ and the noncentrality parameter is given by

$$\delta = \frac{\mathbf{c}\boldsymbol{\beta} - \mathrm{r}}{[\sigma^2\mathbf{c}(\mathbf{x}'\mathbf{x})^{-1}\mathbf{x}'\boldsymbol{\Psi}\mathbf{x}(\mathbf{x}'\mathbf{x})^{-1}\mathbf{c}']^{1/2}}. \tag{14.1.11}$$

An α-level test of H_0 is defined by

$$\text{reject } H_0\colon \mathbf{c}\boldsymbol{\beta} \leq \mathrm{r} \quad \text{if} \quad t \geq t_{1-\alpha}, \tag{14.1.12}$$

where $t_{1-\alpha}$ is the $100(1-\alpha)\%$ quantile of the central T-distribution with $(n-k)$ degrees of freedom. A test of $H_0\colon \mathbf{c}\boldsymbol{\beta} \geq \mathrm{r}$ follows directly via inequality reversals above and the use of $-t_{1-\alpha} = t_\alpha$ in place of $t_{1-\alpha}$ in (14.1.12).

Confidence region estimation procedures can be defined in the usual way through duality with hypothesis testing procedures. We will see that in the more realistic situation where $\boldsymbol{\Psi}$ is unknown (Chapter 15), hypothesis-testing and confidence-region estimation procedures based on the LS estimator are still possible, and the statistics (14.1.8) and (14.1.10) will remain highly relevant.

► **Example 14.1.1:** To demonstrate the statistical performance of the LS–ML estimator when $\boldsymbol{\Psi} \neq \mathbf{I}$, we provide the GAUSS program C14LSML.gss in the examples manual. A set of Monte Carlo exercises is used to simulate the sampling properties of the estimators $\hat{\boldsymbol{\beta}}$ and S^2 for a simple heteroscedastic linear regression model. GAUSS also simulates the sampling properties of the F and T tests under the correct and incorrect matrices for $\mathbf{cov}[\hat{\boldsymbol{\beta}}]$ and under S^2 and S_*^2.

14.2. GLS–ML–Extremum Analysis of the Linear Model: Incorporating a Known Ψ

Reconsider the case of a linear regression model DSP given by

$$\mathbf{Y} = \mathbf{x}\boldsymbol{\beta} + \boldsymbol{\varepsilon}, \qquad \boldsymbol{\varepsilon} \sim \mathrm{N}(\mathbf{0}, \sigma^2\boldsymbol{\Psi}), \tag{14.2.1}$$

where $\boldsymbol{\Psi}$ is assumed to be positive definite, symmetric, and *known*. The corresponding log likelihood function can be specified as

$$\ln \mathrm{L}(\boldsymbol{\beta}, \sigma^2; \mathbf{y}, \mathbf{x}) = -\frac{n}{2}\ln(2\pi) - \frac{n}{2}\ln(\sigma^2) - \frac{1}{2}\ln|\boldsymbol{\Psi}| - \frac{1}{2\sigma^2}(\mathbf{y} - \mathbf{x}\boldsymbol{\beta})'\boldsymbol{\Psi}^{-1}(\mathbf{y} - \mathbf{x}\boldsymbol{\beta}). \tag{14.2.2}$$

In this section, we first solve the likelihood-based estimation problem for the ML estimators of $\boldsymbol{\beta}$ and σ^2 and use the normality assumption to establish the finite sample properties of the estimators. Then, we show that the linear regression model may be transformed to derive an associated least-squares estimator without requiring the normality assumption. For this more general case, we demonstrate the large sample properties of the estimator.

14.2.1. ML–Extremum Estimators for $\boldsymbol{\beta}$ and σ^2

Following the discussion in Chapter 3, we can maximize the log-likelihood function (14.2.2) by solving the first-order conditions

$$\frac{\partial \ln \mathrm{L}(\boldsymbol{\beta}, \sigma^2; \mathbf{y}, \mathbf{x})}{\partial \boldsymbol{\beta}} = \frac{\mathbf{x}'\boldsymbol{\Psi}^{-1}\mathbf{y} - (\mathbf{x}'\boldsymbol{\Psi}^{-1}\mathbf{x})\boldsymbol{\beta}}{\sigma^2} = \mathbf{0} \tag{14.2.3}$$

and

$$\frac{\partial \ln \mathrm{L}(\boldsymbol{\beta}, \sigma^2; \mathbf{y}, \mathbf{x})}{\partial \sigma^2} = \frac{-n}{2\sigma^2} + \frac{1}{2\sigma^4}(\mathbf{y} - \mathbf{x}\boldsymbol{\beta})'\boldsymbol{\Psi}^{-1}(\mathbf{y} - \mathbf{x}\boldsymbol{\beta}) = 0 \tag{14.2.4}$$

The ML estimate of $\boldsymbol{\beta}$ is defined by solving (14.2.3) for $\boldsymbol{\beta}$ obtaining

$$\hat{\mathbf{b}}_{\mathrm{ML}} = (\mathbf{x}'\boldsymbol{\Psi}^{-1}\mathbf{x})^{-1}\mathbf{x}'\boldsymbol{\Psi}^{-1}\mathbf{y}, \tag{14.2.5}$$

and the ML estimate of σ^2 is then defined by solving (14.2.4) for σ^2 to yield

$$\mathrm{s}^2_{\mathrm{ML}} = \frac{(\mathbf{y} - \mathbf{x}\hat{\mathbf{b}}_{\mathrm{ML}})'\boldsymbol{\Psi}^{-1}(\mathbf{y} - \mathbf{x}\hat{\mathbf{b}}_{\mathrm{ML}})}{n}. \tag{14.2.6}$$

We can form the ML estimators $\hat{\boldsymbol{\beta}}_{\mathrm{ML}}$ and $\mathrm{S}^2_{\mathrm{ML}}$ by replacing the observations $\mathbf{y}$ with the random vector $\mathbf{Y}$ in (14.2.5) and (14.2.6) (and replacing $\mathbf{x}$ with $\mathbf{X}$ in the case in which the explanatory variables are stochastic).

Given that the MLE $\hat{\boldsymbol{\beta}}_{\mathrm{ML}}$ is a linear combination of the multivariate normal random vector $\mathbf{Y}$, we know that $\hat{\boldsymbol{\beta}}_{\mathrm{ML}} \sim \mathrm{N}[\boldsymbol{\beta}, \sigma^2(\mathbf{x}'\boldsymbol{\Psi}^{-1}\mathbf{x})^{-1}]$ for all sample sizes n. It follows immediately that the ML estimator is unbiased for $\boldsymbol{\beta}$ and the estimator is asymptotically normal because it is normally distributed for every n. The ML estimator will be consistent if $(\mathbf{x}'\boldsymbol{\Psi}^{-1}\mathbf{x})^{-1} \to \mathbf{0}$ because then mean-square convergence occurs, and

$\hat{\boldsymbol{\beta}}_{\mathrm{ML}} \xrightarrow{\mathrm{m}} \boldsymbol{\beta} \Rightarrow \hat{\boldsymbol{\beta}}_{\mathrm{ML}} \xrightarrow{\mathrm{p}} \boldsymbol{\beta}$. A sufficient condition for $(\mathbf{x}'\boldsymbol{\Psi}^{-1}\mathbf{x})^{-1} \to \mathbf{0}$ is the condition that $n^{-1}(\mathbf{x}'\boldsymbol{\Psi}^{-1}\mathbf{x}) \to \mathbf{m}$ as $n \to \infty$, where $\mathbf{m}$ is a symmetric positive definite matrix.

It can also be shown that $\mathrm{S}^2_{\mathrm{ML}}$ is a biased estimator of σ^2, but the estimator $\mathrm{S}^2_{+} = (\frac{n}{n-k})\mathrm{S}^2_{\mathrm{ML}}$ is unbiased. To see this, note that

$$\begin{aligned}
\mathrm{E}[\mathrm{S}^2_{+}] &= \mathrm{E}\left[\frac{(\mathbf{Y}-\mathbf{x}\hat{\boldsymbol{\beta}}_{\mathrm{ML}})'\boldsymbol{\Psi}^{-1}(\mathbf{Y}-\mathbf{x}\hat{\boldsymbol{\beta}}_{\mathrm{ML}})}{n-k}\right] \\
&= \mathrm{E}\left[\frac{\varepsilon'(\boldsymbol{\Psi}^{-1}-\boldsymbol{\Psi}^{-1}\mathbf{x}(\mathbf{x}'\boldsymbol{\Psi}^{-1}\mathbf{x})^{-1}\mathbf{x}'\boldsymbol{\Psi}^{-1})\varepsilon}{n-k}\right] \\
&= (n-k)^{-1}(\mathrm{tr}[\boldsymbol{\Psi}^{-1}\mathrm{E}[\varepsilon\varepsilon']] - \mathrm{tr}[(\mathbf{x}'\boldsymbol{\Psi}^{-1}\mathbf{x})^{-1}\mathbf{x}'\boldsymbol{\Psi}^{-1}\mathrm{E}[\varepsilon\varepsilon']\boldsymbol{\Psi}^{-1}\mathbf{x}]) \\
&= (n-k)^{-1}(\sigma^2\mathrm{tr}[\mathbf{I}_n] - \sigma^2\mathrm{tr}[(\mathbf{x}'\boldsymbol{\Psi}^{-1}\mathbf{x})^{-1}\mathbf{x}'\boldsymbol{\Psi}^{-1}\mathbf{x}]) \\
&= (n-k)^{-1}(\sigma^2 n - \sigma^2 k) = \sigma^2. \qquad (14.2.7)
\end{aligned}$$

As well, the normality assumption implies that $(n-k)\mathrm{S}^2_{+}/\sigma^2$ is distributed as Chi-square$(n-k, 0)$. This follows because

$$\begin{aligned}
(n-k)\mathrm{S}^2_{+}/\sigma^2 &= (\varepsilon/\sigma)'[\boldsymbol{\Psi}^{-1} - \boldsymbol{\Psi}^{-1}\mathbf{x}(\mathbf{x}'\boldsymbol{\Psi}^{-1}\mathbf{x})^{-1}\mathbf{x}'\boldsymbol{\Psi}^{-1}](\varepsilon/\sigma) \\
&= (\boldsymbol{\Psi}^{-1/2}\varepsilon/\sigma)'[\mathbf{I}_n - \boldsymbol{\Psi}^{-1/2}\mathbf{x}(\mathbf{x}'\boldsymbol{\Psi}^{-1}\mathbf{x})^{-1}\mathbf{x}'\boldsymbol{\Psi}^{-1/2}](\boldsymbol{\Psi}^{-1/2}\varepsilon/\sigma) \\
&= \varepsilon_*'[\mathbf{I}_n - \boldsymbol{\Psi}^{-1/2}\mathbf{x}(\mathbf{x}'\boldsymbol{\Psi}^{-1}\mathbf{x})^{-1}\mathbf{x}'\boldsymbol{\Psi}^{-1/2}]\varepsilon_* \\
&= \varepsilon_*'[\mathbf{p}\boldsymbol{\Lambda}\mathbf{p}']\varepsilon_* = (\mathbf{p}'\varepsilon_*)'\boldsymbol{\Lambda}(\mathbf{p}'\varepsilon_*), \qquad (14.2.8)
\end{aligned}$$

where $\varepsilon_* \equiv (\boldsymbol{\Psi}^{-1/2}\varepsilon/\sigma) \sim \mathrm{N}(\mathbf{0}, \mathbf{I}_n)$, $\mathbf{p}$ and $\boldsymbol{\Lambda}$ are the matrices of eigenvectors and eigenvalues of the symmetric idempotent matrix $[\mathbf{I}_n - \boldsymbol{\Psi}^{-1/2}\mathbf{x}(\mathbf{x}'\boldsymbol{\Psi}^{-1}\mathbf{x})^{-1}\mathbf{x}'\boldsymbol{\Psi}^{-1/2}]$. The idempotent matrix has trace and thus rank $(n-k)$, $\mathbf{p}'\mathbf{p} = \mathbf{p}\mathbf{p}' = \mathbf{I}_n$, and the diagonal entries of $\boldsymbol{\Lambda}$ contain $(n-k)$ 1's and k 0's because of the idempotency rank characteristic of $[\mathbf{I}_n - \boldsymbol{\Psi}^{-1/2}\mathbf{x}(\mathbf{x}'\boldsymbol{\Psi}^{-1}\mathbf{x})^{-1}\mathbf{x}'\boldsymbol{\Psi}^{-1/2}]$. Also, $\mathbf{p}'\varepsilon_* \sim \mathrm{N}(\mathbf{0}, \mathbf{p}'\mathbf{I}\mathbf{p}) = \mathrm{N}(\mathbf{0}, \mathbf{I}_n)$, and it follows that (14.2.8) is the sum of squares of $(n-k)$ iid standard normal random variables in which case $(n-k)\mathrm{S}^2_{+}/\sigma^2$ has a Chi-square$(n-k, 0)$ distribution. Because scalar transformations of Chi-square distributed random variables are gamma distributed, it follows that both S^2_{+} and $\mathrm{S}^2_{\mathrm{ML}}$ are gamma distributed, as Gamma$[\frac{n-k}{2}, \frac{2\sigma^2}{(n-k)}]$ and Gamma $[\frac{n-k}{2}, \frac{2\sigma^2}{(n)}]$, respectively. Additional finite and large sample properties of the ML estimators are discussed ahead.

14.2.2. LS–Extremum Estimators for $\boldsymbol{\beta}$ and σ^2: Transformed Linear Model

If we do not adopt the normality assumption, we can follow the arguments presented in Chapter 5 and derive estimators of $\boldsymbol{\beta}$ and σ^2 that have favorable large-sample properties. The key idea underlying the result is to transform the linear model in a way that satisfies the conditions outlined in Table 5.1 and then to apply the LS estimator to the transformed model. As the reader might anticipate, the LS estimators based on the transformed model are closely related to the ML estimators of $\boldsymbol{\beta}$ and σ^2 derived in the previous subsection.

The transformation we consider is based on the use of the *symmetric square root* of a positive definite symmetric matrix (see the matrix review manual). Recall that for $\boldsymbol{\Psi}$, the symmetric square root is a positive definite symmetric matrix $\boldsymbol{\Psi}^{1/2}$ for which $\boldsymbol{\Psi} = \boldsymbol{\Psi}^{1/2}\boldsymbol{\Psi}^{1/2}$, and $\mathbf{I} = \boldsymbol{\Psi}^{-1/2}\boldsymbol{\Psi}^{1/2} = \boldsymbol{\Psi}^{1/2}\boldsymbol{\Psi}^{-1/2}$, where $\boldsymbol{\Psi}^{-1/2} = (\boldsymbol{\Psi}^{1/2})^{-1}$ denotes the inverse of $\boldsymbol{\Psi}^{1/2}$. Such a matrix always exists for any positive definite symmetric matrix and in particular can be defined as $\boldsymbol{\Psi}^{1/2} = \mathbf{p}\boldsymbol{\Lambda}^{1/2}\mathbf{p}'$, where $\boldsymbol{\Lambda}^{1/2}$ is an $(n \times n)$ diagonal matrix having the square roots of the eigenvalues of $\boldsymbol{\Psi}$ along its diagonal, and $\mathbf{p}$ is an $(n \times n)$ matrix whose columns are the corresponding eigenvectors of $\boldsymbol{\Psi}$. Given the orthogonality of $\mathbf{p}$, so that $\mathbf{I} = \mathbf{p}'\mathbf{p} = \mathbf{p}\mathbf{p}'$ and thus $\mathbf{p}' = \mathbf{p}^{-1}$, it follows that $\boldsymbol{\Psi}^{-1/2} = \mathbf{p}\boldsymbol{\Lambda}^{-1/2}\mathbf{p}'$, where $\boldsymbol{\Lambda}^{-1/2}$ is the inverse of $\boldsymbol{\Lambda}^{1/2}$.

On the basis of the matrix square-root concept, consider the following transformation of the aforementioned linear regression model

$$\boldsymbol{\Psi}^{-1/2}\mathbf{Y} = \boldsymbol{\Psi}^{-1/2}\mathbf{x}\boldsymbol{\beta} + \boldsymbol{\Psi}^{-1/2}\boldsymbol{\varepsilon} \quad \text{or} \quad \mathbf{Y}_* = \mathbf{x}_*\boldsymbol{\beta} + \boldsymbol{\varepsilon}_*. \tag{14.2.9}$$

where $\mathbf{Y}_* \equiv \boldsymbol{\Psi}^{-1/2}\mathbf{Y}$, $\mathbf{x}_* \equiv \boldsymbol{\Psi}^{-1/2}\mathbf{x}$ and $\boldsymbol{\varepsilon}_* \equiv \boldsymbol{\Psi}^{-1/2}\boldsymbol{\varepsilon}$. Clearly, the assumptions presented at the beginning of Chapter 5 apply to the transformed model (14.2.9). In particular, note that $\mathrm{E}[\boldsymbol{\varepsilon}_*] = \mathrm{E}[\boldsymbol{\Psi}^{-1/2}\boldsymbol{\varepsilon}] = \boldsymbol{\Psi}^{-1/2}\mathrm{E}[\boldsymbol{\varepsilon}] = \mathbf{0}$, $\mathbf{cov}(\boldsymbol{\varepsilon}_*) = \boldsymbol{\Psi}^{-1/2}(\sigma^2\boldsymbol{\Psi})\boldsymbol{\Psi}^{-1/2} = \sigma^2\mathbf{I}_n$, $\mathbf{x}_* = \boldsymbol{\Psi}^{-1/2}\mathbf{x}$ is fixed and has full-column rank (because $\boldsymbol{\Psi}^{-1/2}$ is nonsingular), $\mathrm{E}[\mathbf{Y}_*] = \mathbf{x}_*\boldsymbol{\beta}$, and $\mathbf{cov}(\mathbf{Y}_*) = \mathbf{cov}(\boldsymbol{\varepsilon}_*) = \sigma^2\mathbf{I}_n$. These observations fully justify the application of the LS–extremum estimators to (14.2.9) for solving the inverse problem of estimating values of $(\boldsymbol{\beta}, \sigma^2)$ and also justify all of the previous sampling properties attributed to the estimator, and thus nothing more really needs to be said about the point estimation problem. However, we will nonetheless examine the definition and properties of the estimator in more detail to establish a framework for examining the important case in Chapter 15, where $\boldsymbol{\Psi}$ is unknown.

The LS objective function applied to the transformed regression model (14.2.9) can be represented as

$$\mathrm{s}_*(\mathbf{b}, \mathbf{y}, \mathbf{x}) = (\mathbf{y}_* - \mathbf{x}_*\mathbf{b})'(\mathbf{y}_* - \mathbf{x}_*\mathbf{b}) = (\mathbf{y} - \mathbf{x}\mathbf{b})'\boldsymbol{\Psi}^{-1}(\mathbf{y} - \mathbf{x}\mathbf{b}). \tag{14.2.10}$$

By analogy, note that the least-squares objective function measures the distance between $\mathbf{y}$ and $\mathbf{xb}$ in the inverse $\boldsymbol{\Psi}$ metric. As well, (14.2.10) is a strictly monotonically decreasing linear function of the normal log likelihood function (14.2.2). Proceeding as we did in Chapter 5, the first-order conditions for minimizing $\mathrm{s}_*(\mathbf{b}, \mathbf{y}, \mathbf{x})$ with respect to a choice of $\mathbf{b}$ are given by

$$\frac{\partial \mathrm{s}_*(\mathbf{b}, \mathbf{y}, \mathbf{x})}{\partial \mathbf{b}} = 2[(\mathbf{x}_*'\mathbf{x}_*\mathbf{b} - \mathbf{x}_*'\mathbf{y}_*)] = 2[(\mathbf{x}'\boldsymbol{\Psi}^{-1}\mathbf{x})\mathbf{b} - \mathbf{x}'\boldsymbol{\Psi}^{-1}\mathbf{y}] = \mathbf{0} \tag{14.2.11}$$

Solving the first-order conditions for the optimum value of $\mathbf{b}$ yields

$$\hat{\mathbf{b}}_{\mathrm{G}} = (\mathbf{x}_*'\mathbf{x}_*)^{-1}\mathbf{x}_*'\mathbf{y}_* = (\mathbf{x}'\boldsymbol{\Psi}^{-1}\mathbf{x})^{-1}\mathbf{x}'\boldsymbol{\Psi}^{-1}\mathbf{y} \tag{14.2.12}$$

with the associated estimator being defined by

$$\hat{\boldsymbol{\beta}}_{\mathrm{G}} = (\mathbf{x}'\boldsymbol{\Psi}^{-1}\mathbf{x})^{-1}\mathbf{x}'\boldsymbol{\Psi}^{-1}\mathbf{Y} \tag{14.2.13}$$

Clearly, $\hat{\boldsymbol{\beta}}_{\mathrm{G}}$ is identical to the ML estimator $\hat{\boldsymbol{\beta}}_{\mathrm{ML}}$, and in practice the estimation rules are known as the *generalized least-squares* (GLS), *Aitken* (named after A. C. Aitken who first proposed the estimator in 1935), or *weighted least-squares* estimator. The unbiased estimator of σ^2 based on the GLS estimator is

$$S_G^2 = \frac{(\mathbf{Y}_* - \mathbf{x}_*\hat{\boldsymbol{\beta}}_G)'(\mathbf{Y}_* - \mathbf{x}_*\hat{\boldsymbol{\beta}}_G)}{n-k} = \frac{(\mathbf{Y} - \mathbf{x}\hat{\boldsymbol{\beta}}_G)'\boldsymbol{\Psi}^{-1}(\mathbf{Y} - \mathbf{x}\hat{\boldsymbol{\beta}}_G)}{n-k} \tag{14.2.14}$$

Because the GLS estimator is identical to the least-squares estimator applied to the transformed linear model (14.2.9), which adheres to the classical assumptions of the linear regression model, $\hat{\boldsymbol{\beta}}_G$ has all of the finite sample properties associated with the LS estimator from Chapter 5. In particular, $\hat{\boldsymbol{\beta}}_G$ will be unbiased, BLUE, MVUE (under normality), minimax under quadratic risk and minimizes the sum of squared prediction errors. We also know the estimator S^2 applied to the transformed sample data $(\mathbf{y}_*, \mathbf{x}_*)$ will be unbiased and MVUE (under normality) for the parameter σ^2.

We conclude by demonstrating our earlier claim that the LS estimator is inefficient relative to the GLS estimator. In comparing the covariance matrices of $\hat{\boldsymbol{\beta}}$ and $\hat{\boldsymbol{\beta}}_G$, note that

$$\mathbf{cov}(\hat{\boldsymbol{\beta}}) - \mathbf{cov}(\hat{\boldsymbol{\beta}}_G) = \sigma^2 \mathbf{c}\boldsymbol{\Psi}\mathbf{c}' \tag{14.2.15}$$

where $\mathbf{c} = (\mathbf{x}'\mathbf{x})^{-1}\mathbf{x}' - (\mathbf{x}'\boldsymbol{\Psi}^{-1}\mathbf{x})^{-1}\mathbf{x}'\boldsymbol{\Psi}^{-1}$, and thus the difference in asymptotic covariance matrices is at least positive semidefinite and nonzero if $\mathbf{c} \neq \mathbf{0}$ because $\boldsymbol{\Psi}$ is positive definite. Therefore, $\hat{\boldsymbol{\beta}}$ is less efficient than the GLS estimator $\hat{\boldsymbol{\beta}}_G$ *when* $\boldsymbol{\Psi}$ *is known.* However, we emphasize for future reference that the definition of the LS estimator $\hat{\boldsymbol{\beta}}$ does not require knowledge of $\boldsymbol{\Psi}$ in contrast to $\hat{\boldsymbol{\beta}}_G$, which is unknown and unobservable when $\boldsymbol{\Psi}$ is not known.

14.2.3. Asymptotic Properties

If we do not adopt the normality assumption, we can follow the approach taken in Chapter 5 and develop the large sample properties of the GLS estimator. On the basis of Theorem 5.3.2, the GLS estimator $\hat{\boldsymbol{\beta}}_G$ will be consistent if

$$\mathrm{tr}(\mathbf{x}_*'\mathbf{x}_*) = \mathrm{tr}(\mathbf{x}'\boldsymbol{\Psi}^{-1}\mathbf{x}) \to \infty \text{ as } n \to \infty \tag{14.2.16}$$

and

$$\frac{\lambda_L(\mathbf{x}_*'\mathbf{x}_*)}{\lambda_s(\mathbf{x}_*'\mathbf{x}_*)} = \frac{\lambda_L(\mathbf{x}'\boldsymbol{\Psi}^{-1}\mathbf{x})}{\lambda_s(\mathbf{x}'\boldsymbol{\Psi}^{-1}\mathbf{x})} \leq \delta < \infty,$$

where λ_L and λ_s are the largest and smallest eigenvalues, respectively, of the matrix $\mathbf{x}_*'\mathbf{x}_* = \mathbf{x}'\boldsymbol{\Psi}^{-1}\mathbf{x}$. These conditions are no more restrictive than their counterparts in Chapter 5. In particular, note that (see Mittelhammer, Lemma 8.4, p. 454)

$$\mathrm{tr}(\mathbf{x}'\boldsymbol{\Psi}^{-1}\mathbf{x}) = \mathrm{tr}(\boldsymbol{\Psi}^{-1}\mathbf{x}\mathbf{x}') \geq \lambda_s(\boldsymbol{\Psi}^{-1})\mathrm{tr}(\mathbf{x}'\mathbf{x}), \tag{14.2.17}$$

and thus if $\lambda_s(\boldsymbol{\Psi}^{-1}) \geq \zeta > 0$, which means that the smallest eigenvalue of $\boldsymbol{\Psi}^{-1}$ is bounded away from zero (or equivalently, the largest eigenvalue of $\boldsymbol{\Psi}$ is bounded away from infinity), then as $n \to \infty$, $\mathrm{tr}(\mathbf{x}'\boldsymbol{\Psi}^{-1}\mathbf{x}) \to \infty$ if $\mathrm{tr}(\mathbf{x}'\mathbf{x}) \to \infty$, the latter being identical to the condition used in Chapter 5 to establish consistency of $\hat{\boldsymbol{\beta}}$. The lower bound on the smallest eigenvalue of $\boldsymbol{\Psi}^{-1}$ is a very mild restriction on the covariance structure of the noise component and can be assumed to hold widely in practice. For example, if the noise component is heteroscedastic but not autocorrelated, the restriction is equivalent to requiring that the largest variance associated with the noise elements is bounded away from infinity. Likewise, the second condition in (14.2.16) referring to the condition number of the matrix $(\mathbf{x}'\boldsymbol{\Psi}^{-1}\mathbf{x})$ is not very restrictive, only requiring that the columns in $\boldsymbol{\Psi}^{-1/2}\mathbf{x}$ are prevented from becoming too close to exhibiting linear dependence, and thus the matrix $(\mathbf{x}'\boldsymbol{\Psi}^{-1}\mathbf{x})$ is prevented from becoming too close to being singular.

The asymptotic normality of $\hat{\boldsymbol{\beta}}_{\mathrm{G}}$ can be established via an application of Theorem 5.3.3 to the transformed regression model (14.2.9). In particular, if

$$n^{-1}\mathbf{x}_*'\mathbf{x}_* = n^{-1}\mathbf{x}'\boldsymbol{\Psi}^{-1}\mathbf{x} \rightarrow \boldsymbol{\Xi} \text{ as } n \rightarrow \infty$$

and

$$\mathrm{E}|\varepsilon_*[i]|^{2+\delta} = \mathrm{E}|(\boldsymbol{\Psi}^{-1/2}\boldsymbol{\varepsilon})[i]|^{2+\delta} \leq \zeta < \infty, \tag{14.2.18}$$

where $\boldsymbol{\Xi}$ is a finite positive definite symmetric matrix and $\varepsilon_*[i] \equiv (\boldsymbol{\Psi}^{-1/2}\boldsymbol{\varepsilon})[i]$ denotes the ith element of the vector $\boldsymbol{\Psi}^{-1/2}\boldsymbol{\varepsilon}$, and if the elements of $\boldsymbol{\varepsilon}_*$ are independent, then Theorem 5.3.3 applies directly and $n^{1/2}(\hat{\boldsymbol{\beta}}_{\mathrm{G}} - \boldsymbol{\beta}) \xrightarrow{\mathrm{d}} \mathrm{N}(\mathbf{0}, \sigma^2\boldsymbol{\Xi}^{-1})$. Given (14.2.18), an asymptotic distribution for $\hat{\boldsymbol{\beta}}_{\mathrm{G}}$ is given by

$$\hat{\boldsymbol{\beta}}_{\mathrm{G}} \overset{\mathrm{a}}{\sim} \mathrm{N}[\boldsymbol{\beta}, \sigma^2(\mathbf{x}'\boldsymbol{\Psi}^{-1}\mathbf{x})^{-1}], \tag{14.2.19}$$

and the approximation is in fact the actual distribution of $\hat{\boldsymbol{\beta}}_{\mathrm{G}}$ under the assumption that the noise component is multivariate normal. Note that if $\boldsymbol{\varepsilon}_* = \boldsymbol{\Psi}^{-1/2}\boldsymbol{\varepsilon} \sim \mathrm{N}(\mathbf{0}, \sigma^2\mathbf{I})$, the second condition relating to bounded absolute moments of the transformed noise components in (14.2.18) automatically hold because, for example, $\mathrm{E}[\varepsilon_*[i]]^4 = 3\sigma^4 < \infty$. Thus, only the first condition in (14.2.18) represents an additional new assumption. We also note that independence of the elements of $\boldsymbol{\varepsilon}_*$ is by no means necessary for asymptotic normality of $\hat{\boldsymbol{\beta}}_{\mathrm{G}}$. A wide variety of conditions can lead to a central limit theorem (CLT) justifying the asymptotic normality of $n^{-1/2}\mathbf{x}'\boldsymbol{\Psi}^{-1}\boldsymbol{\varepsilon}$, which, when combined with the first condition in (14.2.18), leads to the asymptotic normality of $\hat{\boldsymbol{\beta}}_{\mathrm{G}}$, as in (14.2.19). See White (1984) for a variety of CLTs along these lines.

Theorem 5.4.2 applied to the transformed data (14.2.9) can be used to justify the consistency of the estimator $\mathrm{S}_{\mathrm{G}}^2$ of σ^2. In fact, the reader can demonstrate that the proof of the theorem proceeds identically as before with $\mathbf{x}_*$ and $\boldsymbol{\varepsilon}_*$ replacing $\mathbf{x}$ and $\boldsymbol{\varepsilon}$, respectively. Thus, under the current DSP assumptions represented by (14.2.9) and Table 14.1, $\mathrm{S}_{\mathrm{G}}^2 \rightarrow \sigma^2$.

► **Example 14.2.1:** To compare the asymptotic properties and relative efficiency of the LS and GLS estimators when $\boldsymbol{\Psi} \neq \mathbf{I}$, we provide the GAUSS program C14GLS.gss in the examples manual. In the context of a simple heteroscedastic linear regression model, GAUSS conducts a Monte Carlo exercise to simulate the moments and sampling distributions for the two estimators. As well, GAUSS reports the simulated relative efficiency of the estimators for a range of specifications of $\boldsymbol{\Psi}$ for the heteroscedastic linear model.

14.2.4. Hypothesis Testing and Confidence Regions

Because we are effectively applying either the LS or ML principle to the transformed linear regression model (14.2.9), all of the hypothesis-testing and confidence-region estimation procedures discussed in Chapters 4 and 6 relative to the linear model apply to the GLS–ML estimator $\hat{\boldsymbol{\beta}}_G$. First, for testing the linear $(j \times 1)$ vector hypothesis $H_0: \mathbf{c}\boldsymbol{\beta} = \mathbf{r}$ versus $H_a: \mathbf{c}\boldsymbol{\beta} \neq \mathbf{r}$ and adopting the normality assumption, one can utilize the F-distributed test statistic

$$\mathrm{F} = \frac{(\mathbf{c}\hat{\boldsymbol{\beta}}_G - \mathbf{r})'[\mathbf{c}(\mathbf{x}_*'\mathbf{x}_*)^{-1}\mathbf{c}']^{-1}(\mathbf{c}\hat{\boldsymbol{\beta}}_G - \mathbf{r})}{j S_G^2}$$

$$= \frac{(\mathbf{c}\hat{\boldsymbol{\beta}}_G - \mathbf{r})'[\mathbf{c}(\mathbf{x}'\boldsymbol{\Psi}^{-1}\mathbf{x})^{-1}\mathbf{c}']^{-1}(\mathbf{c}\hat{\boldsymbol{\beta}}_G - \mathbf{r})}{j S_G^2} \sim \mathrm{F}(j, n-k, \lambda), \qquad (14.2.20)$$

where the noncentrality parameter is defined precisely as in (4.3.12) except that $\mathbf{x}'\mathbf{x}$ is replaced by $\mathbf{x}'\boldsymbol{\Psi}^{-1}\mathbf{x}$. An α-level test is conducted in the usual way by defining a critical region as $C^F = [f_{1-\alpha}, \infty)$, where $f_{1-\alpha}$ is the $100(1-\alpha)\%$ quantile of the central F-distribution with j and $(n-k)$ degrees of freedom. Power characteristics of this and all other tests discussed in this section are analogous to those discussed in Section 4.3.

For a scalar hypothesis, be it an equality or inequality hypothesis, the T-statistic

$$\mathrm{T} = \frac{\mathbf{c}\hat{\boldsymbol{\beta}}_G - \mathrm{r}}{\left[S_G^2\mathbf{c}(\mathbf{x}_*'\mathbf{x}_*)^{-1}\mathbf{c}'\right]^{1/2}} = \frac{\mathbf{c}\hat{\boldsymbol{\beta}}_G - \mathrm{r}}{\left[S_G^2\mathbf{c}(\mathbf{x}'\boldsymbol{\Psi}^{-1}\mathbf{x})^{-1}\mathbf{c}'\right]^{1/2}} \sim \mathrm{T}(n-k, \delta) \qquad (14.2.21)$$

can be used, where δ is the noncentrality parameter defined precisely as it was following (4.3.17), except that $\mathbf{x}'\mathbf{x}$ is replaced by $\mathbf{x}'\boldsymbol{\Psi}^{-1}\mathbf{x}$. An α-level test of various hypotheses relating to linear combinations of $\boldsymbol{\beta}$ can be conducted as follows, where $t_{1-\alpha}$ denotes the $100(1-\alpha)\%$ quantile of the central T-distribution with $(n-k)$ degrees of freedom:

H_0	Critical Region
$\mathbf{c}\boldsymbol{\beta} = \mathrm{r}$	$(-\infty, -t_{1-\alpha/2}] \cup [t_{1-\alpha/2}, \infty)$
$\mathbf{c}\boldsymbol{\beta} \leq \mathrm{r}$	$[t_{1-\alpha}, \infty)$
$\mathbf{c}\boldsymbol{\beta} \geq \mathrm{r}$	$(-\infty, t_\alpha]$

(14.2.22)

As we noted in Section 6.2.3, the GLR, Wald, and LM tests are identical to the preceding F-test under normality, and they are equivalent to the T-test when testing a single linear equality restriction on the elements of $\boldsymbol{\beta}$. We will defer discussing tests of nonlinear functions of $\boldsymbol{\beta}$ until Section 14.3.

Confidence intervals and regions can be generated in the usual way using the duality principle. A confidence interval for $\mathbf{c}\boldsymbol{\beta}$ having confidence level $(1-\alpha)$ is defined by the outcome of

$$\mathrm{CR}_{1-\alpha} = \left(\mathbf{c}\hat{\boldsymbol{\beta}}_G - t_{1-\alpha/2}\left[S_G^2\mathbf{c}(\mathbf{x}'\boldsymbol{\Psi}^{-1}\mathbf{x})^{-1}\mathbf{c}'\right]^{1/2}, \mathbf{c}\hat{\boldsymbol{\beta}}_G + t_{1-\alpha/2}\left[S_G^2\mathbf{c}(\mathbf{x}'\boldsymbol{\Psi}^{-1}\mathbf{x})^{-1}\mathbf{c}'\right]^{1/2}\right). \qquad (14.2.23)$$

Upper and lower confidence bounds on the scalar $\mathbf{c}\boldsymbol{\beta}$ having confidence level $(1-\alpha)$ can be defined, respectively, by the outcome of

$$\begin{aligned} \mathrm{CR}_{1-\alpha} &= \left(-\infty, \mathbf{c}\hat{\boldsymbol{\beta}}_{\mathrm{G}} + t_{1-\alpha}\left[\mathrm{S}_{\mathrm{G}}^2\mathbf{c}(\mathbf{x}'\boldsymbol{\Psi}^{-1}\mathbf{x})^{-1}\mathbf{c}'\right]^{1/2}\right) \\ \mathrm{CR}_{1-\alpha} &= \left(\mathbf{c}\hat{\boldsymbol{\beta}}_{\mathrm{G}} - t_{1-\alpha}\left[\mathrm{S}_{\mathrm{G}}^2\mathbf{c}(\mathbf{x}'\boldsymbol{\Psi}^{-1}\mathbf{x})^{-1}\mathbf{c}'\right]^{1/2}, \infty\right). \end{aligned} \tag{14.2.24}$$

A confidence region (ellipse) for the $(j \times 1)$ vector $\mathbf{c}\boldsymbol{\beta}$ having confidence level $(1-\alpha)$ is defined by the outcome of the random set

$$\mathrm{CR}_{1-\alpha} = \left\{\mathbf{r} : (\mathbf{c}\hat{\boldsymbol{\beta}}_{\mathrm{G}} - \mathbf{r})'[\mathbf{c}(\mathbf{x}'\boldsymbol{\Psi}^{-1}\mathbf{x})^{-1}\mathbf{c}']^{-1}(\mathbf{c}\hat{\boldsymbol{\beta}}_{\mathrm{G}} - \mathbf{r}) < j\mathrm{S}_{\mathrm{G}}^2\mathrm{f}_{1-\alpha}\right\}. \tag{14.2.25}$$

When normality does not apply, testing and confidence region estimation can proceed based on the asymptotic normal distribution of the GLS or ML estimator. The testing and confidence region procedures of Chapter 6 can be applied to transformed data $(\mathbf{y}_*, \mathbf{x}_*)$, which replace the untransformed data $(\mathbf{y}, \mathbf{x})$ in the definition of the procedures.

14.3. GLS–ML–Extremum Analysis of the Nonlinear Model: Incorporating a Known $\boldsymbol{\Psi}$

As in the case of the linear model, the nonlinear regression model $\mathbf{Y} = \mathbf{g}(\mathbf{x}, \boldsymbol{\beta}) + \boldsymbol{\varepsilon}$ with $\mathbf{cov}(\boldsymbol{\varepsilon}) = \sigma^2\boldsymbol{\Psi}$ and $\boldsymbol{\Psi}$ known can be transformed into a form that allows the transfer of all of the previous knowledge we have gained in Chapter 8 relating to information recovery in the nonlinear regression model. Specifically, the model

$$\boldsymbol{\Psi}^{-1/2}\mathbf{Y} = \boldsymbol{\Psi}^{-1/2}\mathbf{g}(\mathbf{x}, \boldsymbol{\beta}) + \boldsymbol{\Psi}^{-1/2}\boldsymbol{\varepsilon} \text{ or } \mathbf{Y}_* = \mathbf{g}_*(\mathbf{x}, \boldsymbol{\beta}) + \boldsymbol{\varepsilon}_*, \tag{14.3.1}$$

where $\mathbf{Y}_* \equiv \boldsymbol{\Psi}^{-1/2}\mathbf{Y}$, $\mathbf{g}_*(\mathbf{x}, \boldsymbol{\beta}) \equiv \boldsymbol{\Psi}^{-1/2}\mathbf{g}(\mathbf{x}, \boldsymbol{\beta})$, and $\boldsymbol{\varepsilon}_* \equiv \boldsymbol{\Psi}^{-1/2}\boldsymbol{\varepsilon}$, satisfies all of the assumptions presented at the beginning of Chapter 8. In particular, $\mathrm{E}[\boldsymbol{\varepsilon}_*] = \boldsymbol{\Psi}^{-1/2}\mathrm{E}[\boldsymbol{\varepsilon}] = \mathbf{0}$, $\mathbf{cov}(\boldsymbol{\varepsilon}_*) = \mathbf{cov}(\boldsymbol{\Psi}^{-1/2}\boldsymbol{\varepsilon}) = \boldsymbol{\Psi}^{-1/2}[\sigma^2\boldsymbol{\Psi}]\boldsymbol{\Psi}^{-1/2} = \sigma^2\mathbf{I}_n$, $\mathrm{E}[\mathbf{Y}_*] = \mathbf{g}_*(\mathbf{x}, \boldsymbol{\beta})$, $\mathbf{cov}(\mathbf{Y}_*) = \mathbf{cov}(\boldsymbol{\varepsilon}_*) = \sigma^2\mathbf{I}_n$, $\mathbf{g}_*(\mathbf{x}, \boldsymbol{\beta}) = \boldsymbol{\Psi}^{-1/2}\mathbf{g}(\mathbf{x}, \boldsymbol{\beta})$ is continuously differentiable in $\boldsymbol{\beta}$ if it is assumed that $\mathbf{g}(\mathbf{x}, \boldsymbol{\beta})$ is continuously differentiable and $\boldsymbol{\varepsilon}_* \sim \mathrm{N}(\mathbf{0}, \sigma^2\mathbf{I}_n)$ if $\boldsymbol{\varepsilon} \sim \mathrm{N}(\mathbf{0}, \sigma^2\boldsymbol{\Psi})$.

14.3.1. Estimator Properties

Because the nonlinear model (14.3.1) is in the precise form of the nonlinear regression model discussed in Chapter 8, the nonlinear least-squares estimator of the parameter vector $\boldsymbol{\beta}$ in (14.3.1) will have properties analogous to those established previously. The nonlinear LS-extremum estimate will be defined by the value of $\mathbf{b}$ that minimizes

$$\mathrm{s}_*(\mathbf{b}) = [\mathbf{y}_* - \mathbf{g}_*(\mathbf{x}, \mathbf{b})]'[\mathbf{y}_* - \mathbf{g}_*(\mathbf{x}, \mathbf{b})] = [\mathbf{y} - \mathbf{g}(\mathbf{x}, \mathbf{b})]'\boldsymbol{\Psi}^{-1}[\mathbf{y} - \mathbf{g}(\mathbf{x}, \mathbf{b})]. \tag{14.3.2}$$

Then, if it is assumed that $\boldsymbol{\beta}$ is identified and that the conditions of Theorem 8.9.1 apply with $\mathbf{Y}$ replaced by $\mathbf{Y}_*$ and $\mathbf{g}(\mathbf{x}, \boldsymbol{\beta})$ replaced by $\mathbf{g}_*(\mathbf{x}, \boldsymbol{\beta})$, the nonlinear generalized least-squares (NGLS) estimator $\hat{\boldsymbol{\beta}}_{\mathrm{G}} = \arg\min_{\mathbf{b}}[\mathrm{S}_*(\mathbf{b})]$ is consistent for $\boldsymbol{\beta}$. If the additional assumptions of Theorem 8.9.2 hold, again with $\mathbf{g}(\mathbf{x}, \boldsymbol{\beta})$ replaced by $\mathbf{g}_*(\mathbf{x}, \boldsymbol{\beta})$ then the NGLS estimator $\hat{\boldsymbol{\beta}}_G$ is also asymptotically normally distributed, where

$$\hat{\boldsymbol{\beta}}_G \overset{a}{\sim} N\left(\boldsymbol{\beta}, \sigma^2\left[\frac{\partial \mathbf{g}_*(\mathbf{x}, \boldsymbol{\beta})}{\partial \boldsymbol{\beta}} \frac{\partial \mathbf{g}_*(\mathbf{x}, \boldsymbol{\beta})}{\partial \boldsymbol{\beta}'}\right]^{-1}\right) = N\left(\boldsymbol{\beta}, \sigma^2\left[\frac{\partial \mathbf{g}(\mathbf{x}, \boldsymbol{\beta})}{\partial \boldsymbol{\beta}} \boldsymbol{\Psi}^{-1} \frac{\partial \mathbf{g}(\mathbf{x}, \boldsymbol{\beta})}{\partial \boldsymbol{\beta}'}\right]^{-1}\right). \tag{14.3.3}$$

If the noise component is multivariate normally distributed, the logarithm of the likelihood function for $(\boldsymbol{\beta}, \sigma^2)$ is analogous to (9.1.2) with $\mathbf{g}_*(\mathbf{x}, \boldsymbol{\beta})$ replacing $\mathbf{g}(\mathbf{x}, \boldsymbol{\beta})$. It follows that the ML estimator of $\boldsymbol{\beta}$ and its associated sampling properties are identical to $\hat{\boldsymbol{\beta}}_G$, and we gain the additional ML property that $\hat{\boldsymbol{\beta}}_G$ is generally asymptotically efficient for estimating $\boldsymbol{\beta}$ (recall (9.1.6) and the accompanying discussion). The ML estimator for σ^2 is

$$S_G^2 = \frac{[\mathbf{Y}_* - \mathbf{g}_*(\mathbf{x}, \hat{\boldsymbol{\beta}}_G)]'[\mathbf{Y}_* - \mathbf{g}_*(\mathbf{x}, \hat{\boldsymbol{\beta}}_G)]}{n} = \frac{[\mathbf{Y} - \mathbf{g}(\mathbf{x}, \hat{\boldsymbol{\beta}}_G)]'\boldsymbol{\Psi}^{-1}[\mathbf{Y} - \mathbf{g}(\mathbf{x}, \hat{\boldsymbol{\beta}}_G)]}{n} \tag{14.3.4}$$

(recall (9.1.9)). The typical consistency, asymptotic normality, and asymptotic efficiency properties of ML estimators can be attributed to S_G^2.

14.3.2. Hypothesis Testing and Confidence Regions

Because all of the critical assumptions made in Chapters 8 and 9 (including normality) can be applied to the transformed nonlinear regression model (14.3.1), the hypothesis testing and confidence region procedures discussed heretofore apply to the model. In particular, each of the test statistics in Sections 8.5, 8.7, and 8.9 apply directly with $\frac{\partial \mathbf{g}(\mathbf{x},\boldsymbol{\beta})}{\partial \boldsymbol{\beta}}$ replaced by $\frac{\partial \mathbf{g}_*(\mathbf{x},\boldsymbol{\beta})}{\partial \boldsymbol{\beta}}$.

For example, to test the nonlinear $(j \times 1)$ vector equality hypothesis H_0: $\mathbf{c}(\boldsymbol{\beta}) = \mathbf{r}$, where $\mathbf{c}(\boldsymbol{\beta})$ is some $(j \times 1)$ vector function of $\boldsymbol{\beta}$ having nonredundant coordinate functions, the Wald statistic

$$W = [\mathbf{c}(\hat{\boldsymbol{\beta}}) - \mathbf{r}]'\left[S_G^2 \left.\frac{\partial \mathbf{c}(\boldsymbol{\beta})}{\partial \boldsymbol{\beta}'}\right|_{\hat{\boldsymbol{\beta}}_G} [\mathbf{x}(\hat{\boldsymbol{\beta}}_G)'\boldsymbol{\Psi}^{-1}\mathbf{x}(\hat{\boldsymbol{\beta}}_G)]^{-1} \left.\frac{\partial \mathbf{c}(\boldsymbol{\beta})}{\partial \boldsymbol{\beta}}\right|_{\hat{\boldsymbol{\beta}}_G}\right]^{-1} [\mathbf{c}(\hat{\boldsymbol{\beta}}) - \mathbf{r}]$$
$$\sim \text{Chi-square}(j, \lambda) \tag{14.3.5}$$

can be used, where $\mathbf{x}(\hat{\boldsymbol{\beta}}_G) \equiv \left.\frac{\partial \mathbf{g}(\mathbf{x},\boldsymbol{\beta})}{\partial \boldsymbol{\beta}'}\right|_{\hat{\boldsymbol{\beta}}_G}$. The critical region for an α-level test is defined by $C^w = [\chi^2_{1-\alpha}, \infty)$, where $\chi^2_{1-\alpha}$ is the $100(1-\alpha)\%$ quantile of a central χ^2 distribution with j degrees of freedom. The noncentrality parameter is given by (8.5.6), where $\boldsymbol{\Xi} = \lim_{n\to\infty} n^{-1}[\mathbf{x}(\boldsymbol{\beta}_0)'\boldsymbol{\Psi}^{-1}\mathbf{x}(\boldsymbol{\beta}_0)]$ and $\boldsymbol{\beta}_0$ denotes the true value of $\boldsymbol{\beta}$. Power function characteristics of the Wald test are analogous to those discussed in Section 8.5.4. Applications of the LM and GLR statistics to test H_0: $\mathbf{c}(\boldsymbol{\beta}) = \mathbf{r}$ follow similarly.

Another example is the tests of scalar nonlinear hypotheses, as well as scalar inequalities, that can be performed based on the Z-statistic (8.8.7), again with $\frac{\partial \mathbf{g}(\mathbf{x},\boldsymbol{\beta})}{\partial \boldsymbol{\beta}'}$

replaced by $\frac{\partial \mathbf{g}_*(\mathbf{x},\boldsymbol{\beta})}{\partial \boldsymbol{\beta}'} = \boldsymbol{\Psi}^{-1/2}\frac{\partial \mathbf{g}(\mathbf{x},\boldsymbol{\beta})}{\partial \boldsymbol{\beta}'}$. The Z-statistic is thus

$$Z = \frac{\mathbf{c}(\hat{\boldsymbol{\beta}}_G) - r}{\left[S_G^2 \frac{\partial \mathbf{c}(\boldsymbol{\beta})}{\partial \boldsymbol{\beta}'}\Big|_{\hat{\boldsymbol{\beta}}_G} [\mathbf{x}(\hat{\boldsymbol{\beta}}_G)'\boldsymbol{\Psi}^{-1}\mathbf{x}(\hat{\boldsymbol{\beta}}_G)]^{-1} \frac{\partial \mathbf{c}(\boldsymbol{\beta})}{\partial \boldsymbol{\beta}}\Big|_{\hat{\boldsymbol{\beta}}_G}\right]^{1/2}}, \tag{14.3.6}$$

and critical regions for various α-level hypotheses are as follows, where $z_{1-\alpha}$ is the $100(1-\alpha)\%$ quantile of the standard normal distribution:

H_0	Critical Region
$\mathbf{c}(\boldsymbol{\beta}) = r$	$(-\infty, -z_{1-\alpha/2}] \cup [z_{1-\alpha/2}, \infty)$
$\mathbf{c}(\boldsymbol{\beta}) \le r$	$[z_{1-\alpha}, \infty)$
$\mathbf{c}(\boldsymbol{\beta}) \ge r$	$(-\infty, z_\alpha]$

(14.3.7)

Power characteristics of the test are as described in Section 8.8.1.

Confidence regions for $\mathbf{c}(\boldsymbol{\beta})$ can be obtained using the duality principle linking hypothesis-testing and confidence-region estimation. For example, an asymptotic $(1-\alpha)$-level confidence region for $\mathbf{c}(\boldsymbol{\beta})$ could be based on the W-statistic (14.3.5), in which case the confidence region estimate would be given by an outcome of

$$CR = \left\{\mathbf{r} : [\mathbf{c}(\hat{\boldsymbol{\beta}}_G) - \mathbf{r}]' \left[S_G^2 \frac{\partial \mathbf{c}(\boldsymbol{\beta})}{\partial \boldsymbol{\beta}'}\Big|_{\hat{\boldsymbol{\beta}}_G} [\mathbf{x}(\hat{\boldsymbol{\beta}}_G)'\boldsymbol{\Psi}^{-1}\mathbf{x}(\hat{\boldsymbol{\beta}}_G)]^{-1} \frac{\partial \mathbf{c}(\boldsymbol{\beta})}{\partial \boldsymbol{\beta}}\Big|_{\hat{\boldsymbol{\beta}}_G}\right]^{-1} \times [\mathbf{c}(\hat{\boldsymbol{\beta}}_G) - \mathbf{r}] < \chi^2_{1-\alpha}\right\}. \tag{14.3.8}$$

Confidence regions for $\mathbf{c}(\boldsymbol{\beta})$ could also be generated based on GLR or LM statistics and critical regions for testing H_0: $\mathbf{c}(\boldsymbol{\beta}) = \mathbf{r}$. Confidence intervals and confidence bounds for a scalar $c(\boldsymbol{\beta})$ can be defined based on duality with the Z-statistic and critical regions, as described in Section 7.9.2. The set definitions for such confidence intervals and bounds are left to the reader.

14.3.3. Applying NLS to Untransformed Data

Analogous to our discussion in Section 14.1, one might wonder what the properties of the NLS estimator of $\boldsymbol{\beta}$ would be if $\boldsymbol{\Psi} \neq \mathbf{I}$ were ignored and the standard NLS estimator of Chapter 8 were applied to the untransformed observations $[\mathbf{y}, \mathbf{g}(\mathbf{x}, \boldsymbol{\beta})]$. To facilitate an analysis of this scenario, we recall that $\mathbf{x}(\boldsymbol{\beta}) \equiv \frac{\partial \mathbf{g}(\mathbf{x},\boldsymbol{\beta})}{\partial \boldsymbol{\beta}'}$ and define $\mathbf{x}_*(\boldsymbol{\beta}) \equiv \frac{\partial \mathbf{g}_*(\mathbf{x},\boldsymbol{\beta})}{\partial \boldsymbol{\beta}'} \equiv \boldsymbol{\Psi}^{-1/2}\frac{\partial \mathbf{g}(\mathbf{x},\boldsymbol{\beta})}{\partial \boldsymbol{\beta}'}$.

On the basis of arguments in Section 8.9.3, except that now $\mathbf{cov}(\varepsilon) = \sigma^2\boldsymbol{\Psi}$, it can be shown that the NLS estimator $\hat{\boldsymbol{\beta}} = \arg\min_{\mathbf{b}}[(\mathbf{Y} - \mathbf{g}(\mathbf{x}, \mathbf{b}))'(\mathbf{Y} - \mathbf{g}(\mathbf{x}, \mathbf{b}))]$ is still asymptotically linear in ε because

$$\hat{\boldsymbol{\beta}} = \boldsymbol{\beta} + [\mathbf{x}(\boldsymbol{\beta})'\mathbf{x}(\boldsymbol{\beta})]^{-1}\mathbf{x}(\boldsymbol{\beta})'\varepsilon + \mathbf{o}_p(n^{-1/2}) \tag{14.3.9}$$

and is a consistent estimator of $\boldsymbol{\beta}$. It is then apparent that the asymptotic distribution of the NLS estimator is given by

$$\hat{\boldsymbol{\beta}} \overset{a}{\sim} \mathrm{N}(\boldsymbol{\beta}, \sigma^2[\mathbf{x}(\boldsymbol{\beta})'\mathbf{x}(\boldsymbol{\beta})]^{-1}[\mathbf{x}(\boldsymbol{\beta})'\boldsymbol{\Psi}\mathbf{x}(\boldsymbol{\beta})][\mathbf{x}(\boldsymbol{\beta})'\mathbf{x}(\boldsymbol{\beta})]^{-1}). \tag{14.3.10}$$

In comparing the asymptotic covariance matrices of $\hat{\boldsymbol{\beta}}$ and $\hat{\boldsymbol{\beta}}_{\mathrm{G}}$ note that

$$\mathbf{asycov}(\hat{\boldsymbol{\beta}}) - \mathbf{asycov}(\hat{\boldsymbol{\beta}}_{\mathrm{G}}) = \sigma^2\mathbf{c}\boldsymbol{\Psi}\mathbf{c}' \tag{14.3.11}$$

where $\mathbf{c} = [\mathbf{x}(\boldsymbol{\beta})'\mathbf{x}(\boldsymbol{\beta})]^{-1}\mathbf{x}(\boldsymbol{\beta})' - [\mathbf{x}(\boldsymbol{\beta})'\boldsymbol{\Psi}^{-1}\mathbf{x}(\boldsymbol{\beta})]^{-1}\mathbf{x}(\boldsymbol{\beta})'\boldsymbol{\Psi}^{-1}$ and (14.2.15) is a special case. Thus, the difference in asymptotic covariance matrices is at least positive semidefinite and nonzero if $\mathbf{c} \neq \mathbf{0}$ because $\boldsymbol{\Psi}$ is positive definite. Therefore, $\hat{\boldsymbol{\beta}}$ is relatively less asymptotically efficient than is the NGLS estimator $\hat{\boldsymbol{\beta}}_{\mathrm{G}}$ when $\boldsymbol{\Psi}$ is known. However, note for future reference that the definition of $\hat{\boldsymbol{\beta}}$ does not require knowledge of $\boldsymbol{\Psi}$, whereas the definition of $\hat{\boldsymbol{\beta}}_{\mathrm{G}}$ relies on knowledge of the matrix $\boldsymbol{\Psi}$, and thus $\hat{\boldsymbol{\beta}}_{\mathrm{G}}$ is unknown and unobservable if $\boldsymbol{\Psi}$ is unknown.

Analogous to the linear model case discussed in Section 14.1, the estimator $\mathrm{S}^2 = [\mathbf{Y} - \mathbf{g}(\mathbf{x}, \hat{\boldsymbol{\beta}})]'[\mathbf{Y} - \mathbf{g}(\mathbf{x}, \hat{\boldsymbol{\beta}})]/(n-k)$ is not a consistent estimator of σ^2. However, if $\boldsymbol{\Psi}$ is known, an adjustment similar to the linear model case, namely $\mathrm{S}_*^2 = \xi(\boldsymbol{\Psi})\mathrm{S}^2$, where $\xi(\boldsymbol{\Psi}) = (n-k)/\mathrm{tr}([\mathbf{I} - \mathbf{x}(\hat{\boldsymbol{\beta}})[\mathbf{x}(\hat{\boldsymbol{\beta}})'\mathbf{x}(\hat{\boldsymbol{\beta}})]^{-1}\mathbf{x}(\hat{\boldsymbol{\beta}})']\boldsymbol{\Psi})$, will produce a consistent estimator of σ^2 under general conditions (recall the discussion following (14.1.8)).

Hypothesis-testing and confidence-region estimation procedures can be based on the asymptotic normal distribution (14.3.10) of the NLS estimator applied to untransformed data. In particular, all of the test statistics and their asymptotic distributions presented in Section 14.3.2, as well as the test rules and confidence regions based on them, can be applied directly after making a simple adjustment. In each case, the asymptotic covariance matrix estimator $\mathrm{S}_{\mathrm{G}}^2[\mathbf{x}(\hat{\boldsymbol{\beta}})'\boldsymbol{\Psi}^{-1}\mathbf{x}(\hat{\boldsymbol{\beta}})]^{-1}$ corresponding to the nonlinear GLS estimator must be replaced with an estimator of the LS estimator's asymptotic covariance matrix of the form $\mathrm{S}_*^2[\mathbf{x}(\hat{\boldsymbol{\beta}})'\mathbf{x}(\hat{\boldsymbol{\beta}})]^{-1}[\mathbf{x}(\hat{\boldsymbol{\beta}})'\boldsymbol{\Psi}\mathbf{x}(\hat{\boldsymbol{\beta}})][\mathbf{x}(\hat{\boldsymbol{\beta}})'\mathbf{x}(\hat{\boldsymbol{\beta}})]^{-1}$.

► **Example 14.3.1:** To compare the asymptotic properties and relative efficiency of the NLS and NGLS estimators when $\boldsymbol{\Psi} \neq \mathbf{I}$, we provide the GAUSS program C14NGLS.gss in the examples manual. In the context of a heteroscedastic nonlinear regression model, GAUSS conducts a Monte Carlo exercise to simulate the moments and sampling distributions for the two estimators. GAUSS presents box and whisker plots and EDFs based on the replicated estimates to examine the consistency and asymptotic normality of the estimators. As well, GAUSS reports the simulated relative efficiency of the estimators for a series of specifications of $\boldsymbol{\Psi}$.

14.4. Parametric Specifications of Noise Covariance Matrices

In this section, we examine two parametric models of the covariance matrix for autocorrelated and heteroscedastic noise elements. Although we have maintained the rather unrealistic assumption that the components of the noise covariance matrix are known, our purpose is to concentrate attention on the underlying arguments that lead to a functional specification of the noise covariance matrix. In Chapter 15 we consider cases in which the parameters in these covariance matrices are unknown and consider the inverse problem of using data to recover estimates of these unknowns together with the remaining parameters of the probability model.

14.4.1. Estimation and Inference with AR(1) Noise

Consider the case in which the elements of the noise vector ε are first-order autocorrelated and the ε_i's are also functions of random ν_i's that are iid with a mean of zero, have a variance of σ_ν^2, and are independent of the ε_i's. Let the regression model for **Y** depend on this autocorrelated noise vector as

$$\mathrm{Y}_i = \mathbf{x}_{i.}\boldsymbol{\beta} + \varepsilon_i \qquad (14.4.1)$$

$$\varepsilon_i = \rho\varepsilon_{i-1} + \nu_i, \qquad (14.4.2)$$

where $\mathrm{E}[\nu_i] = 0$, $\mathrm{E}[\nu_i^2] = \sigma_\nu^2$, $\mathrm{E}[\nu_i\nu_j] = 0$ for $j \neq i$, and $|\rho| < 1$. Under this specification, the noise covariance matrix $\mathrm{E}[\varepsilon\varepsilon'] = \sigma_\nu^2\boldsymbol{\Psi}$ is represented by

$$\sigma_\nu^2\boldsymbol{\Psi}(\rho) = \frac{\sigma_\nu^2}{1-\rho^2}\begin{bmatrix} 1 & \rho & \rho^2 & \cdots & \rho^{n-1} \\ \rho & 1 & \rho & \cdots & \rho^{n-2} \\ \rho^2 & \rho & 1 & \cdots & \rho^{n-3} \\ \vdots & \vdots & \vdots & \ddots & \vdots \\ \rho^{n-1} & \rho^{n-2} & \rho^{n-3} & \cdots & 1 \end{bmatrix}. \qquad (14.4.3)$$

To rationalize the functional form of the covariance matrix, first note that the second equation in (14.4.2) implies that

$$\varepsilon_i = \sum_{j=0}^{\infty} \rho^j \nu_{i-j} \qquad (14.4.4)$$

so that by results on the variance of linear combinations of random variables, and given that the ν_i's are iid,

$$\mathrm{var}(\varepsilon_i) = \sigma_\nu^2 \sum_{j=0}^{\infty} \rho^{2j} = \frac{\sigma_\nu^2}{1-\rho^2} \quad \text{if} \quad |\rho| < 1, \ \forall i, \qquad (14.4.5)$$

which justifies the diagonal terms in (14.4.3). Regarding the covariance terms, note that because $\mathrm{E}[\varepsilon_i] = 0\,\forall i$, and recalling equation (14.4.2), we can write the covariance of the ε_i and ε_{i-j} noise elements as

$$\begin{aligned}\mathrm{cov}(\varepsilon_i, \varepsilon_{i-j}) &= \mathrm{E}[(\rho\varepsilon_{i-1} + \nu_i)(\rho\varepsilon_{i-j-1} + \nu_{i-j})] \\ &= \mathrm{E}\left[\left(\rho^{j+1}\varepsilon_{i-j-1} + \sum_{t=0}^{j}\rho^t\nu_{i-t}\right)(\rho\varepsilon_{i-j-1} + \nu_{i-j})\right].\end{aligned} \qquad (14.4.6)$$

Then, because ε_i is independent of any ν_j for $j > i$ and the ν_j's are independent,

$$\begin{aligned}\mathrm{cov}(\varepsilon_i, \varepsilon_{i-j}) &= \mathrm{E}\left[\left(\rho^{j+2}\varepsilon_{i-j-1}^2 + \rho^j\nu_{i-j}^2\right)\right] \\ &= \rho^{j+2}\frac{\sigma_\nu^2}{1-\rho^2} + \rho^j\sigma_\nu^2 = \frac{\sigma_\nu^2\rho^j}{1-\rho^2},\end{aligned} \qquad (14.4.7)$$

which justifies the off-diagonal terms in (14.4.3).

If ρ is known, the estimation and inference procedures of Section 14.2 may be used to estimate the unknown parameters in the regression model. In particular, the known value of ρ would be substituted into the definition of the noise covariance matrix (14.4.3). Then, the GLS estimator (14.2.13) of $\boldsymbol{\beta}$ would be defined as $\hat{\boldsymbol{\beta}}_{\mathrm{G}} = [\mathbf{x}'\boldsymbol{\Psi}(\rho)^{-1}\mathbf{x}]^{-1}\mathbf{x}'\boldsymbol{\Psi}(\rho)^{-1}\mathbf{Y}$. The estimator has mean $\boldsymbol{\beta}$ and covariance matrix given by $\sigma_v^2[\mathbf{x}'\boldsymbol{\Psi}(\rho)^{-1}\mathbf{x}]^{-1}$ and is the BLUE of $\boldsymbol{\beta}$ as well as the MVUE under the normality assumption. Inference follows directly as outlined in Section 14.2.4.

An estimator of $\mathrm{var}(\varepsilon_i) = \frac{\sigma_v^2}{1-\rho^2}$ could be defined based on $\mathrm{S}_{\mathrm{G}}^2$ in (14.2.14), in which case an estimator of σ_v^2 could be defined by $(1-\rho^2)\mathrm{S}_{\mathrm{G}}^2$. The challenge in practice is that the value of the parameter ρ is generally unknown, in which case an estimate of ρ must be used to generate an approximation to the GLS estimator $\hat{\boldsymbol{\beta}}_{\mathrm{G}}$. We take up this issue in the next chapter.

14.4.2. Heteroscedasticity – Structural Specification Known, Parameters Unknown

Consider the pure heteroscedastic specification

$$\mathrm{Y}_i = \mathbf{x}_{i\cdot}\boldsymbol{\beta} + \varepsilon_i \tag{14.4.8}$$

and

$$\mathrm{E}[\varepsilon_i] = 0,\ \mathrm{E}\left[\varepsilon_i^2\right] = \sigma_i^2 = (\mathbf{z}_{i\cdot}\boldsymbol{\alpha})^2,\ \mathrm{E}[\varepsilon_i\varepsilon_j] = 0 \quad \text{for } i \neq j, \tag{14.4.9}$$

so that $\boldsymbol{\Psi} = \mathrm{diag}(\sigma_1^2, \sigma_2^2, \ldots, \sigma_n^2)$. In this specification $\boldsymbol{\alpha}$ is an $(m \times 1)$ vector of unknown parameters and $\mathbf{z}_{i\cdot}$ is a $(1 \times m)$ row vector of fixed and known explanatory variable values that determine the value of the noise component variance and that may be identical to, or functions of, $\mathbf{x}_{i\cdot}$.

The noise component covariance matrix implied by the characterization (14.4.8) and (14.4.9) is given by the diagonal matrix

$$\boldsymbol{\Psi}(\boldsymbol{\alpha}) = \begin{bmatrix} (\mathbf{z}_{1\cdot}\boldsymbol{\alpha})^2 & 0 & \cdots & 0 \\ 0 & (\mathbf{z}_{2\cdot}\boldsymbol{\alpha})^2 & & 0 \\ \vdots & & \ddots & \vdots \\ 0 & 0 & \cdots & (\mathbf{z}_{n\cdot}\boldsymbol{\alpha})^2 \end{bmatrix}. \tag{14.4.10}$$

If the value of $\boldsymbol{\alpha}$ is known, then the value of the covariance matrix $\boldsymbol{\Psi}(\boldsymbol{\alpha})$ is also known, and the GLS estimator $\hat{\beta} = [\mathbf{x}'\boldsymbol{\Psi}(\boldsymbol{\alpha})^{-1}\mathbf{x}]^{-1}\mathbf{x}'\boldsymbol{\Psi}(\boldsymbol{\alpha})^{-1}\mathbf{Y}$ can be used to estimate the parameter vector $\boldsymbol{\beta}$. The GLS estimator in this special case can also be represented as

$$\hat{\beta}_{\mathrm{G}} = \left[\sum_{i=1}^{n}(\mathbf{z}_{i\cdot}\boldsymbol{\alpha})^{-2}\mathbf{x}_{i\cdot}'\mathbf{x}_{i\cdot}\right]^{-1}\sum_{i=1}^{n}(\mathbf{z}_{i\cdot}\boldsymbol{\alpha})^{-2}\mathbf{x}_{i\cdot}\mathrm{Y}_i \tag{14.4.11}$$

This estimator has mean $\boldsymbol{\beta}$ and covariance $(\mathbf{x}'\boldsymbol{\Psi}^{-1}\mathbf{x})^{-1} = [\sum_{i=1}^{n}(\mathbf{z}_{i\cdot}\boldsymbol{\alpha})^{-2}\mathbf{x}_{i\cdot}'\mathbf{x}_{i\cdot}]^{-1}$ and is the BLUE of $\boldsymbol{\beta}$ as well as the MVUE under the normality assumption. Inference follows directly as outlined in Section 14.2.4. If $\boldsymbol{\alpha}$ is unknown, the GLS estimator (14.4.11) is not operational, and the parameter must be estimated and inserted into (14.4.11) in order for estimates to be generated. We examine this situation in Chapter 15.

14.4.3. General Considerations

The general approach to parametric modeling of the noise component covariance matrix of a probability model is analogous to the preceding illustrations. In particular, one begins by positing a parametric functional specification for the random process by which outcomes of the noise component come about. Next, the implications of this posited random process for the parametric structure of the noise covariance matrix are derived, and the parametric definition of the covariance matrix is established, as in (14.4.3) and (14.4.10). If the parameter values in the noise covariance matrix parameterization are known, then the covariance matrix of the noise component is known, and the GLS estimator $\hat{\boldsymbol{\beta}}_{\mathrm{G}}$ can be computed. If the values of the parameters in the noise covariance matrix definition are unknown, they need to be estimated to define an empirical approximation to $\hat{\boldsymbol{\beta}}_{\mathrm{G}}$.

14.5. Sets of Regression Equations

The current context of regression models with non-iid noise components is the appropriate place to introduce the concept of a DSP characterized by a *set* of regression equations and to analyze the inverse problem of recovering information on parameters contained within a set of equations. The set of equations may refer to a collection of demand functions for different commodities consumed by households in a particular market, a set of output supply and input demand functions characterizing the profit maximizing marginal decisions of various firms in an industry, or equations relating to consumption, savings, investment, exports, imports, and other measures of economic activity of a particular country.

In general, it is often unreasonable to presume a priori that all of the noise components across all of the equations in a set of regression equations exhibit precisely the same variance. Some of the dependent variables involved in the set may be inherently more variable than others, or some of the dependent variables may be measured on different scales or in different units of measurement. Further, some of the regression equations may, out of necessity, be specified more parsimoniously than others, relegating more of the variation in the dependent variable to the noise component. In any case, the GLS estimator is an appropriate estimation concept for accommodating heterogeneous noise component variability across equations.

Furthermore, it is possible that noise components may not be independent across regression equations. For example, in the case of a household that is making consumption decisions, it is reasonable to assume that stochastic elements affecting the consumption level of one good in a household's commodity bundle will influence the consumption of other goods. This may be true because overall household utility, and in particular marginal rates of substitution between goods, can be affected by the stochastic elements. Similarly, stochastic elements, uncertainty affecting the usage of a particular input by a firm, or both can affect the productivity, and in particular the marginal rates of substitution, between other inputs utilized in the production technology of a firm. Thus, it is possible for a set of input demand and output supply functions to be related through the noise components. The use of the GLS estimation approach can accommodate cross-equation noise component interdependence as well. Thinking in terms of a set of regression equations also permits us to consider other interesting issues such as pooling (aggregation over data sets) or imposition of cross-equation parameter restrictions.

14.5.1. Sets of Linear Equations

As a modeling innovation, Zellner (1962) introduced the idea of writing a set of m regression equations in the stacked or vertically concatenated form

$$\begin{bmatrix} \mathbf{Y}_1 \\ \mathbf{Y}_2 \\ \vdots \\ \mathbf{Y}_m \end{bmatrix} = \begin{bmatrix} \mathbf{x}_1 & & & \\ & \mathbf{x}_2 & & \\ & & \ddots & \\ & & & \mathbf{x}_m \end{bmatrix} \begin{bmatrix} \boldsymbol{\beta}_1 \\ \boldsymbol{\beta}_2 \\ \vdots \\ \boldsymbol{\beta}_m \end{bmatrix} + \begin{bmatrix} \varepsilon_1 \\ \varepsilon_2 \\ \vdots \\ \varepsilon_m \end{bmatrix} \tag{14.5.1}$$

or, more compactly, as

$$\mathbf{Y} = \mathbf{x}\boldsymbol{\beta} + \varepsilon, \tag{14.5.2}$$

where $\mathbf{Y}$ is a $(mn \times 1)$ vector of random variables representing the possible n sample observations on the m dependent variables; $\mathbf{x}$ is a block diagonal matrix of m explanatory variable matrices, each having dimension $(n \times k_i)$, where $i = 1, 2, \ldots, m$; and $\boldsymbol{\beta}$ is a $(\sum_{i=1}^{m} k_i \times 1)$ vector of unknown parameters (see also Srivastava and Giles (1987)). The $(nm \times 1)$ random vector ε is assumed to have mean vector zero and covariance matrix

$$\mathrm{E}[\varepsilon\varepsilon'] = \begin{bmatrix} \sigma_{11}\mathbf{I}_n & \sigma_{12}\mathbf{I}_n & \cdots & \sigma_{1\mathrm{m}}\mathbf{I}_n \\ \sigma_{21}\mathbf{I}_n & \sigma_{22}\mathbf{I}_n & \cdots & \sigma_{2\mathrm{m}}\mathbf{I}_n \\ \vdots & \vdots & \ddots & \vdots \\ \sigma_{\mathrm{m}1}\mathbf{I}_n & \sigma_{\mathrm{m}2}\mathbf{I}_n & \cdots & \sigma_{\mathrm{mm}}\mathbf{I}_n \end{bmatrix} = \boldsymbol{\Sigma} \otimes \mathbf{I}_n = \sigma^2\boldsymbol{\Psi} \tag{14.5.3}$$

where $\otimes$ denotes the Kronecker product (see the matrix review manual) and Σ is an $(m \times m)$ known positive definite symmetric matrix whose typical (i, j)th entry is given by σ_{ij}. Given a set of sample outcomes $\mathbf{y}$, and because the $(mn \times mn)$ positive definite symmetric matrix $\boldsymbol{\Sigma} \otimes \mathbf{I}_n$ is known under the current assumptions, we may, as in Section 14.2 for the single-equation linear regression model, choose $\mathbf{b}$ to minimize the weighted sum of square function

$$s_{\mathrm{G}}(\mathbf{b}) = (\mathbf{y} - \mathbf{x}\mathbf{b})'(\boldsymbol{\Sigma}^{-1} \otimes \mathbf{I}_n)(\mathbf{y} - \mathbf{x}\mathbf{b}) \tag{14.5.4}$$

(note that $(\mathbf{A} \otimes \mathbf{B})^{-1} = (\mathbf{A}^{-1} \otimes \mathbf{B}^{-1})$, and thus $(\boldsymbol{\Sigma} \otimes \mathbf{I})^{-1} = (\boldsymbol{\Sigma}^{-1} \otimes \mathbf{I})$. Forming the first-order conditions as in Section 14.2 and then solving for $\mathbf{b}$ yields the extremum estimates

$$\hat{\mathbf{b}}_{\mathrm{G}} = [\mathbf{x}'(\boldsymbol{\Sigma}^{-1} \otimes \mathbf{I}_n)\mathbf{x}]^{-1}\mathbf{x}'(\boldsymbol{\Sigma}^{-1} \otimes \mathbf{I}_n)\mathbf{y}, \tag{14.5.5}$$

which represents the Aitken or GLS estimates of the parameter vector $\boldsymbol{\beta}$. The covariance matrix of the GLS estimator $\hat{\boldsymbol{\beta}}_G$ is given by $[\mathbf{x}'(\boldsymbol{\Sigma}^{-1} \otimes \mathbf{I}_n)\mathbf{x}]^{-1}$. The finite sample and asymptotic properties of $\hat{\boldsymbol{\beta}}_G$ are identical to those of the linear regression model based on a known noise covariance matrix, as discussed in Section 14.2. It should be noted that when the explanatory variable matrices are such that $\mathbf{x}_1 = \mathbf{x}_2 = \cdots = \mathbf{x}_m$, or when $\boldsymbol{\Sigma}$ is diagonal so that the covariance matrix $\boldsymbol{\Psi}$ is block diagonal, the GLS estimator applied to (14.5.1) is algebraically identical to the GLS estimator applied separately to each of the m regression equations.

If we add to the DSP specification (14.5.1) the assumption that the noise component is multivariate normally distributed as $\boldsymbol{\varepsilon} \sim \mathrm{N}(\mathbf{0}, \boldsymbol{\Sigma} \otimes \mathbf{I}_n)$ and $\boldsymbol{\Sigma}$ is known, then the maximum likelihood procedures of Chapter 4 may be used to estimate $\boldsymbol{\beta}$. The ML estimator will be identical to the GLS estimator whose outcomes are given by (14.5.5), and in addition the sampling distribution of the estimator will be $\hat{\boldsymbol{\beta}}_G \sim \mathrm{N}(\boldsymbol{\beta}, [\mathbf{x}'(\boldsymbol{\Sigma}^{-1} \otimes \mathbf{I}_n)\mathbf{x}]^{-1})$. A test of the null hypothesis $\mathrm{H}_0\colon \mathbf{c}\boldsymbol{\beta} = \mathbf{r}$ can be based on the Wald statistic

$$\mathrm{W} = [\mathbf{c}\hat{\boldsymbol{\beta}}_G - \mathbf{r}]'[\mathbf{c}(\mathbf{x}'[\boldsymbol{\Sigma}^{-1} \otimes \mathbf{I}_n]\mathbf{x})\mathbf{c}']^{-1}[\mathbf{c}\hat{\boldsymbol{\beta}}_G - \mathbf{r}], \tag{14.5.6}$$

which has a central Chi-square distribution with j degrees of freedom when H_0 is true and when the $(j \times \sum_{i=1}^{m} k_i)$ matrix $\mathbf{c}$ has full-row rank. The critical region for the test is given by $\mathrm{C}^{\mathrm{w}} = [\chi^2_{1-\alpha}, \infty)$, where $\chi^2_{1-\alpha}$ is the $100(1-\alpha)\%$ quantile of the central Chi-square distribution having j degrees of freedom. The distribution of W is noncentral Chi-square with j degrees of freedom and noncentrality $\lambda = \frac{1}{2}\boldsymbol{\delta}'[\mathbf{c}[\mathbf{x}'(\boldsymbol{\Sigma}^{-1} \otimes \mathbf{I})\mathbf{x}]^{-1}\mathbf{c}']^{-1}\boldsymbol{\delta}$ when $\boldsymbol{\delta} = \mathbf{c}\boldsymbol{\beta} - \mathbf{r} \neq \mathbf{0}$; that is, when H_0 is not true.

Tests of scalar equality or inequality hypotheses relating to linear combinations of the elements in $\boldsymbol{\beta}$ can be based on the T-statistic

$$\mathrm{T} = \frac{\mathbf{c}\hat{\boldsymbol{\beta}}_G - \mathrm{r}}{[\mathbf{c}[\mathbf{x}'(\boldsymbol{\Sigma}^{-1} \otimes \mathbf{I}_n)\mathbf{x}]^{-1}\mathbf{c}']^{1/2}}. \tag{14.5.7}$$

Critical regions for the tests are precisely those indicated in (14.2.22). Confidence regions for $\mathbf{c}\boldsymbol{\beta}$ can be generated based on the confidence region estimates indicated in (14.2.23)–(14.2.25) except that $\mathrm{S}_G^2\mathbf{c}[\mathbf{x}'\boldsymbol{\Psi}^{-1}\mathbf{x}]^{-1}\mathbf{c}'$ would be replaced by $\mathbf{c}[\mathbf{x}'(\boldsymbol{\Sigma}^{-1} \otimes \mathbf{I}_n)\mathbf{x}]^{-1}\mathbf{c}'$. The LM and likelihood ratio test and confidence region procedures could be applied in the current context as well, mutatis mutandis.

Suppose one were to ignore that $\boldsymbol{\Sigma} \otimes \mathbf{I}_n \neq \sigma^2\mathbf{I}_{nm}$ and apply the standard LS estimator of Chapters 4 and 5 to the system of equations (14.5.1) under the tacit assumption that the covariance matrix of $\boldsymbol{\varepsilon}$ equals $\sigma^2\mathbf{I}_{nm}$. One would then obtain the individual equation-by-equation LS estimates of the $\boldsymbol{\beta}_i$'s, that is, $\hat{\mathbf{b}}_i = (\mathbf{x}_i'\mathbf{x}_i)^{-1}\mathbf{x}_i'\mathbf{y}_i$, for $i = 1, \ldots, m$. The sampling properties of the estimator then emulate the properties of the LS estimator discussed in Section 14.3.1. In particular, the estimator will be unbiased, consistent, and asymptotically normally distributed, the asymptotic distribution being given by

$$\hat{\boldsymbol{\beta}} \overset{a}{\sim} \mathrm{N}(\boldsymbol{\beta}, [\mathbf{x}'\mathbf{x}]^{-1}\mathbf{x}'(\boldsymbol{\Sigma} \otimes \mathbf{I})\mathbf{x}[\mathbf{x}'\mathbf{x}]^{-1}]. \tag{14.5.8}$$

If the noise component is multivariate normally distributed, then the LS estimator applied to 14.5.1 is multivariate normally distributed as well, but the $\hat{\boldsymbol{\beta}}_i$'s are generally neither MVUE nor asymptotically efficient. Tests and confidence regions can be generated in the usual way based on the asymptotic or finite sample normality of the least-squares estimator (see the discussion ahead for related information on this issue).

► **Example 14.5.1:** To compare the asymptotic properties and relative efficiency of the LS and GLS estimators in a set of linear equations when $\boldsymbol{\Psi} \neq \mathbf{I}$, we provide the GAUSS program C14SetGLS.gss in the examples manual. In the context of two simple linear regression models with contemporaneously correlated noise terms, GAUSS conducts a Monte Carlo exercise to simulate the moments and sampling distributions for the two estimators. Also, GAUSS presents box and whisker plots and the EDFs based on the replicated estimates to compare the sampling properties of the estimators. Finally, GAUSS reports the simulated relative efficiency of the estimators for a range of values for the contemporaneous correlation coefficient.

14.5.2. Sets of Nonlinear Equations

Sets of nonlinear regression functions can be estimated using the nonlinear generalized least-squares procedure. The m regression equations are represented in stacked or vertically concatenated form as

$$\begin{bmatrix} \mathbf{Y}_1 \\ \mathbf{Y}_2 \\ \vdots \\ \mathbf{Y}_m \end{bmatrix} = \begin{bmatrix} \mathbf{g}_1(\mathbf{x}_1, \boldsymbol{\beta}_1) \\ \mathbf{g}_2(\mathbf{x}_2, \boldsymbol{\beta}_2) \\ \vdots \\ \mathbf{g}_m(\mathbf{x}_m, \boldsymbol{\beta}_m) \end{bmatrix} + \begin{bmatrix} \varepsilon_1 \\ \varepsilon_2 \\ \vdots \\ \varepsilon_m \end{bmatrix} \tag{14.5.9}$$

or more compactly as

$$\mathbf{Y} = \mathbf{g}(\mathbf{x}, \boldsymbol{\beta}) + \varepsilon, \tag{14.5.10}$$

where $\mathbf{Y}$ is a $(mn \times 1)$ vector of random variables representing the possible mn sample observations on the m dependent variables, $\mathbf{x}_i$ is a $(n \times k_i)$ *matrix* of explanatory variables for $i = 1, \ldots, m$, $\boldsymbol{\beta}_i$ is a $(k_i \times 1)$ vector of parameters for $i = 1, \ldots, m$, $\boldsymbol{\beta} = (\boldsymbol{\beta}_1', \ldots, \boldsymbol{\beta}_m')'$, $\mathbf{g}_i(\mathbf{x}_i, \boldsymbol{\beta}_i)$ is the $(n \times 1)$ vector function representing the systematic component of the regression function for $\mathbf{Y}_i$, $\mathbf{g}(\mathbf{x}, \boldsymbol{\beta}) = [\mathbf{g}_1(\mathbf{x}_1, \boldsymbol{\beta}_1)', \ldots, \mathbf{g}_m(\mathbf{x}_m, \boldsymbol{\beta}_m)']'$ is the $(nm \times 1)$ vector representing the stacked systematic components across all equations, and ε_i is the $(n \times 1)$ noise component for the ith equation, $i = 1, \ldots, m$.

If the noise component covariance matrix is assumed to be given by (14.5.3), the NGLS estimate of $\boldsymbol{\beta}$ is found by choosing the value of $\mathbf{b}$ as

$$\hat{\mathbf{b}}_{\mathrm{G}} = \arg\min_{\mathbf{b}}[s_{\mathrm{G}}(\mathbf{b})] = \arg\min_{\mathbf{b}}[[\mathbf{y} - \mathbf{g}(\mathbf{x}, \mathbf{b})]'[\boldsymbol{\Sigma}^{-1} \otimes \mathbf{I}_n][\mathbf{y} - \mathbf{g}(\mathbf{x}, \mathbf{b})]]. \tag{14.5.11}$$

The associated estimator $\hat{\boldsymbol{\beta}}_{\mathrm{G}}$ has the same sampling properties that were attributed to the NGLS estimator based on a known noise covariance, as discussed in Section 14.3. In particular, $\hat{\boldsymbol{\beta}}_{\mathrm{G}}$ is consistent and asymptotically normally distributed. As in the case of the linear model, if $\boldsymbol{\Sigma}$ is diagonal so that the covariance matrix of the noise component is block diagonal, the NGLS estimator applied to (14.5.9) is identical to the NGLS estimator applied *separately* to each of the m regression equations.

If ε is multivariate normally distributed, then the ML estimator of $\boldsymbol{\beta}$ is identical to the NGLS estimator $\hat{\boldsymbol{\beta}}_{\mathrm{G}}$ and is asymptotically efficient. With or without normality, under general regularity conditions such as those discussed in Chapters 8, the asymptotic distribution of $\hat{\boldsymbol{\beta}}_{\mathrm{G}}$ can be specified as

$$\hat{\boldsymbol{\beta}}_{\mathrm{G}} \overset{a}{\sim} \mathrm{N}\left(\boldsymbol{\beta}, \left[\frac{\partial \mathbf{g}(\mathbf{x}, \boldsymbol{\beta})}{\partial \boldsymbol{\beta}}[\boldsymbol{\Sigma}^{-1} \otimes \mathbf{I}]\frac{\partial \mathbf{g}(\mathbf{x}, \boldsymbol{\beta})}{\partial \boldsymbol{\beta}'}\right]^{-1}\right). \tag{14.5.12}$$

A test of the null hypothesis H_0: $\mathbf{c}(\boldsymbol{\beta}) = \mathbf{r}$ can then be conducted using Wald, GLR, or LM procedures. For example, the Wald statistic is given by

$$\mathrm{W} = [\mathbf{c}(\hat{\boldsymbol{\beta}}_{\mathrm{G}}) - \mathbf{r}]'\left[\left.\frac{\partial \mathbf{c}(\boldsymbol{\beta})}{\partial \boldsymbol{\beta}'}\right|_{\hat{\boldsymbol{\beta}}_{\mathrm{G}}}\left[\left.\frac{\partial \mathbf{g}(\mathbf{x}, \boldsymbol{\beta})}{\partial \boldsymbol{\beta}}\right|_{\hat{\boldsymbol{\beta}}_{\mathrm{G}}}[\boldsymbol{\Sigma}^{-1} \otimes \mathbf{I}]\left.\frac{\partial \mathbf{g}(\mathbf{x}, \boldsymbol{\beta})}{\partial \boldsymbol{\beta}'}\right|_{\hat{\boldsymbol{\beta}}_{\mathrm{G}}}\right]^{-1}\left.\frac{\partial \mathbf{c}(\boldsymbol{\beta})}{\partial \boldsymbol{\beta}}\right|_{\hat{\boldsymbol{\beta}}_{\mathrm{G}}}\right]^{-1} \times [\mathbf{c}(\hat{\boldsymbol{\beta}}_{\mathrm{G}}) - \mathbf{r}], \tag{14.5.13}$$

and the critical region for an asymptotic level-α test is defined by $\mathrm{C}^{\mathrm{W}} = [\chi^2_{1-\alpha}, \infty)$, where $\chi^2_{1-\alpha}$ is the $100(1-\alpha)\%$ quantile of the central Chi-square distribution with j degrees of freedom. Asymptotically normal Z-statistics can be used to test equality or inequality hypotheses about the scalar $\mathrm{c}(\boldsymbol{\beta})$ as in (14.3.6) and (14.3.7), except the denominator in (14.3.6) would be replaced by the square root of the outer-most bracketed term in (14.5.13). Confidence regions, intervals, and bounds can be based on duality between the hypothesis-testing and confidence-region generation procedures, the details of which are by now familiar and are left to the reader.

If one were to ignore that $\boldsymbol{\Sigma} \otimes \mathbf{I}_n \neq \sigma^2 \mathbf{I}_{nm}$ and proceed to apply NLS to estimate $\boldsymbol{\beta}$ in (14.5.9), one would obtain the individual equation-by-equation NLS estimates of the $\boldsymbol{\beta}_i$'s that is, $\hat{\mathbf{b}}_i = \arg\min_{\mathbf{b}_i}[\mathbf{y}_i - \mathbf{g}_i(\mathbf{x}_i, \mathbf{b}_i)]'[\mathbf{y}_i - \mathbf{g}_i(\mathbf{x}_i, \mathbf{b}_i)]$, for $i = 1, \ldots, m$. The sampling properties of the estimator are then precisely the same as the properties discussed in Section 14.3, namely, consistency and asymptotic normality. The asymptotic normal distribution can be represented as

$$\hat{\boldsymbol{\beta}} \overset{a}{\sim} \mathrm{N}(\boldsymbol{\beta}, [\mathbf{x}(\boldsymbol{\beta})'\mathbf{x}(\boldsymbol{\beta})]^{-1}\mathbf{x}(\boldsymbol{\beta})'[\boldsymbol{\Sigma} \otimes \mathbf{I}]\mathbf{x}(\boldsymbol{\beta})[\mathbf{x}(\boldsymbol{\beta})'\mathbf{x}(\boldsymbol{\beta})]^{-1}), \tag{14.5.14}$$

where $\mathbf{x}(\boldsymbol{\beta}) \equiv \left[\frac{\partial \mathbf{g}(\mathbf{x}, \boldsymbol{\beta})}{\partial \boldsymbol{\beta}}\right]'$. However, as we noted before when the non-iid nature of the noise component was ignored, the ordinary least-squares estimator $\hat{\boldsymbol{\beta}}$ is not as asymptotically efficient as $\hat{\boldsymbol{\beta}}_{\mathrm{G}}$ or $\hat{\boldsymbol{\beta}}_{\mathrm{ML}}$, *if one assumes that* the structure of $\boldsymbol{\Psi}$ is correctly specified *and known*, so that $\hat{\boldsymbol{\beta}}_{\mathrm{G}}$ or $\hat{\boldsymbol{\beta}}_{\mathrm{ML}}$ exist.

Hypothesis-testing and confidence-region estimation can proceed asymptotically using the normal distribution result (14.5.14). For example, the analog to the Wald statistic in (14.5.13) would be

$$\mathrm{W} = [\mathbf{c}(\hat{\boldsymbol{\beta}}) - \mathbf{r}]'\left[\left.\frac{\partial \mathbf{c}(\boldsymbol{\beta})}{\partial \boldsymbol{\beta}'}\right|_{\hat{\boldsymbol{\beta}}} \boldsymbol{\Phi}^{-1}\left.\frac{\partial \mathbf{c}(\boldsymbol{\beta})}{\partial \boldsymbol{\beta}}\right|_{\hat{\boldsymbol{\beta}}}\right]^{-1}[\mathbf{c}(\hat{\boldsymbol{\beta}}) - \mathbf{r}] \tag{14.5.15}$$

where

$$\Phi = \left[\frac{\partial \mathbf{g}(\mathbf{x}, \boldsymbol{\beta})}{\partial \boldsymbol{\beta}} \bigg|_{\hat{\boldsymbol{\beta}}} \frac{\partial \mathbf{g}(\mathbf{x}, \boldsymbol{\beta})}{\partial \boldsymbol{\beta}'} \bigg|_{\hat{\boldsymbol{\beta}}} \right]^{-1} \left[\frac{\partial \mathbf{g}(\mathbf{x}, \boldsymbol{\beta})}{\partial \boldsymbol{\beta}} \bigg|_{\hat{\boldsymbol{\beta}}} [\boldsymbol{\Sigma} \otimes \mathbf{I}] \frac{\partial \mathbf{g}(\mathbf{x}, \boldsymbol{\beta})}{\partial \boldsymbol{\beta}'} \bigg|_{\hat{\boldsymbol{\beta}}} \right]$$
$$\times \left[\frac{\partial \mathbf{g}(\mathbf{x}, \boldsymbol{\beta})}{\partial \boldsymbol{\beta}} \bigg|_{\hat{\boldsymbol{\beta}}} \frac{\partial \mathbf{g}(\mathbf{x}, \boldsymbol{\beta})}{\partial \boldsymbol{\beta}'} \bigg|_{\hat{\boldsymbol{\beta}}} \right]^{-1}. \tag{14.5.16}$$

The critical region for an asymptotic level-α test would be given by $C^{w} = [\chi^2_{1-\alpha}, \infty)$ as before. Asymptotic Z-statistics could be defined similarly for testing inequality restrictions. Confidence region estimation would follow via duality with hypothesis-testing procedures.

► **Example 14.5.2:** To compare the asymptotic properties and relative efficiency of the NLS and NGLS estimators in a set of nonlinear equations when $\boldsymbol{\Psi} \neq \mathbf{I}$, we provide the GAUSS program C14SetNLS.gss in the examples manual. In the context of two simple nonlinear regression models with contemporaneously correlated noise terms, GAUSS conducts a Monte Carlo exercise to simulate the moments and sampling distributions for the two estimators. Also, GAUSS presents box and whisker plots and the EDFs based on the replicated estimates to compare the sampling properties of the estimators. Finally, GAUSS reports the simulated relative efficiency of the estimators for a range of values for the contemporaneous correlation coefficient.

14.6. The Estimating Equations – Quasi-Maximum Likelihood View: A Unified Approach

In this section, we reexamine, in the context of estimating equations, the inverse problem of recovering estimates of $\boldsymbol{\beta}$ and σ^2 from data observations on $(\mathbf{Y}, \mathbf{X})$ under the probability model conditions delineated in Table 14.1. We will see that the LS and ML solutions to the inverse problem discussed in preceding sections can all be subsumed under the estimating equations (EE) approach of Chapter 11 (Basawa, Godambe, and Taylor (1997)). In addition, we will generalize the ML procedure to a quasi-maximum likelihood (QML)–EE approach in which an estimator of $\boldsymbol{\beta}$ with potentially good finite sample and asymptotic sampling properties is available even if $\boldsymbol{\Psi}$ *is unknown.*

14.6.1. EE Estimation of $\boldsymbol{\beta}$ and σ^2 in the Linear Model When $\boldsymbol{\Psi}$ Is Known

We return to the case of the linear model $\mathbf{Y} = \mathbf{x}\boldsymbol{\beta} + \boldsymbol{\varepsilon}$ under the conditions of Table 14.1, so that $E[\boldsymbol{\varepsilon} \mid \mathbf{x}] = \mathbf{0}$ and $\mathbf{cov}(\boldsymbol{\varepsilon} \mid \mathbf{x}) = \sigma^2 \boldsymbol{\Psi}$, where $\boldsymbol{\Psi}$ is a known positive definite symmetric matrix. Consider the problem of finding the optimal linear unbiased estimating function

$$\mathbf{h}(\mathbf{Y}, \mathbf{x}, \boldsymbol{\beta}) = \boldsymbol{\eta}(\mathbf{x}, \boldsymbol{\beta})(\mathbf{Y} - \mathbf{x}\boldsymbol{\beta}) \tag{14.6.1}$$

for estimating the value of $\boldsymbol{\beta}$ (recall Equation (11.3.5) and the surrounding discussion) via a solution of the associated estimating equations as follows:

$$\hat{\boldsymbol{\beta}}_{\mathrm{EE}} = \arg_{\boldsymbol{\beta}}[\mathbf{h}(\mathbf{Y}, \mathbf{x}, \boldsymbol{\beta}) = \mathbf{0}]. \tag{14.6.2}$$

Recall that an unbiased estimating function is one for which $\mathrm{E}[\mathbf{h}(\mathbf{Y}, \mathbf{x}, \boldsymbol{\beta})] = \mathbf{0}$, and $\eta(\mathbf{x}, \boldsymbol{\beta})$ is a $(k \times n)$ matrix. Note that henceforth we will be operating conditionally on the outcome $\mathbf{x}$ of $\mathbf{X}$ if the explanatory variables are stochastic, and it is further assumed that $\mathbf{X}$ is either independent or contemporaneously uncorrelated with ε.

The optimal estimating function (OptEF) estimator of $\boldsymbol{\beta}$ in the class of estimators defined via the unbiased estimating functions–estimating equations (14.6.1) and (14.6.2) is given by the estimating function that minimizes the covariance matrix of the standardized estimating function (recall (11.3.18))

$$\mathbf{h}_{\mathrm{s}}(\mathbf{Y}, \mathbf{x}, \boldsymbol{\beta}) = \left[\mathrm{E}_{\mathbf{Y}}\left[\frac{\partial \mathbf{h}(\mathbf{Y}, \mathbf{x}, \boldsymbol{\beta})}{\partial \boldsymbol{\beta}}\right]\right]^{-1} \mathbf{h}(\mathbf{Y}, \mathbf{x}, \boldsymbol{\beta}). \tag{14.6.3}$$

In the case at hand, this covariance matrix is given by

$$\begin{aligned} \mathbf{cov}[\mathbf{h}_{\mathrm{s}}(\mathbf{Y}, \mathbf{x}, \boldsymbol{\beta})] &= \sigma^2\left(\mathrm{E}_{\mathbf{Y}}\left[\frac{\partial \mathbf{h}(\mathbf{Y}, \mathbf{x}, \boldsymbol{\beta})}{\partial \boldsymbol{\beta}}\right]\right)^{-1} \eta(\mathbf{x}, \boldsymbol{\beta})\boldsymbol{\Psi}\eta(\mathbf{x}, \boldsymbol{\beta})'\left(\mathrm{E}_{\mathbf{Y}}\left[\frac{\partial \mathbf{h}(\mathbf{Y}, \mathbf{x}, \boldsymbol{\beta})}{\partial \boldsymbol{\beta}'}\right]\right)^{-1} \\ &= \sigma^2[\mathbf{x}'\eta(\mathbf{x}, \boldsymbol{\beta})']^{-1}\eta(\mathbf{x}, \boldsymbol{\beta})\boldsymbol{\Psi}\eta(\mathbf{x}, \boldsymbol{\beta})'[\eta(\mathbf{x}, \boldsymbol{\beta})\mathbf{x}]^{-1}, \end{aligned} \tag{14.6.4}$$

and so the OptEF is defined by the choice of $\eta(\mathbf{x}, \boldsymbol{\beta})$ that minimizes (14.6.4). We know from the general proof following (11.4.7) that this optimal choice is given by $\eta_{\mathrm{opt}}(\mathbf{x}, \boldsymbol{\beta}) = \mathbf{x}'(\sigma^2\boldsymbol{\Psi})^{-1}$. Then the OptEF is

$$\mathbf{h}_{\mathrm{opt}}(\mathbf{Y}, \mathbf{x}, \boldsymbol{\beta}) = \mathbf{x}'(\sigma^2\boldsymbol{\Psi})^{-1}(\mathbf{Y} - \mathbf{x}\boldsymbol{\beta}), \tag{14.6.5}$$

in which case the OptEF estimator defined by an application of (14.6.2) to the estimating function $\mathbf{h}_{\mathrm{opt}}(\mathbf{Y}, \mathbf{x}, \boldsymbol{\beta})$ is given by

$$\hat{\boldsymbol{\beta}}_{\mathrm{EE}} = \arg_{\boldsymbol{\beta}}[\mathbf{h}_{\mathrm{opt}}(\mathbf{Y}, \mathbf{x}, \boldsymbol{\beta}) = \mathbf{0}] = (\mathbf{x}'\boldsymbol{\Psi}^{-1}\mathbf{x})^{-1}\mathbf{x}'\boldsymbol{\Psi}^{-1}\mathbf{Y}. \tag{14.6.6}$$

Thus, the OptEF estimator coincides with the GLS estimator $\hat{\boldsymbol{\beta}}_{\mathrm{G}}$ as well as the ML estimator $\hat{\boldsymbol{\beta}}_{\mathrm{ML}}$ under conditional normality for $(\mathbf{Y} \mid \mathbf{x})$. Therefore, in addition to being derived from the best linear unbiased estimating function, $\hat{\boldsymbol{\beta}}_{\mathrm{EE}}$ also shares all of the sampling properties attributed to the GLS and ML estimators.

Note that the asymptotic properties of the EE estimator could also have been established via an appeal to the theorems in Section 11.3 relating to consistency, asymptotic normality, and efficiency upon scaling of the estimating function by n^{-1}. Note further that the inference procedures relating to EE estimators can be applied in the current situation, which then transfers these EE inference results to the GLS and ML contexts as well. We emphasize that in the current situation, a different covariance matrix estimator $\hat{\mathrm{E}}[\mathbf{h}(\mathbf{Y}, \mathbf{x}, \boldsymbol{\beta})\mathbf{h}(\mathbf{Y}, \mathbf{x}, \boldsymbol{\beta})']$ from that indicated previously in Section 11.3 will be required in the test statistic formulas because of the heteroscedasticity, autocorrelation, or both represented by $\boldsymbol{\Psi}$. Noting that

$$\begin{aligned}\mathrm{E}[\mathbf{h}(\mathbf{Y},\mathbf{x},\boldsymbol{\beta})\mathbf{h}(\mathbf{Y},\mathbf{x},\boldsymbol{\beta})'] &= \mathbf{x}'(\sigma^2\boldsymbol{\Psi})^{-1}\mathrm{E}[(\mathbf{Y}-\mathbf{x}\boldsymbol{\beta})(\mathbf{Y}-\mathbf{x}\boldsymbol{\beta})'](\sigma^2\boldsymbol{\Psi})^{-1}\mathbf{x} \\ &= \mathbf{x}'(\sigma^2\boldsymbol{\Psi})^{-1}\mathbf{x}, \end{aligned} \quad (14.6.7)$$

one could use the unbiased estimator S_G^2 defined in (14.2.14) to estimate the unknown σ^2 in (14.6.7), leading to the covariance matrix estimator

$$\hat{\mathrm{E}}[\mathbf{h}(\mathbf{Y},\mathbf{x},\boldsymbol{\beta})\mathbf{h}(\mathbf{Y},\mathbf{x},\boldsymbol{\beta})'] = \mathbf{x}'\left(S_G^2\boldsymbol{\Psi}\right)^{-1}\mathbf{x} \quad (14.6.8)$$

for use in the test statistic and confidence region estimator procedures.

14.6.2. EE Estimation of $\boldsymbol{\beta}$ and σ^2 in the Nonlinear Model When $\boldsymbol{\Psi}$ Is Known

We now examine the case of the nonlinear model $\mathbf{Y} = \mathbf{g}(\mathbf{x},\boldsymbol{\beta}) + \varepsilon$ under the conditions of Table 14.1, where again $\mathrm{E}[\varepsilon \mid \mathbf{x}] = \mathbf{0}$, $\mathbf{cov}(\varepsilon \mid \mathbf{x}) = \sigma^2\boldsymbol{\Psi}$, and $\boldsymbol{\Psi}$ is a known positive definite symmetric matrix. Consider the problem of finding the optimal linear unbiased estimating function

$$\mathbf{h}(\mathbf{Y},\mathbf{x},\boldsymbol{\beta}) = \boldsymbol{\eta}(\mathbf{x},\boldsymbol{\beta})(\mathbf{Y} - \mathbf{g}(\mathbf{x},\boldsymbol{\beta})) \quad (14.6.9)$$

for estimating the value of $\boldsymbol{\beta}$.

The optimal estimating function (OptEF) estimator of $\boldsymbol{\beta}$ in the class of estimators defined via the unbiased estimating function (14.6.9) is again the estimating function that minimizes the covariance matrix of the standardized estimating function (14.6.3). In this case the covariance matrix is given by

$$\mathbf{cov}[\mathbf{h}_s(\mathbf{Y},\mathbf{x},\boldsymbol{\beta})] = \sigma^2\left[\frac{\partial\mathbf{g}(\mathbf{x},\boldsymbol{\beta})}{\partial\boldsymbol{\beta}}\boldsymbol{\eta}(\mathbf{x},\boldsymbol{\beta})'\right]^{-1}\boldsymbol{\eta}(\mathbf{x},\boldsymbol{\beta})\boldsymbol{\Psi}\boldsymbol{\eta}(\mathbf{x},\boldsymbol{\beta})'\left[\boldsymbol{\eta}(\mathbf{x},\boldsymbol{\beta})\frac{\partial\mathbf{g}(\mathbf{x},\boldsymbol{\beta})}{\partial\boldsymbol{\beta}'}\right]^{-1}, \quad (14.6.10)$$

and so the OptEF is defined by the choice of $\boldsymbol{\eta}(\mathbf{x},\boldsymbol{\beta})$ that minimizes (14.6.10). We again know from the general proof following (11.4.7) that the optimal $\boldsymbol{\eta}(\mathbf{x},\boldsymbol{\beta})$ is given by $\boldsymbol{\eta}_{\mathrm{opt}}(\mathbf{x},\boldsymbol{\beta}) = \frac{\partial\mathbf{g}(\mathbf{x},\boldsymbol{\beta})}{\partial\boldsymbol{\beta}}(\sigma^2\boldsymbol{\Psi})^{-1}$. Then the OptEF is

$$\mathbf{h}_{\mathrm{opt}}(\mathbf{Y},\mathbf{x},\boldsymbol{\beta}) = \frac{\partial\mathbf{g}(\mathbf{x},\boldsymbol{\beta})}{\partial\boldsymbol{\beta}}(\sigma^2\boldsymbol{\Psi})^{-1}[\mathbf{Y} - \mathbf{g}(\mathbf{x},\boldsymbol{\beta})], \quad (14.6.11)$$

in which case the OptEF estimator defined by an application of (14.6.2) to the estimating function $\mathbf{h}_{\mathrm{opt}}(\mathbf{Y},\mathbf{x},\boldsymbol{\beta})$ is given by

$$\hat{\boldsymbol{\beta}}_{\mathrm{EE}} = \arg_\beta[\mathbf{h}_{\mathrm{opt}}(\mathbf{Y},\mathbf{x},\boldsymbol{\beta}) = \mathbf{0}] = \arg\min_\beta[[\mathbf{Y} - \mathbf{g}(\mathbf{x},\boldsymbol{\beta})]'\boldsymbol{\Psi}^{-1}[\mathbf{Y} - \mathbf{g}(\mathbf{x},\boldsymbol{\beta})]] = \hat{\boldsymbol{\beta}}_{\mathrm{G}}, \quad (14.6.12)$$

where now $\hat{\boldsymbol{\beta}}_{\mathrm{G}}$ is the *nonlinear* GLS estimator of Section 14.3 because (14.6.11) is proportional to the first-order conditions for minimizing the quadratic form in brackets in (14.6.12). Thus, the OptEF estimator coincides with the nonlinear GLS estimator $\hat{\boldsymbol{\beta}}_{\mathrm{G}}$ as well as the nonlinear ML estimator $\hat{\boldsymbol{\beta}}_{\mathrm{ML}}$ under conditional normality for $(\mathbf{Y} \mid \mathbf{x})$. Therefore, in addition to being derived from the best linear unbiased estimating function,

$\hat{\boldsymbol{\beta}}_{\text{EE}}$ also shares all of the sampling properties attributed to the nonlinear GLS and ML estimators.

As we noted in the previous subsection relating to linear models, the asymptotic properties of the EE estimator could have also been established via an appeal to the Theorems in Section 11.3 relating to consistency, asymptotic normality, and efficiency upon scaling of the estimating function by n^{-1}. Also the inference procedures relating to EE estimators can be applied in the current situation, which again transfers these EE inference results to the nonlinear GLS and ML contexts. As in the linear model case, a different covariance matrix estimator $\hat{\text{E}}[\mathbf{h}(\mathbf{Y}, \mathbf{x}, \boldsymbol{\beta})\mathbf{h}(\mathbf{Y}, \mathbf{x}, \boldsymbol{\beta})']$ from that indicated previously in Section 11.3 will be required in the test statistic formulas because of the heteroscedasticity, autocorrelation, or both represented by $\boldsymbol{\Psi}$. Noting that

$$\begin{aligned}\text{E}[\mathbf{h}(\mathbf{Y}, \mathbf{x},\boldsymbol{\beta})\mathbf{h}(\mathbf{Y}, \mathbf{x},\boldsymbol{\beta})'] &= \frac{\partial \mathbf{g}(\mathbf{x},\boldsymbol{\beta})}{\partial \boldsymbol{\beta}}(\sigma^2\boldsymbol{\Psi})^{-1}\text{E}[[\mathbf{Y} - \mathbf{g}(\mathbf{x},\boldsymbol{\beta})] \\ &\quad \times [\mathbf{Y} - \mathbf{g}(\mathbf{x}, \boldsymbol{\beta})]'](\sigma^2\boldsymbol{\Psi})^{-1}\frac{\partial \mathbf{g}(\mathbf{x},\boldsymbol{\beta})}{\partial \boldsymbol{\beta}'} \\ &= \frac{\partial \mathbf{g}(\mathbf{x},\boldsymbol{\beta})}{\partial \boldsymbol{\beta}}(\sigma^2\boldsymbol{\Psi})^{-1}\frac{\partial \mathbf{g}(\mathbf{x},\boldsymbol{\beta})}{\partial \boldsymbol{\beta}'},\end{aligned} \tag{14.6.13}$$

one could use the consistent estimator S^2_{G} defined in (14.3.4) to estimate the unknown σ^2 in (14.6.13), leading to the covariance matrix estimator

$$\hat{\text{E}}[\mathbf{h}(\mathbf{Y}, \mathbf{x}, \boldsymbol{\beta})\mathbf{h}(\mathbf{Y}, \mathbf{x}, \boldsymbol{\beta})'] = \left.\frac{\partial \mathbf{g}(\mathbf{x}, \boldsymbol{\beta})}{\partial \boldsymbol{\beta}}\right|_{\hat{\boldsymbol{\beta}}_{\text{G}}} \left(\text{S}^2_{\text{G}}\boldsymbol{\Psi}\right)^{-1} \left.\frac{\partial \mathbf{g}(\mathbf{x}, \boldsymbol{\beta})}{\partial \boldsymbol{\beta}'}\right|_{\hat{\boldsymbol{\beta}}_{G}} \tag{14.6.14}$$

for use in the test statistic and confidence-region estimator procedures.

14.6.3. EE Estimation of $\boldsymbol{\beta}$ and σ^2 in the Linear or Nonlinear Normal Parametric Regression Model When $\boldsymbol{\Psi}$ Is Known

Now revisit the case where the regression model is fully parametrically specified such that the conditions of Table 14.1 apply with $(\mathbf{Y} \mid \mathbf{x}) \sim \text{N}(\mathbf{0}, \sigma^2\boldsymbol{\Psi})$, where $\boldsymbol{\Psi}$ is a known positive definite symmetric matrix. We know that in the case of a fully specified likelihood function, the OptEF is given directly by the gradient of the log of the likelihood function with respect to the parameters (recall Section 11.3.2.c), as

$$\mathbf{h}_{\text{opt}}(\mathbf{Y}, \mathbf{x}, \boldsymbol{\theta}) = \frac{\partial \ln \mathbf{L}(\boldsymbol{\theta}; \mathbf{Y}, \mathbf{x})}{\partial \boldsymbol{\theta}}, \tag{14.6.15}$$

where in the case at hand $\boldsymbol{\theta} = \left[\begin{smallmatrix}\boldsymbol{\beta} \\ \sigma^2\end{smallmatrix}\right]$. It is apparent that when the likelihood function is based on the preceding normal distribution, the OptEF estimator defined via an application of (14.6.2) to (14.6.15) yields an estimator that is equivalent to either the linear GLS–ML or nonlinear GLS–ML estimator of $\boldsymbol{\theta}$. The OptEF estimator thus shares all of the sampling properties and inference procedures relating to the GLS–ML estimators, and vice versa, and the related discussion of the preceding two subsections applies. In addition, note that the optimality of the current OptEF estimator is relative to the *entire* class of unbiased estimating functions and is not restricted to the *linear* unbiased class. Recall that this result relates to the finite sample optimality property of the ML–EE estimator discussed in Section 11.3.2.c.

14.6.4. QML–EE Estimation of $\boldsymbol{\beta}$ and σ^2 in the Linear or Nonlinear Regression Model

To this point in the chapter, we have assumed that the value of $\boldsymbol{\Psi}$ is known. The EE approach can proceed even if $\boldsymbol{\Psi}$ is unknown, albeit at the cost of greater imprecision in the EE estimator compared with an EE estimator based on the true value of $\boldsymbol{\Psi}$. We emphasize that this loss of efficiency may be lamentable but largely unavoidable in practice. If $\boldsymbol{\Psi}$ is unknown, the additional efficiency gain is an ideal goal, but the EE based on it is unobservable.

14.6.4.a. Linear Models

We return to the linear model case of Section 14.6.1 and consider the class of linear unbiased estimating function given by

$$\mathbf{h}(\mathbf{Y}, \mathbf{x}, \boldsymbol{\beta}) = \mathbf{x}'\boldsymbol{\Gamma}^{-1}(\mathbf{Y} - \mathbf{x}\boldsymbol{\beta}), \tag{14.6.16}$$

where $\boldsymbol{\Gamma}$ is *any* known symmetric positive definite matrix (compare with (14.6.5)). The matrix $\boldsymbol{\Gamma}$ can represent some approximation or guess relating to the covariance matrix of the noise component of the regression model, but this is not a necessary condition. Defining the EE estimator using (14.6.2) applied to the estimating function (14.6.16) yields

$$\hat{\boldsymbol{\beta}}_{\text{EE}} = \arg_{\boldsymbol{\beta}}[\mathbf{h}(\mathbf{Y}, \mathbf{x}, \boldsymbol{\beta}) = \mathbf{0}] = (\mathbf{x}'\boldsymbol{\Gamma}^{-1}\mathbf{x})^{-1}\mathbf{x}'\boldsymbol{\Gamma}^{-1}\mathbf{Y}, \tag{14.6.17}$$

which is unbiased, consistent, and asymptotically normally distributed as

$$\hat{\boldsymbol{\beta}}_{\text{EE}} \overset{a}{\sim} \text{N}(\boldsymbol{\beta}, \sigma^2[(\mathbf{x}'\boldsymbol{\Gamma}^{-1}\mathbf{x})^{-1}\mathbf{x}'\boldsymbol{\Gamma}^{-1}\boldsymbol{\Psi}\boldsymbol{\Gamma}^{-1}\mathbf{x}(\mathbf{x}'\boldsymbol{\Gamma}^{-1}\mathbf{x})^{-1}]) \tag{14.6.18}$$

(recall Theorem 11.3.2)). The OptEF estimator of $\boldsymbol{\beta}$ is subsumed by (14.6.17) and (14.6.18) when $\boldsymbol{\Gamma}$ is set equal to $\boldsymbol{\Psi}$.

Note that the EE estimator can be interpreted as a QML estimator derived from a multivariate normal specification for the probability distribution of $\mathbf{Y} = \mathbf{x}\boldsymbol{\beta} + \boldsymbol{\varepsilon}$ given by $\text{N}(\mathbf{x}\boldsymbol{\beta}, \boldsymbol{\Gamma})$. This interpretation follows because (14.6.16) is proportional to the first-order conditions for maximizing, with respect to $\boldsymbol{\beta}$, the likelihood function associated with $\text{N}(\mathbf{x}\boldsymbol{\beta}, \boldsymbol{\Gamma})$. The problem is a QML–EE problem of order 1 (recall Section 11.2) applied to the case of potentially nonindependent sample observations. Note White (1994, corollary 5.5, theorem 6.4) extended the work of Gourieroux et al. (1984) and demonstrated that the consistency and asymptotic normality of the order 1 QML–EE estimator follows even when the noise component is autocorrelated, heteroscedastic, or both. Having identified a genuine likelihood function to which the estimating function (14.6.16) refers, we can reverse the direction of association from first-order conditions to likelihood and note that the estimator (14.6.17) can be interpreted as a QML–E (Quasi-Maximum

Likelihood-Extremum) estimator based on the maximization of a misspecified normal likelihood $N(\mathbf{x}\boldsymbol{\beta}, \boldsymbol{\Gamma})$ (as opposed to a "true" likelihood based on $N(\mathbf{x}\boldsymbol{\beta}, \sigma^2\boldsymbol{\Psi})$). Of course, despite the misspecification, this QML–E estimator has all of the aforementioned finite and asymptotic sampling properties identified heretofore.

The asymptotic normality of the EE estimator can be used in the usual way to define hypothesis-testing and confidence-region estimation procedures relating to the value of functions of $\boldsymbol{\beta}$. The procedures identified in Section 11.3 for EE estimators can be adapted to the current situation, but a difficulty in practice is the definition of a consistent estimate of the asymptotic covariance matrix in (14.6.18). Note that when $\boldsymbol{\Psi}$ is unknown, the difficulty is in estimating the value of $\sigma^2(\mathbf{x}'\boldsymbol{\Gamma}^{-1}\boldsymbol{\Psi}\boldsymbol{\Gamma}^{-1}\mathbf{x})$ – the value of $(\mathbf{x}'\boldsymbol{\Gamma}^{-1}\mathbf{x})^{-1}$ is known and need not be estimated. A closely related issue is defining a consistent estimator $\hat{\mathrm{E}}[\mathbf{h}(\mathbf{Y}, \mathbf{x}, \boldsymbol{\beta})\mathbf{h}(\mathbf{Y}, \mathbf{x}, \boldsymbol{\beta})']$ of the covariance matrix

$$\mathrm{E}[\mathbf{h}(\mathbf{Y}, \mathbf{x}, \boldsymbol{\beta})\mathbf{h}(\mathbf{Y}, \mathbf{x}, \boldsymbol{\beta})'] = \sigma^2(\mathbf{x}'\boldsymbol{\Gamma}^{-1}\boldsymbol{\Psi}\boldsymbol{\Gamma}^{-1}\mathbf{x}) = (\mathbf{x}_*'(\sigma^2\boldsymbol{\Psi})\mathbf{x}_*) \tag{14.6.19}$$

of the estimating function (14.6.16) to use in the inference procedures of Section 11.3, where $\mathbf{x}_* \equiv \boldsymbol{\Gamma}^{-1}\mathbf{x}$. Such an estimator can be defined using a procedure introduced by White (1980) and by Newey and West (1987) in the context of heteroscedastic and autocorrelation robust estimators of covariance matrices and will be discussed in Chapter 15.

14.6.4.b. Nonlinear Models

The preceding discussion of QML–EE estimation can readily be extended to the case of nonlinear regression models. The class of linear (in $\mathbf{Y}$) unbiased estimating functions is now characterized by

$$\mathbf{h}(\mathbf{Y}, \mathbf{x}, \boldsymbol{\beta}) = \frac{\partial \mathbf{g}(\mathbf{x}, \boldsymbol{\beta})}{\partial \boldsymbol{\beta}}\boldsymbol{\Gamma}^{-1}[\mathbf{Y} - \mathbf{g}(\mathbf{x}, \boldsymbol{\beta})]. \tag{14.6.20}$$

The EE estimator is then defined by

$$\hat{\boldsymbol{\beta}}_{\mathrm{EE}} = \arg_{\boldsymbol{\beta}}[\mathbf{h}(\mathbf{Y}, \mathbf{x}, \boldsymbol{\beta}) = \mathbf{0}] = \arg\min_{\boldsymbol{\beta}}[[\mathbf{Y} - \mathbf{g}(\mathbf{x}, \boldsymbol{\beta})]'\boldsymbol{\Gamma}^{-1}[\mathbf{Y} - \mathbf{g}(\mathbf{x}, \boldsymbol{\beta})]], \tag{14.6.21}$$

which can be interpreted as a weighted nonlinear least-squares estimator using the known $\boldsymbol{\Gamma}^{-1}$ matrix as the weighting matrix. On the basis of either general results relating to EE estimators (Chapter 11) or extremum estimators (Chapter 7), one can establish that the EE estimator in (14.6.21) is consistent and asymptotically normally distributed. In fact, Equation (14.6.18) and the remaining discussion in the preceding section relating to sampling properties and inference procedures for the EE estimator apply to the current nonlinear model context upon replacement of $\mathbf{x}$ with $\frac{\partial \mathbf{g}(\mathbf{x}, \boldsymbol{\beta})}{\partial \boldsymbol{\beta}'}$ and $\mathbf{x}\boldsymbol{\beta}$ with $\mathbf{g}(\mathbf{x}, \boldsymbol{\beta})$.

14.6.5. EE Estimation of $\boldsymbol{\beta}$ and σ^2 in Systems of Regression Equations

The EE and QML–EE procedures of Sections 14.6.1–14.6.5 can also be readily extended to encompass the problem of estimating the parameters in a system of regression equations like those of Section 14.5. The extension introduces no new difficulties once the system is expressed in stacked or vertically concatenated form, as in (14.5.1) and (14.5.2) in the linear model case or (14.5.9) and (14.5.10) in the nonlinear case, and it is recognized that the covariance matrix of $(\mathbf{Y} \mid \mathbf{x})$ is now given by $\sigma^2 \boldsymbol{\Psi} \equiv \boldsymbol{\Sigma} \otimes \mathbf{I}_n$.

For example, the optimal unbiased estimating function for the system of linear regression equations, analogous to (14.6.5) for the single-equation linear model, is given by

$$\mathbf{h}_{\text{opt}}(\mathbf{Y}, \mathbf{x}, \boldsymbol{\beta}) = \mathbf{x}'(\boldsymbol{\Sigma}^{-1} \otimes \mathbf{I}_n)(\mathbf{Y} - \mathbf{x}\boldsymbol{\beta}), \tag{14.6.22}$$

where $\mathbf{Y}$ and $\mathbf{x}$ are now defined as they were in Section 14.5. Applying (14.6.2) to the optimal linear unbiased estimating function (14.6.22) yields the OptEF estimator

$$\hat{\boldsymbol{\beta}}_{\text{EE}} = [\mathbf{x}'(\boldsymbol{\Sigma}^{-1} \otimes \mathbf{I}_n)\mathbf{x}]^{-1}\mathbf{x}'(\boldsymbol{\Sigma}^{-1} \otimes \mathbf{I}_n)\mathbf{Y}, \tag{14.6.23}$$

which is identical to the seemingly unrelated regression estimator represented by (14.5.5). Thus the EE and seemingly unrelated regression (SUR) estimators share identical sampling properties and inference procedures.

Analogous extensions to nonlinear systems, parametric normal-based systems, and QML–EE interpretations of the systems estimators can be generated directly by utilizing the stacked form of the equation system, and associated covariance matrix of $(\mathbf{Y} \mid \mathbf{x})$, in the arguments presented in previous sections. The details are left to the reader.

14.7. Some Comments

Removing the iid or the identical first and second moment assumption, or both, relative to the equation noise process in the regression model raises many interesting statistical problems that, over time, have inspired some creative solutions. In this chapter we have recognized the possibility of a general known noise covariance matrix being consistent with our state of knowledge relative to the data-sampling process. Assuming that the noise covariance is some *known* positive definite symmetric matrix allows us to define a transformed regression model consistent with the probability model formulations examined in previous chapters. Thus, an auxiliary benefit of this chapter is that by working with the transformed probability model we are provided with a review of the estimation and inference procedures developed in previous chapters while extending the reach of these procedures to dependent noise components and systems of regression equations.

The results in Section 14.6 demonstrate that all of the procedures used to solve the inverse problem of estimating the unknown parameters of regression models in the case in which the covariance matrix $(\mathbf{Y} \mid \mathbf{x})$ is given by the known matrix $\boldsymbol{\Psi} \neq \sigma^2\mathbf{I}$ are subsumed by the estimating equation approach to estimation and inference. It was also shown that the EE approach can be used to produce useful estimation and inference procedures even when $\boldsymbol{\Psi}$ is unknown. We will see that the EE approach continues to be a unifying theme in the specification of most other estimator and inference procedures in subsequent chapters and suggests that the motivation for the large majority of estimators used in practice may be rooted in a common EE theory of estimation and inference.

We are also now better equipped for dealing with the harder problem characterized by an unknown noise covariance matrix. In Chapter 15 we recognize that in many probability models specified to represent the state of knowledge about economic processes normally found in practice, the elements of the noise covariance matrix are unknown. Consequently, we may be faced with the ill-posed, underdetermined inverse problem of trying to recover information on a total of $k + n(n + 1)/2$ unknown $\boldsymbol{\beta}$ and noise covariance matrix parameters from only n data observations. We turn next to the topic of methods for solving this underdetermined inverse problem.

14.8. Exercises

14.8.1. Idea Checklist – Knowledge Guides

---

1. What are some of the characteristics of economic data that may lead to autocorrelated noise components? What are some of the characteristics of economic data that may aid in specifying the order of the process?
2. What are some of the characteristics of economic data that may lead to heteroscedastic noise components? How may this information be used in specifying the heteroscedastic process?
3. What are some of the changes that occur in a DSP when leaving the world of iid noise components?
4. What is the impact of non-iid noise components on the chance for incorrectly specifying the econometric model? What are the statistical consequences of these misspecifications?
5. What are the benefits and costs of ignoring the general covariance structure of a noise-sampling process and always assuming that $\mathbf{cov}(\varepsilon) = \sigma^2\mathbf{I}$?

14.8.2. Problems

14–1 Demonstrate, under the noise specification $\varepsilon \sim (\mathbf{0}, \sigma^2\boldsymbol{\Psi})$ that the estimator $\hat{\boldsymbol{\beta}} = (\mathbf{x}'\boldsymbol{\Psi}^{-1}\mathbf{x})^{-1}\mathbf{x}'\boldsymbol{\Psi}^{-1}\mathbf{Y}$ is a BLUE. Relate this to the problem of *incorrectly* assuming $\varepsilon \sim (\mathbf{0}, \sigma^2\mathbf{I}_n)$.

14–2 Develop the mean and covariance of a first-order autoregressive noise generation process.

14–3 Demonstrate, under the assumption $\varepsilon \sim \mathrm{N}(\mathbf{0}, \sigma^2\boldsymbol{\Psi})$, that $\varepsilon'\boldsymbol{\Psi}^{-1}\mathbf{x}(\mathbf{x}'\boldsymbol{\Psi}^{-1}\mathbf{x})^{-1}\mathbf{x}'\boldsymbol{\Psi}^{-1}\varepsilon/\sigma^2$ is distributed as a Chi-square$(k, 0)$ random variable.

14–4 On the assumption that $\boldsymbol{\Psi}$ is known, develop a best linear unbiased predictor of E[**Y**] and the corresponding covariance matrix of the prediction error matrix.

14–5 Demonstrate, in the case of sets of regression equations, that when $\mathbf{x}_1 = \mathbf{x}_2 = \cdots = \mathbf{x}_m$ or when $\boldsymbol{\Sigma}$ is diagonal so that the covariance matrix of the noise component is block diagonal the single-equation GLS estimator is BLUE.

14.8.3. Computer Exercises

---

1. Write a GAUSS program to simulate the statistical properties of the biased and bias-corrected estimators of σ^2 discussed in Section 14.1.1. How well does the bias-correction factor perform in the statistical model you specify?
2. Using a model based on Table 14.1, conduct a Monte Carlo exercise designed to compare the statistical properties of the hypothesis-test and confidence-region procedures presented in Section 14.2.4 when based on the LS and GLS estimators. (Hint: Use the GAUSS program C15GLS.gss as a guide.) In particular, do the tests and confidence regions based on the LS estimator exhibit the intended size or coverage probabilities? What about the inferential methods based on the GLS estimator?
3. For Theil's consumption data discussed in Chapter 6, assume the model is characterized by the autocorrelated noise process (14.4.1)–(14.4.3) with $\rho = 0.5$. Compute the GLS estimates of $\boldsymbol{\beta}$ and σ^2 and repeat the hypothesis tests conducted in Chapter 6 (Computer Exercise 2). How do the results compare with the results based on the unadjusted LS estimator?

14.9. References

Aitken, A. C. (1935),"On Least Squares and Linear Combination of Observations." *Proceedings of the Royal Society of Edinburgh*, Vol. 55, pp. 42–8.

Basawa, I. V., V. P. Godambe, and R. L. Taylor (1997), *Selected Proceedings of the Symposium on Estimating Equations*, Institute of Mathematical Statistics, Hayward, CA.

Gourieroux, C., A. Monfort, and A. Trognon (1984), "Pseudo-Maximum Likelihood Methods: Theory," *Econometrica*, Vol. 52, pp. 681–700.

Mittelhammer, R. (1996), *Mathematical Statistics for Economics and Business*, New York: Springer–Verlag.

Newey, W. K., and K. D. West (1987), "A Simple, Positive Semi-Definite, Heteroscedasticity and Autocorrelation Consistent Covariance Matrix," *Econometrica*, Vol. 55, pp. 703–8.

Srivastava, V. K., and D. E. Giles (1987), *Seemingly Unrelated Regression Models*, New York: Marcel Dekker.

White, H. (1980), "A Heteroscedasticity-Consistent Covariance Matrix Estimator and a Direct Test for Heteroscedasticity," *Econometrica*, Vol. 48, pp. 817–38.

White, H. (1984). *Asymptotic Theory for Econometricians*, Orlando, FL: Academic Press.

White, H. (1994), *Estimation, Inference and Specification Analysis*, New York: Cambridge University Press.

Zellner, A. (1962), "An Efficient Method of Estimating Seemingly Unrelated Regressions and Tests of Aggregation Bias," *Journal of the American Statistical Association*, Vol 57, pp. 348–68.

CHAPTER 15

Regression Models with an Unknown General Noise Covariance Matrix

IN this chapter, we recognize that the $\boldsymbol{\Psi}$ component of the covariance matrix $\sigma^2\boldsymbol{\Psi}$ may be unknown when we state our knowledge about a data sampling process through the specification of a probability model. Thus, except for the QML estimators discussed in Section 14.6.4, the estimators and inference procedures of Chapter 14 are not directly available to the inverse problems examined in this chapter. In addition to being unknown, the elements of the noise covariance matrix are unobserved and indeed are unobservable. Thus, we again have a basic inverse problem for which we must use information on observable data in an attempt to recover information on the unknown unobservables.

For the inverse problems examined in this chapter, there are usually more unknowns than data observations, and thus the inverse problems are ill-posed and underdetermined. Solving these problems using traditional estimation procedures requires that we add additional structure or side constraints to the problem. Consequently, to establish a basis for contemplating inverse problem solutions in this case, we consider the problem of recovering information about the unknown $\sigma^2\boldsymbol{\Psi}$ from the sample data and examine the statistical implications of defining estimation rules based on estimates of $\sigma^2\boldsymbol{\Psi}$. We also demonstrate the White (1980, 1984) and Newey and West (1987) robust methods of defining consistent estimators for noise component covariance matrices that do not rely on an explicit parametric structural representation of the $\sigma^2\boldsymbol{\Psi}$ matrix. Finally, we examine the inverse problem from the point of view of estimating equations and quasi-maximum likelihood estimation. In this situation we contemplate robust estimation of unknown parameters in the typical case in which it is highly unlikely that the true functional structure of $\boldsymbol{\Psi}$ can be specified, adequately identified, or accurately estimated.

In the discussion ahead we will sometimes find it useful to absorb the σ^2 parameter into a reparameterization of the covariance matrix $\sigma^2\boldsymbol{\Psi} = \boldsymbol{\Phi}$, where $\boldsymbol{\Phi}$ is a $(n \times n)$ symmetric positive definite matrix. Because in the current inverse problem context both σ^2 and $\boldsymbol{\Psi}$ are unknown and unobservable and only $n(n+1)/2$ parameters are needed to represent a covariance matrix fully, no generality is lost by suppressing σ^2 and representing the covariance matrix by $\boldsymbol{\Phi}$. Nonetheless, we will see that a number of model parameterizations of the noise covariance matrix used in practice maintain

Table 15.1. *Regression Models with Unknown General Noise Covariance Structure*

Model Component	Specific Characteristics	
Y	RV Type:	continuous
	Range:	unlimited
	Y_i dimension:	univariate
	Moments:	$E[\mathbf{Y} \mid \mathbf{x}] = \mathbf{x}\boldsymbol{\beta}$ or $\mathbf{g}(\mathbf{x}, \boldsymbol{\beta})$ and $\mathbf{cov}(\mathbf{Y} \mid \mathbf{x}) = \sigma^2\boldsymbol{\Psi} = \boldsymbol{\Phi}$
$\eta(\mathbf{x}, \boldsymbol{\beta}, \varepsilon)$	Functional Form:	linear or nonlinear in **x** and $\boldsymbol{\beta}$, additive in ε
x	RV Type:	degenerate (fixed) or stochastic
	Genesis:	exogenous to the model
$\boldsymbol{\beta}$	RV Type:	degenerate (fixed)
	Dimension:	finite
ε	RV Type:	non-iid
	Moments:	$E[\varepsilon \mid \mathbf{x}] = \mathbf{0}$, and $\mathbf{cov}(\varepsilon \mid \mathbf{x}) = \sigma^2\boldsymbol{\Psi} = \boldsymbol{\Phi}$
Ω	Prior info:	none
$f(\mathbf{e} \mid \mathbf{x}; \psi)$	PDF family:	normal or unspecified

the identity of σ^2 as a scalar multiplier of the matrix $\boldsymbol{\Psi}$, which in turn is parameterized in terms of substantially fewer than $n(n+1)/2$ parameters, say as $\boldsymbol{\Psi}(\gamma)$. Thus, we will maintain alternative parameterizations of the covariance matrix $\sigma^2\boldsymbol{\Psi}$ as appropriate to the context of our discussion.

Building on some basic results that are established in this chapter, we will take up the problem of model discovery in Chapters 18 and 19. For the case of an unknown noise covariance matrix, we acknowledge a range of tests that have been suggested in the literature for assessing the existence and form of heteroscedastic or autocorrelated errors, or both. In that chapter we also provide a critique of the statistical implications of these testing mechanisms as well as comment on the likelihood that the testing approach can be successful in specifying estimators of model parameters.

The specific probability model characteristics that are assumed to hold in this chapter are presented in Table 15.1.

The particular inverse problem associated with the probability model identified in Table 15.1 involves using observations on $(\mathbf{Y}, \mathbf{X})$ to recover information about the values or functions of the unknown and unobservable $\boldsymbol{\beta}$, σ^2, ε, and $\boldsymbol{\Psi}$. Henceforth our arguments will proceed conditionally on outcomes **x** of **X** if the explanatory variables are stochastic.

15.1. Linear Regression Models with Unknown Noise Covariance

In Chapter 14, we assumed that the noise component covariance matrix $\sigma^2\boldsymbol{\Psi}$ or $(\boldsymbol{\Sigma} \otimes \mathbf{I})$ in the case of a system of equations, was known. Thus, we were able to transform our linear or nonlinear regression models to the standard form in which the noise component covariance matrix is proportional to the identity matrix. In practice the noise component covariance matrix is usually unknown, and so we now consider the problem of estimating the unknown covariance matrix parameters to provide a basis for approximating the GLS estimation and inference procedures of Chapter 14.

Given the estimators developed in Chapter 14, intuition might suggest that the way to proceed is to replace the unknown $\boldsymbol{\Psi}$ with an estimate generated by some estimator $\hat{\boldsymbol{\Psi}}$. This would lead, in the case of the single-equation linear regression model, to the *estimated* GLS (EGLS) estimator of β defined by

$$\hat{\boldsymbol{\beta}}_{\text{EG}} = (\mathbf{x}'\hat{\boldsymbol{\Psi}}^{-1}\mathbf{x})^{-1}\mathbf{x}'\hat{\boldsymbol{\Psi}}^{-1}\mathbf{Y}. \tag{15.1.1.a}$$

This estimator has also been aptly called the *feasible* GLS estimator. Although this may seem a reasonable thing to do, the important question to address is what are the statistical implications of this approach? This question becomes especially intriguing in the single-equation case when we realize there are more unknowns, $n(n+1)/2$ in the inverse problem of estimating $\boldsymbol{\Psi}$ than there are data observations $n > 1$. To achieve a solution to the estimation of $\boldsymbol{\Psi}$, one must make restrictive assumptions concerning the number of unknowns involved in representing the structure of the noise covariance matrix.

In practice the elements of $\boldsymbol{\Psi}$ have been assumed most often to be functions, $\boldsymbol{\Psi}(\gamma)$, of a reduced and fixed number of unknown parameters γ that remain unchanged as the sample size increases. The problem then becomes how best to estimate the unknown γ, and much effort has been expended in econometrics and statistics journals on this matter of modeling and mitigating the problems of autocorrelation and heteroscedasticity. In the subsections ahead we develop some general statistical properties of estimators based on estimated noise covariance matrices when the true noise covariance matrix is not proportional to the identity matrix and is unknown. We will address the issue of attempting to detect and model autocorrelation, heteroscedasticity, or both, in Chapter 19 ahead.

Note for future reference that an alternative representation of the EGLS estimator is given by

$$\hat{\boldsymbol{\beta}}_{\text{EG}} = (\mathbf{x}'\hat{\boldsymbol{\Phi}}^{-1}\mathbf{x})^{-1}\mathbf{x}'\hat{\boldsymbol{\Phi}}^{-1}\mathbf{Y}, \tag{15.1.1.b}$$

where $\hat{\boldsymbol{\Phi}}$ denotes an estimate of the full covariance matrix $\sigma^2\boldsymbol{\Psi}$ rather than an estimate of only the $\boldsymbol{\Psi}$ component of it. The representation of the EGLS estimator in (15.1.1.b) follows from the alternative representation of the GLS estimator given by $\hat{\boldsymbol{\beta}}_{\text{GLS}} = (\mathbf{x}'\boldsymbol{\Phi}^{-1}\mathbf{x})^{-1}\mathbf{x}'\boldsymbol{\Phi}^{-1}\mathbf{Y}$ (note that the σ^2 parameter in the representation of the covariance matrix $\boldsymbol{\Phi} = \sigma^2\boldsymbol{\Psi}$ algebraically cancels to establish the equivalence of the two GLS estimator representations).

15.1.1. Single-Equation Semiparametric Linear Regression Model

In this section we examine the case of the semiparametric linear regression model to which the GLS estimator of Section 14.2 could be applied if $\boldsymbol{\Psi}$ were *known*. We will see that under the appropriate conditions, many of the results involving the GLS estimator and associated inference procedures can be preserved when $\mathbf{\Psi}$ is *unknown*.

15.1.1.a. Estimated Generalized Least-Squares Estimator and Unbiasedness

Consider the linear semiparametric regression model with unknown noise covariance matrix $\mathbf{\Psi}$ and the *estimated* generalized least-squares (EGLS) estimator of $\boldsymbol{\beta}$ given by

$$\hat{\boldsymbol{\beta}}_{\text{EG}} = (\mathbf{x}'\hat{\mathbf{\Psi}}^{-1}\mathbf{x})^{-1}\mathbf{x}'\hat{\mathbf{\Psi}}^{-1}\mathbf{Y} = \boldsymbol{\beta} + (\mathbf{x}'\hat{\mathbf{\Psi}}^{-1}\mathbf{x})^{-1}\mathbf{x}'\hat{\mathbf{\Psi}}^{-1}\boldsymbol{\varepsilon}. \tag{15.1.2}$$

Because any estimator of $\mathbf{\Psi}$ will depend on the sample outcomes of $\mathbf{Y} = \mathbf{x}\boldsymbol{\beta} + \boldsymbol{\varepsilon}$, $\hat{\mathbf{\Psi}}$ and $\boldsymbol{\varepsilon}$ will generally be correlated. As a result, the finite sampling distribution of $\hat{\boldsymbol{\beta}}_{\text{EG}}$ is often very complicated, and we must resort to asymptotic distributions or Monte Carlo simulation as a guide for evaluating estimator properties and establishing hypothesis testing and confidence region estimation procedures.

Before venturing into asymptotics, we note one general finite sample property of $\hat{\boldsymbol{\beta}}_{\text{EG}}$ that can be stated under general conditions. If in (15.1.2), $\hat{\mathbf{\Psi}}$ is an *even* function of $\boldsymbol{\varepsilon}$, then $\hat{\boldsymbol{\beta}}_{\text{EG}}$ is an *unbiased* estimator of $\boldsymbol{\beta}$ if it is assumed that the expectation of $\hat{\boldsymbol{\beta}}_{\text{EG}}$ exists and the noise component distribution is continuous and symmetrically distributed around the zero vector. By *even* function we mean that precisely the same outcome of $\hat{\mathbf{\Psi}}$ occurs when the outcome of $\boldsymbol{\varepsilon}$ is $\mathbf{e}$ or $-\mathbf{e}$, for any vector of outcomes $\mathbf{e}$. The motivation for the "unbiasedness" claim under these conditions is relatively straightforward. In particular, first note that because $\hat{\mathbf{\Psi}}(\mathbf{e}) = \hat{\mathbf{\Psi}}(-\mathbf{e})$, substituting $-\boldsymbol{\varepsilon}$ for $\boldsymbol{\varepsilon}$ in (15.1.2) simply changes the sign of $\hat{\boldsymbol{\beta}}_{\text{EG}} - \boldsymbol{\beta}$, yielding instead the value $\boldsymbol{\beta} - \hat{\boldsymbol{\beta}}_{\text{EG}}$. Then, because the probability distributions of $\boldsymbol{\varepsilon}$ and $-\boldsymbol{\varepsilon}$ are identical and centered at zero, the distributions of $\hat{\boldsymbol{\beta}}_{\text{EG}} - \boldsymbol{\beta}$ and $\boldsymbol{\beta} - \hat{\boldsymbol{\beta}}_{\text{EG}}$ are identical and centered at zero as well. Thus, $\hat{\boldsymbol{\beta}}_{\text{EG}}$ is symmetrically distributed around the value of $\boldsymbol{\beta}$, demonstrating unbiasedness if $\mathrm{E}[\hat{\boldsymbol{\beta}}_{\text{EG}}]$ exists. Additional discussion can be found in Kakwani (1967) and Schmidt (1976).

15.1.1.b. Asymptotic Properties of EGLS

To define the asymptotic properties of $\hat{\boldsymbol{\beta}}_{\text{EG}}$, we recall the asymptotic properties of the GLS estimator $\hat{\boldsymbol{\beta}}_{\text{G}}$ and then develop sufficient conditions for $\hat{\boldsymbol{\beta}}_{\text{EG}}$ to have the same asymptotic properties as $\hat{\boldsymbol{\beta}}_{\text{G}}$. This enables the same asymptotically valid testing and confidence procedures developed for $\hat{\boldsymbol{\beta}}_{\text{G}}$ to be applied to $\hat{\boldsymbol{\beta}}_{\text{EG}}$ as well. Proceeding along these lines, we know from Section 14.2 that, under regularity conditions, establishing that

1. $n^{-1}\mathbf{x}'\mathbf{\Psi}^{-1}\mathbf{x} \to \mathbf{m}$ is a finite, symmetric, and positive definite matrix and

2. $n^{-1/2}\mathbf{x}'\mathbf{\Psi}^{-1}\boldsymbol{\varepsilon} \xrightarrow{\text{d}} \mathrm{N}(\mathbf{0}, \sigma^2\mathbf{m})$,

the GLS estimator is such that

$$n^{1/2}(\hat{\boldsymbol{\beta}}_{\text{G}} - \boldsymbol{\beta}) = (n^{-1}\mathbf{x}'\mathbf{\Psi}^{-1}\mathbf{x})^{-1}n^{-1/2}\mathbf{x}'\mathbf{\Psi}^{-1}\boldsymbol{\varepsilon} \xrightarrow{\text{d}} \mathrm{N}(\mathbf{0}, \sigma^2\mathbf{m}^{-1}), \tag{15.1.3}$$

and thus $\hat{\boldsymbol{\beta}}_G \overset{a}{\sim} N(\boldsymbol{\beta}, n^{-1}\sigma^2\mathbf{m}^{-1})$ and $\hat{\boldsymbol{\beta}}_G \xrightarrow{p} \boldsymbol{\beta}$. By adopting exactly the same regularity conditions that establish these properties for $\hat{\boldsymbol{\beta}}_G$, the EGLS estimator will attain the same limiting and asymptotic distributions identified by (15.1.3) and will be a consistent estimator of $\boldsymbol{\beta}$ if the additional conditions

$$n^{-1}\mathbf{x}'\hat{\boldsymbol{\Psi}}^{-1}\mathbf{x} - n^{-1}\mathbf{x}'\boldsymbol{\Psi}^{-1}\mathbf{x} \xrightarrow{p} \mathbf{0}$$

and

$$n^{-1/2}\mathbf{x}'\hat{\boldsymbol{\Psi}}^{-1}\boldsymbol{\varepsilon} - n^{-1/2}\mathbf{x}'\boldsymbol{\Psi}^{-1}\boldsymbol{\varepsilon} \xrightarrow{p} \mathbf{0} \tag{15.1.4}$$

hold. Note the first of these conditions effectively ensures that $n^{-1}\mathbf{x}'\hat{\boldsymbol{\Psi}}^{-1}\mathbf{x}$ can replace $n^{-1}\mathbf{x}'\boldsymbol{\Psi}^{-1}\mathbf{x}$ in the limit, whereas the second condition ensures that the limiting distributions of $n^{-1/2}\mathbf{x}'\hat{\boldsymbol{\Psi}}^{-1}\boldsymbol{\varepsilon}$ and $n^{-1/2}\mathbf{x}'\boldsymbol{\Psi}^{-1}\boldsymbol{\varepsilon}$ are identical.

It should be noted at this point that the ability to estimate the elements of $\boldsymbol{\Psi}$ consistently with an estimator $\hat{\boldsymbol{\Psi}}$ is not equivalent to achieving the conditions listed in (15.1.4). Unfortunately, the conditions (15.1.4) need to be considered on a case-by-case basis. The rationale underlying the lack of equivalence is rooted in the fact that, whereas each element of $\boldsymbol{\Psi}$ may be estimated consistently by the corresponding element of $\hat{\boldsymbol{\Psi}}$, each element of the matrices $n^{-1}\mathbf{x}'\boldsymbol{\Psi}^{-1}\mathbf{x}$ and $n^{-1/2}\mathbf{x}'\boldsymbol{\Psi}^{-1}\boldsymbol{\varepsilon}$ can be a function of all $n(n+1)/2$ unique entries in $\boldsymbol{\Psi}$, and so elementwise convergence in probability of $\hat{\boldsymbol{\Psi}}$ to $\boldsymbol{\Psi}$ need not imply the elementwise convergence in probability required in (15.1.4). For example, the (i, j)th entry in $n^{-1}\mathbf{x}'\hat{\boldsymbol{\Psi}}^{-1}\mathbf{x}$ will be of the form $n^{-1}\sum_{\ell=1}^{n}\sum_{k=1}^{n}\hat{\Psi}^{-1}[\ell,k]\mathrm{x}[\ell,i]\mathrm{x}[k,j]$, where $\hat{\Psi}^{-1}[\ell,k]$ denotes the (ℓ,k)th element of $\hat{\boldsymbol{\Psi}}^{-1}$. Because the number of terms in the sum expand as n increases, the fact that $\hat{\Psi}^{-1}[\ell,k] - \Psi^{-1}[\ell,k] = o_p(1)$ is not sufficient for the preceding sum to converge to $n^{-1}\sum_{\ell=1}^{n}\sum_{k=1}^{n}\Psi^{-1}[\ell,k]\mathrm{x}[\ell,i]\mathrm{x}[k,j]$. So the consistency of $\hat{\boldsymbol{\Psi}}$ for $\boldsymbol{\Psi}$ is not sufficient for (15.1.4).

Note that if convergence of a consistent estimator $\hat{\boldsymbol{\Psi}}^{-1}$ to $\boldsymbol{\Psi}^{-1}$ is *sufficiently rapid*, then $\hat{\boldsymbol{\Psi}} \xrightarrow{p} \boldsymbol{\Psi}$ will be sufficient for condition (15.1.4). For example, if $\hat{\Psi}^{-1}[\ell,k] - \Psi^{-1}[\ell,k] = o_p(n^{-1})\forall \ell, k$, and on the assumption that the elements in the matrix $\mathbf{x}$ are bounded in absolute value, the (i, j)th entry in $n^{-1}\mathbf{x}'(\hat{\boldsymbol{\Psi}}^{-1} - \boldsymbol{\Psi}^{-1})\mathbf{x}$ is such that

$$\begin{aligned} n^{-1}\sum_{\ell=1}^{n}\sum_{k=1}^{n}(\hat{\Psi}^{-1}[\ell,k] - \Psi^{-1}[\ell,k])\mathbf{x}[\ell,i]\mathbf{x}[k,j] &= n^{-1}\sum_{\ell=1}^{n}\sum_{k=1}^{n}o_p(n^{-1}) \\ &= n o_p(n^{-1}) \xrightarrow{p} 0, \ \forall i, j. \end{aligned} \tag{15.1.5}$$

A similar argument applies to the second condition in (15.1.4).

It should also be noted that, although *sufficient* for the asymptotic equivalence of $\hat{\boldsymbol{\beta}}_G$ and $\hat{\boldsymbol{\beta}}_{EG}$, the conditions (15.1.4) on $\hat{\boldsymbol{\Psi}}$ and $\mathbf{x}$ can be unnecessarily strong, especially if $\boldsymbol{\Psi}$ has a special, more restrictive structure. For example, if ε is *only* heteroscedastic and *not* autocorrelated, the entries in $\mathbf{x}$ are bounded, and the variances of the ε_i's are bounded as well, then $\hat{\boldsymbol{\Psi}} \xrightarrow{p} \boldsymbol{\Psi}$ is indeed sufficient for the conditions in (15.1.4) and for the asymptotic equivalence of $\hat{\boldsymbol{\beta}}_G$ and $\hat{\boldsymbol{\beta}}_{EG}$. This follows from the fact that $\hat{\boldsymbol{\Psi}} \xrightarrow{p} \boldsymbol{\Psi} \Rightarrow \hat{\Psi}[\ell,\ell] \xrightarrow{p} \Psi[\ell,\ell], \forall \ell$, and then the (i, j)th entry in $n^{-1}\mathbf{x}'(\hat{\boldsymbol{\Psi}}^{-1} - \boldsymbol{\Psi}^{-1})\mathbf{x}$ is such that

$$n^{-1}\sum_{\ell=1}^{n}\sum_{k=1}^{n}(\hat{\Psi}^{-1}[\ell,k]-\Psi^{-1}[\ell,k])\mathrm{x}[\ell,i]\mathrm{x}[k,j]$$
$$=n^{-1}\sum_{\ell=1}^{n}(\hat{\Psi}^{-1}[\ell,\ell]-\Psi^{-1}[\ell,\ell])\mathrm{x}[\ell,i]\mathrm{x}[\ell,j]n^{-1}\sum_{\ell=1}^{n}\mathrm{o_p}(1)=\mathrm{o_p}(1)\xrightarrow{\mathrm{p}}0 \tag{15.1.6}$$

► **Example 15.1.1:** The GAUSS program C15Conv.gss (provided in the examples manual) is designed to demonstrate the convergence properties discussed in the preceding paragraphs. For autoregressive and heteroscedastic specifications of (selected by the user), GAUSS examines the convergence of $n^{-1}\mathbf{x}'(\hat{\mathbf{\Psi}}^{-1}-\mathbf{\Psi}^{-1})\mathbf{x}$ under cases in which $\hat{\Psi}^{-1}[\ell,k]-\Psi^{-1}[\ell,k]=\mathrm{o_p}(1)$ and $\hat{\Psi}^{-1}[\ell,k]-\Psi^{-1}[\ell,k]=\mathrm{o_p}(n^{-1})$. The user should find that the simulation results agree with the preceding statements as the sample size (n) becomes large.

Assume that $\hat{\mathbf{\Psi}}$ has been defined so as to estimate $\mathbf{\Psi}$ in a way that achieves the conditions in (15.1.4) and assume further that the previously stated GLS regularity conditions 1 and 2 hold. Then, consistency and asymptotic normality properties of $\hat{\boldsymbol{\beta}}_{\mathrm{EG}}$ are attained and coincide with those of $\hat{\boldsymbol{\beta}}_{\mathrm{G}}$. It follows that $\hat{\boldsymbol{\beta}}_{\mathrm{EG}}$ is *asymptotically* more efficient than the LS estimator $\hat{\boldsymbol{\beta}}$. This conclusion follows from a direct comparison of the covariance matrices of the limiting distributions of $n^{1/2}(\hat{\boldsymbol{\beta}}-\boldsymbol{\beta})$ and $n^{1/2}(\hat{\boldsymbol{\beta}}_{\mathrm{EG}}-\boldsymbol{\beta})$. Recall from (14.1.5) that

$$n^{1/2}(\hat{\boldsymbol{\beta}}-\boldsymbol{\beta})\xrightarrow{\mathrm{d}}\mathrm{N}(\mathbf{0},\sigma^2\mathbf{\Xi}^{-1}\mathbf{h}\mathbf{\Xi}^{-1}), \tag{15.1.7}$$

where $\mathbf{h}=\lim_{n\to\infty}n^{-1}\mathbf{x}'\mathbf{\Psi}\mathbf{x}$ and $\mathbf{\Xi}=\lim_{n\to\infty}n^{-1}\mathbf{x}'\mathbf{x}$. Given (15.1.3), we know that the difference in covariance matrices between $\hat{\boldsymbol{\beta}}$ and $\hat{\boldsymbol{\beta}}_{\mathrm{EG}}$ is

$$\begin{aligned}\mathbf{\Xi}^{-1}\mathbf{h}\mathbf{\Xi}^{-1}-\mathbf{m}^{-1} &= \lim_{n\to\infty} n[(\mathbf{x}'\mathbf{x})^{-1}\mathbf{x}'\mathbf{\Psi}\mathbf{x}(\mathbf{x}'\mathbf{x})^{-1}-(\mathbf{x}'\mathbf{\Psi}^{-1}\mathbf{x})^{-1}]\\ &= \lim_{n\to\infty} n\mathbf{c}\mathbf{\Psi}\mathbf{c}',\end{aligned} \tag{15.1.8}$$

where $\mathbf{m}=\lim n^{-1}\mathbf{x}'\mathbf{\Psi}^{-1}\mathbf{x}$ and $c=(\mathbf{x}'\mathbf{x})^{-1}\mathbf{x}'-\left(\mathbf{x}'\mathbf{\Psi}^{-1}\mathbf{x}\right)^{-1}\mathbf{x}'\mathbf{\Psi}^{-1}$. Because the limit of the sequence of $(k\times k)$ positive semidefinite matrices is itself positive semidefinite and will generally differ from a matrix of zeros, it follows that $\hat{\boldsymbol{\beta}}_{\mathrm{EG}}$ is generally *asymptotically more efficient* than $\hat{\boldsymbol{\beta}}$ and in any case is always at least as asymptotically efficient as $\hat{\boldsymbol{\beta}}$.

We emphasize that in order for $\hat{\boldsymbol{\beta}}_{\mathrm{EG}}$ to be asymptotically more efficient than $\hat{\boldsymbol{\beta}}$, one must have correctly anticipated the true structure of $\mathbf{\Psi}$ in the design of the estimator $\hat{\mathbf{\Psi}}$, and the estimator must then also converge to the correct $\mathbf{\Psi}$ in a way that the previously mentioned limiting distribution result is achieved. Otherwise, the preceding claim that $\hat{\boldsymbol{\beta}}_{\mathrm{EG}}$ is asymptotically more efficient than $\hat{\boldsymbol{\beta}}$ is vacuous. We also emphasize that in general there is *no* guarantee that $\hat{\boldsymbol{\beta}}_{\mathrm{EG}}$ is unequivocally better than $\hat{\boldsymbol{\beta}}$ for estimating $\boldsymbol{\beta}$ if $\mathbf{\Psi}$ is unknown. In particular, if *$\hat{\mathbf{\Psi}}$ is not an accurate estimator of $\mathbf{\Psi}$, or if the parametric structure of $\mathbf{\Psi}$ is misspecified or both, and thus the estimator $\hat{\mathbf{\Psi}}$ is incorrectly* *designed, the finite sampling properties of $\hat{\boldsymbol{\beta}}_{\mathrm{EG}}$ can be considerably worse than those of $\hat{\boldsymbol{\beta}}$.* Furthermore, under the latter condition of misspecification of $\boldsymbol{\Psi}$, $\hat{\boldsymbol{\beta}}$ can be superior to $\hat{\boldsymbol{\beta}}_{\mathrm{EG}}$ even asymptotically.

15.1.1.c. Testing and Confidence Regions

If regularity conditions sufficient for the consistency and asymptotic normality of $\hat{\boldsymbol{\beta}}_{\mathrm{G}}$ as well as the conditions for the asymptotic equivalence of $\hat{\boldsymbol{\beta}}_{\mathrm{G}}$ and $\hat{\boldsymbol{\beta}}_{\mathrm{EG}}$ presented above (15.1.3) are assumed, methods for conducting asymptotically valid hypothesis tests and generating asymptotically valid confidence regions based on $\hat{\boldsymbol{\beta}}_{\mathrm{G}}$ can be applied to $\hat{\boldsymbol{\beta}}_{\mathrm{EG}}$ as well. For example, because $[\mathbf{c}(\mathbf{x}'\boldsymbol{\Phi}^{-1}\mathbf{x})^{-1}\mathbf{c}']^{-1/2}\mathbf{c}(\hat{\boldsymbol{\beta}}_{\mathrm{EG}} - \boldsymbol{\beta}) \xrightarrow{d} \mathrm{N}(\mathbf{0}, \mathbf{I})$ by Slutsky's theorem, it follows that the Wald-type statistic

$$\mathrm{W} = [\mathbf{c}\hat{\boldsymbol{\beta}}_{\mathrm{EG}} - \mathbf{r}]'[\mathbf{c}(\mathbf{x}'\hat{\boldsymbol{\Phi}}^{-1}\mathbf{x})^{-1}\mathbf{c}']^{-1}[\mathbf{c}\hat{\boldsymbol{\beta}}_{\mathrm{EG}} - \mathbf{r}] \overset{a}{\sim} \text{Chi-square}(j, \lambda) \quad (15.1.9)$$

can be used to test j linear restriction hypotheses of the form $\mathrm{H}_0\colon \mathbf{c}\boldsymbol{\beta} = \mathbf{r}$, where it is assumed that the estimator of the noise component covariance matrix is such that $n^{-1}\mathbf{x}'\hat{\boldsymbol{\Phi}}^{-1}\mathbf{x} - n^{-1}\mathbf{x}'\boldsymbol{\Phi}^{-1}\mathbf{x} \xrightarrow{p} \mathbf{0}$. The noncentrality parameter is defined as

$$\lambda = \frac{1}{2\sigma^2}\boldsymbol{\delta}'[\mathbf{c}\,\mathbf{m}^{-1}\mathbf{c}']^{-1}\boldsymbol{\delta}, \quad (15.1.10)$$

where $\boldsymbol{\delta}$ is a $(j \times 1)$ vector defining Pitman drift-type hypotheses of the form $\mathrm{H}\colon \mathbf{c}\boldsymbol{\beta} = \mathbf{r} + n^{-1/2}\boldsymbol{\delta}$, and the critical region is $\mathrm{C}^{\mathrm{W}} = [\chi^2_{1-\alpha}, \infty)$ for defining an asymptotic level α test. Recall that $\chi^2_{1-\alpha}$ is the $100(1-\alpha)\%$ quantile of the central Chi-square distribution with j degrees of freedom. An LM test of $\mathrm{H}_0\colon \mathbf{c}\boldsymbol{\beta} = \mathbf{r}$ can be defined similarly and has exactly the same asymptotic Chi-square distribution. The test can be defined in terms of the Lagrange multipliers of the restricted EGLS problem

$$\min_{\boldsymbol{\beta}}[(\mathbf{y} - \mathbf{x}\boldsymbol{\beta})'\hat{\boldsymbol{\Psi}}^{-1}(\mathbf{y} - \mathbf{x}\boldsymbol{\beta}) - \boldsymbol{\gamma}'(\mathbf{c}\boldsymbol{\beta} - \mathbf{r})].$$

Tests of scalar equality or linear inequality hypotheses can be based on the asymptotically normal Z-statistic

$$\mathrm{Z} = \frac{(\mathbf{c}\hat{\boldsymbol{\beta}}_{\mathrm{EG}} - \mathrm{r})}{[\mathbf{c}(\mathbf{x}'\hat{\boldsymbol{\Phi}}^{-1}\mathbf{x})^{-1}\mathbf{c}']^{1/2}} \overset{a}{\sim} \mathrm{N}\left(\frac{\delta}{[\sigma^2\mathbf{c}\,\mathbf{m}^{-1}\mathbf{c}']^{1/2}}, 1\right), \quad (15.1.11)$$

where δ is a scalar defining Pitman drift-type hypotheses such as $\mathrm{H}\colon \mathbf{c}\boldsymbol{\beta} = \mathrm{r} + n^{-1/2}\delta$. The critical regions for various types of tests are analogous to those listed in (14.3.7). In practice some analysts have utilized the student T-distribution quantiles in tests based on the Z-statistic above, in which case the *actual* probability of Type-I error, as well as the actual power of the test, tends to be smaller than the test based on standard normal quantiles. This results in a more conservative criterion for rejecting null hypotheses when using the asymptotic tests.

Confidence regions and bounds can be constructed in the usual way by invoking duality with hypothesis tests. The appropriate set definitions are analogous to (14.2.23)–(14.2.25), with $\hat{\boldsymbol{\beta}}_{\mathrm{EG}}$ replacing $\hat{\boldsymbol{\beta}}_{\mathrm{G}}$, $\hat{\boldsymbol{\Phi}}$ replacing $\boldsymbol{\Psi}$, $\mathrm{S}^2_{\mathrm{G}}$ removed, and $\mathrm{f}_{1-\alpha}$ and $\mathrm{t}_{1-\alpha/2}$ replaced by $\chi^2_{1-\alpha}$ and $\mathrm{z}_{1-\alpha/2}$, respectively.

15.1.2. Single-Equation Parametric Linear Regression Model – The ML Approach

Within the context of the linear statistical model $\mathbf{Y} = \mathbf{x}\boldsymbol{\beta} + \boldsymbol{\varepsilon}$, suppose it is plausible to assume that the probability distribution of the noise component belongs to a specific parametric family, such as $\boldsymbol{\varepsilon} \sim \mathrm{N}(\mathbf{0}, \sigma^2\boldsymbol{\Psi}(\boldsymbol{\gamma}))$. If the matrix $\boldsymbol{\Psi}(\boldsymbol{\gamma})$ is *unknown* but is a *known* function of the *unknown* finite dimensional vector of parameters $\boldsymbol{\gamma}$, then ML estimation and inference procedures may be used. In the case of a normal distribution, we can specify the log-likelihood function as

$$\begin{aligned}\ln \mathrm{L}(\boldsymbol{\beta}, \sigma^2, \boldsymbol{\gamma}; \mathbf{y}, \mathbf{x}) &= -\frac{n}{2}\ln(2\pi\sigma^2) - \frac{1}{2}\ln(\det[\boldsymbol{\Psi}(\boldsymbol{\gamma})]) \\ &\quad - \frac{1}{2\sigma^2}[\mathbf{y} - \mathbf{x}\boldsymbol{\beta}]'[\boldsymbol{\Psi}(\boldsymbol{\gamma})]^{-1}[\mathbf{y} - \mathbf{x}\boldsymbol{\beta}], \qquad (15.1.12)\end{aligned}$$

where $\det[\boldsymbol{\Psi}(\boldsymbol{\gamma})]$ denotes the determinant of $\boldsymbol{\Psi}(\boldsymbol{\gamma})$.

It is evident that maximization of ln L with respect to $\boldsymbol{\beta}$ and σ^2, *conditional* on $\boldsymbol{\gamma}$, yields GLS-like estimates for these parameters given by

$$\mathbf{b}(\boldsymbol{\gamma}) = (\mathbf{x}'[\boldsymbol{\Psi}(\boldsymbol{\gamma})]^{-1}\mathbf{x})^{-1}\mathbf{x}'[\boldsymbol{\Psi}(\boldsymbol{\gamma})]^{-1}\mathbf{y} \text{ and}$$
$$\mathrm{s}^2(\boldsymbol{\gamma}) = [\mathbf{y} - \mathbf{x}\mathbf{b}(\boldsymbol{\gamma})]'[\boldsymbol{\Psi}(\boldsymbol{\gamma})]^{-1}[\mathbf{y} - \mathbf{x}\mathbf{b}(\boldsymbol{\gamma})]/n$$

that depend on the unknown parameter vector $\boldsymbol{\gamma}$. If $\mathbf{b}(\boldsymbol{\gamma})$ and $\mathrm{s}^2(\boldsymbol{\gamma})$ are substituted into (15.1.12) for $\boldsymbol{\beta}$ and σ^2, this results in the *concentrated* (on the parameter vector $\boldsymbol{\gamma}$) log-likelihood function

$$\ln \mathrm{L_c}(\boldsymbol{\gamma}; \mathbf{y}, \mathbf{x}) = -\frac{n}{2}\ln\{[\mathbf{y} - \mathbf{x}\mathbf{b}(\boldsymbol{\gamma})]'[\boldsymbol{\Psi}(\boldsymbol{\gamma})]^{-1}[\mathbf{y} - \mathbf{x}\mathbf{b}(\boldsymbol{\gamma})]\} - \frac{1}{2}\ln(\det[\boldsymbol{\Psi}(\boldsymbol{\gamma})]) + c, \qquad (15.1.13)$$

where $c = -\frac{n}{2}[\ln(2\pi) + 1 - \ln(n)]$. The maximum likelihood estimate for $\boldsymbol{\gamma}$, say $\hat{\boldsymbol{\gamma}}_{\mathrm{ML}}$, is the value of $\boldsymbol{\gamma}$ for which $\ln \mathrm{L_c}(\boldsymbol{\gamma}; \mathbf{y}, \mathbf{x})$ is maximized. In general, computer-driven numerical optimization procedures will be required to identify the value of $\boldsymbol{\gamma}$ that maximizes the concentrated likelihood function (15.1.13). The associated *unconditional* ML estimates of $\boldsymbol{\beta}$ and σ^2 are then defined as

$$\hat{\mathbf{b}}_{\mathrm{ML}} = \mathbf{b}(\hat{\boldsymbol{\gamma}}_{\mathrm{ML}}) = [\mathbf{x}'[\boldsymbol{\Psi}(\hat{\boldsymbol{\gamma}}_{\mathrm{ML}})]^{-1}\mathbf{x}]^{-1}\mathbf{x}'[\boldsymbol{\Psi}(\hat{\boldsymbol{\gamma}}_{\mathrm{ML}})]^{-1}\mathbf{y} \qquad (15.1.14)$$

and

$$\hat{\mathrm{s}}^2_{\mathrm{ML}} = \mathrm{s}^2(\hat{\boldsymbol{\gamma}}_{\mathrm{ML}}) = \frac{[\mathbf{y} - \mathbf{x}\mathbf{b}(\hat{\boldsymbol{\gamma}}_{\mathrm{ML}})]'[\boldsymbol{\Psi}(\hat{\boldsymbol{\gamma}}_{\mathrm{ML}})]^{-1}[\mathbf{y} - \mathbf{x}\mathbf{b}(\hat{\boldsymbol{\gamma}}_{\mathrm{ML}})]}{n}. \qquad (15.1.15)$$

Note that the triad of estimates $\hat{\boldsymbol{\theta}} = (\hat{\mathbf{b}}'_{\mathrm{ML}}, \hat{\mathrm{s}}^2_{\mathrm{ML}}, \hat{\boldsymbol{\gamma}}'_{\mathrm{ML}})'$ obtained by maximizing (15.1.13) to obtain $\hat{\boldsymbol{\gamma}}_{\mathrm{ML}}$ and then utilizing (15.1.14) and (15.1.15) to obtain $\hat{\mathbf{b}}_{\mathrm{ML}}$ and $\hat{\mathrm{s}}^2_{\mathrm{ML}}$ are completely equivalent to the ML-extremum estimate of Chapter 7 defined by

$$\hat{\boldsymbol{\theta}} = \arg\max_{\boldsymbol{\beta}, \sigma^2, \boldsymbol{\gamma}} [\mathrm{L}(\boldsymbol{\beta}, \sigma^2, \boldsymbol{\gamma}; \mathbf{y}, \mathbf{x})]. \qquad (15.1.16)$$

The ML estimators associated with the estimates of $\boldsymbol{\gamma}$, $\boldsymbol{\beta}$, and σ^2 are defined by replacing $\mathbf{y}$ with $\mathbf{Y}$ in (15.1.13)–(15.1.16). Although the estimators $\hat{\boldsymbol{\beta}}_{\mathrm{ML}}$ and $\mathrm{S}^2_{\mathrm{ML}}$

have the same basic form as the EGLS estimator, in this case the estimator for the unknown parameters in $\Psi(\gamma)$ is defined by maximizing (15.1.12) or (15.1.13). The first-order conditions for these maximization problems do not in general result in a closed-form solution for γ, and so numerical methods are necessary to find the maximum likelihood-extremum estimates. The usual asymptotic statements associated with ML-extremum procedures follow and, of particular importance, include the asymptotic efficiency of the ML estimators. Also, because of the asymptotic normal distributions of $\hat{\boldsymbol{\beta}}_{\text{ML}}$ and S^2_{ML}, an asymptotic basis for inference is available. In particular, all of the usual asymptotic Chi-square and asymptotic normal tests and confidence region procedures discussed previously in the context of ML-extremum estimation apply here.

► **Example 15.1.2:** To demonstrate the setup and application of the concentrated ML estimator in (15.1.13), we provide the GAUSS program C15ConML.gss in the examples manual. The DSP used in the demonstration is based on the heteroscedastic linear regression model discussed in Section 14.4.2. For a given sample, the ML estimates of $\boldsymbol{\beta}$, σ^2, and γ are computed by GAUSS. Then, the sampling properties of the ML estimator are simulated by Monte Carlo methods.

15.2. System of Linear Regression Equations

The regression model involving the system of linear regression equations

$$\begin{bmatrix} \mathbf{y}_1 \\ \mathbf{y}_2 \\ \vdots \\ \mathbf{y}_m \end{bmatrix} = \begin{bmatrix} \mathbf{x}_1 & & & \\ & \mathbf{x}_2 & & \\ & & \ddots & \\ & & & \mathbf{x}_m \end{bmatrix} \begin{bmatrix} \boldsymbol{\beta}_1 \\ \boldsymbol{\beta}_2 \\ \vdots \\ \boldsymbol{\beta}_m \end{bmatrix} + \begin{bmatrix} \varepsilon_1 \\ \varepsilon_2 \\ \vdots \\ \varepsilon_m \end{bmatrix}, \tag{15.2.1}$$

or, more compactly,

$$\mathbf{Y} = \mathbf{x}\boldsymbol{\beta} + \varepsilon \tag{15.2.2}$$

(recall (14.5.1)–(14.5.2) for variable definitions and dimensions) is an explicit example of how the parametric structure of the noise component covariance matrix is restricted to reduce the number of unknowns. In the standard seemingly unrelated regression (SUR) context (recall Section 14.5), the noise component elements *across equations* are assumed to be *contemporaneously* correlated. The noise component elements *across observations* are assumed to be uncorrelated, and the noise components within equations are assumed to be homoscedastic. These assumptions imply that the noise covariance matrix parametric structure is $\text{E}[\varepsilon\varepsilon'] = \sigma^2\boldsymbol{\Psi} = \boldsymbol{\Sigma} \otimes \mathbf{I}_n$ (recall (14.5.3)). We remind the reader that this covariance matrix applies to a vertically concatenated set of noise component vectors $[\varepsilon_1', \varepsilon_2', \ldots, \varepsilon_m']'$ composed of the $(n \times 1)$ noise component vector for each equation successively stacked in a single vector for all m equations. Note this covariance matrix assumption reduces the number of unknown covariance matrix parameters from $(nm)(nm + 1)/2$ to $m(m + 1)/2$.

15.2.1. Estimation: Semiparametric Case

If $\boldsymbol{\Sigma}$ is unknown, its elements, the σ_{ij}'s, can be consistently estimated by

$$\hat{\sigma}_{ij} = n^{-1}\hat{\mathbf{e}}_i'\hat{\mathbf{e}}_j; \quad i, j = 1, 2, \ldots, m, \tag{15.2.3}$$

where $\hat{\mathbf{e}}_i = \mathbf{y}_i - \mathbf{x}_i\hat{\mathbf{b}}_i$ and $\hat{\mathbf{b}}_i = (\mathbf{x}_i'\mathbf{x}_i)^{-1}\mathbf{x}_i'\mathbf{y}_i$ is the least-squares estimator of the parameters contained in the ith equation $\mathbf{Y}_i = \mathbf{x}_i\boldsymbol{\beta} + \varepsilon_i$. If the estimator $\hat{\sigma}_{ij}$ replaces the unknown σ_{ij} in the GLS estimator of the set of equations, the EGLS estimator

$$\hat{\boldsymbol{\beta}}_{\mathrm{EG}} = [\mathbf{x}'(\hat{\boldsymbol{\Sigma}}^{-1} \otimes \mathbf{I})\mathbf{x}]^{-1}\mathbf{x}'(\hat{\boldsymbol{\Sigma}}^{-1} \otimes \mathbf{I})\mathbf{Y} \tag{15.2.4}$$

results, where the (i, j)th element of $\hat{\boldsymbol{\Sigma}}$ is given by (15.2.3).

In terms of asymptotic properties, the estimator $\hat{\boldsymbol{\beta}}_{\mathrm{EG}}$ will have the same asymptotic properties as the estimator $\hat{\boldsymbol{\beta}}_{\mathrm{G}}$, which is based on a known positive definite $\boldsymbol{\Sigma}$, if

$$n^{-1}[\mathbf{x}'(\hat{\boldsymbol{\Sigma}}^{-1} \otimes \mathbf{I})\mathbf{x}] - n^{-1}[\mathbf{x}'(\boldsymbol{\Sigma}^{-1} \otimes \mathbf{I})\mathbf{x}] \xrightarrow{\mathrm{p}} \mathbf{0} \tag{15.2.5}$$

and

$$n^{-1/2}[\mathbf{x}'(\hat{\boldsymbol{\Sigma}}^{-1} \otimes \mathbf{I})\varepsilon] - n^{-1/2}[\mathbf{x}'(\boldsymbol{\Sigma}^{-1} \otimes \mathbf{I})\varepsilon] \xrightarrow{\mathrm{p}} \mathbf{0}, \tag{15.2.6}$$

which are the analog conditions to those in the single equation case (15.1.4). Given the special structure of the covariance matrix of ε assumed in this case, sufficient conditions for (15.2.5) and (15.2.6) are

$$\hat{\boldsymbol{\Sigma}} \xrightarrow{\mathrm{p}} \boldsymbol{\Sigma} \quad \text{and} \quad n^{-1}\mathbf{x}_*'\mathbf{x}_* \to \mathbf{q}, \text{ a finite positive semidefinite matrix,} \tag{15.2.7}$$

where $\mathbf{x}_* = [\mathbf{x}_1 \vdots \mathbf{x}_2 \vdots \cdots \vdots \mathbf{x}_m]$. To motivate sufficiency, first let $\hat{\sigma}^{ij}$ and σ^{ij} denote the (i, j)th entries in the matrices $\hat{\boldsymbol{\Sigma}}^{-1}$ and $\boldsymbol{\Sigma}^{-1}$, respectively. Then condition (15.2.5) can be represented as

$$\begin{bmatrix} (\hat{\sigma}^{11} - \sigma^{11})n^{-1}\mathbf{x}_1'\mathbf{x}_1 & (\hat{\sigma}^{12} - \sigma^{12})n^{-1}\mathbf{x}_1'\mathbf{x}_2 & \cdots & (\hat{\sigma}^{1m} - \sigma^{1m})n^{-1}\mathbf{x}_1'\mathbf{x}_m \\ (\hat{\sigma}^{21} - \sigma^{21})n^{-1}\mathbf{x}_2'\mathbf{x}_1 & (\hat{\sigma}^{22} - \sigma^{22})n^{-1}\mathbf{x}_2'\mathbf{x}_2 & \cdots & (\hat{\sigma}^{2m} - \sigma^{2m})n^{-1}\mathbf{x}_2'\mathbf{x}_m \\ \vdots & \vdots & \ddots & \vdots \\ (\hat{\sigma}^{m1} - \sigma^{m1})n^{-1}\mathbf{x}_m'\mathbf{x}_1 & (\hat{\sigma}^{m2} - \sigma^{m2})n^{-1}\mathbf{x}_m'\mathbf{x}_2 & \cdots & (\hat{\sigma}^{mm} - \sigma^{mm})n^{-1}\mathbf{x}_m'\mathbf{x}_m \end{bmatrix} \xrightarrow{\mathrm{p}} \mathbf{0}, \tag{15.2.8}$$

and condition (15.2.6) can be written as

$$\begin{bmatrix} \sum_{j=1}^{m}(\hat{\sigma}^{1j} - \sigma^{1j})n^{-1/2}\mathbf{x}_1'\varepsilon_j \\ \sum_{j=1}^{m}(\hat{\sigma}^{2j} - \sigma^{2j})n^{-1/2}\mathbf{x}_2'\varepsilon_j \\ \vdots \\ \sum_{j=1}^{m}(\hat{\sigma}^{mj} - \sigma^{mj})n^{-1/2}\mathbf{x}_m'\varepsilon_j \end{bmatrix} \xrightarrow{\mathrm{p}} \mathbf{0}. \tag{15.2.9}$$

The conditions (15.2.7) imply that $\lim_{n\to\infty} n^{-1}\mathbf{x}_i'\mathbf{x}_j$ exists and is finite and $\hat{\sigma}^{ij} - \sigma^{ij} \xrightarrow{\mathrm{p}} 0 \,\forall i, j$. It follows from Slutsky's theorem that the probability limit of every element of (15.2.8) is zero, and thus (15.2.5) holds. Furthermore, because $\mathbf{cov}(n^{-1/2}\mathbf{x}_i'\varepsilon_j) = \sigma_{jj}n^{-1}\mathbf{x}_i'\mathbf{x}_i$ converges to a finite positive definite symmetric matrix when $n \to \infty \forall i$ by (15.2.7), then $[\hat{\sigma}^{ij} - \sigma^{ij}][n^{-1/2}\mathbf{x}_i'\varepsilon_j] = [\mathrm{o_p}(1)][\mathrm{O_p}(1)] \xrightarrow{\mathrm{p}} 0 \,\forall i, j$, and thus condition (15.2.9) holds.

If conditions for the asymptotic normality of $\hat{\boldsymbol{\beta}}_{\mathrm{G}}$ and the conditions (15.2.5)–(15.2.7) are assumed, it follows that

$$\hat{\boldsymbol{\beta}}_{\mathrm{EG}} \overset{\mathrm{a}}{\sim} \mathrm{N}(\boldsymbol{\beta}, [\mathbf{x}'(\boldsymbol{\Sigma}^{-1} \otimes \mathbf{I})\mathbf{x}]^{-1}). \tag{15.2.10}$$

In the light of (15.2.5), the asymptotic covariance matrix of $\hat{\boldsymbol{\beta}}_{\mathrm{EG}}$ can be estimated by $[\mathbf{x}(\hat{\boldsymbol{\Sigma}}^{-1} \otimes \mathbf{I})\mathbf{x}]^{-1}$.

15.2.2. Testing and Confidence Regions: Semiparametric Case

Asymptotically valid tests of the hypothesis $\mathrm{H_0}\colon \mathbf{c}\boldsymbol{\beta} = \mathbf{r}$ can be constructed using the asymptotic normal distribution of $\hat{\boldsymbol{\beta}}_{\mathrm{EG}}$. For example, a Wald statistic can be defined as

$$\mathrm{W} = [\mathbf{c}\hat{\boldsymbol{\beta}}_{\mathrm{EG}} - \mathbf{r}]'[\mathbf{c}[\mathbf{x}'(\hat{\boldsymbol{\Sigma}}^{-1} \otimes \mathbf{I})\mathbf{x}]^{-1}\mathbf{c}']^{-1}[\mathbf{c}\hat{\boldsymbol{\beta}}_{\mathrm{EG}} - \mathbf{r}] \overset{\mathrm{a}}{\sim} \text{Chi-square}(j, \lambda) \tag{15.2.11}$$

and the rejection region for an asymptotic level-α test would be given by $\mathrm{C^W} = [\chi^2_{1-\alpha}, \infty)$, where $\chi^2_{1-\alpha}$ is the $100(1-\alpha)\%$ quantile of the central Chi-square distribution with j degrees of freedom. The noncentrality parameter for the test is given by

$$\lambda = \frac{1}{2}\boldsymbol{\delta}'[\mathbf{c}\,\mathbf{m}^{-1}\mathbf{c}']^{-1}\boldsymbol{\delta}, \tag{15.2.12}$$

where now $\mathbf{m} = \lim_{n\to\infty} n^{-1}\mathbf{x}'(\boldsymbol{\Sigma}^{-1} \otimes \mathbf{I})\mathbf{x}$ and $\boldsymbol{\delta}$ is a $(j \times 1)$ vector defining Pitman drift-type hypotheses of the form $\mathrm{H}\colon \mathbf{c}\boldsymbol{\beta} = \mathbf{r} + n^{-1/2}\boldsymbol{\delta}$. An LM test can be based on the Lagrange multipliers associated with the constraints $\mathrm{H_0}\colon \mathbf{c}\boldsymbol{\beta} = \mathbf{r}$ in the extremum problem $\min_{\boldsymbol{\beta}}[(\mathbf{y} - \mathbf{x}\boldsymbol{\beta})'(\hat{\boldsymbol{\Sigma}}^{-1} \otimes \mathbf{I})(\mathbf{y} - \mathbf{x}\boldsymbol{\beta}) - \boldsymbol{\gamma}'(\mathbf{c}\boldsymbol{\beta} - \mathbf{r})]$. Pseudo-likelihood ratio tests can be based on the extremum objective function evaluated at the constrained and unconstrained estimates of $\boldsymbol{\beta}$.

We note that a prominent use of procedures for testing $\mathrm{H_0}\colon \mathbf{c}\boldsymbol{\beta} = \mathbf{r}$ within the systems of equations context relates to testing *cross-equation restrictions*. For example, in the context of demand equation systems, the neoclassical symmetry conditions imply constraints across pairs of demand equations. Another application relates to the possibility of data pooling, where one tests whether the parameters across equations in (15.2.1) are all equal, that is, $\boldsymbol{\beta}_1 = \boldsymbol{\beta}_2 = \cdots = \boldsymbol{\beta}_m$. If in fact the hypothesis were true, then all of the data can be "pooled" into one single-equation regression relationship $\mathbf{Y} = \mathbf{x}\boldsymbol{\beta} + \varepsilon$, where now $\mathbf{x}$ is $(nm \times k)$ with $\mathbf{x}_i$'s in (15.2.1) vertically stacked or concatenated on top of one another, and $\boldsymbol{\beta}$ is a $(k \times 1)$ vector. Note of course that for this pooling to make sense, it is assumed at the outset that $\mathbf{x}_i$ is $(n_i \times k)$, for $i = 1, \ldots, m$.

Tests of scalar linear restrictions or linear inequalities can be based on the asymptotically normally-distributed Z-statistic

$$\mathrm{Z} = [\mathbf{c}\hat{\boldsymbol{\beta}}_{\mathrm{EG}} - \mathrm{r}]/[\mathbf{c}[\mathbf{x}'(\hat{\boldsymbol{\Sigma}}^{-1} \otimes \mathbf{I})\mathbf{x}]^{-1}\mathbf{c}']^{1/2} \overset{\mathrm{a}}{\sim} \mathrm{N}\left(\frac{\delta}{[\mathbf{c}\,\mathbf{m}^{-1}\mathbf{c}']^{1/2}}, 1\right), \tag{15.2.13}$$

where δ is a scalar defining Pitman drift-type hypotheses such as H: $\mathbf{c}\boldsymbol{\beta} = \mathrm{r} + n^{-1/2}\delta$. The critical regions for various hypothesis tests based on (15.2.13) are precisely those presented in Equation (14.3.7). Confidence regions, intervals, and bounds can be obtained in the usual way based on duality with hypothesis tests.

15.2.3. ML Approach: Parametric Case

If the noise component of the system of regression equations is multivariate normally distributed, then the $\boldsymbol{\beta}$ and $\boldsymbol{\Sigma}$ parameters can be estimated using the ML procedure. The log of the likelihood function is given by

$$\begin{aligned}\ln \mathrm{L}(\boldsymbol{\beta}, \boldsymbol{\Sigma}; \mathbf{y}, \mathbf{x}) &= \frac{-nm}{2}\ln(2\pi) - \frac{1}{2}\ln(\det[\boldsymbol{\Sigma} \otimes \mathbf{I}]) - \frac{1}{2}(\mathbf{y} - \mathbf{x}\boldsymbol{\beta})'(\boldsymbol{\Sigma} \otimes \mathbf{I})^{-1}(\mathbf{y} - \mathbf{x}\boldsymbol{\beta}) \\ &= \frac{-nm}{2}\ln(2\pi) - \frac{n}{2}\ln(\det[\boldsymbol{\Sigma}]) - \frac{1}{2}(\mathbf{y} - \mathbf{x}\boldsymbol{\beta})'(\boldsymbol{\Sigma}^{-1} \otimes \mathbf{I})(\mathbf{y} - \mathbf{x}\boldsymbol{\beta}).\end{aligned} \tag{15.2.14}$$

Maximizing $\ln \mathrm{L}(\boldsymbol{\beta}, \boldsymbol{\Sigma} \mid \mathbf{y}, \mathbf{x})$ with respect to $\boldsymbol{\beta}$ and $\boldsymbol{\Sigma}$ yields a maximum likelihood estimate for $\boldsymbol{\beta}$ that is in precisely the same form as (15.2.4) and an ML estimate for $\boldsymbol{\Sigma}$ that has the form (15.2.3) with estimated noise component elements defined by $\hat{\mathbf{e}}_i = \mathbf{y}_i - \mathbf{x}_i\hat{\mathbf{b}}_{\mathrm{ML}i}$. To see this, first note that the log-likelihood function can be rewritten as (recall that $\det[\boldsymbol{\Sigma}^{-1}] = 1/\det[\boldsymbol{\Sigma}]$)

$$\begin{aligned}\ln \mathrm{L}(\boldsymbol{\beta}, \boldsymbol{\Sigma}^{-1}; \mathbf{y}, \mathbf{x}) &= \frac{-nm}{2}\ln(2\pi) + \frac{n}{2}\ln(\det[\boldsymbol{\Sigma}^{-1}]) \\ &\quad - \frac{1}{2}\sum_{i=1}^{n}\mathrm{tr}\left[\boldsymbol{\Sigma}^{-1}(\mathbf{y}_{(i)} - \mathbf{x}_{(i)}\boldsymbol{\beta})(\mathbf{y}_{(i)} - \mathbf{x}_{(i)}\boldsymbol{\beta})'\right] \\ &= \frac{-nm}{2}\ln(2\pi) + \frac{n}{2}\ln(\det[\boldsymbol{\Sigma}^{-1}]) \\ &\quad - \frac{1}{2}\mathrm{tr}\left[\boldsymbol{\Sigma}^{-1}\sum_{i=1}^{n}(\mathbf{y}_{(i)} - \mathbf{x}_{(i)}\boldsymbol{\beta})(\mathbf{y}_{(i)} - \mathbf{x}_{(i)}\boldsymbol{\beta})'\right],\end{aligned} \tag{15.2.15}$$

where $\mathbf{y}_{(i)}$ is an $(m \times 1)$ vector representing the ith observation on the m dependent variables in the system (15.2.1) and $\mathbf{x}_{(i)}$ is an $(m \times k)$ matrix representing the ith observation on the explanatory variables, respectively, corresponding to the elements in $\mathbf{y}_{(i)}$.

Note that (15.2.15) effectively reparameterizes the likelihood function in terms of the parameters in the *inverse* of the contemporaneous covariance matrix $\boldsymbol{\Sigma}^{-1}$ as opposed to the covariance matrix itself, as in (15.2.14). We do this to simplify the first-order conditions with respect to the covariance matrix parameters and to simplify the subsequent identification of the ML estimates. Taking the derivatives of ln L with respect to $\boldsymbol{\beta}$ yields

$$\frac{\partial \ln \mathrm{L}}{\partial \boldsymbol{\beta}} = \mathbf{x}'(\boldsymbol{\Sigma}^{-1} \otimes \mathbf{I})(\mathbf{y} - \mathbf{x}\boldsymbol{\beta}) = \mathbf{0}, \tag{15.2.16}$$

which is most easily seen as the derivative of the quadratic form term in (15.2.14). Taking the derivative of (15.2.15) with respect to the parameter matrix $\boldsymbol{\Sigma}^{-1}$ yields

$$\frac{\partial \ln \mathrm{L}}{\partial \boldsymbol{\Sigma}^{-1}} = \frac{n}{2}\boldsymbol{\Sigma} - \frac{1}{2}\sum_{i=1}^{n}\left(\mathbf{y}_{(i)} - \mathbf{x}_{(i)}\boldsymbol{\beta}\right)\left(\mathbf{y}_{(i)} - \mathbf{x}_{(i)}\boldsymbol{\beta}\right)' = \mathbf{0} \tag{15.2.17}$$

because, for any nonsingular matrix $\mathbf{A}$, $\frac{\partial \ln(\det[\mathbf{A}])}{\partial \mathbf{A}} = [\mathbf{A}^{-1}]'$, and if $\mathbf{B}$ is any other conformable matrix, $\frac{\partial \mathrm{tr}(\mathbf{AB})}{\partial \mathbf{A}} = \mathbf{B}'$ (see the matrix review manual). In the current application of these matrix differentiation formulas, $\mathbf{A} = \boldsymbol{\Sigma}^{-1}$ and $\mathbf{B} = \sum_{i=1}^{n}(\mathbf{y}_{(i)} - \mathbf{x}_{(i)}\boldsymbol{\beta})(\mathbf{y}_{(i)} - \mathbf{x}_{(i)}\boldsymbol{\beta})'$.

Solving (15.2.16) and (15.2.17) for $\boldsymbol{\beta}$ and $\boldsymbol{\Sigma}$ yields

$$\boldsymbol{\beta} = [\mathbf{x}'(\boldsymbol{\Sigma}^{-1} \otimes \mathbf{I})\mathbf{x}]^{-1}\mathbf{x}'(\boldsymbol{\Sigma}^{-1} \otimes \mathbf{I})\mathbf{y} \tag{15.2.18}$$

and

$$\boldsymbol{\Sigma} = \frac{1}{n}\sum_{i=1}^{n}\left(\mathbf{y}_{(i)} - \mathbf{x}_{(i)}\boldsymbol{\beta}\right)\left(\mathbf{y}_{(i)} - \mathbf{x}_{(i)}\boldsymbol{\beta}\right)'. \tag{15.2.19}$$

Note that (15.2.18) and (15.2.19) are not a closed form solution for the parameters because the expression for $\boldsymbol{\beta}$ depends on $\boldsymbol{\Sigma}$ and vice versa. There are two basic methods used in practice to obtain values for the ML estimates. One procedure is to apply computer-driven numerical optimization techniques to (15.2.15). To reduce the dimensionality of the numerical search for a maximum of the likelihood function, one can concentrate the likelihood function by substituting out either $\boldsymbol{\beta}$ or $\boldsymbol{\Sigma}$ via substitution of (15.2.18) or (15.2.19) into (15.2.15). For example, to concentrate the likelihood function so that it is a function of only $\boldsymbol{\beta}$, one can substitute (15.2.19) into (15.2.15) to yield ultimately

$$\ln \mathrm{L}_c(\boldsymbol{\beta}; \mathbf{y}, \mathbf{x}) = \frac{-nm}{2}[\ln(2\pi) + 1] - \frac{n}{2}\ln\left(\det\left[\frac{1}{n}\sum_{i=1}^{n}\left(\mathbf{y}_{(i)} - \mathbf{x}_{(i)}\boldsymbol{\beta}\right)\left(\mathbf{y}_{(i)} - \mathbf{x}_{(i)}\boldsymbol{\beta}\right)'\right]\right) \tag{15.2.20}$$

Then (15.2.20) can be maximized numerically to yield the ML estimate of $\boldsymbol{\beta}$, which can be substituted into (15.2.19) to obtain the ML estimate of $\boldsymbol{\Sigma}$.

An alternative numerical procedure for obtaining the ML estimates of $\boldsymbol{\beta}$ or $\boldsymbol{\Sigma}$ is to iterate between solving (15.2.18) and (15.2.19) until the two solutions are in agreement (within some prespecified degree of accuracy or "tolerance"). To implement this iterative procedure, one begins with an initial estimate of $\boldsymbol{\beta}$, say $\boldsymbol{\beta}^{(1)}$, which generally equals the EGLS estimate of $\boldsymbol{\beta}$. Then this estimate is used in (15.2.19) to produce an estimate of $\boldsymbol{\Sigma}$, say $\boldsymbol{\Sigma}^{(1)}$. The estimate $\boldsymbol{\Sigma}^{(1)}$ is used in (15.2.18) to produce $\boldsymbol{\beta}^{(2)}$, which in turn is used in (15.2.19) to produce $\boldsymbol{\Sigma}^{(2)}$, and so on iteratively, according to the sequence $\boldsymbol{\beta}^{(1)} \to \boldsymbol{\Sigma}^{(1)} \to \boldsymbol{\beta}^{(2)} \to \boldsymbol{\Sigma}^{(2)} \to \boldsymbol{\beta}^{(3)} \to \boldsymbol{\Sigma}^{(3)} \to \cdots$, until (15.2.18) and (15.2.19) are mutually satisfied up to the chosen level of accuracy.

The ML estimators $\hat{\boldsymbol{\beta}}_{\mathrm{ML}}$ and $\hat{\boldsymbol{\Sigma}}_{\mathrm{ML}}$ possesses all of the typical ML asymptotic properties, including consistency, asymptotic normality, and asymptotic efficiency. Furthermore, $\hat{\boldsymbol{\beta}}_{\mathrm{EG}}$ and $\hat{\boldsymbol{\beta}}_{\mathrm{ML}}$ are asymptotically equivalent, as intuition would suggest upon one's noting from (15.2.18) that the functional forms of the ML and EGLS estimators differ only with respect to which estimator is used for the unknown contemporaneous covariance matrix $\boldsymbol{\Sigma}$, and both of these covariance estimators converge to the true $\boldsymbol{\Sigma}$. Because $\hat{\boldsymbol{\beta}}_{\text{EG}}$ and $\hat{\boldsymbol{\beta}}_{\text{ML}}$ are asymptotically equivalent, hypothesis testing and confidence region estimation can proceed precisely as indicated in Section 15.2.2. In addition, procedures based on the generalized likelihood ratio statistic are also applicable in the usual way and result in asymptotic Chi-square-distributed test statistics with the same asymptotic distribution as those based on Wald or LM statistics.

Although the ML and EGLS are asymptotically equivalent, they are not generally equivalent in finite samples. Which of the two estimators is preferred in finite samples is an open question because there are no finite sample results available that establish the unequivocal superiority of one estimator's sampling properties over the other. In fact, there are also no results suggesting that either the ML or EGLS estimator is always preferred to the LS estimator applied equation by equation, which effectively ignores any contemporaneous correlation among noise components. What we do know is that *if the sample size is large enough, if the noise component is multivariate normally distributed, if the linear model specification is true*, and *if the noise component covariance actually has the functional structure* $\boldsymbol{\Sigma} \otimes \mathbf{I}$, then $\hat{\boldsymbol{\beta}}_{\text{ML}}$ will tend to be the most efficient estimator of $\boldsymbol{\beta}$ in the system of equations (15.2.1).

15.3. Nonlinear Regression Models with Unknown Noise Covariance

The EGLS procedure examined in the previous section can be extended to estimate the parameters of single- and multiple-equation nonlinear regression models in the case in which the noise covariance matrix is unknown. We note that the introductory remarks made at the beginning of Section 15.1 apply equally well here, except that the nonlinear least-squares method of estimation would be used in place of the estimator (15.1.1).

15.3.1. Single-Equation Semiparametric Nonlinear Regression Model

In this section we examine the case of the semiparametric nonlinear regression model to which the GLS estimator of Section 14.3 could be applied if $\boldsymbol{\Psi}$ were known. We will see that under the appropriate regularity conditions, many of the results involving the GLS estimator and associated inference procedures apply even when $\boldsymbol{\Psi}$ is unknown.

15.3.2. Estimation

If it is assumed that the conditions of Theorems 8.9.1 and 8.9.2 hold, with $\mathbf{Y}_* = \boldsymbol{\Psi}^{-1/2}\mathbf{Y}$ replacing $\mathbf{Y}$, $\mathbf{g}(\mathbf{x}, \boldsymbol{\beta})$ replaced by $\mathbf{g}_*(\mathbf{x}, \boldsymbol{\beta}) = \boldsymbol{\Psi}^{-1/2}\mathbf{g}(\mathbf{x}, \boldsymbol{\beta})$, and $\frac{\partial \mathbf{g}(\mathbf{x}, \boldsymbol{\beta})}{\partial \boldsymbol{\beta}}$ replaced by $\frac{\partial \mathbf{g}_*(\mathbf{x}, \boldsymbol{\beta})}{\partial \boldsymbol{\beta}} \equiv \frac{\partial \mathbf{g}(\mathbf{x}, \boldsymbol{\beta})}{\partial \boldsymbol{\beta}} \boldsymbol{\Psi}^{-1/2}$, it follows from the theorems that $\hat{\boldsymbol{\beta}}_{\text{G}} \xrightarrow{p} \boldsymbol{\beta}$ and

$$\hat{\boldsymbol{\beta}}_{\text{G}} = \boldsymbol{\beta} + [\mathbf{x}(\boldsymbol{\beta})'\boldsymbol{\Psi}^{-1}\mathbf{x}(\boldsymbol{\beta})]^{-1}\mathbf{x}(\boldsymbol{\beta})'\boldsymbol{\Psi}^{-1}\boldsymbol{\varepsilon} + \mathbf{o}_{\text{p}}(n^{-1/2}) \stackrel{a}{\sim} \text{N}(\boldsymbol{\beta}, \sigma^2[\mathbf{x}(\boldsymbol{\beta})'\boldsymbol{\Psi}^{-1}\mathbf{x}(\boldsymbol{\beta})]^{-1}), \tag{15.3.1}$$

where $\mathbf{x}(\boldsymbol{\beta}) \equiv [\frac{\partial \mathbf{g}(\mathbf{x}, \boldsymbol{\beta})}{\partial \boldsymbol{\beta}}]'$, $n^{-1}[\mathbf{x}(\boldsymbol{\beta})'\boldsymbol{\Psi}^{-1}\mathbf{x}(\boldsymbol{\beta})] \to \boldsymbol{\Xi}$ and $n^{-1/2}\mathbf{x}(\boldsymbol{\beta})'\boldsymbol{\Psi}^{-1}\boldsymbol{\varepsilon} \xrightarrow{d} \mathrm{N}(\mathbf{0}, \sigma^2\boldsymbol{\Xi})$. Similarly, if the conditions of Theorems 8.9.1 and 8.9.2 hold, with $\mathbf{Y}_+ = \hat{\boldsymbol{\Psi}}^{-1/2}\mathbf{Y}$ replacing $\mathbf{Y}$, $\mathbf{g}(\mathbf{x}, \boldsymbol{\beta})$ replaced by $\mathbf{g}_+(\mathbf{x}, \boldsymbol{\beta}) \equiv \hat{\boldsymbol{\Psi}}^{-1/2}\mathbf{g}(\mathbf{x}, \boldsymbol{\beta})$, $\frac{\partial \mathbf{g}(\mathbf{x}, \boldsymbol{\beta})}{\partial \boldsymbol{\beta}}$ replaced by $\frac{\partial \mathbf{g}_+(\mathbf{x}, \boldsymbol{\beta})}{\partial \boldsymbol{\beta}} = \frac{\partial \mathbf{g}(\mathbf{x}, \boldsymbol{\beta})}{\partial \boldsymbol{\beta}}\hat{\boldsymbol{\Psi}}^{-1/2}$, and ordinary convergence replaced by convergence in probability where appropriate, the theorems imply that the *estimated* nonlinear GLS–extremum estimator of $\boldsymbol{\beta}$,

$$\hat{\boldsymbol{\beta}}_{\mathrm{EG}} = \arg\min_{\boldsymbol{\beta}}[[\mathbf{Y} - \mathbf{g}(\mathbf{x}, \boldsymbol{\beta})]'\hat{\boldsymbol{\Psi}}^{-1}[\mathbf{Y} - \mathbf{g}(\mathbf{x}, \boldsymbol{\beta})]], \tag{15.3.2}$$

is such that $\hat{\boldsymbol{\beta}}_{\mathrm{EG}} \xrightarrow{p} \boldsymbol{\beta}$ and

$$\hat{\boldsymbol{\beta}}_{\mathrm{EG}} = \boldsymbol{\beta} + [\mathbf{x}(\boldsymbol{\beta})'\hat{\boldsymbol{\Psi}}^{-1}\mathbf{x}(\boldsymbol{\beta})]^{-1}\mathbf{x}(\boldsymbol{\beta})'\hat{\boldsymbol{\Psi}}^{-1}\boldsymbol{\varepsilon} + \mathbf{o}_{\mathrm{p}}(n^{-1/2}) \overset{a}{\sim} \mathrm{N}(\boldsymbol{\beta}, \sigma^2[\mathbf{x}(\boldsymbol{\beta})'\hat{\boldsymbol{\Psi}}^{-1}\mathbf{x}(\boldsymbol{\beta})]^{-1}), \tag{15.3.3}$$

where $n^{-1}[\mathbf{x}(\boldsymbol{\beta})'\hat{\boldsymbol{\Psi}}^{-1}\mathbf{x}(\boldsymbol{\beta})] \xrightarrow{p} \boldsymbol{\Xi}_+$ and $n^{-1/2}\mathbf{x}(\boldsymbol{\beta})'\hat{\boldsymbol{\Psi}}^{-1}\boldsymbol{\varepsilon} \xrightarrow{d} \mathrm{N}(\mathbf{0}, \sigma^2\boldsymbol{\Xi}_+)$. If $\boldsymbol{\Xi} = \boldsymbol{\Xi}_+$, then the asymptotic properties of $\hat{\boldsymbol{\beta}}_{\mathrm{G}}$ and $\hat{\boldsymbol{\beta}}_{\mathrm{EG}}$ will be identical. Sufficient conditions for this equivalence, which should be compared with (15.1.4), are given by

$$n^{-1}[\mathbf{x}(\boldsymbol{\beta})'\hat{\boldsymbol{\Psi}}^{-1}\mathbf{x}(\boldsymbol{\beta})] - n^{-1}[\mathbf{x}(\boldsymbol{\beta})'\boldsymbol{\Psi}^{-1}\mathbf{x}(\boldsymbol{\beta})] \xrightarrow{p} \mathbf{0}$$

and

$$n^{-1/2}[\mathbf{x}(\boldsymbol{\beta})'\hat{\boldsymbol{\Psi}}^{-1}\boldsymbol{\varepsilon}] - n^{-1/2}[\mathbf{x}(\boldsymbol{\beta})'\boldsymbol{\Psi}^{-1}\boldsymbol{\varepsilon}] \xrightarrow{p} \mathbf{0} \tag{15.3.4}$$

As we noted following (15.1.4), the elementwise consistency of the estimator $\hat{\boldsymbol{\Psi}}$ for $\boldsymbol{\Psi}$ is not sufficient for (15.3.4) to hold. In fact, the previous discussion on this point following (15.1.4) applies equally well here with $\mathbf{x}$ replaced by $\mathbf{x}(\boldsymbol{\beta})$. In addition, the previous point made regarding the asymptotic inefficiency of the nonlinear least-squares estimator $\hat{\boldsymbol{\beta}} \overset{a}{\sim} \mathrm{N}(\boldsymbol{\beta}, \sigma^2[\mathbf{x}(\boldsymbol{\beta})'\mathbf{x}(\boldsymbol{\beta})]^{-1}[\mathbf{x}(\boldsymbol{\beta})'\boldsymbol{\Psi}\mathbf{x}(\boldsymbol{\beta})][\mathbf{x}(\boldsymbol{\beta})'\mathbf{x}(\boldsymbol{\beta})]^{-1})$ also applies here. In particular, given the asymptotic equivalence of $\hat{\boldsymbol{\beta}}_{\mathrm{EG}}$ and $\hat{\boldsymbol{\beta}}_{\mathrm{G}}$, the same argument relating to Equation (15.1.8) can be applied here to demonstrate that $\hat{\boldsymbol{\beta}}_{\mathrm{EG}}$ is no less, and generally more, *asymptotically* efficient than $\hat{\boldsymbol{\beta}}$. However, the reader is asked to reread the paragraph preceding Section 15.1.1.c for a cautionary note on this asymptotic efficiency result that applies equally well to the case at hand.

15.3.3. Testing and Confidence Regions

Hypothesis tests and confidence region estimation can proceed as in Section 14.3.2 with $\boldsymbol{\Psi}$ replaced by $\hat{\boldsymbol{\Psi}}$ and $\mathrm{S}_{\mathrm{G}}^2$ defined via 14.3.4 but with $\hat{\boldsymbol{\Psi}}$ again replacing $\boldsymbol{\Psi}$. As long as the regularity conditions are met, so that $\hat{\boldsymbol{\beta}}_{\mathrm{EG}}$ and $\hat{\boldsymbol{\beta}}_{\mathrm{G}}$ have identical consistency and asymptotic normality properties, the *asymptotic* properties attributed to the test and confidence region procedures when $\boldsymbol{\Psi}$ is known (see Section 14.3.2) also apply when $\boldsymbol{\Psi}$ is estimated by $\hat{\boldsymbol{\Psi}}$ and σ^2 is replaced by $\mathrm{S}_{\mathrm{G}}^2$.

15.3.4. Single-Equation Parametric Nonlinear Regression Model – ML Approach

If the probability distribution of the noise component of the nonlinear regression model can be assumed to belong to the multivariate normal parametric family, or some other parametric family of probability distributions, then the ML procedure can be used to estimate the unknown parameters. We examine the case of multivariate normality and note that the log of the likelihood function can be written in the form

$$\ln \mathrm{L}(\boldsymbol{\beta}, \sigma^2, \gamma; \mathbf{y}, \mathbf{x}) = \frac{-n}{2} \ln(2\pi\sigma^2) - \frac{1}{2} \ln(\det[\boldsymbol{\Psi}(\gamma)]) - \frac{1}{2\sigma^2}[\mathbf{y} - \mathbf{g}(\mathbf{x}, \boldsymbol{\beta})]'[\boldsymbol{\Psi}(\gamma)]^{-1}[\mathbf{y} - \mathbf{g}(\mathbf{x}, \boldsymbol{\beta})], \tag{15.3.5}$$

where $\boldsymbol{\Psi}(\gamma)$ expresses the elements of the $\boldsymbol{\Psi}$ component of the covariance matrix $\sigma^2\boldsymbol{\Psi}$ as a function of a fixed set of parameters γ. Maximizing $\ln \mathrm{L}$ with respect to $\boldsymbol{\beta}$ and γ leads to the ML estimate

$$(\hat{\boldsymbol{\beta}}_{\mathrm{ML}}, \hat{\sigma}^2, \hat{\gamma}_{\mathrm{ML}}) = \arg \max_{\boldsymbol{\beta}, \sigma^2, \gamma} [\ln \mathrm{L}(\boldsymbol{\beta}, \sigma^2, \gamma; \mathbf{y}, \mathbf{x})]. \tag{15.3.6}$$

The ML estimator of $\boldsymbol{\Psi}$ is then given by $\hat{\boldsymbol{\Psi}}_{\mathrm{ML}} = \boldsymbol{\Psi}(\hat{\gamma}_{\mathrm{ML}})$.

Regarding a solution method for obtaining the ML estimates, computer-driven numerical optimization procedures will again be required. The first-order conditions with respect to $\boldsymbol{\beta}$ of the extremum estimation problem (15.3.6) are given by

$$\frac{\partial \ln \mathrm{L}}{\partial \boldsymbol{\beta}} = \frac{1}{\sigma^2} \frac{\partial \mathbf{g}(\mathbf{x}, \boldsymbol{\beta})}{\partial \boldsymbol{\beta}} [\boldsymbol{\Psi}(\gamma)]^{-1}[\mathbf{y} - \mathbf{g}(\mathbf{x}, \boldsymbol{\beta})] = \mathbf{0}. \tag{15.3.7}$$

It is evident, either directly from (15.3.5) or from (15.3.7), that the solution for $\boldsymbol{\beta}$ is given by

$$\boldsymbol{\beta}(\gamma) = \arg \min_{\boldsymbol{\beta}} [[\mathbf{y} - \mathbf{g}(\mathbf{x}, \boldsymbol{\beta})]'[\boldsymbol{\Psi}(\gamma)]^{-1}[\mathbf{y} - \mathbf{g}(\mathbf{x}, \boldsymbol{\beta})]]. \tag{15.3.8}$$

The result (15.3.8) implies that differences in the ML and nonlinear EGLS estimates are exclusively due to differences in the estimates used for $\boldsymbol{\Psi}$ (recall (15.3.2)).

The-first order condition with respect to σ^2 is given by

$$\frac{\partial \ln \mathrm{L}}{\partial \sigma^2} = \frac{-n}{2\sigma^2} + \frac{1}{2\sigma^4} [\mathbf{y} - \mathbf{g}(\mathbf{x}, \boldsymbol{\beta})]' [\boldsymbol{\Psi}(\gamma)]^{-1} [\mathbf{y} - \mathbf{g}(\mathbf{x}, \boldsymbol{\beta})] = \mathbf{0}. \tag{15.3.9}$$

This condition, together with (15.3.8), can be solved for σ^2 to yield

$$\sigma^2(\gamma) = n^{-1} [\mathbf{y} - \mathbf{g}(\mathbf{x}, \boldsymbol{\beta}(\gamma))]' [\boldsymbol{\Psi}(\gamma)]^{-1} [\mathbf{y} - \mathbf{g}(\mathbf{x}, \boldsymbol{\beta}(\gamma))]. \tag{15.3.10}$$

A general statement of the first-order conditions with respect to γ is quite complicated. In particular, the first-order condition with respect to γ_i is given by

$$\frac{\partial \ln \mathrm{L}}{\partial \gamma_i} = \mathrm{tr}\left(\boldsymbol{\Psi}(\gamma) \frac{\partial [\boldsymbol{\Psi}(\gamma)]^{-1}}{\partial \gamma_i}\right) - \frac{1}{2\sigma^2}\left((\mathbf{y} - \mathbf{g}(\mathbf{x}, \boldsymbol{\beta}))' \frac{\partial [\boldsymbol{\Psi}(\gamma)]^{-1}}{\partial \gamma_i} (\mathbf{y} - \mathbf{g}(\mathbf{x}, \boldsymbol{\beta}))\right) = \mathbf{0}. \tag{15.3.11}$$

This result follows from (15.3.5) upon implementing the two general matrix differentiation results $\frac{\partial \ln(\det[\mathbf{A}(\gamma)])}{\partial \gamma_i} = \mathrm{tr}([\mathbf{A}(\gamma)]^{-1} \frac{\partial \mathbf{A}(\gamma)}{\partial \gamma_i})$ and $\frac{\partial \mathrm{tr}(\mathbf{A}(\gamma)\mathbf{B})}{\partial \gamma_i} = \mathrm{tr}([\mathbf{B} \frac{\partial \mathbf{A}(\gamma)}{\partial \gamma_i})$, where the matrix $\mathbf{B}$ is not a function of γ (see the matrix review manual). In general, the first-order conditions for the γ_i's given by (15.3.11) will not admit a closed form solution for γ. It may be possible to simplify these conditions in specific cases, but this depends entirely on the nature of the particular functional specification chosen for $\boldsymbol{\Psi}(\gamma)$. A solution procedure is to concentrate the likelihood function by substituting (15.3.8) and (15.3.10) into (15.3.5), yielding the concentrated likelihood function

$$\begin{aligned}\ln \mathrm{L_c}(\gamma; \mathbf{y}, \mathbf{x}) = &-\frac{n}{2} \ln\{[\mathbf{y} - \mathbf{g}(\mathbf{x}, \mathbf{b}(\gamma))]'[\boldsymbol{\Psi}(\gamma)]^{-1}[\mathbf{y} - \mathbf{g}(\mathbf{x}, \mathbf{b}(\gamma))]\} \\ &-\frac{1}{2} \ln(\det[\boldsymbol{\Psi}(\gamma)]) + \mathrm{c},\end{aligned} \tag{15.3.12}$$

where $\mathrm{c} = -\frac{n}{2}[\ln(2\pi)+1-\ln(n)]$ (compare with (15.1.13)). The concentrated likelihood function is generally maximized using numerical search procedures, and then the ML estimate $\hat{\gamma}_{\mathrm{ML}}$ is substituted into (15.3.8) and (15.3.10) to define the ML estimates of $\boldsymbol{\beta}$ and σ^2.

The results on extremum estimators in Chapter 7 can be used to establish the usual consistency and asymptotic normality properties of the ML estimator. The ML estimator $\hat{\boldsymbol{\beta}}_{\mathrm{ML}}$ will have the same asymptotic properties as either $\hat{\boldsymbol{\beta}}_{\mathrm{G}}$ or $\hat{\boldsymbol{\beta}}_{\mathrm{EG}}$ under the regularity conditions (15.3.4), if it is assumed that $\boldsymbol{\Psi}(\gamma)$ is correctly specified as a function of γ. Given that $\boldsymbol{\varepsilon}$ truly is multivariate normally distributed, $\hat{\boldsymbol{\beta}}_{\mathrm{ML}}$ will also be asymptotically efficient. Hypothesis-testing and confidence-region estimation can proceed as in the case of either $\hat{\boldsymbol{\beta}}_{\mathrm{G}}$ or $\hat{\boldsymbol{\beta}}_{\mathrm{EG}}$. Note that asymptotic Chi-square tests and confidence-region estimation procedures based on the generalized likelihood ratio in the usual way are also available when ML techniques are used to estimate $\boldsymbol{\beta}$.

15.3.5. Sets of Nonlinear Regression Equations

In the case of a multiple equation nonlinear regression model the results of Section 14.5 can be extended to accommodate the case of an unknown noise component covariance matrix.

15.3.5.a. Semiparametric Model

For the semiparametric case, the objective becomes the minimization of the weighted sum of squares presented in (14.5.4), except now $\boldsymbol{\Sigma}$ is replaced by $\hat{\boldsymbol{\Sigma}}$. The estimated GLS estimator that results will be consistent and asymptotically normally distributed under regularity conditions analogous to those assumed in the single-equation case (Section 15.3.1) upon replacing $\hat{\boldsymbol{\Psi}}$ with $(\hat{\boldsymbol{\Sigma}} \otimes \mathbf{I})$, suppressing σ^2, and reinterpreting $\mathbf{Y}$ and $\mathbf{g}(\mathbf{x}, \boldsymbol{\beta})$ as vertically concatenated sets of dependent variable vectors and corresponding systematic components, respectively. In particular, under analogous regularity conditions, it follows that $\hat{\boldsymbol{\beta}}_{\mathrm{EG}} \xrightarrow{\mathrm{p}} \boldsymbol{\beta}$ and

$$\hat{\boldsymbol{\beta}}_{\mathrm{EG}} \overset{\mathrm{a}}{\sim} \mathrm{N}\left(\boldsymbol{\beta}, \left[\frac{\partial \mathbf{g}(\mathbf{x}, \boldsymbol{\beta})}{\partial \boldsymbol{\beta}}(\boldsymbol{\Sigma}^{-1} \otimes \mathbf{I})\frac{\partial \mathbf{g}(\mathbf{x}, \boldsymbol{\beta})}{\partial \boldsymbol{\beta}'}\right]^{-1}\right). \tag{15.3.13}$$

Hypothesis tests and confidence-region estimation can proceed as described in Section 14.5.2, except that $\hat{\Sigma}$ replaces Σ in all cases. For example, a Wald test of the nonlinear null hypothesis H_0: $\mathbf{c}(\boldsymbol{\beta}) = \mathbf{r}$ would be based on the asymptotically Chi-square-distributed statistic

$$\mathrm{W} = [\mathbf{c}(\hat{\boldsymbol{\beta}}) - \mathbf{r}]' \left[\frac{\partial \mathbf{c}(\boldsymbol{\beta})}{\partial \boldsymbol{\beta}'}\bigg|_{\hat{\beta}} \left[\frac{\partial \mathbf{g}(\mathbf{x}, \boldsymbol{\beta})}{\partial \boldsymbol{\beta}}\bigg|_{\hat{\beta}} (\hat{\boldsymbol{\Sigma}}^{-1} \otimes \mathbf{I}) \frac{\partial \mathbf{g}(\mathbf{x}, \boldsymbol{\beta})}{\partial \boldsymbol{\beta}'}\bigg|_{\hat{\beta}} \right]^{-1} \frac{\partial \mathbf{c}(\boldsymbol{\beta})}{\partial \boldsymbol{\beta}}\bigg|_{\hat{\beta}} \right]^{-1} [\mathbf{c}(\hat{\boldsymbol{\beta}}) - \mathbf{r}]. \tag{15.3.14}$$

A confidence region for $\mathbf{c}(\boldsymbol{\beta})$ can again be based on duality with hypothesis tests. For example, a Wald-type $(1 - \alpha)$ level confidence region could be defined as the set of all $\mathbf{r}$ values in (15.3.14) for which $\mathrm{w} < \chi^2_{1-\alpha}$, where $\chi^2_{1-\alpha}$ is the $100(1 - \alpha)\%$ quantile of the central Chi-square distribution with degrees of freedom equal to the number of coordinate functions in $\mathbf{c}(\boldsymbol{\beta})$ (if it is assumed that the coordinate functions are functionally independent).

15.3.5.b. Parametric Model

In a parametric multiple equation model, maximum likelihood procedures could be used to estimate both $\boldsymbol{\beta}$ and the parameter vector γ that determines the noise component covariance matrix $(\boldsymbol{\Sigma}(\gamma) \otimes \mathbf{I})$. Again, if $\mathbf{Y}$ and $\mathbf{g}(\mathbf{x}, \boldsymbol{\beta})$ are interpreted as a vertical concatenation of the dependent variable and systematic component observations across the m equations in a system, the log of the likelihood function for $\boldsymbol{\beta}$ and γ under multivariate normality becomes

$$\begin{aligned} \ln \mathrm{L}(\boldsymbol{\beta}, \gamma; \mathbf{y}, \mathbf{x}) = & \frac{-nm}{2} \ln(2\pi) - \frac{n}{2} \ln(\det[\boldsymbol{\Sigma}(\gamma)]) \\ & - \frac{1}{2} [\mathbf{y} - \mathbf{g}(\mathbf{x}, \boldsymbol{\beta})]' [\boldsymbol{\Sigma}^{-1}(\gamma) \otimes \mathbf{I}] [\mathbf{y} - \mathbf{g}(\mathbf{x}, \boldsymbol{\beta})]. \end{aligned} \tag{15.3.15}$$

Numerical solution issues are analogous to those discussed in Section 15.3.4.

The ML estimator will have the usual asymptotic properties of consistency and asymptotic normality and will be asymptotically equivalent to either $\hat{\boldsymbol{\beta}}_{\mathrm{G}}$ or $\hat{\boldsymbol{\beta}}_{\mathrm{EG}}$ if $\boldsymbol{\Sigma}(\gamma)$ is correctly specified as a function of γ. Given that the noise component is multivariate normally distributed, $\hat{\boldsymbol{\beta}}_{\mathrm{ML}}$ will also be asymptotically efficient. Hypothesis tests and confidence-region estimation can proceed analogously to methods applied in the case of GLS or EGLS estimation with the additional option of using generalized likelihood ratio procedures. Additional theoretical and computational details relating to the estimation of the parameters in the nonlinear system of equations can be found in the seminal work of Barnett (1976, 1981) and Phillips (1976) as well as in Gallant (1987).

15.4. Robust Solution Methods: OLS and Robust Covariance Matrix Estimation

Several approaches have been used in practice for generating solutions to inverse problem for regression models when $\boldsymbol{\Psi}$ is unknown. One approach to solving the inverse problem that has received considerable attention during the last three decades is the triad of modeling, testing, and estimating the precise form of the covariance matrix $\sigma^2\boldsymbol{\Psi}(\boldsymbol{\gamma})$. We examine this approach, along with its major benefits and costs in Chapter 19.

Another approach has been to ignore that $\sigma^2\boldsymbol{\Psi} \neq \sigma^2\mathbf{I}$ and apply ordinary least squares (OLS), as opposed to generalized least squares or ML with a general covariance matrix specification, to generate point estimates either in the linear or nonlinear model context. As we noted previously in Chapter 15, the OLS estimator is at least consistent and asymptotically normal under general regularity conditions. This approach avoids any possibility of model misspecification entering into the inverse problem owing to an incorrect specification of the structure of $\boldsymbol{\Psi}$, its parameterization, or both and thus is of interest when there is substantial uncertainty regarding the appropriate parameterization of the covariance matrix. Furthermore, even though we have seen that the OLS approach is asymptotically inefficient relative to EGLS when $\boldsymbol{\Psi}(\boldsymbol{\gamma})$ is correctly specified and appropriately estimated, this inefficiency is often moot in practice because of the difficulty in correctly specifying or accurately estimating (or both) the parametric form of $\boldsymbol{\Psi}(\boldsymbol{\gamma})$. Fortunately there are methods for consistently estimating the covariance matrix, or asymptotic covariance matrix, of OLS estimators even when the parametric structure of $\boldsymbol{\Psi}$ is unknown. This permits hypothesis testing and confidence region generation to proceed without an explicit specification for $\boldsymbol{\Psi}(\boldsymbol{\gamma})$. In summary, the OLS approach to estimating $\boldsymbol{\beta}$ can be thought of as a robust omnibus approach to handling the problem of a non-iid noise component that has reasonable statistical properties for a wide range of possibilities for the noise covariance matrix $\sigma^2\mathbf{I}$.

In addition to running the risk of being less asymptotically efficient in estimation, the OLS approach can also be less asymptotically powerful in testing, and less asymptotically accurate in confidence region generation relative to EGLS or ML procedures *when* $\boldsymbol{\Psi}(\boldsymbol{\gamma})$ *is perfectly specified and appropriately estimated*. However, we emphasize that the EGLS or ML approach does not *necessarily* have an advantage over the OLS approach in terms of *finite sample* properties, *even when* $\boldsymbol{\Psi}(\boldsymbol{\gamma})$ *is correctly specified.* The ambiguity is due to the inherent finite-sample variability associated with any estimator of $\boldsymbol{\Psi}(\boldsymbol{\gamma})$ used in the definition of the EGLS or ML estimators. Thus, the OLS approach remains a practical alternative for solving inverse problems when the noise component is not iid.

Unfortunately, in practice there is no foolproof method for deciding which particular approach for accommodating $\sigma^2\boldsymbol{\Psi} \neq \sigma^2\mathbf{I}$ is best. The conventional point of view that has largely prevailed over the preceding 30 years of econometric practice is that a valiant effort in producing the best estimate of $\sigma^2\boldsymbol{\Psi}$ possible from the modeling-testing-estimating triad (Chapter 19) will produce an EGLS or ML (based on a general covariance matrix specification) estimator that is superior to OLS. However, we emphasize that there is no reason to conclude that this superiority will always be achieved in a given application – indeed there is no theory to support such an unequivocal point of view, as we will discuss further in Chapter 19. With the relatively recent discovery of robust methods for estimating the covariance matrix of OLS estimators when $\sigma^2\boldsymbol{\Psi} \neq \sigma^2\mathbf{I}$, this opinion that EGLS or ML is always, or even generally, preferred to OLS has been undergoing some reconsideration.

In the discussion ahead, we recognize that, although the OLS estimator is consistent and asymptotically normally distributed under general regularity conditions when $\sigma^2\mathbf{\Psi} \neq \sigma^2\mathbf{I}$ (recall Section 14.1), its true finite sample or asymptotic covariance matrix depends on the unknown $\mathbf{\Psi}$ (see (14.1.2),(14.1.6), and (14.3.3)) and is *not* equal to the standard $\sigma^2(\mathbf{x}'\mathbf{x})^{-1}$ or $\sigma^2[\frac{\partial \mathbf{g}(\mathbf{x},\boldsymbol{\beta})}{\partial \boldsymbol{\beta}}\frac{\partial \mathbf{g}(\mathbf{x},\boldsymbol{\beta})}{\partial \boldsymbol{\beta}'}]^{-1}$ matrices exhibited in Chapter 5 and 8. Thus, without some means of estimating the covariance matrix of the OLS estimator, inference based on the estimator cannot proceed. This raises the question of whether there is a way of estimating $\mathbf{cov}(\hat{\boldsymbol{\beta}})$ when $\sigma^2\mathbf{\Psi} \neq \sigma^2\mathbf{I}$ that avoids the quagmire of modeling, testing, and estimating the form of $\mathbf{\Psi}(\gamma)$. White (1980, 1984) and Newey and West (1987) answered in the affirmative. Testing and confidence-region estimation based on the OLS estimator then proceeds as usual, utilizing the estimates of $\mathbf{cov}(\hat{\boldsymbol{\beta}})$ described ahead.

15.4.1. Heteroscedasticity

White examined the problem of estimating the covariance matrix of the OLS estimator when the noise component is heteroscedastic but not autocorrelated. He noted that, in order to estimate the covariance matrix of the OLS estimator in the linear model case, it is not necessary that one estimate the diagonal matrix $\mathbf{\Psi}$, but rather one needs an estimate of $\sigma^2\mathbf{x}'\mathbf{\Psi}\mathbf{x}$ in the covariance matrix, $\mathbf{cov}(\hat{\boldsymbol{\beta}}) = \sigma^2(\mathbf{x}'\mathbf{x})^{-1}\mathbf{x}'\mathbf{\Psi}\mathbf{x}(\mathbf{x}'\mathbf{x})^{-1}$, of the OLS estimator (recall (14.1.2)). Letting σ_i^2 represent the ith diagonal entry of $\sigma^2\mathbf{\Psi}$, he examined the problem of consistently estimating

$$\sigma^2 n^{-1}(\mathbf{x}'\mathbf{\Psi}\mathbf{x}) = n^{-1}\sum_{i=1}^{n}\sigma_i^2\mathbf{x}[i,.]'\mathbf{x}[i,.] \tag{15.4.1}$$

and suggested the estimator

$$\hat{\mathbf{\Gamma}} = n^{-1}\sum_{i=1}^{n}\hat{\varepsilon}_i^2\mathbf{x}[i,.]'\mathbf{x}[i,.], \tag{15.4.2}$$

where $\hat{\varepsilon}_i = \mathbf{Y}[i] - \mathbf{x}[i,.]\hat{\boldsymbol{\beta}}$ is the estimator for the ith element of the noise component vector. Under general conditions, White applied a weak law of large numbers elementwise to the $k(k+1)/2$ unique elements of the matrix (15.4.2) to demonstrate that $\hat{\mathbf{\Gamma}} - \sigma^2 n^{-1}(\mathbf{x}'\mathbf{\Psi}\mathbf{x}) \xrightarrow{p} \mathbf{0}$. Then, a consistent estimator of the covariance matrix of $n^{1/2}(\hat{\boldsymbol{\beta}} - \boldsymbol{\beta})$ is given by

$$\hat{\mathbf{cov}}[n^{1/2}(\hat{\boldsymbol{\beta}} - \boldsymbol{\beta})] = (n^{-1}\mathbf{x}'\mathbf{x})^{-1}\hat{\mathbf{\Gamma}}(n^{-1}\mathbf{x}'\mathbf{x})^{-1}, \tag{15.4.3}$$

and thus an estimator for $\mathbf{cov}(\hat{\boldsymbol{\beta}})$ is

$$\hat{\mathbf{cov}}(\hat{\boldsymbol{\beta}}) = (\mathbf{x}'\mathbf{x})^{-1}\left[\sum_{i=1}^{n}\hat{\varepsilon}_i^2\mathbf{x}[i,.]'\mathbf{x}[i,.]\right](\mathbf{x}'\mathbf{x})^{-1}. \tag{15.4.4}$$

From (15.4.4) and the asymptotic normality of the least-squares estimator (recall Section 14.1 and (14.1.6)), asymptotically valid Wald, LM, and Z-tests can be constructed as before with asymptotically valid confidence-region estimators derived from them via duality. Although asymptotically valid, MacKinnon and White (1985) and

Davidson and MacKinnon (1993, p. 554) noted that $\hat{\varepsilon}_i^2$ is downward-biased as an estimator of σ_i^2. Consequently, tests based on the covariance matrix (15.4.4) tend to overreject null hypotheses relative to the test's stated level of Type-I error for moderately sized samples. These econometricians investigated three alternatives to (15.4.2) and (15.4.4), which differed in the type of inflation factor that was applied to $\hat{\varepsilon}_i^2$ in (15.4.2) and (15.4.4) to mitigate the bias. The three alternative inflation factors were $n/(n-k)$, $(1-\mathrm{h}_i)^{-1}$, and $(1-\mathrm{h}_i)^{-2}$, where $\mathrm{h}_i = \mathbf{x}[i, .](\mathbf{x}'\mathbf{x})^{-1}\mathbf{x}[i, .]'$. Regarding the rationale for the use of h_i, recall that *under homoscedasticity* $\mathbf{cov}(\hat{\boldsymbol{\varepsilon}}) = \sigma^2[\mathbf{I}-\mathbf{x}(\mathbf{x}'\mathbf{x})^{-1}\mathbf{x}']$, so that $\mathrm{E}[\hat{\varepsilon}_i^2] = \mathrm{var}(\hat{\varepsilon}_i) = \sigma^2(1-\mathrm{h}_i)$, thus, inflating $\hat{\varepsilon}_i^2$ via multiplication by $(1-\mathrm{h}_i)^{-1}$ completely eliminates the bias in $\hat{\varepsilon}_i^2$ as an estimator of σ^2. However, note that *under heteroscedasticity*, inflation by $(1-\mathrm{h}_i)^{-1}$ will generally not eliminate the bias because it is then no longer the case that $\mathbf{cov}(\hat{\boldsymbol{\varepsilon}}) = \sigma^2[\mathbf{I}-\mathbf{x}(\mathbf{x}'\mathbf{x})^{-1}\mathbf{x}']$). Thus, examination of other inflation alternatives is warranted. The first inflation factor was shown by MacKinnon and Davidson in Monte Carlo studies to improve the sampling behavior of Z-tests for small samples, and the second and third inflation factor obtained progressively better results. Chesher and Jewitt (1987), Chesher (1989), and Chesher and Austin (1991) suggest that use of the inflation factor $(1-\mathrm{h}_i)^{-2}$ will not always produce superior results to the use of $(1-\mathrm{h}_i)^{-1}$. Thus, the question remains open as to which inflation factor to apply, although the application of some inflation factor appears warranted and empirically useful to counteract small sample bias in the covariance matrix estimation procedure.

► **Example 15.4.1:** To demonstrate the application of White's estimator under the alternative inflation factors, we provide the GAUSS program C15White.gss in the examples manual. First, the user specifies a heteroscedastic linear regression model, and a pseudorandom sample of observations is generated. The set of three inflation factors are computed and compared, and each is used to form an estimate of $\mathbf{cov}(\hat{\boldsymbol{\beta}})$. Then, GAUSS conducts a Monte Carlo simulation exercise designed to compare the performance of the covariance estimators relative to the known form of the noise covariance structure.

White's approach applies equally well to the nonlinear model case. The appropriate formulas are defined by replacing $\mathbf{x}$ with $[\frac{\partial \mathbf{g}(\mathbf{x}, \boldsymbol{\beta})}{\partial \boldsymbol{\beta}}|_{\hat{\boldsymbol{\beta}}}]'$ in (15.4.1)–(15.4.4), and defining $\hat{\varepsilon}_i = \mathbf{Y}[i] - \mathrm{g}(\mathbf{x}_{i\cdot}, \hat{\boldsymbol{\beta}})$. The issue of applying an inflation factor to $\hat{\varepsilon}_i^2$ also is pertinent in the nonlinear case in which the h_i scalar is defined as before, where again $\mathbf{x}$ is replaced by $[\frac{\partial \mathbf{g}(\mathbf{x}, \boldsymbol{\beta})}{\partial \boldsymbol{\beta}}|_{\hat{\boldsymbol{\beta}}}]'$.

Extensions to systems of regression equations can be made by interpreting either $\mathbf{Y} = \mathbf{x}\boldsymbol{\beta} + \boldsymbol{\varepsilon}$ or $\mathbf{Y} = \mathbf{g}(\mathbf{x}, \boldsymbol{\beta}) + \boldsymbol{\varepsilon}$ as depicting vertically concatenated regression equations as before and reinterpreting $\sigma^2\boldsymbol{\Psi}$ as the $(nm \times nm)$ covariance matrix (often with $\sigma^2 = 1$) applying to all nm elements of the noise component vector of the vertically concatenated system of regression equations. Note in this application that it is often assumed that the noise components across equations are contemporaneously correlated. If the covariance matrix *actually has* the specific structure $(\boldsymbol{\Sigma} \otimes \mathbf{I})$ assumed in preceding sections, with $\boldsymbol{\Sigma}$ non-diagonal, then substituting a direct estimate of $\boldsymbol{\Sigma}$ based on sums of squares and cross products of estimated noise components will generally be the relatively more efficient approach for generating an estimate of the matrix $\mathbf{x}'\boldsymbol{\Psi}\mathbf{x}$. In the absence of specific knowledge that $(\boldsymbol{\Sigma} \otimes \mathbf{I})$ is correct, White's approach remains a viable method for generating estimates of the asymptotic covariance matrix of $\hat{\boldsymbol{\beta}}$.

15.4.2. Heteroscedasticity and Autocorrelation

White and Domowitz (1984) and Newey and West (1987) extended White's robust covariance matrix procedure to encompass autocorrelated as well as heteroscedastic noise components. The problem is still one of consistently estimating the matrix $\sigma^2 n^{-1}\mathbf{x}'\boldsymbol{\Psi}\mathbf{x}$ contained in the covariance matrix

$$\mathbf{cov}[n^{1/2}(\hat{\boldsymbol{\beta}} - \boldsymbol{\beta})] = \sigma^2(n^{-1}\mathbf{x}'\mathbf{x})^{-1}(n^{-1}\mathbf{x}'\boldsymbol{\Psi}\mathbf{x})(n^{-1}\mathbf{x}'\mathbf{x})^{-1}, \tag{15.4.5}$$

except now the previous representation of the middle term in brackets displayed in (15.4.4) is no longer valid because $\boldsymbol{\Psi}$ is no longer diagonal. In fact now

$$\boldsymbol{\Gamma} = \sigma^2 n^{-1}(\mathbf{x}'\boldsymbol{\Psi}\mathbf{x}) = n^{-1}\sum_{i=1}^{n}\sum_{j=1}^{n} \text{cov}(\varepsilon_i\varepsilon_j)\mathbf{x}[i,.]'\mathbf{x}[j,.]. \tag{15.4.6}$$

The purely heteroscedastic case is the special case of (15.4.6), where $\sigma_i^2 = \text{cov}(\varepsilon_i, \varepsilon_i)$ and $\text{cov}(\varepsilon_i, \varepsilon_j) = 0, \forall i \neq j$.

Analogous to White's approach within the linear model context, suppose we replace $\text{cov}(\varepsilon_i, \varepsilon_j)$ with the estimate $\hat{\varepsilon}_i\hat{\varepsilon}_j$, defining the estimator

$$\hat{\boldsymbol{\Gamma}} = n^{-1}\sum_{i=1}^{n}\sum_{j=1}^{n} \hat{\varepsilon}_i\hat{\varepsilon}_j\mathbf{x}[i,.]'\mathbf{x}[j,.], \tag{15.4.7}$$

where $\hat{\varepsilon}_i = \mathbf{Y}[i] - \mathbf{x}[i,.]\hat{\boldsymbol{\beta}}$. Unfortunately without further adjustment $\hat{\boldsymbol{\Gamma}}$ is not useful since the orthogonality of $\hat{\boldsymbol{\varepsilon}}$ and $\mathbf{x}$ implies $\hat{\boldsymbol{\Gamma}} = \mathbf{0}$, and thus the analogy fails. Moreover, in order for a WLLN to apply to (15.4.7) so that $\hat{\boldsymbol{\Gamma}} - \sigma^2 n^{-1}(\mathbf{x}'\boldsymbol{\Psi}\mathbf{x}) \xrightarrow{p} \mathbf{0}$, a pattern in the covariances must exist such that $\text{cov}(\varepsilon_i, \varepsilon_j) \to 0$ as $|i - j|$ increases. In particular, *convergence to zero must be at a rate fast enough* to prevent the n^2 summed terms in (15.4.6) from overpowering the divisor of n so that (15.4.6) does not increase without bound. One case in which convergence is achieved is when the elements of the noise component exhibit *m-dependence*, meaning that $\text{cov}(\varepsilon_i, \varepsilon_j) = 0$ whenever $|i - j| > m$ (see Mittelhammer, p. 281). If so, an additional constraint placed on the summation indices in (15.4.6) and (15.4.7) is that $|i - j| \leq m$, so then only nm summation terms are involved in the double sum. A WLLN can then be applied to (15.4.7) to show that elementwise convergence to $\sigma^2 n^{-1}\mathbf{x}'\boldsymbol{\Psi}\mathbf{x}$ is achieved.

Finally, it is also assumed that the structure of any autocorrelation is such that $\text{cov}(\varepsilon_i, \varepsilon_j) = \tau_{|i-j|}, \forall i, j$. That is, the value of the covariance depends only on the value of $|i - j|$ and not on either i or j per se. For example, in a time series of observations, this implies that noise elements separated by p periods will all have the same covariance value τ_p regardless of when ε_i and ε_j, $|i - j| = p$ occur in time. This characteristic is referred to as *covariance stationarity*. In effect, this characteristic assures that in any sample of size n, there are $(n - p)$ observations $(\hat{\varepsilon}_i, \hat{\varepsilon}_j)$ for which $|i - j| = p$ and $i < j$, which then provide information about τ_p, that is $(n - p)^{-1}\sum_{i=1}^{n-p}\hat{\varepsilon}_i\hat{\varepsilon}_{i+p}$ is a sample estimate of τ_p based on $(n - p)$ observations.

In applications, Newey and West focus their attention on estimators suggested by White and Domowitz of the form

$$\hat{\boldsymbol{\Gamma}} = n^{-1} \sum_{\substack{i=1 \\ |i-j| \leq \mathrm{L}}}^{n} \sum_{j=1}^{n} (\hat{\varepsilon}_i \hat{\varepsilon}_j) \mathbf{x}[i, .]' \mathbf{x}[j, .], \tag{15.4.8}$$

where L is a finite positive integer value. Note that the restriction $|i - j| \leq \mathrm{L}$ is necessary for a WLLN and convergence to apply to $\hat{\boldsymbol{\Gamma}}$. This makes intuitive sense from the standpoint of needing a sufficient number of observations on the product terms $(\hat{\varepsilon}_i \hat{\varepsilon}_j)$ to consistently represent the influence of the $\mathrm{cov}(\varepsilon_i, \varepsilon_j)$ weights separated by L observations or less in the sum (15.4.6). If L is too large, then there are too few possible observations on $(\hat{\varepsilon}_i \hat{\varepsilon}_j)$ with $|i - j| = \mathrm{L}$, and thus the influence of the $\mathrm{cov}(\varepsilon_i, \varepsilon_j)$-weighted terms having $|i - j| = \mathrm{L}$ cannot be consistently represented by the few $(\hat{\varepsilon}_i \hat{\varepsilon}_j)$ values that would appear in (15.4.8). Although L can be a function of n, in general it must be sufficiently less than n to allow convergence of (15.4.8) to occur. A specific suggestion for the choice of L will be provided later.

A problem with the estimator $\hat{\boldsymbol{\Gamma}}$ is that it may *not* be positive semidefinite in finite samples. The reason for the problem is that the matrices being summed in (15.4.8) are generally not all positive semidefinite because, even though the terms $\hat{\varepsilon}_i^2 \mathbf{x}[i, .]' \mathbf{x}[i, .]$ are all necessarily positive semidefinite, $(\hat{\varepsilon}_i \hat{\varepsilon}_j)$ can be positive or negative and $\mathbf{x}[i, .]' \mathbf{x}[j, .]$ can be indefinite, and thus $(\hat{\varepsilon}_i \hat{\varepsilon}_j) \mathbf{x}[i, .]' \mathbf{x}[j, .]$ can be positive semidefinite, negative semidefinite, or neither. Newey and West suggested an alternative estimator that mitigates the problem whereby terms for which $i \neq j$ are progressively down-weighted as the value $|i - j|$ increases. The particular weighting scheme that they suggested is $\mathrm{w}(i - j) \equiv 1 - \frac{|i-j|}{\mathrm{L}+1}$, where L represents the maximum value of $|i - j|$ for which values of $\mathrm{cov}(\varepsilon_i, \varepsilon_j) \neq 0$ are accounted for. In the case of m-dependence, clearly $\mathrm{L} = m$. The weighted estimator of $\sigma^2 n^{-1} \mathbf{x}' \boldsymbol{\Psi} \mathbf{x}$ then becomes

$$\hat{\boldsymbol{\Gamma}} = n^{-1} \sum_{\substack{i=1 \\ |i-j| \leq \mathrm{L}}}^{n} \sum_{j=1}^{n} \mathrm{w}(i - j) \hat{\varepsilon}_i \hat{\varepsilon}_j \mathbf{x}[i, .]' \mathbf{x}[j, .]. \tag{15.4.9}$$

If noise component elements follow *autocorrelation processes*, such as the simple first-order process $\varepsilon_t = \rho \varepsilon_{t-1} + \mathrm{V}_t$, where $|\rho| < 1$ and V_t is independent of the ε_t's with $\mathrm{E}[\mathrm{V}_t] = 0$ and $\mathrm{var}(\mathrm{V}_t) = \sigma^2, \forall t$, then $\mathrm{cov}(\varepsilon_i, \varepsilon_j) \neq 0, \forall i, j$ (recall Section 14.4.1). In this or any other case in which covariances between ε_i and ε_j converge to zero but are not zero for any value of i and j, there is the obvious problem of deciding where to truncate the sum in (15.4.8) and (15.4.9). In order that a WLLN can still be applied to achieve convergence of the estimator to $\boldsymbol{\Gamma}$, the general idea is to truncate terms in the sum for which the magnitude of $\mathrm{cov}(\varepsilon_i, \varepsilon_j)$ is not appreciable in the hope that the omission will have little effect on the estimates of Γ in finite samples but to include more terms as the sample size increases so as to incorporate essentially all of the relevant nonzero covariance terms eventually. This implies that the value of L in (15.4.9) should be a function of the sample size. Newey and West (1991) suggested the value $\mathrm{L} = \mathrm{trunc}(4(n/100)^{2/9})$. Andrews (1991) analyzed several different choices for L as well as different definitions for the weights, $\mathrm{w}(i - j)$. He found that alternative choices of L and

$w(i - j)$ can be advantageous in some cases, but the estimation procedure suggested by Newey and West performs well across a wide variety of problem conditions and can be recommended for use in general practice.

We emphasize that all of the results discussed in this subsection can be applied to nonlinear models as well as to systems of regression equations. For the nonlinear case, $\mathbf{x}$ is replaced by $\frac{\partial \mathbf{g}(\mathbf{x}, \boldsymbol{\beta})}{\partial \boldsymbol{\beta}'}\Big|_{\hat{\boldsymbol{\beta}}}$, and then all of the arguments and formulas apply. For regression equation systems, $\mathbf{Y}$, $\mathbf{x}$, $\mathbf{g}(\mathbf{x}, \boldsymbol{\beta})$, and $\boldsymbol{\varepsilon}$ are interpreted to be in stacked, vertically concatenated form as we have done previously to transform the system into single-equation form. In the stacked system context, one must also account for cross-equation correlation among the noise component elements so that the summation condition $|i - j| \leq \mathrm{L}$ refers to noise elements separated in time by $\leq$L units *with the elements possibly being in different regression equations.*

► **Example 15.4.2:** We provide the GAUSS program C15NW.gss to demonstrate the covariance estimator proposed by Newey and West. First, a set of pseudorandom observations are generated from a linear regression model with autocorrelated or heteroscedastic error terms (specified by the user). For the given sample, GAUSS computes the estimated covariance matrices under the various data-truncation or weighting schemes for the Newey and West estimator. For comparison purposes, GAUSS also reports the estimates based on White's estimator. Then, GAUSS compares the large sample performance of the alternative covariance estimators.

15.5. The Estimating Equations – Quasi-Maximum Likelihood View: A Unified Approach

In this section we reexamine, in the context of estimating equations and QML estimation, the inverse problem of recovering estimates of $\boldsymbol{\beta}$ from data observations on $(\mathbf{Y}, \mathbf{X})$ under the probability model conditions delineated in Table 15.1. We will see that the single and multiple equation GLS and ML solutions to the inverse problem discussed in preceding sections can all be subsumed under the estimating equations (EE) approach of Chapter 11. In addition, we will expand on our discussion of the quasi-maximum likelihood (QML)–EE approach presented in Section 14.6.4 relating to the definition of an estimator of $\boldsymbol{\beta}$ with good finite sample and asymptotic sampling properties when $\boldsymbol{\Psi}$ *is unknown* both in value and in parametric specification.

15.5.1. A Unified EE Characterization of Inverse Problem Solutions

All of the estimation procedures presented in the preceding sections can be characterized as versions of EE estimators appropriate for the probability model characteristics of the respective inverse problems. In particular, the four different estimators spanning the application of EGLS to linear and nonlinear models in the context of both single- and multiple-equation models can all be interpreted as asymptotically OptEF (optimal estimating function) estimators defined in terms of linear unbiased estimating functions

$$\mathbf{h}(\mathbf{Y}, \mathbf{x}, \boldsymbol{\beta}) = \boldsymbol{\eta}(\mathbf{x}, \boldsymbol{\beta})[\mathbf{Y} - \mathbf{g}(\mathbf{x}, \boldsymbol{\beta})], \tag{15.5.1}$$

Table 15.2. *Asymptotic OptEF Specifications Subsuming EGLS Estimators*

Inverse Problem	**$\boldsymbol{\Phi}$ Definition**	$\hat{\mathbf{h}}_{\mathrm{Opt}}(\mathbf{Y}, \mathbf{x}, \boldsymbol{\beta})$
Linear Single Equation	$\boldsymbol{\Psi}$	$\mathbf{x}'\hat{\boldsymbol{\Psi}}^{-1}(\mathbf{Y} - \mathbf{x}\boldsymbol{\beta})$
Nonlinear Single Equation	$\boldsymbol{\Psi}$	$\frac{\partial \mathbf{g}(\mathbf{x}, \boldsymbol{\beta})}{\partial \boldsymbol{\beta}}\hat{\boldsymbol{\Psi}}^{-1}[\mathbf{Y} - \mathbf{g}(\mathbf{x}, \boldsymbol{\beta})]$
Linear Equation System	$\boldsymbol{\Sigma} \otimes \mathbf{I}$	$\mathbf{x}'(\hat{\boldsymbol{\Sigma}} \otimes \mathbf{I})^{-1}(\mathbf{Y} - \mathbf{x}\boldsymbol{\beta})$
Nonlinear Equation System	$\boldsymbol{\Sigma} \otimes \mathbf{I}$	$\frac{\partial \mathbf{g}(\mathbf{x}, \boldsymbol{\beta})}{\partial \boldsymbol{\beta}}(\hat{\boldsymbol{\Sigma}} \otimes \mathbf{I})^{-1}[\mathbf{Y} - \mathbf{g}(\mathbf{x}, \boldsymbol{\beta})]$.

where $\mathbf{g}(\mathbf{x}, \boldsymbol{\beta})$ denotes the conditional expectation of $\mathbf{Y}$ given $\mathbf{x}$. To see this, first recall that in Section 11.4.1 it was proved that the OptEF estimator in the class of estimating equations based on estimating functions of the form (15.5.1) is characterized by the solution to

$$\mathbf{h}_{\mathrm{Opt}}(\mathbf{Y}, \mathbf{x}, \boldsymbol{\beta}) = \frac{\partial \mathbf{g}(\mathbf{x}, \boldsymbol{\beta})}{\partial \boldsymbol{\beta}}\boldsymbol{\Phi}^{-1}[\mathbf{Y} - \mathbf{g}(\mathbf{x}, \boldsymbol{\beta})] = \mathbf{0}, \qquad (15.5.2)$$

where $\boldsymbol{\Phi}$ can be any matrix proportional to the covariance matrix of $(\mathbf{Y} \mid \mathbf{x})$. Then all of the aforementioned EGLS estimators can be characterized as solutions to (15.5.2) with $\boldsymbol{\Phi}$ replaced by a consistent estimator $\hat{\boldsymbol{\Phi}}$, resulting in estimators that are *asymptotically* equivalent to the OptEF estimators for their respective inverse problem characteristics. The specific form of (15.5.2) used in each case is displayed in Table 15.2, where it is understood that $\mathbf{Y}$, $\mathbf{x}$, and $\mathbf{g}(\mathbf{x}, \boldsymbol{\beta})$ denote appropriately stacked or vertically concatenated vectors or matrices in the case of equation systems, and $\frac{\partial \mathbf{g}(\mathbf{x}, \boldsymbol{\beta})}{\partial \boldsymbol{\beta}} = \mathbf{x}'$ in the case of linear models. If the same regularity conditions introduced previously in establishing the asymptotic properties of the EGLS estimators are assumed, or else if Theorems 11.3.1 and 11.3.2 are applied directly, the consistency and asymptotic normality of the EE estimator follows in each of the cases depicted in the table. Inference proceeds precisely in the same way as for the EGLS estimators. Note that in defining a consistent estimator $\hat{\boldsymbol{\Phi}}$ of $\boldsymbol{\Phi}$ one will generally utilize a consistent estimator of the noise component of the regression models based on a preliminary nonoptimal EE estimator. The typical choice for this preliminary estimator is the EE estimator defined by setting $\boldsymbol{\Phi} = \mathbf{I}$ in (15.3.2), which is equivalent to utilizing linear or nonlinear OLS estimators of the regression equations to obtain noise component estimates. We will revisit the issue of estimating the matrix $\boldsymbol{\Phi}$ based on preliminary estimates of the regression models in Chapter 19.

Regarding how the EE approach subsumes all of the ML estimators discussed above, recall that the OptEF in the class of *all* unbiased estimating functions is given by the gradient of the likelihood function when the parametric family of distributions for $(\mathbf{Y} \mid \mathbf{x})$ is known (recall Section 11.3.2, and especially 11.3.2.c). In each of the ML contexts discussed above, it was assumed that the normal distribution was the appropriate parametric family for $(\mathbf{Y} \mid \mathbf{x})$. It follows that the OptEFs are defined directly by the gradients of the likelihood functions with respect to the parameters of each of the preceding inverse problems, in general as $\mathbf{h}_{\mathrm{Opt}}(\mathbf{Y}, \mathbf{x}, \boldsymbol{\theta}) = \frac{\partial \ln \mathrm{L}}{\partial \boldsymbol{\theta}}$. Then, the OptEF estimator is obtained in the usual way by solving $\mathbf{h}_{\mathrm{Opt}}(\mathbf{Y}, \mathbf{x}, \boldsymbol{\theta}) = \mathbf{0}$ for $\boldsymbol{\theta}$, which of course is equivalent to the ML estimator of $\boldsymbol{\theta}$. Again, inference based on the OptEF estimator can proceed using the procedures identified previously for the ML estimator, or else one can deduce appropriate inference procedures from the general results for EE estimators discussed in Chapter 11.

15.5.2. QML–EE Estimation

Recall from Section 14.6.4 that QML–EE estimators for $\boldsymbol{\beta}$ are available via solutions to the linear unbiased estimating equation system

$$\mathbf{h}(\mathbf{Y}, \mathbf{x}, \boldsymbol{\beta}) = \frac{\partial \mathbf{g}(\mathbf{x}, \boldsymbol{\beta})}{\partial \boldsymbol{\beta}} \boldsymbol{\Gamma}^{-1}[\mathbf{Y} - \mathbf{g}(\mathbf{x}, \boldsymbol{\beta})] = \mathbf{0}, \tag{15.5.3}$$

where $\boldsymbol{\Gamma}$ can be any arbitrary fixed symmetric positive definite matrix. The QML–EE solutions correspond to the maximization of a quasi-likelihood based on a multivariate normal distribution $\mathrm{N}(\mathbf{g}(\mathbf{x}, \boldsymbol{\beta}), \boldsymbol{\Gamma})$ as follows:

$$\mathrm{L}(\boldsymbol{\beta}; \mathbf{y}, \mathbf{x}) = \frac{1}{(2\pi)^{n/2}(\det[\boldsymbol{\Gamma}])^{1/2}} \exp\left\{ -\frac{1}{2}[\mathbf{y} - \mathbf{g}(\mathbf{x}, \boldsymbol{\beta})]'\boldsymbol{\Gamma}^{-1}[\mathbf{y} - \mathbf{g}(\mathbf{x}, \boldsymbol{\beta})]\right\}. \tag{15.5.4}$$

The characterization applies to linear and nonlinear models as well as single- and multiple-equation regression models upon appropriate interpretation of the components of (15.5.3) and (15.5.4).

As long as $\mathrm{E}[\mathbf{Y} \mid \mathbf{x}] = \mathbf{g}(\mathbf{x}, \boldsymbol{\beta})$, that is, we have an Order 1 QML–EE problem (recall Section 11.2), we know that the QML–EE estimator defined by maximizing (15.5.4) or solving the estimating Equations (15.5.3) will be consistent and asymptotically normally distributed. The asymptotic properties hold regardless of whether the underlying probability distribution of $(\mathbf{Y} \mid \mathbf{x})$ is actually normally distributed (Gourieroux, Monfort, and Trognon, 1984; White, 1994, pp. 62–70). The general form of the asymptotic distribution of the QML–EE estimator is given by

$$\hat{\boldsymbol{\beta}}_{\mathrm{EE}} \overset{a}{\sim} \mathrm{N}(\boldsymbol{\beta}, [\mathbf{x}(\boldsymbol{\beta})'\boldsymbol{\Gamma}^{-1}\mathbf{x}(\boldsymbol{\beta})]^{-1}\mathbf{x}(\boldsymbol{\beta})'\boldsymbol{\Gamma}^{-1}\boldsymbol{\Phi}\boldsymbol{\Gamma}^{-1}\mathbf{x}(\boldsymbol{\beta})\,[\mathbf{x}(\boldsymbol{\beta})'\boldsymbol{\Gamma}^{-1}\mathbf{x}(\boldsymbol{\beta})]^{-1}), \tag{15.5.5}$$

where $\mathbf{x}(\boldsymbol{\beta}) \equiv \frac{\partial \mathbf{g}(\mathbf{x}, \boldsymbol{\beta})}{\partial \boldsymbol{\beta}'}$ and $\mathbf{cov}(\mathbf{Y} \mid \mathbf{x}) = \boldsymbol{\Phi}$. The asymptotic distribution of the QML–EE estimator justifies the usual types of asymptotically valid inference procedures based on Wald, LM, Z, and pseudo-likelihood ratio statistics.

If the conditional mean function is misspecified so that $\mathrm{E}[\mathbf{Y} \mid \mathbf{x}] \neq \mathbf{g}(\mathbf{x}, \boldsymbol{\beta})$, note that the QML–EE estimator nonetheless provides an estimate of $\boldsymbol{\beta}_*$, the parameter value in (15.5.4) and defines the normal approximation that is closest in Kullback–Leibler distance to the true underlying probability distribution for $(\mathbf{Y} \mid \mathbf{x})$ (recall Section 11.2.2, and see White, 1994, pp. 31–2). The QML–EE estimator is consistent for, and asymptotically normally distributed around, the vector $\boldsymbol{\beta}_*$ (as opposed to $\boldsymbol{\beta}$ in (15.5.5)). In effect, the QML–EE estimator will do the best it can to accommodate the true probability distribution within the confines of the analyst's choice of probability model representation for the DSP. Asymptotic inference can proceed based on the usual statistics, except in this misspecified context one is effectively testing hypotheses about

$\boldsymbol{\beta}_*$ and not $\boldsymbol{\beta}$, and so the economic or other contextual meaning of model parameters and hypotheses about them require special care.

Furthermore, note that the use of OLS as a robust method for estimating $\boldsymbol{\beta}$, as discussed in Section 15.4, is a special case of the QML–EE procedure. In particular, it is the case where $\boldsymbol{\Gamma}$ is set equal to $\mathbf{I}$, in which case solving (15.5.3) or maximizing (15.5.4) is equivalent to applying OLS to the linear or nonlinear regression equations being estimated. The asymptotic distribution of the QML–EE estimator in this case is given by (15.5.5) with $\boldsymbol{\Gamma} = \mathbf{I}$, yielding

$$\hat{\boldsymbol{\beta}}_{\text{EE}} \overset{a}{\sim} \text{N}(\boldsymbol{\beta}, [\mathbf{x}(\boldsymbol{\beta})'\mathbf{x}(\boldsymbol{\beta})]^{-1}\mathbf{x}(\boldsymbol{\beta})'\boldsymbol{\Phi}\mathbf{x}(\boldsymbol{\beta})[\mathbf{x}(\boldsymbol{\beta})'\mathbf{x}(\boldsymbol{\beta})]^{-1}), \tag{15.5.6}$$

which coincides with the asymptotic distribution of the OLS estimator for the case at hand.

15.5.3. EE Extensions

The preceding two subsections demonstrate that all of the OLS, GLS, and ML results presented in previous sections of this chapter are subsumed under the EE approach to inverse problem solutions. In addition to providing a unifying solution paradigm for the types of inverse problems examined in this chapter, the EE approach can also lead to alternative and distinct estimation and inference procedures for inverse problems. These alternative solutions arise naturally in the context of specific parameterizations for the covariance structure of sample observations, and we will encounter some of these cases when we examine such parameterizations in detail in Chapter 19. However, we will briefly foreshadow this extended application of the EE here using the example of a linear single-equation model under a heteroscedastic but nonautocorrelated covariance structure.

Assume that the linear model $\mathbf{Y} = \mathbf{x}\boldsymbol{\beta} + \boldsymbol{\varepsilon}$ applies, where $\mathbf{cov}(\mathbf{Y} \mid \mathbf{x}) = \sigma^2\boldsymbol{\Psi}$ is *diagonal* and the covariance matrix is parameterized in terms of the $\boldsymbol{\beta}$ parameter such as $\boldsymbol{\Psi}(\boldsymbol{\beta})$. For example, one such parameterization that has been often applied in practice is the case in which the variances of the sample observations are presumed to be proportional to the conditional mean of $\mathbf{Y}$, in which case the ith diagonal element of the covariance matrix is represented by $\Psi_{i,i}(\boldsymbol{\beta}) \equiv \sigma^2(\mathbf{x}_{i\cdot}\boldsymbol{\beta})$. This parametric structure implies that the variance of an observation will be higher the higher the value of the conditional mean. Generalizations of this parameterization involve raising the conditional expectation to a power, such as $\Psi_{i,i}(\boldsymbol{\beta}) \equiv \sigma^2(\mathbf{x}_{i\cdot}\boldsymbol{\beta})^{\alpha}$, and will be examined in Chapter 19.

Now consider defining the OptEF estimator of $\boldsymbol{\beta}$ within the class of linear unbiased estimating functions (15.5.1). The general form of the OptEF in this class is given by (15.5.2), which in the case at hand leads to the specific form of estimating equation

$$\mathbf{h}_{\text{Opt}}(\mathbf{Y}, \mathbf{x}, \boldsymbol{\beta}) = \left[\frac{1}{\sigma^2}\right]\mathbf{x}' \begin{bmatrix} \mathbf{x}_{1\cdot}\boldsymbol{\beta} & 0 & \cdots & 0 \\ 0 & \mathbf{x}_{2\cdot}\boldsymbol{\beta} & \cdots & 0 \\ \vdots & \vdots & \ddots & \vdots \\ 0 & 0 & \cdots & \mathbf{x}_{n\cdot}\boldsymbol{\beta} \end{bmatrix}^{-1} (\mathbf{Y} - \mathbf{x}\boldsymbol{\beta}) = \mathbf{0}. \tag{15.5.7}$$

Note that the estimating equations are uninformative with respect to σ^2, and in fact σ^2 can be eliminated from (15.5.7) without affecting the solution for $\boldsymbol{\beta}$. The OptEF estimator for $\boldsymbol{\beta}$ will be defined via the numerical solution to (15.5.7), where the estimator is defined as $\hat{\boldsymbol{\beta}}_{\text{EE}} = \arg_{\boldsymbol{\beta}}[\mathbf{h}_{\text{Opt}}(\mathbf{Y}, \mathbf{x}, \boldsymbol{\beta}) = \mathbf{0}]$.

The OptEF estimator will generally differ from the EGLS or QML (under normality) estimators of $\boldsymbol{\beta}$, as the reader may recall from a similar heteroscedastic model considered in Example 11.3.1. The claim can also be verified by comparing (15.5.7) to either the first-order conditions of the QML problem under the normality assumption or to the definition of the EGLS estimator. In particular, note that the EGLS and OptEF estimates will coincide only if $\hat{\boldsymbol{\beta}}_{\text{EE}}$ is used to estimate $\boldsymbol{\Psi}$, as $\boldsymbol{\Psi}(\hat{\boldsymbol{\beta}}_{\text{EE}})$, in the definition of the EGLS estimator (15.1.1.a). Applications of Theorems 11.3.1 and 11.3.2 establish the consistency and asymptotic normality of the OptEF estimator, and the asymptotic covariance matrix of the OptEF estimator displayed in Theorem 11.3.2 can be used for inference purposes. Moreover, the OptEF estimator is *asymptotically efficient* within the class of estimators that can be derived from linear unbiased estimating functions of the form (15.5.1). This means that the OptEF estimator defined via (15.5.7) is efficient relative to the EGLS estimator (asymptotically), if it is assumed the covariance matrix parameterization defined above is correct, for the EGLS estimator belongs to the class of estimators defined via linear unbiased estimating equations. However, the QML estimator based on both normality and the preceding covariance parameterization does not belong to the linear unbiased estimating equation class, and so asymptotic superiority of the OptEF estimator relative to the QML estimator cannot be claimed. *If* the sampling distribution is in fact normal and *if* the parameterization is correct, QML will be asymptotically efficient in the class of all unbiased estimating functions and thus would be asymptotically superior to the EE estimator derived from (15.5.7). In the absence of omniscience regarding the distribution of $(\mathbf{Y} \mid \mathbf{x})$, the EE estimator remains an attractive alternative for solving the inverse problem under the current heteroscedastic covariance specification.

15.5.4. MEL and MEEL Applications of EE

As one might anticipate from the discussion of EE extensions in the preceding subsection, one can think of applying the maximum empirical likelihood (MEL) and maximum entropy empirical likelihood (MEEL) approaches of Chapters 12 and 13 to models with nonspherical covariance structures. That this might be possible can be anticipated from the work of Owen (1991), Kolacyzk (1994), and Kitamura (1997) on the application of MEL (and by association, MEEL) to the case of non-iid sampling, which we noted in Section 12.5.

It turns out that MEL and MEEL applications in nonspherical problem contexts are largely analogous to the types of applications we have already discussed in Chapters 12 and 13 when sampling is non-iid but independent. The asymptotics of such applications are rationalized by appeals to CLTs for triangular arrays along the lines of Owen and Kolacyzk's results. To illustrate a MEL example in this context, reconsider the illustration discussed in the preceding subsection, where the covariance matrix

$\mathbf{cov}(\mathbf{Y} \mid \mathbf{x}) = \sigma^2\boldsymbol{\Psi}$ is heteroscedastic but not autocorrelated, with variances being proportional to the mean, $\Psi_{i,i}(\boldsymbol{\beta}) \equiv \sigma^2(\mathbf{x}_{i}.\boldsymbol{\beta})$, which can be generalized to a power function of the mean. Recall the OptEF identified in (15.5.7) and note that population moments for this model can be specified as

$$\mathrm{E}[\mathbf{h}(\mathrm{Y}_i, \mathbf{x}_{i}., \boldsymbol{\beta})] = \mathrm{E}\left(\mathbf{x}_{i.}'\left[\frac{1}{\sigma^2(\mathbf{x}_{i}.\boldsymbol{\beta})}\right](\mathrm{Y}_i - \mathbf{x}_{i}.\boldsymbol{\beta})\right) = \mathbf{0}. \tag{15.5.8}$$

Then, a MEL approach for estimating $\boldsymbol{\beta}$ would be to choose $\boldsymbol{\beta}$ so as to maximize empirical likelihood in the moment-constrained problem

$$\max_{\boldsymbol{\beta},\,\mathbf{p}}\left[\sum_{i=1}^{n}\ln(\mathrm{p}_i)\ \text{s.t.}\ \sum_{i=1}^{n}\mathrm{p}_i\left[\mathbf{x}_{i.}'\left(\frac{1}{\sigma^2(\mathbf{x}_{i}.\boldsymbol{\beta})}\right)(\mathbf{Y}_i - \mathbf{x}_{i}.\boldsymbol{\beta})\right] = \mathbf{0}\ \text{and}\ \sum_{i=1}^{n}\mathrm{p}_i = 1\right]. \tag{15.5.9}$$

A MEEL approach to the estimation of $\boldsymbol{\beta}$ can be defined by simply replacing the EL objective function $\sum_{i=1}^{n}\ln(\mathrm{p}_i)$ in (15.5.9) with the entropy objective function $-\sum_{i=1}^{n}\mathrm{p}_i\ln(\mathrm{p}_i)$. The development of the consistency and asymptotic normality results for the MEL or MEEL estimators are analogous to the results in Chapters 12 and 13. The reader is directed to the references for further details on these types of applications.

Extensions to problems involving dependent (autocorrelated) sampling are possible. Given the current technology for this case, an adjustment in the definition of the MEL or MEEL problem along the lines of so-called "observation blocking" is needed to reestablish the usual asymptotic results. We will have more to say about this case in Section 16.4 of the next chapter. The principal references for the dependent sampling case are Kitamura (1997) and Kitamura and Stutzer (1997).

15.6. Some Comments

Removing the assumption that the noise covariance matrix is proportional to the identity matrix in the regression model raises many challenging statistical problems. For one thing, it suddenly becomes very clear just how far-reaching the assumption $\mathbf{cov}(\varepsilon) = \sigma^2\mathbf{I}$ is. This assumption permits us to reduce the dimensionality of the parameter space from $\mathrm{k} + (n+1)n/2$ parameters to $k+1$ parameters. Its absence raises the problem of more potential unknown parameters than data points, resulting in an ill-posed or underdetermined inverse problem. Of course we could ignore the possibility that the noise covariance matrix is not $\sigma^2\mathbf{I}$ and act as if it were true. In that event, the "unbiasedness," consistency, and asymptotic normality properties of the LS or ML (assuming normality) estimator of $\boldsymbol{\beta}$ continue to hold, but our former attractive efficiency results (minimum variance unbiased, asymptotic efficiency, or both) then no longer hold.

If we are to achieve the efficiency properties, we must be able to posit a probability model with a substantially reduced set of unknown parameters that also remains congruent with the data-sampling process. This is a substantial challenge in practice. For example, even if we know that the noise elements are independent, this (zero) restriction on noise covariances would only reduce the number of potential unknowns in the regression model to $(n+k)$. In terms of recovering the unknown parameters, we still have an ill-posed problem unless we can impose even more parameter restrictions on the model specification.

Fortunately, as we have seen in Section 15.4, there are methods for consistently estimating the covariance matrix of OLS estimators that do not require the researcher to specify the functional parametric structure of the unknown covariance matrix of $(\mathbf{Y} \mid \mathbf{x})$. Of course, relative to the best EGLS situation (perfect specification and estimation of the unknown and unobservable covariance structure), we would lose asymptotic efficiency if we were to use the OLS estimator instead. However, robust procedures do offer an attractive, robust way of proceeding when one is faced with a complex set of model choices. And in practice, one cannot expect omniscience in the specification of a noise covariance matrix parameterization and so must admit that the goal of achieving efficient parameter estimation is effectively a straw man.

The estimating equations and quasi-maximum likelihood procedure again provide us with a means of unifying all of the estimators under one estimation paradigm. In addition, the QML–EE approach provides an entire class of consistent and asymptotically normal estimators of unknown parameters of an inverse problem that do not require a specific parameterization of the covariance matrix of $(\mathbf{Y} \mid \mathbf{x})$. Furthermore, the QML context allows one to interpret an estimator as providing the best approximation to the true underlying probability model even when the conditional mean function of $\mathbf{Y}$ is misspecified.

Finally, we note that we have largely ignored an issue that is often given a great deal of attention in empirical practice, the iterative determination of an estimate of $\boldsymbol{\beta}$ based on initial estimates of $\boldsymbol{\Psi}$. Following our discussion of the iterative solution for the ML estimators based on (15.2.18) and (15.2.19), we can replace the initial estimate $\hat{\boldsymbol{\Psi}}$ with a version based on the adjusted estimator of $\boldsymbol{\beta}$ (e.g., $\hat{\boldsymbol{\beta}}_{\mathrm{EG}}$). The iterative process can continue, iteratively updating $\hat{\boldsymbol{\Psi}}$ and $\hat{\boldsymbol{\beta}}_{\mathrm{EG}}$, until the parameter estimates converge under a suitable criterion. For example, we noted in Chapter 7 that the algorithm used to compute MAD estimates is commonly known as iteratively reweighted least squares, which is a special case of EGLS. Conceptually, we may adopt an iterative solution technique for each of the estimators in this chapter that are based on an initial consistent estimate of $\boldsymbol{\Psi}$.

However, the iterative procedures can be computationally expensive in some cases. Moreover, on the basis of recent research, contributors to the literature have noted the result that an estimator based on a single iteration can have the same large sample distribution as the fully iterated estimator. Newey and McFadden (Section 3.4, 1994) review the basic properties of one-step estimators, and the key assumption underlying the result is that the initial estimator is bounded in probability as $n^{1/2}(\hat{\boldsymbol{\beta}} - \boldsymbol{\beta}_0) = \mathrm{O}_{\mathrm{p}}(1)$. If the full set of regularity conditions are met, we may then equivalently (in large samples) rely on the one-step or fully iterated versions of the estimators discussed in this chapter. Which of the estimators has superior sampling properties in finite samples is an open question.

In Chapter 19 we will explicitly examine the issue of modeling, testing for, and estimating covariance structure. At that time we will once again appreciate the difficulty of specifying $\sigma^2\boldsymbol{\Psi}$ and the attractiveness of the robust inverse problem solutions suggested in this chapter.

15.7. Exercises

15.7.1. Idea Checklist – Knowledge Guides

1. What are some of the alternative ways of specifying the noise covariance matrix and using sample information to convert the estimation problem for a general noise covariance structure from an ill-posed, underdetermined problem to a well-posed problem?
2. What is the detrimental impact of incorrectly specifying the noise covariance matrix?
3. What is meant by the concept of a robust covariance matrix estimator? Should analysts always use robust covariance matrix estimators? Why or why not?
4. In a system of regression equations context, what are the statistical implications of imposing t‌ʰ $(\boldsymbol{\Sigma} \otimes \mathbf{I})$ form of noise covariance matrix?
5. In the case of a fixed but unknown noise covariance matrix, how does one go about comr the performance or relative efficiencies of competing EE estimators?

15.7.2. Problems

15–1 Define an LM test for hypotheses of the form $\mathrm{H}_0\colon \mathbf{c}\boldsymbol{\beta} = \mathbf{r}$ in the model context of Section 15.1. Compare the asymptotic distribution of the LM test with the Wal test presented in (15.1.9) and (15.1.10).

15–2 Repeat Exercise 1 in the context of a system of regression equations Section 15.2.

15–3 In the SUR model, define the EGLS estimator and its sampling properties when

a. $\boldsymbol{\Sigma}$ is a diagonal matrix;

b. $\mathbf{x}_1 = \mathbf{x}_2 = \mathbf{x}_3 = \cdots = \mathbf{x}_m$.

15–4 Define an efficient SUR estimator for the case in which the number of data points differs for each regression equation in the system.

15–5 Provide a proof of the consistency of White's heteroscedastic–robust covariance matrix estimator.

15.7.3. Computer Exercises

1. Extend Example 15.1.2 by using the squared predicted values $(\mathbf{x}[i,.]\hat{\mathbf{b}})^2$ from an initial least-squares estimation step to form an EGLS estimator. How do the sampling properties and efficiency of the EGLS estimator compare with the MLE?
2. Repeat Computer Exercise 3 from Chapter 14 using the EGLS estimator for Theil's consumption data. Hint: A simple estimator of ρ can be computed as the sample autocorrelation $\hat{\rho} = \sum_{i=2}^{n} \varepsilon_i \varepsilon_{i-1} / \sum_{i=2}^{n} \varepsilon_i^2$ of the least-squares residuals.
3. Write a GAUSS program designed to compare the sampling properties of the LS and EGLS estimators in a finite sample setting. In particular, compare the relative efficiency of the two estimators as the sample size increases. Also, compare the statistical properties of a particular

test statistic (e.g., Wald) based on the estimators and the correct specification of the covariance matrices. For the model you have selected, does it appear that the EGLS estimator offers any advantages over the LS estimator in finite samples?

4. Adapt the GAUSS program C11WLS.gss to compute the EE estimator of $\boldsymbol{\beta}$ from the estimating equations (15.5.7). An EGLS estimator of $\boldsymbol{\beta}$ may be formed by initially estimating the variances σ_i^2 from the regression $\ln(e_i^2) = \mathbf{x}[i, .]\boldsymbol{\beta} + \mathrm{v}_i$, where $\mathbf{e}$ is the vector of LS residuals. Conduct a Monte Carlo simulation exercise to compare the sampling properties of the EE and EGLS estimators of $\boldsymbol{\beta}$ for this model.

15.8. References

Andrews, D. W. K. (1991), "Heteroskedasticity and Autocorrelation Consistent Covariance Matrix Estimation," *Econometrica*, Vol. 59, pp. 817–58.

Barnett, W. A. (1976), "Maximum Likelihood and Iterated Aitkin Estimation of Nonlinear Systems of Equations," *Journal of the American Statistical Association*, Vol. 71, pp. 354–60.

Barnett, W. A. (1981), *Consumer Demand and Labor Supply*, Chapter 4, Amsterdam: North-Holland.

Chesher, A. (1989), "Hajek Inequalities, Measures of Leverage and the Size of Heteroskedastic Robust Tests," *Econometrica*, Vol. 57, pp. 971–77.

Chesher, A., and G. Austin (1991), "The Finite-Sample Distributions of Heteroskedasticity Robust Wald Tests," *Journal of Econometrics*, Vol. 47, pp. 153–73.

Chesher, A., and I. Jewitt (1987), "The Bias of a Heteroskedasticity Consistent Covariance Matrix Estimator," *Econometrica*, Vol. 55, pp. 1217–22.

Davidson, R., and J. G. MacKinnon (1993), *Estimation and Inference in Econometrics*, New York: Oxford University Press.

Gallant, A. R. (1987), *Nonlinear Statistical Models*, New York: John Wiley and Sons.

Gourieroux, C., A. Monfort, and A. Trognon (1984), "Pseudo-maximum Likelihood Methods: Theory," *Econometrica*, Vol. 52, pp. 681–700.

Judge, G., W. E. Griffiths, R. C. Hill, H. Lütkepohl, and T. C. Lee (1985), *The Theory and Practice of Econometrics*, New York: John Wiley and Sons.

Kakwani, N. (1967), "The Unbiasedness of Zellner's Seemingly Unrelated Regression Equation Estimators," *Journal of the American Statistical Association*, Vol. 62, pp. 141–42.

Kitamura, Y. (1997), "Empirical Likelihood Methods with Weakly Dependent Processes," *Annals of Statistics*, Vol. 25, pp. 2084–2102.

Kitamura, Y., and M. Stutzer (1997), "An Information-Theoretic Alternative to Generalized Method of Moments Estimation," *Econometrica*, Vol. 65, pp. 861–74.

Kolacyzk, E. (1994), "Empirical Likelihood for Generalized Linear Models," *Statistica Sinica*, Vol. 4, pp. 199–218.

MacKinnon, J. G., and H. White (1985), "Some Heteroskedasticity Consistent Covariance Matrix Estimators with Improved Finite Sample Properties," *Journal of Econometrics*, Vol. 29, pp. 305–25.

Mittelhammer, R. C. (1996), *Mathematical Statistics for Economics and Business*, New York: Springer–Verlag.

Newey, W. K., and D. McFadden (1994), "Large Sample Estimation and Hypothesis Testing," Chap. 36, in R. F. Engle, and D. McFadden, (Eds.), *Handbook of Econometrics, Vol. 4*, New York: North–Holland.

Newey, W. K., and K. D. West (1987), "A Simple, Positive Semi-Definite, Heteroskedasticity and Autocorrelation Consistent Covariance Matrix," *Econometrica*, Vol. 55, pp. 703–8.

Owen, A. (1991), "Empirical Likelihood for Linear Models," *The Annals of Statistics*, Vol. 19, pp. 1725–47.

Phillips, P. C. B. (1976), "On the Iterated Minimum Distance Estimator and the Quasi-Maximum Likelihood Estimator," *Econometrica*, Vol. 44, pp. 449–60.

Schmidt, P. (1976), *Econometrics*, New York: Marcel Dekker.

White, H. (1980), "A Heteroskedasticity-Consistent Covariance Matrix Estimator and a Direct Test for Heteroskedasticity," *Econometrica*, Vol. 48, pp. 817–38.

White, H. (1984), *Asymptotic Theory for Econometricians*, Orlando, FL: Academic Press.

White, H. (1994), *Estimation, Inference, and Specification Analysis*, New York: Cambridge University Press.

White, H. and I. Domowitz (1984), "Nonlinear Regression with Dependent Observations," *Econometrica*, Vol. 52, pp. 143–161.

PART SIX

Simultaneous Equation Probability Models and General Moment-Based Estimation and Inference

In Chapter 16 we consider moment-based estimation equations in a framework in which the estimating functions may be biased, the system of estimating equations may overdetermine the parameters, and the sample outcomes resulting from the DSP may not be iid. This leads us to the concepts of instrumental variables and the general method of moments procedure and permits us to again use the EE, MEL, MEEL, and OptEF approaches of earlier chapters. Building on this estimation and inference base, we recognize in Chapter 17 that much economic data are generated from interdependent economic relations that are stochastic, dynamic, and simultaneous and specify a simultaneous equations probability model consistent with this DSP. Given the interdependent nature of economic data, a range of traditional and modern estimation rules and inference procedures are demonstrated and their asymptotic properties evaluated.

CHAPTER 16

Generalized Moment-Based Estimation and Inference

In Chapter 10 we introduced the concept of the method of moments (MOM) and then applied it to iid sample observations in a linear model context, where the orthogonality conditions $E[\mathbf{X}'_{i.}(Y_i - \mathbf{X}_{i.}\boldsymbol{\beta})] = \mathbf{0}$, $\forall i$ are assumed to hold. In the MOM procedure, where the number of empirical moment conditions and the number of unknown parameters are equal, empirical moments are effectively equated to their expectations and then solved for the unknown parameters of interest. In the linear model case, this led to MOM estimator $\hat{\boldsymbol{\beta}}_{\text{MOM}} = \arg_{\beta}[n^{-1}\mathbf{X}'(\mathbf{Y} - \mathbf{X}\boldsymbol{\beta}) = \mathbf{0}]$ that coincides with the least-squares estimator. In Chapters 11–13, we continued to use sample moments as a basis for defining estimating equations (EE) from unbiased estimating functions (EF) and also sought alternative nonuniform weightings of the observations to define optimal estimates of the unknown parameters. The alternative procedures (optimal estimating functions [OptEF], maximum empirical likelihood [MEL], and maximum entropy empirical likelihood [MEEL]) extended the MOM procedure by allowing the number of estimating equations to exceed the number of unknown parameters while still allowing for a unique inverse problem solution for the parameters with optimal asymptotic efficiency.

Building on the concepts of data aggregates and weighted sample moments, in this chapter we contemplate the use of moment-based estimating equations in a more general framework in which the usual estimating equation information may be biased, the system of equations may over-determine the unknown parameters of interest, or the data observations may not be iid. We refer to this case as generalized moment-based estimation and inference. We will see that traditional instrumental variable (IV) and generalized method of moments (GMM) procedures, along with the more recent approaches of EE, MEL, and MEEL, can be used to solve inverse problems such as these.

In terms of the presentation of topics, we initially assume an iid sampling context and revisit and elaborate on issues relating to parameter estimation when the number of unbiased estimating functions, derived from moment relationships, is equal to or larger than the number of unknown parameters of interest. The case in which the number of estimating equations exceeds the number of unknown parameters is referred

Table 16.1. *Probability Model Characteristics*

Model Component	Specific Characteristics	
$\mathbf{Y}$	RV Type:	continuous
	Range: Y_i	unlimited
	dimension:	univariate
	Moments:	$\mathbf{E}[\mathbf{Y} \mid \mathbf{X}] = \mathbf{X}\boldsymbol{\beta} + \mathbf{E}[\varepsilon \mid \mathbf{X}]$, or $= \mathbf{g}(\mathbf{X}, \boldsymbol{\beta}) + \mathbf{E}[\varepsilon \mid \mathbf{X}]$
$\eta(\mathbf{X}, \boldsymbol{\beta}, \varepsilon)$	Functional Form:	linear or nonlinear in $\mathbf{X}$, $\boldsymbol{\beta}$, or both; additive in ε
$\mathbf{X}$	RV Type:	fixed or stochastic, and $\mathbf{X}$ has full-column rank with probability 1
	Genesis:	exogenous to the model, or correlated with the noise component
$\boldsymbol{\beta}$	RV Type:	degenerate (fixed)
	Dimension:	finite
ε	RV Type:	iid or non-iid
	Moments:	$\mathrm{E}[\varepsilon \mid \mathbf{X}] = \eta(\mathbf{X})$, and $\mathbf{cov}(\varepsilon \mid \mathbf{X}) = \sigma^2\mathbf{I}$ or $\sigma^2\boldsymbol{\Psi}$
Ω	Prior info:	none
$\mathrm{f}(\mathbf{e} \mid \mathbf{x}, \varphi)$	PDF family:	unspecified

to as an *overdetermined* model, meaning essentially that we are *over* the number of estimating equations needed to *determine* values of the parameters. The case in which the number of equations is equal to the number of parameters is aptly called the *just-determined* case. We then present a moment basis for estimation and inference when the orthogonality conditions do not hold and the number of estimating equations used for estimation is the same as the number of unknown parameters of interest. This leads to the traditional instrumental variable (IV) estimators, as well as alternative approaches, including OptEF estimators, that have attractive asymptotic properties. Finally, we consider the case in which orthogonality does not hold and the number of estimating equations is greater than the number of unknown parameters. This leads us to the generalized method of moments (GMM) estimator as well as corresponding OptEF and alternative MEL and MEEL approaches.

In terms of the general class of probability models portrayed in Table 2.1, we will be concerned in this chapter with the special case set forth in Table 16.1.

16.1. Parameter Estimation in Just-determined and Overdetermined Models with iid Observations: Back to the Future

In this section we take inventory of methods that we have already examined for solving inverse problems in cases in which the number of unbiased estimating equations, derived from moment-type relationships, is equal to or exceeds the number of parameters. The focus is on the overdetermined case, and the purpose of this review is twofold. First, the review emphasizes that we have already identified procedures equipped to handle the overdetermined case, and thus, in the absence of any additional difficulties, essentially nothing is new in such an inverse problem situation. We will introduce an alternative traditional approach for handling overdetermined systems of estimating equation–moment relations in Section 16.2, called the generalized method of moments (GMM) approach. However, we will see that the GMM approach is not really new either in the sense that the sampling properties of the optimal GMM procedure are anticipated by the OptEF method. Secondly, the review sets the notational and conceptual stage for generalizing procedures to cases in which (1) the explanatory variables are correlated with the noise components of the models, and (2) cases in which the sample observations are not iid.

To begin the review, first consider a linear model context in which $(\mathrm{y}_i, \mathbf{x}_{i\cdot}), i=1, \ldots, n$ are iid outcomes and the orthogonality-moment conditions $\mathrm{E}[\mathbf{X}_{i\cdot}'\varepsilon_i] = \mathrm{E}[\mathbf{X}_{i\cdot}'(\mathrm{Y}_i - \mathbf{X}_{i\cdot}\boldsymbol{\beta})] = \mathbf{0}, \forall i$ hold. Then $\mathbf{h}(\mathbf{Y}, \mathbf{X}, \boldsymbol{\beta}) = n^{-1}\mathbf{X}'\varepsilon = n^{-1}\sum_{i=1}^{n}\mathbf{X}_{i\cdot}'\varepsilon_i = n^{-1}\sum_{i=1}^{n}\mathbf{X}_{i\cdot}'(\mathrm{Y}_i - \mathbf{X}_{i\cdot}\boldsymbol{\beta}) = n^{-1}\mathbf{X}'(\mathbf{Y} - \mathbf{X}\boldsymbol{\beta})$ is an $(m \times 1)$ unbiased estimating function having expectation

$$\mathrm{E}[\mathbf{h}(\mathbf{Y}, \mathbf{X}, \boldsymbol{\beta})] = \mathrm{E}[n^{-1}\mathbf{X}'(\mathbf{Y} - \mathbf{X}\boldsymbol{\beta})] = \mathbf{0} \tag{16.1.1.a}$$

with sample estimating equation–moment analog

$$n^{-1}[\mathbf{x}'(\mathbf{y} - \mathbf{x}\boldsymbol{\beta})] = \mathbf{0}. \tag{16.1.1.b}$$

Note a sufficient condition for the orthogonality condition to hold is that $\mathrm{E}[\varepsilon \mid \mathbf{X}] = \mathbf{0}$, where the double expectation theorem can be applied to yield $\mathrm{E}[\mathbf{X}'\varepsilon] = \mathrm{E}[\mathrm{E}[\mathbf{X}'\varepsilon \mid \mathbf{X}]] = \mathrm{E}[\mathbf{X}'\mathrm{E}[\varepsilon \mid \mathbf{X}]] = \mathrm{E}[\mathbf{X}'\mathbf{0}] = \mathbf{0}$. We previously assumed this condition in Chapter 10 when discussing the impact of stochastic regressors on the analysis of regression models.

Since the $\boldsymbol{\beta}$ parameter vector is $(k \times 1)$, there are exactly the same number of estimating equations as parameters, $m = k$. If it is assumed that the system of equations (16.1.1.b) has full row rank, which is assured by the classical regularity condition that $\mathbf{x}$ has full column rank, the estimating equations can be solved for $\boldsymbol{\beta}$, and the LS–MOM–OptEF estimate $\hat{\mathbf{b}} = (\mathbf{x}'\mathbf{x})^{-1}\mathbf{x}'\mathbf{y}$ is thereby defined. This is an example of a just-determined inverse problem, meaning that there are just enough estimating equations to identify the unknown parameter values. More generally, in either linear or nonlinear model contexts, when there are just enough unbiased estimating equations–moment relationships to solve for unique values of the parameters, we are dealing with a well-posed, just-determined inverse problem. These just-determined inverse problems can be solved, in the iid sampling case, using a variety of procedures already discussed in previous chapters, including the MOM, OptEF, MEL, and MEEL approaches.

Now, assume that the dimension of the $(m \times 1)$ unbiased estimating functions is greater than the number of unknown parameters k, that is, $m > k$. This general situation often arises in economic models that characterize the optimizing behavior of economic agents in terms of first-order conditions applied to an agent's economic objective function. For example, within the iid linear model context, which represents a precursor to more general models in Sections 16.3 and 16.4, assume $m > k$ population moment conditions and further assume there exists a matrix $\mathbf{Z}$ for which the moment conditions $\mathrm{E}[\mathbf{Z}_{i.}'\varepsilon_i] = \mathrm{E}[\mathbf{Z}_{i.}'(\mathrm{Y}_i - \mathbf{X}_{i.}\boldsymbol{\beta})] = \mathbf{0}$ hold for $i = 1, \ldots, n$. Then $\mathbf{h}(\mathbf{Y}, \mathbf{X}, \mathbf{Z}, \boldsymbol{\beta}) = \sum_{i=1}^{n}[n^{-1}\mathrm{Z}_{i.}'(\mathrm{Y}_i - \mathbf{X}_{i.}\boldsymbol{\beta})] = n^{-1}\mathbf{Z}'(\mathbf{Y} - \mathbf{X}\boldsymbol{\beta})]$ is an $m \times 1$ unbiased estimating function because

$$\mathrm{E}[\mathbf{h}(\mathbf{Y}, \mathbf{X}, \mathbf{Z}, \boldsymbol{\beta})] = \mathrm{E}[n^{-1}\mathbf{Z}'(\mathbf{Y} - \mathbf{X}\boldsymbol{\beta})] = \mathbf{0} \tag{16.1.2.a}$$

and a sample estimating equation–moment analog is given by

$$n^{-1}\mathbf{z}'(\mathbf{y} - \mathbf{x}\boldsymbol{\beta}) = \mathbf{0}. \tag{16.1.2.b}$$

Here, $\mathbf{Z}$ is some $(m \times n)$ matrix having full-row rank with probability 1, such that (16.1.2.a) is true, and the vector estimating function $\mathbf{h}(\mathbf{Y}, \mathbf{X}, \mathbf{Z}, \boldsymbol{\beta}) = n^{-1}\mathbf{Z}'(\mathbf{Y} - \mathbf{X}\boldsymbol{\beta})$ is unbiased. It is possible for $\mathbf{Z}$ to contain one or more of the columns in the $\mathbf{X}$ matrix so long as (16.1.2.a) remains true. Note, by the double expectation theorem, a sufficient condition for (16.1.2.a) to be true is that $\mathrm{E}[\varepsilon \mid \mathbf{Z}] = \mathrm{E}[(\mathbf{Y} - \mathbf{X}\boldsymbol{\beta}) \mid \mathbf{Z}] = \mathbf{0}$. Consequently, $\mathbf{Z}$ is a matrix of variables that has no effect on the (zero) value of the conditional expectation of the noise component of the model. We assume this condition for the remainder of this section. We also assume for now that $\mathbf{cov}(\varepsilon \mid \mathbf{Z}) = \mathbf{cov}(\varepsilon \mid \mathbf{Z}) = \sigma^2\mathbf{I}$. We will see in Section 16.3 that the $\mathbf{Z}$ variables are often referred to in practice as *instrumental variables*. Further properties required of the matrix $\mathbf{Z}$ will be identified ahead.

The set of estimating Equations (16.1.2) is overdetermined for estimating $\boldsymbol{\beta}$. Therefore, the inverse problem of estimating $\boldsymbol{\beta}$ is overdetermined, and it will generally be impossible to solve for a vector $\boldsymbol{\beta}$ that will satisfy (16.1.2.b). To solve this problem, we need to reconcile, in some way, the overdetermined nature of the set of estimating equations. There are several different ways we might consider doing this, and in fact we have already examined procedures in previous chapters that can be used to provide solutions. The approaches commonly used in practice for solving this problem generally belong either to the extremum or estimating equations class of estimators, or to both.

The estimating equations approach can be used to seek k linear combinations of the m estimating equations that collectively represent a transformed just-determined system of equations that can be solved uniquely for $\boldsymbol{\beta}$. The linear combinations should be chosen to define an estimator with good, and preferably optimal, finite sample or asymptotic sampling properties. This type of problem is one that we have already examined in Chapter 11 relating to OptEF estimators.

Alternatively, additional unknowns in the form of nonuniform weights on the sample observations can be introduced to define differentially weighted sample moment conditions. Then, using either a maximum empirical likelihood or maximum entropy estimation objective function, one can solve for both the sample weights and unknown parameters via maximization of the estimation objective. In this case, n new unknown sample weight parameters are introduced into the overdetermined inverse problem to redefine the problem effectively into an underdetermined inverse problem relative to the sample weights and unknown parameters. Then, the underidentification problem is resolved by choosing values of the unknowns that maximize an extremum-type estimation objective function. Remarkably, the asymptotic properties of the OptEF, MEL, and MEEL approaches are identical in the iid context, as we have seen in Chapters 11–13.

To establish a conceptual and notational base for the extensions in this chapter, we now provide a brief review of the major considerations underlying the application of the

OptEF, MEL, and MEEL approaches to just-determined and overdetermined inverse problems. We make liberal use of the linear model context as a running illustration. The reader can review Chapters 11–13 for additional details.

16.1.1. OptEF Approach

In the OptEF approach, we know from Section 11.3.2.b that the optimal $(k \times 1)$ linear combination of estimating functions of the form $\mathbf{h}_\nu(\mathbf{y}, \mathbf{x}, \mathbf{z}, \boldsymbol{\beta}) \equiv \boldsymbol{\nu}\mathbf{h}(\mathbf{y}, \mathbf{x}, \mathbf{z}, \boldsymbol{\beta}) = \mathbf{0}$, where $\boldsymbol{\nu}$ is a $(k \times m)$ matrix with full row rank, is given by the choice of $\boldsymbol{\nu}$ that minimizes

$$\left(\mathrm{E}\left[\frac{\partial \mathbf{h}_\nu(\mathbf{Y}, \mathbf{X}, \mathbf{Z}, \boldsymbol{\beta})}{\partial \boldsymbol{\beta}}\right]\right)^{-1} \mathrm{E}[\mathbf{h}_\nu(\mathbf{Y}, \mathbf{X}, \mathbf{Z}, \boldsymbol{\beta})\mathbf{h}_\nu(\mathbf{Y}, \mathbf{X}, \mathbf{Z}, \boldsymbol{\beta})'] \left(\mathrm{E}\left[\frac{\partial \mathbf{h}_\nu(\mathbf{Y}, \mathbf{X}, \mathbf{Z}, \boldsymbol{\beta})}{\partial \boldsymbol{\beta}'}\right]\right)^{-1}. \tag{16.1.3}$$

In the context of a linear model application with estimating equation–moment relations given by (16.1.2), this is equivalent to choosing $\boldsymbol{\nu}$ to minimize

$$\begin{aligned}&[\mathrm{E}[\mathbf{X}'\mathbf{Z}]\boldsymbol{\nu}']^{-1}\mathrm{E}[\boldsymbol{\nu}\mathbf{Z}'(\mathbf{Y} - \mathbf{X}\boldsymbol{\beta})(\mathbf{Y} - \mathbf{X}\boldsymbol{\beta})'\mathbf{Z}\boldsymbol{\nu}'][\boldsymbol{\nu}\mathrm{E}[\mathbf{Z}'\mathbf{X}]]^{-1} \\ &\quad = [\mathrm{E}[\mathbf{X}'\mathbf{Z}]\boldsymbol{\nu}']^{-1}[\sigma^2\boldsymbol{\nu}\mathrm{E}[\mathbf{Z}'\mathbf{Z}]\boldsymbol{\nu}'][\boldsymbol{\nu}\mathrm{E}[\mathbf{Z}'\mathbf{X}]]^{-1}.\end{aligned} \tag{16.1.4}$$

On the basis of an approach similar to that used in Section 11.4.1, it can be shown that (16.1.4) is minimized by choosing $\boldsymbol{\nu} = \mathrm{E}[\mathbf{X}'\mathbf{Z}](\mathbf{E}[\mathbf{Z}'\mathbf{Z}])^{-1}$. Thus, the OptEF in this case is given by

$$\mathbf{h}_{\mathrm{opt}}(\mathbf{Y}, \mathbf{X}, \mathbf{Z}, \boldsymbol{\beta}) = n^{-1}\mathrm{E}[\mathbf{X}'\mathbf{Z}](\mathrm{E}[\mathbf{Z}'\mathbf{Z}])^{-1}\mathbf{Z}'(\mathbf{Y} - \mathbf{X}\boldsymbol{\beta}). \tag{16.1.5}$$

Because in practice the expectations in (16.1.5) will be unknown in general, they will be replaced by the consistent estimators $\hat{\mathrm{E}}\left[n^{-1}\mathbf{X}'\mathbf{Z}\right] = n^{-1}\mathbf{X}'\mathbf{Z}$ and $\hat{\mathrm{E}}\left[n^{-1}\mathbf{Z}'\mathbf{Z}\right] = n^{-1}\mathbf{Z}'\mathbf{Z}$, and thus the (estimated) OptEF estimator of $\boldsymbol{\beta}$ is ultimately defined by

$$\hat{\boldsymbol{\beta}}_{\mathrm{EE}} = \arg_{\boldsymbol{\beta}}[\hat{\mathbf{h}}_{\mathrm{opt}}(\mathbf{Y}, \mathbf{X}, \mathbf{Z}, \boldsymbol{\beta}) = \mathbf{0}] = [\mathbf{X}'\mathbf{Z}(\mathbf{Z}'\mathbf{Z})^{-1}\mathbf{Z}'\mathbf{X}]^{-1}\mathbf{X}'\mathbf{Z}(\mathbf{Z}'\mathbf{Z})^{-1}\mathbf{Z}'\mathbf{Y} \tag{16.1.6}$$

(the estimators used for the expectation terms will be discussed further in Section 16.2.1). If $\mathbf{X}$ and $\mathbf{Z}$ are fixed, or the OptEF can be stated conditionally on values $\boldsymbol{x}$ and $\mathbf{z}$, then the expectations in (16.1.5) can be dropped, and the estimator in (16.1.6) can be expressed in terms of $\mathbf{x}$ and $\mathbf{z}$. Note the similarity in form to the GLS estimator in Chapter 14. In the simultaneous equations context to be examined in Chapter 17, this OptEF estimator has been traditionally referred to as the *two-stage least squares estimator.*

On the basis of its OptEF property, we know from Chapter 11 that $\hat{\boldsymbol{\beta}}_{\mathrm{EE}}$ is asymptotically (and in finite samples if the expectations happen to be known in (16.1.5)) the best estimator in the class of estimators derived from linear unbiased estimating equations defined in terms of moment equations (16.1.2). Furthermore, it is consistent and asymptotically normally distributed in addition to being asymptotically optimal in this class. In particular, the asymptotic distribution of $\hat{\boldsymbol{\beta}}_{\mathrm{EE}}$ is given by $\hat{\boldsymbol{\beta}}_{\mathrm{EE}} \overset{a}{\sim} \mathrm{N}(\mathbf{0}, \boldsymbol{\Sigma})$

where (recall Theorem 11.3.2))

$$\boldsymbol{\Sigma} = \left[\mathrm{E}\left[\frac{\partial \mathbf{h}(\mathbf{Y}, \mathbf{Q}, \boldsymbol{\beta})}{\partial \boldsymbol{\beta}} \bigg|_{\boldsymbol{\beta}_0} \right] (\mathrm{E}[\mathbf{h}(\mathbf{Y}, \mathbf{Q}, \boldsymbol{\beta})\mathbf{h}(\mathbf{Y}, \mathbf{Q}, \boldsymbol{\beta})'|_{\boldsymbol{\beta}_0}])^{-1} \mathrm{E}\left[\frac{\partial \mathbf{h}(\mathbf{Y}, \mathbf{Q}, \boldsymbol{\beta})}{\partial \boldsymbol{\beta}'} \bigg|_{\boldsymbol{\beta}_0} \right] \right]^{-1} \tag{16.1.7}$$

and $\mathbf{Q} \equiv [\mathbf{X}', \mathbf{Z}']'$. In the linear model example, an appropriate representation of the covariance matrix (16.1.7) can be given as (again, using sample moments to approximate the expectation terms as indicated previously)

$$\boldsymbol{\Sigma} = \sigma^2 [\mathbf{x}'\mathbf{z}(\mathbf{z}'\mathbf{z})^{-1}\mathbf{z}'\mathbf{x}]^{-1}, \tag{16.1.8}$$

which is consistently estimated by replacing σ^2 with $s_{\mathrm{EE}}^2 = (\mathbf{y} - \mathbf{x}\hat{\mathbf{b}}_{\mathrm{EE}})'(\mathbf{y} - \mathbf{x}\hat{\mathbf{b}}_{\mathrm{EE}})/n$. Note that the overdetermined nature of the inverse problem has been resolved through a rank k linear transformation, leading to a set of k optimal estimating functions in the class of linear unbiased estimating functions based on (16.1.2). Testing and confidence-region estimation can proceed as usual based on the statistics for the EE approach presented in Chapter 11. We point out that for the estimator and covariance matrix to be well defined for large n, it is assumed that $n^{-1}\mathbf{Z}'\mathbf{Z}$ and $n^{-1}\mathbf{X}'\mathbf{Z}$ converge to finite nonsingular and full-row rank matrices, respectively, or else at least the nonsingularity and rank conditions are maintained uniformly for all n. We will discuss these properties further ahead.

► **Example 16.1.1:** To develop a numerical procedure for computing the two-stage least-squares estimator, we provide the GAUSS program C162SLS.gss in the examples manual. The program implements formulae (16.1.6) and (16.1.8) in calculating 2SLS estimates and their estimated standard errors. Note that the σ^2 parameter is replaced by the estimate indicated below (16.1.8) when estimating the asymptotic covariance matrix. Based on observed outcomes of a dependent variable $\mathbf{y}$, explanatory variables $\mathbf{x}$, and instruments $\mathbf{z}$, the 2SLS procedure is applied and the results are reported to the user.

16.1.2. Empirical Likelihood Approaches

In the MEL or MEEL approach, the overdetermined nature of the estimating equations is resolved in general by solving the extremum-type problem

$$\max_{\mathbf{p}, \boldsymbol{\beta}} \left[\sum_{i=1}^{n} \ln(p_i) \right] \quad \text{or} \quad \max_{\mathbf{p}, \boldsymbol{\beta}} \left[-\sum_{i=1}^{n} p_i \ln(p_i) \right] \tag{16.1.9}$$

subject to the empirical moment restrictions

$$\sum_{i=1}^{n} p_i \mathbf{h}(y_i, \mathbf{q}_{i\cdot}, \boldsymbol{\beta}) = \mathbf{0} \tag{16.1.10}$$

and

$$\sum_{i=1}^{n} p_i = 1, \tag{16.1.11}$$

where we let $\mathbf{q}$ represent any other variables besides $\mathbf{y}$ that appear in the estimating equations. Note that by introducing the unknown sample weights $\mathbf{p}$ in place of the known uniform weights n^{-1} in the representation of the empirical moment conditions (16.1.10), an underdetermined inverse problem of recovering values of $\mathbf{p}$ and $\boldsymbol{\beta}$ is now defined. In contrast to the overdetermined linear model example (16.1.2), the empirical moment restrictions (16.1.10) are now given specifically by

$$\sum_{i=1}^{n} \mathrm{p}_i \mathbf{h}(\mathrm{y}_i, \mathbf{q}_{i\cdot}, \boldsymbol{\beta}) = \sum_{i=1}^{n} \mathrm{p}_i \mathbf{z}'_{i\cdot}(\mathrm{y}_i - \mathbf{x}_{i\cdot}\boldsymbol{\beta}) = \mathbf{0}. \tag{16.1.12}$$

The solution for the MEL or MEEL estimate is then obtained by solving the extremum problem (16.1.9), (16.1.11), and (16.1.12) numerically, and the characterizations of the solutions have been discussed in detail in Chapters 12 and 13.

Under general regularity conditions that include the assumption that the sample observations are iid, the resulting MEL and MEEL estimators share the same asymptotic properties and, moreover, are consistent, asymptotically normally distributed, and asymptotically efficient. Furthermore, as we have also noted in both Chapters 12 and 13, the MEL and MEEL estimators in the iid case have the same asymptotic properties as the OptEF estimator of the previous subsection. The initial overdetermined nature of the inverse problem was resolved by first transforming the problem into an underdetermined inverse problem via the introduction of unknown sample weights. Then, the full set of unknowns in the augmented problem is estimated by solving an extremum estimation problem based on either an MEL or MEEL estimation objective. Testing and confidence region estimation can proceed as usual based on the statistics for the MEL and MEEL approaches discussed in Chapters 12 and 13.

16.1.3. Summary and Foreword

In effect, our preceding review of the EE, MEL, and MEEL approaches goes a long way toward indicating how overdetermined inverse problems defined in terms of unbiased estimating equations can be solved. In the remainder of this chapter, we first expand our inventory of methods for solving these types of overdetermined inverse problems by introducing the traditional generalized method of moments (GMM) approach. We then focus on a new regression problem situation in which the explanatory variable matrix $\mathbf{X}$ is correlated with the noise component ε so that the usual estimating equations derived from moment-type relationships such as $\mathbf{h}(\mathbf{Y}, \mathbf{X}, \boldsymbol{\beta}) = n^{-1}\mathbf{X}'(\mathbf{Y} - \mathbf{X}\boldsymbol{\beta})$ are biased. In this new problem context, we first examine a just-determined estimating equation system and present the traditional instrumental variable method of solution. We then allow the estimating equation system to be overdetermined and see how the GMM, OptEF, MEL, and MEEL approaches can be applied to this problem. In the process we subsume the IV and GMM approaches under the OptEF approach.

► **Example 16.1.2:** The moment-based estimation methods may also be applied to just-identified inverse problems with nonlinear (in $\boldsymbol{\beta}$) estimating equations of the form $\mathrm{E}[\mathbf{h}(\mathbf{Y}, \mathbf{X}, \mathbf{Z}, \boldsymbol{\beta})] = \mathrm{E}[n^{-1}\mathbf{Z}'\mathbf{g}(\mathbf{Y}, \mathbf{X}, \boldsymbol{\beta})] = \mathbf{0}$, where $\mathbf{g}(\mathbf{Y}, \mathbf{X}, \boldsymbol{\beta})$ is a nonlinear specification such that $\mathrm{E}[\mathrm{g}(\mathrm{Y}_i, \mathbf{X}_{i\cdot}, \boldsymbol{\beta})] = \mathbf{0}$. The GAUSS program C16HS.gss (provided in the examples manual) demonstrates the solution of a nonlinear just-determined equation of the preceding form. For a given set of observations on the dependent, explanatory, and instrumental variables relating to a just-determined nonlinear (in $\boldsymbol{\beta}$) estimating equation associated with a nonlinear regression model, the C16HS.gss program calculates the unknown $\boldsymbol{\beta}$ parameters of the regression relationship and also calculates the approximate standard errors. The program also reports the outcomes of hypothesis tests on the parameters. Confidence regions could also be generated, and are left to the reader as an exercise.

16.2. GMM Solutions for Unbiased Estimating Equations in the Overdetermined Case

In this section we analyze an extension of the ordinary MOM approach to cases where the number of estimating equation–moment conditions m exceeds the number of unknown parameters k that we seek to recover. When $m > k$ and the inverse problem is overdetermined, it is not generally possible to find a value of the parameter vector that simultaneously sets all of the sample moment conditions exactly equal to zero. In effect there are more equations than unknown parameters, and the system of moment condition equations is overdetermined. The solution proposed by Hansen (1982) is to choose model parameters that set the moment functions as close to zero as possible, where closeness is measured in terms of weighted Euclidean distance. Although each weighting scheme may provide a different consistent estimator, the weights may be selected to achieve a consistent estimator that is asymptotically normally distributed within a broad class of alternative estimators.

16.2.1. GMM Concept

The GMM framework extends the MOM procedure by considering a $(m \times 1)$ random vector function of the form $\mathbf{h}_*(\mathrm{Y}_i, \mathbf{Q}_{i\cdot}, \boldsymbol{\beta})]$ that has moments

$$\mathrm{E}[\mathbf{h}_*(\mathrm{Y}_i, \mathbf{Q}_{i\cdot}, \boldsymbol{\beta})] = \mathbf{0}, \qquad \text{for} \quad i = 1, \ldots, n, \tag{16.2.1}$$

where $(\mathbf{Y}, \mathbf{Q})$ has some joint probability distribution on which the expectations in (16.2.1) are based. In anticipation of generalizations later in the chapter, we let $\mathbf{Q}$ be a matrix representing all variables in the model other than $\mathbf{Y}$. The dimension of $\mathbf{h}_*$ may be greater than the number of unknown parameters. Consequently, there may not exist a unique parameter vector $\boldsymbol{\beta}$ that solves the sample moment conditions via the ordinary MOM approach, which attempts to find a $\boldsymbol{\beta}$ that satisfies

$$\mathbf{h}(\mathbf{Y}, \mathbf{Q}, \boldsymbol{\beta}) \equiv n^{-1} \sum_{i=1}^{n} \mathbf{h}_*(\mathrm{Y}_i, \mathbf{Q}_{i\cdot}, \boldsymbol{\beta}) = \mathbf{0}. \tag{16.2.2}$$

Under the GMM approach, we choose the parameter vector for which the sample moment conditions are as close to the zero vector as possible. In pursuit of this objective we use the following weighted Euclidean distance (i.e., weighted squared distance) as our measure of closeness:

$$\min_{\boldsymbol{\beta}}[\mathrm{m}(\boldsymbol{\beta}, \mathbf{Y}, \mathbf{Q})] = \min_{\boldsymbol{\beta}}\left[\left[n^{-1}\sum_{i=1}^{n}\mathbf{h}_*(\mathrm{Y}_i, \mathbf{Q}_{i\cdot}, \boldsymbol{\beta})\right]'\mathbf{W}\left[n^{-1}\sum_{i=1}^{n}\mathbf{h}_*(\mathrm{Y}_i, \mathbf{Q}_{i\cdot}, \boldsymbol{\beta})\right]\right]$$
$$= \min_{\boldsymbol{\beta}}[\mathbf{h}(\mathbf{Y}, \mathbf{Q}, \boldsymbol{\beta})'\mathbf{W}\,\mathbf{h}(\mathbf{Y}, \mathbf{Q}, \boldsymbol{\beta})], \qquad (16.2.3)$$

where $\mathbf{W}$ is an $(m \times m)$ positive definite symmetric weight matrix.

Note that the form of the estimation objective is very similar to the nonlinear least-squares estimator, where instead of minimizing the weighted squared distance between $[\mathbf{Y} - \mathbf{g}(\mathbf{X}, \boldsymbol{\beta})]$ and $\mathbf{0}$, the estimator seeks to minimize the weighted squared distance between $\mathbf{h}(\mathbf{Y}, \mathbf{Q}, \boldsymbol{\beta})$ and $\mathbf{0}$. Note further that the fundamental rationale for choosing $\boldsymbol{\beta}$ to satisfy the sample moment conditions (16.2.2) as closely as possible is analogous to the (ordinary) method of moments. Namely, we are assuming that an appropriate uniform law of large numbers applies so that $n^{-1}\sum_{i=1}^{n}\mathbf{h}_*(\mathrm{Y}_i, \mathbf{Q}_{i\cdot}, \boldsymbol{\beta}) \xrightarrow{\mathrm{p}} \mathbf{0}$ uniquely when $\boldsymbol{\beta}$ is set equal to the true value $\boldsymbol{\beta}_0$ of the parameter vector. Then, solving the sample moment conditions for $\boldsymbol{\beta}$ leads to a sequence of solutions $\{\hat{\boldsymbol{\beta}}_n\}$ for which $\hat{\boldsymbol{\beta}}_n \xrightarrow{\mathrm{p}} \boldsymbol{\beta}_0$ as $n \to \infty$ so that the estimator so defined is consistent. We discuss sampling properties of GMM estimators in more detail in Section 16.2.2.

Another illuminating way to view the GMM approach to the problem of solving overdetermined sets of sample moment conditions is through the necessary conditions for the minimization of (16.2.3) given by

$$\frac{\partial \mathrm{m}(\boldsymbol{\beta}, \mathbf{Y}, \mathbf{Q})}{\partial \boldsymbol{\beta}} = \left[n^{-1}\sum_{i=1}^{n}\frac{\partial \mathbf{h}_*(\mathrm{Y}_i, \mathbf{Q}_{i\cdot}, \boldsymbol{\beta})}{\partial \boldsymbol{\beta}}\right]\mathbf{W}\left[n^{-1}\sum_{i=1}^{n}\mathbf{h}_*(\mathrm{Y}_i, \mathbf{Q}_{i\cdot}, \boldsymbol{\beta})\right]$$
$$= \left[\frac{\partial \mathbf{h}(\mathbf{Y}, \mathbf{Q}, \boldsymbol{\beta})}{\partial \boldsymbol{\beta}}\right]\mathbf{W}\,\mathbf{h}(\mathbf{Y}, \mathbf{Q}, \boldsymbol{\beta}) = \mathbf{0}. \qquad (16.2.4)$$

The conditions (16.2.4) indicate that the nonuniqueness problem is overcome by forming a $(k \times 1)$ linear combination of the moment conditions. In effect, we use the $(k \times m)$ matrix $[\frac{\partial \mathbf{h}(\mathbf{Y}, \mathbf{Q}, \boldsymbol{\beta})}{\partial \boldsymbol{\beta}}]\mathbf{W}$ to project the moment conditions from m-space down to k-space so that we produce a transformed, just-determined inverse problem with as many equations as unknowns, allowing a unique solution to the inverse problem to be calculated. As we choose alternative weight matrices $\mathbf{W}$, we alter the projection and generally the solution to the problem.

The major difficulty in implementing the GMM estimator is the choice of the weighting matrix $\mathbf{W}$, which has an effect on the relative efficiency of the estimator. In fact, for any given set of estimating equations–moment conditions, (16.2.3) identifies an entire uncountably infinite class of estimators as a function of $\mathbf{W}$, and the efficient choice of $\mathbf{W}$, though theoretically defined, is almost always unknown in practice. We address the choice of $\mathbf{W}$ in subsequent sections.

16.2.2. GMM Linear Model Estimation

Referring to the overdetermined linear model context discussed in Section 16.1, GMM moment conditions in the case of the linear model can be represented by (let $\mathbf{Q} \equiv [\mathbf{X}', \mathbf{Z}']'$

in Section 16.2.1)

$$\mathrm{E}[\mathbf{h}_*(\mathrm{Y}_i, \mathbf{Q}_{i\cdot}, \boldsymbol{\beta})] = \mathrm{E}[\mathbf{Z}'_{i\cdot}(\mathrm{Y}_i - \mathbf{X}_{i\cdot}\boldsymbol{\beta})] = \mathbf{0}, \quad i = 1, \ldots, n, \tag{16.2.5}$$

and the sample moment counterpart is

$$\mathbf{h}(\mathbf{Y}, \mathbf{Q}, \boldsymbol{\beta}) = n^{-1} \sum_{i=1}^{n} \mathbf{h}_*(\mathrm{Y}_i, \mathbf{Q}_{i\cdot}, \boldsymbol{\beta}) = n^{-1}\mathbf{Z}'(\mathbf{Y} - \mathbf{X}\boldsymbol{\beta}) = \mathbf{0}, \tag{16.2.6}$$

as they were before. We implement the GMM approach by defining, in an extremum estimation context, a weighted Euclidean distance-based estimation objective function and define a GMM estimator as

$$\hat{\boldsymbol{\beta}}(\mathbf{W}) = \arg\min_{\boldsymbol{\beta}}[\mathrm{m}(\boldsymbol{\beta}, \mathbf{Y}, \mathbf{Q})] = \arg\min_{\boldsymbol{\beta}}[n^{-2}(\mathbf{Y} - \mathbf{X}\boldsymbol{\beta})'\mathbf{Z}\mathbf{W}\mathbf{Z}'(\mathbf{Y} - \mathbf{X}\boldsymbol{\beta})]. \tag{16.2.7}$$

Differentiating $m(\boldsymbol{\beta}, \mathbf{Y}, \mathbf{Q})$ in (16.2.7) with respect to $\boldsymbol{\beta}$ yields the following first-order conditions (representing a specific instance of (16.2.4)):

$$\frac{\partial \mathrm{m}(\boldsymbol{\beta}, \mathbf{Y}, \mathbf{Q})}{\partial \boldsymbol{\beta}} = -2n^{-2}\mathbf{X}'\mathbf{Z}\mathbf{W}\mathbf{Z}'(\mathbf{Y} - \mathbf{X}\boldsymbol{\beta}) = \mathbf{0}, \tag{16.2.8}$$

which can be solved for the GMM estimator

$$\hat{\boldsymbol{\beta}}(\mathbf{W}) = [\mathbf{X}'\mathbf{Z}\mathbf{W}\mathbf{Z}'\mathbf{X}]^{-1}\mathbf{X}'\mathbf{Z}\mathbf{W}\mathbf{Z}'\mathbf{Y}. \tag{16.2.9}$$

In (16.2.8) we have used the $(k \times m)$ matrix $\mathbf{X}'\mathbf{Z}\mathbf{W}$ to project the m moment conditions (16.2.6) to a set of k equations in k unknowns. This transformation produces a just-determined inverse problem that can be solved uniquely for $\boldsymbol{\beta}$.

16.2.2.a. Optimal GMM Weight Matrix

Of course, to make the GMM estimator operational we need to choose a weight matrix **W**, and we would prefer to make an optimal choice of **W** if such a choice is available. The work of Hansen (1982) indicates that the choice of **W** that defines the most efficient estimator of the form (16.2.7) is to set **W** equal to the *inverse* of the covariance matrix $\mathbf{cov}(n^{-1/2}\mathbf{Z}'\boldsymbol{\varepsilon})$. Assuming that $\mathrm{E}[n^{-1}\mathbf{Z}'\mathbf{Z}]$ exists as a finite positive definite matrix, say $\mathbf{a}^n_{\mathbf{ZZ}}$, we can apply the double expectation theorem to express the optimal $\mathbf{W}^{-1}$ as

$$\begin{aligned}\mathbf{w}_*^{-1} &= \mathbf{cov}(n^{-1/2}\mathbf{Z}'\boldsymbol{\varepsilon}) = n^{-1}\mathrm{E}_{\mathbf{Z}}[\mathrm{E}[\mathbf{Z}'\boldsymbol{\varepsilon}\boldsymbol{\varepsilon}'\mathbf{Z} \mid \mathbf{Z}]] \\ &= n^{-1}\mathrm{E}_{\mathbf{Z}}[\mathbf{Z}'(\sigma^2\mathbf{I})\mathbf{Z}] = n^{-1}\sigma^2\mathrm{E}(\mathbf{Z}'\mathbf{Z}) = \sigma^2\mathbf{a}^n_{\mathbf{ZZ}},\end{aligned} \tag{16.2.10}$$

where we have used the assumption that $\mathrm{E}(\boldsymbol{\varepsilon}\boldsymbol{\varepsilon}' \mid \mathbf{Z}) = \sigma^2\mathbf{I}$. Note that $\mathbf{a}^n_{\mathbf{ZZ}}$ is a finite sample expectation, which we emphasize through the use of the superscript n.

The intuition in support of this optimal choice of **W** is analogous to the observation-weighting arguments underlying the GLS context of Chapter 14. The extremum estimation problem exhibited in (16.2.7) is actually equivalent to a least-squares problem of the form $\mathbf{V}'\mathbf{W}\mathbf{V}$, where $\mathbf{V} \equiv \mathbf{Z}'(\mathbf{Y} - \mathbf{X}\boldsymbol{\beta}) \equiv \mathbf{Y}_* - \mathbf{X}_*\boldsymbol{\beta}$ (the scaling by n^{-2} is superfluous to the optimal value of $\boldsymbol{\beta}$ in (16.2.7). It is apparent that the random variables in **V** are generally heteroscedastic and autocorrelated, where $\mathbf{cov}(\mathbf{V}) = \sigma^2\mathrm{E}(\mathbf{Z}'\mathbf{Z})$.

Under these circumstances we know from Chapter 14 that it is the GLS estimator, obtained by choosing $\boldsymbol{\beta}$ to minimize the *weighted* sum of squares $\mathbf{V}'[\mathbf{cov}(\mathbf{V})]^{-1}\mathbf{V}$, that is optimal. The weight matrix $[\mathbf{cov}(\mathbf{V})]^{-1}$ accounts for the inherent differential variability in the m moment conditions in the current application, effectively providing more weight to those moment conditions with more information or less variability. Except for a scaling factor, which has no effect on the solved value of $\boldsymbol{\beta}$ in (16.2.7), this is precisely the optimal weighting matrix identified by Hansen in the GMM context.

In practice, both σ^2 and $\mathrm{E}(n^{-1}\mathbf{Z}'\mathbf{Z}) = \mathbf{a}_{ZZ}^n$ are unknown, and so we have an operational dilemma analogous to the case of the EGLS estimator encountered in Chapter 16. To define an estimated optimal GMM (EOGMM) estimator, we can insert consistent estimators in place of σ^2 and $\mathrm{E}(n^{-1}\mathbf{Z}'\mathbf{Z})$ in the definition of $\mathbf{w}_*$. Furthermore, σ^2 can actually be eliminated from the definition of the weight matrix because the optimal $\hat{\boldsymbol{\beta}}(\mathbf{W})$ obtained from (16.2.7) is completely unaffected if the weight matrix is multiplied by any positive scalar, that is, $\hat{\boldsymbol{\beta}}(\mathbf{W}) = \hat{\boldsymbol{\beta}}(c\mathbf{W})$ for any $c > 0$.

If the $\mathbf{Z}_{i\cdot}$'s are iid, then $\mathbf{a}_{ZZ}^n = \mathbf{a}_{ZZ} = \mathrm{E}[\mathbf{Z}'_{1\cdot}\mathbf{Z}_{1\cdot}]\ \forall n$, and a simple consistent estimator of $\mathbf{a}_{ZZ}$ is given by

$$\hat{a}_{ZZ}^n = n^{-1}\sum_{i=1}^{n}\mathbf{Z}'_{i\cdot}\mathbf{Z}_{i\cdot} = n^{-1}\mathbf{Z}'\mathbf{Z}. \tag{16.2.11}$$

If the $\mathbf{Z}_{i\cdot}$'s are not iid, then so long as $n^{-1}\mathbf{Z}'\mathbf{Z} - \mathbf{a}_{ZZ}^n \xrightarrow{p} \mathbf{0}$ as $n \to \infty$, $\hat{\mathbf{a}}_{ZZ}^n$ can still be used to define the EOGMM estimator. Various laws of large numbers can be invoked to ensure that such convergence of $n^{-1}\mathbf{Z}'\mathbf{Z}$ will occur for non-iid sequences. For convergence, the main requirement is that any dependence among the sample observations dissipates sufficiently fast as observations become further separated in the sample sequence (see Mittelhammer, pp. 261–2, and White, 1984, Chapter 3 for results along these lines). For example, such convergence can be expected from typical convergent autocorrelated–heteroscedastic sample sequences.

Substituting the sample estimator of the optimal weighting matrix $\hat{\mathbf{W}} \propto [n^{-1}\mathbf{Z}'\mathbf{Z}]^{-1}$ into (16.2.7)–(16.2.9) yields the EOGMM estimator,

$$\hat{\boldsymbol{\beta}}_{\mathrm{GMM}} = [\mathbf{X}'\mathbf{Z}(\mathbf{Z}'\mathbf{Z})^{-1}\mathbf{Z}'\mathbf{X}]^{-1}\mathbf{X}'\mathbf{Z}(\mathbf{Z}'\mathbf{Z})^{-1}\mathbf{Z}'\mathbf{Y}, \tag{16.2.12}$$

which is identical to the OptEF estimator defined in (16.1.6). In Section 16.2.2.c, we show that this GMM estimator is *asymptotically* efficient relative to the class of all estimators formed by alternative choices of the weighting matrix $\mathbf{W}$ in (16.2.7).

16.2.2.b. GMM Linear Model Estimation When $\mathbf{cov}(\varepsilon) \neq \sigma^2\mathbf{I}$

We can extend the GMM estimator to account for the possibility of a generalized covariance structure for the noise component by making an appropriate choice of the weight matrix. Suppose the model noise component has a zero mean vector and a covariance structure

$$\mathbf{cov}(\varepsilon \mid \mathbf{Z}) = \mathrm{E}[\varepsilon\varepsilon' \mid \mathbf{Z}] = \boldsymbol{\Phi} \neq \sigma^2\mathbf{I}_n. \tag{16.2.13}$$

On the basis of regularity conditions similar to those discussed in the context of EGLS estimation in Chapter 15, it can be argued that the GMM estimator (16.2.9) is consistent and asymptotically normally distributed.

First of all, if $\mathbf{\Phi} = \sigma^2 \mathbf{I}_n$ and the weight matrix is chosen optimally as defined in (16.2.10), it follows that

$$n^{1/2}(\hat{\boldsymbol{\beta}}_{\text{GMM}} - \boldsymbol{\beta}) \xrightarrow{\text{d}} \text{N}\left[\mathbf{0}, \sigma^2 \left(\mathbf{a}_{\text{XZ}} \mathbf{a}_{\text{ZZ}}^{-1} \mathbf{a}_{\text{ZX}}\right)^{-1}\right], \qquad (16.2.14)$$

where we assume the average cross-product matrices $\mathbf{Z}'\mathbf{Z}$ and $\mathbf{Z}'\mathbf{X}$ are such that $n^{-1}\mathbf{Z}'\mathbf{Z} \xrightarrow{\text{p}} \mathbf{a}_{\text{ZZ}}$ and $n^{-1}\mathbf{Z}'\mathbf{X} \xrightarrow{\text{p}} \mathbf{a}_{\text{ZX}}$, with $\mathbf{a}_{\text{ZZ}}$ and $\mathbf{a}_{\text{ZX}}$ being finite and nonsingular. We can use $n^{-1}\mathbf{Z}'\mathbf{Z}$ and $n^{-1}\mathbf{Z}'\mathbf{X}$ to estimate $\mathbf{a}_{\text{ZZ}}$ and $\mathbf{a}_{\text{ZX}}\mathbf{a}'_{\text{XZ}}$ consistently and $s^2_{\text{GMM}} = (\mathbf{y} - \mathbf{x}\hat{\mathbf{b}}_{\text{GMM}})'(\mathbf{y} - \mathbf{x}\hat{\mathbf{b}}_{\text{GMM}})/n$ to estimate σ^2 consistently in order to form an estimate of the covariance matrix in (16.2.14).

In the more general case in which $\mathbf{\Phi} \neq \sigma^2 \mathbf{I}$, the asymptotically efficient GMM estimator is still the one for which $\mathbf{W}$ is chosen to equal $[\mathbf{cov}(n^{-1/2}\mathbf{Z}'\varepsilon)]^{-1}$. However, the heteroscedasticity or autocorrelation in the noise component, or both now complicate the estimation of the weight matrix. A consistent estimate can be generated based on the heteroscedasticity and autocorrelation robust covariance matrix estimators suggested by White and by Newey and West, as discussed in Section 15.4.

The procedure is a three-step process. First, a consistent estimator of the noise component is required. In practice, this is obtained by setting $\mathbf{W} = \mathbf{I}$ (any arbitrarily chosen positive definite symmetric matrix can be chosen for $\mathbf{W}$ to obtain a consistent estimator of $\boldsymbol{\beta}$) and calculating $\hat{\boldsymbol{\beta}}(\mathbf{I})$ in (16.2.9). The estimated noise component can be consistently estimated by $\hat{\varepsilon} = \mathbf{Y} - \mathbf{X}\hat{\boldsymbol{\beta}}(\mathbf{I})$. In the second step either White's or Newey-West's robust covariance matrix estimator (recall Section 15.4; see Andrews, 1991a for other possibilities) can be applied to the estimated noise component to obtain a consistent estimator of

$$\mathbf{w}_{\text{n}}^{-1} = \mathbf{cov}(n^{-1/2}\mathbf{Z}'\varepsilon) = \text{E}[n^{-1}\mathbf{Z}'\mathbf{\Phi}\mathbf{Z}]. \qquad (16.2.15)$$

For example, White's estimator for the case in which ε is heteroscedastic but not autocorrelated would be defined by

$$\hat{\mathbf{W}}_{\text{n}}^{-1} = \mathbf{C\hat{O}V}(n^{-1/2}\mathbf{Z}'\varepsilon) = \hat{\text{E}}[n^{-1}\mathbf{Z}'\mathbf{\Phi}\mathbf{Z}] = n^{-1}\sum_{i=1}^{n} \hat{\varepsilon}_i^2(\mathbf{Z}'_{i\cdot}\mathbf{Z}_{i\cdot}). \qquad (16.2.16)$$

The Newey–West estimator can be applied similarly to accommodate autocorrelation. The third step consists of replacing $\mathbf{W}$ with $\hat{\mathbf{W}}_n$ in (16.2.9) and calculating the EOGMM estimator of $\boldsymbol{\beta}$. The resulting estimator will be of the form

$$\hat{\boldsymbol{\beta}}_{\text{GMM}} = (\mathbf{X}'\mathbf{Z}\hat{\mathbf{W}}_n\mathbf{Z}'\mathbf{X})^{-1}\mathbf{X}'\mathbf{Z}\hat{\mathbf{W}}_n\mathbf{Z}'\mathbf{Y}. \qquad (16.2.17)$$

One might also consider reestimating the noise component based on $\hat{\boldsymbol{\beta}}(\hat{\mathbf{W}}_n)$, recalculating the weight matrix, and iteratively updating the estimate of the weight matrix, but asymptotic efficiency is unaffected, and any benefits of such an iterative scheme in finite samples is an open question. Additional readings relating to consistent estimation of the optimal weight matrix are found in Andrews (1991b) and White (1994).

16.2.2.c. Sampling Properties of EOGMM Estimator

In order to establish consistency of the EOGMM estimator, note that we can rewrite the estimator as

$$\hat{\boldsymbol{\beta}}(\hat{\mathbf{W}}_n) = \boldsymbol{\beta} + [\mathbf{X}'\mathbf{Z}\hat{\mathbf{W}}_n\mathbf{Z}'\mathbf{X})]^{-1}\mathbf{X}'\mathbf{Z}\hat{\mathbf{W}}_n\mathbf{Z}'\varepsilon. \tag{16.2.18}$$

Given that $\hat{\mathbf{W}}_n - \mathbf{w} \xrightarrow{\text{p}} \mathbf{0}$, where $\mathbf{w}$ is a finite positive definite symmetric matrix, we can make repeated use of Slutsky's theorem to demonstrate that

$$\begin{aligned} \text{p}\lim \hat{\boldsymbol{\beta}}(\hat{\mathbf{W}}_n) &= \boldsymbol{\beta} + \text{plim}\left(\left[\left(\frac{\mathbf{X}'\mathbf{Z}}{n}\right)\hat{\mathbf{W}}_n\left(\frac{\mathbf{Z}'\mathbf{X}}{n}\right)\right]^{-1}\left(\frac{\mathbf{X}'\mathbf{Z}}{n}\right)\hat{\mathbf{W}}_n\left(\frac{\mathbf{Z}'\varepsilon}{n}\right)\right) \\ &= \boldsymbol{\beta} + [\mathbf{a}_{\mathbf{XZ}}\mathbf{w}\mathbf{a}_{\mathbf{ZX}}]^{-1}\mathbf{a}_{\mathbf{XZ}}\mathbf{w}\mathbf{0} = \boldsymbol{\beta} \end{aligned} \tag{16.2.19}$$

under the prevailing assumptions. It is important to note that if the weight matrix must be consistently estimated, even if a nonoptimal weight matrix is used or if ε is heteroscedastic, autocorrelated, or both the GMM estimator is a consistent estimator of $\boldsymbol{\beta}$.

We can establish the asymptotic normality of the GMM estimator under the assumption

$$n^{-1/2}\mathbf{Z}'\varepsilon \xrightarrow{\text{d}} \text{N}[\mathbf{0}, \boldsymbol{\Delta}], \tag{16.2.20}$$

which may be justified by an appropriate central limit theorem (e.g., Lindeberg–Levy if $\mathbf{Z}'_{i.}\varepsilon_i, i = 1, \ldots, n$ were iid). Note (16.2.20) is analogous to the condition used in previous chapters to establish asymptotic normality of least-squares estimators, except here it is applied to the variables $\mathbf{Z}$ as opposed to $\mathbf{X}$. Accordingly, we may utilize the expression in (16.2.20) to define

$$n^{1/2}[\hat{\boldsymbol{\beta}}(\hat{\mathbf{W}}_n) - \boldsymbol{\beta}] = \left[\left(\frac{\mathbf{X}'\mathbf{Z}}{n}\right)\hat{\mathbf{W}}_n\left(\frac{\mathbf{Z}'\mathbf{X}}{n}\right)\right]^{-1}\left(\frac{\mathbf{X}'\mathbf{Z}}{n}\right)\hat{\mathbf{W}}_n(n^{-1/2}\mathbf{Z}'\varepsilon). \tag{16.2.21}$$

Then, using Slutsky's theorem, we can state that

$$n^{1/2}[\hat{\boldsymbol{\beta}}(\hat{\mathbf{W}}_n) - \boldsymbol{\beta}] \xrightarrow{\text{d}} (\mathbf{a}_{\mathbf{XZ}}\mathbf{w}\mathbf{a}_{\mathbf{ZX}})^{-1}\mathbf{a}_{\mathbf{XZ}}\mathbf{w}\mathbf{V}, \tag{16.2.22}$$

where $\mathbf{V} \sim \text{N}(\mathbf{0}, \boldsymbol{\Delta})$, so that

$$n^{1/2}[\hat{\boldsymbol{\beta}}(\hat{\mathbf{W}}_n) - \boldsymbol{\beta}] \xrightarrow{\text{d}} \text{N}(\mathbf{0}, (\mathbf{a}_{\mathbf{xz}}\mathbf{w}\mathbf{a}_{\mathbf{zx}})^{-1}\mathbf{a}_{\mathbf{XZ}}\mathbf{w}\boldsymbol{\Delta}\mathbf{w}\mathbf{a}_{\mathbf{ZX}}(\mathbf{a}_{\mathbf{XZ}}\mathbf{w}\mathbf{a}_{\mathbf{ZX}})^{-1}). \tag{16.2.23}$$

Finally, because we are using the EOGMM estimator, so that $\mathbf{cov}(n^{-1/2}\mathbf{Z}'\varepsilon) \to \mathbf{w}^{-1} = \boldsymbol{\Delta} = \text{p}\lim(n^{-1}\mathbf{Z}'\boldsymbol{\Phi}\mathbf{Z})$ under the current assumptions, the asymptotic distribution of the EOGMM estimator implied by (16.2.23) simplifies to

$$\hat{\boldsymbol{\beta}}(\hat{\mathbf{W}}_n) \overset{\text{a}}{\sim} \text{N}(\boldsymbol{\beta}, n^{-1}(\mathbf{a}_{\mathbf{XZ}}\boldsymbol{\Delta}^{-1}\mathbf{a}_{\mathbf{ZX}})^{-1}). \tag{16.2.24}$$

The asymptotic covariance matrix of the EOGMM estimator in (16.2.24) can be estimated by the matrix

$$\hat{\mathbf{cov}}[\hat{\boldsymbol{\beta}}(\hat{\mathbf{W}}_n)] = n^{-1}[(n^{-1}\mathbf{x}'\mathbf{z})\hat{\mathbf{w}}_n(n^{-1}\mathbf{z}'\mathbf{x})]^{-1}, \tag{16.2.25}$$

where $\hat{\mathbf{w}}_n^{-1}$ is the outcome of a consistent estimator of $\mathbf{cov}(n^{-1/2}\mathbf{Z}'\varepsilon)$. Asymptotic normality can be established using other weaker conditions, and the reader is referred to Hansen (1982) and Newey and McFadden (1994) for results and references along these lines.

16.2.2.d. Hypothesis Testing and Confidence Regions

As one has come to expect by now, testing hypotheses regarding values of functions of the parameter vector $\boldsymbol{\beta}$ can be accomplished using Wald, LM, pseudolikelihood ratio, or Z-statistics. The statistics will have asymptotic Chi-square or normal distributions based on the asymptotic normality of the estimator $\hat{\boldsymbol{\beta}}(\hat{\mathbf{W}}_n)$. Confidence region estimates can be generated via duality with hypothesis tests.

16.2.2.e. Alternative Moment Conditions and Optimality of EOGMM When $\mathbf{cov}(\varepsilon) = \boldsymbol{\Phi} \neq \sigma^2\mathbf{I}$

Note that it is at least theoretically possible to define alternative moment conditions to $n^{-1}\mathbf{Z}'(\mathbf{Y} - \mathbf{X}\boldsymbol{\beta}) = \mathbf{0}$ that can result in a more asymptotically efficient GMM estimator than the GMM estimators discussed in the previous subsections. We examine here the case in which $\mathbf{Z}$ is taken as given and defer the question of an optimal choice of $\mathbf{Z}$ to Section 16.4.7. We also assume that $\mathbf{cov}(\varepsilon) = \boldsymbol{\Phi}$. We will see that the redefinition of the moment conditions to account for the nonspherical noise component, and the subsequent asymptotic efficiency gains attained by the GMM estimator, parallel the model transformation and subsequent efficiency gains that are possible by applying GLS as opposed to OLS when the noise component is nonspherical (Chapter 14). Note this result does *not* contradict our claims of optimality made for the GMM estimator defined in the preceding subsections because optimality is established *conditionally* on a specific set of moment conditions. Here we are considering changing the moment conditions, which in effect changes the class of GMM estimators from that discussed in the previous subsections.

In an attempt to achieve a more efficient GMM estimator, consider the alternative moment conditions defined by $\mathrm{E}[n^{-1}\mathbf{Z}'\boldsymbol{\Phi}^{-1}(\mathbf{Y} - \mathbf{X}\boldsymbol{\beta})] = \mathbf{0}$, the sample analog being $n^{-1}[\mathbf{z}'\boldsymbol{\Phi}^{-1}(\mathbf{y} - \mathbf{x}\boldsymbol{\beta})] = \mathbf{0}$. The optimal weighting matrix $\mathbf{W}$ for GMM estimation in this case is defined by $\mathbf{W}_n^{-1} = \mathbf{COV}(n^{-1/2}\mathbf{Z}'\boldsymbol{\Phi}^{-1}\varepsilon) = \mathrm{E}[n^{-1}\mathbf{Z}'\boldsymbol{\Phi}^{-1}\mathbf{Z}]$. Then, through use of the alternative moments and approximation of $\mathbf{W}_n^{-1}$ by $n^{-1}\mathbf{Z}'\boldsymbol{\Phi}^{-1}\mathbf{Z}$, the GMM estimator in this case is given by

$$\hat{\boldsymbol{\beta}}^*_{\mathrm{GMM}} = [(\mathbf{X}'\boldsymbol{\Phi}^{-1}\mathbf{Z})(\mathbf{Z}'\boldsymbol{\Phi}^{-1}\mathbf{Z})^{-1}(\mathbf{Z}'\boldsymbol{\Phi}^{-1}\mathbf{X})]^{-1}(\mathbf{X}'\boldsymbol{\Phi}^{-1}\mathbf{Z})(\mathbf{Z}'\boldsymbol{\Phi}^{-1}\mathbf{Z})^{-1}\mathbf{Z}'\boldsymbol{\Phi}^{-1}\mathbf{Y}. \tag{16.2.26}$$

Although perhaps not apparent at first glance, the estimator is not as complicated in concept as it may at first appear. Defining $\mathbf{Y}_* = \boldsymbol{\Phi}^{-1/2}\mathbf{Y}$, $\mathbf{Z}_* = \boldsymbol{\Phi}^{-1/2}\mathbf{Z}$, and $\mathbf{X}_* = \boldsymbol{\Phi}^{-1/2}\mathbf{X}$, the estimator can be restated as

$$\hat{\boldsymbol{\beta}}^*_{\mathrm{GMM}} = [(\mathbf{X}_*'\mathbf{Z}_*)(\mathbf{Z}_*'\mathbf{Z}_*)^{-1}(\mathbf{Z}_*'\mathbf{X}_*)]^{-1}(\mathbf{X}_*'\mathbf{Z}_*)(\mathbf{Z}_*'\mathbf{Z}_*)^{-1}\mathbf{Z}_*'\mathbf{Y}_*, \tag{16.2.27}$$

which makes it apparent that the GMM estimator is simply the OptEF or two-stage least-squares estimator defined previously in (16.1.6) applied to transformed data. The transformation that was applied to the original data is precisely the GLS transformation used in Chapter 14 to transform nonspherical data into spherical form. It can be shown that the asymptotic distribution of $\hat{\boldsymbol{\beta}}^*_{\mathrm{GMM}}$ is given by

$$\hat{\boldsymbol{\beta}}^*_{\mathrm{GMM}} \overset{a}{\sim} \mathrm{N}(\boldsymbol{\beta}, n^{-1}[\mathbf{a}_{\mathbf{X}_*\mathbf{Z}_*}\boldsymbol{\Delta}_*^{-1}\mathbf{a}_{\mathbf{Z}_*\mathbf{X}_*}]^{-1}), \tag{16.2.28}$$

where $n^{-1}\mathbf{Z}_*'\mathbf{Z}_* = n^{-1}\mathbf{Z}'\boldsymbol{\Phi}^{-1}\mathbf{Z} \overset{p}{\to} \boldsymbol{\Delta}_*$ and $n^{-1}\mathbf{Z}_*'\mathbf{X}_* = n^{-1}\mathbf{Z}'\boldsymbol{\Phi}^{-1}\mathbf{X} \overset{p}{\to} \mathbf{a}_{\mathbf{Z}_*\mathbf{X}_*}$, with $\boldsymbol{\Delta}_*$ and $\mathbf{a}_{\mathbf{Z}_*\mathbf{X}_*}$ being finite and nonsingular. It can be further shown that the covariance matrix in (16.2.28) is smaller than the covariance matrix in (16.2.24) by a positive semidefinite matrix. Thus, by redefining the moment conditions, we were able to define an alternative GMM estimator that exhibits an increase in asymptotic efficiency.

Why would one wish to use $\hat{\boldsymbol{\beta}}_{\mathrm{GMM}}$ instead of $\hat{\boldsymbol{\beta}}^*_{\mathrm{GMM}}$? There are in fact some good reasons to do so. First, and most obviously, $\boldsymbol{\Phi}$ is generally unknown, and so $\hat{\boldsymbol{\beta}}^*_{\mathrm{GMM}}$ is not calculable in practice. Of course, not knowing $\boldsymbol{\Phi}$ is also a problem for the definition of $\hat{\boldsymbol{\beta}}_{\mathrm{GMM}}$, for $\boldsymbol{\Phi}$ is used in the definition of the optimal weight matrix in that case. However, $\hat{\boldsymbol{\beta}}_{\mathrm{GMM}}$ relies on $\boldsymbol{\Phi}$ only in the form $\mathrm{E}[n^{-1}\mathbf{Z}'\boldsymbol{\Phi}\mathbf{Z}]$, and even in the absence of knowledge relating to an appropriate parametric structure for $\boldsymbol{\Phi}$, the matrix $\mathrm{E}[n^{-1}\mathbf{Z}'\boldsymbol{\Phi}\mathbf{Z}]$ can be estimated robustly based on the White or Newey–West approaches (recall 16.2.16). On the other hand, $\hat{\boldsymbol{\beta}}^*_{\mathrm{GMM}}$ relies on $\boldsymbol{\Phi}$ in the form $n^{-1}\mathbf{Z}'\boldsymbol{\Phi}^{-1}\mathbf{Z}$, whose expectation or probability limit cannot be estimated effectively without consistently estimating $\boldsymbol{\Phi}$ itself. Thus, the information required to implement each of the procedures empirically is notably different, with a greater potential for misspecification existing for $\hat{\boldsymbol{\beta}}^*_{\mathrm{GMM}}$. Furthermore, in addition to the sampling properties deterioration in $\hat{\boldsymbol{\beta}}^*_{\mathrm{GMM}}$ that is likely from misspecification, there is no guarantee that $\hat{\boldsymbol{\beta}}^*_{\mathrm{GMM}}$ is superior to $\hat{\boldsymbol{\beta}}_{\mathrm{GMM}}$ in finite samples even under correct specification. In effect, we have an analog to the use of OLS in place of GLS in the case of nonspherical noise components.

16.2.2.f. Summary and Foreword: GMM Approach in the Linear Model Context

The GMM approach applied within the linear model context provides a way of extending the ordinary MOM approach to the case in which there are more estimating equations–moment conditions than unknown $\boldsymbol{\beta}$ elements. For a given set of moment conditions, the GMM procedure actually defines an entire family of consistent and asymptotically normally distributed estimators as a function of the weight matrix $\mathbf{W}$. A theoretically optimal choice for the weight matrix exists, but it is generally unknown in practice and must be consistently estimated from the data. Although *asymptotically* optimal, the resulting EOGMM estimator, defined as a two-step estimator in which the first step involves the construction of some consistent estimator of the optimal weight matrix, is not necessarily optimal in finite samples. Moreover, the finite sample properties of the EOGMM estimator depend on the choice of weight matrix estimator, for which there are many possibilities analogous to the dilemma of specifying and estimating the covariance matrix of the noise component for use in the estimated GLS procedure of Chapter 16. Thus, there is still reason to consider alternative estimation procedures in the overdetermined linear model case, and we do so in Sections 16.3 and 16.4.

Our principal focus in the preceding discussion of GMM was on the overdetermined nature of the estimating equation system. We note at this point that in our discussion of applications within the linear model context, we were not explicit about the status of the orthogonality condition between the explanatory variable matrix **X** and the noise component ε. In fact, the preceding discussion of the GMM method applied within the linear model context follows through whether or not orthogonality holds. However, we will see ahead that it is actually only in the case in which **X** and ε are nonorthogonal that the notion of using an overdetermined set of moment conditions such as $n^{-1}\mathbf{Z}'(\mathbf{Y}-\mathbf{X}\boldsymbol{\beta})$ will be of benefit, for in the orthogonal case, $\mathbf{Z}=\mathbf{X}$ will turn out to be the asymptotically optimal choice of **Z** (see Section 16.4.7), resulting in a *just-determined* system being the optimal choice of estimating equations. Thus, it follows that using any other choice of **Z** than **X** in the preceding GMM estimator definitions produces an inferior estimator in the orthogonal case, although this conclusion does not necessarily hold in the nonorthogonal case.

► **Example 16.2.1:** To demonstrate the GMM estimation concepts in the context of the linear regression model, we provide the GAUSS program C16GMM1.gss in the examples manual. The user chooses the sample size and the weight matrix, **W**, to use in calculating GMM estimates of the parameters of a regression model. Then GMM estimates are reported to the user as well as associated confidence regions for each of the parameters of the model. Finally, the program conducts a Monte Carlo simulation exercise to compare the sampling properties of the EOGMM estimator to other GMM estimators defined by alternative weight matrices, **W**.

16.2.3. GMM Estimators – General Properties

One important aspect of the GMM estimation procedure is that it can be applied to a myriad of other estimation contexts besides the linear model context of Section 16.2.2. We sketch here some of the general properties that can be attributed to the GMM estimator. These properties will be established alternatively through association with OptEF estimators in Section 16.4. It may be useful to return to this section and reread its contents after completing Section 16.4. For additional information, see section 8.4 in Mittelhammer (1996), Chapter 3 of Gallant (1987), Sections 2.5 and 3.3 in Newey and McFadden (1994), Bates and White (1985, 1988), and Gallant and White (1988).

Recall that, in general, the GMM estimator is found by minimizing the quadratic form (16.2.3) with respect to the choice of $\boldsymbol{\beta}$. For purposes of defining consistent and asymptotically normal estimators, the weight matrix **W** can be set equal to any positive definite symmetric matrix, and the moment conditions (16.2.1) can be based on a variety of moment conditions of the form $\mathrm{E}[\mathbf{h}_*(\mathrm{Y}_i, \mathbf{Q}_{i\cdot}, \boldsymbol{\beta})] = \mathbf{0}$ thought to hold for the data-sampling process under investigation. In practice, when the number of moment conditions exceeds the number of parameters, one will generally seek to utilize an estimate of the optimal weight matrix for **W**. The choice of **W** that results in the asymptotically most efficient estimator within the class of GMM estimators based on a given set of estimating equations–moment conditions is the inverse of the covariance matrix $\mathbf{cov}[n^{1/2}\mathbf{h}(\mathbf{Y}, \mathbf{Q}, \boldsymbol{\beta})] \equiv \mathbf{cov}(n^{-1/2}\sum_{i=1}^{n}\mathbf{h}_*(\mathrm{Y}_i, \mathbf{Q}_{i\cdot}, \boldsymbol{\beta}))$ if it is assumed the estimating equation–moment relations are expressed in the form (16.2.2) (see Hansen, 1982; Andrews, 1999). Optimality in the current context refers to choosing a **W** matrix in the definition of the GMM estimator

$$\hat{\boldsymbol{\beta}}_{\mathrm{GMM}}(\mathbf{W}) = \arg\min_{\boldsymbol{\beta}}[\mathbf{h}(\mathbf{Y}, \mathbf{Q}, \boldsymbol{\beta})'\mathbf{W}\,\mathbf{h}(\mathbf{Y}, \mathbf{Q}, \boldsymbol{\beta})] \tag{16.2.29}$$

such that $\hat{\boldsymbol{\beta}}_{\mathrm{GMM}}(\mathbf{W})$ has the smallest *asymptotic* covariance matrix. Because the optimal weight matrix implied by $\mathbf{w}_*^{-1} = \mathbf{cov}[n^{1/2}\mathbf{h}(\mathbf{Y}, \mathbf{Q}, \boldsymbol{\beta})]$ is generally unknown, and thus $\hat{\boldsymbol{\beta}}_{\mathrm{GMM}}(\mathbf{w}_*)$ is not operational, a consistent estimator, $\hat{\mathbf{W}}_n$, of $\mathbf{w}_*$ is used; then the estimated optimal GMM (EOGMM) estimator is defined by $\hat{\boldsymbol{\beta}}_{\mathrm{GMM}}(\hat{\mathbf{W}}_n)$.

16.2.3.a. Consistency

The EOGMM estimator will be consistent under general conditions. The principal condition leading to the consistency property is that the objective function of the GMM procedure $\mathbf{h}(\mathbf{Y}, \mathbf{Q}, \boldsymbol{\beta})'\hat{\mathbf{W}}_n\,\mathbf{h}(\mathbf{Y}, \mathbf{Q}, \boldsymbol{\beta})$ converge uniformly in probability to a continuous nonstochastic function $\bar{\mathbf{h}}(\boldsymbol{\beta})'\,\mathbf{w}\bar{\mathbf{h}}(\boldsymbol{\beta})$ that has a unique minimum at the true value of the parameter vector $\boldsymbol{\beta}_0$. The uniform convergence ensures that the minimum of the limit function $\bar{\mathbf{h}}(\boldsymbol{\beta})'\,\mathbf{w}\bar{\mathbf{h}}(\boldsymbol{\beta})$ is equal to the limit of the sequence of minimums of $\mathbf{h}(\mathbf{Y}, \mathbf{Q}, \boldsymbol{\beta})'\hat{\mathbf{W}}_n\,\mathbf{h}(\mathbf{Y}, \mathbf{Q}, \boldsymbol{\beta})$ in probability, so that $\hat{\boldsymbol{\beta}}_{\mathrm{GMM}} \xrightarrow{p} \boldsymbol{\beta}_0$. Sufficient conditions for this convergence to occur include the following:

1. The parameter space for $\boldsymbol{\beta}$ is nonempty, closed, and bounded (i.e., compact);
2. $\mathbf{h}(\mathbf{Y}, \mathbf{Q}, \boldsymbol{\beta})$ is continuous in $\boldsymbol{\beta}$;
3. $\mathbf{h}(\mathbf{Y}, \mathbf{Q}, \boldsymbol{\beta}) \xrightarrow{p} \bar{\mathbf{h}}(\boldsymbol{\beta})$ uniformly in $\boldsymbol{\beta}$, $\bar{\mathbf{h}}(\boldsymbol{\beta})$ being continuous;
4. $\hat{\mathbf{W}}_n \xrightarrow{p} \mathbf{w}$, a positive definite symmetric matrix; and
5. $\bar{\mathbf{h}}(\boldsymbol{\beta})'\,\mathbf{w}\bar{\mathbf{h}}(\boldsymbol{\beta})$ is uniquely minimized at $\boldsymbol{\beta}_0$.

We emphasize that it is not necessary for $\hat{\mathbf{W}}_n$ to be estimating the optimal weighting matrix for consistency to be obtained. All that is required in the preceding argument is that $\hat{\mathbf{W}}_n$ converge to some positive definite symmetric matrix. Thus, there generally exist many choices of consistent GMM estimators.

As noted by Newey and McFadden (1994), some of the conditions may be altered under appropriate assumptions on the probability model of the data-sampling process. For example, the compactness requirement may be eliminated if it can be shown that the GMM objective function is strictly concave in $\boldsymbol{\beta}$ for all adequately large sample sizes. The reader is referred to the cited references for other possibilities.

16.2.3.b. Asymptotic Normality

Under general regularity conditions in addition to those leading to consistency, the GMM estimator will be asymptotically normally distributed. The general approach to demonstrating asymptotic normality relies on expanding the first-order conditions for the minimization problem (16.2.3) in a Taylor series about the true $\boldsymbol{\beta}_0$. Depending on the degree of continuous differentiability with respect to $\boldsymbol{\beta}$ assumed for the moment function $\mathbf{h}(\mathbf{Y}, \mathbf{Q}, \boldsymbol{\beta})$, the demonstration can proceed on the basis of either a first- or second-order Taylor series. We sketch the first-order approach here.

The first-order conditions require that $\hat{\boldsymbol{\beta}}$ be chosen to satisfy

$$\frac{\partial \mathbf{h}(\mathbf{Y}, \mathbf{Q}, \hat{\boldsymbol{\beta}})}{\partial \boldsymbol{\beta}} \hat{\mathbf{W}}\, \mathbf{h}(\mathbf{Y}, \mathbf{Q}, \hat{\boldsymbol{\beta}}) = \mathbf{0}, \tag{16.2.30}$$

where $\hat{\mathbf{W}}$ denotes some choice of weight matrix that converges in probability to a fixed positive definite symmetric matrix $\mathbf{w}$, and henceforth $\frac{\partial \mathbf{h}(\mathbf{Y}, \mathbf{Q}, \hat{\boldsymbol{\beta}})}{\partial \boldsymbol{\beta}} \equiv \frac{\partial \mathbf{h}(\mathbf{Y}, \mathbf{Q}, \boldsymbol{\beta})}{\partial \boldsymbol{\beta}}\Big|_{\boldsymbol{\beta}=\hat{\boldsymbol{\beta}}}$. Expanding $\mathbf{h}(\mathbf{Y}, \mathbf{Q}, \hat{\boldsymbol{\beta}})$ in a first-order Taylor series about $\boldsymbol{\beta}_0$, substituting this expansion for the $\mathbf{h}(\mathbf{Y}, \mathbf{Q}, \hat{\boldsymbol{\beta}})$ term that postmultiplies $\hat{\mathbf{W}}$ in (16.2.30), and then solving for $n^{1/2}(\hat{\boldsymbol{\beta}} - \boldsymbol{\beta}_0)$ yields

$$n^{1/2}(\hat{\boldsymbol{\beta}} - \boldsymbol{\beta}_0) = -\left[\frac{\partial \mathbf{h}(\mathbf{Y}, \mathbf{Q}, \hat{\boldsymbol{\beta}})}{\partial \boldsymbol{\beta}} \hat{\mathbf{W}} \frac{\partial \mathbf{h}(\mathbf{Y}, \mathbf{Q}, \boldsymbol{\beta}_*)}{\partial \boldsymbol{\beta}'}\right]^{-1} \frac{\partial \mathbf{h}(\mathbf{Y}, \mathbf{Q}, \hat{\boldsymbol{\beta}})}{\partial \boldsymbol{\beta}} \hat{\mathbf{W}} n^{1/2} \mathbf{h}(\mathbf{Y}, \mathbf{Q}, \boldsymbol{\beta}_0), \tag{16.2.31}$$

where $\boldsymbol{\beta}_*$ is a convex combination of $\hat{\boldsymbol{\beta}}$ and $\boldsymbol{\beta}_0$ and may be different for each row in (16.2.31). Consistency of the GMM estimator implies that $\hat{\boldsymbol{\beta}} \xrightarrow{p} \boldsymbol{\beta}_0$, and thus also $\boldsymbol{\beta}_* \xrightarrow{p} \boldsymbol{\beta}_0$. Then, if $\frac{\partial \mathbf{h}(\mathbf{Y}, \mathbf{Q}, \hat{\boldsymbol{\beta}})}{\partial \boldsymbol{\beta}}$, and thus also $\frac{\partial \mathbf{h}(\mathbf{Y}, \mathbf{Q}, \boldsymbol{\beta}_*)}{\partial \boldsymbol{\beta}}$ both converge in probability to a function $\frac{\partial \bar{\mathbf{h}}(\boldsymbol{\beta}_0)}{\partial \boldsymbol{\beta}}$, and if $n^{1/2}\mathbf{h}(\mathbf{Y}, \mathbf{Q}, \boldsymbol{\beta}_0) \xrightarrow{d} \mathrm{N}(\mathbf{0}, \mathbf{v})$, it follows that

$$n^{1/2}(\hat{\boldsymbol{\beta}} - \boldsymbol{\beta}_0) \xrightarrow{d} \mathrm{N}\left(\mathbf{0}, \left[\frac{\partial \bar{\mathbf{h}}(\boldsymbol{\beta}_0)}{\partial \boldsymbol{\beta}} \mathbf{w} \frac{\partial \bar{\mathbf{h}}(\boldsymbol{\beta}_0)}{\partial \boldsymbol{\beta}'}\right]^{-1}\right.$$

$$\left. \times \frac{\partial \bar{\mathbf{h}}(\boldsymbol{\beta}_0)}{\partial \boldsymbol{\beta}} \mathbf{w}\, \mathbf{v}\, \mathbf{w} \frac{\partial \bar{\mathbf{h}}(\boldsymbol{\beta}_0)}{\partial \boldsymbol{\beta}'} \left[\frac{\partial \bar{\mathbf{h}}(\boldsymbol{\beta}_0)}{\partial \boldsymbol{\beta}} \mathbf{w} \frac{\partial \bar{\mathbf{h}}(\boldsymbol{\beta}_0)}{\partial \boldsymbol{\beta}'}\right]^{-1}\right) \tag{16.2.32}$$

if it is assumed that the inverse matrices exist, which will be true if $\frac{\partial \bar{\mathbf{h}}(\boldsymbol{\beta}_0)}{\partial \boldsymbol{\beta}}$ has full-row rank.

If the EOGMM estimator, say $\hat{\boldsymbol{\beta}}_*$, is being used, so that $\hat{\mathbf{W}} \xrightarrow{p} \mathbf{w} = \mathbf{v}^{-1}$, then the covariance matrix of the limiting distribution in (16.2.32) simplifies substantially as follows:

$$n^{1/2}(\hat{\boldsymbol{\beta}}_* - \boldsymbol{\beta}) \xrightarrow{d} \mathrm{N}\left(\mathbf{0}, \left[\frac{\partial \bar{\mathbf{h}}(\boldsymbol{\beta}_0)}{\partial \boldsymbol{\beta}} \mathbf{v}^{-1} \frac{\partial \bar{\mathbf{h}}(\boldsymbol{\beta}_0)}{\partial \boldsymbol{\beta}'}\right]^{-1}\right). \tag{16.2.33}$$

The asymptotic efficiency of $\hat{\boldsymbol{\beta}}_*$ can be motivated by the fact that the covariance matrix in (16.2.32) exceeds the covariance matrix in (16.2.33) by a positive semidefinite matrix. The proof can be constructed analogously to the proof of the asymptotic efficiency of the OptEF estimator demonstrated in Section 11.4.1. In practice, the EOGMM is calculated by first obtaining a consistent estimator of $\boldsymbol{\beta}$, usually by setting $\mathbf{W} = \mathbf{I}$ and calculating $\hat{\boldsymbol{\beta}}(\mathbf{I})$. Then, on the assumption that sample observations are independent, $\mathbf{v}$ is estimated by an outcome of $\hat{\mathbf{V}} = n^{-1} \sum_{i=1}^{n} \mathbf{h}_*[\mathrm{Y}_i, \mathbf{Q}_{i\cdot}, \hat{\boldsymbol{\beta}}(\mathbf{I})]\mathbf{h}_*[\mathrm{Y}_i, \mathbf{Q}_{i\cdot}, \hat{\boldsymbol{\beta}}(\mathbf{I})]'$, and $\hat{\mathbf{W}}$ is defined as $\hat{\mathbf{W}} = \hat{\mathbf{V}}^{-1}$. If observations are autocorrelated, then a Newey–West type estimator may be used to provide a robust estimator for the covariance matrix $\mathbf{v}$, or else if a parametric structure for **v** is known, **v** can be estimated in terms of consistently estimated values of its parametric representation. Finally the EOGMM estimator is defined as $\hat{\boldsymbol{\beta}}(\hat{\mathbf{W}})$. An estimate of the covariance matrix in (16.2.33) can be obtained by calculating the outcome of $[\frac{\partial \mathbf{h}(\mathbf{Y},\mathbf{Q},\hat{\boldsymbol{\beta}}(\hat{\mathbf{W}}))}{\partial \boldsymbol{\beta}}\hat{\mathbf{W}}\frac{\partial \mathbf{h}(\mathbf{Y},\mathbf{Q},\hat{\boldsymbol{\beta}}(\hat{\mathbf{W}}))}{\partial \boldsymbol{\beta}'}]^{-1}$, where the calculation of $\hat{\mathbf{W}}$ can be updated using the outcome of the EOGMM estimator.

16.2.3.c. Hypothesis Testing and Confidence Regions

Hypothesis tests can be based on Wald, LM, pseudolikelihood ratio (using values of constrained and unconstrained GMM estimation objective functions), or Z-statistics in the usual way utilizing the asymptotic normality of the EOGMM estimator. Confidence regions can be defined based on duality with hypothesis tests. Further results along these lines will be discussed in Section 16.4.

► **Example 16.2.2:** To demonstrate the GMM estimation concepts in the context of a nonlinear regression model, we provide the GAUSS program C16GMM2.gss in the examples manual. The program extends the approach utilized in example 16.1.2 to the case of an over-identified extimating equation. For a given set of observations on the dependent, explanatory, and instrumental variables relating to an over-determined nonlinear (in $\boldsymbol{\beta}$) estimating equation associated with a nonlinear regression model, the C16GMM2.gss program calculates the unknown $\boldsymbol{\beta}$ parameters of the regression relationship and also calculates the approximate standard errors. The program also reports the outcomes of hypothesis tests on the parameters. Confidence regions could also be generated, and are left to the reader as an exercise.

16.3. IV Solutions in the Just-determined Case When $\mathrm{E}[\mathbf{X}'\varepsilon]\neq\mathbf{0}$

In this section we focus explicit attention on the problem situation in which the zero correlation or orthogonality assumption $\mathrm{E}[\mathbf{X}'\varepsilon]=\mathbf{0}$ *does not hold.* We will henceforth refer to this model as the nonorthogonal model. In this case, the conditional expectation $\mathrm{E}[\varepsilon \mid \mathbf{X}]=\eta(\mathbf{X})$ *will depend* on the values of the $(n \times k)$ explanatory variable matrix **X** such that the unconditional expectation of $n^{-1}\mathbf{X}'\varepsilon$ is $\mathrm{E}[n^{-1}\mathbf{X}'\varepsilon]=n^{-1}\mathrm{E}[\mathbf{X}'\eta(\mathbf{X})]=\upsilon_n\neq\mathbf{0}$ and

$$\mathrm{plim}(n^{-1}\mathbf{X}'\varepsilon)=\bar{\upsilon}\neq\mathbf{0} \tag{16.3.1}$$

for some nonzero vector $\bar{\upsilon}$. Thus, **X** is correlated with ε, and the LS estimator in the linear model, $\hat{\boldsymbol{\beta}}=(\mathbf{X}'\mathbf{X})^{-1}\mathbf{X}'\mathbf{Y}$, will have unconditional expectation $\mathrm{E}[\hat{\boldsymbol{\beta}}]=\boldsymbol{\beta}+\mathrm{E}[(\mathbf{X}'\mathbf{X})^{-1}\mathbf{X}'\varepsilon]=\boldsymbol{\beta}+\mathrm{E}[(\mathbf{X}'\mathbf{X})^{-1}\mathbf{X}'\eta(\mathbf{X})]\neq\boldsymbol{\beta}$. Therefore $\hat{\boldsymbol{\beta}}$ is a biased estimator of the $(k \times 1)$ parameter vector $\boldsymbol{\beta}$. Furthermore, if it is assumed that $\mathrm{plim}(n^{-1}\mathbf{X}'\mathbf{X})=\boldsymbol{\Gamma}$, a positive definite and symmetric matrix, then $\mathrm{plim}(\hat{\boldsymbol{\beta}})=\boldsymbol{\beta}+\boldsymbol{\Gamma}^{-1}\bar{\upsilon}\neq\boldsymbol{\beta}$, and $\hat{\boldsymbol{\beta}}$ is also an inconsistent estimator of $\boldsymbol{\beta}$.

A prominent case in which the orthogonality condition will fail, and one case that provided the motivation for the development of the IV approach (Reiersol, 1941), is the problem of measurement error in the observed sample data. To illustrate the problem, consider the simple linear model $\mathbf{Y} = \mathbf{X}\boldsymbol{\beta} + \varepsilon$ in which the ε_i's are iid with mean zero and variance σ^2 and $\mathbf{X}$ is a vector. Suppose that $\mathbf{X}$ is observed with error so that what we actually observe is the outcome of the vector $\mathbf{X}_*$, where $\mathbf{X}_* = \mathbf{X} + \mathbf{V}$ and outcomes of $\mathbf{V}$ represent unobservable measurement errors. Assume further that the vector $\mathbf{V}$ consists of iid observations with a mean of zero and a variance of τ^2 and that $\mathbf{V}$ is independent of both $\mathbf{X}$ and ε. Then the linear model, represented in terms of observable dependent and explanatory variables, is given by $\mathbf{Y} = \mathbf{X}_*\beta + \varepsilon_*$, where $\varepsilon_* = \varepsilon - \mathbf{V}\beta$. It follows that

$$\mathbf{E}[\mathbf{X}_*'\varepsilon_*] = \mathbf{E}[(\mathbf{X} - \mathbf{V})'(\varepsilon - \mathbf{V}\beta)] = -n\tau^2\beta \neq 0, \tag{16.3.2}$$

and thus orthogonality fails. Of course the same nonorthogonal result can occur based on a variety of more elaborate models and more complex unobservable measurement error situations.

The purpose of this section is to define a family of moment-based estimators that may be used to avoid inconsistency problems in cases in which the inverse problem of estimating $\boldsymbol{\beta}$ is just-determined and $\mathbf{X}$ is correlated with ε. Note the ideas introduced in this section serve as a precursor to more general approaches that can be applied to overdetermined nonorthogonal models.

16.3.1. Traditional Instrumental Variable Estimator in the Linear Model

When the inconvenient property (16.3.1) applies, a traditional approach has been to seek k random variables whose n potential observations, represented by the $(n \times k)$ random matrix $\mathbf{Z}$, are correlated with outcomes of the $(n \times k)$ matrix $\mathbf{X}$ but uncorrelated with ε. Specific properties relating to $\mathbf{Z}$ that are assumed to hold include $\mathrm{E}[\mathbf{Z}'\varepsilon] = \mathbf{0}$, $\mathrm{E}[\varepsilon \mid \mathbf{Z}] = \mathbf{0}$, $\mathbf{cov}(\varepsilon \mid \mathbf{Z}) = \mathrm{E}[\varepsilon\varepsilon' \mid \mathbf{Z}] = \sigma^2\mathbf{I}$, $\mathrm{E}[\mathbf{Z}'\mathbf{Z}]$ exists as a $(k \times k)$ finite positive definite matrix, and $\mathbf{Z}'\mathbf{X}$ is uniformly nonsingular with probability 1 (i.e., $\det(\mathbf{Z}'\mathbf{X}) > \delta$ for some $\delta > 0$ and all n with probability 1). The matrix $\mathbf{Z}$ is referred to as a matrix of instrumental variables essentially because they lead to a transformation of the original model that is *instrumental* to solving the current inverse problem in which the orthogonality between $\mathbf{X}$ and ε does not hold.

In practice, the instrumental variables, or instruments, are chosen to be variables whose outcomes are thought to be unrelated to the outcomes of the noise component but that track, either positively or inversely, outcomes of $\mathbf{X}$. Note that some of the variables in $\mathbf{X}$ would be excellent candidates for instruments if they were orthogonal to ε. We emphasize that it is not necessarily the case that all of the $\mathbf{X}$ variables must be correlated with ε for the nonorthogonality condition to fail. Thus, $\mathbf{Z}$ might contain a number of columns identical to columns in $\mathbf{X}$. In the Hansen and Singleton model, the instrumental variables are simply lagged values of the variables in the model; therefore, the instruments are predetermined and thus uncorrelated with the current noise components. Additional rationale for the existence of $\mathbf{Z}$ will be developed further in the next chapter, but for now we focus on the statistical model at hand and assume that such a $\mathbf{Z}$ is available. To utilize this new information, we transform the linear model $\mathbf{Y} = \mathbf{X}\boldsymbol{\beta} + \varepsilon$ as follows:

$$\mathbf{Z}'\mathbf{Y} = \mathbf{Z}'\mathbf{X}\boldsymbol{\beta} + \mathbf{Z}'\varepsilon \quad \text{or} \quad \mathbf{Y}_* = \mathbf{X}_*\boldsymbol{\beta} + \varepsilon_*, \tag{16.3.3}$$

where $E[\varepsilon_*] = E[\mathbf{Z}'\varepsilon] = \mathbf{0}$, and $\mathbf{cov}(\varepsilon_*) = \mathbf{cov}(\mathbf{Z}'\varepsilon) = \sigma^2 E[\mathbf{Z}'\mathbf{Z}]$ by the double expectation theorem.

Given the form of (16.3.3), it may have occurred to the reader that it is possible at this point to apply a MOM approach to estimate $\boldsymbol{\beta}$. The implementation of the procedure would rely on the assumption of the random variables $(Y_i, \mathbf{X}_{i\cdot}, \mathbf{Z}_{i\cdot})$, $i = 1, \ldots, n$ as iid, and then an analog to the approach in Section 10.6.3 could be followed to define the MOM estimator. By now this process should be familiar, and so we will proceed to examine a more general context in which the $(Y_i, \mathbf{X}_{i\cdot}, \mathbf{Z}_{i\cdot})$'s are not necessarily iid.

In developing the instrumental variables (IV) estimation procedure, first note that moment conditions involving $\boldsymbol{\beta}$ that reflect the orthogonality between $\mathbf{Z}$ and ε are represented by $E[\mathbf{h}(\mathbf{Y}, \mathbf{X}, \mathbf{Z}, \boldsymbol{\beta})] = E[n^{-1}\mathbf{Z}'(\mathbf{Y} - \mathbf{X}\boldsymbol{\beta})] = \mathbf{0}$ when $\boldsymbol{\beta}$ equals the true value of the parameter. The corresponding sample analog of the moment conditions is $\mathbf{h}(\mathbf{y}, \mathbf{x}, \mathbf{z}, \boldsymbol{\beta}) = n^{-1}[\mathbf{z}'\mathbf{y} - \mathbf{z}'\mathbf{x}\boldsymbol{\beta}] = \mathbf{0}$. Note, unlike the ordinary MOM approach, we are *not* necessarily assuming that the $(Y_i, \mathbf{X}_{i\cdot}, \mathbf{Z}_{i\cdot})$'s underlying these moment conditions are iid. Rather, we are assuming that the moment assumptions apply to the joint distribution of $(\mathbf{Y}, \mathbf{X}, \mathbf{Z})$. Thus, regarding the sample analog to the moment conditions, we have in mind that a law of large numbers justifies that

$$n^{-1}[\mathbf{Z}'(\mathbf{Y} - \mathbf{X}\boldsymbol{\beta})] \xrightarrow{p} \mathbf{0}, \tag{16.3.4}$$

when $\boldsymbol{\beta}$ equals the true value of the parameter, and thus that the sample moment condition is indeed meaningful as a sample analog to the true moment condition based on the joint distribution of $(\mathbf{Y}, \mathbf{X}, \mathbf{Z})$. Therefore, *although the specification of true and sample analog moment conditions is MOM-like, we emphasize that the current IV procedure is potentially more general in terms of the data-sampling processes that it can be applied to.*

Given the uniformly nonsingular nature of $\mathbf{Z}'\mathbf{X}$, the sample moment equations

$$n^{-1}[\mathbf{Z}'(\mathbf{Y} - \mathbf{X}\boldsymbol{\beta})] = \mathbf{0} \tag{16.3.5}$$

can be solved, regardless of the value of n, for a unique value of $\boldsymbol{\beta}$. The solution identifies the IV estimator of $\boldsymbol{\beta}$ as

$$\hat{\boldsymbol{\beta}}_{IV} = (\mathbf{Z}'\mathbf{X})^{-1}\mathbf{Z}'\mathbf{Y}. \tag{16.3.6}$$

Note this estimator coincides with the OptEF estimator (16.1.6) in the case where $m = k$.

The IV estimator $\hat{\boldsymbol{\beta}}_{IV}$ is a consistent estimator of $\boldsymbol{\beta}$ under general regularity conditions. To see this, assume the average cross-product matrices $\mathbf{Z}'\mathbf{Z}$ and $\mathbf{Z}'\mathbf{X}$ are such that $n^{-1}\mathbf{Z}'\mathbf{Z} \xrightarrow{p} \mathbf{a}_{ZZ}$ and $n^{-1}\mathbf{Z}'\mathbf{X} \xrightarrow{p} \mathbf{a}_{ZX}$, where $\mathbf{a}_{ZZ}$ and $\mathbf{a}_{ZX}$ are finite and nonsingular. It follows directly upon substituting $\mathbf{Y} = \mathbf{X}\boldsymbol{\beta} + \varepsilon$ that

$$\begin{aligned} \text{p}\lim(\boldsymbol{\beta}_{IV}) &= \text{p}\lim[(n^{-1}\mathbf{Z}'\mathbf{X})^{-1}(n^{-1}\mathbf{Z}'\mathbf{Y})] \\ &= \boldsymbol{\beta} + \text{plim}[(n^{-1}\mathbf{Z}'\mathbf{X})^{-1}(n^{-1}\mathbf{Z}'\varepsilon)] \\ &= \boldsymbol{\beta} + \mathbf{a}_{ZX}^{-1} \cdot \mathbf{0} = \boldsymbol{\beta} \end{aligned} \tag{16.3.7}$$

because $n^{-1}\mathbf{Z}'\varepsilon \xrightarrow{p} \mathbf{0}$. Again, because the $\mathbf{Z}$ *variables were instrumental* in defining a transformation of the original model that led to a consistent estimator of $\boldsymbol{\beta}$, the estimator has come to be called an *instrumental variable (IV) estimator.*

The IV estimator is shown to be asymptotically normally distributed by first applying an appropriate central limit theorem so that $n^{-1/2}\mathbf{Z}'\varepsilon \overset{a}{\sim} \mathrm{N}[\mathbf{0}, \sigma^2 \mathbf{a}_{ZZ}]$. Then we can determine via Slutsky's theorem that (recall (16.3.7))

$$n^{1/2}(\hat{\boldsymbol{\beta}}_{\mathrm{IV}} - \boldsymbol{\beta}) \equiv (n^{-1}\mathbf{Z}'\mathbf{X})^{-1}(n^{-1/2}\mathbf{Z}'\varepsilon) \overset{a}{\sim} \mathrm{N}\left[\mathbf{0}, \sigma^2 \mathbf{a}_{ZX}^{-1}\mathbf{a}_{ZZ}\mathbf{a}_{XZ}^{-1}\right], \qquad (16.3.8)$$

where $\mathbf{a}_{XZ} = \mathbf{a}'_{ZX}$. The covariance matrix in (16.3.8) may be estimated by $s_{\mathrm{IV}}^2[(n^{-1}\mathbf{z}'\mathbf{x})^{-1}(n^{-1}\mathbf{z}'\mathbf{z})(n^{-1}\mathbf{x}'\mathbf{z})^{-1}]$, where $s_{\mathrm{IV}}^2 = (\mathbf{y} - \mathbf{x}\hat{\mathbf{b}}_{\mathrm{IV}})'(\mathbf{y} - \mathbf{x}\hat{\mathbf{b}}_{\mathrm{IV}})/n$. Thus, an estimate of the asymptotic covariance matrix of $\hat{\boldsymbol{\beta}}_{\mathrm{IV}}$ itself is given by $s_{\mathrm{IV}}^2[(\mathbf{z}'\mathbf{x})^{-1}(\mathbf{z}'\mathbf{z})(\mathbf{x}'\mathbf{z})^{-1}]$, where it is important to note that this is equivalent to the OptEF result (16.1.8) when $m = k$.

Although the IV estimator exhibits the usual large sample properties, we cannot claim that $\hat{\boldsymbol{\beta}}_{\mathrm{IV}}$ is unbiased because at least some of the columns of $\mathbf{Z}$ and $\mathbf{X}$ are stochastic. Consequently, it is not necessarily the case that $\mathrm{E}[(\mathbf{Z}'\mathbf{X})^{-1}\mathbf{Z}'\varepsilon] = \mathbf{0}$ because of the dependence of the conditional expectation of ε on the value of $\mathbf{X}$.

The sample analog $n^{-1}[\mathbf{z}'\mathbf{y} - \mathbf{z}'\mathbf{x}\boldsymbol{\beta}] = \mathbf{0}$ of the moment condition also suggests an alternative extremum estimation criterion for estimating $\boldsymbol{\beta}$ based on squared Euclidean distance between $n^{-1}[\mathbf{Z}'\mathbf{Y} - \mathbf{Z}'\mathbf{X}\boldsymbol{\beta}]$ and $\mathbf{0}$. Moving in this direction and ignoring n^{-1}, we can define the estimator in GMM-like (equivalent to GMM with $\mathbf{W} = \mathbf{I}$) fashion as

$$\hat{\boldsymbol{\beta}}_* = \arg\min_{\boldsymbol{\beta}}[(\mathbf{Z}'\mathbf{Y} - \mathbf{Z}'\mathbf{X}\boldsymbol{\beta})'(\mathbf{Z}'\mathbf{Y} - \mathbf{Z}'\mathbf{X}\boldsymbol{\beta})], \qquad (16.3.9)$$

which has first-order necessary conditions given by

$$-2\mathbf{X}'\mathbf{Z}\mathbf{Z}'\mathbf{Y} + 2\mathbf{X}'\mathbf{Z}\mathbf{Z}'\mathbf{X}\boldsymbol{\beta} = \mathbf{0}. \qquad (16.3.10)$$

Because, under the current assumptions, $(\mathbf{Z}'\mathbf{X})$ is square and invertible with probability 1, the resulting IV estimator is

$$\hat{\boldsymbol{\beta}}_* = \hat{\boldsymbol{\beta}}_{\mathrm{IV}} = (\mathbf{Z}'\mathbf{X})^{-1}(\mathbf{X}'\mathbf{Z})^{-1}(\mathbf{X}'\mathbf{Z})\mathbf{Z}'\mathbf{Y} = (\mathbf{Z}'\mathbf{X})^{-1}\mathbf{Z}'\mathbf{Y}, \qquad (16.3.11)$$

which is identical to (16.3.6) and to the OptEF estimator (16.1.6) when $m = k$ and therefore has sampling properties identical to the OptEF estimator.

16.3.2. GLS as an IV Estimator

The IV estimation concepts also have use in cases in which the orthogonality condition $\mathrm{E}[\mathbf{X}'\varepsilon] = \mathbf{0}$ holds but other statistical complications arise. Suppose the assumption of iid noise component elements does not hold and we are faced with the situation in which $\mathrm{var}(\varepsilon_i) \neq \mathrm{var}(\varepsilon_j)$ (heteroscedasticity) or $\mathrm{cov}(\varepsilon_i, \varepsilon_j) \neq 0$ (autocorrelation), or both, for at least some values of $i \neq j$. Consequently, the assumption $\mathbf{cov}(\varepsilon) = \sigma^2\mathbf{I}_n$ does not hold, and we must cope with a noise component that has a generalized covariance structure, as in Chapters 14 and 15 and Section 16.2.2.b. To characterize the linear regression model with $\mathbf{cov}(\varepsilon) \neq \sigma^2\mathbf{I}_n$, we write

$$\mathbf{Y} = \mathbf{X}\boldsymbol{\beta} + \varepsilon; \qquad \mathrm{E}[\varepsilon\varepsilon'] = \boldsymbol{\Phi}, \qquad (16.3.12)$$

where $\boldsymbol{\Phi}$ is an $(n \times n)$ symmetric and positive definite covariance matrix. Now transform the linear model (16.3.12) as follows:

$$\boldsymbol{\Phi}^{-1/2}\mathbf{Y} = \boldsymbol{\Phi}^{-1/2}\mathbf{X}\boldsymbol{\beta} + \boldsymbol{\Phi}^{-1/2}\varepsilon, \qquad (16.3.13)$$

where $\mathbf{cov}(\boldsymbol{\Phi}^{-1/2}\varepsilon) = \mathbf{I}_n$. Applying the LS rule to the transformed model yields the GLS estimator

$$\hat{\boldsymbol{\beta}}_{\mathrm{GLS}} = (\mathbf{X}'\boldsymbol{\Phi}^{-1}\mathbf{X})^{-1}\mathbf{X}'\boldsymbol{\Phi}^{-1}\mathbf{Y}. \tag{16.3.14}$$

In terms of the IV estimation context, we can view $\mathbf{Z} \equiv \boldsymbol{\Phi}^{-1}\mathbf{X}$ as the instrumental variables applied to (16.3.12) that lead to an efficient estimator, where $\hat{\boldsymbol{\beta}}_{\mathrm{GLS}}$ has the same form as (16.3.11). If $\boldsymbol{\Phi}$ is unknown but can be expressed in a known parametric functional form (e.g., first-order autocorrelation), then if a consistent estimator of the parameters that define $\boldsymbol{\Phi}$ can be found with which to construct $\hat{\boldsymbol{\Phi}}$, an asymptotically efficient EGLS estimator is possible. This will be examined further in Chapter 19.

16.3.3. Extensions: Nonlinear IV Formulations and Non-iid Sampling

As a generalization of the linear IV problem, consider a stochastic $\mathbf{X}$ variant of the nonlinear statistical model from Chapter 8,

$$\mathrm{Y}_i = \mathrm{g}(\mathbf{X}_{i\cdot}, \boldsymbol{\beta}) + \varepsilon_i, \qquad i = 1, \ldots, n, \tag{16.3.15}$$

where $\mathrm{E}[\varepsilon] = \mathbf{0}$ and $\mathbf{cov}(\varepsilon) = \sigma^2\mathbf{I}$. If we assume again that we have an $(n \times k)$ instrumental variable matrix $\mathbf{Z}$, we may then state the nonlinear equivalent of the moment conditions as $\mathrm{E}[n^{-1}\mathbf{Z}'(\mathbf{Y} - \mathbf{g}(\mathbf{X}, \boldsymbol{\beta}))] = \mathbf{0}$. The corresponding sample moment conditions are $n^{-1}[\mathbf{z}'\mathbf{y} - \mathbf{z}'\mathbf{g}(\mathbf{x}, \boldsymbol{\beta})] = \mathbf{0}$, and the nonlinear IV estimator is obtained by solving the sample moment conditions–estimating equations, expressed in terms of random variables, for $\boldsymbol{\beta}$ as follows:

$$\hat{\boldsymbol{\beta}}_{\mathrm{IV}} = \arg_{\boldsymbol{\beta}}[\mathbf{Z}'\mathbf{Y} - \mathbf{Z}'\mathbf{g}(\mathbf{X}, \boldsymbol{\beta})] = \mathbf{0}. \tag{16.3.16}$$

The solution to (16.3.16) would also be the solution to the GMM-like extremum estimation problem (completely equivalent to GMM when $\mathbf{W} = \mathbf{I}$) based on squared Euclidean distance between $[\mathbf{Z}'\mathbf{Y} - \mathbf{Z}'\mathbf{g}(\mathbf{X}, \boldsymbol{\beta})]$ and $\mathbf{0}$ as follows:

$$\hat{\boldsymbol{\beta}}_{\mathrm{IV}} = \arg\min_{\boldsymbol{\beta}}[[\mathbf{Y} - \mathbf{g}(\mathbf{X}, \boldsymbol{\beta})]'\mathbf{Z}\mathbf{Z}'[\mathbf{Y} - \mathbf{g}(\mathbf{X}, \boldsymbol{\beta})]]. \tag{16.3.17}$$

The optimization problem can be viewed as an NLS problem for the model $\mathbf{Y}_* = \mathbf{g}_*(\mathbf{X}, \boldsymbol{\beta}) + \mathbf{V}$, where $\mathbf{Y}_* \equiv \mathbf{Z}'\mathbf{Y}$ and $\mathbf{g}_*(\mathbf{X}, \boldsymbol{\beta}) \equiv \mathbf{Z}'\mathbf{g}(\mathbf{X}, \boldsymbol{\beta})$. Note that it is because the system is just-determined that the solution to (16.3.17) and (16.3.16) will coincide, and the NLS objective function will in fact be zero at the least-squares solution. Under regularity conditions applied to $\mathbf{Y}_*$ and $\mathbf{g}_*(\mathbf{X}, \boldsymbol{\beta})$ analogous to those introduced in the NLS context of Chapter 8, replacing lims with plims where appropriate, we have that $\hat{\boldsymbol{\beta}}_{\mathrm{IV}} \xrightarrow{\mathrm{p}} \boldsymbol{\beta}$, and thus the nonlinear IV estimator is consistent and asymptotically normal as follows:

$$\hat{\boldsymbol{\beta}}_{\mathrm{IV}} \overset{\mathrm{a}}{\sim} \mathrm{N}\left(\boldsymbol{\beta}, \sigma^2\left[\left[\mathbf{z}'\frac{\partial\mathbf{g}(\mathbf{x}, \boldsymbol{\beta})}{\partial\boldsymbol{\beta}'}\right]^{-1}\mathbf{z}'\mathbf{z}\left[\frac{\partial\mathbf{g}(\mathbf{x}, \boldsymbol{\beta})}{\partial\boldsymbol{\beta}}\mathbf{z}\right]^{-1}\right]\right). \tag{16.3.18}$$

The special case of the linear model is reestablished when $\mathbf{g}(\mathbf{x}, \boldsymbol{\beta}) \equiv \mathbf{x}\boldsymbol{\beta}$ and thus $\frac{\partial\mathbf{g}(\mathbf{x}, \boldsymbol{\beta})}{\partial\boldsymbol{\beta}} \equiv \mathbf{x}'$.

In cases in which sampling is not iid and the sample observations exhibit heteroscedasticity, autocorrelation, or both, so that $\mathbf{cov}(\varepsilon) = \mathbf{\Phi}$, the asymptotic distribution of the IV estimator can be represented as

$$\hat{\boldsymbol{\beta}}_{\mathrm{IV}} \overset{a}{\sim} \mathrm{N}\left(\boldsymbol{\beta}, \left[\left[\mathbf{z}'\frac{\partial \mathbf{g}(\mathbf{x}, \boldsymbol{\beta})}{\partial \boldsymbol{\beta}'}\right]^{-1} \mathbf{z}'\mathbf{\Phi}\mathbf{z}\left[\frac{\partial \mathbf{g}(\mathbf{x}, \boldsymbol{\beta})}{\partial \boldsymbol{\beta}}\mathbf{z}\right]^{-1}\right]\right). \tag{16.3.19}$$

Note in the special case of the orthogonal linear model, and if $\mathbf{z} \equiv \mathbf{x}$, this result is precisely the distribution of the ordinarily least-squares estimator applied in the context of non-iid sampling, as discussed in Chapter 14. Questions of estimating the covariance matrices in (16.3.18) or (16.3.19) for purposes of testing or confidence region estimation are addressed ahead.

16.3.4. Hypothesis Testing and Confidence Regions

Hypothesis tests relating to the value of $\mathbf{c}(\boldsymbol{\beta})$ can be based on the usual Wald, LM, or Z-statistics possibly adjusted for heteroscedasticity, autocorrelation, or both if necessary. The test statistics are asymptotically Chi-square or normally distributed based on the asymptotic normality of the IV estimator. Note that a pseudolikelihood ratio test based on the optimized values of estimation objective function in (16.3.9) or (16.3.17) is *not* available because the unconstrained minimums of these functions are identically zero.

For an example of a testing procedure in the IV context, a Wald test of a nonlinear hypothesis H_0: $\mathbf{c}(\boldsymbol{\beta}) = \mathbf{r}$ in the case of a linear model with $\mathbf{cov}(\varepsilon) = \sigma^2\mathbf{I}$ would be defined in terms of the statistic

$$\mathrm{W} = [\mathbf{c}(\hat{\boldsymbol{\beta}}_{\mathrm{IV}}) - \mathbf{r}]'\left[\left.\frac{\partial \mathbf{c}(\boldsymbol{\beta})}{\partial \boldsymbol{\beta}'}\right|_{\hat{\boldsymbol{\beta}}_{\mathrm{IV}}}\left[\mathrm{S}^2_{\mathrm{IV}}(\mathbf{z}'\mathbf{x})^{-1}(\mathbf{z}'\mathbf{z})(\mathbf{x}'\mathbf{z})^{-1}\right]\left.\frac{\partial \mathbf{c}(\boldsymbol{\beta})}{\partial \boldsymbol{\beta}}\right|_{\hat{\boldsymbol{\beta}}_{\mathrm{IV}}}\right]^{-1}[\mathbf{c}(\hat{\boldsymbol{\beta}}_{\mathrm{IV}}) - \mathbf{r}]$$

$$\overset{a}{\sim} \text{Chi-square}(j, \lambda). \tag{16.3.20}$$

(recall the definition of $\mathrm{S}^2_{\mathrm{IV}}$ given following (16.3.8)). In the case of the nonlinear regression model and IV estimator, the Wald test would be based on (16.3.19) as well, except that $\mathbf{X}$ would be replaced by $\frac{\partial \mathbf{g}(\mathbf{X}, \boldsymbol{\beta})}{\partial \boldsymbol{\beta}'}|_{\hat{\boldsymbol{\beta}}_{\mathrm{IV}}}$. In either the linear or nonlinear case, if sample observations exhibit heteroscedasticity, autocorrelation, or both so that $\mathbf{cov}(\varepsilon) = \mathbf{\Phi}$, then the $(\mathbf{z}'\mathbf{z})$ term in (16.3.20) is replaced by $(\mathbf{z}'\mathbf{\Phi}\mathbf{z})$, and $\mathrm{S}^2_{\mathrm{IV}}$ is deleted. Because $(\mathbf{z}'\mathbf{\Phi}\mathbf{z})$ is generally unknown, it must be consistently estimated from the sample data to render (16.3.20) operational. If $\mathbf{\Phi}$ is known to be a function of parameters such as $\mathbf{\Phi}(\alpha)$, and if these parameters can be consistently estimated, then $[\mathbf{z}'\mathbf{\Phi}(\hat{\alpha})\mathbf{z}]$ can be used to estimate the unknown $(\mathbf{z}'\mathbf{\Phi}\mathbf{z})$ term. Otherwise, one may consider the use, of a White- or Newey–West-type heteroscedasticity, autocorrelation robust estimator, or both of $(\mathbf{z}'\mathbf{\Phi}\mathbf{z})$.

Confidence regions for $\mathbf{c}(\boldsymbol{\beta})$ could be constructed based on the duality between hypothesis tests and confidence regions. The reader is asked to contemplate the various possibilities.

16.3.5. Summary: IV Approach to Estimation and Inference

The IV approach allows one to proceed with consistent estimation of model parameters and make asymptotically valid inferences about parameter values in nonorthogonal models in which the usual moment conditions–estimating equations in linear or nonlinear models are *biased*. The IV approach relies on the existence of instrumental variables that provide the means for specifying a just-determined set of *unbiased* estimating equations in place of the original biased set.

We emphasize that, as described in this section, the IV approach applies only to *just-determined* sets of unbiased estimating equations formed with the aid of instrumental variables. This feature of the approach is actually more restrictive than the approaches discussed in the previous sections, which are applicable to overdetermined models as well. The IV method will be extended to overdetermined systems in the next section, where we discuss GMM, MEL, MEEL, and OptEF alternatives for estimating nonorthogonal linear and nonlinear models.

A useful source of additional readings on the IV approach is the work of Bowden and Turkington (1984).

► **Example 16.3.1:** To demonstrate the instrumental variable concept, we provide the GAUSS program C16IV.gss in the examples manual. The program calculates instrumental variable estimates and their estimated covariance matrix based on equations 16.3.6 and 16.3.8, utilizing an estimated value of σ^2. Based on outcomes from a linear regression relationship where $E[\mathbf{X}'\varepsilon] \neq \mathbf{0}$, the program calculates IV estimates and standard errors for the parameters of the model. A Monte Carlo exercise is used to simulate the sampling properties of the LS and IV estimators.

16.4. Solutions in the Overdetermined Case When $E[\mathbf{X}'\varepsilon] \neq \mathbf{0}$

In this section we generalize the basic IV concept introduced in Section 16.3 to cases in which the system of estimating equations–moment conditions *overdetermine* the unknown parameters being estimated. We will see that all of the previous methods we have examined for solving systems of estimating equations, including the OptEF, MEL, MEEL, and now GMM procedures can be applied to the case in which $\mathbf{X}$ and ε are correlated and the equation system is overdetermined. All of the approaches share a common foundation in that they are based on the existence of moment conditions that can be used to form unbiased estimating functions for the parameters. This basis prevails even though $\mathbf{X}$ and ε are correlated so that the typical moment conditions–estimating equations such as $\mathbf{h}(\mathbf{Y}, \mathbf{X}, \boldsymbol{\beta}) = n^{-1}\mathbf{X}'(\mathbf{Y} - \mathbf{X}\boldsymbol{\beta})$ in the case of linear models or $\mathbf{h}(\mathbf{Y}, \mathbf{X}, \boldsymbol{\beta}) = n^{-1}\mathbf{X}'[\mathbf{Y} - \mathbf{g}(\mathbf{X}, \boldsymbol{\beta})]$ in the case of nonlinear models, are biased. As in the just-determined case of Section 16.3, the procedures rely on the existence of instrumental variables for defining a valid system of unbiased estimating equations, where in the current context this system will be overdetermined for estimating $\boldsymbol{\beta}$. Each of the alternative procedures defines a unique estimate of $\boldsymbol{\beta}$ by effectively converting an initial overdetermined system of estimating equations–moment conditions to a just-determined system. The procedures are differentiated on the basis of how this conversion is accomplished.

We examine essentially three different approaches for obtaining inverse problem solutions in the overdetermined nonorthogonal case: (1) GMM, (2) MEL and MEEL, and (3) OptEF. As seen in Sections 16.1 and 16.2, these approaches differ in terms of the method by which they resolve the overdetermined nature of a system of estimating equations when solving for parameter estimates. In GMM, the unbiased estimating equations are drawn as close to zero in weighted Euclidean distance as possible. In the MEL or MEEL approach, additional unknown weights on each of the sample observations are introduced to define initially an *underdetermined* inverse problem consisting of unknown parameters and unknown sample weights. Then the underdetermined nature of the estimating equations is resolved by choosing values for all of the unknowns (sample weights and parameters) that solve an extremum problem having a maximum empirical likelihood or maximum entropy objective function. The OptEF approach transforms the original overdetermined set of estimating equations into a new just-determined set by forming an optimal linear combination of estimating equations. The optimal just-determined set of estimating equations can then be solved directly for the parameter estimates.

We will see later that actually all of the procedures can ultimately be viewed as reducing the overdetermined system of estimating equations to just-determined systems via either fixed or stochastic linear transformations. In the final analysis, all of the procedures can effectively be subsumed by the OptEF approach in the sense that the optimal estimator produced by each alternative procedure is at best equal to the OptEF estimator in terms of asymptotic efficiency. Moreover, as the sample size increases to infinity, the outcomes generated by all of the estimators will coincide with the OptEF estimator outcomes. However, outcomes of the estimators will differ in finite samples for some of the estimators, as will their finite sampling properties, and work remains to be done in assessing the relative merits of the procedures in small samples.

In terms of small sample properties, the OptEF approach (based on true and not approximated expectation terms if any appear in its definition) produces an estimator based on estimating functions that have the smallest finite-sample standardized variance or covariance matrix within whatever class of estimating functions is being considered. This imparts a small-sample optimality property to the estimating equations used in the OptEF approach (you may wish to reread Section 11.3.2 for a discussion of this property and its implications). OptEF estimates are solutions to a set of unbiased estimating functions having the smallest random variability among all possible sets of unbiased estimating equations producible from within a given class of estimating equations. Consequently, one might expect the solutions to these equations to reside closer to the true parameter values than outcomes of other estimators whose outcomes solve estimating equations exhibiting more random variability.

16.4.1. Unbiased Estimating Equations Basis for Inverse Problem Solutions When $\mathrm{E}[\mathbf{X}'\varepsilon] \neq \mathbf{0}$

Fundamental to all of the approaches we will examine for solving overdetermined inverse problems in cases in which explanatory variables $\mathbf{X}$ are correlated with the noise component ε is the existence of a collection of $m > k$ moment conditions on the sample data that can be used to specify unbiased estimating equations. In practice the most common source of these types of moment relationships is instrumental variable specifications of the type introduced in our discussion of IV estimation in Section 16.3. Thus, we have in mind $m > k$ estimating equation–moment relationships of the form $E[\mathbf{h}(\mathbf{Y}, \mathbf{X}, \mathbf{Z}, \boldsymbol{\beta})] = \mathbf{0}$ with estimating functions defined in the case of linear models as $\mathbf{h}(\mathbf{Y}, \mathbf{X}, \mathbf{Z}, \boldsymbol{\beta}) = n^{-1}\mathbf{Z}'(\mathbf{Y} - \mathbf{X}\boldsymbol{\beta})$ or $\mathbf{h}(\mathbf{Y}, \mathbf{X}, \mathbf{Z}, \boldsymbol{\beta}) = n^{-1}\mathbf{Z}'[\mathbf{Y} - \mathbf{g}(\mathbf{X}, \boldsymbol{\beta})]$ for nonlinear models. As indicated in the previous section, two important general features of the $(n \times m)$ instrumental variables matrix $\mathbf{Z}$ are that the variables are orthogonal to the noise component and that they are also correlated with the explanatory variables $\mathbf{X}$. Other specific characteristics of the instruments were presented in Section 16.3 and will be evident in the derivations ahead.

16.4.2. GMM Approach

The GMM solution to the inverse problem in the case of an overdetermined nonorthogonal linear or nonlinear model is given by

$$\hat{\boldsymbol{\beta}}(\mathbf{W}) = \arg\min_{\boldsymbol{\beta}}[\mathrm{m}(\boldsymbol{\beta}, \mathbf{Y}, \mathbf{Q})] = \arg\min_{\boldsymbol{\beta}}[n^{-2}[\mathbf{Y} - \mathbf{g}(\mathbf{X}, \boldsymbol{\beta})]'\mathbf{Z}\mathbf{W}\mathbf{Z}'[\mathbf{Y} - \mathbf{g}(\mathbf{X}, \boldsymbol{\beta})]], \tag{16.4.1}$$

where $\mathbf{W}$ is a positive definite symmetric weighting matrix, as discussed in Section 16.2, and $\mathbf{g}(\mathbf{X}, \boldsymbol{\beta}) = \mathbf{X}\boldsymbol{\beta}$ in the case of the linear model (recall (16.2.7)). As we noted previously in Section 16.2.2.a, the optimal GMM estimator is defined by choosing the weight matrix $\mathbf{W}$ to satisfy

$$\begin{aligned}\mathbf{W}^{-1} &= \mathbf{w}_*^{-1} = \mathbf{cov}(n^{-1/2}\mathbf{Z}'[\mathbf{Y} - \mathbf{g}(\mathbf{X}, \boldsymbol{\beta})]) = \mathbf{cov}(n^{-1/2}\mathbf{Z}'\varepsilon),\\ &= n^{-1}E_Z[E[\mathbf{Z}'\varepsilon\varepsilon'\mathbf{Z} \mid \mathbf{Z}]] = n^{-1}E[\mathbf{Z}'\boldsymbol{\Phi}\mathbf{Z}],\end{aligned} \tag{16.4.2}$$

where we allow for possible heteroscedasticity or autocorrelation in the noise component, or both, so that the noise covariance matrix is represented by $\mathbf{cov}(\varepsilon \mid \mathbf{Z}) = \boldsymbol{\Phi}$. The first-order conditions to the extremum problem in (16.4.1), with $\mathbf{W} = \mathbf{w}_*$, are given by

$$\begin{aligned}\frac{\partial \mathrm{m}(\boldsymbol{\beta}, \mathbf{Y}, \mathbf{Q})}{\partial \boldsymbol{\beta}} &= \left[\frac{\partial \mathbf{h}(\mathbf{Y}, \mathbf{Q}, \boldsymbol{\beta})}{\partial \boldsymbol{\beta}}\right]\mathbf{w}_*\,\mathbf{h}(\mathbf{Y}, \mathbf{Q}, \boldsymbol{\beta})\\ &= -2\left[n^{-1}\frac{\partial \mathbf{g}(\mathbf{X}, \boldsymbol{\beta})}{\partial \boldsymbol{\beta}}\mathbf{Z}\right]\mathbf{w}_*\,(n^{-1}\mathbf{Z}'[\mathbf{Y} - \mathbf{g}(\mathbf{X}, \boldsymbol{\beta})]) = \mathbf{0}.\end{aligned} \tag{16.4.3}$$

Finding the solution to the extremum problem, and thereby satisfying the first-order conditions, will often require numerical methods in the case of nonlinear models. In the linear model case the solution is in closed form and given by (16.2.9) with $\mathbf{W} = \mathbf{w}_*$. For comparisons with the alternative inverse solution procedures presented ahead, note that the outcome of (16.4.3) is in the general form $\mathbf{h}_\nu(\mathbf{y}, \mathbf{x}, \mathbf{z}, \boldsymbol{\beta}) \equiv \boldsymbol{\nu}\mathbf{h}(\mathbf{y}, \mathbf{x}, \mathbf{z}, \boldsymbol{\beta}) = \mathbf{0}$, where $\mathbf{h}(\mathbf{y}, \mathbf{x}, \mathbf{z}, \boldsymbol{\beta}) \equiv n^{-1}\mathbf{z}'[\mathbf{y} - \mathbf{g}(\mathbf{x}, \boldsymbol{\beta})]$ and $\boldsymbol{\nu} \equiv -2[n^{-1}\frac{\partial \mathbf{g}(\mathbf{x}, \boldsymbol{\beta})}{\partial \boldsymbol{\beta}}\mathbf{z}]\mathbf{w}_*$. That is, the estimating equations are in the form of a dimension-reducing linear transformation of the original overdetermined set, going from m to k estimating equations.

Because the optimal weighting matrix will generally be unknown in practice, an estimated optimal GMM (EOGMM) can be defined by substituting a consistent estimator $\hat{\mathbf{W}}$ for $\mathbf{w}_*$ into the definition (16.4.1) of the GMM estimator, resulting in the EOGMM estimator $\hat{\boldsymbol{\beta}}(\hat{\mathbf{W}})$ that will have the same asymptotic properties as the optimal

GMM estimator. This is analogous to the asymptotic equivalence of GLS and EGLS presented in Chapter 15. Unless the specific parametric functional form of the heteroscedasticity, autocorrelation, or both is known, the estimator $\hat{\mathbf{W}}$ will generally be defined based on either White's heteroscedastic robust estimator or else a Newey–West-type heteroscedasticity–autocorrelation robust estimator, as discussed in Section 15.4. Also following our discussion in Chapter 15, one can iterate between calculating the covariance matrix estimate, calculating $\hat{\boldsymbol{\beta}}(\hat{\mathbf{W}})$, refining the estimate of $\hat{\mathbf{W}}$ based on updated noise component estimates, reestimating $\hat{\boldsymbol{\beta}}(\hat{\mathbf{W}})$, and so on until convergence. For recent work and references along these lines, see Hansen, Heaton, and Yaron (1996).

Asymptotic sampling properties and inference procedures for the EOGMM and OptEF estimators are closely related because of the relationship between (16.4.3) and the estimating equations defining the OptEF estimator. These properties are discussed in Section 16.4.4.

16.4.3. MEL and MEEL Approaches

The standard MEL or MEEL solution to the inverse problem in the case of an overdetermined nonorthogonal linear or nonlinear model is given by the solution to the extremum-type problem (recall Section 16.1.2)

$$\begin{aligned}\boldsymbol{\beta} &= \arg\max_{\boldsymbol{\beta},\,\mathbf{p}}\left[\varphi(\mathbf{p})\text{ s.t. }\sum_{i=1}^{n}\mathrm{p}_i\mathbf{z}_{i\cdot}'[\mathrm{Y}_i-\mathbf{g}(\mathbf{X}_{i\cdot},\boldsymbol{\beta})]=\mathbf{0}\text{ and }\sum_{i=1}^{n}\mathrm{p}_i=1\right]\\ &= \arg\max_{\boldsymbol{\beta},\,\mathbf{p}}[\varphi(\mathbf{p})\text{ s.t. }(\mathbf{p}\odot\mathbf{z})'[\mathbf{Y}-\mathbf{g}(\mathbf{X},\boldsymbol{\beta})]=\mathbf{0}\text{ and }\mathbf{p}'\mathbf{1}=1],\end{aligned} \tag{16.4.4}$$

where $\odot$ denotes a Hadamard (elementwise) product, $\mathbf{g}(\mathbf{X},\boldsymbol{\beta})=\mathbf{X}\boldsymbol{\beta}$ in the case of the linear model, and the estimation objective function is either $\varphi(\mathbf{p})\equiv\sum_{i=1}^{n}\ln(\mathrm{p}_i)$ or $-\sum_{i=1}^{n}\mathrm{p}_i\ln(\mathrm{p}_i)$, depending on whether we are defining the MEL or MEEL estimator, respectively. Calculating the solution to either the MEL or MEEL estimation problem will generally require that a computer-driven maximization algorithm be employed. The reader is referred to Chapters 12 and 13 for solution characterizations relating to each of the estimators. An excellent recent discussion regarding calculations of solutions to these types of problems can be found in Imbens, Spady, and Johnson (1998).

16.4.3.a. iid Sampling

In the case of iid sampling, we have already seen in Chapters 12 and 13 that both MEL and MEEL estimators are consistent, asymptotically normally distributed, and as asymptotically efficient as the asymptotically optimal OptEF estimator given the estimating equations–moment conditions under consideration. In fact, both estimators remain consistent and asymptotically normal even if the sampling is *not* iid, and in particular the estimators retain these properties under general types of heteroscedastic, autocorrelated, or both data-sampling processes often considered in empirical work. In particular, Kitamura (1997, 1998) and Kitamura and Stutzer (1997) present such results for situations in which sample observations are allowed to follow the general dependence relationship known as strong or α-mixing. This form of dependence effectively encompasses all DSPs whose outcomes are asymptotically independent, meaning that dependence among observations dissipates to zero as the separation between observations in a sequence becomes arbitrarily large (see White, 1984, on mixing and asymptotic independence concepts). However, without modification, the usual calculated versions of the MEL and MEEL test and confidence-region statistics introduced in Chapters 12 and 13 do not have the usual asymptotic Chi-square or normal distributions. Furthermore, the MEL and MEEL estimators are no longer asymptotically optimal when sampling is not iid, and in particular they are generally less asymptotically efficient than the OptEF estimator in this case. We now introduce modifications that reestablish both asymptotic optimality and the validity of the usual asymptotic Chi-square or normal-based tests and confidence-region estimation procedures.

16.4.3.b. Non-iid Sampling

Kitamura (1997, 1998) and Kitamura and Stutzer (1997) have suggested a relatively straightforward modification of the MEL and MEEL approaches that accommodates dependence in the data and leads to asymptotically valid test and confidence-region statistics. In effect, what they suggest is that the moments be smoothed using some moving average of successive sample outcomes of the moment conditions, and then the MEL or MEEL approach is applied to the smoothed moment-estimating equations. Although a variety of different types of moving averages could be contemplated, the type of averaging that has received a detailed investigation in this literature is the simple moving average of the form

$$\bar{\mathbf{h}}(\mathrm{t}, \boldsymbol{\beta}) \equiv (2\tau + 1)^{-1} \sum_{i=-\tau}^{\tau} \mathbf{h}_*(\mathrm{y}_{t-i}, \mathbf{q}_{t-i}, \boldsymbol{\beta}), \qquad t = \tau + 1, \ldots, n - \tau. \tag{16.4.5}$$

In the linear or nonlinear model case, the averaged moments would take the form

$$\bar{\mathbf{h}}(\mathrm{t}, \boldsymbol{\beta}) \equiv (2\tau + 1)^{-1} \sum_{i=-\tau}^{\tau} \mathbf{z}'_{i\cdot}(\mathrm{y}_{t-i} - \mathrm{g}(\mathbf{x}_{t-i\cdot}, \boldsymbol{\beta})), \qquad t = \tau + 1, \ldots, n - \tau. \tag{16.4.6}$$

Then the MEL and MEEL estimators are obtained by solving the extremum-type problem

$$\hat{\boldsymbol{\beta}} = \arg\min_{\boldsymbol{\beta}, \mathbf{p}} \left[\varphi(\mathbf{p}) \text{ s.t. } \sum_{t=\tau+1}^{n-\tau} \mathrm{p}_i \bar{\mathbf{H}}(t, \boldsymbol{\beta}) = \mathbf{0} \text{ and } \sum_{t=\tau+1}^{n-\tau} \mathrm{p}_i = 1 \right], \tag{16.4.7}$$

which is an ordinary application of the MEL or MEEL estimation procedure to the averaged moment conditions–unbiased estimating functions.

The value of τ, often referred to as the *bandwidth* parameter, must be chosen in (16.4.6) and (16.4.7) to make the estimators operational. For asymptotic efficiency to be obtained, the value of τ must be such that $\tau \to \infty$ as $n \to \infty$, but τ must increase at a rate less than n. Kitamura and Stutzer (1997) suggest that τ be chosen so that $n^{-1}\tau^2 \to 0$ as $n \to \infty$. Kitamura (1998) suggests that the sampling properties of the estimator are relatively insensitive to the choice of τ, but work remains to be done on the effects of choosing different values for τ. Furthermore, there is an additional issue relating to the degree to which the moving average terms should contain sample observations that overlap, and alternative definitions of (16.4.5)–(16.4.7) are available that vary the amount of this observation overlap (Kitamura, 1997). The degree of overlap does not affect asymptotic properties but can impact finite sampling properties of the estimator in ways that are not yet clear.

16.4.3.c. Asymptotic Properties

The demonstrations of the asymptotics of the MEL or MEEL estimators, especially in the case of dependent sample observations, are very involved. We provide a heuristic view of the asymptotic properties here to yield additional insights into the connections between the MEL and MEEL approaches and the OptEF approach to be discussed ahead. The discussion applies equally well to either iid or non-iid sampling. In the latter case, one will need to interpret the moment conditions ahead as smoothed moments as defined in the previous section, and the summations ahead will be applied to the reduced number of observations available on the smoothed moment conditions. The reader is directed to Kitamura (1997, 1998), Kitamura and Stutzer (1997), and Qin and Lawless (1994) for additional details and formal demonstrations of results.

Suppose that we are dealing with unbiased estimating functions that adhere to a uniform weak law of large numbers, so that $n^{-1}\sum_{i=1}^{n}\mathbf{h}_*(\mathbf{Y}_i, \mathbf{Q}_i, \boldsymbol{\beta}_0) \xrightarrow{p} \mathbf{0}$, and convergence to zero occurs only for the true value of the parameter vector, denoted by $\boldsymbol{\beta}_0$. Note this is the principal condition that makes the estimating equation–moment approach to estimation viable and the resultant estimators consistent. *We emphasize that such convergence does not require that the sample observations be iid.*

Consider the solution for the sample weights $\mathbf{p}$ that would result from solving the following extremum-type problem:

$$\max_{\mathbf{p}}\left[\varphi(\mathbf{p})\ \text{s.t.} \sum_{i=1}^{n} \mathrm{p}_i \mathbf{h}_*(\mathbf{Y}_i, \mathbf{Q}_{i\cdot}, \boldsymbol{\beta}_0) = \mathbf{0} \text{ and } \sum_{i=1}^{n} \mathrm{p}_i = 1\right]. \qquad (16.4.8)$$

Note this is similar to the MEL or MEEL optimization problem, but it is conditioned on the true value $\boldsymbol{\beta}_0$ of the parameter vector. Both the MEL and MEEL objective functions achieve their unconstrained maximum values when $\mathrm{p}_i = n^{-1}\ \forall i$, and this value actually becomes feasible with probability converging to 1 as $n \to \infty$ because, as assumed above, $n^{-1}\sum_{i=1}^{n}\mathbf{h}_*(\mathbf{Y}_i, \mathbf{Q}_i, \boldsymbol{\beta}_0) \xrightarrow{p} \mathbf{0}$. Consequently, as $n \to \infty$, the optimized empirical moment conditions in (16.4.8) effectively emulate the form of the ordinary sample moment conditions $n^{-1}\sum_{i=1}^{n}\mathbf{h}_*(\mathbf{Y}_i, \mathbf{Q}_i, \boldsymbol{\beta}_0) = \mathbf{0}$ with the optimum values of the sample weights, conditional on $\boldsymbol{\beta}_0$, approaching the form $\mathrm{p}_i(\boldsymbol{\beta}_0) = n^{-1}\ \forall i$. Now because the MEL or MEEL estimator is consistent for the true value of the parameter vector, we know that $\hat{\boldsymbol{\beta}} \xrightarrow{p} \boldsymbol{\beta}_0$. If we denote the unconditional optimal sample weights as $\mathrm{p}_i(\hat{\boldsymbol{\beta}})$, we can conclude that, as $n \to \infty$, the unconditional values of the sample weights also tend to uniformity as $\mathrm{p}_i(\hat{\boldsymbol{\beta}}) \xrightarrow{p} \mathrm{p}_i(\boldsymbol{\beta}_0) = n^{-1}$. Thus, we expect the unconditional solution to the MEL or MEEL extremum problem to satisfy $n^{-1}\sum_{i=1}^{n}\mathbf{h}_*(\mathbf{Y}_i, \mathbf{Q}_i, \boldsymbol{\beta}_0) = \mathbf{0}$ as $n \to \infty$. We emphasize that this is the form in which the overdetermined system of estimating equations is used in the OptEF and GMM approaches to the estimation problem.

Now, leaving the asymptotic context temporarily, we consider the finite sample solution to the MEL or MEEL problem of the form

$$\hat{\boldsymbol{\beta}} = \arg\max_{\boldsymbol{\beta},\mathbf{p}} \left[\varphi(\mathbf{p}) \text{ s.t. } \sum_{i=1}^{n} \mathrm{p}_i \mathbf{h}_*(\mathbf{Y}_i, \mathbf{Q}_{i\cdot}, \boldsymbol{\beta}) = \mathbf{0} \text{ and } \sum_{i=1}^{n} \mathrm{p}_i = 1 \right]. \quad (16.4.9)$$

Given values of the optimal sample weights, say $\hat{\mathbf{p}}$, obtained from solving (16.4.9) for a given sample of data outcomes, the value of the MEL or MEEL estimator can be obtained by finding the value of $\boldsymbol{\beta}$ that solves the set of $m > k$ empirical moment equations

$$\hat{\mathbf{h}}(\mathbf{y}, \mathbf{q}, \boldsymbol{\beta}) \equiv \sum_{i=1}^{n} \hat{\mathrm{p}}_i \mathbf{h}_*(\mathbf{y}_i, \mathbf{q}_{i\cdot}, \boldsymbol{\beta}) = \mathbf{0}. \quad (16.4.10)$$

Note that this is possible, despite there being more equations than unknowns, because at the optimal solution to the MEL or MEEL optimization problem, the moment equations must be satisfied. This implies that the m equations in (16.4.10) are in fact *functionally dependent* (or else there would be no value of $\boldsymbol{\beta}$ for which (16.4.10) is satisfied, and the MEL or MEEL could not have been solved), with $m - k$ functions being redundant. In fact, *this is precisely how the MEL or MEEL approach rectifies the overdetermined nature of the original estimating equation – the sample weights form a convex combination of the n observations on the* $(m \times 1)$ *moment equations so as to produce a functionally dependent system of equations,* $\hat{\mathbf{h}}(\mathbf{y}, \mathbf{q}, \boldsymbol{\beta})$, *in which* $m - k$ *equations are redundant.* The functional dependence effectively removes the overdetermined nature of the equation system, and in effect the $m > k$ estimating equations actually represent a just-determined system of estimating equations for calculating $\boldsymbol{\beta}$.

The preceding observation indicates that it is permissible to project the m MEL or MEEL estimating equations in (16.4.10) down to a k-dimension set by premultiplying the m equations by a $(k \times m)$ matrix, say $\boldsymbol{\nu}$, having full-row rank, as

$$\mathbf{h}_{\nu}(\mathbf{y}, \mathbf{q}, \boldsymbol{\beta}) \equiv \boldsymbol{\nu}\hat{\mathbf{h}}(\mathbf{y}, \mathbf{q}, \boldsymbol{\beta}) = \sum_{i=1}^{n} \hat{\mathrm{p}}_i [\boldsymbol{\nu}\mathbf{h}_*(\mathbf{y}_i, \mathbf{q}_{i\cdot}, \boldsymbol{\beta})] = \mathbf{0}. \quad (16.4.11)$$

In particular, there is no reason why $\boldsymbol{\nu}$ cannot be set equal to the matrix that represents the optimal $(k \times m)$ linear transformation of the original m moment conditions, $n^{-1}\sum_{i=1}^{n} \mathbf{h}_*(\mathbf{Y}_i, \mathbf{Q}_i, \boldsymbol{\beta}) = \mathbf{0}$, used by the OptEF procedure. *The resulting estimating equations (16.4.11) are effectively a just-determined system that can be solved for precisely the same optimal value of* $\boldsymbol{\beta}$ *that solves (16.4.10).*

Now, to complete the heuristic argument, recall that as $n \to \infty$, $\hat{\mathbf{h}}(\mathbf{y}, \mathbf{q}, \boldsymbol{\beta})$ will emulate $n^{-1}\sum_{i=1}^{n} \mathbf{h}_*(\mathbf{Y}_i, \mathbf{Q}_i, \boldsymbol{\beta}) = \mathbf{0}$, and thus the MEL or MEEL solution obtained from (16.4.11) will emulate the solution to the estimating equations

$$\left[n^{-1} \sum_{i=1}^{n} \boldsymbol{\nu}\mathbf{h}_*(\mathbf{Y}_i, \mathbf{Q}_i, \boldsymbol{\beta}) \right] = \mathbf{0}, \quad (16.4.12)$$

which is the $(m \times 1)$ set of estimating equations defining the OptEF estimator. Then, for large enough n, the MEL or MEEL solution closely emulates the outcome of the OptEF estimator, and we expect that the sampling properties of the MEL or MEEL estimator will emulate those of the OptEF estimator as well. Indeed this is the case, as the rigorous proofs of Kitamura (1997) and Kitamura and Stutzer (1997) demonstrate – *the asymptotic properties of the MEL, MEEL and OptEF estimators are equivalent*, as (16.4.12) suggests. We provide the details of the asymptotic distribution in Section 16.4.5.

16.4.4. OptEF–Quasi–ML Approach: Asymptotic Unification of Inverse Solution Methods

The OptEF solution to the inverse problem in the case of an overdetermined nonorthogonal linear or nonlinear model is given by the solution to a just-determined set of estimating equations–moment conditions formed by the optimal $(k \times m)$ linear transformation of the original m estimating equations as follows:

$$\hat{\mathbf{b}}_{\text{opt}} \equiv \arg_{\boldsymbol{\beta}}[\mathbf{h}_{\nu}(\mathbf{y}, \mathbf{x}, \mathbf{z}, \boldsymbol{\beta}) = \mathbf{0}] = \arg_{\boldsymbol{\beta}}[\boldsymbol{\nu}\, \mathbf{h}(\mathbf{y}, \mathbf{x}, \mathbf{z}, \boldsymbol{\beta}) = \mathbf{0}] \qquad (16.4.13)$$

where

$$\mathbf{h}(\mathbf{y}, \mathbf{x}, \mathbf{z}, \boldsymbol{\beta}) \equiv n^{-1}\mathbf{z}'[\mathbf{y} - \mathbf{g}(\mathbf{x}, \boldsymbol{\beta})]. \qquad (16.4.14)$$

We know from our examination of the OptEF estimator in Chapter 11 that the (estimated) optimal linear transformation is defined by the matrix

$$\boldsymbol{\nu} \equiv \left[n^{-1} \frac{\partial \mathbf{g}(\mathbf{x}, \boldsymbol{\beta})}{\partial \boldsymbol{\beta}} \mathbf{z} \right] \mathbf{w}_*, \qquad (16.4.15)$$

where $\mathbf{w}_*^{-1} = \mathbf{cov}(n^{-1/2}\mathbf{Z}'[\mathbf{Y} - \mathbf{g}(\mathbf{X}, \boldsymbol{\beta})])$ and expectations have already been approximated by sample moments such as $\hat{\mathrm{E}}[n^{-1} \frac{\partial \mathbf{g}(\mathbf{X}, \boldsymbol{\beta})}{\partial \boldsymbol{\beta}} \mathbf{Z}] = n^{-1} \frac{\partial \mathbf{g}(\mathbf{x}, \boldsymbol{\beta})}{\partial \boldsymbol{\beta}} \mathbf{z}$. A Comparison of (16.4.13)–(16.4.15) with the first-order conditions for the linear and nonlinear GMM extremum problems given by (16.2.8) and (16.4.3) makes it apparent that the OptEF and the optimal GMM estimators coincide. If it is assumed that one uses the same consistent estimator of $\mathbf{w}_*$ in either the OptEF or GMM cases, the estimated versions of these estimators will also be identical. A case of non-iid sampling can be accommodated in the OptEF–GMM approach by using an appropriate heteroscedastic, or autocorrelation robust estimator, or both of $\mathbf{w}_*$, as discussed in Sections 16.2.2.b and 15.4. A parametric estimate of $\mathbf{w}_*$ could also be utilized if a parametric functional form were known to apply to $\mathbf{w}_*$ and the parameters could be consistently estimated (see Chapter 19). All asymptotic tests and confidence-region procedures appropriate for the OptEF context are also appropriate for the GMM context, and vice versa. Of course, the OptEF estimator also subsumes the IV approach for just-determined linear or nonlinear models as a special case (recall that the IV approach is just a special case of the GMM approach).

It is also apparent from the form of the OptEF estimating equations (16.4.13)–(16.4.15) that the OptEF–GMM estimator can be viewed as a quasi-maximum likelihood (QML) estimator of the parameter $\boldsymbol{\beta}$. The quasi-likelihood is based on a multivariate normal probability distribution for the transformed sample data $n^{-1/2}\mathbf{Z}'\mathbf{Y}$, the distribution being $\mathrm{N}(n^{-1/2}\mathbf{Z}'\mathbf{g}(\mathbf{X}, \boldsymbol{\beta}), \mathbf{w}_*)$. Thus, all tests and confidence-region procedures appropriate for the QML estimator apply. Furthermore, one can interpret the value of the OptEF–GMM–QML estimator as the choice that identifies the particular multivariate normal distribution of the form $\mathrm{N}(n^{-1/2}\mathbf{Z}'\mathbf{g}(\mathbf{X}, \boldsymbol{\beta}), \mathbf{w}_*)$ that is the closest in Kullback–Leibler distance to the true underlying distribution of $n^{-1/2}\mathbf{Z}'\mathbf{Y}$, as discussed in Section 11.2.2.

From the heuristic asymptotic argument of Section 16.4.3, and based rigorously on the work of Kitamura (1997, 1998), Kitamura and Stutzer (1997), Qin and Lawless (1994), and Imbens, Spady, and Johnson (1998), both the MEL and MEEL estimators are also asymptotically equivalent to the OptEF estimator, either in the iid or non-iid DSP cases (if it is assumed in the latter case that moment-smoothing techniques such as those described in Section 16.4.3.b are utilized when implementing MEL or MEEL). Thus, in an asymptotic context, the OptEF approach unifies all of the alternative approaches (GMM, QML, MEL, and MEEL) within one inverse problem-solution paradigm.

Implementation of the OptEF estimator in practice will be accomplished by replacing the unknown optimal linear transformation matrix ν in (16.4.15) by a consistent estimate. As noted, the parenthetical term on the right-hand side of (16.4.15) is simply evaluated at the outcome values of $\mathbf{x}$ and $\mathbf{z}$. The asymptotic covariance term underlying the definition of $\mathbf{w}_*$ must be consistently estimated. If the covariance matrix $\boldsymbol{\Phi}$ of the noise component ε is known to be of a specific parametric functional form $\boldsymbol{\Phi}(\boldsymbol{\alpha})$, and the parameters $\boldsymbol{\alpha}$ can be consistently estimated from observations on $\hat{\varepsilon}$, then $\mathbf{w}_*$ can be estimated parametrically as $\boldsymbol{\Phi}(\hat{\boldsymbol{\alpha}})$. This leads to a parametric estimate of the optimal linear transformation matrix of the form

$$\nu \equiv \left[n^{-1} \frac{\partial \mathbf{g}(\mathbf{x}, \boldsymbol{\beta})}{\partial \boldsymbol{\beta}} \mathbf{z} \right] [n^{-1}\mathbf{z}'\boldsymbol{\Phi}(\hat{\boldsymbol{\alpha}})\mathbf{z}]^{-1}. \tag{16.4.16}$$

Alternatively, $\mathbf{w}_*$ can be estimated using a heteroscedastic, or autocorrelation robust covariance matrix estimator, or both, as described in Section 15.4.

16.4.5. Asymptotic Sampling Properties and Inference

Because all of the inverse problem solutions examined above are asymptotically equivalent to the OptEF approach, all of the asymptotic testing and confidence-region generation procedures that apply to the OptEF context apply to the GMM, QML, MEL, and MEEL contexts as well. In effect, one can implement an OptEF test or confidence-region procedure but utilize GMM, QML, MEL, or MEEL estimates when calculating the outcomes of test statistics or confidence-region estimators. Then, all of the tests and confidence-region procedures discussed in Section 11.3.5 can be applied, taking proper care to replace the unknown covariance matrix utilized in the test statistics with an appropriately consistent estimator. Note further that the converse also holds – tests and confidence-region procedures appropriate for one of the other estimation procedures are asymptotically applicable to OptEF estimators as well (with p_i's replaced by n^{-1} when one attempts to utilize procedures originating in the MEL or MEEL contexts).

The asymptotic distribution of the OptEF estimator, as well as all of the other approaches asymptotically equivalent to it, can be characterized via Theorem 11.3.2, in the case of linear or nonlinear models, as

$$\hat{\boldsymbol{\beta}} \overset{a}{\sim} \mathrm{N}\left(\mathbf{0}, \left[\left(\frac{\partial \mathbf{g}(\mathbf{x}, \boldsymbol{\beta})}{\partial \boldsymbol{\beta}}\mathbf{z}\right)(\mathbf{z}'\boldsymbol{\Phi}\mathbf{z})^{-1}\left(\frac{\partial \mathbf{g}(\mathbf{x}, \boldsymbol{\beta})}{\partial \boldsymbol{\beta}}\mathbf{z}\right)'\right]^{-1}\right). \qquad (16.4.17)$$

Other representations of the asymptotic covariance matrix are possible based on the generally nonuniform sample weights used in either the MEL or MEEL contexts, and the reader is directed to Chapters 12 and 13 for details of these covariance matrix expressions.

16.4.6. Testing Moment Equation Validity

Of particular interest in the current instrumental variable-type context is the validity of the moment conditions on which the unbiased estimating equations for any of the inverse problem solutions are based. It is possible to test the validity of estimating equations used to define an OptEF estimator (or to define any of the other estimators for that matter) in the *overdetermined* case, where validity in this context means the unbiasedness of the estimating functions. The test is based on the asymptotic normal distribution of the estimating functions themselves. In particular, if $\boldsymbol{\Psi}^{-1/2}\mathbf{h}(\mathbf{Y}, \mathbf{q}, \boldsymbol{\beta}_0) \xrightarrow{d} \mathrm{N}(0, \mathbf{I})$, where $\boldsymbol{\Psi} = \mathbf{cov}[\mathbf{h}(\mathbf{Y}, \mathbf{x}, \boldsymbol{\beta}_0)] = \mathrm{E}[\mathbf{h}(\mathbf{Y}, \mathbf{x}, \boldsymbol{\beta}_0)\mathbf{h}(\mathbf{Y}, \mathbf{x}, \boldsymbol{\beta}_0)']$, as assumed in Theorem 11.3.2, then it follows via Slutsky's theorem that

$$\mathbf{h}(\mathbf{Y}, \mathbf{q}, \boldsymbol{\beta}_0)'[\mathrm{E}[\mathbf{h}(\mathbf{Y}, \mathbf{q}, \boldsymbol{\beta}_0)\mathbf{h}(\mathbf{Y}, \mathbf{q}, \boldsymbol{\beta}_0)']]^{-1}\mathbf{h}(\mathbf{Y}, \mathbf{q}, \boldsymbol{\beta}_0) \xrightarrow{d} \text{Chi-square}(\mathrm{m}, 0) \text{ under } \mathrm{H}_0. \qquad (16.4.18)$$

The expectation term in (16.4.18) can be consistently estimated by (11.3.27) in the case of independent sample observations or based on a Newey–West-type estimator to accommodate heteroscedasticity, autocorrelation, or both. If a parametric representation of the expectation term is known, a parametric estimate may be possible. Then, the term $\mathbf{h}(\mathbf{Y}, \mathbf{q}, \boldsymbol{\beta}_0)$ is replaced by the observable quantity $\mathbf{h}(\mathbf{Y}, \mathbf{q}, \hat{\boldsymbol{\beta}}_{\mathrm{EE}})$ to define an observable version of (16.4.18). However, note that there is a loss of degrees of freedom in the asymptotic Chi-square distribution of the *estimated* statistic

$$\hat{\mathrm{W}} = \mathbf{h}(\mathbf{Y}, \mathbf{q}, \hat{\boldsymbol{\beta}}_{\mathrm{EE}})'[\hat{\mathrm{E}}[\mathbf{h}(\mathbf{Y}, \mathbf{q}, \hat{\boldsymbol{\beta}}_{00})\mathbf{h}(\mathbf{Y}, \mathbf{q}, \hat{\boldsymbol{\beta}}_{00})']]^{-1}\mathbf{h}(\mathbf{Y}, \mathbf{q}, \hat{\boldsymbol{\beta}}_{\mathrm{EE}}). \qquad (16.4.19)$$

This occurs in the current application because there are k restrictions on the m estimating equations induced by applying the OptEF linear transformation $\boldsymbol{\nu}\mathbf{h}(\mathbf{y}, \mathbf{q}, \boldsymbol{\beta}) = \mathbf{0}$ to the estimating equations when solving for the OptEF estimator $\hat{\boldsymbol{\beta}}_{\mathrm{EE}}$. In effect there are only $m - k$ freely varying dimensions of the estimating equations available, and once the values of these $m - k$ of the estimating equations are known, the remaining k can be solved for through use of the k optimal linear restrictions $\boldsymbol{\nu}\mathbf{h}(\mathbf{y}, \mathbf{q}, \boldsymbol{\beta}) = \mathbf{0}$. In fact, the number of degrees of freedom is reduced by precisely the k number of equality restrictions applied to the estimated moments, leading to the asymptotic distribution $\hat{\mathrm{W}} \overset{a}{\sim} \text{Chi-square}(m - k, 0)$. The test of moment validity is then conducted in the usual way, where if the outcome exceeds the $100(1 - \alpha)\%$ quantile of the central Chi-square distribution with $m - k$ degrees of freedom, the validity of the estimating equations is rejected at the asymptotic level α.

Within the linear or nonlinear model OptEF context, an asymptotic Chi-square-distributed test of moment-equation validity can be conducted based on the statistic

$$[n^{-1}\mathbf{Z}'[\mathbf{Y} - \mathbf{g}(\mathbf{X}, \hat{\boldsymbol{\beta}}_{EE})]]'\hat{W}_*[n^{-1}\mathbf{Z}'[\mathbf{Y} - \mathbf{g}(\mathbf{X}, \hat{\boldsymbol{\beta}}_{EE})]] \xrightarrow{d} \text{Chi-square}(m-k, 0) \tag{16.4.20}$$

under H_0. We emphasize that the null hypothesis of moment-equation validity in this context refers to both the orthogonality of the instruments relative to the noise component and the proper characterization of the noise component itself in terms of $\varepsilon = \mathbf{Y} - \mathbf{g}(\mathbf{X}, \boldsymbol{\beta})$, which includes the specification of $\mathbf{g}(\mathbf{X}, \boldsymbol{\beta})$. Rejection of the null hypothesis can signal a violation in one or both of these conditions.

16.4.7. Relationship Between Estimator Efficiency and the Number and Type of Estimating Equations

We begin this subsection by emphasizing that the concept of efficiency utilized in reference to all of the preceding alternative methods of solving overdetermined, nonorthogonal inverse problems is defined *relative to a given set of moment conditions–estimating equations*. For a specific empirical problem in which the moment information is stated and given, the procedures we have discussed above make asymptotically optimal use of the information. This means we are working with optimal information-processing rules, and this is a very important and useful property for any estimator to possess. Fortunately, the alternative estimators discussed in this chapter possess this property.

A different important model specification question relates to the choice of the moment conditions. In the current context this is tantamount to asking which instrumental variables should be used in specifying the initial set of estimating equations. A related question along these lines is, How many estimating equations or instrumental variables should be used; that is, are more better than less? We address these questions in reverse order.

Regarding the number of estimating equations or instruments to use, asymptotic efficiency comparisons suggest more is better than less. Before motivating this statement further, we note that the question may be moot in any given application if the analyst is using all of the information at his or her disposal and there is no prospect of increasing the information base further. Presuming the idea of considering additional moment conditions–instruments is relevant, consider with reference to linear models and (16.4.17) the case in which $\mathbf{Z}_*$ is a full-column rank matrix of instrumental variables that is equal to the instrumental variable matrix $\mathbf{Z}$ plus an *additional* one or more columns of variables. Then

$$[(\mathbf{x}'\mathbf{z})(\mathbf{z}'\boldsymbol{\Phi}\mathbf{z})^{-1}(\mathbf{x}'\mathbf{z})']^{-1} - [(\mathbf{x}'\mathbf{z}_*)(\mathbf{z}_*'\boldsymbol{\Phi}\mathbf{z}_*)^{-1}(\mathbf{x}'\mathbf{z}_*)']^{-1} \tag{16.4.21}$$

is positive semidefinite, implying that the estimator based on the larger set of estimating equations–moment conditions is asymptotically more efficient.

Unfortunately, it is not necessarily the case that more instruments–estimating equations are better than less in terms of finite sampling properties. In fact, there is a tendency for finite sample bias to increase as more estimating equations are used for estimation.

This tendency is perhaps clearest to see in the case of the linear model and the OptEF estimator (16.1.6). Note that we can rewrite this estimator as

$$\begin{aligned}\hat{\boldsymbol{\beta}}_{\text{EE}} &= [\mathbf{X}'\mathbf{Z}(\mathbf{Z}'\mathbf{Z})^{-1}\mathbf{Z}'\mathbf{Z}(\mathbf{Z}'\mathbf{Z})^{-1}\mathbf{Z}'\mathbf{X}]^{-1}\mathbf{X}'\mathbf{Z}(\mathbf{Z}'\mathbf{Z})^{-1}\mathbf{Z}'\mathbf{Y} \\ &= (\hat{\mathbf{X}}'\hat{\mathbf{X}})^{-1}\hat{\mathbf{X}}'\mathbf{Y}, \qquad (16.4.22)\end{aligned}$$

where $\hat{\mathbf{X}} \equiv \mathbf{Z}(\mathbf{Z}'\mathbf{Z})^{-1}\mathbf{Z}'\mathbf{X}$ is effectively the prediction of $\mathbf{X}$ based on a linear least-squares fit utilizing explanatory variables $\mathbf{Z}$. It is clear that the more explanatory variables contained in $\mathbf{Z}$, the better the prediction of $\mathbf{X}$, and the predictions will be perfect if $m = n$. Thus, by adding instruments, the OptEF estimator eventually emulates a least-squares procedure applied to explanatory variables that are equal to the $\mathbf{X}$ variables themselves, which, if the original model is nonorthogonal, exhibits the full least-squares bias that the approaches in this chapter were designed to mitigate. Unfortunately, the number of instruments required to optimize finite-sample properties of the estimator cannot be calculated because the finite-sample properties of the estimators are generally not calculable. Some degree of judgment by the analyst in terms of the reasonableness of the resulting estimates is inescapable if there is a large set of estimating equations–instruments from which to choose. We address this issue further in the next chapter.

Regarding the question of which instruments to use in a given inverse problem, we first note that *theoretically*, there is a *globally* optimal set of instruments $\mathbf{Z}_*$ that is precisely equal in dimension to the dimension of the $\mathbf{X}$ matrix. The ith column of this optimal set in the case of the linear model is defined by

$$\mathbf{Z}_*[.,i] \equiv \mathbf{X}[.,i] - \mathbf{cov}(\mathbf{X}[.,i], \mathbf{Y} - \mathbf{X}\boldsymbol{\beta}_0)\boldsymbol{\Phi}^{-1}(\mathbf{Y} - \mathbf{X}\boldsymbol{\beta}_0), \qquad (16.4.23)$$

where $\boldsymbol{\beta}_0$ denotes the true value of the parameter vector (Singh and Rao, 1998, Section 3.3). The use of this optimal set of instruments for $\mathbf{Z}$ in any of the procedures that we have reviewed in this chapter results in an estimator with the smallest asymptotic covariance matrix among all possible choices for the moment conditions–estimating equations derived from moments of the form $\mathrm{E}[\mathbf{Z}'(\mathbf{Y} - \mathbf{X}\boldsymbol{\beta})] = \mathbf{0}$.

Unfortunately, these optimal instruments are not observable and are also generally not even estimable because they depend not only on the true value of $\boldsymbol{\beta}$ but also on the inverse covariance matrix $\boldsymbol{\Phi}^{-1}$. Consistent estimators for the covariance matrix do not generally exist unless a parametric functional form for $\boldsymbol{\Phi}$ is known that can be consistently estimated. Furthermore, the covariance matrix between $\mathbf{X}[.,i]$ and $\varepsilon = \mathbf{Y} - \mathbf{X}\boldsymbol{\beta}_0$ is unobservable and inestimable except under substantial parametric restrictions requiring knowledge not generally available in practice. As a very special case, note that in the orthogonal situation, the latter covariance matrix is the zero matrix. Thus, the optimal instruments implied by (16.4.23) are $\mathbf{Z}_* \equiv \mathbf{X}$, and this leads to the ordinary least-squares result in the linear model case under standard assumptions. Extensions of this argument to the nonlinear model case follow directly upon replacing $\mathbf{X}\boldsymbol{\beta}$ with $\mathbf{g}(\mathbf{X}, \boldsymbol{\beta})$ and replacing $\mathbf{X}[.,i]$ with $\frac{\partial \mathbf{g}(\mathbf{X}, \boldsymbol{\beta})'}{\partial \boldsymbol{\beta}_i}$. Singh and Rao (1998, p. 188) use the concept of optimal instruments to define a relative efficiency measure for a given estimator derived from instrument-based moment conditions.

In practice, because the optimal instruments are unobservable and also generally inestimable, instruments must be obtained elsewhere. We have discussed the sampling properties that are required of such instruments. In the next chapter, we discuss further the possible origin of such instruments.

► **Example 16.4.1:** To demonstrate the impact of adding additional instruments in the orthogonal case, we provide the GAUSS program C16ORTH.gss in the examples manual. To begin, GAUSS uses the 2sls() procedure (constructed in Example 16.1.1) to compute OptEF estimates of $\boldsymbol{\beta}$ using several sets of instrumental variables $\mathbf{Z}$, including $\mathbf{Z} = \mathbf{X}$. Then, the program conducts a Monte Carlo simulation exercise designed to approximate the sampling properties of the OptEF estimators based on various numbers of instruments (samples sizes and m selected by the user). The user should find that the simulation results confirm that the addition of instrumental variables ($m > k$) does not improve the performance of the estimator relative to $\mathbf{Z} = \mathbf{X}$.

16.5. Concluding Comments

In this chapter we have enlarged the set of estimation and inference procedures to include methods based on sets of overdetermined moment conditions–estimating equations that do not rely on strong distributional assumptions. In this context, we examined estimators under the conditions that the orthogonality assumption $E[\mathbf{X}'\boldsymbol{\varepsilon}] = \mathbf{0}$, the iid sampling condition *do* and *do not* hold, or all of these conditions. In each case, the estimators are, in general, functions of sample moments, have the desirable properties of consistency and asymptotic normality, and also are asymptotically efficient under certain problem conditions. Hypothesis-testing and confidence-region estimation followed the usual asymptotic approach based on the asymptotic normality of the estimators.

Using the theory of estimating equations as a unifying principle, and introducing the concept of instrumental variables, this chapter has provided a review of efficient estimation and inference procedures for just-determined and overdetermined models in iid and non-iid sample settings. In the traditional GMM approach for solving either the orthogonal or nonorthogonal overdetermined inverse problem, a two-step procedure is used in which the optimal weighting matrix is estimated from the sample data in the first step. The GMM estimator is asymptotically optimal, but the finite sample properties of the estimator can be sensitive to how the optimal weighting matrix is estimated from the data. Finite sample properties of GMM estimators are not well-understood, and how these properties compare with the finite sampling properties of alternative estimators is an area of ongoing research.

Alternative empirical likelihood procedures (MEL and MEEL) were introduced for solving orthogonal or nonorthogonal overdetermined systems of estimating equations. These methods are one-step procedures based on generalized moment conditions–estimating equations defined in terms of differential nonuniform sample weights. In the case of independent sample observations, these one-step empirical likelihood methods do not require any preestimation of weighting matrices or specification of any other user-defined constants or parameters in their implementation. Furthermore, they result in consistent and asymptotically normally distributed estimators even if the observations are heteroscedastic. However, given current known results, achieving asymptotic efficiency requires either that the data-sampling process be iid or else that the user employ moment-smoothing techniques. Although asymptotic efficiency will be achieved over a wide range of different smoothing techniques, the finite sample sensitivity of the estimators to the pattern of moving average weights used in the smoothing is currently not well understood.

The OptEF estimation procedure is another alternative method for solving orthogonal or nonorthogonal overdetermined estimating equations systems. *The OptEF approach utilizes an optimal linear combination of the overdetermined estimating equations to define a transformed just-determined set of estimating equations that can be solved directly for the asymptotically optimal estimator of* $\boldsymbol{\beta}$. The best candidates from among the GMM, MEL, and MEEL classes of procedures for solving overdetermined inverse problems for either linear or nonlinear models are asymptotically equivalent to the OptEF approach. This means that all of the alternative procedures inherit the asymptotic optimality property of OptEF, and the OptEF procedure subsumes the alternatives asymptotically. However, like the GMM approach, empirical implementation of the OptEF approach generally requires a two-step procedure in which the optimal linear transformation matrix must be consistently estimated from the data in the first step. The finite sample sensitivity of the OptEF estimator to the choice of the first step estimator is not well understood.

Overall, the procedures examined in this section represent a useful collection of methods that allow estimation of β to proceed in linear or nonlinear models under relatively weak distributional assumptions in which regressors may or may not be stochastic, orthogonality conditions may not hold, and the data-sampling process may not be iid. There are some unresolved questions relating to the finite sample properties of the estimators relative to each other and relative to the choice of first-step estimation or moment-smoothing procedures used in the definition of the estimators. However these questions disappear as sample sizes increase, for all approaches make optimal use of the moment information for solving the inverse problem for large enough samples of data.

Using the data based information theoretic estimation model in section 13.6, van Akkeren, Judge and Mittelhammer (1999) have developed a generalized moment based estimator (GMBE) that, relative to traditional competitions, provides an improved basis for estimation and inference. The estimating criterion for the GMB formulation provides for the possibility of a dual loss function. The risk gains of GMBE appear to be especially significant when the variables in statistical model of the system of interest are highly correlated, a situation normally found in economic practice.

We should note that the emphasis in this chapter has been with just and over determined specifications. There is the nagging question concerning what can be said in an estimation and inference context if the moment conditions are under determined. There is a growing literature and this and some alternative formulations for coping with this type of ill-posed inverse problem are discussed in electronic Chapter E3.

In the chapter ahead we consider the simultaneous equation econometric model that involves an instantaneous feedback mechanism among some of the model variables and provides a basis for defining the origin of instrumental variables. Fortunately, the framework developed in this chapter provides us with a modern way to think about and analyze this econometric model involving endogenous, jointly determined variables and a system of simultaneous stochastic relationships that define the underlying sample data.

16.6. Exercises

16.4.1. Idea Checklist – Knowledge Guides

---

1. What do you see as the statistical implications of the fact that most estimators are functions of moment-based sample information?
2. What is the primary motivation for defining estimation and testing procedures in terms of solutions to moment-type equations?
3. Does the analyst lose information, or condition the type of information that can be recovered, when he or she transforms from the data to the moments and utilizes only moment information in the definition of estimators and testing procedures?
4. What is an instrumental variable, and what is instrumental about its purpose?
5. What is the rationale underlying Hansen and Sargent's (1980) use of moment estimating functions in their estimation work?
6. Does efficient information recovery in essence involve how best to weight or reweight the data, the moments, or both?

16.4.2. Problems

16–1 Demonstrate that the choice of weight matrix $\mathbf{w}$ in (16.2.9) that results in an estimator with the smallest asymptotic covariance matrix is given by $\mathbf{w} = [\mathbf{cov}(n^{-1/2}\mathbf{Z}'\varepsilon)]^{-1}$.

16–2 Demonstrate that the asymptotic covariance matrix of the EOGMM indicated in (16.2.33) is smaller than the asymptotic covariance matrix of the GMM indicated in (16.2.32) by a positive semidefinite matrix.

16–3 Define how you would generate a consistent estimate of the optimal weight matrix for the EOGMM estimator in the case in which the noise component is subject to heteroscedasticity and autocorrelation of unknown and unspecified form.

16–4 Suppose that you want to estimate the unknown parameters of a consumption function represented by

$$\mathrm{c}_t^* = \beta_1 + \beta_2 \mathrm{y}_t^* + \varepsilon_t,$$

where c_t^* and y_t^* denote the true but unobservable levels of consumption and income, respectively. Observable values of consumption and income are subject to measurement errors as represented by

$$\mathrm{c}_t = \mathrm{c}_t^* + \mathrm{v}_t \quad \text{and} \quad \mathrm{y}_t = \mathrm{y}_t^* + \mathrm{w}_t,$$

where v_t and w_t, $i = 1, \ldots, n$, are each iid outcomes from some probability distribution having mean zero.

a. Can the parameters of the consumption function be consistently estimated based on the observable data relating to consumption and income?

b. Describe how you would estimate the parameters of the model if the two instruments i_t (investment) and g_t (government spending) were available.

16–5 Prove that Equation (16.4.21) is positive semidefinite.

16.4.3. Computer Exercises

---

1. For a linear regression model, suppose we conduct a Wald test of the hypothesis H_0: $\boldsymbol{\beta} = \mathbf{0}$ based on the LS estimator when $E[\mathbf{X}'\boldsymbol{\varepsilon}] \neq \mathbf{0}$. How will this test perform in repeated samples? To assist you in answering the question, conduct a Monte Carlo exercise designed to simulate the null distribution of the Wald test statistic as well as the power function.
2. Using the 2sls() or IV() procedures developed in this chapter, write a GAUSS program designed to simulate the sampling properties of the OptEF (16.1.6) or instrumental variable (IV) estimators for a particular linear regression model.
3. Extend the GAUSS program provided for Example 16.1.2 (C16HS.gss) to compute the parameter estimates by MEL and MEEL. Also, for a relatively small sample size (n), simulate the sampling properties of the OptEF, MEL, and MEEL by paired bootstrap resampling. How well do the estimators compare? Next, simulate the DSP by Monte Carlo replication and compare the estimators as n increases. Do your findings agree with the claim that the three estimators are asymptotically equivalent?
4. On the basis of Example 16.2.2, test the null hypothesis H_0: $\alpha = -1$ (i.e., risk neutrality) under the Z-test criterion. Use a Monte Carlo exercise to simulate the power function for the Z-test. Repeat the simulation exercise for the one-sided null hypothesis H_0: $\alpha < -1$ (i.e., risk aversion).

16.7. References

van Akkeren, M., G. Judge, and R. Mettelhammer (1999), "Generalized Moment Based Estimation and Inference," working paper, University of California, Berkeley.

Andrews, D. W. K. (1999), "Consistent Moment Selection Procedures for Generalized Method of Moments Estimation," *Econometrica*, 67, pp. 543–64.

Andrews, D. W. K. (1991a), "Heteroskedasticity and Autocorrelation Consistent Covariance Matrix Estimation," *Econometrica*, Vol. 59, pp. 817–58.

Andrews, D. W. K. (1991b), "An Empirical Process Central Limit Theorem for Dependent Nonidentically Distributed Random Variables," *Journal of Multivariate Analysis*, Vol. 38, pp. 187–203.

Bates, C., and H. White (1985), "A Unified Theory of Consistent Estimation for Parametric Models," *Econometric Theory*, Vol. 1, pp. 151–78.

Bates, C., and H. White (1988), "Efficient Instrumental Variable Estimation of Systems of Implicit Heterogeneous Nonlinear Dynamic Equations with Nonspherical Errors," in W. A. Barnett, E. R. Berndt, and H. White (Eds.), *Proceedings of the Third International Symposium in Economic Theory and Econometrics*, pp. 3–26.

Bowden, R. J., and D. A. Turkington (1984), *Instrumental Variables*, Cambridge, UK: Cambridge University Press.

Gallant, R. (1987), *Nonlinear Statistical Models*, New York: John Wiley and Sons.

Gallant, R., and H. White (1988), *A Unified Theory of Estimation and Inference for Nonlinear Dynamic Models*, Oxford, UK: Basil Blackwell.

Godambe, V., and C. Heyde (1987), "Quasi-likelihood and Optimal Estimation," *International Statistical Review*, Vol. 55, pp. 231–44.

Hansen, L. (1982), "Large Sample Properties of Generalized Method of Moments Estimators," *Econometrica*, Vol. 50, pp. 1029–54.

Hansen, L., and T. Sargent (1980), "Formulating and Estimating Dynamic Linear Rational Expectations Models," *Journal of Economic Dynamics and Control*, Vol. 2, pp. 7–46.

Hansen, L., and K. Singleton (1982), "Generalized Instrumental Variables Estimators of Nonlinear Rational Expectations Models," *Econometrica*, Vol. 50, pp. 1269–86.

Hansen, L., P. J. Heaton, and A. Yaron (1996), "Finite Sample Properties of Some Alternative GMM Estimators," *Journal of Business and Economic Statistics*, Vol. 14, pp. 262–80.

Imbens, G. W., R. H. Spady, and P. Johnson (1998), "Information Theoretic Approaches to Inference in Moment Condition Models," *Econometrica*, Vol. 66, pp. 333–57.

Kitamura, Y. (1997), "Empirical Likelihood Methods with Weakly Dependent Processes," *Annals of Statistics*, Vol. 25, pp. 2084–2102.

Kitamura, Y. (1998), "Empirical Likelihood and the Bootstrap for Time Series Regressors," working paper, January, Department of Economics, University of Wisconsin.

Kitamura, Y., and M. Stutzer (1997), "An Information–Theoretic Alternative to Generalized Method of Moments Estimation," *Econometrica*, Vol. 65, pp. 861–74.

Mittelhammer, R. C. (1996), *Mathematical Statistics for Economics and Business*, New York: Springer–Verlag.

Nelder, J. A., and Y. Lee (1992), "Likelihood, Quasi-likelihood and Pseudo-likelihood: Some Comparisons," *Journal of the Royal Statistical Society, Series B*, Vol. 54, pp. 273–84.

Newey, W., and D. McFadden (1994), "Estimation in Large Samples," In R. Engle and D. McFadden (Eds.), *Handbook of Econometrics, Vol. IV*, pp. 2111–245, Amsterdam: North–Holland.

Qin, J., and J. Lawless (1994), "Empirical Likelihood and General Estimating Equations," *Annals of Statistics*, Vol. 22, pp. 300–25.

Reirsol, O. (1941), "Confluence Analysis by Means of Lag Moments and Other Methods of Confluence Analysis," *Econometrica*, Vol. 9, pp. 1–24.

Singh, A. C., and R. P. Rao (1998), "Optimal Instrumental Variable Estimation for Linear Models with Stochastic Regressors Using Estimating Functions," in Godambe, V. P. (ed.), Institute of Mathematical Statistics Symposium on Estimating Functions, N.Y., pp. 177–92.

White, H. (1984), Asymptotic Theory for Econometricians, Academic Press, Orlando, FL.

White, H. (1994), *Estimation, Inference and Specification Analysis*, New York: Cambridge University Press.

CHAPTER 17

Simultaneous Equations Econometric Models: Estimation and Inference

IN Chapter 16 we considered the interesting modeling situation in which the orthogonality condition $E[\mathbf{X}'\boldsymbol{\varepsilon}] = \mathbf{0}$ was *not* satisfied. In this case instrumental variables were used to define unbiased estimating equation–moment conditions that led to estimates of the unknown parameters that had often asymptotically optimal sampling properties. An important question that arises when implementing instrumental variable-based procedures is, where do (instrumental) variables that are correlated with the **X**'s but uncorrelated with the noise components come from? In this chapter we provide a conceptual basis for defining these variables that links them, in terms of econometric history, to a very important probability–econometric model. The resulting econometric model was developed from the idea that the sampling process underlying the observed economic data can be viewed as coming from a system of economic relations that are stochastic, possibly dynamic, and simultaneous. If the results of econometric analyses are to reflect desirable properties in estimation and inference, there must be consistency between the statistical model employed and the underlying data-sampling process, and thus a variety of simultaneous equation statistical models have emerged.

Although the resulting probability models were capable of reflecting the stochastic, dynamic, and simultaneous nature of economic data, it was the instantaneous feedback and jointly interdependent nature of the economic data-sampling processes that were the principal foci of model development efforts in this area. For example, partial equilibrium econometric models involving a demand and supply relation and a relation to express the equilibrium condition for the market became a way to characterize an instantaneous feedback sampling process and to frame the corresponding estimation and inference problem. As a case in point, consider the following equilibrium demand and supply system of equations:

$$\mathbf{Y}_1 = \mathbf{Y}_3\gamma_1 + \mathbf{X}_1\boldsymbol{\beta}_1 + \boldsymbol{\varepsilon}_1 = \mathbf{M}_1\boldsymbol{\delta}_1 + \boldsymbol{\varepsilon}_1 \qquad (17.0.1)$$

$$\mathbf{Y}_2 = \mathbf{Y}_3\gamma_2 + \mathbf{X}_2\boldsymbol{\beta}_2 + \boldsymbol{\varepsilon}_2 = \mathbf{M}_2\boldsymbol{\delta}_2 + \boldsymbol{\varepsilon}_2 \qquad (17.0.2)$$

$$\mathbf{Y}_1 = \mathbf{Y}_2, \qquad (17.0.3)$$

where $E[\varepsilon_1] = E[\varepsilon_2] = \mathbf{0}$, $\mathbf{cov}(\varepsilon_1) = \sigma_1^2\mathbf{I}$, $\mathbf{cov}(\varepsilon_2) = \sigma_2^2\mathbf{I}$, $\mathbf{Y}_1$ and $\mathbf{Y}_2$ represent quantity demanded and supplied, $\boldsymbol{\delta}_i \equiv [\gamma_i, \boldsymbol{\beta}_i']'$, $\mathbf{Y}_3$ represents the price variable, $\mathbf{M}_1 \equiv [\mathbf{Y}_3, \mathbf{X}_1]$ and $\mathbf{M}_2 \equiv [\mathbf{Y}_3, \mathbf{X}_2]$ represent the model's right-hand-side explanatory variables residing in Equations (17.0.1) and (17.0.2) respectively, and $\mathbf{X}_1$ and $\mathbf{X}_2$ are explanatory variable matrices that appear in the respective equations *and that are orthogonal* to the noise components of each equation. The equation system (17.0.1)–(17.0.3) jointly determines the values of $\mathbf{Y} \equiv [\mathrm{Y}_1, \mathrm{Y}_2, \mathrm{Y}_3]$ in terms of both the values of the explanatory variables $\mathbf{X} = [\mathbf{X}_1, \mathbf{X}_2]$ and values of the noise components $\varepsilon \equiv [\varepsilon_1, \varepsilon_2]$. In particular, note that if we set (17.0.1) and (17.0.2) equal to each other, which is admissible by (17.0.3), and solve for $\mathbf{Y}_3$, it is apparent that $\mathbf{Y}_3$ is a function of *both* ε_1 and ε_2 as follows:

$$\mathbf{Y}_3 = (\gamma_1 - \gamma_2)^{-1}[\mathbf{X}_2\boldsymbol{\beta}_2 - \mathbf{X}_1\boldsymbol{\beta}_1 + \varepsilon_2 - \varepsilon_1]. \tag{17.0.4}$$

The values of $\mathbf{Y}_1$ and $\mathbf{Y}_2$ can then be determined by substituting (17.0.4) into (17.0.1) and (17.0.2).

Because $\mathbf{M}_1$ and $\mathbf{M}_2$ contain a variable $\mathbf{Y}_3$ that is jointly dependent with the left-hand variables and, moreover, is functionally dependent on $\varepsilon \equiv [\varepsilon_1, \varepsilon_2]$, the orthogonality conditions $E[\mathbf{M}_1'\varepsilon_1] = \mathbf{0}$ and $E[\mathbf{M}_2'\varepsilon_2] = \mathbf{0}$ *do not hold.* Thus, if we proceed in a traditional way to use ordinary least-squares procedures to recover $\boldsymbol{\delta}_1$ and $\boldsymbol{\delta}_2$ from the data, the resulting estimators would be biased *and* inconsistent. However, if we interpret the explanatory variables $\mathbf{X}_1$ and $\mathbf{X}_2$ as instrumental variables in the context of Chapter 16, this should point to estimating-moment equation possibilities for coping with the estimation and inference problems underlying statistical models of this type. To place the econometric models and procedures discussed in this chapter into historical perspective, a brief historical view of economics and econometrics during thc birth of simultaneous-equations statistical models is given in the chapter appendix.

In the sections ahead we first focus on economic models that involve an instantaneous feedback mechanism and the underlying data-sampling process that it implies. We then state what this means in terms of probability–econometric models and investigate traditional and nontraditional estimation and inference procedures that may be used to solve associated inverse problems. The general class of probability models that we will be concerned with are identified in Table 17.1. As usual, the inverse problems we investigate involve recovering the unknown unobservables from the observables – the data.

17.1. Linear Simultaneous Equations Models

In this section we specify a basic linear probability–econometric model that is consistent with a simultaneous equations data-sampling process (DSP). This implies that we visualize the outcomes of economic variables as being simultaneously determined by a system of economic relations. This is the type of situation that economists analyze in partial equilibrium, general equilibrium, and aggregate economic settings in which

Table 17.1. *Simultaneous Equations Regression Models*

Model Component	Specific Characteristics	
$\mathbf{Y}$	RV Type:	continuous
	Range:	unlimited
	$\mathbf{Y}_i$ dimension:	multivariate
	Moments:	$\mathrm{E}[\mathbf{Y} \mid \mathbf{X}] = \mathbf{X}\boldsymbol{\pi}(\boldsymbol{\delta})$ or $\mathbf{g}(\mathbf{X}, \boldsymbol{\delta}, \boldsymbol{\varphi})$
		$\mathbf{cov}(\mathbf{Y}) = \boldsymbol{\Psi}_{\mathbf{Y}}$
$\eta(\mathbf{X}, \boldsymbol{\delta}, \boldsymbol{\varepsilon})$	Functional	$\eta(\mathbf{X}, \boldsymbol{\delta}, \boldsymbol{\varepsilon}) = \mathbf{X}\boldsymbol{\pi}(\boldsymbol{\delta}) + \mathbf{V}(\boldsymbol{\varepsilon})$ (linear model)
	Form:	$\eta(\mathbf{X}, \boldsymbol{\delta}, \boldsymbol{\varepsilon})$ (nonlinear model)
$\mathbf{X}$	RV Type:	stochastic or degenerate
	Genesis:	predetermined
$\boldsymbol{\beta}$	RV Type:	degenerate (fixed)
	Dimension:	finite
$\boldsymbol{\varepsilon}$	RV Type:	iid, or non-iid
	Moments:	$\mathrm{E}[\boldsymbol{\varepsilon} \mid \mathbf{X}] = \mathbf{0}$, and $\mathbf{cov}(\boldsymbol{\varepsilon} \mid \mathbf{X}) = \boldsymbol{\Psi}_{\boldsymbol{\varepsilon}}$
Ω	Prior info:	none
$\mathrm{f}(\mathbf{e} \mid \mathbf{x}, \boldsymbol{\varphi})$	PDF family:	unspecified or specified

the economic variable outcomes are jointly or interdependently determined. In this context, interdependence and instantaneous feedback determine outcomes for a set of dependent variables. We now visualize in detail a probability–econometric model that involves the following:

1. *Endogenous variables*, whose outcomes are jointly or interdependently determined within the system through interaction with other variables in the system. Examples are prices and quantities in a market in which supply and demand are simultaneously determined.
2. *Exogenous variables*, whose outcome values are determined outside and independently of the simultaneous system under study but that condition the outcome of the endogenous variables.
3. *Predetermined variables*, including such variables as lagged endogenous variables and exogenous variables whose values in the current period are predetermined and unaffected by outcomes of noise components in the current and future periods.
4. Unobservable equation noise.

Thus, we envision a system of equations in which two or more economic variables are determined jointly within the system as functions of exogenous variables, predetermined variables and equation noise. We now examine how to use the data in the representation of the joint distribution of the endogenous variables, conditional on exogenous or predetermined variables, or both, to solve inverse problems.

To represent the simultaneous equations associated with a DSP, consider the following linear statistical model:

$$\mathbf{Y\Gamma} = \mathbf{XB} + \varepsilon, \tag{17.1.1}$$

where $\mathbf{Y}$ is a $(n \times q)$ matrix of n potential outcomes on q observable jointly determined–endogenous random variables; $\mathbf{X}$ is a $(n \times k)$ matrix of observable or known explanatory–exogenous, predetermined, or both variables; ε is now a $(n \times q)$ *matrix* of unobservable random variables (noise components), and $\mathbf{\Gamma}$ and $\mathbf{B}$ are $(q \times q)$ and $(k \times q)$ matrices of unknown parameters, respectively. Given this specification and the preceding definitions, assume the following initially:

1. The $(1 \times q)$ random noise vectors $\varepsilon[i, .]$, for $i = 1, \ldots, n$, are iid with mean vector zero and have an unknown positive definite contemporaneous $(q \times q)$ covariance matrix $\mathbf{\Sigma}$. Thus, $\mathrm{E}[\varepsilon] = \mathbf{0}$ and $\mathrm{E}[\varepsilon[i, \cdot]'\varepsilon[i, \cdot]] = \mathrm{E}[n^{-1}\varepsilon'\varepsilon] = \mathbf{\Sigma}$.
2. The explanatory variables $\mathbf{X}[i, .]$ and the equation noise vector $\varepsilon[i + j, \cdot]$ are statistically independent $\forall j \geq 0$ so that $\mathrm{E}[\varepsilon[i + j, \cdot] \,|\, \mathbf{X}[i, \cdot]] = \mathbf{0}, \forall j \geq 0$. This independence condition for $j \geq 0$ is the fundamental characterization of *predetermined variables*. The set of predetermined variables subsumes *exogenous variables* as well, which are variables that are fully independent of the noise component. That is, $\mathbf{X}[\cdot, j]$ is an *exogenous variable* if $\mathbf{X}[\cdot, j]$ and ε are statistically independent, and thus $\mathrm{E}[\varepsilon[i + j, \cdot] \,|\, \mathbf{X}[i, \cdot]] = \mathbf{0}, \forall j$.
3. The explanatory variables $\mathbf{X}$ have rank k and $\mathrm{plim}[n^{-1}\mathbf{X}'\mathbf{X}]$ exists as a finite positive definite symmetric matrix, say $\mathbf{q}_{\mathrm{xx}}$.
4. The $(q \times q)$ parameter matrix $\mathbf{\Gamma}$ is nonsingular.

For future reference, note that the preceding assumptions imply that $\mathrm{p\,lim}(n^{-1}\mathbf{X}'\varepsilon) = \mathrm{E}[n^{-1}\mathbf{X}'\varepsilon] = \mathbf{0}$. As we work our way through a range of estimation and inference problems, we will weaken or strengthen some of these assumptions. For example, we will later add the assumption that the random noise is multivariate normally distributed, and we will relax the iid assumption of the rows of ε.

In the structural equation model (17.1.1) there are $q^2 + qk$ unknown parameters and q equations, not counting the $q(q+1)/2$ unknown parameters in the symmetric contemporaneous covariance matrix $\mathbf{\Sigma}$. Under traditional methods of estimating the unknown parameters, additional structure or restrictions must be imposed on the equations to estimate the unknown parameters. One restriction that involves no loss of generality is to *normalize* $\mathbf{\Gamma}$ by setting $\Gamma_{\mathrm{ii}} = 1$ for $i = 1, 2, \ldots, q$. That is, we assume the diagonal elements of $\mathbf{\Gamma}$ take on unit values, which produce an observationally equivalent set of equations with fewer unknowns, $(q^2 + qk - q)$. Note that the normalization may be accomplished by dividing each equation by the associated Γ_{ii}, and thus the restriction also rescales the contemporaneous covariance matrix Σ of the noise component if the value of Γ_{ii} was not originally equal to 1. Any additional parameter restrictions must come from a priori knowledge concerning the parameters $\mathbf{\Gamma}$ and $\mathbf{B}$ and the covariance structure of ε.

For a specific example of a linear simultaneous equations model, consider the following model specification in which the parameters have been rescaled by normalizing the coefficient of one endogenous variable in each equation to 1 and in which some parameter values have been set to zero a priori:

$$\begin{aligned}
\mathbf{Y}_{\cdot 1} + \mathbf{Y}_{\cdot 2}\gamma_{21} + \mathbf{0} &= \mathbf{X}_{\cdot 1}\beta_{11} + \mathbf{0} + \mathbf{X}_{\cdot 3}\beta_{31} + \mathbf{0} + \mathbf{X}_{\cdot 5}\beta_{51} + \boldsymbol{\varepsilon}_{\cdot 1} \\
\mathbf{Y}_{\cdot 1}\gamma_{12} + \mathbf{Y}_{\cdot 2} + \mathbf{Y}_{\cdot 3}\gamma_{32} &= \mathbf{X}_{\cdot 1}\beta_{12} + \mathbf{X}_{\cdot 2}\beta_{22} + \mathbf{0} + \mathbf{0} + \mathbf{X}_{\cdot 5}\beta_{52} + \boldsymbol{\varepsilon}_{\cdot 2} \\
\mathbf{Y}_{\cdot 1}\gamma_{13} + \mathbf{0} + \mathbf{Y}_{\cdot 3} &= \mathbf{X}_{\cdot 1}\beta_{13} + \mathbf{0} + \mathbf{X}_{\cdot 3}\beta_{33} + \mathbf{X}_{\cdot 4}\beta_{43} + \mathbf{0} + \boldsymbol{\varepsilon}_{\cdot 3}
\end{aligned} \tag{17.1.2}$$

We pause here to consider what is implied by the DSP characterized by the model (17.1.1) or (17.1.2) and the assumption set on which it is built. One fact that distinguishes (17.1.2) from models in earlier chapters is that there is a distinct difference in the direction of any causality relating to the sampling process underlying the economic data. Obviously, this is not a statistical model that would be useful in any experiment in which the outcomes of $\mathbf{Y}_{\cdot 1}$, $\mathbf{Y}_{\cdot 2}$, and $\mathbf{Y}_{\cdot 3}$ appear to be process or time-ordered. Rather, we now envision a sampling situation in which economic data are outcomes of experiments carried out by society and result in observable economic variables such as prices, quantities, consumption, and income that are jointly and interdependently determined within the time frame of an observation. Thus, it is a statistical model consistent with the notion that the sampling process underlying the economic data is described by a system of concurrent, interdependent economic relations. Consequently, the endogenous nature of sample outcomes should be taken into account in the estimation and inference process. In the context of (17.1.2), the sample outcomes of $\mathbf{Y}_{\cdot 1}$, $\mathbf{Y}_{\cdot 2}$, and $\mathbf{Y}_{\cdot 3}$ are envisioned as occurring *simultaneously*.

To achieve a greater appreciation for what is implied by a simultaneous equations model, it would be useful at this point for the reader to consider a micro or macro economic problem of interest and write down an econometric model that expresses the corresponding simultaneous, stochastic, and possibly dynamic DSP. After having specified one or more econometric models consistent with the DSP (17.1.1), and upon achieving an appreciation for the interdependent, simultaneous nature of these types of sampling processes, one is naturally led to the question of how to recover information about the unknown parameters from a sample of observables from such a process. Before facing this interesting estimation problem, we examine how to rewrite (17.1.1) in two equivalent and useful ways.

17.1.1. An Equivalent Vectorized System of Equations

Because not all variables appear in every equation, some of the elements in $\boldsymbol{\Gamma}$ and $\mathbf{B}$ are zero, and these zero values are often referred to as *exclusion restrictions* because they effectively exclude variables from one or more equations in the system. In this context, we can rewrite (17.1.1) in a more familiar form so that the left-hand side is a column vector rather than a matrix. Not counting the normalized (to 1) coefficient in each equation, let $-\boldsymbol{\gamma}_i$ be those elements in the ith column of $\boldsymbol{\Gamma}$ that are *nonzero*, which correspond to all of the endogenous variables, other than the one with the normalized coefficient ($\mathbf{Y}_{\cdot i}$), that appear in the ith equation. Likewise, let $\boldsymbol{\beta}_i$ be those parameters in the ith column of $\mathbf{B}$ that are *nonzero*, which are the coefficients of the predetermined–explanatory variables that appear in the ith equation. For example, $-\boldsymbol{\gamma}_2' = [\gamma_{12}, \gamma_{32}]$

from the second column of the matrix $\boldsymbol{\Gamma}$ and $\boldsymbol{\beta}_2' = [\beta_{12}, \beta_{22}, \beta_{52}]$ from the second column of $\mathbf{B}$ in (17.1.2).

Accordingly, letting $\mathbf{Y}_{(i)}$ and $\mathbf{X}_{(i)}$ represent the matrices of endogenous and predetermined variables that appear in the ith equation with coefficients that are neither zero nor the normalized coefficient, we can write the ith equation of (17.1.1) as

$$\begin{aligned}\mathbf{Y}_{\cdot i} &= \mathbf{Y}_{(i)}\gamma_i + \mathbf{X}_{(i)}\boldsymbol{\beta}_i + \varepsilon_{\cdot i} \\ &= \mathbf{M}_{(i)}\boldsymbol{\delta}_i + \varepsilon_{\cdot i},\end{aligned} \tag{17.1.3}$$

where $\mathbf{M}_{(i)} = [\mathbf{Y}_{(i)}, \mathbf{X}_{(i)}]$, $\boldsymbol{\delta}_i = \left[\begin{smallmatrix}\gamma_i \\ \boldsymbol{\beta}_i\end{smallmatrix}\right]$, and the number of columns of $\mathbf{Y}_{(i)}$ and $\mathbf{X}_{(i)}$ are q_i and k_i, respectively. Finally, given (17.1.3), the system of Equations (17.1.1) may be expressed as a $(qn \times 1)$ vector representing n observations on each of the q equations in the system, as

$$\mathbf{Y}_{\mathrm{v}} = \mathbf{M}\boldsymbol{\delta} + \varepsilon_{\mathrm{v}} \tag{17.1.4.a}$$

with vertically concatenated or stacked vectors

$$\begin{aligned}\mathbf{Y}_{\mathrm{v}} &= (\mathbf{Y}_{\cdot 1}', \mathbf{Y}_{\cdot 2}', \ldots, \mathbf{Y}_{\cdot q}')' = \mathrm{vec}(\mathbf{Y}) \\ \boldsymbol{\delta} &= (\boldsymbol{\delta}_1', \boldsymbol{\delta}_2', \ldots, \boldsymbol{\delta}_q')' \\ \varepsilon_{\mathrm{v}} &= (\varepsilon_{\cdot 1}', \varepsilon_{\cdot 2}', \ldots, \varepsilon_{\cdot q}')' = \mathrm{vec}(\varepsilon)\end{aligned} \tag{17.1.4.b}$$

and a block diagonal $\mathbf{M}$ matrix, with ith block given by $\mathbf{M}_{(i)}$, as

$$\mathbf{M} = \begin{bmatrix}\mathbf{M}_{(1)} & & & \\ & \mathbf{M}_{(2)} & & \\ & & \ddots & \\ & & & \mathbf{M}_{(q)}\end{bmatrix}. \tag{17.1.4.c}$$

The corresponding noise covariance matrix is $\mathbf{cov}(\varepsilon_{\mathrm{v}}) = \boldsymbol{\Psi} = \mathrm{E}[\varepsilon_{\mathrm{v}}\varepsilon_{\mathrm{v}}'] = \boldsymbol{\Sigma} \otimes \mathbf{I}_n$. We can now see that the system of equations is represented in the seemingly unrelated regression form of Section 14.5. The difference, of course, is that each of the $\mathbf{M}_{(i)}$'s in (17.1.4) may contain one or more *endogenous* variables.

17.1.2. The Reduced-Form Regression Model

Because we have assumed that the $\boldsymbol{\Gamma}$ matrix is nonsingular, we may postmultiply both sides of (17.1.1) by $\boldsymbol{\Gamma}^{-1}$ to obtain an observationally equivalent representation of the outcomes of $\mathbf{Y}$ given by

$$\begin{aligned}\mathbf{Y}\boldsymbol{\Gamma}\boldsymbol{\Gamma}^{-1} &= \mathbf{X}\mathbf{B}\boldsymbol{\Gamma}^{-1} + \varepsilon\boldsymbol{\Gamma}^{-1} \\ \mathbf{Y} &= \mathbf{X}\boldsymbol{\pi} + \mathbf{V},\end{aligned} \tag{17.1.5}$$

where $\boldsymbol{\pi} \equiv \mathbf{B}\boldsymbol{\Gamma}^{-1}$ is a $(k \times q)$ matrix of reduced-form parameters, $\mathbf{V} \equiv \varepsilon\boldsymbol{\Gamma}^{-1}$, and $\mathrm{E}[\mathbf{V}] \equiv \mathrm{E}[\varepsilon\boldsymbol{\Gamma}^{-1}] = \mathrm{E}[\varepsilon]\boldsymbol{\Gamma}^{-1} = \mathbf{0}\boldsymbol{\Gamma}^{-1} = \mathbf{0}$. The statistical model (17.1.5) represents n potential observations on the q endogenous variables in terms of *reduced-form* equations. In the reduced-form of a system of simultaneous equations, each endogenous variable is expressed in terms of predetermined variables and noise component elements only – no current endogenous variables appear on the right-hand side of reduced-form equations. The n observations on the ith equation of the system of reduced-form equations may be written as

$$\mathbf{Y}_{\cdot i} = \mathbf{X}\boldsymbol{\pi}_{\cdot i} + \mathbf{V}_{\cdot i}, \tag{17.1.6}$$

and the system of n potential observations on each of the q reduced form equations may be written in vertically concatenated or stacked, seemingly unrelated regression form as

$$\mathbf{Y}_{\mathrm{v}} = (\mathbf{I}_{\mathrm{q}} \otimes \mathbf{X})\boldsymbol{\pi}_{\mathrm{v}} + \mathbf{V}_{\mathrm{v}} \tag{17.1.7.a}$$

where $\mathbf{V}_{\mathrm{v}} = \mathrm{vec}(\mathbf{V})$, $\boldsymbol{\pi}_{\mathrm{v}} = \mathrm{vec}(\boldsymbol{\pi})$,

$$\mathrm{E}[\mathbf{V}_{\mathrm{v}}] = \mathbf{0} \quad \text{and} \quad \mathbf{cov}(\mathbf{V}_{\mathrm{v}}) = \boldsymbol{\Xi} \otimes \mathbf{I}_n \tag{17.1.7.b}$$

with $\boldsymbol{\Xi} \equiv (\boldsymbol{\Gamma}^{-1})'\boldsymbol{\Sigma}\boldsymbol{\Gamma}^{-1}$.

In this representation, only *predetermined* explanatory variables appear on the right-hand side of the equations and, as we noted previously, we assume that the scaled cross-product matrix $n^{-1}\mathbf{X}'\mathbf{X}$ converges in probability to a *finite* positive definite moment matrix, say $\mathbf{q}_{\mathrm{xx}}$. Note that $\mathbf{X}$ is *contemporaneously* uncorrelated with the elements in ε, and this leads to $\mathbf{X}$ also being contemporaneously uncorrelated with the reduced form noise component $\mathbf{V}$, leading to the conditions

$$\mathrm{E}[n^{-1}\mathbf{X}'\mathbf{V}] = \mathrm{E}[n^{-1}\mathbf{X}'\varepsilon]\boldsymbol{\Gamma}^{-1} = \mathbf{0}\boldsymbol{\Gamma}^{-1} = \mathbf{0} \tag{17.1.8}$$

and

$$\mathrm{plim}(n^{-1}\mathbf{X}'\mathbf{V}) = \mathrm{p}\lim(n^{-1}\mathbf{X}'\varepsilon)\boldsymbol{\Gamma}^{-1} = \mathbf{0}\boldsymbol{\Gamma}^{-1} = \mathbf{0}. \tag{17.1.9}$$

In other words, the scaled cross-product matrix $n^{-1}\mathbf{X}'\mathbf{V}$ has a mean value equal to a zero matrix and converges in probability to a zero matrix as well.

Having defined the reduced form of a set of simultaneous equations, we henceforth refer to the original system of equations (17.1.1) in which multiple endogenous variables appear within equations and endogenous variables are specified in interdependent and jointly determined ways, as the *structural form* of the simultaneous equations system. Using this terminology, the parameters represented by $\boldsymbol{\pi}$ are then referred to as *reduced-form parameters*, whereas $\boldsymbol{\Gamma}$ and $\mathbf{B}$ are referred to as *structural parameters*.

► **Example 17.1.1:** Using the system of equations (17.1.2) as a guide, the GAUSS program C17DSP.gss (provided in the examples manual) generates pseudorandom observations for a simultaneous system of equations. The program first asks the user to supply values for the nonzero and nonnormalized elements of $\boldsymbol{\Gamma}$ and the elements of $\boldsymbol{\Sigma}$ (the elements of $\mathbf{B}$ are given). Then, the program computes $\boldsymbol{\pi}$ and generates observations for $\mathbf{X}$ and $\mathbf{V}_{\mathrm{v}}$ and obtains outcomes for the dependent variables $\mathbf{Y}_{\mathrm{v}}$. The program may be extended to generate pseudorandom samples for other systems of linear equations considered in this chapter.

17.1.3. Estimating the Reduced-Form Coefficients

The reduced-form model is in the form of the linear regression model considered in Chapters 3–6, and the least-squares estimator for $\boldsymbol{\pi}_{\cdot i}$ in Equation (17.1.6) is given by

$$\hat{\boldsymbol{\pi}}_{\cdot i} = (\mathbf{X}'\mathbf{X})^{-1}\mathbf{X}'\mathbf{Y}_{\cdot i}. \tag{17.1.10}$$

This estimator is consistent because

$$\begin{aligned}\text{p}\lim(\hat{\boldsymbol{\pi}}_{\cdot i}) &= \boldsymbol{\pi}_{\cdot i} + \text{p}\lim(n^{-1}\mathbf{X}'\mathbf{X})^{-1}\text{p}\lim(n^{-1}\mathbf{X}'\mathbf{V}_{\cdot i})\\ &= \boldsymbol{\pi}_{\cdot i} + \mathbf{q}_{\text{xx}}\cdot\mathbf{0}\\ &= \boldsymbol{\pi}_{\cdot i},\end{aligned} \tag{17.1.11}$$

where $\text{p}\lim(n^{-1}\mathbf{X}'\mathbf{V}_{\cdot i}) = \mathbf{0}$. If the $\mathbf{X}$ matrix consists only of exogenous variables, then the least-squares estimator (17.1.10) is unbiased. To see this, apply the double expectation theorem in the usual way to yield

$$\text{E}[\hat{\boldsymbol{\pi}}_{\cdot i}] = \boldsymbol{\pi}_{\cdot i} + \text{E}[(\mathbf{X}'\mathbf{X})^{-1}\mathbf{X}'\mathbf{V}_{\cdot i}] = \boldsymbol{\pi}_{\cdot i} + \text{E}_{\mathbf{x}}[(\mathbf{X}'\mathbf{X})^{-1}\mathbf{X}'\text{E}[\mathbf{V}_{\cdot i}\,|\,\mathbf{X}]] = \boldsymbol{\pi}_{\cdot i} \tag{17.1.12}$$

because $\text{E}[\mathbf{V}_{\cdot i}\,|\,\mathbf{X}] = \mathbf{0}$. However, if $\mathbf{X}$ is predetermined but not exogenous, with one or more columns of $\mathbf{X}$ containing lagged endogenous variables, then the first expectation term on the right-hand side of (17.1.12) is not generally the zero matrix. The matrix $(\mathbf{X}'\mathbf{X})^{-1}\mathbf{X}'$, being a function of some of the variables in the matrix $\mathbf{Y}$, is functionally dependent on some of the same structural noise component elements as $\mathbf{V}_{\cdot i}$. Relatedly, the value of $\text{E}[\mathbf{V}_{\cdot i}\,|\,\mathbf{X}]$ in (17.1.12) is not generally a zero vector because of the mutual dependency of elements of $\mathbf{V}_{\cdot i}$ and $\mathbf{X}$ on common elements of $\boldsymbol{\varepsilon}$.

If we view the system of reduced-form equations within the context of the seemingly unrelated regression format, the generalized least-squares estimator of Chapter 14 applied to (17.1.7) is

$$\begin{aligned}\hat{\boldsymbol{\pi}}_{\text{v}} &= [(\mathbf{I}_q\otimes\mathbf{X})'(\boldsymbol{\Xi}\otimes\mathbf{I}_n)^{-1}(\mathbf{I}_q\otimes\mathbf{X})]^{-1}(\mathbf{I}_q\otimes\mathbf{X})'(\boldsymbol{\Xi}\otimes\mathbf{I}_n)^{-1}\mathbf{Y}_{\text{v}}\\ &= [\boldsymbol{\Xi}^{-1}\otimes\mathbf{X}'\mathbf{X}]^{-1}(\boldsymbol{\Xi}^{-1}\otimes\mathbf{X}')\mathbf{Y}_{\text{v}}\\ &= [\boldsymbol{\Xi}\otimes(\mathbf{X}'\mathbf{X})^{-1}](\boldsymbol{\Xi}^{-1}\otimes\mathbf{X}')\mathbf{Y}_{\text{v}}\\ &= [\mathbf{I}_{\text{q}}\otimes(\mathbf{X}'\mathbf{X})^{-1}\mathbf{X}']\mathbf{Y}_{\text{v}}.\end{aligned} \tag{17.1.13}$$

Owing to the Kronecker product in the final expression of (17.1.13), it is evident that $\hat{\boldsymbol{\pi}}_{\text{v}}$ is identical to a vertical concatenation or stacking of linear least-squares estimators applied to each equation separately. Note that the equivalence of LS and GLS is due to each of the m reduced-form equations having *precisely the same explanatory variable matrix* $\mathbf{X}$.

Because $\hat{\boldsymbol{\pi}}_{\text{v}} = \boldsymbol{\pi}_{\text{v}} + [\mathbf{I}_{\text{q}}\otimes(\mathbf{X}'\mathbf{X})^{-1}\mathbf{X}']\mathbf{V}_{\text{v}}$, it follows from (17.1.7b) and an application of the double expectation theorem that the covariance matrix of $\hat{\boldsymbol{\pi}}_{\text{v}}$ is given by

$$\begin{aligned}\text{E}[(\hat{\boldsymbol{\pi}}_{\text{v}}-\boldsymbol{\pi}_{\text{v}})(\hat{\boldsymbol{\pi}}_{\text{v}}-\boldsymbol{\pi}_{\text{v}})'] &= \text{E}[(\mathbf{I}_q\otimes(\mathbf{X}'\mathbf{X})^{-1}\mathbf{X}')\mathbf{V}_{\text{v}}\mathbf{V}_{\text{v}}'(\mathbf{I}_q\otimes\mathbf{X}(\mathbf{X}'\mathbf{X})^{-1})]\\ &= \text{E}[(\mathbf{I}_q\otimes(\mathbf{X}'\mathbf{X})^{-1}\mathbf{X}')(\boldsymbol{\Xi}\otimes\mathbf{I}_n)(\mathbf{I}_q\otimes\mathbf{X}(\mathbf{X}'\mathbf{X})^{-1})]\\ &= \boldsymbol{\Xi}\otimes\text{E}(\mathbf{X}'\mathbf{X})^{-1},\end{aligned} \tag{17.1.14}$$

when $\mathbf{X}$ is purely exogenous. The $(q \times q)$ unknown contemporaneous covariance matrix Ξ can be consistently estimated by $\hat{\Xi}$, whose elements are defined by

$$\hat{\Xi}_{ij} = \frac{\hat{\mathbf{V}}'_{.i}\hat{\mathbf{V}}_{.j}}{n} \quad \text{for} \quad i, j = 1, 2, \ldots, q, \tag{17.1.15}$$

where $\hat{\mathbf{V}}_{.i} \equiv \mathbf{Y}_{.i} - \mathbf{X}\hat{\pi}_{.i}$, and the unknown $\mathrm{E}(\mathbf{X}'\mathbf{X})^{-1}$ term can be replaced in applications by $(\mathbf{X}'\mathbf{X})^{-1}$. The covariance matrix of the reduced-form parameter estimator $\hat{\pi}_{\mathrm{v}}$ may be estimated by $\hat{\mathbf{cov}}(\hat{\pi}_{\mathrm{v}}) = \hat{\Xi} \otimes (\mathbf{X}'\mathbf{X})^{-1}$ in finite samples.

In the case in which $\mathbf{X}$ contains lagged endogenous variables, the first line of (17.1.14) remains valid, but the approach of conditioning on $\mathbf{X}$ and using the double expectation cannot be used to yield the remaining terms. To proceed, first note that

$$\mathbf{cov}([\mathbf{I}_q \otimes (n^{-1}\mathbf{X}'\mathbf{X})]n^{1/2}\hat{\pi}_{\mathrm{v}}) = \mathrm{E}[n^{-1}(\mathbf{I}_q \otimes \mathbf{X}')\mathbf{V}_{\mathrm{v}}\mathbf{V}'_{\mathrm{v}}(\mathbf{I}_q \otimes \mathbf{X})] \tag{17.1.16}$$

because $[\mathbf{I}_q \otimes (\mathbf{X}'\mathbf{X})](\hat{\pi}_{\mathrm{v}} - \pi_{\mathrm{v}}) = [\mathbf{I}_q \otimes \mathbf{X}']\mathbf{V}_{\mathrm{v}}$. A consistent estimator for (17.1.16) is given by $n^{-1}[\sum_{i=1}^{n}(\hat{\mathbf{V}}[i, .]' \otimes \mathbf{X}[i, \cdot]')(\hat{\mathbf{V}}[i, \cdot] \otimes \mathbf{X}[i, \cdot])]$ (recall the definition of $\mathbf{V}$ in (17.1.5) and the definition of $\hat{\mathbf{V}}$ following (17.1.15); see Gallant, 1987, Section 6.3 for additional details). Then a consistent estimator for the covariance matrix of $\hat{\pi}_{\mathrm{v}}$ can be defined by

$$\widehat{\mathbf{cov}}(\pi_{\mathrm{v}}) = [(\mathbf{I}_{\mathrm{q}} \otimes (\mathbf{X}'\mathbf{X})^{-1})\Bigg[\sum_{i=1}^{n}(\hat{\mathbf{V}}[i, \cdot]' \otimes \mathbf{X}[i, \cdot]') \times (\hat{\mathbf{V}}[i, \cdot]' \otimes \mathbf{X}[i, \cdot]')'](\mathbf{I}_q \otimes (\mathbf{X}'\mathbf{X})^{-1})\Bigg] \tag{17.1.17}$$

Note that the estimator (17.1.17) is *robust to heteroscedasticity* across sample observations, and in fact can be viewed as a systems-of-equations extension of White's heteroscedasticity-robust covariance matrix estimator (let $q = 1$ and compare with (15.4.4)). This estimator can also be used in the case in which $\mathbf{X}$ is exogenous and a heteroscedastic robust covariance matrix estimator is desired. Having noted this robustness, it turns out that in the current case where it is assumed that the $(q \times 1)$ noise component vectors $\varepsilon_{i\cdot}$, $i = 1, \ldots, n$ are in fact iid, n times (17.1.17) will converge to $n[\hat{\mathbf{cov}}(\hat{\pi}_{\mathrm{v}})] = \hat{\Xi} \otimes (n^{-1}\mathbf{X}'\mathbf{X})^{-1}$ as $n \to \infty$ (Schmidt, 1976, pp. 98–9, 259). Therefore, the simpler estimator for the covariance matrix of $\hat{\pi}_{\mathrm{v}}$, $\hat{\mathbf{cov}}(\hat{\pi}_{\mathrm{v}}) = \hat{\Xi} \otimes (\mathbf{X}'\mathbf{X})^{-1}$, which is also generally the more accurate estimator in the absence of heteroscedasticity, is preferred in the iid case.

Under general regularity conditions analogous to those discussed in the linear model context of Chapter 5 and the SUR context of Chapter 14, the estimator $\hat{\pi}_{\mathrm{v}}$ is asymptotically normally distributed. Its asymptotic mean is π and its asymptotic covariance matrix can be estimated by either $\hat{\mathbf{cov}}(\hat{\pi}_{\mathrm{v}}) = \hat{\Xi} \otimes (\mathbf{X}'\mathbf{X})^{-1}$ or (17.1.17), depending on whether the disturbances are homoscedastic across observations. Note further that in the case where $\mathbf{X}$ is purely exogenous, the Gauss–Markov theorem can be applied to conclude that $\hat{\pi}_{\mathrm{v}}$ is the BLUE estimator of π, which the reader will be asked to prove in the problems section.

17.1.4. The Identification Problem

The reduced form (17.1.5) is easily recognized as a member of the class of linear models discussed in Chapters 3–6 and Chapter 14, and we now have a least-squares estimator for the qk unknown reduced form parameter $\boldsymbol{\pi}$ that has several good sampling properties. However, the inverse problem of recovering information on $\boldsymbol{\Gamma}$ and $\mathbf{B}$ from $\boldsymbol{\pi}$ is ill-posed because we cannot obtain unique estimates of the $q^2 + qk - q$ unknown structural $\boldsymbol{\Gamma}$ and $\mathbf{B}$ parameters from the qk coefficients of the reduced form if $q > 1$; that is $\boldsymbol{\pi}\boldsymbol{\Gamma} = \mathbf{B}$ cannot be solved uniquely for $\boldsymbol{\Gamma}$ and $\mathbf{B}$ as functions of $\boldsymbol{\pi}$. Thus, to derive a consistent estimator of the structural parameters from the consistent estimator of $\boldsymbol{\pi}$, additional restrictions must be imposed on $\boldsymbol{\Gamma}$ and $\mathbf{B}$.

More generally, relative to the issue of identification, first note that if one had knowledge of the reduced form parameter $\boldsymbol{\pi}$, one then would have complete knowledge of how an observation on the $(q \times 1)$ endogenous variable vector $\mathbf{Y}_{i\cdot}$ is obtained from the values of predetermined variables and outcomes of the noise component. Would this knowledge of the DSP allow us to identify the unique value of the structural parameters $\boldsymbol{\Gamma}$ and $\mathbf{B}$ and thereby identify the structural form characterization of the DSP? The argument in the preceding paragraph suggests the answer is no without further restrictions on the structural parameters. Thus, in the absence of this additional information, the structural parameters are *not identified* because there would then be an infinite number of structural model parameter specifications consistent with the known DSP.

To provide additional details regarding the identification problem, examine the ith equation in the system of q equations. The unknown parameters in the ith equation in (17.1.1) are related to the parameters of the reduced form (17.1.5) as follows:

$$\boldsymbol{\pi}\boldsymbol{\Gamma}_{\cdot i} - \mathbf{I}_k\boldsymbol{\beta}_{\cdot i} = [\boldsymbol{\pi}, -\mathbf{I}_k]\begin{bmatrix}\boldsymbol{\Gamma}_{\cdot i}\\ \boldsymbol{\beta}_{\cdot i}\end{bmatrix} = \boldsymbol{\Phi}'\begin{bmatrix}\boldsymbol{\Gamma}_{\cdot i}\\ \boldsymbol{\beta}_{\cdot i}\end{bmatrix} = \mathbf{0}, \tag{17.1.18}$$

where the matrix $\boldsymbol{\Phi}' \equiv [\boldsymbol{\pi}, -\mathbf{I}_k]$ is of dimension $k \times (q + k)$ and clearly has full-row rank because of the presence of the $(k \times k)$ identity matrix. In the absence of any restrictions on the parameters, this system of linear equations contains $q + k$ unknowns and only k linearly independent equations, and so it is clear that no unique solution for $\boldsymbol{\Gamma}_{\cdot i}$ and $\boldsymbol{\beta}_{\cdot i}$ will be possible. To obtain a solution, and thereby identify the structural parameters, *at least* q nonredundant restrictions on the parameters will be required, and these restrictions can be in the form of exclusion, linear, and nonlinear restrictions on the values of $(\boldsymbol{\Gamma}_{\cdot i}, \boldsymbol{\beta}_{\cdot i})$. We focus our attention henceforth on exclusion restrictions.

First of all, recall that the normalization $\Gamma_{ii} = 1$ can be imposed on each structural equation, and so our excess of unknown parameters in (17.1.18) is actually only $q - 1$. Taking this normalization into consideration, we can rewrite (17.1.18) as

$$\boldsymbol{\Phi}'_*\begin{bmatrix}\boldsymbol{\Gamma}^*_{\cdot i}\\ \boldsymbol{\beta}_{\cdot i}\end{bmatrix} = -\boldsymbol{\pi}_{\cdot i} \tag{17.1.19}$$

where $\boldsymbol{\Phi}'_*$ and $\boldsymbol{\Gamma}^*_{\cdot i}$ are identically $\boldsymbol{\Phi}'$ and $\boldsymbol{\Gamma}_{\cdot i}$ with their ith column and ith row removed, respectively. Now note that setting elements of the vectors $\boldsymbol{\Gamma}^*_{\cdot i}$, $\boldsymbol{\beta}_{\cdot i}$ or both to 0 effectively removes the corresponding column vectors in $\boldsymbol{\Phi}'_*$ from consideration in the linear equation system (17.1.19). If q_i and k_i are, respectively, the number of *explanatory* (or right-hand-side) endogenous and predetermined variables that appear in the specification of equation i, then $q - q_i - 1$ of the elements in $\boldsymbol{\Gamma}^*_{\cdot i}$ are set to 0 and $k - k_{\cdot i}$ of the elements in $\boldsymbol{\beta}_{\cdot i}$ are zero-valued. Letting $\boldsymbol{\Gamma}^{*0}_{\cdot i}$ and $\boldsymbol{\beta}^0_{\cdot i}$ denote the vectors $\boldsymbol{\Gamma}^*_{\cdot i}$ and $\boldsymbol{\beta}_{\cdot i}$ after zero values are removed, and letting $\boldsymbol{\Phi}^{0'}_*$ denote $\boldsymbol{\Phi}'_*$ after the columns have been removed that correspond to the zero-valued entries in $\boldsymbol{\Gamma}^*_{\cdot i}$ and $\boldsymbol{\beta}_{\cdot i}$, we have the reduced linear system

$$\boldsymbol{\Phi}^{0'}_* \begin{bmatrix} \boldsymbol{\Gamma}^{*0}_{\cdot i} \\ \boldsymbol{\beta}^0_{\cdot i} \end{bmatrix} = -\boldsymbol{\pi}_{\cdot i}. \tag{17.1.20}$$

All of the possible solutions to (17.1.20) can be characterized as follows (Graybill, 1984, p. 153; also see the Linear Equations topic in the matrix review manual):

$$\begin{bmatrix} \boldsymbol{\Gamma}^{*0}_{\cdot i} \\ \boldsymbol{\beta}^0_{\cdot i} \end{bmatrix} = -(\boldsymbol{\Phi}^{0'}_*)^- \boldsymbol{\pi}_{\cdot i} + [\mathbf{I}_{q_i+k_i} - (\boldsymbol{\Phi}^{0'}_*)^-(\boldsymbol{\Phi}^{0'}_*)]\mathbf{h}, \tag{17.1.21}$$

where $\mathbf{h}$ is an *arbitrary* $(q_i + k_i) \times 1$ vector of real numbers and $(\boldsymbol{\Phi}^{0'}_*)^-$ denotes the *generalized* inverse of $\boldsymbol{\Phi}^{0'}_*$. Because the generalized inverse of a matrix is unique, it is clear that the solution for the unknown structural parameters will be unique iff the bracketed matrix premultiplying $\mathbf{h}$ in (17.1.21) is the zero matrix. The condition $(\boldsymbol{\Phi}^{0'}_*)^-(\boldsymbol{\Phi}^{0'}_*) = \mathbf{I}_{q_i+k_i}$ requires that $\boldsymbol{\Phi}^{0'}_*$ have full-column rank (Graybill, p. 112), and because $\boldsymbol{\Phi}^{0'}_*$ has dimension $k \times (q_i + k_i)$, a necessary condition for the identification of the structural parameters in terms of the reduced form parameters is that $\boldsymbol{\Phi}^{0'}_*$ have at least as many rows as columns,

$$k \geq (q_i + k_i) \text{ or } (k - k_i) \geq q_i. \tag{17.1.22}$$

That is, *the number of predetermined variables excluded from the ith equation must be at least as large as the number of included endogenous variables minus 1* (the "minus 1" is the dependent variable whose coefficient has been normalized to 1). This is called the *order* condition for identification because it deals with the orders of matrices involved in solving for the structural parameters.

The necessary *and sufficient* condition for uniquely identifying the structural parameters in terms of the reduced form parameters, which subsumes the necessary order condition (17.1.22), is the *rank condition*

$$\operatorname{rank}(\boldsymbol{\Phi}^{0'}_*) = \operatorname{rank}(\boldsymbol{\pi}^0_*, -\mathbf{I}^0_k) = q_i + k_i, \tag{17.1.23}$$

where $\boldsymbol{\pi}^0_*$ and $\mathbf{I}^0_k$ are matrices consisting of the columns of $\boldsymbol{\Phi}^{0'}_*$ corresponding to $\boldsymbol{\Gamma}^{*0}_{\cdot i}$ and $\boldsymbol{\beta}^0_{\cdot i}$ in (17.1.20), respectively.

There is an equivalent alternative version of the rank condition (17.1.23) that can be stated. First note that by construction, $\mathbf{I}^0_k$ is a $k \times (k - k_i)$ matrix containing $k - k_i$ rows of zeros and k_i rows containing a single unit value, with the rest of the elements being zero. By reordering the rows in $\mathbf{I}^0_k$, the rank condition (17.1.23) can be represented as

$$\operatorname{rank}\begin{bmatrix} \boldsymbol{\pi}^0_{*1} & -\mathbf{I}_{k_i} \\ \boldsymbol{\pi}^0_{*0} & \mathbf{0} \end{bmatrix} = q_i + k_i, \tag{17.1.24}$$

where $\boldsymbol{\pi}^0_{*1}$ are the rows of $\boldsymbol{\pi}^0_*$ corresponding to equations in (17.1.19) having nonzero $\boldsymbol{\beta}_{\cdot i}$ elements, and $\boldsymbol{\pi}^0_{*0}$ are the rows of $\boldsymbol{\pi}^0_*$ corresponding to equations in (17.1.19) for which the elements of $\boldsymbol{\beta}_{\cdot i}$ were set to zero. Because the negative of the $(k_i \times k_i)$ identity matrix, $-\mathbf{I}_{k_i}$, has rank k_i, implying that the upper k_i rows of (17.1.24) have full-row rank k_i, and the lower set of rows $[\boldsymbol{\pi}^0_{*0}\ \mathbf{0}]$ will necessarily be linearly independent from the upper set because of the presence of the zero matrix in the lower right corner of the bracketed matrix in (17.1.24), it is clear that the rank condition is equivalent to

$$\operatorname{rank}\left(\boldsymbol{\pi}^0_{*0}\right) = q_i \tag{17.1.25}$$

Three distinct possibilities for the rank and order conditions, and the identifiability of parameters in the ith structural equation, are now apparent. These are as follows:

Order Condition +	Rank Condition ⇒	Identification
$(k - k_i) \gtreqless q_i$	not met	underidentified
$(k - k_i) = q_i$	met	just-identified
$(k - k_i) > q_i$	met	overidentified

It is clear that in the underidentified case there is no hope of recovering the structural parameters via a function of the reduced-form parameters, whereas in the just and overidentified cases, such a solution is possible. What is the difference between the just and overidentified cases? In the just-identified case, the number of equations in the system (17.1.20) is precisely equal to the number of unknowns, whereas in the overidentified case there is an excess of $k - k_i - q_i$ equations over the number of unknowns. Thus, in the overidentified case, if the rank condition is met, one can select various subsets of the k equations in (17.1.18) made up of $k_i + q_i$ equations and thereby define systems of equations that can be solved analogously as in (17.1.19)–(17.1.21) for the values of the structural parameters. Note the number of different systems of equations that can be constructed equals the combinatorial value $\binom{k}{k_i+q_i}$. Thus, the finite collection of alternative functional mappings from $\boldsymbol{\pi}$ to the $k_i + q_i$ nonzero and nonunit-valued entries in $\boldsymbol{\Gamma}_{\cdot i}$ and $\boldsymbol{\beta}_{\cdot i}$ generate as many as $\binom{k}{k_i+q_i}$ alternative solutions for the structural parameters for a given value of the reduced form parameters. This creates a dilemma in the problem of estimating the structural parameters: Which if any of the structural-reduced form parameter mappings should be used to represent the unknown structural parameters?

We now examine methods of estimating the structural parameters of an econometric model when the equations in the system are identified. In particular, we will see how the excess of parameter-identifying equations in the overidentified case can be addressed.

► **Example 17.1.2:** The GAUSS program C17Ident.gss (provided in the examples manual) constructs a procedure SEIdent() that checks the identification conditions for each equation in a system of simultaneous equations. The matrices $\boldsymbol{\Gamma}$ and $\mathbf{B}$ are input as arguments to the procedure, and GAUSS checks the rank and order conditions for each equation and reports the results. To demonstrate the procedure, the program asks the user to provide values for the elements of $\boldsymbol{\Gamma}$ and $\mathbf{B}$ in (17.1.2) and reports the identification character of the specified system of equations.

17.2. Least-Squares and GMM Estimation: The Semiparametric Case

Given the presence of one or more right-hand-side random variables in (17.1.1) that are not independent of the noise component, one might anticipate that the least-squares rule applied to each equation (17.1.3) or to the whole system of equations (17.1.4) will have unfavorable statistical consequences. Early econometricians identified the resulting estimation problem as "least-squares bias." Their concern is readily seen if we use the statistical model (17.1.3), which we repeat here for convenience as follows:

$$\mathbf{Y}_{\cdot i} = \mathbf{M}_{(i)}\boldsymbol{\delta}_i + \boldsymbol{\varepsilon}_{\cdot i}. \tag{17.2.1}$$

Under this formulation $\mathbf{M}_{(i)}$ contains one or more endogenous variables and the linear least-squares (LS) procedure yields the estimator

$$\hat{\boldsymbol{\delta}}_i^{\mathrm{LS}} = \left(\mathbf{M}'_{(i)}\mathbf{M}_{(i)}\right)^{-1}\mathbf{M}'_{(i)}\mathbf{Y}_{\cdot i}, \tag{17.2.2}$$

which has mean

$$\mathrm{E}\big[\hat{\boldsymbol{\delta}}_i^{\mathrm{LS}}\big] = \boldsymbol{\delta}_i + \mathrm{E}\big[\left(\mathbf{M}'_{(i)}\mathbf{M}_{(i)}\right)^{-1}\mathbf{M}'_{(i)}\boldsymbol{\varepsilon}_{\cdot i}\big]. \tag{17.2.3}$$

Consequently, $\mathrm{E}[\hat{\boldsymbol{\delta}}_i^{\mathrm{LS}}] \neq \boldsymbol{\delta}_i$ and, in terms of convergence in probability,

$$\mathrm{plim}\big(\hat{\boldsymbol{\delta}}_i^{\mathrm{LS}}\big) = \boldsymbol{\delta}_i + \mathrm{plim}\left(\mathrm{n}^{-1}\mathbf{M}'_{(i)}\mathbf{M}_{(i)}\right)^{-1}\mathrm{plim}\left(\mathrm{n}^{-1}\mathbf{M}'_{(i)}\boldsymbol{\varepsilon}_{\cdot i}\right) \neq \boldsymbol{\delta}_i \tag{17.2.4}$$

because the random variables $\mathbf{Y}_{(i)}$ contained in $\mathbf{M}_{(i)}$ are not independently distributed of, and are functionally related to, the structural noise component $\boldsymbol{\varepsilon}_{\cdot i}$. Thus, to achieve the important property of consistency, we must seek a different method of estimation.

In contrast to the structural form of the model, the reduced-form version of the model yields the set of individual equations

$$\mathbf{Y}_{\cdot i} = \mathbf{X}\boldsymbol{\pi}_{\cdot i} + \mathbf{V}_{\cdot i}, \quad \text{for} \quad i = 1, \ldots, q, \tag{17.2.5}$$

or for the complete equation system,

$$\mathbf{Y}_{\mathrm{v}} = (\mathbf{I}_q \otimes \mathbf{X})\boldsymbol{\pi}_{\mathrm{v}} + \mathbf{V}_{\mathrm{v}}, \tag{17.2.6}$$

where the right-hand-side variables are all predetermined and thus contemporaneously uncorrelated with the noise component. Consequently, the LS approach (or the maximum likelihood (ML) approach if the noise is normally distributed, as discussed in Section 17.3) yields estimators of the reduced form coefficients $\boldsymbol{\pi}$ that have desirable statistical properties, including "unbiasedness" and BLUE (if X is purely exogenous), consistency, and asymptotic normality under standard regularity conditions (recall Section 17.1.2). In the next subsection, we use the LS estimator of $\boldsymbol{\pi}$ in the just-identified case to obtain estimates of the structural parameters.

17.2.1. Estimators of Parameters for a Just-Identified Structural Equation

In this subsection, we examine two different procedures for estimating parameters contained in a just-identified structural equation, indirect least squares and instrumental variables/GMM. Although the initial motivations for the two procedures are seemingly different, the procedures ultimately produce the same estimates of structural parameters.

17.2.1.a. Indirect Least-Squares Approach

On the basis of the relationship between the reduced form and structural parameters given by $\boldsymbol{\pi}\boldsymbol{\Gamma} = \mathbf{B}$, or more directly for the individual ith equation by (17.1.18) and (17.1.19), we are in a position to recover estimates of $\boldsymbol{\delta}_i = (\boldsymbol{\gamma}_i', \boldsymbol{\beta}_i')'$ directly from the consistent reduced-form parameter estimates when the ith equation within the system of equations is *just* identified. An estimator defined as the solution to (17.1.18) for structural parameters in the just-identified case is called an *indirect least-squares* (ILS) *estimator*. Consequently, if an equation within the system of equations is just identified, we may obtain unique estimates of the structural parameters in the ith equation from estimates of the reduced-form parameters by solving (17.1.20) as $\begin{bmatrix} \hat{\boldsymbol{\Gamma}}_{.i}^{*0} \\ \hat{\boldsymbol{\beta}}_{.i}^{0} \end{bmatrix} = -[\boldsymbol{\Phi}_*^{o'}]^{-1}\hat{\boldsymbol{\pi}}_{.i}$. Note this is possible because the matrix $\hat{\boldsymbol{\Phi}}_*^{0'} = [\hat{\boldsymbol{\pi}}_*^0, -\mathbf{I}_k^0]$ is then $(k \times k)$ and nonsingular (assuming the rank condition holds), where $k = k_i + q_i$.

The ILS estimator of the structural parameters is consistent. This follows directly from the consistency of the reduced-form parameter estimator and because the ILS estimates are continuous functions of the reduced-form parameters estimates in the just-identified case (recall that plim f($\mathbf{X}$) = f(plim $\mathbf{X}$) if f($\mathbf{X}$) is a continuous function of $\mathbf{X}$). The ILS estimator can also be shown to be asymptotically normally distributed, which follows from the asymptotic normality of $\hat{\boldsymbol{\pi}}$ and because the ILS estimates are continuously differentiable functions of the reduced form parameters. The derivation of the asymptotic normal distribution in this way is complicated and is omitted. We will instead examine a method of moments approach ahead that applies to the just-identified case and, unlike the ILS estimation approach, can be generalized to the overidentified case as well. When an equation is just identified, the ILS approach and the moment approach examined in the following paragraphs are numerically equivalent, and thus the asymptotic properties of the ILS estimator can be deduced from those presented for the moment approach.

17.2.1.b. Instrumental Variables Approach

At this point it is instructive to recall from Chapter 16 the linear model in which some of the right-hand-side explanatory variables were not independent of the noise component. To provide a consistent estimator in this situation, we introduced the concept of instrumental variables that were correlated with the offending columns of $\mathbf{X}$ but were uncorrelated with the noise components of the models. We did not say much in Chapter 16 about the origins of these instruments. Now, within the current context of the simultaneous equations model, we can define instrumental variables in terms of the predetermined variables of the system of equations such as $\mathbf{Z} \equiv \mathbf{X}$. Focusing on the ith equation (17.1.3), we can write k moment conditions as

$$\mathrm{E}\left[\mathbf{Z}'\left(\mathbf{Y}_{\cdot i} - \mathbf{M}_{(i)}\boldsymbol{\delta}_i\right)\right] = \mathrm{E}\left[\mathbf{X}'\left(\mathbf{Y}_{\cdot i} - \mathbf{M}_{(i)}\boldsymbol{\delta}_i\right)\right] = \mathbf{0} \tag{17.2.7}$$

If the number of predetermined variables outside of the ith equation, $k - k_i$, is such that the number of moments in (17.2.7), k, is equal to the number of unknown parameters in δ_i, $q_i + k_i$, as it will be in the just-identified case, and if the usual regularity conditions are satisfied, then we have a traditional instrumental variable (IV)-generalized method of moments (GMM) estimator (see Section 16.3) whose statistical properties coincide with those of the ILS estimator. The ILS–IV–GMM estimator in this just-identified case is given by

$$\hat{\boldsymbol{\delta}}_i = \left(\mathbf{X}'\mathbf{M}_{(i)}\right)^{-1}\mathbf{X}'\mathbf{Y}_{\cdot i}. \tag{17.2.8}$$

The standard expressions for the asymptotic covariance matrix of the estimator, as well as asymptotic statistical tests and confidence-region procedures, are as indicated in Section 16.3.

Thus, if the DSP underlying the sample observations is such that an equation from the structural equation representation of the DSP is just identified, then an estimator that has the desirable statistical property of consistency, asymptotic normality, and asymptotic efficiency (relative to the given moment information) exists. In addition, the standard asymptotic Chi-square testing and confidence-region procedures are available to form inferential decisions. However, in applications we often encounter situations where the structural equations of interest are overidentified. Consequently, we have the interesting problem of developing a basis for coping with this situation, and this is the topic to which we now turn.

17.2.2. GMM Estimator of Parameters for an Overidentified Structural Equation

In dealing with overidentified structural equations, consider the problem of estimating the unknown parameters of the ith equation (17.1.3) and assume the rank condition is satisfied. Remember in this formulation that there are k predetermined variables in the system of equations, and there are $k - k_i$ predetermined variables in the system that appear only outside of the ith equation. Considering the predetermined variables as instruments, we can, in a GMM context, again write down the k moment conditions and their sample moment counterparts as

$$\mathrm{E}\left[n^{-1}\mathbf{X}'\left(\mathbf{Y}_{\cdot i} - \mathbf{M}_{(i)}\boldsymbol{\delta}_i\right)\right] = \mathbf{0} \tag{17.2.9.a}$$

and

$$n^{-1}\mathbf{x}'\left(\mathbf{y}_{\cdot i} - \mathbf{m}_{(i)}\boldsymbol{\delta}_i\right) = \mathbf{0}. \tag{17.2.9.b}$$

In the overidentified case the order condition implies $k > q_i + k_i$, and thus there are more moment conditions in (17.2.9) than unknown parameters in $\boldsymbol{\delta}_i = [\boldsymbol{\gamma}_i', \boldsymbol{\beta}_i']'$. This looks quite like the problem in Chapter 16 that we characterized in a general method of moments (GMM) context, and in fact it is identical to it. Thus, given the moment conditions, we can formulate the estimation problem in the context of an extremum problem.

Recall that to obtain an asymptotically optimal GMM estimates it is necessary in this case to define a consistent estimate of the covariance matrix of the scaled moment condition $n^{-1/2}\mathbf{X}'(\mathbf{Y}_{\cdot i}-\mathbf{M}_{(i)}\boldsymbol{\delta}_i)$. When $\mathbf{X}$ is purely exogenous, a straightforward application of the double expectation theorem yields

$$\begin{aligned}\mathbf{cov}\left[n^{-1/2}\mathbf{X}'\left(\mathbf{Y}_{\cdot i}-\mathbf{M}_{(i)}\boldsymbol{\delta}_i\right)\right] &= \mathrm{E}_x\left[n^{-1}\mathbf{X}'\mathrm{E}\left[\left(\mathbf{Y}_{\cdot i}-\mathbf{M}_{(i)}\boldsymbol{\delta}_i\right)\left(\mathbf{Y}_{\cdot i}-\mathbf{M}_{(i)}\boldsymbol{\delta}_i\right)' \mid \mathbf{X}\right]\mathbf{X}\right] \\ &= \sigma_{ii}\mathrm{E}[n^{-1}\mathbf{X}'\mathbf{X}] \qquad (17.2.10)\end{aligned}$$

Then the asymptotically optimal GMM estimator can be defined by solving the extremum problem (recall Section 16.2)

$$\arg\min_{\boldsymbol{\delta}_i}\left[n^{-1}\left(\mathbf{Y}_{\cdot i}-\mathbf{M}_{(i)}\boldsymbol{\delta}_i\right)'\mathbf{X}(\sigma_{ii}\mathbf{X}'\mathbf{X})^{-1}\mathbf{X}'\left(\mathbf{Y}_{\cdot i}-\mathbf{M}_{(i)}\boldsymbol{\delta}_i\right)\right], \qquad (17.2.11)$$

where $n^{-1}\mathbf{X}'\mathbf{X}$ is used to estimate $\mathrm{E}[n^{-1}\mathbf{X}'\mathbf{X}]$. Note that the noise variance σ_{ii} can be eliminated from (17.2.13) without having any effect on the solved value of the GMM estimate, and so for purposes of estimating $\boldsymbol{\delta}_i$ it is not necessary to estimate σ_{ii} from the data. The first-order conditions for solving the minimization problem require that

$$\mathbf{M}_{(i)}{}'\mathbf{X}(\mathbf{X}'\mathbf{X})^{-1}\mathbf{X}'\left(\mathbf{Y}_{\cdot i}-\mathbf{M}_{(i)}\hat{\boldsymbol{\delta}}_i\right)=\mathbf{0}. \qquad (17.2.12)$$

Solving (17.2.12) for $\hat{\boldsymbol{\delta}}_i$ yields the estimated optimal GMM (EOGMM) estimator

$$\hat{\boldsymbol{\delta}}_i=\left[\mathbf{M}'_{(i)}\mathbf{X}(\mathbf{X}'\mathbf{X})^{-1}\mathbf{X}'\mathbf{M}_{(i)}\right]^{-1}\mathbf{M}'_{(i)}\mathbf{X}(\mathbf{X}'\mathbf{X})^{-1}\mathbf{X}'\mathbf{Y}_{\cdot i}. \qquad (17.2.13)$$

Note in the special case where the ith equation is just-identified, $\mathbf{M}'_{(i)}\mathbf{X}$ is a square nonsingular matrix, resulting in the aforementioned ILS–IV estimator

$$\hat{\delta}_i=\left(\mathbf{X}'\mathbf{M}_{(i)}\right)^{-1}\mathbf{X}'\mathbf{Y}_{\cdot i}, \qquad (17.2.14)$$

as in (17.2.8).

When $\mathbf{X}$ is not purely exogenous but is rather only predetermined and contains one or more lagged endogenous variables, the covariance matrix of the scaled moment condition needed for defining the asymptotically optimal GMM estimator cannot be derived via (17.2.10). However, it can be shown based on central limit theorems for dependent random variables that the limiting distribution of $n^{-1/2}\mathbf{X}'(\mathbf{Y}_{\cdot i}-\mathbf{M}_{(i)}\boldsymbol{\delta}_i)$ is normal, with a covariance matrix equal to $\sigma_{ii}\mathbf{q}_{\mathrm{xx}}=\sigma_{ii}\mathrm{plim}(n^{-1}\mathbf{X}'\mathbf{X})$ (Schmidt, 1976, pp. 98–9, 259). Therefore, even in the case where $\mathbf{X}$ contains lagged dependent variables, the preceding GMM estimation approach can be applied to define an asymptotically optimal GMM estimator of the structural parameters.

Under the usual regularity conditions, including $\mathrm{plim}(n^{-1}\mathbf{X}'\boldsymbol{\varepsilon}_{\cdot i})=\mathbf{0}$ and $\mathrm{plim}(n^{-1}\mathbf{X}'\mathbf{X})=\mathbf{q}_{\mathrm{xx}}$ exists and is finite and nonsingular, the estimator (17.2.13) is consistent and

$$n^{1/2}(\hat{\boldsymbol{\delta}}_i-\boldsymbol{\delta}_i)\xrightarrow{\mathrm{d}}\mathrm{N}\left(\mathbf{0},\sigma_{ii}\mathrm{plim}\left[\left(n^{-1}\mathbf{M}'_{(i)}\mathbf{X}(\mathbf{X}'\mathbf{X})^{-1}\mathbf{X}'\mathbf{M}_{(i)}\right)^{-1}\right]\right). \qquad (17.2.15)$$

Because in practice σ_{ii} is unknown, it is generally replaced by outcomes of the consistent estimator

$$\hat{\sigma}_{ii}=\left(\mathbf{Y}_{\cdot i}-\mathbf{M}_{(i)}\hat{\boldsymbol{\delta}}_i\right)'\left(\mathbf{Y}_{\cdot i}-\mathbf{M}_{(i)}\hat{\boldsymbol{\delta}}_i\right)/n. \qquad (17.2.16)$$

As before, the plim(·) in (17.2.15) is consistently estimated by outcomes of $(n^{-1}\mathbf{M}'_{(i)}\mathbf{X}(\mathbf{X}'\mathbf{X})^{-1}\mathbf{X}'\mathbf{M}_{(i)})^{-1}$. Then, the usual asymptotic tests and confidence-region procedures can be based on the asymptotic normal limiting distribution (17.2.15) with unknowns replaced by consistent estimates.

It was noted in Section 16.3 that the GMM estimator (17.2.15) leads to what has been called in the literature the *two-stage least-squares (2SLS) estimator*. In the 2SLS interpretation of the formulation, the least-squares estimates of the reduced form equations are used to predict the endogenous variables (*first stage*). Then, the values of the right-hand-side endogenous variables are replaced by the predictions, and a *second-stage* least-squares estimation is performed to recover estimates of $\boldsymbol{\delta}_i = [\boldsymbol{\gamma}'_i, \boldsymbol{\beta}'_i]'$. This interpretation of the estimator is directly motivated by writing the estimator (17.2.13) equivalently as

$$\begin{aligned}\hat{\boldsymbol{\delta}}_i &= \left[\mathbf{M}'_{(i)}\mathbf{X}(\mathbf{X}'\mathbf{X})^{-1}\mathbf{X}'\mathbf{X}(\mathbf{X}'\mathbf{X})^{-1}\mathbf{X}'\mathbf{M}_{(i)}\right]^{-1}\mathbf{M}'_{(i)}\mathbf{X}(\mathbf{X}'\mathbf{X})^{-1}\mathbf{X}'\mathbf{Y}_{\cdot i} \\ &= \left[\left[\hat{\mathbf{Y}}_{(i)}\ \mathbf{X}_{(i)}\right]'\left[\hat{\mathbf{Y}}_{(i)}\ \mathbf{X}_{(i)}\right]\right]^{-1}\left[\hat{\mathbf{Y}}_{(i)}\ \mathbf{X}_{(i)}\right]'\mathbf{Y}_{\cdot i}, \qquad (17.2.17)\end{aligned}$$

where $\hat{\mathbf{M}}_{(i)} = [\hat{\mathbf{Y}}_{(i)}\ \mathbf{X}_{(i)}] \equiv \mathbf{X}(\mathbf{X}'\mathbf{X})^{-1}\mathbf{X}'\mathbf{M}_{(i)}$ is the ordinary least-squares-based predictions of the columns of $\mathbf{M}_{(i)} = [\mathbf{Y}_{(i)}\ \ \mathbf{X}_{(i)}]$ using the explanatory variables $\mathbf{X}$. The asymptotic properties of the 2SLS estimator are of course identical to those of the GMM estimator (for further reading on the traditional 2SLS estimator, see Judge et al., pp. 644–6).

17.2.3. Estimation of a Complete System of Equations

We now consider a complete system of equations in vertically concatenated, or "stacked" form as

$$\mathbf{Y}_{\mathrm{v}} = \mathbf{M}\boldsymbol{\delta} + \boldsymbol{\varepsilon}_{\mathrm{v}}, \qquad (17.2.18)$$

where $\mathbf{Y}_{\mathrm{v}}$, $\mathbf{M}$, $\boldsymbol{\delta}$, and $\boldsymbol{\varepsilon}_{\mathrm{v}}$ are as defined in (17.1.4). We assume that by the rank and order conditions each of the equations in the system are just- or overidentified. The current problem is to develop an estimator for the entire parameter vector $\boldsymbol{\delta}$ and thus an estimator for all of the parameters contained in $\boldsymbol{\delta}_i = [\boldsymbol{\gamma}'_i, \boldsymbol{\beta}'_i]'$ for each of the equations in the complete system of equations. This problem was first investigated by Zellner and Theil (1962), when they proposed a three-stage least-squares (3SLS) estimator solution. Given Chapter 16 and Section 17.2.2, the most straightforward way to derive the estimator and its asymptotic properties is to consider the $k \times q$ *matrix* of moment conditions

$$\mathrm{E}[n^{-1}\mathbf{X}'(\mathbf{Y}\boldsymbol{\Gamma} - \mathbf{X}\mathbf{B})] = \mathbf{0} \qquad (17.2.19)$$

and apply GMM procedures to the complete system of simultaneous equations.

To define empirical counterparts to the moment conditions (17.2.19) in the context of the stacked simultaneous equations system (17.2.18), subtract $\mathbf{M}\boldsymbol{\delta}$ from both sides of the system and then premultiply the system by $n^{-1}(\mathbf{I}_q \otimes \mathbf{X}')$ to obtain

$$n^{-1}(\mathbf{I}_q \otimes \mathbf{X}')(\mathbf{Y}_{\mathrm{v}} - \mathbf{M}\boldsymbol{\delta}) = n^{-1}(\mathbf{I}_q \otimes \mathbf{X}')\boldsymbol{\varepsilon}_{\mathrm{v}}. \qquad (17.2.20)$$

Note for subsequent use in defining the asymptotically optimal GMM estimator that the covariance matrix of $n^{-1/2}(\mathbf{I}_q \otimes \mathbf{X}')\boldsymbol{\varepsilon}_{\mathrm{v}}$ is given in the case of purely exogenous $\mathbf{X}$ by an application of the double expectation theorem analogous to (17.2.10), yielding

$$\begin{aligned} \mathrm{E}[n^{-1}(\mathbf{I}_q \otimes \mathbf{X}')\boldsymbol{\varepsilon}_{\mathrm{v}}\boldsymbol{\varepsilon}_{\mathrm{v}}'(\mathbf{I}_q \otimes \mathbf{X})] &= \mathrm{E}[n^{-1}(\mathbf{I}_q \otimes \mathbf{X}')(\boldsymbol{\Sigma} \otimes \mathbf{I}_n)(\mathbf{I}_q \otimes \mathbf{X})] \\ &= \boldsymbol{\Sigma} \otimes \mathrm{E}[n^{-1}\mathbf{X}'\mathbf{X}], \end{aligned} \tag{17.2.21}$$

where $\boldsymbol{\Sigma}$ is an unknown $(q \times q)$ matrix representing the contemporaneous covariance matrix of the noise component elements across equations. If the usual convergence assumption is adopted, $n^{-1}\mathbf{X}'\mathbf{X}$ will be a consistent estimator of $\mathrm{E}[n^{-1}\mathbf{X}'\mathbf{X}]$, and thus asymptotically we can replace (17.2.21) by $\boldsymbol{\Sigma} \otimes n^{-1}\mathbf{X}'\mathbf{X}$. Note further that in the case in which $\mathbf{X}$ is only predetermined and contains lagged endogenous variables, $\boldsymbol{\Sigma} \otimes n^{-1}\mathbf{X}'\mathbf{X}$ can still be used asymptotically to represent the covariance matrix of the scaled moment conditions $n^{-1/2}(\mathbf{I}_q \otimes \mathbf{X}')(\mathbf{Y}_{\mathrm{v}} - \mathbf{M}\boldsymbol{\delta})$ by an appeal to central limit theorems for dependent random variables (Schmidt, 1976, pp. 98–9, 259).

If one proceeds as in Section 17.2.2, an asymptotically valid estimation objective function for defining the asymptotically optimal GMM estimator is given by

$$\arg_{\boldsymbol{\delta}} \min[n^{-1}(\mathbf{Y}_{\mathrm{v}} - \mathbf{M}\boldsymbol{\delta})'(\mathbf{I}_{\mathrm{q}} \otimes \mathbf{X})(\boldsymbol{\Sigma} \otimes \mathbf{X}'\mathbf{X})^{-1}(\mathbf{I}_{\mathrm{q}} \otimes \mathbf{X})'(\mathbf{Y}_{\mathrm{v}} - \mathbf{M}\boldsymbol{\delta})] \tag{17.2.22}$$

with first-order minimizing conditions requiring that

$$\mathbf{M}'(\mathbf{I}_{\mathrm{q}} \otimes \mathbf{X})(\boldsymbol{\Sigma} \otimes \mathbf{X}'\mathbf{X})^{-1}(\mathbf{I}_{\mathrm{q}} \otimes \mathbf{X}')(\mathbf{Y}_{\mathrm{v}} - \mathbf{M}\boldsymbol{\delta}) = \mathbf{0}. \tag{17.2.23}$$

The solution to (17.2.23) yields the GMM or 3SLS systems estimator

$$\begin{aligned} \boldsymbol{\delta}_{\mathrm{GMM}} &= \{\mathbf{M}'(\mathbf{I} \otimes \mathbf{X})[\boldsymbol{\Sigma}^{-1} \otimes (\mathbf{X}'\mathbf{X})^{-1}](\mathbf{I} \otimes \mathbf{X}')\mathbf{M}\}^{-1} \\ &\quad \times \mathbf{M}'(\mathbf{I} \otimes \mathbf{X})[\boldsymbol{\Sigma}^{-1} \otimes (\mathbf{X}'\mathbf{X})^{-1}](\mathbf{I} \otimes \mathbf{X}')\mathbf{Y}_{\mathrm{v}} \\ &= \{\mathbf{M}'[\boldsymbol{\Sigma}^{-1} \otimes \mathbf{X}(\mathbf{X}'\mathbf{X})^{-1}\mathbf{X}']\mathbf{M}\}^{-1}\mathbf{M}'[\boldsymbol{\Sigma}^{-1} \otimes \mathbf{X}(\mathbf{X}'\mathbf{X})^{-1}\mathbf{X}']\mathbf{Y}_{\mathrm{v}}. \end{aligned} \tag{17.2.24}$$

In practice $\boldsymbol{\Sigma}$ is unknown. To make (17.2.24) fully operational, a consistent estimate of $\boldsymbol{\Sigma}$ must be defined. This is analogous to the method of defining a feasible GLS estimator in Chapter 15. In this regard it is useful to note that if we ignore that the equation errors are contemporaneously correlated, and therefore specify $\boldsymbol{\Sigma}$ to be the identity matrix, the system GMM estimator (17.2.24) reduces to the equation-by-equation GMM estimator $\hat{\boldsymbol{\delta}}_i$ defined in (17.2.13). Note this estimator, with $\boldsymbol{\Sigma}$ replaced by $\mathbf{I}_q$, is consistent and asymptotically normal because it is effectively a GMM estimator with a given (nonoptimal) weight matrix $\mathbf{W} = (\mathbf{I}_q \otimes n^{-1}\mathbf{X}'\mathbf{X})^{-1} = \mathbf{I}_q \otimes (n^{-1}\mathbf{X}'\mathbf{X})^{-1}$. To make the GMM (3SLS) estimator operational, we can use this GMM equation-by-equation estimator $\hat{\boldsymbol{\delta}}_i$ as a basis for estimating the σ_{ij} elements of $\boldsymbol{\Sigma}$ as follows:

$$\hat{\sigma}_{ij} = n^{-1}\left(\mathbf{Y}_{\cdot i} - \mathbf{M}_{(i)}\hat{\boldsymbol{\delta}}_i\right)'\left(\mathbf{Y}_{\cdot j} - \mathbf{M}_{(j)}\hat{\boldsymbol{\delta}}_j\right), \tag{17.2.25}$$

and thus obtain a consistent estimator $\hat{\boldsymbol{\Sigma}}$ for $\boldsymbol{\Sigma}$. Substituting $\hat{\boldsymbol{\Sigma}}$ for $\boldsymbol{\Sigma}$ in (17.2.24) yields the estimated optimal GMM and 3SLS estimator of $\boldsymbol{\delta}$, say $\hat{\boldsymbol{\delta}}_{\mathrm{GMM}}$.

Consistency of $\hat{\boldsymbol{\delta}}_{\mathrm{GMM}}$ follows directly from the assumption that $\mathrm{plim}[n^{-1}(\mathbf{I}_{\mathrm{q}} \otimes \mathbf{X}')\boldsymbol{\varepsilon}_{\mathrm{v}}] = \mathbf{0}$ together with the usual assumption that the probability limits of $n^{-1}\mathbf{X}'\mathbf{X}$ and $n^{-1}(\mathbf{I} \otimes \mathbf{X}')\mathbf{M}$ exist and are finite and $\hat{\boldsymbol{\Sigma}}$ is consistent for $\boldsymbol{\Sigma}$, as the reader can demonstrate. In terms of the asymptotic distribution of $\hat{\boldsymbol{\delta}}_{\text{GMM}}$, it follows from

$$n^{1/2}(\hat{\boldsymbol{\delta}}_{\text{GMM}} - \boldsymbol{\delta}) = [n^{-1}\mathbf{M}'(\mathbf{I}_q \otimes \mathbf{X})[\hat{\boldsymbol{\Sigma}}^{-1} \otimes (n^{-1}\mathbf{X}'\mathbf{X})^{-1}]n^{-1}(\mathbf{I}_q \otimes \mathbf{X}')\mathbf{M}]^{-1} \cdot n^{-1}\mathbf{M}'(\mathbf{I}_q \otimes \mathbf{X})[\hat{\boldsymbol{\Sigma}}^{-1} \otimes (n^{-1}\mathbf{X}'\mathbf{X})^{-1}]n^{-1/2}(\mathbf{I}_q \otimes \mathbf{X}')\boldsymbol{\varepsilon}_v \quad (17.2.26)$$

and the asymptotic normality of $n^{-1/2}(\mathbf{I}_q \otimes \mathbf{X}')\boldsymbol{\varepsilon}_v$ that

$$n^{1/2}(\hat{\boldsymbol{\delta}}_{\text{GMM}} - \boldsymbol{\delta}) \xrightarrow{d} \text{N}(\mathbf{0}, \text{plim}[n^{-1}\mathbf{M}'(\boldsymbol{\Sigma}^{-1} \otimes \mathbf{X}(\mathbf{X}'\mathbf{X})^{-1}\mathbf{X}')\mathbf{M}]^{-1}). \quad (17.2.27)$$

The asymptotic covariance matrix for the GMM estimator $\boldsymbol{\delta}$ can then be estimated using

$$\mathbf{cov}(\hat{\boldsymbol{\delta}}_{\text{GMM}}) = \left[\mathbf{M}'[\hat{\boldsymbol{\Sigma}}^{-1} \otimes \mathbf{X}(\mathbf{X}'\mathbf{X})^{-1}\mathbf{X}']\mathbf{M}\right]^{-1}. \quad (17.2.28)$$

If we make an asymptotic comparison of the covariance matrices of the GMM or 3SLS systems estimator $\hat{\boldsymbol{\delta}}_{\text{GMM}}$ and the equation-by-equation GMM (2SLS) estimator $\hat{\boldsymbol{\delta}}_i$, it is possible to show that the difference in the covariance matrices of the limiting distributions of $\hat{\boldsymbol{\delta}}_{\text{GMM}}$ and $\hat{\boldsymbol{\delta}}_{\text{2SLS}} = [\hat{\boldsymbol{\delta}}_1', \hat{\boldsymbol{\delta}}_2', \ldots, \hat{\boldsymbol{\delta}}_m']'$ results in a negative semidefinite matrix, which establishes the gain in asymptotic efficiency in using $\hat{\boldsymbol{\delta}}_{\text{GMM}}$ relative to $\hat{\boldsymbol{\delta}}_{\text{2SLS}}$.

Regarding the historical reason why the GMM estimator was called a *three-stage* least-squares estimator, the estimator can be thought of as being constructed in three stages. The first stage is identical to the first stage of 2SLS, whereby the values of right-hand-side endogenous variables are replaced by predictions based on ordinary least-squares estimation of the reduced form. The second stage consists of equation-by-equation 2SLS estimation of the parameters in the system, resulting in $\hat{\boldsymbol{\delta}}_{\text{2SLS}} = (\hat{\boldsymbol{\delta}}_1', \hat{\boldsymbol{\delta}}_2', \ldots, \hat{\boldsymbol{\delta}}_m')'$. The third stage consists of estimating $\boldsymbol{\Sigma}$ based on $\hat{\boldsymbol{\delta}}_{\text{2SLS}}$ and (17.2.25) and then applying the feasible SUR procedure to the system of equations in which right-hand-side endogenous variable values have been replaced by their reduced-form predicted values. To demonstrate that this "last stage" is analogous to feasible SUR estimation, note that the GMM–3SLS estimator (17.2.24) can be equivalently written, albeit in a protracted form, as

$$\hat{\boldsymbol{\delta}}_{\text{GMM}} = [\mathbf{M}'[\mathbf{I} \otimes \mathbf{X}(\mathbf{X}'\mathbf{X})^{-1}\mathbf{X}'](\hat{\boldsymbol{\Sigma}}^{-1} \otimes \mathbf{I})[\mathbf{I} \otimes \mathbf{X}(\mathbf{X}'\mathbf{X})^{-1}\mathbf{X}']\mathbf{M}]^{-1} \cdot \mathbf{M}'[\mathbf{I} \otimes \mathbf{X}(\mathbf{X}'\mathbf{X})^{-1}\mathbf{X}'](\hat{\boldsymbol{\Sigma}}^{-1} \otimes \mathbf{I})\mathbf{Y}_v. \quad (17.2.29)$$

Because

$$\hat{\mathbf{M}} = [\mathbf{I} \otimes \mathbf{X}(\mathbf{X}'\mathbf{X})^{-1}\mathbf{X}']\mathbf{M} = \begin{bmatrix} \hat{\mathbf{M}}_{(1)} & & & \\ & \hat{\mathbf{M}}_{(2)} & & \\ & & \ddots & \\ & & & \hat{\mathbf{M}}_{(q)} \end{bmatrix}, \quad (17.2.30)$$

where $\hat{\mathbf{M}}_{(i)} = [\hat{\mathbf{Y}}_{(i)}\ \mathbf{X}_{(i)}]$ as in (17.2.17), it is then apparent that the effective "third stage" in conceptualizing the calculation of

$$\hat{\boldsymbol{\delta}}_{\text{GMM}} = [\hat{\mathbf{M}}'(\hat{\boldsymbol{\Sigma}}^{-1} \otimes \mathbf{I})\hat{\mathbf{M}}]^{-1}\hat{\mathbf{M}}'(\hat{\boldsymbol{\Sigma}}^{-1} \otimes \mathbf{I})\mathbf{Y}_v, \quad (17.2.31)$$

is the application of the feasible SUR procedure to a system of linear equations whose right-hand-side explanatory variable values for the ith equation consist of $\hat{\mathbf{M}}_{(i)}$ (compare with the SUR estimation procedure in Section 15.2).

So far we have not assumed that we know the underlying parametric family of distributions of the random variables in the linear simultaneous equations models. In the next section we make a normality assumption and revisit the ML procedure as it applies to the current model.

17.3. Maximum Likelihood Estimation in the Linear Model: The Parametric Case

We now assume that the equation noise components for the linear simultaneous equations model (LSEM) are multivariate normally distributed. This means we can summarize the information in the data and model by a likelihood function and, using procedures first introduced in Chapter 3, produce ML estimators that have some desirable statistical properties.

17.3.1. Full-Information Maximum Likelihood (FIML)

We continue to represent the LSEM in the stacked, vertically concatenated form

$$\mathbf{Y}_v = \mathbf{M}\boldsymbol{\delta} + \boldsymbol{\varepsilon}_v, \tag{17.3.1}$$

where $\boldsymbol{\varepsilon}_v$ is now assumed to be a multivariate *normal* random vector with mean $\mathbf{0}$ and covariance $\boldsymbol{\Sigma} \otimes \mathbf{I}$. This means, following the approach of Chapter 3, that we can write the joint-density function for $\boldsymbol{\varepsilon}$ as

$$\mathrm{f}(\boldsymbol{\varepsilon}_v; \boldsymbol{\Sigma}) = (2\pi)^{-qn/2}[\det(\boldsymbol{\Sigma} \otimes \mathbf{I})]^{-1/2} \exp\left[-\frac{1}{2}\boldsymbol{\varepsilon}_v'(\boldsymbol{\Sigma} \otimes \mathbf{I})^{-1}\boldsymbol{\varepsilon}_v\right], \tag{17.3.2}$$

where, as one may recall, the notation $\det(\boldsymbol{\Sigma} \otimes \mathbf{I})$ denotes the determinant of the matrix $\boldsymbol{\Sigma} \otimes \mathbf{I}$. If we replace $\boldsymbol{\varepsilon}_v$ by $\mathbf{Y}_v - \mathbf{M}\boldsymbol{\delta}$ and note that the Jacobian of the transformation from $\boldsymbol{\varepsilon}_v$ to $\mathbf{Y}_v$ is $\boldsymbol{\Gamma} \otimes \mathbf{I}_n$ (recall the definitions of $\mathbf{M}$ and $\boldsymbol{\delta}$ in (17.1.4)), an application of the change of variables approaches obtains the joint distribution of $\mathbf{Y}_v$ as

$$\begin{aligned}\mathrm{f}(\mathbf{Y}_v; \mathbf{X}, \boldsymbol{\delta}, \boldsymbol{\Sigma}) &= (2\pi)^{-qn/2}[\det(\boldsymbol{\Sigma} \otimes \mathbf{I})]^{-1/2}|\det(\boldsymbol{\Gamma})|^n \\ &\quad \times \exp\left[-\frac{1}{2}(\mathbf{Y}_v - \mathbf{M}\boldsymbol{\delta})'(\boldsymbol{\Sigma} \otimes \mathbf{I})^{-1}(\mathbf{Y}_v - \mathbf{M}\boldsymbol{\delta})\right],\end{aligned} \tag{17.3.3}$$

where the notation $|\det(\boldsymbol{\Gamma})|$ will be used henceforth to denote the *absolute value* of the determinant of $\boldsymbol{\Gamma}$. The log-likelihood function is then

$$\begin{aligned}\ln \mathrm{L}(\boldsymbol{\delta}, \boldsymbol{\Sigma}; \mathbf{Y}_v, \mathbf{X}) &= -\frac{qn}{2}\ln(2\pi) - \frac{n}{2}\ln(\det(\boldsymbol{\Sigma})) + n\ln(|\det(\boldsymbol{\Gamma})|) \\ &\quad - \frac{1}{2}(\mathbf{Y}_v - \mathbf{M}\boldsymbol{\delta})'(\boldsymbol{\Sigma}^{-1} \otimes \mathbf{I})(\mathbf{Y}_v - \mathbf{M}\boldsymbol{\delta})\end{aligned} \tag{17.3.4}$$

or, equivalently, in terms of the original nonvectorized form of the model (17.1.1)

$$\ln \mathrm{L}(\boldsymbol{\Gamma}, \mathbf{B}, \boldsymbol{\Sigma}; \mathbf{Y}, \mathbf{X}) = -\frac{qn}{2} \ln(2\pi) - \frac{n}{2} \ln(\det(\boldsymbol{\Sigma})) + n \ln(|\det(\boldsymbol{\Gamma})|) - \frac{1}{2} \operatorname{tr}(\boldsymbol{\Sigma}^{-1}(\mathbf{Y}\boldsymbol{\Gamma} - \mathbf{XB})'(\mathbf{Y}\boldsymbol{\Gamma} - \mathbf{XB})). \tag{17.3.5}$$

The maximum likelihood estimators of $\boldsymbol{\delta}$, and $\boldsymbol{\Sigma}$, or $\boldsymbol{\Gamma}$, $\mathbf{B}$, and $\boldsymbol{\Sigma}$ are then the values that maximize (17.3.4) or (17.3.5) subject to the zero and normalization restrictions on $\boldsymbol{\delta}$, or equivalently on $\mathbf{B}$ and $\boldsymbol{\Gamma}$. This estimator is known in the literature as the *full-information ML (FIML) estimator*.

For purposes of calculating a maximum likelihood solution, it is often helpful to define the *concentrated* likelihood function, which involves differentiating (17.3.5) with respect to $\boldsymbol{\Sigma}$ and solving this subset of the first-order conditions for the optimal $\boldsymbol{\Sigma}$ in terms of $\boldsymbol{\Gamma}$ and $\mathbf{B}$ as

$$\boldsymbol{\Sigma} = n^{-1}(\mathbf{Y}\boldsymbol{\Gamma} - \mathbf{XB})'(\mathbf{Y}\boldsymbol{\Gamma} - \mathbf{XB}). \tag{17.3.6}$$

When (17.3.6) is substituted for $\boldsymbol{\Sigma}$ in (17.3.5), we have concentrated the log-likelihood function on the $\boldsymbol{\Gamma}$, $\mathbf{B}$ parameters as follows:

$$\ln \mathrm{L_c}(\boldsymbol{\Gamma}, \mathbf{B}; \mathbf{Y}, \mathbf{X}) = \frac{-qn}{2}[1 + \ln(2\pi)] + n \ln(|\det(\boldsymbol{\Gamma})|) - \frac{n}{2} \ln\left(\det\left[\frac{1}{n}(\mathbf{Y}\boldsymbol{\Gamma} - \mathbf{XB})'(\mathbf{Y}\boldsymbol{\Gamma} - \mathbf{XB})\right]\right) \tag{17.3.7}$$

or equivalently, after the application of some matrix algebra,

$$\begin{aligned}\ln \mathrm{L_c}(\boldsymbol{\Gamma}, \mathbf{B}; \mathbf{Y}, \mathbf{X}) &= \tau - \frac{n}{2} \ln\left(\det\left[\frac{1}{n}(\boldsymbol{\Gamma}')^{-1}\boldsymbol{\Gamma}'(\mathbf{Y} - \mathbf{XB}\boldsymbol{\Gamma}^{-1})'(\mathbf{Y} - \mathbf{XB}\boldsymbol{\Gamma}^{-1})\boldsymbol{\Gamma}\boldsymbol{\Gamma}^{-1}\right]\right) \\ &= \tau - \frac{n}{2} \ln\left(\det\left[\frac{1}{n}\mathbf{Y} - \mathbf{XB}\boldsymbol{\Gamma}^{-1})'(\mathbf{Y} - \mathbf{XB}\boldsymbol{\Gamma}^{-1})\right]\right),\end{aligned} \tag{17.3.8}$$

where terms not related to unknown parameters in (17.3.8) have been represented collectively by τ. The latter representation of the likelihood function establishes a relationship with both the nonlinear regression models introduced in previous chapters and the corresponding numerical solution procedures for those models.

In terms of asymptotic properties, if we let $\mathbf{B}_0$ and $\boldsymbol{\Gamma}_0$ represent the true values of $\mathbf{B}$ and $\boldsymbol{\Gamma}$, and if we substitute $\mathbf{Y} = \mathbf{XB}_0\boldsymbol{\Gamma}_0^{-1} + \mathbf{V}$, into (17.3.8), then, given that the identification conditions and other general regularity conditions hold, $\operatorname{plim} \mathrm{L_c}(\cdot)$ is minimized at $\mathbf{B} = \mathbf{B}_0$, $\boldsymbol{\Gamma} = \boldsymbol{\Gamma}_0$, and the ML estimators of $\mathbf{B}$ and $\boldsymbol{\Gamma}$ are consistent. It also follows that the ML estimator of $\boldsymbol{\Sigma}$ obtained by substituting the ML estimators for $\boldsymbol{\Gamma}$ and $\mathbf{B}$ into (17.3.6), is consistent. Given the consistency of the ML estimators of $\boldsymbol{\Gamma}$, $\mathbf{B}$ and $\boldsymbol{\Sigma}$, it follows under general regularity conditions that

$$n^{1/2}(\boldsymbol{\delta}_{\mathrm{ML}} - \boldsymbol{\delta}) \xrightarrow{d} \mathrm{N}(\mathbf{0}, \operatorname{plim}(n^{-1}\tilde{\mathbf{M}}'[\boldsymbol{\Sigma}^{-1} \otimes \mathbf{I}]\tilde{\mathbf{M}})^{-1}), \tag{17.3.9}$$

where $\tilde{\mathbf{M}} = \operatorname{diag}[\tilde{\mathbf{M}}_{(1)}, \ldots, \tilde{\mathbf{M}}_{(m)}]$, $\tilde{\mathbf{M}}_{(i)} = [\tilde{\mathbf{Y}}_{(i)}, \tilde{\mathbf{X}}_{(i)}]$, $\tilde{\mathbf{Y}} = \mathbf{XB}\boldsymbol{\Gamma}^{-1}$, and $\tilde{\mathbf{Y}}_{(i)}$ is a matrix consisting of the columns of $\tilde{\mathbf{Y}}$ that correspond to the right-hand-side endogenous variables appearing in the ith equation. The asymptotic covariance matrix is estimated by replacing $\mathbf{\Sigma}$, $\mathbf{B}$, and $\mathbf{\Gamma}$ by their FIML estimates and, in particular, replacing $\tilde{\mathbf{M}}$ by $\hat{\mathbf{M}}$, where the columns of $\tilde{\mathbf{Y}}$ used in the definition of $\tilde{\mathbf{M}}$ are replaced by the appropriate columns of $\hat{\mathbf{Y}} = \mathbf{X}\hat{\mathbf{B}}\hat{\mathbf{\Gamma}}^{-1}$ to define $\hat{\mathbf{M}}$. Details of the derivation of the asymptotic covariance matrix of the FIML estimator of $\boldsymbol{\delta}$ can be found in Hausman (1975), who also demonstrates that FIML has an instrumental variable estimator interpretation. It is apparent from the preceding limiting distribution result, and the consistency of $\hat{\mathbf{B}}$ and $\hat{\mathbf{\Gamma}}$, that the GMM systems (3SLS) estimator of Section 17.2 and FIML are asymptotically equivalent *when the noise component is multivariate normally distributed.* If the normality assumption is correct, the FIML, and hence the GMM–3SLS estimator, are asymptotically efficient.

The usual Wald, Lagrange multiplier, and likelihood ratio tests are available for making tests relating to the values of functions of model parameters. In addition, interest sometimes centers on the validity of the overidentifying parameter restrictions for the system. To make such a test we can, for example, use the likelihood ratio test that compares the restricted (by exclusion restrictions) likelihood function (17.3.8) with the unrestricted likelihood function value based on the reduced-form noise component representation $\mathbf{V} = \mathbf{Y} - \mathbf{X}\boldsymbol{\pi}$, which amounts to replacing $\mathbf{B}\mathbf{\Gamma}^{-1}$ in (17.3.8) by the unrestricted ML estimates $\hat{\boldsymbol{\pi}}$. Twice the *difference* between the unrestricted and the restricted likelihood functions is asymptotically distributed as a χ^2 random variable with degrees of freedom equal to the number of *overidentifying* restrictions.

► **Example 17.3.1:** To demonstrate an application of the FIML estimator, we provide the GAUSS program C17FIML.gss in the examples manual. The program uses the concept of a concentrated log-likelihood function (17.3.8)-(17.3.8) to solve for the parameters of a structural model and to derive an estimate of the contemporaneous covariance matrix. The program generates a pseudo-random sample consistent with a version of the DSP (17.3.3) and then computes the FIML parameter estimates and the associated estimated standard errors, and also calculates 3SLS estimates for comparison purposes. Finally, the program conducts a hypothesis test and reports a confidence region for a subset of the model parameters.

Note that the FIML obtained by maximizing (17.3.3) can be applied even when the noise component is not assumed to be multivariate normally distributed. In this case, the FIML becomes a quasi-maximum likelihood (QML) estimator of model parameters. The QML is generally consistent and asymptotically normally distributed in this case, but it generally no longer has the asymptotic efficiency property of maximum likelihood estimation when the true underlying sampling distribution is not the normal distribution.

17.3.2. Limited Information Maximum Likelihood (LIML)

Consistent with Section 17.3.1, there is also a maximum likelihood basis for estimating *one* structural equation, or a proper subset of structural equations from a system of equations. Such a procedure, called *limited information ML* (LIML), was proposed by Anderson and Rubin in 1949 and was the method of choice used by applied researchers until 2SLS was discovered in the 1950s. In this context, assume we are interested in estimating the first equation of a system, which we write as

$$\mathbf{Y}_{.1} = \mathbf{Y}_{(1)}\gamma_1 + \mathbf{X}_{(1)}\boldsymbol{\beta}_1 + \varepsilon_{.1} = \mathbf{M}_{(1)}\boldsymbol{\delta}_1 + \varepsilon_{.1}. \tag{17.3.10}$$

Using information from the remainder of the system of equations, we can write the unrestricted reduced-form equations for the right-hand-side endogenous variables $\mathbf{Y}_{(1)}$ as

$$\mathbf{Y}_{(1)} = \mathbf{X}_{(1)}\boldsymbol{\pi}_1 + \mathbf{X}_{(-1)}\boldsymbol{\pi}_2 + \mathbf{V}_{(1)}, \tag{17.3.11}$$

where $\mathbf{X}_{(-1)}$ denotes the predetermined variables in the system that are *not* in the first equation. Note that the information contained in endogenous variables that are not in the first equation is not directly used in the formulation, which is why the approach is referred to as a *limited information* approach.

The LIML estimator of γ_1 and $\boldsymbol{\beta}_1$, or $\boldsymbol{\delta}_1$, is obtained by maximizing (under the normality assumption) the joint probability density of $\mathbf{Y}_{.1}$ and $\mathbf{Y}_{(1)}$ with respect to choices of $\boldsymbol{\delta}_1$, $\boldsymbol{\pi}_1$, $\boldsymbol{\pi}_2$ and the elements of the covariance matrix associated with the noise components $\varepsilon_{.1}$ and $\mathbf{V}_{.1}$ represented by $\boldsymbol{\Sigma}(\varepsilon_{.1}, \mathbf{V}_{.1})$. The resulting estimator does not make use of all the information in the system and is not as efficient as FIML when the normality assumptions is true. The LIML has asymptotic properties that are equivalent to the single-equation GMM and 2SLS estimators, and thus testing and confidence-region estimation can proceed as in the case of GMM based on asymptotic Chi-square and normal statistics. Some Monte Carlo evidence exists indicating that LIML has better finite sample properties than its 2SLS counterpart *when the noise component is truly multivariate normally distributed.* In terms of testing over-identifying restrictions, as in FIML, the likelihood ratio test statistic involving the restricted and unrestricted reduced forms of the joint density may be used to form a Chi-square test with degrees of freedom equal to the degree to which the restrictions overidentify the parameters.

► **Example 17.3.2:** To demonstrate an application of the LIML estimator, we provide the GAUSS program C17LIML.gss in the examples manual. The method of estimation utilized in the program is based on equations (17.3.10)–(17.3.11) and the discussion in the preceding paragraph. Following Example 17.3.1, the program generates a random sample consistent with a version of the DSP (17.3.3) and then computes the LIML parameter estimates and the associated estimated standard errors, and also calculates 2SLS estimates for comparison purposes. Finally, the program conducts a hypothesis test and reports a confidence region for a subset of the model parameters. By increasing the number of sample observations used in the analysis, the user should find that the LIML and 2SLS estimates of model parameters converge to each other.

17.4. Nonlinear Simultaneous Equations

Characterizations of DSPs sometimes require nonlinear model specifications, and in these situations linear models may, at best, be only first-order approximations. In a more general nonlinear context, we can write the *system of simultaneous equations as*

$$\mathbf{Y}_{\text{v}} = \mathbf{g}(\mathbf{M}, \boldsymbol{\delta}) + \varepsilon_{\text{v}}, \tag{17.4.1}$$

where $\mathbf{g}(\mathbf{M}, \boldsymbol{\delta}) \equiv [\mathbf{g}_1(\mathbf{M}_{(1)}, \boldsymbol{\delta}_1)', \mathbf{g}_2(\mathbf{M}_{(2)}, \boldsymbol{\delta}_2)', \ldots, \mathbf{g}_q(\mathbf{M}_{(q)}, \boldsymbol{\delta}_q)']'$ is a $(nq \times 1)$ vector function of endogenous variables, predetermined variables and parameters (or both), $\mathbf{Y}_{.i} = \mathbf{g}_i(\mathbf{M}_{(i)}, \boldsymbol{\delta}_i) + \varepsilon_{.i}$ denotes n potential observations on the ith equation of the system, and the remaining variables and parameters are as defined in (17.1.4.b) and (17.1.4.c). In this case, the nonlinearities can be handled through a GMM formulation that begins with nonlinear moment conditions.

17.4.1. Single-Equation Estimation: Semiparametric Case

The estimation and testing procedures that have been used most often in practice for analyzing nonlinear simultaneous equation models are members of the GMM class of procedures. To sketch the fundamental ideas involved, first consider the case of estimating one nonlinear equation in a system of simultaneous equations, the equation of interest being, say,

$$\mathbf{Y}_{.i} = \mathbf{g}_i\left(\mathbf{Y}_{(i)}, \mathbf{X}_{(i)}, \boldsymbol{\delta}_{(i)}\right) + \varepsilon_{.i}. \tag{17.4.2}$$

Here $\mathbf{g}_i(\cdot)$ is a continuous function of its arguments and is twice continuously differentiable in the $(k_i \times 1)$ parameter vector $\boldsymbol{\delta}_i$. Note that in the current context k_i refers to the total number of unknown parameters in $\mathbf{g}_i(\cdot)$ and not just to parameters associated with predetermined variables. We assume that some $(n \times m)$ matrix of instrumental variables, say $\mathbf{Z}$, exists that can be used to define the m moment conditions

$$\mathrm{E}\left[n^{-1}\mathbf{Z}'\left[\mathbf{Y}_{.i} - \mathbf{g}_i\left(\mathbf{Y}_{(i)}, \mathbf{X}_{(i)}, \boldsymbol{\delta}_{(i)}\right)\right]\right] = \mathbf{0}. \tag{17.4.3}$$

The instruments can consist of predetermined variables $\mathbf{X}$ in the system of equations, functions of them, or both.

17.4.1.a. Estimated Optimal GMM Estimation

To implement GMM estimation of $\boldsymbol{\delta}_i$, empirical moments corresponding to (17.4.3) are specified as

$$\bar{\mathbf{H}}_i(\boldsymbol{\delta}_i) \equiv n^{-1}\mathbf{Z}'\left[\mathbf{Y}_{.i} - \mathbf{g}_i\left(\mathbf{Y}_{(i)}, \mathbf{X}_{(i)}, \boldsymbol{\delta}_i\right)\right] = \mathbf{0}. \tag{17.4.4}$$

The asymptotically optimal GMM weighting matrix is defined in terms of the inverse of the asymptotic covariance matrix of $n^{-1/2}\mathbf{Z}'[\mathbf{Y}_{.i} - \mathbf{g}(\mathbf{Y}_{(i)}, \mathbf{X}_{(i)}, \boldsymbol{\delta}_i)]$ (recall Section 16.2). If the entries in $\varepsilon_{.i}$ are independent with mean zero and variance σ^2, $\sigma^2 n^{-1}\mathbf{Z}'\mathbf{Z}$ converges to this asymptotic covariance matrix (recall Section 17.2.2 and note the heteroscedastic–robust alternative representation in (17.1.16)). Then, because σ^2 is a positive scalar multiplier of the asymptotically optimal weight matrix, it can be suppressed in the objective function used to define the GMM estimator, and the estimated optimal GMM (EOGMM) estimator is obtained by solving the GMM extremum problem

$$\begin{aligned}\hat{\boldsymbol{\delta}}_{i,\text{EOGMM}} &= \arg\min_{\delta_i}[[n^{-1}\mathbf{Z}'[\mathbf{Y}_{\cdot i} - \mathbf{g}_i(\boldsymbol{\delta}_i)]]'(n^{-1}\mathbf{Z}'\mathbf{Z})^{-1}[n^{-1}\mathbf{Z}'[\mathbf{Y}_{\cdot i} - \mathbf{g}_i(\boldsymbol{\delta}_i)]]] \\ &= \arg\min_{\delta_i}[[\mathbf{Y}_{\cdot i} - \mathbf{g}_i(\boldsymbol{\delta}_i)]'\mathbf{Z}(\mathbf{Z}'\mathbf{Z})^{-1}\mathbf{Z}'[\mathbf{Y}_{\cdot i} - \mathbf{g}_i(\boldsymbol{\delta}_i)]], \end{aligned} \quad (17.4.5)$$

where to simplify notation we henceforth define $\mathbf{g}_i(\boldsymbol{\delta}_i) \equiv \mathbf{g}_i(\mathbf{Y}_{(i)}, \mathbf{X}_{(i)}, \boldsymbol{\delta}_i)$, and we have suppressed the n^{-1} terms in (17.4.5), which has no effect on the EOGMM solution.

In the context of a simultaneous equations system, a typical choice for the instrumental variables is the matrix of predetermined variables $\mathbf{X}$. Setting $\mathbf{Z} \equiv \mathbf{X}$, the EOGMM estimator of $\boldsymbol{\delta}_i$ is defined by

$$\hat{\boldsymbol{\delta}}_{i,\text{EOGMM}} = \arg\min_{\delta_i}[[\mathbf{Y}_{\cdot i} - \mathbf{g}(\boldsymbol{\delta}_i)]'\mathbf{X}(\mathbf{X}'\mathbf{X})^{-1}\mathbf{X}'[\mathbf{Y}_{\cdot i} - \mathbf{g}(\boldsymbol{\delta}_i)]]. \quad (17.4.6)$$

Amemiya (1974) called the GMM estimator in (17.4.6) the *nonlinear two-stages least-squares estimator*. However, the name is somewhat misleading because, unlike the case of linear models, the estimator (17.4.6) cannot be conceptualized as being constructed in "two steps." Note, however, that in the special linear-model case in which $\mathbf{g}_i(\boldsymbol{\delta}_i) \equiv \mathbf{M}_{(i)}\boldsymbol{\delta}_i$, it follows that

$$\hat{\boldsymbol{\delta}}_{i,\text{EOGMM}} \equiv \hat{\boldsymbol{\delta}}_{i,2\text{SLS}} = \left[\mathbf{M}_{(i)}'\mathbf{X}(\mathbf{X}'\mathbf{X})^{-1}\mathbf{X}'\mathbf{M}_{(i)}\right]^{-1}\mathbf{M}_{(i)}'\mathbf{X}(\mathbf{X}'\mathbf{X})^{-1}\mathbf{X}'\mathbf{Y}_{\cdot i}, \quad (17.4.7)$$

and thus the EOGMM estimator is identically the two-stage least-squares estimator for linear models, which has the "two-stages" interpretation.

The EOGMM estimator (17.4.6) inherits all of the general GMM properties, including consistency and asymptotic normality, where

$$n^{1/2}(\hat{\boldsymbol{\delta}}_{i,\text{EOGMM}} - \boldsymbol{\delta}_i) \xrightarrow{d} N\left(\mathbf{0}, \left[\frac{\partial \mathbf{h}_i^0(\boldsymbol{\delta}_i)}{\partial \boldsymbol{\delta}_i}[\sigma^2 \text{plim}(n^{-1}\mathbf{X}'\mathbf{X})]^{-1}\frac{\partial \mathbf{h}_i^0(\boldsymbol{\delta}_i)}{\partial \boldsymbol{\delta}_i'}\right]^{-1}\right) \quad (17.4.8)$$

with $\mathbf{h}_i^0(\boldsymbol{\delta}_i) = \text{plim}[\bar{\mathbf{H}}_i(\boldsymbol{\delta}_i)]$ (recall (17.4.4) and also Section 16.2.3.b with straightforward notational changes). The asymptotic covariance matrix of $\hat{\boldsymbol{\delta}}_{i,\text{EOGMM}}$ can then be estimated by

$$\widehat{\mathbf{cov}}(\hat{\boldsymbol{\delta}}_{i,\text{EOGMM}}) = \frac{\hat{\sigma}^2}{n}\left[\left.\frac{\partial \bar{\mathbf{H}}_i(\boldsymbol{\delta}_i)}{\partial \boldsymbol{\delta}_i}\right|_{\hat{\delta}_{i,\text{EOGMM}}}(n^{-1}\mathbf{X}'\mathbf{X})^{-1}\left.\frac{\partial \bar{\mathbf{H}}_i(\boldsymbol{\delta}_i)}{\partial \boldsymbol{\delta}_i'}\right|_{\hat{\delta}_{i,\text{EOGMM}}}\right]^{-1} \quad (17.4.9)$$

where $\hat{\sigma}^2 = n^{-1}(\hat{\varepsilon}_{\cdot i}{}'\hat{\varepsilon}_{\cdot i})$ and $\hat{\varepsilon}_{\cdot i} = \mathbf{Y}_{\cdot i} - \mathbf{g}_i(\hat{\boldsymbol{\delta}}_{i,\text{EOGMM}})$. Note that in the case of the linear model, (17.4.9) equals

$$\widehat{\mathbf{cov}}(\hat{\boldsymbol{\delta}}_{i,2\text{SLS}}) = \hat{\sigma}^2\left[\mathbf{M}_{(i)}'\mathbf{X}(\mathbf{X}'\mathbf{X})^{-1}\mathbf{X}'\mathbf{M}_{(i)}\right]^{-1}. \quad (17.4.10)$$

As usual, the asymptotic normality of $\hat{\boldsymbol{\delta}}_{i,\text{EOGMM}}$ can be used to construct asymptotically valid Wald, LM, or pseudolikelihood ratio tests of the value of functions of the parameter vector δ_i. Duality can be used to produce confidence-region estimates.

17.4.1.b. Accommodating Heteroscedasticity and Autocorrelation

Heteroscedasticity and autocorrelation can be accommodated by an appropriate redefinition of the optimal weighting matrix in the definition of the GMM estimator. For example, if the noise component is heteroscedastic, then the optimal EOGMM weighting matrix can be estimated by the inverse of White's Heteroscedasticity robust estimator of the asymptotic covariance matrix of $n^{-1/2}\mathbf{Z}'[\mathbf{Y}_{\cdot i} - \mathbf{g}_i(\boldsymbol{\delta}_i)]$ given by $n^{-1}\sum_{j=1}^{n} \hat{\varepsilon}_{ji}^2 \mathbf{Z}_{j\cdot}'\mathbf{Z}_{j\cdot}$. The EOGMM estimator can then be defined by

$$\hat{\boldsymbol{\delta}}_{i,\mathrm{EOGMM}} = \arg\min_{\boldsymbol{\delta}_i} \left[[n^{-1}\mathbf{Z}'[\mathbf{Y}_{\cdot i} - \mathbf{g}_i(\boldsymbol{\delta}_i)]]' \left(n^{-1} \sum_{j=1}^{n} \hat{\varepsilon}_{ji}^2 \mathbf{Z}_{j\cdot}'\mathbf{Z}_{j\cdot} \right)^{-1} \times [n^{-1}\mathbf{Z}'[\mathbf{Y}_{\cdot i} - \mathbf{g}_i(\boldsymbol{\delta}_i)]] \right]. \tag{17.4.11}$$

Note that $\hat{\boldsymbol{\varepsilon}}_{\cdot i}$ will be obtained from a consistent estimate of $\boldsymbol{\delta}_i$ generated from a GMM estimator based on a weighting matrix of $\mathbf{W} = \mathbf{I}$ (or possibly some other fixed choice of positive definite symmetric weight matrix).

Autocorrelation, with or without heteroscedasticity, can be accommodated using a Newey–West type estimator of the asymptotic covariance matrix of $n^{-1/2}\mathbf{Z}'[\mathbf{Y}_{\cdot i} - \mathbf{g}_i(\boldsymbol{\delta}_i)]$ in place of White's estimator. However, we note a complication that can arise in practice if the noise components of the equations in the system are autocorrelated *and* the $\mathbf{X}$ matrix contains lagged dependent variables. In particular, one cannot use lagged dependent variables contained in $\mathbf{X}$ as instruments when defining the $\mathbf{Z}$ matrix because these lagged dependent variables are correlated with subsequent noise component elements of the model. In effect lagged dependent variables are *not* actually predetermined variables when the noise component of the model is autocorrelated (recall the definition of predetermined variables in Section 17.1), and so these variables cannot serve as instruments. Relatedly, the moment conditions (17.4.3) are no longer valid if lagged dependent variables are used in the definition of the $\mathbf{Z}$ matrix. In practice, lagged values of the truly predetermined variables contained in $\mathbf{X}$ are often used in place of the lagged dependent variables when defining the instrumental variables matrix $\mathbf{Z}$. Then, given these instruments, the GMM estimator based on the weight matrix of $\mathbf{W} = \mathbf{I}$ is used to generate a consistent estimator of model parameters, and a consistent estimate of the model's noise component is calculated. The noise component estimates are finally used in a Newey–West type estimator to estimate the asymptotic covariance matrix of the scaled moment conditions, the inverse of which is used as the weight matrix in defining the EOGMM estimator. For additional information on the problem of defining instruments when autocorrelation is present, see Hatanaka (1974, 1976).

In the unlikely event that the analyst is fortunate enough actually to know the appropriate parametric structure of any heteroscedasticity, autocorrelation, or both, the model specification can be altered to accommodate this structure, and the autocorrelation and heteroscedasticity problems thereby mitigated asymptotically (as discussed in Chapter 15). We emphasize that the robust and parametric procedures for accommodating heteroscedasticity, autocorrelation, or both, apply equally well in the special case in which $\mathbf{g}_i(\boldsymbol{\delta}_i)$ represents a *linear* model.

17.4.2. Complete System Estimation: Semiparametric Case

To estimate the parameters of a complete system of nonlinear equations, we again turn to the GMM class of procedures. We now represent the n observations on q structural equations in vertically concatenated or "stacked" form

$$\mathbf{Y}_{\mathrm{v}} = \mathbf{g}(\mathbf{M}, \boldsymbol{\delta}) + \boldsymbol{\varepsilon}_{\mathrm{v}}, \tag{17.4.12}$$

as defined in (17.4.1). The $\mathbf{g}_i(\cdot)$'s contained in $\mathbf{g} = (\mathbf{g}_1', \ldots, \mathbf{g}_q')'$ are assumed to be continuous functions of their arguments and twice continuously differentiable in the parameter vector. We again assume that some $(n \times m)$ matrix of instrumental variables, $\mathbf{Z}$, is available that can be used to define the mq moment conditions

$$\mathrm{E}[n^{-1}(\mathbf{I}_q \otimes \mathbf{Z}')[\mathbf{Y}_{\mathrm{v}} - \mathbf{g}(\mathbf{M}, \boldsymbol{\delta})]] = \mathbf{0}. \tag{17.4.13}$$

The corresponding set of mq empirical moment conditions are given by

$$\bar{\mathbf{H}}(\boldsymbol{\delta}) \equiv n^{-1}(\mathbf{I}_q \otimes \mathbf{Z}')[\mathbf{Y}_{\mathrm{v}} - \mathbf{g}(\mathbf{M}, \boldsymbol{\delta})] = \mathbf{0}. \tag{17.4.14}$$

If the rows of the unstacked $(n \times q)$ noise component matrix $\boldsymbol{\varepsilon}$ are independent with covariance matrix $\boldsymbol{\Sigma}_i$, for $i = 1, \ldots, n$, then the asymptotic covariance matrix of $n^{-1/2}(\mathbf{I}_q \otimes \mathbf{Z}')[\mathbf{Y}_{\mathrm{v}} - \mathbf{g}(\mathbf{M}, \boldsymbol{\delta})]$ is consistently estimated by

$$\begin{aligned}\hat{\mathbf{W}}_n^{-1} &= n^{-1}\sum_{i=1}^{n}(\mathbf{I}_q \otimes \mathbf{Z}_{i\cdot}')\hat{\boldsymbol{\varepsilon}}_{i\cdot}'\hat{\boldsymbol{\varepsilon}}_{i\cdot}(\mathbf{I}_q \otimes \mathbf{Z}_{i\cdot}) \\ &= n^{-1}\sum_{i=1}^{n}(\hat{\boldsymbol{\varepsilon}}_{i\cdot} \otimes \mathbf{Z}_{i\cdot})'(\hat{\boldsymbol{\varepsilon}}_{i\cdot} \otimes \mathbf{Z}_{i\cdot}),\end{aligned} \tag{17.4.15}$$

where $\hat{\boldsymbol{\varepsilon}}$ is the $(n \times q)$ unstacked form of $\hat{\boldsymbol{\varepsilon}}_{\mathrm{v}} = \mathbf{Y}_{\mathrm{v}} - \mathbf{g}(\mathbf{M}, \hat{\boldsymbol{\delta}})$, and $\hat{\boldsymbol{\delta}}$ is a consistent estimator of $\boldsymbol{\delta}$ (Gallant, 1987, pp. 444–5). The estimator (17.4.15) is a generalization of White's heteroscedastic robust covariance matrix estimator and is identical to the estimator discussed in Section 15.4 when $q = 1$. The EOGMM estimator of $\boldsymbol{\delta}$ is then defined by

$$\begin{aligned}\hat{\boldsymbol{\delta}}_{\mathrm{EOGMM}} = \arg\min_{\boldsymbol{\delta}}&[n^{-1}(\mathbf{I}_q \otimes \mathbf{Z}')[\mathbf{Y}_{\mathrm{v}} - \mathbf{g}(\mathbf{M}, \boldsymbol{\delta})]]' \\ &\times \hat{\mathbf{W}}_n[n^{-1}(\mathbf{I}_q \otimes \mathbf{Z}')[\mathbf{Y}_{\mathrm{v}} - \mathbf{g}(\mathbf{M}, \boldsymbol{\delta})]].\end{aligned} \tag{17.4.16}$$

Note that in calculating a consistent estimator of $\boldsymbol{\delta}$ to use in defining the estimated noise component appearing in (17.4.15), a consistent GMM estimator is often used based on (17.4.16) with $\hat{\mathbf{W}}_n$ replaced by $\mathbf{I}_{qm}$.

In the context of a simultaneous equations system, a logical choice for the instrumental variables is the matrix of predetermined variables $\mathbf{X}$, in which case $\mathbf{Z} \equiv \mathbf{X}$ in (17.4.13)–(17.4.16). On the basis of the usual EOGMM properties, the estimator is a consistent estimator of $\boldsymbol{\delta}$ and is asymptotically normally distributed with a mean of $\boldsymbol{\delta}$ and an asymptotic covariance matrix that is consistently estimated by

$$\mathbf{c\hat{o}v}(\hat{\boldsymbol{\delta}}_{\mathrm{EOGMM}}) = n^{-1}\left[\left.\frac{\partial \bar{\mathbf{H}}(\boldsymbol{\delta})}{\partial \boldsymbol{\delta}}\right|_{\hat{\boldsymbol{\delta}}_{\mathrm{EOGMM}}} \hat{\mathbf{W}}_n \left.\frac{\partial \bar{\mathbf{H}}(\boldsymbol{\delta})}{\partial \boldsymbol{\delta}'}\right|_{\hat{\boldsymbol{\delta}}_{\mathrm{EOGMM}}}\right]^{-1}. \tag{17.4.17}$$

Asymptotic tests and confidence-region estimation procedures can be based on the asymptotic normality of $\hat{\boldsymbol{\delta}}_{\mathrm{EOGMM}}$ in the usual way.

In the special case in which the rows of the noise component matrix are independent with common variance matrix $\mathbf{\Sigma}$, the optimal weight matrix $\mathbf{W}_n$ is given by $(\mathbf{\Sigma} \otimes [n^{-1}\mathbf{Z}'\mathbf{Z}])^{-1}$. If $\mathbf{\Sigma}$ is replaced with a consistent estimator $\hat{\mathbf{\Sigma}}$, the EOGMM estimator can be defined in this case by

$$\hat{\delta}_{\text{EOGMM}} = \arg\min_{\delta}[[\mathbf{Y}_{\text{v}} - \mathbf{g}(\mathbf{M}, \delta)]'[\hat{\mathbf{\Sigma}}^{-1} \otimes \mathbf{Z}(\mathbf{Z}'\mathbf{Z})^{-1}\mathbf{Z}'][\mathbf{Y}_{\text{v}} - \mathbf{g}(\mathbf{M}, \delta)]], \tag{17.4.18}$$

which Jorgenson and Laffont (1974) called the *nonlinear three-stage least-squares estimator*, although there is nothing akin to "three stages" in the calculation of $\hat{\delta}_{\text{EOGMM}}$. A consistent estimator of $\hat{\mathbf{\Sigma}}$ can be defined by $n^{-1}\sum_{i=1}^{n}\hat{\varepsilon}'_{\cdot i}\hat{\varepsilon}_{\cdot i}$, where $\hat{\varepsilon}_{\cdot i}$ is the estimated noise component value for observation i based on parameter estimates from (17.4.18) with $\hat{\mathbf{\Sigma}}^{-1}$ replaced by $\mathbf{I}_q$. In the even more specialized linear model case in which $\mathbf{g}(\mathbf{M}, \delta) = \mathbf{M}\delta$, and with $\mathbf{Z} \equiv \mathbf{X}$, the EOGMM estimator (17.4.18) is identically equal to the (linear) three-stage least-squares estimator discussed in Section 17.3.

Autocorrelation, either with or without heteroscedasticity, can be accommodated by using a Newey–West-type procedure for defining a consistent estimator of the asymptotic covariance matrix of $n^{-1/2}([\mathbf{I}_q \otimes \mathbf{Z}'][\mathbf{Y}_{\text{v}} - \mathbf{g}(\mathbf{M}, \delta)])$ and then using its inverse as the weight matrix in defining the EOGMM. The complication of not being able to use lagged dependent variables in the definition of the instrumental variable matrix when the noise component is autocorrelated is analogous to the discussion following (17.4.11). As we noted previously, lagged dependent variables effectively cease to be predetermined variables in such cases.

In the unlikely event that the analyst knows the functional parametric structure of any heteroscedasticity, autocorrelation, or both in the simultaneous equations system, a parametric estimation of the scaled moment covariance matrix can be pursued. Informative readings on the parameterization of autocorrelation in the context of systems of equations include Berndt and Savin (1975) and Srivastava and Giles (1987, Chapter 7).

17.4.3. Nonlinear Maximum Likelihood Estimation: Parametric Case

If a specific parametric family of probability distributions can be assumed for the noise component of the nonlinear simultaneous equations model, then one can proceed to use maximum likelihood (ML) estimation to estimate the model parameters. Assuming that the rows of ε are independent $\text{N}(\mathbf{0}, \mathbf{\Sigma})$, we then have that

$$[\mathbf{Y}_{\text{v}} - \mathbf{g}(\mathbf{M}, \delta)] \sim \text{N}(\mathbf{0}, \mathbf{\Sigma} \otimes \mathbf{I}_q). \tag{17.4.19}$$

The logarithm of the likelihood function for the parameters of the problem is then

$$\ln \text{L}(\delta, \mathbf{\Sigma}; \mathbf{y}_{\text{v}}, \mathbf{x}_{\text{v}}) = -\frac{nq}{2}\ln(2\pi) + \sum_{i=1}^{n}\ln(|\det(\mathbf{J}_i)|) - \frac{n}{2}\ln(\det[\mathbf{\Sigma}])$$
$$- \frac{1}{2}[\mathbf{y}_{\text{v}} - \mathbf{g}(\mathbf{m}, \delta)]'(\mathbf{\Sigma}^{-1} \otimes \mathbf{I}_q)[\mathbf{y}_{\text{v}} - \mathbf{g}(\mathbf{m}, \delta)], \tag{17.4.20}$$

where $\mathbf{J}_i$ is the Jacobian of the transformation from $\varepsilon_{i\cdot}$ to $\mathbf{Y}_i$, and $|\det(\mathbf{J}_i)|$ denotes the absolute value of the determinant of $\mathbf{J}_i$. The ML estimator of $\boldsymbol{\delta}$ and $\boldsymbol{\Sigma}$ is then

$$(\hat{\boldsymbol{\delta}}, \hat{\boldsymbol{\Sigma}}) = \arg \max_{\boldsymbol{\delta},\boldsymbol{\Sigma}} [\ln \mathrm{L}(\boldsymbol{\delta}, \boldsymbol{\Sigma}; \mathbf{Y}, \mathbf{X})]. \quad (17.4.21)$$

The ML estimator will be consistent, asymptotically normally distributed, and asymptotically efficient under general regularity conditions. The asymptotic covariance matrix of $(\hat{\boldsymbol{\delta}}, \hat{\boldsymbol{\Sigma}})$ can then be estimated in the usual way based on first- or second-order derivatives of $\ln \mathrm{L}$ evaluated at the ML estimates, as described in Chapter 4. Note that unlike the linear model case, the FIML and the complete system EOGMM (NL3SLS) estimators are *not* generally asymptotically equivalent.

It should be noted that unlike the linear case, the QML estimator is generally *not* consistent in the nonlinear simultaneous equations case. The interested reader can consult Amemiya (1977) for further details on this inconsistency problem. Thus, although ML provides the efficient estimator for structural parameters in a simultaneous equations system when the distribution of the noise component can be specified parametrically, it is not robust to misspecification of this distribution. Furthermore, computation of the estimator can be numerically quite challenging. For these reasons, GMM is used more often than ML in applications despite the fact that FIML is generally more asymptotically efficient *if normality of* $\boldsymbol{\varepsilon}$ *is true.*

Computationally, there is a large literature, dating back to Eisenpress and Greenstadt (1966) on algorithms that can be used to maximize the likelihood function in a nonlinear FIML problem. An informative presentation concerning related NLS computational problems is contained in Chapter 8 of Amemiya (1985).

► **Example 17.4.1:** The GAUSS program C17NL.gss (provided in the examples manual) demonstrates an application of the nonlinear two-stage and three-stage least-squares estimators, (17.4.5) and (17.4.16), and the nonlinear FIML estimator (17.4.21). For a simple nonlinear system of equations (partly specified by the user), the program generates a pseudorandom set of observations and computes the parameter estimates and the estimated covariance matrices. The program then conducts a series of hypothesis tests to compare the inferential decisions formed in each case.

17.4.4. Identification in Nonlinear Systems of Equations

To this point we have not discussed the issue of parameter identification in nonlinear simultaneous equation systems. Unfortunately, conditions for identification are generally much more complicated in the nonlinear case than in the linear case discussed previously. In particular, identification cannot generally be verified by examining order or rank conditions involving only the parameters of the simultaneous equations system, and in fact the very idea of reduced-form parameters may be ill-defined because reduced forms of nonlinear systems may not even exist in closed form.

We will briefly mention a few results that can be helpful when contemplating the identifiability of parameters in a system. Additional details relating to various parameter identification concepts can be found in the works of Fisher (1966), Gabrielsen (1978), Rothenberg (1971), and the summary in Greenberg and Webster (1983, Chapter 9).

First of all, it is helpful to note that the existence of a consistent estimator for a parameter vector $\boldsymbol{\delta}$ implies the identification of the parameter vector. Thus, if regularity conditions hold that ensure the consistency of an estimator of $\boldsymbol{\delta}$, such as those that can be stated for GMM or ML estimators, then these regularity conditions are also sufficient conditions for the identification of the parameter vector. This result was demonstrated in the informative short article by Gabrielsen (1978).

On a general level, identification of a parameter vector $\boldsymbol{\theta}$ is concerned with whether a parameterized model is such that $\mathrm{f}(\mathbf{y};\boldsymbol{\theta}_0) \neq \mathrm{f}(\mathbf{y};\boldsymbol{\theta}_1)$ when $\boldsymbol{\theta}_0 \neq \boldsymbol{\theta}_1$. Parameter vectors $\boldsymbol{\theta}_0$ and $\boldsymbol{\theta}_1$ are *observationally equivalent* when $\mathrm{f}(\mathbf{y};\boldsymbol{\theta}_0) = \mathrm{f}(\mathbf{y};\boldsymbol{\theta}_1)$ with probability 1, in which case neither $\boldsymbol{\theta}_0$ nor $\boldsymbol{\theta}_1$ is identifiable because differences in the behavior of sample outcomes, $\mathbf{y}$ do not relate to differences in the parameter values $\boldsymbol{\theta}_0$ and $\boldsymbol{\theta}_1$. A parameter vector $\boldsymbol{\theta}_0$ is *globally* identifiable if there is no other parameter vector $\boldsymbol{\theta}$ to which it is observationally equivalent. The parameter vector $\boldsymbol{\theta}_0$ is *locally* identified if there is no other $\boldsymbol{\theta}$ in an open neighborhood of $\boldsymbol{\theta}_0$ to which $\boldsymbol{\theta}_0$ is observationally equivalent.

Rothenberg (1971) settles the issue of local identification when the support of the probability density $\mathrm{f}(\mathbf{y};\boldsymbol{\theta})$ does not depend on $\boldsymbol{\theta}$ and the information matrix $\mathrm{I}(\boldsymbol{\theta}) \equiv \mathrm{E}[\frac{\partial \ln \mathrm{f}(\mathbf{Y};\boldsymbol{\theta})}{\partial \boldsymbol{\theta}} \frac{\partial \ln \mathrm{f}(\mathbf{Y};\boldsymbol{\theta})}{\partial \boldsymbol{\theta}'}]$ exists and is continuous in $\boldsymbol{\theta}$. In this case, $\boldsymbol{\theta}_0$ is locally identifiable if $\mathrm{I}(\boldsymbol{\theta})$ is nonsingular in a neighborhood of $\boldsymbol{\theta}_0$. Note in the context of ML estimation that this condition relates to the nonsingularity of the covariance matrix of the estimator. If it can be further assumed that $\mathrm{f}(\mathbf{y};\boldsymbol{\theta})$ is a member of the exponential class of densities, and if in addition $\mathrm{I}(\boldsymbol{\theta})$ has full rank for all $\boldsymbol{\theta}$ in some convex set of parameter values Ω, then the parameter vector $\boldsymbol{\theta}$ is globally identified on Ω.

As a practical matter, identification conditions will generally depend on unknown parameters and will not be verifiable with certainty. In practice, when dealing with nonlinear systems, one generally presumes that if an estimate of a parameter vector is found that optimizes the estimation objective function of GMM, ML, or some other accepted estimation procedure, and if the estimate is not blatantly imprecise as evidenced by an inordinately large asymptotic covariance matrix estimate, then the parameter vector is identified in the model being estimated. The rationale is that, if $\boldsymbol{\theta}$ was not identified in the model, such a solution would not exist for the estimation problem. Of course, such a decision rule is far from foolproof because, in nonlinear estimation situations, numerical anomalies can prevent solutions or else even create solutions in cases in which none should theoretically exist. But by and large, the existence of a sensible solution to a nonlinear estimation problem is generally good evidence that a parameter vector is indeed identified.

17.5. Information Theoretic Procedures

Having studied Chapters 12, 13, and 16, one might suspect that there are information theoretic alternatives to the traditional GMM or ML class of estimators that have the same data requirements and computational feasibility and that are also comparable in terms of the inference procedures available. Although GMM and ML procedures can produce useful estimates and inferences, there are reasons why it is indeed prudent to consider alternative approaches. In the case of ML, the information requirement is stringent – the analyst must have knowledge of the functional form characterizing the parametric family of distributions underlying the data sampling process. In practice the analyst is most often in a semiparametric environment in which knowledge of the functional form of the appropriate parametric probability distribution family is not available. The analyst is then relegated to a QML analysis for which the full set of sampling properties attributable to the ML approach generally does not apply. We henceforth concentrate on the semiparametric environment.

Regarding the GMM approach, Hansen and Singleton (1982) demonstrated a basis for estimating the EOGMM weight matrix, leading to consistent estimators with a minimum *asymptotic* covariance matrix *for a given set of moment restrictions*. However, Altonji and Segal (1994), reporting the results of a simulation study, noted that the resulting two-stage estimators are biased in small samples "because sampling errors in the second moments are correlated with sampling errors in the estimate of the covariance matrix of the sample moments." Furthermore, they found in some cases that the use of the asymptotically nonoptimal identity matrix in place of an *estimate* of the asymptotically optimal weight matrix produced a GMM with better finite sample properties than the EOGMM. Thus, the finite sample performance of the EOGMM is open to question. It therefore seems reasonable to examine information theoretic alternatives that avoid the data-dependent two-stage tuning associated with asymptotic covariance matrix estimation. In effect, the discussion ahead provides a review and extension of the MEEL and MEL approaches of Chapters 12, 13, and 16 as they apply to the simultaneous equations inverse problem context of this chapter.

17.5.1. Minimum KLIC Approach: MEEL and MEL

Within the context of Chapters 12, 13, and 16, one information theoretic alternative to GMM estimation is to use a minimum Kullback–Leibler information criterion (KLIC) in place of the GMM criterion to estimate model parameters. In sketching the procedure, first note, as in previous chapters, that the minimum KLIC–MEEL–MEL procedure begins with the same basic theoretical moment conditions as the GMM procedure, namely, the moment conditions

$$\mathrm{E}\big[n^{-1}\mathbf{Z}'\big[\mathbf{Y}_{\cdot i} - \mathbf{g}_i\big(\mathbf{Y}_{(i)}, \mathbf{X}_{(i)}, \delta_i\big)\big]\big] = \mathbf{0} \tag{17.5.1}$$

in the single equation case, or

$$\mathrm{E}[n^{-1}(\mathbf{I}_q \otimes \mathbf{Z}')[\mathbf{Y}_{\mathrm{v}} - \mathbf{g}(\mathbf{M}, \delta)]] = \mathbf{0} \tag{17.5.2}$$

in the case of a system of equations (recall Equations (17.4.3) and (17.4.13)). However, the translation to *empirical* moment conditions does not follow the GMM approach in (17.4.3) and (17.4.13). Instead, for the single (ith) equation case, the moment conditions are given by

$$\sum_{j=1}^{n} \mathrm{p}_j \mathbf{Z}'_{j.}\big[\mathbf{Y}_{ji} - \mathrm{g}_i\big(\mathbf{Y}_{(i)}[j, .], \mathbf{X}_{(i)}[j, .], \delta\big)\big] = \mathbf{0}, \tag{17.5.3}$$

or equivalently

$$(\mathbf{p} \odot \mathbf{Z})'\left[\mathbf{Y}_{\cdot i} - g_i\left(\mathbf{Y}_{(i)}, \mathbf{X}_{(i)}, \boldsymbol{\delta}_i\right)\right] = \mathbf{0}, \tag{17.5.4}$$

where $\odot$ denotes the Hadamard (elementwise) product operator and $\mathbf{p} = (\mathrm{p}_1, \mathrm{p}_2, \ldots, \mathrm{p}_n)'$, with $\mathbf{1}'\mathbf{p} = 1$ and $\mathrm{p}_i \geq 0\,\forall_i$. For the case of an entire system of simultaneous equations, the empirical moment conditions are given by (17.5.3) for $i = 1, \ldots, q$, or equivalently by

$$[\mathbf{I}_q \otimes (\mathbf{p} \odot \mathbf{Z})'][\mathbf{Y}_{\mathrm{v}} - \mathbf{g}(\mathbf{M}, \boldsymbol{\delta})] = \mathbf{0}. \tag{17.5.5}$$

Thus, the essential difference in the empirical representation of the moment conditions is the replacement of the equal sample observation weights implied by the classical empirical distribution function $n^{-1}\mathbf{1}$ with a more flexible distribution of sample observation weights $(\mathrm{p}_1, \mathrm{p}_2, \ldots, \mathrm{p}_n)$.

For clarity of exposition we temporarily focus attention on a single equation contained within a simultaneous linear system of equations, so that $\mathbf{g}_i(\mathbf{Y}_{(i)}, \mathbf{X}_{(i)}, \boldsymbol{\delta}_i) \equiv \mathbf{M}_{(i)}\boldsymbol{\delta}_i$ with $\mathbf{M}_{(i)} \equiv [\mathbf{Y}_{(i)}, \mathbf{X}_{(i)}]$, but the procedure applies equally well to the general cases of (17.5.4) and (17.5.5) mutatis mutandis. We will return to the more general nonlinear equations and systems of equations cases ahead and summarize what is involved in making these extensions.

The estimation objective in the minimum KLIC–MEEL–MEL approach is to choose values of both $\mathbf{p}$ and $\boldsymbol{\delta}$ to minimize the KL information discrepancy between the $\mathbf{p}$-distribution and the empirical uniform distribution of weights n^{-1}, $\forall i$ subject to the generalized empirical moment constraints and the probability distribution normalization constraint. Whether the KLIC is specified as $\varphi(\mathbf{p}) \equiv \mathrm{KL}(\mathbf{p}, n^{-1}\mathbf{1})$ or $\varphi(\mathbf{p}) \equiv \mathrm{KL}(n^{-1}\mathbf{1}, \mathbf{p})$ determines whether the MEEL or the MEL approach will be used to solve the inverse problem, respectively. This leads to the extremum problem

$$\min_{\mathrm{p},\delta}\left[\varphi(\mathbf{p}) \equiv \sum_{j=1}^{n} \mathrm{p}_j \ln(\mathrm{p}_j/n^{-1}) \text{ or } \sum_{j=1}^{n} n^{-1} \ln(n^{-1}/\mathrm{p}_j)\right] \tag{17.5.6}$$

subject to

$$(\mathbf{p} \odot \mathbf{Z})'\left(\mathbf{Y}_{\cdot i} - \mathbf{M}_{(i)}\boldsymbol{\delta}_i\right) = \mathbf{0}, \tag{17.5.7}$$

$$\mathbf{1}'\mathbf{p} = 1, \quad \text{and} \quad \mathrm{p}_j \geq 0, \forall_j. \tag{17.5.8}$$

Regarding the equivalence of the extremum problems stated in terms of the KLIC and the MEL–MEEL estimation objectives, note that the first of the objective functions in (17.5.6) characterizes the MEEL problem because the value of $\mathbf{p}$ that minimizes $\sum_{j=1}^{n} \mathrm{p}_j \ln(\mathrm{p}_j/n^{-1}) \equiv \sum_{j=1}^{n} \mathrm{p}_j \ln(\mathrm{p}_j) + \ln(n)$ is precisely the same value of $\mathbf{p}$ that maximizes entropy $-\sum_{j=1}^{n} \mathrm{p}_j \ln(\mathrm{p}_j)$ (note $\ln(n)$ is simply an added constant in the KLIC objective). The second KLIC objective function in (17.5.6) characterizes the MEL problem because $\sum_{j=1}^{n} n^{-1} \ln(n^{-1}/\mathrm{p}_j) \equiv -n^{-1}\sum_{j=1}^{n} \ln(\mathrm{p}_j) - \ln(n)$, and so precisely the same value of $\mathbf{p}$ that maximizes the EL objective function $n^{-1}\sum_{j=1}^{n} \ln(\mathrm{p}_j)$ minimizes the KLIC objective function (again note that $\ln(n)$ is simply a subtracted constant in the KLIC objective). We henceforth allow the KLIC objective function to refer generically to either the MEEL or MEL objective. We will be explicit in our discussion when we wish to refer to either the MEL or MEEL special case.

We pause here to emphasize a fundamental difference between the GMM and the minimum KLIC estimation criterion. Recall that in GMM estimation attention is focused on the inability of values of parameter vectors to satisfy the moment conditions. In practice, the expectations defining the empirical moment conditions are effectively based on the a priori fixed empirical distribution that assigns the equal weight n^{-1} to each observation, and then the parameter estimate is the value of the parameter vector that satisfies these moment conditions *as closely as possible*. Closeness is measured in a weighted quadratic loss or weighted Euclidean distance metric.

The minimum KLIC estimation criterion focuses attention on the difference between the empirical distribution function weights n^{-1} and the alternative distribution of probability weights $\mathbf{p}$ assigned to the data observations. In applications of the minimum KLIC approach, it is the probability distribution $\mathbf{p}$ that is used in defining the expectations that form the empirical moment conditions and not the empirical distribution function weights n^{-1}. The minimum KLIC method then focuses attention on the inability of the values of the empirical probability weights $\mathbf{p}$ to equal the empirical distribution function weights n^{-1} in order for the values of the parameter vector $\boldsymbol{\delta}$ to satisfy the empirical moment conditions (based on $\mathbf{p}$) *exactly*. The minimum KLIC estimator for $\boldsymbol{\delta}$ is the value of $\boldsymbol{\delta}$ that both satisfies the empirical moment conditions exactly and that concomitantly allows the elements of the $\mathbf{p}$ distribution defining the empirical moments to be chosen as close to n^{-1} as possible. Closeness is measured in terms of the Kullback–Leibler information discrepancy. The orientation of the discrepancy measure, being either $\varphi(\mathbf{p}) \equiv \text{KL}(\mathbf{p}, n^{-1}\mathbf{1})$ or $\varphi(\mathbf{p}) \equiv \text{KL}(n^{-1}\mathbf{1}, \mathbf{p})$, differentiates the MEEL from the MEL approach. Regarding this orientation, recall that the KLIC–MEEL objective $\text{E}_{\text{p}}[\ln(p/n^{-1})] \equiv \sum_{j=1}^{n} \text{p}_j \ln(\text{p}_j/n^{-1})$ can be interpreted as an empirical expectation of a log ratio of EL to empirical distribution function sample weights, the empirical expectation being based on the EL weights $\mathbf{p}$. The KLIC–MEL objective $\text{E}_{n^{-1}\mathbf{1}}[(n^{-1}/\text{p})] \equiv \sum_{j=1}^{n} n^{-1} \ln(n^{-1}/\text{p}_j)$ can be interpreted as an empirical expectation of the inverted (compared with the MEEL) log ratio of empirical distribution function to EL sample weights, the empirical expectation being based on the empirical distribution function weights $n^{-1}\mathbf{1}$.

In summary, the principal difference between the GMM and minimum KLIC procedure for choosing $\boldsymbol{\delta}$ is that the former focuses on closeness of estimated sample moments to their theoretical zero values, whereas the latter focuses on closeness of the estimated probability distribution of the observations to their theoretical values as reflected by the EDF. In particular, in the minimum KLIC case, note that the empirical distribution function converges to the true probability distribution of the observations under general conditions, and the KLIC procedure draws the empirical $\mathbf{p}$-distribution as closely as possible to the empirical distribution function while satisfying the empirical moment conditions exactly. Given that the theoretical moment conditions are in fact true when evaluated at the true value of $\boldsymbol{\delta}$, we would expect that as $n \to \infty$, $\hat{\boldsymbol{\delta}} \xrightarrow{\text{p}} \boldsymbol{\delta}$, $\mathbf{p}$ is drawn to the true underlying population distribution, and the *theoretical* as well as empirical moment conditions hold in the limit. In fact, as we noted in Chapters 12, 13, and 16, these results hold under general regularity conditions, making the minimum KLIC approach a viable alternative to GMM estimation.

17.5.2. MEEL Estimation and Inference

Returning to the basic MEEL approach first introduced in Chapter 13, We recall for purposes of setting up the Lagrange form of the problem (17.5.6)–(17.5.8) for the KLIC–MEEL objective that the objective function (17.5.6) can be written as

$$\sum_{j=1}^{n} \mathrm{p}_j \ln(\mathrm{p}_j) - \sum_{j=1}^{n} \mathrm{p}_j \ln(n^{-1}) = \sum_{j=1}^{n} \mathrm{p}_j \ln(\mathrm{p}_j) + \ln(n) \qquad (17.5.9)$$

because $\mathbf{1}'\mathbf{p} = \sum_{j=1}^{n} \mathrm{p}_j = 1$. Then, for purposes of calculating the optimal values of $\mathbf{p}$ and $\boldsymbol{\delta}$, (17.5.9) can be replaced by simply $\sum_{j=1}^{n} \mathrm{p}_j \ln(\mathrm{p}_j)$, which differs from (17.5.9) only by the subtraction of a scalar constant $\ln(n)$.

17.5.2.a. MEEL Estimation in the Single Linear Equation Case

The Lagrange function for calculating the KLIC-minimizing optimal $\mathbf{p}$ and $\boldsymbol{\delta}$ can be specified as

$$\mathrm{L}(\mathbf{p}, \boldsymbol{\delta}, \boldsymbol{\lambda}, \eta) = \sum_{j=1}^{n} \mathrm{p}_j \ln(\mathrm{p}_j) - \boldsymbol{\lambda}'\left[(\mathbf{p} \odot \mathbf{Z})'(\mathbf{Y}_{\cdot i} - \mathbf{M}_{(i)}\boldsymbol{\delta}_i)\right] + \eta \left(\sum_{j=1}^{n} \mathrm{p}_j - 1\right). \qquad (17.5.10)$$

The first-order conditions are

$$\frac{\partial \mathrm{L}}{\partial \mathrm{p}_j} = 1 + \ln(\mathrm{p}_j) - \boldsymbol{\lambda}'\left[\mathbf{Z}'_{j\cdot}\left(\mathrm{Y}_{ji} - \mathbf{M}_{(i)}[j, \cdot]\boldsymbol{\delta}_i\right)\right] + \eta = 0 \qquad (17.5.11)$$

$$\frac{\partial \mathrm{L}}{\partial \delta_{il}} = \boldsymbol{\lambda}'(\mathbf{p} \odot \mathbf{Z})'\mathbf{M}_{(i)}[\cdot, l] = 0 \qquad (17.5.12)$$

plus the conditions (17.5.7) and (17.5.8). It is evident from (17.5.11) that

$$\mathrm{p}_j = \exp\left[\boldsymbol{\lambda}'(\mathbf{Z}'_{j\cdot}\left[\mathrm{Y}_{ji} - \mathbf{M}_{(i)}[j, \cdot]\boldsymbol{\delta}_i\right]) - \eta - 1\right] \qquad (17.5.13)$$

and because, $\mathbf{1}'\mathbf{p} = 1$ (17.5.13) can be expressed equivalently as

$$\mathrm{p}_j(\boldsymbol{\lambda}, \boldsymbol{\delta}_i) = \frac{\exp\left[\boldsymbol{\lambda}'(\mathbf{Z}'_{j\cdot}\left[\mathrm{Y}_{ji} - \mathbf{M}_{(i)}[j, \cdot]\boldsymbol{\delta}_i\right])\right]}{\sum_{j=1}^{n} \exp\left[\boldsymbol{\lambda}'(\mathbf{Z}'_{j\cdot}\left[\mathrm{Y}_{ji} - \mathbf{M}_{(i)}[j, \cdot]\boldsymbol{\delta}_i\right])\right]}. \qquad (17.5.14)$$

The p_j's can be concentrated out of the minimization problem by substituting (17.5.14) into (17.5.10).

To solve for the optimal $\boldsymbol{\lambda}$, fix $\boldsymbol{\delta}_i = \boldsymbol{\delta}_i^0$ and define $\varepsilon_{ji}(\boldsymbol{\delta}_i^0) \equiv \mathrm{Y}_{ji} - \mathbf{M}_{(i)}[j,\cdot]\boldsymbol{\delta}_i^0$. Then the conditional-on-$\boldsymbol{\delta}_i^0$ concentrated Lagrange objective function obtained by substituting $\mathbf{p}(\boldsymbol{\lambda}, \boldsymbol{\delta}_i^0)$ and $\boldsymbol{\delta}_i^0$ into (17.5.10) becomes

$$\begin{aligned}
\mathrm{L_c}(\boldsymbol{\lambda} \mid \boldsymbol{\delta}_i^0) &= \sum_{j=1}^{n} \mathrm{p}_j(\boldsymbol{\lambda}, \boldsymbol{\delta}_i^0) \ln (\mathrm{p}_j(\boldsymbol{\lambda}, \boldsymbol{\delta}_i^0)) - \boldsymbol{\lambda}'[(\mathbf{p}(\boldsymbol{\lambda}, \boldsymbol{\delta}_i^0) \odot \mathbf{Z})'(\mathbf{Y}_{\cdot i} - \mathbf{M}_{(i)}\boldsymbol{\delta}_i)] \\
&= \sum_{j=1}^{n} \mathrm{p}_j(\boldsymbol{\lambda}, \boldsymbol{\delta}_i^0)[\boldsymbol{\lambda}'[\mathbf{Z}'_{j\cdot}\varepsilon_{ji}(\boldsymbol{\delta}_i^0)]] - \ln(\Omega(\boldsymbol{\lambda})) - \boldsymbol{\lambda}'[[\mathbf{p}(\boldsymbol{\lambda}, \boldsymbol{\delta}_i^0) \odot \mathbf{Z}]'\varepsilon_{\cdot i}(\boldsymbol{\delta}_i^0)] \\
&= -\ln(\Omega(\boldsymbol{\lambda})),
\end{aligned} \qquad (17.5.15)$$

where $\Omega(\boldsymbol{\lambda}) \equiv \sum_{j=1}^{n} \exp[\boldsymbol{\lambda}'[\mathbf{Z}'_{j\cdot}(\mathrm{Y}_{ji} - \mathbf{M}_{(i)}[j,\cdot]\boldsymbol{\delta}_i)]]$, and η is dropped from (17.5.10) because $\mathbf{1}'\mathbf{p}(\boldsymbol{\lambda}, \boldsymbol{\delta}_\mathrm{i}^0) \equiv 1$. At this point it is important to recall that solving the Lagrange form (17.5.10) of the minimization problem is a *saddle-point problem* in which we *minimize* through choice of the $\boldsymbol{\delta}_i$ values but *maximize* through choice of the Lagrange multiplier values. Thus, in order to optimize $\boldsymbol{\lambda}$ in (17.5.10), we must *maximize* (17.5.15) with respect to $\boldsymbol{\lambda}$. Note that there is a substantial computational benefit in concentrating and then conditioning the Lagrange function, as in (17.5.15), because the maximization problem is *unconstrained* with respect to $\boldsymbol{\lambda}$. Maximization of (17.5.15) with respect to $\boldsymbol{\lambda}$ can be accomplished using standard iterative techniques such as the Newton–Raphson algorithm. The resulting optimal $\boldsymbol{\lambda}$ value is conceptually a function of the conditioning $\boldsymbol{\delta}_i^0$ values such as $\boldsymbol{\lambda}(\boldsymbol{\delta}_i^0)$.

To solve finally for the minimum KLIC–MEEL estimates of the structural parameters $\boldsymbol{\delta}_i$, one substitutes $\boldsymbol{\lambda}(\boldsymbol{\delta}_i^0)$ for $\boldsymbol{\lambda}$ in the concentrated-conditional Lagrange function (17.5.15) and then minimizes with respect to the $\boldsymbol{\delta}_i^0$ value. The minimum KLIC–MEEL estimate can then be represented as

$$\hat{\boldsymbol{\delta}}_{i,\mathrm{MEEL}} = \arg\min_{\boldsymbol{\delta}_i^0}\left[\mathrm{L_c}(\boldsymbol{\lambda}(\boldsymbol{\delta}_i^0)|\boldsymbol{\delta}_i^0)\right] = \arg\min_{\boldsymbol{\delta}_i^0}\left[\max_{\boldsymbol{\lambda}}\left[\mathrm{L_c}(\boldsymbol{\lambda} \mid \boldsymbol{\delta}_i^0)\right]\right]. \qquad (17.5.16)$$

Further results concerning the existence and dual nature of this solution to the minimum KLIC–MEEL problem can be found in Kitamura and Stutzer (1997, p. 864), Golan, Judge, and Miller (1996), and Ben-Tal (1985, pp. 268–72). Once $\hat{\boldsymbol{\delta}}_i$ is obtained, it can be substituted into $\boldsymbol{\lambda}(\hat{\boldsymbol{\delta}}_i)$ to yield the KLIC–MEEL estimate $\hat{\boldsymbol{\lambda}}_{\mathrm{MEEL}} = \boldsymbol{\lambda}(\hat{\boldsymbol{\delta}}_i)$ for the Lagrange multipliers, and then $\hat{\boldsymbol{\delta}}_{i,\mathrm{MEEL}}$ and $\hat{\boldsymbol{\lambda}}_{\mathrm{MEEL}}$ can be substituted into (17.5.14) to obtain the KLIC estimate of $\mathbf{p}$.

► **Example 17.5.1:** To demonstrate an application of the KLIC–MEEL estimator, we provide the GAUSS program C17MEEL1.gss in the examples manual. Using a DSP associated with a nonlinear regression model, the program generates a random sample of observations and then computes KLIC-MEEL estimates of the model parameters together with an estimate of the associated covariance matrix appropriate for the KLIC-MEEL procedure (see Theorem 17.5.1 ahead). Then, the program reports the result of a hypothesis test on the parameters of the model and generates a confidence region outcome based on the Wald criterion.

17.5.2.b. Complete System Estimation and Nonlinear Models

All of the preceding results relating to the MEEL approach to estimation can be extended to encompass both the estimation of a complete system of simultaneous equations and nonlinear models. The only essential differences are the addition of moment conditions that encompass the remainder of equations in the system and the replacement of linear functions with nonlinear functions of the parameters of the model. The Lagrangian form of the KLIC–MEEL extremum problem in the nonlinear simultaneous equations inverse problem is given by

$$\begin{aligned} L(\mathbf{p}, \boldsymbol{\delta}, \boldsymbol{\lambda}, \eta) = \sum_{j=1}^{n} p_j \ln(p_j) - \boldsymbol{\lambda}'([\mathbf{I}_q \otimes (\mathbf{p} \odot \mathbf{Z})'] \\ \times [\mathbf{Y}_v - \mathbf{g}(\mathbf{M}, \boldsymbol{\delta})]) + \eta\left(\sum_{j=1}^{n} p_j - 1\right), \end{aligned} \tag{17.5.17}$$

where now the Lagrangian multiplier vector $\boldsymbol{\lambda}$ is of dimension $(mq \times 1)$ instead of dimension $(m \times 1)$ as in the single-equation case, m being the number of instrumental variables. A simultaneous equation system with linear equations is subsumed by (17.5.17) upon setting $\mathbf{g}(\mathbf{M}, \boldsymbol{\delta}) \equiv \mathbf{M}\boldsymbol{\delta}$.

To draw close analogies with the previous development of the single-equation case, define the elements of the $\boldsymbol{\lambda}$ vectors in a way that makes clear which equation an element refers to as follows:

$$\begin{aligned} \boldsymbol{\lambda} &\equiv [\lambda_1[1], \ldots, \lambda_1[m], \lambda_2[1], \ldots, \lambda_2[m], \ldots, \lambda_q[1], \ldots, \lambda_q[m]]' \\ &\equiv [\boldsymbol{\lambda}_1', \boldsymbol{\lambda}_2', \ldots, \boldsymbol{\lambda}_q']', \end{aligned} \tag{17.5.18}$$

and thus $\lambda_i[j]$ is the Lagrange multiplier for the jth moment condition on the ith equation, and the vector $\boldsymbol{\lambda}_i$ is the $(m \times 1)$ vector of Lagrange multipliers on the m moment conditions associated with equation i. Then the Lagrange form of the KLIC–MEEL extremum problem (17.5.17) can be written, in the case of a linear system of equations, equivalently as

$$L(\mathbf{p}, \boldsymbol{\delta}, \boldsymbol{\lambda}, \eta) = \sum_{j=1}^{n} p_j \ln(p_j) - \sum_{i=1}^{q} \boldsymbol{\lambda}_i'\left[(\mathbf{p} \odot \mathbf{Z})'\left(\mathbf{Y}_{\cdot i} - \mathbf{M}_{(i)}\boldsymbol{\delta}_i\right)\right] + \eta\left(\sum_{j=1}^{n} p_j - 1\right). \tag{17.5.19}$$

The first-order conditions and the solution for $\mathbf{p}$, which are extended-system analogues to (17.5.11)–(17.5.14) for the single-equation case, are then

$$\frac{\partial L}{\partial p_j} = 1 + \ln(p_j) - \sum_{i=1}^{q} \boldsymbol{\lambda}_i'\left[\mathbf{Z}_{j\cdot}'\left(\mathbf{Y}_{ji} - \mathbf{M}_{(i)}[j, \cdot]\boldsymbol{\delta}_i\right)\right] + \eta = 0 \tag{17.5.20}$$

$$\frac{\partial L}{\partial \delta_{i\ell}} = \boldsymbol{\lambda}_i'(\mathbf{p} \odot \mathbf{Z})' \frac{\partial \mathbf{g}_i\left(\mathbf{Y}_{(i)}, \mathbf{X}_{(i)}, \boldsymbol{\delta}_i\right)}{\partial \delta_{i\ell}} = 0 \tag{17.5.21}$$

plus the conditions $(\mathbf{p} \odot \mathbf{Z})'(\mathbf{Y}_{\cdot i} - \mathbf{M}_{(i)}\boldsymbol{\delta}_i) = 0$ for $i = 1, \ldots, q$, $\mathbf{1}'\mathbf{p} = \mathbf{1}$, and $p_j \geq 0$, $\forall j$, where $\mathbf{g}_i(\mathbf{Y}_{(i)}, \mathbf{X}_{(i)}, \boldsymbol{\delta}_i) \equiv \mathrm{M}_{(i)}\boldsymbol{\delta}_i$ in this linear case. It is evident from (17.5.21) that

$$\mathrm{p}_j = \exp\left[\sum_{i=1}^{q} \boldsymbol{\lambda}_i'[\mathbf{Z}_{j\cdot}'(\mathbf{Y}_{ji} - \mathbf{M}_{(i)}[j,\cdot]\boldsymbol{\delta}_i)] - \eta - 1\right] \qquad (17.5.22)$$

and since $\mathbf{1}'\mathbf{p} = 1$, (17.5.22) can be expressed equivalently as

$$\mathrm{p}_j(\boldsymbol{\lambda}, \boldsymbol{\delta}) = \frac{\exp\left[\sum_{i=1}^{q} \boldsymbol{\lambda}_i'[\mathbf{Z}_{j\cdot}'(\mathbf{Y}_{ji} - \mathbf{M}_{(i)}[j,\cdot]\boldsymbol{\delta}_i)]\right]}{\sum_{j=1}^{n} \exp\left[\sum_{i=1}^{q} \boldsymbol{\lambda}_i'[\mathbf{Z}_{j\cdot}'(\mathbf{Y}_{ji} - \mathbf{M}_{(i)}[j,\cdot]\boldsymbol{\delta}_i)]\right]} \qquad (17.5.23)$$

The p_j's can be concentrated out of the minimization problem by substituting (17.5.23) into (17.5.19).

To solve for the optimal $\boldsymbol{\lambda}$, fix $\boldsymbol{\delta}_i = \boldsymbol{\delta}_i^0$ for every i and define $\varepsilon_{ji}(\boldsymbol{\delta}_i^0) \equiv (\mathbf{Y}_{ji} - \mathbf{M}_{(i)}[j,\cdot]\boldsymbol{\delta}_i^0)$. Then the conditional-on-$\boldsymbol{\delta}^0$ concentrated Lagrange objective function obtained by substituting $\mathbf{p}(\boldsymbol{\lambda}, \boldsymbol{\delta}^0)$ and $\boldsymbol{\delta}^0$ into (17.5.19) becomes

$$\begin{aligned}
\mathrm{L}_c(\boldsymbol{\lambda} \mid \boldsymbol{\delta}^0) &= \sum_{j=1}^{n} \mathrm{p}_j(\boldsymbol{\lambda}, \boldsymbol{\delta}^0)\ln(\mathrm{p}_j(\boldsymbol{\lambda}, \boldsymbol{\delta}^0)) - \sum_{i=1}^{q} \boldsymbol{\lambda}_i'\left[[\mathbf{p}(\boldsymbol{\lambda}, \boldsymbol{\delta}^0) \odot \mathbf{Z}]'(\mathbf{Y}_{\cdot i} - \mathbf{M}_{(i)}\boldsymbol{\delta}_i^0)\right] \\
&= \sum_{j=1}^{n} \mathrm{p}_j(\boldsymbol{\lambda}, \boldsymbol{\delta}^0)\left[\sum_{i=1}^{q} \boldsymbol{\lambda}_i'[\mathbf{Z}_{j\cdot}'\varepsilon_{ji}(\boldsymbol{\delta}_i^0)]\right] \\
&\quad - \ln(\Omega(\boldsymbol{\lambda})) - \sum_{i=1}^{q} \boldsymbol{\lambda}_i'\left[[\mathbf{p}(\boldsymbol{\lambda}, \boldsymbol{\delta}^0) \odot \mathbf{Z}]'\boldsymbol{\varepsilon}_{\cdot i}(\boldsymbol{\delta}_i^0)\right] \\
&= -\ln(\Omega(\boldsymbol{\lambda}))
\end{aligned} \qquad (17.5.24)$$

where $\Omega(\boldsymbol{\lambda}) \equiv \sum_{j=1}^{n} \exp[\sum_{i=1}^{q} \boldsymbol{\lambda}_i'(\mathbf{Z}_{j\cdot}'[\mathbf{Y}_{ji} - \mathbf{M}_{(i)}[j,\cdot]\boldsymbol{\delta}_i])]$, and η is dropped from (17.5.19) because $\mathbf{1}'\mathbf{p}(\boldsymbol{\lambda}, \boldsymbol{\delta}^0) \equiv 1$. At this point it is again important to recall that solving the Lagrange form (17.5.19) of the minimization problem is a *saddle-point problem* in which we *minimize* through choice of the $\boldsymbol{\delta}$ values but *maximize* through choice of the Lagrange multiplier values. Thus, in order to optimize $\boldsymbol{\lambda}$ in (17.5.19), we must *maximize* (17.5.24) with respect to $\boldsymbol{\lambda}$. We note, as we did in the single-equation case, that there is a substantial computational benefit in concentrating and then conditioning the Lagrange function, as in (17.5.24), because the maximization problem is *unconstrained* with respect to $\boldsymbol{\lambda}$. Maximization of (17.5.24) with respect to $\boldsymbol{\lambda}$ can be accomplished using standard iterative techniques, such as the Newton–Raphson algorithm. The resulting optimal $\boldsymbol{\lambda}$ value is conceptually a function of the conditioning $\boldsymbol{\delta}^0$ values such as $\boldsymbol{\lambda}(\boldsymbol{\delta}^0)$.

The minimum KLIC–MEEL estimates of the structural parameters $\boldsymbol{\delta}$ can be solved for by substituting $\boldsymbol{\lambda}(\boldsymbol{\delta}^0)$ for $\boldsymbol{\lambda}$ in the concentrated-conditional Lagrange function (17.5.24) and then minimizing with respect to the $\boldsymbol{\delta}^0$ value. The minimum KLIC–MEEL estimate can then be represented as

$$\hat{\boldsymbol{\delta}}_{\mathrm{MEEL}} = \arg\min_{\boldsymbol{\delta}^0}[\mathrm{L}_c(\boldsymbol{\lambda}(\boldsymbol{\delta}^0) \mid \boldsymbol{\delta}^0)] = \arg\min_{\boldsymbol{\delta}^0}[\max_{\boldsymbol{\lambda}}[\mathrm{L}_c(\boldsymbol{\lambda} \mid \boldsymbol{\delta}^0)]]. \qquad (17.5.25)$$

Further results concerning the existence and dual nature of this solution to the minimum KLIC–MEEL problem can be found in the references cited following (17.5.16). Once $\hat{\boldsymbol{\delta}}_{\text{MEEL}}$ is obtained, it can be substituted into $\boldsymbol{\lambda}(\hat{\boldsymbol{\delta}}_{\text{MEEL}})$ to yield the KLIC–MEEL estimate $\hat{\boldsymbol{\lambda}}_{\text{MEEL}} = \boldsymbol{\lambda}(\hat{\boldsymbol{\delta}}_{\text{MEEL}})$ for the Lagrange multipliers, and then $\hat{\boldsymbol{\delta}}_{\text{MEEL}}$ and $\hat{\boldsymbol{\lambda}}_{\text{MEEL}}$ can be substituted into (17.5.23) to obtain the KLIC estimate of $\mathbf{p}$.

The preceding development encompassing equations (17.5.19)–(17.5.25) extends directly to the case of a system of nonlinear equations. The essential difference in the argument is the replacement of $\mathbf{M}\boldsymbol{\delta}$ with $\mathbf{g}(\mathbf{M}, \boldsymbol{\delta})$ appropriately throughout the development.

17.5.2.c. Asymptotic Distribution and Inference

Hall and Horowitz (1996) have noted that in sample sizes typically found in practice, the finite sample properties of tests based on the GMM procedure can sometimes be questionable and not closely reflective of their asymptotic properties. It is therefore useful to investigate alternative inference procedures based on the minimum KLIC–MEEL approach. Under general regularity conditions akin to those imposed in GMM estimation (see Chapter 16 and Kitamura and Stutzer, 1997, p. 866), the minimum KLIC–MEEL estimator is consistent and asymptotically normally distributed. Regarding the specifics of the asymptotic distribution, we have the following theorem that encompasses inverse problems relating to single equations contained within a simultaneous equations system as well as the complete system of equations. In particular, it is admissible to interpret $\hat{\boldsymbol{\delta}}_{\text{MEEL}}$ in Theorem 17.5.1 as either the estimator for the parameters of a single equation or for the entire parameter vector of the simultaneous equations model.

Theorem 17.5.1 (Asymptotic Properties of Minimum KLIC–MEEL Estimator): *Under general regularity conditions, the minimum KLIC–MEEL estimator is consistent and asymptotically normally distributed as* $n^{1/2}(\hat{\boldsymbol{\delta}}_{MEEL} - \boldsymbol{\delta}) \xrightarrow{d} \mathrm{N}(\mathbf{0}, \boldsymbol{\Xi})$. *The definition of the covariance matrix of the limiting distribution is given by*

$$\boldsymbol{\Xi} = [\mathbf{d}'\mathbf{a}^{-1}\mathbf{d}]^{-1},$$

if sampling is iid or

$$\boldsymbol{\Xi} = [\mathbf{d}'\mathbf{a}^{-1}\mathbf{d}]^{-1}(\mathbf{d}'\mathbf{a}^{-1}\boldsymbol{\Phi}\mathbf{a}^{-1}\mathbf{d})[\mathbf{d}'\mathbf{a}^{-1}\mathbf{d}]^{-1},$$

if sampling is not iid, where

$$\mathbf{d} = \operatorname{plim}\left[n^{-1}\frac{\partial \mathbf{h}(\boldsymbol{\delta})}{\partial \boldsymbol{\delta}'}\right], \quad \mathbf{a} = \operatorname{plim}\left[n^{-1}\sum_{j=1}^{n}\mathbf{h}_j(\boldsymbol{\delta})\mathbf{h}_j(\boldsymbol{\delta})'\right],$$

$$\mathbf{h}(\boldsymbol{\delta}) \equiv \sum_{j=1}^{n}\mathbf{h}_j(\boldsymbol{\delta}) \equiv \sum_{j=1}^{n}\left(\mathbf{Z}'_{j\cdot}\left[\mathrm{Y}_{ji} - \mathbf{g}_i\left(\mathbf{Y}_{(i)}[j,\cdot], \mathbf{X}_{(i)}[j,\cdot], \boldsymbol{\delta}_i\right)\right]\right)$$

$$= \mathbf{Z}'\left[\mathbf{Y}_{\cdot i} - \mathbf{g}_i\left(\mathbf{Y}_{(i)}, \mathbf{X}_{(i)}, \boldsymbol{\delta}_i\right)\right]$$

for the single ith equation case,

$$\mathbf{h}(\boldsymbol{\delta}) \equiv \sum_{j=1}^{n} \mathbf{h}_j(\boldsymbol{\delta}) \equiv \sum_{j=1}^{n} \left(\begin{bmatrix} \mathrm{Y}_{j1} - \mathbf{g}_1\left(\mathbf{Y}_{(1)}[j,\cdot], \mathbf{X}_{(1)}[j,\cdot], \boldsymbol{\delta}_1\right) \\ \mathrm{Y}_{j2} - \mathbf{g}_2\left(\mathbf{Y}_{(2)}[j,\cdot], \mathbf{X}_{(2)}[j,\cdot], \boldsymbol{\delta}_2\right) \\ \vdots \\ \mathrm{Y}_{jq} - \mathbf{g}_q\left(\mathbf{Y}_{(q)}[j,\cdot], \mathbf{X}_{(q)}[j,\cdot], \boldsymbol{\delta}_q\right) \end{bmatrix} \otimes \mathbf{Z}[j,\cdot]' \right)$$

$$= (\mathbf{I}_q \otimes \mathbf{Z}')[\mathbf{Y}_{\mathrm{v}} - \mathbf{g}(\mathbf{M}, \boldsymbol{\delta}])$$

for complete systems of equations, and

$$\boldsymbol{\Phi} \equiv \lim_{n\to\infty} \mathbf{cov}(n^{-1/2}\mathbf{h}(\boldsymbol{\delta}_i)).$$

PROOF: Kitamura and Stutzer (1997, pp. 871–3).

Estimates of the asymptotic covariances in Theorem 17.5.1 can be obtained by replacing parameter values by their minimum KLIC–MEEL estimates and basing plim terms on either sample averages (moments) or expectations with respect to the MEEL estimated $\hat{\mathbf{p}}$ distribution. For example, in the case of estimating the $\mathbf{a}$ matrix, one could use either $\hat{\mathbf{a}} = [n^{-1}\sum_{i=1}^{n} \mathbf{h}_i(\hat{\boldsymbol{\delta}})\mathbf{h}_i(\hat{\boldsymbol{\delta}})']$ or $\hat{\mathbf{a}} = [\sum_{i=1}^{n} \hat{\mathrm{p}}_i \mathbf{h}_i(\hat{\boldsymbol{\delta}})\mathbf{h}_i(\hat{\boldsymbol{\delta}})']$. Test statistics can be based on the asymptotic normal distribution of $\hat{\boldsymbol{\delta}}_{\mathrm{MEEL}}$ in the usual way. For example, the Wald statistic for the test of the restriction $\mathrm{H}_0 : \mathbf{c}\boldsymbol{\delta} = \mathbf{r}$ is given by

$$\mathrm{W} = n(\mathbf{c}\hat{\boldsymbol{\delta}} - \mathbf{r})'[\mathbf{c}\hat{\boldsymbol{\Xi}}\mathbf{c}']^{-1}(\mathbf{c}\hat{\boldsymbol{\delta}} - \mathbf{r}) \overset{a}{\sim} \text{Chi-square}(j, 0) \text{ under } \mathrm{H}_0, \qquad (17.5.26)$$

where j equals the number of rows in $\mathbf{c}$ (assumed to be full-row rank), and $\hat{\boldsymbol{\Xi}}$ is a consistent estimator of the covariance matrix given in Theorem 17.5.1. Additional details relating to hypothesis-testing procedures, including pseudolikelihood ratio and Lagrange multiplier tests, can be found in Kitamura and Stutzer (1997). As usual, confidence-region estimation can be based on duality with hypothesis tests.

► **Example 17.5.2:** Following the GAUSS demonstration in Example 17.5.1, we extend the KLIC–MEEL estimator to a system of equations in the program C17MEEL2.gss (provided in the examples manual). For a given sample of observations, the program computes the parameter estimates and the estimated covariance matrix for $\hat{\boldsymbol{\delta}}_{\mathrm{MEEL}}$. The program then conducts a Wald test based on (17.5.26) of a set of cross-equation restrictions on the model parameters.

17.5.3. MEL Estimation

The entire development of the minimum KLIC–MEEL estimation procedure given in Section 17.5.2 could be repeated by reversing the roles of the $\mathbf{p}$-distribution and empirical distribution function $n^{-1}\mathbf{1}\ \forall i$ in the specification of the objective function (17.5.6) and then proceeding to minimize the objective function subject to the moment constraints (17.5.7). What results is the estimation procedures, estimation results, and inference approach for the maximum empirical likelihood (MEL) estimation approach. The conceptual steps are in fact precisely the same as in the preceding section, and the arguments and sequence of equations can be revised one by one to reflect the different estimation objective function, but identical remaining problem components, associated with the MEL approach. We emphasize that Theorem 17.5.1 applies equally well to the MEL estimation context, and indeed the asymptotics of MEL and MEEL are the same. The derivations and results presented in Chapter 12, relating to the MEL approach are closely related to the derivations and results needed here, and given the previous section of this chapter and Chapter 12, a template is in place for providing the MEL results in the current problem context. Therefore, we will not present further details here, and we ask the reader to fill in the algebraic details in the problems section.

The MEL approach to estimating the structural parameters, $\boldsymbol{\delta}_i$ or $\boldsymbol{\delta}$ represents an alternative to both GMM and minimum KLIC–MEEL estimation. Asymptotically, MEEL, MEL, and EOGMM all have identical asymptotic distributional properties (if the use of smoothed moment conditions is assumed in the MEEL and MEL approaches in the case of *non-iid* sampling, as discussed in Section 16.3). The literature is as of yet unsettled regarding which, if any, of the procedures is superior to the others with respect to finite sampling properties, although the ability of both the MEL and MEEL procedures to avoid the preestimation of covariance matrices associated with the empirical moments in the GMM approach is a distinct advantage that may favor small-sample superiority of MEL and MEEL estimators.

17.5.4. The KLIC–MEEL–MEL Procedures: Critique

Estimation and inference in simultaneous equations econometric models usually reduce to a problem of imposing a set of moment conditions on the economic data. These conditions reflect orthogonality conditions corresponding to a set of unbiased estimating equations with dimensions often larger than the number of unknown parameters. Given this overidentified situation, the general estimation and inference objective is to find an efficient method of recovering the unknowns. Consequently, the estimating equations approach developed in Chapter 16 is a natural framework to use with overidentified simultaneous equation models.

The generalized estimating equations approach of MEEL and MEL incorporates information on the overidentifying restrictions relating to the parameters and results in a transformed, *effectively* just-identified set of estimating functions, such as $(\hat{\mathbf{p}} \odot \mathbf{Z}')(\mathbf{Y}_{\cdot i} - \mathbf{M}_{(i)}\boldsymbol{\delta}_i) = \mathbf{0}$ for a single-equation estimator, that can be solved for parameter estimates. Thus, by redefining or transforming the estimating equations appropriately an overidentified inverse problem can be treated as a just-identified one. The estimating equations in the MEEL–MEL *one-step* approach have many appealing theoretical features in the form of asymptotic efficiency, robustness, and computational tractability. In contrast, in the EOGMM–2SLS–3SLS approach to this inverse problem the search for the optimum weight matrix depends on two-steps, one of which relates to the recovery of an additional unknown covariance matrix of scaled moments. Unfortunately, as we argued in Chapter 16, estimates obtained from the resulting two-step EOGMM estimator can be sensitive to the way in which the optimal weight matrix is estimated from the data. Consequently, the finite-sample properties of the EOGMM–2SLS–3SLS type estimators can be effected. The MEEL–MEL approaches are free of the first-step complication.

On the other hand, the standard MEL–MEEL approaches achieve their asymptotic optimal equivalence to the asymptotically optimal GMM approach only in the case in which sampling is independent from observation to observation. When sample observations exhibit dependence, as in the case of autocorrelated noise elements, then it is the *smoothed* moment-type estimators of Kitamura and Stutzer (1997) (and recall Section 16.3) that achieves asymptotic optimality and asymptotic equivalence to the estimated optimal GMM estimators. The smoothed moment estimators require an initial decision with regard to the degree and type of smoothing, which affects finite sample properties of the estimation procedures just as the choice of covariance matrix estimators affects the sampling properties of the GMM estimator. Additional work is needed in sorting out whether a preferred approach exists with regard to finite sample properties in cases in which sample observations are not independent.

17.6. OptEF Estimation and Inference

In this section we present a brief discussion of the OptEF–QML solution to the simultaneous equations inverse problem to provide additional insights into estimation alternatives as well as to offer a means for asymptotically unifying the EOGMM–MEEL–MEL approaches. As in the case of the previous MEL–MEEL section, the conceptual foundation for applying the OptEF–QML approach to simultaneous equations models is already in place, and Chapter 11 and Sections 15.5 and 16.4 provide the needed concepts. In this section, we focus on how the OptEF concepts are applied in the simultaneous equations context.

17.6.1. The OptEF Estimator in Simultaneous Equations Models

All of the estimation procedures presented in the preceding sections are asymptotically equivalent to an asymptotically OptEF (optimal estimating function) estimator defined in terms of linear unbiased estimating functions belonging to the class of estimating functions

$$\mathbf{h}(\mathbf{Y}, \mathbf{X}, \mathbf{Z}, \boldsymbol{\delta}) = \boldsymbol{\nu}[n^{-1}(\mathbf{I}_{\mathrm{q}} \otimes \mathbf{Z}')[\mathbf{Y}_{\mathrm{v}} - \mathbf{g}(\mathbf{M}, \boldsymbol{\delta})]]. \tag{17.6.1}$$

By asymptotically equivalent, we mean that the asymptotic distributions of the EOGMM, MEEL, and MEL estimators are in fact the same. Note that letting $q = 1$, and replacing $\mathbf{Y}_{\mathrm{v}}$ and $\mathbf{g}(\mathbf{M}, \boldsymbol{\delta})$ with $\mathbf{Y}_i$ and $\mathbf{g}_i(\mathbf{M}_{(i)}, \boldsymbol{\delta}_i)$, respectively, represents the case in which only the parameters of one equation of a simultaneous system are being estimated.

To derive the asymptotically OptEF estimator in the simultaneous equations case, first recall Section 11.3.2.b, from which it follows that the OptEF estimator in the class of estimating equations based on estimating functions of the form (17.6.1) is characterized by setting $\boldsymbol{\nu} = \mathrm{E}[n^{-1}\frac{\partial[(\mathbf{I}_q \otimes \mathbf{Z}')[\mathbf{Y}_{\mathrm{v}} - \mathbf{g}(\mathbf{M}, \boldsymbol{\delta})]]}{\partial \boldsymbol{\delta}}]\boldsymbol{\Phi}^{-1}$ (see also Vijayan, 1991, and Vinod, 1997, p. 222). Here $\boldsymbol{\Phi}$ can be any $(mq \times mq)$ matrix proportional to the covariance matrix of the limiting distribution of $n^{-1/2}[(\mathbf{I}_q \otimes \mathbf{Z}')(\mathbf{Y}_{\mathrm{v}} - \mathbf{g}(\mathbf{M}, \boldsymbol{\delta}))]$. After the expectation term in the definition of ν is replaced by the sample moments, the OptEF solution is then defined via the solution to the estimating equations

$$\mathbf{h}_{\text{Opt}}(\mathbf{Y}, \mathbf{X}, \mathbf{Z}, \boldsymbol{\delta}) = -\left[n^{-1}\frac{\partial \mathbf{g}(\mathbf{M}, \boldsymbol{\delta})}{\partial \boldsymbol{\delta}}(\mathbf{I}_q \otimes \mathbf{Z})\right]\boldsymbol{\Phi}^{-1}[n^{-1}(\mathbf{I}_q \otimes \mathbf{Z}')[\mathbf{Y}_{\text{v}} - \mathbf{g}(\mathbf{M}, \boldsymbol{\delta})]] = \mathbf{0} \tag{17.6.2}$$

Under general regularity conditions, including the assumption that the $(n \times q)$ noise component $\boldsymbol{\varepsilon}$ of the system of simultaneous equations has a covariance matrix equal to $\boldsymbol{\Sigma} \otimes \mathbf{I}$, it follows that $\boldsymbol{\Phi} = \boldsymbol{\Sigma} \otimes \text{plim}(n^{-1}\mathbf{Z}'\mathbf{Z})$. Then, using a consistent estimator $\hat{\boldsymbol{\Sigma}}$ of $\boldsymbol{\Sigma}$ and using $n^{-1}\mathbf{Z}'\mathbf{Z}$ to estimate $\text{plim}(n^{-1}\mathbf{Z}'\mathbf{Z})$ consistently, the OptEF (17.6.2) can be asymptotically characterized as (suppressing a minus sign and superfluous multipliers involving n)

$$\mathbf{h}_{\text{Opt}}(\mathbf{Y}, \mathbf{X}, \mathbf{Z}, \boldsymbol{\beta}) = \left[\frac{\partial \mathbf{g}(\mathbf{M}, \boldsymbol{\delta})}{\partial \boldsymbol{\delta}}(\hat{\boldsymbol{\Sigma}}^{-1} \otimes \mathbf{Z}(\mathbf{Z}'\mathbf{Z})^{-1}\mathbf{Z}')[\mathbf{Y}_{\text{v}} - \mathbf{g}(\mathbf{M}, \boldsymbol{\delta})]\right] = \mathbf{0}. \tag{17.6.3}$$

Note that the OptEF estimator

$$\hat{\boldsymbol{\delta}}_{\text{OptEF}} = \arg_{\boldsymbol{\delta}}[\mathbf{h}_{\text{Opt}}(\mathbf{Y}, \mathbf{X}, \mathbf{Z}, \boldsymbol{\delta}) = \mathbf{0}] \tag{17.6.4}$$

obtained using the optimal estimating function defined in (17.6.3) is precisely equal to the nonlinear 3SLS estimator defined by Jorgenson and Laffont (1974) and characterized by (17.4.18) in EOGMM or extremum estimation form. In the special case in which only one equation is being estimated, (17.6.3) is equivalent to the nonlinear 2SLS estimator of Amemiya (1974) characterized in the EOGMM or extremum estimator context by (17.4.6). The standard 3SLS and 2SLS estimators for simultaneous systems of linear equations are defined by setting $\mathbf{g}(\mathbf{M}, \boldsymbol{\delta}) \equiv \mathbf{M}\boldsymbol{\delta}$ or $\mathbf{g}_i(\mathbf{M}_{(i)}, \boldsymbol{\delta}_i) \equiv \mathbf{M}_{(i)}\boldsymbol{\delta}_i$, respectively. Thus, all of the linear and nonlinear 2SLS and 3SLS estimators, as well as the EOGMM estimator, are subsumed under the OptEF approach to estimating the parameters of simultaneous equations systems.

Note in the case in which the noise component of the simultaneous equations model is heteroscedastic, autocorrelated, or both that the OptEF estimator characterized by (17.6.2) and (17.6.4) still applies. However, the covariance matrix $\boldsymbol{\Phi}$ of the scaled moment conditions then must reflect the general covariance structure of the noise component. In the absence of knowledge relating to the functional parametric structure of $\boldsymbol{\Phi}$, robust estimation of the covariance matrix can be pursued via White or Newey–West-type procedures, as discussed in Sections 17.4.1 and 17.4.2 in the context of a two-step estimation scheme. Consistent parametric estimation of $\boldsymbol{\Phi}$ could be attempted in cases in which the parametric structure of $\boldsymbol{\Phi}$ happens to be known.

17.6.2. OptEF Asymptotic Unification of Inverse Problem Solutions

The asymptotics of the OptEF estimator and inference procedures based on the asymptotic distribution coincide with the results noted above for the 2SLS–3SLS–EOGMM estimators. Moreover, the asymptotics of the OptEF estimation approach discussed in Section 11.4 can be applied, which subsumes all of the results in this chapter as special cases. The asymptotic distributions of MEEL and MEL estimators defined in Theorem 17.5.1 are in fact coincident with the asymptotic distributions of OptEF–EOGMM–2SLS–3SLS estimators, as can be demonstrated by applying the formulas for Ξ in that theorem. Thus, asymptotically, the MEEL and MEL distributional results are also anticipated by the OptEF estimation context, implying that all of the procedures examined in this chapter for solving the simultaneous equations inverse problem are consistent, asymptotically normal, and asymptotically efficient. The estimators are also asymptotically equivalent given the types of moment conditions, as defined above.

Work remains in comparing the small-sample behavior of the various approaches to estimation and inference in the simultaneous equations context based on the preceding types of moment conditions. Although the OptEF estimation approach subsumes the asymptotics of all of the other approaches, MEL and MEEL are one-step methods, whereas the applications of OptEF–EOGMM–3SLS–2SLS estimators are two-step procedures for which the first step involves the estimation of the covariance matrix of scaled moment conditions. Which approach is superior in small samples and under what conditions such superiority can be expected are open questions.

17.7. Concluding Comments

This chapter has focused on estimation and inference procedures that may by used to recover information when there is a joint-simultaneous-feedback mechanism at work between some of the variables. The chapter is important for several reasons. For one thing this chapter enforces our continued emphasis on how characteristics of the underlying DSP condition both the specification of the econometric model and the appropriate estimation and inference procedures for solving the associated inverse problems. This chapter lets us build on the moment-type estimators developed in Chapters 10 through 13 and Chapter 16 and shows how these estimators based on unbiased estimating equations can be a unifying framework for estimation and inference. Also introduced are estimators identified historically under the labels of 2SLS, 3SLS, LIML and FIML that are placed in perspective with corresponding moment-based estimators.

In spite of the attractive results that have been achieved during the last five decades, some nagging problems relating to the application of moment-based estimators remain. One prominent problem relates to the lack of invariance of estimated values to the choice of left-hand-side or dependent variables in the specification of a simultaneous equations model. Another relates to the finite sampling properties of estimators as well as the existence of second- (and higher-) order moments of estimators in finite samples. An MEEL–MEL formulation that would mitigate the invariance problem looms as a possibility but has yet to be realized.

17.8. Exercises

17.8.1. Idea Checklist – Knowledge Guides

1. Depending on the span of time to which sample observations refer (i.e., hourly, daily, weekly, monthly, and yearly), an econometric model may or may not need to be in the form of a *simultaneous* equations model. Do you agree?
2. What is the difference between endogenous, exogenous, and predetermined variables?
3. For a conceptual econometric model of an economic problem of interest to you, defend the classification of explanatory variables claimed to be exogenous.
4. How does the endogenous–predetermined–exogenous classification of variables condition the basis for estimation of unknown parameters?
5. Some would argue that in an econometric macromodel of the entire United States economy all variables are endogenous, and thus the model is not estimable by standard econometric estimation procedures. Do you agree?
6. Are the right-hand sides of both the structural and reduced-form representations of a simultaneous equations model equivalent representations of the expectation of **Y** conditional on the explanatory variables in the model?
7. Because the FIML estimation procedure is more efficient than the 3SLS–GMM procedure, does this mean that one should generally use the maximum likelihood approach for estimating simultaneous equations models in practice?
8. Because asymptotically optimal GMM–MEEL–MEL–OptEF estimators derived from moment condition information are all equivalent, how would you go about choosing among the alternatives?

17.8.2. Problems

17–1 For the system of Equations (17.1.2), define examples of the three-equation system in which the parameters of the first equation are

a. underidentified,
b. just-identified, and
c. overidentified.

17–2 Identify estimation procedures that could be used to estimate the parameters in a through c of problem 1 above.

17–3 In the context of testing a hypothesis about the value of a linear combination of the parameters in an overidentified structural equation, define a test statistic you could use for this purpose and then define the test rule. Define a confidence-region estimator based on your hypothesis test and the duality principle.

17–4 How would your response to the preceding problem change if the hypothesis referred to the value of a differentiable nonlinear function of the parameters of the equation?

17–5 How would your answers to problems 3 and 4 change if the linear combination or nonlinear function of the parameters involved parameters appearing in two or more equations of the equation system?

17–6 Assume normality of the noise component and answer problems 3 through 5 based on a likelihood ratio statistic.

17–7 Show that in the case of a linear model the asymptotic covariance matrix of the single-equation EOGMM estimation (17.4.9) simplifies to the 2SLS asymptotic covariance matrix (17.4.10).

17–8 Show that the asymptotic covariance matrix of the multiequation EOGMM estimator (17.4.16) simplifies to the asymptotic covariance matrix of the linear 3SLS estimator when the regression model is linear and the moment conditions are based on $\mathbf{Z} \equiv \mathbf{X}$.

17–9 Make an asymptotic comparison of the covariance matrices of the GMM or 3SLS systems estimator $\hat{\delta}_{\text{GMM}}$ and the equation-by-equation GMM (2SLS) estimator $\hat{\delta}_{\text{2SLS}}$ showing that the difference in the covariance matrices of the limiting distributions results in a negative semidefinite matrix that establishes the gain in asymptotic efficiency in using $\hat{\delta}_{\text{GMM}}$ relative to $\hat{\delta}_{\text{2SLS}}$.

17–10 In the case in which $\mathbf{X}$ is purely exogenous, show that the Gauss–Markov theorem can be applied to conclude that $\hat{\pi}_{\text{v}}$ is the BLUE estimator of the π parameter vector of the reduced form of a simultaneous equations system.

17–11 On the basis of the same conceptual steps as in Section 17.5.2 for the case of MEEL estimation in the simultaneous equations problem context, derive the Lagrangian form of the extremum problem, first order conditions, and estimation results for the MEL approach.

17.8.3. Computer Problems

17–1 Using the GAUSS program C17DSP.gss to generate pseudorandom samples for an LSEM of your choice, conduct a Monte Carlo exercise designed to demonstrate the bias of the least-squares estimator (17.2.2) applied to the structural equations (17.2.1).

17–2 On the basis of the development of the 2sls() procedure in Chapter 16, write a GAUSS procedure (named 3sls()) that computes the 3SLS or GMM estimator (17.2.29) and its estimated covariance matrix. Then, use the 2sls() and 3sls() procedures to conduct a Monte Carlo simulation designed to compare the sampling properties of the two estimators. For the LSEM model you specify, do you find that the 3SLS estimator exhibits improved efficiency (see Problem 9 in this chapter) relative to the single-equation 2SLS estimator?

17–3 Use the GAUSS program for Example 17.3.3 (C17LIML.gss) as a guide to conduct a Monte Carlo exercise designed to compare the LIML and 2SLS estimators under normal and nonnormal noise distributions. Do your findings agree with the claim that LIML performs better than 2SLS when the noise term is normally distributed? How do the estimators compare under the nonnormal noise process?

17–4 The files C17LSEM1.dat, C17LSEM2.dat, and C17LSEM3.dat (provided on the CD) contain observations generated from different probability models. The definitions of the variables in the data sets, including possible exclusion restrictions, are noted in the files. For each case, specify a system of simultaneous equations and estimate the parameters using 2SLS or 3SLS, LIML or FIML, and an information theoretic procedure. Do you believe your models are correctly specified? How well do the estimates compare across the different estimation procedures?

17.9. References

Altonji, J., and L. Segal (1996), "Small-Sample Bias in GMM Estimation of Covariance Structures," *Journal of Business and Economic Statistics*, Vol. 14, pp. 353–66.

Amemiya, T. (1977), "The Maximum Likelihood Estimator and the Nonlinear Three-Stage Least Squares Estimator in the General Nonlinear Simultaneous Equation Model," *Econometrica*, Vol. 45, pp. 955–68.

Amemiya, T. (1985), *Advanced Econometrics*, Cambridge, MA: Harvard University Press.

Anderson, T. W., and H. Rubin (1949), "Estimation of the Parameters of a Single Equation in a Complete System of Stochastic Equations," *Annals of Mathematical Statistics*, Vol. 20, pp. 546–63.

Anderson, T. W., and H. Rubin (1950), "The Asymptotic Properties of Estimators of Estimates of the Parameters of a Single Equation in a Complete System of Stochastic Equations," *Annals of Mathematical Statistics*, Vol. 21, pp. 570–82.

Ben-Tal, A. (1985), "The Entropic Penalty Approach to Stochastic Programming," *Mathematics of Operations Research*, Vol. 10, pp. 263–79.

Berndt, E. R., and N. E. Savin (1975), "Estimation and Hypothesis Testing in Singular Equation Systems with Autoregressive Disturbances," *Econometrica*, Vol. 43, pp. 937–57.

Eisenpress, H., and Greenstadt (1966), "The Estimation of Nonlinear Econometric Systems," *Econometrica*, Vol. 34, pp. 851–61.

Fisher, F. M. (1966), *The Identification Problem in Econometrics*, Huntington, NY: Krieger.

Gabrielson, A. (1978), "Consistency and Identifiability," *Journal of Econometrics*, Vol. 8, pp. 261–3.

Gallant, A. R. (1987), Nonlinear Statistical Models. New York: John Wiley.

Gallant, A. R., and A. Holly (1980), "Statistical Inference in an Implicit, Nonlinear, Simultaneous Equation Model in the Context of Maximum Likelihood Estimation," *Econometrica*, Vol. 48, pp. 697–720.

Golan, A., G. Judge, and D. Miller (1996), Maximum Entropy Econometrics, New York: John Wiley.

Golan, A., G. Judge, and D. Miller (1998), "Information Recovery in Simultaneous-Equations' Statistical Models," In A. Ullah and D. Giles (Ed.), *Handbook of Applied Economic Statistics*, New York: Marcel Dekker, pp. 365–81.

Graybill, F. A. (1983), Matrices with Applications in Statistics, Belmont, California: Wadsworth.

Greenberg, E., and C. E. Webster (1983), *Advanced Econometrics: A Bridge to the Literature*, New York: John Wiley and Sons.

Hall, P., and J. Horowitz (1996), "Bootstrap Critical Values for Tests Based on Generalized-Method-of-Moments Estimators," *Econometrica*, Vol. 64, pp. 891–916.

Hansen, L. (1982), "Large Sample Properties of Generalized Method of Moments Estimators," *Econometrica*, Vol. 50, pp. 1029–54.

Hansen, L. P., and K. J. Singleton (1982), "Generalized Instrumental Variables Estimation of Nonlinear Rational Expectations Models," *Econometrica*, Vol. 50, pp. 1269–86.

Hatanaka, M. (1974), "An Efficient Two-Step Estimator for the Dynamic Adjustment Model with Autoregressive Errors," *Journal of Econometrics*, Vol. 2, pp. 199–220.

Hatanaka, M. (1976), "Several Efficient Two-Step Estimators for the Dynamic Simultaneous Equations Model with Autoregressive Disturbances," *Journal of Econometrics*, Vol. 4, pp. 189–204.

Hendry, D. F. (1976), "The Structure of Simultaneous Equations Estimators," *Journal of Econometrics*, Vol. 4, pp. 51–88.

Jorgenson, D. W. and J. J. Laffont (1974), "Efficient Estimation of Nonlinear Simultaneous Equations with Additive Disturbances," Annals of Economic and Social Measurement, Vol. 3, pp. 615–40.

Judge, G. G., W. E. Griffiths, R. C. Hill, H. Lütkepohl, and T.-C. Lee (1985), *The Theory and Practice of Econometrics*, (2nd ed.), New York: John Wiley and Sons.

Judge, G. G., R. C. Hill, W. E. Griffiths, H. Lütkepohl, and T.-C. Lee (1988), *Introduction to the Theory and Practice of Econometrics*, (2nd ed.), New York: John Wiley and Sons.

Kitamura, Y., and M. Stutzer (1997), "An Information-Theoretic Alternative to Generalized Method of Moments Estimation," *Econometrica*, Vol. 65, pp. 861–74.

Koopmans, T. C., and W. C. Hood (1953), "The Estimation of Simultaneous Linear Economic Relationships," In W. C. Hood and T. C. Koopmans (Eds.), *Studies in Econometric Method*, New Haven: Yale University Press, pp. 112–99.

Prucha, I. R., and H. H. Kelejian (1984), "The Structure of Simultaneous Equations Estimators: A Generalization Toward Nonnormal Disturbances," *Econometrica*, Vol. 52, pp. 721–36.

Rothenberg, T. J. (1971), Identification in Parametric Models. Econometrica, Vol. 39, pp. 577–91.

Rothenberg, T. J. (1974), "Bayesian Analysis of Simultaneous Equations Models," In S. E. Fienberg and A. Zellner (Eds.), *Studies in Bayesian Econometrics and Statistics*, (pp. 405–24), Amsterdam: North–Holland.

Srivastava, V. K., and D. E. A. Giles (1987), *Seemingly Unrelated Regression Equations Models*, New York: Marcel Dekker.

Schmidt, P. (1976), *Econometrics*, New York: Marcel Dekker.

Vijayan, K. (1991), "Estimating Functions in Survey Sampling: Estimation of Super-Population Regression Parameters," Chapter 17 in V. P. Godambe (Ed.), Estimating Functions. Clorenden, Clarendon Press, Oxford.

Vinod, H. (1997), "Using Godambe-Durbin Estimating Functions in Econometrica " in Selected Proceedings of the Symposium on Estimating Equations, Institute of Mathematical Statistics, pp. 215–38.

Zellner, A. (1998), "The Finite Sample Properties of Simultaneous Equations' Estimates and Estimators: Bayesian and Non-Bayesian Approaches," *Journal of Econometrics*, Annals Issue in Honor of Carl F. Christ, (L. R. Klein, Ed.), Vol. 83, pp. 185–212.

Zellner, A., and H. Theil (1962), "Three Stage Least Squares: Simultaneous Estimation of Simultaneous Equations," *Econometrica*, Vol. 30, pp. 54–78.

17.10. Appendix: Historical Perspective

In this appendix we present a brief historical overview of the intellectual activity that spawned the econometric models discussed in this chapter. In many ways the early 1940s, when the statistical implications of simultaneity were first raised, mark the beginning of the era of modern econometrics. The conceptual problems raised by E. J. Working (1926), Frisch (1934), Tinbergen (1938), and others emphasized among other things that economic data are generated by systems of economic relations that are stochastic, possibly dynamic, and simultaneous. This type of DSP pointed to many unsolved problems of statistical inference – from characterizations of the generation of the observed data to estimating the unknown parameters of relevant economic relations. It was fully realized that if the results of econometric analyses were to reflect desirable properties in estimation and inference, there must be consistency between the statistical model employed and the sampling model by which the data were generated.

In formulating statistical models consistent with the way economic data are visualized as being generated, a milestone was reached in 1943 when two articles that recognized the characteristics of economic data were published in *Econometrica* by Haavelmo and by Mann and Wald. About the same time Einstein was asserting that God did not play dice with the universe, Haavelmo wrote a monograph entitled *The Probability Approach to Econometrics* (1944). Haavelmo converted the economist's simultaneous equation model to a statistical model by assuming a random noise component for each equation and specifying the joint probability distribution of these random variables. This specification resulted in the so-called simultaneous system of equations statistical model. Mann and Wald suggested a large-sample solution to the estimation problem arising from the new systems of equations formulations.

Anderson and Rubin (1949) developed the "limited information" maximum likelihood estimators for estimating the parameters of an equation contained in a system of equations and derived corresponding large-sample properties and statistical tests. Koopmans (1949) tackled the parameter identification problem first raised by Working (1926) and developed necessary and sufficient conditions for identifying each mathematical equation as a separate economic relation and for discriminating between alternative competing structures. The work of the 1940s, which was based squarely on economic and statistical theory, was to a large extent centered at the Cowles Commission at the University of Chicago. A monograph edited by Koopmans (1950) summarized the state of the tools of quantitative knowledge after the developments of the 1940s.

In the applied econometrics area, Girshick and Haavelmo (1947) integrated economic theory and inferential statistics beautifully in their classic five-equation model concerned with the demand for food. Haavelmo (1947) made use of a system of equations in estimating the parameters of the consumption function. Klein (1950) completed his work on a sophisticated macroeconometric model of the United States economy. Computational burdens with the new techniques were significant because the desk calculator was still the main tool of researchers.

Concurrently, Samuelson published his book entitled *Foundations of Economic Analysis* (1948), Von Neumann and Morgenstern (1947) introduced the profession to game theory, Wald (1950) developed statistical decision theory and started us viewing econometrics as the study of statistical decision problems under uncertainty, Dantzig (1951a,b) developed the simplex algorithm for use with linear optimizing models, and Koopmans (1951) and his cohorts identified the conceptual basis for the activity analysis approach to price and allocation problems in economics. Each of these creative efforts had a significant impact on the demand for, and structure of, econometric efforts in the 1950s. At the end of this period there was great optimism that we were on the road to making mathematical economics and econometrics into tools that would serve the needs and aspirations of the discipline and society. On the basis of these intellectual gifts, the fundamental principles underlying the analysis of simultaneous equations models were born.

PART SEVEN

Model Discovery

PERHAPS you have been wondering, as we have worked our way through a wide range of sampling models, where do econometric models come from? Perhaps it has also been apparent to you that the econometric problem of developing a plausible basis for reasoning in situations of partial–incomplete information also extends in a real-world context beyond the recovery of information about parameter values or unknown components of a model to the specification of the econometric–probability model itself. Because the basic form and specific characteristics of the probability–econometric model are fundamental to framing the inverse problem and devising estimation and inference procedures, in Chapters 18 and 19 we now face up to how one goes about using sample and nonsample information to attempt to solve this model-discovery problem. As we work our way through this difficult model selection problem, we first consider the statistical consequences of model misspecification and then we go on to evaluate a range of model discovery procedures that have evolved in the statistics and econometric literature. We hope the results of this tour will help the reader appreciate the statistical implications of, and the care required, in the model-discovery phase of the information recovery process.

CHAPTER 18

Model Discovery: The Problem of Variable Selection and Conditioning

18.1. Introduction

We have, to this point, viewed econometrics in the context of developing a plausible basis for reasoning in situations involving incomplete–partial (sample) information. Prior chapters have dealt primarily with situations in which the probability–econometric model of a DSP was assumed to encompass an accurate representation of the actual sampling process that led to data outcomes. Estimation, testing, and confidence-region procedures were then developed that were generally *conditional* on the assumption that the probability–econometric model actually encompassed an acceptable characterization of the DSP underlying the data. Indeed, much of the current established econometric theory relates to this context of defining good or optimal estimation and testing procedures *conditional* on given characteristics of the DSP. *In this chapter we explicitly recognize that the problem of incomplete information extends to the specification of the underlying probability–econometric model itself.*

Because the functional and stochastic characteristics of a probability–econometric model are fundamental to devising estimation and inference procedures, we now face the problem of using information in the observed data to discover properties that collectively define the probability–econometric model. In other words, the properties of the model specifications are to be inferred from the data. Unfortunately, this is an area of econometric inquiry in which there has been little success in devising plausible methods of resolution.

Building on the conceptual knowledge that exists about the DSP in a given research problem, how does one *infer appropriate probability–econometric model characteristics from an observed sample of information?* A finite sample of data is generally insufficient for discovering or specifying a full representation of the probability distribution underlying the DSP. In effect, one generally cannot expect to observe, experience, or infer all of the features of a probability distribution underlying a data-sampling process from just a limited or finite set of observations from the process. Thus, the idea that model discovery procedures can recover some "true" underlying probability–econometric model must be tempered to the objective of seeking a model that captures as many valid data-restricting constraints as possible. The very idea that there exists a "true" probability–econometric model to be discovered may be ill conceived, and the concept may actually be detrimental to reaching our estimation and inference objectives.

Probability–econometric models are conceptual devices invented by researchers to provide a context in which to interpret both the data and the sampling process underlying the data. The values of model parameters that we seek are not only unobserved, but they are also generally unobservable (consider the difficulty associated with collecting a bet from a colleague on the value of an unknown model parameter). Although searching for the "true model" may be an empty exercise, seeking a useful model that helps narrow the possibilities regarding the implications of a particular theory or the characteristics of a DSP are worthy goals of applied econometrics. Even if we view the probability–econometric model as only a conceptual tool, and the objective is only to provide a working model of a theory, a DSP, or both, the uncertainty underlying the specification process remains all too apparent.

18.1.1. Experiments in Nonexperimental Model Building

In economics, much of the data underlying the search for data-constraining properties of probability–econometric models are not the result of a controlled experimental design. This leads to a situation in which

1. there are typically many plausible specifications of probability–econometric models that do not contradict our knowledge of human behavior or of the economic and institutional processes from which economic data are sampled, and
2. we must proceed through the model-discovery phase of an econometric analysis using a strategy of nonexperimental model building. Therefore, in most econometric analyses there is significant uncertainty regarding an appropriate specification of many of the components underlying an econometric model. Correspondingly, given the possibility of model misspecification, there is uncertainty concerning the appropriate choice and the performance of estimation and inference procedures.

What makes the model selection problem especially challenging is that in most instances we must use a given finite sample of data to accomplish many objectives at once, including

1. choosing model-restricting constraints relating unknowns to sample data,
2. choosing an appropriate estimation procedure for recovering values of unknowns,
3. estimating the unknown parameters,
4. choosing appropriate inference procedures for assessing hypotheses, generating confidence regions about unknowns, or both, and
5. making inference decisions.

Although we often enter into econometric analyses with some nonsample information about characteristics of the inverse problem and the underlying range of possible models, the goal of achieving all of the varied objectives (1–5) still places a large burden of information recovery on one finite sample of data. Note that in preceding chapters, our focus has been on the problems inherent in objectives (2–5) above, *given* a set of choices relating to the first objective. In fact most of econometric theory proceeds in this context. Much work remains relating to the difficult problems associated with the first objective, and we discuss some of these vexing problems ahead in this and the next chapter.

In working our way through various forms of models in the preceding chapters, we have already examined some concepts and procedures that have been used in practice in attempts to help identify an appropriate model specification. For examples of conceptual tools, recall that in Chapter 15 we identified a possible source of probability model uncertainty represented by unknown nonspherical noise covariance matrices that was reflective of a situation in which information about sampling characteristics of the equation noise component was notably partial or incomplete. Another example was in the multiple–simultaneous equation model context in which we developed a conceptual basis for classifying variables as to their endogeneity or predeterminedness and investigated the implication for parameter identification in the model. Regarding procedural tools, over a range of chapters we have noted finite and asymptotic hypothesis-testing procedures that have been used by analysts to check model-defining characteristics relating to values of parameters and to asses the adequacy of the specification of a probability–econometric model. In particular, in moment-based estimation, we considered procedures for evaluating the validity of overdetermined moment constraints, which also encompassed a general evaluation of the validity of regression model specifications both in terms of functional form and in variable content.

Thus, we do not come into this chapter devoid of concepts or procedures that have been used in econometric practice to facilitate model specification. The purpose of this and the next chapter is to focus and amplify issues relating to two of the arguably most pervasive model specification issues, namely, the issues of explanatory variable selection and condition (addressed in this chapter) and noise covariance specification (Chapter 19).

18.1.2. The Chapter Format

In this chapter we focus explicitly on fundamental model discovery issues relating to variable selection. Model discovery issues relating to characteristics of the noise component of the probability model will be analyzed in Chapter 19. The organization of this chapter is as follows: We first discuss the fundamental statistical consequences of incorrect variable selection. Next we examine statistical implications of using classical testing procedures to select right-hand-side variables and to determine the consistency between sample and nonsample information. We acknowledge that in applied econometrics some type of hypothesis-testing strategy is the most widely used variable selection technique, but we question the interpretation and inference basis that results when testing is used for this purpose. Because many analysts nonetheless desire and use systematic recipes in their attempts to find good interpretable econometric models, we then discuss variable selection procedures that have evolved over time involving both goodness-of-fit assessments and penalties for model complexity. We then review procedures that do not select a particular subset of variables but rather shrink coefficients of explanatory variables without eliminating any of them from the model. Noting that much economic data are nonexperimental in nature, we next review procedures for coping with the problem of ill-conditioned matrices of explanatory variable. Finally, we provide a few comments regarding the general testing-for-model specification concepts and philosophy that practitioners often use for selecting their models and recognize the currently inadequate nature of these procedures for model–variable discovery.

18.2. Variable Selection Problem in a Loss or MSE Context

The concepts we examine in this section are readily applicable to a wide range of parametric and semiparametric econometric models, but to establish a formal basis for analyzing the variable selection and estimation problems, we begin by focusing on the following simple noisy inverse problem that often arises in practice. Assume we are unable to measure the unknown k-dimensional parameter vector $\boldsymbol{\beta}$ from a set $\Omega_{\boldsymbol{\beta}}$ of possible parameter vectors directly and instead observe an n-dimensional vector of noisy sample outcomes from the random vector $\mathbf{Y}=[\mathrm{Y}_1, \mathrm{Y}_2, \ldots, \mathrm{Y}_n]'$ that are consistent with the underlying data-sampling process

$$\mathbf{Y} = \mathbf{x}\boldsymbol{\beta} + \varepsilon, \tag{18.2.1}$$

where $\mathbf{x}$ is a known $(n \times k)$ matrix of explanatory variables having full-column rank. The unobservable components of the model are $\boldsymbol{\beta}=[\beta_1, \beta_2, \ldots, \beta_k]'$, a vector of k unknown parameters, the n-dimensional noise vector ε, which is an $(n \times 1)$ random vector having a multivariate (possibly normal) probability distribution with a mean vector of zero, a covariance matrix $\boldsymbol{\Sigma}_\varepsilon = \sigma^2\mathbf{I}_n$, and a noise component variance σ^2.

Given the random sample $\mathbf{Y}$ defined in (18.2.1), the problem is to find an estimator $\hat{\eta} = \hat{\eta}(\mathbf{Y})$ of the unknowns and unobservables of interest that has good sampling properties or that, in a decision theoretic context, yields small risk. The definition of the risk function depends on the researcher's perceptions of loss as well as the researcher's information recovery objectives. If, for example, the objective is estimating the conditional expectation of $\mathbf{Y}$, $\mathrm{E}[\mathbf{Y} \mid \mathbf{x}] = \mathbf{x}\boldsymbol{\beta}$, the expected squared-error loss function

$$\rho(\hat{\eta}, \mathbf{x}\boldsymbol{\beta}) = \mathrm{E}\|\hat{\eta}(\mathbf{Y}) - \mathbf{x}\boldsymbol{\beta}\|^2 = \mathrm{E}[[\hat{\eta}(\mathbf{Y}) - \mathbf{x}\boldsymbol{\beta}]'[\hat{\eta}(\mathbf{Y}) - \mathbf{x}\boldsymbol{\beta}]] \tag{18.2.2}$$

is relevant and is known as *conditional mean forecasting risk* (Judge and Bock, 1978, p. 33). If, instead, primary interest is focused on estimating the values of the parameters $\boldsymbol{\beta}$ then the *mean-squared error risk* function

$$\rho(\hat{\eta}, \boldsymbol{\beta}) = \mathrm{E}\|\hat{\eta}(\mathbf{Y}) - \boldsymbol{\beta}\|^2 = \mathrm{E}[[\hat{\eta}(\mathbf{Y}) - \boldsymbol{\beta}]'[\hat{\eta}(\mathbf{Y}) - \boldsymbol{\beta}]] \tag{18.2.3}$$

could be utilized. Weighted risk functions could also be considered if the analyst wished to treat the elements of $\boldsymbol{\beta}$, or of $\mathbf{x}\boldsymbol{\beta}$, asymmetrically (Judge and Bock, 1978, p. 30). When ε is a multivariate normal random vector, when $\mathbf{x}$ has full-column rank, and when the model (18.2.1) is congruent with the true underlying data-sampling process, the maximum likelihood (ML)–least squares (LS) estimator

$$\hat{\eta} = \hat{\boldsymbol{\beta}} = (\mathbf{x}'\mathbf{x})^{-1}\mathbf{x}'\mathbf{Y} \sim \mathrm{N}(\boldsymbol{\beta}, \sigma^2(\mathbf{x}'\mathbf{x})^{-1}) \tag{18.2.4}$$

is a minimum variance unbiased estimator and, under the risk measure (18.2.3), is also minimax with a constant mean-squared error risk $\rho(\hat{\boldsymbol{\eta}}, \boldsymbol{\beta}) = \sigma^2 \text{tr}(\mathbf{x}'\mathbf{x})^{-1}$ (recall Chapter 3). The estimator $\mathbf{x}\hat{\boldsymbol{\beta}}$ of the conditional mean $\mathbf{x}\boldsymbol{\beta}$ has conditional mean forecasting risk equal to $\sigma^2 k$.

In reality, an appropriate specification of the explanatory variable matrix $\mathbf{x}$ may be unknown. Consequently, within the context of an econometric model based on (18.2.1), the *variable selection problem* may be described as follows: An investigator has a given sample of data and wants to estimate the unknown parameters of a statistical model that lies within the parameter space $\Omega_{\boldsymbol{\beta}}$, where $\boldsymbol{\beta}$ is a parameter vector in $\Omega_{\boldsymbol{\beta}}$. However, the investigator suspects the relationship may be characterized by a lower-dimensional parameter space $\Omega_{\boldsymbol{\beta}_0}$, where $\Omega_{\boldsymbol{\beta}_0}$ is a proper subspace of $\Omega_{\boldsymbol{\beta}}$. Consequently, we visualize a k-dimensional parameter space that, by assumption, includes some set of k_0 relevant variables, plus $k - k_0$ extraneous ones, where k_0 is generally unknown. Therefore, the explanatory variable matrix congruent with the data-sampling process is a submatrix of the initial explanatory variable matrix. In terms of variable selection, there are 2^k possible models that can be defined based on the general model (18.2.1) and that are candidates for a regression model representation of the observed vector $\mathbf{y}$. Consequently, these 2^k alternative models make up a nested set of alternatives for describing the explanatory variables consistent with $\mathbf{y}$.

Given the size-2^k model possibility space, the next question is, Why should we be concerned in a statistical context with this subset-nested model choice problem?

18.2.1. Bias-Variance Trade-Off in Incorrect Variable Selection

The conventional trade-off to consider in the variable selection problem posed in Section 18.2 is that of bias versus variance. Parameter estimators based on the higher-dimensional parameter space $\Omega_{\boldsymbol{\beta}}$ will be unbiased but may have large variance if the model is overspecified (i.e., includes irrelevant explanatory variables and parameters). Conversely, estimators restricted to the smaller dimensional parameter space $\Omega_{\boldsymbol{\beta}_0}$ may have smaller variances but nonzero bias (if relevant explanatory variables and parameters are omitted). To see the underlying basis for this statement, consider the regressor choice problem within the context of two sets of regressors. In this context, we make use of the linear regression model (18.2.1) in the form

$$\mathbf{y} = \mathbf{x}_1\boldsymbol{\beta}_1 + \mathbf{x}_2\boldsymbol{\beta}_2 + \boldsymbol{\varepsilon}, \tag{18.2.5}$$

where $\mathbf{x}_1$ and $\mathbf{x}_2$ are known matrices of dimension $(n \times k_1)$ and $(n \times k_2)$, respectively, with $k_1 + k_2 = k$, and $\boldsymbol{\beta}$ is a k-dimensional vector of unknown parameters partitioned comformably into components $\boldsymbol{\beta}_1$ and $\boldsymbol{\beta}_2$. If we generically let $\mathbf{x}_1$ represent the included variables and $\mathbf{x}_2$ represent the excluded or omitted variables, where $k_1 \leq k$, the regression model (18.2.5) can be made to represent all of the possible subsets (combinations) of $\mathbf{x}$ by varying the column dimensions and content of $\mathbf{x}_1$ and $\mathbf{x}_2$ and setting $\boldsymbol{\beta}_2 = \mathbf{0}$.

Now consider only the $\mathbf{x}_1$ subset of $\mathbf{x}$, and assume that the $\mathbf{x}_2$ set of variables is omitted, so that $\boldsymbol{\beta}_2$ in Equation (18.2.5) is set equal to a zero vector. Thus, perhaps on the basis of nonsample information, if we assume the $\mathbf{x}_2$ variables are extraneous and are then omitted from the regression model, we can represent this information by the set of linear restrictions

$$\mathbf{c}\boldsymbol{\beta} = [\mathbf{0} \quad \mathbf{I}_{k_2}] \begin{bmatrix} \boldsymbol{\beta}_1 \\ \boldsymbol{\beta}_2 \end{bmatrix} = \mathbf{r} = \mathbf{0}_{k_2}, \tag{18.2.6}$$

where $\mathbf{c}$ is a $(k_2 \times k)$ matrix of rank k_2 and $\mathbf{0}_{k_2}$ is a k_2-dimensional zero vector. Under this scenario, the general restricted ML–LS estimator is defined by

$$\hat{\boldsymbol{\beta}}^* = \hat{\boldsymbol{\beta}} - (\mathbf{x}'\mathbf{x})^{-1}\mathbf{c}'[\mathbf{c}(\mathbf{x}'\mathbf{x})^{-1}\mathbf{c}']^{-1}(\mathbf{c}\hat{\boldsymbol{\beta}} - \mathbf{r}) \tag{18.2.7}$$

with expectation

$$\mathrm{E}[\hat{\boldsymbol{\beta}}^*] = \boldsymbol{\beta} - (\mathbf{x}'\mathbf{x})^{-1}\mathbf{c}'[\mathbf{c}(\mathbf{x}'\mathbf{x})^{-1}\mathbf{c}']^{-1}(\mathbf{c}\boldsymbol{\beta} - \mathbf{r}) \tag{18.2.8}$$

and covariance matrix

$$\begin{aligned} \mathrm{E}[(\hat{\boldsymbol{\beta}}^* - \mathrm{E}[\hat{\boldsymbol{\beta}}^*])(\hat{\boldsymbol{\beta}}^* - \mathrm{E}[\hat{\boldsymbol{\beta}}^*])'] &= \sigma^2[(\mathbf{x}'\mathbf{x})^{-1} - (\mathbf{x}'\mathbf{x})^{-1}\mathbf{c}'[\mathbf{c}(\mathbf{x}'\mathbf{x})^{-1}\mathbf{c}']^{-1}\mathbf{c}(\mathbf{x}'\mathbf{x})^{-1}] \\ &= \begin{bmatrix} \sigma^2(\mathbf{x}_1'\mathbf{x}_1)^{-1} & \mathbf{0} \\ \mathbf{0} & \mathbf{0}_{k_2} \end{bmatrix}. \end{aligned} \tag{18.2.9}$$

The difference between the covariance matrices for $\hat{\boldsymbol{\beta}}$ and $\hat{\boldsymbol{\beta}}^*$ is the nonzero positive semidefinite matrix

$$\mathbf{cov}(\hat{\boldsymbol{\beta}}) - \mathbf{cov}(\hat{\boldsymbol{\beta}}^*) = \sigma^2(\mathbf{x}'\mathbf{x})^{-1}\mathbf{c}'[\mathbf{c}(\mathbf{x}'\mathbf{x})^{-1}\mathbf{c}']^{-1}\mathbf{c}(\mathbf{x}'\mathbf{x})^{-1}, \tag{18.2.10}$$

and thus the restricted estimator always has the smaller covariance matrix.

An estimator of σ^2 that uses the restricted least-squares estimator $\hat{\boldsymbol{\beta}}^*$, and thereby incorporates the restrictions, is

$$\hat{\sigma}^{2*} = \frac{(\mathbf{Y} - \mathbf{x}\hat{\boldsymbol{\beta}}^*)'(\mathbf{Y} - \mathbf{x}\hat{\boldsymbol{\beta}}^*)}{n - k_1} = \frac{\mathbf{Y}'(\mathbf{I}_n - \mathbf{x}_1(\mathbf{x}_1'\mathbf{x}_1)^{-1}\mathbf{x}_1')\mathbf{Y}}{n - k_1}, \tag{18.2.11a}$$

and its expectation is given by

$$\mathrm{E}[\hat{\sigma}^{2*}] = \sigma^2 + \frac{\boldsymbol{\beta}_2'\mathbf{x}_2'[\mathrm{I} - \mathbf{x}_1(\mathbf{x}_1'\mathbf{x}_1)^{-1}\mathbf{x}_1']\mathbf{x}_2\boldsymbol{\beta}_2}{n - k_1}. \tag{18.2.11b}$$

Therefore, unless it is true that $\boldsymbol{\beta}_2 = \mathbf{0}$ so that the restricted model is a valid regression model, $\hat{\sigma}^{2*}$ yields a biased estimator of σ^2. Also, for purposes of inference, when $\boldsymbol{\beta}_2 \neq \mathbf{0}$, the ratio $(n - k_1)\hat{\sigma}^{2*}/\sigma^2$ is distributed as a *noncentral* Chi-square random variable with $n - k_1$ degrees of freedom on the assumption that the noise component in (18.2.5) is multivariate normally distributed with mean zero and $\mathbf{cov}(\varepsilon) = \sigma^2\mathbf{I}_n$.

These results identify the following statistical consequences of using a subset $\mathbf{x}_1$ of the original set of explanatory variable values $\mathbf{x}$:

1. The estimator $\hat{\boldsymbol{\beta}}^*$ is a biased estimator of $\boldsymbol{\beta}$ unless it is true that $\mathbf{c}\boldsymbol{\beta} = \boldsymbol{\beta}_2 = \mathbf{0}$.
2. The estimator $\hat{\boldsymbol{\beta}}_1^*$ is a biased estimator of $\boldsymbol{\beta}_1$ unless it is true that $\mathbf{c}\boldsymbol{\beta} = \boldsymbol{\beta}_2 = \mathbf{0}$ *or* $\mathbf{x}_1$ and $\mathbf{x}_2$ are orthogonal (note that (18.2.8) implies that $\mathbf{E}[\hat{\boldsymbol{\beta}}^*] = \mathrm{E}[\hat{\boldsymbol{\beta}}_1]$ when $\mathbf{x}_1'\mathbf{x}_2 = \mathbf{0}$ and $\mathbf{c}\boldsymbol{\beta} = \boldsymbol{\beta}_2 = \mathbf{r}$).
3. Whether or not it is true that $\boldsymbol{\beta}_2 = \mathbf{0}$, the unrestricted least-squares estimator of $\boldsymbol{\beta}_1$, where both $\mathbf{x}_1$ and $\mathbf{x}_2$ *are included* in the regression model specification, generally has a larger

covariance matrix than the estimator of $\boldsymbol{\beta}_1$ based on the restricted model. Consequently, the sampling variability of $\hat{\boldsymbol{\beta}}_1^*$ is generally less than the sampling variability of $\hat{\boldsymbol{\beta}}_1$.

4. The subset (restricted) model estimator $\hat{\sigma}^{2*}$ has a positive bias unless either $\boldsymbol{\beta}_2 = \mathbf{0}$, or $\mathbf{x}_2'[\mathbf{I} - \mathbf{x}_1(\mathbf{x}_1'\mathbf{x}_1)^{-1}\mathbf{x}_1']\mathbf{x}_2 = \mathbf{0}$, or both.
5. If it is true that $\boldsymbol{\beta}_2 \neq \mathbf{0}$, then either $\hat{\boldsymbol{\beta}}_1^*$ is biased, or $\hat{\sigma}^{2*}$ is biased, or both are biased.

► **Example 18.2.1:** To demonstrate the results stated in this section, we provide the GAUSS program C18Model.gss in the examples manual. The user selects parameter values $(\boldsymbol{\beta}, \sigma^2)$ and a sample size (n) for a linear regression model and determines the subsets of the $\boldsymbol{\beta}$ vector, $\boldsymbol{\beta}_1$ and $\boldsymbol{\beta}_2$. Then, GAUSS conducts a Monte Carlo simulation exercise based on the four possible cases ($\boldsymbol{\beta}_2$ correctly included, $\boldsymbol{\beta}_2$ correctly excluded, $\boldsymbol{\beta}_2$ incorrectly included, $\boldsymbol{\beta}_2$ incorrectly excluded). For each case, GAUSS reports the estimated bias and variance of the associated LS estimators. The user should find that results confirm the statements appearing in the preceding list.

18.2.2. Statistical Implications under an MSE Matrix Measure

The preceding conclusions focus the consequences for correct model choice on a bias-variance trade-off. The mean-square error measure, which is a function of the levels of both variance and bias, provides a performance basis for evaluating the trade-off between bias and variance.

Within the context of (18.2.5), if $\boldsymbol{\beta}_2 \neq \mathbf{0}$ and thus $\boldsymbol{\delta} \equiv \mathbf{c}\boldsymbol{\beta} - \mathbf{r} \neq \mathbf{0}$ when $\mathbf{c}\boldsymbol{\beta} = \boldsymbol{\beta}_2$ and $\mathbf{r} = \mathbf{0}$, then $\hat{\boldsymbol{\beta}}^*$ is a biased estimator of $\boldsymbol{\beta}$ with *mean-square error (MSE) matrix*

$$\begin{aligned}\mathbf{mse}(\hat{\boldsymbol{\beta}}^*) &\equiv \mathrm{E}[(\hat{\boldsymbol{\beta}}^* - \boldsymbol{\beta})(\hat{\boldsymbol{\beta}}^* - \boldsymbol{\beta})'] \\ &= \sigma^2(\mathbf{x}'\mathbf{x})^{-1} - \sigma^2(\mathbf{x}'\mathbf{x})^{-1}\mathbf{c}'[\mathbf{c}(\mathbf{x}'\mathbf{x})^{-1}\mathbf{c}']^{-1}\mathbf{c}(\mathbf{x}'\mathbf{x})^{-1} \\ &\quad + (\mathbf{x}'\mathbf{x})^{-1}\mathbf{c}'[\mathbf{c}(\mathbf{x}'\mathbf{x})^{-1}\mathbf{c}']^{-1}\boldsymbol{\delta}\boldsymbol{\delta}'[\mathbf{c}(\mathbf{x}'\mathbf{x})^{-1}\mathbf{c}']^{-1}\mathbf{c}(\mathbf{x}'\mathbf{x})^{-1}, \end{aligned} \qquad (18.2.12)$$

which is the sum of the covariance matrix of $\hat{\boldsymbol{\beta}}^*$ and the outer product of the *bias vector* associated with $\hat{\boldsymbol{\beta}}^*$ defined by

$$\mathbf{bias}(\hat{\boldsymbol{\beta}}^*) \equiv \mathrm{E}[\hat{\boldsymbol{\beta}}^*] - \boldsymbol{\beta} = -(\mathbf{x}'\mathbf{x})^{-1}\mathbf{c}'[\mathbf{c}(\mathbf{x}'\mathbf{x})^{-1}\mathbf{c}']^{-1}\boldsymbol{\delta}. \qquad (18.2.13)$$

The restricted estimator $\hat{\boldsymbol{\beta}}^*$ is said to be *strong mean-square error* (SMSE) superior to the unrestricted estimator $\hat{\boldsymbol{\beta}}$ iff $\mathbf{mse}(\hat{\boldsymbol{\beta}}) - \mathbf{mse}(\hat{\boldsymbol{\beta}}^*)$ is a positive semidefinite (psd) matrix, so that the MSE matrix of $\hat{\boldsymbol{\beta}}^*$ is no larger, and generally smaller, than the MSE matrix of $\hat{\boldsymbol{\beta}}$.

From (18.2.12) it follows that

$$\begin{aligned}\mathbf{mse}(\hat{\boldsymbol{\beta}}) - \mathbf{mse}(\hat{\boldsymbol{\beta}}^*) &= (\mathbf{x}'\mathbf{x})^{-1}\mathbf{c}'[\mathbf{c}(\mathbf{x}'\mathbf{x})^{-1}\mathbf{c}']^{-1}[\sigma^2\mathbf{c}(\mathbf{x}'\mathbf{x})^{-1}\mathbf{c}' - \boldsymbol{\delta}\boldsymbol{\delta}'] \\ &\quad \times [\mathbf{c}(\mathbf{x}'\mathbf{x})^{-1}\mathbf{c}']^{-1}\mathbf{c}(\mathbf{x}'\mathbf{x})^{-1}. \end{aligned} \qquad (18.2.14a)$$

Because $(\mathbf{x}'\mathbf{x})^{-1}\mathbf{c}'[\mathbf{c}(\mathbf{x}'\mathbf{x})^{-1}\mathbf{c}']^{-1}$ is a $(k \times j)$ matrix of rank j, (18.2.14a) is psd, and the restricted estimator is SMSE superior to the unrestricted estimator, iff $[\sigma^2\mathbf{c}(\mathbf{x}'\mathbf{x})^{-1}\mathbf{c}' - \boldsymbol{\delta}\boldsymbol{\delta}']$ is psd, which in turn is psd by definition iff

$$\boldsymbol{\tau}'[\sigma^2\mathbf{c}(\mathbf{x}'\mathbf{x})^{-1}\mathbf{c}' - \boldsymbol{\delta}\boldsymbol{\delta}']\boldsymbol{\tau} \geq 0 \quad \forall \boldsymbol{\tau}. \tag{18.2.14b}$$

Because $\boldsymbol{\tau}'[\sigma^2\mathbf{c}(\mathbf{x}'\mathbf{x})^{-1}\mathbf{c}']\boldsymbol{\tau} > 0\ \forall \boldsymbol{\tau} \neq \mathbf{0}$, a condition equivalent to (18.2.14b) is that

$$\frac{\boldsymbol{\tau}'\boldsymbol{\delta}\boldsymbol{\delta}'\boldsymbol{\tau}}{\boldsymbol{\tau}'[\sigma^2\mathbf{c}(\mathbf{x}'\mathbf{x})^{-1}\mathbf{c}']\boldsymbol{\tau}} \leq 1 \quad \forall \boldsymbol{\tau} \neq \mathbf{0}. \tag{18.2.14c}$$

The maximum of the left-hand side of (18.2.14c) with respect to the choice of $\boldsymbol{\tau}$ can be shown to equal $\frac{\boldsymbol{\delta}'[\mathbf{c}(\mathbf{x}'\mathbf{x})^{-1}\mathbf{c}']^{-1}\boldsymbol{\delta}}{\sigma^2}$. Therefore,

$$\mathbf{mse}(\hat{\boldsymbol{\beta}}) - \mathbf{mse}(\hat{\boldsymbol{\beta}}^*) \text{ is psd} \quad \text{iff} \quad \lambda \leq \frac{1}{2}, \tag{18.2.15a}$$

where

$$\lambda \equiv \frac{\boldsymbol{\delta}'[\mathbf{c}(\mathbf{x}'\mathbf{x})^{-1}\mathbf{c}']^{-1}\boldsymbol{\delta}}{2\sigma^2}. \tag{18.2.15b}$$

If the restricted estimator $\hat{\boldsymbol{\beta}}^*$ is SMSE superior to $\hat{\boldsymbol{\beta}}$, then every linear combination of the elements of $\hat{\boldsymbol{\beta}}^*$ has MSE equal to or smaller than the corresponding linear combination of the elements of $\hat{\boldsymbol{\beta}}$, making $\boldsymbol{\tau}'\hat{\boldsymbol{\beta}}^*$ superior to $\boldsymbol{\tau}'\hat{\boldsymbol{\beta}}$ for estimating $\boldsymbol{\tau}'\boldsymbol{\beta}$. Superiority is seen to depend on the magnitude of the constraint error $\boldsymbol{\delta} = \mathbf{c}\boldsymbol{\beta} - \mathbf{r}$ being small enough in terms of the value of the quadratic distance-from-zero measure (18.2.15b). An important point to emphasize is that the constraints *do not have to be correct* for the restricted estimator to be superior to the unrestricted estimator, they just need to be "close enough" to correct as gauged by $\lambda \leq \frac{1}{2}$.

The value of λ in (18.2.15b) is recognized as the noncentrality parameter of the Chi-square-distributed Wald test of the j restrictions H_0: $\mathbf{c}\boldsymbol{\beta} = \mathbf{r}$ (see Chapters 4 and 6). It is therefore possible to test SMSE superiority asymptotically by testing whether $\lambda \leq \frac{1}{2}$, which is accomplished by the test rule

$$\text{reject SMSE superiority if } \mathrm{w} = (\mathbf{c}\hat{\mathbf{b}} - \mathbf{r})'[\mathrm{s}^2\mathbf{c}(\mathbf{x}'\mathbf{x})^{-1}\mathbf{c}']^{-1}(\mathbf{c}\hat{\mathbf{b}} - \mathbf{r}) \geq \chi^2_{1-\alpha}(j, .5), \tag{18.2.16}$$

where $\chi^2_{1-\alpha}(j, .5)$ is the $(1-\alpha)^{\text{th}}$ quantile of the *noncentral* Chi-square distribution with j degrees of freedom and noncentrality parameter $\lambda = .5$. In the event that the noise component of (18.2.1) is multivariate normally distributed, the SMSE test can be made exact (as opposed to being only asymptotically valid) by using the F-statistic $\mathrm{F} = \mathrm{W}/j$ and testing whether $\mathrm{f} \geq \mathrm{f}_{1-\alpha}(j, n-k, .5)$, where $f_{1-\alpha}(j, n-k, .5)$ is the $(1-\alpha)^{\text{th}}$ quantile of the noncentral F-distribution with noncentrality of $\lambda = .5$, j being the number of independent restrictions being tested. We emphasize that the preceding results apply for a general specification of the matrix $\mathbf{c}$ used to define the linear restrictions being tested, and so the SMSE superiority and testing implications extend well beyond the case of exclusion restrictions on the regression model specification.

Lest the reader jump to conclusions about the SMSE superiority test being a perfectly general *model selection* procedure whereby one would choose an SMSE superior model on the basis of the outcome of the SMSE test, we emphasize some significant conceptual difficulties. First of all, if the final specification of the regression model is selected on the basis of the outcome of an SMSE superiority test, the final model specification is itself random, and the estimator that is then applied to this random specification is a *pretest estimator*. The sampling properties of a pretest estimator are neither those of the restricted or unrestricted estimator but are rather a generally complicated probabilistic mixture of these properties, the mixture being dependent on the respective probabilities that the restricted and unrestricted models will be chosen as the final regression model in repeated sampling. Secondly, if $\mathbf{X}$ does not contain all of the relevant explanatory variables such that $\hat{\boldsymbol{\beta}}$ is unbiased, the preceding MSE comparison is misspecified and irrelevant. Thirdly, even if $\mathbf{X}$ does contain all of the relevant explanatory variables so that $\hat{\boldsymbol{\beta}}$ is unbiased, the test decision itself will be wrong with positive probability based on the usual Type-I and Type-II errors associated with any hypothesis-testing procedure. Finally, in the absence of a normally distributed noise component, the finite sample behavior of the SMSE test is generally unknown, and the test is only asymptotically valid and thus subject to finite sample approximation error. Thus, choosing the final model on the basis of the outcome of a SMSE test does not guarantee an SMSE superior model.

► **Example 18.2.2:** The GAUSS program C18SMSE.gss (provided in the examples manual) conducts a Monte Carlo simulation exercise designed to examine the properties of a pretest estimator based on the SMSE test. First, GAUSS simulates the quadratic risk of the pretest estimator based on the Wald version of the SMSE test and compares the estimated risk function to the quadratic risks of the LS and RLS estimators. Then, GAUSS simulates the power function of the SMSE test under normal and nonnormal noise components. In the normal case, the test is based on the exact F test, and the associated Wald test is used in the nonnormal setting.

18.2.3. Statistical Implications under a Quadratic Risk Function Measure

Now instead of using an SMSE criterion, consider using the conditional mean forecasting risk function measure concerned with estimating $\mathbf{x}\boldsymbol{\beta}$, which represents the expected values of the elements of $\mathbf{Y}$ at the sample points in $\mathbf{x}$. The risk of the maximum likelihood estimator $\mathbf{x}\hat{\boldsymbol{\beta}}$ under squared-error loss is (recall (18.2.2))

$$\begin{aligned}\mathrm{E}[(\hat{\boldsymbol{\beta}}-\boldsymbol{\beta})'\mathbf{x}'\mathbf{x}(\hat{\boldsymbol{\beta}}-\boldsymbol{\beta})] &= \sigma^2\,\mathrm{tr}(\mathbf{x}(\mathbf{x}'\mathbf{x})^{-1}\mathbf{x}') = \sigma^2\,\mathrm{tr}(\mathbf{x}'\mathbf{x}(\mathbf{x}'\mathbf{x})^{-1})\\ &= \sigma^2\mathrm{tr}(\mathbf{I}_k) = \sigma^2 k, \end{aligned} \tag{18.2.17}$$

which is an increasing function of the number of variables k. The corresponding risk for the restricted estimator $\mathbf{x}\hat{\boldsymbol{\beta}}^*$ is given by (recall (18.2.12))

$$\begin{aligned}\mathrm{E}[(\hat{\boldsymbol{\beta}}^*-\boldsymbol{\beta})'\mathbf{x}'\mathbf{x}(\hat{\boldsymbol{\beta}}^*-\boldsymbol{\beta})] &= \mathrm{tr}\,\mathrm{E}[(\hat{\boldsymbol{\beta}}^*-\boldsymbol{\beta})(\hat{\boldsymbol{\beta}}^*-\boldsymbol{\beta})'\mathbf{x}'\mathbf{x}]\\ &= \mathrm{tr}(\sigma^2\mathbf{I}_k - \sigma^2(\mathbf{x}'\mathbf{x})^{-1}\mathbf{c}'[\mathbf{c}(\mathbf{x}'\mathbf{x})^{-1}\mathbf{c}']^{-1}\mathbf{c}\\ &\quad + (\mathbf{x}'\mathbf{x})^{-1}\mathbf{c}'[\mathbf{c}(\mathbf{x}'\mathbf{x})^{-1}\mathbf{c}']^{-1}\boldsymbol{\delta}\boldsymbol{\delta}'[\mathbf{c}(\mathbf{x}'\mathbf{x})^{-1}\mathbf{c}']^{-1}\mathbf{c})\\ &= \sigma^2 k - \sigma^2 k_2 + \boldsymbol{\delta}'[\mathbf{c}(\mathbf{x}'\mathbf{x})^{-1}\mathbf{c}']^{-1}\boldsymbol{\delta}\\ &= \sigma^2 k_1 + \boldsymbol{\beta}_2'[\mathbf{x}_2'\mathbf{x}_2 - \mathbf{x}_2'\mathbf{x}_1(\mathbf{x}_1'\mathbf{x}_1)^{-1}\mathbf{x}_1'\mathbf{x}_2]\boldsymbol{\beta}_2, \end{aligned} \tag{18.2.18}$$

where partitioned inversion and the special form of **c** and **r** have been used (recall (18.2.6)). One can interpret $\sigma^2 k_1$ as the risk penalty for the number of included variables (complexity), whereas the quadratic-form term can be viewed as the risk penalty for misspecification (incorrect variable selection).

A comparison between the risk of the unrestricted estimator (18.2.17) and the risk of the restricted estimator (18.2.18) yields the result that

$$\mathrm{E}[(\hat{\boldsymbol{\beta}} - \boldsymbol{\beta})'\mathbf{x}'\mathbf{x}(\hat{\boldsymbol{\beta}} - \boldsymbol{\beta})] - \mathrm{E}[(\hat{\boldsymbol{\beta}}^{*} - \boldsymbol{\beta})'\mathbf{x}'\mathbf{x}(\hat{\boldsymbol{\beta}}^{*} - \boldsymbol{\beta})] \geq 0 \qquad (18.2.19)$$

iff

$$\frac{\boldsymbol{\delta}'[\mathbf{c}(\mathbf{x}'\mathbf{x})^{-1}\mathbf{c}']^{-1}\boldsymbol{\delta}}{2\sigma^2} \leq \frac{k_2}{2}. \qquad (18.2.20)$$

Thus one would select the restricted model based on $\mathbf{x}_1$ over the complete model involving $\mathbf{x}_1$ and $\mathbf{x}_2$ if one knew that the risk (18.2.18) is less than the risk (18.2.17), or equivalently, if one knew that (18.2.20) were true. Since the specification error $\boldsymbol{\delta}$ depends on $\boldsymbol{\beta}_2$, which is unknown, in practice one does not know whether (18.2.20) holds. Recalling from Section 18.2.2 that the left hand side of (18.2.20) is in the form of the noncentrality parameter associated with the Wald Chi-square test of the restrictions $\mathbf{c}\boldsymbol{\beta} = \mathbf{r}$, one can conceive of a conditional mean forecasting risk superiority test analogous to the SMSE test of the previous section. In fact the only difference from the previous test would be that now the critical $(1-\alpha)^{\text{th}}$ quantile of the noncentral Chi-square distribution is based on a noncentrality of $k_2/2$, and not $1/2$. However, used as a *model selection* procedure, the test suffers from all of the same difficulties that were discussed relative to the SMSE superiority test. Therefore, for variable selection purposes, the procedure has conceptual difficulties and leads to an estimator with generally complicated sampling properties. The search for other model selection rules is the subject of the next sections ahead.

We note that other measures of performance based on the elements of the MSE matrix have been used in practice. These include the weak mean-square error criterion, which is based on the squared-error risk function $\mathrm{E}[(\hat{\boldsymbol{\beta}} - \boldsymbol{\beta})'(\hat{\boldsymbol{\beta}} - \boldsymbol{\beta})]$. See Judge and Bock (1978) for further details.

18.2.4. Extensions to Nonlinear Models, General Covariance Structures, and Systems of Equations

All of the preceding results, including the limitations of the approach in model selection contexts, can be extended to the context of nonlinear models and systems of equations. The results may also be extended to problem situations in which the covariance matrix of the noise component and/or dependent variable of the model are not proportional to the identity matrix. In the extension of the preceding results to nonlinear models, one must generally rely on asymptotic criteria and the fact that the nonlinear least squares approach results in an estimator that is asymptotically linear (recall section 8.9.3). In effect the preceding mean square error matrix and quadratic risk comparisons apply, to order $o_p(n^{-1/2})$, to the asymptotic distributions of the respective estimators. In this context, $\boldsymbol{\delta}$ refers to the direction vector associated with Pitman drift alternatives of the form $\mathbf{c}\boldsymbol{\beta} = \mathbf{r} + n^{-1/2}\boldsymbol{\delta}$ and $\mathbf{x}$ in the preceding discussion would generally be replaced by the gradient $\mathbf{x}(\boldsymbol{\beta}) \equiv \frac{\partial \mathbf{g}(\mathbf{x}, \boldsymbol{\beta})}{\partial \boldsymbol{\beta}'}$ relating to the nonlinear model $\mathbf{Y} = \mathbf{g}(\mathbf{x}, \boldsymbol{\beta}) + \varepsilon$.

For example, it is still the case that, to order $o_p(n^{-1/2})$, $\mathbf{mse}(\hat{\boldsymbol{\beta}}) - \mathbf{mse}(\hat{\boldsymbol{\beta}}^*)$ is psd iff $\lambda \leq \frac{1}{2}$, where now in the nonlinear context, $\lambda \equiv \frac{\boldsymbol{\delta}'[\mathbf{c}(\mathbf{x}(\boldsymbol{\beta})'\mathbf{x}(\boldsymbol{\beta}))^{-1}\mathbf{c}']^{-1}\boldsymbol{\delta}}{2\sigma^2}$ (recall (18.2.15.b)). An asymptotic test of the SMSE superiority of the restricted NLS estimator relative to the unrestricted NLS estimator can proceed on the basis of the Wald statistic as

$$\mathrm{w} = (\mathbf{c}\hat{\mathbf{b}} - \mathbf{r})'[s^2\mathbf{c}(\mathbf{x}(\boldsymbol{\beta})'\mathbf{x}(\boldsymbol{\beta}))^{-1}\mathbf{c}']^{-1}(\mathbf{c}\hat{\mathbf{b}} - \mathbf{r}) \geq \chi^2_{1-\alpha}(j, .5) \qquad (18.2.21)$$

where $\chi^2_{1-\alpha}(j, .5)$ is the $(1-\alpha)^{\text{th}}$ quantile of the *noncentral* Chi-square distribution with j degrees of freedom and noncentrality parameter $\lambda = .5$ (recall (18.2.16)). Furthermore, results can be extended to nonlinear restrictions on the parameter vector of the form $\mathbf{c}(\boldsymbol{\beta}) = \mathbf{r} + n^{-1/2}\boldsymbol{\delta}$, mutatis mutandis.

Extensions to problems involving general covariance matrices can be made by first transforming the linear or nonlinear model into a form in which the covariance matrix is again proportional to the identity matrix, and then applying the preceding results to the transformed model. For example, in the case where $\mathbf{Y} = \mathbf{x}\boldsymbol{\beta} + \varepsilon$ and $\mathbf{cov}(\varepsilon) = \sigma^2\boldsymbol{\Psi}$, all of the previous results relating to MSE and risk comparisons between restricted and unrestricted models applies to the transformed model

$$\mathbf{Y}_* = \boldsymbol{\Psi}^{-1/2}\mathbf{Y} = \boldsymbol{\Psi}^{-1/2}\mathbf{x}\boldsymbol{\beta} + \boldsymbol{\Psi}^{-1/2}\varepsilon = \mathbf{x}_*\boldsymbol{\beta} + \varepsilon_*. \qquad (18.2.22)$$

In particular, all of the preceding formulas apply directly with $\mathbf{Y}_*$ and $\mathbf{x}_*$ replacing $\mathbf{Y}$ and $\mathbf{x}$. In the typical case, where $\boldsymbol{\Psi}$ is unknown and consistently estimated, all of the stated results hold in sufficiently large samples.

Extensions to systems of equations can be made by applying the preceding single-equation results to a stacked, vertically concatenated representation of the system of equations that has been effectively transformed into the single-equation form, as in Chapter 17. The nonspherical nature of the noise covariance matrix of a stacked system can be addressed via transformation as in the preceding paragraph. Simultaneity in the stacked system of equations can be accommodated through the use of instrumental variables, also as in Chapter 17.

18.3. Fisherian Testing and Model Choice: Critique

Given the dimensionality problem in nested model-discovery relating to the 2^k possible regression models that can be specified based on a set of k explanatory variables, along with the bias-variance trade-off that model choice produces, many analysts have used various test mechanisms based on an accept–reject dichotomy to develop rules that lead to a choice of the "best subset" of explanatory variables, such as those examined in the previous section. In the selection of model dimensionality, several ad hoc methods that have a testing basis and that separate the estimation and inference problems have evolved and are commonly used.

One procedure that is built into many statistical software packages is the forward and backward "stepwise" methods that use the outcomes of simple hypothesis tests involving F and T statistics of the significance of regression parameters to provide a choice rule for adding, deleting, or retaining variables. These methods can sometimes lead to interpretable models. However, the results can be erratic because the model search is based on a discrete process in which variables are either retained or dropped from the model in a stepwise fashion. The variable choices are based on probabilities relating to Type-I and Type-II error probabilities associated with the test rules used at each step.

Furthermore, repeated and generally nonindependent tests are performed stepwise based on the same sample of data. Consequently, the stated Type-I and Type-II error probabilities associated with any single test used at any stage in the stepwise procedure are not indicative of the operating characteristics of the joint test represented by the intersection of all of the individual tests used in the variable discovery process. It is generally very difficult if not impossible to ascribe probabilistic justification to the final model chosen via such a stepwise procedure, regardless of whether a model produced in any given application of the approach is ultimately interpretable or not. In addition, small changes in the data can result in very different stepwise paths and models being selected with corresponding impacts on precision, bias, and model interpretation. Even in relatively simple problems choices can get complicated quickly, as anyone who has gotten lost in a tangle of forward and backward stepwise regression programs based on varying test criteria can attest.

More generally, any model choice strategies based on several individual tests of parameter significance yield algorithms involving generally unknown joint significance levels across the collection of tests that result in final model choices. In these cases the final model choice(s) cannot be defended probabilistically despite the model's seemingly rigorous test-based genesis. Commenting on these ad hoc procedures, Breiman (1992) notes, "... this usage [stepwise methods] has long been a quiet scandal in the statistical community. It is clear that selecting a sequence of submodels in terms of an optimum or suboptimum fit to the data can produce severe biases in all statistical measures used for the classical linear model (p. 738)."

In terms of model selection, testing theory built on the traditional Fisherian base represents little more than a possible starting point for *comparing* models. This approach treats the problems of 1) model selection and estimation and 2) evaluation and testing of models as if they were separate problems and continues the practice of the last 60 years in which these two clearly interdependent phases of a statistical–econometric analysis are nonetheless artificially separated. The sampling properties of pretest estimators discussed in previous chapters attest to the negative statistical implications of this approach when it is used for model selection. Compounding the difficulties in interpreting results is the fact that many of the tests used in practice are necessarily of an asymptotic variety, whereas model selection problems evolve from small sample considerations. This exacerbates the problem of devising a probabilistic and sampling theory justification for a final model choice obtained purely via mechanistic application of test criteria.

It should be noted that diagnostic testing of econometric models has developed into a major component of current applied econometric modeling practice. Invariably this diagnostic exercise is based on a battery of hypothesis tests with each test having documented statistical properties relating to the specific hypothesis for which it was designed. Underlying this process is the maintained hypothesis that the model contains a specification that is congruent with the underlying DSP. However, purveyors of new tests are largely silent as to the corresponding statistical implications of using their tests for model selection rather than for testing the validity of a particular isolated hypothesis. And even when such tests are applied to the specific hypotheses for which they were designed, the significance of any collection of decisions implied by these tests is called into question if many such tests are all applied to the same data. Understandably, this generally leads to a degradation of the Type-I error probability to trivial levels that virtually assure rejections of one or more hypotheses regardless of their validity.

In any event, the problem of hypothesis testing is not the same problem as model selection despite the attempts of many to make it serve this purpose. At the outset of a modeling exercise, a maintained hypothesis has already been selected that in a sense delineates a favorite and plausible encompassing model, and this model will be abandoned only when it is not compatible with, or fundamentally fails to explain, an available data set. This is as opposed to model–variable selection in which all 2^k models are on equal footing and the objective is to choose the one that conforms best to the constraints of the data. We will ultimately see ahead that given the current state of affairs, any plausible strategy of model choice will depend in a significant way on the use of prior information and professional judgment.

18.4. Estimated Risk Criteria and Model Choice: Mallows C_p Criterion

In an attempt to avoid the stepwise-testing approach to model selection in the context of linear models, many analysts have used the C_p criterion of Mallows (1973) as a solution to the variable selection problem. The criterion is based on the conditional mean forecasting risk measure discussed earlier in Section 18.2. For the restricted model $\mathbf{y} = \mathbf{x}_1\boldsymbol{\beta}_1 + \varepsilon_1$, where $\varepsilon_1 = \mathbf{x}_2\boldsymbol{\beta} + \varepsilon$, this criterion may be defined as

$$\begin{aligned}\rho(\mathbf{x}\hat{\boldsymbol{\beta}}^*, \mathbf{x}\boldsymbol{\beta}) &= \mathrm{E}[(\mathbf{x}\hat{\boldsymbol{\beta}}^* - \mathbf{x}\boldsymbol{\beta})'(\mathbf{x}\hat{\boldsymbol{\beta}}^* - \mathbf{x}\boldsymbol{\beta})] \\ &= \sigma^2 k_1 + \boldsymbol{\beta}_2'\mathbf{x}_2'[\mathrm{I} - \mathbf{x}_1(\mathbf{x}_1'\mathbf{x}_1)^{-1}\mathbf{x}_1']\mathbf{x}_2\boldsymbol{\beta}_2, \qquad (18.4.1)\end{aligned}$$

where the quadratic term on the right-hand side of the second equality is the sum of the squared biases in using the elements of $\mathbf{x}\hat{\boldsymbol{\beta}}^*$ to estimate the corresponding elements of $\mathbf{x}\boldsymbol{\beta}$. The representation follows from the fact that $\hat{\boldsymbol{\beta}}_1^* = \boldsymbol{\beta}_1 + (\mathbf{x}_1'\mathbf{x}_1)^{-1}\mathbf{x}_1'\mathbf{x}_2\boldsymbol{\beta}_2 + (\mathbf{x}_1'\mathbf{x}_1)^{-1}\mathbf{x}_1'\varepsilon$ because $\mathbf{y} = \mathbf{x}_1\boldsymbol{\beta}_1 + \mathbf{x}_2\boldsymbol{\beta}_2 + \varepsilon$ and $\hat{\boldsymbol{\beta}}_2^* = \mathbf{0}$. Because (18.4.1) contains unknown parameters, a way to proceed is to use an estimate of the unknowns and choose the model with the smallest estimated risk.

Let $\hat{\sigma}_1^{2*} \equiv (n - k_1)^{-1}(\mathbf{Y} - \mathbf{x}_1\hat{\boldsymbol{\beta}}_1^*)'(\mathbf{Y} - \mathbf{x}_1\hat{\boldsymbol{\beta}}_1^*)$ denote the restricted estimator of the noise variance and note that

$$\begin{aligned}\mathrm{E}[(\mathbf{Y} - \mathbf{x}_1\hat{\boldsymbol{\beta}}_1^*)'(\mathbf{Y} - \mathbf{x}_1\hat{\boldsymbol{\beta}}_1^*)] &= \mathrm{E}[(n - k_1)\hat{\sigma}_1^{2*}] \\ &= \boldsymbol{\beta}_2'\mathbf{x}_2'[\mathrm{I} - \mathbf{x}_1(\mathbf{x}_1'\mathbf{x}_1)^{-1}\mathbf{x}_1']\mathbf{x}_2\boldsymbol{\beta}_2 + \sigma^2(n - k_1). \qquad (18.4.2)\end{aligned}$$

Consequently,

$$\boldsymbol{\beta}_2'\mathbf{x}_2'[\mathbf{I} - \mathbf{x}_1(\mathbf{x}_1'\mathbf{x}_1)^{-1}\mathbf{x}_1']\mathbf{x}_2\boldsymbol{\beta}_2 = \mathrm{E}\big[(n - k_1)\hat{\sigma}_1^{2*}\big] - (n - k_1)\sigma^2, \qquad (18.4.3)$$

which leads to the measure of standardized (by σ^2) risk given by (recall 18.4.1)

$$\rho_s(\mathbf{x}\hat{\boldsymbol{\beta}}^*, \mathbf{x}\boldsymbol{\beta}) \equiv \frac{\rho(\mathbf{x}\hat{\boldsymbol{\beta}}^*, \mathbf{x}\boldsymbol{\beta})}{\sigma^2} = \frac{\mathrm{E}\big[(n - k_1)\hat{\sigma}_1^{2*}\big]}{\sigma^2} + (2k_1 - n). \qquad (18.4.4)$$

If the unknown parameter σ^2 in (18.4.4) is replaced by an outcome of the unbiased estimator $\hat{\sigma}^2 = (\mathbf{Y} - \mathbf{x}\hat{\boldsymbol{\beta}})'(\mathbf{Y} - \mathbf{x}\hat{\boldsymbol{\beta}})/(n - k)$, we can define an estimator of the standardized risk as

$$\mathrm{C_p} = \hat{\rho}_s(\mathbf{x}\hat{\boldsymbol{\beta}}^*, \mathbf{x}\boldsymbol{\beta}) = \frac{(n - k_1)\hat{\sigma}_1^{2*}}{\hat{\sigma}^2} + (2k_1 - n), \qquad (18.4.5)$$

which is Mallows' criterion. When the restricted model has small bias, which in the current context means that $\boldsymbol{\beta}_2$ is close to zero, then $\hat{\sigma}_1^{2*}$ is approximately equal to $\hat{\sigma}^2$ on average (recall (18.2.11.b)), and $\mathrm{C_p}$ is then likewise approximately equal to the value k_1. One strategy that is sometimes followed in practice is to calculate all 2^k potential regression models formed from all possible combinations of the explanatory variables and then choose the model whose $\mathrm{C_p}$ value is closest to k_1. The thinking here is to search for the model with smallest bias from among all of the potential models. Alternatively, one can think of choosing the model with the smallest $\mathrm{C_p}$ value, the idea being to search for the model with the smallest conditional mean forecasting risk. In this latter case, one must be willing at the outset to accept some bias in return for variance reductions with the hope of ultimately reducing risk.

Unfortunately, the model selection strategy based on choosing a final model on the basis of a minimum $\mathrm{C_p}$, or on the basis of the proximity of $\mathrm{C_p}$ to k_1, shares all of the negative performance consequences of the stepwise and testing-based model selection rules and thus contributes to Breiman's scandal. The final model choice is a probabilistic mix of subset models with complicated, generally intractable sampling characteristics and with no guarantee of choosing a risk-superior model. Other selection criteria along these lines are, of course, possible, and a discussion of some of these rules is included in Judge et al., 1985, pp. 862–8. All of these alternative criteria are functions of the equation error sum of squares in some way and thus are related. Because all of the procedures lead in practice to a pretest estimator in one form or another, they all lead, under a squared-error loss measure, to estimators whose sampling properties are complex and generally unknown. Furthermore, it is known that these estimators are inadmissible when the noise component is multivariate normally distributed. Consequently, interpretation of inferences derived from estimators chosen on the basis of any of these model search procedures should be viewed with caution and interpreted with more than a little suspicion by the applied researcher.

18.5. An Information Theoretic Model Selection Criterion: Akaike Information

Over the last three decades, the Akaike information criterion (AIC), which makes use of the Kullback–Leibler information criterion (KLIC) introduced in Chapter 13, has occupied the conceptual high ground in terms of statistical model-discovery procedures. The criterion is widely used in practice and is reported by a wide variety of statistical and econometric computing packages. However, AIC, which can be characterized as a bias correction to the logarithm of the maximized likelihood function, can provide a biased estimate of the expected KL information discrepancy between the true and candidate model being evaluated. Consequently, several variants of the measure have appeared over time, each promising to improve model choice performance in small samples.

18.5.1. Basic Rationale for the AIC and Variants

The rationale for the AIC and its variants is roughly as follows, where we initially focus on a classical linear regression model to clarify ideas. Assume the data-sampling process is actually given by

$$\mathbf{Y} = \mathbf{x}_0\boldsymbol{\beta}_0 + \varepsilon_0, \qquad (18.5.1)$$

and there exists a family of candidate models

$$\mathbf{Y} = \mathbf{x}\boldsymbol{\beta} + \varepsilon, \qquad (18.5.2)$$

where $\mathbf{cov}(\varepsilon_0) = \sigma_0^2\mathbf{I}$ and $\mathbf{cov}(\varepsilon) = \sigma^2\mathbf{I}$, the distributions of $\mathbf{Y}$ under the respective models are $\mathrm{f}(\mathbf{y}; \boldsymbol{\beta}_0, \sigma_0)$ and $\mathrm{f}(\mathbf{y}; \boldsymbol{\beta}, \sigma)$, respectively, and we have notationally suppressed references to $\mathbf{x}_0$ and $\mathbf{x}$ in the distributions. Here $\mathbf{x}_0$ and $\mathbf{x}$ are $n \times k_0$ and $n \times k$ matrices of explanatory variables, $\boldsymbol{\beta}_0$ and $\boldsymbol{\beta}$ are $k_0 \times 1$ and $k \times 1$ vectors of unknown regression function parameters, and σ_0 and σ are scale parameters. In general the DSP represented by (18.5.1) and the candidate models (18.5.2) may differ in terms of both location, $\mathrm{E}[\mathbf{Y}]$, and scale σ. Given the data and candidate models, assume the unknown parameters are estimated via the maximum likelihood approach as follows:

$$(\hat{\boldsymbol{\beta}}, \hat{\sigma}) \equiv \arg\max_{\boldsymbol{\beta},\sigma}[\mathrm{f}(\mathbf{y}; \boldsymbol{\beta}, \sigma)] = \arg\max_{\boldsymbol{\beta},\sigma}[\mathrm{L}(\boldsymbol{\beta}, \sigma; \mathbf{y})] \qquad (18.5.3)$$

On the assumption that the model can be represented in the form of a family of potential probability-sampling distributions as above, the objective is to provide a simultaneous solution to the model selection and estimation problems and thus to avoid the traditional and questionable separation of estimation and testing activities. In this context, Akaike (1974) reasoned that, if one had an objective measure of the divergence between the probability model and the true sampling distribution, then a good strategy, both in terms of model selection and estimation, would be to make this divergence as small as possible. As a basis for assessing the divergence between the true distribution and the candidate probability models, one possibility is to use the Kullback–Liebler information criterion of Chapter 13, defined in the current context as

$$\text{KLIC}(\mathrm{g}(\mathbf{y}), \mathrm{f}(\mathbf{y};\hat{\boldsymbol{\theta}})) = \int_{\mathbf{y}} \mathrm{g}(\mathbf{y}) \ln\left(\frac{\mathrm{g}(\mathbf{y})}{\mathrm{f}(\mathbf{y};\hat{\boldsymbol{\theta}})}\right) d\mathbf{y} = \mathrm{E}_{\mathrm{g}}\left[\ln\left(\frac{\mathrm{g}(\mathbf{y})}{\mathrm{f}(\mathbf{y};\hat{\boldsymbol{\theta}})}\right)\right]$$

$$= \int_{\mathbf{y}} \mathrm{g}(\mathbf{y}) \ln(\mathrm{g}(\mathbf{y}))\, d\mathbf{y} - \int_{\mathbf{y}} \mathrm{g}(\mathbf{y}) \ln(\mathrm{f}(\mathbf{y};\hat{\boldsymbol{\theta}}))\, d\mathbf{y}, \qquad (18.5.4)$$

where $\mathrm{g}(\mathbf{y})$ denotes the true sampling distribution of $\mathbf{Y}$, $\mathrm{E}_{\mathrm{g}}[\,]$ denotes an expectation taken with respect to the distribution g, and $\mathrm{f}(\mathbf{y};\boldsymbol{\theta})$ is a parametric family of probability-sampling distributions defined by a probability model. In the context of our linear model example (18.5.1) and (18.5.2), $\hat{\mathbf{b}}$ and $\hat{\mathrm{s}}$ are the ML estimates of $\boldsymbol{\beta}$ and σ, with $\boldsymbol{\theta} = \binom{\boldsymbol{\beta}}{\sigma}$, and $\hat{\boldsymbol{\theta}} = \binom{\hat{\mathbf{b}}}{\hat{\mathrm{s}}}$, the true and candidate models are $\mathrm{g}(\mathbf{y}) \equiv \mathrm{f}(\mathbf{y};\boldsymbol{\beta}_0, \sigma_0)$ and $\mathrm{f}(\mathbf{y};\boldsymbol{\beta},\sigma)$, respectively. Thus (18.5.4) provides a KLIC measure of discrepancy between the true distribution relative to some other estimated candidate distribution, and the KLIC attains its minimum value of zero when the candidate distribution $\mathrm{f}(\mathbf{y};\hat{\boldsymbol{\theta}})$ and true sampling distribution $\mathrm{g}(\mathbf{y})$ coincide.

Because the first term on the right-hand side of the second equality in (18.5.4) is independent of any particular model, minimizing (18.5.4) with respect to the choice of probability density f is equivalent to

$$\min_{\mathrm{f}}[\mathrm{m}(\mathrm{f})] = \min_{\mathrm{f}}\left[-\int_{\mathbf{y}} \mathrm{g}(\mathbf{y}) \ln \mathrm{f}(\mathbf{y};\hat{\boldsymbol{\theta}})\, d\mathbf{y}\right]. \qquad (18.5.5)$$

Minimizing $\mathrm{m}(\mathrm{f}) \equiv -\int \mathrm{g}(\mathbf{y}) \ln \mathrm{f}(\mathbf{y};\hat{\boldsymbol{\theta}})\, d\mathbf{y}$ in (18.5.5) is not feasible because $\mathrm{g}(\mathbf{y})$ is unknown. Akaike shows that m(f) can be estimated by

$$\text{AIC} = \hat{\mathrm{m}}(\mathrm{f}) = -2 \ln \mathrm{f}(\mathbf{y};\hat{\boldsymbol{\theta}}) + 2j, \qquad (18.5.6)$$

which is known as the *Akaike information criterion* (AIC) (see also Amemiya (1980)). Here j is the dimension of the parameter vector. The criterion can be interpreted as the (negative of) the likelihood function, penalized (by the addition of $2j$) for the degree of parameterization, representing model complexity. Akaike suggests calculating the AIC for the alternative possible models under consideration. In the explanatory variable selection problem for the linear model context above, this amounts to calculating (18.5.6) with various subsets of the elements of $\boldsymbol{\beta}$ restricted to zero. Akaike then chooses the model that minimizes AIC, which is effectively choosing the model, within the candidate set of models that has the smallest (estimated) KLIC divergence from the true but unknown probability distribution. Although we focused on the linear model context at the outset of the discussion, we emphasize that it is apparent from (18.5.3)–(18.5.6) that the AIC applies more generally to a probability model in which a set of probability distribution candidates is defined. Thus, the AIC can be applied equally well to nonlinear models and even systems of equations. Moreover, a restriction to spherical covariance structures is not necessary so long as consistent maximum likelihood estimates of the parameters of the unknown covariance structure are possible.

Many analysts have noted that there can be an appreciable bias in the AIC estimate (18.5.6) and as a result the AIC may not provide an effective model selection rule. This has inspired a great deal of work to find a better estimator of (18.5.5) and recently has led Hurvich and Tsai (1991) to devise and substitute the term

$$j + \frac{(j+1)(j+2)}{n-j-2} \tag{18.5.7}$$

for $2j$ in the AIC when applied to models based on normal distributions. In the context of more general probability models based on (18.5.2), Shi and Tsai (1998) propose a generalized KLIC formulation and develop three robust model selection criteria that encompass nonnormally distributed noise components. Their procedure does not rely on the maximum likelihood estimation approach, or even on the specification of a likelihood function, and can be applied to a broad class of extremum estimators.

As Sclove (1987) and Dayton (1998) have observed, algebraically the AIC and its variants can be viewed as a penalized log likelihood function that can be written in the general form

$$\mathrm{L_p} = -2\ \ln[\mathrm{f}(\mathbf{y}; \hat{\theta})] + \mathrm{a}(n)j, \tag{18.5.8}$$

where $\mathrm{a}(n)$ is a function involving a tuning parameter that may depend on sample size. In AIC the tuning parameter $\mathrm{a}(n)$ is equal to 2 for all n, and as a result this criterion does not have the asymptotic property of consistency in the sense that the true model will be selected with probability converging to 1 as $n \to \infty$. Bozdogan (1987) has developed a consistent version of AIC, where the probability of selecting the true model does approach 1 as n increases (on the presumption that the probability model *actually contains the true model*). Dayton (1998) has suggested how the information criteria may be used in the paired model comparison problem to avoid the usual computing and interpreting of conventional statistics.

In a similar context, Golan and Judge (1996) have used the KLIC criterion and the maximum entropy principle (Chapters 12 and electronic Chapter E3) to formulate a simultaneous model selection, estimation, and inference formulation. The procedure appears to have good finite sample properties and does not involve evaluating the 2^k subset model possibilities (with respect to the choice of the $k \times 1$ vector β). We should also note that cross validation (Brieman and Specter, 1992) offers a possible viable selection solution, but its usefulness appears limited in the case of small samples of data.

► **Example 18.5.1:** The GAUSS program C18CPAIC.gss (provided in the examples manual) conducts a Monte Carlo simulation exercise designed to examine the properties of pretest estimators based on the Mallow's $\mathrm{C_p}$ and AIC criteria. For a set of three candidate regression models, GAUSS simulates the quadratic risk of the pretest estimators based on the $\mathrm{C_p}$ (18.4.5), AIC (18.5.6), and Hurvich–Tsai generalized AIC (18.5.7) criteria. For comparison purposes, the estimated pretest risk functions are plotted with the estimated risk functions for the quadratic risks of the LS and RLS estimators.

18.5.2. A Comment

Although there is a certain intuitive appeal and logic to AIC and many of the ad hoc informal model selection rules that have been suggested, we should not forget (1) their heuristic base, (2) the "penalties" imposed for including additional variables that differ according to the variable selection rule, (3) that their sampling properties are virtually unknown, and (4) their practical utility is mainly demonstrated by numerical examples. Consequently, there is in the background the nagging question of applicability of the results to broader types of data-sampling processes. Moreover, there remains the difficulty of determining to what extent, if any, the final model chosen from such a procedure is interpretable in a sampling theory-probability context.

18.6. Shrinkage as a Basis for Dealing with Variable Uncertainty

In the previous sections of this chapter we have focused on the selection of a subset of explanatory variables as a basis for econometric model discovery. We have noted that, because subset selection is a discrete process, small changes in the data can lead to very different statistical models, and we have discussed the possible unfavorable sampling characteristics of these variable choice rules. In this section we focus on procedures involving a continuous process that "shrinks" the coefficients but does not eliminate variables or set any parameter equal to zero. Relative to the discrete variable choice procedures, the shrinkage estimators are more stable, but they generally do not yield easily interpretable econometric models. Moreover, most of the known sampling property results for shrinkage estimators relate to the case in which the noise component of the model is multivariate normally distributed.

We continue to consider the traditional noisy inverse problem in which we are unable to measure the unknown k-dimensional vector $\boldsymbol{\beta}$ directly and instead observe an n-dimensional vector of noisy observations $\mathbf{y} = (\mathrm{y}_1, \mathrm{y}_2, \ldots, \mathrm{y}_\mathrm{n})'$ that are consistent with the underlying data-sampling process (DSP)

$$\mathbf{Y} = \mathbf{x}\boldsymbol{\beta} + \varepsilon, \tag{18.6.1}$$

where $\mathbf{x}$ is a $(n \times k)$ matrix of explanatory variable values. The unobservable components are $\boldsymbol{\beta} = (\beta_1, \beta_2, \ldots, \beta_k)'$, a vector of k unknown parameters, the n-dimensional noise vector ε is drawn from a multivariate (generally normal) distribution with mean zero and covariance matrix $\Sigma_\varepsilon = \sigma^2\mathbf{I}_n$, and the parameter σ^2 is unknown. We note that the shrinkage methods discussed ahead can be applied in the context of nonlinear models as well.

18.6.1. Stein-Like Shrinkage Estimators

As we noted in Chapter 6, when estimating $\boldsymbol{\beta}$ in the multivariate normal linear regression model Stein (1955) proved, for the special case in which the sample data have been scaled so that $\mathbf{x}'\mathbf{x} = \mathbf{I}_k$, $\sigma^2 = 1$, and $\mathbf{cov}(\hat{\boldsymbol{\beta}}) = \sigma^2(\mathbf{x}'\mathbf{x})^{-1} = \sigma^2\mathbf{I}_k$ that the conventional ML–LS estimator $\hat{\boldsymbol{\beta}}$ is inadmissible with respect to quadratic loss when $k \geq 3$. James and Stein (1960) demonstrated for this case that the estimator

$$\tau_s(\hat{\boldsymbol{\beta}}) \equiv \left(1 - \frac{k-2}{\|\hat{\boldsymbol{\beta}}\|^2}\right)\hat{\boldsymbol{\beta}} \tag{18.6.2}$$

has uniformly smaller squared-error risk than $\hat{\boldsymbol{\beta}}$, where $\|\hat{\boldsymbol{\beta}}\| \equiv [\hat{\boldsymbol{\beta}}'\hat{\boldsymbol{\beta}}]^{1/2}$ denotes the standard Euclidean distance of $\hat{\boldsymbol{\beta}}$ from the zero vector. Baranchik (1964) and Stein (1966) developed a positive-part Stein rule estimator

$$\hat{\tau}_s^+(\hat{\boldsymbol{\beta}}) \equiv (1 - \min[1, (k-2)/\hat{\boldsymbol{\beta}}'\hat{\boldsymbol{\beta}}])\hat{\boldsymbol{\beta}}$$

$$\equiv \mathrm{I}_{(k-2,\,\infty)}(\hat{\boldsymbol{\beta}}'\hat{\boldsymbol{\beta}})\left(1 - \frac{(k-2)}{\hat{\boldsymbol{\beta}}'\hat{\boldsymbol{\beta}}}\right)\hat{\boldsymbol{\beta}}, \tag{18.6.3}$$

where $\mathrm{I}_{(k-2,\,\infty)}(\hat{\boldsymbol{\beta}}'\hat{\boldsymbol{\beta}})$ is an indicator function with $(\hat{\boldsymbol{\beta}}'\hat{\boldsymbol{\beta}})$ as the argument, that demonstrated the inadmissibility of both $\hat{\boldsymbol{\beta}}$ and $\tau_s(\hat{\boldsymbol{\beta}})$ (see Judge and Bock 1978, p. 183).

Given this work, much interest has centered on the use of minimax shrinkage estimators for the symmetric shrinkage case (Berger, 1983). However, for an application of the Stein-type estimators to result in significant risk improvement, one must be able to identify the region or subspace in which $\boldsymbol{\beta}$ lies or is thought likely to lie a priori, and then shrink towards a point in this region (as opposed to shrinking always towards the zero vector). For example, in the normal symmetric case, assuming $\mathbf{cov}(\hat{\boldsymbol{\beta}}) = \sigma^2(\mathbf{x}'\mathbf{x})^{-1} = \mathbf{I}_k$, if we consider a Stein-like shrinkage estimator of the form

$$\hat{\tau}_2(\hat{\boldsymbol{\beta}}, \mathbf{r}) \equiv \left[1 - \frac{k-2}{\|\hat{\boldsymbol{\beta}} - \mathbf{r}\|^2}\right](\hat{\boldsymbol{\beta}} - \mathbf{r}) + \mathbf{r} \tag{18.6.4}$$

that shrinks outcomes of $\hat{\boldsymbol{\beta}}$ toward the target vector $\mathbf{r} \in \mathbf{R}^k$, then, when $\boldsymbol{\beta}$ is in a small neighborhood surrounding $\mathbf{r}$, $\hat{\tau}_s$ yields very small risk that approaches 2. Unfortunately, when $\boldsymbol{\beta}$ is far from this neighborhood or if this prior information or shrinkage vector $\mathbf{r}$ is misspecified for a few of the coordinates in $\boldsymbol{\beta}$, then the Stein rules are such that their risk will virtually be the same as the risk for $\hat{\boldsymbol{\beta}}$, which equals k, the number of coordinates. This result holds even if the prior-information shrinkage vector $\mathbf{r}$ for some of the coordinates is correct or nearly correct and could otherwise lead to an improved basis for estimation and inference.

Typically, $\mathbf{r}$ is a prior guess as to the location of $\boldsymbol{\beta}$. Because different estimators do well in different regions of the parameter space, it is crucial to have a basis for differentiating *among* estimators. In practice, the location vector $\boldsymbol{\beta}$ is unknown, and, as noted by Anderson (1984, p. 91), consequently the risk-minimizing region or the appropriate shrink point or vector is unknown. Because the form of the estimator must be selected before examining the data, the selection of a Stein-like estimator, or equivalently the selection of the shrinkage vector or risk improvement region, is typically based on prior information. Consequently, many minimax or near-minimax shrinkage estimators have been proposed corresponding to the use of different types of prior information.

18.6.2. Multiple Shrinkage Estimator

In this section we expand the generality of our search for how to best make use of both nonsample and sample information under model uncertainty and a squared-error loss measure. We now consider the problem of selecting a shrinkage estimator when conflicting or vague prior information concerning the location vector suggests that *one or more* of a broad class of estimators with $m \geq 2$ potential shrinkage points may be worthy of consideration for attaining the risk-minimizing objective. Minimax or near-minimax shrinkage estimators are proposed that incorporate this prior information about the potential shrinkage points in a multiple shrinkage context and that use the data and an entropy metric to identify a risk-effective estimator that shrinks to the desired but unknown region where $\boldsymbol{\beta}$ lies.

Following our previous discussion of shrinkage estimators, it may seem natural to raise the question, what if I do not know how to choose the shrinkage point? In some cases, we may in fact be able to identify two or more points or subspaces in the parameter space that appear as plausible restrictions on the model. The problem of combining multiple estimators into a composite point estimation rule was addressed in a series of articles by George (1986a and b). Following Stein (1981), who recognized that some priors are better than others in terms of the sampling properties of estimators that incorporate the prior information, George considers the set of normal (Gaussian) probability models based on m different shrinkage points $\boldsymbol{\beta}_m$, $m = 1, \ldots, M$ and shows that the optimal Bayes estimator (see Chapters 22–24) for each alternative shrinkage point takes the form

$$\tilde{\boldsymbol{\beta}}_m = \hat{\boldsymbol{\beta}} + \frac{\partial \ln[\mathrm{f}_m(\boldsymbol{\beta})]}{\partial \boldsymbol{\beta}}, \tag{18.6.5}$$

where f_m represents the unconditional density of the sample (i.e., the marginalized likelihood function) with respect to the prior specification represented by the mth shrinkage point. As such, the optimal Bayes rule reflects an adjustment of the unrestricted normal maximum likelihood estimator $\hat{\boldsymbol{\beta}}$. Discrete probability weights q_m may be used to describe our prior subjective beliefs regarding the relative plausibility of the alternative models. Estimators of the form (18.6.5) are commonly known as pseudo-Bayesian estimators, and Brown (1971) proved that all admissible estimators of $\boldsymbol{\beta}$ for the Gaussian (normal) DSP must take this form.

The composite point estimator is then assembled as

$$\tilde{\boldsymbol{\beta}} = \sum_{m=1}^{M} \mathrm{p}_m \tilde{\boldsymbol{\beta}}_m, \tag{18.6.6}$$

where the set of discrete probability weights p_m adaptively reflect the fit of the alternative models. George shows that the optimal weights take the form

$$\mathrm{p}_m = \frac{\mathrm{q}_m \mathrm{f}_m(\tilde{\boldsymbol{\beta}}_m)}{\sum_{m=1}^{M} \mathrm{q}_m \mathrm{f}_m(\tilde{\boldsymbol{\beta}}_m)}, \tag{18.6.7}$$

where the unconditional likelihood terms are inversely proportional to the predictive fit of the candidate estimator obtained by minimizing $(\mathbf{y} - \mathbf{x}\tilde{\boldsymbol{\beta}}_m)'(\mathbf{y} - \mathbf{x}\tilde{\boldsymbol{\beta}}_m)$. That is, we assign greater weight to models with larger predata weights or those that provide a better fit to the data.

18.7. The Problem of an Ill-Conditioned Explanatory Variable Matrix

In economics, where we typically work with nonexperimentally generated data, the probability model may often be ill-posed in the sense that there is insufficient information contained in the ill-conditioned explanatory variable matrix and the noisy data observations $\mathbf{y}$ to permit meaningful recovery of the unknown parameters by traditional estimation methods. More generally, the problem is one of attempting to infer an unknown regression function based on insufficient data information and prior information that specifies only a *feasible* set of regression functions. In this case, the issue of model selection can be muddled with effectively no choice of explanatory variable subset representing a meaningful, interpretable, and defensible model.

The ill-posed aspect may arise in practice because, for example, (1) the number of unknown parameters exceeds the number of data points, (2) the data are mutually inconsistent, or (3) the experiment may be badly designed or the data nonexperimentally generated, causing the columns of the design or explanatory variable matrix $\mathbf{x}$, or the columns of the gradient matrix $\mathbf{x}(\boldsymbol{\beta}) \equiv \frac{\partial \mathbf{g}(\mathbf{x}, \boldsymbol{\beta})}{\partial \boldsymbol{\beta}'}$ in the case of nonlinear models, to be linearly dependent or nearly so. Therefore, if traditional estimation procedures are used (1) there may be arbitrary unidentified parameters, (2) the estimator solution may be undefined, and (3) the estimates can be highly unstable, giving rise to high variance or low precision for the recovered parameter information.

Given this result, one alternative for facilitating model choice is to rely on nonsample information as a way of enhancing the information base and defining a well-posed problem. In this context, many applied analysts have made use of the shrinkage properties of the ridge regression estimator (Hoerl and Kennard, 1970), which is a method of regularization (MOR) (O'Sullivan, 1986; Titterington, 1985). In general, MOR estimators fit the data $\mathbf{y}$ by optimizing an estimation objective function subject to an added penalty function (i.e., penalized extremum estimator approach) and can be formulated as the solution of an optimization problem involving both a measure of the lack of fit (prediction) of the data and a convex measure of roughness or plausibility relative to prior information or constraints imposed on the estimates. A parameter, called the *regularization, tuning, or smoothing parameter*, is specified to define the trade-off between the lack of fit and roughness criteria in determining the final MOR estimates. Thus, regularization procedures involve the use of both the data and prior notions about the unknown parameters.

In general, the MOR-ridge estimator can be defined as

$$\hat{\boldsymbol{\beta}}_{\mathrm{MOR}}(\lambda_{\mathrm{R}}) \equiv \arg\min_{\boldsymbol{\beta}}[\delta(\mathbf{Y}, \boldsymbol{\beta}) + \lambda_{\mathrm{R}}\phi(\boldsymbol{\beta})], \tag{18.7.1}$$

where $\delta(\mathbf{y}, \boldsymbol{\beta})$ is some measure of the lack of fit (quality of prediction) relative to the data, $\phi(\boldsymbol{\beta})$ is a convex measure of roughness or plausibility of the estimates relative to some prior information or constraints, and λ_{R} is a regularization, tuning, or smoothing parameter. Equivalently, $\phi(\boldsymbol{\beta})$ may be interpreted as a restriction on the minimization of $\delta(\mathbf{y}, \boldsymbol{\beta})$, and λ_{R} is then the Lagrange multiplier on the restriction. If $\lambda_{\mathrm{R}} = 0$, then we have a purely data-driven estimate for $\boldsymbol{\beta}$, and, as $\lambda_{\mathrm{R}} \to \infty$, the penalty $\phi(\boldsymbol{\beta})$ dominates the definition of the estimate. In practice an intermediate value of λ_R is generally chosen to make use of the data and provide a stable estimate [see, for example, Thompson et al., 1991], which begs the question of what basis to use for choosing the smoothing or Lagrange parameter λ_R. We emphasize that the approach is equally applicable to linear and nonlinear model contexts.

To make things more familiar and operational, consider again the inverse problem associated with the linear regression model and the following quadratic regularization method, which seeks a solution to the following optimization problem:

$$\min_{\boldsymbol{\beta}}[\|\mathbf{y} - \mathbf{x}\boldsymbol{\beta}\|^2 + \lambda_R \boldsymbol{\beta}'\mathbf{c}\boldsymbol{\beta}], \tag{18.7.2}$$

where $\mathbf{c}$ is a *specified* positive semidefinite matrix. The solution to (18.7.2) is

$$\hat{\mathbf{b}}_{\text{MOR}}(\lambda_R) = (\mathbf{x}'\mathbf{x} + \lambda_R\mathbf{c})^{-1}\mathbf{x}'\mathbf{y} = \mathbf{v}\mathbf{y}, \tag{18.7.3}$$

where the inverse in (18.7.3) is assumed to exist. This regularization rule is also known in the literature under such names as *penalized likelihood, damped least-squares*, and *generalized ridge regression*. In terms of a conventional ridge regression scenario, one might alternatively write the problem as

$$\min_{\boldsymbol{\beta}}[\|\mathbf{y} - \mathbf{x}\boldsymbol{\beta}\|^2] \tag{18.7.4}$$

subject to

$$\boldsymbol{\beta}'\mathbf{c}\boldsymbol{\beta} = \text{s}. \tag{18.7.5}$$

Given (18.7.4) and (18.7.5), a Lagrangian function representation of the minimization problem can be specified as

$$\text{L} = \|\mathbf{y} - \mathbf{x}\boldsymbol{\beta}\|^2 - \lambda_R(s - \boldsymbol{\beta}'\mathbf{c}\boldsymbol{\beta}), \tag{18.7.6}$$

which yields first-order conditions with respect to $\boldsymbol{\beta}$ that are identical to those for the original MOR problem (18.7.2) and leads to the solution

$$\hat{\mathbf{b}}_{\text{MOR}}(\hat{\lambda}_R) = (\mathbf{x}'\mathbf{x} + \hat{\lambda}_R\mathbf{c})^{-1}\mathbf{x}'\mathbf{y}. \tag{18.7.7}$$

Given (18.7.5) and (18.7.6), choosing a value for s is equivalent to choosing a value for λ_R. As is evident from the ridge literature (Hoerl, Kennard, and Baldwin, 1975), given a sampling performance measure for any particular problem, there is the question of how to choose an appropriate value for the tuning constants λ_R or s (Le Cessie and van Houwelingen, 1992).

18.7.1. Penalized Estimation

To provide a more general example of the regularization concept for the general linear model, consider a formulation within the context of a penalized estimation objective function. It may be useful in understanding this criterion to recall that in Section 18.5 we interpreted AIC as a penalized likelihood criterion. For the penalized problem, the usual weighted least-squares estimation criterion is augmented by the weighted Euclidean distance of $\boldsymbol{\beta}$ from some point in the parameter space $\bar{\boldsymbol{\beta}}$, yielding the extremum estimation problem and associated estimator definition

$$\hat{\boldsymbol{\beta}}_{\mathrm{MOR}}(\lambda_{\mathrm{R}}) \equiv \arg\min_{\boldsymbol{\beta}}[(\mathbf{Y}-\mathbf{x}\boldsymbol{\beta})'\mathbf{w}(\mathbf{Y}-\mathbf{x}\boldsymbol{\beta}) + \lambda_{\mathrm{R}}(\boldsymbol{\beta}-\bar{\boldsymbol{\beta}})'\mathbf{q}(\boldsymbol{\beta}-\bar{\boldsymbol{\beta}})]. \quad (18.7.8)$$

The weighted least-squares component $(\mathbf{y}-\mathbf{x}\boldsymbol{\beta})'\mathbf{w}(\mathbf{y}-\mathbf{x}\boldsymbol{\beta})$ of the estimation objective function provides a measure of the degree to which the estimator fits the data, whereas the squared, weighted Euclidean distance between $\boldsymbol{\beta}$ and $\bar{\boldsymbol{\beta}}$ measures the closeness of the estimator to the point $\bar{\boldsymbol{\beta}}$ in the parameter space. The trade-off between the two estimation criteria is provided by the value of the smoothing or tuning parameter $\lambda_{\mathrm{R}} > 0$. As λ_{R} increases from zero, the criterion provides increasing incentive for closer proximity of estimates to the point $\bar{\boldsymbol{\beta}}$, and the fit of the estimator to the data becomes less important. In this fashion, the sample and nonsample information can be combined without having to make an explicit discrete choice between $\bar{\boldsymbol{\beta}}$ and the unrestricted alternative.

There exists a unique solution to the problem if $\mathbf{x}$ has full-column rank and if $\mathbf{w}$ and $\mathbf{q}$ are symmetric positive definite matrices because then the estimation objective function (18.7.8) is strictly convex in $\boldsymbol{\beta}$ (note that the Hessian matrix with respect to $\boldsymbol{\beta}$ is given by $2(\mathbf{x}'\mathbf{wx} + \lambda_{\mathrm{R}}\mathbf{q})$, which is the sum of two symmetric positive definite matrices and thus is itself symmetric and positive definite). The explicit solution to the problem is

$$\hat{\mathbf{b}}_{\mathrm{MOR}}(\lambda_{\mathrm{R}}) = [\mathbf{x}'\mathbf{wx} + \lambda_{\mathrm{R}}\mathbf{q}]^{-1}(\mathbf{x}'\mathbf{wy} + \lambda_{\mathrm{R}}\mathbf{q}\bar{\boldsymbol{\beta}}). \quad (18.7.9)$$

Clearly, the estimator reduces to the standard weighted least-squares estimator if $\lambda_{\mathrm{R}} = 0$. If the weight matrices $\mathbf{w}$ and $\mathbf{q}$ and the ridge parameter are subjectively selected or known (nonstochastic) quantities, we may compute the finite-sample bias and variance of the ridge estimator. However, if we employ some estimated covariance matrix $\hat{\mathbf{W}}$ to weight the observations, as in the feasible generalized least-squares case discussed in Chapter 15, the finite sample properties of the estimator are generally intractable but may be approximated by Monte Carlo simulation. In large samples, it can be shown that the ridge estimator is inconsistent unless either λ_{R} approaches zero at a suitable rate or else $\bar{\boldsymbol{\beta}}$ happens to coincide with the true value of $\boldsymbol{\beta}$. Intuitively, λ_{R} approaching zero implies that we place greater emphasis on the sample information as the sample size increases. Several authors have proposed data-based methods for choosing optimal values (in some sense) for the ridge parameter, and a summary is provided by Amemiya (1985, Section 2.2).

The ridge regression estimator may also be derived as a restricted least-squares estimator subject to the inequality constraint $(\boldsymbol{\beta}-\bar{\boldsymbol{\beta}})'\mathbf{q}(\boldsymbol{\beta}-\bar{\boldsymbol{\beta}}) \leq r$. In this case, we have explicitly restricted the estimator to an elliptical subset of the parameter space (centered at $\bar{\boldsymbol{\beta}}$), and the squared, weighted Euclidean distance of $\boldsymbol{\beta}$ from $\bar{\boldsymbol{\beta}}$ is restricted to be no greater than r. The ridge parameter is now the Lagrange multiplier on the inequality constraint, and $\lambda_{\mathrm{R}} = 0$ if the unrestricted estimator satisfies the inequality. Also, note that in Chapter 22 we demonstrate that the ridge estimator is the Bayesian posterior mean under a normal likelihood function and a $\mathrm{N}[\bar{\boldsymbol{\beta}}, \lambda_{\mathrm{R}}^{-1}\mathbf{q}^{-1}]$ prior distribution for the parameter vector $\boldsymbol{\beta}$. As our prior beliefs become more uninformative for the parameter space, the variance of the prior distribution should increase. Accordingly, λ_{R} becomes smaller and the posterior mean (ridge estimator) approaches the optimal Bayes estimator under an uninformative prior, which is the normal maximum likelihood estimator.

The ridge regression estimator has been used in well-posed estimation problems as a treatment for estimator instability caused by collinearity among the columns of $\mathbf{x}$ or other shortcoming of the available data. The ridge estimator discussed previously is an example of a *Type-1 MOR*, which refers to an application of MOR in the case in which the estimation problem is well-posed, and the MOR approach seeks to improve the sampling properties of the estimator. For comparison purposes, suppose the data are so poorly conditioned that the set of regressors are rank deficient (i.e., linearly dependent), and the least-squares estimator is therefore not uniquely defined. In this case, we can derive a *Type-2* (referring to ill-posed estimation contexts) *MOR* solution to the least-squares estimation problem by minimizing the squared, weighted Euclidean distance $(\boldsymbol{\beta}-\bar{\boldsymbol{\beta}})'\mathbf{q}(\boldsymbol{\beta}-\bar{\boldsymbol{\beta}})$ subject to the least-squares first-order or estimating equations $\mathbf{x}'(\mathbf{y}-\mathbf{x}\boldsymbol{\beta})=\mathbf{0}$. The associated Lagrangian expression is

$$\mathrm{L}(\boldsymbol{\beta}, \lambda) = (\boldsymbol{\beta}-\bar{\boldsymbol{\beta}})'\mathbf{q}(\boldsymbol{\beta}-\bar{\boldsymbol{\beta}}) + \boldsymbol{\lambda}'\mathbf{x}'(\mathbf{y}-\mathbf{x}\boldsymbol{\beta}), \tag{18.7.10}$$

and the optimum solution to the Type-2 problem is

$$\tilde{\boldsymbol{\beta}} = \bar{\boldsymbol{\beta}} + \frac{1}{2}\mathbf{q}^{-1}\mathbf{x}'\mathbf{x}\tilde{\boldsymbol{\lambda}}, \tag{18.7.11}$$

where $\tilde{\boldsymbol{\lambda}}$ is the optimum value of the Lagrange multiplier vector. As expected, the estimate $\tilde{\boldsymbol{\beta}}$ is equivalent to the predata value $\bar{\boldsymbol{\beta}}$ if $\bar{\boldsymbol{\beta}}$ satisfies the least-squares first-order on estimating equations. Otherwise, the solution is the value $\tilde{\boldsymbol{\beta}}$ that is closest to $\bar{\boldsymbol{\beta}}$ in terms of the distance norm $(\boldsymbol{\beta}-\bar{\boldsymbol{\beta}})'\mathbf{q}(\boldsymbol{\beta}-\bar{\boldsymbol{\beta}})$ within the subspace of parameter vectors that satisfy the first-order estimating equations.

18.7.2. Finite Sample Performance

In this section, we report the results of limited Monte Carlo sampling experiments that reflect the small sample performance of the penalized likelihood criterion-shrinkage estimators for both well-posed and ill-conditioned problems. Ill-conditioning is measured by the condition number $\kappa(\mathbf{x}'\mathbf{x}) = \pi_1/\pi_k$, which is the ratio of the largest and smallest singular values of $\mathbf{x}'\mathbf{x}$ (equivalently, the largest and smallest eigenvalues of $\mathbf{x}'\mathbf{x}$). As $\kappa(\mathbf{x}'\mathbf{x})$ increases, traditional methods of solving the linear inverse problem with noise may be unstable and have low precision. For a more complete report of these types of sampling results, see Golan, Judge and Miller (1996, pp. 133–7).

The sampling experiment involves a (10×4) design matrix sampled from a normal distribution such that the condition number $\kappa(\mathbf{x}'\mathbf{x})$ has a prescribed value and $\mathrm{tr}(\mathbf{x}'\mathbf{x}) = k = 4$. Noise outcomes were obtained from an iid N(0, 1) pseudorandom number generator, the parameter vector $\boldsymbol{\beta} = [1, 2, -3, 2]'$, and $\kappa(\mathbf{x}'\mathbf{x}) = 1, 10, 20, \ldots, 100$. The shrinkage point is the zero vector, that is, $\boldsymbol{\beta} = \mathbf{0}$, and the weight matrix is $\mathbf{q} = \mathbf{I}$. A ridge smoothing parameter

$$\hat{\lambda}_{\mathrm{R}} = \frac{k\mathrm{S}^2}{\hat{\boldsymbol{\beta}}'\hat{\boldsymbol{\beta}}} \tag{18.7.12}$$

was used to provide a data-based method of regularizing the ill-conditioned inverse problem, where $\hat{\boldsymbol{\beta}}$ and S^2 are the standard least-squares estimators of $\boldsymbol{\beta}$ and σ^2. For

Table 18.1. *MSE from 5000 Replications of ML and Ridge Estimators*

$\kappa(\mathbf{x}'\mathbf{x})$	LS	Ridge
1	3.98	4.54
10	7.95	6.46
20	12.74	7.92
30	17.71	8.98
40	22.47	10.01
50	27.99	10.86
60	33.22	11.39
70	38.27	12.37
80	42.13	12.80
90	46.68	14.12
100	54.20	14.07

each of 5000 trials, the LS and ridge estimates were computed, and the associated average empirical MSE (risk) $\|\tilde{\boldsymbol{\beta}} - \boldsymbol{\beta}\|^2$ is presented in Table 18.1.

For the LS rule, the calculated empirical risk for $\kappa(\mathbf{x}'\mathbf{x}) = 1$ is 3.98, which is close to the theoretical risk of 4. Correspondingly, the ridge estimator has an empirical risk of 4.54, indicating its inferior relative performance in this well-posed situation. When $\kappa(\mathbf{x}'\mathbf{x}) = 100$, in which case the design matrix is notably ill-conditioned, the empirical LS risk is 54.20, whereas the empirical risk of the penalized likelihood–ridge estimator is 14.07.

▶ **Example 18.7.1:** The impact of an ill-conditioned design matrix on the LS and ridge estimators is examined in the GAUSS program C18Ridge.gss (provided in the examples manual). To begin, GAUSS describes the procedure used to generate ill-conditioned or collinear data with a particular condition number. Then, the program conducts a Monte Carlo simulation experiment designed to estimate the quadratic risk of the LS, ridge, and James–Stein (18.6.2) estimators. For comparison purposes, the estimated quadratic risk functions are plotted, and the user should observe a risk pattern similar to the results reported in Table 18.1.

18.8. Final Comments and Critique

As we noted in Chapter 1, some years ago Erich Lehmann wrote an article titled "Where Do Statistical Models Come From?" The article caused quite a stir with his colleagues and served to remind statisticians and econometricians that statistical and econometric models, like the mathematical–probability systems on which they are based, are invented rather than discovered. It was a reminder that such things as Gaussian random variables, probability distributions, stochastic processes, and expected values – things that are sometimes viewed as if they were real properties having physical existence in nature – are actually only conceptual tools that are rooted in the logic provided by probability theory. The article also reminds us, in facing the problem of information recovery, that we have much discretion in the specification of our econometric models as to what we assume and what we leave as unknown and seek to discover. This goes to the heart of the question of the use of prior or nonsample information in the econometric research process.

Prior to this chapter we have been concerned primarily with how best to reason and process data information conditional on the model. We handled the question raised by Lehmann by stating, what if our sample information comes from the following DSP encompassed by a given probability model? We then focused, conditional on the model, on effective way(s) to carry through the estimation and inference process. In doing so, we have endeavored in the preceding chapters to make clear the assumptions that are consistent with the DSP and the unknowns contained in the statistical model. In fact, much of econometric theory is focused on the problem of producing good or optimal information-processing rules *with the specification of the econometric model taken as given and on the assumption that the model encompasses an instance that is compatible with the true underlying data-sampling process*. Despite the efforts of many statisticians and econometricians and the monumental number of suggested and applied approaches appearing in the literature, procedures for model specification and selection are nonetheless burdened with conceptual and interpretational difficulties.

As we progress to an econometric model that may reflect a DSP based on experimentally or nonexperimentally generated sample information, or both, we immediately face questions concerning the relationship between the actual and the assumed DSPs. By necessity, the specification of an econometric model, which purports to encompass an actual DSP, involves a large amount of nonsample information as well as simplifications, or parsimonious representations of reality, or both. In recognition of this, we often read about "false or incorrect econometric models." The phrase in quotes is not generally meant to be interpreted literally. What is usually meant is that the underlying DSP for a particular problem is not, or may not be, encompassed by the simplified, assumed probability model used for econometric analysis purposes. Because this occurs often in econometric practice, it also suggests that we need a basis for estimation and inference that recognizes incorrectly or incompletely specified models.

It might be useful to think back, starting with Chapter 2, to the range of probability models that we have specified and evaluated. Each was based on a particular set of assumptions and, in relation to a real-world data sample, one or more of the assumptions may be violated. The assumptions underlying an econometric model are not made for the purpose of convenience. They are supposed to represent the best information that the analyst has about the DSP underlying the data sample. Unfortunately statistical model misspecification can have negative statistical consequences, not only for sampling properties of estimators and hypothesis-testing procedures but also for sampling properties of model discovery procedures and the testing of economic theories.

It should be apparent by now that the specification of an econometric model appropriate for a particular economic problem must, by necessity, involve a good measure of both sample and nonsample information. Any specified econometric model reflects a range of dogmatic priors, and we should not delude ourselves into thinking otherwise. We have no choice but to make use of prior nonsample information in model specification. Consequently, the real question is how we incorporate such information in an intelligent and defensible way. We must also be aware that we are working with only a sample of observations and that a finite sample will often not capture all of the salient distributional features of an underlying DSP. So just as there is a significant probability that estimates of the values of continuous parameters based on observed data will miss the exact mark, so too is there a notable probability that the discrete problem of model selection from observed data will result in misspecified models. Unfortunately, none of the existing recipes for model selection offers much hope or confidence that the problem can be solved. In facing the model choice problem, the relevant criterion is not whether a certain procedure can be implemented but whether the analyst can give the result of such a procedure a reasonable and defensible statistical interpretation. We suggest that use of this criterion would relegate to history a great deal of diagnostic testing for the purposes of model selection and specification.

The focus in this chapter has been on a basis for choosing among nested statistical models. There is in the background the harder problem that deals with a choice among nonnested parametric families of models. In this situation one model cannot be obtained by imposing appropriate restrictions on another. The procedures we have discussed in this chapter for model choice do not in general apply to the nonnested case. In the nonnested case the problem is cast as follows: for a data sampling process, a set of alternative probability models are nonnested and thus unranked in terms of generality. Each of the models M_i is considered equally likely, and the objective is to see if any or none is consistent with the data. At this point, there are differences among statisticians as to the appropriate way to perform the evaluation of the alternative, unranked models and how to interpret the probability model that emerges. See Judge et al. (1985), Pollack and Wales (1991), McAleer (1987), and McAleer, Pesaran, and Bera (1990) for additional details and references to this literature. The specification-testing foundations for the nonnested case are even more insecure than for the nested case.

In Chapter 22 we introduce the Bayesian approach to estimation and inference, which recognizes explicitly the problem of making use of both sample and nonsample information. In Chapter 23 we couch the Bayes estimators in the family of shrinkage estimators. This then raises the question, in both Bayesian and sampling theory contexts, of how to capture or represent the data-restricting constraints and best achieve the process of learning from a sample of data while avoiding the usual statistical pitfalls. The Bayes, empirical Bayes, Stein-like (shrinkage), MOR, multiple shrinkage–maximum entropy, and equality and inequality constrained and pretest (estimator) estimators reflect ideas for coping with the process of model discovery. However, they are only ideas.

Model choice is an area of probability–econometric research that deals with the most basic of estimation and inference problems. A conceptual breakthrough is definitely needed. One hopes that historical precedent will not guide future practice, and we will decide that this is *not* an area in which we can substitute capital for thinking and use machine learning to handle these decision–choice problems.

18.9. Exercises

18.9.1. Idea Checklist – Knowledge Guides

---

1. What are the different components of econometric model uncertainty?
2. What is the difference between the problems of hypothesis testing and econometric model discovery?
3. What are the pitfalls of focusing on only one component of model uncertainty?
4. What are the differences and similarities between hypothesis testing and Stein-like estimation?
5. How do you make a choice among alternative penalty or loss function in reaching model-discovery decisions?
6. Contrast the different routes to experimental and nonexperimental model discovery.
7. What is the connection between the overdetermined inverse problems of Chapters 16 and 17 and the problem of variable selection focused on in this chapter?

18.9.2. Problems

18–1 Show that the maximum value of the left-hand side of (18.2.14c) is given by $\frac{\boldsymbol{\delta}'[\mathbf{c}(\mathbf{x}'\mathbf{x})^{-1}\mathbf{c}]^{-1}\boldsymbol{\delta}}{\sigma^2}$.

18–2 Show that if the restricted estimator $\hat{\boldsymbol{\beta}}^*$ is SMSE superior to $\hat{\boldsymbol{\beta}}$, then every linear combination of the elements of $\hat{\boldsymbol{\beta}}^*$ has MSE equal to or smaller than the corresponding linear combination of the elements of $\hat{\boldsymbol{\beta}}$, making $\boldsymbol{\tau}'\hat{\boldsymbol{\beta}}^*$ superior to $\boldsymbol{\tau}'\hat{\boldsymbol{\beta}}$ for estimating $\boldsymbol{\tau}'\boldsymbol{\beta}$.

18–3 Demonstrate a Stein-like version of (18.6.2) when the scale parameter σ^2 is unknown and interpret the result.

18–4 Suppose you use hypothesis testing to reach a decision concerning the addition or deletion of a right-hand-side variable. Write down the resulting estimator and go as far as you can in developing its sampling properties.

18–5 What are the implications in a linear model context for variable selection based on using the criterion of maximizing the multiple correlation coefficient $R^2 \equiv 1 - \frac{\hat{\mathbf{e}}'\hat{\mathbf{e}}}{(\mathbf{y}-\mathbf{1}\bar{\mathbf{y}})'(\mathbf{y}-\mathbf{1}\bar{\mathbf{y}})}$?

18–6 Use the partitioned inverse approach to derive equation (18.2.9). Verify the expected value stated in equation (18.2.11b).

18.9.3. Computer Problems

18–1 Using the GAUSS program provided for Example 18.2.2 (C18SMSE.gss) as a guide, repeat the model selection simulation exercise for the test developed under the quadratic risk criterion.

18–2 For a data set of your choice, specify two or more alternative model specifications and use one of the model selection criteria (e.g., AIC) to identify a final version of the model. Do you find that the explanatory variables included in the final model match your predata expectations? Construct a Monte Carlo simulation exercise that replicates your model-selection decision process. How well does the pretest estimation rule associated with your decision process perform in repeated samples?

18–3 Select two or more shrinkage points for each of the parameters in the regression model for Theil's consumption data. Use the multiple shrinkage procedure to estimate the parameter vector and compare the results to the LS estimates.

18–4 Write a GAUSS procedure to compute the multiple shrinkage estimator based on data and shrinkage points reported by the user.

18–5 Conduct a Monte Carlo exercise designed to simulate the sampling properties of the MOR (ridge) estimator (18.7.9). How do the sampling properties of the estimator change as you alter **w**, **q**, or λ_R?

18.10. References

Akaike, H. (1974), "A New Look at the Statistical Model Identification," *IEEE Transactions on Automatic Control*, Vol. 19, pp. 716–23.

Amemiya, T. (1980), "Selection of Regressors," *International Economic Review*, Vol. 21, pp. 331–54.

Amemiya, T. (1985), *Advanced Econometrics*, Cambridge, MA: Harvard University Press.

Anderson, T. W. (1984), *An Introduction to Multivariate Statistical Analysis*, New York: John Wiley and Sons.

Baranchik, A. J. (1964), "Multiple Regression and the Estimation of the Mean of a Multivariate Normal Distribution," (Technical Report No. 51), Department of Statistics, Stanford University, Stanford, CA.

Berger, J. (1983), "The Stein Effect," In S. Kotz and Johnson (Eds.), *Encyclopedia of Statistical Sciences*, New York: John Wiley and Sons.

Bozdogan, H. (1987), "Model Selection and AIC," *Psychometrika*, Vol. 52, pp. 345–70.

Breiman, L. (1992), "The Little Bootstrap and other Methods for Dimensionality Selection in Regression: X-Fixed Prediction Error," *Journal of the American Statistical Association*, Vol. 87, pp. 738–54.

Breiman, L. (1995), "Better Subset Regression Using the Nonnegative Garrote," *Technometrics*, Vol. 37, pp. 373–84.

Breiman, L., and P. Spector (1992), "Submodel Selection and Evaluation in Regression. The X-Random Case," *International Statistical Institute Review*, Vol. 60, pp. 291–319.

Brown, L. D. (1971), "Admissible Estimators, Recurrent Diffusion and Insoluble Boundary Value Problems," *Annals of Mathematical Statistics*, Vol. 42, pp. 855–903.

Dayton, C. M. (1998), "Information Criteria for Paired Comparisons Problem," *American Statistician*, Vol. 52, pp. 144–51.

Efron, B. (1998), "R. A. Fisher in the 21st Century," *Statistical Science*, Vol. 13, pp. 95–122.

George, E. I. (1986a), "Combining Minimax Shrinkage Estimators," *Journal of the American Statistical Association*, Vol. 81, pp. 437–45.

George, E. I. (1986b), "Minimax Multiple Shrinkage Estimation," *Annals of Statistics*, Vol. 14, pp. 188–205.

George, E., and R. McCulloch (1993), "Variable Selection in Gibbs Sampling," *Journal of the American Statistical Association*, Vol. 88(423), pp. 881–9.

Golan, A., and G. Judge (1996), "A Simultaneous Estimation and Variable Selection Rule," (unpublished paper), University of California, Berkeley.

Golan, A., G. G. Judge, and D. Miller (1996), *Maximum Entropy Econometrics: Robust Estimation with Limited Data*, New York: John Wiley and Sons.

Hocking, R. R. (1976), "The Analysis and Selection of Variables in Linear Regression," *Biometrics*, Vol. 32, pp. 1–51.

Hoerl, A. E., and R. W. Kennard (1970), "Ridge Regression: Biased Estimation for Non-orthogonal Problems," *Technometrics*, Vol. 1, pp. 55–67.

Hoerl, A., R. Kennard, and K. Baldwin (1975), "Ridge Regression: Some Simulations," *Communications in Statistics*, Vol. 5, pp. 105–23.

Hurvich, C. M., and C.-L. Tsai (1991), "Bias of the Corrected AIC Criterion for Underfitted Regression and Time Series Models," *Biometrika*, Vol. 78, pp. 499–509.

James, W., and C. Stein (1960), "Estimation with Quadratic Loss," in *Proceedings of the Fourth Berkeley Symposium on Mathematical Statistics and Probability*, University of California Press, Berkeley, CA, pp. 361–79.

Judge, G. G., and M. E. Bock (1978), *The Statistical Implications of Pre-Test and Stein-Rule Estimators in Econometrics*, Amsterdam: North–Holland.

Judge, G. G., W. E. Griffiths, R. C. Hill, H. Lütkepohl, and T.-C. Lee (1985), *The Theory and Practice of Econometrics*, (2nd ed.), New York: John Wiley and Sons.

Judge, G., G. Yi, T. Yancey, and T. Teräsvirta (1987), "The Extended Stein Procedure for Simultaneous Model Selection and Parameter Estimation," *Journal of Econometrics*, Vol. 35, pp. 375–91.

Kullback, J. (1959), *Information Theory and Statistics*, New York: John Wiley and Sons.

Le Cessie, S., and J. C. van Houwelingen (1992), "Ridge Estimators in Logistic Regression," *Journal of Applied Statistics*, Vol. 41, pp. 191–201.

Mallows, C. L. (1973), "Some Comments on C_P," *Technometrics*, Vol. 15, pp. 671–6.

McAleer, M. J. (1987), "Specification Tests for Separate Models: A Survey," in *Specification Analysis in the Linear Model*, M. L. King and D. E. A. Giles (Eds.), London: Routledge and Kegan Paul.

McAleer, M. J., M. H. Pesaran, and A. K. Bera (1990), "Alternative Approaches to Testing Non-nested Models with Autocorrelated Disturbances: An Application to Models of U.S. Unemployment," *Communications in Statistics, Series A*, Vol. 19, pp. 3619–44.

Miller, A. J. (1990), *Subset Selection in Regression*, London: Chapman and Hall.

O'Sullivan, F. (1986), "A Statistical Perspective on Ill-Posed Inverse Problems," *Statistical Science*, Vol. 1, pp. 502–27.

Pollack, R. A., and T. J. Wales (1991), "The Likelihood Dominance Criterion: A New Approach to Model Selection," *Journal of Econometrics*, Vol. 47, pp. 227–42.

Schwarz, G. (1978), "Estimating the Dimensions of a Model," *The Annals of Statistics*, Vol. 6, pp. 461–4.

Sclove, S. (1987), "Application of Selection Criteria to Some Problems in Multivariate Analysis," *Psychometrika*, Vol. 52, pp. 333–43.

Shi, P., and T. Tsai (1998), "A Note on the Unification of Akaike Information Criteria," *Journal of the Royal Statistical Society, Series B*, Vol. 60, pp. 551–8.

Stein, C. (1955), "Inadmissibility of the Usual Estimator for the Mean of a Multivariate Normal Distribution," in *Proceedings of the Third Berkeley Symposium on Mathematical Statistics and Probability*, University of California Press, Berkeley, CA, pp. 197–206.

Stein, C. (1966), "An Approach to the Recovery of Interblock Information in Balanced Incomplete Block Designs," in F. N. David (Ed.), *Research Papers in Statistics*, New York: John Wiley and Sons, pp. 351–66.

Stein, C. (1981), "Estimation of the Mean of a Multivariate Normal Distribution," *The Annals of Statistics*, Vol. 9, pp. 1135–51.

Thompson, A. M., J. C. Brown, J. W. McKay, and D. M. Titterington (1991), "A Study of Methods of Choosing the Smoothing Parameter in Image Restoration by Regularization," *IEEE Transactions on Pattern Analysis and Machine Intelligence*, Vol. 13, pp. 326–39.

Tibshirani, R. (1996), "Regression Shrinkage and Selection via the Lasso," *Journal of the Royal Statistical Society, Series B*, Vol. 58, pp. 267–88.

Titterington, D. M. (1985), "Common Structures of Smoothing Techniques in Statistics," *International Statistical Review*, Vol. 53, pp. 141–70.

Zaman, A. (1984), "Avoiding Model Selection by the Use of Shrinkage Techniques," *Journal of Econometrics*, Vol. 25, pp. 73–86.

Zhang, P. (1992), "On the Distributional Properties of Model Selection Criteria," *Journal of the American Statistical Association*, Vol. 87, pp. 732–7.

Zheng, X., and W.-Y. Loh (1995), "Consistent Variable Selection in Linear Models," *Journal of the American Statistical Association*, Vol. 90, pp. 151–6.

CHAPTER 19

Model Discovery: The Problem of Noise Covariance Matrix Specification

19.1. Introduction

This chapter continues the analysis relating to the specification or discovery of the underlying probability–econometric model. The specific issue in this chapter is the specification of the particular parametric form of the fixed but unknown covariance matrix of the noise component of an econometric model. This is different from the unknown covariance matrix situations examined in Chapter 15. In that chapter, either the parametric form of the covariance matrix was completely unknown and robust methods of accounting for the nonspherical nature of the noise components were examined, or the parametric functional form of the covariance matrix was fully known, in which case the inverse problem reduced to one of estimating the unknown parameters of the functional form. The current problem is much more difficult and has as its objective both the discovery of the appropriate parametric specification of the covariance matrix as well as the estimation of the value of the covariance matrix. On this score, it is important to emphasize, as we did in the previous chapter, that concepts such as random variables, probability distributions, stochastic processes, and covariance matrices – concepts that underlie models of noise component outcomes and DSPs – are only tools that are rooted in, and derive their interpretation from, the logic of probability theory. These conceptual devices do not originate as entities having physical existence in nature or in the economic process being analyzed but are rather conceptual properties having existence as postulated components of models. Thus the search for "the true" covariance matrix may be akin to a search for the Holy Grail – both being noble, mystic, and elusive objectives. It is perhaps more reasonable to view the former search as seeking covariance matrix specifications coinciding with probability models that serve as good working descriptors of how data outcomes are sampled.

Over the past few decades, econometricians have invested a substantial amount of effort in proposing and applying a wide range of procedures for identifying–discovering covariance matrix specifications. Nonetheless, the problem of covariance matrix discovery, and the closely related problems of model choice and estimation, remains largely insoluble unless substantial prior information relating to the structure of the covariance matrix is available. The general conceptual difficulties involved are analogous to those discussed in the introduction to Chapter 18 and include (1) that a finite sample of data is not a census and will generally not reflect all of the idiosyncratic characteristics of the particular distribution underlying a DSP, and (2) that a myriad of different probability distributions are consistent with the noisy estimates of characteristics that can be inferred from the data. As a result, the information in a sample of data is inherently insufficient to refute or discriminate among a large variety of covariance matrix contingencies – especially because the covariance matrix involves a rather substantial number, $n(n+1)/2$, of unknowns that will often greatly exceed the number of data observations n. Thus, unless structure can be imposed on the covariance matrix, inferring the values of its elements is an ill-posed problem.

If the analyst seeks to utilize a battery of hypothesis tests as a strategy for discovering the "true" structure of the covariance matrix, there is a plethora of hypotheses specifications that are possible in the absence of prior information to the contrary. In this case there are $2^{n(n-1)/2}$ possible contingencies for nonzero covariance values (autocorrelation) in addition to 2^n different possibilities regarding unequal variance values (heteroscedasticity). Related to this dimensionality problem is that all possible $2^{n+n(n-1)/2}$ contingencies cannot possibly be tested based on one finite sample of data without degrading the joint (across all tests) Type-I error probabilities. In effect, such a testing strategy for purposes of covariance matrix discovery is virtually certain to "detect" nonsphericity in the noise component for even relatively small values of n with no discernible degree of assurance that the correct covariance matrix specification will result.

In deciding how to proceed in the quest to discover the covariance matrix specification, it is important to pause and contemplate why one should attempt this discovery process in the first place. In the absence of the use of lagged dependent variables as explanatory variables, the conceptual issue is basically the opportunity cost of not achieving efficiency in parameter estimation when the nonspherical parametric structure of the covariance matrix is ignored. When lagged dependent variables are included in the model as explanatory variables, the opportunity cost also generally includes the cost of not achieving consistency in parameter estimation if the nonsphericity involves an autocorrelation component. The traditional way to proceed in this situation has been to posit a nonspherical covariance structure (e.g., a first-order autoregressive noise process is quite "popular" among practitioners) and perform a hypothesis test to determine whether sphericity is rejected in favor of the nonspherical alternative. If the answer is yes, one then transforms the sample observations using the posited nonspherical covariance matrix representation and utilizes an EGLS estimator, appropriately parameterizes an ML estimation approach, or uses some other estimator that corrects for the assumed type of nonsphericity.

Even if the "true" covariance structure were accidentally discovered by the postulation–testing–transformation process, the covariance matrix value ultimately used in the transformation–estimation stage is only an estimate. The estimators defined as functions of estimates will generally not achieve the efficiency properties attributable to the conceptually ideal estimator based on the actual nonspherical covariance matrix except asymptotically. In terms of finite sampling properties, whether or not the correct covariance matrix specification is fortuitously postulated and then used, there exists the real possibility that the postulation–testing–transformation estimator will perform more poorly than an estimator that ignores the nonsphericity problem entirely. In practice, because one cannot expect omniscience in the specification of a noise covariance matrix parameterization or even in the specification of a noise covariance matrix *hypothesis*, one must admit that the goal of achieving efficiency in estimation is effectively a straw man. And though we may lament the loss of consistency, the loss may be unavoidable in the absence of prior knowledge relating to the appropriate structural covariance matrix specification to test or implement.

The preceding discussion begs the question of why one should bother with testing hypotheses relating to covariance matrix specifications at all. One answer is that there is historical precedent for it, and to be able to comprehend and critique the massive theoretical and applied literature dealing with this issue, it is important that the reader have at least a fundamental understanding of the basic logic underlying the principal tests suggested and utilized in this area. A more substantive answer is that when interpreted properly within the conditional and often rarified context in which the tests directly apply, they serve to identify whether postulates are contradicted by the data, albeit one cannot interpret a nonrejected postulate as representing truth.

Having said all of this, in this chapter we think it is important to acknowledge that a range of tests have been suggested in the literature for assessing the existence of heteroscedastic or autocorrelated errors, or both. We review the basic principles underlying these tests, and the statistical implications of these testing mechanisms for covariance matrix discovery are critiqued.

19.2. Specific Parametric Specifications of the Noise Covariance Matrix: Estimation and Inference

In this section we reexamine two parametric noise covariance matrix specifications first presented in Section 14.4 in the context of the linear regression model. The purpose of this reexamination is to illustrate the traditional approach for estimating values of unknown parameters contained in a postulated specification. We also indicate the typical way practitioners then proceed with inference in these situations. These cases are representative of the historical approach that has been followed in solving inverse problems characterized by a wide variety of parametric noise covariance specifications.

19.2.1. AR(1) Noise

In this case the dependent variable $\mathbf{Y}$ is assumed to depend on an autocorrelated noise vector in the following way:

$$\mathrm{Y}_i = \mathbf{x}_{i.}\boldsymbol{\beta} + \varepsilon_i \tag{19.2.1}$$

$$\varepsilon_i = \rho\varepsilon_{i-1} + \nu_i, \tag{19.2.2}$$

where $E[\nu_i]=0$, $E[\nu_i^2]=\sigma_\nu^2$, $E[\nu_i\nu_j]=0$ for $j \neq i$, and $|\rho|<1$. Under this specification, the noise covariance matrix $E[\boldsymbol{\varepsilon\varepsilon}']=\sigma_\nu^2\boldsymbol{\Psi}$ is represented by

$$\sigma_\nu^2\boldsymbol{\Psi}(\rho)=\frac{\sigma_\nu^2}{1-\rho^2}\begin{bmatrix} 1 & \rho & \rho^2 & \cdots & \rho^{n-1} \\ \rho & 1 & \rho & \cdots & \rho^{n-2} \\ \rho^2 & \rho & 1 & \cdots & \rho^{n-3} \\ \vdots & \vdots & \vdots & \ddots & \vdots \\ \rho^{n-1} & \rho^{n-2} & \rho^{n-3} & \cdots & 1 \end{bmatrix}. \tag{19.2.3}$$

19.2.1.a. NLS and ML Estimation

When ρ is unknown in the noise covariance matrix specification corresponding to an AR(1) process, and if the distribution of the noise component is unknown, one possibility is to use the least-squares estimation objective and, within a nonlinear LS–extremum estimator context, estimate $\boldsymbol{\beta}$ and ρ using the estimator

$$\begin{aligned}[\hat{\boldsymbol{\beta}}_G' \vdots \hat{\rho}_G]' &\equiv \arg\min_{\boldsymbol{\beta},\rho}[(\mathbf{Y}-\mathbf{x}\boldsymbol{\beta})'\boldsymbol{\Psi}(\rho)^{-1}(\mathbf{Y}-\mathbf{x}\boldsymbol{\beta})] \\ &\equiv \arg\min_{\boldsymbol{\beta},\rho}\Bigg[(1-\rho^2)(\mathrm{y}_1-\mathbf{x}_{1\cdot}\boldsymbol{\beta})^2 \\ &\quad + \sum_{i=2}^{n}[(\mathrm{y}_i-\rho\mathrm{y}_{i-1})-(\mathbf{x}_{i\cdot}-\rho\mathbf{x}_{i-1\cdot})\boldsymbol{\beta}]^2\Bigg].\end{aligned} \tag{19.2.4}$$

Note that the second line in (19.2.4) follows from the fact that

$$\boldsymbol{\Psi}(\rho)^{-1} \equiv \begin{bmatrix} 1 & -\rho & 0 & \cdots & 0 & 0 \\ -\rho & 1+\rho^2 & -\rho & \cdots & 0 & 0 \\ 0 & -\rho & 1+\rho^2 & \cdots & 0 & 0 \\ \vdots & \vdots & \vdots & \ddots & \vdots & \vdots \\ 0 & 0 & 0 & \cdots & 1+\rho^2 & -\rho \\ 0 & 0 & 0 & \cdots & -\rho & 1 \end{bmatrix}, \tag{19.2.5}$$

which has a Cholesky decomposition $\boldsymbol{\Psi}(\rho)^{-1} \equiv \mathbf{c}(\rho)'\mathbf{c}(\rho)$ with $\mathbf{c}(\rho)$ defined as

$$\mathbf{c}(\rho) \equiv \begin{bmatrix} \sqrt{1-\rho^2} & 0 & 0 & \cdots & 0 & 0 \\ -\rho & 1 & 0 & \cdots & 0 & 0 \\ 0 & -\rho & 1 & \cdots & 0 & 0 \\ \vdots & \vdots & \vdots & \ddots & \vdots & \vdots \\ 0 & 0 & 0 & \cdots & 1 & 0 \\ 0 & 0 & 0 & \cdots & -\rho & 1 \end{bmatrix}. \tag{19.2.6}$$

Then, expressing $(\mathbf{Y}-\mathbf{x}\boldsymbol{\beta})'\boldsymbol{\Psi}(\rho)^{-1}(\mathbf{Y}-\mathbf{x}\boldsymbol{\beta}) \equiv (\mathbf{Y}-\mathbf{x}\boldsymbol{\beta})'\mathbf{c}'\mathbf{c}(\mathbf{Y}-\mathbf{x}\boldsymbol{\beta})$ in scalar notation leads directly to the second line in (19.2.4).

Under this formulation, the values of $\boldsymbol{\beta}$ and ρ that solve (19.2.4) may be simultaneously computed by nonlinear least-squares (NLS). In applied work, iterative procedures that make use of an initial estimate of ρ have often been used to solve (19.2.4). One such approach is the procedure by Cochrane and Orcutt (1949), who used a series of least-squares fits beginning with $\hat{\rho} = \sum_{i=1}^{n} \hat{\varepsilon}_i \hat{\varepsilon}_{i-1} / \sum_{i=2}^{n} \hat{\varepsilon}_i^2$ to solve (19.2.4), where $\hat{\varepsilon}_i$'s are estimated noise component elements obtained from a standard least-squares estimate of the linear model $\mathbf{Y} = \mathbf{x}\boldsymbol{\beta} + \varepsilon$. Under this approach, $\hat{\rho}$ replaces the unknown ρ in (19.2.4) and then $\hat{\boldsymbol{\beta}}(\hat{\rho})$ is obtained by solving (19.2.4) conditional on $\rho = \hat{\rho}$. Then $\hat{\varepsilon}$ is recalculated based on $\hat{\boldsymbol{\beta}}(\hat{\rho})$, $\hat{\rho}$ is updated based on the new $\hat{\varepsilon}$, $\hat{\boldsymbol{\beta}}$ is updated based on the new $\hat{\rho}$, and the process continues sequentially until the estimates converge. However, with the advent of powerful desktop computing, it is currently quite feasible to solve (19.2.4) directly.

► **Example 19.2.1:** To demonstrate the setup and application of the NLS estimator for the AR(1) model, we provide the GAUSS program C19ARNLS.gss in the examples manual. For a given sample of data, GAUSS computes the NLS estimates of $\boldsymbol{\beta}$, σ^2, and ρ by directly minimizing (19.2.4). Then, the sampling properties of the NLS estimator are simulated by a Monte Carlo exercise.

If the parametric family of the noise distribution is known, then the likelihood function can be specified, and the maximum likelihood (ML) approach can be used. For example, if the normal assumption is appropriate, then the likelihood function can be represented as

$$\mathrm{L}(\boldsymbol{\beta}, \sigma_v^2, \rho; \mathbf{y}) = \mathrm{f}(\mathrm{y}_1) \cdot \mathrm{f}(\mathrm{y}_2 \mid \mathrm{y}_1) \cdots \mathrm{f}(\mathrm{y}_n \mid \mathrm{y}_{n-1}), \tag{19.2.7}$$

where

$$\mathrm{f}(\mathrm{y}_1) = (2\pi)^{-1/2} \sqrt{\frac{1-\rho^2}{\sigma_v^2}} \cdot \exp\left[-\left(\frac{1-\rho^2}{2\sigma_v^2}\right)(\mathrm{y}_1 - \mathbf{x}_{1\cdot}\boldsymbol{\beta})^2\right], \tag{19.2.8}$$

and

$$\mathrm{f}(\mathrm{y}_i \mid \mathrm{y}_{i-1}) = \left(2\pi\sigma_v^2\right)^{-1/2} \exp\left[-\frac{1}{2\sigma_v^2}(\mathrm{y}_i - \rho \mathrm{y}_{i-1} - \mathbf{x}_{i\cdot}\boldsymbol{\beta} + \rho \mathbf{x}_{i-1\cdot}\boldsymbol{\beta})^2\right], \tag{19.2.9}$$

where $i = 2, 3, \ldots, n$. Thus,

$$\begin{aligned}\mathrm{L}(\boldsymbol{\beta}, \sigma_v^2, \rho; \mathbf{y}) = \frac{\sqrt{1-\rho^2}}{\left(2\pi\sigma_v^2\right)^{n/2}} \exp\Bigg\{-\frac{1}{2\sigma_v^2}\Bigg[&(\mathrm{y}_1\sqrt{1-\rho^2} - \mathbf{x}_{1\cdot}\boldsymbol{\beta}\sqrt{1-\rho^2})^2 \\ &+ \sum_{i=2}^{n}(\mathrm{y}_i - \rho\mathrm{y}_{i-1} - \mathbf{x}_{i\cdot}\boldsymbol{\beta} + \rho\mathbf{x}_{i-1\cdot}\boldsymbol{\beta})^2\Bigg]\Bigg\}\end{aligned} \tag{19.2.10}$$

The ML estimates $\boldsymbol{\beta}$, σ_v^2, are ρ found by maximizing (19.2.10), generally using numerical computational procedures, leading to the extremum estimator

$$\left(\hat{\boldsymbol{\beta}}_{\mathrm{ML}}, \hat{\sigma}_{v\mathrm{ML}}^2, \hat{\rho}_{\mathrm{ML}}\right)' = \arg\max_{\boldsymbol{\beta}, \sigma_v^2, \rho} \left[\mathrm{L}(\boldsymbol{\beta}, \sigma_v^2, \rho; \mathbf{Y})\right]. \tag{19.2.11}$$

► **Example 19.2.2:** To demonstrate the setup and application of the ML estimator for the AR(1) model, we provide the GAUSS program C19ARML.gss in the examples manual.

For a given sample of data, the ML estimates of $\boldsymbol{\beta}$, σ^2, and ρ are computed by GAUSS. Then, the sampling properties of the ML estimator are simulated by a Monte Carlo exercise.

In terms of sampling properties, if mild regularity conditions hold, including the condition that the explanatory variables do not contain lagged values of the dependent variable, then for either the NLS or ML estimator of $\boldsymbol{\beta}$,

$$n^{1/2}(\hat{\boldsymbol{\beta}} - \boldsymbol{\beta}) \xrightarrow{d} \mathrm{N}[\mathbf{0}, \sigma^2 \lim(n^{-1}\mathbf{x}'\boldsymbol{\Psi}^{-1}\mathbf{x})^{-1}]. \tag{19.2.12}$$

Therefore, the NLS and ML estimators have the same asymptotic normal distribution. Estimation in the case of a lagged dependent explanatory variable can proceed by using an instrumental variable approach to mitigate the correlation between the explanatory variable and the noise component, where typically current and lagged values of the exogenous explanatory variables are used as instruments (see Hatanaka, 1974).

19.2.1.b. Inference

To test the null hypothesis of no-first-order autocorrelation, the null hypothesis H_0: $\rho = 0$ can be tested against the alternative H_0: $\rho \neq 0$. Under regularity conditions, which again include the condition that the explanatory variables do not contain lagged values of the dependent variable, it can be shown that $\hat{\rho}$ is approximately normally distributed with mean ρ and variance $(1 - \rho^2)/n$. It follows that the statistic

$$\mathrm{Z} = (\hat{\rho} - \rho)/\sqrt{(1 - \hat{\rho}^2)/n} \overset{a}{\sim} \mathrm{N}(0, 1) \tag{19.2.13}$$

can be used in the usual way to construct an asymptotic level-α test of the null hypothesis H_0: $\rho = 0$, where the critical regions is defined in terms of quantiles of the standard normal distribution. When the noise distribution is multivariate normal, we can use the more powerful test developed by Durbin and Watson (1950, 1951, 1971). Finally, the usual Wald, Lagrange multiplier, and pseudo-likelihood ratio tests may be used to test hypotheses and generate confidence regions for functions of the model parameters. Unfortunately, little is known as to the small sample properties of the procedures because analytical results are difficult to achieve. We discuss specific autocorrelation tests and their associated properties in much greater detail in Section 19.4.

19.2.2. Heteroscedastic Noise: $\sigma_i^2 = (\mathbf{z}_{i\cdot}\boldsymbol{\alpha})^2$

In this case the dependent variable $\mathbf{Y}$ is assumed to be heteroscedastic with variances depending on the square of a linear combination of explanatory variables such as

$$\mathrm{Y}_i = \mathbf{x}_{i\cdot}\boldsymbol{\beta} + \varepsilon_i \tag{19.2.14}$$

$$\mathrm{var}(\varepsilon_i) = \sigma_i^2 = (\mathbf{z}_{i\cdot}\boldsymbol{\alpha})^2. \tag{19.2.15}$$

Under this specification, the noise covariance matrix $E[\varepsilon\varepsilon'] = \boldsymbol{\Psi}$ is represented by

$$\boldsymbol{\Psi} = \begin{bmatrix} (\mathbf{z}_{1\cdot}\boldsymbol{\alpha})^2 & 0 & \cdots & 0 \\ 0 & (\mathbf{z}_{2\cdot}\boldsymbol{\alpha})^2 & \cdots & 0 \\ \vdots & \vdots & \ddots & \vdots \\ 0 & 0 & \cdots & (\mathbf{z}_{n\cdot}\boldsymbol{\alpha})^2 \end{bmatrix}. \tag{19.2.16}$$

19.2.2.a. NLS and ML Estimation

When $\boldsymbol{\alpha}$ is unknown in the heteroscedastic noise covariance matrix specification, nonlinear estimation procedures may be used to recover the unknown parameters and provide a basis for inference. For example, one possibility is to define a nonlinear LS estimator for $\boldsymbol{\alpha}$ that involves minimizing $\sum_{i=1}^{n}[\hat{\varepsilon}_i^2 - (\mathbf{z}_{i\cdot}\boldsymbol{\alpha})^2]^2$, where the estimated noise component elements are generated by a (ordinary) least-squares fit as $\hat{\varepsilon}_i = \mathbf{Y}_i - \mathbf{x}_{i\cdot}\hat{\boldsymbol{\beta}}_{\mathrm{LS}}$. Then, the NLS–extremum estimator of $\boldsymbol{\alpha}$, $\hat{\boldsymbol{\alpha}} = \min_{\boldsymbol{\alpha}}[\hat{\boldsymbol{\varepsilon}}^2 - (\mathbf{z}\boldsymbol{\alpha})^2]'[\hat{\boldsymbol{\varepsilon}}^2 - (\mathbf{z}\boldsymbol{\alpha})^2]$, can be used to replace $\boldsymbol{\alpha}$ in (19.2.16), leading to the EGLS estimator of $\hat{\boldsymbol{\beta}}$ represented by

$$\hat{\boldsymbol{\beta}}_{\mathrm{G}} = (\mathbf{x}'\boldsymbol{\Psi}(\hat{\boldsymbol{\alpha}})^{-1}\mathbf{x})^{-1}\mathbf{x}'\boldsymbol{\Psi}(\hat{\boldsymbol{\alpha}})^{-1}\mathbf{Y} = \left(\sum_{i=1}^{n}(\mathbf{z}_{i\cdot}\hat{\boldsymbol{\alpha}})^{-2}\mathbf{x}_{i\cdot}'\mathbf{x}_{i\cdot}\right)^{-1}\sum_{i=1}^{n}(\mathbf{z}_{i\cdot}\hat{\boldsymbol{\alpha}})^{-2}\mathbf{x}_{i\cdot}\mathrm{Y}_i. \tag{19.2.17}$$

Alternatively, if the ε_i's are independent and normally distributed, the log of the likelihood function (where c is a constant) is

$$\ln \mathrm{L}(\boldsymbol{\beta}, \boldsymbol{\alpha}; \mathbf{y}, \mathbf{x}, \mathbf{z}) = \mathrm{c} - \sum_{i=1}^{n}\ln(\mathbf{z}_{i\cdot}\boldsymbol{\alpha}) - \left(\frac{1}{2}\right)\sum_{i=1}^{n}\left(\frac{\mathrm{y}_i - \mathbf{x}_{i\cdot}\boldsymbol{\beta}}{\mathbf{z}_{i\cdot}\boldsymbol{\alpha}}\right)^2. \tag{19.2.18}$$

The ML estimates are obtained from the extremum estimator defined by maximizing (19.2.18) with respect to the unknown $\boldsymbol{\beta}$ and $\boldsymbol{\alpha}$.

19.2.2.b. Inference

Multivariate normality of the noise component allows for the use of generalized likelihood ratio statistics for generating asymptotically valid tests and confidence regions for values of the parameters of the model. For example, if $\mathrm{z}[i, 1] = 1\ \forall i$ in the heteroscedastic specification above, an asymptotic test of the hypothesis of no heteroscedasticity can be performed in the usual way based on -2 times the log of the ratio of the restricted likelihood function reflecting the null hypotheses $\boldsymbol{\alpha}[2\colon \mathrm{m}] = \mathbf{0}$ divided by the likelihood functions evaluated at the unrestricted ML estimates of $\boldsymbol{\alpha}$ and $\boldsymbol{\beta}$. The test would be an asymptotically valid Chi-square test based on $m - 1$ degrees of freedom. Of course Wald, LM and Z-tests and confidence-region estimation procedures remain applicable in the ML context as well.

Note also that the use of (19.2.18) can be considered even in the case in which it is not known that the ε_i's are independent and normally distributed, in which case the procedure can be interpreted as a quasi-likelihood approach to the problem. Moreover, the NL approach, with or without normality of the noise component, leads to the usual asymptotic tests and confidence-region procedures, as discussed in Section 14.3.2, with $\boldsymbol{\Psi}$ replaced by $\boldsymbol{\Psi}(\hat{\boldsymbol{\alpha}})$.

19.3. Tests for Heteroscedasticity: Rationale and Application

There are two basic reasons for attempting to detect the presence of heteroscedasticity. One obvious reason is to discern whether there is any justification for using either the robust or parametric estimates of the noise covariance matrix, such as those introduced above and in Chapter 15, to perform inference, or to implement EGLS estimation, or to do both. A second reason is to attempt to discover the particular structure of the noise covariance matrix for use in the definition of an EGLS estimator or inference procedure. Most of the test procedures used in practice are *constructive* tests, meaning that if a test indicates that the noise covariance matrix is not equal to $\sigma^2\mathbf{I}$, the test procedure also specifies a particular parametric representation of the nonspherical covariance matrix together with a method for estimating the values of the unknowns in the parameterization.

Virtually all of the tests for heteroscedasticity that are currently used in practice can be represented in the form of auxiliary regression equations that have some function of estimated noise component outcomes as dependent variables and various functions of the explanatory variables as right-hand-side variables. We note that in several of the original papers, the tests were not presented in auxiliary regression form but were represented as LR, Wald, or Chi-square test statistics having asymptotic Chi-square distributions. Engle (1979a,b; 1984) was apparently the first to point out that the auxiliary regression approach provides heteroscedasticity tests that are asymptotically equivalent to previous tests based on LR, Wald, or Chi-square test statistics. Koenker (1981) showed that the auxiliary regression form of testing is actually more robust than alternative forms when the noise component is not normally distributed.

There is literally an infinite number of possibilities for the functional specification of the covariance associated with heteroscedastic (or autocorrelated) noise components of a regression model. One is only limited by his or her imagination as to this set of possibilities, and unfortunately it is often the case in practice that prior information is quite limited regarding the true form of the parametric representation of $\mathbf{cov}(\boldsymbol{\varepsilon})$. In this section we provide a brief unifying review of some tests for heteroscedasticity that applied analysts have utilized in empirical work. Our review is not exhaustive, but the tests discussed here are the ones that appear to have been applied most often in the literature. Discussion of these and other tests abound in other econometric texts and in the journal literature. The reader is referred to Judge et al. (1988, pp. 351–409) and to Godfrey (1988, Sections 4.5 and 5.4) for extensive details and references.

We emphasize to the reader that if these tests are used to *choose* the form of an EGLS-type estimator, then the analyst is actually *not* using a particular EGLS estimator to solve the inverse problem at hand but rather is utilizing a pretest estimator. The details of pretest estimation in this context are discussed ahead in Section 19.5. This fact is almost universally ignored when discussing the properties of EGLS or ML estimators used in empirical work. We also add that with the built-in propensity for all statistical tests to commit Type-I and Type-II errors with positive probability, one can be quite confident of eventually rejecting or accepting a null hypothesis of no heteroscedasticity (or autocorrelation), regardless of its validity, if a sufficient number of alternative tests are applied. Thus, in the complete absence of prior information relating to the parametric structure of $\mathbf{cov}(\varepsilon)$, a strategy of performing a dense set of tests with the aim of uncovering an appropriate specification of $\mathbf{\Psi}$ is ill-advised. In these cases, one might be better served by an ordinary LS estimator together with the use of a robust estimate of its covariance matrix for inference purposes.

19.3.1. Types of Heteroscedasticity Tests

As we noted previously, virtually all of the tests for heteroscedasticity currently used in practice can be represented in the form of auxiliary regression equations that have some function of the estimated noise component outcomes as dependent variables and various functions of explanatory variables as right-hand-side variables. Table 19.1 provides a catalog of the most popular tests used in empirical work.

The tests are based on articles by Breusch and Pagan (1979), Glejser (1969), Godfrey (1978), Harvey (1976), White (1980), and Engle (1982). We again emphasize that in many of these original articles, the tests were not presented in auxiliary regression form but rather as GLR, Wald, or Chi-square test statistics having asymptotic Chi-square distributions. As noted earlier, Engle (1979a,b; 1984) motivated the asymptotically equivalent auxiliary regression form of these type of tests, and Koenker (1981) showed that the auxiliary regression tests tend to be more robust when the noise component is not normally distributed. We emphasize that the tests can be applied in both linear and nonlinear model contexts.

19.3.2. Motivation for Tests Based on $\hat{\varepsilon}_t^2$

To provide some common motivation for all of the tests in Table 19.1 that utilize $\hat{\varepsilon}_t^2$ for the dependent variable of the auxiliary regression and $n\mathrm{R}_\mathrm{a}^2$ for the test statistic, first consider the following null and alternative hypotheses:

$$\mathrm{H}_0\colon \sigma_t^2 = \sigma^2, \quad \forall t \text{ versus } \mathrm{H}_\mathrm{a}\colon \sigma_t^2 = \alpha_0 + \mathbf{z}[t,.]\boldsymbol{\alpha}, \tag{19.3.1}$$

where $\mathbf{z}[t,.]$ is a $(1 \times m)$ vector of variables thought to explain the level of the variance for observation t, and $\boldsymbol{\alpha}$ is a $(m \times 1)$ vector of parameters. Note that setting $\boldsymbol{\alpha} = \mathbf{0}$ in H_a implies H_0, that is, homoscedasticity is implied because then $\sigma_t^2 = \alpha_0 = \sigma^2\ \forall t$. Now consider the following regression-like representation of H_a:

$$\begin{aligned}\varepsilon_t^2 &= \alpha_0 + \mathbf{z}[t,.]\boldsymbol{\alpha} + \left(\varepsilon_t^2 - \sigma_t^2\right) \\ &= \alpha_0 + \mathbf{z}[t,.]\boldsymbol{\alpha} + \mathbf{V}_t,\end{aligned} \tag{19.3.2}$$

where $\mathbf{V}_t \equiv \varepsilon_t^2 - \sigma_t^2$, so that $\mathrm{E}\mathbf{V}_t = 0$ and $\mathrm{E}\varepsilon_t^2 = \sigma_t^2 = \alpha_0 + \mathbf{z}[t,.]\boldsymbol{\alpha}$. If observations on outcomes of ε_t^2 were available, it is clear that the parameters in (19.3.2) could be estimated by least squares, and then the hypothesis $\boldsymbol{\alpha} = \mathbf{0}$ could be tested using, say, a Wald or LM test. If an appropriate family of probability distributions for $\mathbf{V}_t$ could be assumed, a GLR test of $\boldsymbol{\alpha} = \mathbf{0}$ could also be performed.

Table 19.1. *Heteroscedasticity Tests[a] Based on Auxiliary Linear Regressions*

Name	Dependent Variable	Explanatory Variables	Asymptotic Chi-square Test Statistics	D.F.
Breusch–Pagan–Godfrey (BPG)	$\hat{\varepsilon}_t^2$	$z_t(1 \times m)$	nR_a^2	m
Harvey	$\ln(\hat{\varepsilon}_t^2)$	$z_t(1 \times m)$	$RSS_a/4.9348$	m
Glejser	$\lvert\hat{\varepsilon}_t\rvert$	$z_t(1 \times m)$	$RSS_a/\left[\left(1-\frac{2}{\pi}\right)\hat{\sigma}_a^2\right]$	m
Autoregressive Conditional	$\hat{\varepsilon}_t^2$	$\hat{\varepsilon}_{t-1}^2$	nR_a^2	1
Mean Conditional	$\hat{\varepsilon}_t^2$	$\hat{Y}_t$	nR_a^2	1
Squared-Mean Conditional	$\hat{\varepsilon}_t^2$	$\hat{Y}_t^2$	nR_a^2	1
Log Squared-Mean Conditional	$\hat{\varepsilon}_t^2$	$\ln(\hat{Y}_t^2)$	nR_a^2	1
White	$\hat{\varepsilon}_t^2$	Linear, squares, and cross products of columns in the $(1 \times k)x_t$, dropping any resulting linearly dependent vectors	nR_a^2	$\frac{k(k+1)}{2} - 1$

[a] All auxiliary regression models are assumed to have an intercept term. In White's test, if $\mathbf{x}_t$ does not initially include a 1, it is added and counted as one of the k entries in $\mathbf{x}_t$. The R_a^2, regression sum of squares $(RSS)_a$, and noise component variance estimates, $\hat{\sigma}_a^2$, all refer to the estimated auxiliary regression. The R_a^2 value is defined as $1 - (\hat{\mathbf{e}}_a'\hat{\mathbf{e}}_a/TSS_a)$, where TSS_a is the adjusted (by the mean) total sum of squares of the dependent variable in the auxiliary regression and $\hat{\mathbf{e}}_a$ is the estimated noise component of the auxiliary regression model. The regression sum of squares is equal to $TSS_a - \hat{\mathbf{e}}_a'\hat{\mathbf{e}}_a$. The $\hat{Y}_t = \mathbf{x}_{t\cdot}\hat{\boldsymbol{\beta}}$ or $g(\mathbf{x}_{t\cdot}, \hat{\boldsymbol{\beta}})$ refers to the original linear or nonlinear regression model.

To see why nR_a^2 can be used as an appropriate asymptotic Chi-square statistic, first recall that the Wald, GLR, and LM tests of $\boldsymbol{\alpha} = \mathbf{0}$ are asymptotically equivalent. Also recall that the LM test statistic can be written as

$$LM = \frac{\hat{\mathbf{V}}_r'\mathbf{w}(\mathbf{w}'\mathbf{w})^{-1}\mathbf{w}'\hat{\mathbf{V}}_r}{S_r^2} \overset{a}{\sim} \text{Chi-square}(m, 0), \tag{19.3.3}$$

where $\hat{\mathbf{V}}_r$ represents the estimated noise component of (19.3.2) under the restriction that $\boldsymbol{\alpha} = \mathbf{0}$, that is, $\hat{\mathbf{V}}_r = \varepsilon^2 - \hat{\alpha}_0\mathbf{1}$ with $\mathbf{1}$ a $(n \times 1)$ unit vector; S_r^2 is the restricted estimator of the noise component variance $\sigma^2 = \alpha_0$ under H_0, that is, $S_r^2 = n^{-1}\hat{\mathbf{V}}_r'\hat{\mathbf{V}}_r$, and $\mathbf{w} \equiv [\mathbf{1} \vdots \mathbf{z}]$. Now because the least-squares estimator of α_0 under the restriction $\boldsymbol{\alpha} = \mathbf{0}$ is given by $\hat{\alpha}_{0r} = \bar{\varepsilon}^2 = n^{-1}\sum_{i=1}^n \varepsilon_i^2$, it follows immediately that S_r^2 represents the total sum of squares ($\mathrm{TSS_a}$) of ε_i^2's around their mean divided by n, that is,

$$\mathrm{S}_{\mathrm{r}}^2 = n^{-1} \sum_{i=1}^{n} \left(\varepsilon_i^2 - \bar{\varepsilon}^2\right)^2 = n^{-1}\mathrm{TSS_a} \tag{19.3.4}$$

The numerator in (19.3.3) is equivalent to the regression sum of squares ($\mathrm{RSS_a}$) for the least-squares estimate of (19.3.2). To see this, first note that using the partitioned inverse of $(\mathbf{w}'\mathbf{w})$,

$$\hat{\mathbf{V}}_{\mathrm{r}}'\mathbf{w}(\mathbf{w}'\mathbf{w})^{-1}\mathbf{w}'\hat{\mathbf{V}}_{\mathrm{r}} = \hat{\mathbf{V}}_{\mathrm{r}}'[\mathbf{1} \,\vdots\, \mathbf{z}] \begin{bmatrix} \tau_{11} & \tau_{12} \\ \tau_{21} & \tau_{22} \end{bmatrix} \begin{bmatrix} \mathbf{1}' \\ \mathbf{z}' \end{bmatrix} \hat{\mathbf{V}}_{\mathrm{r}}, \tag{19.3.5}$$

where

$$\tau_{22} = [\mathbf{z}'\mathbf{z} - \mathbf{z}'\mathbf{1}(\mathbf{1}'\mathbf{1})^{-1}\mathbf{1}'\mathbf{z}]^{-1} = [\mathbf{z}'[\mathbf{I} - \mathbf{1}(\mathbf{1}'\mathbf{1})^{-1}\mathbf{1}']\mathbf{z}]^{-1} = [\mathbf{z}'\mathbf{m}_1\mathbf{z}]^{-1}. \tag{19.3.6}$$

Then, because $\hat{\mathbf{V}}_{\mathrm{r}}'\mathbf{1} = 0$,

$$\hat{\mathbf{V}}_{\mathrm{r}}'\mathbf{w}(\mathbf{w}'\mathbf{w})^{-1}\mathbf{w}'\hat{\mathbf{V}}_{\mathrm{r}} = \hat{\mathbf{V}}_{\mathrm{r}}'\mathbf{z}[\mathbf{z}'\mathbf{m}_1\mathbf{z}]^{-1}\mathbf{z}'\hat{\mathbf{V}}_{\mathrm{r}}. \tag{19.3.7}$$

Now note the following theorem:

Theorem 19.3.1 (Frisch–Waugh–Lovell (FWL) Theorem): *The LS estimates of $\boldsymbol{\beta}_2$, the estimates of the noise components, and the values of the error sum of squares for the models*

a. $\mathbf{Y} = \mathbf{x}_1\boldsymbol{\beta}_1 + \mathbf{x}_2\boldsymbol{\beta}_2 + \varepsilon$

b. $\mathbf{m}_1\mathbf{Y} = \mathbf{m}_1\mathbf{x}_2\boldsymbol{\beta}_2 + \mathbf{V},\ \mathbf{m}_1 = \mathbf{I} - \mathbf{x}_1(\mathbf{x}_1'\mathbf{x}_1)^{-1}\mathbf{x}_1'$,

are identical, where $\mathbf{x}_1$ and $\mathbf{x}_2$ are mutually exclusive submatrices of $\mathbf{x} = [\mathbf{x}_1, \mathbf{x}_2]$.

PROOF: Davidson and MacKinnon (1993), pp. 19–24.

The FWL theorem can be applied to (19.3.2) upon defining $\mathbf{Y} \equiv \varepsilon^2$, $\mathbf{x}_1 \equiv \mathbf{1}$, and $\mathbf{x}_2 \equiv \mathbf{z}$. Then, on the basis of part b of the FWL theorem, the error sum of squares ($\mathrm{ESS_a}$) of (19.3.2) can be represented as

$$\begin{aligned} \mathbf{ESS_a} &= [\mathbf{m}_1\varepsilon^2 - \mathbf{m}_1\mathbf{z}(\mathbf{z}'\mathbf{m}_1\mathbf{z})^{-1}\mathbf{z}'\mathbf{m}_1\varepsilon^2]'[\mathbf{m}_1\varepsilon^2 - \mathbf{m}_1\mathbf{z}(\mathbf{z}'\mathbf{m}_1\mathbf{z})^{-1}\mathbf{z}'\mathbf{m}_1\varepsilon^2] \\ &= [\hat{\mathbf{V}}_{\mathrm{r}} - \mathbf{m}_1\mathbf{z}(\mathbf{z}'\mathbf{m}_1\mathbf{z})^{-1}\mathbf{z}'\hat{\mathbf{V}}_{\mathrm{r}}]'[\hat{\mathbf{V}}_{\mathrm{r}} - \mathbf{m}_1\mathbf{z}(\mathbf{z}'\mathbf{m}_1\mathbf{z})^{-1}\mathbf{z}'\hat{\mathbf{V}}_{\mathrm{r}}] \\ &= \hat{\mathbf{V}}_{\mathrm{r}}'\hat{\mathbf{V}}_{\mathrm{r}} - \hat{\mathbf{V}}_{\mathrm{r}}'\mathbf{z}(\mathbf{z}'\mathbf{m}_1\mathbf{z})^{-1}\mathbf{z}'\hat{\mathbf{V}}_{\mathrm{r}}, \end{aligned} \tag{19.3.8}$$

where the second equality follows because $\hat{\mathbf{V}}_{\mathrm{r}} \equiv \mathbf{m}_1\varepsilon^2$, and the third equality is true because $\mathbf{m}_1\hat{\mathbf{V}}_{\mathrm{r}} \equiv \hat{\mathbf{V}}_{\mathrm{r}}$ because $\mathbf{1}'\hat{\mathbf{V}}_{\mathrm{r}} = 0$. Finally, because $\hat{\mathbf{V}}_{\mathrm{r}}'\hat{\mathbf{V}}_{\mathrm{r}}$ is the $\mathrm{TSS_a}$ for the dependent variable in (19.3.2), as demonstrated by (19.3.4), it follows that the regression sum of squares corresponding to (19.3.2) is given by

$$\mathrm{RSS_a} = \hat{\mathbf{V}}_{\mathrm{r}}'\hat{\mathbf{V}}_{\mathrm{r}} - \mathrm{ESS_a} = \hat{\mathbf{V}}_{\mathrm{r}}'\mathbf{z}[\mathbf{z}'\mathbf{m}_1\mathbf{z}]^{-1}\mathbf{z}'\hat{\mathbf{V}}_{\mathrm{r}}. \tag{19.3.9}$$

Then, from (19.3.3)–(19.3.9),

$$n\mathrm{R}_\mathrm{a}^2 = \mathrm{RSS_a}/[n^{-1}\mathrm{TSS_a}] = \mathrm{LM}. \tag{19.3.10}$$

Therefore, the LM test value is identical to the value of $n\mathrm{R}_\mathrm{a}^2$, and so an asymptotic level τ test of $\mathrm{H_0}: \sigma_t^2 = \sigma^2\ \forall t$ versus $\mathrm{H_a}: \sigma_t^2 = \alpha_0 + \mathbf{z}[t, .]\boldsymbol{\alpha}$ (recall 19.3.1) can be based on the test rule

$$\text{reject } \mathrm{H_0} \quad \text{iff} \quad n\mathrm{R}_\mathrm{a}^2 \geq \chi^2_{1-\tau,m},$$

where $\chi^2_{1-\tau,m}$ is the $100(1-\tau)\%$ quantile of the central Chi-square distribution with m degrees of freedom.

Of course the outcomes of ε_t^2, $t = 1, \ldots, n$ are generally unknown. To make the preceding test procedure operational, outcomes of ε_t^2 are estimated by the least-squares estimates, which in the case of a linear model are given by $\hat{\varepsilon}_t^2 = (\mathbf{Y}[t] - \mathbf{x}[t, .]\hat{\boldsymbol{\beta}})^2,\ \forall t$. The asymptotic properties of the test are unaltered by the substitution of $\hat{\varepsilon}_t^2$ for ε_t^2 under general regularity conditions assumed to hold in practice, whereby $\hat{\varepsilon}_t^2 \xrightarrow{p} \varepsilon_t^2,\ \forall t$.

Table 19.2 indicates the types of explanatory variables that enter the specification of the auxiliary regression (19.3.2). In these auxiliary regressions, $\hat{\mathbf{Y}}_t$ is a proxy for $\mathrm{E}[\mathbf{Y}_t]$, and $\hat{\varepsilon}_{t-1}^2$ is a proxy for ε_{t-1}^2 and σ_{t-1}^2. The underlying specification of $\mathrm{H_a}$ corresponding to each of these tests is given in Table 19.2. It is assumed in the table that when White's test is implemented, $\mathbf{x}$ contains a column of unit values, and if not, 1 is inserted before performing the test. Subsequent estimates of $\boldsymbol{\beta}$ based on an $\mathrm{H_a}$ in Table 19.2 are defined by utilizing estimates of the α_0's, $\boldsymbol{\alpha}$'s or $\mathbf{a}$, or all three, generating $\hat{\alpha}_t^2$'s from them, and then substituting the implied $\hat{\boldsymbol{\Psi}}$ into an EGLS estimator, or else under a normality assumption, estimating the parameters simultaneously by maximizing an appropriately parameterized likelihood function.

Table 19.2. *Alternative Hypotheses for Heteroscedasticity Tests*

TEST	$\mathrm{H_a}$
BPG	$\sigma_t^2 = \alpha_0 + \mathbf{z}[t, .]\boldsymbol{\alpha}$
Autoregressive Conditional	$\sigma_t^2 = \alpha_0 + \alpha_1\varepsilon_{t-1}^2$
Mean Conditional	$\sigma_t^2 = \alpha_0 + \alpha_1\mathrm{E}\mathbf{Y}_t$
Squared-Mean Conditional	$\sigma_t^2 = \alpha_0 + \alpha_1(\mathrm{E}\mathbf{Y}_t)^2$
Log Squared-Mean Conditional	$\sigma_t^2 = \alpha_0 + \alpha_1\ln(\mathrm{E}\mathbf{Y}_t^2)$
White[a]	$\sigma_t^2 = \mathbf{x}[t, .]\mathbf{a}\,\mathbf{x}[t, .]'$, where $\mathbf{a}$ is a symmetric $(k \times k)$ matrix.
Harvey	$\ln(\sigma_t^2) = \alpha_0 + \mathbf{z}[t, .]\boldsymbol{\alpha}$
Glejser	$\sigma_t = \alpha_0 + \mathbf{z}[t, .]\boldsymbol{\alpha}$

[a] It is assumed that $\mathbf{x}[t, .]$ contains a unit value in the implementation of White's test. If not, 1 is added so that the quadratic form subsumes an intercept term as well as linear functions of the nonunit values in $\mathbf{x}[t, .]$.

19.3.3. Motivation for the Test Based on $\ln(\hat{\varepsilon}_t^2)$

The form of the test statistic suggested by Harvey is much more closely tied to the assumption of normality than are the tests based on $\hat{\varepsilon}_t^2$. The initial form of the auxiliary regression for Harvey's test can be represented as

$$\begin{aligned}\ln(\varepsilon_t^2) &= \alpha_0 + \mathbf{z}[t,.]\boldsymbol{\alpha} + \ln\left(\varepsilon_t^2/\sigma_t^2\right)\\ &= \alpha_0 + \mathbf{z}[t,.]\boldsymbol{\alpha} + \mathrm{V}_t. \qquad (19.3.11)\end{aligned}$$

On the assumption that $\varepsilon_t \sim \mathrm{N}(0, \sigma_t^2)$ and also that the ε_t's are independent, it follows immediately that

$$\mathrm{E}(\mathrm{V}_t) = \mathrm{E}\left[\ln\left(\chi_1^2\right)\right] = -1.2704$$

and

$$\mathrm{var}(\mathrm{V}_t) = \mathrm{var}\left(\ln\left[\chi_1^2\right]\right) = 4.9348, \qquad (19.3.12)$$

where χ_1^2 is a central Chi-square random variable with 1 degree of freedom. We can then transform (19.3.11) so that it has a noise component with zero expectation as follows:

$$\begin{aligned}\ln(\varepsilon_t^2) &= (\alpha_0 - 1.2704) + \mathbf{z}[t,.]\boldsymbol{\alpha} + (\mathrm{V}_t + 1.2704)\\ &= \alpha_0^* + \mathbf{z}[t,.]\boldsymbol{\alpha} + \mathrm{V}_t^*, \qquad (19.3.13)\end{aligned}$$

and thus $\mathrm{E}(\mathrm{V}_t^*) = 0$ and $\mathrm{var}(\mathrm{V}_t^*) = 4.9348$. If it is assumed temporarily that outcomes of $\ln(\varepsilon_t^2)$ are observable, the least-square estimate of $\boldsymbol{\alpha}^* = (\alpha_0^* \vdots \boldsymbol{\alpha}')'$ is $\hat{\boldsymbol{\alpha}}^* = (\mathbf{w}'\mathbf{w})^{-1}\mathbf{w}'\ln(\boldsymbol{\varepsilon}^2)$ and $\mathbf{cov}(\hat{\boldsymbol{\alpha}}^*) = 4.9348(\mathbf{w}'\mathbf{w})^{-1}$, where $\mathbf{w} = (\mathbf{1} \vdots \mathbf{z})$.

A Wald test of H_0: $\boldsymbol{\alpha} = \mathbf{0}$, which coincides with the null hypothesis of homoscedasticity, can be defined by

$$\mathrm{W} = (\mathbf{c}\hat{\boldsymbol{\alpha}}^*)'[\mathbf{c}\,\mathbf{cov}(\hat{\boldsymbol{\alpha}}^*)\mathbf{c}']^{-1}(\mathbf{c}\hat{\boldsymbol{\alpha}}^*) = \hat{\boldsymbol{\alpha}}'[\mathbf{c}(\mathbf{w}'\mathbf{w})^{-1}\mathbf{c}']^{-1}\hat{\boldsymbol{\alpha}}/4.9348 \sim \text{Chi-square}(m, \lambda), \qquad (19.3.14)$$

where $\mathbf{c} = [\mathbf{0} \vdots \mathbf{I}_m]$, m is the number of columns in the z matrix, and $\hat{\boldsymbol{\alpha}}$ is $\hat{\boldsymbol{\alpha}}^*$, with the first element referring to the intercept parameter removed. The FWL theorem can be used analogously to the way it was used previously to demonstrate that the numerator of the Wald statistic in (19.3.14) is identical to the $\mathrm{RSS}_\mathbf{a}$ associated with the auxiliary regression model (19.3.13). Therefore, the Harvey test rule is given by

$$\text{reject } \mathrm{H}_0 \quad \text{iff} \quad \mathbf{w} = \mathrm{RSS}_\mathbf{a}/4.9348 \geq \chi^2_{1-\tau,\mathrm{m}}, \qquad (19.3.15)$$

where $\chi^2_{1-\tau,\mathrm{m}}$ is the $100(1-\tau)\%$ quantile of the central Chi-square distribution with m degrees of freedom.

Replacing $\ln(\varepsilon_t^2)$ with $\ln(\hat{\varepsilon}_t^2)$ maintains the asymptotic Chi-square distribution validity of the test under regularity conditions generally assumed to hold in practice, and because outcomes of $\ln(\varepsilon_t^2)$ are virtually never known, it is the asymptotically valid form of the test that is used in empirical work. In the absence of normality, the variance of V_t^* is not necessarily 4.9348, nor is the distribution of (19.3.14) necessarily Chi-square. The robustness of Harvey's test to departures from normality is open to question.

19.3.4. Motivation for Test Based on $|\hat{\varepsilon}_t|$

Like Harvey's test, the form of Glejser's test is also closely tied to the normality assumption. The form of the auxiliary regression for Glejser's test can be written initially as

$$|\varepsilon_t| = \alpha_0 + \mathbf{z}[t,.]\boldsymbol{\alpha} + (|\varepsilon_t| - \sigma_t). \tag{19.3.16}$$

On the assumption that $\varepsilon_t \sim \mathrm{N}(0, \sigma_t^2)$ and that the ε_t's are independent, it follows from properties of the normal distribution that

$$\mathrm{E}(|\varepsilon_t|) = (2/\pi)^{1/2}\sigma_t = \mathrm{a}\,\sigma_t, \tag{19.3.17}$$

and thus that $\mathrm{E}[|\varepsilon_t| - \sigma_t] = (\mathrm{a}-1)\sigma_t$. We can then transform (19.3.16) into a form in which the noise component has zero expectation as follows:

$$\begin{aligned} |\varepsilon_t| &= [\alpha_0 + (\mathrm{a}-1)\sigma_t] + \mathbf{z}[t,.]\boldsymbol{\alpha} + \mathrm{V}_t \\ &= [\alpha_0 + (\mathrm{a}-1)[\alpha_0 + \mathbf{z}[t,.]\boldsymbol{\alpha}]] + \mathbf{z}[t,.]\boldsymbol{\alpha} + \mathrm{V}_t \\ &= \mathrm{a}\,\alpha_0 + \mathbf{z}[t,.](\mathrm{a}\boldsymbol{\alpha}) + \mathrm{V}_t \\ &= \alpha_0^* + \mathbf{z}[t,.]\boldsymbol{\alpha}^* + \mathrm{V}_t, \end{aligned} \tag{19.3.18}$$

where $\mathrm{V}_t = |\varepsilon_t| - \mathrm{a}\,\sigma_t$. The hypothesis $\mathrm{H}_0\colon \boldsymbol{\alpha}^* = \mathbf{0}$ is thus equivalent to the hypothesis of homoscedasticity in Glejser's testing framework.

The noise component of the auxiliary regression model (19.3.18) is such that $\mathrm{E}[\mathrm{V}_t] = 0$ and, under the normality assumption,

$$\begin{aligned} \mathrm{var}(\mathrm{V}_t) = \mathrm{EV}_t^2 &= \mathrm{E}[|\varepsilon_t| - \mathrm{a}\sigma_t]^2 \\ &= \mathrm{E}(\varepsilon_t^2) - 2\mathrm{a}\sigma_t\mathrm{E}(|\varepsilon_t|) + \mathrm{a}^2\sigma_t^2 \\ &= \sigma_t^2(1-\mathrm{a}^2) \\ &= [\alpha_0 + \mathbf{z}[t,.]\boldsymbol{\alpha}]^2(1-\mathrm{a}^2). \end{aligned} \tag{19.3.19}$$

Then, under $\mathrm{H}_0\colon \alpha = 0$, it follows that $\mathrm{var}(\mathrm{V}_t) = \sigma^2(1-\mathrm{a}^2) = \alpha_0^2(1-\mathrm{a}^2)$, $\forall t$. Therefore, under H_0 the LS estimator of $\boldsymbol{\alpha}_\# = (\alpha_0^* \vdots \boldsymbol{\alpha}^{*\prime})'$ in (19.3.18), $\hat{\boldsymbol{\alpha}}_\# = (\mathbf{w}'\mathbf{w})^{-1}\mathbf{w}'|\varepsilon|$, is such that $\mathbf{cov}(\hat{\boldsymbol{\alpha}}_\#) = \alpha_0^2(1-\mathrm{a}^2)(\mathbf{w}'\mathbf{w})^{-1}$. A Wald test of $\boldsymbol{\alpha}^* = \mathbf{0}$, which is equivalent to a test of $\boldsymbol{\alpha} = \mathbf{0}$, can be defined as

$$\begin{aligned} \mathrm{w} &= (\mathbf{c}\hat{\boldsymbol{\alpha}}_\#)'[\mathbf{c}\,\mathbf{cov}(\hat{\boldsymbol{\alpha}}_\#)\mathbf{c}']^{-1}(\mathbf{c}\hat{\boldsymbol{\alpha}}_\#) \\ &= \frac{\hat{\boldsymbol{\alpha}}^{*\prime}[\mathbf{c}(\mathbf{w}'\mathbf{w})^{-1}\mathbf{c}']^{-1}\hat{\boldsymbol{\alpha}}^*}{\alpha_0^2(1-\mathrm{a}^2)} \\ &= \frac{\hat{\boldsymbol{\alpha}}^{*\prime}[\mathbf{c}(\mathbf{w}'\mathbf{w})^{-1}\mathbf{c}']^{-1}\hat{\boldsymbol{\alpha}}^*}{\alpha_0^2\left(1-\frac{2}{\pi}\right)}. \end{aligned} \tag{19.3.20}$$

Because under H_0 the equality $\sigma_t^2 = \sigma^2$ is true, we can use the estimated noise component of the auxiliary regression to estimate α_0^2 as $\hat{\alpha}_0^2 = \hat{\sigma}^2 = (\hat{\mathbf{V}}'\hat{\mathbf{V}})/[n(1-\frac{2}{\pi})]$.

In practice, the unobservable $|\varepsilon_t|$ is replaced by $|\hat{\varepsilon}_t|$, and α_0^2 is replaced by $\hat{\alpha}_0^2$, resulting in an asymptotically valid Chi-square test of homoscedasticity. Using the FWL theorem analogous to its previous two applications, one can show that the numerator of the Wald statistic (19.3.20) is the $\text{RSS}_{\mathbf{a}}$ for the estimated auxiliary regression (19.3.18), and thus the asymptotically valid τ-level test rule can be stated as

$$\text{reject } \text{H}_0 \quad \text{iff} \quad \mathbf{w} = \text{RSS}_{\mathbf{a}} \Big/ \left[\hat{\sigma}^2\left(1 - \frac{2}{\pi}\right)\right] \geq \chi^2_{1-\tau,\,\text{m}} \qquad (19.3.21)$$

where m is the number of (linearly independent) columns in z.

19.3.5. More Tests

Still other tests for heteroscedasticity exist. Two notable examples are the Goldfeld–Quandt test and the "peaks" test, which was also introduced by Goldfeld and Quandt (1965). The interested reader can consult Judge et al. (1985), Chapter 11, and Section 19.5.2, for further details. See also McCullough and Renfro (1999).

We emphasize that all of the preceding tests can be applied in the context of both linear and nonlinear regression models. The only essential difference in the application of these tests between applying them in linear and nonlinear model contexts is the genesis of the estimated noise component. The values for $\hat{\varepsilon}_t$ are obtained from a nonlinear least-squares or maximum likelihood estimator in the case of nonlinear models rather than from the ordinary linear least-squares estimator in the case of the linear model.

Although we have reviewed the principal heteroscedasticity tests used in empirical applications, there are many more possibilities for the specification of auxiliary regressions for modeling the structure of heteroscedasticity across observations. Unfortunately, this presents a formidable dilemma in practice, because if too many alternative models are tested, the analyst will eventually reject the hypothesis of homoscedasticity one or more times owing to an accumulation of Type-I error probabilities whether or not the noise component is truly heteroscedastic. Furthermore, it is possible that the analyst will conclude his or her testing exercise with more than one model being deemed acceptable by the hypothesis tests, but at most, only one can be correct. We remind the reader that there is always the option of using heteroscedasticity robust methods of testing hypothesis about $\boldsymbol{\beta}$ that avoid the necessity of specifying and making a decision about a specific structure for the heteroscedasticity. Otherwise, the analyst must at least be cognizant of the real possibility that he or she will be working with incorrectly specified probability models even after the testing process concludes.

► **Example 19.3.1:** The GAUSS program (C19Het.gss) examines the implications of using a battery of heteroscedasticity tests to detect the presence and type of shifts in the variance of the noise process. To begin, GAUSS briefly introduces a class of procedures designed to report the test statistics and asymptotic p-values for the tests described in Tables 19.1 and 19.2. Then, the user is asked to specify the type of heteroscedastic noise present in a linear regression model, and GAUSS reports the observed test statistics and asymptotic p-values for a single data sample. Next, the program conducts a Monte Carlo simulation of the probability of null hypothesis rejection for each test under the specified model. Finally, GAUSS simulates the probability that at least one of the tests will reject the null hypothesis under a homoscedastic probability model.

19.4. Tests for Autocorrelation: Rationale and Application

As in the case of heteroscedasticity, there are two basic reasons why analysts test for the presence of autocorrelation. One reason is to discern if there is any reason for using either the robust or parametric estimates of the noise covariance matrix, such as those introduced above and in Chapter 15, to perform inference or to implement EGLS estimation, or to do both. The other is to identify a particular structure of the autocorrelation for use in defining an EGLS estimator of the parameters of the model. If autocorrelation is deemed to exist in some form, one also has the option of using the Newey–West or other autocorrelation–heteroscedasticity robust covariance matrix estimators for testing and confidence-region estimation, which avoid the need for a particular specification of the autocorrelation–heteroscedasticity structure.

19.4.1. Autocorrelation Processes

Unlike the case of heteroscedasticity, there is more agreement among applied econometricians regarding the form of the alternative hypothesis if the null hypothesis of no autocorrelation in the noise component is rejected. In particular, the alternative hypotheses are generally taken to be some *autocorrelation process* of order m, AR(m), which is represented by

$$\varepsilon_t = \sum_{i=1}^{m} \rho_i \varepsilon_{t-i} + \mathrm{V}_t, \tag{19.4.1}$$

where V_t's are iid random variables with $\mathrm{EV}_t = 0$ and $\mathrm{var}(\mathrm{V}_t) = \sigma^2\ \forall t$, and the ρ_i's satisfy conditions that ensure that the difference equation inherent in (19.4.1) is convergent. Under these conditions the ε_t's are homoscedastic. Heteroscedasticity in the ε_t's is possible if the V_t's exhibit heteroscedasticity.

We note before proceeding further that, although there is significant professional consensus that autocorrelation processes represent interesting parametric representations for nonspherical covariance matrices, these are by no means the only alternative specifications possible for representing or parameterizing correlation dependence among the noise component elements of a model. The analyst is again only limited by his or her imagination as to the types of nonspherical covariance structures that might be hypothesized. In the absence of prior information to the contrary, the true pattern of noise-component dependence may not be defined by an autocorrelation process, regardless of whether the process happens to be used as the alternative hypothesis relative to a rejected null hypothesis of sphericity.

19.4.1.a. AR(1) Process

The way in which the parameters of the AR(m) in (19.4.1) relate to the covariance matrix of ε can be quite complicated, especially for large values of m. In particular, the process of establishing this relationship involves solving the difference equation (19.4.1) so as to express ε_t in terms of V_{t-i}'s, $i = 0, 1, 2 \ldots$, and then using this representation of the ε_t's to establish variances and covariances of the noise elements as expectations of functions of the V_{t-i}'s. For small values of m, the difference equation solution can be obtained via repeated backward substitution.

To illustrate the substitution procedure, consider the AR(1) case

$$\begin{aligned}
\varepsilon_t &= \rho\varepsilon_{t-1} + \mathrm{V}_t \\
&= \rho\,\underbrace{[\rho\varepsilon_{t-2} + \mathrm{V}_{t-1}]}_{\varepsilon_{t-1}} + \mathrm{V}_t \\
&= \rho\left[\underbrace{\rho\,\underbrace{[\rho\varepsilon_{t-3} + \mathrm{V}_{t-2}]}_{\varepsilon_{t-2}} + \mathrm{V}_{t-1}}_{\varepsilon_{t-1}}\right] + \mathrm{V}_t \\
&\;\;\vdots \\
&= \sum_{i=0}^{\infty} \rho^i \mathrm{V}_{t-i} \quad \text{if } \rho^i \to 0 \text{ as } i \to \infty. \qquad (19.4.2)
\end{aligned}$$

It is evident that for the solution in (19.4.2) to exist, or in other words for the difference equation to be convergent, the condition $|\rho| < 1$ is necessary and sufficient.

From the solution in (19.4.2), we can now derive the relationship between the parameters in (19.4.2) and the parameterization of the entries in $\mathbf{cov}(\varepsilon) = \boldsymbol{\Psi}(\rho)$ for an autoregressive process with $m = 1$. Regarding the diagonal variance entries, because $\mathrm{E}\varepsilon_t = \sum_{i=0}^{\infty} \rho^i \mathrm{E}\mathrm{V}_{t-i} = 0$, we have by the iid nature of the V_t's that

$$\mathrm{cov}(\varepsilon_t, \varepsilon_{t-j}) = \mathrm{E}\left[\left(\sum_{i=0}^{\infty} \rho^i \mathrm{V}_{t-i} \sum_{i=0}^{\infty} \rho^i \mathrm{V}_{t-j-i}\right)\right] = \sigma^2 \sum_{i=0}^{\infty} \rho^{j+2i} = \sigma^2\left(\frac{\rho^j}{1-\rho^2}\right), \quad \forall j \geq 1 \qquad (19.4.3)$$

Note the bandlike pattern of the entries in the covariance matrix $\boldsymbol{\Psi}(\rho)$, which has already been displayed in (19.2.3). The diagonal elements of the matrix (where $j = 0$) are all equal to $\sigma^2(1-\rho^2)^{-1}$. The first "band" of entries parallel and either above or below the diagonal (where $j = 1$) are all equal to $\sigma^2\rho/(1-\rho^2)$. The second band of entries above and below the diagonal (where $j = 2$) are all equal to $\sigma^2\rho^2/(1-\rho^2)$; and so on. Such a special banded matrix is called a *Toeplitz* matrix.

19.4.1.b. AR(m) Process

The Toeplitz nature of the $\boldsymbol{\Psi}(\rho)$ matrix under AR(m) for $m = 1$ models also applies when $m > 1$. In particular, under all convergent AR(m) models of the type (19.4.1) the value of the covariance between ε_t and ε_{t-j} will depend only on the value of j. This property is referred to as *covariance stationarity*. An overview of the general method for defining the relationship between the parameters of a convergent AR(m) process and the entries in $\boldsymbol{\Psi}(\rho)$ is as follows. First of all, the necessary and sufficient condition for the difference equation (19.4.1) to possess a convergent solution is that the roots,

$\tau_1, \ldots, \tau_m$, of the polynomial equation (define $\rho_0 \equiv 1$)

$$\tau^m - \sum_{i=1}^{m} \rho_i \tau^{m-i} = \tau^m - \rho_1 \tau^{m-1} - \rho_2 \tau^{m-2} - \cdots - \rho_m = 0 \qquad (19.4.4)$$

are such that

$$|\tau_i| < 1 \qquad \text{for } i = 1, 2, \ldots, m. \qquad (19.4.5)$$

When $m = 1$, the convergence condition is equivalent to $|\rho| < 1$, and when $m = 2$ the convergence condition is equivalent to $\rho_1 + \rho_2 < 1$, $\rho_2 - \rho_1 < 1$, and $\rho_2 > -1$. Note that the values of the roots of a polynomial equation such as (19.4.4) can be obtained numerically, such as through the use of the polyroot() procedure in GAUSS.

Under the convergence conditions (19.4.4) and (19.4.5) the solution to the difference Equation (19.4.1) has the form

$$\varepsilon_t = \sum_{i=0}^{\infty} \zeta_i(\boldsymbol{\rho}) \mathrm{V}_{t-i}, \qquad (19.4.6)$$

where the $\boldsymbol{\zeta}(\boldsymbol{\rho})$ values are functions of the $(m \times 1)$ vector $\boldsymbol{\rho} = (\rho_1, \rho_2, \ldots, \rho_m)'$. The elements of $\boldsymbol{\zeta}(\boldsymbol{\rho})$ can be determined by solving the following set of linear equations:

$$\begin{aligned}
&\zeta_0 &&= 1 \\
&\zeta_1 - \rho_1 \zeta_0 &&= 0 \\
&\zeta_2 - \rho_1 \zeta_1 - \rho_2 \zeta_0 &&= 0 \\
& &&\ \vdots \\
&\zeta_m - \rho_1 \zeta_{m-1} \ldots - \rho_{m-2} \zeta_2 - \rho_{m-1} \zeta_1 - \rho_m \zeta_0 &&= 0 \\
&\zeta_{m+\tau} - \sum_{i=1}^{m} \rho_i \zeta_{m-i+\tau} &&= 0, \quad \text{for } \tau = 1, 2, 3, \ldots.
\end{aligned} \qquad (19.4.7)$$

The equations can be solved recursively for the ζ_i values. If we return to the case in which $m = 1$, and let $\rho_1 = \rho$, the solutions prescribed by (19.4.7) take the form $\zeta_0 = 1$, $\zeta_1 = \rho\zeta_0 = \rho$, $\zeta_2 = \rho\zeta_1 = \rho^2$, and in general, $\zeta_j = \rho^j$. Then the solution to the AR(1) process suggested by (19.4.6) equals $\varepsilon_t = \sum_{i=0}^{\infty} \rho^i \mathrm{V}_{t-i}$, which is identical to our solution obtained via backward substitution earlier and implies the covariance matrix structure for ε given by (19.4.3) and (19.2.3).

Analytical solutions to higher-order autoregressive processes get progressively more complex, as the reader will discover should he or she define the convergent solution to the case where $m = 2$ or larger (see Judge et al., 1985, pp. 293–99, for additional details). However, *numerical* solutions for the ζ_i's, given a value of $\boldsymbol{\rho}$, are not difficult because $|\zeta_i| \to 0$ as $i \to \infty$ for convergent solutions, and thus the recursive solution for the ζ_i's can be halted for large enough i to achieve solutions within an a priori prescribed level of tolerance. In the general AR(m) case the entries in $\mathbf{cov}(\varepsilon) = \boldsymbol{\Psi}(\boldsymbol{\rho})$ are characterized by

$$\mathrm{var}(\varepsilon_t) = \sigma^2 \sum_{i=0}^{\infty} \zeta_i^2(\boldsymbol{\rho}) \qquad (19.4.8)$$

and

$$\operatorname{cov}(\varepsilon_t, \varepsilon_{t-j}) = \sigma^2 \sum_{i=0}^{\infty} \zeta_i(\rho)\zeta_{i-j}(\rho), \tag{19.4.9}$$

where both infinite sums in (19.4.8) and (19.4.9) converge to a fixed finite limit, and $\operatorname{cov}(\varepsilon_t, \varepsilon_{t+j}) \to 0$ as $j \to \infty$ so that noise component elements spaced far enough apart in the sequence $\{\varepsilon_n\}$ approach zero correlation (as well as independence under multivariate normality).

► **Example 19.4.1:** To demonstrate the concepts related to AR(m) processes, we provide the GAUSS program C19ARM.gss on the CD. First, the user is asked to select the number of lags (m) and the associated vector ρ, and GAUSS uses the polyroot() procedure to check the stationarity of the specified process. Then, the elements of $\zeta(\rho)$ are determined by the recursive relationship (19.4.7). Finally, we recover the matrix $\Psi(\rho)$ from the provided information and show how the matrix can be used to generate pseudorandom noise components consistent with the AR(m) process.

19.4.2. Estimation

On the assumption that the analyst had prior information about the appropriate noise component lags required to specify the structure of the autocorrelation process correctly and also if it is assumed that a consistent estimator $\hat{\rho}$ of the vector ρ is available, EGLS estimation of $\boldsymbol{\beta}$ could be performed based on the estimated covariance matrix $\Psi(\hat{\rho})$. Alternatively, ρ and $\boldsymbol{\beta}$ could be estimated simultaneously based on NLS or ML procedures applied to the transformed model

$$[\Psi(\rho)]^{-1/2}\mathbf{Y} = [\Psi(\rho)]^{-1/2}\mathbf{x}\boldsymbol{\beta} + [\Psi(\rho)]^{-1/2}\varepsilon. \tag{19.4.10}$$

Further details on estimating (19.4.10) for $m = 1$ or 2 can be found in Section 19.2.1.a and Judge et al., 1985, Section 10.2.

The preceding approach applies equally well to nonlinear regression models. In fact, all that would need to be changed is the very last expression (19.4.10), where the transformed model would become

$$[\Psi(\rho)]^{-1/2}\mathbf{Y} = [\Psi(\rho)]^{-1/2}\mathbf{g}(\mathbf{x}, \boldsymbol{\beta}) + [\Psi(\rho)]^{-1/2}\varepsilon. \tag{19.4.11}$$

Extensions to systems of linear or nonlinear regression equations can also be readily accomplished, in which case the preceding discussion, as well as the transformation of the model analogous to (19.4.10) and (19.4.11) would be interpreted in a blockwise fashion, each block representing an equation in the system. Allowances for intercorrelations of noise components across equations can also be introduced into the autocorrelation process. Some results for the AR(1) case, as well as additional references, can be found in Judge et al., 1985, Section 12.3.

Having discussed some of the principal properties of AR(m) processes and associated noise covariance matrix parameterizations, we now turn to some testing procedures that have been used in practice in attempts to obtain information about the existence or structure, or both, of the autocorrelation process associated with the noise component.

19.4.3. Autocorrelation Tests

A substantial amount of literature has been devoted to devising tests for the presence of autocorrelation in the noise component of regression models. As originally presented, these tests were in the form of various specialized test statistics whose asymptotic distributions were either Chi-square or some other specific distribution. However, unlike the literature devoted to heteroscedasticity tests in which a myriad of different forms for the alternative hypotheses are deemed possible, focusing attention on the set of specific alternative hypotheses of the form (19.4.1) leads to an objective of devising the best type of test (i.e., the most powerful) against alternatives of the AR(m) form. Suffice it to say that no particular test has yet been judged to be unequivocally best, and thus the analyst is still in the unenviable position of considering a varied collection of test procedures for detecting the presence or structure, or both, of autocorrelation. Before proceeding, we repeat that, although autocorrelation processes have been the most popular alternatives to sphericity when analyzing dependence among noise component elements, popularity does not necessarily equate to validity. It is important to realize that there are a myriad of other specifications of dependence that are conceptually possible.

There are principally two different types of auxiliary regression models that are most often used to test for the presence of mth order autocorrelation in the linear model case. In the case of linear models, these auxiliary regression specifications are given by

$$\mathbf{Y}_t = \mathbf{x}_{t}.\boldsymbol{\beta} + \sum_{i=1}^{m} \rho_i \varepsilon_{t-i} + \mathrm{V}_t \tag{19.4.12}$$

and

$$\varepsilon_t = \rho_i \varepsilon_{t-i} + \mu_t. \tag{19.4.13}$$

Under the null hypothesis of no autocorrelation, $\rho_i = 0,\ \forall i$, in which case $\mathrm{V}_t = \mu_t = \varepsilon_t$ in (19.4.12) and (19.4.13).

If the outcomes of ε_{t-i} were observable, one could then obtain the LS or ML estimate of (19.4.12) and (19.4.13) and test the hypothesis H_0: $\rho_1 = \rho_2 = \cdots = \rho_m = 0$ using a Wald, GLR, or LM test. In the absence of observations on ε_{t-i}, consistent estimates of the noise component outcomes are used in place of ε_{t-i} outcomes such as the estimates based on a least-square fit to the model $\hat{\boldsymbol{\varepsilon}} = \mathbf{Y} - \mathbf{x}\hat{\boldsymbol{\beta}}_{\mathrm{LS}}$. Given that observations for $\mathbf{y}_t$ and $\mathbf{x}_t$. exist only for $t = 1, \ldots, n$, it is clear that $\hat{\varepsilon}_0, \hat{\varepsilon}_{-1}, \ldots, \hat{\varepsilon}_{-m}$ will not be available. In this case, the missing ε_{t-i}'s can be replaced by their expected value of zero. Define $\hat{\boldsymbol{\varepsilon}}_{(-i)}$ to be the $(n \times 1)$ vector for which

$$\hat{\varepsilon}_{(-i)}[j] = \begin{cases} \hat{\varepsilon}_{j-i} & \text{if } j > i \\ 0 & \text{otherwise} \end{cases} \tag{19.4.14}$$

so that, for example, $\hat{\varepsilon}_{(-2)} = [0\,0\,\hat{\varepsilon}_1\hat{\varepsilon}_2 \cdots \hat{\varepsilon}_{n-2}]'$. The auxiliary regression used to test H_0 is then

$$\mathbf{Y} = \mathbf{x}\boldsymbol{\beta} + \sum_{i=1}^{m} \rho_i \hat{\varepsilon}_{(-i)} + \mathbf{V}. \tag{19.4.15}$$

The test statistics used to test hypotheses about $\boldsymbol{\rho}$, and thus about the order of the autocorrelation process, are the standard ones discussed in Chapters 4 and 6 and are asymptotically valid.

► **Example 19.4.2:** To demonstrate the autocorrelation test based on the auxiliary regression model (19.4.15), we provide the GAUSS program C19AUX.gss in the examples manual. For a given sample, the estimated noise components $\hat{\varepsilon}$, the auxiliary regression results, and the Wald test of H_0 are reported by GAUSS. Then, the power function of the Wald test is estimated by Monte Carlo simulation and compared with the limiting power function for $n \to \infty$.

Breusch (1978) and Godfrey (1978) suggested a variation on the use of (19.4.15) in which $\mathbf{x}\hat{\boldsymbol{\beta}}$ is subtracted from both sides of (19.4.15) to yield

$$\hat{\varepsilon} = \mathbf{x}\boldsymbol{\tau} + \sum_{i=1}^{m} \rho_i \hat{\varepsilon}_{(-i)} + \mathbf{V}, \tag{19.4.16}$$

where $\boldsymbol{\tau} = \boldsymbol{\beta} - \hat{\boldsymbol{\beta}}$. By using the FWL theorem analogously to how it was utilized in deriving (19.3.10), it follows that the LM test of H_0: $\rho_i = 0,\ \forall i$ can be conducted using the R_a^2 from the fit of the auxiliary regression (19.4.16) as follows:

$$\text{reject } H_0 \quad \text{iff} \quad nR_a^2 \geq \chi^2_{1-\tau,m}, \tag{19.4.17}$$

where $\chi^2_{1-\tau,m}$ is the $(1-\tau)$th quantile of the central Chi-square distribution with m degrees of freedom. Engle (1984, p. 806) notes that because $\operatorname{p\,lim}(\mathbf{x}'\hat{\varepsilon}_{(-i)}) = \mathbf{0}$ as $n \to \infty$ for $i = 1, 2, \ldots,$ so that $\mathbf{X}$ and the $\hat{\varepsilon}_{(-i)}$'s are asymptotically orthogonal the $\mathbf{x}$ matrix can be dropped from the right-hand side of (19.4.16) without having any effect on the asymptotic properties of the test. Monte Carlo evidence provided by Mizon and Hendry (1980) suggest that the Breusch–Godfrey test behaves quite favorably in small samples. However, Kiviet (1986) and Spencer (1975) recommend the use of an F-statistic and quantiles of the F-distribution with m and $(n-m)$ degrees of freedom instead of (19.4.17) on the basis of superior Monte Carlo performance when the systematic component of the regression model is overspecified.

Durbin and Watson (1950, 1951) defined a test for *first-order* autocorrelation based originally on the test statistic

$$D = \sum_{i=2}^{n} (\hat{\varepsilon}_i - \hat{\varepsilon}_{i-1})^2 \Big/ \sum_{i=1}^{n} \hat{\varepsilon}_i^2 = \hat{\varepsilon}'\mathbf{a}\hat{\varepsilon}/\hat{\varepsilon}'\hat{\varepsilon} \tag{19.4.18}$$

and assumed *normality* for the noise component. The matrix $\mathbf{a}$ is a Toeplitz-like $(n \times n)$ banded matrix with -1's on the first off-diagonal bands, 2's on the diagonal band except for unit values in the (1, 1) and (n, n) positions, and zeros everywhere else, as follows:

$$\mathbf{a} \equiv \begin{bmatrix} 1 & -1 & & & & & \\ -1 & 2 & -1 & & & & \\ & -1 & 2 & \ddots & & & \\ & & -1 & \ddots & -1 & & \\ & & & \ddots & 2 & -1 & \\ & & & & -1 & 2 & -1 \\ & & & & & -1 & 1 \end{bmatrix}. \tag{19.4.19}$$

The finite sample distribution of DW under H_0 is quite complicated and depends on the value of the **x** matrix, which is assumed *not* to contain lagged values of the dependent variable. Durbin and Watson (1951) provided tables of bounds for the statistic to facilitate applications of the test. However, these table values include inconclusive ranges of values for DW in which no decision regarding H_0 can be made. The DW test is a two-sided test that rejects the null hypothesis of no first-order autocorrelation if DW is *outside of* the range $(d_\ell, 4 - d_\ell)$, where the interval bounds are available in DW tables (Durbin and Watson, 1951) and $d_\ell < 2$. For example, the test rejects the null hypothesis under the alternative hypothesis of positive autocorrelation if $d < d_\ell$. The test has an "inconclusive" region represented by the interval $(d_u, 4 - d_u)$, the central tendency of DW being asymptotically 2.

From results presented by Imhof (1961) and given the power of modern PCs, it is now not difficult to calculate cumulative distribution function values for DW under the normality assumption and thus determine the exact probability values of DW tests. In particular, for a given value of $d \in [0, 4]$ (this interval represents the asymptotically admissible range of d),

$$\mathrm{P}(\mathrm{DW} \leq d) = \frac{1}{2} - \frac{1}{\pi} \int_0^\infty \frac{\sin[\mathrm{e(w)}]}{\mathrm{wg(w)}}\, \mathrm{dw} \tag{19.4.20}$$

where

$$\begin{aligned} \mathrm{e(w)} &\equiv \frac{1}{2} \sum_{i=1}^{n} [\tan^{-1}(\lambda_i \mathrm{w})] \\ \mathrm{g(w)} &\equiv \left[\prod_{i=1}^{n} \left(1 + \lambda_i^2 \mathrm{w}^2\right) \right]^{.25}, \end{aligned} \tag{19.4.21}$$

and the λ_i's are the n eigenvalues of the matrix $\mathbf{h} = \mathbf{mam} - \mathrm{d}\mathbf{m}$, with $\mathbf{m} = \mathbf{I} - \mathbf{x}(\mathbf{x}'\mathbf{x})^{-1}\mathbf{x}'$ and **a** as defined in (19.4.19). In the numerical calculation of (19.4.20), one can truncate ∞ to the value

$$u = \left[\frac{\zeta \sum_{i=1}^{n_r} |\lambda_i|^{1/2} \pi n_r}{2} \right]^{-(2/n_r)}, \tag{19.4.22}$$

where n_r is the number of nonzero λ_i's with the assurance that $\mathrm{P}(\mathrm{DW} \leq d)$ is calculated to within ζ (e.g., $\zeta = .001$) of the true value, that is, less than ζ of the value of the integral has been truncated. In calculating the integrand values in (19.4.20), it is also useful to note that $\lim_{w \to 0} \frac{\sin[e(w)]}{wg(w)} = (\sum_{i=1}^{n_r} \lambda_i)/2$.

► **Example 19.4.3:** The purpose of the GAUSS program C19DW.gss provided in the examples manual is to demonstrate the computation of DW tail probabilities with the DW() procedure. Then, a Monte Carlo exercise is used to simulate the tail probabilities of the test statistic for a given AR(1) model, and the results are compared to the results from (19.4.20).

The reader is reminded that both the tabled bounds and the preceding exact CDF calculations for DW are based on the assumption that under H_0, the ε_t's are iid $N(0, \sigma^2)$. Thus, even the exact CDF calculations become *approximate* when normality for ε does not hold. The accuracy of the approximation in such cases is unknown unless prior information about the distribution of the noise component is available so that the accuracy of the approximation can be investigated.

Asymptotically, the DW test is equivalent to a test based on an inverse auxiliary regression relative to (19.4.1) with $m = 1$. To see this, note that the DW statistic can be written as

$$DW = \frac{\sum_{t=2}^{n} \left(\hat{\varepsilon}_t + \hat{\varepsilon}_{t-1}^2 - 2\hat{\varepsilon}_t\hat{\varepsilon}_{t-1}\right)}{\sum_{t=1}^{n} \hat{\varepsilon}_t^2}. \tag{19.4.23}$$

Because $\sum_{t=2}^{n} \hat{\varepsilon}_t^2 / \sum_{t=1}^{n} \hat{\varepsilon}_t^2$ and $\sum_{t=2}^{n} \hat{\varepsilon}_{t-1}^2 / \sum_{t=1}^{n} \hat{\varepsilon}_t^2$ each $\to 1$ as $n \to \infty$, and because $\sum_{t=2}^{n} \hat{\varepsilon}_t\hat{\varepsilon}_{t-1} / \sum_{t=1}^{n} \hat{\varepsilon}_t^2 \to \hat{r}$, then $DW \approx 2(1 - \hat{r})$, where $\hat{r}$ is the LS estimate of r in the inverse auxiliary regression model

$$\hat{\varepsilon}_{(-1)} = r\hat{\varepsilon} + \mathbf{V}. \tag{19.4.24}$$

Testing $H_0: r = 0$ is then (asymptotically) equivalent to testing that DW is significantly different from the value 2, which is effectively Durbin and Watson's original test for AR(1) noise. We note that testing the significance of r in (19.4.24) *does not require normality*, which suggests that an asymptotic Z or T-test (based on 19.4.24) may be preferred when the normality assumption is not appropriate. A variation on the DW test is available, called the Durbin h test, for models containing lagged dependent variables as explanatory variables (see Durbin, 1970), and in this case (19.4.24) also applies given consistent estimates of the noise component elements, which will generally be obtained via an application of an instrumental variable procedure (recall the comments made at the end of Section 19.2.1.a).

Box and Pierce (BP) (1970) and Ljung and Box (BL) (1978) suggested tests of H_0: $\rho_i = 0, i = 1, \ldots, m$ that are also asymptotically equivalent to tests based on inverse auxiliary regression models of the form

$$\hat{\varepsilon}_{(-i)} = r_i\hat{\varepsilon} + V_i, \quad i = 1, 2, \ldots, m. \tag{19.4.25}$$

As in the case of the DW test, the original BP and BL tests rely on the normality of ε for their small sample properties and assume no lagged dependent explanatory variables. Box and Pierce show that

$$\mathrm{BP} = n \sum_{i=1}^{m} \hat{\mathrm{R}}_i^2 \overset{a}{\sim} \chi^2_m, \tag{19.4.26}$$

where $\hat{\mathrm{R}}_i$ is the LS estimator of r_i in the inverse auxiliary regression (19.4.25). The test of H_0 is conducted based on the decision rule

$$\text{reject } \mathrm{H}_0 \quad \text{iff} \quad \mathrm{BP} \geq \chi^2_{(1-\tau),\, m} \tag{19.4.27}$$

resulting in an asymptotic level-τ test of H_0.

Ljung and Box (1978) introduced a modified test of H_0 whose finite sample distribution is more closely approximated by the central Chi-square distribution under H_0. In particular, the BL statistic is defined by

$$\mathrm{BL} = n(n+2) \sum_{i=1}^{n} \left[\hat{\mathrm{R}}_i^2/(n-i)\right] \overset{a}{\sim} \text{Chi-square}(m, 0) \text{ under } \mathrm{H}_0. \tag{19.4.28}$$

The test of H_0 would be conducted as in (19.4.27) with BL replacing BP. Given the closer adherence to its asymptotic distribution, the BL test is generally preferable to the BP test for applied work involving relatively small sample sizes.

All of the preceding autocorrelation tests can be applied to nonlinear models. The only changes required are that the estimated noise components be obtained from NLS or nonlinear ML estimation, and terms of the general form $\mathbf{x}\boldsymbol{\tau}$, as in (19.4.12) or (19.4.16), be replaced by $\mathbf{g}(\mathbf{x}, \boldsymbol{\tau})$. Furthermore, the exact CDF results for the DW statistic can no longer be applied, and thus the DW approach becomes approximate even under normality. Applications to equation systems can be made either by applying the procedures blockwise to each equation in the system if noise components are uncorrelated across equations or else by extending the procedures to accommodate cross-equation correlation. See Judge et al. (1985), Section 12.3, and Srivastava and Giles (1987, Chapter 7) for additional details. Additional tests continue to be developed, and a promising new type of autocorrelation test based on partial sums of lagged cross products of regression residuals has recently been suggested by Gooijer and MacNeill (1999).

19.5. Pretest Estimators Defined by Heteroscedasticity or Autocorrelation Testing

To provide cautionary insights relative to the use of heteroscedasticity and autocorrelation tests for statistical model selection, we now report some of the statistical implications of making use of these tests in finite samples for model selection. We examine two cases. In the first case we specify and evaluate, under a squared-error loss measure, the sampling properties of alternative estimators for the parameter vector of a system of two linear regression equations involving two samples of data with unknown and possibly different scale parameters. In the second case, we examine empirical issues relating to a single-equation linear regression model when attempting to choose an autocorrelation model structure based on a preliminary test of an autocorrelation hypothesis.

19.5.1. Two-Equation Linear System with Potential Heteroscedasticity

Consider the following linear model:

$$\mathbf{Y} = \begin{bmatrix} \mathbf{Y}_1 \\ \mathbf{Y}_2 \end{bmatrix} = \begin{bmatrix} \mathbf{x}_1 \\ \mathbf{x}_2 \end{bmatrix} \boldsymbol{\beta} + \begin{bmatrix} \varepsilon_1 \\ \varepsilon_2 \end{bmatrix} = \mathbf{x}\boldsymbol{\beta} + \varepsilon. \tag{19.5.1}$$

For expository purposes, we assume each of the observable normally distributed random vectors $\mathbf{Y}_1$ and $\mathbf{Y}_2$ has dimension $(n \times 1)$ and that each of the known $(n \times k)$ explanatory variable matrices $\mathbf{x}_1$ and $\mathbf{x}_2$ have been transformed to satisfy the orthonormal condition $\mathbf{x}_1'\mathbf{x}_1 = \mathbf{x}_2'\mathbf{x}_2 = \mathbf{I}_k$. In addition, $\boldsymbol{\beta}$ is a $(k \times 1)$ vector of unknown parameters, and ε_1 and ε_2 are unobservable $(n \times 1)$ normal random vectors with mean vector 0 and covariance matrix

$$\mathrm{E}[\varepsilon\varepsilon'] = \boldsymbol{\Psi} = \begin{bmatrix} \sigma_1^2\mathbf{I}_n & 0 \\ 0 & \sigma_2^2\mathbf{I}_n \end{bmatrix}, \tag{19.5.2}$$

or compactly $\varepsilon \sim \mathrm{N}(\mathbf{0}, \boldsymbol{\Psi})$.

If $\sigma^2 = \sigma_1^2 = \sigma_2^2$, the maximum likelihood (ML) estimator of $\boldsymbol{\beta}$ is $\hat{\boldsymbol{\beta}} = (\tilde{\boldsymbol{\beta}}_1 + \tilde{\boldsymbol{\beta}}_2)/2$ and is distributed $\mathrm{N}[\boldsymbol{\beta}, (\sigma^2/2)\mathbf{I}_k]$, where $\tilde{\boldsymbol{\beta}}_i = \mathbf{x}_i'\mathbf{Y}_i$. For this traditional specification, $\hat{\boldsymbol{\beta}}$ is minimum variance unbiased and, under squared-error loss, is minimax with risk equal to

$$\rho(\boldsymbol{\beta}, \hat{\boldsymbol{\beta}}) = \mathrm{E}[(\hat{\boldsymbol{\beta}} - \boldsymbol{\beta})'(\hat{\boldsymbol{\beta}} - \boldsymbol{\beta})] = (\sigma^2/2)k. \tag{19.5.3}$$

If we let $\lambda = \sigma_1^2/\sigma_2^2$, then, when $\lambda \neq 1$, the ML–LS estimator $\hat{\boldsymbol{\beta}}$ is distributed as

$$\hat{\boldsymbol{\beta}} \sim \mathrm{N}\big[\boldsymbol{\beta}, \big[(\sigma_1^2 + \sigma_2^2)/4\big]\mathrm{I}_k\big] = \mathrm{N}\big[\boldsymbol{\beta}, \sigma_2^2[(1+\lambda)/4]\mathrm{I}_k\big] \tag{19.5.4}$$

and under squared-error loss has risk

$$\rho(\boldsymbol{\beta}, \hat{\boldsymbol{\beta}}) = \sigma_2^2[(1+\lambda)/4]k. \tag{19.5.5}$$

If the variance parameters are known, the GLS estimator

$$\begin{aligned} \hat{\boldsymbol{\beta}}_{\mathrm{G}}(\boldsymbol{\Psi}) &= (\mathbf{x}'\boldsymbol{\Psi}^{-1}\mathbf{x})^{-1}\mathbf{x}'\boldsymbol{\Psi}^{-1}\mathbf{Y} \\ &= \big[\sigma_1^2\sigma_2^2/(\sigma_1^2 + \sigma_2^2)\big]\big[(1/\sigma_1^2)\mathbf{x}_1'\mathbf{Y}_1 + (1/\sigma_2^2)\mathbf{x}_2'\mathbf{Y}_2\big] \end{aligned} \tag{19.5.6}$$

is distributed

$$\hat{\boldsymbol{\beta}}_{\mathrm{G}} \sim \mathrm{N}\big[\boldsymbol{\beta}, \big[\sigma_1^2\sigma_2^2/(\sigma_1^2 + \sigma_2^2)\big]\mathbf{I}_k\big] = \mathrm{N}\big[\boldsymbol{\beta}, \big[\sigma_2^2\lambda/(1+\lambda)\big]\mathbf{I}_k\big]. \tag{19.5.7}$$

This estimator (19.5.6) is a minimum variance unbiased estimator of $\boldsymbol{\beta}$ under the stated problem conditions. Under a squared-error loss measure of performance, the estimator $\hat{\boldsymbol{\beta}}_{\mathrm{G}}$ has risk

$$\rho(\boldsymbol{\beta}, \hat{\boldsymbol{\beta}}_{\mathrm{G}}) = \big[\sigma_2^2\lambda/(1+\lambda)\big]k. \tag{19.5.8}$$

When the variance parameters are equal, the risk simplifies to $(\sigma^2/2)k$ and equals the risk for the ML–LS estimator $\hat{\boldsymbol{\beta}}$. When $0 \leq (\sigma_1^2/\sigma_2^2) = \lambda < \infty$, these risk results imply that

$$\rho(\boldsymbol{\beta}, \hat{\boldsymbol{\beta}}_{\mathrm{G}}) = \sigma_2^2[\lambda/(1+\lambda)]k \leq \rho(\boldsymbol{\beta}, \hat{\boldsymbol{\beta}}) = \sigma_2^2[(1+\lambda)/4]k \tag{19.5.9}$$

or

$$\rho(\boldsymbol{\beta}, \hat{\boldsymbol{\beta}})/\rho(\boldsymbol{\beta}, \hat{\boldsymbol{\beta}}_G) \geq 1. \qquad (19.5.10)$$

If the scale parameters are unknown so that the use of $\hat{\boldsymbol{\beta}}_G$ is not feasible, and if one suspects $\lambda \neq 1$, one possibility is to use the sample data as a basis for estimating the unknown scale parameters. This process leads to the two-step estimated GLS (2SEGLS) estimator

$$\begin{aligned}\hat{\boldsymbol{\beta}}(\hat{\boldsymbol{\Psi}}) &= (\mathbf{x}'\hat{\boldsymbol{\Psi}}^{-1}\mathbf{x})^{-1}\mathbf{x}'\hat{\boldsymbol{\Psi}}^{-1}\mathbf{Y} \\ &= \left(\hat{\sigma}_1^2\hat{\sigma}_2^2/(\hat{\sigma}_1^2+\hat{\sigma}_2^2)\right)\left[\left(1/\hat{\sigma}_1^2\right)\mathbf{x}_1'\mathbf{Y}_1 + \left(1/\hat{\sigma}_2^2\right)\mathbf{x}_2'\mathbf{Y}_2\right], \qquad (19.5.11)\end{aligned}$$

where the first stage commonly uses $\hat{\sigma}_i^2 = (\mathbf{Y}_i - \mathbf{x}_i\tilde{\boldsymbol{\beta}}_i)'(\mathbf{Y}_i - \mathbf{x}_i\tilde{\boldsymbol{\beta}}_i)/(n-k)$ to estimate the σ_i^2's in $\boldsymbol{\Psi}$. Taylor (1977, 1978) has analyzed a reparameterized version of this regression model and has shown that under appropriate conditions the 2SEGLS estimator $\hat{\boldsymbol{\beta}}(\hat{\boldsymbol{\Psi}})$ is consistent and asymptotically efficient with the same asymptotic covariance matrix as $\hat{\boldsymbol{\beta}}_G$.

19.5.2. A Heteroscedasticity Pretest Estimator

The results for the cases analyzed above contain no surprises when the scale parameters are known. However, what are we to expect for the case in which the scale parameters are unknown and the outcome of a test of the hypothesis $H_0 : \sigma_1^2 = \sigma_2^2$ is used to determine whether to choose the ML–LS or EGLS estimator of $\boldsymbol{\beta}$? Greenberg (1980) and Judge and Yanccy (1986), building on the work of Taylor (1977, 1978), used a test procedure suggested by Goldfeld and Quandt (1965) to investigate the finite sample properties of a pretest estimator $\bar{\boldsymbol{\beta}}$ that makes use of $\hat{\boldsymbol{\beta}}$ if the hypothesis of homoscedasticity is accepted and $\hat{\boldsymbol{\beta}}(\hat{\boldsymbol{\Psi}})$ otherwise. The preliminary test or pretest estimator is defined specifically by

$$\bar{\boldsymbol{\beta}} = \begin{cases} \hat{\boldsymbol{\beta}} & \text{if } H_0\colon \sigma_1^2 = \sigma_2^2 \text{ is not rejected} \\ \hat{\boldsymbol{\beta}}(\hat{\boldsymbol{\Psi}}) & \text{if } H_0\colon \sigma_1^2 = \sigma_2^2 \text{ is rejected.} \end{cases} \qquad (19.5.12)$$

As a basis for testing the null hypothesis

$$H_0\colon \sigma_1^2 = \sigma_2^2 \qquad (19.5.13)$$

against

$$H_a\colon \sigma_1^2 \neq \sigma_2^2 \qquad (19.5.14)$$

we know that

$$\frac{(n_i - k)\hat{\sigma}_i^2}{\sigma_i^2} \sim \text{Chi-square}(n_i - k, 0) \quad i = 1, 2, \qquad (19.5.15)$$

and, thus, that

$$\frac{\hat{\sigma}_1^2}{\sigma_1^2} \Big/ \frac{\hat{\sigma}_2^2}{\sigma_2^2} \sim \text{F}(n_1 - k, n_2 - k, 0). \qquad (19.5.16)$$

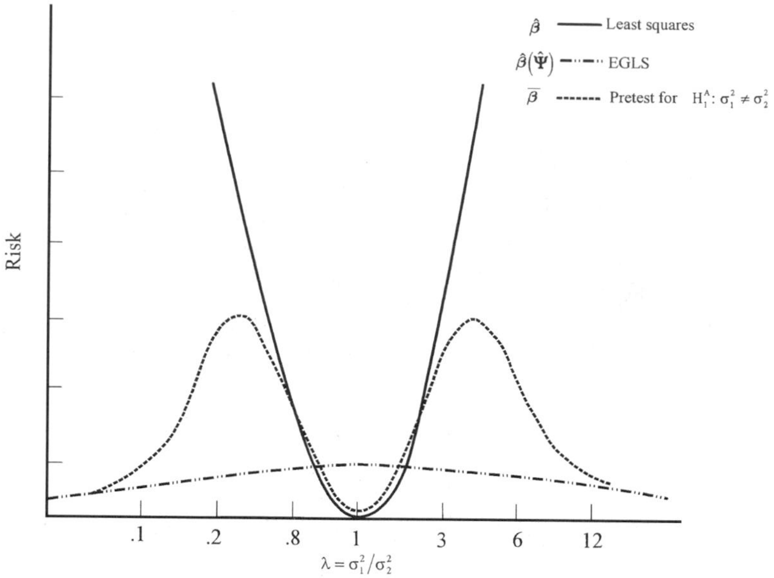

Figure 19.1: Relative risk characteristics of $\hat{\boldsymbol{\beta}}$, $\bar{\boldsymbol{\beta}}$ and $\hat{\boldsymbol{\beta}}(\hat{\boldsymbol{\Psi}})$.

Under the null hypothesis $\mathrm{H}_0: \sigma_1^2 = \sigma_2^2$,

$$\frac{\hat{\sigma}_1^2}{\hat{\sigma}_2^2} \sim \mathrm{F}(n_1 - k, n_2 - k, 0). \qquad (19.5.17)$$

The test is carried out by computing $(\hat{\sigma}_1^2/\hat{\sigma}_2^2)$ and comparing this value with quantiles of the central F-distribution.

The general sampling-risk function characteristics of the estimators $\hat{\boldsymbol{\beta}}$, $\hat{\boldsymbol{\beta}}_{\mathrm{G}}$ and $\hat{\boldsymbol{\beta}}(\hat{\boldsymbol{\Psi}})$ are given in Figure 19.1. All risk comparisons are made relative to the risk of the GLS estimator $\hat{\boldsymbol{\beta}}_{\mathrm{G}}$.

As expected, when the variance parameters of the two samples are equal ($\lambda = 1$), the ML–LS and GLS estimators have the same risk. At this point, the relative risk of the 2SEGLS estimator $\hat{\boldsymbol{\beta}}(\hat{\boldsymbol{\Psi}})$ reaches a maximum. For departures away from $\lambda = \sigma_1^2/\sigma_2^2 \neq 1$, the relative risk of the ML–LS estimator $\hat{\boldsymbol{\beta}}$ rises dramatically. As the degree to which $\sigma_1^2/\sigma_2^2 \neq 1$ increases, the risk of the 2SEGLS estimator $\hat{\boldsymbol{\beta}}(\hat{\boldsymbol{\Psi}})$ decreases, becomes relative risk superior to $\hat{\boldsymbol{\beta}}$, and approaches the risk of the GLS estimator $\hat{\boldsymbol{\beta}}_{\mathrm{G}}$. The pretest estimator $\bar{\boldsymbol{\beta}}$ is risk inferior to $\hat{\boldsymbol{\beta}}$ over part of the parameter space and risk inferior to $\hat{\boldsymbol{\beta}}(\hat{\boldsymbol{\Psi}})$ over a large part of the parameter space. Thus, neither $\bar{\boldsymbol{\beta}}$, $\hat{\boldsymbol{\beta}}$ nor $\hat{\boldsymbol{\beta}}(\hat{\boldsymbol{\Psi}})$ are risk dominant, but the risk functions provide a good perspective on the consequences of estimator choice and on the unsatisfactory nature of the pretest estimator $\bar{\boldsymbol{\beta}}$.

► **Example 19.5.2:** To demonstrate the relative risk characteristics of the estimators depicted in Figure 19.1, we provide the GAUSS program C19HPT.gss in the examples manual. For a given sample, the LS and EGLS estimates and the test decision under rule (19.5.12) are reported by GAUSS. Then, the quadratic risk functions of the two estimators plus the associated pretest estimator are simulated by a Monte Carlo exercise.

19.5.3. An Autocorrelation Pretest Estimator

When we use the outcome of an autocorrelation test statistic as a basis for choosing the specification of a probability model, the focus must again turn to the statistical properties of the resulting pretest estimator. For example, when a choice between the LS estimator $\hat{\boldsymbol{\beta}}$ and the EGLS estimator $\hat{\boldsymbol{\beta}}(\hat{\boldsymbol{\Psi}})$ is made on the basis of, say, a test for first-order autocorrelation, a pretest estimator is born. On the basis of Judge and Bock (1978), if positively or negatively autocorrelated noise is a possibility, then the pretest estimator is defined by

$$\bar{\boldsymbol{\beta}} = \begin{cases} \hat{\boldsymbol{\beta}} \text{ if } \mathrm{c}_\ell < \mathrm{c} < \mathrm{c}_\mathrm{u} \\ \hat{\boldsymbol{\beta}}(\hat{\boldsymbol{\Psi}}) \text{ if } \mathrm{c} \leq \mathrm{c}_\ell \text{ or } \mathrm{c} \geq \mathrm{c}_\mathrm{u}, \end{cases}$$

where c_ℓ and c_u are the lower and upper critical values for an autocorrelation test such as the Durbin–Watson test and c is the outcome of the test statistic used. A typical relative squared-error risk relationship between LS, EGLS, and pretest estimators is as portrayed in Figure 19.2.

As seems reasonable, when $\rho = 0$ the probability model having iid noise elements is correct and the ML–LS estimator $\hat{\boldsymbol{\beta}}$ is the MVUE when the noise component is multivariate normally distributed. Alternatively, note at the origin, even if $\rho = 0$, the null hypothesis will be rejected τ percent of the time. Consequently, τ percent of the time the econometrician will use the wrong probability model and utilize the estimator $\hat{\boldsymbol{\beta}}(\hat{\boldsymbol{\Psi}})$, and the risk of the resulting pretest estimator $\bar{\boldsymbol{\beta}}$ is greater than that of $\hat{\boldsymbol{\beta}}$. If the econometrician assumes $\rho \neq 0$ and *always* uses $\hat{\boldsymbol{\beta}}(\hat{\boldsymbol{\Psi}})$, then at the origin the risk of $\hat{\boldsymbol{\beta}}(\hat{\boldsymbol{\Psi}})$ is greater than $\bar{\boldsymbol{\beta}}$ and $\hat{\boldsymbol{\beta}}$. As $|\rho|$ becomes larger, there are risk consequences for *always* using $\hat{\boldsymbol{\beta}}$ that become effective, where the risks of $\bar{\boldsymbol{\beta}}$ and $\hat{\boldsymbol{\beta}}(\hat{\boldsymbol{\Psi}})$ are superior to

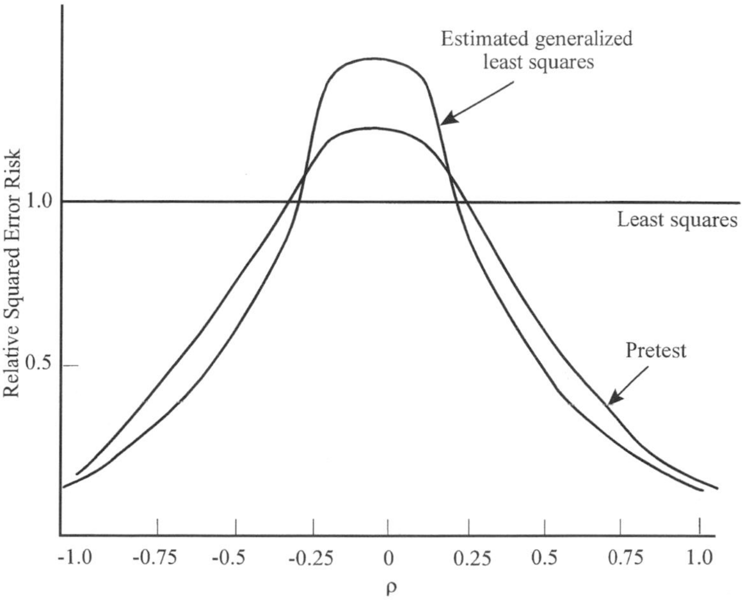

Figure 19.2: Relative risk functions for $\hat{\boldsymbol{\beta}}$, $\hat{\boldsymbol{\beta}}(\hat{\boldsymbol{\Psi}})$, and $\bar{\boldsymbol{\beta}}$.

that of $\hat{\boldsymbol{\beta}}$. As $|\rho|$ becomes larger over part of the ρ parameter space, the risk of $\hat{\boldsymbol{\beta}}(\hat{\boldsymbol{\Psi}})$ is superior to that of both $\bar{\boldsymbol{\beta}}$ and $\hat{\boldsymbol{\beta}}$. Finally, when $|\rho|$ becomes large and the probability of Type-II errors is small, the risks of $\bar{\boldsymbol{\beta}}$ and $\hat{\boldsymbol{\beta}}(\hat{\boldsymbol{\Psi}})$ are essentially identical, and for sufficiently large ρ, both $\bar{\boldsymbol{\beta}}$ and $\hat{\boldsymbol{\beta}}(\hat{\boldsymbol{\Psi}})$ have risks that are superior to $\hat{\boldsymbol{\beta}}$. This suggests that if the econometrician has prior information that a notable degree of positive or negative autocorrelated errors reflect the appropriate statistical model, then the "always correct-for-nonsphericity estimator" $\hat{\boldsymbol{\beta}}(\hat{\boldsymbol{\Psi}})$ is a good strategy. We emphasize, however, that in this comparison there is the important assumption that the analyst has used the correct functional specification of $\boldsymbol{\Psi}$ when constructing the EGLS estimator.

► **Example 19.5.3:** To demonstrate the relative risk characteristics of the estimators depicted in Figure 19.2, we provide the GAUSS program C19ARPT.gss in the examples manual. For a given sample, the LS and EGLS estimates and the test decision are reported by GAUSS. Then, the quadratic risk functions of the two estimators plus the associated pretest estimator are simulated by a Monte Carlo exercise.

19.6. Concluding Comments

In this chapter we have reviewed the basic rationale, implementation, and interpretation of some of the most popular types of procedures that have been used in practice to attempt to decide whether the noise component of an econometric model exhibits heteroscedasticity, autocorrelation, or both and to determine the particular form of nonspherical covariance matrix. Given the large number of possible specifications for the error covariance matrix $\boldsymbol{\Psi}$, the postulation–testing–transformation process leads eventually to selecting a probability model on the basis of the final conclusion of a series of hypothesis tests. This spawns a pretest estimator and leaves much to be desired in terms of how to interpret the sampling properties of the final estimator utilized to estimate model parameters.

Moreover, one must question the genesis of the particular nonspherical covariance matrix specification tested and its factual status: What basis is there for affording the particular covariance matrix specification defined by the alternative (to sphericity) hypothesis the status of "truth" if it is simply the postulated alternative to a *rejected* null hypothesis? What about alternative plausible (or agnostic) specifications of the covariance structure? If prior information is not available that anoints the alternative hypothesis with the special status of being the only relevant alternative nonspherical specification to consider, then why should we claim to have discovered the appropriate covariance matrix specification as a result of the hypothesis test outcome? And in the absence of prior information that isolates a particular nonspherical specification as the only viable alternative, why should one think that the end decision of a long string of tests on a menu of nonspherical alternatives will discover the "true" one with any appreciable protection against test-decision error?

In fact, for a long enough list of alternatives, the latter strategy will almost certainly lead to a rejection of a null hypothesis of sphericity, regardless of its validity, and will often lead to spurious "discoveries" of covariance matrix structure. To summarize the current state of affairs, the postulation–testing–transformation approach to nonspherical model discovery is generally doomed to failure without strong prior knowledge of the relevant alternative nonspherical contingency to test.

When substantial uncertainty exists regarding the structure of the noise covariance matrix, and in place of a strategy that will likely often lead to a decision of nonsphericity and to a specification of some generally incorrect form of covariance matrix, one prudent alternative is to revert to robust representations of the covariance structure such as the White or Newey–West-type approaches discussed in Chapter 15, which at least consistently estimate both spherical and nonspherical contingencies.

19.7. Exercises

19.7.1. Idea Checklist – Knowledge Guides

1. What are the potential pitfalls of using a battery of tests to search for heteroscedastic or autocorrelated noise components?
2. If you wish to use more than one diagnostic test, is it possible to adjust the individual test procedures to control the overall size of the joint test?
3. Can you think of any alternatives to the AR(m) specifications to represent dependent or correlated noise components?

19.7.2. Problems

19–1 Verify that (19.2.5) and (19.2.6) are related as $\boldsymbol{\Psi}(\rho)^{-1} \equiv \mathbf{c}(\rho)'\mathbf{c}(\rho)$.

19–2 Derive the likelihood function (19.2.10) from the conditional likelihood function statements (19.2.7)–(19.2.9).

19–3 Try to derive analytical solutions for $\boldsymbol{\alpha}$ and $\boldsymbol{\beta}$ in the NLS and ML estimation problems in Section 19.2.2.a, equation (19.2.18). Are you able to compose closed-form or explicit solutions? Are you able to derive an intermediate solution and form a concentrated NLS or ML problem?

19.7.3. Computer Problems

19–1 Use the program provided for Example 19.2.1 (C19ARNLS.gss) as a guide to write a GAUSS procedure that computes the parameter estimates by the iterative Cochrane–Orcutt procedure. Do the NLS and Cochran–Orcutt methods provide the same estimates for a given sample? If not, do you observe any differences in the sampling properties of the estimators in repeated samples? Which computational method do you prefer?

19–2 Write a GAUSS program designed to compute NLS and ML estimates for the heteroscedastic formulations in Section 19.2.2.a equation (19.2.18). For a heteroscedastic linear regression model of your choice, conduct a Monte Carlo simulation exercise to compare the sampling properties of the estimators. How do the estimators compare in terms of sampling properties? How do the estimators compare in terms of computation time?

19–3 Use Bonferroni's inequality to adjust the GAUSS program provided for Example 19.3.1 (C19Het.gss) to control the overall size of the joint test for heteroscedasticity at level α. Repeat the Monte Carlo exercise and compare the probabilities of rejection to the results generated in the original version of the program.

19–4 Following the discussion in Section 19.5, write a GAUSS program to form a pretest estimator based on one of the heteroscedasticity tests listed in Table 19.1 or 19.2. Then, simulate the quadratic risk function of this estimator and compare it with the risk of the EGLS estimator based on White's robust estimator of the covariance matrix. (Hint: Use the GAUSS program C19HPT.gss as a guide.)

19.8. References

Box, G. E. P., and D. A. Pierce (1970), "Distribution of Residual Autocorrelations in Autoregressive-Integrated Moving Average Time Series Models," *Journal of the American Statistical Association*, Vol. 65, pp. 1509–26.

Breusch, T. S. (1978), "Testing for Autocorrelation in Dynamic Linear Models," *Australian Economic Papers*, Vol. 17, pp. 334–55.

Breusch, T. S., and A. R. Pagan (1979), "A Simple Test for Heteroskedasticity and Random Coefficient Variation," *Econometrica*, Vol. 47, pp. 1287–94.

Cochrane, D., and G. H. Orcutt (1949), "Application of Least Squares Regressions to Relationships Containing Autocorrelated Error Terms," *Journal of the American Statistical Association*, Vol. 44, pp. 32–61.

Davidson, R., and J. MacKinnon (1993), *Estimation and Inference in Econometrics*, Oxford, UK: Oxford University Press.

Durbin, J. (1970), "Testing for Serial Correlation in Least Squares Regression When Some of the Regressors are Lagged Dependent Variables," Econometrica, Vol. 38, pp. 410–21.

Durbin, J., and G. S. Watson (1950), "Testing for Serial Correlation in Least Squares Regressions I," *Biometrika*, Vol. 37, pp. 409–28.

Durbin, J., and G. S. Watson (1951), "Testing for Serial Correlation in Least Squares Regressions II," *Biometrika*, Vol. 38, pp. 159–78.

Durbin, J., and G. S. Watson (1971), "Testing for Serial Correlation in Least Squares Regressions III," *Biometrika*, Vol. 37, pp. 1–42.

Engle, R. F. (1979a), "A General Approach to the Construction of Model Diagnostics Based on the Lagrange Multiplier Principle," USCD discussion paper No. 79–43.

Engle, R. F. (1979b),"Estimation of the Price Elasticity of Demand Facing Metropolitan Producers," *Journal of Urban Economics*, Vol. 6, pp. 42–64.

Engle, R. F. (1982), "A General Approach to Lagrange Multiplier Model Diagnostics," *Journal of Econometrics*, Vol. 20, pp. 83–104.

Engle, R. F. (1984), "Wald, Likelihood Ratio, and Lagrange Multiplier Tests in Econometrics," Chapter 13 in *Handbook of Econometrics*, Vol. 2, Z. Griliches, and M. Intrilligator (Eds.), Amsterdam: North–Holland, pp. 775–826.

Glejser, H. (1969), "A New Test for Heteroskedasticity," *Journal of the American Statistical Association*, Vol. 64, pp. 316–23.

Godfrey, L. G. (1978), "Testing for Multiplicative Heteroskedasticity," *Journal of Econometrics*, Vol. 8, pp. 227–36.

Godfrey, L. G. (1988), Misspecification Tests in Econometrics: The Lagrange Multiplier Principle and Other Approaches, Cambridge, UK: Cambridge University Press.

Goldfeld, S. M., and R. E. Quandt (1965), "Some Tests for Homoskedasticity," *Journal of the American Statistical Association*, Vol. 60, pp. 539–47.

Gooijer, J. G., and I. B. MacNeill (1999), "Lagged Regression Residuals and Serial-Correlation Tests," *Journal of Business and Economic Statistics*, Vol. 17, pp. 236–47.

Greenberg, E. (1980), "Finite Sample Moments of a Preliminary-Test Estimator in the Case of Possible Heteroskedasticity," *Econometrica*, Vol. 48, pp. 1805–13.

Harvey, A. C. (1976), "Estimating Regression Models with Multiplicative Heteroskedasticity," *Econometrica*, Vol. 44, pp. 461–5.

Hatanaka, M. (1974), "An Efficient Two-Step Estimator for the Dynamic Adjustment Model with Autoregressive Errors," *Journal of Econometrics*, Vol. 2, pp. 199–220.

Judge, G. G., and M. E. Bock (1978), *Statistical Implications of Pre-Test and Stein-Rule Estimators in Econometrics*, Amsterdam: North–Holland.

Judge, G. G., and T. A. Yancey (1986), *Improved Methods of Inference in Econometrics*, Amsterdam: North–Holland.

Judge, G. G., W. E. Griffiths, R. C. Hill, and T.-C. Lee (1985), *The Theory and Practice of Econometrics*, New York: John Wiley and Sons.

Judge, G. G., R. C. Hill, W. E. Griffiths, H. Lutkepohl, and T.-C. Lee (1988), *Introduction to the Theory and Practice of Econometrics*, New York: John Wiley and Sons.

Kiviet, J. (1986), "On the Rigour of Some Specification Tests for Modelling Dynamic Relationships," *Review of Economic Studies*, Vol. 53, pp. 241–62.

Koenker, R. (1981), "A Note on Studentizing a Test for Heteroskedasticity," *Journal of Econometrics*, Vol. 17, pp. 107–12.

Ljung, G. M., and G. E. P. Box (1978), "On a Measure of Lack of Fit in Time Series Models," *Biometrika*, Vol. 65, pp. 297–303.

McCullough, B. D., and C. G. Renfro (1999), "Benchmarks and Software Standards: A Case Study of GARCH Procedure," *Journal of Economic and Social Measurement*, in press.

McCullough, B. D., and C. G. Renfro (2000), "Some Numerical Aspects of Nonlincar Estimation," *Journal of Economic and Social Measurement*, in press.

Mizon, G. E., and D. F. Hendry (1980), "An Empirical Application and Monte Carlo Analysis of Tests of Dynamic Specification," *Review of Economic Studies*, Vol. 47, pp. 21–45.

Spencer, B. G. (1975), "The Small Sample Bias of Durbin's Tests for Serial Correlation When One of the Regressors is the Lagged Dependent Variable and the Null Hypothesis is True," *Journal of Econometrics*, Vol. 3, pp. 249–54.

Srivastava, V. K., and D. E. A. Giles (1987), *Seemingly Unrelated Regression Equations Models: Estimation and Inference*, New York: Marcel Dekker.

Taylor, W. E. (1977), "Small Sample Properties of a Class of Two-Stage Aitken Estimators," *Econometrica*, Vol. 45, pp. 497–508.

Taylor, W. E. (1978), "The Heteroskedastic Linear Model: Exact Finite Sample Results," *Econometrica*, Vol. 46, pp. 663–75.

White, H. (1980), "A Heteroskedastic-Consistent Covariance Matrix and a Direct Test for Heteroskedasticity," *Econometrica*, Vol. 48, pp. 421–48.

PART EIGHT

Special Econometric Topics

In Part VIII we focus on probability models and estimation and inference procedures that may be used to cope with a range of special econometric problems. As a first example, in Chapter 20 we consider dependent variables representing responses that are discrete rather than continuous or that have various mixed discrete–continuous components. Maximum likelihood and information theoretic criteria are used as a basis for recovering the relevant unknown parameters of these binary–multinomial response models and their censored-limited dependent variable cousins. Asymptotics is the basis for gauging the sampling properties of the ML–extremum estimators and associated inference procedures.

In a second econometric topics context, we recognize that, although theoretical economic constructs typically include or exclude variables and imply monotonicity, concavity or homogeneity in various forms, economic theory is seldom specific in terms of the functional forms that may apply to the variables involved in economic interrelationships. The econometric techniques we have considered thus far have required a significant degree of functional parametric input. In contrast, in nonparametric regression, little else is specified about the shape of the regression function beyond the assumption of some degree of smoothness. Consequently, in Chapter 21 we provide an introduction to nonparametric techniques in which the regression specification serves only to identify which explanatory variables condition the mean of $\mathbf{Y}$, but no specific parametric family of functional forms is imposed on the relationship.

Finally, we include electronic Chapter E3 on the CD-ROM where we consider a class of finite, discrete stochastic linear additive ill-posed inverse problems that are not amenable to traditional estimation and inference procedures. Information theoretic procedures that are discussed in Chapters 13 and 16 are used for processing and recovering information in these ill-posed situations, which may be more the general rule than the exception in economics. The methods of analysis examined in Chapter E3 are in a state of development, and refinements are currently underway.

CHAPTER 20

Qualitative–Censored Response Models

So far in each chapter of this book, we have specified particular classes of data-sampling process (DSPs) and associated probability–econometric models of the DSPs and then we led the reader step by step through corresponding estimation and inference procedures appropriate for recovering information on unknowns and unobservables in the model. The goal of this approach has been to have the reader accumulate knowledge and experience in specifying a variety of probability and econometric models and in devising estimation and inference procedures that have useful statistical interpretations and properties. In nearly all of the cases examined heretofore, the DSPs referred to dependent variable outcomes of some *continuous* random variable generally conditioned on the values of other explanatory variables that could be measured on either a continuous or discrete scale. We now use this knowledge and experience to begin thinking in creative ways about notably different alternative forms of DSPs that result in data that may require more specialized probability models and tools in the information recovery process.

In the probability models we have considered to this point, the dependent variable **Y** was considered to be a continuous random variable and this implied that an observed outcome of **Y** could logically be any value in a continuum on the real line. In this chapter, we examine DSPs for which the range of possible outcomes of the dependent variable is restricted in some way. In particular, one important case that we will examine concerns a dependent variable that can take on only a finite–discrete set of values. Consideration of observations in this form seems reasonable because much of our work in economics involves developing a rational basis for choosing between or among a finite set of alternatives or discrete qualitative outcomes. In particular, producer and consumer actions or reactions depend on decisions taken when choosing between or among two or more alternatives in a choice space.

One can easily envision a myriad of binary choice situations in the real world. A firm decides whether or not to pursue a business loan. A consumer decides whether to buy a car or a home. A couple decides whether to marry or perhaps whether to stay married or seek a divorce. These are all examples of binary choices or responses, and it seems reasonable to suspect that various explanatory variables may have been involved in the determination of these decisions or choices. Consequently, it is easy to see the importance of considering the specification and analysis of probability–econometric models of binary choices that might help us understand and make predictions about the outcomes of relevant binary discrete random variables.

When more than two choices are involved, we leave the context of binomial random variables and enter the world of multinomial responses in which again we may suspect certain explanatory variables affect the observed choices or decisions. For example, in traveling from Berkeley to San Francisco, one has the option of traveling by bus, car, or BART (subway). An undergraduate must make a choice among several fields in which to major. An individual may want to choose among various recreation sites for a weekend getaway. A bond rating firm will be concerned with the choice among AAA, AA, A, . . . ratings to assign to a bond. A student will make choices regarding whether to pursue a B.S., M.S., or Ph.D. The first three examples represent *unordered* multinomial choice problems, whereas the last two examples illustrate *ordered* multinomial choice situations. Whether the choice problem is ordered or not depends on whether there is a unique natural ordering to the responses or decisions under investigation. In bond ratings, there is clearly an ascending scale of bond quality to be assigned, and in the choice of education, there is a clear hierarchy in the choice among the three degrees. Without additional information, no unique natural ordering of choices in the other illustrations appears to be relevant.

Another important case that will be examined in this chapter involves response variables that may have both continuous and discrete components. Tobin (1958), in analyzing the demand for durable goods, found that most households report zero expenditures on automobiles or other durable goods in any given year. He then reasoned that if a regression model is to be used in an econometric analysis of durables, then some formal recognition of the discontinuity in the distribution of responses must be an integral characteristic of the model. The idea of a mixed discrete–continuous, censored, or limited dependent random variable was thereby introduced into the econometric literature.

Finally, and relatedly, consider the prototypical situation of a loan officer at Bank of America in Pullman, Washington, who has two decisions to make: whether to make a loan to a student specializing in econometrics and, if so, how large the loan should be. This decision process involves first the outcome of a discrete yes or no response variable and then, if (conditional on) yes, the outcome of a continuous response variable regarding how much to loan. Taking into account factors based on the historical experience of a large number of loan applications in an attempt to help explain bank profitability of loans made to various types of individuals, it is interesting to ponder how to model and analyze such a loan decision process econometrically.

Given these interesting choice and decision situations involving discrete or mixed discrete–continuous response variables, the purpose of this chapter is to introduce a range of econometric models, together with estimation and inference procedures, that may be used as a basis for coping with dependent variables that represent choices that are discrete rather than continuous or that have various discrete–continuous components. In terms of the general class of statistical models portrayed in Table 2.1, we examine the special case identified in Table 20.1. The particular inverse problem associated with the statistical models delineated in this chapter is represented by $(\mathbf{Y}, \mathbf{x}) \Rightarrow (\boldsymbol{\beta}, \sigma^2, \varepsilon)$.

Table 20.1. *Limited Dependent Variable Statistical Model*

Model Component	Specific Characteristics	
$\mathbf{Y}$	RV Type:	mixed discrete–continuous
	Range:	limited
	Y_i dimension:	univariate
	Moments:	$E[\mathbf{Y} \mid \mathbf{x}] = \mathbf{h}(\mathbf{x}, \boldsymbol{\beta}, \sigma)$
		$\mathbf{cov}(\mathbf{Y} \mid \mathbf{x}) = \Sigma_{\mathbf{Y}}(\mathbf{x}, \boldsymbol{\beta}, \sigma)$
$\eta(\mathbf{x}, \boldsymbol{\beta}, \varepsilon)$	Functional Form:	nonlinear transformation of continuous random noise component ε into a mixed discrete–continuous random function of $\mathbf{x}$ and $\boldsymbol{\beta}$.
$\mathbf{x}$	RV Type:	degenerate (fixed)
	Genesis:	exogenous to the model
$\boldsymbol{\beta}$	RV Type:	degenerate (fixed)
	Dimension:	finite
ε	RV Type:	iid
	Moments:	$E[\varepsilon \mid \mathbf{x}] = \mathbf{0}$, and $\mathbf{cov}\ (\varepsilon \mid \mathbf{x}) = \sigma^2\mathbf{I}$
Ω	Prior info:	none
$f(\mathbf{e} \mid \mathbf{x}, \varphi)$	PDF family:	specified or unspecified

We begin our investigation with a simple econometric model, which in this case reflects a binary-choice–discrete-random-variable situation.

20.1. Binary–Discrete Choice Response Models

Consider an experiment with n individuals, $i = 1, 2, \ldots, n$, where each individual is faced with a binary yes or no decision or choice, $j = 0, 1$. How should we go about modeling choice behavior when the individual outcomes or responses can be represented by

$$Y_i = \begin{cases} 1 \text{ if one alternative is chosen (yes)} \\ 0 \text{ if the other alternative is chosen (no)} \end{cases} \qquad (20.1.1)$$

so that Y_i is a discrete dichotomous random variable?

Because our information is in the form of dichotomous outcomes or responses, it is appropriate to assign discrete probabilities to each of the two outcomes and treat these probabilities as parameters in the model of the underlying data-sampling process. If the outcome space is defined as in (20.1.1), the outcomes for Y_i can be coded as $j = 0$ or 1, and the probabilities of the respective binary responses can be defined by the corresponding discrete probabilities $P(y_i = j)$. Consequently, if $p_i = P(y_i = 1)$ is the probability that Y_i takes the value 1, and $1 - p_i$ is the probability that Y_i is 0, then we can express this probabilistic information on Y_i in the form of a Bernoulli random variable and corresponding Bernoulli probability distribution, as

$$Y_i \sim f(y_i) = p_i^{y_i}(1 - p_i)^{1-y_i} \quad \text{for} \quad y = 0, 1, \quad p_i \in [0, 1]. \tag{20.1.2}$$

It follows that $E[Y_i] = 1 \times P(y_i = 1) + 0 \times P(y_i = 0) = P(y_i = 1) = p_i$ and $\text{var}(Y_i) = P(y_i = 1)(1 - P(y_i = 1)) = p_i(1 - p_i)$. Given this way of modeling the choice response information, interest centers on the individual attributes that will allow us to recover or predict the choice probability p_i from the observable information-data.

20.1.1. A Linear Probability Model

We begin the conceptualization of an econometric model of the binary choice problem by postulating that the choice made by each of the n individuals chosen randomly from a large population can be represented by an observed outcome of the dichotomous random variable Y_i, which takes the value 0 or 1. Furthermore, we postulate that the observed choice is affected, or partially explained, by a collection of observable explanatory variables $\mathbf{x}_{i\cdot}$, and we specify the linear regression model

$$Y_i = \mathbf{x}_{i\cdot}\boldsymbol{\beta} + \varepsilon_i, \tag{20.1.3}$$

where $\boldsymbol{\beta}$ is a $(k \times 1)$ vector of unknown and unobservable parameters, and ε_i is an unobserved and unobservable random noise variable with $E[\varepsilon_i] = 0$. If we then draw the logical conclusion from the Bernoulli nature of Y_i that $E[Y_i] = p_i = P(y_i = 1 \mid \mathbf{x}_{i\cdot}) = \mathbf{x}_{i\cdot}\boldsymbol{\beta}$, then it would seem that we have the makings of a linear regression model to use as the basis for recovering the unknown $\boldsymbol{\beta}$ and the unknown probabilities $P(y_i = 1 \mid \mathbf{x}_{i\cdot})$, $i = 1, \ldots, n$ that are consistent with the observed data. Indeed, this formulation of the discrete data generation process suggests that it may be possible to specify this problem as a regression model with a dichotomous dependent variable.

Now let us look more critically at this regression specification. First, because the probability p_i is a linear function of $\mathbf{x}_{i\cdot}\boldsymbol{\beta}$, for $i = 1, \ldots, n$, and since the value of $\mathbf{x}_{i\cdot}\boldsymbol{\beta}$ is not inherently constrained to the interval [0, 1] in which the value of any probability must lie, we have an internal logical contradiction in our regression model specification. Furthermore, because the outcome Y_i can only assume the dichotomous values 1 and 0, the associated noise component is also dichotomous, and the internal logic of our current regression requires that

$$\varepsilon_i = \begin{cases} 1 - \mathbf{x}_{i\cdot}\boldsymbol{\beta} \text{ with probability } \mathbf{x}_{i\cdot}\boldsymbol{\beta} \\ -\mathbf{x}_{i\cdot}\boldsymbol{\beta} \text{ with probability } 1 - \mathbf{x}_{i\cdot}\boldsymbol{\beta} \end{cases} \tag{20.1.4}$$

Consequently, the random noise elements cannot be identically distributed and in fact are heteroscedastic with variances logically given by $\sigma_i^2 = (\mathbf{x}_{i\cdot}\boldsymbol{\beta})(1 - \mathbf{x}_{i\cdot}\boldsymbol{\beta})$ for $i = 1, \ldots, n$. This raises estimation and inference issues relating to a non-iid data-sampling process and a general noise covariance matrix specification (see Chapters 14 and 15).

Despite the logical and statistical complications identified above, the linear probability model is still used in practice by some analysts. The principal advantages of the model are the relative ease of computation and interpretation. Although the model has a heteroscedastic noise component, the functional form of the heteroscedasticity is known and suggests that maximum likelihood methods or feasible generalized least-squares might be utilized for estimation and inference. The interpretation of the model is of the standard linear regression model variety. Regarding the problem of $\mathbf{x}_{i\cdot}\boldsymbol{\beta}$'s not restricting values to the [0, 1] interval, one might adopt the pragmatic view that the model is still applicable to problems in which the variation in $\mathbf{x}_{i\cdot}$ values is sufficiently small so that $\mathbf{x}_{i\cdot}\boldsymbol{\beta} \in [0, 1]$ for all, or almost all observations, and use as post hoc evidence the fact that $\mathbf{x}_{i\cdot}\hat{\mathbf{b}} \in [0, 1]$ for all or almost all i.

Although legitimate arguments can be made in defense of its pragmatic use, we now consider within a likelihood context a model of the binary choice process that mitigates the logical and statistical problems associated with the linear probability model. The additional cost of such a specification derives from the need for slightly more complicated procedures of estimation and inference, and the additional effort required in interpreting the meaning of the estimated model.

20.1.2. A Reformulated Binary Response Model

Consider a reformulated econometric model of binary choice that postulates that for each individual i chosen randomly from a large population, the associated observable dichotomous random choice variable Y_i is related to a $(k \times 1)$ vector of observable explanatory variables $\mathbf{x}_{i\cdot}$ by the statistical model

$$Y_i = I_{(0,\infty)}(Y_i^*), \qquad Y_i^* = \mathbf{x}_{i\cdot}\boldsymbol{\beta} + \varepsilon_i, \tag{20.1.5}$$

or equivalently by

$$Y_i = I_{(0,\infty)}(\mathbf{x}_{i\cdot}\boldsymbol{\beta} + \varepsilon_i), \tag{20.1.6}$$

where $I_A(z)$ is the standard indicator function for which $I_A(z) = 1$ if $z \in A$ and $I_A(z) = 0$ otherwise. It follows that

$$y_i = \begin{Bmatrix} 1 \\ 0 \end{Bmatrix} \quad \text{iff} \quad Y_i^* = \mathbf{x}_{i\cdot}\boldsymbol{\beta} + \varepsilon_i \begin{Bmatrix} > \\ \leq \end{Bmatrix} 0, \tag{20.1.7}$$

where $\boldsymbol{\beta}$ is a $(k \times 1)$ vector of unknown and unobservable parameters and ε_i is an unobserved and unobservable random variable $E[\varepsilon_i] = 0$. In this formulation Y_i^* can be viewed as a *latent* variable that summarizes the influence of explanatory variables on the dichotomous outcome of Y_i, the summary measure being expressed in the form of a real-valued scalar index. Note that the latent variable can be generalized to be a *nonlinear* function of $\mathbf{x}_{i\cdot}$, but linearity has been adopted in most applications, and we continue to focus on the linear case for the sake of clarity of exposition.

We pause to emphasize at this point that the nature of the observable data on $\mathbf{Y}$ in the current inverse problem has changed to finite–discrete outcomes as opposed to previous chapters in which the outcomes were presumed to be measurable on a continuous scale. Furthermore, in representing the discrete nature of the observable data, an additional unknown and unobservable component has been introduced into the model that has not been encountered heretofore – namely, the latent variable Y_i^*. The latent variable approach appears in many qualitative choice-censored response models, and it is important to understand the rationale for introducing such a latent variable into the probability model of a DSP as well as the approach for handling this unknown and unobservable variable when solving the inverse problem.

One way of motivating the reformulated latent variable model is to associate choice with utility and assume individual i receives utility U_{ij} when alternative j ($=0$ or 1 in the current choice situation) is chosen. If utility maximizing behavior is assumed, individual i then chooses the alternative coded by $Y_i = 1$, if $U_{i1} > U_{i0}$. If we assume utility satisfies the separable specification $U_{ij} = \mathbf{w}'_{ij}\boldsymbol{\beta} + V_{ij}$, where $\mathbf{w}_{ij}$ is the value of the column vector of explanatory variables associated with individual i and choice j, then on the basis of the random utilities U_{i1} and U_{i0}, the ith individual will choose alternative 1 if the unobservable latent random variable $Y_i^* = U_{i1} - U_{i0}$ is such that $y_i^* > 0$. In this case the outcome of the *observable* dichotomous random variable Y_i is visualized as being determined by

$$y_i = \begin{cases} 1 \text{ if } y_i^* > 0 \text{ or } u_{i1} > u_{i0} \\ 0 \text{ if } y_i^* \leq 0 \text{ or } u_{i0} \leq u_{i1} \end{cases}. \tag{20.1.8}$$

Letting $\mathbf{x}'_{i.} \equiv \mathbf{w}_{i1} - \mathbf{w}_{i0}$ and $\varepsilon_i \equiv V_{i1} - V_{i0}$, we have the linear regression model

$$Y_i^* = \mathbf{x}_{i.}\boldsymbol{\beta} + \varepsilon_i, \tag{20.1.9}$$

where now the ε_i's are iid unobservable random variables. Equation (20.1.5) transforms (20.1.9) into a zero–one indicator functional form that is characteristic of empirical binary response models. In the current utility function context, the elements of the $(k \times 1)$ vector $\boldsymbol{\beta}$ reflects the marginal utilities associated with the respective explanatory variables in $\mathbf{x}_{i.}$. The random unobservable ε_i represents unobserved factors affecting the level of utility.

In the context of this so-called *discrete choice model* (Quandt (1966) and McFadden (1976)), we can represent the probability that $y_i = 1$ as

$$p_i = P(y_i = 1) = P(y_i^* > 0) = P(\varepsilon_i > -\mathbf{x}_{i.}\boldsymbol{\beta}). \tag{20.1.10}$$

At this point, to establish an explicit functional linkage between p_i and $\mathbf{x}_{i.}\boldsymbol{\beta}$, the standard approach is to specify a parametric family of probability distributions for the unobservable noise component ε_i. By doing so, a functional linkage between p_i and $\mathbf{x}_{i.}\boldsymbol{\beta}$ is defined through the functional form of the CDF, $F(\varepsilon_i)$ of ε_i as follws:

$$p_i = P(\varepsilon_i > -\mathbf{x}_{i.}\boldsymbol{\beta}) = 1 - F(-\mathbf{x}_{i.}\boldsymbol{\beta}). \tag{20.1.11}$$

If the family of PDFs chosen for ε_i is symmetric around a mean of zero, as is often the case in practice, then (20.1.11) is equivalent to

$$p_i = P(\varepsilon_i > -\mathbf{x}_{i.}\boldsymbol{\beta}) = P(\varepsilon_i < \mathbf{x}_{i.}\boldsymbol{\beta}) = F(\mathbf{x}_{i.}\boldsymbol{\beta}), \tag{20.1.12}$$

where we assume that $F(\varepsilon_i)$ is continuous. Note that because $F(z) \in [0, 1]$, which is a standard property of CDFs, the range of possible values for p_i is functionally constrained to the appropriate [0, 1] interval. Note further that by specifying a parametric PDF family for ε_i, the maximum likelihood approach for estimation and inference is enabled.

20.1.2.a. PDF Choices for Functionally Linking p_i and $\mathbf{x}_{i.}\boldsymbol{\beta}$

Two parametric families of PDFs that have been often used in empirical discrete choice modeling are the standard normal and logistic distributions. Both distributions are symmetric around zero-valued means, and the distributions closely mimic each other in general shape, except that the logistic distribution has fatter tails. The variance of the standard logistic distribution is $\pi^2/3$ compared with a variance of 1 for the standard normal distribution.

If the logistic distribution is used in specifying the discrete choice model, the model is referred to as a *logit* model. In this case, the specific functional relationship between p_i and $\mathbf{x}_{i.}\boldsymbol{\beta}$ is given by (recall (20.1.12))

$$p_i = F_{LOG}(\mathbf{x}_{i.}\boldsymbol{\beta}) = \frac{\exp(\mathbf{x}_{i.}\boldsymbol{\beta})}{1 + \exp(\mathbf{x}_{i.}\boldsymbol{\beta})}, \tag{20.1.13}$$

where $F_{LOG}(\cdot)$ is the CDF of the logistic distribution. Alternatively, if the standard normal distribution is used in the discrete choice model, the model is referred to as a *probit* (also historically referred to as *normit*) model, and is given by

$$p_i = F_{NORM}(\mathbf{x}_{i.}\boldsymbol{\beta}) = \int_{-\infty}^{\mathbf{x}_{i.}\boldsymbol{\beta}} (2\pi)^{-1/2} \exp\left(-\frac{z^2}{2}\right) dz, \tag{20.1.14}$$

where $F_{NORM}(\cdot)$ is the CDF of the standard normal distribution. It is apparent that the logit model has a computational advantage over the probit model in the sense that the functional representation of p_i is a closed-form analytical function of $\mathbf{x}_{i.}\boldsymbol{\beta}$ in (20.1.13), but only an integral expression in (20.1.14). This computational advantage, plus the general similarity of the standard logistic and normal distributions, accounts for the popularity of the logit model in empirical work. We remind the reader, however, that a myriad of choices for $F(\mathbf{x}_{i.}\boldsymbol{\beta})$ are possible – the logistic and normal CDFs are only two, albeit very popular, choices.

We pause to address an issue that the reader may have identified when contemplating the use of the standard normal distribution in the discrete, choice model: namely, why use the *standard* normal? Could we contemplate the use of say, an $N(0, \sigma^2)$ distribution? More generally, should we allow for an unknown variance in *any* of the choices of $F(\cdot)$ that we might make in specifying the functional form of p_i through (20.1.11) or (20.1.12)? The answer is no, and the issue here is parameter identification. Note that

$$p_i = P(\varepsilon_i > -\mathbf{x}_{i.}\boldsymbol{\beta}) = P(\varepsilon_i/\sigma > -\mathbf{x}_{i.}\boldsymbol{\beta}/\sigma) = P(\varepsilon_i^* > -\mathbf{x}_{i.}\boldsymbol{\beta}_*) = 1 - F(-\mathbf{x}_{i.}\boldsymbol{\beta}_*), \tag{20.1.15}$$

where $\boldsymbol{\beta}_* \equiv \boldsymbol{\beta}/\sigma$ and $\varepsilon_i^* \equiv \varepsilon_i/\sigma$, and thus discrete choice models based on CDFs that differ only with respect to scaling (variances) are indistinguishable, and the parameter σ is therefore unidentifiable. Thus, we lose no generality by choosing $\sigma = 1$, or any other constant, within a parametric family of distributions.

20.1.2.b. Marginal Effect on p_i of Changes in x_{ij}

The effect that changes in explanatory variable values has on the probabilities of the discrete choice outcomes is of course dependent on the functional form linking p_i and $\mathbf{x}_{i\cdot}\boldsymbol{\beta}$. In general, for any choice of symmetric probability distribution represented by the differentiable CDF $F(\cdot)$, we have the derivative relationship

$$\frac{\partial p_i}{\partial x_{ij}} = \frac{\partial F(\mathbf{x}_{i\cdot}\boldsymbol{\beta})}{\partial x_{ij}} = f(\mathbf{x}_{i\cdot}\boldsymbol{\beta})\beta_j, \tag{20.1.16}$$

where $f(\cdot)$ is the probability density function associated with the CDF $F(\cdot)$. Then, for the logit and probit discrete choice models, we have

$$\frac{\partial p_i}{\partial x_{ij}} = \frac{\partial F_{LOG}(\mathbf{x}_{i\cdot}\boldsymbol{\beta})}{\partial x_{ij}} = f_{LOG}(\mathbf{x}_{i\cdot}\boldsymbol{\beta})\beta_j = \frac{\exp(\mathbf{x}_{i\cdot}\boldsymbol{\beta})}{[1+\exp(\mathbf{x}_{i\cdot}\boldsymbol{\beta})]^2}\beta_j \tag{20.1.17}$$

and

$$\frac{\partial p_i}{\partial x_{ij}} = \frac{\partial F_{NORM}(\mathbf{x}_{i\cdot}\boldsymbol{\beta})}{\partial x_{ij}} = f_{NORM}(\mathbf{x}_{i\cdot}\boldsymbol{\beta})\beta_j = (2\pi)^{-1/2}\exp\left[-\frac{1}{2}(\mathbf{x}_{i\cdot}\boldsymbol{\beta})^2\right]\beta_j, \tag{20.1.18}$$

where $f_{LOG}(\cdot)$ and $f_{NORM}(\cdot)$ are the probability density functions for the logit and standard normal distributions, respectively.

Maximum likelihood estimates of these derivatives are obtained by replacing the unknown $\boldsymbol{\beta}$ by an ML estimate. Given the alternative ways of modeling a discrete random variable whose outcomes represent dichotomous choices, we next consider the problem of estimation and inference in the discrete choice model.

20.2. Maximum Likelihood Estimation and Inference for the Discrete Choice Model

Given the parametric specification of the discrete choice model, including the choice of a CDF with which to establish the functional linkage between p_i and $\mathbf{x}_{i\cdot}\boldsymbol{\beta}$, a likelihood function for the parameters of the model can be specified as

$$L(\boldsymbol{\beta};\mathbf{y}) = \prod_{i=1}^{n} p_i^{y_i}(1-p_i)^{1-y_i} = \prod_{i=1}^{n}[1-F(-\mathbf{x}_{i\cdot}\boldsymbol{\beta})]^{y_i}F(-\mathbf{x}_{i\cdot}\boldsymbol{\beta})^{(1-y_i)} \tag{20.2.1}$$

The corresponding log likelihood function is given by

$$\begin{aligned}\ln[L(\boldsymbol{\beta};\mathbf{y})] &= \sum_{i=1}^{n}[y_i\ln(p_i)+(1-y_i)\ln(1-p_i)]\\ &= \sum_{i=1}^{n}[y_i\ln(1-F(-\mathbf{x}_{i\cdot}\boldsymbol{\beta}))+(1-y_i)\ln(F(-\mathbf{x}_{i\cdot}\boldsymbol{\beta}))].\end{aligned} \tag{20.2.2}$$

20.2.1. Logit Model

If we use the logit CDF in (20.1.13) and recall (20.1.12) and (20.2.2), the log likelihood function for the logit discrete choice model may be expressed as

$$\ln[\mathrm{L}(\boldsymbol{\beta};\mathbf{y})] = \sum_{i=1}^{n}\left[\mathrm{y}_i \ln\left(\frac{\mathrm{e}^{\mathbf{x}_{i\cdot}\boldsymbol{\beta}}}{1+\mathrm{e}^{\mathbf{x}_{i\cdot}\boldsymbol{\beta}}}\right) + (1-\mathrm{y}_i)\ln\left(\frac{1}{1+\mathrm{e}^{\mathbf{x}_{i\cdot}\boldsymbol{\beta}}}\right)\right]$$

$$= \sum_{i=1}^{n}[\mathrm{y}_i\mathbf{x}_{i\cdot}\boldsymbol{\beta} - \ln(1+\mathrm{e}^{\mathbf{x}_{i\cdot}\boldsymbol{\beta}})]. \qquad (20.2.3)$$

The corresponding first-order conditions characterizing the maximum of the log-likelihood function are given by

$$\frac{\partial \ln[\mathrm{L}(\boldsymbol{\beta};\mathbf{y})]}{\partial \boldsymbol{\beta}} = \sum_{i=1}^{n}\left(\mathrm{y}_i\mathbf{x}_{i\cdot}' - \frac{\mathrm{e}^{\mathbf{x}_{i\cdot}\boldsymbol{\beta}}}{1+\mathrm{e}^{\mathbf{x}_{i\cdot}\boldsymbol{\beta}}}\mathbf{x}_{i\cdot}'\right) = \sum_{i=1}^{n}[\mathrm{y}_i - \mathrm{p}_i(\boldsymbol{\beta})]\mathbf{x}_{i\cdot}' = \mathbf{0}, \qquad (20.2.4)$$

where $\mathrm{p}_i(\boldsymbol{\beta}) \equiv \mathrm{F}_{\mathrm{LOG}}(\mathbf{x}_{i\cdot}\boldsymbol{\beta}) \equiv \frac{\mathrm{e}^{\mathbf{x}_{i\cdot}\boldsymbol{\beta}}}{1+\mathrm{e}^{\mathbf{x}_{i\cdot}\boldsymbol{\beta}}}$ is equal to $\mathrm{p}(\mathrm{y}_i = 1)$. These first-order conditions look similar to the estimating–normal equations for the ML estimator that we have encountered in previous chapters. It is apparent that these estimating equations are highly nonlinear functions of $\boldsymbol{\beta}$ and cannot be solved analytically. Regarding the existence of a solution, note that the Hessian matrix of second-order derivatives is given by

$$\frac{\partial \mathbf{h}(\boldsymbol{\beta})}{\partial \boldsymbol{\beta}} = \frac{\partial^2 \ln[\mathrm{L}(\boldsymbol{\beta};\mathbf{y})]}{\partial \boldsymbol{\beta}\partial \boldsymbol{\beta}'} = -\sum_{i=1}^{n}\frac{\mathrm{e}^{\mathbf{x}_{i\cdot}\boldsymbol{\beta}}}{(1+\mathrm{e}^{\mathbf{x}_{i\cdot}\boldsymbol{\beta}})^2}\mathbf{x}_{i\cdot}'\mathbf{x}_{i\cdot}. \qquad (20.2.5)$$

If $\mathbf{x}$ has full-column rank, then $\frac{\partial \mathbf{h}(\boldsymbol{\beta})}{\partial \boldsymbol{\beta}}$ is negative definite, and an ML solution exists and is unique.

Note that the solution for $\boldsymbol{\beta}$ obtained from (20.2.4) is the optimal estimating function (OptEF) estimator for $\boldsymbol{\beta}$ described in Section 11.3.2.c. Therefore, as discussed in Section 11.3.2.b, the use of the estimating function given by (20.2.4) has an asymptotic optimality justification. In particular, the specification solves the problem of seeking the unbiased estimating function that produces the consistent estimating equation (EE) estimator of $\boldsymbol{\beta}$ with the smallest asymptotic covariance matrix. Furthermore, the ML estimator has the finite sample optimality property of representing the estimating function (20.2.4) with the smallest standardized covariance matrix (recall Section 11.3.2.b). We emphasize that these optimality results are predicated on the assumption that the logistic distribution underlying the likelihood specification is in fact the correct parametric family of distributions underlying the DSP.

Under standard regularity conditions, the ML estimator of the logit model will have the usual asymptotic properties of ML estimation, including consistency, asymptotic normality, and asymptotic efficiency. Specifically, the asymptotic distribution is defined by

$$\hat{\boldsymbol{\beta}}_{\mathrm{ML}} \overset{\mathrm{a}}{\sim} \mathrm{N}[\boldsymbol{\beta}, \boldsymbol{\Sigma}_{\hat{\boldsymbol{\beta}}_{\mathrm{ML}}}(\boldsymbol{\beta})], \qquad (20.2.6)$$

where the asymptotic covariance matrix is given by the negative of the inverse of the expected Hessian matrix as

$$\boldsymbol{\Sigma}_{\hat{\boldsymbol{\beta}}_{\mathrm{ML}}}(\boldsymbol{\beta}) = -\left[\mathrm{E}\left[\frac{\partial^2 \ln(\mathrm{L}(\boldsymbol{\beta};\mathbf{Y}))}{\partial\boldsymbol{\beta}\partial\boldsymbol{\beta}'}\right]\right]^{-1} = -\left[\mathrm{E}\left[\frac{\partial \mathbf{H}(\boldsymbol{\beta})}{\partial\boldsymbol{\beta}}\right]\right]^{-1}$$

$$= \left[\sum_{i=1}^{n} \frac{\mathrm{e}^{\mathbf{x}_{i.}\boldsymbol{\beta}}}{\left(1+\mathrm{e}^{\mathbf{x}_{i.}\boldsymbol{\beta}}\right)^2}\mathbf{x}_{i.}'\mathbf{x}_{i.}\right]^{-1} \tag{20.2.7}$$

A sufficient condition for consistency is that $\boldsymbol{\Sigma}_{\hat{\boldsymbol{\beta}}_{\mathrm{ML}}}(\boldsymbol{\beta}) \to \mathbf{0}$ as $n \to \infty$, which can be expected to occur in general. For example if $(\mathbf{x}'\mathbf{x})^{-1} \to \mathbf{0}$, as we assumed previously in establishing the consistency of linear least-squares estimators of $\boldsymbol{\beta}$, and given that

$$0 < \tau_{\mathrm{L}} \leq \frac{\mathrm{e}^{\mathbf{x}_{i.}\boldsymbol{\beta}}}{(1+\mathrm{e}^{\mathbf{x}_{i.}\boldsymbol{\beta}})^2} = \mathrm{p}_i\left(1-\mathrm{p}_i\right) \leq .25,\ \forall i, \tag{20.2.8}$$

then

$$\tau_{\mathrm{L}}^{-1}(\mathbf{x}'\mathbf{x})^{-1} \succeq \boldsymbol{\Sigma}_{\hat{\boldsymbol{\beta}}_{\mathrm{ML}}}(\boldsymbol{\beta}) \succeq 4(\mathbf{x}'\mathbf{x})^{-1}, \tag{20.2.9}$$

where $\succeq$ denotes "larger than by a positive semidefinite matrix." Because $\tau_{\mathrm{L}} > 0$, and given $(\mathbf{x}'\mathbf{x})^{-1} \to \mathbf{0}$, it is clear that $\boldsymbol{\Sigma}_{\hat{\boldsymbol{\beta}}_{\mathrm{ML}}}(\boldsymbol{\beta}) \to \mathbf{0}$ and $\hat{\boldsymbol{\beta}}_{\mathrm{ML}} \xrightarrow{\mathrm{p}} \boldsymbol{\beta}$.

Asymptotically valid Wald tests of hypotheses, as well as dual-associated confidence-region estimators, can be based on the asymptotic normality of $\hat{\boldsymbol{\beta}}_{\mathrm{ML}}$ and the consistent asymptotic covariance matrix estimator defined by $\hat{\boldsymbol{\Sigma}}_{\hat{\boldsymbol{\beta}}_{\mathrm{ML}}} \equiv \boldsymbol{\Sigma}_{\hat{\boldsymbol{\beta}}_{\mathrm{ML}}}(\hat{\boldsymbol{\beta}}_{\mathrm{ML}})$. Of course, likelihood ratio tests and confidence regions based on asymptotic Chi-square distributions are also applicable, as are Lagrange multiplier procedures. The reader can revisit the definitions of these procedures in our general discussion of maximum likelihood methods in earlier chapters.

► **Example 20.2.1:** A GAUSS procedure logit() designed to compute maximum likelihood parameter estimates for the logit model is provided in the examples manual. The purpose of the program C20Logit.gss is to illustrate the computational steps involved in the computer program and to identify and explain the various components of the logit() procedure.

► **Example 20.2.2:** To demonstrate the computation and use of ML estimates for a logistic model of discrete choice data, we provide the GAUSS program C20MLLog.gss in the examples manual. On the basis of parameters and a sample size provided by the user, pseudorandom data are generated for both the latent regression model and the associated binary observations. The ML parameter estimates, approximate standard errors, and estimated marginal effects (see Section 20.3.1.d) are reported to the user, and the predictive fit of the model is compared with the results from the linear probability model. The estimated covariance matrix can be used in hypothesis testing and is left to the reader as an exercise.

20.2.2. Probit Model

If the noise components in the discrete choice model (20.1.7) are assumed to be standard normally distributed, then the probit model and corresponding ML solution results. The steps required to obtain the ML estimates of $\boldsymbol{\beta}$, to characterize the asymptotic normal distribution of $\hat{\boldsymbol{\beta}}_{ML}$, and to define hypothesis-testing and confidence-region estimation procedures are analogous to those followed for the logit model. For completeness, we review these steps ahead.

Using the probit CDF in (20.1.14) and recalling (20.1.12) and (20.2.2), we may express the log likelihood function for the probit discrete choice model as

$$\ln[\mathrm{L}(\boldsymbol{\beta};\mathbf{y})] = \sum_{i=1}^{n}[\mathrm{y}_i \ln(1 - \mathrm{F}_{\mathrm{NORM}}(-\mathbf{x}_{i.}\boldsymbol{\beta})) + (1-\mathrm{y}_i)\ln(\mathrm{F}_{\mathrm{NORM}}(-\mathbf{x}_{i.}\boldsymbol{\beta}))]. \tag{20.2.10}$$

The corresponding first-order conditions characterizing the maximum of the log-likelihood function are given by

$$\frac{\partial \ln[\mathrm{L}(\boldsymbol{\beta};\mathbf{y})]}{\partial \boldsymbol{\beta}} = \sum_{i=1}^{n}\left[\frac{[\mathrm{y}_i - \mathrm{F}_{\mathrm{NORM}}(\mathbf{x}_{i.}\boldsymbol{\beta})]}{[\mathrm{F}_{\mathrm{NORM}}(\mathbf{x}_{i.}\boldsymbol{\beta})[1-\mathrm{F}_{\mathrm{NORM}}(\mathbf{x}_{i.}\boldsymbol{\beta})]]}\right]\mathrm{f}_{\mathrm{NORM}}(\mathbf{x}_{i.}\boldsymbol{\beta})\mathbf{x}_{i.}'$$

$$= \sum_{i=1}^{n}[\mathrm{y}_i - \mathrm{p}_i(\boldsymbol{\beta})]\xi(\mathbf{x}_{i.}\boldsymbol{\beta})\mathbf{x}_{i.}' = \mathbf{0}, \tag{20.2.11}$$

where $\mathrm{p}_i(\boldsymbol{\beta}) \equiv \mathrm{F}_{\mathrm{NORM}}(\mathbf{x}_{i.}\boldsymbol{\beta}) \equiv \int_{-\infty}^{\mathbf{x}_{i.}\boldsymbol{\beta}}(2\pi)^{-1/2}\exp(-\frac{z^2}{2})\,dz$, and

$$\xi(\mathbf{x}_{i.}\boldsymbol{\beta}) \equiv \left[\frac{\mathrm{f}_{\mathrm{NORM}}(\mathbf{x}_{i.}\boldsymbol{\beta})}{[\mathrm{F}_{\mathrm{NORM}}(\mathbf{x}_{i.}\boldsymbol{\beta})[1-\mathrm{F}_{\mathrm{NORM}}(\mathbf{x}_{i.}\boldsymbol{\beta})]]}\right]. \tag{20.2.12}$$

These first-order conditions look similar to the estimating–normal equations for the ML estimator that we have encountered in previous chapters. As in the logit case, it is apparent that these estimating equations are highly nonlinear functions of $\boldsymbol{\beta}$ and cannot be solved analytically. Regarding the existence of a solution, note that the Hessian matrix of second-order derivatives is given by

$$\frac{\partial \mathbf{h}(\boldsymbol{\beta})}{\partial \boldsymbol{\beta}} = \frac{\partial^2 \ln(\mathrm{L}(\boldsymbol{\beta};\mathbf{y}))}{\partial \boldsymbol{\beta}\partial \boldsymbol{\beta}'} = -\sum_{i=1}^{n}\lambda_i(\mathbf{x}_{i.}\boldsymbol{\beta})[\lambda_i(\mathbf{x}_{i.}\boldsymbol{\beta}) + \mathbf{x}_{i.}\boldsymbol{\beta}]\mathbf{x}_{i.}'\mathbf{x}_{i.}, \tag{20.2.13}$$

where

$$\lambda_i(\mathbf{x}_{i.}\boldsymbol{\beta}) \equiv \mathrm{y}_i\left[\frac{\mathrm{f}_{\mathrm{NORM}}(\mathbf{x}_{i.}\boldsymbol{\beta})}{\mathrm{F}_{\mathrm{NORM}}(\mathbf{x}_{i.}\boldsymbol{\beta})}\right] + (1-\mathrm{y}_i)\left[\frac{-\mathrm{f}_{\mathrm{NORM}}(\mathbf{x}_{i.}\boldsymbol{\beta})}{1-\mathrm{F}_{\mathrm{NORM}}(\mathbf{x}_{i.}\boldsymbol{\beta})}\right]. \tag{20.2.14}$$

Although not obvious, the terms $\lambda_i(\mathbf{x}_{i.}\boldsymbol{\beta})[\lambda_i(\mathbf{x}_{i.}\boldsymbol{\beta}) + \mathbf{x}_{i.}\boldsymbol{\beta}]$ are all contained in the interval (0, 1) for all values of $\boldsymbol{\beta}$ (Amemiya (1985, pp. 273–4)). It follows that if $\mathbf{x}$ has full-column rank, then $\frac{\partial \mathbf{h}(\boldsymbol{\beta})}{\partial \boldsymbol{\beta}}$ is negative definite, and an ML solution exists and is unique.

Note that the solution for $\boldsymbol{\beta}$ obtained from (20.2.11) is the optimal estimating function (OptEF) estimator for $\boldsymbol{\beta}$ described in Section 11.3.2.c. Therefore, as discussed in Section 11.3.2.b, the use of the estimating function given by (20.2.11) has an asymptotic optimality justification. In particular, the specification solves the problem of seeking the unbiased estimating function that produces the consistent estimating equation (EE) estimator of $\boldsymbol{\beta}$ with the smallest asymptotic covariance matrix. Furthermore, the ML estimator has the finite sample optimality property of representing the estimating function (20.2.11) with the smallest standardized covariance matrix (recall Section 11.3.2.b). We emphasize that these optimality results are predicated on the assumption that the normal distribution underlying the likelihood specification is in fact the correct parametric family of distributions underlying the DSP.

Under standard regularity conditions, the ML estimator of the normal model will have the usual asymptotic properties of ML estimation, including consistency, asymptotic normality, and asymptotic efficiency. Specifically, the asymptotic distribution is defined by

$$\hat{\boldsymbol{\beta}}_{\mathrm{ML}} \overset{a}{\sim} \mathrm{N}\left[\boldsymbol{\beta}, \boldsymbol{\Sigma}_{\hat{\boldsymbol{\beta}}_{\mathrm{ML}}}(\boldsymbol{\beta})\right], \tag{20.2.15}$$

where the asymptotic covariance matrix is given by the negative of the inverse of the expected Hessian matrix as follows:

$$\begin{aligned}\boldsymbol{\Sigma}_{\hat{\boldsymbol{\beta}}_{\mathrm{ML}}}(\boldsymbol{\beta}) &= -\left[\mathrm{E}\left[\frac{\partial^2 \ln(\mathrm{L}(\boldsymbol{\beta};\mathbf{Y}))}{\partial\boldsymbol{\beta}\partial\boldsymbol{\beta}'}\right]\right]^{-1} = -\left[\mathrm{E}\left[\frac{\partial\mathbf{H}(\boldsymbol{\beta})}{\partial\boldsymbol{\beta}}\right]\right]^{-1} \\ &= \left[\sum_{i=1}^{n} \frac{[\mathrm{f}_{\mathrm{NORM}}(\mathbf{x}_{i\cdot}\boldsymbol{\beta})]^2}{\mathrm{F}_{\mathrm{NORM}}(\mathbf{x}_{i\cdot}\boldsymbol{\beta})[1-\mathrm{F}_{\mathrm{NORM}}(\mathbf{x}_{i\cdot}\boldsymbol{\beta})]}\mathbf{x}_{i\cdot}'\mathbf{x}_{i\cdot}\right]^{-1}.\end{aligned} \tag{20.2.16}$$

A sufficient condition for consistency is that $\boldsymbol{\Sigma}_{\hat{\boldsymbol{\beta}}_{\mathrm{ML}}}(\boldsymbol{\beta}) \to \mathbf{0}$ as $n \to \infty$, which can be expected to occur in general. For example if $(\mathbf{x}'\mathbf{x})^{-1} \to \mathbf{0}$, as we assumed previously in establishing the consistency of linear least-squares estimators of $\boldsymbol{\beta}$, and given that

$$0 < \tau_{\mathrm{L}} \leq \frac{[\mathrm{f}_{\mathrm{NORM}}(\mathbf{x}_{i\cdot}\boldsymbol{\beta})]^2}{\mathrm{F}_{\mathrm{NORM}}(\mathbf{x}_{i\cdot}\boldsymbol{\beta})[1-\mathrm{F}_{\mathrm{NORM}}(\mathbf{x}_{i\cdot}\boldsymbol{\beta})]} \leq \tau_{\mathrm{H}} < \infty, \forall i, \tag{20.2.17}$$

then

$$\tau_{\mathrm{L}}^{-1}(\mathbf{x}'\mathbf{x})^{-1} \succeq \boldsymbol{\Sigma}_{\hat{\boldsymbol{\beta}}_{\mathrm{ML}}}(\boldsymbol{\beta}) \succeq \tau_{\mathrm{H}}^{-1}(\mathbf{x}'\mathbf{x})^{-1}, \tag{20.2.18}$$

where $\succeq$ denotes "larger than by a positive semidefinite matrix." Then, if $(\mathbf{x}'\mathbf{x})^{-1} \to \mathbf{0}$, it is clear that $\Sigma_{\hat{\boldsymbol{\beta}}_{\mathrm{ML}}}(\boldsymbol{\beta}) \to \mathbf{0}$ and $\hat{\boldsymbol{\beta}}_{\mathrm{ML}} \overset{p}{\to} \boldsymbol{\beta}$.

Asymptotically valid Wald tests of hypotheses, as well as dual-associated confidence-region estimators, can be based on the asymptotic normality of $\hat{\boldsymbol{\beta}}_{\mathrm{ML}}$ and the consistent asymptotic covariance matrix estimator defined by $\hat{\Sigma}_{\hat{\boldsymbol{\beta}}_{\mathrm{ML}}} \equiv \Sigma_{\hat{\boldsymbol{\beta}}_{\mathrm{ML}}}(\hat{\boldsymbol{\beta}}_{\mathrm{ML}})$. Of course, likelihood ratio tests and confidence regions based on asymptotic Chi-square distributions are also applicable, as are Lagrange multiplier procedures. The reader can revisit the definitions of these procedures in our general discussion of maximum likelihood methods in earlier chapters.

► **Example 20.2.3:** A GAUSS procedure probit() designed to compute maximum likelihood parameter estimates for the probit model is provided in the examples manual. The purpose of the program C20Pbit.gss is to identify and explain the various components of the probit procedure. The key difference between this example and Example 20.2.1 is the use of the normal CDF procedure (cdfn() in GAUSS) to form the log-likelihood function and the estimated large-sample covariance matrix.

► **Example 20.2.4:** To demonstrate the computation and use of ML estimates for a normal model of discrete choice data, we provide the GAUSS program C20MLPbt.gss in the examples manual. On the basis of parameters and a sample size provided by the user, pseudorandom data are generated for the latent regression model and the associated binary observations. The ML parameter estimates, approximate standard errors, and estimated marginal effects are reported to the user, and the predictive fit of the model is compared with the results from the linear probability model. The estimated covariance matrix can be used in hypothesis testing and is left as an exercise.

20.2.3. Probit or Logit?

As we noted earlier, the logistic and normal DSP specifications are similar. Both are symmetric around zero, and both lead to models whose functional representations of probabilities are confined to the unit interval. The tails of the logistic distribution are fatter than those of the normal distribution, and thus there is a scaling difference in the parameter estimates (see Maddala, 1983, p. 23). In the binary case, both formulations are computationally tractable. However, we will see that the logit formulation is more tractable than probit as the category dimensions increase. In applications, the distribution choice has often been based on the availability of computer software.

► **Example 20.2.5:** To compare and contrast the logit and probit estimation methods, we provide the GAUSS program C20LvsP.gss in the examples manual. The program reports parameter estimates, approximate standard errors, and predictive fits for both estimators when the mechanism used to transform the latent variables to the observed variables is logistic or normal.

20.3. Multinomial Discrete Choice

We now expand the alternatives–categories space and envision a situation in which an individual is faced with $J > 2$ choices or relevant descriptive categories. As will be apparent when the multinomial problem is specified, the binary case of the preceding section generalizes directly to the multinomial case. Unfortunately, computational tractability of the normal–probit formulation does not extend directly. Consequently, in this section we will focus on the multinomial logit model whose solution can be expressed in closed form. Research continues to be directed toward developing a computationally tractable basis for handling the multinomial probit (McFadden, 1989; Hajivassilou and McFadden, 1998; and Kimhi, 1999).

The general *unordered* multinomial discrete choice problem can be described as follows. We begin with an experiment consisting of n random trials or n randomly selected individuals. The outcome for the ith trial or individual is a $(J \times 1)$ vector, $(\mathrm{y}_{i1}, \ldots, \mathrm{y}_{iJ})$, where Y_{ij} is a binary random variable that can assume only the value 0 or 1, $\mathrm{y}_{ij} = 1$ indicates that alternative j was chosen by individual i or occurred on trial i, and $\mathrm{y}_{ij} = 0$ indicates that alternative j was not chosen or did not occur. It is assumed that the choice situation is such that only one of the J alternatives can be chosen on trial i, and the J alternatives exhaust the choice possibilities, which then implies that $\sum_{j=1}^{J} \mathrm{y}_{ij} = 1, \forall i$. If p_{ij} denotes, the probability that alternative j is chosen or occurs on the ith trial, the probability distribution across alternative outcomes for individual i can be represented by the multinomial distribution

$$\mathrm{f}_i(\mathrm{y}_{i1}, \ldots, \mathrm{y}_{iJ}) = \prod_{j=1}^{J} \mathrm{p}_{ij}^{\mathrm{y}_{ij}} \quad \text{for} \quad \mathrm{y}_{ij} = 0 \text{ or } 1, \quad \sum_{j=1}^{J} \mathrm{y}_{ij} = 1. \tag{20.3.1}$$

It follows that if we have an independent random sample of n individuals, then the joint probability distribution across all J alternative choice outcomes and all n individuals is given by

$$\mathrm{f}(\mathrm{y}_{11}, \ldots, \mathrm{y}_{nJ}) = \prod_{i=1}^{n} \mathrm{f}_i(\mathrm{y}_{i1}, \ldots, \mathrm{y}_{iJ}) = \prod_{i=1}^{n} \prod_{j=1}^{J} \mathrm{p}_{ij}^{\mathrm{y}_{ij}}. \tag{20.3.2}$$

We now assume that the choice probabilities depend on the values of explanatory variables. Operating analogously to the binary choice situation in Section 20.2, we make the general assumption that the multinomial probabilities p_{ij}, in (20.3.2) are represented by parametric functions

$$\mathrm{p}_{ij} = \mathrm{g}_{ij}(\mathbf{x}_{i\cdot}\boldsymbol{\beta}_j), \qquad j = 1, \ldots, J. \tag{20.3.3}$$

Given the standard properties of probabilities, we know that

$$\mathrm{g}_{ij}(\mathbf{x}_{i\cdot}\boldsymbol{\beta}_j) \in [0, 1] \quad \text{and} \quad \sum_{j=1}^{J} \mathrm{g}_{ij}(\mathbf{x}_{i\cdot}\boldsymbol{\beta}_j) = 1. \tag{20.3.4}$$

Any specific choice of $\mathrm{g}_{ij}(\cdot)$ that satisfies (20.3.4) will define a legitimate multinomial response model. We also note that we need not restrict the argument of $\mathrm{g}_{ij}(\cdot)$ to be a linear scalar index of the explanatory variable values, and the more general form $\mathrm{g}_{ij}(\mathbf{x}_{i\cdot}, \boldsymbol{\beta}_j)$ could be used. Nonetheless, we focus on the basic model (20.3.3) and note that it has by far been the most popular form used in empirical work.

20.3.1. Multinomial Logit

The specific functional choice

$$\mathrm{g}_{ij}(\mathbf{x}_{i\cdot}\boldsymbol{\beta}_j) \equiv \frac{\mathrm{e}^{\mathbf{x}_{i\cdot}\boldsymbol{\beta}_j}}{\sum_{k=1}^{J} \mathrm{e}^{\mathbf{x}_{i\cdot}\boldsymbol{\beta}_k}}, \qquad \text{for } i = 1, \ldots, n \quad \text{and} \quad j = 1, \ldots, J \tag{20.3.5}$$

satisfies the desired properties in (20.3.4) and defines the multinomial response model most often applied in practice, namely, the *multinomial logit* model. Note that the binary logit model can be thought of as a special case of the multinomial logit model where $J = 2$ and $\boldsymbol{\beta}_1 \equiv \mathbf{0}$ in (20.3.5). We will see ahead that there is compelling rationale based on parameter identification issues for the parameter constraint $\boldsymbol{\beta}_1 \equiv \mathbf{0}$ in both the binary and multinomial logit models.

20.3.1.a. Utility Maximization Motivation

As in the case of binary choice, one way of motivating the multinomial logit model is through a utility theory argument. Specifically, let the utility of alternative j for individual i be represented by

$$\mathrm{Y}_{ij}^* = \mathbf{x}_{i\cdot}\boldsymbol{\beta}_j + \varepsilon_{ij}. \tag{20.3.6}$$

On the assumption of utility maximization, alternative j will be chosen by individual i if $\mathrm{Y}_{ij}^* > \mathrm{Y}_{ik}^*\ \forall\, k \neq j$. If the ε_{ij}'s are iid, each with the *extreme value* distribution

$$\mathrm{f(z)} = \mathrm{e}^{-z}\,\mathrm{e}^{-\mathrm{e}^{-z}} \quad \text{and} \quad \mathrm{F}(z) = \mathrm{e}^{-\mathrm{e}^{-z}}, \tag{20.3.7}$$

then it follows that

$$\begin{aligned} \mathrm{P}(\mathrm{y}_{ij} = 1) &= \mathrm{P}(\mathrm{Y}_{ij}^* > \mathrm{Y}_{ik}^*, \forall k \neq j) \\ &= \mathrm{P}[\varepsilon_{ij} - \varepsilon_{ik} > -\mathbf{x}_{i\cdot}(\boldsymbol{\beta}_j - \boldsymbol{\beta}_k), \forall k \neq j] = \frac{\mathrm{e}^{\mathbf{x}_{i\cdot}\boldsymbol{\beta}_j}}{\sum_{j=1}^{J} \mathrm{e}^{\mathbf{x}_{i\cdot}\boldsymbol{\beta}_j}}. \end{aligned} \tag{20.3.8}$$

A proof of (20.3.8) is provided in the chapter appendix. If, instead, the ε_{ij}'s were assumed to be iid standard normal, then the multinomial probit model is defined. We note again that the probit model is computationally difficult except in cases in which alternatives are restricted to 3 or less.

Note, as in the binary case, the multinomial logit model can be applied in situations other than those characterized by utility maximizing choice. For example, the model might be used to model whether employees in a firm undergoing downsizing are laid off, fired, offered the opportunity for retraining, or kept in their current positions. In this case, the explanatory variables might include an employee's education, job performance rating, years with the company, age, sex, and the like.

In some applications of the qualitative choice models, the explanatory variables describe characteristics of the choices rather than the decision-makers. For example, the decision among transportation choices available to a Bay Area commuter may depend on the location of the person's home in Berkeley. The explanatory variables may include measures of the relative commuting time or cost of each alternative for a set of locations. The latent regression model may be stated as $\mathrm{Y}_{ij}^* = \mathbf{z}_{ij}\gamma + \varepsilon_{ij}$, and McFadden (1974) refers to this formulation as the conditional logit model. Of course, the multinomial logit model developed in this section may represent a latent model combining choice-specific and individual-specific explanatory variables such as $\mathrm{Y}_{ij}^* = \mathbf{x}_{i\cdot}\boldsymbol{\beta}_j + \mathbf{z}_{ij}\gamma + \varepsilon_{ij}$.

20.3.1.b. Identification Restriction

Regarding the estimation of the parameters of the multinomial logit model, we first must consider a fundamental identification problem with the model. Suppose that we add the vector **d** to each of the parameter vectors $\boldsymbol{\beta}_k$, $k = 1, \ldots, J$ in (20.3.5). Note that the value of (20.3.5) remains unchanged because

$$g_{ij}(\mathbf{x}_{i\cdot}(\boldsymbol{\beta}_j + \mathbf{d})) = \frac{e^{\mathbf{x}_{i\cdot}(\boldsymbol{\beta}_j + \mathbf{d})}}{\sum_{k=1}^{J} e^{\mathbf{x}_{i\cdot}(\boldsymbol{\beta}_k + \mathbf{d})}} = \frac{e^{\mathbf{x}_{i\cdot}\mathbf{d}}}{e^{\mathbf{x}_{i\cdot}\mathbf{d}}} \cdot \frac{e^{\mathbf{x}_{i\cdot}\boldsymbol{\beta}_j}}{\sum_{k=1}^{J} e^{\mathbf{x}_{i\cdot}\boldsymbol{\beta}_k}} = g_{ij}(\mathbf{x}_{i\cdot}\boldsymbol{\beta}_j). \qquad (20.3.9)$$

This implies that the set of parameter vectors $\boldsymbol{\beta}_k$, $k = 1, \ldots, J$ are *not identified* in the multinomial logit model, and thus it is not possible to devise an estimator of them. In practice the identification problem is mitigated by restricting the first parameter vector to zero (i.e., $\boldsymbol{\beta}_1 = \mathbf{0}$), in which case the remaining parameters are identified (one could just as well normalize $\boldsymbol{\beta}_1$ to any other vector of values). After this identification restriction is imposed, the representation of the multinomial probabilities becomes

$$\begin{aligned} p_{ij} = g^*_{ij}(\mathbf{x}_{i\cdot}\boldsymbol{\beta}_j) &= \frac{e^{\mathbf{x}_{i\cdot}\boldsymbol{\beta}_j}}{1 + \sum_{k=2}^{J} e^{\mathbf{x}_{i\cdot}\boldsymbol{\beta}_k}} \quad \text{for } j \geq 2 \\ &= \frac{1}{1 + \sum_{k=2}^{J} e^{\mathbf{x}_{i\cdot}\boldsymbol{\beta}_k}} \quad \text{for } j = 1. \end{aligned} \qquad (20.3.10)$$

It is now clear that (20.3.10) subsumes the binary choice case when $J = 2$.

20.3.1.c. Maximum Likelihood Estimation and Inference

Substituting (20.3.10) into (20.3.2) and taking logarithms, we can represent the log-likelihood function for the multinomial logit model by (recall $\sum_{j=1}^{J} y_{ij} = 1$)

$$\ln(L(\boldsymbol{\beta}; \mathbf{y})) = \sum_{i=1}^{n} \left[\sum_{j=2}^{J} y_{ij}[\mathbf{x}_{i\cdot}\boldsymbol{\beta}_j] - \ln\left(1 + \sum_{k=2}^{J} e^{\mathbf{x}_{i\cdot}\boldsymbol{\beta}_k}\right)\right], \qquad (20.3.11)$$

where $\boldsymbol{\beta} \equiv \text{vec}([\boldsymbol{\beta}_1, \boldsymbol{\beta}_2, \ldots, \boldsymbol{\beta}_J])$ is a column-vectorized representation of model parameters. If we let $y(i) \in \{1, 2, \ldots, J\}$ equal the number of the alternative chosen by the ith individual and recall that $\boldsymbol{\beta}_1 = \mathbf{0}$, the log-likelihood can be written equivalently as

$$\ln(L(\boldsymbol{\beta}; \mathbf{y})) = \sum_{i=1}^{n} \left[\mathbf{x}_{i\cdot}\boldsymbol{\beta}_{y(i)} - \ln\left(1 + \sum_{k=2}^{J} e^{\mathbf{x}_{i\cdot}\boldsymbol{\beta}_k}\right)\right]. \qquad (20.3.12)$$

The ML estimator of the $\boldsymbol{\beta}_k$'s is defined by maximizing (20.3.12), yielding

$$\hat{\boldsymbol{\beta}}_{\text{ML}} = \arg\max_{\boldsymbol{\beta}}[\ln(L(\boldsymbol{\beta}; \mathbf{Y}))]. \qquad (20.3.13)$$

Alternatively, the maximum likelihood estimates can be obtained by solving the estimating equations (first-order conditions)

$$\begin{aligned}\frac{\partial \ln(\mathrm{L}(\boldsymbol{\beta};\mathbf{y}))}{\partial \boldsymbol{\beta}_j} &= \sum_{i=1}^{n}\left(\mathrm{y}_{ij}\mathbf{x}_{i.}' - \frac{e^{\mathbf{x}_{i.}\boldsymbol{\beta}_j}}{1+\sum_{k=2}^{J} e^{\mathbf{x}_{i.}\boldsymbol{\beta}_k}}\mathbf{x}_{i.}'\right)\\ &= \sum_{i=1}^{n}[\mathrm{y}_{ij} - \mathrm{p}_i(\boldsymbol{\beta}_j)]\mathbf{x}_{i.}' = \mathbf{0}, \qquad j = 2,\ldots,J, \qquad (20.3.14)\end{aligned}$$

where $\mathrm{p}_i(\boldsymbol{\beta}_j) \equiv \frac{e^{\mathbf{x}_{i.}\boldsymbol{\beta}_j}}{1+\sum_{k=2}^{J} e^{\mathbf{x}_{i.}\boldsymbol{\beta}_k}} = \mathrm{p}(\mathrm{y}_{ij} = 1)$. As in the case of the binary logit model, the solution for $\boldsymbol{\beta}$ obtained from (20.3.14) (with $\boldsymbol{\beta}_1 = \mathbf{0}$) is the optimal estimating function (OptEF) estimator for $\boldsymbol{\beta}$ described in Section 11.3.2.c. The estimating function given by (20.3.14) is asymptotically optimal in the sense that it solves the problem of seeking the unbiased estimating function that produces the consistent estimating equation (EE) estimator of $\boldsymbol{\beta}$ with the smallest asymptotic covariance matrix (recall Section 11.3.2.b). Furthermore, the ML estimator has the finite sample optimality property of representing the estimating function (20.3.14) with the smallest standardized covariance matrix (again recall Section 11.3.2.b). We emphasize that these optimality results are predicated on the assumption that the logistic–extreme value distribution assumption underlying the likelihood specification is in fact the correct parametric family of distributions underlying the DSP.

The usual ML asymptotic properties apply in general, and thus $\hat{\boldsymbol{\beta}}^*_{\mathrm{ML}}$ is consistent, asymptotically normal, and asymptotically efficient, with

$$\hat{\boldsymbol{\beta}}^*_{\mathrm{ML}} \overset{a}{\sim} \mathrm{N}\left(\boldsymbol{\beta}^*, -\left[\mathrm{E}\frac{\partial^2 \ln(\mathrm{L}(\boldsymbol{\beta}^*;\mathbf{Y}))}{\partial \boldsymbol{\beta}^* \partial \boldsymbol{\beta}^{*\prime}}\right]^{-1}\right), \qquad (20.3.15)$$

where the * denotes that $\boldsymbol{\beta}_1$ has been removed from the parameter vector $\boldsymbol{\beta}$ (see (20.3.32) for the functional form of the asymptotic covariance matrix in (20.3.15)). All of the usual asymptotically valid Chi-square test and confidence-region methods can be applied, including Wald, likelihood ratio, and Lagrange multiplier procedures based on standard ML-based formulas. The asymptotic covariance matrix can be estimated in the usual way by eliminating the expectation operator and evaluating the Hessian matrix at $\boldsymbol{\beta} = \hat{\mathbf{b}}_{\mathrm{ML}}$ and $\mathbf{Y} = \mathbf{y}$.

20.3.1.d. Marginal Effects on Probabilities of Explanatory Variables

The individual parameters in the specification of the logit model are not easily interpretable. The parameters act in concert to parameterize the marginal effects of explanatory variables on the probabilities of the various choices in the multinomial decision problem. The marginal effects are given for a continuous explanatory variable by the partial derivatives of the probabilities (20.3.3) with respect to the explanatory variables, yielding (recall (20.3.5))

$$\frac{\partial \mathrm{p}_{ij}}{\partial \mathbf{x}_{i\cdot}} = \mathrm{p}_{ij}\left[\boldsymbol{\beta}_j - \sum_{k=2}^{J} \mathrm{p}_{ik}\boldsymbol{\beta}_k\right]. \tag{20.3.16}$$

The maximum likelihood estimates of these partial derivatives are obtained on the basis of the ML invariance principle, by replacing unknown parameters in (20.3.16) by ML estimates. Asymptotic standard errors for the estimated derivatives in (20.3.16) can be calculated based on the usual method for approximating standard errors relating to nonlinear functions of parameters (Chapter 8). Likewise, the trio of Wald, likelihood ratio, and Lagrange multiplier statistics can be used to test hypotheses and generate confidence regions for the derivatives (20.3.16), albeit the tests are asymptotic and not exact.

One can also define log-odds ratios, which are less complicated in functional form than the partial derivatives in (20.3.16). Specifically, normalizing on Alternative 1 and recalling that $\boldsymbol{\beta}_1 \equiv \mathbf{0}$, one can calculate log-odds ratios as follows:

$$\ln\left(\frac{\mathrm{p}_{ij}}{\mathrm{p}_{i1}}\right) = \mathbf{x}_{i\cdot}\boldsymbol{\beta}_j. \tag{20.3.17}$$

One can normalize on other alternatives besides the first, leading to the general log-odds formula

$$\ln\left(\frac{\mathrm{p}_{ij}}{\mathrm{p}_{ik}}\right) = \mathbf{x}_{i\cdot}(\boldsymbol{\beta}_j - \boldsymbol{\beta}_k). \tag{20.3.18}$$

Maximum likelihood estimates, standard errors, testing, and confidence-region estimation for the log-odds ratios are analogous to those described following (20.3.16).

► **Example 20.3.1:** To demonstrate an application of the multinomial logit estimator, we provide the GAUSS program C20Mult.gss in the examples manual. Using multinomial choice data provided on the CD (mlogit.dat), the program uses the GAUSS procedure mlogit() (also provided on the CD) to compute the ML parameter estimates as well as the approximate standard errors and the predicted choice probabilities. The estimated covariance matrix can be used for hypothesis testing and is left as an exercise.

20.3.1.e. Independence of Irrelevant Alternatives

The definition of the log-odds ratios (20.3.17) and (20.3.18) in the preceding subsection indicates that these ratios are independent of all alternatives other than the two explicitly involved in the ratio. This property of multinomial logit models is known as the *independence of irrelevant alternatives* (IIA) property. The property follows from the original assumption that the elements of the noise component vector are independent random variables.

The IIA property implies choice behavior that may not be plausible in all circumstances. In particular, adding another alternative to the choice set contained in the model will have no effect on the odds ratios relating to alternatives that were previously in the model. Hausman and McFadden (1984) and McFadden (1987) devised asymptotically valid Chi-square tests of the validity of IIA. If the property is rejected, then one alternative is to devise an alternative model of multinomial choice that does not assume independence of noise component elements, a natural alternative being the multivariate probit. However, as we stated previously, if J is large, the probit model is computationally prohibitive. Research is ongoing relating to more general and tractable alternatives to the multinomial logit model, including computational methods for making the multivariate probit more tractable (Hajivassilou and McFadden, 1998).

20.3.2. Information Theoretic Estimation of the Multinomial Decision Model

For cases in which the analyst is uncomfortable making distributional assumptions, it is interesting to examine the possibility of making use of the information theoretic procedures that were developed in Chapter 13 to analyze the multinomial choice problem. Thus, the task is to formulate the multinomial problem in terms of an estimation objective function and constraints that will result in the recovery of the unknown inverse probabilities and model parameters. In so doing, we will see a striking connection with the multinomial logit formulation. Building on the information theoretic approach introduced in Chapter 13, in the multinomial formulation to follow, we make use of Shannon's (1948) entropy measure

$$\mathrm{H}(\mathrm{p}) = -\sum_j \mathrm{p}_j \ln(\mathrm{p}_j) \tag{20.3.19}$$

and use Jaynes' (1957a,b) maximum entropy principle as a basis for assigning or recovering the unknown probabilities. In this approach to multinomial response problems, a solution to the inverse problem is sought by maximizing the entropy measure (20.3.19) subject to appropriate information–moment relations and adding up (normalization) constraints relating to the probabilities. As a result, we have a nonparametric method of estimation that is similar to EL and resampling (bootstrap) methods with an inference basis analogous to the parametric methods discussed previously.

To begin the maximum entropy conceptualization, we follow Golan, Judge, and Perloff (1996) and represent the multinomial choice outcomes in the following very general form:

$$\mathrm{y}_{ij} = \mathrm{p}_{ij} + \varepsilon_{ij}, \qquad \forall i \text{ and } j. \tag{20.3.20}$$

Then, we rewrite (20.3.20) in matrix form by defining the $(\mathrm{nJ}\times 1)$ vector $\mathbf{y} = [\mathrm{y}_{11}, \ldots, \mathrm{y}_{n1}, \mathrm{y}_{12}, \ldots, \mathrm{y}_{n2}, \ldots, \mathrm{y}_{1J}, \ldots, \mathrm{y}_{nJ}]'$, with $\mathbf{p}$ and ε defined accordingly, so that

$$\mathbf{y} = \mathbf{p} + \varepsilon. \tag{20.3.21}$$

Next, we introduce explanatory variable information in the form of moment restrictions. Specifically, the multinomial choice model (20.3.21) is transformed as

$$(\mathbf{I}_{\mathrm{J}} \otimes \mathbf{x}')\mathbf{y} = (\mathbf{I}_{\mathrm{J}} \otimes \mathbf{x}')\mathbf{p} + (\mathbf{I}_{\mathrm{J}} \otimes \mathbf{x}')\varepsilon, \tag{20.3.22}$$

where $\mathbf{I}_{\mathrm{J}}$ is a $(\mathrm{J}\times\mathrm{J})$ identity matrix and $\mathbf{x}$ is an $(n \times k)$ matrix of explanatory variable values, the ith row containing the appropriate values for individual or observation i.

Regarding the noise component term in (20.3.22), note that $E[\mathbf{I}_J \otimes \mathbf{x}']\varepsilon = \mathbf{0}$. From the perspective of our discussion of estimating equations in Chapter 11, we can remove this term, and the remainder is a set of unbiased estimating functions for $\mathbf{p}$. The restricted and transformed multinomial choice model is then

$$(\mathbf{I}_J \otimes \mathbf{x}')\,\mathbf{y} = (\mathbf{I}_J \otimes \mathbf{x}')\,\mathbf{p}, \tag{20.3.23}$$

which is a pure (i.e., noise suppressed) moment formulation of the problem. In this case, the number of estimating equations, kJ, is less than the number of unknown choice probabilities nJ (on the assumption, as is usual in practice, that $k < n$).

Under the foregoing specification (20.3.23), the multinomial probabilities $\mathbf{p}$ *cannot* be determined by direct inversion of (20.3.23) because the problem is ill-posed and the data points may be consistent with a variety of different values for $\mathbf{p}$. This means we must use an ill-posed formulation and seek non-traditional solutions to the estimation problem. As noted in electronic Chapter E3 for cases in which multiple solutions are possible, under the principle of maximum entropy, *out of the possible multinomial probability distributions consistent with the data*, the maximally noncommittal choice is to select the $\mathbf{p}$ with minimum information content for the multinomial problem. This leads to the pure inverse maximum entropy formulation

$$\max_{\mathbf{p}}[-\mathbf{p}'\ln(\mathbf{p})] \tag{20.3.24}$$

subject to the information-moment constraints

$$(\mathbf{I}_J \otimes \mathbf{x}')\mathbf{y} = (\mathbf{I}_J \otimes \mathbf{x}')\mathbf{p} \tag{20.3.25}$$

and the n normalization (adding-up) conditions

$$(\mathbf{1}_J' \otimes \mathbf{I}_n)\mathbf{p} = \mathbf{1}, \tag{20.3.26}$$

where $\mathbf{1}_j$ is a $(J \times 1)$ vector of 1's. Note that maximization of (20.3.24), subject to the moment constraints (20.3.25) and the adding up-normalization conditions (20.3.26), is equivalent to minimization of the Kullback–Leibler cross-entropy function relative to a uniform distribution for each vector of probabilities $(p_{i1}, \ldots, p_{iJ})$, $i = 1, \ldots, n$ and subject to the same moment constraints.

First-order conditions for the Lagrangian form of the optimization problem (20.3.24)–(20.3.26) form a basis for recovering the unknown $\mathbf{p}$ and the Lagrange multipliers. In particular, the Lagrangian for the maximum entropy optimization problem is

$$L = -\mathbf{p}'\ln(\mathbf{p}) + \boldsymbol{\lambda}'[(\mathbf{I}_J \otimes \mathbf{x}')(\mathbf{p} - \mathbf{y})] + \boldsymbol{\tau}'[(\mathbf{1}_J' \otimes \mathbf{I}_n)\mathbf{p} - \mathbf{1}]. \tag{20.3.27}$$

The solution to this optimization problem is

$$\hat{p}_{ij} = \frac{\exp(-\mathbf{x}_{i\cdot}\hat{\boldsymbol{\lambda}}_j)}{\Omega_i(-\hat{\boldsymbol{\lambda}})} = \frac{\exp(\mathbf{x}_{i\cdot}\hat{\boldsymbol{\beta}}_j)}{\Omega_i(\hat{\boldsymbol{\beta}})} = \frac{\exp(\mathbf{x}_{i\cdot}\hat{\boldsymbol{\beta}}_j)}{1 + \sum_{k=2}^{J}\exp(\mathbf{x}_{i\cdot}\hat{\boldsymbol{\beta}}_k)}, \tag{20.3.28}$$

where $\hat{\boldsymbol{\lambda}}_j$ refers to the $(k \times 1)$ vector of elements of $\hat{\boldsymbol{\lambda}}$ associated with alternative j,

$$\Omega_i(\hat{\boldsymbol{\beta}}) \equiv 1 + \sum_{k=2}^{J}\exp(\mathbf{x}_{i\cdot}\hat{\boldsymbol{\beta}}_k), \tag{20.3.29}$$

$\hat{\boldsymbol{\beta}}_j \equiv -\hat{\boldsymbol{\lambda}}_j$ measures the impact of the explanatory variables on the p_{ij}'s, and we also assume henceforth that the standard identification condition $\hat{\boldsymbol{\beta}}_1 = \mathbf{0}$ is imposed. The $\Omega_i(\hat{\boldsymbol{\beta}})$ term is a normalization factor. The unknown $\boldsymbol{\beta}_j$'s that link the p_{ij} to the $\mathbf{x}_{i\cdot}$ are the negative of the kJ Lagrange multiplier parameters that are chosen so that the optimum solution p^*_{ij} satisfies the constraints (20.3.25). Given the Lagrangian and the corresponding first-order conditions, the Hessian is characterized by elements

$$\frac{\partial^2 \mathrm{L}(\cdot)}{\partial \mathrm{p}_{ij} \partial \mathrm{p}_{ij}} = -\frac{\Omega_i(\boldsymbol{\beta})}{\exp(\mathbf{x}_{i\cdot}\boldsymbol{\beta}_j)} = -\frac{1}{\mathrm{p}_{ij}}, \tag{20.3.30}$$

where all off-diagonal elements are zero. The result is a negative definite Hessian matrix that ensures a unique global solution for the p_{ij}'s.

Defining 1_j to be a $(J \times 1)$ unit vector with one in row j and summing over the J alternatives yields

$$\mathrm{I}(\mathbf{p}_i)_{\mathrm{ME}} = \sum_j \frac{1}{p_{ij}} \mathbf{1}_\mathrm{j} \mathbf{1}'_\mathrm{j} \tag{20.3.31}$$

where $\mathbf{p}_i$ is the vector of probabilities related to observation i for all J alternatives. Finally, by transformation from $\mathbf{p}_i$ to $\boldsymbol{\beta}_j$ space (see Lehmann and Casella 1998, p. 115),

$$\begin{aligned} \mathrm{I}(\boldsymbol{\beta}_l, \boldsymbol{\beta}_m)_{\mathrm{ME}} &= \sum_i \left(\frac{\partial \mathbf{p}_i}{\partial \boldsymbol{\beta}'_l}\right)' \mathrm{I}(\mathbf{p}_i)_{\mathrm{ME}} \left(\frac{\partial \mathbf{p}_i}{\partial \boldsymbol{\beta}'_m}\right) \\ &= \sum_i [p_{im} \mathbf{1}'_l \mathbf{1}_\mathrm{m} - \mathrm{p}_{\mathrm{il}} \mathrm{p}_{\mathrm{im}}] \mathbf{x}'_{i\cdot} \mathbf{x}_{i\cdot} = \mathrm{I}(\boldsymbol{\beta}_l, \boldsymbol{\beta}_m)_{\mathrm{ML}}, \end{aligned} \tag{20.3.32}$$

where (20.3.32) is the (l, m) block of $(J-1)^2$ blocks of dimension $(k \times k)$ referring to all parameter vectors other than the fixed $\boldsymbol{\beta}_1 = \mathbf{0}$. The $[k(\mathrm{J}-1)] \times [k(\mathrm{J}-1)]$ matrix having (20.3.32) for its diagonal blocks is identical to the ML multinomial logit information matrix for $\boldsymbol{\beta}$ in (20.3.15). The asymptotic covariance matrix of $\hat{\boldsymbol{\beta}}$ can be estimated using the inverse of the information matrix evaluated at the classical ME–logit estimates.

Although the conceptual bases for the traditional maximum likelihood (ML) multinomial logit and the classical maximum entropy (ME) formulation are different, and under the classical ME formulation no particular functional form linking the p_{ij} and the $\mathbf{x}_{i\cdot}\boldsymbol{\beta}_j$ was specified, the resulting ML logit and classical ME solutions and information matrices are equivalent, and the usual ML asymptotic properties follow. An intuitive explanation for the correspondence between the classical ME and ML logit solutions is that (1) the estimating equations or moment constraints in the ME formulation are the ML logit first-order conditions, and (2) the ME solution resulting from the optimization has the same mathematical form as the logistic multinomial probabilities. To show this correspondence explicitly, the classic ME approach can be reformulated as an unconstrained problem. Combining the Lagrangian (20.3.27) and the solution for the p_{ij}'s (20.3.28), we may rewrite the ME problem in an unconstrained or concentrated form as the *minimization* problem with respect to $\boldsymbol{\lambda}$ of

$$\mathrm{M}(\boldsymbol{\lambda}) = -\mathbf{y}'(\mathrm{I} \otimes \mathbf{x})\boldsymbol{\lambda} + \sum_i \ln[\Omega_i(-\boldsymbol{\lambda})], \tag{20.3.33}$$

which is equivalent to *maximizing* the multinomial log-likelihood function

$$\begin{aligned}
\ln(\mathrm{L}(\boldsymbol{\beta};\mathbf{y})) &= \sum_i \sum_j \mathrm{y}_{ij} \ln \mathrm{p}_{ij} \\
&= \sum_i \sum_j \mathrm{y}_{ij} \ln \left[\frac{\exp(\mathbf{x}_{i\cdot}\boldsymbol{\beta}_j)}{\sum_j \exp(\mathbf{x}_{i\cdot}\boldsymbol{\beta}_j)} \right] \\
&= \sum_i \sum_j \mathrm{y}_{ij}[\mathbf{x}_{i\cdot}\boldsymbol{\beta}_j] - \sum_i \ln[\Omega_i(\boldsymbol{\beta})],
\end{aligned} \tag{20.3.34}$$

where $\boldsymbol{\beta} = -\boldsymbol{\lambda}$. Consequently, the usual asymptotic properties follow. As discussed in electronic Chapter E3, the concentrated approach substantially reduces computational complexity.

20.3.3. Ordered Multinomial Choice

Up to this point we have not been concerned with the order of the discrete choice alternatives or categories. In some cases, such as the bond rating example cited in the introduction to this chapter, utilities or preferences relate to discrete outcomes that can be expressed in a unique natural order. Fortunately, the estimation and inference procedures that we have developed to handle the unordered discrete case provide a basis for handling the ordered case. In general our objective will be to transform the discrete case into a continuous one in which, given a distribution function, we can then make use of ML procedures. One useful way of thinking about the ordered case is to let the values of a latent variable Y_i^* correspond to a partition of the real line and let the partition be used to indicate which of the ordered alternatives is chosen. More specifically, we consider an unobservable–latent random variable $\mathrm{Y}_i^* = \mathbf{x}_{i\cdot}\boldsymbol{\beta} + \varepsilon_i$ that can take on values over the real line and that determines the outcome of Y_i by the rule

$$\mathrm{Y}_i = j \quad \text{if} \quad \alpha_j < \mathrm{Y}_i^* \leq \alpha_{j+1}; \qquad j = 1, 2, \ldots, J-1 \tag{20.3.35}$$

and $\mathrm{Y}_i = 0$ if $\mathrm{Y}_i^* \leq \alpha_1$ or $\mathrm{Y}_i = \mathrm{J}$ if $\mathrm{Y}_i^* > \alpha_\mathrm{J}$. For example, assume that what we observe is a discrete random variable Y_i that takes on only the three values

$$\begin{aligned}
\mathrm{Y}_i &= 0 \quad \text{if} \quad \mathrm{Y}_i^* \leq \alpha_1 \\
\mathrm{Y}_i &= 1 \quad \text{if} \quad \alpha_1 < \mathrm{Y}_i^* \leq \alpha_2 \\
\mathrm{Y}_i &= 2 \quad \text{if} \quad \alpha_2 < \mathrm{Y}_i^*.
\end{aligned} \tag{20.3.36}$$

Thus, the ordered model involves the unknown threshold parameters α_1 and α_2 as well as the parameter vector $\boldsymbol{\beta}$. Then, the probability that $\mathbf{Y}_i = 0$ is

$$\begin{aligned}
\mathrm{P}(\mathrm{y}_i = 0) &= \mathrm{P}(\mathrm{y}_i^* \leq \alpha_1) = \mathrm{P}(\mathbf{x}_{i\cdot}\boldsymbol{\beta} + \varepsilon_i \leq \alpha_1) \\
&= \mathrm{F}_{\varepsilon_i}(\alpha_1 - \mathbf{x}_{i\cdot}\boldsymbol{\beta})
\end{aligned} \tag{20.3.37}$$

and similarly for the other discrete outcomes. Therefore, in most applications the ordered model takes the simple form

$$P(Y_i = j \mid \mathbf{x}_{i\cdot}, \boldsymbol{\alpha}, \boldsymbol{\beta}) = F_{\varepsilon_i}(\alpha_{j+1} - \mathbf{x}_{i\cdot}\boldsymbol{\beta}) - F_{\varepsilon_i}(\alpha_j - \mathbf{x}_{i\cdot}\boldsymbol{\beta}), \tag{20.3.38}$$

where $j = 0, 1, 2, \ldots, J, \alpha_0 = -\infty, \alpha_j \leq \alpha_{j+1}$, and $\alpha_{J+1} = \infty$.

If the ε_i's are N(0, 1), then maximizing the likelihood function results in the ordered multinomial probit ML estimator. Correspondingly, if the ε_i's are iid logistic, the ordered multinomial ML estimator results. Both formulations have solutions that can be characterized by optimal estimating functions (represented by the first-order conditions for the maximum of the likelihood) and so the estimators have the usual asymptotic and OptEF properties accorded ML estimators. Also, the usual contingent of asymptotic Chi-square test and confidence region procedures can be applied.

The application of ordered multinomial response models seems to be the exception rather than the rule. However, it is useful to have this model in reserve for analysis purposes when it is important to rank or order discrete alternatives. Also, this model is related to our next topic involving censored response models.

20.4. Censored Response Data

Many econometric models are born when someone encounters a problem applying a traditional probability model to a particular type of sample observation and sets out to remedy the problem. For example, when Tobin (1958) was analyzing household expenditures on durable goods with a regression model, he recognized that the sample observations could not logically be negative. Thus, the regression model involved limited dependent variable response data, where the sample outcomes were constrained in some way. Note that a fundamental difference between the response data modeled in previous sections and the data modeled here is that the current situation involves response variables whose range is limited but *continuous*, whereas previously the range of the response variables was limited and *discrete*.

20.4.1. Censoring Versus Truncation

Before proceeding to a discussion of the details of Tobin's model and some of its extensions, we clarify the difference between a *censored* dependent variable and a *truncated* dependent variable. Suppose $(y_1^*, \ldots, y_n^*)$ is a sample outcome of size n relating to some dependent variable of interest. If a constant c is chosen and then the sample outcomes are recorded as

$$y_i = \begin{Bmatrix} y_i^* \\ c \end{Bmatrix} \quad \text{if} \quad y_i^* \begin{Bmatrix} > \\ \leq \end{Bmatrix} c, \tag{20.4.1}$$

the recorded sample values constitute a *censored* sample, the outcomes being (singly) censored at the lower bound c. Censoring can occur at lower bounds or upper bounds (single censoring) or at both lower and upper bounds (a doubly censored sample). As a concrete example, if $\mathbf{y}^* = [-1, 1, 0, 2, 4, 0, 5, 3, -1, 4]$, and if the recorded sample is (singly) censored at the lower bound 1, then the recorded sample of outcomes would be $\mathbf{y} = [1, 1, 1, 2, 4, 1, 5, 3, 1, 4]$.

The use of a censoring mechanism in defining a recorded sample will generally have a notable effect on the form of the joint density of the random sample and associated likelihood function for parameters associated with a DSP model. For example, suppose the Y_i^*'s in the random sample $\mathbf{Y}^* = (Y_1^*, \ldots, Y_n^*)'$ are iid $N(\mu, \sigma^2)$, and the recorded sample is censored at the lower bound c. Then, the joint density of $\mathbf{Y}^*$ and the likelihood function for μ and σ^2 are given by

$$L_*(\mu, \sigma^2; \mathbf{y}^*) = f_{NORM}(\mathbf{y}^*; \mu, \sigma^2) = \prod_{i=1}^{n} \frac{1}{(2\pi)^{1/2}\sigma} \exp\left[-\frac{1}{2\sigma^2}(y_i^* - \mu)^2\right]$$
$$= \frac{1}{\sigma^n} \prod_{i=1}^{n} f_{NORM}\left(\frac{y_i^* - \mu}{\sigma}\right) \tag{20.4.2}$$

On the other hand, the recorded sample based on (20.4.1) has a joint density and associated likelihood function given by

$$L(\mu, \sigma^2; \mathbf{y}) = f(\mathbf{y}; \mu, \sigma^2)$$
$$= \left[\prod_{\{y_i\text{'s}>c\}} \frac{1}{(2\pi)^{1/2}\sigma} \exp\left(-\frac{1}{2\sigma^2}(y_i - \mu)^2\right)\right]\left[\prod_{\{y_i\text{'s}=c\}} \int_{-\infty}^{c} \frac{1}{(2\pi)^{1/2}\sigma} \times \exp\left(-\frac{1}{2\sigma^2}(y_i - \mu)^2\right)\right]$$
$$= \left[\frac{1}{\sigma^{\#(y_i\text{'s}>c)}} \prod_{y_i\text{'s}>c} f_{NORM}\left(\frac{y_i - \mu}{\sigma}\right)\right]\left[F_{NORM}\left(\frac{c - \mu}{\sigma}\right)\right]^{\#(y_i\text{'s}=c)}, \tag{20.4.3}$$

where $\#(y_i\text{'s} > c)$ and $\#(y_i\text{'s} = c)$ are the number of outcomes in $(y_1, \ldots, y_n)$ whose values exceed c and equal c, respectively. Also, the second bracketed term in the middle line of (20.4.3) is the probability of observing the set of censored values. Note that, although the Y_i^*'s are *continuous* random variables in this illustration, the Y_i's are *mixed discrete–continuous* random variables, where

$$f(y_i) = \begin{Bmatrix} \frac{1}{(2\pi)^{1/2}\sigma} \exp\left(-\frac{1}{2\sigma^2}(y_i - \mu)^2\right) \\ p(y_i = c) = F_{NORM}\left(\frac{c - \mu}{\sigma}\right) \end{Bmatrix} \quad \text{if} \quad y_i \begin{Bmatrix} > c \\ = c \end{Bmatrix} \tag{20.4.4}$$

Now consider a sampling situation in which, *before* the sample is taken, we truncate the distribution from which the sample is drawn, meaning that we eliminate a subset of the support of the distribution so that no observations are sampled from this discarded subset. For example, in studying the consumption behavior of households, we might sample only households whose incomes exceed \$5000. The key operational difference between censoring and truncation is that, under censoring, we record either the censored value or the actual value of a sample outcome to produce a recorded sample from an original (uncensored) sample, whereas under truncation, we alter the support of the sampling distribution before sampling begins.

As in the case of censoring, the truncation procedures will generally have a notable effect on the form of the joint probability distribution associated with the observed and recorded sample. Examine the case in which Y_i^*'s are iid $N(\mu, \sigma^2)$ random variables, and suppose that prior to sampling, the distribution is truncated by eliminating all potential observations $\leq c$. Then the sampled random variables, say the Y_i's, have a *truncated* normal distribution defined by

$$y_i \sim f(y_i^* \mid y_i^* > c) = \frac{(2\pi\sigma^2)^{-1/2} \exp\left(-\frac{1}{2\sigma^2}(y_i^* - \mu)^2\right)}{1 - F_{NORM}\left(\frac{c-\mu}{\sigma}\right)} \quad \text{for } y_i^* > c$$

$$= 0 \qquad \text{elsewhere.} \tag{20.4.5}$$

Note that $1 - F_{NORM}(\frac{c-\mu}{\sigma})$ is the normalizing constant that rescales the $N(\mu, \sigma^2)$ density so that it integrates to 1 over the restricted support (c, ∞). It is clear that the joint density of the truncated iid random sample, which would equal the product (20.4.5) over all $i = 1, \ldots, n$, is notably different from the joint PDF of the untruncated sample (20.4.2). Note further that the random variables in the truncated random sample are all still *continuous* random variables as opposed to the random variables in the censored random sample, which were *mixed discrete–continuous* random variables.

20.4.2. Tobit Model

Tobin (1958) devised a model and estimation procedure that is appropriate for censored samples. To appreciate why special models and estimation procedures are generally needed when sample data are censored, consider the case in which

$$Y_i^* = \mathbf{x}_{i\cdot}\boldsymbol{\beta} + \varepsilon_i^*, \qquad \varepsilon_i^* \sim \text{iid } N(0, \sigma^2) \tag{20.4.6}$$

and the recorded sample of data is censored at a lower bound of $c = 0$ using (20.4.1). The observed data then satisfy

$$y_i = \begin{Bmatrix} y_i^* \\ 0 \end{Bmatrix} \text{ if } \begin{Bmatrix} y_i^* > 0 \\ y_i^* \leq 0 \end{Bmatrix}. \tag{20.4.7}$$

It follows that

$$E[Y_i] = \int_{-\mathbf{x}_{i\cdot}\boldsymbol{\beta}}^{\infty} (\mathbf{x}_{i\cdot}\boldsymbol{\beta} + \varepsilon_i) N(\varepsilon_i; 0, \sigma^2)\, d\varepsilon_i + 0 \cdot P(\varepsilon_i \leq -\mathbf{x}_{i\cdot}\boldsymbol{\beta})$$

$$= [\mathbf{x}_{i\cdot}\boldsymbol{\beta} + E[\varepsilon_i \mid \varepsilon_i > -\mathbf{x}_{i\cdot}\boldsymbol{\beta}]] P(\varepsilon_i > -\mathbf{x}_{i\cdot}\boldsymbol{\beta})$$

$$= (\mathbf{x}_{i\cdot}\boldsymbol{\beta}) F_{NORM}\left(\frac{\mathbf{x}_{i\cdot}\boldsymbol{\beta}}{\sigma}\right) + \sigma f_{NORM}\left(\frac{\mathbf{x}_{i\cdot}\boldsymbol{\beta}}{\sigma}\right) \tag{20.4.8}$$

because, upon substituting $z = \varepsilon_i/\sigma$,

$$\begin{aligned} E[\varepsilon_i \mid \varepsilon_i > -\mathbf{x}_{i\cdot}\boldsymbol{\beta}]\,P(\varepsilon_i > -\mathbf{x}_{i\cdot}\boldsymbol{\beta}) &= \int_{-\mathbf{x}_{i\cdot}\boldsymbol{\beta}}^{\infty} \varepsilon_i \frac{1}{(2\pi)^{1/2}\sigma} \exp\left(-\frac{\varepsilon_i^2}{2\sigma^2}\right) d\varepsilon_i \\ &= \sigma \int_{-\mathbf{x}_{i\cdot}\boldsymbol{\beta}/\sigma}^{\infty} z \frac{1}{(2\pi)^{1/2}} \exp\left(-\frac{z^2}{2}\right) dz \\ &= \sigma f_{\mathrm{NORM}}\left(\frac{\mathbf{x}_{i\cdot}\boldsymbol{\beta}}{\sigma}\right). \end{aligned} \tag{20.4.9}$$

The marginal effect of a change in a continuous explanatory variable on the expected value of Y_i can be defined as (recall (20.4.8))

$$\frac{\partial E[Y_i]}{\partial \mathbf{x}'_{i\cdot}} = \boldsymbol{\beta}\, F_{\mathrm{NORM}}\left(\frac{\mathbf{x}_{i\cdot}\boldsymbol{\beta}}{\sigma}\right). \tag{20.4.10}$$

Note that this derivative refers specifically to a Tobit model whose response variable is censored at a lower bound of zero. More generally, if the response variables are censored from below at the value c_1 and from above at the value c_2, the appropriate derivative expression will be given by

$$\frac{\partial E[Y_i]}{\partial \mathbf{x}'_{i\cdot}} = \boldsymbol{\beta}\left[F_{\mathrm{NORM}}\left(\frac{c_2 - \mathbf{x}_{i\cdot}\boldsymbol{\beta}}{\sigma}\right) - F_{\mathrm{NORM}}\left(\frac{c_1 - \mathbf{x}_{i\cdot}\boldsymbol{\beta}}{\sigma}\right)\right] \tag{20.4.11}$$

(see Nakamura and Nakamura (1983)). Close examination of (20.4.10) and (20.4.11) indicates that the marginal effects of continuous explanatory variables are given by the associated elements of $\boldsymbol{\beta}$ scaled by the probability that the response variable is *not censored.*

Maximum likelihood estimation of (20.4.10) or (20.4.11) can be performed by replacing unknowns by ML estimates and appealing to the invariance property of ML estimation. Calculating asymptotic standard errors, tests, and confidence regions can proceed as usual based on standard results applicable in ML contexts involving nonlinear functions of parameters.

It is apparent that an application of least squares to data generated from $(\mathbf{Y}, \mathbf{x})$ results in $\hat{\boldsymbol{\beta}} = (\mathbf{x}'\mathbf{x})^{-1}\mathbf{x}'\mathbf{Y}$ for which

$$E[\hat{\boldsymbol{\beta}}] = (\mathbf{x}'\mathbf{x})^{-1}\mathbf{x}'[(\mathbf{x}\boldsymbol{\beta}) \odot F_{\mathrm{NORM}}(\mathbf{x}\boldsymbol{\beta}/\sigma) + \sigma f_{\mathrm{NORM}}(\mathbf{x}\boldsymbol{\beta}/\sigma)] \neq \boldsymbol{\beta}, \tag{20.4.12}$$

where $F_{\mathrm{NORM}}(\mathbf{x}\boldsymbol{\beta}/\sigma) \equiv [F_{\mathrm{NORM}}(\mathbf{x}_{1\cdot}\boldsymbol{\beta}/\sigma), \ldots, F_{\mathrm{NORM}}(\mathbf{x}_{n\cdot}\boldsymbol{\beta}/\sigma)]'$, $f_{\mathrm{NORM}}(\mathbf{x}\boldsymbol{\beta}/\sigma) \equiv [f_{\mathrm{NORM}}(\mathbf{x}_{1\cdot}\boldsymbol{\beta})/\sigma, \ldots, f_{\mathrm{NORM}}(\mathbf{x}_{n\cdot}\boldsymbol{\beta}/\sigma)]'$, and $\odot$ denotes the Hadamard (elementwise) product. Thus, the LS estimator is biased. There is also no reason to expect the bias to dissipate as $n \to \infty$, and so the estimator is not consistent. Finally, if the values of the vectors $F_{\mathrm{NORM}}(\mathbf{x}\boldsymbol{\beta}/\sigma)$ and $f_{\mathrm{NORM}}(\mathbf{x}\boldsymbol{\beta}/\sigma)$ were known, it is evident from (20.4.8) that upon defining $\mathbf{x}_* \equiv [\mathbf{x} \odot F_{\mathrm{NORM}}(\mathbf{x}\boldsymbol{\beta}/\sigma) \,\vdots\, f_{\mathrm{NORM}}(\mathbf{x}\boldsymbol{\beta}/\sigma)]$ and $\boldsymbol{\beta}_* = [\boldsymbol{\beta}' \,\vdots\, \sigma]'$, we could define the model

$$\mathbf{Y} = \mathbf{x}_*\boldsymbol{\beta}_* + \mathbf{V}, \tag{20.4.13}$$

and then the LS estimator $\hat{\boldsymbol{\beta}}_* = (\mathbf{x}'_*\mathbf{x}_*)^{-1}\mathbf{x}'_*\mathbf{Y}$ would be an unbiased and consistent estimator. Of course, we generally do not know $F_{\mathrm{NORM}}(\mathbf{x}\boldsymbol{\beta}/\sigma)$ or $f_{\mathrm{NORM}}(\mathbf{x}\boldsymbol{\beta}/\sigma)$ owing to the presence of the unknown parameters σ and $\boldsymbol{\beta}$.

20.4.2.a. ML Estimation and Inference for the Tobit Model

To develop the ML approach to estimation and inference in the Tobit model we continue to examine the censoring defined by (20.4.7), and we also maintain the normality assumption (20.4.6). Now note that $P(y_i = 0) = P(y_i^* \le 0) = P(\varepsilon_i^* \le -\mathbf{x}_{i\cdot}\boldsymbol{\beta}) = P(\varepsilon_i^*/\sigma \le -\mathbf{x}_{i\cdot}\boldsymbol{\beta}/\sigma)$, in which case the likelihood function associated with a sample outcome $(y_1, \ldots, y_n)$ is given by

$$L(\boldsymbol{\beta}, \sigma; \mathbf{y}) = \prod_{\{i: y_i = 0\}} F_{\mathrm{NORM}}(-\mathbf{x}_{i\cdot}\boldsymbol{\beta}/\sigma) \prod_{\{i: y_i > 0\}} \sigma^{-1} f_{\mathrm{NORM}}(y_i - \mathbf{x}_{i\cdot}\boldsymbol{\beta}/\sigma). \quad (20.4.14)$$

As in our discussion of censoring in Section 20.4.1, the likelihood function represents the mixed discrete–continuous nature of y_i, which takes the value 0 with *probability* $F_{\mathrm{NORM}}(-\mathbf{x}_{i\cdot}\boldsymbol{\beta}/\sigma)$ and takes on a value $y_i > 0$ with *probability density* $\sigma^{-1} f_{\mathrm{NORM}}(\mathbf{x}_{i\cdot}\boldsymbol{\beta}/\sigma)$. The first term in (20.4.14) looks very much like the corresponding term in the likelihood function for the probit model, which inspired Goldberger to label the model to which $L(\boldsymbol{\beta}, \sigma^2; \mathbf{y})$ refers as the Tobit model.

The maximum likelihood estimate of $\boldsymbol{\beta}$ and σ is obtained by maximizing $L(\boldsymbol{\beta}, \sigma; \mathbf{y})$ or, equivalently, maximizing $\ln(L(\boldsymbol{\beta}, \sigma; \mathbf{y}))$. Amemiya (1973) demonstrated that the usual consistency and asymptotic normality properties of ML estimators hold for this model. The asymptotic normal distribution of the ML estimator can be estimated in the usual way as

$$\hat{\boldsymbol{\theta}}_{\mathrm{ML}} \overset{a}{\sim} N\left(\boldsymbol{\theta}, -\left[\left.\frac{\partial^2 \ln(L(\boldsymbol{\theta}; \mathbf{y}))}{\partial \boldsymbol{\theta} \partial \boldsymbol{\theta}'}\right|_{\hat{\boldsymbol{\theta}}_{\mathrm{ML}}}\right]^{-1}\right), \quad (20.4.15)$$

where $\boldsymbol{\theta} \equiv \binom{\boldsymbol{\beta}}{\sigma}$. The usual asymptotic Chi-square testing and confidence-region estimation procedures applied in the ML context follow directly.

20.4.2.b. Two-Step (Heckman) Estimation of the Tobit Model

We noted earlier that if the values of the vectors $F_{\mathrm{NORM}}(\mathbf{x}\boldsymbol{\beta}/\sigma)$ and $f_{\mathrm{NORM}}(\mathbf{x}\boldsymbol{\beta}/\sigma)$ were known, we could estimate the Tobit model using the least-squares estimator applied to the linear model (20.4.13). Heckman (1976) demonstrated a consistent estimation procedure for the Tobit model based on a two-step procedure in which the first step entails obtaining consistent estimates of $F_{\mathrm{NORM}}(\mathbf{x}\boldsymbol{\beta}/\sigma)$ and $f_{\mathrm{NORM}}(\mathbf{x}\boldsymbol{\beta}/\sigma)$ and the second step uses these estimates in place of the unknowns in the least-squares estimation of (20.4.13).

The first step of the procedure consists of estimating a probit model for the binary variables

$$z_i = \begin{Bmatrix} 1 \\ 0 \end{Bmatrix} \quad \text{if} \quad y_i^* = \mathbf{x}_{i\cdot}\boldsymbol{\beta} + \varepsilon_i^* \begin{Bmatrix} >0 \\ \le 0 \end{Bmatrix}, \qquad \text{for } j = 1, \ldots, n. \quad (20.4.16)$$

The likelihood function for the probit model is given by

$$L(\boldsymbol{\beta}/\sigma; \mathbf{z}) = \prod_{z_i\text{'s}=1} F_{\mathrm{NORM}}(\mathbf{x}_{i\cdot}\boldsymbol{\beta}/\sigma) \prod_{z_i\text{'s}=0} (1 - F_{\mathrm{NORM}}(\mathbf{x}_{i\cdot}\boldsymbol{\beta}/\sigma)), \quad (20.4.17)$$

where we have expressed the parameters as $\boldsymbol{\beta}/\sigma$ because only the ratios defined by $\boldsymbol{\beta}/\sigma$ are identifiable in the probit model, as discussed in Section 20.1.2. Maximizing the likelihood or log-likelihood function of (20.4.17) with respect to the choice of $\boldsymbol{\beta}/\sigma$ yields the consistent ML estimate of the ratio $\boldsymbol{\beta}/\sigma$, say $(\widehat{\boldsymbol{\beta}/\sigma})_{\mathrm{ML}}$. Then, by the ML invariance principle, ML estimates of $\mathrm{F_{NORM}}(\mathbf{x}_{i\cdot}\boldsymbol{\beta}/\sigma)$ and $\mathrm{f_{NORM}}(\mathbf{x}_{i\cdot}\boldsymbol{\beta}/\sigma)$ are defined by

$$\hat{\mathrm{F}}_{\mathrm{NORM},\,i} \equiv \mathrm{F_{NORM}}(\mathbf{x}_{i\cdot}(\widehat{\boldsymbol{\beta}/\sigma})_{\mathrm{ML}}) \ \text{ and } \ \hat{\mathrm{f}}_{\mathrm{NORM},\,i} \equiv \mathrm{f_{NORM}}(\mathbf{x}_{i\cdot}(\widehat{\boldsymbol{\beta}/\sigma})_{\mathrm{ML}}), \quad i=1,\ldots,n, \tag{20.4.18}$$

and these estimates are consistent. Substituting the estimates (20.4.18) into (20.4.13) yields the linear model

$$\mathbf{Y} = [\mathbf{x} \odot \hat{\mathrm{F}}_{\mathrm{NORM}} \,\vdots\, \hat{\mathrm{f}}_{\mathrm{NORM}}] \begin{bmatrix} \boldsymbol{\beta} \\ \cdots \\ \sigma \end{bmatrix} + \mathbf{W}, \tag{20.4.19}$$

and least squares applied to (20.4.19) yields consistent estimates of the parameters $\boldsymbol{\beta}$ and σ. The usual asymptotic tests and confidence region estimation procedures can be used for inference relating to parameter values.

We note that it is possible to define a two-step estimator that is based on a model that relates to only the nonzero (more generally noncensored) observations. The reader can demonstrate that

$$\begin{aligned} \mathrm{E}[\mathrm{Y}_i \mid \mathrm{y}_i > 0] &= \mathbf{x}_{i\cdot}\boldsymbol{\beta} + \mathrm{E}[\varepsilon_i^* \mid \varepsilon_i^* > -\mathbf{x}_{i\cdot}\boldsymbol{\beta}] \\ &= \mathbf{x}_{i\cdot}\boldsymbol{\beta} + \sigma \left[\frac{\mathrm{f_{NORM}}(\mathbf{x}_{i\cdot}\boldsymbol{\beta}/\sigma)}{\mathrm{F_{NORM}}(\mathbf{x}_{i\cdot}\boldsymbol{\beta}/\sigma)} \right], \end{aligned} \tag{20.4.20}$$

where the bracketed expression postmultiplying σ in (20.4.20) is referred to as the *Mill's ratio*. Therefore,

$$\mathrm{Y}_i = \mathbf{x}_{i\cdot}\boldsymbol{\beta} + \sigma \left[\frac{\mathrm{f_{NORM}}(\mathbf{x}_{i\cdot}\boldsymbol{\beta}/\sigma)}{\mathrm{F_{NORM}}(\mathbf{x}_{i\cdot}\boldsymbol{\beta}/\sigma)} \right] + \mathrm{V}_i, \quad i = 1, \ldots, n \tag{20.4.21}$$

would be a linear regression model in the parameters $\boldsymbol{\beta}$ and σ if the values of the bracketed expression were known. As one might expect by now, the bracketed expression can be estimated based on the ML probit estimates of $(\boldsymbol{\beta}/\sigma)$, and through these estimates in (20.4.21), $\boldsymbol{\beta}$ and σ can then be consistently estimated via least squares.

► **Example 20.4.1:** To compare the estimation procedures for the censored regression model, we provide the GAUSS program C20Tobit.gss in the examples manual. For a given set of censored data, estimates of $\boldsymbol{\beta}$ and σ^2 are computed by Tobin's MLE, Heckman's two-stage estimator, and the regression procedure based on the noncensored observations. GAUSS reports the parameter estimates and approximate standard errors for each of the alternatives.

20.4.3. Extensions of the Tobit Formulation

One direct extension to the Tobit formulation is a model to accommodate double or multiple censoring. For example, to return to the basic latent variable model

$$\mathrm{Y}_i^* = \mathbf{x}_{i\cdot}\boldsymbol{\beta} + \varepsilon_i; \quad \varepsilon_i \overset{\text{iid}}{\sim} \mathrm{N}(0, \sigma^2), \quad i = 1, \ldots, n, \tag{20.4.22}$$

consider a situation in which there are J censored values that are observable, as defined by $J - 1$ threshold or boundary points

$$\begin{aligned} \mathrm{Y}_i &= 0 \quad \text{if } \mathrm{Y}_i^* \leq \mu_1 \\ \mathrm{Y}_i &= 1 \quad \text{if } \mu_1 < \mathrm{Y}_i^* \leq \mu_2 \\ &\vdots \\ \mathrm{Y}_i &= J - 1 \quad \text{if } \mathrm{Y}_i^* > \mu_{J-1}, \end{aligned} \tag{20.4.23}$$

where the threshold or boundary parameters $\mu_1, \ldots, \mu_{J-1}$ may be known or unknown. This multiple censoring transformation (20.4.23) is a variant of the ordered multinomial response model (Zavoina and McElvey, 1975; Beggs, Cardell, and Hausman, 1981; and Greene, 1993). Another variation on this theme is the case in which the Y_i variable is continuous on one or more of the intervals in (20.4.23) and is only censored on a subset of the intervals.

Alternatively, within this context, consider the case in which observations on the variable $\mathrm{Y}_i^* = \mathbf{x}_{i\cdot}\boldsymbol{\beta} + \varepsilon_i$ are generated by random censoring in which one observes $\mathrm{Y}_i, \mathrm{d}_i, \mathbf{x}_{i\cdot}$ with

$$\mathrm{Y}_i = \max(\mathrm{Y}_i^*, \mu_i), \quad \mathrm{d}_i = \mathrm{I}_{(\mathrm{y}_i, \infty)}(\mu_i), \quad i = 1, 2, \ldots, n, \tag{20.4.24}$$

and μ_i is an outcome of a random variable that is independent of $\mathbf{x}_{i\cdot}$ and ε_i. The function $\mathrm{I}_{(\mathrm{y}_i, \infty)}(\mu_i)$ is a zero–one indicator function that equals 1 if censoring occurs. Miller (1976), Buckley and James (1979), Koul, Susarla, and Van Ryzin (1981), and Honoré and Powell (1994) have proposed estimators to accommodate such random censoring. An alternative random censoring model has been proposed by Cheng and Wu (1994), where $\mu_i = \mathrm{g}(\mathbf{x}_{i\cdot}, \mathrm{v}_i)$ and v_i is a random error.

Still another interesting extension to the Tobit model entails multiple equations. Consider, for example, the two-equation Tobit model in which

$$\begin{aligned} \mathrm{Y}_{1i}^* &= \mathbf{x}_{1i}'\boldsymbol{\beta}_1 + \varepsilon_{1i} \\ \mathrm{Y}_{2i}^* &= \mathbf{x}_{2i}'\boldsymbol{\beta}_2 + \varepsilon_{2i} \\ \mathrm{Y}_{2i} &= \mathrm{Y}_{2i}^* \text{ if } \mathrm{Y}_{1i}^* > 0 \\ \mathrm{Y}_{2i} &= 0 \text{ if } \mathrm{Y}_{1i}^* \leq 0 \end{aligned} \tag{20.4.25}$$

for $i = 1, 2, \ldots, n$, where $(\varepsilon_{1i}, \varepsilon_{2i})$ are iid drawings from a bivariate normal distribution with mean zero and covariance matrix $\boldsymbol{\Sigma}$, and $\mathbf{x}_{1i}$ and $\mathbf{x}_{2i}$ are column vectors of explanatory variable values associated with the ith observation. Only the sign of Y_{1i}^* is assumed observed, and Y_{2i}^* is only observed when $\mathrm{Y}_{1i}^* > 0$. The explanatory variables

$\mathbf{x}'_{2i}$ need not be observed when $Y^*_{1i} \leq 0$. In defining the likelihood function for use in ML estimation and inference, the likelihood function then involves $P(Y^*_{1i} \leq 0)$, the joint conditional density $f(Y^*_{2i} \mid Y^*_{1i} > 0)$, and $P(Y^*_{1i} > 0)$. The likelihood function for this formulation can be represented in general form by

$$\begin{aligned} L(\boldsymbol{\beta}; \mathbf{y}) &= \prod_{\{i:y_{2i}=0\}} p(y^*_{1i} \leq 0) \prod_{\{i:y_{2i}\neq 0\}} f(y_{2i} \mid y^*_{1i} > 0) p(y^*_{1i} > 0) \\ &= \prod_{\{i:y_{2i}=0\}} p(y^*_{1i} \leq 0) \prod_{\{i:y_{2i}\neq 0\}} \int_0^\infty f(y^*_{1i} \mid y_{2i}) f(y_{2i})\, dy^*_{1i} \qquad (20.4.26) \end{aligned}$$

Then, because under the current normality assumptions the conditional distribution of Y^*_{1i}, given $y^*_{2i} = y_{2i}$, is also normally distributed with mean $\mathbf{x}'_{1i}\boldsymbol{\beta}_1 + \Sigma_{12}\Sigma_{22}^{-1}(y_{2i} - \mathbf{x}'_{2i}\boldsymbol{\beta}_2)$ and covariance matrix (scalar variance in this case) $\Sigma_{11} - \Sigma_{12}\Sigma_{22}^{-1}\Sigma_{21}$ (see electronic Chapter E1), the likelihood function can finally be expressed as

$$L(\boldsymbol{\beta}; \mathbf{y}) = \prod_{\{i:y_{2i}=0\}} \left[1 - F_{NORM}\left(\mathbf{x}'_{1i}\left(\boldsymbol{\beta}_1 / \Sigma_{11}^{1/2}\right)\right)\right] \prod_{\{i:y_{2i}\neq 0\}}$$

$$\times \left[F_{NORM}\left(\frac{\left[\mathbf{x}'_{1i}\boldsymbol{\beta}_1 + \Sigma_{12}\Sigma_{22}^{-1}(y_{2i} - \mathbf{x}'_{2i}\boldsymbol{\beta}_2)\right]}{\left(\Sigma_{11} - \Sigma_{12}\Sigma_{22}^{-1}\Sigma_{21}\right)^{1/2}} \right) f_{NORM}\left((y_{2i} - \mathbf{x}'_{2i}\boldsymbol{\beta}_2)/\Sigma_{22}^{1/2}\right) \right] \qquad (20.4.27)$$

In the current specification of the model, the parameter Σ_{11} is not identified. The usual practice is to set $\Sigma_{11} = 1$; then the rest of the model parameters can be estimated, and testing and confidence region estimation can proceed, using the usual ML approach. If there are additional restrictions on model parameters (for example, if one or more of the elements in $\boldsymbol{\beta}_1$ and $\boldsymbol{\beta}_2$ are constrained to be equal), then Σ_{11} is identifiable and need not be normalized to 1.

One application of the formulation (20.4.25) relates back to the loan agent problem that addresses the discrete question of whether or not to make a loan and, conditional on making the loan, how large the loan should be. Many other interesting possibilities exist for being creative with regression models involving censored or truncated observations. At this point in our study the reader should be able to propose a scenario involving censored–truncated response variables and devise a corresponding probability model and estimation rule. In fact, an exercise at the end of the chapter will encourage the reader in this direction.

20.5. Concluding Remarks

In this chapter we have examined the interesting problem of how to deal with discrete or mixed discrete–continuous rather than continuous response data. In each of the formulations we have considered we have used a latent variable Y^*_i, which can take on values over the real line, to transform the statistical model to a form that is tractable, given the tools developed in previous chapters. Following tradition, in general we associated the latent variable Y_i^* with a particular distribution that permitted us to use ML procedures and thus utilize estimation and inference procedures that have good asymptotic properties. However, in a nontraditional, nonparametric context we have also formulated the multinomial response problem in a maximum entropy framework involving an estimation objective function with side constraints that yield results analogous to parametric methods. The latter approach was suggestive of a whole set of possible nonparametric alternative specifications of qualitative response and limited dependent variable models that deserve the attention of future research.

This chapter provides only an introduction to some of the problems and ideas dealing with discrete response data. The discrete, choice-limited, dependent literature is massive, and there are many interesting and important topics that have been given little or no exposure in this introduction. We have made the choice to concentrate on the basic formulations so that the reader will have a foundation to build on as his or her interest in this area grows. The references at the end of the chapter should help the reader to become further immersed in this vast literature.

Before closing, we note in both the censored regression and binary–multinomial response models that the focus is on recovering information about the underlying unknown parameters. For these models, the various traditional estimation procedures differ mainly in terms of the knowledge assumed about the noise distribution. If knowledge of the underlying data-sampling process is available and the correct likelihood is specified, the maximum likelihood (ML) estimator is consistent and asymptotically efficient. However, knowledge of the underlying data-sampling process is seldom available, and thus models relying on the specification of parametric distributions may be subject to distributional misspecifications, which may then lead to inconsistent or inefficient estimates. If there are missing observations, or the noise distribution is other than the normal or logistic, the likelihood function may be complicated and the task of maximizing the likelihood function burdensome.

To avoid the statistical consequences of one or more of these potential problems, in the Tobit-censored regression model, Powell (1984, 1986a,b), Newey (1989), Nawata (1990), and Newey and Powell (1990) have weakened or relaxed the traditional parametric restriction on the form of the distribution of the underlying errors and have proposed consistent estimators that require only weak sampling conditions.

Using the objective of not employing distributional information that we do not possess, Golan, Judge, and Perloff (1997) reformulated the parameter recovery problem under weak sampling assumptions and used a generalization of the maximum entropy (GME) and cross entropy (GCE) estimation methods of Chapter 13 to recover the unknown and unobservable parameters (see electronic Chapter E3). Unlike ML procedures in which the estimators are defined in terms of moments of the data and the emphasis is on prediction, in the GME–GCE approaches the *entire* set of sample points, along with any nonsample information that is natural to include, is used to recover the unknown parameters and unobservable parameters $\boldsymbol{\beta}$ and ε, and the aim is to maximize a dual objective function emphasizing both estimation precision and prediction.

20.6. Exercises

20.6.1. Idea Checklist – Knowledge Guides

---

1. How are latent variables used to transform problems characterized by a discrete or mixed discrete–continuous response (e.g., binary, multinomial, Tobit models) into a form that is amenable to ML estimation? What is "latent" about the latent variables used in these contexts?
2. Consider the case of the demand for a durable good as Tobin did when he first presented the model that has now become known as the Tobit model. Why could the response variable not be modeled as a no-purchase or how-much-purchased outcome, with the response variable having a truncated (at zero) normal, logistic, or some other continuous distribution? In other words, what does censoring introduce that truncation would not in this modeling context?
3. How should one measure the marginal impact of a change in a dummy or indicator (0–1) explanatory variable on the probability of a zero outcome in a binary, multinomial, or Tobit model (if it is assumed zero is an outcome or response that has nonzero probability)? Why can one simply not use the derivative of the predicted probability with respect to a change in the explanatory variable?
4. In multinomial discrete choice problems with relatively large numbers of choices, what makes the assumption of normality so computationally difficult?
5. When, if at all, should an analyst prefer a two-step estimator over a maximum likelihood estimator in analyzing a Tobit-type model?
6. How would you implement the bootstrap resampling procedures for a model with mixed discrete–continuous observations? Would it be easier to use parametric or nonparametric bootstrap procedures for the models discussed in this chapter?

20.6.2. Problems

20–1 Define an asymptotic Wald test for testing an hypothesis about the value of the derivative with respect to a continuous explanatory variable of the probability of a unit outcome in the binary choice problem (see Equations (20.1.16)–(20.1.18)). Use duality to define a confidence region for the value of the derivative.

20–2 Repeat the preceding problem for likelihood ratio and Lagrange multiplier tests and confidence regions.

20–3 Within a Tobit model context in which normality is assumed and the observations are censored at the value zero (e.g., modeling the purchase decision regarding a consumer good), consider using maximum likelihood to estimate the parameters of the model when we are using only the *nonzero* observations in the sample. Develop the maximum likelihood estimation procedure in this case and concurrently show that estimation proceeds on the basis of a *truncated* normal distribution as opposed to a mixed discrete–continuous distribution induced by censoring of the response variable.

20–4 For a particular multinomial logit model, suppose we have two plausible sets of explanatory variables $\mathbf{x}_1$ and $\mathbf{x}_2$ with associated parameter vectors $\boldsymbol{\beta}_1$ and $\boldsymbol{\beta}_2$. Suggest at least three test procedures that may be used to evaluate the null hypothesis $\mathrm{H}_0\colon \boldsymbol{\beta}_2 = \mathbf{0}$. State the relevant test statistics and the associated limiting distributions under the null hypothesis.

20–5 Suppose the covariance matrix for the logit ML estimator is $\boldsymbol{\Sigma}$. Derive the approximate large-sample covariance matrix for the marginal effects (20.3.16) on the assumption $J = 2$ and $k > 1$. Devise an appropriate test statistic (or set of statistics) for the null hypothesis H_0: $\partial p_{i1}/\partial x_{i1} < 0$ and $\partial p_{i1}/\partial x_{i2} < 0$ (i.e., the marginal effects of the first two explanatory variables are negative).

20–6 Under the same assumptions stated in Problem 5, derive a 90% asymptotic confidence interval for the predicted choice probability $g(\mathbf{x}_{i\cdot}\hat{\boldsymbol{\beta}})$ for a particular $\mathbf{x}_{i\cdot}$. How would you form a joint confidence region (with overall coverage probability of 90%) for a subset of the n predicted choice probabilities in the sample?

20.6.3. Computer Problems

20–1 Using the GAUSS program C20MLLog.gss (Example 20.2.2) as a guide, design a Monte Carlo simulation exercise to demonstrate the statistical pitfalls of using the linear probability model. In particular, do the sample moments and empirical distribution (or histogram) of the simulated parameter estimates indicate that the estimator may be biased, consistent, or asymptotically normal?

20–2 Extend the GAUSS program C20Tobit.gss (Example 20.4.1) to include a Monte Carlo sampling experiment designed to simulate the statistical properties of the various censored regression estimators. On the basis of your findings, what can you say about the relative performance of the ML and two-step estimators of the Tobit model?

20–3 Construct a DSP for a censored regression model. Using pseudorandom censored observations generated from this model, simulate the statistical properties of the unadjusted and weighted least-squares estimators. Do the simulation results conform to your expectations based on the discussion in this chapter? How well does the least-squares estimator perform when the parameter estimates are only computed from the uncensored observations?

20–4 You are given the following data on $\mathbf{Y}$ and $\mathbf{x}$:

$$\begin{aligned}\mathbf{y}' &= [0 \quad 0 \quad 1 \quad 0 \quad 1 \quad 1 \quad 0 \quad 1 \quad 0 \quad 0] \\ \mathbf{x}' &= [9 \quad 7 \quad 2 \quad 6 \quad 3 \quad 5 \quad 4 \quad 2 \quad 7 \quad 8]\end{aligned}.$$

a. Estimate probit and logit models and test the hypothesis that the explanatory variable is not effective in determining the probability that the dependent variable takes an outcome of 1.

b. On the basis of the data in Computer Problem 3 above, use a maximum entropy approach to estimate the probabilities associated with the binary choice problem.

20.7. References

Amemiya, T. (1973), "Regression Analysis When the Dependent Variable Is Truncated Normal," *Econometrica*, Vol. 41, pp. 997–1016.

Amemiya, T. (1978), "The Estimation of a Simultaneous Equation Generalized Probit Model," *Econometrica*, Vol. 46, pp. 1193–1205.

Amemiya, T. (1981), "Qualitative Response Models: A Survey," *Journal of Economic Literature*, Vol. 19, pp. 1483–1536.

Amemiya, T. (1984), "Tobit Models: A Survey," *Journal of Econometrics*, Vol. 24, pp. 3–61.

Amemiya, T. (1985), *Advanced Econometrics*, Cambridge, MA: Harvard University Press.

Beggs, S., S. Cardell, and J. Hausman (1981), "Assessing the Potential Demand for Electric Cars," *Journal of Econometrics*, Vol. 17, pp. 1–19.

Buckley, J., and I. James (1979), "Linear Regression with Censored Data," *Biometrika*, Vol. 66, pp. 429–36.

Cheng, K. F., and J. W. Wu (1994), "Adjusted Least Squares Estimates for the Scaled Regression Coefficients with Censored Data," *Journal of the American Statistical Association*, Vol. 89, pp. 1483–91.

Denzau, A. T., P. C. Gibbons, and E. Greenberg (1989), "Bayesian Estimation of Proportions with a Cross-Entropy Prior," *Communications in Statistics-Theory and Methods*, Vol. 18, pp. 1843–61.

Golan, A., G. Judge, and J. Perloff (1996), "A Maximum Entropy Approach to Recovering Information from Multinomial Response Data," *Journal of the American Statistical Association*, Vol. 91, pp. 841–53.

Golan, A., G. Judge, and A. Perloff (1997), "Estimation and Inference with Censored and Multinomial Response Data," *Journal of Econometrics*, Vol. 79, pp. 23–51.

Greene, W. H. (1981), "On the Asymptotic Bias of the Ordinary Least Squares Estimator of the Tobit Model," *Econometrica*, Vol. 49, pp. 505–13.

Greene, W. H. (1983), "Estimation of Limited Dependent Variable Models and the Method of Moments," *Journal of Econometrics*, Vol. 21, pp. 195–212.

Greene, W. H. (1993), *Econometric Analysis*, New York: Macmillan.

Hajivassilou, V., and D. McFadden (1998), "The Method of Simulated Scores for the Estimation of LDV Models," *Econometrica*, Vol. 66, pp. 863–96.

Hausman, J., and D. McFadden (1984), "A Specification Test for the Multinomial Logit Model," *Econometrica*, Vol. 52, pp. 1219–40.

Heckman, J. (1976), "The Common Structure of Statistical Models of Truncation, Sample Selection and Limited Dependent Variables and a Simple Estimator for Such Models," *Annals of Economic and Social Measurement*, Vol. 5, pp. 475–92.

Honoré, B., and J. L. Powell (1994), "Quantile Regression under Random Censoring," unpublished paper, University of California, Berkeley.

Ichimura, H., and T. S. Thompson (1998), "Maximum Likelihood Estimation of a Binary Choice Model with Random Coefficients of Unknown Parameters," *Journal of Econometrics*, Vol. 86, pp. 269–95.

Jaynes, E. T. (1957a), "Information Theory and Statistical Mechanics," *Physics Review*, Vol. 106, pp. 620–30.

Jaynes, E. T.(1957b), "Information Theory and Statistical Mechanics II," *Physics Review*, Vol. 108, pp. 171–90.

Kimhi, A. (1999), "On the Tradeoff Between Computational Simplicity and Asymptotic Properties in Multivariate Probit," *Computational Economics*, Vol. 13, pp. 93–101.

Koul, H., V. Susarla, and J. Van Ryzin (1981), "Regression Analysis with Randomly Right-Censored Data," *Annals of Statistics*, Vol. 9, pp. 1276–88.

Lehmann, E. L., and G. Casella (1998), *Theory of Point Estimation*, New York: Springer–Verlag.

Maddala, G. S. (1983), *Limited Dependent and Qualitative Variables in Econometrics*, Cambridge, UK: Cambridge University Press.

Manski, D., and D. McFadden (Eds.) (1981), *Structural Analysis of Discrete Data with Econometric Applications*, Cambridge, MA: MIT Press.

McFadden, D. (1974), "Conditional Logit Analysis of Qualitative Choice Behavior," in *Frontiers of Econometrics*, P. Zarembka (Ed.), New York: Academic Press, pp. 105–42.
McFadden, D. (1976), "Quantal Choice Analysis: A Survey," *Annals of Economic and Social Measurement*, Vol. 5, pp. 363–90.
McFadden, D. (1987), "Regression Based Specification Tests for the Multinomial Logit Model," *Journal of Econometrics*, Vol. 34, pp. 63–82.
McFadden, D. (1989), "A Method of Simulated Moments for Estimation of Discrete Response Models Without Numerical Interpolation," *Econometrica*, Vol. 57, pp. 995–1024.
Miller, R. G. (1976), "Least Squares Regression with Censored Data," *Biometrika*, Vol. 63, pp. 449–64.
Nakamura, A., and M. Nakamura (1983), "Part-Time and Full-Time Work Behavior of Married Women: A Model with a Doubly Truncated Dependent Variable," *Canadian Journal of Economics*, Vol. 16, pp. 201–18.
Nawata, K. (1990), "Robust Estimation Based on Group-Adjusted Data in Censored Regression Models," *Journal of Econometrics*, Vol. 43, pp. 337–62.
Newey, W. K. (1989), "Efficient Estimation of Tobit Models Under Symmetry," in W. A. Barnett, J. L. Powell, and G. Tauchen (Eds.), *Nonparametric and Semiparametric Methods in Econometrics and Statistics*, Cambridge, UK: Cambridge University Press.
Newey, W. K., and J. L. Powell (1990), "Efficient Estimation of Linear and Type I Censored Regression Models Under Conditional Quantile Restrictions," *Economic Theory*, Vol. 6, pp. 295–317.
Powell, J. L. (1984), "Least Absolute Deviations Estimation for the Censored Regression Model," *Journal of Econometrics*, Vol. 25, pp. 303–25.
Powell, J. L. (1986a), "Censored Regression Quantiles," *Journal of Econometrics*, Vol. 32, pp. 143–55.
Powell, J. L. (1986b), "Symmetrically Trimmed Least Squares Estimation for Tobit Models," *Econometrica*, Vol. 54, pp. 1435–60.
Quandt, R. (1966), "Probabilistic Theory of Consumer Behavior," *Quarterly Journal of Economics*, Vol. 70, pp. 507–36.
Shannon, C. E. (1948), "A Mathematical Theory of Communication," *Bell System Technical Journal*, Vol. 27, pp. 379–423.
Soofi, E. S. (1992), "A Generalizable Formulation of Conditional Logit with Diagnostics," *Journal of the American Statistical Association*, Vol. 87, pp. 812–16.
Tobin, J. (1958), "Estimation of Relationships for Limited Dependent Variables," *Econometrica*, Vol. 26, pp. 24–36.
Zavoina, R., and W. McElvey (1975), "A Statistical Model for the Analysis of Ordinal Level Dependent Variables," *Journal of Mathematical Sociology*, Vol. 4, pp. 103–20.

20.8. Appendix

PROOF OF EQUATION (20.3.8): First note that

$$\mathrm{y}_{ij} = 1 \Leftrightarrow \varepsilon_{ik} < \varepsilon_{ij} + \mathbf{x}_{i\cdot}(\boldsymbol{\beta}_j - \boldsymbol{\beta}_k)\ \forall k \neq j \tag{20.8.1}$$

Then, because (with any conditioning on $\mathbf{x}$ suppressed)

$$\mathrm{p}(\mathrm{y}_{ij} = 1) = \mathrm{E}_{\varepsilon_{ij}}[\mathrm{p}(\mathrm{y}_{ij} = 1 \mid \varepsilon_{ij})], \tag{20.8.2}$$

it follows that (recall (20.3.7))

$$\begin{aligned}
\mathrm{p}(\mathrm{y}_{ij} = 1) &= \int_{-\infty}^{\infty} \mathrm{f(z)} \prod_{k \neq j} \mathrm{F}[\mathbf{x}_{i\cdot}(\boldsymbol{\beta}_j - \boldsymbol{\beta}_k) + z]\,\mathrm{dz} \\
&= \int_{-\infty}^{\infty} \mathrm{e}^{-\mathrm{z}} \exp\left(-\mathrm{e}^{-\mathrm{z}}\left[1 + \sum_{k \neq j} \mathrm{e}^{\mathbf{x}_{i\cdot}(\boldsymbol{\beta}_k - \boldsymbol{\beta}_j)}\right]\right) \mathrm{dz} \\
&= \int_{-\infty}^{\infty} \left[\frac{\mathrm{e}^{-[\mathrm{z}-\ln(\xi)]} - \exp\left(-\mathrm{e}^{-[\mathrm{z}-\ln(\xi)]}\right)}{\xi}\right] \mathrm{dz}, \qquad (20.8.3)
\end{aligned}$$

where $\xi \equiv 1 + \sum_{k \neq j} \mathrm{e}^{\mathbf{x}_{i\cdot}(\boldsymbol{\beta}_j - \boldsymbol{\beta}_k)}$. Then, making the substitution $\mathrm{w} = \mathrm{z} - \ln(\xi)$ in (20.8.3) results in

$$\begin{aligned}
\mathrm{p}(\mathrm{y}_{ij} = 1) &= \frac{1}{\xi} \underbrace{\int_{-\infty}^{\infty} \mathrm{e}^{-\mathrm{w}} \mathrm{e}^{-\mathrm{e}^{-\mathrm{w}}} \mathrm{dw}}_{=1} \\
&= \xi^{-1} = \frac{\mathrm{e}^{\mathbf{x}_{i\cdot}\boldsymbol{\beta}_j}}{\sum_{j=1}^{J} \mathrm{e}^{\mathbf{x}_{i\cdot}\boldsymbol{\beta}_j}}. \qquad (20.8.4)
\end{aligned}$$

CHAPTER 21

Introduction to Nonparametric Density and Regression Analysis

In the preceding chapters our focus has been on parametric or semiparametric models in which the expectation of the dependent variable was specified as a function of the data. A principal maintained assumption in these types of models is that the form of the relationship between the expected value of the dependent variable and the explanatory variables belongs to, or is well-approximated by, a finite-dimensional class of parametric functional forms. In particular, we have specified linear and nonlinear models of the form

$$\mathbf{Y} = \mathbf{g}(\mathbf{X}, \boldsymbol{\beta}) + \varepsilon \tag{21.0.1}$$

in which $\mathbf{g}(\cdot)$ is a *known* function of the explanatory variables $\mathbf{X}$ and an unspecified and unknown k-vector $\boldsymbol{\beta}$. When the probability distribution of ε in (21.0.1) is also specified as a particular parametric family of probability distributions, the full model is known except for a finite number of model parameters. In the linear case, this means the conditional expectation of $\mathbf{Y}$ given $\mathbf{x}$ is defined by $\mathrm{E}[\mathbf{Y} \mid \mathbf{x}] = \mathbf{x}\boldsymbol{\beta}$. If the parametric family of the probability distributions of ε is left unspecified, the model is a semiparametric model with parametric component $\mathbf{g}(\mathbf{X}, \boldsymbol{\beta})$.

In the case of nonparametric models, we attempt to estimate $\mathrm{E}[\mathbf{Y} \mid \mathbf{x}]$ without specifying the functional form of the conditional expectation and examine regression specifications

$$\mathbf{Y} = \mathbf{g}(\mathbf{X}) + \varepsilon, \tag{21.0.2}$$

where now $\mathbf{g}(\mathbf{X})$ is left *unspecified*. Under the model assumption that $\mathrm{E}[\varepsilon \mid \mathbf{x}] = \mathbf{0}$, the conditional expectation (regression function) of $\mathbf{Y}$ given $\mathbf{x}$ equals $\mathrm{E}[\mathbf{Y} \mid \mathbf{x}] = \mathbf{g}(\mathbf{x}) = \int \mathbf{y}\mathrm{f}(\mathbf{y} \mid \mathbf{x})dy$ for the continuous case. Consequently, if we can estimate $\mathrm{f}(\mathbf{y} \mid \mathbf{x})$ in a nonparametric sense, then we can obtain a nonparametric estimate of $\mathrm{E}[\mathbf{Y} \mid \mathbf{x}]$, as well.

In the nonparametric case, the regression specification (21.0.2) serves only to identify which explanatory variables are assumed to affect the conditional mean of $\mathbf{Y}$, but no parametric family of functional shapes is imposed on $\mathbf{g}(\mathbf{X})$. This is not to say that $\mathbf{g}(\mathbf{X})$ must necessarily be left totally without any specified characteristics. In fact, it is most often the case in practice that $\mathbf{g}(\mathbf{X})$ is assumed to be continuous or even to be a

Table 21.1. *Nonparametric Regression Model*

Model Component	Specific Characteristics	
$\mathbf{Y}$	RV Type:	Continuous
	Range:	Unlimited
	Y_i dimension:	Univariate
	Moments:	$E[\mathbf{Y} \mid \mathbf{x}] = \mathbf{g}(\mathbf{x})$ and $\mathbf{cov}(\mathbf{Y} \mid \mathbf{x}) = \sigma^2\mathbf{I}$
$\eta(\mathbf{x}, \varepsilon)$	Functional Form:	$\eta(\mathbf{x}, \varepsilon) \equiv \mathbf{g}(\mathbf{x}) + \varepsilon$, $\mathbf{g}(\mathbf{x})$ functional form unspecified
$\mathbf{x}$	RV Type:	degenerate (fixed)
	Genesis:	exogenous to the model
$\boldsymbol{\beta}$	RV Type:	unspecified
	Dimension:	unspecified
ε	RV Type:	iid or independent
	Moments:	$E[\varepsilon \mid \mathbf{x}] = \mathbf{0}$, and $\mathbf{cov}(\varepsilon \mid \mathbf{x}) = \sigma^2\mathbf{I}$
Ω	Prior info:	none
$f(\mathbf{e} \mid \mathbf{x}, \varphi)$	PDF family:	unspecified

differentiable function of **X**. But other than such smoothness assumptions, the form of **g(X)** is left quite general. In terms of the general class of statistical models portrayed in Table 2.1, the type of models that we focus on in this chapter are summarized in Table 21.1.

The benefits of nonparametric models are perhaps obvious to the reader. By not having to restrict the functional form of $E[\mathbf{Y} \mid \mathbf{x}]$ via parametric specifications, we can mitigate the problem of misspecification of the form of the regression relationship. We can thereby avoid the bias, imprecision, and inconsistency in estimation and testing that can be induced by the misspecification of the functional form of the regression function. Nonparametric analyses can also be used to enhance parametric analyses by providing a means for very general exploratory investigations of the relationship between dependent and explanatory variables as well as providing diagnostic checks on estimated parametric models.

The substantial generality of nonparametric analyses is not without some notable costs. Although the nonparametric estimators used in practice are typically consistent and asymptotically normally distributed, just like their parametric and semiparametric alternatives, the nonparametric estimators typically converge at slower rates. In particular, although the parametric and semiparametric cases generally exhibit $\sqrt{n}$ or "root n" convergence to a true regression function value, nonparametric models generally converge at a rate slower than root n. Thus, larger sample sizes are generally required to obtain precise nonparametric estimates of regression functions than for parametric or semiparametric models. Moreover, nonparametric estimates tend to be less precise than estimates for parametric or semiparametric models at given sample sizes. However, these statements are predicated on the assumption that the true regression function is encompassed by the functional form of the parametric regression function. If this is not the case, it is then possible for nonparametric estimates to be MSE superior for a given common sample size.

The plan for the remainder of the chapter is as follows: We begin our introduction to nonparametric methods in the next section by discussing the concept of kernel density estimation, which is a general nonparametric procedure for estimating the probability distribution associated with the random variables in a random sample of data. We then discuss the concept of a nonparametric kernel regression estimator, which is defined in terms of the kernel density estimator and the familiar concept of conditional expectation. In the third section we extend the kernel regression idea to the concept of local polynomial regression in which polynomial approximations to the unknown regression function are locally fit to each data point in the observed sample. For those readers who wish to begin their study of nonparametric density and regression estimation at a more fundamental level, we include a discussion of the foundation concepts of local weighted averages and histograms in Section 21.4, which are conceptual precursors to the ideas of kernel density and nonparametric regression estimators.

21.1. Density Estimation via Kernels

In this section we examine a nonparametric method of estimating the PDF of a continuous random variable **Z** called a kernel density estimator. We will begin by examining the case in which Z is a scalar. We examine multivariate extensions in Section 21.1.5.

To motivate the definition of a kernel density estimator, first recall that the probability density function of a continuous scalar random variable Z at the point z_0 can be represented as

$$\mathrm{f}(z_0) = \lim_{h\to 0} \frac{1}{2h} \mathrm{P}(z \in (z_0 - h, z_0 + h)) \tag{21.1.1}$$

Then, for small h and large n, and because as $n \to \infty$ the strong law of large numbers implies that $\frac{\#\{Z_i\text{'s} \in (z_0-h,\, z_0+h)\}}{n} \overset{\text{as}}{\to} \mathrm{P}(z \in (z_0 - h, z_0 + h))$. A natural estimate of $\mathrm{f}(z_0)$ is given by

$$\hat{\mathrm{f}}(z_0; \mathbf{z}) = \frac{\#\{z_i\text{'s} \in (z_0 - h, z_0 + h)\}}{2hn}, \tag{21.1.2}$$

where the numerator in (21.1.2) denotes the number of the iid outcomes in $\mathbf{z} = [z_1, \ldots, z_n]'$ that are contained in the interval $(z_0 - h, z_0 + h)$. We can rewrite (21.1.2) in an equivalent way that is typical of the form of a kernel density estimate as

$$\hat{\mathrm{f}}(z_0; \mathbf{z}) = \frac{1}{nh} \sum_{i=1}^{n} \mathrm{K}\left(\frac{z_0 - z_i}{h}\right), \tag{21.1.3}$$

where

$$K(\mu) = \frac{1}{2} I_{(-1,\,1)}(\mu). \tag{21.1.4}$$

The estimate $\hat{f}(z_0; \mathbf{z})$ in (21.1.2) or equivalently in (21.1.3) would coincide with a histogram estimate of $f(z_0)$ if z_0 were at the center of a bin, the bin width were *2h*, and no observations occurred precisely on the boundaries of the bin (a probability 1 event for continuous Z). The interested reader can see the histogram discussion in Section 21.4.5 for more details. Note further that (21.1.2) and (21.1.3) can be applied $\forall z_0$ on the real line. Thus, the estimate $\hat{f}(z_0; \mathbf{z})$ can be viewed as a procedure that defines a collection of histogram-type estimates, one for each $z_0 \in R$, where each of these estimates has a bin width of $2h$ and a bin centered at z_0. This estimate clearly mitigates the typical problem with histograms of choosing bin locations, for these locations are automatically and uniquely defined by centering a bin on z_0, $\forall z_0$. Furthermore, we will see that the asymptotic integrated mean-square error (AIMSE) using this type of estimation procedure converges to zero at rate $O(n^{-4/5})$, which is more rapid than the fixed-bin histogram estimator of Section 21.4.5. The AIMSE is a standard measure of density estimator performance and will be defined in detail later. Thus, the estimation approach of (21.1.2) and (21.1.3) addresses two known deficiencies of simple and familiar histogram estimators. However, note that the estimate (21.1.2) and (21.1.3) still exhibits discontinuities and will necessarily be zero-valued outside of a finite range of values because of the kernel definition in (21.1.4). These last two characteristics can be changed so that $\hat{f}(z_0; \mathbf{z})$ will be continuous, even differentiable, or have infinite support (or all of these characteristics), by choosing the $K(\mu)$ function, called the *kernel function*, appropriately.

21.1.1. Kernels

The function (21.1.4) is one example of a kernel function. The following definition delineates general characteristics of such functions.

Definition 21.1.1 (Kernel Functions (scalar case)): A kernel function is any real-valued function, $K(\mu)$ that

1. is symmetric around $\mu = 0$, so that $K(\mu) = K(-\mu)$;
2. is piecewise continuous;
3. integrates to 1, as $\int_{-\infty}^{\infty} K(\mu)\, d\mu = 1$;
4. is nonnegative-valued.

Note that Condition 4 is not actually necessary to construct effective kernel density estimators, but it is virtually always assumed in empirical work, and so we adopt it here.

Any density function estimate of the form (21.1.3) that uses a kernel function for $K(\cdot)$, as defined in Definition 21.1.1, with $h > 0$, will be a genuine probability density function itself. To see this, first note that because $K(\mu) \geq 0$, then $\hat{f}(z_0; \mathbf{z}) \geq 0\, \forall z_0$.

Furthermore, through a change of variables to $\mu = (z_0 - z_i)/h$,

$$\int_{-\infty}^{\infty} \hat{\mathrm{f}}(z_0; \mathbf{z})\, dz_0 = \frac{1}{nh}\sum_{i=1}^{n}\int_{-\infty}^{\infty} \mathrm{K}\left(\frac{z_0 - z_i}{h}\right)\mathrm{d}z_0$$
$$= \frac{1}{nh}\sum_{i=1}^{n}\int_{-\infty}^{\infty} \mathrm{K}(\mu)h\, \mathrm{d}\mu$$
$$= \frac{1}{n}\sum_{i=1}^{n} 1 = \frac{n}{n} = 1 \qquad (21.1.5)$$

Thus, the function $\hat{\mathrm{f}}(z_0; \mathbf{z})$ satisfies the sufficient conditions for a function to be a continuous probability density function.

The kernel function clearly governs the weight given to each observation z_i in the definition of the density function estimate $\hat{\mathrm{f}}(z_0; \mathbf{z})$. The weight depends on (1) the distance of z_i from the point of evaluation z_0, (2) the scaling of this distance by the choice of h, and (3) the particular functional form of the kernel. The kernel functions most often used in empirical work assign declining weight to observations the more distant the observation is from z_0 and kernels that we examine will all exhibit this property. The scale factor h is referred to in kernel density literature as the *window width, bandwidth,* or *smoothing parameter*. The smaller the bandwidth, the less weight is assigned to a point $z_i \neq z_0$, and the smaller will be the neighborhood of data points around z_0 that contribute effectively to the estimate of $\hat{\mathrm{f}}(z_0; \mathbf{z})$. Larger values of h produce larger data neighborhoods around z_0 that contribute significantly to the estimate of $\mathrm{f}(z_0)$. Kernel density estimates of the form (21.1.3) tend to have a "smoother" appearance the larger the value of h. This is because a larger proportion of the observations $z_1, \ldots, z_n$ then contribute effectively to the calculation of each $\hat{\mathrm{f}}(z_0; \mathbf{z})$ value, muting the influence of both individual observations and shifting weight values as z_0 is changed; hence, the name "smoothing parameter" is used for h.

The rationale for the kernel density estimator given previously in (21.1.1)–(21.1.4) is clear, and one may question why we should consider deviating from it by considering kernel functions different from (21.1.4). To provide some intuition for considering alternatives, first note that (21.1.2) or (21.1.3) established the density estimate for $\mathrm{f}(z_0)$ by estimating the probability of the event $\mathrm{z} \in (z_0 - h, z_0 + h)$ with the empirical probability measure $\#\{z_i\text{'s} \in (z_0 - h, z_0 + h)\}/n$. In effect, this probability is treated as being *uniformly* distributed across all of the points in the interval $(z_0 - h, z_0 + h)$. In this case, once the bandwidth h is *set*, the distribution of the sample outcomes throughout the window $(z_0 - h, z_0 + h)$ has no impact on the estimated value $\hat{\mathrm{f}}(z_0; \mathbf{z})$. However, for example, one might intuitively expect that if the observations within the window are more densely clustered around z_0, this should imply that the density function at z_0 has a higher value than if the z_i's were concentrated elsewhere in the window. The principal reason for examining alternative kernels is so that the relative density of observations close to z_0 within a window can have a demonstrable influence on the estimated value of $\mathrm{f}(z_0)$. We will see later that kernels that differentially weight the observations around z_0 according to their distance from z_0 can reduce the AIMSE compared with kernels that do not.

21.1.2. IMSE, AIMSE, and Kernel Choice

In this section we define the MSE of the kernel density estimator $\hat{f}(z_0; \mathbf{Z})$ as well as its integrated MSE (IMSE) and asymptotic integrated MSE (AIMSE). On the basis of these measures of estimation effectiveness, we can then investigate what effect the choice of kernel has on the efficiency of the kernel density estimator of the PDF. We can also examine the impact of bandwidth choice on kernel density estimator properties.

How good is the density estimator $\hat{f}$? To answer this question, we need to specify a measure of closeness between the estimated and actual PDF of Z. The measure most often used for this purpose in nonparametric density estimation applications is the integrated mean square error (IMSE) criterion defined by

$$\begin{aligned} \mathrm{IMSE}(\hat{f}) &= \int_{-\infty}^{\infty} \mathrm{E}[\hat{f}(z_0; \mathbf{Z}) - f(z_0)]^2 dz_0 \\ &= \int_{-\infty}^{\infty} [[\mathrm{bias}(\hat{f}(z_0; \mathbf{Z}))]^2 + \mathrm{var}(\hat{f}(z_0; \mathbf{Z}))]\, dz_0 \end{aligned} \qquad (21.1.6)$$

Note that $\mathrm{E}[\cdot]$ denotes the expectation taken with respect to the true joint probability distribution of the random sample $\mathbf{Z} = [Z_1, \ldots, Z_n]'$, and thus $\mathrm{IMSE}(\hat{f})$ represents the *expected* squared difference between $\hat{f}(z_0; \mathbf{Z})$ and $f(z_0)$ integrated over *all* possible points of evaluation z_0. We emphasize that in (21.1.6), $\hat{f}(z_0; \mathbf{Z})$ is random, whereas $f(z_0)$ is fixed. It is the estimated value of $f(z_0)$ represented by the outcome of $\hat{f}(z_0; \mathbf{Z})$ that changes from sample to sample and not the point of evaluation z_0. The *asymptotic* IMSE, denoted by AIMSE, is a first-order approximation to the IMSE defined in (21.1.6) that becomes an ever more accurate representation of IMSE as $n \to \infty$, $h \to 0$, and $nh \to \infty$. The AIMSE is obtained by approximating the bias and variance terms in (21.1.6) using first-order Taylor series expansions (see Section 21.4.5 and the appendix for a detailed derivation in the context of histograms).

To derive the various MSE measures for the kernel density estimator, we assume, in addition to Conditions 1–4 of definition 21.1.1, that $\int \mu^2 K(\mu)\, d\mu = \sigma_K^2 > 0$. Given the standard properties of the kernel function, this additional property is analogous to requiring that a PDF (here, the weighting function represented by the kernel function) have a defined, positive variance. Furthermore, we assume that $\int [K(\mu)]^2\, d\mu < \infty$, and thus we are assuming that the kernel function is *square integrable*. Note that both of these additional assumptions can always be achieved in practice because the choice of $K(\mu)$ is under the control of the analyst.

Regarding the underlying population distribution, we assume that $\frac{\partial^2 f(z)}{\partial z^2}$ is absolutely continuous and the square of $\frac{\partial^2 f(z)}{\partial z^2}$ is integrable. Then, using Taylor series approximations (see Section 21.4.5 and the appendix for a detailed derivation in the case of the histogram estimator) we have that

$$\mathrm{bias}(\hat{f}(z_0; \mathbf{Z})) = \frac{\sigma_K^2 h^2}{2} \left[\frac{\partial^2 f(z_0)}{\partial z^2} \right] + O(h^{>2}), \qquad (21.1.7)$$

where $O(h^{>2})$ denotes terms of order of magnitude greater than h^2, and henceforth $\frac{\partial^2 f(z_0)}{\partial z^2} \equiv \frac{\partial^2 f(z)}{\partial z^2}\big|_{z_0}$. In addition,

$$\text{var}[\hat{f}(z_0; \mathbf{Z})] = \frac{f(z_0)R(K)}{nh} + o((nh)^{-1}) \tag{21.1.8}$$

where $R(K) \equiv \int_{-\infty}^{\infty} [K(\mu)]^2 d\mu$ (Tapia and Thompson, 1978; Silverman, 1986, pp. 38–40). It follows that the MSE of $\hat{f}(z_0; \mathbf{Z})$ as an estimator of $f(z_0)$ is given by (variance plus the square of the bias)

$$\text{MSE}(\hat{f}(z_0; \mathbf{Z})) = \frac{f(z_0)R(K)}{nh} + \frac{h^4\sigma_K^4}{4}\left[\frac{\partial^2 f(z_0)}{\partial z^2}\right]^2 + o((nh)^{-1}) + O(h^{>4}) \tag{21.1.9}$$

Integrating $\text{MSE}(\hat{f}(z_0; \mathbf{Z}))$ over the real line defines the *integrated MSE* as

$$\text{IMSE}(\hat{f}) = \int_{-\infty}^{\infty} \text{MSE}(\hat{f}(z_0; \mathbf{Z}))\, dz_0 = \frac{R(K)}{nh} + \frac{h^4\sigma_K^4}{4} \times \int_{-\infty}^{\infty}\left[\frac{\partial^2 f(z_0)}{\partial z^2}\right]^2 dz_0 + o((nh)^{-1}) + O(h^{>4}) \tag{21.1.10}$$

The leading terms of $\text{IMSE}(\hat{f})$ define the asymptotic integrated mean-square error (AIMSE) as

$$\text{AIMSE}(\hat{f}) = \frac{R(K)}{nh} + \frac{h^4\sigma_K^4}{4}\int_{-\infty}^{\infty}\left[\frac{\partial^2 f(z_0)}{\partial z^2}\right]^2 dz_0 \tag{21.1.11}$$

Then, the asymptotically optimal bandwidth, defined as the bandwidth that minimizes $\text{AIMSE}(\hat{f})$, can be found by setting the first derivative of (21.1.11) with respect to h equal to zero and solving for h, yielding

$$h_* = \left[\frac{R(K)}{\sigma_K^4 \int_{-\infty}^{\infty}\left[\frac{\partial^2 f(z_0)}{\partial z^2}\right]^2 dz_0}\right]^{1/5} n^{-1/5} \tag{21.1.12}$$

Finally, by substituting (21.1.12) into (21.1.11), the minimal $\text{AIMSE}(\hat{f})$ is given by

$$\text{AIMSE}(\hat{f})_* = 1.25[\sigma_K R(K)]^{4/5}\left[\int_{-\infty}^{\infty}\left[\frac{\partial^2 f(z_0)}{\partial z^2}\right]^2 dz_0\right]^{1/5} n^{-4/5}. \tag{21.1.13}$$

It is apparent that the choice of kernel function has an effect on the $\text{AIMSE}(\hat{f})_*$. It is then logical to consider whether a kernel function can be found that minimizes $\text{AIMSE}(\hat{f})_*$. Given the conditions on the kernel function assumed heretofore, such an optimum kernel function can be determined, and it is the Epanechnikov kernel defined by

$$\begin{aligned} K(\mu) &= .75(1-\mu^2) \quad &&\text{for } \mu \in [-1, 1] \\ &= 0 &&\text{elsewhere} \end{aligned} \tag{21.1.14}$$

(Epanechnikov, 1969).

Table 21.2. *Relative Asymptotic Efficiencies of Alternative Kernels*

Kernel	Definition	Relative Asymptotic Efficiency (Optimal Efficiency = 1)
Epanechnikov	$.75(1-\mu^2)$ for $\|\mu\| < 1$ 0 otherwise	1
Biweight	$\frac{15}{16}(1-\mu^2)^2$ for $\|\mu\| < 1$ 0 otherwise	.9939
Triweight	$\frac{35}{32}(1-\mu^2)^3$ for $\|\mu\| < 1$ 0 otherwise	.9867
Gaussian	$(2\pi)^{-1/2}\exp(-\mu^2/2)$	.9512
Uniform	$\frac{1}{2}$ for $\|\mu\| < 1$ 0 otherwise	.9295

Now that the optimal kernel function has been identified, it is informative to examine how sensitive the AIMSE$(\hat{\text{f}})_*$ measure is to other choices of kernels. Table 21.2 lists a number of kernel functions that have been used in practice along with their relative (to optimal) asymptotic efficiency. The values in the right-most column in the table are calculated by forming the ratio of the AIMSE (21.1.13) for the optimal Epanechnikov kernel to the AIMSE for the kernel listed in the left-most column of the table.

It is apparent that the value of AIMSE$(\hat{\text{f}})_*$ is rather insensitive to the choice of kernel function. Thus, the choice of kernel function is often made based on other considerations such as what the kernel implies relative to the continuity, differentiability, or the density support (or all of these considerations) associated with the estimate $\hat{\text{f}}$. We also note that, regardless of the choice of the kernel function, the kernel density estimator (21.1.3) has a notably more rapid convergence of AIMSE$(\hat{\text{f}})$ to zero than the histogram estimator, the former converging at the rate $\text{O}(n^{-4/5})$, whereas the latter converges at the rate $\text{O}(n^{-2/3})$ (see Section 21.4.5).

► **Example 21.1.1:** To compare the properties of the kernel functions in Table 21.2, we provide the GAUSS program C21Kern.gss in the examples manual. For a kernel function selected by the user, GAUSS plots the function and illustrates the impact of changes in $|z_0 - z|$ and the bandwidth parameter h. Then, GAUSS briefly summarizes the steps involved in programming the kernel density procedure, kernel(), which is also provided on the CD. Finally, GAUSS generates a small sample of observations and plots the kernel density estimate using the kernel function selected by the user.

21.1.3. Bandwidth Choice

We have already provided a solution to the problem of finding an asymptotically optimal bandwidth for a given kernel function via the definition of h_* in (21.1.12). It was shown that the magnitude of the optimal bandwidth is inversely related to the value of $\int_{-\infty}^{\infty}[\frac{\partial^2 f(z_0)}{\partial z^2}]^2 dz_0$, which can be viewed as a measure of the amount of changing curvature, or roughness, of the graph of the underlying true PDF. This implies the intuitively reasonable relationship that the more changes or roughness in the graph of the PDF, and thus the more difficult it is to estimate the graph, the smaller the bandwidth must be to capture the curvature effectively.

Unfortunately, the definition of the optimal bandwidth is functionally dependent on the unknown PDF and cannot be directly calculated. One approach followed in practice is to choose h_* on the basis of some reference distribution, which is then used in the calculation of $\int_{-\infty}^{\infty}[\frac{\partial^2 f(z_0)}{\partial z^2}]^2 dz_0$ to define h_*. A reference distribution may be chosen because it is thought to resemble the true f(z) in terms of basic shape and moment characteristics. For example, if the Gaussian kernel function is used, and if the reference PDF is assumed to be N(0, σ^2), then $\int_{-\infty}^{\infty}[\frac{\partial^2 f(z_0)}{\partial z^2}]^2 dz_0 = \frac{3}{8}\pi^{-1/2}\sigma^{-5} \approx 0.212\sigma^{-5}$, and the optimal bandwidth is $h_* = 1.059\sigma n^{-1/5}$. A numerical estimate of h_* can then be obtained by replacing σ with a consistent estimate such as the sample standard deviation.

Another procedure for calculating h, which is entirely data-based, is the method of *cross-validation*. In this method, a "leave one observation out" density estimate is defined as

$$\hat{f}_{-i}(z_0; \mathbf{z}) = \frac{1}{(n-1)h} \sum_{\substack{j=1 \\ j \neq i}}^{n} K\left(\frac{z_0 - z_j}{h}\right), \forall i. \tag{21.1.15}$$

Then h is chosen to minimize

$$m(h) = \int_{-\infty}^{\infty} \hat{f}(z_0; \mathbf{z})^2 \, dz_0 - 2n^{-1} \sum_{i=1}^{n} \hat{f}_{-i}(z_0; \mathbf{z}), \tag{21.1.16}$$

defining what is called the least-squares cross-validation (LSCV) estimate of h (Rudemo, 1982 and Bowman, 1984).

Why should $\hat{h} = \arg\min_h[m(h)]$ produce a good estimate of h? The integrated squared error (ISE) of $\hat{f}(z_0; \mathbf{z})$ when estimating f(z) is given by

$$\begin{aligned} \text{ISE}(\hat{f}) &\equiv \int_{-\infty}^{\infty} [\hat{f}(z_0; \mathbf{z}) - f(z_0)]^2 dz_0 \\ &\equiv \int_{-\infty}^{\infty} [\hat{f}(z_0; \mathbf{z})]^2 \, dz_0 - 2\int_{-\infty}^{\infty} \hat{f}(z_0; \mathbf{z}) f(z_0) dz_0 + \int_{-\infty}^{\infty} [f(z_0)]^2 dz_0 \end{aligned} \tag{21.1.17}$$

Because the trailing term in the second line of (21.1.17) does not depend on the choice of $\hat{f}(z_0; \mathbf{z})$, the ISE is minimized by the $\hat{f}(z_0; \mathbf{z})$ that minimizes

$$q(\hat{f}) \equiv \int_{-\infty}^{\infty} [\hat{f}(z_0; \mathbf{z})]^2 \, dz_0 - 2\int_{-\infty}^{\infty} \hat{f}(z_0; \mathbf{z}) f(z_0) \, dz_0. \tag{21.1.18}$$

It can be shown that

$$E\left[n^{-1} \sum_{i=1}^{n} \hat{f}_{-i}(z_i; \mathbf{Z})\right] = E\left[\int_{-\infty}^{\infty} \hat{f}(z_0; \mathbf{Z}) f(z_0) \, dz_0\right] \tag{21.1.19}$$

(Silverman, 1986, p. 49), and thus that $E[M(h)] = E[Q(\hat{f})]$. Then, it also follows from (21.1.16)–(21.1.19) that $m(h) + \int [f(z_0)]^2 dz_0$ would be an unbiased estimate of the integrated mean squared error of $\hat{f}$. Therefore, minimizing $m(h)$ is effectively minimizing an unbiased estimate of the integrated mean-squared error because $\int [f(z_0)]^2 dz_0$ is constant for all h.

There is an even stronger asymptotic justification for the LSCV estimate of h. In particular, if $f(z)$ is bounded, then as $n \to \infty$, the LSCV method of estimating h results in the best possible choice of bandwidth in terms of minimizing $ISE(\hat{f})$ (Stone, 1984). Marron (1987) discusses a pseudolikelihood cross-validation method of calculating h as well as other purely data-based methods for determining h.

► **Example 21.1.2:** To demonstrate the computation of the LSCV estimate for the bandwidth, we provide the GAUSS program C21CVH.gss in the examples manual. For a given sample of observations, GAUSS calculates the function $m(h)$ on a grid of bandwidth values. Then, GAUSS plots the function and selects the value of h that minimizes $\hat{m}(h)$ as an estimate of $\hat{h}$. Finally, GAUSS uses the estimated $\hat{h}$ to compute a kernel density estimate for the observations.

21.1.4. Other Properties and Issues

It is apparent from (21.1.9) that if $h \to 0$, $n \to \infty$, and $nh \to \infty$, then the kernel density estimator $\hat{f}(z_0; \mathbf{Z})$ defined in (21.1.3) is a consistent estimator of $f(z)$. Parzen (1962) showed that $\hat{f}(z_0; \mathbf{Z})$ is also asymptotically normally distributed. In particular, if $\frac{\partial^2 f(z)}{\partial z^2}$ is continuous and bounded in a neighborhood of z_0 and if $(nh)^{1/2} h^2 \to 0$ as $n \to \infty$, then

$$(nh)^{1/2}[\hat{f}(z_0; \mathbf{Z}) - f(z_0)] \xrightarrow{d} N\left(0, f(z_0) \int_{-\infty}^{\infty} [K(\mu)]^2 \, d\mu\right). \tag{21.1.20}$$

Refinements can be added to the kernel density approach to improve the quality of estimates in several ways. These refinements include reducing the level of bias in the tails of $\hat{f}(z)$, allowing for varying bandwidths to be used throughout the range of Z, and using more general forms of kernel functions. The reader is directed to Izenman (1991) and Simonoff (1996) for additional discussion and a substantial number of references relating to kernel and other methods of density estimation.

► **Example 21.1.3:** The GAUSS program C21Bands.gss demonstrates the formation of confidence bands for a kernel density estimate. For a given sample, GAUSS computes and plots the kernel density estimate for a kernel function selected by the user. Then, the estimated large sample variance in (21.1.20) is used to form 90% confidence bands at various points in the support of the distribution. It is also important to note that the bands ignore the finite sample bias in the kernel density estimator. An alternative approach for obtaining confidence bands is to resample the data via bootstrapping and base the bands on quantiles of the empirical bootstrap distribution of kernel density outcomes.

21.1.5. Multivariate Extensions

The kernel density estimation procedure can be extended to estimate multivariate probability distributions. Assume now that $\mathbf{z} = [\mathbf{z}_1, \ldots, \mathbf{z}_n]$ is a $(m \times n)$ matrix consisting of n independent sample outcomes of an m-dimensional random variable having an m-variate probability density function $\mathrm{f}(\mathbf{z}_0)$, where $\mathbf{z}_0$ is an $(m \times 1)$ vector. The general form of the kernel density estimate of $\mathrm{f}(\mathbf{z}_0; \mathbf{z})$ is given by

$$\hat{\mathrm{f}}(\mathbf{z}_0; \mathbf{z}) = \frac{1}{n \det(\mathbf{h})} \sum_{i=1}^{n} \mathrm{K}(\mathbf{h}^{-1}(\mathbf{z}_0 - \mathbf{z}_i)), \tag{21.1.21}$$

where $\mathbf{h}$ is a nonsingular $(m \times m)$ bandwidth matrix. Note the univariate case is subsumed by (21.1.21) upon interpreting $\mathbf{h}$ as the scalar matrix $h > 0$. The multivariate kernel function $\mathrm{K}(\cdot)$ in (21.1.21) is assumed to adhere to Definition 21.1.1 interpreted within a multivariate context. In practice, the kernel function is most often simplified by defining $\mathbf{h}$ to be a diagonal matrix, defining $\mathrm{K}(\boldsymbol{\mu})$ to be a product of univariate kernel functions, or both. We will concentrate on the case of a diagonal $\mathbf{h}$ and defer generalizations to further reading (see Scott, 1992; Simonoff, 1996, Section 4.2; and Wand, 1992).

Consider the case in which the bandwidth matrix is defined as $\mathbf{h} = \mathrm{h}\mathbf{I}$, for $h > 0$, which implies that the same degree of smoothing is used for each of the m-dimensions of the multivariate kernel density estimate. In practice, this approach will generally produce good results if the multivariate data being analyzed are roughly spherical, so that the m elements in each of the $\mathbf{Z}_i$'s are equivalent in scale and have zero covariances. If not, and if the m elements in each of the $\mathbf{Z}_i$'s are uncorrelated, one first performs a scale transformation, dividing each of the m variables by their respective (generally estimated) standard deviations before applying the density estimation procedure. More generally, if the $\mathbf{Z}_i$'s have a nonspherical covariance matrix $\boldsymbol{\Sigma}$, one transforms each of the $\mathbf{Z}_i$'s to sphericity through premultiplication by (a generally estimated) $\boldsymbol{\Sigma}^{-1/2}$, as $\boldsymbol{\Sigma}^{-1/2}\mathbf{Z}_i, i = 1, \ldots, n$ prior to applying the density estimation procedure.

To derive an expression for the AIMSE, we assume that the analyst's choice of kernel function is such that $\int_{\mathrm{R}^m} \boldsymbol{\mu}\boldsymbol{\mu}'\mathrm{K}(\boldsymbol{\mu})\, \mathrm{d}\boldsymbol{\mu} = \sigma_K^2 \mathbf{I}_m$ for $\sigma_K^2 > 0$, which is the analog to our assumption that $\int_{-\infty}^{\infty} \mu^2 \mathrm{K}(\mu)\, \mathrm{d}\mu = \sigma_K^2 > 0$ in the univariate case. We also assume that $\mathrm{f}(\mathbf{z}_0)$ is twice continuously (at least piecewise) differentiable and the second partial derivatives are square integrable. Then it can be shown via Taylor series approximations that (Cacoullos, 1966; Epanechnikov, 1969; Scott, 1992, Section 6.3.2)

$$\mathrm{AIMSE}(\hat{\mathrm{f}}) = \frac{\mathrm{R(K)}}{nh^m} + \frac{h^4 \sigma_K^4}{4} \int_{\mathrm{R}^m} \left[\mathrm{tr}\left(\frac{\partial^2 \mathrm{f}(\mathbf{z}_0)}{\partial \mathbf{z} \partial \mathbf{z}'} \right) \right]^2 \mathrm{d}z_0, \tag{21.1.22}$$

where $\mathrm{R(K)} \equiv \int_{\mathrm{R}^m} [\mathrm{K}(\boldsymbol{\mu})]^2 \mathrm{d}\boldsymbol{\mu}$, $\frac{\partial^2 \mathrm{f}(\mathbf{z}_0)}{\partial \mathbf{z} \partial \mathbf{z}'} \equiv \left.\frac{\partial^2 \mathrm{f}(\mathbf{z})}{\partial \mathbf{z} \partial \mathbf{z}'}\right|_{\mathbf{z}_0}$, and the two summed terms in (21.1.22) represent the asymptotic variance and asymptotic squared-bias terms, respectively. Then the optimal bandwidth in terms of minimizing AIMSE($\hat{\mathrm{f}}$) is the value of h that sets the first derivative of (21.1.22) with respect to h equal to zero and is given by

$$h_* = \left[\frac{m R(K)}{\sigma_K^4 \int_{\mathrm{R}^m} \left[\mathrm{tr}\left(\frac{\partial^2 \mathrm{f}(\mathbf{z}_0)}{\partial \mathbf{z} \partial \mathbf{z}'} \right) \right]^2 \mathrm{d}z_0} \right]^{\frac{1}{m+4}} n^{-\left(\frac{1}{m+4}\right)}. \tag{21.1.23}$$

The optimal bandwidth (21.1.23) can be substituted into (21.1.22) to obtain the optimized AIMSE($\hat{\mathrm{f}}$). Doing so results in AIMSE$(\hat{\mathrm{f}})_* = \mathrm{O}(n^{-4/(m+4)})$, which makes clear that the convergence rate of multivariate kernel density estimators is *slowed* by increasing dimensionality, often referred to as the "curse of dimensionality." Nonetheless, it is also clear that so long as $n \to \infty$, $h \to 0$, and $nh^m \to \infty$, the multivariate kernel density estimator will consistently estimate $\mathrm{f}(\mathbf{z}_0)$.

21.1.5.a. Kernel Choice

On kernel choice, the discussion for the univariate case remains relevant. The optimal kernel choice, in terms of minimizing AIMSE$(\hat{\mathrm{f}})_*$, is the *multivariate* Epanechnikov kernel

$$\begin{aligned} \mathrm{K}_{\mathrm{EPAN}}(\boldsymbol{\mu}) &= \frac{1}{2}\mathrm{c}_m^{-1}(m+2)(1-\boldsymbol{\mu}'\boldsymbol{\mu}) \quad \text{for } \boldsymbol{\mu}'\boldsymbol{\mu} \leq 1 \\ &= 0 \quad \text{otherwise,} \end{aligned} \tag{21.1.24}$$

where c_m is the volume of the m-dimensional unit sphere (which equals 2, π, and $4\pi/3$ for one, two, and three dimensions, respectively, and in general, $\mathrm{c}_m = [\pi^{m/2}/[\Gamma(\frac{m}{2}+1)]]$, where $\Gamma(\cdot)$ is the gamma function (Izenman, 1991, p. 210)). However, just as in the univariate case, the value of the AIMSE$(\hat{\mathrm{f}})_*$ is not very sensitive to the choice of kernel, and thus often other kernels are utilized to obtain the estimator properties of continuity, differentiability, unbounded supports, and even computational simplifications (Izenman, 1991; Marron and Nolan, 1987). A popular alternative kernel function choice has been the multivariate normal kernel

$$\mathrm{K}_{\mathrm{NORM}}(\boldsymbol{\mu}) = (2\pi)^{-m/2} \exp\left(-\frac{1}{2}\boldsymbol{\mu}'\boldsymbol{\mu}\right) \tag{21.1.25}$$

(see Silverman, 1986, Section 4.21, for others). Often the multivariate kernel function is defined as the product of univariate kernels as $\mathrm{K}(\boldsymbol{\mu}) = \Pi_{i=1}^m \mathrm{K}_i(\mu_i)$ (note that $\mathrm{K}_{\mathrm{NORM}}(\boldsymbol{\mu})$ can be represented as the product of m standard normal kernel functions).

21.1.5.b. Bandwidth Choice

Just as in the univariate case, the optimal bandwidth (21.1.23) depends on the unknown probability density function $\mathrm{f}(\mathbf{z}_0)$ and so is not calculable. One way of proceeding is to utilize a reference distribution for calculating the unknown integral in (21.1.23), which is analogous to the univariate case. For example, if one adopts a multivariate normal distribution for the reference distribution and it is assumed the data have been standardized to have unit variances, then the optimal bandwidth for a normal kernel (21.1.25) is given by

$$h_* = \left(\frac{4}{m+2}\right)^{\frac{1}{m+4}} n^{-\frac{1}{m+4}}. \tag{21.1.26}$$

Other reference distribution and kernel function pairings are accommodated by calculating (often numerically) the appropriate $R(K)$ and integral terms in (21.1.23) and then determining the value of h_*.

Least-squares cross-validation methods can also be used to choose h in the multivariate case analogously to the way it was used in the univariate case. In particular, h is chosen to minimize (21.1.16), where now the kernel estimates $\hat{\mathrm{f}}(\mathbf{z}_0; \mathbf{z})$ and $\hat{\mathrm{f}}_{-i}(\mathbf{z}_0; \mathbf{z})$ (recall (21.1.15)) are *multivariate* in the *vector* $\mathbf{z}_0$ and the *matrix* $\mathbf{z}$. The rationale in defense of the LSCV estimate of h is precisely as before and relates to Equations (21.1.16)–(21.1.19), and thus $\hat{\mathrm{h}}$ based on the LSCV criterion minimizes an unbiased estimate of the integrated mean-square error of $\hat{\mathrm{f}}$. Furthermore, the LSCV-based $\hat{\mathrm{h}}$ is also asymptotically the best bandwidth choice in terms of minimizing $\mathrm{ISE}(\hat{\mathrm{f}})$.

► **Example 21.1.4:** To demonstrate an application of multivariate kernel density estimation, we consider the problem of estimating a bivariate normal density. The GAUSS program C21Mult.gss (provided in the examples manual) generates n pairs (x, y) from the $\mathrm{N}(\boldsymbol{\mu}, \boldsymbol{\Sigma})$ distribution with the user selecting the bandwidth, either an Epanechnikov or normal kernel, and the parameter of the normal distribution. Then, GAUSS computes the bivariate kernel density estimate and plots the surface of the estimated PDF. As the user alters the parameters of the mixture distribution, GAUSS generates a new pseudorandom sample and computes a revised bivariate kernel density estimate.

21.2. Kernel Regression Estimators

In this section we extend the concept of kernel density estimation to encompass the estimation of regression functions. In principle, such an extension is rather straightforward if the random vector $(\mathrm{Y}, \mathbf{X})$ has a joint $(k+1)$ dimensional probability distribution $\mathrm{f}(\mathrm{Y}, \mathbf{X})$. Then, the true regression function is by definition

$$\mathrm{E}(\mathrm{Y} \mid \mathbf{x}) = \mathrm{g}(\mathbf{x}) = \int_{-\infty}^{\infty} \mathrm{y} \left[\frac{\mathrm{f}(\mathrm{y}, \mathbf{x})}{\mathrm{f}(\mathbf{x})}\right] d\mathrm{y}. \tag{21.2.1}$$

One can then imagine that if the joint PDF $\mathrm{f}(\mathrm{y}, \mathbf{x})$ and marginal PDF $\mathrm{f}(\mathbf{x})$ in (21.2.1) could each be replaced by estimates based on kernel density estimators, then the integral in (21.2.1) could be calculated, producing an estimate of the regression function of Y on $\mathbf{X}$. It is precisely this idea that underlies the basic concept of a kernel regression estimator. Furthermore, the procedure can be applied even if $\mathbf{X}$ is fixed, so that $f(\mathbf{x})$ is degenerate on a point. Because kernel density estimators are involved in defining a kernel regression estimator, it is not surprising that problems of kernel function choice and bandwidth selection will arise in the regression context.

21.2.1. Nonparametric Regression Model Specification

Before examining the details of the implementation of kernel regression estimators, we discuss here a fundamental distinction between model specification, or misspecification, in the nonparametric versus parametric or semiparametric cases. We begin the discussion by noting that *whatever* the set of explanatory variables chosen by the analyst, so long as $(Y_i, \mathbf{X}_{i\cdot})$ has a $(k+1)$ dimensional PDF $f(y_i, \mathbf{x}_{i\cdot})$ and $E|Y_i| < \infty$, then the conditional expectation $E[Y_i \mid \mathbf{X}_{i\cdot}]$ exists and has the general form

$$E(Y_i|\mathbf{X}_{i\cdot}) = g(\mathbf{X}_{i\cdot}) \tag{21.2.2}$$

for *some* real-valued function $g(\cdot)$. Furthermore, $g(\mathbf{X}_{i\cdot})$ is itself a random variable (degenerate if $\mathbf{x}$ is degenerate; see Chung, 1974, Theorems 9.1.1 and 9.1.2). It follows that the random variable Y_i can be represented in standard regression form as

$$Y_i = g(\mathbf{X}_{i\cdot}) + \varepsilon_i, \qquad E[\varepsilon_i] = 0, \tag{21.2.3}$$

where $E[\varepsilon_i \mid \mathbf{X}_{i\cdot}] = 0$ with probability 1, which implies $E[\varepsilon_i] = 0$.

The importance of the preceding simple observation is that a nonparametric regression model is quite generally *correctly* specified in the sense of there being a legitimate regression-type relationship between Y_i and $\mathbf{X}_{i\cdot}$, regardless of how $\mathbf{X}_{i\cdot}$ is specified by the analyst. One can think of any other explanatory variables not explicitly contained in the vector $\mathbf{X}_{i\cdot}$ as having been marginalized (integrated) out of a higher-dimensional joint PDF to yield the joint PDF $f(y_i, \mathbf{x}_{i\cdot})$ being analyzed. So long as the conditional expectation $E[Y_i \mid \mathbf{X}_{i\cdot}]$ *exists*, a nonparametric regression model of the type (21.2.2) is applicable. Furthermore, because the functional form of $g(\cdot)$ is left completely general in the nonparametric approach, the form of the conditional expectation function is encompassed and cannot be "misspecified." We emphasize that the true unknown functional form of $g(\cdot)$ can change as elements are added or removed from the explanatory variable vector $\mathbf{X}_{i\cdot}$, but this does not alter either the legitimacy of the general regression relationship (21.2.2) or the ability of the nonparametric regression model to accommodate the form of the conditional expectation function.

As the reader will recall from Chapter 18, the model specification situation is quite different for parametric regression models, or for semiparametric regression models with parametric component $E[Y_i \mid \mathbf{X}_{i\cdot}] = g(\mathbf{X}_{i\cdot}, \boldsymbol{\beta})$ for $\boldsymbol{\beta} \in \Omega$. For these models to be correctly specified, in the sense that the regression relationship (21.2.3) is applicable, the parametric family of functions represented by $g(\mathbf{x}_{i\cdot}, \boldsymbol{\beta})$, for $\boldsymbol{\beta} \in \Omega$ must be such that $g(\mathbf{x}_{i\cdot}) \equiv g(\mathbf{x}_{i\cdot}, \boldsymbol{\beta})\ \forall \mathbf{x}_{i\cdot}$, for some $\boldsymbol{\beta} \in \Omega$. If not, the conditional expectation function is misspecified, and the damage such misspecification causes to the properties of the estimates of conditional expectations and the parameters of the model depends on characteristics of the PDF of $f(y_i, \mathbf{x}_{i\cdot})$ as well as how closely (or poorly) $g(\mathbf{X}_{i\cdot}, \boldsymbol{\beta})$ approximates $g(\mathbf{X}_{i\cdot})$ in the $\mathbf{X}_{i\cdot}$ dimension. It is apparent that the propensity to misspecify parametric or semiparametric regression models is substantially greater than for nonparametric regression models.

Although the nonparametric approach affords considerable protection against misspecification of a regression function in a statistical sense, this is not to say that the regression relationship specified is appropriate for the analyst's research objectives. In economics, one is often interested in ceteris paribus–type analyses in which a certain set of explanatory factors are explicitly held constant while one examines the marginal effects on the dependent variable of a change in a particular explanatory variable of interest. Obviously an explanatory variable must be included explicitly in the vector $\mathbf{X}_{i\cdot}$ if the analyst expects to condition on a value of it in a ceteris paribus analysis. If such explanatory variables are not explicitly conditioned upon, then any marginal effect on the expectation of the dependent variable due to a change in, say, x_{ij}, may not be isolated from the effects of other uncontrolled explanatory variables that are not independent of x_{ij}. In particular any *estimated* marginal effects of changes in x_{ij} obtained from a nonparametric regression analysis could also be accounting for the effects of omitted explanatory variables that are correlated and change with x_{ij}.

The point is that there are more general model specification issues than just the statistical issue of whether a theoretically legitimate regression relationship has been specified, and this more general specification issue effects both nonparametric and other regression models. This more general specification issue is specific to the analyst's research objectives and also depends on the availability of data with which to specify the set of explanatory variables and perform the regression analysis. We will not pursue this regression interpretation issue further here. We end this subsection by emphasizing to the reader that, although he or she will quite generally be dealing with correctly specified regression relationships *in the statistical sense* when performing nonparametric regression analysis, one should nevertheless think carefully about interpreting the meaning of the effects of marginal changes in explanatory variables within the context of the particular economic problem being analyzed.

21.2.2. Nadaraya–Watson Kernel Regression: Alias Zero-Order Local Polynomial Regression

Let $(\mathrm{y}_i, \mathbf{x}_{i\cdot})$, $i = 1, \ldots, n$ be an iid random sample outcome from the $(k+1)$-dimensional continuous PDF $\mathrm{f}(\mathrm{y}_*, \mathbf{x}_*)$, where the $(k+1)$-dimensional random vector $(\mathrm{Y}_*, \mathbf{X}_*')$ is used to denote the population random vector. Furthermore, let

$$\hat{\mathrm{f}}(\mathrm{y}_0, \mathbf{x}_0; \mathrm{y}, \mathbf{x}) = \frac{1}{nh^{k+1}} \sum_{j=1}^{n} \mathrm{K}_* \left(\frac{\mathrm{y}_0 - \mathrm{y}_j}{h}, \frac{\mathbf{x}_0 - \mathbf{x}_{j\cdot}'}{h} \right) \tag{21.2.4}$$

be a kernel density estimate of $\mathrm{f}(\mathrm{y}_0, \mathbf{x}_0)$ conditional on observations $(\mathrm{y}, \mathbf{x})$. The kernel function is assumed to adhere to the multivariate version of Definition 21.1.1 so that K_* is symmetric around zero in its first argument, and thus $\int_{-\infty}^{\infty} \mathrm{z}\mathrm{K}_*(\mathrm{z}, \frac{\mathbf{x}_0 - \mathbf{x}_{j\cdot}'}{h})\, d\mathrm{z} = 0$. The (marginal) kernel function for the k-dimensional $\mathbf{x}_0$ vector is given by $\int_{-\infty}^{\infty} \mathrm{K}_*(\frac{\mathrm{y}_0 - \mathrm{y}_j}{h}, \frac{\mathbf{x}_0 - \mathbf{x}_{j\cdot}'}{h})\, d\mathrm{y}_0 = h\mathrm{K}(\frac{\mathbf{x}_0 - \mathbf{x}_{j\cdot}'}{h})$.

Now recall the regression function definition in (21.2.1), replace the unknown $f(y_0, \mathbf{x}_0)$ by the kernel density estimate (21.2.4), and replace the unknown $f(\mathbf{x}_0)$ by the marginal kernel density estimate

$$\hat{f}(\mathbf{x}_0; \mathbf{x}) = \int_{-\infty}^{\infty} \hat{f}(y_0, \mathbf{x}_0; \mathbf{y}, \mathbf{x})\, dy_0 = \frac{1}{nh^k} \sum_{j=1}^{n} K\left(\frac{\mathbf{x}_0 - \mathbf{x}'_{j.}}{h}\right) \tag{21.2.5}$$

to obtain

$$\hat{g}(\mathbf{x}_0; \mathbf{x}) = \int_{-\infty}^{\infty} y_0 \left[\frac{\frac{1}{nh^{k+1}} \sum_{j=1}^{n} K_*\left(\frac{y_0 - y_j}{h}, \frac{\mathbf{x}_0 - \mathbf{x}'_{j.}}{h}\right)}{\frac{1}{nh^k} \sum_{j=1}^{n} K\left(\frac{\mathbf{x}_0 - \mathbf{x}'_{j.}}{h}\right)} \right] dy_0. \tag{21.2.6}$$

If one makes a change of variables to $z = (y_0 - y_j)/h$ in the jth term of the numerator sum in the integrand of (21.2.6), and recalls the properties of the kernel stated below (21.2.4), the integral (21.2.6) simplifies to

$$\hat{g}(\mathbf{x}_0; \mathbf{x}) = \frac{\sum_{j=1}^{n} y_j K\left(\frac{\mathbf{x}_0 - \mathbf{x}'_{j.}}{h}\right)}{\sum_{j=1}^{n} K\left(\frac{\mathbf{x}_0 - \mathbf{x}'_{j.}}{h}\right)} = \sum_{j=1}^{n} w_j(\mathbf{x}_0) y_j \tag{21.2.7}$$

where $w_j(\mathbf{x}_0) \equiv \frac{K(\frac{\mathbf{x}_0 - \mathbf{x}'_{j.}}{h})}{\sum_{j=1}^{n} K(\frac{\mathbf{x}_0 - \mathbf{x}'_{j.}}{h})}$, $\sum_{j=1}^{n} w_j(\mathbf{x}_0) = 1$ and $w_j(\mathbf{x}_0) \geq 0$ for $j = 1, \ldots, n$. The estimate in (21.2.7) is called the Nadaraya–Watson (NW) kernel regression estimator and was named after Nadaraya (1964) and Watson (1964). The estimate is a weighted average of the observed y_j values, the weights being supplied by the kernel $K(\cdot)$ normalized by the kernel sum in (21.2.7). This estimate is in the form of a locally weighted average and can also be interpreted as a local-weighted least-squares estimate of an intercept or mean value parameter, as developed in Section 21.4.3, Equations (21.4.11)–(21.4.14). Equivalently, the NW estimator can be thought of as a 0th order local polynomial approximation to the true regression function at the point of evaluation $\mathbf{x}$, as defined in Sections 21.3 and 21.4.4.

21.2.2.a. Asymptotic Properties

Under general regularity conditions, the NW kernel regression estimator is a consistent and asymptotically normally distributional estimator of $E[Y \mid \mathbf{x}_0]$. Regarding motivation for the consistency of the NW estimator, we assume that the properties of kernel functions listed in Definition 21.1.1 apply. Rescale the numerator and denominator in (21.2.7) by $(nh^k)^{-1}$ and note that the scaled denominator term is such that

$$\hat{f}(\mathbf{x}_0; \mathbf{X}) = \left(nh^k\right)^{-1} \sum_{j=1}^{n} K\left(\frac{\mathbf{x}_0 - \mathbf{X}'_{j.}}{h}\right) \xrightarrow{P} f(\mathbf{x}_0) \tag{21.2.8}$$

given the consistency of the kernel density estimator for the PDF of $\mathbf{X}$.

The scaled (by $(nh^k)^{-1}$) numerator term in (21.2.7), upon substitution of $g(\mathbf{X}_{j\cdot}) + \varepsilon_j$ for y_j from (21.2.3), can be written as

$$\xi_n(\mathbf{x}_0; \mathbf{X}) = (nh^k)^{-1} \sum_{j=1}^{n} K\left(\frac{\mathbf{x}_0 - \mathbf{X}'_{j\cdot}}{h}\right) [g(\mathbf{X}_{j\cdot}) + \varepsilon_j]. \tag{21.2.9}$$

Given that the $\mathbf{X}_{j\cdot}$'s are iid, and because $E[\varepsilon_j \mid \mathbf{X}_{j\cdot}] = 0$, the expectation of (21.2.9) can be written as

$$E\left[\xi_n(\mathbf{x}_0; \mathbf{X})\right] = h^{-k} E\left[K\left(\frac{\mathbf{x}_0 - \mathbf{X}'_{1\cdot}}{h}\right) g(\mathbf{X}_{1\cdot})\right] = \int_{R^k} K(\mathbf{z}) g(\mathbf{x}_0 - h\mathbf{z}) f(\mathbf{x}_0 - h\mathbf{z})\, d\mathbf{z}, \tag{21.2.10}$$

where we have used the change of variables $\mathbf{z} = (\mathbf{x}_0 - \mathbf{x}'_{1\cdot})/h$. Assuming that $g(\cdot)$ and $f(\cdot)$ are each twice continuously differentiable with bounded derivatives, we can expand the integral (21.2.10) in a Taylor series around $h = 0$ as

$$E\left[\xi_n(\mathbf{x}_0; \mathbf{X})\right] = g(\mathbf{x}_0) f(\mathbf{x}_0) + O(h^2), \tag{21.2.11}$$

and thus $E[\xi_n(\mathbf{x}_0; \mathbf{X})] \to g(\mathbf{x}_0) f(\mathbf{x}_0)$ when the bandwidth h converges to zero.

It can be shown via further use of Taylor series expansions that the variance of $\xi_n(\mathbf{x}_0; \mathbf{X})$ is given by

$$\operatorname{var}(\xi_n(\mathbf{x}_0; \mathbf{X})) = (nh^k)^{-1} \left[[g^2(\mathbf{x}_0) + \sigma^2] f(\mathbf{x}_0) \int_{R^k} [K(\mathbf{z})]^2\, d\mathbf{z} + O(1) \right] = O(n^{-1} h^{-k}), \tag{21.2.12}$$

where $\sigma^2 = \operatorname{var}(\varepsilon_i)$ (Lee, 1996, p. 147) and it is assumed that $K(\mathbf{z})$ is square integrable. Then if $h \to 0$ and $nh^k \to \infty$, it follows from (21.2.11), (21.2.12), and mean-square convergence that

$$\hat{g}(\mathbf{x}_0) = \frac{\xi_n(\mathbf{x}_0; \mathbf{X})}{\hat{f}(\mathbf{x}_0; \mathbf{x})} \xrightarrow{p} \frac{g(\mathbf{x}_0) f(\mathbf{x}_0)}{f(\mathbf{x}_0)} = g(\mathbf{x}_0), \tag{21.2.13}$$

and thus the NW estimator is a consistent estimator of $E(Y \mid \mathbf{x}_0)$ at each point $\mathbf{x}_0$.

Regarding asymptotic normality of the NW estimator, first note that

$$\hat{g}(\mathbf{x}_0; \mathbf{X}) - g(\mathbf{x}_0) = (nh^k)^{-1} \left[\sum_{j=1}^{n} K\left(\frac{\mathbf{x}_0 - \mathbf{X}'_{j\cdot}}{h}\right) [Y_j - g(\mathbf{x}_0)] \right] \Big/ \hat{f}(\mathbf{x}_0; \mathbf{X}). \tag{21.2.14}$$

Then, substituting $Y_i = g(\mathbf{X}_{i\cdot}) + \varepsilon_i$ and scaling by $(nh^k)^{1/2}$ yields

$$(nh^k)^{1/2} [\hat{g}(\mathbf{x}_0; \mathbf{X}) - g(\mathbf{x}_0)] = (nh^k)^{-1/2} [\hat{f}(\mathbf{x}_0; \mathbf{X})]^{-1} \left[\sum_{j=1}^{n} K\left(\frac{\mathbf{x}_0 - \mathbf{X}'_{j\cdot}}{h}\right) \times [g(\mathbf{X}_{j\cdot}) - g(\mathbf{x}_0) + \varepsilon_j] \right], \tag{21.2.15}$$

and it can be shown via central limit theory that this scaled sum of iid random variables has a normal limiting distribution of the form (Lee, 1996, p. 151; Bierens, 1985, pp. 105–11)

$$(nh^k)^{1/2}[\hat{g}(\mathbf{x}_0;\mathbf{X}) - g(\mathbf{x}_0)] \xrightarrow{d} N\left(0, \frac{\sigma^2}{f(\mathbf{x}_0)}\int_{R^k}[K(\mathbf{z})]^2\, d\mathbf{z}\right) \tag{21.2.16}$$

so long as $nh^{k+4} \to 0$. If $nh^{k+4} \not\to 0$, then a zero mean is not obtained in (21.2.16), and the NW estimator exhibits an asymptotic bias such that

$$(nh^k)^{1/2}\left[\hat{g}(\mathbf{x}_0;\mathbf{X}) - g(\mathbf{x}_0) - \sigma_K^2 \sum_{j=1}^{k}\left[\frac{\partial g(\mathbf{x}_0)}{\partial x_0[j]}\frac{\partial f(\mathbf{x}_0)}{\partial x_0[j]} f(\mathbf{x}_0)^{-1} + \frac{1}{2}\frac{\partial^2 g(\mathbf{x}_0)}{\partial x_0[j]^2}\right] h^2\right] \tag{21.2.17}$$

achieves the normal limiting distribution in (21.2.16), where it is assumed that $\sigma_K^2 > 0$ and $\int_{R^k} \mathbf{z}\mathbf{z}' K(\mathbf{z})\, d\mathbf{z} = \sigma_K^2 \mathbf{I}$.

It is useful to note that asymptotically, $(nh^k)^{1/2}[\hat{g}(\mathbf{x}_0;\mathbf{X}) - g(\mathbf{x}_0)]$ and $(nh^k)^{1/2}$ $[\hat{g}(\mathbf{x}_*;\mathbf{X}) - g(\mathbf{x}_*)]$ have zero covariance whenever $\mathbf{x}_0 \neq \mathbf{x}_*$. Thus, a multivariate version of (21.2.16) applies to the vector estimator$[\hat{g}(\mathbf{x}_{1\cdot};\mathbf{X}), \ldots, \hat{g}(\mathbf{x}_{m\cdot};\mathbf{X})]$ in which the $(m \times m)$ covariance matrix is a diagonal matrix whose (j, j)th element is given by $\frac{\sigma^2}{f(\mathbf{x}_{j\cdot})}\int_{R^k}[K(\mathbf{z})]^2 d\mathbf{z}$.

In practice, estimates for σ^2 and $f(\mathbf{x}_0)$ are needed to use the asymptotic normal limiting distribution result (21.2.16) for hypothesis testing and confidence-region estimation purposes. An estimate of $f(\mathbf{x}_0)$ can be obtained from the outcome of the kernel density estimator $\hat{f}(\mathbf{x}_0;\mathbf{X})$. An estimate for the noise component variance σ^2 is given straightforwardly by

$$\hat{\sigma}^2 = n^{-1}\sum_{j=1}^{n}[y_j - \hat{g}(\mathbf{x}_{j\cdot};\mathbf{x})]^2, \tag{21.2.18}$$

where $\hat{g}(\mathbf{x}_{j\cdot};\mathbf{x})$ is the NW estimator evaluated at $\mathbf{x}_{j\cdot}$.

21.2.2.b. Choosing the Kernel and Bandwidth

Our discussion of the choice of kernel function and bandwidth in Sections 21.1.2 and 21.1.3 remains largely relevant here, which is of course not surprising because kernel density estimators are central components of the NW estimator definition. The choice of kernel function can proceed as in the density estimation case by choosing an optimality criterion and then seeking a kernel function that optimizes the criterion (see Muller, 1988). However, as in the case of density estimation, the choice of the kernel function does not have large impacts on estimates, and it is generally felt that the choice of bandwidth is the much more important task. Thus, in practice the choice of kernel function is often driven by the desire to impart continuity, differentiability, infinite support, or other characteristics to the kernel density estimators underlying the definition of the nonparametric regression estimator.

Regarding bandwidth choice, the cross-validation approach is most often used in practice, as was the case in density estimation as well. In the regression case, the least-squares cross-validation (LSCV) procedure is to choose h as

$$h_* = \arg\min_{h} \left[\sum_{j=1}^{n} [y_j - \hat{g}_{-j}(\mathbf{x}_{j\cdot};\mathbf{x})] \right]^2, \tag{21.2.19}$$

where $\hat{g}_{-j}(\mathbf{x}_{j\cdot};\mathbf{x})$ is the "leave one out" NW estimator of $g(\mathbf{x}_{j\cdot})$ based on bandwidth h in which the jth observation is eliminated from the definition of the NW estimator (21.2.7). Asymptotically, the LSCV choice of h_* can be shown to minimize the integrated squared error of $\hat{g}(\mathbf{x}_0;\mathbf{x})$ as an estimator of $g(\mathbf{x}_0)$ defined by

$$\text{ISE}(\hat{g}, g) = \int_{R^k} [\hat{g}(\mathbf{x}_0;\mathbf{x}) - g(\mathbf{x}_0)]^2 f(\mathbf{x}_0)\, d\mathbf{x}_0 \tag{21.2.20}$$

as well as the AIMSE (Stone, 1974; Hardle and Marron, 1985).

► **Example 21.2.1:** The GAUSS program C21NW.gss (provided in the examples manual) demonstrates an application of the Nadaraya–Watson kernel regression estimator. In the spirit of the first example presented by Vinod and Ullah (1988), GAUSS generates a pseudorandom set of capital–labor inputs and the associated output from a translog production function. The parametric regression function is estimated in log-linear form by LS, and the nonparametric regression function is estimated by the Nadaraya–Watson procedure. For comparison purposes, GAUSS generates a surface plot for each of the two estimated regression functions.

21.2.2.c. Estimating and Testing Derivatives of $g(\mathbf{x}_0)$

Analysts are often interested in assessing the marginal impacts of changes in explanatory variables on the expected value of the dependent variable, and these changes are represented by the partial derivatives of the regression function with respect to explanatory variables. These marginal effects, which are also often referred to as *response coefficients* (Ullah, 1988) are represented by the β_i's and $\partial g(\mathbf{x}_0, \boldsymbol{\beta})/\partial x_0[i]$'s in linear and nonlinear parametric (or semiparametric) models, respectively. In nonparametric models, such a marginal effect is represented by $\partial g(\mathbf{x}_0)/\partial x_0[i]$.

A direct method of estimating the marginal effect of an explanatory variable is to differentiate the NW kernel estimator with respect to the variable and use the resulting outcome of the derivative as an estimate of the marginal effect. Thus, the response coefficient for the ith explanatory variable, evaluated at the point $\mathbf{x}_0$, is given by

$$\hat{\beta}_i(\mathbf{x}_0;\mathbf{x}) = \partial \hat{g}(\mathbf{x}_0;\mathbf{x})/\partial x_0[i] = \sum_{j=1}^{n} y_j \frac{\partial w_j(\mathbf{x}_0)}{\partial x_0[i]} \tag{21.2.21}$$

(recall (21.2.7)). We emphasize that the estimator (21.2.21) is only appropriate for continuous explanatory variables, or else the partial derivative $\partial g(\mathbf{x}_0)/\partial x_0[i]$ does not exist, and the estimator (21.2.21) does not make sense.

The estimator (21.2.21) is consistent and asymptotically normal under general conditions (see Pagan and Ullah, 1999, Section 4.5.1, for proofs). In particular, if $(\mathbf{x}_{j\cdot}, \varepsilon_j)$,

$j = 1, \ldots, n$ are iid, $\mathbf{x}_{j.}$ is independent of ε_j, $\mathrm{E}[\varepsilon_j] = 0\,\forall j$, $|\mathrm{z}|\mathrm{K}(\mathbf{z}) \to 0$ as $|\mathrm{z}| \to \infty$, and $\sup(\mathrm{K}(\mathbf{z})) < \infty$, then if $h \to 0$ and $nh^3 \to \infty$,

$$\hat{\beta}_i(\mathbf{x}_0; \mathbf{X}) \xrightarrow{p} \beta_i(\mathbf{x}_0) \equiv \partial \mathrm{g}(\mathbf{x}_0)/\partial \mathrm{x}_0[i], \tag{21.2.22}$$

and thus the response coefficient estimator is consistent. Under additional assumptions relating to the existence and boundedness of third-order partial derivatives of $\mathrm{f}(\mathbf{x}_0)$, $\mathrm{g}(\mathbf{x}_0)$, and $\mathrm{v}(\mathbf{x}_0) = \int \mathrm{y}^2 \mathrm{f}(\mathrm{y}, \mathbf{x}_0)d\mathrm{y}$, on the assumption that $\mathrm{E}|\varepsilon_j|^{2+\delta}$ exists for some $\delta > 0$, and given that the kernel function is chosen so that both $\int_{\mathrm{R}^k} |\mathrm{K}(\mathbf{z})|^{2+\xi} d\mathbf{z} < \infty$ for some $\xi > 0$ and $\int_{\mathrm{R}^k} \mathrm{z}_j^2 \mathrm{K}(\mathbf{z})d\mathbf{z} < \infty\,\forall j$, it follows from central limit theory that if $nh^7 \to 0$, then

$$(nh^{2+k})^{1/2}[\hat{\boldsymbol{\beta}}(\mathbf{x}_0; \mathbf{X}) - \boldsymbol{\beta}(\mathbf{x}_0)] \xrightarrow{d} \mathrm{N}(\mathbf{0}, \boldsymbol{\Sigma}_{\hat{\beta}}), \tag{21.2.23}$$

where $\Sigma_{\hat{\beta}} = \frac{\sigma^2}{\mathrm{f}(\mathbf{x}_0)} \int_{\mathrm{R}^k} [\frac{\partial \mathrm{K}(\mathbf{z})}{\partial \mathbf{z}} \frac{\partial \mathrm{K}(\mathbf{z})}{\partial \mathbf{z}'}] d\mathbf{z}$, $\boldsymbol{\beta}(\mathbf{x}_0) \equiv \partial \mathrm{g}(\mathbf{x}_0)/\partial \mathbf{x}_0$ is the $k \times 1$ vector of response coefficients, and $\hat{\boldsymbol{\beta}}(\mathbf{x}_0; \mathbf{X}) \equiv \partial \hat{\mathrm{g}}(\mathbf{x}_0; \mathbf{X})/\partial \mathbf{x}_0$ is the $k \times 1$ vector estimator of the response coefficients.

To perform hypothesis tests and generate confidence region estimates based on the asymptotic normality of $\hat{\boldsymbol{\beta}}(\mathbf{x}_0; \mathbf{X})$, the unknowns σ^2 and $\mathrm{f}(\mathbf{x}_0)$ in the definition of the asymptotic covariance matrix, $\boldsymbol{\Sigma}_{\hat{\beta}}$ must be replaced by estimates. As was suggested when estimating the regression function via the NW estimator, $\mathrm{f}(\mathbf{x}_0)$ can be replaced by the kernel density estimate, $\hat{\mathrm{f}}(\mathbf{x}_0; \mathbf{x})$, and σ^2 can be estimated using (21.2.18). Then, asymptotic Chi-square–type testing and confidence region estimation can proceed as usual. For example, to test the linear hypothesis H_0: $\mathbf{c}\boldsymbol{\beta}(\mathbf{x}_0) = \mathbf{r}$, one could utilize the Wald statistic

$$\mathrm{W} = [\mathbf{c}\hat{\boldsymbol{\beta}}(\mathbf{x}_0; \mathbf{X}) - \mathbf{r}]'(\mathbf{c}[(nh^{2+k})^{-1}\hat{\boldsymbol{\Sigma}}_{\hat{\beta}}]\mathbf{c}')^{-1}[\mathbf{c}\hat{\boldsymbol{\beta}}(\mathbf{x}_0; \mathbf{X}) - \mathbf{r}] \overset{a}{\sim} \text{Chi-square}(j, 0), \tag{21.2.24}$$

where j is the number of rows in $\mathbf{c}$ (it is assumed that $\mathbf{c}$ has full-row rank). Confidence regions can be constructed in the usual way via duality with hypothesis tests. Other informative references relating to testing hypotheses within the nonparametric framework include the works of Lavergne and Vuong (1996) and Fan and Li (1996). See also Rilstone and Ullah (1989) for a finite difference method of derivative estimation.

► **Example 21.2.2:** To demonstrate an application of the estimation and testing of response coefficients in a nonparametric regression function, we provide the GAUSS program C21RC.gss in the examples manual. Continuing the analysis of production data from Example 21.2.1, the program computes the marginal product of labor, evaluated at a given level of capital, and for a given set of evaluation points relating to the level of labor. Then GAUSS uses (21.2.23) to form a 90% confidence interval for the marginal product of the labor input. Finally, the program uses the Wald statistic (21.2.24) to conduct a test of the hypothesis that the marginal product of labor, given the level of capital, equals the value 1.

21.2.2.d. Testing Global Significance of Explanatory Variables

We emphasize that in the nonparametric model, the response coefficient is permitted to vary over the different evaluation points for $\mathbf{x}_0$. This has important implications for testing the significance of explanatory variables in a nonparametric model. In particular, the null hypothesis H_0: $\beta_j(\mathbf{x}_0) = 0$ is not a test of the significance of the explanatory variable $\mathbf{x}[., j]$ in the regression model but rather tests the marginal effect of a change in $\mathbf{x}[i, j]$ at the evaluation point $\mathbf{x}[i, .] = (\mathbf{x}[i, 1], \mathbf{x}[i, 2], \ldots, \mathbf{x}[i, k])$. An explanatory variable will be insignificant or irrelevant in a nonparametric model only when $\beta_j(\mathbf{x}_0) = 0 \ \forall \mathbf{x}_0$.

Racine (1997) suggests a procedure for testing the significance of a group of explanatory variables in the nonparametric regression context. The null and alternative hypotheses are

$$\begin{aligned} H_0 &: \frac{\partial g(\mathbf{x}_0)}{\partial x_0[j]} = 0 \ \forall j \in J \quad \text{and} \quad \forall \mathbf{x}_0 \in \text{Range}(\mathbf{X}_0) \\ H_a &: \frac{\partial g(\mathbf{x}_0)}{\partial x_0[j]} \neq 0 \quad \text{for some } j \in J \text{ and some } \mathbf{x}_0 \in \text{Range}(\mathbf{X}_0), \end{aligned} \tag{21.2.25}$$

where J is an index set containing the indices of the explanatory variables whose significance is being tested and Range $(\mathbf{X}_0)$ is the set of values representing the support of $\mathbf{X}$. Racine transforms these hypotheses into

$$\begin{Bmatrix} H_0 \\ H_a \end{Bmatrix} : \sum_{j \in J} \left[\frac{\partial g(\mathbf{x}_0)}{\partial \mathbf{x}_0[j]} \right]^2 \begin{Bmatrix} = \\ > \end{Bmatrix} 0. \tag{21.2.26}$$

Then, a random variable used as a test statistic to assess the validity of H_0 is constructed by defining sample analogs to each of the bracketed terms involved in the sum of squares in (21.2.26), the random variable outcome being

$$\hat{\lambda} = n^{-1} \sum_{i=1}^{n} \sum_{j \in J} [\hat{\beta}_j(\mathbf{x}_{i\cdot}; \mathbf{x}) / s(\hat{\beta}_j(\mathbf{x}_{i\cdot}; \mathbf{x}))]^2, \tag{21.2.27}$$

where $s[\hat{\beta}_j(\mathbf{x}_{i\cdot}; \mathbf{x})]$ denotes the estimated asymptotic standard error of $\hat{\beta}_j(\mathbf{x}_{i\cdot}; \mathbf{X})$ obtained from the square roots of the diagonal entries in $(nh^{2+k})^{-1}\hat{\boldsymbol{\Sigma}}_{\hat{\beta}}$.

The test statistic outcome used to test H_0 is then given by

$$\hat{\tau} = \hat{\lambda} / s(\hat{\lambda}), \tag{21.2.28}$$

where $s(\hat{\lambda})$ is an estimate of the standard error of $\hat{\lambda}$. The finite sample distribution of $\hat{\tau}$ outcomes is unknown. To base a test on $\hat{\tau}$, Racine estimates the sampling distribution of $\hat{\tau}$ outcomes under the null hypothesis via a nested bootstrap resampling scheme. For iid sample outcomes, the bootstrap algorithm for estimating the null sampling distribution of $\hat{\tau}$ outcomes is given next (see Kunsch, 1989 for bootstrap sampling with non-iid data), where $\mathbf{x}_{iJ}$ is a vector denoting the ith observation on the explanatory variables indexed by J, $\mathbf{x}_{iJ^c}$ is the ith observation on the remaining explanatory variables (the complement of $\mathbf{x}_{iJ}$), and $\bar{\mathbf{x}}_J = n^{-1} \sum_{i=1}^{n} \mathbf{x}_{iJ}$.

Nested Bootstrap Algorithm for $\hat{\tau}$ Outcome Distribution

1. Estimate the *restricted* conditional means $\hat{g}(\bar{\mathbf{x}}_J, \mathbf{x}_{iJ^c}; \mathbf{x}), \equiv \hat{E}(Y \mid \bar{\mathbf{x}}_J, \mathbf{x}_{iJ^c}), i = 1, \ldots, n$.
2. Calculate residuals $\hat{v}_i = y_i - \hat{g}(\bar{\mathbf{x}}_J, \mathbf{x}_{iJ^c}; \mathbf{x})$, and then center them as $\hat{v}_i^c = \hat{v}_i - n^{-1} \sum_{i=1}^n \hat{v}_i$, $i = 1, \ldots, n$.
3. Randomly sample n residuals from $\{\hat{v}_1^c, \ldots, \hat{v}_n^c\}$ with replacement, resulting in the bootstrap sample $\{\hat{\varepsilon}_1^*, \ldots, \hat{\varepsilon}_n^*\}$.
4. Generate n bootstrapped outcomes of the dependent variable as

$$y_i^* = \hat{g}(\bar{\mathbf{x}}_J, \mathbf{x}_{iJ^c}; \mathbf{x}) + \hat{\varepsilon}_i^*, \quad i = 1, \ldots, n,$$

   and define a *bootstrap sample* as $\{y_i^*, \mathbf{x}_{i\cdot}\}$, $i = 1, \ldots, n$, where the $\mathbf{x}_{i\cdot}$, $i = 1, \ldots, n$ of the bootstrap sample are now the *original* observations on all of the explanatory variables.
5. Using the bootstrap sample data from step 4, calculate $\hat{\boldsymbol{\beta}}(\mathbf{x}_{i\cdot}; \mathbf{x})^*$ and $\mathbf{std}[\hat{\boldsymbol{\beta}}(\mathbf{x}_{i\cdot}; \mathbf{x})]^*$ for $i = 1, \ldots, n$, where **std**( ) denotes the vector of standard deviations, and then calculate a bootstrapped outcome of (21.2.27), resulting in $\hat{\lambda}^*$.
   - **a.** Draw an iid random sample, with replacement, of $(k+1)$-dimensional *vectors* $(y_\ell^*, \mathbf{x}_{\ell\cdot})$ from the set of vectors $\{y_i^*, \mathbf{x}_{i\cdot}\}$, $i = 1, \ldots, n$, yielding the resampled pairs $\{y_i^{**}, \mathbf{x}_{i\cdot}^*\}$, $i = 1, \ldots, n$.
   - **b.** Calculate an outcome of $\hat{\lambda}$ from the resampled data in **a**, yielding $\hat{\lambda}^{**}$.
   - **c.** Repeat **a.** and **b.** B_2 times, producing a sample of B_2 values $\hat{\lambda}_1^{**}, \ldots, \hat{\lambda}_{B_2}^{**}$, and use these values to calculate a sample standard deviation for $\hat{\lambda}$, yielding $\text{std}(\hat{\lambda})^*$.
6. Calculate a bootstrapped outcome of $\hat{\tau}$ as $\hat{\tau}^* = \hat{\lambda}^*/\text{std}(\hat{\lambda})^*$.
7. Repeat steps 3–6 B_1 times to obtain B_1 sampled $\hat{\tau}$ values, $\hat{\tau}_1^*, \ldots, \hat{\tau}_{B_1}^*$, representing outcomes of the bootstrapped null distribution of $\hat{\tau}$.

Given the bootstrapped null distribution of $\hat{\tau}$ outcomes, bootstrap critical values can be obtained by ordering the $\hat{\tau}_i^*$'s from lowest to highest and then choosing the $\hat{\tau}_\ell^*$ value representing the appropriate $(1-\alpha)$th quantile of the bootstrap distribution. By letting $\tau_{1-\alpha}^*$ represent the appropriate bootstrap outcome associated with the $(1-\alpha)$th quantile of the bootstrap distribution, a size-α test is conducted as

$$\text{reject } H_0 \quad \text{if } \hat{\tau} \geq \tau_{1-\alpha}^*. \tag{21.2.29}$$

Racine recommends bootstrap sample sizes of $B_1 \geq 1000$ and $B_2 \geq 100$. Monte Carlo analyses of his testing procedure suggests that the approach is remarkably insensitive to the choice of bandwidth underlying the kernel regression estimator and that the empirical test size obtained when using an LSCV-determined bandwidths is very close to the specified nominal size of the test, α . Furthermore, the test was shown to have good power characteristics.

21.2.2.e. Estimating and Testing Higher-Order Derivatives of g(x)

Estimation of higher-order derivatives of the regression function can be accomplished by taking higher-order derivatives of the kernel regression estimator. Such estimators, say $\hat{\beta}_i^{(q)}(\mathbf{x}_0)$ for the qth order derivative with respect to $x_0[i]$, are both consistent and asymptotically normally distributed under general conditions. The relevant limiting distribution result for the full $(k \times 1)$ vector derivative estimator is given by

$$(nh^{k+2q})^{1/2}\left[\hat{\boldsymbol{\beta}}^{(q)}(\mathbf{x}_0;\mathbf{X}) - \boldsymbol{\beta}^{(q)}(\mathbf{x}_0)\right] \xrightarrow{d} \mathrm{N}\left(\mathbf{0}, \boldsymbol{\Sigma}_{\hat{\beta}}^{(q)}\right), \tag{21.2.30}$$

where $\boldsymbol{\beta}^{(q)}(\mathbf{x}_0)$ denotes the vector of qth order derivatives of $\mathrm{g}(\mathbf{x}_0)$ with respect to $\mathbf{x}_0$, and

$$\boldsymbol{\Sigma}_{\hat{\beta}}^{(q)} \equiv \frac{\sigma^2}{\mathrm{f}(\mathbf{x}_0)} \int_{\mathrm{R}^k} \left[\frac{\partial^q \mathrm{K}(\mathbf{z})}{\partial \mathbf{z}^q}\left(\frac{\partial^q \mathrm{K}(\mathbf{z})}{\partial \mathbf{z}^q}\right)'\right] d\mathbf{z} \tag{21.2.31}$$

(see Pagan and Ullah, 1999, Section 5.5.3 for further discussion of these and other results relating to higher-order derivative estimation). Hypothesis tests relating to values of $\boldsymbol{\beta}^{(q)}(\mathbf{x}_0)$, or any linear or differentiable function of the elements in $\boldsymbol{\beta}^{(q)}(\mathbf{x}_0)$, can be based on the asymptotic normality of $\hat{\boldsymbol{\beta}}^{(q)}(\mathbf{x}_0;\mathbf{X})$. For example the Wald test defined in (21.2.24) applies analogously to hypotheses of the form H_0: $\mathbf{c}\boldsymbol{\beta}^{(q)}(\mathbf{x}_0) = \mathbf{r}$ upon replacement of the asymptotic covariance matrix with $(nh^{k+2q})^{-1}\hat{\boldsymbol{\Sigma}}_{\hat{\beta}}^{(q)}$, where σ^2 is replaced by $\hat{\sigma}^2$, as before. Confidence-region estimates follow via duality with the hypothesis tests.

It should be noted that when estimating derivatives, the *optimal* window width for minimizing MSE to first-order terms is $\mathrm{h}_* \propto \mathrm{n}^{-1/(k+4+2q)}$, where q is the order of the derivatives being estimated. The point is that different window widths are needed for (asymptotically) *optimal* estimation of regression functions and progressively higher-order derivatives. The window width generally widens the higher the order of the derivative (Pagan and Ullah, 1999, Section 5.7). Nonetheless, it is often the case in practice that h is chosen via the application of LSCV applied to the estimation of the regression function itself, and this same (suboptimal for derivative estimation) bandwidth is then used in the estimation of derivatives.

21.2.2.f. Other Issues and Extensions

The literature on kernel regression estimation is vast and growing, and many additional issues and extensions have been examined or are in the process of being addressed. In the case in which some of the explanatory variables in the regression model are discrete rather than continuous, Bierens (1985, Section 3.2) notes that the kernel regression estimator can be used precisely as before, and the estimator continues to be consistent and asymptotically normal. However, it should be noted that the covariance matrix of the normal limiting distribution (21.2.16) must be changed by replacing k with m, and $\int_{\mathrm{R}^k}[\mathrm{K}(z)]^2\,d\mathbf{z}$ by $\int_{\mathrm{R}^m}[\mathrm{K}(z_1,\mathbf{0})]^2\,d\mathbf{z}_1$, where $\mathbf{x}_0 = [x_0[1], \ldots, x_0[m], x_0[m+1], \ldots, x_0[k]]'$ is such that $(x_0[1], \ldots, x_0[m])$ are continuous and $(x_0[m+1], \ldots, x_0[k])$ are discrete, which correspond to the $\mathbf{z}_1$ and $\mathbf{z}_2 = \mathbf{0}$ entries in the kernel function, respectively. In the case in which all explanatory variables are discrete, the limiting distribution result becomes simply $n^{1/2}[\hat{\mathrm{g}}(\mathbf{x}_0;\mathbf{X}) - \mathrm{g}(\mathbf{x}_0)] \xrightarrow{d} \mathrm{N}[0, \sigma^2/\mathrm{f}(\mathbf{x}_0)]$ (note the scaling factor $n^{1/2}$, so that convergence in the all-discrete case is at the same rate as parametric models (Bierens, 1985, p. 117).

In the case in which the explanatory variables are fixed, as opposed to random, the kernel regression approach again applies directly and produces consistent and asymptotically normal estimates. In this case the derivations of estimator properties are considerably simplified because the kernel regression estimator (21.2.7) is then simply a weighted sum of Y_j's with nonstochastic fixed, as opposed to random, weights. In fact, the estimator is then of the familiar GLS form (see 21.4.15), and thus standard methods of analyzing GLS estimator properties, as identified in Chapter 14 for a known weight matrix $\mathbf{\Phi}$, apply to the kernel regression estimator.

The kernel regression method can be extended to cases in which the noise component of the model is heteroscedastic, autocorrelated, or both. In fact, the same kernel regression estimator used in the iid case will produce consistent and asymptotically normally distributed estimates in the non-iid case. All that is required is that the degree of dependence among sample observations be limited appropriately, and the usual convergent autocorrelation processes that arise in applied work are allowed. The asymptotic covariance matrix of the normal limiting distribution of the kernel regression estimator is of course affected by dependence of the observations, and the reader can consult Bierens (1985), Robinson (1983), and Pagan and Ullah (1999) for further discussion and references.

Extensions of the kernel regression estimator to systems of equations, including simultaneous equations, are currently being developed. A discussion of recent results and references can be found in Pagan and Ullah (1998, Chapter 6). There is also a growing literature in the use of nonparametric regression estimators for assessing the adequacy of parametric models, and a summary of results and references can be found in Pagan and Ullah (1999, Section 4.13). It is also possible to impose restrictions on $g(\mathbf{x}_0)$ in estimation, as described in Section 5.4 of Pagan and Ullah (1999). Finally, it is possible to develop a nonparametric local maximum likelihood estimation procedure for estimating nonparametric regression models that is based on kernel function weighting procedures, as presented in Fan, Farmen, and Gijbels (1998) and Pagan and Ullah (1999, Section 3.2.8).

Finally, a recent contribution by Zhao (1999) presents a promising and relatively straightforward procedure for improving the asymptotic efficiency of nonparametric regression estimators such as the NW estimator, regardless of the type of kernel used or the bandwidth chosen. The approach utilizes a particular type of data-determined linear transformation of the estimator to achieve the asymptotic efficiency gains, and this method can be applied in certain types of semiparametric estimation contexts as well. The reader is referred to Zhao's article for details.

21.3. Local Polynomial Regression

From the discussion following Equation (21.2.7), we know that the NW estimator can be viewed as a 0th order local polynomial (i.e., constant) least-squares approximation to the regression function $g(\mathbf{x}_0)$ at the point of evaluation $\mathbf{x}_0$. In the quest for generating more accurate approximations to the regression function at $\mathbf{x}_0$, higher-order local polynomial approximations to the regression function could be considered. This is the intent of the local polynomial regression procedure.

A local linear (first-order polynomial) regression (LLR) estimator, where now a kernel function provides the weights, is defined by

$$\hat{\boldsymbol{\beta}}_{\mathrm{LLR}}(\mathbf{x}_0;\mathbf{x}) \equiv \arg\min_{\mathrm{a,b}} \left[\sum_{i=1}^{n} [\mathrm{y}_i - \mathrm{a} - (\mathbf{x}_{i\cdot} - \mathbf{x}_0')\mathbf{b}]^2 \mathrm{K}((\mathbf{x}_{i\cdot} - \mathbf{x}_0')/h) \right] \tag{21.3.1}$$

(see Section 21.4.4 for additional background information). The value of $\hat{\mathrm{a}}(\mathbf{x}_0;\mathbf{x})$ obtained from (21.3.1) is the LLR estimate of the regression function evaluated at $\mathbf{x}_0$, $\mathrm{g}(\mathbf{x}_0)$. The value of $\hat{\mathbf{b}}(\mathbf{x}_0;\mathbf{x})$ obtained from (21.3.1) is the LLR estimate of the vector of first-order partial derivatives of $\mathrm{g}(\mathbf{x}_0)$ with respect to $\mathbf{x}_0$.

An immediate advantage of LLR over the NW estimator is apparent – the first-order LLR produces a ready-made estimate of the first-order derivatives of the regression function. There are several additional advantages as well. First, it can be shown that the bias of the LLR estimator is unaffected by the value of $\partial \mathrm{g}(\mathbf{x}_0)/\partial \mathbf{x}_0$, whereas the bias of the NW estimator is generally affected, as is evident from (21.2.17). In addition, LLR exhibits less bias at the boundary of the data range owing to the local linear, as opposed to constant, approximation (see Hastie and Loader, 1993). Furthermore, Fan (1992, 1993) shows that in the class of "linear smoothers" of the form $\hat{\mathrm{g}}_{\mathrm{L}}(\mathbf{x}_0;\mathbf{x}) = \sum_{j=1}^{n} \mathrm{w}_j(\mathbf{x}_0;\mathbf{x})\mathrm{Y}_j$ where the w_j's are functions of the explanatory variables, the LLR minimizes the maximum expected squared difference between $\hat{\mathrm{g}}_{\mathrm{L}}(\mathbf{x}_0;\mathbf{x})$ and $\mathrm{g}(\mathbf{x}_0)$.

Regarding the LLR estimator $\hat{\mathrm{a}}(\mathbf{x}_0;\mathbf{X})$ of $\mathrm{g}(\mathbf{x}_0)$, Ruppert and Wand (1994, p. 1351) show under general regularity conditions that the asymptotic bias of $\hat{\mathrm{a}}(\mathbf{x}_0;\mathbf{X})$ in estimating $\mathrm{g}(\mathbf{x}_0)$ is given by

$$\mathrm{ABias}(\hat{\mathrm{a}}(\mathbf{x}_0;\mathbf{X})) = \frac{\sigma_{\mathrm{K}}^2 h^2}{2} \mathrm{tr}\left[\frac{\partial^2 \mathrm{g}(\mathbf{x}_0)}{\partial \mathbf{x}_0 \partial \mathbf{x}_0'}\right] \tag{21.3.2}$$

and the asymptotic variance is

$$\mathrm{AVar}\,(\hat{\mathrm{a}}(\mathbf{x}_0;\mathbf{X})) = \frac{\sigma^2}{n h^{\mathrm{k}} \mathrm{f}(\mathbf{x}_0)} \int_{\mathrm{R}^{\mathrm{k}}} [\mathrm{K}(\mathbf{z})]^2 \, d\mathbf{z}, \tag{21.3.3}$$

where the evaluation point $\mathbf{x}_0$ is any point in the interior of the support of $\mathrm{f}(\mathbf{x})$ and $\sigma_{\mathrm{K}}^2 > 0$ satisfies $\int_{\mathrm{R}^{\mathrm{k}}} \mathbf{z}\mathbf{z}'\mathrm{K}(\mathbf{z})d\mathbf{z} = \boldsymbol{\sigma}_{\mathrm{K}}^2\mathbf{I}$. Comparing (21.3.2) and (21.3.3) with (21.2.16) and (21.2.17) reveals that the asymptotic variances of the LLR and NW estimators of $\mathrm{g}(\mathbf{x}_0)$ are precisely the same, whereas the asymptotic bias terms differ only by the NW estimator's inclusion of a summation term involving first-order derivatives of $\mathrm{g}(\mathbf{x}_0)$ and $\mathrm{f}(\mathbf{x}_0)$, as we mentioned in the preceding paragraph.

It is apparent from (21.3.2) that the asymptotic bias of the LLR estimator is zero if the underlying true regression function is actually linear in $\mathbf{X}$, regardless of the value of the bandwidth h. Such is generally not the case for the NW estimator because of the dependence of the asymptotic bias (21.2.17) on first-order derivatives. It is also interesting to note that the asymptotic bias of the LLR estimator is unaffected by the form of the PDF for $\mathbf{X}$, whereas such is not the case for the NW estimator because the asymptotic bias depends on both $\mathrm{f}(\mathbf{x}_0)$ and $\partial \mathrm{f}(\mathbf{x}_0)/\partial \mathbf{x}_0$. Thus, the bias component of the LLR is stable across $\mathbf{X}$-distributions. In any case, under general regularity conditions, and on the assumption $nh^{k+4} \to 0$, the limiting distributions of the LLR and NW estimators of $g(\mathbf{x}_0)$ will be identical, as given in (21.2.16). The unknown components of the asymptotic distribution can be estimated, as we described in discussing (21.2.16), to construct hypothesis tests and generate confidence intervals.

Regarding the estimator $\hat{b}(\mathbf{x}_0; \mathbf{X})$ of the first derivatives of $g(\mathbf{x}_0)$ with respect to $\mathbf{x}_0$, the approach of Rupert and Wand (1994) can again be used to derive the asymptotic bias and variance expressions. When $k = 1$ (one regressor), the asymptotic bias and variance for the LLR estimator $\hat{b}(\mathbf{x}_0; \mathbf{X})$ are given by

$$\text{ABias}[\hat{b}(x_0; X)] = h^2 \left(\frac{\mu_4}{\mu_2} \left[\frac{g'''(x_0)}{6} + \frac{g''(x_0)f'(x_0)}{2f(x_0)} \right] - \frac{\mu_2}{2} \left[\frac{g''(x_0)f'(x_0)}{f(x_0)} \right] \right) \tag{21.3.4}$$

$$\text{AVar}[\hat{b}(x_0; X)] = \frac{\sigma^2 \int_{-\infty}^{\infty} z^2 [K(z)]^2 dz}{nh^3 f(x_0) \mu_2^2}, \tag{21.3.5}$$

where the number of prime superscripts denotes the order of the derivative, and $\mu_r = \int_{-\infty}^{\infty} z^r K(z)\, dz$. It is apparent from (21.3.4) that, unlike the LLR estimator $\hat{a}(x_0; X)$, the asymptotic bias of the LLR estimator $\hat{b}(\mathbf{x}_0; \mathbf{X})$ is affected by the PDF of $\mathbf{X}$ and its derivatives. It is thus unclear whether the LLR estimator of derivatives is superior in terms of asymptotic bias to the NW estimator of derivatives.

Regarding asymptotic variance comparisons, it is apparent upon comparing (21.3.5) and (21.2.23) that whether LLR is superior to NW for estimating $\partial g(x_0)/\partial x_0$ depends entirely on characteristics of the kernel function. For example, if a standard normal kernel is used, the estimators have identical asymptotic variances. In general, the variances will differ. Which of the two methods for estimating $\partial g(x_0)/\partial x_0$ is superior is currently not settled.

Asymptotic bias and variance expressions for the multivariate case can be based on the approach of Ruppert and Wand (1994). Bandwidth selection can be made using the LSCV approach, but such bandwidths will not necessarily be optimal for derivative estimation. Procedures for setting the bandwidths of LLR estimators are still being researched. Higher-order polynomials than the first order can be used to define estimators of $g(\mathbf{x}_0)$ and $\frac{\partial^r g(\mathbf{x}_0)}{\partial \mathbf{x}_0^r}$ with possibly more accuracy than the LLR, but widely accepted methods of choosing an optimal order of polynomial are not yet available. For further information on derivative estimation using local polynomial regression and other methods, see Pagan and Ullah (1998), Chapter 5, and the references therein.

21.4. Prequel of Fundamental Concepts: Local Weighted Averages, Local Linear Regressions, and Histograms

In this section we review some fundamental concepts relating to local weighted averages, local linear regressions, and the estimation of histograms. These concepts are the precursors and foundation on which kernel density estimation and nonparametric regression estimation procedures are built. This more fundamental discussion is provided for those readers who desire a more basic discussion of the concepts underlying the previous three sections of this chapter.

21.4.1. Nonparametric Regression under Repeated Sampling: Simple Sample Means

The objective of estimating the regression relationship between **Y** and **X** is the problem of estimating $\mathrm{E}[\mathbf{Y} \mid \mathbf{x}] = \mathbf{g}(\mathbf{x})$. This problem has a very simple nonparametric solution *if* interest centers on a given set of different **x**-values *and* repeated sampling at each of the **x**-values is possible.

Suppose one were interested in the values of the regression relationship between **Y** and **X** at the distinct explanatory variable values $\mathbf{x}_{1\cdot}, \mathbf{x}_{2\cdot}, \ldots, \mathbf{x}_{n\cdot}$. Furthermore, suppose it were possible to sample outcomes of the dependent variable repeatedly for each of the n-values of the explanatory variable vector. In particular, suppose that one could obtain m sample outcomes of the dependent variable for each $\mathbf{x}_{i\cdot}$. Then, a natural nonparametric estimator of the n regression function values $\mathrm{E}[\mathbf{Y}_i \mid \mathbf{x}_{i\cdot}]$, $i = 1, \ldots, n$, is given by the vector of sample means

$$\hat{\mathrm{E}}[\mathbf{Y} \mid \mathbf{x}] = \begin{bmatrix} \hat{\mathrm{E}}\,[\mathbf{Y}_1 \mid \mathbf{x}_{1\cdot}] \\ \vdots \\ \hat{\mathrm{E}}\,[\mathbf{Y}_n \mid \mathbf{x}_{n\cdot}] \end{bmatrix} \begin{bmatrix} m^{-1} \sum_{j=1}^{m} \mathrm{Y}_{1j} \\ \vdots \\ \mathrm{m}^{-1} \sum_{j=1}^{m} \mathrm{Y}_{nj} \end{bmatrix} \begin{bmatrix} \bar{\mathrm{Y}}_1 \\ \vdots \\ \bar{\mathrm{Y}}_n \end{bmatrix}, \tag{21.4.1}$$

where $\mathbf{Y}_{\cdot 1}, \mathbf{Y}_{\cdot 2}, \ldots \mathbf{Y}_{\cdot m}$ denotes the sample of m $(n \times 1)$ dependent variable vectors.

If the repeated sampling underlying (21.4.1) is iid, then we know at once that

$$\hat{\mathrm{E}}\,[\mathrm{Y}_i \mid \mathbf{x}_{i\cdot}] \overset{a}{\sim} \mathrm{N}(\mathrm{E}[\mathrm{Y}_i \mid \mathbf{x}_{i\cdot}], \sigma_i^2(\mathbf{x}_{i\cdot})/m), \tag{21.4.2}$$

where $\sigma_i^2(\mathbf{x}_{i\cdot})$ is the variance of $(\mathbf{Y}_i \mid \mathbf{x}_{i\cdot})$. This result follows straightforwardly from the usual asymptotic properties of sample means. An estimator for the variance can be defined in the usual way as

$$\hat{\sigma}^2(\mathrm{x}_{i\cdot}) = (m-1)^{-1} \sum_{j=1}^{m} (\mathrm{Y}_{ij} - \bar{\mathrm{Y}}_i)^2. \tag{21.4.3}$$

If the dependent variable were known to be homoscedastic for all explanatory variable values, so that

$$\mathrm{var}(\mathrm{Y}_i \mid \mathbf{x}_{i\cdot}) = \sigma_i^2(\mathbf{x}_{i\cdot}) = \sigma^2 \,\forall i, \tag{21.4.4}$$

then a more efficient pooled variance estimator could be defined as

$$\widehat{\mathrm{var}}(\mathrm{Y}_i \mid \mathbf{x}_{i\cdot}) = \hat{\sigma}^2 = (nm-n)^{-1} \sum_{i=1}^{n} \sum_{j=1}^{m} (\mathrm{Y}_{ij} - \bar{\mathrm{Y}}_i)^2. \tag{21.4.5}$$

Asymptotically valid tests relating to the value of $\mathrm{E}(\mathrm{Y}_i \mid \mathbf{x}_{i\cdot})$ could be conducted in the usual way based on the asymptotic normality of $\hat{\mathrm{E}}[\mathrm{Y}_i \mid \mathbf{x}_{i\cdot}]$. Confidence regions for the value of $E[Y_i \mid \mathbf{x}_{i\cdot}]$ could be defined using the standard duality relationship with hypothesis tests.

There are two main reasons why the simple nonparametric regression estimator outlined above is not often used in practice. The first and obvious reason is that it is often the case that we only have one observation (or only very few observations) on the dependent variable for each distinct value of the explanatory variable vector, making the application of (21.4.1) ineffective and the asymptotic results (21.4.2) irrelevant. Although one might argue that a single outcome of Y_i, for a given value of $\mathbf{X}_{i\cdot}$, is a legitimate estimate of $E[Y_i \mid \mathbf{x}_{i\cdot}]$, this will generally be a very noisy estimate, having variance $\sigma_i^2(\mathbf{x}_{i\cdot})$. Secondly, the estimator in (21.4.1) makes no provision for extrapolating estimates of $E[Y \mid \mathbf{x}_0]$, where $\mathbf{x}_0$ is *not* an observed outcome of the explanatory variables. Thus, although we have estimates of the regression function at a given set of points of evaluation using (21.4.1), we really do *not* have an estimate of the regression *function* if the domain of this function is larger than the set $\{\mathbf{x}_{1\cdot}, \mathbf{x}_{2\cdot}, \ldots, \mathbf{x}_{n\cdot}\}$. We therefore seek a more general type of nonparametric regression estimator ahead.

21.4.2. Local Sample Means: Using Data Neighborhoods

Suppose that we know or expect that the regression relationship between $\mathbf{Y}$ and $\mathbf{X}$ is smooth, and thus when the points $\mathbf{x}_{i\cdot}$ and $\mathbf{x}_{j\cdot}$ are close together, the values of the regression functions $E[Y_i \mid \mathbf{x}_{i\cdot}]$ and $E[Y_j \mid \mathbf{x}_{j\cdot}]$ are close together as well. We might then consider using observations on $(Y_k \mid \mathbf{x}_{k\cdot})$, for values of $\mathbf{x}_{k\cdot}$ in a *neighborhood* of $\mathbf{x}_0$, to form a sample mean estimate of $E[Y \mid \mathbf{x}_0]$. The logic would be that these outcomes are approximately from a distribution with mean $E[Y \mid \mathbf{x}_0]$ because all of the $E[Y_k \mid \mathbf{x}_{k\cdot}]$ values are close to $E[Y \mid \mathbf{x}_0]$ given that all of the $\mathbf{x}_{k\cdot}$'s are close to (i.e., are in the neighborhood of) $\mathbf{x}_0$. Letting $N(\mathbf{x}_0)$ denote a neighborhood of $\mathbf{x}_0$, the nonparametric regression estimator under consideration would be

$$\hat{\mu}(\mathbf{x}_0) \equiv \hat{E}[Y \mid \mathbf{x}_0] = m_0^{-1} \sum_{j \in N(\mathbf{x}_0)} Y_j, \tag{21.4.6}$$

where m_0 represents the number of data observations contained in the neighborhood $N(\mathbf{x}_0)$ of $\mathbf{x}_0$.

The estimator (21.4.6) overcomes the problem of having only one or no observation on the dependent variable for a given value $\mathbf{x}_0$ of the explanatory variable by effectively acting as if the m_0 values of $(y_i \mid \mathbf{x}_{i\cdot})$ encompassed by the neighborhood of $\mathbf{x}_0$ are a repeated sampling of dependent variable values associated with the explanatory variable value $\mathbf{x}_0$. At this point in the reader's study, he or she no doubt suspects that there are statistical trade-offs in the design of the estimator (21.4.6). On the one hand, one would suspect that the variance of the estimator can be reduced by adding observations to the sample on which the sample mean calculation is based. On the other hand, we are combining observations from probability distributions that have means, $E[Y_i \mid \mathbf{x}_{i\cdot}]$, which, although close to $E[Y \mid \mathbf{x}_0]$, do not all exactly equal $E[Y \mid \mathbf{x}_0]$. Thus, one suspects a mean–variance or mean-square error trade-off is involved here. Adding observations by expanding the size of the neighborhood can decrease variance, and at the same time the bias may be expanded by including outcomes of $(Y_i \mid \mathbf{x}_{i\cdot})$ whose means are quite divergent from $E[Y \mid \mathbf{x}_0]$.

To be more specific about the trade-offs involved, assume m_0 and $\mathbf{x}$ are fixed, let $\mu(\mathbf{x}_{i\cdot}) \equiv E[Y_i \mid \mathbf{x}_{i\cdot}]$, and define $V(\mathbf{x}_{i\cdot}) \equiv Y_i - \mu(\mathbf{x}_{i\cdot})$. Then, the estimator (21.4.6) can be written as

$$\hat{\mu}(\mathbf{x}_0) = \mu(\mathbf{x}_0) + m_0^{-1} \sum_{j \in N(\mathbf{x}_0)} [\mu(\mathbf{x}_{j\cdot}) - \mu(\mathbf{x}_0)] + m_0^{-1} \sum_{j \in N(\mathbf{x}_0)} V(\mathbf{x}_{j\cdot}). \quad (21.4.7)$$

It is apparent from (21.4.7) that the bias in the estimator (21.4.6) is given by

$$\text{bias}(\hat{\mu}(\mathbf{x}_0)) = E[\hat{\mu}(\mathbf{x}_0) - \mu(\mathbf{x}_0)] = m_0^{-1} \sum_{j \in N(\mathbf{x}_0)} [\mu(\mathbf{x}_{j\cdot}) - \mu(\mathbf{x}_0)], \quad (21.4.8)$$

whereas the variance of the estimator, on the assumption the $(Y_i \mid \mathbf{x}_{i\cdot})$'s are independent, is given by

$$\text{var}(\hat{\mu}(\mathbf{x}_0)) = m_0^{-2} \sum_{j=1}^{m_0} \sigma_j^2(\mathbf{x}_{j\cdot}). \quad (21.4.9)$$

Therefore, the nonparametric regression estimator (21.4.6) based on observations in the neighborhood of $\mathbf{x}_0$ is an improvement, in terms of MSE, over an estimator based on only outcomes of $(Y \mid \mathbf{x}_0)$ if the variance of the estimator, (21.4.9) decreases more than the square of the bias (21.4.8) increases when observations in the neighborhood $N(\mathbf{x}_0)$ are used. Similar analyses apply if m_0, $\mathbf{X}$, or both are random.

There are two basic methods of choosing the neighborhood in current applications of nonparametric regression. The *nearest neighbor* approach fixes the value of the sample size m_0 and then defines the neighborhood as the collection of the m_0 values of the explanatory variable, $\mathbf{x}_{i\cdot}, i = 1, \ldots, n$ that are *nearest* in Euclidean distance to the evaluation point of interest $\mathbf{x}_0$. We note that in the nonparametric regression literature the term *span* is synonymous with the value of the sample size m_0 associated with the neighborhood of data used in the calculation of the nonparametric estimate. Given that the span is held constant across all points of evaluation, it follows that all estimated regression values in the nearest neighbor approach will be based on the same sample size and will exhibit the same sample variability if the $(Y_i \mid \mathbf{x}_{i\cdot})$'s are homoscedastic.

Another method of choosing the neighborhood is by specifying the distance from $\mathbf{x}_0$ to the boundary of the neighborhood and then including all of the $(Y_i \mid \mathbf{x}_{i\cdot})$ observations in the calculation of (21.4.6) that have $\mathbf{x}_{i\cdot}$'s contained within this distance from $\mathbf{x}_0$. In this case, if it is assumed $\mathbf{x}$ is fixed, the span m_0 of observations used in the calculation of (21.4.6) can change at different points of evaluation. Whether and how much m_0 changes at different points of evaluation depend on the distribution of $\mathbf{x}_{i\cdot}$ outcomes. As the distance defining neighborhoods is increased, the span will tend to increase, the variance of the estimator will tend to decrease, and the bias of the estimator will generally increase. Similar analyses can be applied to cases in which m_0, $\mathbf{X}$, or both are random.

At this point, a logical question to consider would be how one chooses the span, distance, or both from $\mathbf{x}_0$ that defines the neighborhood used in the calculation of the nonparametric regression estimate. We defer this question until we also consider a further generalization of the procedure that involves using weighted averages when defining the means of observations within neighborhoods. Weighted averaging can reduce the bias in the nonparametric regression estimator and is the approach most often used in practice.

21.4.3. Local Weighted Averages within Data Neighborhoods: Local Least-Squares Regressions

Assuming, as we have before, that $g(\mathbf{x}_0)$ is a smooth function of the explanatory variables, we have confidence that values of $E(Y_i \mid \mathbf{x}_{i\cdot})$ will be close to $E[Y \mid \mathbf{x}_0]$ if $\mathbf{x}_{i\cdot}$ is close to $\mathbf{x}_0$, but we have no such confidence for values of $\mathbf{x}_{i\cdot}$ that are not close to $\mathbf{x}_0$. We have already examined methods for *eliminating* $(y_i \mid \mathbf{x}_{i\cdot})$ observations when $\mathbf{x}_{i\cdot}$ is not close to $\mathbf{x}_0$; namely, we eliminate all observations too far away from $\mathbf{x}_0$ in Euclidean distance, or else only keep m_0 of the observations that are nearest to $\mathbf{x}_0$. An alternative approach, which can be defined in a way so as to subsume the Euclidean distance and nearest-neighbor approaches as special cases, is to define a nonparametric regression estimator as a weighted average of the sample observations as

$$\hat{\mu}(\mathbf{x}_0) = \hat{E}(Y \mid \mathbf{x}_0) = \sum_{i=1}^{n} w_i Y_i, \tag{21.4.10}$$

where $\sum_{i=1}^{n} w_i = 1$ and $w_i \geq 0 \ \forall i$. The idea here is to define the weights w_i, $i = 1, \ldots, n$, so that observations $(y_i \mid \mathbf{x}_{i\cdot})$ for which $\mathbf{x}_{i\cdot}$ is close to $\mathbf{x}_0$ get higher weight, whereas observations for which $\mathbf{x}_{i\cdot}$ is more distant from $\mathbf{x}_0$ get lower weight.

Note that in the case of the nearest-neighbor procedure in Section 21.4.2, $w_i = m_0^{-1} \ \forall y_i$ for which $\mathbf{x}_{i\cdot}$ is one of the m_0 values closest to $\mathbf{x}_0$, and $w_i = 0$ otherwise. Similarly, through the use of Euclidean distance to define the neighborhood of data observations $w_i = m_0^{-1} \ \forall y_i$ for which $d(\mathbf{x}_{i\cdot}, \mathbf{x}_0) \leq \delta$ and $w_i = 0$ otherwise, where $d(.,.)$ denotes Euclidean distance, δ is the distance level specified, and m_0 is the number of explanatory variable values that are within δ-distance of $\mathbf{x}_0$.

There exists a myriad of different weighting schemes that can be applied to define nonparametric regression estimators representing alternatives to those examined in Section 21.4.2. The most understood of these alternatives, in terms of statistical properties of the resultant estimators, bases the weighting schemes on kernel functions, which we examined in detail in previous sections of this chapter.

Regardless of the weighting scheme used to define the nonparametric regression estimator (21.4.10), such an estimator can be defined as a local weighted least-squares (WLS) regression estimator. The weights in the WLS estimator are the same as those in (21.4.10), and the regression is local in the sense of being specific to a point of evaluation $\mathbf{x}_0$ for the regression function. Specifically, consider the simple regression model that expresses $\mathbf{Y}$ as a function of only an intercept or mean-level parameter β

and a noise vector $\mathbf{V}$, as

$$\mathbf{Y} = \mathbf{1}\beta + \mathbf{V}. \tag{21.4.11}$$

Now let $\mathbf{x}_0$ be the point of evaluation for the regression function, and let $\mathrm{w}_1(\mathbf{x}_0;\mathbf{x}), \ldots, \mathrm{w}_n(\mathbf{x}_0;\mathbf{x})$ be the weights assigned to the n sample observations when we are considering the data neighborhood of the point $\mathbf{x}_0$. Finally, consider estimating β by minimizing the weighted least-squares objective function

$$\sum_{i=1}^{n} \mathrm{w}_i(\mathbf{x}_0;\mathbf{x})[\mathrm{y}_i - \beta]^2. \tag{21.4.12}$$

The first-order condition for the minimum is given by

$$-2\sum_{i=1}^{n} \mathrm{w}_i(\mathbf{x}_0;\mathbf{x})[\mathrm{y}_i - \beta] = 0, \tag{21.4.13}$$

and because $\sum_{i=1}^{n} \mathrm{w}_i(\mathbf{x}_0;\mathbf{x}) = 1$, it follows that

$$\hat{\beta} = \sum_{i=1}^{n} \mathrm{w}_i(\mathbf{x}_0;\mathbf{x})\mathrm{Y}_i. \tag{21.4.14}$$

Thus, the nonparametric regression estimator (21.4.10) is a local weighted least-squares estimator of an intercept or mean-value parameter. The estimator (21.4.14) can be expressed in the familiar GLS form of Chapter 14 by letting $\mathbf{z} = \mathbf{1}$ and $\boldsymbol{\Phi}$ be the $(n \times n)$ diagonal matrix whose ith diagonal element is $\mathrm{w}_i(\mathbf{x}_0;\mathbf{x})$, in which case

$$\hat{\beta} = (\mathbf{z}'\boldsymbol{\Phi}\mathbf{z})^{-1}\mathbf{z}'\boldsymbol{\Phi}\mathbf{Y}. \tag{21.4.15}$$

Rather than locally approximating the regression function at $\mathbf{x}_0$ by only the constant, $\hat{\beta}$, one might consider a local linear, quadratic, or even higher-order polynomial regression approximation. The rationale is based on the idea that a local constant generally only makes sense as an approximation to a function over a very small neighborhood of the point of evaluation, whereas polynomials can approximate functions over a larger neighborhood of a point. This is the subject of our final subsection in this evolution of fundamental ideas underlying nonparametric regression.

21.4.4. Local Polynomial Regressions

Building on the idea that a nonparametric regression estimator can be viewed as a local WLS estimator of the parameter β in the local approximation $\mathrm{Y} = \beta + \mathrm{V}$ of the regression function evaluated at $\mathbf{x}_0$, we now consider improving the local approximation through the use of higher-order local polynomials. We will concentrate here on the linear (first-order polynomial) approximation, but extensions of the approach to quadratic and higher-order polynomials is straightforward. In practice, first-order approximations are generally a good compromise between increased accuracy of the approximation and proliferation of unknown coefficients in the local polynomial approximations.

Again, letting $\mathrm{w}_1(\mathbf{x}_0;\mathbf{x}), \ldots, \mathrm{w}_n(\mathbf{x}_0;\mathbf{x})$ denote the observation weights when considering the regression function estimate at the evaluation point $\mathbf{x}_0$, we now consider the local WLS estimator of the local linear approximation of the unknown regression function. This approximation is given by

$$\mathbf{Y} = \mathbf{1}\beta_0 + \sum_{j=1}^{k}(\mathbf{x}_{.j} - \mathbf{1}x_{0j})\beta_j + \mathbf{V}, \tag{21.4.16}$$

where x_{0j} denotes the jth element of the vector $\mathbf{x}_0$. We define $\hat{\boldsymbol{\beta}}$ as the vector that minimizes the weighted sum of squares

$$\sum_{i=1}^{n} w_i(\mathbf{x}_0; \mathbf{x}) \left[y_i - \beta_0 - \sum_{j=1}^{k}(x_{ij} - x_{0j})\beta_j \right]^2. \tag{21.4.17}$$

Defining $\boldsymbol{\Phi}$ as we did preceding (21.1.15), and now letting $\mathbf{z}$ be defined as

$$\mathbf{z} = \begin{bmatrix} 1 & (x_{11} - x_{01}) & \cdots & (x_{1k} - x_{0k}) \\ \vdots & \vdots & & \vdots \\ 1 & (x_{n1} - x_{01}) & \cdots & (x_{nk} - x_{0k}) \end{bmatrix}, \tag{21.4.18}$$

the $\hat{\boldsymbol{\beta}}$ vector is again given by (21.4.15).

In addition to the potential of increasing the accuracy of the approximation of the regression function, the local polynomial regression approach has another valuable practical advantage in analyzing the characteristics of the true regression function. Specifically, the approach incorporates built-in natural estimators for partial derivatives of the regression surface evaluated at $\mathbf{x}_0$. For example, using the linear approximation, the estimator $\hat{\beta}_i$ of β_i in (21.4.16) is a natural estimator for the partial derivative of the regression function with respect to the ith explanatory variable evaluated at the point $\mathbf{x}_0$. The reader can contemplate the representation of higher-order derivatives afforded by higher-order polynomial approximations.

There is another advantage to the use of first and higher-order approximations compared to 0th order (constant) approximations when one is attempting to analyze the true regression function at a point of evaluation $\mathbf{x}_0$ for which there is a substantially asymmetric distribution of $\mathbf{x}_{i.}$ values in the data neighborhood of $\mathbf{x}_0$. An extreme case of such an asymmetric distribution is when $\mathbf{x}_0$ is at a boundary of the range of data points. In this case bias can be accentuated for the 0th order approximation because the value of the approximation is essentially pulled in the direction of the Y_i values associated with the concentration of $\mathbf{x}_{i}$. values. By extrapolating a curve through the data points, the higher-order polynomial approximations are generally less sensitive to asymmetric data clustering in the neighborhood of $\mathbf{x}_0$.

21.4.5. Histograms: Precursor to Kernel Density Estimation

In this section we examine the concept of histograms, which can be thought of as a precursor to modern nonparametric methods of estimating probability distributions. Our principal interest in histograms is in motivating the *kernel density estimation* procedure. We are interested in the latter topic for two principal reasons. First of all, kernel density estimation is useful in its own right as a general method of estimating the probability distribution of a random vector **Z** when the analyst has insufficient information to specify a parametric family for **Z**'s distribution. Secondly, kernel density estimates can provide a direct way of defining weights with which to calculate nonparametric regression estimates. Recall that the regression function of $\mathbf{Y}_i$ on $\mathbf{X}_{i\cdot}$ is given by (continuous case)

$$g(\mathbf{x}_{i\cdot}) \equiv E(Y_i \mid \mathbf{x}_{i\cdot}) \equiv \int y_i \, dF(y_i \mid \mathbf{x}_{i\cdot}) \equiv \int y_i \left[\frac{f(y_i, \mathbf{x}_{i\cdot})}{f(\mathbf{x}_{i\cdot})} \right] dy_i. \qquad (21.4.19)$$

Therefore, if we can construct accurate nonparametric estimates of the joint PDF of $(\mathbf{Y}_i, \mathbf{X}_{i\cdot})$ and the marginal density of $\mathbf{X}_{i\cdot}$, then substituting these estimates for the unknown densities in (21.4.19) and integrating over y_i produces a nonparametric estimate of $g(\mathbf{x}_{i\cdot})$.

We will begin the discussion by focusing on the univariate case. We will then note extensions to the estimation of multivariate density functions. In both cases, we assume that the random variables whose distribution we are estimating are continuous random variables.

Regarding the discrete distribution case, note that nonparametric estimates of the discrete probability values of the probability distribution are relatively straightforward. In particular, one can simply use the observed relative frequency of occurrence of each of the countable outcomes of the discrete random variable as an estimate of the probability of occurrence of that outcome. The reader can demonstrate that each probability estimate is then Bernoulli distributed with a mean equal to the true probability value, say p_i, and variance equal to $p_i(1 - p_i)/n$. The estimator is also consistent and asymptotically normally distributed.

21.4.5.a. Histogram Concept

Histograms have historically been the most widely used estimators of probability density functions. They also are the simplest and most easily understood density estimator. Although most readers may be familiar with the concept of histograms, we nonetheless review the concept in some detail to lay the groundwork for the more sophisticated and generally more accurate kernel density estimator. Additional details can be found in Scott (1979) and Freedman and Diaconis (1981).

Let Φ be a set of potential random variable values that are of interest in a particular problem. If the PDF of the random variable Z under study has a fixed finite support, Φ might be set equal to this support. It is often the case in practice that Φ is set equal to the interval $[\min(z_1, \ldots, z_n), \max(z_1, \ldots, z_n)]$, where $(z_1, \ldots, z_n)$ is the observed outcome of a random sample of size n. In any case, it is presumed that Φ is a finite length interval.

Now partition the interval of interest into k equal-length (this length equality can be relaxed) subintervals of length h as follows:

$$\Phi = \bigcup_{j=1}^{k} (b_j, b_{j+1}], \qquad (21.4.20)$$

where $b_{j+1} - b_j = h, \forall j$. Because Z is a continuous random variable, it makes no difference to any probability analysis as to whether the points b_1, b_{k+1}, or both are included in the set (21.4.20), and thus Φ can be a closed, open, or half-open–closed interval by appropriately adjusting the definition of the first and kth subintervals in (21.4.20). In histogram parlance, the subintervals are called *bins*, and the common length or width of the intervals is called the *bin width*.

The histogram estimate of the PDF of Z, based on the random sample outcome $(z_1, \ldots, z_n)$, is defined by

$$\hat{f}(z_0; \mathbf{z}) = \frac{\#\{z_i\text{'s} \leq b_{j+1}\} - \#\{z_i\text{'s} \leq b_j\}}{nh} \quad \text{for } z_0 \in (b_j, b_{j+1}], \qquad (21.4.21)$$

where $\#\{z_i\text{'s} \leq c\}$ denotes the number of outcomes among $(z_1, \ldots, z_n)$ that are $\leq c$. Note that $\hat{f}(z_0; \mathbf{z})$ is a piecewise continuous function of z, the only points of discontinuity occurring at the boundaries of the bins. The histogram is nonnegative-valued, just as a continuous probability density function is supposed to be. Also, $\hat{f}(z_0; \mathbf{z})$ integrates to 1, as a continuous PDF is required to do. To see this latter point, note that

$$\int_{b_1}^{b_{k+1}} \hat{f}(z_0; \mathbf{z})\, dz_0 = \sum_{j=1}^{k} \int_{b_j}^{b_{j+1}} \frac{(n_{j+1} - n_j)}{nh}\, dz_0 = \sum_{j=1}^{k} \frac{(n_{j+1} - n_j)(b_{j+1} - b_j)}{nh} = \frac{n}{n} = 1 \qquad (21.4.22)$$

because $b_{j+1} - b_j = h$, where $n_j \equiv \#\{z_i\text{'s} \leq b_j\}$. Thus, $\hat{f}(z_0; \mathbf{z})$ exhibits all of the necessary properties for it to be a continuous probability density function.

► **Example 21.4.1:** To demonstrate the computation of a histogram estimator, we provide the GAUSS program C21Hist1.gss in the examples manual. For a DSP and sample size selected by the user, GAUSS generates a pseudo-random sample of n iid observations. Using the number of equal-length subintervals or bins also selected by the user, GAUSS computes and plots the histogram and compares it to the underlying PDF of the true probability model. The user can alter the number of bins as well as the sample size to observe the impact on the estimated histogram.

21.4.5.b. Integrated Mean-Squared Error

How well does the estimator $\hat{f}(z_0; \mathbf{z})$ perform? To answer this question, we need to specify a measure of closeness between the estimated and actual PDF of Z. A measure often used for this purpose is the integrated mean-square error (IMSE) criterion defined by

$$\text{IMSE}(\hat{f}) = \int_{-\infty}^{\infty} \text{E}[\hat{f}(z_0; \mathbf{Z}) - f(z_0)]^2 dz_0. \qquad (21.4.23)$$

Note that $\text{E}[\cdot]$ denotes the expectation taken with respect to the true joint distribution of the random sample $\mathbf{Z} = [Z_1, \ldots, Z_n]'$, and thus $\text{IMSE}(\hat{f})$ represents the *expected* squared difference between $\hat{f}(z_0; \mathbf{Z})$ and $f(z_0)$ integrated over *all* possible points of evaluation z_0. Note carefully regarding the bracketed expression in (21.4.23) that

$\hat{f}(z_0; \mathbf{Z})$ is random, whereas $f(z_0)$ is fixed. It is the estimated value $\hat{f}(z_0; \mathbf{z})$ in (21.4.23) that changes from sample to sample and not the point of evaluation z_0.

To evaluate the IMSE of the histogram, it will prove beneficial to represent the histogram in an alternative but equivalent way. In particular, (21.4.21) is equivalent to

$$\hat{f}(z_0; \mathbf{z}) = n^{-1} \sum_{j=1}^{n} w(z_j, z_0), \tag{21.4.24}$$

where $w(z_j, z_0) = \begin{cases} h^{-1} & \text{if } z_j \text{ and } z_0 \text{ are in the same bin} \\ 0 & \text{otherwise} \end{cases}$, as the reader can readily demonstrate.

Now note that

$$E[\hat{f}(z_0; \mathbf{Z}) - f(z_0)]^2 = \text{var}(\hat{f}(z_0; \mathbf{Z})) + (E[\hat{f}(z_0; \mathbf{Z})] - f(z_0))^2 \tag{21.4.25}$$

because the left-hand side of (21.4.25) is clearly the MSE of the estimator $\hat{f}(z_0; \mathbf{Z})$ in estimating $f(z_0)$, and the MSE can be decomposed into the sum of the variance and the squared bias of the estimator. Examine the bias term first, and note that because the Z_i's are iid

$$\begin{aligned} E[\hat{f}(z_0; \mathbf{Z})] &= n^{-1} E\left[\sum_{j=1}^{n} w(Z_j, z_0)\right] = E\left[w(Z_1, z_0)\right] = \int_{b_j}^{b_{j+1}} \frac{1}{h} f(z_1)\, dz_1 \\ &= \frac{1}{h}[F(b_{j+1}) - F(b_j)] \quad \text{for } z_0 \in \left(b_j, b_{j+1}\right], \end{aligned} \tag{21.4.26}$$

where F(c) is the CDF of Z. We can expand F(c) in a Taylor Series around $\mathbf{z}_0$ as

$$F(c) = F(z_0) + f(z_0)(c - z_0) + \frac{1}{2}\frac{\partial f(z_0)}{\partial z_0}(c - z_0)^2 + \cdots, \tag{21.4.27}$$

which, when substituted into (21.4.26) for both $F(b_{j+1})$ and $F(b_j)$ and then subtracting $f(z_0)$ yields

$$\begin{aligned} \text{bias}(\hat{f}(z_0; \mathbf{Z})) &= E[\hat{f}(z_0; \mathbf{Z})] - f(z_0) \\ &= [h^{-1} f(z_0)(b_{j+1} - b_j) - f(z_0)] \\ &\quad + \frac{1}{2h}\frac{\partial f(z_0)}{\partial z_0}[(b_{j+1} - z_0)^2 - (b_j - z_0)^2] + \cdots \\ &= \frac{1}{2h}\frac{\partial f(z_0)}{\partial z_0}\left[b_{j+1}^2 - b_j^2 - 2z_0(b_{j+1} - b_j)\right] + \cdots \\ &= \frac{1}{2h}\frac{\partial f(z_0)}{\partial z_0}[h(2b_j + h) - 2z_0 h] + \cdots \\ &= \frac{1}{2}\frac{\partial f(z_0)}{\partial z_0}[h - 2(z_0 - b_j)] + O(h^2) \end{aligned} \tag{21.4.28}$$

Two characteristics of the bias term are apparent from (21.4.28). First of all, the bias does *not* depend on the sample size n. Secondly, the bias *does* depend on the bin width h. In fact, as $h \to 0$, the bias goes to zero (note $h \to 0 \Rightarrow (z_0 - b_j) \to 0$).

Now consider the variance of $\hat{f}(z_0; \mathbf{Z})$. Again, using the representation of $\hat{f}(z_0; \mathbf{Z})$ presented in (21.4.24), we have

$$\begin{aligned}
\operatorname{var}(\hat{f}(z_0; \mathbf{Z})) &= E\left[\left(n^{-1}\sum_{j=1}^{n} w(Z_j, z_0)\right)^2\right] - (E[\hat{f}(z_0; \mathbf{Z})])^2 \\
&= n^{-2}E\left[\sum_{j=1}^{n} w(Z_j, z_0)^2 + \sum_{i \neq j}\sum w(Z_i, z_0)w(Z_j, z_0)\right] - (E[\hat{f}(z_0; \mathbf{Z})])^2 \\
&= n^{-2}[nE[w(Z_1, z_0)^2] + n(n-1)(E[w(Z_1, z_0)])^2] - (E[w(Z_1, z_0)])^2 \\
&= n^{-1}[E[w(Z_1, z_0)^2] - (E[w(Z_1, z_0)])^2] \\
&= \frac{1}{nh^2}[F(b_{j+1}) + F(b_j) - [F(b_{j+1}) - F(b_j)]^2], \qquad (21.4.29)
\end{aligned}$$

where we have also used the fact that the Z_i's are iid. Substituting the Taylor series representation (21.4.27) for the CDF terms in (21.4.29) finally yields

$$\operatorname{var}(\hat{f}) = \frac{f(z_0)}{nh} + O(n^{-1}). \qquad (21.4.30)$$

The bias and variance representations (21.4.28) and (21.4.30) can be used to define sufficient conditions for the consistent estimation of $f(z_0)$. In particular, $\operatorname{MSE}(\hat{f}(z_0; \mathbf{Z})) \to 0$, so that plim $\hat{f}(z_0; \mathbf{z}) = f(z_0)$, if both $h \to 0$ and $nh \to \infty$. Thus, as the sample size increases, the bin width should decrease to zero but at a rate slow enough so that it is still true that $nh \to \infty$, that is, h will be $o(n^{-\delta})$ for $\delta < 1$.

► **Example 21.4.2:** To examine the sampling performance of the histogram estimator, we provide the GAUSS program C21Hist2.gss in the examples manual. For sample sizes (n), bandwidth, and true probability model selected by the user, GAUSS generates pseudo-random observations and computes histogram estimates of density values. The bias and variance of the histogram estimator are estimated based on a Monte Carlo simulation of the DSP and on a given evaluation point. By varying the bandwidth and sample size, the user can observe the effects on histogram bias and variance.

Adding together the variance term (21.4.30) and the square of the bias term, (21.4.28) and then integrating the resultant MSE expression over all z_0, or equivalently integrating over each bin and then summing the results bin by bin, yields the IMSE for $\hat{f}$ as

$$\operatorname{IMSE}(\hat{f}) = \frac{1}{nh} + \frac{h^2}{12}\int_{-\infty}^{\infty}\left[\frac{\partial f(z_0)}{\partial z_0}\right]^2 dz_0 + O(n^{-1}) + O(h^3) \qquad (21.4.31)$$

(see the chapter appendix for further details regarding the derivation of (21.4.31)). It is apparent that the minimization of $\operatorname{IMSE}(\hat{f})$ involves a trade-off between variance and bias as the bin width h is changed. As $h \to 0$, the bias limits to zero with $\hat{f}$ approaching spikes at each observation, but variability increases. As h increases, more observations are associated with the bins and less variance is associated with $\hat{f}$, but bias increases.

21.4.5.c. Asymptotically Optimal Bin Width

The leading terms in the representation of the IMSE represent the *asymptotic* IMSE as follows:

$$\mathrm{AIMSE}(\hat{\mathrm{f}}) = \frac{1}{nh} + \frac{h^2}{12} \int_{-\infty}^{\infty} \left[\frac{\partial \mathrm{f}(z_0)}{\partial z_0} \right]^2 \mathrm{d}z_0. \tag{21.4.32}$$

We can then find an asymptotically optimal bin width by minimizing AIMSE $(\hat{\mathrm{f}})$ with respect to h. The first-order condition for the minimum can be solved for the optimal bin width

$$h_* = n^{-1/3} \left[\frac{6}{\int_{-\infty}^{\infty} \left[\frac{\partial \mathrm{f}(z_0)}{\partial z_0} \right]^2 \mathrm{d}z_0} \right]^{1/3}. \tag{21.4.33}$$

Substituting this bin width into (21.4.32) identifies the minimum AIMSE as

$$\mathrm{AIMSE}(\hat{\mathrm{f}})_* = \left[\frac{9 \int_{-\infty}^{\infty} \left[\frac{\partial \mathrm{f}(z_0)}{\partial z_0} \right]^2 \mathrm{d}z_0}{16} \right]^{1/3} n^{-2/3}. \tag{21.4.34}$$

From an empirical point of view, (21.4.33) has a clear defect – the value of h_* depends on the first derivative of the unknown probability distribution $f(z_0)$. In practice, it is often the case that the analyst will choose a particular family of PDFs for $\mathrm{f}(z_0)$ he or she feels will exhibit characteristics that will emulate characteristics of the true distribution and thereby approximate, in an a priori sense, the optimal bin width. Such a PDF is called a *reference distribution.* As one might expect, the normal distribution has been a popular choice. The following are examples of specific optimal bin widths:

$\mathrm{f}(z_0)$	h_*
$\mathrm{N}(\mu, \sigma^2)$	$3.49\, \sigma n^{-1/3}$
Exponential (λ)	$2.28\, \lambda n^{-1/3}$

The unknown standard deviations σ and λ in the above table can be estimated using a consistent estimate such as the sample standard deviation. The value of h_* for other choices of $\mathrm{f}(z_0)$ can be found directly from (21.4.33) – often by using numerical integration for finding the value of the integral in the definition of h_*.

21.4.5.d. Histogram Deficiencies

Although the histogram is no doubt a useful tool for exploring the form of the probability distribution of a sample of data, the histogram exhibits several characteristics or deficiencies that might prompt one to investigate whether improvements can be achieved. First of all, it is apparent from (21.4.34) that the *optimal* rate of AIMSE convergence to zero is only $\mathrm{O}(n^{-2/3})$. This is slower than the convergence rate of $\mathrm{O}(n^{-1})$

we have seen for the majority of the parametric estimators encountered previously. In fact, if the parametric family of probability distributions were actually known, the $O(n^{-1})$ rate of convergence could actually be achieved by substituting root-n consistent estimators for the unknown parameters and using the resultant estimated density to estimate $f(z_0)$. Boyd and Steele (1978) showed this $O(n^{-1})$ rate of convergence is actually the fastest rate possible for density estimation. In essence, the slower rate of histogram convergence is a price that must be paid for using a nonparametric approach for estimating $f(z_0)$. But one may wonder whether this rate can be improved upon. The answer is yes, and the kernel density estimators that we examined earlier in this chapter can provide such an improvement.

There are at least three other reasons why the histogram should not be considered the final word on density estimation. First of all, the histogram exhibits discontinuities at the boundary points of the bins even though the underlying population distribution is continuous. Secondly, the histogram is zero-valued outside of a finite range of values, even if the underlying density does not have finite support. Finally, histograms can be sensitive to the choice of bin location on the real line in addition to the choice of bin width (Silverman, 1986, Section 2.2). The kernel density can mitigate some or all of these problems, and the reader is directed back to the previous sections of this chapter for details relating to the kernel density approach.

21.5. Concluding Comments

In this chapter we have revisited the problem of observing data $y_1, y_2, \ldots y_n$, from the regression model $y_i = g(\mathbf{x}_{i\cdot}) + \varepsilon_i$, where g is a smooth regression function, and the ε_i's are uncorrelated random noise elements with 0 mean and variance σ^2. Our interesting new objective was to estimate the regression function without constraining it a priori to a parametric class of functional forms. To accomplish this estimation objective, we used the methods of kernel estimators and local polynomial approximations. In applying these and other methods such as smoothing splines (Donoho and Johnstone, pp. 425–55, 1994), a basic problem involves selecting the estimator's smoothing parameter. The ultimate solution to this problem is to develop a data-based, one-step smoothing parameter estimate. For kernel and local linear estimation this appears to be the cross-validation method proposed by Hart and Yi (1998, pp. 620–31).

Before closing our discussion of nonparametrics we should mention a new formulation that has evolved over the last decade that is concerned with wavelet regression. Consider the nonparametric regression problem in which we have observations at 2^m regularly spaced points η_i of some unknown function g that is subject to noise as $y_i = g(\eta_i) + \varepsilon_i$, where the ε_i's are independent $N(0, \sigma^2)$ random variables. The basic wavelet approach to the estimation of g proceeds by taking the discrete wavelet transform of the data y_i, processing the coefficients to remove noise, and then transforming back to obtain the estimate. In this respect the wavelet transform is a tool that cuts data or functions into frequency components and then studies each component individually. The underlying notion is that the resulting unknown function g has a wavelet expression where g is well approximated by a function with a relatively small proportion of nonzero wavelet coefficients. There is an interesting connection between wavelet regression, $Y_i = \theta_i + \varepsilon_i, i = 1, \ldots, n$, where many of the nonzero θ_i coefficients may be zero. In a model selection context the nonzero θ_i's correspond to parameters that actually enter the model, and the others are noisy observations that are mostly zero. For a discussion of wavelets, see Bock (1999), Donoho et al. (1995), Daubeches (1992), Johnstone and Silverman (1999) and Vidakovic (1999).

Another interesting new development that represents an approach to estimation and inference that is a hybrid of parametric and nonparametric approaches and that does not a priori constrain the regression function to a fixed parametric class of functional forms have been introduced by Hamilton (1999). In effect the unknown regression function specification itself is considered a random outcome of a stochastic process. The approach does not use kernel estimation and thus avoids the problem of selecting kernels and bandwidths but relies on relatively more stringent stochastic assumptions on the DSP underlying the data. The reader is directed to Hamilton's paper for details.

We end our discussion by emphasizing that this chapter is only an introduction to the vast literature on nonparametric estimation and inference issues. Some recommended journal articles and books that permit you to continue your reading in this important and advancing area are listed in the references.

21.6. Exercises

21.6.1. Idea Checklist – Knowledge Guides

1. Contrast the benefits and costs of the use of parametric, semiparametric, and nonparametric statistical models.
2. It is generally felt that larger sample sizes are needed to achieve precise nonparametric estimates than for parametric estimates. Why may this be the case? Will this always be the case? Do you agree with the statement?
3. What advantages may there be in using a kernel density approach for estimating a PDF instead of an empirical distribution function type of approach? Are there disadvantages?
4. Nonparametric regression is often described as method based on local weighted averages. What is meant by this? Why does such a method make sense as a means of calculating a regression value?
5. Discuss why one might think that a local linear regression procedure for calculating the value of a regression surface at a point may be an improvement over the use of a local weighted average. In particular, why may this be the case at the boundary of the data set?

21.6.2. Problems

21–1 Using the expressions for the asymptotic bias and variance in (21.3.2) and (21.3.3), calculate the optimal bandwidth in terms of minimum MSE for the LLR estimator. Can the optimal h be estimated? If so, how?

21–2 Verify the asymptotic efficiency values (relative to the Epanechnikov kernel) stated in Table 21.1.

21–3 In the LSCV method of choosing the bandwidth, the jth sample observation is left out when calculating the nonparametric estimate of the regression function value evaluated at $\mathbf{x}_{j.}$ (see (21.2.19)). Would the LSCV approach in (21.2.19) work properly if all observations were used for each $\mathbf{x}_{j.}$, $j = 1, \ldots, n$? Why or why not?

21–4 Define a test statistic appropriate for testing a hypothesis about a nonlinear function of the response coefficients of a nonparametric regression model evaluated at a point $\mathbf{x}_0$, say as H_0: $\mathbf{c}[\boldsymbol{\beta}(\mathbf{x}_0)] = \mathbf{r}$. Describe how you would calculate the value of the test statistic and interpret the meaning of a test statistic outcome.

21–5 Consider the case in which the explanatory variable values are fixed. Use the GLS representation of the Nadaraya–Watson estimator of the regression function evaluated at $\mathbf{x}_0$ (recall (21.4.15) to identify the statistical properties that apply to the estimator. In particular, is the estimator unbiased, consistent, or asymptotically normal?

21–6 Repeat the preceding problem for the case of the local linear regression model when the explanatory variable values are fixed.

21.6.3. Computer Problems

21–1 Extend the production example considered in Example 21.2.1 by generating a third input that does not enter the translog production function. Write a GAUSS program designed to compute the estimated regression function of output conditional on the three inputs. Then, implement the nested bootstrap algorithm for the test (21.2.28) for the null hypotheses that the marginal products of labor and the third input are zero. Repeat the test for the null hypothesis that the marginal product of the third input is zero. How well does the test perform in these cases?

21–2 Using the GAUSS programs C21NW.gss and C21RC.gss as guides, collect a set of data for a demand relationship (e.g., quantities, prices, and income) and estimate a nonparametric demand relationship with the Nadaraya–Watson regression estimator. Compute a 90% confidence interval for the own-price elasticity of demand. Use a Z test to evaluate the null hypothesis that demand is income inelastic at the mean level of the data. Is the demand relation homogeneous of degree zero for various price–income pairs?

21–3 Repeat the preceding problem for the LLR estimator. Compare regression function estimates and test and confidence region results for the N–W and LLR estimators.

21–4 For each of the price series in the file C21Price.dat, estimate a kernel density estimate of the marginal PDFs. Then, compute the multivariate kernel density estimate for the full set of prices. Is the estimated joint density sensitive to the choice of kernel? Bandwidth? Finally, how could you fit a conditional density function (i.e., the probability density of one price given the value of another price)? If you want, select two of the price series and try to estimate the conditional density function.

21.7. References

Bierens, H. J. (1985), "Kernel Estimators of Regression Functions." in *Advances in Econometrics*, (5th World Congress, Volume I), T. F. Bewley (Ed.), Cambridge, UK: Cambridge University Press.

Bock, M. E. (1999), "Using Wavelets for Denoising Data," working paper, Department of Statistics, Purdue University.

Bowman, A. W. (1984), "An Alternative Method of Cross-Validation for the Smoothing of Density Estimates," *Biometrika*, Vol. 71, pp. 353–60.

Boyd, D. W., and J. M. Steele (1978), "Lower Bounds for Nonparametric Density Estimation Rates," *Annals of Statistics*, Vol. 6, pp. 932–34.

Cacoullos, T. (1966), "Estimation of a Multivariate Density," *Annals of the Institute of Statistical Mathematics*, Vol. 18, pp. 179–89.

Chung, K. L. (1974), *A Course in Probability Theory*, New York: Academic Press.

Daubeches, I. (1992), *The Lectures on Wavelets*, SIAM, Philadelphia, PA.

Donoho, D. L., and I. M. Johnstone (1994), "Ideal Spatial Adaptation via Wavelet Shrinkage," *Biometrika*, Vol. 81, pp. 425–55.

Donoho, D. L., I. M. Johnstone, G. Kerkyacharian, and D. Picard (1995), "Wavelet Shrinkage: Asymptopia?," *Journal of the Royal Statistical Society, Series B*, Vol. 57, pp. 301–69.

Epanechnikov, V. A. (1969), "Non-parametric Estimation of a Multivariate Probability Density," *Theory of Probability and Its Applications*, Vol. 14, pp. 153–58.

Fan, J. (1992), "Design-Adaptive Nonparametric Regression." *Journal of the American Statistical Association*, Vol. 87, pp. 998–1004.

Fan, J. (1993), "Local Linear Regression Smoothers and Their Minimax Efficiencies," *Annals of Statistics*, Vol. 21, pp. 196–216.

Fan, J. (1998), "Test of Significance When Data are Curves," *Journal of the American Statistical Association*, Vol. 93, pp. 1007–21.

Fan, J., M. Farmen, and I. Gijbels (1998), "Local Maximum Likelihood Estimation and Inference," *Journal of the Royal Statistical Society, Series B*, Vol. 60, pp. 591–608.

Fan, Y., and Q. Li (1996), "Consistent Model Specification Tests: Omitted Variables and Semiparametric Functional Forms," *Econometrica*, Vol. 64, pp. 865–90.

Freedman, D., and P. Diaconis (1981), "On the Histogram as a Density Estimator: L_2 Theory." *Zeitschrift für Wahrscheinlichkeitstheorie und verwandte Gebiete*, Vol. 57, pp. 453–76.

Hamilton, J. D. (1999), "A Parametric Approach to Flexible Nonlinear Inference," Discussion Paper No. 99-03, University of California, San Diego.

Härdle, W., and J. S. Marron (1985), "Optimal Bandwidth Selection in Nonparametric Regression Function Estimation," *Annals of Statistics*, Vol. 13, pp. 1465–81.

Hart, J. D., and S. Yi (1998), "One-Sided Cross Validation," *Journal of the American Statistical Association*, Vol. 93, pp. 620–31.

Hastie, T., and C. Loader (1993), "Local Regression: Automatic Kernel Carpentry (with discussion)," *Statistical Science*, Vol. 8, pp. 120–43.

Izenman, A. J. (1991), "Recent Developments in Nonparametric Density Estimation," *Journal of the American Statistical Association*, Vol. 86, pp. 205–24.

Johnstone, I. M., and D. Silverman (1999), "Empirical Bayes Approaches to Mixture Problems and Wavelet Regression," working paper, Stanford University.

Künsch, H. R. (1989), "The Jack Knife and the Bootstrap of General Stationary Observations," *Annals of Statistics*, Vol. 17, No. 3, pp. 1217–45.

Lavergne, P., and Q. Vuong (1996), "Nonparametric Selection of Regressions: The Non-nested Case," *Econometrica*, 64, 207–19.

Lee, M. (1996), *Methods of Moments and Semiparametric Econometrics for Limited Dependent Variables*, New York: Springer–Verlag.

Marron, J. S. (1987), "A Comparison of Cross-Validation Techniques in Density Estimation," *Annals of Statistics*, Vol. 15, pp. 152–62.

Marron, J. S., and Nolan (1987), "Partitioned Cross-Validation," *Econometric Reviews*, Vol. 6, pp. 271–83.

Müller, H. G. (1988), *Nonparametric Regression Analysis of Longitudinal Data*, Lecture Notes in Statistics, No. 46, New York: Springer–Verlag.

Nadaraya, E. A. (1964), "On Estimating Regression," *Theory of Probability and Its Applications*, Vol. 10, pp. 186–90.

Pagan, A., and A. Ullah (1999), *Nonparametric Econometrics*, New York: Cambridge University Press.
Parzen, E. (1962), "On Estimation of a Probability Density Function and Mode," *Annals of Mathematical Statistics*, Vol. 33, pp. 1065–76.
Racine, J. (1997), "Consistent Significance Testing for Nonparametric Regression," *Journal of Business and Economic Statistics*, Vol. 15, No. 3.
Rilstone, P., and A. Ullah (1989), "Nonparametric Estimation of Response Coefficients," *Communications in Statistics, Theory and Methods*, Vol. 18, pp. 2615–27.
Robinson, P. M. (1983), "Nonparametric Estimators for Time Series," *Journal of Time Series Analysis*, Vol. 4, pp. 185–207.
Rudemo, M. (1982), "Empirical Choice of Histograms and Kernel Density Estimators," *Scandinavian Journal of Statistics*, Vol. 9, pp. 65–78.
Rupert, D., and M. P. Wand (1994), "Multivariate Locally Weighted Least Squares Regression," *Annals of Statistics*, Vol. 22, pp. 1346–70.
Scott, D. W. (1979), "On Optimal and Data-Based Histograms," *Biometrika*, Vol. 66, pp. 605–10.
Scott, D. W. (1992), *Multivariate Density Estimation: Theory, Practice, and Visualization*, New York: John Wiley.
Silverman, B. W. (1985), "Some Aspects of the Spline Smoothing Approach to Nonparametric Regression Curve Fitting (with discussion)." *Journal of the Royal Statistical Society, Series B*, Vol. 47, pp. 1–52.
Silverman, B. W. (1986), *Density Estimation for Statistics and Data Analysis*, London: Chapman and Hall.
Simonoff, J. S. (1996), *Smoothing Methods in Statistics*, New York: Springer–Verlag.
Stone, M. (1974), "Cross-Validatory Choices and Assessment of Statistical Predictions (with discussion)," *Journal of the Royal Statistical Society, Series. B*, Vol. 36, pp. 111–47.
Stone, C. J. (1984), "An Asymptotically Optimal Window Selection Rule for Kernel Density Estimates," *Annals of Statistics*, Vol. 12, pp. 1285–97.
Tapia, R. A., and J. R. Thompson (1978), *Nonparametric Probability Density Estimation*, Baltimore: Johns Hopkins University Press.
Ullah, A. (1988), *Semiparametric and Nonparametric Econometrics*, Heidelberg: Physics–Verlag.
Vidakovic, B. (1999), *Wavelets*, New York: John Wiley and Sons.
Vinod, H. D., and A. Ullah (1988), "Flexible Production Function Estimation by Nonparametric Kernel Estimators," in *Advances in Econometrics*, Vol. 7, G. F. Rhodes, Jr., and T. B. Fomby (Eds.), Greenwich, CT: JAI Press, Inc., pp. 139–60.
Wand, M. P. (1992), "Error Analysis for General Multivariate Kernel Estimators," *Journal of Nonparametric Statistics*, Vol. 2, pp. 1–15.
Watson, G. S. (1964), "Smooth Regression Analysis." *Sankhyā*, *Ser. A*, Vol. 26, pp. 359–72.
Zhao, L. H. (1999), "Improved Estimators in Nonparametric Regression Problems," *Journal of the American Statistical Association*, Vol. 94, pp. 164–73.

21.8. Appendix: Derivation of Equation (21.4.31)

From (21.4.28) and (21.4.30), the mean-squared error can be written for $z_0 \in (\mathrm{b}_j, \mathrm{b}_{j+1}]$, as follows:

$$\begin{aligned}\mathrm{MSE}(\hat{\mathrm{f}}) = {}& \frac{\mathrm{f}(z_0)}{nh} + \frac{h^2}{4}[\mathrm{f}'(z_0)]^2 + [\mathrm{f}'(z_0)]^2(z_0 - \mathrm{b}_j)^2 - h[\mathrm{f}'(z_0)]^2(z_0 - \mathrm{b}_j) \\ & + \mathrm{O}(n^{-1}) + \mathrm{O}(h^3) \qquad (21.8.1)\end{aligned}$$

where $f'(z_0) \equiv \frac{\partial f(z_0)}{\partial z_0}$. Integrating (21.8.1) over all bins yields the integrated mean-squared error

$$\mathrm{IMSE}(\hat{f}) = \frac{1}{nh} + \int \frac{h^2}{4}[f'(z_0)]^2 dz_0 + \sum_j \int_{b_j}^{b_{j+1}} [f'(z_0)]^2 (z_0 - b_j)^2 dz_0$$

$$- h \sum_j \int_{b_j}^{b_{j+1}} [f'(z_0)]^2 (z_0 - b_j)\, dz_0 + O(n^{-1}) + O(h^3) \qquad (21.8.2)$$

Making the substitution $y = z_0 - b_j$ in each of the integrals in the third and fourth terms of (21.8.2), the sum of these two terms can be represented as

$$\sum_j \int_0^h [f'(y + b_j)]^2 y^2 dy - h \sum_j \int_0^h [f'(y + b_j)]^2 y\, dy + O(h^3) \qquad (21.8.3)$$

Now, using the relationship $f'(y + b_j) = f'(b_j) + O(h)$, one can rewrite (21.8.3) as

$$\sum_j \int_0^h [f'(b_j)]^2 y^2 dy - h \sum_j \int_0^h [f'(b_j)]^2 y\, dy + O(h^3)$$

$$= \sum_j \frac{h^3}{3}[f'(b_j)]^2 - \sum_j \frac{h^3}{2}[f'(b_j)]^2 + O(h^3)$$

$$= \frac{h^2}{3} \int_{-\infty}^{\infty} [f'(z_0)]^2 dz - \frac{h^2}{2} \int_{-\infty}^{\infty} [f'(z_0)]^2 dz_0 + O(h^3), \qquad (21.8.4)$$

where we have used the numerical approximation result that as $n \to \infty$ and $h \to 0$, $\sum_j g(b_j)(b_{j+1} - b_j) = \sum_j g(b_j)h \to \sum_j \int_{b_j}^{b_{j+1}} g(z_0)dz_0$. Then, from substitution of (21.8.4) for the third and fourth terms in (21.8.2), Equation (21.4.31) in the text results.

PART NINE

Bayesian Estimation and Inference

In the previous parts of the book we have emphasized the classical sampling theory approach to estimation and inference, and the focus has been to a large extent on how to reason in a predata, repeated sampling context. In this part of the book we focus on the Bayesian method of reasoning that emphasizes a subjective basis for probability theory and a postdata basis for inference that is conditioned on the particular observed sample of data. Because Bayesian inference is not covered or developed sufficiently in many courses in theoretical statistics and econometrics, in Chapters 22 through 24 we review the basic concepts underlying the Bayesian approach to estimation and inference and demonstrate these procedures for a range of situations in the context of stochastic linear additive inverse problems. Traditional Bayesian analysis is extended to include empirical Bayes, the Bayesian method of moments, and how one may deal with the problem of unfriendly posterior distributions.

CHAPTER 22

Bayesian Estimation: General Principles with a Regression Focus

22.1. Introduction

In the previous parts of the book we have emphasized the sampling theory approach to estimation and inference, and the focus has been to a large extent on how to reason in a predata context. In this part of the book we focus on Bayesian reasoning that emphasizes a subjective basis for probability theory and a postdata basis of inference. As such it links work on rational behavior under uncertainty and statistical decision making. Because Bayesian inference reflects a new basis for reasoning in situations involving partial–incomplete information and is not developed in many courses in theoretical statistics and econometrics, we have included in this chapter a discussion of inverse probability and the general principles of Bayesian estimation and inference with particular emphasis on the regression model context.

The term "Bayesian," as applied in statistical inference, recognized the contributions of the seventeenth-century English clergyman Thomas Bayes. His seminal ideas on inverse probability were presented in two papers published after his death in the *Philosophical Transactions* (1763 and 1764). These seminal ideas were extended, and the initial elements of a formalized theory of Bayesian inference can be seen in the work of P. S. de Laplace in the early 1800s. However, interest in the approach subsequently dissipated, and it was not until the 1930s that interest in the Bayesian approach was rekindled. Some of the prominent early contributors to the development of a formal theory of Bayesian inference include F. Y. Edgeworth, F. P. Ramsey, H. Jeffreys, D. V. Lindley, B. de Finetti, L. J. Savage, and I. J. Good. The work of Arnold Zellner, beginning in the 1960s, is largely responsible for the introduction of the principles of Bayesian inference into the practice of econometrics. As with the classical approach, research into the theory and application of Bayesian principles for solving problems of statistical inference is ongoing.

To begin to establish a formal basis for our discussion of Bayesian reasoning, let $\{Y_1, Y_2, \ldots, Y_m\}$ represent a set of equally likely outcomes or propositions for an experiment. If the event A represents some subset of the possibility space that identifies an event of interest for the experiment, the probability of the event is defined, via the classical probability concept, as $P(A) = n(A)/m$, where $n(A)$ is the number of elements in A. Following Bernoulli, if we acquire n independent outcomes from the experiment, and if we find that A occurs t times, it is of interest to compare observed relative frequencies of occurrence t/n with the conceptual, true fixed probability of the occurrence of event A, P(A). The random relative frequency T/n is, in a predata classical sense, a minimum variance unbiased estimator (MVUE) of P(A). The MVUE property is relevant in the context of all hypothetically possible outcomes of T/n that are possible prior to data being actually observed.

22.1.1. Bayes Theorem

In contrast to the classical approach, Bayes inverted the classical reasoning and focused his attention on the problem of inferring the probabilities that P(A) takes on various values, given what *has been observed* for the sample outcome of T/n. Thus, in the problem posed by Bayes, we observe data, and thereby know the values of the data outcomes, and wish to know what probabilities are consistent with these outcomes. His concept has been given the name *inverse probability* because of his inversion of the classical approach of assigning probabilities to sample observations, given a value of the parameter vector, to the approach of assigning probabilities to parameter values given a sample observation. Given propositions A and B and the rules of conditional probability, Bayes' principle of inverse probability (Bayes theorem)

$$P(A \mid B) = \frac{P(B \mid A)P(A)}{P(B)} \tag{22.1.1}$$

reflects what we know about A after making use of the (new) information in B.

The analog to Bayes theorem when we are dealing with probability densities, and not necessarily probabilities, is then given by the natural representation

$$f(x \mid y) = \frac{f(y \mid x)f_X(x)}{f_Y(y)}, \tag{22.1.2}$$

where $f_X(x)$ and $f_Y(y)$ are the marginal probability density functions of X and Y. Note that the validity of (22.1.2) in fact follows immediately from the definition of the conditional probability density function $f(x \mid y) \equiv \frac{f(x,y)}{f_Y(y)}$ when one recalls the probability multiplication rule $f(x, y) = \frac{f(x,y)}{f_X(x)} f_X(x) = f(y \mid x)f_X(x)$.

Consider applying Bayes' logic to a coin-tossing experiment. Let the outcome of the random variable T represent the number of heads observed in n independent tosses of the coin, so that $Y = T/n$ represents the relative frequency of heads. We can represent the probability distribution of potential outcomes Y for the relative frequency of heads, as

$$L(\theta \mid y) \equiv f(y \mid \theta) = \binom{n}{ny} \theta^{ny}(1-\theta)^{n-ny} I_{\{0,1,\ldots,n\}}(ny), \quad \theta \in [0, 1], \tag{22.1.3}$$

where θ denotes a possible value for P(H), the probability of a head on any coin toss. Note that (22.1.3) follows directly from the fact that T has a binomial distribution, and thus Y is then a binomial random variable that has been scaled by n. Now let the PDF $p(\theta)$, for $\theta \in [0, 1]$, be our prior (previous to observing the outcome $y = t/n$)

information representing the distribution of probabilities (or degrees of belief) that the various values of θ represent the true value of P(H). Then, setting $x \equiv \theta$ and $f_X(x) \equiv p(\theta)$ in the statement (22.1.2) of Bayes theorem leads to the following representation of the probability distribution of θ, given that the value $y = t/n$ *has been observed*, as

$$p(\theta \mid y) = \frac{L(\theta \mid y)p(\theta)}{f_Y(y)} = \frac{f(y \mid \theta)p(\theta)}{f_Y(y)} \propto f(y \mid \theta)p(\theta). \tag{22.1.4}$$

We emphasize that the term $f_Y(y)$ in (22.1.4) is the value of the marginal probability distribution of $Y = T/n$, evaluated at $y = t/n$, and $\propto$ denotes "proportional to". Note that the marginal distribution of Y can be defined by

$$f_Y(y) = \int_0^1 f(y \mid \theta)p(\theta)\, d\theta \tag{22.1.5}$$

because, again, by the probability multiplication rule, $f(y, \theta) = f(y \mid \theta)p(\theta)$ is the joint probability distribution of the pair (Y, Θ). The distribution (22.1.4) is referred to as the *posterior* distribution of Θ because it reflects that our information about θ is posterior to, or after, the observed data information has been incorporated into the information base. Thus, Bayes has inferred a probability distribution on potential values of $\theta \in [0, 1]$ of P(H) from prior and data information on the sampling process underlying the data.

If new data information were to become available, we could treat (22.1.4) as the prior (i.e., prior to the *new* data information) distribution on potential P(H) values, and we could again follow the information updating process (22.1.3) and (22.1.4) to obtain an updated posterior distribution for θ. In the updating process the conditional and marginal distributions $f(y \mid \theta)$ and $f_Y(y)$ would then refer to probability distributions of the *new* data information, but otherwise the updating process is identical to the one described previously. Such updating can occur whenever new information becomes available. The association of probability with incomplete information about events or propositions is a principal feature of Bayes' use of probability.

As a concrete illustration of a posterior distribution, suppose that in our coin-tossing experiment we have no a priori information that any value for the probability of heads is any more likely to be the true value than any other value. We represent this prior state of ignorance by specifying the uniform prior distribution $p(\theta) = I_{(0,1)}(\theta)$, where $I_{(0,1)}(\theta)$ is the indicator function equaling 1 when $\theta \in (0, 1)$ and 0 otherwise. Suppose further that the coin-tossing experiment consisted of 10 coin tosses, of which 4 came up heads. Then setting $y = .4$ in (22.1.3) and (22.1.4) yields the posterior distribution result

$$p(\theta \mid y = .4) \propto \theta^4(1 - \theta)^6, \quad \theta \in (0, 1), \tag{22.1.6}$$

which is recognized as a Beta distribution, Beta (5, 7).

22.1.2. A Format for Bayesian Reasoning

On the basis of the conceptual foundation of the preceding subsection, the fundamental components of Bayesian inference consist of the sample data, prior density of the parameters, the posterior density of the parameters, a loss function and the corresponding optimal posterior risk-minimizing postdata Bayes estimate, and the predictive distribution of observations outside of the sample. These components, now stated in the context of data and parameter vectors, translate into

1. sample information $\mathbf{y} = (y_1, y_2, \ldots, y_n)$ having a joint probability density function $f(\mathbf{y} \mid \boldsymbol{\theta})$ and associated likelihood function $L(\boldsymbol{\theta} \mid \mathbf{y})$, $\boldsymbol{\theta} \in \Omega$,
2. prior information in the form of a prior probability density $p(\boldsymbol{\theta})$, $\boldsymbol{\theta} \in \Omega$ for the parameter $\boldsymbol{\theta}$ in the sampling–probability model $f(\mathbf{y} \mid \boldsymbol{\theta})$, $\boldsymbol{\theta} \in \Omega$, and
3. the likelihood function $L(\boldsymbol{\theta} \mid \mathbf{y})$ and prior density $p(\boldsymbol{\theta})$ combined by Bayes theorem (22.1.4) to yield the posterior density of $\boldsymbol{\theta}$.

From this posterior, which is the foundation for Bayesian inference, a conditional postdata basis for inferences about $\boldsymbol{\theta}$ is summarized in the form of a joint distribution of probabilities. From these fundamental components, the Bayesian approach to inference may be illustrated as follows:

The Probability–Sampling Model

$$f(\mathbf{y} \mid \boldsymbol{\theta}), \ \boldsymbol{\theta} \in \Omega$$

$$\downarrow$$

The Sample Observations

$$\mathbf{y} = (y_1, y_2, \ldots, y_n) \text{ from density } f(\mathbf{y} \mid \boldsymbol{\theta})$$

$$\downarrow$$

The Prior Information Density

$$p(\boldsymbol{\theta}), \ \boldsymbol{\theta} \in \Omega$$

$$\downarrow$$

The Posterior Density

$$p(\boldsymbol{\theta} \mid \mathbf{y}) = \frac{f(\mathbf{y} \mid \boldsymbol{\theta}) p(\boldsymbol{\theta})}{\int_{\boldsymbol{\theta} \in \Omega} f(\mathbf{y} \mid \boldsymbol{\theta})\, p(\boldsymbol{\theta})\, d\boldsymbol{\theta}} \propto f(\mathbf{y} \mid \boldsymbol{\theta}) p(\boldsymbol{\theta}) = L(\boldsymbol{\theta} \mid \mathbf{y}) p(\boldsymbol{\theta})$$

posterior PDF $\propto$ (likelihood function) $\times$ (prior PDF)

$$\downarrow$$

Posterior Inferences

$$\downarrow$$

Parameter Estimation   Prediction   Hypothesis Evalution

This diagram not only illustrates the basic components of Bayesian inference but also suggests a format for carrying through an applied Bayesian analysis. These ideas are presented in a more complete and formal way in Table 22.1.

Before turning to the principles of Bayesian estimation, let us be clear about a semantic trap that seems to have clouded the interpretation and acceptance of the Bayesian approach. Given a posterior distribution for, say, a parameter, some may initially suppose that the Bayesian interpretation of the statistical model necessarily implies that model parameters are inherently random variables. However, *the posterior distribution describes our postdata information about the parameters* and not the stochastic properties of the parameter, which is typically an unknown fixed constant. Consequently, in the

Table 22.1. *General Bayesian Model Components and Characteristics*

Model Component	Specific Characteristics	
	Y RV Type:	continuous or discrete
Likelihood Function:	**Y** Range:	limited or unlimited
$L(\boldsymbol{\theta} \mid \boldsymbol{y}) \equiv f(\boldsymbol{y} \mid \boldsymbol{\theta})$	Moments:	$E[\mathbf{Y} \mid \boldsymbol{\theta}] = \boldsymbol{\mu}_{\mathbf{Y}}(\boldsymbol{\theta})$ and $\mathbf{cov}(\mathbf{Y} \mid \boldsymbol{\theta}) = \Sigma_{\mathbf{Y}}(\boldsymbol{\theta})$
	PDF Family:	normal or any other parametric family satisfying moment conditions
Prior Distribution:	$\boldsymbol{\Theta}$ RV Type:	continuous or discrete
$p(\boldsymbol{\theta})$	$\boldsymbol{\Theta}$ Range:	limited or unlimited
	Moments:	$E[\boldsymbol{\Theta}] = \boldsymbol{\mu}_{\Theta}$ and $\mathbf{cov}(\boldsymbol{\Theta}) = \Sigma_{\Theta}$
	PDF Family:	conjugate or nonconjugate
	Normalization:	proper: $\int_{\boldsymbol{\theta} \in \Omega} p(\boldsymbol{\theta})\, d\boldsymbol{\theta} = 1$ or $\sum_{\boldsymbol{\theta} \in \Omega} p(\boldsymbol{\theta}) = 1$ improper: $\int_{\boldsymbol{\theta} \in \Omega} p(\boldsymbol{\theta})\, d\boldsymbol{\theta} = \infty$ or $\sum_{\boldsymbol{\theta} \in \Omega} p(\boldsymbol{\theta}) = \infty$
Marginal Distribution of **Y**:	**Y** RV Type:	continuous or discrete
$f_{\mathbf{Y}}(\mathbf{y}) = \int_{\boldsymbol{\theta} \in \Omega} f(\boldsymbol{y} \mid \boldsymbol{\theta})$	**Y** Range:	limited or unlimited
$\times\, p(\boldsymbol{\theta})\, d\boldsymbol{\theta}$ or	Moments:	$E[\mathbf{Y}] = \boldsymbol{\mu}_{\mathbf{Y}}$ and $\mathbf{cov}(\mathbf{Y}) = \Sigma_{\mathbf{Y}}$
$f_{\mathbf{Y}}(\boldsymbol{y}) = \sum_{\boldsymbol{\theta} \in \Omega} f(\boldsymbol{y} \mid \boldsymbol{\theta}) p(\boldsymbol{\theta})$	PDF Family:	normal or any other parametric family satisfying moment conditions
Posterior Distribution:	$\boldsymbol{\Theta}$ RV Type:	continuous or discrete
$p(\boldsymbol{\theta} \mid \mathbf{y}) = \frac{L(\boldsymbol{\theta} \mid \mathbf{y}) p(\boldsymbol{\theta})}{f_{\mathbf{Y}}(\mathbf{y})}$	$\boldsymbol{\Theta}$ Range:	limited or unlimited
$\propto L(\boldsymbol{\theta} \mid \mathbf{y}) p(\boldsymbol{\theta})$	Moments:	$E[\boldsymbol{\Theta} \mid \mathbf{y}] = \boldsymbol{\mu}_{\Theta}(\mathbf{y})$ and $\mathbf{cov}(\boldsymbol{\Theta} \mid \mathbf{y}) = \Sigma_{\Theta}(\mathbf{y})$
	PDF Family:	normal or any other parametric family satisfying moment conditions

context of the prior information and the data, the posterior summarizes this information in the form of a joint distribution of probabilities for a collection of possible values for the unknown fixed quantity of interest. It is also important to emphasize that the focus on the posterior, and the conditional-postdata inferences derived from it, leads to conclusions about events that are based on only data that actually happened, as evidenced by the realized sample observations, and not on data that might have happened but did not, as in the classical paradigm.

The overall objective of this chapter is to clarify the meaning of the model components in Table 22.1 as they relate to Bayesian estimation in general and the regression model in particular. In the process, we will review some underlying Bayes' theory and discover its implications in a focused regression model setting.

22.2. Bayesian Probability Models and Posterior Distributions

Before proceeding to an analysis of regression models we elaborate on some of the concepts introduced in Section 22.1. In the Bayesian approach, unknown and unobservable elements of the statistical model underlying an inverse problem, *including parameters*, are treated operationally as if they are random variables. As we noted in Section 22.1, this is not to say that a parameter is actually a random variable. Rather, this is a conceptual device that allows the analyst to identify the possible values considered as candidates for the generally fixed unknown parameter value as well as the corresponding probabilities, or degrees of belief, relating to the validity of these values.

As in the classical approach, the random behavior of the observable sample outcomes is characterized by the joint PDF of the random sample $f(\mathbf{y} \mid \boldsymbol{\theta})$, where we are using the conditional-on-parameters notation in Bayesian analyses, as opposed to the classical semicolon notation $f(\mathbf{y}; \boldsymbol{\theta})$, to denote that the PDF for $\mathbf{Y}$ is defined *given* or *conditional on* a specific value $\boldsymbol{\theta}$ of the *random* parameter vector $\boldsymbol{\Theta}$. Note that the functional specification of $f(\mathbf{y} \mid \boldsymbol{\theta})$ is precisely the same as in the classical case – it is simply the joint PDF of $\mathbf{Y}$. However, in the Bayesian context, the joint PDF of the random sample is interpreted as a *conditional* PDF because $\boldsymbol{\Theta}$ is a random vector and we are then conditioning on a specific outcome $\boldsymbol{\theta}$ when referring to a specific parameter value. Note further that just as in the classical case, $L(\boldsymbol{\theta} \mid \mathbf{y}) \equiv f(\mathbf{y} \mid \boldsymbol{\theta})$ can be interpreted as the likelihood function for $\boldsymbol{\theta}$ given the sample outcome $\mathbf{y}$, where we again utilize conditional notation, as opposed to the classical semicolon notation $L(\boldsymbol{\theta}; \mathbf{y})$, to emphasize the random nature of both $\boldsymbol{\Theta}$ and $\boldsymbol{Y}$ and the concomitant conditioning that must then underlie the interpretation of $L(\boldsymbol{\theta} \mid \mathbf{y})$ as a likelihood function for $\boldsymbol{\theta}$ *given* $\mathbf{y}$.

22.2.1. Prior Distributions

The Bayesian approach, like maximum likelihood-based methods, uses the likelihood function to provide a linkage between the information contained in a sample of data and the value of the unknown parameters of a statistical model. In addition, the Bayesian method factors additional information into inverse problem solutions via the specification of a *prior* PDF, $p(\boldsymbol{\theta})$, on the parameter vector of the statistical model. The information represented by $p(\boldsymbol{\theta})$ can be objective, subjective, or a combination of the two. It is presumed that if $p(\boldsymbol{\theta})$ represents subjective information, then the analyst has adhered to the axioms of probability in defining $p(\boldsymbol{\theta})$ so that the function is indeed a legitimate probability measure on $\boldsymbol{\theta}$ values. Berger (1985, Section 3.2), as if responding to the question 'Where do priors come from?' provides an informative discussion of methods used to form or elicit subjective prior distributions, and specific examples and selections of prior distributions are provided in Kass and Wasserman (1996).

Given that the classical approach is the most commonly taught statistical method in introductory statistics courses, many readers may be unaccustomed to associating probabilities with model parameters. Regarding the randomness of parameters, one develops the stochastic characterization of parameters in terms of the *prior* distribution representing the degree of predata (i.e., *prior* to observing the data) uncertainty about the value of parameters in the probability model. In this vein, there is no loss of generality in viewing the prior distribution as representing information that is introduced at the stage in the statistical analysis at which a probability model *has already been defined*, the inverse problem *has already been identified*, and a solution to the inverse problem is then being contemplated. The analyst can therefore view the specification of the probability model itself and the inverse problem identified by the model in precisely the same way, regardless of whether a Bayesian or a classical approach is ultimately adopted for solving the inverse problem. In any case, one should keep in mind that the statistical model and the associated parameters are merely convenient abstract representations of some real-world DSP and only exist owing to the mutual agreement of interested researchers. By formalizing uncertainty regarding model parameters in the form of prior probability distributions, the Bayesian approach allows differing beliefs about the plausible values of these parameters to be incorporated explicitly into inverse problem solutions.

22.2.2. Posterior Probability Distributions

Because, within the Bayesian paradigm, both $\mathbf{Y}$ and $\boldsymbol{\Theta}$ are considered to be random variables, one can then conceive of a joint probability distribution, say $\mathrm{f}(\boldsymbol{y}, \boldsymbol{\theta})$, existing for the pair $(\mathbf{Y}, \boldsymbol{\Theta})$. Letting $\mathrm{f}_{\mathbf{Y}}(\boldsymbol{y})$ represent the *marginal* probability distribution of the random sample, it follows directly from the definition of conditional PDFs that we can represent the joint PDF of $(\mathbf{Y}, \boldsymbol{\Theta})$ as

$$\mathrm{f}(\boldsymbol{y}, \boldsymbol{\theta}) = \mathrm{f}(\boldsymbol{y} \mid \boldsymbol{\theta})\mathrm{p}(\boldsymbol{\theta}) = \mathrm{p}(\boldsymbol{\theta} \mid \boldsymbol{y})\mathrm{f}_{\mathbf{Y}}(\boldsymbol{y}). \tag{22.2.1}$$

The probability distribution of the parameter vector, conditional on the observed data, is given by

$$\mathrm{p}(\boldsymbol{\theta} \mid \boldsymbol{y}) = \frac{\mathrm{f}(\boldsymbol{y}, \boldsymbol{\theta})}{\mathrm{f}_{\mathbf{Y}}(\boldsymbol{y})}. \tag{22.2.2}$$

Given (22.2.2), the conditional PDF of the parameter vector can be represented in terms of only a *kernel* of the PDF. Noting that $\mathrm{f}_{\mathbf{Y}}(\boldsymbol{y})$ is a constant when we are conditioning on $\mathbf{y}$, we can represent the PDF up to a positive scale factor as

$$\mathrm{p}(\boldsymbol{\theta} \mid \boldsymbol{y}) \propto \mathrm{f}(\boldsymbol{y} \mid \boldsymbol{\theta})\mathrm{p}(\boldsymbol{\theta}) \equiv \mathrm{L}(\boldsymbol{\theta} \mid \boldsymbol{y})\mathrm{p}(\boldsymbol{\theta}). \tag{22.2.3}$$

This follows from both (22.2.1) and (22.2.2) and the definition $\mathrm{L}(\boldsymbol{\theta} \mid \boldsymbol{y}) \equiv \mathrm{f}(\boldsymbol{y} \mid \boldsymbol{\theta})$, where again $\propto$ denotes "proportional to." Note that the scale factor needed to transform the kernel into a proper PDF can be recovered by taking the inverse of the integral (or inverse of the sum in the discrete case) of the kernel over all $\boldsymbol{\theta}$ values in the support of the PDF. In the continuous case, the integral of the kernel is $\mathrm{f}_{\mathbf{Y}}(\boldsymbol{y}) = \int_{\boldsymbol{\theta} \in \Omega} \mathrm{f}(\boldsymbol{y} \mid \boldsymbol{\theta})\mathrm{p}(\boldsymbol{\theta})\, d\boldsymbol{\theta}$, and thus the scale factor is $[\mathrm{f}_{\mathbf{Y}}(\boldsymbol{y})]^{-1}$, as one would expect from (22.2.2).

The conditional PDF $\mathrm{p}(\boldsymbol{\theta} \mid \boldsymbol{y})$ is called the *posterior* distribution of the parameters because it is defined after observing the data (i.e., postdata) and incorporates the data information into the distribution of $\boldsymbol{\Theta}$. The result (22.2.3) is *Bayes theorem*, which can be expressed in words as

$$\text{posterior PDF} \propto (\text{likelihood function}) \times (\text{prior PDF}). \tag{22.2.4}$$

One can view either (22.2.3) or (22.2.4) as defining an information processing, input–output procedure in which the prior information on the parameters is updated by the information contained in the observed data ultimately to obtain the posterior information on the parameters. Note that the posterior distribution in a Bayesian analysis represents all of the information available about the parameters of the problem and thus narrows the uncertainty about the value of $\boldsymbol{\theta}$ to the maximal extent possible given the information available relating to the inverse problem.

22.3. The Bayesian Linear–Regression-Based Probability Model

In terms of the general class of statistical models portrayed in Table 2.1, we focus our primary attention on the special case of the linear regression model as delineated in Table 22.2. To facilitate the representation of probabilistic information about the possible values of the parameters of the model, we introduce the capital beta notation, $\mathbf{B}$, to denote the conceptually random vector whose outcomes $\boldsymbol{\beta}$ represent candidates for the parameter vector of explanatory variable coefficients. We use the capital sigma notation Σ to denote the conceptually random scalar whose outcomes σ denote possible values of the standard deviation of the noise component. We assume that a linear regression model with *fixed* parameters $\boldsymbol{\beta}_0$ and σ_0 characterizes the true DSP underlying the sample data. The randomization of the parameter vectors, via the use of the random vector $(\mathbf{B}, \Sigma)$, is then a conceptual device for representing prior and posterior information about the linear regression model parameters in probabilistic form.

We emphasize that in previous chapters we have been careful to distinguish between cases of fixed $\mathbf{x}$ and stochastic $\mathbf{X}$ regressors. This is important in the classical

Table 22.2. *Bayesian Linear Regression*

Model Component	Specific Characteristics	
$\mathbf{Y}$	RV Type:	continuous
	Range:	unlimited
	Y_i dimensions:	univariate
	Moments:	$E[\mathbf{Y} \mid \mathbf{x}, \boldsymbol{\beta}, \sigma] = \mathbf{x}\boldsymbol{\beta}$ and $\mathbf{cov}(\mathbf{Y} \mid \mathbf{x}, \boldsymbol{\beta}, \sigma) = \sigma^2\mathbf{I}$
$\eta(\mathbf{x}, \boldsymbol{\beta}, \varepsilon)$	Functional Form:	linear in $\mathbf{x}$ and $\boldsymbol{\beta}$, additive in ε, as $\mathbf{x}\boldsymbol{\beta} + \varepsilon$
$\mathbf{x}$ or $\mathbf{X}$	RV Type:	fixed or random
	Genesis:	exogenous to the model
$\mathbf{B}$	RV Type:	conceptually random
	Dimension:	finite
ε	RV Type:	iid or independent
	Moments:	$E[\varepsilon \mid \mathbf{x}, \boldsymbol{\beta}, \sigma] = \mathbf{0}$, and $\mathbf{cov}(\varepsilon \mid \mathbf{x}, \boldsymbol{\beta}, \sigma) = \sigma^2\mathbf{I}$
$\boldsymbol{\Omega}$	Prior info:	$(\mathbf{B}, \Sigma) \sim p(\boldsymbol{\beta}, \sigma)$, a proper or improper PDF, for $(\boldsymbol{\beta}, \sigma) \in \boldsymbol{\Omega}$.
$f(\mathbf{e} \mid \mathbf{x}, \varphi)$	PDF family:	normal or any other parametric family satisfying moment conditions

repeated-sampling context because the stochastic nature of $\mathbf{X}$ affects the definition of the sample space over which repeated-sampling properties are evaluated. In the Bayesian approach, both $\mathbf{Y}$ and $\mathbf{X}$ constitute data, and the posterior distribution is developed by conditioning on outcomes of both. Consequently, in the Bayesian approach, methods of inference, and the inferences themselves, are identical regardless of whether the regressors are fixed or stochastic.

22.3.1. Bayesian Regression Analysis under Normality and Uninformative Priors

Because applications of the traditional Bayesian method require that a parametric family of joint probability density functions, or equivalently the likelihood function, be specified, we will begin our discussion with a return to the normal distribution–based regression models of Chapter 4 and specify the parametric regression model of the DSP in the familiar form

$$\mathbf{Y} = \mathbf{x}\boldsymbol{\beta} + \boldsymbol{\varepsilon}, \tag{22.3.1}$$

where

$$\mathbf{Y} \sim \mathrm{N}(\mathbf{x}\boldsymbol{\beta}, \sigma^2\mathbf{I}_n) \tag{22.3.2}$$

and

$$\boldsymbol{\varepsilon} \sim \mathrm{N}(\mathbf{0}, \sigma^2\mathbf{I}_n). \tag{22.3.3}$$

We make the usual assumptions here that the parameters $\boldsymbol{\beta}$ and σ are fixed unknown constants, and we represent the DSP conditional on an outcome for the explanatory variable matrix $\mathbf{x}$. As before, the covariance matrix of $\mathbf{Y}$ or $\boldsymbol{\varepsilon}$ is assumed *known* up to the constant of proportionality σ^2.

Given the regression model, we denote the joint probability density function that encompasses the sample of observations $\mathbf{y}$ as well as the values of $\mathbf{x}$, $\boldsymbol{\beta}$, and σ by $\mathrm{f}(\mathbf{y}, \mathbf{x}, \boldsymbol{\beta}, \sigma)$. The corresponding likelihood function is then

$$\mathrm{L}(\boldsymbol{\beta}, \sigma \mid \mathbf{y}, \mathbf{x}) = (2\pi\sigma^2)^{-n/2} \exp\left[\frac{-(\mathbf{y} - \mathbf{x}\boldsymbol{\beta})'(\mathbf{y} - \mathbf{x}\boldsymbol{\beta})}{2\sigma^2}\right]. \tag{22.3.4}$$

We use the conditional-on-data notation for the likelihood function to emphasize that we are now in the Bayesian context in which the parameters are *conceptually* randomized for purposes of representing information about parameters in probabilistic form. In Chapter 3 we used the sample information represented by the likelihood function to define a maximum likelihood (ML) estimator of $\boldsymbol{\beta}$ as

$$\hat{\boldsymbol{\beta}} = (\mathbf{x}'\mathbf{x})^{-1}\mathbf{x}'\mathbf{Y} \sim \mathrm{N}(\boldsymbol{\beta}, \sigma^2(\mathbf{x}'\mathbf{x})^{-1}). \tag{22.3.5}$$

Under a squared-error loss measure,

$$\ell(\boldsymbol{\beta}, \hat{\boldsymbol{\beta}}) = \|\boldsymbol{\beta} - \hat{\boldsymbol{\beta}}\|^2 = (\boldsymbol{\beta} - \hat{\boldsymbol{\beta}})'(\boldsymbol{\beta} - \hat{\boldsymbol{\beta}}), \tag{22.3.6}$$

the ML estimator is, in addition to a host of other sampling properties, minimax and has constant risk $\mathrm{E}[\|\boldsymbol{\beta} - \hat{\boldsymbol{\beta}}\|^2] = \sigma^2\mathrm{tr}(\mathbf{x}'\mathbf{x})^{-1}$ given the value of σ^2.

Now, within the context of the normal regression model, consider the case in which our conceptual–prior information about model parameters is vague (uninformative, diffuse). To represent this vague information on the values of $\boldsymbol{\beta}$ and σ in a Bayesian analysis it is standard practice to characterize the randomization of the parameters (i.e., **B** and Σ) by specifying their probability distribution as

$$(\mathbf{B}, \Sigma) \sim p(\boldsymbol{\beta}, \sigma) \equiv p(\boldsymbol{\beta})p(\sigma) \propto \frac{1}{\sigma}, \quad \text{for } \sigma \in (0, \infty) \text{ and } \boldsymbol{\beta} \in R^k, \tag{22.3.7}$$

where

$$p(\boldsymbol{\beta}) \propto c \quad \text{and} \quad p(\sigma) \propto \frac{1}{\sigma}. \tag{22.3.8}$$

The rationale in support of the improper PDF (i.e., a PDF that does not integrate to 1) specification in (22.3.7) and (22.3.8) is rooted in considerations of invariance of vague information under transformations of the parameter space. This is discussed ahead, and by Zellner (1971, pp. 41–53) and Berger (1985, Section 3.3).

22.3.2. Uninformative Priors and Proper Marginal Posteriors

To provide some motivation for the prior PDF specification (22.3.7)–(22.3.8), first focus on the parameter vector $\boldsymbol{\beta}$. Note that the purpose of the value of $\boldsymbol{\beta}$ in the regression model is to parameterize, or determine, the mean, $\mathbf{x}\boldsymbol{\beta}$ of the vector **Y**. Thus, our interpretation of the meaning of $\boldsymbol{\beta}$ is derived from its role in determining E[**Y**], and we would be ignorant of the value of $\boldsymbol{\beta}$ iff we were ignorant of the value of E[**Y**]. Ignorance of the value of E[**Y**] would imply indifference regarding whether $\mathbf{x}\boldsymbol{\beta}$ or $\mathbf{x}[\boldsymbol{\beta} + \boldsymbol{\xi}]$ is the true value of E[**Y**], for any choice of the $(k \times 1)$ vector $\boldsymbol{\xi}$. This line of reasoning then suggests **B** should be uniformly distributed on R^k a priori, because $p(\boldsymbol{\beta}) = p(\boldsymbol{\beta} + \boldsymbol{\xi})\ \forall \boldsymbol{\xi}$. Because no *proper* prior distribution (i.e., a PDF that integrates to 1) exists that can represent such a uniform weighting on all of the elements of R^k, Bayesians adopt, as in (22.3.8), the *improper* prior PDF $p(\boldsymbol{\beta}) \propto c$, for $\boldsymbol{\beta} \in R^k$ and $c > 0$, to represent the uniformity of prior weights. An admissible and common choice for c is $c = 1$.

Regarding the choice of prior for σ, note that the purpose of the value of σ in the regression model is to parameterize, or determine, the standard deviation σ of the Y_i's. Our interpretation of the meaning of σ is thus derived from its role in representing this standard deviation of the elements of **Y**. Lack of information concerning the standard deviation of Y_i must then also imply a lack of information concerning the standard deviation of τY_i, $\tau > 0$, which is represented by $\tau\sigma$. It follows in this situation that the prior probability we assign to $\sigma \in A$ should be no different than the prior probability we assign to $\tau\sigma \in A$ because elements of A are then no more likely to be the value of σ than the value of $\tau\sigma$. Then, because $\tau\sigma \in A$ iff $\sigma \in \tau^{-1}A$, where the set $\tau^{-1}A$ denotes the elements in A each divided by the positive constant τ, we conclude our prior PDF must be such that

$$\int_A p(\sigma)\, d\sigma = \int_{\tau^{-1}A} p(\sigma)\, d\sigma = \int_A p(\tau^{-1}\sigma)\tau^{-1}\, d\sigma \tag{22.3.9}$$

for every choice of event A, the last integral in (22.3.9) following from an application of the change of variables method. This finally implies that the prior PDF should be of the form

$$p(\sigma) = \tau^{-1} p(\tau^{-1}\sigma)\ \forall \sigma, \tag{22.3.10}$$

which is satisfied by the family of functions $p(z) \propto z^{-1}$. Consequently, as indicated in (22.3.8), our prior PDF on σ is of the form $p(\sigma) \propto \sigma^{-1}$. Assuming independence of prior information on $\boldsymbol{\beta}$ and σ then leads naturally to the joint prior PDF specification indicated in (22.3.7).

Although the improper PDF in (22.3.7) is the standard prior used when the prior information about the regression model parameters is diffuse or uninformative, we note that there are other possibilities for representing ignorance that might be defended on grounds other than the property of invariance under parameter transformations. For example, if the improper uniform prior $p(\boldsymbol{\beta}, \sigma) = 1$ is assumed, so that all values of $(\boldsymbol{\beta}, \sigma) \in R^k \times R_{\geq 0}$ (recall $\sigma \geq 0$) are assumed to be equally plausible as the true value of the model parameters, then the posterior distribution of the model parameters would be identical to the likelihood function of the parameters. One could then argue that the data information represented by the likelihood function is completely unaffected by the prior information (or lack of prior information) when moving to the posterior distribution via Bayes rule, which is surely another defensible notion of a diffuse prior. It turns out that in the case at hand, the difference in posterior inferences between using the former and latter prior distribution is very small for even relatively small sample sizes ($n \approx 20$), and the difference rapidly becomes negligible as n increases. We will revisit this issue ahead.

22.3.3. Posterior Distribution under an Uninformative Prior

On the basis of the standard diffuse prior for $\boldsymbol{\beta}$ and σ defined in (22.3.7), we can proceed to define the posterior distribution of the parameters in the linear regression model (22.3.1)–(22.3.3). First, given the normality assumption (22.3.2)–(22.3.4), the likelihood function for the parameters can be represented up to a factor of proportionality by

$$\begin{aligned} L(\boldsymbol{\beta}, \sigma \mid \mathbf{y}, \mathbf{x}) &\propto \frac{1}{\sigma^n} \exp\left[-\frac{1}{2\sigma^2}(\mathbf{y} - \mathbf{x}\boldsymbol{\beta})'(\mathbf{y} - \mathbf{x}\boldsymbol{\beta})\right] \\ &\propto \frac{1}{\sigma^n} \exp\left[-\frac{1}{2\sigma^2}[(n-k)\hat{\sigma}^2 + (\boldsymbol{\beta} - \hat{\mathbf{b}})'\mathbf{x}'\mathbf{x}(\boldsymbol{\beta} - \hat{\mathbf{b}})]\right], \end{aligned} \tag{22.3.11}$$

where $\hat{\sigma}^2 = (\mathbf{y} - \mathbf{x}\hat{\mathbf{b}})'(\mathbf{y} - \mathbf{x}\hat{\mathbf{b}})/(n-k)$ and $\hat{\mathbf{b}} = (\mathbf{x}'\mathbf{x})^{-1}\mathbf{x}'\mathbf{y}$. After combination of the prior PDF (22.3.7) and the likelihood function-data PDF (22.3.11) using Bayes theorem, the joint posterior PDF for $\mathbf{B}$ and Σ is then defined to be

$$p(\boldsymbol{\beta}, \sigma \mid \mathbf{y}, \mathbf{x}) \propto \frac{1}{\sigma^{n+1}} \exp\left[-\frac{1}{2\sigma^2}[(n-k)\hat{\sigma}^2 + (\boldsymbol{\beta} - \hat{\mathbf{b}})'\mathbf{x}'\mathbf{x}(\boldsymbol{\beta} - \hat{\mathbf{b}})]\right]. \tag{22.3.12}$$

It follows directly from the definition of a conditional probability density function that the *conditional* posterior PDF for **B**, given σ, is a k-dimensional multivariate normal PDF with mean **B** and covariance $\sigma^2(\mathbf{x}'\mathbf{x})^{-1}$,

$$\mathrm{p}(\boldsymbol{\beta} \mid \sigma, \mathbf{y}, \mathbf{x}) \propto \exp\left[-\frac{(\boldsymbol{\beta}-\hat{\mathbf{b}})'\mathbf{x}'\mathbf{x}(\boldsymbol{\beta}-\hat{\mathbf{b}})}{2\sigma^2}\right]. \qquad (22.3.13)$$

► **Example 22.3.1:** Consider the statistical model $\mathrm{Y}_i = \theta + \varepsilon_i$ and $\varepsilon_i \sim \text{iid}\,\mathrm{N}(0, 1)$ for $i = 1, 2, \ldots, n$. Assume our prior information on θ is diffuse and use the improper uniform prior $\mathrm{p}(\theta) \propto \mathrm{c}$. The likelihood function can be expressed as

$$\mathrm{L}(\theta \mid \mathbf{y}) = (2\pi)^{-n/2} \exp\left\{-\frac{1}{2}[(n-1)\hat{\sigma}^2 + n(\theta - \bar{y})^2]\right\},$$

where $\bar{y} = n^{-1}\sum_{i=1}^{n} \mathrm{y}_i$ and $\hat{\sigma}^2 = \sum_{i=1}^{n}(\mathrm{y}_i - \bar{y})^2/(n-1)$. The kernel of the posterior PDF for θ can be expressed as

$$\mathrm{p}(\theta \mid \mathbf{y}) \propto \exp[-n(\theta - \bar{\mathrm{y}})^2/2],$$

which is in the form of a normal distribution with posterior mean $\bar{\mathrm{y}}$. Note that the posterior mean is equal to the ML estimate of θ, and the posterior variance equals $1/n$. Note further that, although the prior indicates that all of the values on the real line are equally plausible for the value of θ, the posterior distribution for θ is very informative regarding the value of θ, even for moderate sample sizes. For example, according to the posterior PDF, if $n = 25$, the value of θ is contained in the interval $[\bar{\mathrm{y}} - .4, \bar{\mathrm{y}} + .4]$ with posterior probability .95. The GAUSS program C22Scalr.gss (provided in the examples manual) graphically presents the posterior PDF and outlines other properties of the postdata distribution.

22.3.4. Marginal Posteriors

Because σ is unknown, we may integrate (22.3.12) with respect to σ, using the substitution $z = \sigma^{-2}$ and noting that $\int_0^\infty z^c \mathrm{e}^{-\mathrm{a}z}\,\mathrm{d}z = \frac{\Gamma(c+1)}{a^{c+1}}$ for $c > -1$ $a > 0$ and gamma function $\Gamma(\cdot)$, to obtain the *marginal* posterior PDF for the random vector **B** as

$$\begin{aligned}\mathrm{p}(\boldsymbol{\beta} \mid \mathbf{y}, \mathbf{x}) &= \int_0^\infty \mathrm{p}(\boldsymbol{\beta}, \sigma \mid \mathbf{y}, \mathbf{x})\,\mathrm{d}\sigma \\ &\propto [(n-k)\hat{\sigma}^2 + (\boldsymbol{\beta}-\hat{\mathbf{b}})'\mathbf{x}'\mathbf{x}(\boldsymbol{\beta}-\hat{\mathbf{b}})]^{-n/2} \\ &\propto [v + (\boldsymbol{\beta}-\hat{\mathbf{b}})'\hat{\sigma}^{-2}\mathbf{x}'\mathbf{x}(\boldsymbol{\beta}-\hat{\mathbf{b}})]^{-(v+k)/2},\end{aligned} \qquad (22.3.14)$$

which is in the form of a multivariate **T** PDF with mean vector $\hat{\mathbf{b}}$, covariance matrix $\frac{\hat{\sigma}^2(n-k)}{(n-k-2)}(\mathbf{x}'\mathbf{x})^{-1}$, and $v = n-k$ degrees of freedom. To be specific, note that the k-variate multivariate **T**-distribution with v degrees of freedom is characterized in general by the kernel

$$\mathrm{p}(\boldsymbol{\beta}) = \mathrm{Mult}\mathbf{T}(\boldsymbol{\beta} \mid \boldsymbol{\mu}, \mathbf{h}, v, \mathrm{k}) \propto [v + (\boldsymbol{\beta}-\boldsymbol{\mu})'\mathbf{h}(\boldsymbol{\beta}-\boldsymbol{\mu})]^{-(v+k)/2} \qquad (22.3.15)$$

where

$$\mathrm{E}(\mathbf{B}) = \boldsymbol{\mu} \quad \text{for } v > 1, \tag{22.3.16}$$

$$\mathbf{cov}(\mathbf{B}) = \frac{v}{v-2}\mathbf{h}^{-1} \quad \text{for } v > 2, \tag{22.3.17}$$

and the matrix $\mathbf{h}$ is positive definite symmetric. In the case at hand, $v = n - k$ and $\mathbf{h} = \hat{\sigma}^{-2}\mathbf{x}'\mathbf{x}$, which then justifies why (22.3.14) is in the form of a multivariate **T**-distribution and also justifies the previous definition of the posterior covariance matrix for **B**.

The marginal posterior for **B** can be used to make posterior inferences about subsets or functions of the parameter vector $\boldsymbol{\beta}$ without having to consider σ, which is a *nuisance parameter* in this context. The marginal PDF for making inferences about individual parameter vector elements β_i can be obtained by integrating $\mathrm{p}(\boldsymbol{\beta} \mid \mathbf{y}, \mathbf{x})$ with respect to every β_j, $j \neq i$, and the result is a univariate student's T-distribution with $n - k$ degrees of freedom. Specifically, the marginal posterior distribution of $(\mathrm{B}_j - \mu_j)/[h^{-1}[j, j]]^{1/2}$ values is a student's (central) T-distribution with $(n - k)$ degrees of freedom, $[h^{-1}[j, j]]^{1/2}$ being the square root of the (j, j)th entry in $\mathbf{h}^{-1}$.

More generally, for purposes of generating inference relating to values of $\boldsymbol{\beta}$ or $\mathbf{c}\boldsymbol{\beta}$, for any conformable matrix $\mathbf{c}$ with full-row rank j, it can be shown that

$$k^{-1}(\mathbf{B} - \hat{\mathbf{b}})'\hat{\sigma}^{-2}\mathbf{x}'\mathbf{x}(\mathbf{B} - \hat{\mathbf{b}}) \sim \mathrm{F}(k, n - k, 0), \tag{22.3.18}$$

$$j^{-1}[\mathbf{c}(\mathbf{B} - \hat{\mathbf{b}})]'[\hat{\sigma}^2\mathbf{c}(\mathbf{x}'\mathbf{x})^{-1}\mathbf{c}']^{-1}[\mathbf{c}(\mathbf{B} - \hat{\mathbf{b}})] \sim \mathrm{F}(j, n - k, 0), \tag{22.3.19}$$

and

$$\mathbf{B}_* \equiv \mathbf{cB} - \mathbf{r} \sim \mathrm{MultT}(\boldsymbol{\beta}_* \mid \mathbf{c}\boldsymbol{\mu} - \mathbf{r}, [\mathbf{ch}^{-1}\mathbf{c}']^{-1}, v, j). \tag{22.3.20}$$

This follows from two fundamental results relating to properties of multivariate **T**-distributed random variables. First, if a k-variate random variable **B** has the multivariate **T** distribution with v degrees of freedom, as in (22.3.15), then $k^{-1}(\mathbf{B} - \boldsymbol{\mu})'\mathbf{h}(\mathbf{B} - \boldsymbol{\mu}) \sim \mathrm{F}(k, v, 0)$ (see Zellner (1971), p. 385). Second, if **B** has the multivariate **T**-distribution in (22.3.15), it follows that

$$\mathbf{B}_* \equiv \mathbf{cB} - \mathbf{r} \sim \mathrm{p}(\boldsymbol{\beta}_*) \propto [v + [\boldsymbol{\beta}_* - (\mathbf{c}\boldsymbol{\mu} - \mathbf{r})]'[\mathbf{ch}^{-1}\mathbf{c}']^{-1}[\boldsymbol{\beta}_* - (\mathbf{c}\boldsymbol{\mu} - \mathbf{r})]]^{-(v+k)/2}, \tag{22.3.21}$$

which is a multivariate **T**-distribution with $\mathbf{h}$ replaced by $[\mathbf{ch}^{-1}\mathbf{c}']^{-1}$ and $\boldsymbol{\mu}$ replaced by $\mathbf{c}\boldsymbol{\mu} - \mathbf{r}$. In general, linear combinations of multivariate **T**-distributed random variables are themselves multivariate **T**-distributed with means and covariance matrix equal to what would be expected from standard moment results relating to linear combinations of random variables (Johnson, 1987, p. 108).

Note that the distributional results in (22.3.18) and (22.3.19) are similar to the classical F-test results for the linear regression model with a normally distributed noise component. Of course the interpretation of (22.3.18) and (22.3.19) is in a Bayesian conditional-postdata context, the F-distribution being the posterior distribution of the quadratic function of **B** or **cB**.

The marginal PDF for σ may be computed in similar fashion by integrating $\boldsymbol{\beta}$ out of the joint posterior (22.3.12) by means of

$$\begin{aligned} p(\sigma \mid \mathbf{y}, \mathbf{x}) &= \int_{R^k} p(\boldsymbol{\beta}, \sigma \mid \mathbf{y}, \mathbf{x})\, d\boldsymbol{\beta} \\ &\propto \sigma^{-(n-k+1)} \exp\left[-\frac{(n-k)\hat{\sigma}^2}{2\sigma^2}\right], \end{aligned} \tag{22.3.22}$$

which is the kernel of an inverted-square root gamma PDF and thus the distribution of $W = Z^{-1/2}$, when Z is gamma distributed. This marginal posterior PDF can be used to form posterior inferences about the unknown noise variance parameter.

We note here that, if the analyst had adopted the prior distribution $p(\boldsymbol{\beta}, \sigma) = 1$ instead of $p(\boldsymbol{\beta}, \sigma) \propto \sigma^{-1}$, the only thing that would change in the definition of the marginal posterior distribution for $\boldsymbol{\beta}$ (22.3.14) is that the exponent of the bracketed expression would be $(n - 1)/2$ instead of $n/2$. Consequently, the degrees of freedom become $v = n - k - 1$ instead of $v = n - k$. It follows that the covariance matrix of the multivariate $\mathbf{T}$ distribution would then become $\frac{\hat{\sigma}^2(n-k-1)}{(n-k-3)}(\mathbf{x}'\mathbf{x})^{-1}$ instead of $\frac{\hat{\sigma}^2(n-k)}{(n-k-2)}(\mathbf{x}'\mathbf{x})^{-1}$ with the $\mathbf{T}$ distribution having $n - k - 1$ instead of $n - k$ degrees of freedom. It would be useful for the reader to demonstrate these results and indicate the minor degrees of freedom changes that are then necessary in the F-distribution results (22.3.18) and (22.3.19). It is clear that any differences in posterior inferences between Bayesian analyses based on the two different prior distributions will be small even for moderate n and will vanish as n increases.

► **Example 22.3.2:** To demonstrate the interpretation of posterior distributions based on diffuse or flat prior distributions, we provide the GAUSS program C22Flat.gss in the examples manual. For a given sample of data for a linear regression model (sample size selected by the user), GAUSS plots the marginal posterior distributions for elements of $\boldsymbol{\beta}$ and σ. The program also examines some of the characteristics (e.g., tail probabilities) of the posterior distributions.

Given this basic Bayesian result for the linear regression model, we next examine the more interesting case of an informative prior distribution on some of the parameters.

22.4. Bayesian Regression Analysis under Normality and Conjugate Informative Priors

Given the general procedures for combining prior and sample information that were developed in Section 22.3, we now assume that we have an informative prior PDF for values of the unknown $\boldsymbol{\beta}$ vector and σ parameter based on conceptual or preexperiment information of some form. In particular, we assume that the prior distribution is of the form

$$p(\boldsymbol{\beta}, \sigma) \propto \sigma^{-m} \exp\left\{-\frac{1}{2\sigma^2}[\eta + (\boldsymbol{\beta} - \boldsymbol{\mu})'\boldsymbol{\Psi}^{-1}(\boldsymbol{\beta} - \boldsymbol{\mu})]\right\}, \tag{22.4.1}$$

where $\eta > 0$ and $\boldsymbol{\Psi}$ is symmetric positive definite. This family of joint prior density functions represents the *conjugate family* of prior density functions for the normal distribution-based likelihood function (22.3.11).

By *conjugate family* of priors, we mean a family of prior distributions that, when combined with the likelihood function via Bayes theorem, result in a posterior distribution that is of the same parametric family of distributions as the prior distribution. Note this is a useful property for a prior distribution to possess if the prior distribution function is a tractable function of $(\boldsymbol{\beta}, \sigma)$ in terms of integration operations, for then the posterior distribution will inherit this tractability. Conjugate priors are sometimes referred to as *convenience priors* in recognition of this integration facilitation, which makes posterior analysis analytically "convenient." In the case at hand, the prior distribution (22.4.1), although not particularly simple to integrate with respect to $\boldsymbol{\beta}$, σ, or both, is nonetheless at least analytically tractable with respect to integration. As will be evident ahead, the use of the conjugate prior (22.4.1) allows the posterior distribution to inherit this tractability.

To provide some additional motivation for the interpretation and use of the joint prior (22.4.1), first note that this prior can be represented as the product of the conditional prior on $\boldsymbol{\beta}$ values, $\mathrm{p}(\boldsymbol{\beta} \mid \sigma)$, and the marginal prior on σ values, $\mathrm{p}(\sigma)$, as

$$\mathrm{p}(\boldsymbol{\beta}, \sigma) = \mathrm{p}(\boldsymbol{\beta} \mid \sigma)\mathrm{p}(\sigma), \tag{22.4.2}$$

where

$$\mathrm{p}(\boldsymbol{\beta} \mid \sigma) = \frac{1}{(2\pi)^{k/2}\sigma^k[\det(\boldsymbol{\Psi})]^{1/2}} \exp\left[-\frac{1}{2\sigma^2}(\boldsymbol{\beta} - \boldsymbol{\mu})'\boldsymbol{\Psi}^{-1}(\boldsymbol{\beta} - \boldsymbol{\mu})\right] \tag{22.4.3}$$

and

$$\mathrm{p}(\sigma) \propto \sigma^{-(m-k)} \exp\left[-\frac{\eta}{2\sigma^2}\right], \quad \text{for } \sigma > 0, \tag{22.4.4}$$

where $m > k + 1$ and $\eta > 0$. The kernel of the prior distribution on σ values is of the inverted-square root gamma form, that is, this is the distribution of $\mathrm{W} = \mathrm{Z}^{-1/2}$ when Z has a gamma distribution. The prior conditional distribution (22.4.3) on $\boldsymbol{\beta}$ values, given σ, is multivariate normal with prior mean vector $\boldsymbol{\mu}$ and covariance matrix $\sigma^2\boldsymbol{\Psi}$.

The marginal prior distribution of $\mathbf{B}$ can be found by integrating σ out of (22.4.1), using the substitution $z = \sigma^{-2}$, and noting that $\int_0^\infty z^c \mathrm{e}^{-\mathrm{a}z}\,dz = \frac{\Gamma(c+1)}{\mathrm{a}^{c+1}}$ for $c > -1$ and $\mathrm{a} > 0$, where $\Gamma(\cdot)$ is the gamma function, to yield

$$\begin{aligned}\mathrm{p}(\boldsymbol{\beta}) &\propto [\eta + (\boldsymbol{\beta} - \boldsymbol{\mu})'\boldsymbol{\Psi}^{-1}(\boldsymbol{\beta} - \boldsymbol{\mu})]^{-(m-1)/2} \\ &\propto \left[v + (\boldsymbol{\beta} - \boldsymbol{\mu})'\frac{v}{\eta}\boldsymbol{\Psi}^{-1}(\boldsymbol{\beta} - \boldsymbol{\mu})\right]^{-(v+k)/2}.\end{aligned} \tag{22.4.5}$$

This marginal prior is of the multivariate **T**-distribution form, as can be verified by again referring to the general multivariate **T**-distribution representation discussed in (22.3.15)–(22.3.17). In particular, in the case at hand $v = m - k - 1$ and $\mathbf{h} = (\frac{m-k-1}{\eta})\boldsymbol{\Psi}^{-1}$. Therefore, the kernel (22.4.5) represents a multivariate **T**-distribution with mean and covariance matrix given by

$$\mathrm{E}(\mathbf{B}) = \boldsymbol{\mu} \quad \text{for } m > k + 2, \tag{22.4.6}$$

and

$$\mathbf{cov}(\mathbf{B}) = \left(\frac{\eta}{m-k-3}\right)\boldsymbol{\Psi} \quad \text{for} \quad m > k+3. \tag{22.4.7}$$

The marginal prior distribution of $(\mathrm{B}_j - \mu_j)/[h^{-1}[j,j]]^{1/2}$ is a student's (central) T-distribution with $(m-k-1)$ degrees of freedom, $[h^{-1}[j,j]]^{1/2}$ being the square root of the (j, j)th entry in $\mathbf{h}^{-1}$.

In practice, the analyst must specify the parameters of the prior distribution $\mathrm{p}(\boldsymbol{\beta}, \sigma)$. This involves setting the parameters m and η in the inverted gamma distribution (22.4.4) as well as specifying the mean vector $\boldsymbol{\mu}$ and the positive definite symmetric $\boldsymbol{\Psi}$ matrix that determines the covariance matrix (22.4.7) of the multivariate **T**-distribution (22.4.5). In the case of the *empirical Bayes procedure*, which we discuss later, these parameters are estimated from the data.

22.4.1. The Joint Posterior Distribution under the Conjugate Prior

Combining the prior information represented by the conjugate prior (22.4.1) with the sample information represented by the likelihood function (22.3.11) through an application of Bayes theorem, the joint posterior distribution of $(\mathbf{B}, \Sigma)$ is given by

$$\mathrm{p}(\boldsymbol{\beta}, \sigma \mid \mathbf{y}, \mathbf{x}) \propto \frac{1}{\sigma^{n+m}} \exp\left[-\frac{1}{2\sigma^2}[(n-k)\hat{\sigma}^2 + (\boldsymbol{\beta} - \hat{\mathbf{b}})'\mathbf{x}'\mathbf{x}(\boldsymbol{\beta} - \hat{\mathbf{b}})]\right]$$
$$\times \exp\left[-\frac{1}{2\sigma^2}[\eta + (\boldsymbol{\beta} - \boldsymbol{\mu})'\boldsymbol{\Psi}^{-1}(\boldsymbol{\beta} - \boldsymbol{\mu})]\right], \tag{22.4.8}$$

where $\hat{\sigma}^2 = (\mathbf{y} - \mathbf{x}\hat{\mathbf{b}})'(\mathbf{y} - \mathbf{x}\hat{\mathbf{b}})/(n-k)$ and $\hat{\mathbf{b}} = (\mathbf{x}'\mathbf{x})^{-1}\mathbf{x}'\mathbf{y}$. The expression for the posterior distribution can be rewritten in the algebraically equivalent form

$$\mathrm{p}(\boldsymbol{\beta}, \sigma \mid \mathbf{y}, \mathbf{x}) \propto \frac{1}{\sigma^{n+m}} \exp\left\{-\frac{1}{2\sigma^2}[(\boldsymbol{\beta} - \boldsymbol{\beta}_*)'(\boldsymbol{\Psi}^{-1} + \mathbf{x}'\mathbf{x})(\boldsymbol{\beta} - \boldsymbol{\beta}_*) + \xi]\right\}, \tag{22.4.9}$$

where

$$\boldsymbol{\beta}_* = (\boldsymbol{\Psi}^{-1} + \mathbf{x}'\mathbf{x})^{-1}(\boldsymbol{\Psi}^{-1}\boldsymbol{\mu} + \mathbf{x}'\mathbf{x}\hat{\mathbf{b}}), \tag{22.4.10}$$

and

$$\xi = \eta + (n-k)\hat{\sigma}^2 + \boldsymbol{\mu}'\boldsymbol{\Psi}^{-1}\boldsymbol{\mu} + \hat{\mathbf{b}}'\mathbf{x}'\mathbf{x}\hat{\mathbf{b}} - \boldsymbol{\beta}_*'(\boldsymbol{\Psi}^{-1} + \mathbf{x}'\mathbf{x})\boldsymbol{\beta}_*. \tag{22.4.11}$$

A proof of the equivalence of (22.4.9) and (22.4.8) can be obtained directly by expanding the exponents of both expressions and noting that they match term for term.

22.4.2. The Marginal Posteriors

The marginal posterior distribution for **B** can be obtained by integrating out σ from (22.4.9), using the substitution $z = \sigma^{-2}$, and noting that $\int_0^\infty z^c \mathrm{e}^{-\mathrm{a}z}\mathrm{d}z = \frac{\Gamma(c+1)}{\mathrm{a}^{c+1}}$ for $c > -1$

and $a > 0$, to yield

$$\mathrm{p}(\boldsymbol{\beta}\,|\,\mathbf{y}) \propto [\xi + (\boldsymbol{\beta} - \boldsymbol{\beta}_*)'(\boldsymbol{\Psi}^{-1} + \mathbf{x}'\mathbf{x})(\boldsymbol{\beta} - \boldsymbol{\beta}_*)]^{-(n+m-1)/2}$$
$$\propto \left[v + (\boldsymbol{\beta} - \boldsymbol{\beta}_*)'\frac{v}{\xi}(\boldsymbol{\Psi}^{-1} + \mathbf{x}'\mathbf{x})(\boldsymbol{\beta} - \boldsymbol{\beta}_*)\right]^{-(v+k)/2}, \qquad (22.4.12)$$

where $v = n + m - k - 1$. Analagous to (22.3.15)–(22.3.17), the posterior is a multivariate **T**-distribution with

$$\mathrm{E}(\mathbf{B}\,|\,\mathbf{y}) = \boldsymbol{\beta}_* \quad \text{for} \quad (n + m - k) > 2, \qquad (22.4.13)$$

and

$$\mathbf{cov}(\mathbf{B}\,|\,\mathbf{y}) = \left(\frac{\xi}{n + m - k - 3}\right)(\boldsymbol{\Psi}^{-1} + \mathbf{x}'\mathbf{x})^{-1} \quad \text{for } n + m - k > 3, \qquad (22.4.14)$$

with $\mathbf{h} = [\frac{v}{\xi}(\boldsymbol{\Psi}^{-1} + \mathbf{x}'\mathbf{x})]$. The marginal posterior distribution of $(\mathrm{B}_j - \beta_{*j})/[h^{-1}[j, j]]^{1/2}$ is a student's (univariate) T-distribution with $v = (n + m - k - 1)$ degrees of freedom. It can also be shown that

$$\frac{(n + m - k - 1)}{k\xi}(\mathbf{B} - \boldsymbol{\beta}_*)'(\boldsymbol{\Psi}^{-1} + \mathbf{x}'\mathbf{x})(\mathbf{B} - \boldsymbol{\beta}_*) \sim \mathrm{F}(k, v, 0), \qquad (22.4.15)$$

$$\frac{(n + m - k - 1)}{j\xi}[\mathbf{c}(\mathbf{B} - \boldsymbol{\beta}_*)]'[\mathbf{c}(\boldsymbol{\Psi}^{-1} + \mathbf{x}'\mathbf{x})^{-1}\mathbf{c}']^{-1}[\mathbf{c}(\mathbf{B} - \boldsymbol{\beta}_*)] \sim \mathrm{F}(j, v, 0), \qquad (22.4.16)$$

and

$$\mathbf{B}_c \equiv \mathbf{cB} - \mathbf{r} \sim \mathrm{Mult}\mathbf{T}(\boldsymbol{\beta}_c\,|\,\mathbf{c}\boldsymbol{\beta}_* - \mathbf{r}, [\mathbf{c}(\boldsymbol{\Psi}^{-1} + \mathbf{x}'\mathbf{x})^{-1}\mathbf{c}']^{-1}, v, j). \qquad (22.4.17)$$

This again follows from the general results relating to multivariate **T**-distributions discussed earlier (22.3.20). Posterior analysis of propositions relating to $\boldsymbol{\beta}$, including posterior credible regions and hypothesis tests (see Chapter 24), can be based on the preceding posterior distribution results. The marginal posterior distribution of σ is obtained by integrating out $\boldsymbol{\beta}$ from the joint posterior (22.4.9), as in (22.3.22).

► **Example 22.4.1:** To demonstrate the interpretation of posterior distributions based on informative prior distributions, we provide the GAUSS program C22Info.gss in the examples manual. For a given sample of data for a linear regression model (sample size selected by the user), GAUSS plots the marginal posterior distributions for elements of $\boldsymbol{\beta}$ and σ^2. The program also examines some of the characteristics (e.g., tail probabilities) of the posterior distributions and compares these with the posterior distribution for the diffuse or flat prior case.

22.5. Bayesian Point Estimates

Given the posterior PDF for $\boldsymbol{\Theta}$, if a point estimate for the parameter vector $\boldsymbol{\theta}$ is desired, the Bayesian approach is to choose a nonrandom estimate $\hat{\boldsymbol{\theta}} = \hat{\boldsymbol{\theta}}(\mathbf{y})$ so as to minimize the posterior expectation of an appropriate loss function $\ell(\mathbf{\Theta}, \hat{\boldsymbol{\theta}})$. The Bayes criterion is thus to find the $\hat{\boldsymbol{\theta}}$ that solves

$$\min_{\hat{\theta}} \mathrm{E}[\ell(\mathbf{\Theta}, \hat{\boldsymbol{\theta}})] = \min_{\hat{\theta}} \left[\int_{\theta \in \Omega} \ell(\boldsymbol{\theta}, \hat{\boldsymbol{\theta}}) \mathrm{p}(\boldsymbol{\theta} \mid y)\, \mathrm{d}\boldsymbol{\theta} \right]. \tag{22.5.1}$$

The value of $\hat{\boldsymbol{\theta}}$ that minimizes (22.5.1), say $\hat{\boldsymbol{\theta}}(\boldsymbol{y})$, is called the optimal posterior or post-data Bayes estimate of $\boldsymbol{\theta}$. If, for example, a quadratic loss function $\ell(\mathbf{\Theta}, \hat{\boldsymbol{\theta}}) = (\mathbf{\Theta} - \hat{\boldsymbol{\theta}})'$ $(\mathbf{\Theta} - \hat{\boldsymbol{\theta}})$ is used, the optimal Bayes estimate is the mean vector of the posterior probability distribution of $\mathbf{\Theta}$. This follows from the first-order necessary conditions for the Bayesian point estimation problem (defining by differentiating the integral in (22.5.1) with respect to $\hat{\boldsymbol{\theta}}$), which require that

$$\int_{\theta \in \Omega} (\boldsymbol{\theta} - \hat{\boldsymbol{\theta}}) \mathrm{p}(\boldsymbol{\theta} \mid \boldsymbol{y})\, \mathrm{d}\boldsymbol{\theta} = \mathbf{0}, \tag{22.5.2}$$

and thus the optimal decision rule is the mean vector of the posterior distribution

$$\hat{\boldsymbol{\theta}} = \int_{\theta \in \mathrm{R}^k} \boldsymbol{\theta} \mathrm{p}(\boldsymbol{\theta} \mid \boldsymbol{y})\, \mathrm{d}\boldsymbol{\theta}. \tag{22.5.3}$$

The posterior mean is also readily shown to be the optimal Bayes point estimate under the more general weighted quadratic loss function $\ell(\mathbf{\Theta}, \hat{\boldsymbol{\theta}}) = (\mathbf{\Theta} - \hat{\boldsymbol{\theta}})' \mathbf{m} (\mathbf{\Theta} - \hat{\boldsymbol{\theta}})$, where $\mathbf{m}$ is any fixed positive definite symmetric weighting matrix.

We emphasize that the functional form of the optimal Bayes estimate will generally change with the choice of the loss function. For example, if θ is a scalar, $\mathrm{p}(\theta \mid \boldsymbol{y})$ is a continuous posterior PDF with finite support, and the absolute value loss function, $\ell(\theta, \hat{\theta}) = |\theta - \hat{\theta}|$ is utilized, then the value of $\hat{\theta}$ that minimizes expected posterior loss (22.5.1) is the *median*, not the mean, of the posterior distribution (see Exercise 22.3). Alternatively, the value of $\hat{\theta}$ that minimizes expected posterior loss is the *mode* of the posterior distribution under the zero-one loss function, $\ell(\theta, \hat{\theta}) = 1 - \mathrm{I}_{\theta}(\hat{\theta})$.

In terms of the regression model, the posterior mean, which is the Bayes estimator of $\boldsymbol{\beta}$ under squared-error loss, is seen from (22.4.10) to be a matrix-weighted average of the prior mean $\boldsymbol{\mu}$ and the least-squares or MLE estimate, $\hat{\mathbf{b}}$. The relative weights in forming the average depend on the conditional (on σ) prior covariance matrix of $\boldsymbol{\beta}$ and the covariance matrix of the data-based MLE $\hat{\boldsymbol{\beta}}$. Because (22.4.10) minimizes expected quadratic risk and the prior distribution is proper, the Bayes estimator is an admissible estimator under this risk function (see Section (22.5.2)). The form of the Bayes estimator (22.4.10) suggests it can be viewed as a shrinkage-type estimator. Note, for example, how $\boldsymbol{\beta}_*$ shrinks the ML estimate $\hat{\mathbf{b}}$ towards the prior mean vector $\boldsymbol{\mu}$ in a manner controlled by the choice of the prior covariance matrix $\mathbf{\Psi}$. In terms of the ridge estimator (Hoerl and Kennard, 1970) discussed in Chapter 18, we can see that (22.4.10) is a generalized ridge estimator for $\boldsymbol{\beta}$. If we also let $\boldsymbol{\mu} = \mathbf{0}$ and $\mathbf{\Psi} = \mathrm{k}^{-1}\mathbf{I}_{\mathrm{k}}$, then the conventional ridge estimator results.

22.5.1. Minimum Expected Risk

In addition to minimizing posterior expected loss, the Bayesian point estimator has several additional attractive properties. Although not necessarily of interest to the pure Bayesian, consider the predata risk function

$$R_{\hat{\theta}}(\boldsymbol{\theta}) = \int_{R^n} \ell(\boldsymbol{\theta}, \hat{\boldsymbol{\theta}}(\mathbf{y}))f(\mathbf{y} \mid \boldsymbol{\theta})\, d\mathbf{y}, \quad \text{for } \boldsymbol{\theta} \in \Omega. \tag{22.5.4}$$

Note that the predata risk function is averaging loss over all possible contingencies for the sample data outcome $\mathbf{y}$ and is thus very much a classical, predata concept. It is relatively straightforward to show that the Bayesian estimator minimizes the expected risk

$$\begin{aligned} ER_{\hat{\theta}}(\boldsymbol{\theta}) &= \int_{\Omega} \left[\int_{R^n} \ell(\boldsymbol{\theta}, \hat{\boldsymbol{\theta}}(y))f(y \mid \boldsymbol{\theta})\, dy \right] p(\boldsymbol{\theta})\, d\boldsymbol{\theta} \\ &= \int_{\Omega} \int_{R^n} \ell(\boldsymbol{\theta}, \hat{\boldsymbol{\theta}}(y))p(\boldsymbol{\theta} \mid y)f_Y(y)\, dy\, d\boldsymbol{\theta} \\ &= \int_{R^n} \left[\int_{\Omega} \ell(\boldsymbol{\theta}, \hat{\boldsymbol{\theta}}(y))p(\boldsymbol{\theta} \mid y)\, d\boldsymbol{\theta} \right] f_Y(y)\, dy. \end{aligned} \tag{22.5.5}$$

Note the second equality follows because $p(\boldsymbol{\theta} \mid y)f_Y(y) \equiv f(y \mid \boldsymbol{\theta})p(\boldsymbol{\theta})$, and the third equality follows upon reversing the order of integration, which is allowable, for example, if $\ell(\cdot)$ is nonnegative valued and integrable and $p(\boldsymbol{\theta})$ is a proper PDF. The Bayesian estimator minimizes expected risk because the bracketed expression following the third equality in (22.5.5) is expected posterior loss and is minimized $\forall \boldsymbol{\theta}$ by the Bayesian estimator $\hat{\boldsymbol{\theta}}(\mathbf{Y})$. The Bayesian estimator then necessarily minimizes the integral of this expected posterior loss for $\boldsymbol{\theta} \in \Omega$, which of course also minimizes expected risk by the equality in (22.5.5).

22.5.2. Admissibility

The fact that the Bayes estimator minimizes expected risk implies that the estimator is *admissible* relative to the risk function based on $\ell(\boldsymbol{\theta}, \hat{\boldsymbol{\theta}})$. This follows by contradiction. For example, suppose that the Bayes estimator was not admissible and thus that there was an alternative estimator that uniformly (i.e., for all $\boldsymbol{\theta} \in \Omega$) dominated the Bayes estimator in terms of risk (22.5.4). It would then necessarily follow that the alternative estimator had lower expected risk, which contradicts our previous observation that the Bayes estimator minimizes expected risk. Thus, the Bayes estimator is admissible. For the argument to be unequivocally true, we must insist that the prior distribution be proper. Sometimes the expected risk in the case of improper priors is *infinite*, even though the expected posterior loss is finite and minimized by the Bayes estimator.

22.5.3. Consistency and Asymptotic Normality

Bayes estimators are generally *consistent* for estimating finite-dimensional parameter vectors. Doob (1949) was apparently the first to prove this result formally, and his results were extended and proven under more general conditions by Schwartz (1965, Theorem 3.2) and Schervish and Seidenfeld (1990, Theorem 2). Their results indicate that if there exists *some* function of the sample data, say $\boldsymbol{t}(\boldsymbol{y})$, for which $\boldsymbol{t}(\boldsymbol{Y}) \stackrel{p}{\rightarrow} \boldsymbol{\theta}_0$, where $\boldsymbol{\theta}_0$ is the true value of the finite-dimensional parameter vector $\boldsymbol{\theta}$, then

$$\lim_{n\to\infty} \int_{\theta \in A} dP(\boldsymbol{\theta} \mid \mathbf{Y}) \stackrel{as}{\rightarrow} 1 \tag{22.5.6}$$

for every integrable open neighborhood set A of parameter values around $\boldsymbol{\theta}_0$, where it is assumed that $\boldsymbol{\theta}_0$ is in the support of the prior distribution on $\boldsymbol{\theta}$. Intuitively, this result means that so long as *some* consistent estimator (in the classical sense) of $\boldsymbol{\theta}$ *exists*, the posterior distribution of the parameter vector will concentrate on $\boldsymbol{\theta}_0$ with probability 1. It follows that the Bayes estimator (e.g., mean, median, mode, or some other function of the sample data, depending on the loss function chosen) will generate estimates that converge in probability to the true value of $\boldsymbol{\theta}$, and thus the Bayes estimator will consistently estimate $\boldsymbol{\theta}_0$.

The posterior distribution on $\boldsymbol{\theta}$ values is also quite generally *asymptotically normal.* In this context, we simply note the essence of a theorem relating to the asymptotic nature of the posterior distribution, whose proof can be found in Schervish (1995, pp. 437–41), which states that under general conditions, *conditional on* $\mathbf{y}$,

$$\hat{\boldsymbol{\Sigma}}^{-1/2}(\boldsymbol{\Theta} - \hat{\boldsymbol{\theta}}_{\text{MLE}}) \stackrel{d}{\rightarrow} N(\mathbf{0}, \mathbf{I}), \tag{22.5.7}$$

where $\hat{\boldsymbol{\Sigma}}$ is the observed (estimated) MLE covariance matrix

$$\hat{\boldsymbol{\Sigma}} = -\left[\left. \frac{\partial^2 \ln L(\boldsymbol{\theta} \mid \mathbf{y})}{\partial \boldsymbol{\theta} \partial \boldsymbol{\theta}'} \right|_{\hat{\boldsymbol{\theta}}_{\text{MLE}}} \right]^{-1}. \tag{22.5.8}$$

Note carefully that this result relates to the *posterior* distribution of $\boldsymbol{\Theta}$ and is *conditional on the data* $\mathbf{y}$, and thus this is not a direct analog to classical results in which estimators of $\boldsymbol{\theta}$ of the form $\boldsymbol{t}(\boldsymbol{Y})$ are asymptotically normally distributed. However, the result does indicate that as $n \to \infty$, inferences in both the classical and Bayesian contexts will be based ultimately on multivariate normal distribution theory with numerically equivalent covariances matrices.

The previous asymptotic normality result also leads to another large sample similarity between classical and Bayesian estimation and inference procedures. In particular, because $\hat{\boldsymbol{\Sigma}} \to \mathbf{0}$ as $n \to \infty$, it follows that as $\boldsymbol{\Theta} - \hat{\boldsymbol{\theta}}_{\text{MLE}} \stackrel{p}{\rightarrow} \mathbf{0}$ as $n \to \infty$. Thus, as sample sizes increase, estimates based on Bayes estimators and MLEs will converge to one another and be identical in the limit with probability converging to 1. Thus, as $n \to \infty$, Bayesians and classicists will eventually reach the same conclusions regarding the true value of $\boldsymbol{\theta}$.

22.5.4. Comments on Bayes Estimator Properties

Perhaps conspicuous by its absence has been a discussion of the bias properties of Bayes estimators. We emphasize that to a pure Bayesian, the concept of unbiasedness is irrelevant because the idea of a weighted average value of estimator outcomes over all of the potential *predata* possibilities for these outcomes is irrelevant – Bayesians deal with *postdata* inferences. Nonetheless, if one were to contemplate how the Bayes estimator would perform for repeated samples and a fixed prior distribution, there is nothing inherent in the approach that necessarily guarantees unbiasedness across samples – just as in the case of the MLE. Thus, unbiasedness cannot be claimed, although it is possible that unbiasedness is achieved in special cases.

Regarding asymptotics of Bayes estimators, we emphasize that a necessary condition for the Bayes estimator to achieve the asymptotic properties discussed in this section is that the support of the prior distribution contains the true value of $\boldsymbol{\theta}$. This follows because the support of the *posterior* distribution on $\boldsymbol{\theta}$-values cannot be any larger than that of the *prior* distribution, and if the prior distribution does not encompass $\boldsymbol{\theta}_0$, neither does the posterior. Remarkably, other than the positivity and continuity of the prior distribution at $\boldsymbol{\theta}_0$, there is essentially no other functional restriction on the prior needed to achieve all of the asymptotic properties discussed heretofore, and even continuity is not necessary to achieve the consistency property. Thus, the implication for empirical work is that the analyst should take care to specify the support of the prior widely enough to encompass the true $\boldsymbol{\theta}_0$ with substantial confidence. A more complete discussion of Bayesian asymptotics, as it applies to specific cases and general cases, is given in the appendix to this chapter.

22.6. On the Use of Conjugate Priors and Coincidence of Classical and Bayesian Estimates

In Section 22.4 we examined an important but special case in which the likelihood function was analytically tractable and the prior distribution belonged to a tractable conjugate family of distributions, and thus the posterior remained tractable. In applications, it certainly may be the case that a conjugate prior can effectively portray the prior information available for the problem, and tractable posterior analyses will follow. However, one should not opt for convenience at the expense of improperly representing the prior information available. We will examine in Chapter 23 the case of so-called unfriendly priors that result in complex or analytically intractable posteriors. We emphasize that the Bayesian approach outlined in the previous subsections remains intact, except posterior analyses may require computer techniques such as Monte Carlo simulation as opposed to direct analytical solutions.

Although it seems fashionable to emphasize the difference between the Bayes and classical approaches, we now utilize the conjugate prior formulation of Section 22.4 together with the diffuse prior approach of Section 22.3 to underscore the possibility that the two approaches can lead to similar results in finite samples. We consider the case in which the prior information arises from a previous sample from the same DSP as the current data sample and the classical econometrician wishes to combine the two samples for purposes of estimating the $\boldsymbol{\beta}$ parameters of the underlying regression model.

► **Example 22.6.1 (Coincidence of Classical and Bayesian Estimates):** Let $\mathbf{x}_1$ be the explanatory variable values pertaining to a prior sample of data with $\mathbf{x}_2$ then referring to the explanatory variable values corresponding to the current sample of data. Both samples of data are assumed to have arisen from the same linear regression model DSP having iid normal noise components. The sampling model is represented in stacked vertically concatenated form as

$$\begin{bmatrix}\mathbf{y}_1\\ \mathbf{y}_2\end{bmatrix} = \begin{bmatrix}\mathbf{x}_1\\ \mathbf{x}_2\end{bmatrix}\boldsymbol{\beta} + \begin{bmatrix}\varepsilon_1\\ \varepsilon_2\end{bmatrix}. \tag{22.6.1}$$

Given that $\text{var}(\varepsilon_1[i]) = \text{var}(\varepsilon_2[i]) = \sigma^2\ \forall i$, the LS–ML estimate of $\boldsymbol{\beta}$ is

$$\hat{\mathbf{b}} = (\mathbf{x}_1'\mathbf{x}_1 + \mathbf{x}_2'\mathbf{x}_2)^{-1}(\mathbf{x}_1'\mathbf{y}_1 + \mathbf{x}_2'\mathbf{y}_2). \tag{22.6.2}$$

Given the likelihood function pertaining to the first sample of data based on the normality of the noise component of $\mathbf{Y}_1 = \mathbf{x}_1\boldsymbol{\beta} + \varepsilon_1$, the approach of Section 22.3 relating to diffuse or uniformative priors can be followed to derive the posterior of $(\boldsymbol{\beta}, \sigma)$. This leads to the posterior distribution of the form (22.3.12) with $\mathbf{x} = \mathbf{x}_1$ and $\hat{\mathbf{b}} = \hat{\mathbf{b}}_1$. Now, consider this posterior as a *prior distribution* for $(\boldsymbol{\beta}, \sigma)$, and combine this prior with the normal-based likelihood function implied by $\mathbf{Y}_2 = \mathbf{x}_2\boldsymbol{\beta} + \varepsilon_2$ just as we did in Section 22.4 for the case of informative priors. We are then led, as the reader can verify, to the (updated) joint posterior for $(\boldsymbol{\beta}, \sigma)$ of the form (22.4.9) with $\boldsymbol{\Psi}^{-1} = \mathbf{x}_1'\mathbf{x}_1$, $\mathbf{x} = \mathbf{x}_2$, and $\boldsymbol{\mu} = (\mathbf{x}_1'\mathbf{x}_1)^{-1}\mathbf{x}_1'\mathbf{y}_1$. It follows that the posterior mean of the (updated) marginal posterior distribution for $\boldsymbol{\beta}$, (22.4.10) and (22.4.12), is *precisely* the same as the LS–ML estimate (22.6.2), that is, $\boldsymbol{\beta}_* = \hat{\mathbf{b}}$. Thus, the Bayesian and the classical analysts produce exactly the same point estimate for $\boldsymbol{\beta}$, although of course the Bayesian postdata and classical predata interpretations of the meaning of the point value are notably different.

22.7. Concluding Remarks

In the quest to develop a basis for reasoning in situations involving incomplete–partial information, the sampling theory approach to inference currently occupies the high ground. However, Bayes theorem, which encourages us to make use of all of our conceptual and realized information in the learning and decision process, has many attractive features. The basic tenets of Bayesian reasoning involve a probabilistic model of observable quantities, the use of prior or subjective judgments, or both in the form of a PDF, and the use of Bayes theorem for updating knowledge in the light of new information. When information about the DSP exists in the form of a well-defined likelihood function and a natural conjugate prior, this leads to tractable posterior distributions. In this case the Bayes approach to estimation and inference provides a tractable and logically consistent approach for combining data and prior information to make postdata inferences about model parameters. In addition, as we will see in Chapter 23, alternative Bayesian formulations, such as empirical Bayes procedures, exist where it is possible to do well simultaneously in terms of estimation and inference from both Bayesian postdata and classical predata perspectives.

Some who embrace the Classical sampling theory–frequentist approach to estimation and inference do so because of their reluctance to use subjective probability, which is often a component of Bayesian analyses. Others point to the difficulty in assessing or specifying informative prior distributions on model parameters. In the final analysis, whether one takes the classical or Bayesian approach, any statistical analysis generally involves a great deal of prior–nonsample information imposed on the problem by the analyst. So perhaps the question is not *whether* to use prior–nonsample information but *how* best to combine this type of information with sample information in the information recovery process. In this context, the Bayes approach offers a systematic, internally consistent method of proceeding that contains both learning and decision processes.

► **Example 22.7.1:** The GAUSS program C22Comp.gss (provided in the examples manual) is designed to compare the properties and interpretation of Bayes and ML estimates. First, GAUSS requests a sample size (n) and asks the user about the informative prior distribution to be used in the Bayesian analysis. Then, GAUSS reports the ML estimate of $\boldsymbol{\beta}$ and σ^2 as well as the posterior mean of the marginal posterior distributions under diffuse and informative priors. Moreover, the sampling distribution of the ML estimator and the marginal prior and posterior distributions are plotted for comparison purposes.

For those who, in previous study, did not get beyond Bayes theorem, we hope this chapter has provided an understanding of some of the basic components of Bayesian estimation problems and the inverse probability reasoning process. The Bayesian approach can be extended to the analysis of multiple equations, simultaneous equations, nonlinear equations, models with nonspherical noise components, and time series models. The interested reader is directed to the works of Zellner (1997) and Dorfman (1998) for additional reading and references.

22.8. Exercises

22.8.1. Idea Checklist – Knowledge Guides

---

1. What are inverse probabilities and how do they relate to the inverse problem introduced in Chapter 2?
2. What are the differences in the Bayesian and sampling theory approaches to learning from a sample of data?
3. In the Bayesian approach to estimation of parameters in the multivariate normal DSP, can you provide a heuristic explanation for why the posterior mean is a Bayes estimate?
4. In the context of Question 2 and through use of an informative conjugate prior for which the prior mean is zero and the prior covariance is $\gamma^2 \mathbf{I}_k$, what are the characteristics of the resulting estimator?

22.8.2. Problems

22–1 Prove that the posterior *mean* is the optimal Bayes point estimate under the weighted quadratic loss function

$$\ell(\Theta, \hat{\theta}) = (\Theta - \hat{\theta})' \mathbf{m} (\Theta - \hat{\theta}),$$

where $\mathbf{m}$ is any fixed positive definite symmetric weighting matrix.

22–2 Prove that the posterior *median* is the optimal Bayes point estimate of a scalar parameter θ when the loss function is of the absolute error loss type $\ell(\Theta, \hat{\theta}) = |\Theta - \hat{\theta}|$.

22–3 Consider the location and known scale version of the regression model for which $\mathbf{y} \sim \mathrm{N}(\mathbf{x}\beta, \sigma^2\mathbf{I})$ and $\mathbf{x}'\mathbf{x} = 1$. Let the prior density be $\beta \sim \mathrm{N}(0, \sigma^2)$.

a. Develop a sufficient statistic for the data.
b. Develop the Bayes estimator.
c. In general, the Bayes estimator is biased toward the zero prior mean. Derive the mean-squared error of the Bayes estimator and the ML estimator.
d. Discuss the risk characteristics of the resulting estimator.

22–4 The generalized ridge or Type 2 MOR estimator presented in Equation (18.7.9) is $\hat{\mathbf{b}}_{\mathrm{MOR}}(\lambda_{\mathrm{R}}) = [\mathbf{x}'\mathbf{w}\mathbf{x} + \lambda_{\mathrm{R}}\,\mathbf{q}]^{-1}(\mathbf{x}'\mathbf{w}\mathbf{y} + \lambda_{\mathrm{R}}\,\mathbf{q}\,\bar{\boldsymbol{\beta}})$. Under what conditions is $\hat{\mathbf{b}}_{\mathrm{MOR}}(\lambda_{\mathrm{R}})$ equal to the posterior mean (22.4.10)? Discuss the appropriateness of the implied prior for many economic DSP's.

22–5 Use (22.4.10) and (22.4.11) to show that the posterior result in (22.4.9) can be derived from (22.4.8).

22–6 Derive the marginal posterior distribution for σ under the conjugate informative prior (Section 22.4) and compare it with (22.3.22).

22.8.3. Computer Problems

22–1 Identify an economic problem and data set of interest to you and specify a parametric model for the underlying DSP. For this likelihood function, select one or more prior distributions for the model parameters. Using the GAUSS program provided for Example 22.7.1 (C22Comp.gss) as a guide, compute the ML parameter estimates and derive the Bayesian posterior distributions for the parameters. Determine the corresponding Bayesian point estimates under squared-error loss and compare them with the ML estimates.

22–2 For the data you used to complete Problem 1, form two partitions of the sample $(\mathbf{y}_1, \mathbf{x}_1)$ and $(\mathbf{y}_2, \mathbf{x}_2)$. On the basis of the discussion in Example 22.6.1, derive the Bayesian posterior PDF based only on the sample information in the first partition as well as the posterior for the full sample. Using GAUSS, plot one or more of the marginal posterior PDFs based on the first partition and the full sample. How does the introduction of the second set of data alter the posterior distribution? Finally, verify that the Bayesian posterior mean for the full sample is identical with the ML estimate of $\boldsymbol{\beta}$.

22–3 Write a GAUSS program designed to demonstrate the consistency and asymptotic normality properties presented in Sections 22.10.1a and 22.10.1b. In particular, conduct a Monte Carlo simulation of the Bayesian posterior mean and form the box plots and the empirical distribution function (EDFs) of the replicated posterior mean for increasing n. Does the posterior mean appear to converge in probability to the true value of $\boldsymbol{\beta}$? Does the EDF converge to the limiting posterior distribution?

22–4 Given that the inverted-square root gamma distribution is not symmetric, we know that the mean, median, and mode of the posterior distribution for σ (e.g., (22.3.22)) are not identical. For an inverted-square root gamma PDF in generic form

$$\mathrm{f}(y; \alpha, \beta) = \frac{2}{\beta^{\alpha}\Gamma(\alpha)} y^{-(2\alpha+1)} e^{-1/\beta y^2}$$

where $y > 0$ and $\alpha, \beta > 0$. Write a GAUSS procedure designed to return the Bayesian point estimate of σ based on user-provided input of the required sample and prior information as well as an indicator of the loss function (quadratic or zero–one). Also, can you extend the procedure to report the posterior median under the absolute error loss function?

22.9. References

Berger, J. O. (1985), *Statistical Decision Theory and Bayesian Analysis*, (2nd ed.), New York: Springer–Verlag.

Bernardo, J. M., and A. F. M. Smith (1994), *Bayesian Theory*, New York: John Wiley and Sons.

de Groot, M. (1970), *Optimal Statistical Decisions*, New York: McGraw–Hill.

Doob, J. L. (1949), "Application of the Theory of Martingales," in Le Calcul des Probabilite's et ses Applications (pp. 23–7). Paris: Colloques Internationaux du Centre National de la Recherche Scientifique.

Dorfman, J. (1998), *Bayesian Economics Through Numerical Methods: A Guide to Econometrics and Decision-Making with Prior Information*, New York: Springer–Verlag.

Hoerl, A. E., and R. W. Kennard (1970), "Ridge Regression: Biased Estimation for Non-orthogonal Problems," *Technometrics*, Vol. 1, pp. 55–67.

Johnson, M. (1987), *Multivariate Statistical Simulation*, New York: John Wiley and Sons.

Judge, G. G., W. E. Griffiths, R. C. Hill, H. Lütkepohl, and T.-C. Lee (1985), *The Theory and Practice of Econometrics*, (2nd ed.), New York: John Wiley and Sons.

Judge, G. G., R. C. Hill, W. E. Griffiths, H. Lütkepohl, and T.-C. Lee (1988), *Introduction to the Theory and Practice of Econometrics*, (2nd ed.), New York: John Wiley and Sons.

Kass, R. E., and L. Wasserman (1996), "The Selection of Prior Distributions by Formal Rules," *Journal of the American Statistical Association*, Vol. 97, pp. 1343–70.

Schervish, M. J., and T. Seidenfeld (1990), "An Approach to Consensus and Certainty with Increasing Evidence," *Journal of Statistical Planning and Inference*, Vol. 25, pp. 401–14.

Schwartz, L. (1965), "On Bayes Procedures," Zeitschrift für Wahrscheinlich Keits theorie, Vol. 4, pp. 10–26.

Zellner, A. (1971), *An Introduction to Bayesian Inference in Econometrics*, New York: John Wiley and Sons. Reprinted by Krieger Publishing Co., 1987 and by Wiley, 1996.

Zellner, A. (1997), *Bayesian Analysis in Econometrics and Statistics: The Zellner View and Papers*, Cheltenham, UK: Edward Elgar Publishing Ltd.

22.10. Appendix: Bayesian Asymptotics

Regarding the asymptotic behavior of the marginal posterior distribution of $\mathbf{B}$, the posterior PDF will generally tend towards normality as $n \to \infty$. Furthermore, the posterior will generally collapse to a degenerate distribution on the posterior mean, which will coincide with the true value of $\boldsymbol{\beta}$. Thus, Bayes estimators will generally converge to the true value of $\boldsymbol{\beta}$ as the data sample size increases, which is analogous to consistent classical estimators of $\boldsymbol{\beta}$.

In this section we first illustrate the basic concept of Bayesian asymptotics through an examination of the asymptotic behavior of the posterior distributions and the Bayes estimators of $\boldsymbol{\beta}$ in the cases discussed in previous sections in which specific likelihood functions and prior PDFs were involved. Then we provide a more general discussion of Bayesian asymptotics for those readers interested in learning more about the general arguments that lead to the asymptotic normality of posteriors and the consistency of Bayes estimators.

22.10.1. Bayesian Asymptotics: Specific Cases

In this section we examine the asymptotics of marginal posteriors and Bayes estimators of $\boldsymbol{\beta}$ in the cases in which the noise component is normally distributed and the prior distribution on model parameters is the parameter transformation–invariant uninformative prior or the conjugate prior. The posterior distribution and Bayes estimate pairs we examine are then given respectively by (22.3.14) and $\hat{\mathbf{b}} = (\mathbf{x}'\mathbf{x})^{-1}\mathbf{x}'\mathbf{y}$, (22.4.12), and (22.4.10).

It turns out that a few fundamental assumptions and a distributional convergence result relating to the multivariate **T**-distribution unify the asymptotic discussion of all of the aforementioned cases. We first assume that the classical linear model assumptions delineated in Chapter 4 hold. We also assume that $(\mathbf{x}'\mathbf{x})^{-1} \to \mathbf{0}$ so that the LS or MLE estimator $\hat{\boldsymbol{\beta}}$ consistently estimates $\boldsymbol{\beta}$ under the classical assumptions. Finally, we note that, just as the univariate student's **T**-distribution converges to the standard normal distribution as $n \to \infty$, so too does the multivariate **T**-distribution converge to the multivariate normal distribution. Specifically, the convergence result is

$$\text{if } \mathbf{Z} \sim \text{Mult}\mathbf{T}(\mathbf{z} \mid \boldsymbol{\mu}, \mathbf{h}, v, k), \quad \text{then } \mathbf{Z} \xrightarrow{d} \text{N}(\boldsymbol{\mu}, \mathbf{h}^{-1}) \text{ as } v \to \infty. \tag{22.10.1}$$

The validity of (22.10.1) can be established directly by examining a distributional result that we use in our algorithm for generating iid outcomes from the multivariate **T**-distribution in Section 23.4.1b ahead. We note in the construction of the algorithm that $\mathbf{T} = \boldsymbol{\mu} + \mathbf{W}[\frac{Z^2}{v}]^{-1/2}$ has the $\text{Mult}\mathbf{T}(\mathbf{z} \mid \boldsymbol{\mu}, \mathbf{h}, v, k)$ distribution if $\mathbf{W} \sim \text{N}(\mathbf{0}, \mathbf{h}^{-1})$, $Z^2 \sim \text{Chi-square}(v, 0)$, and $\mathbf{W}$ and Z^2 are independent. Now, because $(Z^2/v) \xrightarrow{p} 1$, then $\mathbf{T} \xrightarrow{p} \boldsymbol{\mu} + \mathbf{W} \sim \text{N}(\boldsymbol{\mu}, \mathbf{h}^{-1})$, and because convergence in probability implies convergence in distribution, (22.10.1) is justified.

22.10.1.a. Diffuse Prior Case

Given the preceding results, consider the posterior analysis of Section 22.3 in which the standard uninformative prior $\text{p}(\boldsymbol{\beta}, \sigma) \propto \sigma^{-1}$ was used in obtaining the marginal posterior of $\mathbf{B}$, given by $\text{p}(\boldsymbol{\beta} \mid \mathbf{y}, \mathbf{x}) = \text{Mult}\mathbf{T}(\boldsymbol{\beta} \mid \hat{\mathbf{b}}, \hat{\sigma}^{-2}\mathbf{x}'\mathbf{x}, n - k, k)$. It follows from (22.3.20) that

$$[\hat{\sigma}^2(\mathbf{x}'\mathbf{x})^{-1}]^{-1/2}(\mathbf{B} - \hat{\mathbf{b}}) \sim \text{Mult}\mathbf{T}(\mathbf{0}, \mathbf{I}, n - k, k) \tag{22.10.2}$$

and thus from (22.10.1)

$$[\hat{\sigma}^2(\mathbf{x}'\mathbf{x})^{-1}]^{-1/2}(\mathbf{B} - \hat{\mathbf{b}}) \xrightarrow{d} \text{Normal}(\mathbf{0}, \mathbf{I}) \text{ as } n \to \infty. \tag{22.10.3}$$

Therefore,

$$\mathbf{B} \overset{a}{\sim} \text{Normal}(\hat{\mathbf{b}}, \hat{\sigma}^2(\mathbf{x}'\mathbf{x})^{-1}) \tag{22.10.4}$$

so that the posterior distribution is asymptotically normal. Furthermore, because $(\mathbf{x}'\mathbf{x})^{-1} \to \mathbf{0}$, we have that

$$\mathbf{B} - \hat{\mathbf{b}} \overset{d}{\to} \mathbf{0} \quad \text{and} \quad \hat{\mathbf{b}} \overset{p}{\to} \boldsymbol{\beta}_0 \Rightarrow \mathbf{B} \overset{p}{\to} \boldsymbol{\beta}_0 \tag{22.10.5}$$

so that the Bayes estimator is a consistent estimator of $\boldsymbol{\beta}_0$. Consistency of the Bayes estimator can be proven more directly simply by noting that $\text{E}[\mathbf{B}] \equiv \hat{\mathbf{b}} \overset{p}{\to} \boldsymbol{\beta}_0$, where we are assuming as before that a quadratic loss function is being used in the analysis.

22.10.1.b. Conjugate Prior Case

Now consider the case of the conjugate prior in Section 22.4, where the marginal posterior distribution of $\mathbf{B}$ was given by $\text{p}(\boldsymbol{\beta} \mid \mathbf{y}, \mathbf{x}) = \text{Mult}\mathbf{T}(\boldsymbol{\beta} \mid \mu, \frac{v}{\xi}(\boldsymbol{\Psi}^{-1} + \mathbf{x}'\mathbf{x}), v, k)$. It follows from (22.3.20) that

$$\left(\frac{\xi}{v}\right)^{-1/2} (\boldsymbol{\Psi}^{-1} + \mathbf{x}'\mathbf{x})^{1/2}(\mathbf{B} - \boldsymbol{\beta}_*) \sim \text{Mult}\mathbf{T}(\mathbf{0}, \mathbf{I}, v, k), \tag{22.10.6}$$

where $v = n + m - k - 1$. Then, (22.10.1) implies that

$$\left(\frac{\xi}{v}\right)^{-1/2} (\boldsymbol{\Psi}^{-1} + \mathbf{x}'\mathbf{x})^{1/2}(\mathbf{B} - \boldsymbol{\beta}_*) \overset{d}{\to} \text{N}(\mathbf{0}, \mathbf{I}) \text{ as } n \to \infty, \tag{22.10.7}$$

and $\mathbf{B}$ is asymptotically distributed as

$$\mathbf{B} \overset{a}{\sim} \text{N}\left(\boldsymbol{\beta}_*, \frac{\xi}{v}(\boldsymbol{\Psi}^{-1} + \mathbf{x}'\mathbf{x})^{-1}\right). \tag{22.10.8}$$

Consistency of the Bayes estimator $\boldsymbol{\beta}_*$ can be shown by recalling (22.4.10) and noting that because $(\mathbf{ab})^{-1} = \mathbf{b}^{-1}\mathbf{a}^{-1}$,

$$\boldsymbol{\beta}_* = \underbrace{(\mathbf{I} + \boldsymbol{\Psi}\mathbf{x}'\mathbf{x})^{-1}}_{\to \mathbf{0}} \mu + \underbrace{[(\mathbf{x}'\mathbf{x})^{-1}\boldsymbol{\Psi}^{-1} + \mathbf{I}]^{-1}}_{\to \mathbf{I}} \hat{\mathbf{b}} \to \hat{\mathbf{b}} \overset{p}{\to} \boldsymbol{\beta}_0 \text{ as } n \to \infty. \tag{22.10.9}$$

Regarding convergence of the first term in the sum to $\mathbf{0}$, note that $(\mathbf{I} + \boldsymbol{\Psi}\mathbf{x}'\mathbf{x})^{-1} = \mathbf{I} - [\mathbf{I} + (\mathbf{x}'\mathbf{x})^{-1}\boldsymbol{\Psi}^{-1}]^{-1}$, and because $\boldsymbol{\Psi}$ is a fixed $(k \times k)$ matrix and $(\mathbf{x}'\mathbf{x})^{-1} \to \mathbf{0}$, this inverse matrix converges to $\mathbf{I} - \mathbf{I} = \mathbf{0}$. The inverse matrix expression can be derived from the general matrix inverse result $(\mathbf{a} + \mathbf{b})^{-1} = \mathbf{a}^{-1} - \mathbf{a}^{-1}(\mathbf{a}^{-1} + \mathbf{b}^{-1})^{-1}\mathbf{a}^{-1}$. Convergence of the second term of the sum follows from similar reasoning as well as from the consistency of the LS–MLE estimator $\hat{\boldsymbol{\beta}}$. Consistency can also be shown from the asymptotic normality result (22.10.8) upon noting that $(\boldsymbol{\Psi}^{-1} + \mathbf{x}'\mathbf{x})^{-1} \to \mathbf{0}$ and ξ/v is $\text{O}_\text{p}(1)$.

► **Example 22.10.1:** To examine the large sample properties of Bayesian estimators, we provide the GAUSS program C22Asy.gss in the examples manual. For a series of sample sizes (n) selected by the user, GAUSS compares the marginal posterior distributions for the parameters of a linear regression model to the limiting normal posterior PDF. The user should find that the demonstration supports the result presented in (22.10.1) as applied to the diffuse and informative prior cases.

22.10.1.c. Summary Comments

In summary, the posterior distribution of $\boldsymbol{\beta}$ values is asymptotically normal, and the posterior distribution degenerates to the true value of $\boldsymbol{\beta}$ as $n \to \infty$ in all of our posterior analyses, regardless of whether an uninformative or conjugate prior is used in the analysis. These are asymptotic properties of Bayes estimators that hold quite generally assuming of course that the likelihood is correctly specified. We also found that because $\boldsymbol{\beta}_* \to \hat{\mathbf{b}}$, it is also true that Bayes and LS–ML estimates of $\boldsymbol{\beta}$ become indistinguishable as $n \to \infty$, again regardless of the type of prior PDF used.

22.10.2. Bayesian Asymptotics: General Considerations

There are three basic reasons for considering large sample results in the Bayesian context. First of all, the likelihood component $\mathrm{L}(\boldsymbol{\theta} \mid \boldsymbol{y})$ of the posterior distribution $\mathrm{p}(\boldsymbol{\theta} \mid \boldsymbol{y})$ generally dominates any fixed continuous prior PDF $\mathrm{p}(\boldsymbol{\theta})$ as $n \to \infty$. As such, the large sample behavior of the likelihood function holds the key to the limiting behavior of the posterior distribution, and the asymptotic approximation may provide a convenient yet reasonably accurate representation of the posterior distribution. Second, most researchers share a natural tendency to compare classical and Bayes estimators and test procedures, and one source of common ground is to consider the behavior of the decision rules as the sample becomes infinitely large. Third, although the Bayesian approach to estimation and inference is conditional on the observed sample, one means of evaluating unfriendly posterior distributions is based on asymptotic approximations.

The earliest asymptotic approximations of posterior distributions may be traced back nearly 200 hundred years to Laplace (1812), who proved that posterior distributions for many Bayes problems converge in distribution to a multivariate normal distribution as $n \to \infty$. In time, Laplace's result became known as the Bernstein–von Mises theorem, and a modern proof of the general result was first presented by Le Cam (1953). A large literature on the topic has evolved since Le Cam's early work, and advanced summaries of the relevant literature are presented by Bernardo and Smith (1994, Section 5.3), Hartigan (1983, Chapter 11), Le Cam (1986, Chapter 12), and Lehmann and Casella (1998, Chapter 6). For a basic introduction to the key ideas, readers may wish to consult Section 11 in Lindley (1971). Although the idea of considering sampling performance for unobserved outcomes generally runs against the Bayesian grain, statisticians have used the results to prove that many Bayes estimators are consistent, asymptotically efficient, and asymptotically equivalent to the maximum likelihood estimator.

22.10.2.a. Basic Convergence Result

To examine the limiting posterior distribution in the Bayesian context, we consider a Taylor series expansion of the logarithm of the posterior distribution. We omit the technical details of the argument and focus on the key steps in the proof by Bernardo and Smith (interested readers may also refer to Hartigan, Le Cam, or Lehmann and Casella for alternative proofs). To simplify matters, we assume the observations are independent and identically distributed so that the log-posterior may be stated as

$$\ln(\mathrm{p}(\boldsymbol{\theta} \mid \mathbf{y})) = \ln(\mathrm{p}(\boldsymbol{\theta})) + \sum_{i=1}^{n} \ln(\mathrm{L}(\boldsymbol{\theta} \mid \mathrm{y}_i)). \qquad (22.10.10)$$

To evaluate the right-hand-side terms, we use a second-order Taylor series expansion of the log-prior about the modal value $\bar{\boldsymbol{\theta}}$ and the log-likelihood function about the maximum likelihood estimator $\hat{\boldsymbol{\theta}}_n$ (which are assumed to exist). After reducing terms, the approximation to (22.10.10) may be stated as

$$\ln(\mathrm{p}(\boldsymbol{\theta} \mid \mathbf{y})) = \ln(\mathrm{p}(\bar{\boldsymbol{\theta}})) + \sum_{i=1}^{n} \ln(\mathrm{L}(\hat{\boldsymbol{\theta}}_n \mid \mathrm{y}_i)) + \frac{1}{2}(\boldsymbol{\theta} - \bar{\boldsymbol{\theta}})' \left[\left. \frac{\partial^2 \mathrm{p}(\boldsymbol{\theta})}{\partial \boldsymbol{\theta} \partial \boldsymbol{\theta}'} \right|_{\theta = \bar{\theta}} \right] (\boldsymbol{\theta} - \bar{\boldsymbol{\theta}})$$
$$+ \frac{1}{2}(\boldsymbol{\theta} - \hat{\boldsymbol{\theta}}_n)' \left[\sum_{i=1}^{n} \left. \frac{\partial^2 \ln(\mathrm{L}(\boldsymbol{\theta} \mid \mathrm{y}_i))}{\partial \boldsymbol{\theta} \partial \boldsymbol{\theta}'} \right|_{\theta = \hat{\theta}_n} \right] (\boldsymbol{\theta} - \hat{\boldsymbol{\theta}}_n) \qquad (22.10.11)$$

If we denote the quadratic forms on the right-hand-side of (22.10.11) as Q_1 and Q_{2n}, note that Q_{2n} dominates Q_1 such that $(\mathrm{Q}_1 + \mathrm{Q}_{2n})/\mathrm{Q}_{2n} \to 1$ as $n \to \infty$. Therefore, conditional on the data, the limiting posterior distribution is proportional to

$$\mathrm{p}(\boldsymbol{\theta} \mid \mathbf{y}) \propto \exp\left[\frac{1}{2}(\boldsymbol{\theta} - \hat{\boldsymbol{\theta}}_n)' \left[\sum_{i=1}^{n} \left. \frac{\partial^2 \ln(\mathrm{L}(\boldsymbol{\theta} \mid \mathrm{y}_i))}{\partial \boldsymbol{\theta} \partial \boldsymbol{\theta}'} \right|_{\theta = \hat{\theta}_n} \right] (\boldsymbol{\theta} - \hat{\boldsymbol{\theta}}_n) \right]. \qquad (22.10.12)$$

Thus, the posterior distribution converges to a multivariate normal distribution with mean $\hat{\boldsymbol{\theta}}_n$ and covariance matrix

$$\mathbf{cov}(\boldsymbol{\theta} \mid \mathbf{y}) = -\left(\sum_{i=1}^{n} \left. \frac{\partial^2 \ln(\mathrm{L}(\boldsymbol{\theta} \mid \mathrm{y}_i))}{\partial \boldsymbol{\theta} \partial \boldsymbol{\theta}'} \right|_{\theta = \hat{\theta}_n} \right)^{-1} = [n\mathbf{I}(\hat{\boldsymbol{\theta}}_n)]^{-1}, \qquad (22.10.13)$$

where $\mathbf{I}(\hat{\boldsymbol{\theta}}_n)$ is the sample analog to the Fisher information matrix (under the iid assumption). Of course, the limiting Bayesian posterior is interpreted in a much different fashion than in the case of the corresponding ML result. First, the observed ML estimate $\hat{\boldsymbol{\theta}}_n$ is the asymptotic mean of the Bayesian posterior, not the true parameter value. Second, as noted by Lindley, the Bayesian covariance matrix $[n\mathbf{I}(\hat{\boldsymbol{\theta}}_n)]^{-1}$ is based on the observed sample rather than the Fisher information matrix, which is a matrix of expected values. We would violate the likelihood principle if we used the Fisher (expected) information matrix because unobserved pre-data outcomes in the sample space would then be involved.

22.10.2.b. Regularity Conditions

As in our earlier statements of large sample results, a formal proof requires some regularity conditions on the prior distribution and the likelihood function to avoid technical pitfalls. For our purposes, we consider an abridged list of the regularity conditions stated by Hartigan (1983, Section 11.2):

A1. The likelihood function $L(\boldsymbol{\theta} \mid \mathbf{y})$ has a unique maxima $\boldsymbol{\theta}_0$.

A2. The prior distribution satisfies $p(\boldsymbol{\theta}_0) > 0$ and is continuous at $\boldsymbol{\theta}_0$.

A3. The posterior distribution $p(\boldsymbol{\theta} \mid \mathbf{y})$ becomes concentrated at $\boldsymbol{\theta}_0$ such that $\Pr[\|\boldsymbol{\theta} - \boldsymbol{\theta}_0\| > \varepsilon \mid \mathbf{y}] \to 0$ (almost surely) for some $\varepsilon > 0$ as $n \to \infty$.

A4. $L(\boldsymbol{\theta} \mid \mathbf{y})$ is twice continuously differentiable in a neighborhood of $\boldsymbol{\theta}_0$.

In general, conditions A1 and A4 are similar to those required for asymptotic normality of the maximum likelihood estimator. Although we have implicitly focused on real-valued parameter spaces with absolutely continuous priors, asymptotic posterior normality may also be proven for models in which the parameter space $\boldsymbol{\Theta}$ is a countable set.

Several researchers have derived alternative sets of sufficient conditions (e.g., Proposition 5.15, Bernardo and Smith, 1994), although some are difficult to verify in practice. In the case of conjugate analysis, we may rely on Proposition 5.16 provided by Bernardo and Smith (1994, p. 293) to show that posterior distributions derived from likelihood functions and conjugate priors in the canonical exponential family are asymptotically normal.

22.10.3. Appendix References

Bernardo, J. M., and A. F. M. Smith (1994), *Bayesian Theory*, New York: John Wiley and Sons.

Hartigan, J. A. (1983), *Bayes Theory*, New York: Springer–Verlag.

LaPlace, P. S. (1812), Théorie Analytique des Probabilités. Reprinted as Volume 7 of Oeuvres de LaPlace (1847). Paris: Imprimerie Royale.

Le Cam, L. M. (1953), "On Some Asymptotic Properties of Maximum Likelihood Estimates and Related Bayes Estimates," University of California Publications in Statistics, Vol. 1, pp. 277–330.

Le Cam, L. (1986), *Asymptotic Methods in Statistical Decision Theory*, New York: Springer–Verlag.

Le Cam, L., and G. L. Yang (1990), *Asymptotics in Statistics: Some Basic Concepts*, New York: Springer–Verlag.

Lehmann, E., and G. Casella (1998), *Theory of Point Estimation*, New York: Springer–Verlag.

Lindley, D. V. (1971), Bayesian Statistics: A Review, Philadelphia: Society for Industrial and Applied Mathematics.

Poirier, D. J. (1995), *Intermediate Statistics and Econometrics*, MIT Press, Cambridge.

Schervish, M. J. (1995), *Theory of Statistics*, New York: Springer–Verlag.

CHAPTER 23

Alternative Bayes Formulations for the Regression Model

IN Chapter 22 we introduced some basic Bayesian concepts and focused on a Bayesian analysis of the normal regression model under a conjugate informative prior. Given a corresponding posterior distribution, Bayesian point estimates were developed and their sampling properties reviewed. In this chapter we leave the world of well-defined likelihood functions, natural conjugate priors, and tractable posterior distributions, and, with an eye toward applicability, consider a range of extensions to the basic Bayesian regression formulation.

First we consider a specific form of natural conjugate informative prior for the $\boldsymbol{\beta}$ parameters of a normal linear regression model, called g-priors, that permits an attractive basis for specifying the covariance matrix of the prior probability distribution. Next, we examine empirical Bayes procedures. In Bayesian posterior analysis it is often the case that one or more of the parameters of the prior distribution are unknown. To mitigate this problem, an alternative is to make use of a parametric Bayes procedure to estimate the unknown parameters of the prior. Then point estimates are inserted in place of the unknown parameters of the prior and treated as if they were the known values of the parameters, and posterior analysis proceeds.

We then consider the case in which it is not practicable to use a conjugate prior distribution on the regression parameters and closed-form analytical results are not available. In this case Bayesian posterior estimation and inference must rely on numerical or Monte Carlo techniques. Finally, in some cases we may lack information necessary to specify the likelihood function. We then make use of the Bayesian method of moments to present a way to avoid having to specify the underlying likelihood function. This may remind you of how in Chapter 12 we used the empirical likelihood concept to profile a likelihood function.

The general class of statistical models to which these Bayesian extensions apply are portrayed in Table 23.1. The notation and definitions used in Chapter 22 continue for this chapter.

Table 23.1. *Bayesian Linear Regression*

Model Component	Specific Characteristics	
$\mathbf{Y}$	RV Type:	continuous
	Range:	unlimited
	Y_i dimension:	univariate
	Moments:	$E[\mathbf{Y} \mid \mathbf{x}, \boldsymbol{\beta}, \sigma] = \mathbf{x}\boldsymbol{\beta}$ and $\mathbf{cov}(\mathbf{Y} \mid \mathbf{x}, \boldsymbol{\beta}, \sigma) = \sigma^2\mathbf{I}$
$\eta(\mathbf{x}, \boldsymbol{\beta}, \varepsilon)$	Functional Form:	linear in $\mathbf{x}$ and $\boldsymbol{\beta}$, additive in ε, as $\mathbf{x}\boldsymbol{\beta} + \varepsilon$
$\mathbf{x}$ or $\mathbf{X}$	RV Type:	fixed or random
	Genesis:	exogenous to the model
$\mathbf{B}$	RV Type:	conceptually random
	Dimension:	finite
ε	RV Type:	iid or independent
	Moments:	$E[\varepsilon \mid \mathbf{x}, \boldsymbol{\beta}, \sigma] = \mathbf{0}$, and $\mathbf{cov}(\varepsilon \mid \mathbf{x}, \boldsymbol{\beta}, \sigma) = \sigma^2\mathbf{I}$
Ω	Prior info:	$(\mathbf{B}, \Sigma) \sim p(\boldsymbol{\beta}, \sigma)$, a proper or improper PDF, for $(\boldsymbol{\beta}, \sigma) \in \Omega$.
$f(\mathbf{e} \mid \mathbf{x}, \varphi)$	PDF family:	normal or any other parametric family satisfying moment conditions

23.1. *g*-Priors

For the linear regression model, we may have a number of sources for the prior–conceptual information about the individual elements of $\boldsymbol{\beta}$. Relatedly, the specification of the covariance matrix $\boldsymbol{\Psi}$ of a prior probability distribution may be difficult to justify or visualize. In recognition of this limitation, one simple approach to this covariance specification is to follow Zellner (1980, 1986) and use the concept of "g-priors," where the significance of the "g" adjective will become evident as we develop this concept.

23.1.1. A Family of *g*-Priors and Associated Posteriors

A g-prior is a specific form of natural conjugate informative prior for the $\boldsymbol{\beta}$ parameters of a linear regression model having a normally distributed noise component. The marginal prior distribution for values of σ is defined to be the standard parameter transformation–invariant diffuse prior $p(\sigma) \propto \sigma^{-1}$, and so ignorance of the noise component variance is assumed. Because the joint prior distribution on $(\boldsymbol{\beta}, \sigma)$ values can be conceptualized as $p(\boldsymbol{\beta} \mid \sigma)p(\sigma)$, we then focus attention on the specification of the conditional prior distribution $p(\boldsymbol{\beta} \mid \sigma)$.

The conditional g-prior family of prior distributions for $\mathbf{B}$, given σ, is defined by

$$p(\boldsymbol{\beta} \mid \sigma) \equiv N(\boldsymbol{\mu}, g^{-1}\sigma^2(\mathbf{x}'\mathbf{x})^{-1}) \propto \frac{1}{\sigma^k} \exp\left[\frac{-g}{2\sigma^2}(\boldsymbol{\beta} - \boldsymbol{\mu})'\mathbf{x}'\mathbf{x}(\boldsymbol{\beta} - \boldsymbol{\mu})\right] \quad (23.1.1)$$

in which case the joint prior distribution of $(\boldsymbol{\beta}, \sigma)$ values is

$$p(\boldsymbol{\beta}, \sigma) \equiv p(\boldsymbol{\beta} \mid \sigma)p(\sigma) \propto \frac{1}{\sigma^{k+1}} \exp\left[\frac{-g}{2\sigma^2}(\boldsymbol{\beta} - \boldsymbol{\mu})'\mathbf{x}'\mathbf{x}(\boldsymbol{\beta} - \boldsymbol{\mu})\right]. \tag{23.1.2}$$

The inclusion of the "g" parameter in the specification of the prior distributions is the reason for affixing the name "g-prior" to these distributions.

Comparing Zellner's g-prior with the conditional conjugate prior for $\mathbf{B}$ defined in (22.4.3) indicates that the two conditional priors are identical when $\boldsymbol{\Psi}^{-1} = g\mathbf{x}'\mathbf{x}$. Furthermore, the use of the joint g-prior in a Bayesian linear regression analysis can be considered a limiting case of the conjugate posterior analysis of Section 22.4. In particular, if we set $m = k+1$ on the righthand side of the definition for $p(\sigma)$ given in (22.4.4), and let $\eta \to 0$, this improper ignorance prior, $p(\sigma) \propto \sigma^{-1}$ is implied. This allows us to derive the posterior probability distribution of $\mathbf{B}$, as well as the Bayes estimate of $\boldsymbol{\beta}$, as a special limiting case of the posterior results derived for the conjugate prior analysis in Section 22.4. We caution the reader, however, that the limiting cases of our previous results (22.4.5)–(22.4.7) relating to the marginal prior of $\boldsymbol{\beta}$ are not applicable because (22.4.5) is not a proper prior probability density when $m = k + 1$.

For convenience, we review the major posterior results in the remainder of this section. First of all, the posterior distribution of $(\mathbf{B}, \Sigma)$ is given by (22.4.9) with $\boldsymbol{\Psi}^{-1} = g\mathbf{x}'\mathbf{x}$, $m = k+1$, and the value of η in the definition of ξ (22.4.11) set to zero. In addition, the posterior mean is given by (22.4.10) with the same substitution for $\boldsymbol{\Psi}^{-1}$ being made. The relevant expressions are then

$$p(\boldsymbol{\beta}, \sigma \mid \mathbf{y}, \mathbf{x}) \propto \frac{1}{\sigma^{n+k+1}} \exp\left\{-\frac{1}{2\sigma^2}[(\boldsymbol{\beta} - \boldsymbol{\beta}_*)'[(1+g)\mathbf{x}'\mathbf{x}](\boldsymbol{\beta} - \boldsymbol{\beta}_*) + \xi]\right\} \tag{23.1.3}$$

where

$$\boldsymbol{\beta}_* = [(1+g)\mathbf{x}'\mathbf{x}]^{-1}[\mathbf{x}'\mathbf{x}(\hat{\mathbf{b}} + g\boldsymbol{\mu})] = \frac{\hat{\mathbf{b}} + g\boldsymbol{\mu}}{(1+g)}, \tag{23.1.4}$$

and

$$\xi = (n-k)\hat{\sigma}^2 + g\boldsymbol{\mu}'\mathbf{x}'\mathbf{x}\boldsymbol{\mu} + \hat{\mathbf{b}}'\mathbf{x}'\mathbf{x}\hat{\mathbf{b}} - \boldsymbol{\beta}_*'[(1+g)\mathbf{x}'\mathbf{x}]\boldsymbol{\beta}_*. \tag{23.1.5}$$

The marginal posterior for $\mathbf{B}$ is given by (22.4.12) with the appropriate substitutions delineated above having been made, yielding

$$p(\boldsymbol{\beta} \mid \mathbf{y}) \propto \left[n + (\boldsymbol{\beta} - \boldsymbol{\beta}_*)'\frac{n}{\xi}[(1+g)\mathbf{x}'\mathbf{x}](\boldsymbol{\beta} - \boldsymbol{\beta}_*)\right]^{-(n+k)/2}, \tag{23.1.6}$$

which is in the familiar multivariate $\mathbf{T}$ distribution form. The Bayes estimate of $\boldsymbol{\beta}$ is then equal to the posterior mean $\boldsymbol{\beta}_*$ defined in (23.1.4) under quadratic loss, and the posterior covariance matrix is given by the specialized version of (22.4.14)

$$\mathbf{cov}(\mathbf{B} \mid \mathbf{y}) = \left(\frac{\xi}{n-2}\right)[(1+g)\mathbf{x}'\mathbf{x}]^{-1} \quad \text{for } n > 2. \tag{23.1.7}$$

Upon examination of the posterior distribution results associated with the g-prior, it is apparent that the posterior mean for $\mathbf{B}$ is a simple weighted average of the prior mean $\boldsymbol{\mu}$ and the pure data-based ML–LS estimate of $\boldsymbol{\beta}$ given by $\hat{\mathbf{b}}$. In the limit when $g \to 0$, the marginal posterior for $\mathbf{B}$ converges to (22.3.14) with $v = n$, the posterior mean is such that $\mathrm{E}[\mathbf{B} \mid \mathbf{y}] \to \hat{\mathbf{b}}$, and $\mathbf{cov}(\mathbf{B} \mid \mathbf{y}) \to \frac{\hat{\sigma}^2 n}{(n-2)}(\mathbf{x}'\mathbf{x})^{-1}$. The posterior covariance matrix becomes indistinguishable from the covariance matrix estimate for the ML–LS estimator as n increases. It is interesting to note that these limiting posterior results could be achieved following an approach analogous to the diffuse prior approach of Section 22.3, except that the prior $\mathrm{p}(\boldsymbol{\beta}, \sigma) \propto \sigma^{-(k+1)}$ would be used in place of the prior $\mathrm{p}(\boldsymbol{\beta}, \sigma) \propto \sigma^{-1}$. In the limit as $g \to \infty$, the marginal posterior for $\mathbf{B}$ becomes degenerate on the vector $\boldsymbol{\mu}$, with $\mathrm{E}[\mathbf{B} \mid \mathbf{y}] \to \boldsymbol{\mu}$ and $\mathbf{cov}(\mathbf{B} \mid \mathbf{y}) \to \mathbf{0}$, which the reader can also verify. Thus, the choice of the value of the g parameter defines the convex combination that governs where the posterior mean is located between $\boldsymbol{\mu}$ and $\hat{\mathbf{b}}$, and the parameter g also determines the scale of the posterior covariance matrix for $\mathbf{B}$. On the latter point, it is helpful to note that the conditional-on-σ *posterior* covariance matrix of $\mathbf{B}$ is given simply by $\mathbf{cov}(\mathbf{B} \mid \sigma, \mathbf{y}) = [\frac{\sigma^2}{1+g}](\mathbf{x}'\mathbf{x})^{-1}$. This is immediately evident from the conditional normal form of the kernel of the joint posterior (23.1.3), and this means that the elements of the conditional posterior covariance decrease monotonically as g is increased.

23.1.2. Rationalizing and Specifying g-priors

It is clear from the posterior results obtained in Section 23.1.1 that g-priors lead to simple and easily interpretable results relating to how sample and prior information are combined into posterior distributions and moments. Apart from the ease of use and interpretation, what else can we say in defense of the use of g-priors?

Consider the following reasoning. In the absence of any prior information about the model parameters, we have already seen in Section 22.3 that the use of the standard ignorance prior on regression model parameters leads to a multivariate $\mathbf{T}$-distributed posterior with covariance matrix proportional to $(\mathbf{x}'\mathbf{x})^{-1}$. Thus, in the absence of any additional prior information, we know that the elements of $\mathbf{B}$ will be correlated, and their covariances will be proportional to the off-diagonal elements of $(\mathbf{x}'\mathbf{x})^{-1}$. Now suppose that the analyst feels it is possible to specify some prior information *marginally* on each of the elements of $\boldsymbol{\beta}$, but he or she feels unable to specify the correlation structure between the B_i's because of a lack of prior information to this effect. Then it seems reasonable to adopt the correlation structure of Section 22.3 that is known to apply under an uninformed situation; namely, the correlation structure implied by $(\mathbf{x}'\mathbf{x})^{-1}$. This is precisely what the g-prior distribution does, as is evident from the conditional g-prior (23.1.1) in which the *prior* covariance matrix for $\mathbf{B}$, conditional on σ, is given by $\mathbf{cov}(\mathbf{B} \mid \sigma, \mathbf{y}) = [\frac{\sigma^2}{g}](\mathbf{x}'\mathbf{x})^{-1}$.

Regarding the choice of the $\boldsymbol{\mu}$ and g parameters in the g-prior distribution, Zellner presumes that the analyst can provide "anticipated values" or best prior guesses for the elements in $\mathbf{B}$, and consistent with the Bayesian approach and on the assumption of quadratic loss, the prior mean $\boldsymbol{\mu}$ is set equal to these anticipated values. The value of g can then be set so that the marginal prior univariate $\mathbf{T}$-distributions for the B_i's implied by (23.1.6) are consistent with the analyst's prior information concerning probable intervals of values for the β_i's. Alternatively, a prior distribution could be specified for the value of g, which could be an improper ignorance prior or an informative prior, and then the g parameter could be integrated out of the posterior distribution for the regression model parameters (note the concept of hierarchical prior distributions in the section ahead). Zellner (1986) suggests still another method of assessing g based on conceptual samples, and the reader is directed to Zellner's article for further details.

► **Example 23.1.1:** To demonstrate the specification, use, and interpretation of Zellner's g-prior, we provide the GAUSS example C23G.gss in the examples manual. First, the user is asked to select the sample size (n) and the prior mean ($\boldsymbol{\mu}$) for the parameter vector $\boldsymbol{\beta}$ of the linear regression model. For a series of g-values (also selected by the user), GAUSS plots the marginal posterior densities and reports the posterior means and variances for a given sample. As indicated in this section, the user should find that the influence of the prior information on the posterior distribution increases as $g \to \infty$.

23.2. An Empirical Bayes Estimator

In attempting to perform Bayesian posterior analyses it is sometimes the case that one or more parameters of the prior distribution are unknown. For example, it might be the case that the g parameter of the g-prior distribution of the previous section is an unknown prior parameter. In typical Bayesian fashion, one could contemplate using conceptual knowledge in assigning a prior distribution to the prior distribution parameters, such as g in the g-prior, and then the parameters could be integrated out of the prior to define $p(\boldsymbol{\beta})$. For example, let $p(\boldsymbol{\mu}, g)$ be a prior distribution on the parameters $(\boldsymbol{\mu}, g)$ of a prior distribution. The prior distribution for $\boldsymbol{\beta}$, with $\boldsymbol{\mu}$ and g integrated out, is given by

$$p(\boldsymbol{\beta}) = \int_{\boldsymbol{\mu},g} p(\boldsymbol{\beta} \mid \boldsymbol{\mu}, g) p(\boldsymbol{\mu}, g) \, \mathrm{d}\boldsymbol{\mu} \, \mathrm{d}g. \tag{23.2.1}$$

In this type of problem, where the parameters *of the priors* are treated as random variables for the purpose of representing prior information about them, the parameters are referred to as *hyperparameters* of the inference problem. The prior distributions on hyperparameters are referred to as *hierarchical priors*.

If the prior distribution $p(\boldsymbol{\beta})$ defined via the use of hyperparameters and hierarchical priors is inappropriate, then the Bayes estimator can perform quite poorly from a frequentist point of view. To address this problem, one alternative approach is to make use of the parametric empirical Bayes procedures suggested by Efron and Morris (1973), Berger (1980), and Casella (1985). In the empirical Bayes procedure, data are used to estimate the unknown parameters in the prior, and these point estimates are then inserted into the prior and treated as if they were known.

To illustrate the empirical Bayes procedure, we revisit the g-prior analysis of the previous section. First of all, we reparameterize the problem by setting $\tau^2 \equiv \sigma^2/g$ so that conditional on σ and on the assumption that μ has been specified by the analyst, the prior distribution on $\boldsymbol{\beta}$ is given by $p(\boldsymbol{\beta} \mid \tau) = \mathrm{N}[\mu, \tau^2(\mathbf{x}'\mathbf{x})^{-1}]$ (recall Equation (23.1.1). The conditional distribution of the ML–LS estimator $\hat{\boldsymbol{\beta}}$ is given by $p(\hat{\mathbf{b}} \mid \boldsymbol{\beta}, \sigma) = \mathrm{N}(\boldsymbol{\beta}, \sigma^2(\mathbf{x}'\mathbf{x})^{-1})$. Then, by integrating out $\boldsymbol{\beta}$ from the joint posterior $p(\boldsymbol{\beta}, \hat{\mathbf{b}} \mid \tau, \sigma) \equiv p(\hat{\mathbf{b}} \mid \boldsymbol{\beta}, \sigma)p(\boldsymbol{\beta} \mid \tau)$ following the approach of Berger (1985, p. 127), the marginal distribution for $\hat{\boldsymbol{\beta}}$ is defined as

$$\mathrm{m}(\hat{\mathbf{b}} \mid \tau, \sigma) = \mathrm{N}(\mu, (\sigma^2 + \tau^2)(\mathbf{x}'\mathbf{x})^{-1}) \tag{23.2.2}$$

Therefore,

$$\frac{(\hat{\boldsymbol{\beta}} - \mu)'\mathbf{x}'\mathbf{x}(\hat{\boldsymbol{\beta}} - \mu)}{\sigma^2 + \tau^2} \sim \text{Chi-square}(k, 0), \tag{23.2.3}$$

and because

$$\mathrm{E}\left[1/\chi^2_{(k)}\right] = (k-2)^{-1}, \tag{23.2.4}$$

where $\chi^2_{(k)} \sim \text{Chi-square}(k, 0)$, it follows that

$$\mathrm{E}\left[\frac{k-2}{(\hat{\boldsymbol{\beta}} - \mu)'\mathbf{x}'\mathbf{x}(\hat{\boldsymbol{\beta}} - \mu)}\right] = (\sigma^2 + \tau^2)^{-1}. \tag{23.2.5}$$

Therefore,

$$(\widehat{\sigma^2 + \tau^2})^{-1} = (k-2)/(\hat{\boldsymbol{\beta}} - \mu)'\mathbf{x}'\mathbf{x}(\hat{\boldsymbol{\beta}} - \mu) \tag{23.2.6}$$

is an unbiased estimator of $(\sigma^2 + \tau^2)^{-1}$.

Now note that under the new parameterization for the g-prior, the posterior mean of **B**, displayed above as (23.1.4) under the original parameterization, can be represented by

$$\begin{aligned}\boldsymbol{\beta}_* &= \frac{\sigma^2}{\sigma^2 + \tau^2}\mu + \frac{\tau^2}{\sigma^2 + \tau^2}\hat{\mathbf{b}} \\ &= \mu + \left(\frac{\tau^2}{\sigma^2 + \tau^2}\right)(\hat{\mathbf{b}} - \mu) \\ &= \hat{\mathbf{b}} - \frac{\sigma^2}{\sigma^2 + \tau^2}(\hat{\mathbf{b}} - \mu)\end{aligned} \tag{23.2.7}$$

If, for the unknown σ^2 in (23.2.7), we substitute the estimator $(n-k)\hat{\sigma}^2/(n-k+2)$, which is the *best* (minimum MSE) *quadratic* (i.e., representable in the form $\varepsilon'\mathbf{Q}\varepsilon$) estimator of σ^2, and if we also substitute the unbiased estimator (23.2.6) for $(\sigma^2+\tau^2)^{-1}$, we have the empirical Bayes estimator

$$\begin{aligned}\boldsymbol{\beta}_{\mathrm{EB}} &= \hat{\boldsymbol{\beta}} - \left[\frac{\xi(k-2)}{(n-k+2)(\hat{\boldsymbol{\beta}} - \mu)'\mathbf{x}'\mathbf{x}(\hat{\boldsymbol{\beta}} - \mu)}(\hat{\boldsymbol{\beta}} - \mu)\right], \\ &= \left[1 - \frac{(n-k)\hat{\sigma}^2(k-2)}{(n-k+2)(\hat{\boldsymbol{\beta}} - \mu)'\mathbf{x}'\mathbf{x}(\hat{\boldsymbol{\beta}} - \mu)}\right](\hat{\boldsymbol{\beta}} - \mu) + \mu\end{aligned} \tag{23.2.8}$$

where $\xi \equiv (n-k)\hat{\sigma}^2$. The estimator $\boldsymbol{\beta}_{\text{EB}}$ is an empirical *approximation* to the mean of the Bayes posterior distribution.

In some cases the mean vector $\boldsymbol{\mu}$ in the prior for $\boldsymbol{\beta}$ is also unknown. Suppose we let $\boldsymbol{\mu} = \mathbf{0}$ and therefore adopt the prior $\text{p}(\boldsymbol{\beta} \mid \tau) = \text{N}(\mathbf{0}, \tau^2(\mathbf{x}'\mathbf{x})^{-1})$. The empirical Bayes estimator (the conditional posterior mean of $\boldsymbol{\beta}$) then reduces to

$$\boldsymbol{\beta}_{\text{EB}}^{\mu=0} = \left(1 - \frac{\xi(k-2)}{(n-k+2)\hat{\boldsymbol{\beta}}'\mathbf{x}'\mathbf{x}\hat{\boldsymbol{\beta}}}\right)\hat{\boldsymbol{\beta}}. \tag{23.2.9}$$

In the orthonormal case where $\mathbf{x}'\mathbf{x} = \mathbf{I}_k$, (23.2.9) reduces to a James and Stein-like estimator introduced in Chapter 3. The empirical Bayes estimator $\boldsymbol{\beta}_{\text{EB}}^{\mu=0}$ has Bayes risk

$$\text{E}\big[\rho\big(\boldsymbol{\beta}, \boldsymbol{\beta}_{\text{EB}}^{\mu=0}\big)\big] = \sigma^2 \text{tr}(\mathbf{x}'\mathbf{x})^{-1} - \frac{\sigma^4(n-k)(k-2)}{(\sigma^2+\tau^2)(n-k+2)k}\text{tr}(\mathbf{x}'\mathbf{x})^{-1}. \tag{23.2.10}$$

For large τ^2, where the prior $\text{p}(\boldsymbol{\beta} \mid \tau)$ is essentially diffuse, the Bayes and empirical Bayes estimators have approximately the same risk. Judge and Bock (1978, Chapter 10) have shown that if $(k-2) \leq 2[\text{tr}(\mathbf{x}'\mathbf{x})^{-1}\text{d}_{\text{L}}^{-1} - 2]$, where d_{L} is the largest characteristic root of $(\mathbf{x}'\mathbf{x})^{-1}$, then the empirical Bayes–Stein type estimator (23.2.9) is minimax and dominates the maximum likelihood estimator $\hat{\boldsymbol{\beta}}$.

If, as a special case, we work with the orthonormal linear statistical model in which $\mathbf{x}'\mathbf{x} = \mathbf{I}_k$, $\boldsymbol{\mu} = \mathbf{0}$, and the scale parameter is known to be $\sigma^2 = 1$ and used in place of the previous substitution of $(n-k)\hat{\sigma}^2/(n-k+2)$, then the empirical Bayes estimator (23.2.9) reduces to

$$\boldsymbol{\beta}_{\text{EB}}^{**} = [1 - (k-2)/\hat{\boldsymbol{\beta}}'\hat{\boldsymbol{\beta}}]\hat{\boldsymbol{\beta}}, \tag{23.2.11}$$

which is an approximation to the mean of the posterior probability density function for $\boldsymbol{\beta}$ and is identical in form to the James and Stein estimator introduced in Chapter 3. The average risk for this empirical Bayes–James and Stein estimator is

$$\text{E}[\rho(\boldsymbol{\beta}, \boldsymbol{\beta}_{\text{EB}}^{**})] = k - (k-2)/(1+\tau^2), \tag{23.2.12}$$

where the expectation is taken over $\boldsymbol{\beta}$ and $\hat{\boldsymbol{\beta}}$. When $\mathbf{x}'\mathbf{x} = \mathbf{I}_k$ and $\sigma^2 = 1$, the risk differs from the minimum Bayes risk

$$\text{E}[\text{p}(\boldsymbol{\beta}, \boldsymbol{\beta}_*)] = \sigma^2\text{tr}(\mathbf{x}'\mathbf{x})^{-1} - \left(\frac{\sigma^2}{\tau^2+\sigma^2}\right)\text{tr}(\mathbf{x}'\mathbf{x})^{-1} \tag{23.2.13}$$

by the quantity $2/(1+\tau^2)$. Thus, for large τ^2 the Bayes and empirical Bayes estimators have approximately the same risk. One advantage of the empirical Bayes estimator is that it makes it possible to avoid the potentially large estimation errors of the Bayes estimator if τ^2 is misspecified.

The risk performance of the Bayes, empirical Bayes, and ML estimators is summarized in Figure 23.1. Fortunately, as we have demonstrated, it is possible for the empirical Bayes estimation procedure to perform well from both a Bayesian and sampling theory point of view.

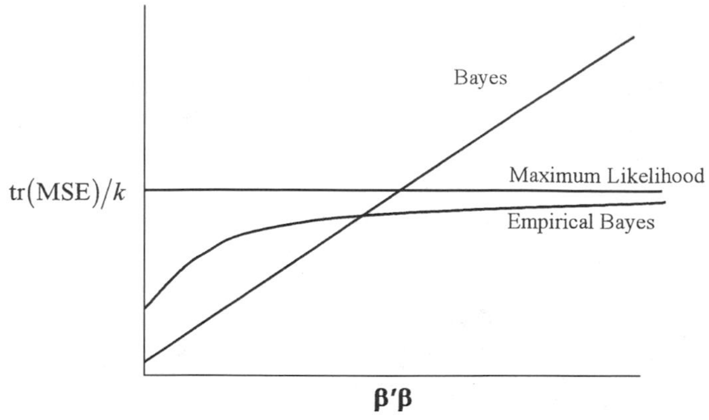

Figure 23.1: The characteristics of risk functions for Bayes, empirical Bayes, and maximum likelihood estimators.

► **Example 23.2.1:** To compare the various empirical Bayes estimators discussed in this section, we provide the GAUSS program C23EB.gss in the examples manual. First, GAUSS asks the user to specify the sample size (n) as well as the appropriate prior information for the Bayes estimator. For a given sample, the ML estimator and the Bayes and empirical Bayes posterior means are reported and compared. Then, GAUSS conducts a Monte Carlo simulation exercise designed to replicate the quadratic risk results reported in Figure 23.1.

23.3. General Bayesian Regression Analysis with Nonconjugate Informative–Uninformative Prior

In this section we consider the case in which the analyst is unable or unwilling to use a convenient conjugate prior distribution to represent prior information on regression model parameters. In addition, we consider the most common situation in practice in which the prior distribution on $\boldsymbol{\beta}$ is informative but the prior information on σ is vague. In this case, closed-form analytical results like those in the previous two sections are not generally available, and Bayesian posterior inference then relies on numerical or Monte Carlo techniques.

23.3.1. Normal Noise Component

In this subsection we continue to assume normality for the noise component of the regression model, as in Section 22.3. Regarding the prior distribution on model parameters, we also continue to assume that the prior information on $\boldsymbol{\beta}$ and σ values is independent. Furthermore, the prior PDF on $\boldsymbol{\beta}$ values is assumed to be some proper probability distribution on R^k, which we denote by $p(\boldsymbol{\beta})$. The PDF p($\boldsymbol{\beta}$) is now completely general, and for example the PDF could represent prior information in the form of inequality restrictions on the model parameters such as $\boldsymbol{\beta}_i \in [\mathrm{a}_i, \mathrm{b}_i]$, for $i = 1, \ldots, k$. In this case the analyst could specify the functional form of $\mathrm{p}(\boldsymbol{\beta})$ as uniform

$$p(\boldsymbol{\beta}) = \left[\prod_{i=1}^{k} [\mathrm{b}_i - \mathrm{a}_i]^{-1}\right] \mathrm{I}_{\mathrm{A}}(\boldsymbol{\beta}), \qquad \text{where } \mathrm{A} = \times_{i=1}^{k} [\mathrm{a}_i, \mathrm{b}_i], \tag{23.3.1}$$

where $\mathrm{I}_{\mathrm{A}}(\boldsymbol{\beta})$ is the standard indicator function taking the value 1 when $\boldsymbol{\beta} \in \mathrm{A}$ and 0 otherwise. Because we are not requiring the use of conjugate priors, the possibilities for the prior PDF on $\boldsymbol{\beta}$ values are literally endless.

If we adopt the parameter transformation–invariant ignorance prior $p(\sigma) \propto \sigma^{-1}$ for the prior PDF on σ, the joint prior distribution on the regression model parameters can then be represented in the form

$$p(\boldsymbol{\beta}, \sigma) \propto \sigma^{-1} p(\boldsymbol{\beta}). \tag{23.3.2}$$

Combining this prior distribution with the normal distribution-based likelihood function (22.3.11) via Bayes rule yields the posterior distribution for $(\boldsymbol{\beta}, \sigma)$ values given by

$$p(\boldsymbol{\beta}, \sigma \mid \mathbf{y}, \mathbf{x}) \propto \frac{1}{\sigma^{n+1}} \exp\left[-\frac{1}{2\sigma^2}[(n-k)\hat{\sigma}^2 + (\boldsymbol{\beta} - \hat{\mathbf{b}})'\mathbf{x}'\mathbf{x}(\boldsymbol{\beta} - \hat{\mathbf{b}})]\right] p(\boldsymbol{\beta}). \tag{23.3.3}$$

The marginal posterior distribution for $\mathbf{B}$ can be derived from (23.3.3) in the usual way by integrating out the nuisance parameter σ. The integration procedure is precisely the same as the approach described preceding (22.3.14) and results in

$$\begin{aligned} \mathrm{p}(\boldsymbol{\beta} \mid \mathbf{y}, \mathbf{x}) &= \int_0^{\infty} \mathrm{p}(\boldsymbol{\beta}, \sigma \mid \mathbf{y}, \mathbf{x})\, d\sigma \\ &\propto [(n-k)\hat{\sigma}^2 + (\boldsymbol{\beta} - \hat{\mathbf{b}})'\mathbf{x}'\mathbf{x}(\boldsymbol{\beta} - \hat{\mathbf{b}})]^{-n/2} \mathrm{p}(\boldsymbol{\beta}) \\ &\propto [v + (\boldsymbol{\beta} - \hat{\mathbf{b}})'\hat{\sigma}^{-2}\mathbf{x}'\mathbf{x}(\boldsymbol{\beta} - \hat{\mathbf{b}})]^{-(v+k)/2} \mathrm{p}(\boldsymbol{\beta}) \end{aligned} \tag{23.3.4}$$

where $v = n - k$. It is apparent that the marginal posterior PDF of $\mathbf{B}$ is in the form of a multivariate $\mathbf{T}$-distribution multiplied by the prior distribution of $\boldsymbol{\beta}$ values. In general, posterior analysis based on (23.3.4) will require numerical or Monte Carlo techniques of PDF evaluation.

23.3.1.a. Posterior Based on Prior Inequality Restrictions on $\boldsymbol{\beta}$

Consider the special but important case of prior inequality restrictions on the elements of $\boldsymbol{\beta}$ represented by the uniform prior distribution on $\boldsymbol{\beta}$ values displayed in (23.3.1). Because the uniform distribution is constant on the hyperrectangular set A defined in (23.3.1), we can rewrite the kernel of the marginal posterior PDF of $\boldsymbol{\beta}$ values in this special case as

$$\begin{aligned} p(\boldsymbol{\beta} \mid \mathbf{y}, \mathbf{x}) &\propto [(n-k)\hat{\sigma}^2 + (\boldsymbol{\beta} - \hat{\mathbf{b}})'\mathbf{x}'\mathbf{x}(\boldsymbol{\beta} - \hat{\mathbf{b}})]^{-n/2} \mathrm{I}_{\mathrm{A}}(\boldsymbol{\beta}) \\ &\propto [v + (\boldsymbol{\beta} - \hat{\mathbf{b}})'\hat{\sigma}^{-2}\mathbf{x}'\mathbf{x}(\boldsymbol{\beta} - \hat{\mathbf{b}})]^{-(v+k)/2} \mathrm{I}_{\mathrm{A}}(\boldsymbol{\beta}). \end{aligned} \tag{23.3.5}$$

It is apparent from the density kernel that the marginal posterior distribution is a *truncated* multivariate **T**-distribution, the truncation being defined by the new restricted support represented by the set A.

The Bayesian estimate of $\boldsymbol{\beta}$ under a quadratic loss function is, as usual, the mean of the posterior distribution. However, the posterior mean of a truncated multivariate **T**-distribution is not generally the value $\hat{\mathbf{b}}$, as it was for the untruncated distribution, and there is no simple analytical procedure for deriving the posterior mean of (23.3.5). Furthermore, integrals of (23.3.5) for purposes of assigning posterior probabilities to propositions as well as determining credible regions from the PDF (23.3.5) are complex undertakings that are difficult analytically. We must resort to the computer to facilitate posterior analysis of $\boldsymbol{\beta}$ in the case at hand.

23.3.1.b. Posterior Analysis with an Unfriendly Prior: Inequality Restrictions

We consider the use of Monte Carlo (MC) techniques for performing posterior analyses on $\boldsymbol{\beta}$ based on the truncated multivariate **T** posterior distribution displayed in (23.3.5). This case serves as a focused introduction to the use of MC techniques for performing posterior analyses in cases in which unfriendly (nonconjugate) priors result in posterior distributions that are difficult or intractable to deal with analytically.

Suppose that we could find a way to generate iid outcomes from the truncated multivariate **T**-distribution in (23.3.5). We could then rely on laws of large numbers and use sample averages to calculate the expectation of any function for which an expectation existed. That is, if $\mathrm{E}[\mathbf{g}(\mathbf{B})]$ exists, where $\mathrm{E}[\cdot]$ is an expectation taken with respect to the posterior distribution $\mathrm{p}(\boldsymbol{\beta} \mid \mathbf{y}, \mathbf{x})$, and if $\boldsymbol{\beta}^*_{(i)}$, $i = 1, \ldots, n^*$ is a set of iid outcomes from $\mathrm{p}(\boldsymbol{\beta} \mid \mathbf{y}, \mathbf{x})$, then by the strong law of large numbers,

$$\hat{\mathrm{E}}[\mathbf{g}(\mathbf{B})] = \frac{1}{n^*}\sum_{i=1}^{n^*} \mathbf{g}\big(\boldsymbol{\beta}^*_{(i)}\big) \xrightarrow{\text{as}} \mathrm{E}[\mathbf{g}(\mathbf{B})]. \tag{23.3.6}$$

We would then have a method of estimating $\mathrm{E}[\mathbf{g}(\mathbf{B})]$ that converges to the true expected value with probability 1, and all we would have to do is to generate a sufficiently large number of iid outcomes to estimate $\mathrm{E}[\mathbf{g}(\mathbf{B})]$ with the desired level of precision. The generality of the approach would allow the posterior mean to be estimated by setting $\mathbf{g}(\mathbf{B}) \equiv \mathbf{B}$, thereby providing a method of calculating the Bayes estimate of $\boldsymbol{\beta}$ under quadratic loss. The posterior probability of any event C could be estimated by setting $\mathrm{g}(\mathbf{B}) \equiv \mathrm{I_C}(\mathbf{B})$. Furthermore, the set C would be a credible region having posterior probability equal to $\mathrm{E}[\mathrm{g}(\mathbf{B})] \equiv \mathrm{E}[\mathrm{I_C}(\mathbf{B})]$ (see Chapter 24 for a discussion of credible regions).

It turns out that in this case, there is a relatively simple computer algorithm available for generating iid outcomes from the truncated multivariate **T**-distribution. The steps are given ahead. Note steps 1–3 generate iid outcomes from a Mult $\mathbf{T}(\boldsymbol{\mu}, \mathbf{h}, \mathrm{v}, \mathrm{k})$ distribution. Step 4 is the truncation step.

Algorithm: iid Truncated MultT(μ, h, v, k) Outcomes on the Support $\boldsymbol{\beta} \in$ A

1. Generate a $k \times 1$ outcome **w** of **W** distributed as $\mathbf{W} \sim \mathrm{N}(\mathbf{0}, \mathbf{h}^{-1})$.

2. Generate an outcome z^2 of the scalar $\mathrm{Z}^2 \sim$ Chi-square(v, 0) (independently of **W**).

3. Calculate $\mathbf{t} = \mu + \mathbf{w}[\frac{z^2}{v}]^{-1/2}$.

4. Keep the outcome only if $\mathbf{t} \in$ A.

(See Johnson, 1987, Chapter 6, p. 118, and note the correction made here in step 3 regarding v; Johnson and Kotz (1972, p. 133)

Steps 1–4 can be repeated as often as necessary to obtain as large a random sample from Mult $\mathbf{T}(\mu, \mathbf{h}, \mathrm{v}, \mathrm{k})$ as desired. The multivariate normal outcomes can be generated via linear transformations of iid N(0, 1) outcomes, where the latter can be obtained using a pseudorandom number generator such as rndn() in GAUSS. In particular, if $\mathbf{Y} \sim \mathrm{N}(\mathbf{0}, \mathbf{I})$, then both $\mathbf{W} = \mathbf{h}^{-1/2}\mathbf{Y}$ and $\mathbf{W} = \mathbf{c}'\mathbf{Y}$ are distributed as $\mathrm{N}(\mathbf{0}, \mathbf{h}^{-1})$, where $\mathbf{h}^{-1/2}$ is the symmetric square root of $\mathbf{h}^{-1}$, and **c** is the Cholesky factor such that $\mathbf{c}'\mathbf{c} = \mathbf{h}^{-1}$. The required iid Chi-square outcomes can be generated directly using a pseudorandom number generator such as the gamma random generator rndgam() in GAUSS.

Regarding the problem of knowing when one has generated enough random numbers to achieve the level of convergence or accuracy desired for the calculation in (23.3.6), one can simply calculate the standard deviation of the sample mean $\frac{1}{n^*}\sum_{i=1}^{n^*} \mathbf{g}(\boldsymbol{\beta}^*_{(i)})$ in the usual way, that is, by taking the square root of $\frac{1}{n^*(n^*-1)}\sum_{i=1}^{n^*}(\mathrm{z}_i - \bar{\mathrm{z}})^2$ where $\mathrm{z}_i \equiv \mathrm{g}(\boldsymbol{\beta}^*_{(i)})$. By central limit theory, the sample mean will be asymptotically normally distributed, and one then knows that ± 1.96 standard deviations around the sample mean will encompass the true expected value with .95 probability. Then once this interval becomes small enough, implying that the expectation has been estimated accurately enough, one can cease adding iid outcomes of **g(B)** to the mean calculation.

The preceding MC procedure can be refined several ways to speed convergence. One of the most useful ways is to use the method of antithetic sampling, as described by Geweke (1986). In short, antithetic sampling is a method that uses pairs of homoscedastic and *dependent* random sample outcomes with negative covariances in the sample mean calculation instead of using only independent outcomes. On the basis of linear combinations of random variables theory, one can argue that the sum of pairs of negatively correlated homoscedastic random variables has a smaller variance than the sum of the same number of independent homoscedastic random variables. This is, of course, based on the assumption that all of the random variables involved have the same variance to begin with. It is then possible to speed convergence of mean calculations (i.e., lower the variance of the mean) through the use of antithetic sampling. Antithetic pairs in the case at hand consist of $\mathbf{t}_1 = \boldsymbol{\mu} + \mathbf{w}[\frac{z^2}{v}]^{-1/2}$ and $\mathbf{t}_2 = \boldsymbol{\mu} - \mathbf{w}[\frac{z^2}{v}]^{-1/2}$, where it can be shown that $\mathbf{t}_2$ is also an outcome of the multivariate **T**-distribution MultT(μ, **h**, v, k), but the two variables are clearly not independent, and in fact are negatively correlated. The idea is then to generate these multivariate **T** outcomes in antithetic pairs and then use all of the paired outcomes in the estimation of posterior moments. More advanced MC concepts are discussed in the book appendix on MC methods.

If there are many inequality constraints, and/or if the likelihood function is concentrated outside the set A, then the preceding algorithm may not be practical because few or no outcomes will be retained in Step 4. Under these circumstances, a metropolis algorithm can be used to generate observations from the truncated PDF. For an example in the context of a set of regression equations model (Chapter 15), see Griffiths and Chotikapanich (1997).

Finally, using the change of variables approach, we can show that $[\hat{\sigma}^2(\mathbf{x}'\mathbf{x})^{-1}]^{-1/2}(\mathbf{B}-\hat{\mathbf{b}}) \sim \text{Mult}\mathbf{T}(\mathbf{0}, \mathbf{I}, n-k, k)$ *truncated* to $[\hat{\sigma}^2(\mathbf{x}'\mathbf{x})^{-1}]^{-1/2}(\boldsymbol{\beta}-\hat{\mathbf{b}}) \in \text{A}_*$. Then (22.10.1) of Chapter 22 implies that as $n \to \infty$, $[\hat{\sigma}^2(\mathbf{x}'\mathbf{x})^{-1}]^{-1/2}(\mathbf{B}-\hat{\mathbf{b}}) \xrightarrow{d} \text{N}(\mathbf{0}, \mathbf{I})$ *truncated* to $[\hat{\sigma}^2(\mathbf{x}'\mathbf{x})^{-1}]^{-1/2}(\boldsymbol{\beta}-\hat{\mathbf{b}}) \in \text{A}_*$, in which case the posterior distribution is asymptotically truncated normal as $\mathbf{B} \overset{a}{\sim} \text{Normal}\,(\hat{\mathbf{b}}, \hat{\sigma}^2(\mathbf{x}'\mathbf{x})^{-1})$ *truncated* to $\boldsymbol{\beta} \in \text{A}$. So long as the true $\boldsymbol{\beta}$, say $\boldsymbol{\beta}_0$, is contained within the truncated support A, the distribution will degenerate to the value that $\hat{\mathbf{b}}$ converges to, namely $\boldsymbol{\beta}_0$.

23.3.1.c. Posterior Analysis Based on a General Prior PDF, p($\boldsymbol{\beta}$)

In this subsection we consider posterior analyses of $\boldsymbol{\beta}$ values when the prior PDF is some general proper PDF. This discussion subsumes all of the previous discussions of posterior analyses, based on proper priors, as special cases, and so the procedures considered here can be applied to the previous cases as well.

In this case, the marginal posterior distribution is defined by the PDF displayed in (23.3.4). The distribution is often analytically intractable, and so we are again in the position of needing to resort to computer techniques for conducting posterior analyses based on $\text{p}(\boldsymbol{\beta} \mid \mathbf{y}, \mathbf{x})$. It turns out that we can build on the techniques introduced in Section 23.3.1b to perform such posterior analyses. To see the connection, first note that the conceptual definition of the marginal posterior distribution of $\mathbf{B}$ relating to (23.3.4) is given by

$$\text{p}(\boldsymbol{\beta} \mid \mathbf{y}, \mathbf{x}) = \frac{\text{Mult}\mathbf{T}(\boldsymbol{\beta} \mid \hat{\mathbf{b}}, \hat{\sigma}^{-2}\mathbf{x}'\mathbf{x}, n-k, k)p(\boldsymbol{\beta})}{\int_{\text{R}^k} \text{Mult}\mathbf{T}(\boldsymbol{\beta} \mid \hat{\mathbf{b}}, \hat{\sigma}^{-2}\mathbf{x}'\mathbf{x}, n-k, k)p(\boldsymbol{\beta})\,\text{d}\boldsymbol{\beta}}. \tag{23.3.7}$$

It follows that the expectation of $\mathbf{g}(\mathbf{B})$ with respect to the posterior distribution $\text{p}(\boldsymbol{\beta} \mid \mathbf{y}, \mathbf{x})$ is defined conceptually by

$$\text{E}[\mathbf{g}(\mathbf{B})] = \int_{\text{R}^k} \left[\frac{\mathbf{g}(\boldsymbol{\beta})\,\text{Mult}\mathbf{T}(\boldsymbol{\beta} \mid \hat{\mathbf{b}}, \hat{\sigma}^{-2}\mathbf{x}'\mathbf{x}, n-k, k)p(\boldsymbol{\beta})}{\int_{\text{R}^k} \text{Mult}\mathbf{T}(\boldsymbol{\beta} \mid \hat{\mathbf{b}}, \hat{\sigma}^{-2}\mathbf{x}'\mathbf{x}, n-k, k)p(\boldsymbol{\beta})\,\text{d}\boldsymbol{\beta}} \right] \text{d}\boldsymbol{\beta}. \tag{23.3.8}$$

Letting $\text{E}_{\text{T}}[\cdot]$ denote an expectation taken with respect to the multivariate $\mathbf{T}$ distribution $\text{Mult}\mathbf{T}(\hat{\mathbf{b}}, \hat{\sigma}^{-2}\mathbf{x}'\mathbf{x}, n-k, k)$, we now make the important observation that the posterior expectation in (23.3.8) can be rewritten as

$$\text{E}[\mathbf{g}(\mathbf{B})] = \frac{\text{E}_{\text{T}}[\mathbf{g}(\mathbf{B})p(\mathbf{B})]}{\text{E}_{\text{T}}[\text{p}(\mathbf{B})]}. \tag{23.3.9}$$

Then if we had a set of iid outcomes $\boldsymbol{\beta}^*_{(i)}$, $i = 1, \ldots, n^*$, from $\text{Mult}\mathbf{T}(\hat{\mathbf{b}}, \hat{\sigma}^{-2}\mathbf{x}'\mathbf{x}, n - k, k)$, we could again rely on laws of large numbers to estimate the expectation arbitrarily closely as

$$\hat{\mathrm{E}}[\mathbf{g}(\mathbf{B})] = \frac{\frac{1}{n^*}\sum_{i=1}^{n^*} \mathbf{g}(\boldsymbol{\beta}^*_{(i)})\mathrm{p}(\boldsymbol{\beta}^*_{(i)})}{\frac{1}{n^*}\sum_{i=1}^{n^*} \mathrm{p}(\boldsymbol{\beta}^*_{(i)})} \overset{\text{as}}{\rightarrow} \mathrm{E}[\mathbf{g}(\mathbf{B})]. \tag{23.3.10}$$

Clearly the $1/n^*$ terms in (23.3.10) are redundant and can be removed from the calculation.

As we noted, the generality of the approach would allow the posterior mean to be estimated by setting $\mathbf{g}(\mathbf{B}) \equiv \mathbf{B}$, the posterior probability of any event C could be estimated by setting $\mathrm{g}(\mathbf{B}) \equiv \mathrm{I}_{\mathrm{C}}(\mathbf{B})$, and the set C would be a credible region having posterior probability equal to $\mathrm{Eg}(\mathbf{B}) \equiv \mathrm{E}[\mathrm{I}_{\mathrm{C}}(\mathbf{B})]$ (see Chapter 24).

Given our algorithm for generating iid outcomes from the multivariate **T**-distribution described above, the procedure defined in (23.3.10) is in fact operational and can be used to perform posterior analyses when the prior is a general nonconjugate PDF. Of course, the procedure can also be used when $\mathrm{p}(\boldsymbol{\beta})$ is a conjugate PDF – the numerical approach is completely general. Also, as we discussed above, the accuracy of the approximation can be judged by calculating the standard deviations of the numerator and denominator sample mean calculations in (23.3.10); the number of iid outcomes is sufficient when confidence intervals about the sample mean calculations are sufficiently small. Also Geweke (1989) derived an accuracy measure for the calculated value of $\hat{\mathrm{E}}[\mathbf{g}(\mathbf{B})]$. See example 23.3.1 for an application.

23.3.2. Nonnormal Noise Component

In the case of a nonnormal noise component, we generally lose the multivariate **T**-distribution component of the posterior distribution derivation, and in fact little can be said in the way of specifics regarding how Bayesian posterior analyses can proceed. However, the general approach followed in previous sections still applies, including the MC method of estimating posterior expectations.

In the general case the marginal posterior distribution for **B** will be represented by

$$p(\boldsymbol{\beta} \mid \mathbf{y}, \mathbf{x}) = \frac{\int_0^\infty \mathrm{L}(\boldsymbol{\beta}, \sigma \mid \mathbf{y}, \mathbf{x}) p(\boldsymbol{\beta}, \sigma)\, \mathrm{d}\sigma}{\int_{\mathrm{R}^k} \left[\int_0^\infty \mathrm{L}(\boldsymbol{\beta}, \sigma \mid \mathbf{y}, \mathbf{x}) p(\boldsymbol{\beta}, \sigma)\, \mathrm{d}\sigma\right] \mathrm{d}\boldsymbol{\beta}} \tag{23.3.11}$$

for some choice of likelihood function $\mathrm{L}(\boldsymbol{\beta}, \sigma \mid \mathbf{y}, \mathbf{x})$ and prior PDF $\mathrm{p}(\boldsymbol{\beta}, \sigma)$. If we continue to assume that the prior on $\boldsymbol{\beta}$ values is independent of the prior on σ values, so that our prior PDF is of the form $\mathrm{p}(\boldsymbol{\beta}, \sigma) \equiv p(\boldsymbol{\beta})p(\sigma)$, then the marginal posterior on $\boldsymbol{\beta}$ can be simplified to

$$p(\boldsymbol{\beta} \mid \mathbf{y}, \mathbf{x}) = \frac{\mathrm{L}_*(\boldsymbol{\beta} \mid \mathbf{y}, \mathbf{x}) p(\boldsymbol{\beta})}{\int_{\mathrm{R}^k} [\mathrm{L}_*(\boldsymbol{\beta} \mid \mathbf{y}, \mathbf{x}) \mathrm{p}(\boldsymbol{\beta})]\, \mathrm{d}\boldsymbol{\beta}} \tag{23.3.12}$$

where

$$\mathrm{L}_*(\boldsymbol{\beta} \mid \mathbf{y}, \mathbf{x}) = \int_0^\infty \mathrm{L}(\boldsymbol{\beta}, \sigma \mid \mathbf{y}, \mathbf{x}) \mathrm{p}(\sigma)\, \mathrm{d}\sigma \tag{23.3.13}$$

is the expectation of the likelihood function taken with respect to the prior PDF on σ. Note that (23.3.12) is (23.3.7) with the Mult$\mathbf{T}(\cdot)$ distribution replaced by $L_*(\boldsymbol{\beta} \mid \mathbf{y}, \mathbf{x})$.

If, as is often the case, α properly scaled $L_*(\boldsymbol{\beta} \mid \mathbf{y}, \mathbf{x})$ is a PDF from which iid random outcomes $\boldsymbol{\beta}^*_{(i)}$, $i = 1, \ldots, n^*$, can be generated, then we can rely on the fact that posterior expectations of $\mathbf{g}(\mathbf{B})$ can be represented as

$$\mathrm{E}[\mathbf{g}(\mathbf{B})] = \frac{\mathrm{E}_{L_*}[\mathbf{g}(\mathbf{B})p(\mathbf{B})]}{\mathrm{E}_{L_*}[p(\mathbf{B})]} \tag{23.3.14}$$

to estimate $\mathrm{E}[\mathbf{g}(\mathbf{B})]$ using the method defined by (23.3.10). More sophisticated MC methods can be used to estimate expectations when it is not possible to sample from a scaled $L_*(\boldsymbol{\beta} \mid \mathbf{y}, \mathbf{x})$ directly or when $L_*(\boldsymbol{\beta} \mid \mathbf{y}, \mathbf{x})$ itself is difficult to define (see the book appendix on computer simulation and the next example).

► **Example 23.3.1:** To demonstrate the application of Monte Carlo methods to the calculation of properties of the posterior distribution, we provide the GAUSS program C23MC.gss in the examples manual. Following the discussion in this section, we consider posterior distributions based on normal and nonnormal likelihood functions and on a prior distribution selected by the user. For various sizes of the Monte Carlo sample, GAUSS reports the sample average and standard deviation for the simulated posterior outcomes designed to represent a truncated parameter space. The program also demonstrates importance sampling and a stopping rule for the Monte Carlo simulation procedure.

23.3.3. Summary Comments

Depending on the problem, various forms of prior distributions could be appropriate for the parameters, and various likelihood representations could be relevant for the realized data sample. However, in general, all Bayesian estimation and inference procedures evolve from the same basic and common framework presented in this and previous sections of Chapters 22 (and also Chapter 24), and the technical issues should not obscure the relevance of this learning–information recovery process. If, for example, interest centers on estimation, then, whatever the posterior distribution of model parameters, and however this posterior is defined, we consistently do what is natural: We choose a loss function (say, quadratic loss) and find the estimator that minimizes expected posterior loss. If interest centers on evaluating particular propositions, then, regardless of how the posterior was derived, we consider the posterior probabilities of these propositions. In all of this we must be fully cognizant of the conditional postdata interpretation of the Bayes estimation rule and posterior probabilities.

23.4. Bayesian Method of Moments

In Chapters 10–13 we examined, in a traditional sampling theory context, an array of MOM-type estimators for a range of probability–econometric models. In this section we introduce the Bayesian method of moments (BMOM) to permit the computation of postdata densities for parameters when we lack adequate information to specify the likelihood function appropriately. In economics, many times we have only one sample of data and are not sure of the underlying DSP. Thus, it may be hard to justify the traditional sampling assumptions necessary to support the specification of a likelihood function and to implement conventional likelihood and Bayes approaches. In this situation the BMOM idea introduced by Zellner (1996) is quite important because it may permit us to avoid the likelihood specification that is a basic component of the traditional Bayes reasoning process.

In developing the BMOM approach to information recovery, we make use of the regression model $\mathbf{y} = \mathbf{x}\boldsymbol{\beta} + \varepsilon$, where $\mathbf{y}$ and $\mathbf{x}$ are observed values. At the outset, we introduce assumptions that permit us to obtain posterior moments involving the unknown and unobservable $\boldsymbol{\beta}$ and ε and generate estimates of $\boldsymbol{\beta}$ and σ^2. We then use a continuous version of the maximum entropy formalism that was demonstrated in Chapters 13 and electronic Chapter E3 to obtain postdata densities.

In developing BMOM, Zellner reasons as follows: Given a sample of data $\mathbf{y}$, the least-squares estimate of $\boldsymbol{\beta}$ is

$$\hat{\mathbf{b}} = (\mathbf{x}'\mathbf{x})^{-1}\mathbf{x}'\mathbf{y} = \boldsymbol{\beta} + (\mathbf{x}'\mathbf{x})^{-1}\mathbf{x}'\varepsilon \tag{23.4.1}$$

We assume that the columns of $\mathbf{x}$ are orthogonal to ε, and we define $\mathrm{E}[\varepsilon \mid \mathrm{D}]$, where E is a postdata expectation operator with $\mathrm{D} = (\mathbf{y}, \mathbf{x})$. Given $\mathbf{y} = \mathbf{x}\boldsymbol{\beta} + \varepsilon$, we can then write its postdata expectation as $\mathbf{y} = \mathbf{x}\mathrm{E}[\boldsymbol{\beta} \mid \mathrm{D}] + \mathrm{E}(\varepsilon \mid \mathrm{D})$. Thus, because *the posterior moment condition* $\mathbf{x}'\mathrm{E}(\varepsilon \mid \mathrm{D}) = \mathbf{0}$ *is assumed to hold*, the observed vector $\mathbf{y}$ can be viewed as the sum of two *orthogonal* vectors $\mathbf{x}\mathrm{E}[\boldsymbol{\beta} \mid \mathrm{D}]$ and $\mathrm{E}(\varepsilon \mid \mathrm{D})$. Taking the postdata expectations of both sides of (23.4.1), we then have

$$\hat{\mathbf{b}} = (\mathbf{x}'\mathbf{x})^{-1}\mathbf{x}'\mathbf{y} = \mathrm{E}[\boldsymbol{\beta} \mid \mathrm{D}] + \underbrace{(\mathbf{x}'\mathbf{x})^{-1}\mathbf{x}'\mathrm{E}(\varepsilon \mid \mathrm{D})}_{=\mathbf{0}}. \tag{23.4.2}$$

Consequently, the postdata mean of $\boldsymbol{\beta}$, represented by $\mathrm{E}[\boldsymbol{\beta} \mid \mathrm{D}]$, is equal to the least-squares estimate of $\boldsymbol{\beta}$, which under a squared-error loss measure minimizes expected posterior loss.

The postdata mean of the noise component vector is given by

$$\mathrm{E}(\varepsilon \mid \mathrm{D}) = \mathbf{y} - \mathbf{x}\mathrm{E}(\boldsymbol{\beta} \mid \mathrm{D}) = \mathbf{y} - \mathbf{x}\hat{\mathbf{b}} = \hat{\varepsilon}, \tag{23.4.3}$$

which is recognized as the standard LS-based noise component estimate. In addition, the postdata covariance matrix of ε is of the general form $\mathbf{cov}(\varepsilon \mid \mathrm{D}) = \mathrm{E}[\sigma^2 \mid \mathrm{D}]\mathbf{x}(\mathbf{x}'\mathbf{x})^{-1}\mathbf{x}'$. To see this, first note that from (23.4.1)

$$\varepsilon - \hat{\varepsilon} = -\mathbf{x}(\boldsymbol{\beta} - \hat{\mathbf{b}}) = \mathbf{x}(\mathbf{x}'\mathbf{x})^{-1}\mathbf{x}'(\varepsilon - \hat{\varepsilon}) \tag{23.4.4}$$

because $\mathbf{x}'\hat{\varepsilon} = \mathbf{0}$. Therefore, the posterior covariance matrix of ε must satisfy the functional equation

$$\begin{aligned}\mathbf{cov}(\varepsilon \mid \mathrm{D}, \sigma) &= \mathrm{E}[(\varepsilon - \hat{\varepsilon})(\varepsilon - \hat{\varepsilon})' \mid \mathrm{D}, \sigma] \\ &= \mathbf{x}(\mathbf{x}'\mathbf{x})^{-1}\mathbf{x}'\mathrm{E}[(\varepsilon - \hat{\varepsilon})(\varepsilon - \hat{\varepsilon})' \mid \mathrm{D}, \sigma]\mathbf{x}(\mathbf{x}'\mathbf{x})^{-1}\mathbf{x}'.\end{aligned} \tag{23.4.5}$$

Solutions to (23.4.5) are of the form

$$\mathbf{cov}(\varepsilon \mid \mathrm{D}, \sigma) = \sigma^2 \mathbf{x}(\mathbf{x}'\mathbf{x})^{-1}\mathbf{x}' \quad \text{for any } \sigma^2 > 0, \tag{23.4.6}$$

which can be straightforwardly verified by substitution into (23.4.5). By taking the expectation of (23.4.6) with respect to the posterior distribution of σ, the unconditional (not conditioned on σ) posterior covariance matrix of ε is given by

$$\mathbf{cov}(\varepsilon \mid \mathrm{D}) = \mathrm{E}[\sigma^2 \mid \mathrm{D}]\mathbf{x}(\mathbf{x}'\mathbf{x})^{-1}\mathbf{x}'. \tag{23.4.7}$$

It follows from (23.4.6) and $\boldsymbol{\beta} = \hat{\boldsymbol{\beta}} - (\mathbf{x}'\mathbf{x})^{-1}\mathbf{x}'\varepsilon$ that the conditional-on-σ, posterior covariance matrix of $\boldsymbol{\beta}$ is given by

$$\mathbf{cov}(\boldsymbol{\beta} \mid \mathrm{D}, \sigma) = \sigma^2(\mathbf{x}'\mathbf{x})^{-1}. \tag{23.4.8}$$

Because σ^2 is unknown, we need the unconditional posterior covariance matrix of $\boldsymbol{\beta}$ to perform effective posterior inference. In particular, taking the expectation of (23.4.8) with respect to σ yields the unconditional covariance matrix that we seek,

$$\mathbf{cov}(\boldsymbol{\beta} \mid \mathrm{D}) = \mathrm{E}_\sigma[\mathbf{cov}(\boldsymbol{\beta} \mid \mathrm{D}, \sigma)] = \mathrm{E}[\sigma^2 \mid \mathrm{D}](\mathbf{x}'\mathbf{x})^{-1}. \tag{23.4.9}$$

To link the posterior expectation of σ^2 with the observed data, another posterior moment assumption is now introduced. In particular, Zellner assumes the moment condition

$$\mathrm{E}[n^{-1}\varepsilon'\varepsilon \mid \mathrm{D}] \equiv \mathrm{E}[\sigma^2 \mid \mathrm{D}], \tag{23.4.10}$$

which is consistent with the predata-based moment condition $\mathrm{E}[\varepsilon_i^2] = \sigma^2, \forall i$. It follows that

$$\mathrm{E}[\sigma^2 \mid \mathrm{D}] = \mathrm{E}[n^{-1}\varepsilon'\varepsilon \mid \mathrm{D}] = \mathrm{E}[n^{-1}((\varepsilon - \hat{\varepsilon})'(\varepsilon - \hat{\varepsilon}) + \hat{\varepsilon}'\hat{\varepsilon}) \mid \mathrm{D}] = n^{-1}[\mathrm{k}\,\mathrm{E}[\sigma^2 \mid \mathrm{D}] + \hat{\varepsilon}'\hat{\varepsilon}] \tag{23.4.11}$$

because from (23.4.6)

$$\mathrm{E}[(\varepsilon - \hat{\varepsilon})'(\varepsilon - \hat{\varepsilon}) \mid \mathrm{D}] = \mathrm{tr}[\mathbf{cov}(\varepsilon \mid \mathrm{D})] = \mathrm{E}[\sigma^2 \mid \mathrm{D}]k. \tag{23.4.12}$$

Then, solving (23.4.11) for the posterior expectation of σ^2, we obtain

$$\mathrm{E}[\sigma^2 \mid \mathrm{D}] = (n - k)^{-1}\hat{\varepsilon}'\hat{\varepsilon} = \hat{\sigma}^2. \tag{23.4.13}$$

Finally, the posterior covariance matrix for $\boldsymbol{\beta}$ implied by the BMOM procedure under the posterior moment assumptions made heretofore is

$$\mathbf{cov}(\boldsymbol{\beta} \mid \mathrm{D}) = \hat{\sigma}^2(\mathbf{x}'\mathbf{x})^{-1}. \tag{23.4.14}$$

The correspondence between the values of the ML–LS and BMOM (posterior mean) estimates of $\boldsymbol{\beta}$, as well as the relationship between the predata covariance matrix of $\hat{\boldsymbol{\beta}}$ and the postdata posterior covariance matrix of $\boldsymbol{\beta}$, is striking – they are numerically identical. However, we again emphasize that their respective predata and postdata interpretations are quite different.

Given the preceding posterior first- and second-moment information, we now need a basis for utilizing this information to specify a posterior density function for $[\boldsymbol{\beta} \mid \mathrm{D}]$. The reader may recall how we made use of first- and second-empirical-moment information in Chapters 10–13. Under the Bayesian scenario, we need a basis for computing a density function from the given moment conditions, just as we needed a basis in Chapter 12 for using moment information to produce an empirical likelihood function. Working toward this end, we first take a short detour and elaborate on a continuous rather than a discrete entropy formulation.

23.4.1. Continuous Entropy Formulation

So far in terms of the entropy formulations in Chapter 13, we have focused our attention on a finite discrete set of outcomes. We now consider uncountable sets of outcomes. Let $m \to \infty$, replace $\sum_{k=1}^{m}$ by integrals, and define $\mathrm{f}(x)$ as a continuous probability density. In the continuous probability density case, following Jaynes (1982), Zellner (1996), and Golan, Judge, and Miller (1996), we define continuous entropy as

$$\mathrm{H} = -\int \mathrm{f}(x) \ln \mathrm{f}(x)\, \mathrm{dx}, \tag{23.4.15}$$

which is a measure of the (negative) average or expected log height of a density function. Maximizing H without constraints via the choice of $f(\cdot)$, as in the discrete case, leads to a uniform or constant probability distribution on X.

Suppose information exists that the support of the random variable X is the nonnegative part of the real line $(0, \infty)$, and the expectation of the distribution is known to be

$$\int_0^{\infty} x\mathrm{f}(x)\, \mathrm{dx} = \alpha. \tag{23.4.16}$$

Then the corresponding maximum entropy choice for $\mathrm{f}(x)$, given the moment condition (23.4.16), is given by the solution to the extremum problem

$$\max_{\mathrm{f}} \left[\mathrm{H} = -\int_0^{\infty} \mathrm{f}(x) \ln \mathrm{f}(x)\, \mathrm{dx} \right] \tag{23.4.17}$$

subject to

$$\int_0^{\infty} x\mathrm{f}(x)\, \mathrm{dx} = \alpha \tag{23.4.18}$$

and the PDF normalization condition

$$\int_0^{\infty} \mathrm{f}(x)\, \mathrm{dx} = 1. \tag{23.4.19}$$

Forming the Lagrangian, we can use the calculus of variations and solve the resulting Euler equation, leading to the optimal solution

$$\hat{\mathrm{f}}(x) = (1/\alpha) \exp(-x/\alpha), \qquad \text{for } x \geq 0, \tag{23.4.20}$$

which is an exponential distribution with mean α and variance α^2.

Now suppose the support of the random variable X is the entire real line. If first- and second-moment restrictions such as mean zero and variance σ^2 are imposed on $f(x)$, and specified as

$$\int_{-\infty}^{\infty} x f(x)\, dx = 0 \tag{23.4.21}$$

$$\int_{-\infty}^{\infty} x^2 f(x)\, dx = \sigma^2, \tag{23.4.22}$$

then the Lagrangian expression for objective function (23.4.17), subject to constraints (23.4.19) now integrated over $(-\infty, \infty)$, (23.4.21), and (23.4.22), is

$$\begin{aligned} L = &-\int_{-\infty}^{\infty} f(x) \ln f(x)\, dx + \mu \left[1 - \int_{-\infty}^{\infty} f(x)\, dx\right] \\ &+ \lambda_1 \left(0 - \int_{-\infty}^{\infty} x f(x)\, dx\right) + \lambda_2 \left[\sigma^2 - \int_{-\infty}^{\infty} x^2 f(x)\, dx\right] \\ = &\ \mu + \lambda_2 \sigma^2 - \int_{-\infty}^{\infty} [\ln f(x) + \mu + \lambda_1 x + \lambda_2 x^2] f(x)\, dx, \end{aligned} \tag{23.4.23}$$

and the optimal solution for $f(x)$ that maximizes constrained entropy is (Zellner and Highfield (1988))

$$\hat{f}(x) = \exp\left(-1 - \hat{\mu} - \hat{\lambda}_1 x - \hat{\lambda}_2 x^2\right) = (2\pi\sigma^2)^{-1/2} \exp[-x^2/(2\sigma^2)], \tag{23.4.24}$$

where

$$\hat{\mu} = (1/2) \ln(2\pi\sigma^2) - 1, \qquad \hat{\lambda}_1 = 0, \qquad \hat{\lambda}_2 = 1/(2\sigma^2). \tag{23.4.25}$$

Thus, X is normally distributed with mean zero and variance σ^2.

These results have been generalized by Zellner and Highfield (1988) to include higher-order moment constraints $\int x^r f(x) = \mu_r$. By adding moment constraints, one may derive a more general class of densities. If the moments are unknown, sample moments may be used as estimates of μ_r, and Bayesian and frequentist interpretations are provided by Ryu (1993).

In the BMOM setting, we use the continuous entropy approach to avoid specifying a likelihood function and to allow the shape of the posterior density to be determined by the data through the postdata moment conditions. Given the maximum entropy basis for defining a continuous probability density function and the postdata moment conditions developed in (23.4.2) and (23.4.14), we now make use of this information to produce a postdata posterior density function for $\boldsymbol{\beta}$ from the BMOM moment information.

23.4.2. A Posterior Density Function

Given the results of Section 23.4.1 and the postdata moment constraints (23.4.2) and (23.4.14), the corresponding entropy-maximizing proper posterior finite sample density is a multivariate normal

$$p(\boldsymbol{\beta} \mid \mathrm{D}) = \mathrm{N}(\hat{\mathbf{b}}, \hat{\sigma}^2(\mathbf{x}'\mathbf{x})^{-1}). \tag{23.4.26}$$

As before, this posterior density can be used to compute optimal point estimates, marginal densities, credible sets, posterior odds ratios, and in general to develop conditional inferences (see Chapter 24 for a discussion of inference procedures). If higher moment conditions exist, this information may be imposed as additional constraints within the maximum entropy context. Also, if certain information exists that would permit one or more of the β_i's to be bounded, this nonsample information could be introduced in the form of inequality constraints. The Monte Carlo integration procedures discussed in Section 23.3 and in the Monte Carlo appendix chapter could then be used to evaluate the truncated posterior density.

► **Example 23.4.1:** The GAUSS program C23BMOM.gss (provided in the examples manual) presents an application of the BMOM estimator to the linear regression model. For a given sample of size n (selected by the user), GAUSS computes the moments of the posterior distribution (23.4.26) and compares the interpretation of the BMOM results to the corresponding LS–ML estimates. Then, GAUSS extends the BMOM procedure to derive the posterior distribution given three post-data moments for the parameter of a simple location model.

23.5. Concluding Remarks

When information about the DSP exists in the form of a well-defined likelihood function and natural conjugate priors exist that lead to tractable posterior distributions, then the Bayes approach to estimation and inference provides a tractable and logically consistent approach for combining data and prior information to make postdata inferences about model parameters. In fact, alternative Bayesian formulations, such as empirical Bayes procedures, provide a basis for estimation and inference solutions that perform well when viewed from both Bayesian postdata and classical predata perspectives. Finally, all posterior distributions may not be friendly, and thus analytical solutions to posterior calculations may not be possible. In situations like this, Monte Carlo procedures, such as those demonstrated in Section 23.3, Example 23.3.1, and in the Monte Carlo book appendix, are available to solve these analytically intractable cases.

When all of the components of the traditional Bayesian approach are not available, the creative efforts of many over time have combined to provide effective alternative approaches for information recovery. When it is difficult to make sampling assumptions that lead to an explicit specification of a likelihood function, the Bayesian method of moments approach (demonstrated in Section 23.4) provides a basis for proceeding. Alternatively, the empirical Bayes approach of Section 23.2 can be used when some parameters of the prior distribution cannot be specified, in which case they are estimated based on observed data.

Given this variety of alternative Bayesian formulations with an estimation objective, we turn in Chapter 24 to the important topic of Bayesian inference.

23.6. Exercises

23.6.1. Idea Checklist – Knowledge Guides

---

1. Why do you think everyone is not a Bayesian? Alternatively, why does the sampling theory approach seem to hold the high ground with econometricians?
2. What is the basis for the empirical Bayes estimator and how does it differ from the traditional Bayes estimator?
3. How would you analyze a likelihood-prior posterior combination when the prior is not conjugate? How would you proceed if the integrals defining the posterior are analytically intractable?
4. When there is uncertainty concerning the prior hyperparameters, how would you make use of the hierarchical Bayes estimator and the possibility of using Monte Carlo methods to compute hierarchical Bayes estimates?
5. What are the statistical implications of the risk functions presented in Figure 23.1?

23.6.2. Problems

23–1 The performance of the Bayes rule depends critically on the choice of the prior variance, and usually we have limited guidance as to how to specify it. Develop a basis for introducing and coping with this uncertainty about the prior.

23–2 Assume production outcomes can be described by the normal linear regression model $y_t = \beta_1 + x_{t2}\beta_2 + x_{t3}\beta_3 + \varepsilon_t$, where output y_t and the inputs x_t are measured on a log scale. Assume your prior beliefs can be expressed in the form of a conjugate prior, that your nonsample knowledge indicates the production process is expected to operate under constant returns to scale, and that you are relatively uncertain about the individual impacts of x_{t2} and x_{t3} on output. Suppose we follow Judge et al. (1988, pp. 288–94) and finalize this presample information as

$$E[\beta_2] = E[\beta_3] = 0.5;\ E[\beta_2 + \beta_3] = 1$$

$$P(0.9 < \beta_2 + \beta_3 < 1.1 \mid \sigma = 0.3) = 0.9$$

$$P(0.2 < \beta_2 < 0.8 \mid \sigma = 0.3) = 0.9$$

$$P(0.2 < \beta_3 < 0.8 \mid \sigma = 0.3) = 0.9$$

Express your presample information on the intercept as

$$E[\beta_1] = 5;\quad P(-10 < \beta_1 < 20 \mid \sigma = .3) = 0.9$$

Assume initially the scale parameter σ^2 is known, $\sigma^2 = 0.09$, and that our information on β_1, β_2, and β_3 can be represented in normal form.

a. Given this presample information, develop the hierarchical parameters of the prior mean and covariance.

b. Using a pseudorandom sample of 20 observations that you generate, derive the posterior PDF and the corresponding mean and covariance matrix. Derive the marginal

PDF for β_2 and β_3 and interpret. Compute the probability that $\beta_3 < 0.35$ and interpret the result.

c. Assume the scale parameter σ^2 is unknown. How would you proceed in carrying through a Bayesian analysis and the corresponding interpretation?

23–3 Demonstrate the expected quadratic risk for the empirical Bayes–Stein-like estimator (23.2.11). Contrast the Bayes and sampling theory statistical interpretations of this shrinkage estimator.

23–4 Suppose you have a sample of n iid observations for the Poisson(λ) model. The conjugate prior distribution for $\lambda > 0$ is the Gamma(α, β) family.

a. Derive the posterior distribution for λ.

b. If we view the posterior mean as a classical estimator, can we say that the estimator is consistent and asymptotically normal?

c. Suppose you can specify a value for the prior parameter α but remain uncertain about β. If you use a hierarchical Gamma(γ, δ) prior distribution to represent your beliefs about $\boldsymbol{\beta}$, what is the joint posterior distribution for β and λ?

d. Show that you can factor the joint posterior distribution as the product of the conditional posterior distributions $\mathrm{p}(\lambda \mid \beta, \alpha, \mathbf{y}) = \mathrm{Gamma}\,(\alpha + n\bar{y}, \beta + n)$ and $\mathrm{p}(\beta \mid \lambda, \alpha, \gamma, \delta, \mathbf{y}) = \mathrm{Gamma}(\alpha + \gamma, \lambda + \delta)$.

23–5 Suppose we observe a random sample of n observations $\mathbf{y}$ from the N(μ, 1) distribution and we express our limited information about μ with a Cauchy(δ) prior distribution

$$\mathrm{p}(\mu) = \frac{1}{\pi[1 + (\mu - \delta)^2]}.$$

Further, suppose we place an improper prior on the hyperparameter δ. State the posterior distribution $\mathrm{p}(\boldsymbol{\theta} \mid \mathbf{y})$ for $\boldsymbol{\theta}' = (\mu, \delta)$. Can you identify the joint posterior or the conditional posteriors as members of a familiar parametric family?

23.6.3. Computer Problems

23–1 For the Bayesian posterior problem described in Problem 4, suppose we observe $n\,\bar{y}_n = 15$ for $n = 5$ and select $\alpha = 2$, $\gamma = 3$, and $\delta = 2$. Write a GAUSS program to simulate the posterior mean of λ and β by applying the Gibbs sampling algorithm (see the Monte Carlo appendix chapter) to the conditional posterior distributions in Problem 4d. Conduct the sampling exercise with $m = 250$, 500, and 1000 pseudo-random draws.

23–2 For the Bayesian linear regression model, state the conditional posterior distributions $\mathrm{p}(\boldsymbol{\beta} \mid \sigma, \mathbf{y}, \mathbf{x})$ and $\mathrm{p}(\sigma \mid \boldsymbol{\beta}, \mathbf{y}, \mathbf{x})$. List the specific steps in a Gibbs sampling algorithm used to generate pseudorandom observations from the posterior distribution.

23–3 For the Cauchy in Problem 5, write a GAUSS program to implement the Metropolis–Hastings algorithm (see the Monte Carlo appendix chapter) used to simulate $\mathrm{p}(\boldsymbol{\theta} \mid \mathbf{y})$. On the basis of Chib and Greenberg (1995), note that one plausible means of generating candidate parameter values is to set $\boldsymbol{\theta}^{m+1} = \boldsymbol{\theta}^m + \boldsymbol{\nu}$ where $\boldsymbol{\nu} \sim \mathrm{N}(\mathbf{0}, \tau^2\mathbf{I}_k)$ for some $\tau > 0$. In this case, the Markov probability of accepting the new variate reduces to $\alpha(\boldsymbol{\theta}^{m+1}, \boldsymbol{\theta}^m) = \min[\mathrm{p}(\boldsymbol{\theta}^{m+1} \mid \mathbf{y})/\mathrm{p}(\boldsymbol{\theta}^m \mid \mathbf{y}), 1]$ because $\pi(\boldsymbol{\theta}^{m+1} \mid \boldsymbol{\theta}^m)$ is symmetric. Finally, how does an increase in the value of τ^2 affect $\alpha(\boldsymbol{\theta}^{m+1}, \boldsymbol{\theta}^m)$?

23.7. References

Berger, J. (1980), "A Robust Generalized Bayes Estimator and Confidence Region for a Multivariate Normal Mean," *Annals of Statistics*, Vol. 8, pp. 716–61.

Berger, J. O. (1985), "Statistical Decision Theory and Bayesian Analysis (2nd Edition)," New York: Springer–Verlag.

Casella, G. (1985), "An Introduction to Empirical Bayes Data Analysis," *The American Statistician*, Vol. 39, pp. 83–7.

Casella, G., and E. I. George (1994), "Explaining the Gibbs Sampler," *The American Statistician*, Vol. 46, pp. 167–74.

Chib, S., and E. Greenberg (1995), "Understanding the Metropolis–Hastings Algorithm," *The American Statistician*, Vol. 49, pp. 327–35.

Cowles, M. K., and B. P. Carlin (1996), "Markov Chain Monte Carlo Convergence Diagnostics: A Comparative Review," *Journal of the American Statistical Association*, Vol. 91, pp. 883–904.

Efron, B., and C. Morris (1973), "Stein's Estimation Rule and Its Competitors – An Empirical Bayes Approach," *Journal of the American Statistical Association*, Vol. 68, pp. 117–30.

Geman, S., and D. Geman (1984), "Stochastic Relaxation, Gibbs Distributions, and the Bayesian Restoration of Images," *IEEE Transactions on Pattern Analysis and Machine Intelligence*, Vol. 6, pp. 721–41.

Geweke, J. (1986), "Exact Inference in the Inequality Constrained Normal Linear Regression Model," *Journal of Applied Econometrics*, Vol. 1, pp. 127–41.

Geweke, J. (1989), "Exact Predictive Density for Linear Models with ARCH Distributions," *Journal of Econometrics*, Vol. 40, pp. 63–86.

Golan, A., G. G. Judge, and D. Miller (1996), *Maximum Entropy Econometrics: Robust Estimation with Limited Data*, New York: John Wiley and Sons.

Griffiths, W. E., and D. Chotikapanich (1997), "Bayesian Methodology for Imposing Inequality Constraints on a Linear Expenditures System with Demographic Factors," *Australian Economic Papers*, Vol. 36, pp. 321–41.

Hastings, W. (1970), "Monte Carlo Sampling Methods Using Markov Chains and Their Applications," *Biometrika*, Vol. 57, pp. 97–109.

Hoerl, A. E., and R. W. Kennard (1970), "Ridge Regression: Biased Estimation for Nonorthogonal Problems," *Technometrics*, Vol. 1, pp. 55–67.

Jaynes, E. T. (1982), "On the Rationale of Maximum-Entropy Methods," *Proceedings of the IEEE*, Vol. 70, pp. 939–52.

Johnson, M. (1987), *Multivariate Statistical Simulation*, New York: John Wiley and Sons.

Johnson, N. L., and S. Kotz (1972), "Distributions in Statistics: Continuous Multivariate Distribution," New York: John Wiley and Sons.

Judge, G. G., and M. E. Bock (1978), *The Statistical Implications of Pre-Test and Stein–Rule Estimators in Econometrics*, Amsterdam: North–Holland.

Judge, G., R. C. Hill, W. E. Griffiths, H. Lütkepohl, and T.-C. Lee (1988), *Introduction to the Theory and Practice of Econometrics*, (2nd Ed.), New York: John Wiley and Sons.

Judge, G. G., W. E. Griffiths, R. C. Hill, H. Lütkepohl, and T.-C. Lee (1985), *The Theory and Practice of Econometrics*, (2nd ed.), New York: John Wiley and Sons.

Kass, R. E., B. P. Carlin, A. Gelman, and R. M. Neal (1998), "Markov Chain Monte Carlo in Practice: A Roundtable Discussion," *The American Statistician*, Vol. 52, pp. 93–100.

Metropolis, N., A. Rosenbluth, W. Rosenbluth, M. Teller, and E. Teller (1953), "Equations of State Calculations by Fast Computing Machines," *The Journal of Chemical Physics*, Vol. 21, pp. 1087–91.

Poirier, D. (1995), Intermediate Statistics and Econometrics, Cambridge, MA: MIT Press.

Ryu, H. (1993), "Maximum Entropy Estimation of Density and Regression Functions," *Journal of Econometrics*, Vol. 56, pp. 397–440.

Tierney, L. (1994), "Markov Chains for Exploring Posterior Distributions," *The Annals of Statistics*, Vol. 22, pp. 1701–62.

Zellner, A. (1980), "On Bayesian Regression Analysis with g-Prior Distributions," Paper presented at the Econometric Society Meeting, September, 1980, Denver, Colorado.

Zellner, A. (1986), "On Assessing Prior Distributions and Bayesian Regression Analysis with g-prior Distributions," In P. Goel and A. Zellner (Eds.), *Bayesian Inference and Decision Techniques*, (pp. 233–43), Amsterdam: North–Holland.

Zellner, A. (1996), "Bayesian Method of Moments/Instrumental Variable (BMOM/IV) Analysis of Mean and Regression Models," In J. C. Lee, W. O. Johnson, and A. Zellner (Eds.), *Modeling and Prediction: Honoring Seymour Geisser*, New York: Springer–Verlag.

Zellner, A., and R. A. Highfield (1988), "Calculation of Maximum Entropy Distributions and Approximation of Marginal Posterior Distributions," *Journal of Econometrics*, Vol. 37, pp. 195–209.

CHAPTER 24

Bayesian Inference

AS an introduction to this final Bayes chapter, and to reemphasize the sharp contrast between the classical sampling theory and Bayesian approaches to solving inverse problems, reconsider the noisy inverse problem first introduced in Chapter 3. Recall that we were unable to measure the unknown k-dimensional vector $\boldsymbol{\beta}$ directly and instead observed an n-dimensional vector of noisy sample observations $\mathbf{y} = (y_1, y_2, \ldots, y_n)'$ consistent with the underlying linear regression model data-sampling process (DSP)

$$\mathbf{Y} = \mathbf{x}\boldsymbol{\beta} + \varepsilon, \tag{24.0.1}$$

where $\mathbf{x}$ is a $(n \times k)$ design matrix known to the experimenter or the analyst. The unobservable components are a $(k \times 1)$ vector of unknown parameters $\boldsymbol{\beta} = (\beta_1, \beta_2, \ldots, \beta_k)'$, and the n-dimensional noise vector ε that has a multivariate normal distribution with mean zero and covariance matrix $\sigma^2\mathbf{I}_n$. Under this sampling model, the maximum likelihood estimator (MLE)

$$\hat{\boldsymbol{\beta}} = (\mathbf{x}'\mathbf{x})^{-1}\mathbf{x}'\mathbf{Y} \sim \mathrm{N}(\boldsymbol{\beta}, \sigma^2(\mathbf{x}'\mathbf{x})^{-1}) \tag{24.0.2}$$

is a minimum variance unbiased estimator (MVUE). Under the squared-error loss measure, $\rho(\boldsymbol{\beta}, \hat{\boldsymbol{\beta}}) = \mathrm{E}\|\hat{\boldsymbol{\beta}} - \boldsymbol{\beta}\|^2$, the MLE is minimax and has constant risk $\rho(\boldsymbol{\beta}, \hat{\boldsymbol{\beta}}) = \sigma^2\mathrm{tr}(\mathbf{x}'\mathbf{x})^{-1}$. If the scale parameter σ^2 is unknown, it can be estimated by the minimum variance unbiased estimator $\mathrm{S}^2 = (\mathbf{Y} - \mathbf{x}\hat{\boldsymbol{\beta}})'(\mathbf{Y} - \mathbf{x}\hat{\boldsymbol{\beta}})/(n-k)$, where $(n-k)\mathrm{S}^2/\sigma^2$ has a Chi-square$(n-k, 0)$ distribution. The distribution and MVUE properties of the estimators are defined within a predata, conceptual, repeated-sampling framework, which represents sampling properties relative to a universal set of hypothetical outcomes thought to be possible before data are sampled.

In contrast, for purposes of representing information about the model parameters, it is typical in the Bayesian context to assume a joint prior distribution for $\mathbf{B}$ and Σ (where $(\boldsymbol{\beta}, \sigma)$ is now viewed as an outcome of the conceptual random variable $(\mathbf{B}, \Sigma)$). It is then meaningful to conceptualize a conditional distribution for $\mathbf{B}$ given σ, which in the case of a normal distribution can be expressed as $\mathrm{p}(\boldsymbol{\beta} \mid \sigma) = \mathrm{N}(\boldsymbol{\mu}, \sigma^2\boldsymbol{\Psi})$, with $\boldsymbol{\Psi}$ a specified positive definite matrix. If the scale parameter σ^2 is unknown, we may use an appropriate marginal prior distribution for Σ, for example the inverted-square root gamma conjugate prior (22.4.4), to represent information about σ^2. The posterior conditional distribution for **B** given σ, $p(\boldsymbol{\beta} \mid \sigma, \mathbf{y}, \mathbf{x})$, is normal with mean

$$\boldsymbol{\beta}_* = (\boldsymbol{\Psi}^{-1} + \mathbf{x}'\mathbf{x})^{-1}(\mathbf{x}'\mathbf{x}\hat{\mathbf{b}} + \boldsymbol{\Psi}^{-1}\boldsymbol{\mu}) \qquad (24.0.3)$$

and with covariance matrix $\sigma^2(\boldsymbol{\Psi}^{-1} + \mathbf{x}'\mathbf{x})^{-1}$ (see (22.4.9) and (22.4.10)). Under a squared-error loss measure, the minimum risk-point estimator is the posterior mean of **B**. This assessment is postdata and does not consider hypothetically possible but not-yet-observed sample information.

Building on basic Bayesian concepts such as these, in Chapters 22 and 23 we examined the definition of Bayesian posterior distributions in a variety of situations and investigated their use in recovering information about unknown parameters. In this chapter we extend our understanding of the Bayesian approach to include inference and discuss Bayesian credible regions and hypothesis testing in general and their application to the linear regression model in particular. Consistent with Chapters 22 and 23, we note that the definition and interpretation of Bayes inference statements proceed in a conditional, postdata What *did* happen? context rather than the classical predata What *could have* happened? sense. The relevant Bayesian model and regression components and characteristics for this discussion were delineated in Tables 22.1 and 22.2.

24.1. Credible Regions

Credible regions are the Bayesian counterpart to the concept of confidence regions in classical statistical analysis in the sense that both concepts are an attempt to contain the unknown parameter vector within a set of values with a known probability. However, the interpretation of the Bayesian confidence set is *posterior* to or conditional on the observed data, and the known probability refers to the posterior probability that $\boldsymbol{\theta}$ is contained within a given set of values. Alternatively, as we have noted previously, the interpretation of a classical confidence region occurs in a predata repeated-sampling context, and the known probability refers to the predata propensity of a set estimator to generate sets of values that would actually contain $\boldsymbol{\theta}$. We emphasize that the containment propensity, or classical *confidence level*, is determined and applies *prior to* any data's actually being observed.

24.1.1. General Principles

Bayesian interval estimates are based on the posterior PDF for the conceptually random parameter vector of the model $\boldsymbol{\Theta}$. The $100(1-\alpha)\%$ Bayes upper-bounded credible interval for the jth element of $\boldsymbol{\theta}$ is given by $(-\infty, \mathrm{u}_\alpha(\mathbf{y})]$, where

$$P(\theta_j \le \mathrm{u}_\alpha(\mathbf{y}) \mid \mathbf{y}) = \int_{-\infty}^{\mathrm{u}_\alpha(\mathbf{y})} p(\theta_j \mid \mathbf{y})\, d\theta_j = 1 - \alpha, \qquad (24.1.1)$$

$p(\theta_j \mid \mathbf{y})$ is the marginal posterior PDF of Θ_j, and the sample outcome is observed to be $\mathbf{y}$. A $100(1-\alpha)\%$ Bayes lower-bounded credible interval for θ_j is similarly defined by $[\ell_\alpha(\mathbf{y}), \infty)$, where

$$P(\theta_j \geq \ell_\alpha(\mathbf{y}) \mid \mathbf{y}) = \int_{\ell_\alpha(\mathbf{y})}^{\infty} p(\theta_j \mid \mathbf{y})\, d\theta_j = 1 - \alpha. \tag{24.1.2}$$

A $100(1-\alpha)\%$ Bayesian two-sided credible interval for θ_j is an interval set derived from the marginal posterior PDF for Θ_j as $[\ell_\alpha(\mathbf{y}), u_\alpha(\mathbf{y})]$, where

$$P(\ell_\alpha(\mathbf{y}) \leq \theta_j \leq u_\alpha(\mathbf{y}) \mid \mathbf{y}) = \int_{\ell_\alpha(\mathbf{y})}^{u_\alpha(\mathbf{y})} p(\theta_j \mid \mathbf{y})\, d\theta_j = 1 - \alpha. \tag{24.1.3}$$

► **Example 24.1.1:** Following Example 22.3.1, consider a sample of n iid $N(\theta, 1)$ observations and a diffuse prior for Θ. The posterior distribution is a $N(\bar{y}, n^{-1})$ PDF, $p(\theta \mid \mathbf{y}) \propto \exp\{-n(\theta - \bar{y})^2/2\}$. Thus, $Z = \sqrt{n}(\Theta - \bar{y})$ is N(0, 1) a posteriori. To derive upper- and lower-bounded credible intervals, note that a constant can be found such that $P(z \leq u_\alpha(\bar{y}) \mid \bar{y}) = 1 - \alpha$ or $P(z \geq \ell_\alpha(\bar{y}) \mid \bar{y}) = 1 - \alpha$. For example, if $\alpha = .05$, then $u_\alpha(\bar{y}) = -\ell_\alpha(\bar{y}) = 1.645$, and the upper- and lower-bounded credible intervals for θ are given by $\theta \leq \bar{y} + 1.645n^{-1/2}$ and $\theta \geq \bar{y} - 1.645n^{-1/2}$, respectively.

To define a two-sided credible interval we can find constants $u_\alpha(\bar{y})$ and $\ell_\alpha(\bar{y})$ such that $P(z \leq u_\alpha(\bar{y}) \mid \bar{y}) = 1 - (\alpha/2)$ and $P(z \geq \ell_\alpha(\bar{y}) \mid \bar{y}) = 1 - (\alpha/2)$, and these constants will satisfy (24.1.3). For example, if $\alpha = .05$, then $u_\alpha(\bar{y}) = -\ell_\alpha(\bar{y}) = 1.96$ and the credible interval for Θ is given by $\bar{y} - 1.96n^{-1/2} \leq \theta \leq \bar{y} + 1.96n^{-1/2}$. Intervals constructed in this fashion are known as *equal-tail* credible intervals. However, unlike the case of the Bayes lower- and upper-bounded credible intervals, the choice of the lower and upper bounds in the two-sided interval case (24.1.3) is not necessarily unique. In fact, there will be an infinite number of alternative choices in the case at hand. To resolve the uniqueness issue, we examine the concept of *highest posterior density* credible regions in the next subsection.

Credible regions in higher dimensions are general sets of parameter values, say A, in which $\boldsymbol{\Theta}$ lies with posterior probability $1-\alpha$. In the continuous case, any $100(1-\alpha)\%$ credible region for the $(k \times 1)$ parameter vector $\boldsymbol{\theta}$ satisfies

$$\int_{\boldsymbol{\theta} \in A} p(\boldsymbol{\theta} \mid \mathbf{y})\, d\boldsymbol{\theta} = 1 - \alpha \tag{24.1.4}$$

with summation replacing integration in the discrete case. Note that A is not necessarily unique in (24.1.4) and is analogous to the two-sided credible interval for $\boldsymbol{\theta}$ in Example 24.1.1.

24.1.2. Highest Posterior Density Credible Regions

The most common solution to the problem of nonunique credible regions is to utilize the credible region whose elements are assigned *highest posterior density* (HPD). A $100(1-\alpha)\%$ credible region, A, is an HPD region if $p(\boldsymbol{\theta} \mid \mathbf{y}) > p(\boldsymbol{\theta}_0 \mid \mathbf{y})$ for all $\boldsymbol{\theta} \in A$ and $\boldsymbol{\theta}_0 \notin A$, and $\int_A p(\boldsymbol{\theta} \mid \mathbf{y})\, d\boldsymbol{\theta} = 1 - \alpha$ (we provide an alternative equivalent characterization in (24.1.6) and (24.1.7)). This means that all of the $\boldsymbol{\theta}$ values that are contained within the credible region are assigned higher posterior density weightings than the $\boldsymbol{\theta}$

values that are not contained in the credible region, which accounts for the name highest posterior density credible region. In the common case in which the posterior PDF is *unimodal*, the problem of finding the $100(1-\alpha)\%$ two-sided HPD credible interval for scalar θ is equivalent to finding the smallest-length interval of θ values that is assigned posterior probability $(1-\alpha)$. In particular, the highest posterior density credible region is defined by $\{\ell_\alpha^{\text{HPD}}, \text{u}_\alpha^{\text{HPD}}\} = \arg\min_{\ell_\alpha, \text{u}_\alpha}[(\text{u}_\alpha - \ell_\alpha) \text{ s.t} \int_{\ell_\alpha}^{\text{u}_\alpha} \text{p}(\theta \mid \mathbf{y})\, \text{d}\theta = 1-\alpha]$. For *symmetric unimodal* posterior distributions and scalar θ, the bounds of the HPD credible interval are equal to the $100(\alpha/2)\%$ and $100(1-\alpha/2)\%$ quantiles of the posterior distribution, which is an equal-tail interval. In Example 24.1.1, choosing $[\ell_\alpha(\bar{y}), \text{u}_\alpha(\bar{y})]$ so that $\text{P}(z \le \text{u}_\alpha(\bar{y}) \mid \bar{y}) = 1-\alpha/2$ and $\text{P}(z \ge \ell_\alpha(\bar{y}) \mid \bar{y}) = 1-\alpha/2$ defines the two-sided HPD credible interval for θ. Outside of the symmetric and unimodal cases, the formation of HPD regions in multiple parameter settings can be computationally burdensome and is not often attempted in practice.

24.1.3. Credible Regions in the Regression Model

A $100(1-\alpha)\%$ credible region for the parameter vector $\boldsymbol{\beta}$ in the regression model is a subset A of $\boldsymbol{\beta}$-values for which (we suppress the $\mathbf{x}$ argument henceforth)

$$\text{p(A)} = \int_{\text{A}} \text{p}(\boldsymbol{\beta} \mid \mathbf{y})\, \text{d}\boldsymbol{\beta} = 1-\alpha. \tag{24.1.5}$$

In words, (24.1.5) indicates that the posterior probability of $\boldsymbol{\beta} \in \text{A}$ is $1-\alpha$. We emphasize that we are actually referring to the *probability* that $\boldsymbol{\beta}$ is in A, where A is a fixed set of values. In contrast, the classical confidence region corresponding to A is a random set, and we then evaluate the probability that an *outcome* of A, which has not yet been observed, will cover or contain $\boldsymbol{\beta}$. Hence, $1-\alpha$ is also referred to as the *coverage probability* of the confidence region in the classical setting.

In order for the credible set to be as informative about $\boldsymbol{\beta}$ as possible, it is desirable to minimize the length (in one dimension), area (in two dimensions), or volume of the credible set. To accomplish this objective, one seeks to include in the credible set only those values of $\boldsymbol{\beta}$ that have the highest posterior density weightings. This leads to the concept of the $100(1-\alpha)\%$ HPD credible set for the regression model parameters $\boldsymbol{\beta}$ given by

$$\text{A} = \{\boldsymbol{\beta} : \text{p}(\boldsymbol{\beta} \mid \mathbf{y}) \ge k(\alpha)\}, \tag{24.1.6}$$

where $k(\alpha)$ is the largest positive constant for which

$$\text{p}(\text{A} \mid \mathbf{y}) = 1-\alpha. \tag{24.1.7}$$

In some cases, defining the HPD credible set is straightforward. For example, consider the linear regression model with normal likelihood function and natural conjugate informative prior. As stated in Section 22.4, the standardized value of B_j, $(\text{B}_j - \beta_{*j})/[h^{-1}[j, j]]^{1/2}$, has a student's (univariate) T-distribution with $v = (n+m-k-1)$ degrees of freedom, where β_{j*} denotes the mean of the posterior distribution of B_j (the definition of $\mathbf{h}$ is given following (22.4.14)). The symmetric unimodal nature of the student's T distribution implies that an HPD credible set can be characterized in terms of the probability of an event of the symmetric tail form

$$\mathrm{P}\left(\left|\frac{\beta_j - \beta_{j*}}{(h^{-1}[j,j])^{1/2}}\right| \le t_{1-\alpha/2} \,|\, \mathbf{y}\right) = 1 - \alpha, \tag{24.1.8}$$

where $t_{1-\alpha/2}$ is the $(1-\alpha/2)$ quantile of the student's T distribution. The $100(1-\alpha)\%$ HPD credible set is then

$$\beta_j \in [\beta_{j*} - t_{1-\alpha/2}(h^{-1}[j,j])^{1/2}, \beta_{j*} + t_{1-\alpha/2}(h^{-1}[j,j])^{1/2}]. \tag{24.1.9}$$

The HPD credible set looks remarkably similar to a classical confidence interval with confidence coefficient $(1-\alpha)$. However, we again emphasize that the Bayes interval is *fixed,* not random as in the classical case, and thus the interpretation of the interval is markedly different than for the classical confidence interval case.

In higher dimensions, HPD confidence regions for linear regression parameters are fairly straightforward to compute if the noise component is normally distributed and the prior distribution is either the standard ignorance prior (Section 22.3) or the standard conjugate prior (Section 22.4). In these cases we have already observed that a multidimensional credible region can be based on the standard F-distribution (recall (22.3.18), (22.3.19), (22.4.15) and (22.4.16)). It can be shown, on the basis of functional form of the multivariate **T**-distribution, that these credible regions are in fact HPD regions. However, for general noise component distributions, for unfriendly priors, or both, the computation of HPD credible regions can present a significant computational challenge. In these cases, the definition of HPD regions is generally not attempted for more than three dimensions because, in any case, visualization of the set becomes difficult. Instead, one often resorts to simple, more tractable credible set definitions, such as equal tail-type sets. Some computer-based procedures that can be used for evaluating credible regions are demonstrated in the Monte Carlo book appendix.

► **Example 24.1.2:** The GAUSS program C24CSet.gss (provided in the examples manual) compares Bayesian credible regions for parameters of the linear regression model. Given a sample of observations, the posterior distributions are derived under several prior distributions and the multivariate normal likelihood function. GAUSS reports the upper and lower bounds for $100(1-\alpha)\%$ credible regions based on several posterior criteria (i.e., upper-bounded, lower-bounded, asymmetric two-tailed, and HPD) as well as the $100(1-\alpha)\%$ classical confidence intervals. GAUSS then describes the interpretation of the Bayesian and classical sets.

24.2. Hypothesis Evaluation and Decision

Hypothesis testing is considered a problem of decision making under uncertainty in the Bayesian approach. The assumption of a random parameter vector $\boldsymbol{\Theta}$ together with its associated posterior PDF that reflects the uncertainty relating to the value of $\boldsymbol{\theta}$ provides the ingredients for comparing null and alternate hypotheses in probabilistic terms.

24.2.1. General Principles

To motivate the Bayesian approach to evaluating hypotheses, consider the statistical model, $y_i = \theta + \varepsilon_i$ previously examined in Examples 22.3.1 and 24.1.1. For the scalar parameter θ, suppose we are interested in evaluating the hypothesis $H_0: \theta \geq 0$ versus the alternative hypothesis $H_a: \theta < 0$. On the basis of a proper prior distribution for Θ, the *predata* probability assigned to the null hypothesis can be calculated from the prior distribution as

$$P(H_0) = \int_0^\infty p(\theta)\, d\theta \tag{24.2.1}$$

and $P(H_a) = 1 - P(H_0)$. To compare the predata beliefs regarding the two hypotheses, we can use the *prior odds ratio* $P(H_0)/P(H_a)$. After the predata beliefs are updated with the observed sample information, we can compute the posterior probability for the hypotheses as

$$P(H_0 \mid \mathbf{y}) = \int_0^\infty p(\theta \mid \mathbf{y})\, d\theta, \tag{24.2.2}$$

and $P(H_a \mid \mathbf{y}) = 1 - P(H_0 \mid \mathbf{y})$. Accordingly, the *posterior odds ratio* is

$$P(H_0 \mid \mathbf{y})/P(H_a \mid \mathbf{y}). \tag{24.2.3}$$

The posterior odds ratio represents the relative postdata credibility of the two hypotheses, and values of the odds ratio that are greater than or less than 1 provide more or less support for the null hypothesis, respectively.

In determining the optimal decision in a test of H_0 versus H_a, the Bayesian approach also assigns costs, penalties, or losses to each possible outcome. As in our previous applications of decision theory, a loss function $\ell(H_i, H_j)$ describes the penalty assigned to decision H_j when hypothesis H_i is correct. In the Bayesian approach, the optimal decision corresponds to the hypothesis associated with the smallest posterior expected loss. For the typical "two-state, two-action" testing problem, we have the general loss function representation

		TRUTH	
		H_0	H_a
DECISION	H_0	$\ell(H_0, H_0) = 0$	$\ell(H_a, H_0) > 0$
	H_a	$\ell(H_0, H_a) > 0$	$\ell(H_a, H_a) = 0$

Thus, the analyst assigns positive losses, $\ell(H_0, H_a)$ and $\ell(H_a, H_0)$, to Type-I and Type-II errors, respectively.

We can evaluate the posterior expected losses associated with the two possible decisions in the following way:

$$\begin{aligned} \mathrm{E}[\ell(\mathrm{H}, \mathrm{H}_0)] &= \ell(\mathrm{H}_0, \mathrm{H}_0)\mathrm{P}(\mathrm{H}_0 \mid \mathbf{y}) + \ell(\mathrm{H}_a, \mathrm{H}_0)\mathrm{P}(\mathrm{H}_a \mid \mathbf{y}) \\ &= \ell(\mathrm{H}_a, \mathrm{H}_0)\mathrm{P}(\mathrm{H}_a \mid \mathbf{y}) \end{aligned} \tag{24.2.4}$$

$$\begin{aligned} \mathrm{E}[\ell(\mathrm{H}, \mathrm{H}_a)] &= \ell(\mathrm{H}_0, \mathrm{H}_a)\mathrm{P}(\mathrm{H}_0 \mid \mathbf{y}) + \ell(\mathrm{H}_a, \mathrm{H}_a)\mathrm{P}(\mathrm{H}_a \mid \mathbf{y}) \\ &= \ell(\mathrm{H}_0, \mathrm{H}_a)\mathrm{P}(\mathrm{H}_0 \mid \mathbf{y}), \end{aligned} \tag{24.2.5}$$

where the expectation operator (E) indicates the expectation is taken with respect to the posterior distribution of the hypothesis H, which can take the two values H_0 and H_a with probabilities $\mathrm{P}(\mathrm{H}_0 \mid \mathbf{y}) = \int_{\theta \in \mathrm{H}_0} \mathrm{p}(\theta \mid \mathbf{y})\, d\theta$ and $\mathrm{P}(\mathrm{H}_a \mid \mathbf{y}) = \int_{\theta \in \mathrm{H}_a} \mathrm{p}(\theta \mid \mathbf{y})\, d\theta$, respectively (summation replaces integration in the discrete case). Then, decisions are made based on the following rule:

$$\text{If } \mathrm{E}[\ell(\mathrm{H}, \mathrm{H}_0)] \begin{Bmatrix} < \\ > \end{Bmatrix} \mathrm{E}[\ell(\mathrm{H}, \mathrm{H}_a)], \qquad \text{then } \begin{Bmatrix} \text{choose } \mathrm{H}_0 \\ \text{choose } \mathrm{H}_a \end{Bmatrix}. \tag{24.2.6}$$

Note that if the symmetric "0–k" loss function (i.e., $\ell(\mathrm{H}_0, \mathrm{H}_a) = \ell(\mathrm{H}_a, \mathrm{H}_0) = k$) is used, as is often the explicit or implicit case in both classical and Bayesian practice, then the Bayesian decision rule is equivalent to choosing the hypothesis with the larger posterior probability. In this situation, the rule (24.2.6) can be defined equivalently in terms of the posterior odds ratio as follows:

$$\text{if } \mathrm{P}(\mathrm{H}_0 \mid \mathbf{y})/\mathrm{P}(\mathrm{H}_a \mid \mathbf{y}) \begin{Bmatrix} > \\ < \end{Bmatrix} 1 \qquad \text{then } \begin{Bmatrix} \text{choose } \mathrm{H}_0 \\ \text{choose } \mathrm{H}_a \end{Bmatrix}. \tag{24.2.7}$$

We emphasize that the approach outlined between (24.2.4) and (24.2.7) is general and is not tied to the simple scalar hypothesis that was introduced at the outset of this section. In particular, the approach applies to both scalar and multiparameter hypotheses.

24.3. General Hypothesis Testing and Credible Sets in the Regression Model

In practice the posterior odds ratio is the measure most often used in the Bayesian approach for comparing and testing hypotheses in a regression context. Note, however, that more general loss functions than the "0–k" type can be used to evaluate hypotheses, in which case making decisions on the basis of the posterior odds ratio does not necessarily coincide with choosing the hypothesis that minimizes posterior expected loss.

24.3.1. Evaluating Composite Hypotheses about $\boldsymbol{\beta}$ and Bayes Factors

When both the null hypothesis H_0 and alternative hypothesis H_a about $\boldsymbol{\beta}$ are composite, the posterior odds ratio can be defined as (we suppress the $\mathbf{x}$ argument henceforth)

$$\xi = \frac{\mathrm{p}(\mathrm{H}_0 \mid \mathbf{y})}{\mathrm{p}(\mathrm{H}_a \mid \mathbf{y})} = \frac{\int_{\mathrm{H}_0} \mathrm{p}(\boldsymbol{\beta} \mid \mathbf{y})\, d\boldsymbol{\beta}}{\int_{\mathrm{H}_a} \mathrm{p}(\boldsymbol{\beta} \mid \mathbf{y})\, d\boldsymbol{\beta}}, \tag{24.3.1}$$

where $p(\boldsymbol{\beta} \mid \mathbf{y})$ is the marginal posterior distribution of $\boldsymbol{\beta}$. Under the symmetric "0–k" loss function, the optimal decision is H_0 or H_a iff ξ is >1 or <1, respectively. In general, the higher the posterior odds ratio, the greater the posterior support in favor of H_0 and against H_a.

In the case of a normal likelihood function, and for either uninformative or conjugate-informative priors on the parameters of the linear regression model, the posterior odds ratio can be calculated with integrals of the full or truncated multivariate **T**-distribution (recall (22.3.14), (22.4.12), and (23.3.5)). When evaluating hypotheses about individual elements of the $\boldsymbol{\beta}$ vector, the calculation of particular posterior probabilities is generally straightforward. It is based on integrals of the ordinary (central) student's **T**-distribution after standardizing the coefficient, as we have done previously. For example, if one were testing the inequality hypotheses $H_0\colon \beta_j \leq a$ versus $H_a\colon \beta_j > a$, and β_{j*} denotes the posterior mean of β_j, then

$$Z = \frac{B_j - \beta_{j*}}{[h^{-1}[j, j]]^{1/2}} \sim \text{Tdist}(z; v, 0), \tag{24.3.2}$$

where $v = n - k$ or $v = n + m - k + 1$, depending on whether the prior is diffuse (Section 22.3) or conjugate (Section 22.4). The posterior odds ratio could then be defined as

$$\xi = \frac{\int_{-\infty}^{(a-\beta_{j*})/[h^{-1}[j,j]]^{1/2}} \text{Tdist}(z; v, 0)\, dz}{\int_{(a-\beta_{j*})/[h^{-1}[j,j]]^{1/2}}^{\infty} \text{Tdist}(z; v, 0)\, dz}. \tag{24.3.3}$$

The integrals in (24.3.3) can be calculated on the computer using the procedure cdftc(·) in GAUSS. For hypotheses involving higher-dimensional subsets of the elements in $\boldsymbol{\beta}$, it may be possible to integrate the multivariate **T**-distribution numerically. Another alternative is to use Monte Carlo integration techniques to calculate the appropriate posterior probabilities in (24.3.1). Of course, when the likelihood function is based on a distribution other than the normal, as in Section 23.3.2, the integrands of the integrals defining the posterior odds ratio will generally not be in the multivariate **T**-distribution family. In these cases the analyst often must resort to computerized methods, discussed in the Monte Carlo book appendix, for calculating or approximating posterior probabilities.

The posterior odds ratio can be rewritten in a way that facilitates an illuminating contrast between classical likelihood ratio test procedures and the Bayesian approach. In particular, an equivalent representation of the posterior odds ratio (24.3.1) is

$$\xi = p(H_0 \mid \mathbf{y})/p(H_a \mid \mathbf{y}) = \frac{\int_{H_0} \int_0^{\infty} L(\boldsymbol{\beta}, \sigma \mid \mathbf{y}) p(\boldsymbol{\beta}, \sigma)\, d\sigma\, d\boldsymbol{\beta}}{\int_{H_a} \int_0^{\infty} L(\boldsymbol{\beta}, \sigma \mid \mathbf{y}) p(\boldsymbol{\beta}, \sigma)\, d\sigma\, d\boldsymbol{\beta}}$$

$$= \frac{p(H_0) E_{p_0}[L(\boldsymbol{\beta}, \sigma \mid \mathbf{y})]}{p(H_a) E_{p_a}[L(\boldsymbol{\beta}, \sigma \mid \mathbf{y})]} \tag{24.3.4}$$

where

$$p(H_i) = \int_{H_i} \int_0^{\infty} p(\boldsymbol{\beta}, \sigma)\, d\sigma\, d\boldsymbol{\beta}, \quad \text{for } i = 0 \text{ or a} \tag{24.3.5}$$

are the *prior* probabilities of hypotheses H_0 and H_a. The expression $E_{p_i}[\cdot]$ denotes an expectation taken with respect to the prior density assigned to the parameter values in the hypothesis H_i, if H_i is assumed to be true, this prior being

$$p_i(\boldsymbol{\beta}, \sigma) = p(\boldsymbol{\beta}, \sigma)/p(H_i) \quad \text{for } \boldsymbol{\beta} \in H_i, i = 0 \text{ or a}. \tag{24.3.6}$$

As such, the $p_i(\boldsymbol{\beta}, \sigma)$ are *truncated* prior probability distributions for **B** and Σ restricted to $\boldsymbol{\beta} \in H_0$ or $\boldsymbol{\beta} \in H_a$, and $E_{p_i}[L(\boldsymbol{\beta}, \sigma \mid \mathbf{y})]$ is the expected likelihood for values of $(\boldsymbol{\beta}, \sigma)$ consistent with $\boldsymbol{\beta} \in H_i$. Thus, the numerator and denominator of ξ may be expressed in terms of prior (predata) and likelihood (sample) components.

As previously noted, the optimal Bayes decision is H_0 if $\xi > 1$ under symmetric 0-k loss. Equivalently, the Bayes procedure chooses H_0 if the ratio of *expected* likelihood components exceeds the prior odds ratio in favor of H_a, $p(H_a)/p(H_0)$. In contrast, note that the classical likelihood ratio test uses the ratio of *maximized* likelihood function values to test H_0 instead of averaged likelihood functions. Further, the critical value of the test is selected to achieve a given probability of Type-I error over all of the potential test statistic outcomes that could happen.

The ratio of the expected likelihood components is commonly known as the *Bayes factor* in favor of H_0

$$BF = \frac{E_{p_0}[L(\boldsymbol{\beta}, \sigma \mid \mathbf{y})]}{E_{p_a}[L(\boldsymbol{\beta}, \sigma \mid \mathbf{y})]}, \tag{24.3.7}$$

which from (24.3.4) may also be defined as

$$BF = \frac{\text{posterior odds ratio}}{\text{prior odds ratio}} = \frac{p(H_0 \mid \mathbf{y})/p(H_a \mid \mathbf{y})}{p(H_0)/p(H_a)}. \tag{24.3.8}$$

The value of the Bayes factor is a measure of the degree to which sample information alters the prior odds in favor of H_0. As the value of BF deviates from 1, the data information alters prior evidence either in favor of ($BF > 1$), or against ($BF < 1$) H_0.

► **Example 24.3.1:** To demonstrate the conduct of Bayesian tests under composite null and alternative hypotheses, we provide the GAUSS program C24Comp.gss in the examples manual. For a consumer demand model specified in linear regression form, the user is asked to specify the prior odds ratio regarding the own-price and income elasticities of demand. The user is also asked to specify the losses assigned to Type-I and -II errors. Then, a pseudorandom sample is generated from the underlying DSP, and GAUSS reports the Bayes factor, the posterior odds ratios, and the optimal decisions for the Bayesian hypothesis tests.

24.3.2. Evaluating Simple Hypotheses about $\boldsymbol{\beta}$

In principle, testing simple hypotheses about $\boldsymbol{\beta}$, such as H_0: $\boldsymbol{\beta} = \mathbf{r}$, is no different than indicated in the preceding section. One calculates the posterior odds ratio in favor of H_0, and then the validity of the hypothesis is assessed accordingly. However, a simple null hypothesis is completely uninteresting in the Bayesian context if the prior is a continuous distribution. In this case the prior distribution assigns zero probability to the point $\mathbf{r}$. Consequently, the posterior will also assign zero probability to $\mathbf{r}$, and rejecting H_0 is a foregone conclusion.

For a simple null (or alternative) hypothesis about $\boldsymbol{\beta}$ to be interesting, nonzero prior probability must be assigned to H_0. When the alternative hypothesis is composite and consists of a continuum of values, this effectively means that $p(\boldsymbol{\beta})$ must be a mixed discrete–continuous probability distribution assigning positive probability to the *point value* for $\boldsymbol{\beta}$ implied by H_0 and distributing the remaining probability throughout the rest of the continuum of possibilities for $\boldsymbol{\beta}$ values.

To examine the case of simple hypotheses in more formal detail, suppose H_0: $\boldsymbol{\beta} = \mathbf{r}$, $p(H_0) = \pi_0 > 0$, and $p(H_a) = \pi_a = 1 - \pi_0$. Let $g_a(\boldsymbol{\beta})$ be a proper probability distribution that indicates the distribution of the probability π_a over the outcomes of $\boldsymbol{\beta}$ for which $\boldsymbol{\beta} \neq \mathbf{r}$. Then, the prior PDF is

$$p(\boldsymbol{\beta}) = \pi_0 I_{\mathbf{r}}(\boldsymbol{\beta}) + \pi_a g_a(\boldsymbol{\beta})[1 - I_{\mathbf{r}}(\boldsymbol{\beta})], \tag{24.3.9}$$

where $I_{\mathbf{r}}(\cdot)$ is an indicator function such that $I_{\mathbf{r}}(\boldsymbol{\beta}) = 1$ if $\boldsymbol{\beta} = \mathbf{r}$ and $I_{\mathbf{r}}(\boldsymbol{\beta}) = 0$ otherwise. In interpreting $p(\boldsymbol{\beta})$, its mixed discrete–continuous nature must be kept firmly in mind, and thus $p(\mathbf{r}) = \pi_0$ denotes a *probability*, whereas $p(\mathbf{r}_*) = \pi_a g_a(\mathbf{r}_*)$ denotes a *probability density* for $\mathbf{r}_* \neq \mathbf{r}$ (if it is assumed $g_a(\cdot)$ is a continuous PDF). The mixed discrete–continuous posterior distribution for $\boldsymbol{\beta}$ values, on the assumption of independent prior information on σ given by $p(\sigma)$, is then given by Bayes theorem as

$$p(\boldsymbol{\beta} \mid \mathbf{y}) \propto \pi_0 L(\mathbf{r} \mid \mathbf{y}) I_{\mathbf{r}}(\boldsymbol{\beta}) + \pi_a L(\boldsymbol{\beta} \mid \mathbf{y}) g_a(\boldsymbol{\beta})[1 - I_{\mathbf{r}}(\boldsymbol{\beta})], \tag{24.3.10}$$

where $L(\boldsymbol{\beta} \mid \mathbf{y}) \equiv \int_0^\infty L(\boldsymbol{\beta}, \sigma \mid \mathbf{y}) p(\sigma)\, d\sigma$.

The posterior odds in favor of H_0: $\boldsymbol{\beta} = \mathbf{r}$ is then given by

$$\xi = \frac{p(H_0 \mid \mathbf{y})}{p(H_a \mid \mathbf{y})} = \frac{\pi_0 L(\mathbf{r} \mid \mathbf{y})}{\pi_a \int_{H_a} L(\boldsymbol{\beta} \mid \mathbf{y}) g_a(\boldsymbol{\beta})\, d\boldsymbol{\beta}} \tag{24.3.11}$$

(compare with (24.3.4)). Under symmetric "0–k" loss, H_0 or H_a is chosen iff $\xi > 1$ or <1, respectively. The Bayes factor (24.3.7)–(24.3.8) in this situation is equal to

$$BF = \frac{p(H_0 \mid \mathbf{y})/\pi_0}{p(H_a \mid \mathbf{y})/\pi_a} = \frac{L(\mathbf{r} \mid \mathbf{y})}{\int_{H_a} L(\boldsymbol{\beta} \mid \mathbf{y}) g_a(\boldsymbol{\beta})\, d\boldsymbol{\beta}} \tag{24.3.12}$$

When one evaluates a simple null hypothesis that involves only a subset or linear combinations of the elements of $\boldsymbol{\beta}$, the preceding analysis can be applied analogously based on the appropriate marginal posterior distribution of the subset or linear combination of $\boldsymbol{\beta}$-elements.

▶ **Example 24.3.2:** To demonstrate the conduct of a Bayesian test with a simple null hypothesis, we provide the GAUSS program C24Simp.gss in the examples manual. Following Example 24.3.1, we consider the null hypotheses of unitary elastic own-price and income consumer demand. The user selects the prior probabilities for these cases as well as the losses assigned to Type-I and -II errors. Then, a pseudorandom sample is generated from the underlying DSP, and GAUSS reports the Bayes factor, the posterior odds ratio, and the decision resulting from the Bayesian hypothesis tests.

24.4. A Comment

By now it should be apparent how inverse probability in the form of Bayes theorem, when combined with the sample PDF-likelihood function, produces a posterior PDF that can then be used for postdata-conditional estimation and inference. The contrast to the classical approach in terms of how to go about information processing and recovery is quite striking. In particular, although classical procedures appear to be a varied collection of specialized procedures applied to a collection of special cases in a predata interpretative context, a common set of Bayes principles can be applied across a wide range of cases and is postdata in interpretation. Given the effectiveness of Bayes theorem as an information processing rule, the reader may be wondering why more analysts are not Bayesian as they go about the job of learning from a sample of data.

We hope this introduction to Bayesian inference will provide a foundation on which the reader can build a an expanded understanding and basis for reasoning in problems based on partial–incomplete information.

24.5. Exercises

24.5.1. Idea Checklist – Knowledge Guides

---

1. What are the differences in the Bayesian and sampling theory approaches to inference?
2. What are the differences in interpretation and construction between a classical confidence interval and a Bayesian credible interval? Ask a friend to define a confidence interval and critically evaluate what you have heard.
3. What are the differences in interpretation and construction between a classical and a Bayesian test of hypothesis?
4. Why isn't every econometrician a Bayesian?
5. What are the positive and negative aspects of the Bayesian approach to estimation and inference?
6. P values: What are they and what are they not in terms of credibility of hypotheses?

24.5.2. Problems

24–1 Derive the general form for the posterior odds ratio and the Bayes factor for a test of a simple null hypothesis versus a simple alternate hypothesis.

24–2 Suppose we use an asymmetric loss function that assigns $\ell(\mathrm{H_0}, \mathrm{H_a}) = 2k$ and $\ell(\mathrm{H_a}, \mathrm{H_0}) = k$. Derive the optimal decision rule for (24.2.4) and (24.2.5) based on the relative magnitudes of the prior odds ratio and the Bayes factor. Can you think of a situation in which you would assign asymmetric loss?

24–3 For the production function problem (Problem 2, Section 23.6.2), do the following:

a. Compute a highest posterior density 90% interval for β_3 and interpret.
b. Calculate the posterior odds in favor of constant returns to scale.
c. Evaluate the evidence in favor of constant returns to scale in terms of the

hypotheses

$$\text{H}_0: \beta_2 + \beta_3 = 1$$
$$\text{H}_a: \beta_2 + \beta_3 \neq 1.$$

24.5.3. Computer Problems

24–1 Repeat Example 24.3.1 after imposing appropriate inequality restrictions on the demand elasticities (i.e., nonpositive own-price and nonnegative income responses).

24–2 Repeat Example 24.3.1 using a nonconjugate prior distribution for the regression parameters. Do you find that the computations are significantly more burdensome to compute relative to the conjugate results presented in the example? What do you conclude regarding the practical feasibility of using nonconjugate priors?

24–3 For the production function example continued in Problem 1, how would you actually simulate the posterior distribution under the null hypothesis (i.e., $\beta_1 + \beta_2 = 1$) as well as the restriction of positive production responses (i.e., $\beta_1 > 0$ and $\beta_2 > 0$)? After listing the required steps, write a GAUSS program to implement the algorithm.

24.6. References

Berger, J. (1980), "A Robust Generalized Bayes Estimator and Confidence Region for a Multivariate Normal Mean," *Annals of Statistics*, Vol. 8, pp. 716–61.

Berger, J. O. (1985), *Statistical Decision Theory and Bayesian Analysis* (2nd ed.), New York: Springer–Verlag.

Bernardo, J. M., and A. F. M. Smith (1994), *Bayesian Theory*, New York: John Wiley and Sons.

de Groot, M. (1970), *Optimal Statistical Decisions*, New York: McGraw–Hill.

Hartigan, J. A. (1983), *Bayes Theory*, New York: Springer–Verlag.

Judge, G. G., W. E. Griffiths, R. C. Hill, H. Lütkepohl, and T.-C. Lee (1985), *The Theory and Practice of Econometrics* (2nd ed.), New York: John Wiley and Sons.

Judge, G. G., R. C. Hill, W. E. Griffiths, H. Lütkepohl, and T.-C. Lee (1988), *Introduction to the Theory and Practice of Econometrics* (2nd ed.), New York: John Wiley and Sons.

Lehmann, E., and G. Casella (1998), *Theory of Point Estimation*, New York: Springer–Verlag.

Poirier, D. J. (1995), *Intermediate Statistics and Econometrics*, Cambridge, MA: MIT Press.

Schervish, M. (1996), "P Values: What They Are and What They Are Not," *The American Statistician*, Vol. 50, pp. 243–46.

Zellner, A. (1971), *An Introduction to Bayesian Inference in Econometrics*, New York: John Wiley and Sons. Reprinted by Krieger Publishing Co., 1987.

Zellner, A. (1997), *Bayesian Analysis in Econometrics and Statistics*, Cheltenham, UK: Edward Elgar Publishing Ltd.

PART TEN

Epilogue

The previous 24 chapters, and the three electronic chapters ("Probability Theory," "Principles of Estimation and Inference" and "Ill-Posed Underdetermined Inverse Problems") on the accompanying CD, have as their objectives the development of a plausible basis for reasoning in situations involving partial–incomplete economic information. Building on probability theory, which we viewed as providing the logic of the sciences, and classical inference, which we viewed as providing the primary tools for economic information recovery, we have faced a succession of What if? questions regarding the underlying data-sampling processes and their corresponding probability model representation. In each case we have then gone on to provide one or more rules for making use of the data to estimate unknown components of the probability model and make inferences. In each case we have tried to be very explicit about the statistical implications of the choices we have made. Consequently, at this point you have a solid understanding of a range of data-sampling processes, probability models, and estimation and inference tools.

Although we may have told you more than you wanted to know about several probability models, we are far from spanning the space of interesting econometric problem areas. In some areas, such as discrete choice and nonparametrics, we have done little more than provide an introduction to the topic. In other areas, such as time series analysis, we have not even introduced the problem and the solution possibilities.

It is tempting to try to write a book that covers the subject area of econometrics and sets the mind in order in this area for a time. Perhaps 50 years ago one could have written a fairly satisfactory book on the scope and method of econometrics. Both Tintner (1952) and Klein (1953) had a very good go at it. We suspect no one in their right mind would make such an attempt today. The addition to our store of econometric knowledge over the last five decades is nothing short of astounding, and the additions continue at an exponential rate. Although we may have stopped short of making you a complete econometrician, we have attempted to give you enough of the basics so that you can read and begin making sense of econometric journal articles or know when someone is talking sense or nonsense in an econometric seminar. We also, of course, hope that we have provided a broad enough foundation for you to take on an econometric problem of your choosing, specify the corresponding probability model that you think describes the DSP, and then proceed to think your way through the estimation, inference, and implementation stages. We hope by now that the computer is a full partner in this learning–reasoning process.

It is fashionable in some circles to debunk econometrics. Critics point to the fact that we either can not or do not choose to perform controlled experiments and that, as a result, our data are of questionable quality for the questions that we pose, that the inferential basis for information recovery has a shaky foundation, that the number of relevant conditioning variables is virtually infinite and many are unobservable, that many of our forecasts are inferior to the naïve one that says that tomorrow will be like today, that .... Each of these items has a certain amount of truth, and each goes a long way toward defining the econometric problems and the corresponding challenges that lie ahead. A decade from now, when we write the preface for a future edition of this book, it will be interesting to identify the changes that have occurred. The direction and magnitude of these changes in econometric knowledge will depend on how creative we have been in building on productive ideas laid down by our twentieth-century precursors. Perhaps your name will be included in the reference lists of future editions, where new contributions to econometric knowledge are recognized.

APPENDIX

Introduction to Computer Simulation and Resampling Methods

Beginning with Chapter 2, we made extensive use of GAUSS programs to simulate outcomes from data-sampling processes to examine the statistical properties of associated estimation and inference tools. In many cases, the programs were designed to demonstrate finite sample or asymptotic results that may be analytically derived (e.g., expected values, variances, coverage probabilities, and limiting distributions). However, as your econometric knowledge and experience grow, you will find that some of the most interesting and challenging problems may not have tractable solutions, even with the use of asymptotic theory. Moreover, the implications of large sample theory may not adequately represent actual statistical performance in finite samples. Through GAUSS or other statistical software, we may use numerical tools to simulate the solutions to difficult problems or to provide more refined approximations to sampling behavior.

The purpose of this appendix is to review some fundamental concepts and procedures that may be used to conduct numerical simulation exercises. The appendix is organized as follows: We begin with a brief review of the basic methods that may be used to generate numbers that behave as outcomes from some stochastic process. Next, we review the fundamental concepts underlying the Monte Carlo simulation exercises used throughout this book. For the past several decades, the Monte Carlo approach has been the primary tool used by researchers to approximate the values of integral-type expressions quickly and tractably, including means, variances, and other statistical functions. Then, we introduce a data-based simulation method known as the bootstrap. In general, bootstrap simulation procedures do not require explicit assumptions about the true probability model and may provide more refined approximations to the sampling distribution than first-order asymptotic results. We conclude with a brief review of simulation methods that are designed to solve Bayesian estimation and inference problems.

A.1. Pseudorandom Number Generation

Computer programs designed to simulate outcomes of a stochastic process are based on numerical rules or algorithms. Given some starting value, the algorithm generates a sequence of numbers $y_1, y_2, \ldots, y_n$ that behave *as if* drawn from a particular probability distribution F. If we know the starting value and the algorithm used to generate a set of numbers, we can exactly replicate the sequence of outcomes. Thus, computer-generated outcomes are actually deterministic and not truly random. For this reason, numerically generated outcomes are said to be pseudorandom numbers.

GAUSS and other computing packages provide commands and procedures that generate pseudorandom draws from many common parametric families. However, we believe it is important to understand the steps involved in generating pseudorandom numbers in case you encounter nonstandard simulation problems and cannot rely on the preprogrammed numerical tools. In addition, you may be able to avoid some pitfalls in the application of pseudorandom number generators if you understand their structure. We begin our discussion with the U(0,1) distribution. Although probability models of economic behavior are rarely based on uniform distributions, the U(0,1) distribution serves as an important basis for simulating the outcomes of other nonuniform random variables. We then show how pseudorandom U(0,1) outcomes can be transformed to represent outcomes from other nonuniform probability distributions.

A.1.1. Generating U(0,1) Pseudorandom Numbers

Numerical analysts have devised several algorithms designed to simulate pseudorandom outcomes from the U(0,1) distribution. To demonstrate the basic mechanics of generating U(0,1) pseudorandom numbers, we focus on a particular algorithm known as the linear congruential generator.

In simplest terms, the linear congruential rule generates a set of n values $y_1, \ldots, y_n$ in the (0,1) interval by forming the ratio of two integers I_t/m and reporting the fractional remainder y_t for $t = 1, \ldots, n$. The integer in the denominator (m) is a fixed value known as the *modulus*. To form a sequence of pseudorandom numbers, the integer in the numerator (I_t) changes for each number in the sequence. The numerator sequence begins from a starting value I_0, which is known as the *seed*. Subsequent integers are generated by the linear progression $I_t = \alpha + \beta I_{t-1}$ for $t = 1, \ldots, n$ and fixed integers α and β. Thus, a different sequence of numbers may be generated by changing the seed (I_0) or one of the other constants (α, β or m).

Owing to the finite number of integers that may be represented on a modern 32-bit computer, the linear congruential algorithm will eventually repeat the sequence for adequately large n. The *period* of an algorithm is an integer s such that $Y_t = Y_{t+s}$ for each t. This characteristic is a limitation of the computer hardware and not the software, and thus virtually all numerical pseudorandom number generation algorithms have a finite period. Well-written algorithms will have a period that is long enough to avoid the problem of repeating sequences in typical applications. However, to avoid repetition of the generated numbers with the linear congruential method, a new linear congruential rule should be used if the number of pseudorandom draws exceeds m.

The GAUSS procedure rndu() generates pseudorandom outcomes for the U(0,1) distribution and is based on the linear congruential rule. The parameters α, β, and m can be set with the rndcon(), rndmult(), and rndmod() procedures. The seed (starting value) is automatically reset when the GAUSS program is started and is updated each time the rndu()

or rndn() procedures are called. The seed can also be set by the user with the rndseed() procedure. If a large number of pseudorandom draws will be generated in a single GAUSS session, the users can reset the parameters using the preceding commands to define a new congruential rule. Under the default options, GAUSS uses the largest possible modulus for 32-bit computers ($m = 2^{31} - 1 = 2{,}147{,}483{,}647$), and the period ($s$) equals the modulus ($m$).

A.1.2. Generating Continuous Nonuniform Pseudorandom Numbers

Given a reliable means for generating U(0,1) pseudorandom variables, we may be able to use our knowledge of probability theory to transform U(0,1) outcomes in ways that produce random outcomes from other continuous probability distributions. An approach that is commonly used in practice is based on the *probability integral transformation*. On the basis of Theorem 6.22 in Mittelhammer (1996), if X is a continuous random variable with distribution function F(x), then Y = F(X) is a U(0,1) random variable. By the converse to the theorem (Mittelhammer, 1996, Theorem 6.23), the random variable $X_* = F^{-1}(Y)$ for $Y \sim$ U(0,1) has distribution function F(x) if $F^{-1}(y)$ exists. Thus, given the inverse CDF, we can transform U(0,1) outcomes to represent outcomes from distribution F. If the inverse CDF does not exist, then $x_* = \min_x\{x : F(x) \geq y\}$ for U(0,1) outcome y represents an outcome from random variable X_* with distribution function F.

► **Example A.1.1:** The distribution function for a Logistic(0,1) random variable is $F(x) = \exp(-x)/[1 + \exp(x)]$, and the inverse CDF is $F^{-1}(y) = \ln[y/(1-y)]$. To simulate iid Logistic(0,1) random variables, we can transform iid pseudorandom U(0,1) outcomes y to generate $x_* = \ln[y/(1-y)]$. To demonstrate an application of the probability integral transformation to the Logistic distribution, we provide the GAUSS program AppLog.gss in the examples manual. The program describes the internal procedures used to represent the PDF and inverse CDF of the distribution. Then, GAUSS generates a pseudorandom sample of size n (selected by the user) and compares the sample moments to the Logistic(0,1) population moments. GAUSS also computes the kernel density estimate of the PDF and plots it with the actual PDF for comparison purposes.

Most commercial software packages include procedures for the inverse distribution functions of some common continuous random variables. For example, GAUSS provides the inverse standard normal CDF in the cdfni() procedure and the inverse Chi-square CDF in the cdfchii() procedure. Additionally, the cdftci() procedure returns the inverse of the complement to the distribution function $G(x) = 1 - F(x)$ for the students (central) T-distribution. For $Y \sim$ U(0,1), note that $X_* = G^{-1}(Y)$ is a student's t random variable because G(X) is also a U(0,1) random variable and the student's T-distribution is symmetric. Thus, we can use the GAUSS command cdftci(rndu(n,1), k) to generate n iid outcomes for the student's T-distribution with k degrees of freedom.

► **Example A.1.2:** To generate iid standard normal pseudorandom numbers in GAUSS, we may directly employ the rndn() procedure, or we can apply the probability integral transformation in two steps. First, we use the rndu() procedure to generate pseudorandom U(0,1) outcomes **y**. Then, we use the cdfni() procedure to transform **y** to N(0,1) pseudorandom numbers. To generate n iid N(0,1) outcomes by the transformation approach, we may use the composite GAUSS command cdfni(rndu(n,1)).

Given that the inverse CDF of the normal distribution cannot be stated in explicit form, researchers have devised other methods to generation N(0,1) pseudorandom numbers. One of the most popular algorithms is known as the Box–Muller or polar method (see Box and Muller (1958)), which relies on the functional relationship between U(0,1) and N(0,1) random variables under a change of variables to polar coordinates. Suppose Y_1 and Y_2 are independent U(0,1) random variables. Then, we can show that

$$X_1 = \cos(2\pi Y_1)[-2\ln(Y_2)]^{1/2} \quad \text{and} \quad X_2 = \sin(2\pi Y_1)[-2\ln(Y_2)]^{1/2} \tag{A.1.1}$$

are independent N(0,1) random variables. Therefore, we can generate pairs of pseudorandom U(0,1) numbers and convert them to represent N(0,1) outcomes with these equations.

Although the Box–Muller formulas provide a convenient means for generating standard, normal pseudorandom numbers, GAUSS actually uses another algorithm for generating pseudorandom normal variables known as the acceptance–rejection method. This approach is especially useful if we know the form of the *target* density function f(x) but cannot easily generate pseudorandom numbers from this distribution. The basic idea is to generate pseudorandom numbers from a *source* distribution G with density function g(x) from which we can readily generate outcomes. On the basis of Geweke (1996), the necessary condition to use G as a source distribution is

$$\sup_x[f(x)/g(x)] = a < \infty, \tag{A.1.2}$$

where the support of distribution F is a subset of the support, s, of distribution G. Then, the acceptance–rejection algorithm may be summarized as

1. Generate a pseudorandom outcome of $Y \sim U(0,1)$ and outcome of Z from distribution G.
2. If $y > f(z)/[g(z)a]$, repeat Step 1.
3. Otherwise, use the outcome $x = z$.

Geweke shows that the unconditional probability of accepting the outcome is

$$\int_S \left[\frac{f(z)}{g(z)a}\right] g(z)\, dz = a^{-1}, \tag{A.1.3}$$

and the unconditional probability of accepting an outcome with value at most c is

$$\int_{-\infty}^{c} \left[\frac{f(z)}{g(z)a}\right] g(z)\, dz = a^{-1}F(c) \tag{A.1.4}$$

Thus, the probability distribution function for the accepted outcomes is the target distribution F. The efficiency of the procedure improves with the probability of acceptance, and thus we should choose g(x) to be as close to f(x) as possible.

► **Example A.1.3:** To demonstrate the acceptance–rejection algorithm, we provide the GAUSS program AppAR.gss in the examples manual. To begin, the GAUSS program presents the user with a list of target and source distributions. For the case selected by the user, the program plots the PDFs for the target and source distributions and implements the acceptance–rejection algorithm to generate a set of n pseudorandom numbers. To evaluate the performance of the algorithm, GAUSS compares the sample moments and estimated kernel density function for the pseudorandom sample to the moments and PDF of the target distribution. To indicate the efficiency of the procedure, GAUSS also reports the number of candidates rejected.

Marsaglia and Bray (1964) used an acceptance–rejection method to form a modified polar method. The steps used to generate pairs of standard normal pseudorandom outcomes under the modified algorithm are as follows:

1. Generate two pseudorandom U(0,1) outcomes y_1 and y_2 and transform to represent U(−1,1) outcomes as $\mathrm{x}_i = 2\mathrm{y}_i - 1 \quad \text{for } i = 1, 2$.
2. If $v = x_1^2 + x_2^2 \geq 1$, return to Step 1.
3. Otherwise, let $z_i = \mathrm{x}_i \sqrt{-2\ln(v)/v} \quad \text{for } i = 1, 2$.

The values z_1 and z_2 represent a pair of iid. N(0,1) outcomes. Marsaglia and Bray claim that this algorithm is more efficient than the Box–Muller method, and Computer Problem 2 in Section A.6.3 provides you an opportunity to verify their claim.

Additional transformation methods may be used to generate outcomes for one nonuniform distribution from outcomes representing another nonuniform distribution. In many cases, the transformations are based on known relationships among families of random variables. For example, if Z is an N(0,1) random variable, then Z^2 is distributed as a central Chi-square(1,0) random variable. Further, the sum of k squared, independent, standard normal variables is Chi-square(k,0). Random variables in the T, F, and Lognormal families may be composed in similar fashion. GAUSS provides procedures for generating pseudorandom numbers from the Beta, Gamma, Normal, Uniform, and von Mises distributions. Some methods of generating pseudorandom numbers are based on results from asymptotic theory, and the procedure that is considered in Problem 1 of Section A.6.2 is an example. For other methods of generating nonuniform pseudorandom numbers, see Devroye (1986).

A.1.3. Generating Discrete Pseudorandom Numbers

To simulate pseudorandom draws for a discrete random variable with distribution function F supported on a countable set, we can extend the idea underlying the probability integral transformation for a CDF to a step function. Suppose we have a discrete random variable X supported on the ordered set $\{\mathrm{x}_1, \mathrm{x}_2, \ldots\}$ with associated probabilities $\mathbf{p} = (\mathrm{p}_1, \mathrm{p}_2, \ldots)$ such that $\sum_{i=1}^{\infty} \mathrm{p}_i = 1$. The right-continuous distribution function F for X is given by the step function

$$\mathrm{F(x)} = \sum_{i=1}^{\infty} \mathrm{p}_i \mathrm{I}(\mathrm{x}_i \leq x), \tag{A.1.5}$$

where $\mathrm{I}(\mathrm{x}_i \leq x)$ is an indicator function that equals 1 if $\mathrm{x}_i \leq x$ and is 0 otherwise. As in the continuous case, we can apply the "inverse step function" to U(0,1) outcomes to generate pseudorandom outcomes x_* with distribution F.

More formally, let y be an outcome from the U(0,1) distribution. We then generate $x_* = x_1$ if $y \leq F(x_1)$, and in general

$$x_* = x_i \quad \text{if} \quad F(x_{i-1}) < y \leq F(x_i) \quad \text{for } i \geq 2. \tag{A.1.6}$$

If the support is a finite ordered set with k elements, then we generate $x_* = x_k$ if $F(x_{k-1}) < y$. GAUSS only provides procedures for generating discrete pseudorandom numbers for the Poisson and Negative Binomial distributions, and thus this approach may be useful in a variety of simulation exercises. For example, we can use (A.1.6) to generate observations for the qualitative choice models in Chapter 20 in which F is the logistic (logit) or normal (probit) CDF. Moreover, we may wish to generate pseudorandom replicates of the sample using nonuniform weights on the sample elements in applications of the nonparametric bootstrap procedure (discussed in Section A.3). In particular, the nonuniform weights may be the optimal MEL or MEEL weights based on a set of estimating functions, or the weights may reflect the assumptions of a null hypothesis.

► **Example A.1.4:** Efron and Tibshirani (1993, p. 235) consider the problem of generating replicated samples from a set of n observations $\mathbf{x} = (x_1, \ldots, x_n)'$ such that the distribution has mean $E[X] = \mu \neq \bar{x}$. Thus, we cannot simply draw observations from $\mathbf{x}$ with replacement because the expected value of the replicated samples will be $\bar{x}$ (refer to the discussion of the simple nonparametric bootstrap in Section A.3). Efron and Tibshirani suggest redistributing the mass on the elements of $\mathbf{x}$ by selecting the maximum entropy distribution with mean μ. Following our discussion of entropy in Chapters 13 and electronic Chapter E3, we know that the maximum entropy distribution will be closest to the discrete uniform distribution subject to the mean condition.

The GAUSS program AppMEEL.gss (provided in the examples manual) demonstrates a simple application of this procedure. First, GAUSS plots distribution functions for continuous and discrete random variables to illustrate the conceptual similarities between pseudorandom number generation in these cases. Then, for a given sample $\mathbf{x}$, the user is asked to specify the hypothesized mean μ. GAUSS computes the maximum entropy solution and uses the associated distribution function to generate a set of outcomes from the reweighted distribution using Rule (A.1.5). Then, GAUSS repeats the exercise numerous times and compares the mean of the replicated samples with the mean imposed by maximum entropy μ.

A.1.4. Evaluating the Performance of Pseudorandom Number Generators

In general, commercial pseudorandom number generators perform as expected and produce sequences of nonrepetitive numbers that behave as if drawn from the target distribution. However, owing to the deterministic nature of pseudorandom number generation, some algorithms may not provide sequences of numbers that mimic independent or identically distributed outcomes. If the results of a simulation exercise are especially sensitive to the properties of the pseudorandom numbers, or if you have some reason to doubt the quality of an algorithm, you should evaluate the performance of the software.

To check the properties of a particular algorithm, researchers have devised a large number of diagnostic techniques, and many of these tools are adapted from the literature on nonparametric statistics. For example, one of the most commonly used diagnostic tools is Pearson's χ^2 test

$$\chi^2 = \sum_{i=1}^{k} \frac{(\mathrm{o}_i - \mathrm{e}_i)^2}{\mathrm{e}_i} \tag{A.1.7}$$

The sample space for the target distribution is divided in k bins, o_i is the number of *observed* outcomes in the ith bin, and e_i is the number of *expected* outcomes in the ith bin under the target distribution. For example, to evaluate a U(0,1) pseudorandom number generator, we could divide the unit interval in $k = 10$ bins so that $e_i = n/10$ for a sample of n pseudorandom numbers and $i = 1, \ldots, 10$. As $n \to \infty$, the statistic is asymptotically Chi-square$(k - 1, 0)$ under the null hypothesis that the sample was generated by the target distribution. Under the multinomial probability model, the likelihood ratio test statistic for this hypothesis $2 \sum_{i=1}^{k} o_i \ln(o_i/e_i)$ equals the scaled KLIC (cross-entropy) measure and has the same limiting distribution as Pearson's test statistic.

Alternative goodness-of-fit measures include the Kolmogorov–Smirnov and Shapiro–Wilks (for normality) tests, and other diagnostic tools may be used to evaluate particular characteristics of samples drawn from pseudorandom number generators. For example, dependence among the outcomes may be evaluated with the Wald–Wolfowitz runs test or by examining the sample autocorrelation function. For additional details on these and other tests, the reader is encouraged to consult Section 10.8 in Mittelhammer (1996). If a particular pseudorandom number generator algorithm exhibits unintended properties, we still may be able to use the software. For example, we may be able to diminish the impact of serial correlation among the generated numbers by reordering or shuffling the outcomes.

► **Example A.1.5:** To demonstrate an application of the diagnostic tools to a candidate algorithm, we provide the GAUSS program AppTest.gss in the examples manual. For a sample size n selected by the user, GAUSS generates a pseudorandom N(0,1) sample using the algorithm considered in Problem 1 of Section A.6.2. To evaluate the performance of the algorithm, GAUSS reports a set of diagnostic measures computed from the observed sample. The user is reminded that the application of two or more tests to the same sample of data may distort the overall size of the joint test, and the Bonferroni adjustment may be used to control the probability of committing a Type-I error. Finally, given the asymptotic justification of the algorithm, GAUSS then repeats the demonstration for a series of samples sizes (also selected by the user).

A.2. Monte Carlo Simulation

Monte Carlo simulation methods were originally devised to evaluate integral functions that do not have tractable solutions, and the origins of the Monte Carlo approach are commonly attributed to Metropolis and Ulam (1949). Although our discussion of estimation and inference may seem far removed from the domain of integral calculus, note that many of the properties of estimators and test statistics can be stated as integral functions defined with respect to some probability distribution. In the sampling theoretic setting, we generally consider integrals of the form

$$\mathrm{E}[g(\mathbf{Y};\boldsymbol{\theta})] = \int g(\mathbf{y};\boldsymbol{\theta})\,\mathrm{f}(\mathbf{y};\boldsymbol{\theta})\,d\mathbf{y}, \tag{A.2.1}$$

where $\mathrm{f}(\mathbf{y};\boldsymbol{\theta})$ is a parametric PDF and $g(\mathbf{y};\boldsymbol{\theta})$ is a measurable function. For example, suppose

$$g(\mathbf{y};\boldsymbol{\theta}) = -\frac{\partial^2 \ln(L(\boldsymbol{\theta};\mathbf{y}))}{\partial\boldsymbol{\theta}\,\partial\boldsymbol{\theta}'} \tag{A.2.2}$$

so that $\mathrm{E}[g(\mathbf{Y};\boldsymbol{\theta})]$ is the information matrix $\mathrm{I}(\boldsymbol{\theta})$. From Chapter 4, recall that the power function for an α-level F-test with j and $n-k$ degrees of freedom is given by the integral

$$\pi(\lambda) = \int_{\mathrm{f}_{1-\alpha}}^{\infty} \mathrm{F}(z; j, n-k, \lambda)\,\mathrm{d}z. \tag{A.2.3}$$

In the Bayesian context, the key issues of estimation and inference focus on integrals computed with respect to the prior or posterior distribution. For example, the posterior risk function is

$$\int_{\Omega} \ell(\boldsymbol{\theta},\hat{\boldsymbol{\theta}})\,\mathrm{p}(\boldsymbol{\theta}\mid\mathbf{y})\,d\boldsymbol{\theta} \tag{A.2.4}$$

under loss function $\ell(\boldsymbol{\theta},\hat{\boldsymbol{\theta}})$.

A.2.1. Background and Conceptual Motivation

To solve intractable integration problems, researchers have proposed several numerical methods that may be used to approximate the value of the integral function. Conceptually, the integral (A.2.1) may be approximated by an associated Riemann sum, which may be stated as

$$\int \mathrm{g}(\mathrm{y};\boldsymbol{\theta})\mathrm{f}(\mathrm{y};\boldsymbol{\theta})\,\mathrm{dy} \approx \sum_{i=1}^{m} \mathrm{g}(\mathrm{y}_i;\boldsymbol{\theta})\mathrm{f}(\mathrm{y}_i;\boldsymbol{\theta})(\mathrm{a}_i - \mathrm{a}_{i-1}) \tag{A.2.5}$$

for the univariate case. Here, $\{\mathrm{a}_0 < \mathrm{a}_1 < \cdots < \mathrm{a}_m\}$ is a partition of the domain of g and each $\mathrm{y}_i \in [\mathrm{a}_{i-1}, \mathrm{a}_i]$. The Riemann sum partitions the integral into a finite number of pieces to approximate the corresponding areas under the graph of $\mathrm{g}(\mathrm{y};\boldsymbol{\theta})$. A large number of numerical integration methods, including Simpson's rule for univariate integrals and Gaussian quadrature in multiple dimensions (see Press et al., 1992, Section 4.5), are based on extensions of this simple idea. The numerical integration routines in GAUSS are based on a method known as Gauss–Legendre quadrature.

Note that the Riemann sum may be viewed as an expected value under a discrete distribution with histogram-type weights $\mathrm{f}(\mathrm{y}_i;\boldsymbol{\theta})(\mathrm{a}_i - \mathrm{a}_{i-1})$. The mass assigned to $\mathrm{g}(\mathrm{y}_i;\boldsymbol{\theta})$ is based on bin height $\mathrm{f}(\mathrm{y}_i;\boldsymbol{\theta})$ and bin width $(\mathrm{a}_i - \mathrm{a}_{i-1})$ (recall our discussion of histograms in Chapter 21). When viewed as an expected value with respect to the distribution F, we can see that the Riemann sum will exactly equal the left-hand side of (A.2.5) if F is a discrete distribution and the domain partition is appropriately chosen. For continuous distributions, the weights in the Riemann sum serve as a discrete approximation of the expectation taken with respect to F. Clearly, the accuracy of the approximation depends on the choice of the points $\{a_0 < a_1 < \cdots < a_m\}$.

Monte Carlo integration methods avoid the problem of partition choice by evaluating the integral at m randomly generated points in the domain. If each of the points is equally weighted, we can use the sample average of the function values as an estimate of the integral value

$$\hat{E}[g(Y;\boldsymbol{\theta})] = m^{-1} \sum_{i=1}^{m} g(y_i;\boldsymbol{\theta}), \tag{A.2.6}$$

where $(y_1, \ldots, y_m)$ are iid outcomes drawn from distribution F. Although the discrete weights in the Riemann sum are replaced with uniform weights, the points at which the integral is approximated reflect the density of the underlying probability distribution. Non-iid sampling procedures have also been devised, and thus simulations based on iid sampling are commonly known as the simple Monte Carlo method.

A.2.2. Key Assumptions

On the basis of our brief description, we can see that the Monte Carlo simulation of an integral can be quickly and easily computed if the function is convenient to evaluate and if we can generate pseudorandom outcomes from F. Morc formally, the key assumptions required for Monte Carlo simulation of an integral are as follows:

1. The relevant probability distribution $F(\mathbf{y};\boldsymbol{\theta})$ is known.
2. The integral exists such that $E[g(\mathbf{Y};\boldsymbol{\theta})] < \infty$ for all $\theta \in \boldsymbol{\Omega}$.
3. We can generate iid observations that behave as if they were drawn from F.

For conceptual purposes, the first assumption is most restrictive in estimation and inference problems. Note that much of the content of this book focuses on semiparametric and nonparametric models because we rarely know which probability model underlies the data-sampling process. Although the lack of a fully parametric model did not hamper our development of estimation and inference methods, this is commonly viewed as a key drawback of the Monte Carlo approach. For now, we proceed as if we are able to specify F for our Monte Carlo simulation exercises. The bootstrap procedure introduced in Section A.3 is designed to overcome this limitation of traditional Monte Carlo simulation methods.

The second assumption is rarely addressed in applications of the Monte Carlo approach, but we emphasize that an integral must exist for the simulation results to have any meaning. To illustrate this point, consider the well-known example of a Cauchy(0,1) random variable that does not have a finite expected value. In GAUSS, we can simulate pseudorandom outcomes from the Cauchy(0,1) distribution by forming the ratio of iid N(0,1) outcomes. A vector of n iid Cauchy(0,1) outcomes may be generated with the GAUSS command rndn(n,1)./rndn(n,1), and the reader is encouraged to perform this operation in GAUSS. You should find that the sample mean of n simulated Cauchy(0,1) outcomes will be finite, but the estimate will effectively be meaningless.

Although the third assumption points to the practical challenges of Monte Carlo simulation, we can use the methods discussed in Section A.1 to generate pseudorandom outcomes for many common distributions. If the numerical tools cannot be used to simulate draws from F, we may be able to rely on a method known as *importance sampling*. Suppose we are able to simulate pseudorandom outcomes from a distribution with density function $h(\mathbf{y})$ supported on S, which includes the support of $f(\mathbf{y}; \boldsymbol{\theta})$ as a subset. Note that we can rewrite (A.2.1) in terms of $h(\mathbf{y})$ as

$$E[g(\mathbf{Y}; \boldsymbol{\theta})] = \int_S g(\mathbf{y}; \boldsymbol{\theta}) f(\mathbf{y}; \boldsymbol{\theta})\, d\mathbf{y} = \int_S \left[\frac{g(\mathbf{y}; \boldsymbol{\theta}) f(\mathbf{y}; \boldsymbol{\theta})}{h(\mathbf{y})}\right] h(\mathbf{y})\, d\mathbf{y} \qquad \text{(A.2.7)}$$

Then, the importance sampler approximates (A.2.7) by generating iid outcomes from distribution H(y) and computing

$$\hat{E}[\mathbf{g}(\mathbf{Y}; \boldsymbol{\theta})] = \hat{E}_h\left[\frac{g(\mathbf{y}; \boldsymbol{\theta}) f(\mathbf{y}; \boldsymbol{\theta})}{h(\mathbf{y})}\right] = m^{-1} \sum_{i=1}^{m} \frac{g(\mathbf{y}_i; \boldsymbol{\theta}) f(\mathbf{y}_i; \boldsymbol{\theta})}{h(\mathbf{y}_i)}, \qquad \text{(A.2.8)}$$

which is analogous to (A.2.6), where $E_h[\cdot]$ denotes an expectation taken with respect to the density h. Thus, we may use the importance sampler to approximate the integral provided we can evaluate the density function of F. In general, the distribution H should be selected to be as close to F as possible to minimize the variance of the estimator.

A.2.3. Basic Properties of Monte Carlo Simulation Estimators

If $E[g(\mathbf{Y}; \boldsymbol{\theta})] < \infty$, integral estimates based on Monte Carlo simulation may be justified by direct application of an appropriate weak law of large numbers. In general,

$$\bar{g}_m(\boldsymbol{\theta}) = m^{-1} \sum_{i=1}^{m} g(\mathbf{y}_i; \boldsymbol{\theta}) \xrightarrow{p} E[g(\mathbf{Y}; \boldsymbol{\theta})] \quad \forall \boldsymbol{\theta} \in \boldsymbol{\Omega} \qquad \text{(A.2.9)}$$

as $m \to \infty$ for iid outcomes $\mathbf{y}_1, \ldots, \mathbf{y}_m$ drawn from F. Moreover Monte Carlo estimators often satisfy strong laws of large numbers so that the sample mean converges almost surely to the integral value. Thus, if we can generate random vectors that reflect the properties of the assumed sampling distribution, the sample mean of the integrand is a consistent estimator of the integral.

In practice, Monte Carlo estimates are based on a finite number of trials (m), and the integral estimator will behave like any other point estimator and exhibit some sampling error. Note that estimator (A.2.9) is a sample average, and thus we may use an appropriate central limit theorem (CLT) to evaluate the sampling properties of the integral estimator as $m \to \infty$. Under iid sampling, the Lindeberg–Levy CLT may be used to approximate the large sample distribution of the integral estimator. If $E[\mathbf{g}(\mathbf{Y}; \boldsymbol{\theta})] < \infty$ and

$$\mathbf{cov}[\mathbf{g}(\mathbf{Y}; \boldsymbol{\theta})] = \boldsymbol{\Xi} \qquad \text{(A.2.10)}$$

is a finite positive definite matrix, then the multivariate Lindeberg–Levy CLT implies that

$$m^{1/2}(\bar{\mathbf{g}}_m(\boldsymbol{\theta}) - E[\mathbf{g}(\mathbf{Y}; \boldsymbol{\theta})]) \xrightarrow{d} N(\mathbf{0}, \boldsymbol{\Xi}) \qquad \text{(A.2.11)}$$

In practice, we are not likely to know the covariance of the integrand Ξ but can use the consistent estimator based on the sample covariance of the Monte Carlo replicates

$$\widehat{\mathbf{cov}}[\mathbf{g}(\mathbf{Y};\boldsymbol{\theta})] = m^{-1}\sum_{i=1}^{m}[\mathbf{g}(\mathbf{y}_i;\boldsymbol{\theta}) - \bar{\mathbf{g}}_m(\boldsymbol{\theta})][\mathbf{g}(\mathbf{Y}_i;\boldsymbol{\theta}) - \bar{\mathbf{g}}_m(\boldsymbol{\theta})]'. \tag{A.2.12}$$

The large sample properties of other Monte Carlo procedures may be derived in similar fashion. For example, Evans and Swartz (1995, Section 4) describe the convergence and asymptotic normality of the importance sampling estimator. Given the asymptotic normality of the integral estimator, standard asymptotic confidence intervals can be constructed to assess the precision of the integral estimate.

► **Example A.2.1:** We provide the GAUSS program AppMC.gss in the examples manual to demonstrate the basic steps involved in a Monte Carlo simulation exercise. Suppose we observe n iid observations $y_1, \ldots y_n$ from the N(μ,1) distribution and use the sample average $\bar{y}$ to estimate μ. Although we can easily verify that the estimator is unbiased, suppose we are not able to determine this property analytically. For values of m and n selected by the user, GAUSS describes the steps involved in computing estimates of $E[\bar{Y}]$ by Monte Carlo simulation for several values of μ. The program reports the sample moments of the replicated samples and plots the response function for the expected value. Then, for fixed n and a series of m values, GAUSS repeats the simulation exercise to examine the impact of m on the sampling variation. In each case, GAUSS compares the properties of the estimated expectation to the actual properties under the normal distribution.

Numerical analysts have devised several important ways to reduce the sampling variation in Monte Carlo simulation exercises. One of the most commonly used techniques is the method of antithetic sampling, which can be used to reduce computation time as well as the variance of Monte Carlo estimators. Suppose we draw outcome y_{1t} from a continuous distribution that is symmetric about the point μ. Then, $y_{2t} = 2\mu - y_{1t}$ represents another outcome drawn from the same distribution. Thus, we can generate two pseudorandom numbers, called *antithetic pairs*, for each number drawn, and we guarantee that the observations mimic the symmetry of the underlying distribution.

The variance reduction achieved depends on the character of the function $\mathbf{g}(\mathbf{y};\boldsymbol{\theta})$. On the basis of Geweke (1996), the limiting variance of the Monte Carlo estimator under antithetic sampling is

$$\frac{1}{2}[\text{var}(g(y_{1i};\boldsymbol{\theta})) + \text{cov}(g(y_{1i};\boldsymbol{\theta}), g(y_{2i};\boldsymbol{\theta}))] \tag{A.2.13}$$

If $\mathbf{g}(\mathbf{y};\boldsymbol{\theta})$ is linear in y, then $\text{cov}(g(y_{1i};\boldsymbol{\theta}), g(y_{2i};\boldsymbol{\theta})) = -\text{var}(g(y_{1i};\boldsymbol{\theta})$ and the variance is fully reduced. To see this point, consider the linear case in which F is symmetric about μ and the integral estimator of interest is

$$\bar{g}_{2m}(\mu) = m^{-1}\sum_{i=1}^{m} y_{1i} + m^{-1}\sum_{i=1}^{m} y_{2i} = \mu \tag{A.2.14}$$

For each m, the estimated integral is simply equal to μ, and there is no sampling variation in the estimator. For nonlinear $g(y; \boldsymbol{\theta})$, the antithetic sampling procedure reduces the variance of the estimator provided $\text{cov}(g(y_{1i}; \boldsymbol{\theta}), g(y_{2i}; \boldsymbol{\theta})) < 0$. For further details on antithetic sampling and other variance reduction methods, the reader should refer to Geweke (1996).

Finally, we note that the Monte Carlo integration techniques have a key advantage over quadrature and other numerical integration tools when used to solve integration problems in several dimensions. Press et al. (1992, Section 4.6) show that a k-dimensional integral evaluated as m pieces by Gaussian quadrature requires $O(m^k)$ function evaluations, and the error in the approximation is $O(m^{-2/k})$. Thus, the number of points required to achieve a fixed-error bound increases exponentially in k, and high-dimensional integrals are very costly to approximate by Gaussian quadrature. Alternatively, the approximation error for most Monte Carlo approximations is $O(m^{-1/2})$, and thus the method is more accurate than Gaussian quadrature for $k > 4$. In summary, the number of function evaluations required to achieve a given level of accuracy with Gaussian quadrature increases rapidly with the dimension, but the cost of computing Monte Carlo simulations is roughly constant. Of course, the practical advantages of using Monte Carlo methods have increased with advances in computing power and in the pseudorandom number generation and variance reduction techniques.

Readers interested in further study of the Monte Carlo methods may wish to consult one of the well-known references such as Hammersley and Handscomb (1964), Davis and Rabinowitz (1975), Niederreiter (1992), or Sobol (1994). A survey of Monte Carlo methods designed for an econometric audience is provided by Hendry (1984).

A.3. Bootstrap Resampling

In this section, we review the conceptual foundations and basic properties of another simulation method known as the bootstrap resampling procedure. The bootstrap approach views the observed sample as a population. The distribution function for this population is the EDF of the sample, and parameter estimates based on the observed sample are treated as the actual model parameters in the bootstrap world. Conceptually, we can then examine the properties of estimators or test statistics in repeated samples drawn from a tangible data-sampling process that mimics the actual DSP. Although simulation results based on the bootstrap DSP do not represent the exact finite sample properties of estimators and test statistics under the actual DSP, the bootstrap provides an approximation that improves as the size of the observed sample increases.

In recent years, the bootstrap procedure has gained acceptance in applied research for several reasons. First, the bootstrap avoids most of the strong distributional assumptions required of traditional Monte Carlo simulation exercises. As such, researchers can simulate the DSP without having to specify a parametric probability model. Second, like the Monte Carlo methods, the bootstrap procedure may be used to solve intractable estimation and inference problems by computation rather than reliance on asymptotic approximations, which may be very complicated in nonstandard problems. Third, bootstrap approximations are often equivalent to first-order asymptotic results in large samples, and, as we shall see, the bootstrap may dominate the first-order asymptotic results in some cases.

A.3.1. Basic Properties of the Bootstrap

To begin, we introduce a more general set of notation to help the reader fully appreciate the properties and structure of the bootstrap. Consider a sample of n observations $\mathbf{y}$ with distribution function $F(\mathbf{y}, \boldsymbol{\theta})$. Suppose we are interested in the sampling properties of a statistic or *root* T_n, which may be an estimator, test statistic, or some other random variable of interest that is based on outcomes of the DSP. To indicate the relationship between $F(\mathbf{y}, \boldsymbol{\theta})$ and the statistic, we denote the distribution of T_n as $G_n(F)$. Even if we assume we know F, as in the case of a fully parametric model, we may only be able to derive the distribution G_n in a limited number of cases. For example, we know that the test statistic (4.3.11) has a central F-distribution with j and $n - k$ degrees of freedom under on H_0: $\mathbf{c}\boldsymbol{\beta} = \mathbf{r}$, but you should note that such cases are relatively rare in this book. In general, we have to use the sample to tell us about F in order to recover information subsequently about G_n. As such, the inverse problem may be stated in two stages as $\mathbf{Y} \Rightarrow F \Rightarrow G_n$.

For parametric and semiparametric models, we can use an estimator $\hat{\boldsymbol{\theta}}$ to provide some information about F and ultimately G_n. One approach that we have used throughout this book is to approximate G_n in large samples by using derived asymptotic properties of $\hat{\boldsymbol{\theta}}$ and F (and perhaps other regularity conditions). In the bootstrap literature, the asymptotic distribution is commonly denoted G_∞, and an operational version of the large-sample approximation to G_n is based on $\hat{\boldsymbol{\theta}}$. For example, consider the Wald test statistic (i.e., $T_n =$ W) for H_0: $\mathbf{c}\boldsymbol{\beta} = \mathbf{r}$ based on the LS estimator of $\boldsymbol{\beta}$ in the semiparametric linear regression model. Although we were unable to derive the finite sample distribution of W, we were able to show that $G_\infty = \text{Chi-square}(j,0)$ under H_0 and other regularity conditions.

Alternatively, Efron (1979) devised a data-based approximation to G_n known as the bootstrap. To approximate $G_n(F)$, the bootstrap replaces F with the EDF, $F_n(y) = n^{-1}\sum_{i=1}^{n} I(y_i \le y)$, of the observed sample. For finite n, we may (at least conceptually) enumerate each possible sample of size n that may be generated with replacement from F_n. The distribution of the statistic T_n derived from the full set of conceptual samples is the bootstrap distribution, $G_n(F_n)$. The number of distinct conceptual samples that may be generated is $(2n - 1)!/[n!(n - 1)!]$ (i.e., $2n - 1$ choose n), and thus complete enumeration of F_n is rarely possible in practice (Beran and Ducharme, 1991, recognize two special cases). Nonetheless, the repeated sampling operation provides the conceptual link between the bootstrap DSP and the actual DSP it is designed to emulate.

In practice, the bootstrap distribution is approximated by Monte Carlo simulation, and we denote the approximate bootstrap distribution as $\hat{G}_n(F_n)$. As we note in the next subsection, there are several ways to implement the Monte Carlo approximation to $G_n(F_n)$. The simplest procedure is the *nonparametric* bootstrap estimate, which is computed by drawing m samples of size n from F_n with replacement. The bootstrap samples $y_1^*, y_2^*, \ldots, y_m^*$ are used to compute replicated outcomes of the statistics $T_{n1}^*, T_{n2}^*, \ldots, T_{nm}^*$, and the approximate bootstrap distribution is the EDF

$$\hat{G}_n(\tau, F_n) = m^{-1}\sum_{i=1}^{m} I(T_{ni}^* \le \tau). \tag{A.3.1}$$

As discussed in our previous applications of the EDF, $\hat{G}_n(F_n) \xrightarrow{p} G_n(F_n)$ as $m \to \infty$ by the Glivenko–Cantelli theorem. As in traditional Monte Carlo simulation, the choice of m is often determined by the time available to run computer programs, and authors in the bootstrap literature often recommend values of the order $m = 1000$ for most applications.

We emphasize that the bootstrap approximation $G_n(F_n)$ is not identical to the finite sample distribution of T_n, $G_n(\mathrm{F})$, because it is the empirical distribution function, and not the true cumulative distribution function, that is being used in the approximation. However, the accuracy of the approximation should improve as the sample size increases. Beran and Ducharme (1991, Propositions 1.2 and 1.3) show that $G_n(F_n) \xrightarrow{\mathrm{p}} \mathrm{G}_\infty(\mathrm{F})$ as $n \to \infty$ under a rather mild set of regularity conditions. In particular, the key conditions are $F_n \xrightarrow{\mathrm{p}} \mathrm{F}$ uniformly in y as $n \to \infty$ and $G_n(\tau, \mathrm{F}) \xrightarrow{\mathrm{p}} \mathrm{G}_\infty(\tau, \mathrm{F})$, where the limiting distribution is continuous in τ. In most applications, the first condition is met under the Glivenko–Cantelli theorem, and the second condition is satisfied if T_n has a continuous limiting distribution (e.g., asymptotically normal or Chi-square).

Given the bootstrap approximation $\hat{G}_n(F_n)$, we can use this distribution to form estimates or inferences in the same way we would use a finite sample or limiting distribution. For example, we may use the sample mean $\bar{T}_n^* = m^{-1} \sum_{i=1}^m T_{ni}^*$ as an estimator of $\mathrm{E}[T_n]$, and the bootstrap estimator of bias$[T_n]$ is $\bar{T}_n^* - \hat{T}_n$ where $\hat{T}_n$ is the value of the statistic computed from the observed sample. The variance of the statistic is estimated as from the Monte Carlo samples by

$$\widehat{\mathrm{var}}[T_n] = (m-1)^{-1} \sum_{i=1}^{m} (T_{ni}^* - \bar{T}_n^*)^2, \tag{A.3.2}$$

and the square root of (A.3.2) is the estimated standard error of T_n. In general, Monte Carlo approximations to bootstrap estimators of moments may be computed with relatively small simulation sample sizes m. Many authors report that estimators based on sample sizes on the order of $m = 100$ perform very well, and thus the Monte Carlo approximation of the moments of $G_n(F_n)$ may be computationally inexpensive.

The quantiles of $\hat{G}_n(F_n)$ may be used to form bootstrap $100(1-\alpha)\%$ confidence intervals or critical values for α-level bootstrap hypothesis tests, and researchers have devised several alternative procedures. For example, confidence intervals based on the percentile method are formed directly from $\hat{G}_n(F_n)$ by

$$\left[\hat{G}_n^{-1}(\alpha/2), \hat{G}_n^{-1}(1-\alpha/2)\right], \tag{A.3.3}$$

where $\hat{G}_n^{-1}(\alpha)$ is "inverse" of the EDF for the bootstrap samples evaluated at α. Given that the EDF is a step function, $\hat{G}_n^{-1}(\alpha)$ is the $[\alpha m]$ element of the ordered bootstrap observations. For example, a 90% percentile confidence interval is based on elements 5 and 95 in the vector of ordered outcomes, $(T_{n(1)}^*, \ldots, T_{n(m)}^*)$, for $m = 100$. Although $m = 100$ may be adequate for moment estimation, we can see that the Monte Carlo sample size for the percentile procedure should be relatively large to represent the tails of G_n adequately (again, many authors recommend $m = 1000$).

An alternative method for forming a $100(1-\alpha)\%$ confidence interval is known as the bootstrap-t procedure, which is analogous to the traditional approach to interval estimation. The bootstrap-T approach considers the empirical distribution of the studentized statistic

$$Z^*_{ni} = \frac{T^*_{ni} - \hat{T}_n}{[\hat{\text{var}}(T_n)]^{1/2}} \tag{A.3.4}$$

with distribution $H_n(F_n)$. To form $\hat{H}_n(F_n)$, the values $Z^*_{nl}, \ldots, Z^*_{nm}$ are ordered, and the quantiles $\hat{H}_n^{-1}(\alpha/2)$ and $\hat{H}_n^{-1}(1-\alpha/2)$ are the $[\alpha m/2]$ and $[(1-\alpha/2)m]$ elements of the list. The bootstrap-t confidence interval is then

$$\left[\hat{T}_n - \hat{H}_n^{-1}(1-\alpha/2)\hat{\sigma}_n, \hat{T}_n - \hat{H}_n^{-1}(\alpha/2)\hat{\sigma}_n\right], \tag{A.3.5}$$

where $\hat{\sigma}_n$ is an estimate of the standard error of T_n based on the observed sample.

Following the large-sample properties of the bootstrap distributions, the coverage probabilities of the bootstrap confidence intervals converge to $(1-\alpha)$ in large samples. Moreover, asymptotically correct critical values may be derived from the bootstrap distributions in similar fashion. However, the confidence intervals and the associated rejection regions may be biased in small samples, and several bias-correction procedures have been proposed to overcome this problem. For further details on the bias correction and other adjustment procedures, as well as comparisons of the alternative methods, readers should refer to Efron and Tibshirani (1993) or Shao and Tu (1995).

In applications of the bootstrap to hypothesis testing, we can show that the bootstrap may actually be more accurate than the first-order asymptotic approximations used throughout this book. Although the technical details are beyond the scope of our discussion, we follow the very clear discussion provided by Horowitz (1997) for the simple case of a two-sided symmetric test. The problem is to choose a critical value $z_{n\alpha}$ such that $G_n(z_{n\alpha}, F) - G_n(-z_{n\alpha}, F) = 1-\alpha$. Using the first-order asymptotic approximation to G_n(F) the critical value $z_{\infty\alpha}$ is selected to satisfy $G_\infty(z_{\infty\alpha}, F) - G_\infty(-z_{\infty\alpha}, F) = 1-\alpha$. For example, we would use this approach to compute the critical value from the N(0,1) distribution for an asymptotic two-sided Z-test. Under suitable regularity conditions, we can show that the critical value of the asymptotic test has the property $\Pr[|T_n| > z_{\infty\alpha}] = \alpha + o_p(n^{-1/2})$. In general, the bootstrap critical value z^*_α selected to satisfy $G_n(z^*_\alpha, F_n) - G_n(-z^*_\alpha, F_n) = 1-\alpha$ has an error of the same stochastic order.

However, if the test statistic T_n is asymptotically pivotal and G_∞ does not depend on F in large samples (e.g., the usual asymptotics based on standard normal, Chi-square), the bootstrap critical value has an error of the order $\Pr[|T_n| > z^*_\alpha] = \alpha + o_p(n^{-1})$. Thus, the error converges to zero more rapidly than the asymptotic test. This does not mean that the bootstrap test always dominates the asymptotic test or that it always performs well in finite samples, but it does imply that the bootstrap test is generally more accurate than the asymptotic test. Although many of the test statistics considered in this book are asymptotic pivots, there are well-known cases in which the limiting distribution depends on F.

For such cases, Beran (1987, 1988) proposes a procedure called prepivoting that generates an asymptotic U(0,1) statistic (and thus pivotal) by using the EDF (A.4.1) to form a probability integral transformation. Prepivoting is implemented with an extension of the bootstrap procedure known as the double or iterated bootstrap. For a summary of the relevant literature and a clear discussion of the method and applications, readers should refer to the article by McCullough and Vinod (1998). Finally, we note that the bootstrap may perform very poorly, and Horowitz (1997, p. 200) notes a few well-known cases of "bootstrap failure." For additional details on the asymptotic properties of the bootstrap, we encourage the interested reader to consult Beran and Ducharme (1991), Hall (1992), or Shao and Tu (1995).

A.3.2. Bootstrap Simulation Procedures for Regression Models

In the preceding subsection, we noted that the simplest way to implement the Monte Carlo approximation to the bootstrap distribution is known as the nonparametric bootstrap. That is, the replicated samples are drawn with replacement from the set of observed data. Since Efron published his seminal article in 1979, researchers have devised many ways to generate bootstrap samples that are designed to accommodate special features of the probability model (i.e., dependence). In this section, we consider extensions of the simple nonparametric bootstrap that may be used to resample data for a linear regression model, and bootstrap procedures for nonlinear, qualitative choice, and simultaneous equations models may be constructed in similar fashion.

For the semiparametric linear regression model with fixed **x**, the bootstrap DSP is often constructed from the estimated residuals and model parameters. The bootstrap distribution of some statistic T_n is derived by conceptually evaluating all possible samples that may be generated with replacement from the residual vector, which represents the population for the bootstrap noise-sampling process. The systematic component of the model is simply the vector of predicted values, and the bootstrap-dependent variables are the sum of these two components. For an application of residual resampling to a model estimated by LS, suppose we wish to simulate the bootstrap distribution of the LS estimator. The steps of the Monte Carlo approximation procedure are as follows:

1. Compute the LS estimate of $\boldsymbol{\beta}$, $\hat{\mathbf{b}}$, and the LS noise component estimate ê.
2. Draw n pseudorandom errors, $\hat{\mathbf{e}}_i^*$ from $\hat{\mathbf{e}}$ with replacement and form the n bootstrap sample observations $\mathbf{y}_i^* = \mathbf{x}[i, .]\,\hat{\mathbf{b}} + \hat{\mathbf{e}}_i^*$, $i = 1, \ldots, n$.
3. Compute and save the LS estimate, $\hat{\mathbf{b}}^*$, obtained from the replicated sample $(\mathbf{y}^*, \mathbf{x})$.
4. Repeat Steps 2 and 3 m times, yielding $\hat{\mathbf{b}}^*_{(1)}, \hat{\mathbf{b}}^*_{(2)}, \ldots, \hat{\mathbf{b}}^*_{(m)}$.

We can use the set of replicated LS estimates to approximate the sampling distribution of $\hat{\boldsymbol{\beta}}$. For example, the Monte Carlo approximation to the bootstrap expected value of $\hat{\boldsymbol{\beta}}$ is $\hat{\mathrm{E}}[\hat{\boldsymbol{\beta}}] = m^{-1} \sum_{i=1}^{m} \hat{\mathbf{b}}^*_{(i)}$. Therefore, the residual resampling scheme is relatively quick and easy to implement. Clearly, the stated problem is only illustrative and not a case in which the bootstrap application is particularly interesting because we can analytically determine the expected value of the LS estimator for a broad class of error distributions.

Before proceeding, we should note that residual resampling procedure may present interesting examples of bootstrap failure, or cases in which the bootstrap does not perform as intended. First, note that the LS residuals have the same expected value as the unobserved errors $\mathrm{E}[\hat{e}_i] = \mathrm{E}[\hat{e}_i^*] = \mathrm{E}[\varepsilon_i] = 0$, but the covariance matrices are different because

$$\mathbf{cov}[\hat{\mathbf{e}}] = \sigma^2[\mathbf{I}_n - \mathbf{x}(\mathbf{x}'\mathbf{x})^{-1}\mathbf{x}'] \neq \sigma^2 \mathrm{I}_n = \mathbf{cov}[\varepsilon]. \tag{A.3.6}$$

Thus, the LS residuals are dependent and heteroscedastic. The dependence issue may be overcome by iid sampling in the Monte Carlo simulation procedure. The variance issue may be addressed in a variety of ways. First, we may simply choose to ignore the heteroscedasticity by noting that $\hat{\varepsilon}[\mathrm{i}] \xrightarrow{p} \varepsilon[\mathrm{i}]$ as $n \to \infty$, and thus the problem is insignificant in large samples. Alternatively, many authors recommend scaling the LS residuals to homoscedasticity before generating the bootstrap samples (see Shao and Tu, 1995, p. 290). A potentially greater problem may arise if the sample average of the residuals is nonzero (i.e., LS estimation without an intercept term). In this case, the residuals must be recentered (i.e., subtract the sample mean) before resampling so the noise process for the bootstrap DSP satisfies $\mathrm{E}[\hat{\mathrm{e}}_i^*] = \mathrm{E}[\varepsilon_i] = 0$.

► **Example A.3.1:** To demonstrate the basic steps involved in a bootstrap simulation exercise for a linear regression model, we provide the GAUSS exercise named AppSLR.gss in the examples manual. In the context of a simple linear regression (SLR or slope–intercept) model, we resample the residuals, form replicated versions of $\mathbf{Y}$, and compare the bootstrap simulated statistical properties of the least-squares estimator to the theoretical large-sample properties. GAUSS then forms an estimated model in which the residuals are uncentered and the program demonstrates the unintended properties of the bootstrap estimator.

The residual resampling procedure typically works very well in cases for which the regressors $\mathbf{x}$ are fixed in repeated samples. However, if the regressors are stochastic, the residual resampling algorithm ignores the sampling variation in $\mathbf{X}$. To accommodate linear regression models with potentially stochastic regressors, we can use a procedure known as paired sampling. The steps of the Monte Carlo approximation procedure under paired sampling are as follows:

1. Compute the LS estimate of $\boldsymbol{\beta}$, $\hat{\mathbf{b}}$, and the LS noise component estimate $\hat{\mathbf{e}}$.
2. Draw n pseudorandom pairs, $(\mathrm{y}_i^*, \boldsymbol{x}^*[i, .])$, $i = 1, \ldots, n$, with replacement from the rows of $(\mathbf{y}, \mathbf{x})$.
3. Compute and save the LS estimate, $\hat{\mathbf{b}}^*$, obtained from the replicated sample $(\mathbf{y}^*, \mathbf{x}^*)$.
4. Repeat Steps 2 and 3 m times, yielding $\hat{\mathbf{b}}^*_{(1)}, \hat{\mathbf{b}}^*_{(2)}, \ldots, \hat{\mathbf{b}}^*_{(m)}$.

Thus, the paired sampling procedure is similar to the simple nonparametric bootstrap discussed earlier, and it reflects the joint stochastic character of $(\mathbf{Y}, \mathbf{X})$. In addition, the paired bootstrap is less sensitive to model specification errors than is the residual sampling algorithm. However, one potential drawback of this approach is that the bootstrap design matrix $\mathbf{x}^*$ may not have full-column rank even if $\mathbf{x}$ has full rank.

The bootstrap may also be applied to linear regression models under a fully parametric specification. Following our discussion in Chapter 3, suppose we assume $\boldsymbol{\varepsilon} \sim \mathrm{N}(\mathbf{0}, \sigma^2\mathbf{I}_n)$ so that the LS–ML estimator of the vector $\boldsymbol{\beta}$ is $\hat{\boldsymbol{\beta}} = (\mathbf{x}'\mathbf{x})^{-1}\mathbf{x}'\mathbf{Y} \sim \mathrm{N}(\boldsymbol{\beta}, \sigma^2(\mathbf{x}'\mathbf{x})^{-1})$. Although we can derive a large number of finite sample properties under the normality assumption, we may have reason to simulate the properties of some statistics for which such derivations are quite complicated. For example, suppose $T_n = \phi(\hat{\boldsymbol{\beta}})$ where ϕ is some nonlinear function of the LS–ML estimator. To estimate $\mathrm{E}[\phi(\hat{\boldsymbol{\beta}})]$, we may use a simulation procedure known as the *parametric* bootstrap:

1. Compute the LS–ML estimates $\hat{\mathbf{b}}$ and s^2.
2. Draw n pseudorandom outcomes, y_i^*, $i = 1, \ldots, n$, from the $N(\mathbf{x}\hat{\mathbf{b}}, s^2\mathbf{I}_n)$ distribution.
3. Compute and save the ML estimate, $\hat{\mathbf{b}}^*$, from the replicated sample $(\mathbf{y}^*, \mathbf{x})$.
4. Repeat Steps 2 and 3 m times, yielding $\hat{\mathbf{b}}^*_{(1)}, \hat{\mathbf{b}}^*_{(2)}, \ldots, \hat{\mathbf{b}}^*_{(m)}$.

We can then use the bootstrapped values collected in Step 4 to simulate outcomes of $T_n = \phi(\hat{\boldsymbol{\beta}})$ as $T^*_{ni} = \phi(\hat{\mathbf{b}}^*_{(i)})$, $i = 1, \ldots, m$ and estimate the expected value of T_n as $\hat{E}[T_n] = m^{-1}\sum_{i=1}^{m}\phi(\hat{\mathbf{b}}^*_{(i)})$. In general, the large sample properties of the parametric bootstrap follow those of the nonparametric case under the same regularity conditions stated earlier. In particular, note that $F_n \xrightarrow{p} F$ as $n \to \infty$ because the ML estimators are consistent, and thus we only require the continuity of G_∞ to hold. Clearly, the parametric bootstrap is very closely related to traditional Monte Carlo simulation procedures.

Finally, we note that the external or wild bootstrap (Wu, 1986) may be used to maintain temporal properties of the residuals such as heteroscedasticity that would be disrupted by resampling. In this case, the scaled (for homoscedasticity) or unscaled residuals are multiplied by outcomes $\tilde{e}_i$ drawn from a distribution with mean zero and unit variance. The resulting bootstrap noise components $e_i^* = \hat{e}_i \cdot \tilde{e}_i$ are used to form the replicated observations as in the residual resampling procedure. For further details on bootstrap theory and methods for other models, readers may wish to consult introductory references such as Efron (1982), Efron and Tibshirani (1993), or Horowitz (1997). Readers interested in a more advanced treatment of the bootstrap should refer to Beran and Ducharme (1991), Hall (1992, 1994), and Shao and Tu (1995).

A.4. Numerical Tools for Evaluating Posterior Distributions

Given recent advances in computing power, Bayesian researchers have been able to move beyond the conjugate families and use numerical methods to approximate the properties of unfriendly posterior distributions. For example, suppose we wish to compute the mean of the posterior distribution $p(\boldsymbol{\theta} \mid \mathbf{y})$. Following our discussion in Section A.2, we can estimate the mean by generating m pseudorandom draws from $p(\boldsymbol{\theta} \mid \mathbf{y})$ and computing the sample average $\bar{\boldsymbol{\theta}}_m$. Under appropriate assumptions on the Monte Carlo sampling process, we can prove that $\bar{\boldsymbol{\theta}}_m$ is a consistent estimator of the true posterior mean as $m \to \infty$. If we cannot generate samples directly from $p(\boldsymbol{\theta} \mid \mathbf{y})$ we may be able to use importance sampling or acceptance–rejection methods to estimate means and other functionals of $p(\boldsymbol{\theta} \mid \mathbf{y})$. Regardless, the Monte Carlo methods discussed in Section A.2 may be applied to Bayesian posterior analysis. The key distinction is that the pseudorandom outcomes are parameter values rather than sample data elements.

Unfortunately, many of the same problems that hamper numerical quadrature can also cause problems in Bayesian applications of Monte Carlo integration. Potential problems may arise if the elements of the posterior distribution are highly correlated or if there are many parameters. An alternative approach to the numerical integration problem is known as the class of Markov Chain Monte Carlo (MCMC) methods. The origins of the MCMC literature are often traced back to the seminal work of Metropolis, et al. (1953), and the methods have only recently appeared in statistical applications.

As in Monte Carlo integration methods, the MCMC algorithms generate a large number of pseudorandom numbers to represent the posterior distribution numerically. However, each MCMC replication is conditional on the last draw, and thus the draws are serially correlated. The stochastic properties of the conditional relationship are described by a stationary Markov chain, which explains the name given to this class of numerical algorithms. For our purposes, we review two basic MCMC formulations known as the Gibbs sampling algorithm and the Metropolis–Hastings algorithm.

A.4.1. The Gibbs Sampling Algorithm

The Gibbs sampler is one of the most widely used MCMC algorithms and was introduced to the statistics literature by Geman and Geman (1984). The first use of the Gibbs sampler to solve Bayesian integration problems was reported by Gelfand and Smith (1990). Although the advanced literature on the Gibbs sampler draws heavily on stochastic process theory, Casella and George (1992) provide a clearly written introduction to the algorithm. To review thc basic components of the algorithm, consider a posterior distribution $\mathrm{p}(\boldsymbol{\theta} \mid \mathbf{y})$ for a k-vector of unknown model parameters. We first represent a set of univariate conditional distributions, one for each element of $\boldsymbol{\theta}$, as

$$\begin{gathered} \mathrm{p}(\theta_1 \mid \theta_2, \theta_3, \ldots, \theta_k, \mathbf{y}) \\ \mathrm{p}(\theta_2 \mid \theta_1, \theta_3, \ldots, \theta_k, \mathbf{y}) \\ \vdots \\ \mathrm{p}(\theta_k \mid \theta_1, \theta_2, \ldots, \theta_{k-1}, \mathbf{y}). \end{gathered} \tag{A.4.1}$$

Under the Gibbs sampling algorithm, the conditional distributions are used to generate sequences of univariate pseudorandom parameter values, one for each element in $\boldsymbol{\theta}$. By operating with univariate distributions at each step, we may be able to eliminate the practical difficulties associated with high-dimensional Monte Carlo integration.

Given the set of conditional posterior distributions (A.4.1), the Gibbs sampling algorithm is initiated by specifying a set of starting values for the parameters $\boldsymbol{\theta}^0$. Then, the next set of parameter values is sequentially generated by drawing the elements of $\boldsymbol{\theta}$ from the conditional distributions

$$\begin{gathered} \mathrm{p}\left(\theta_1^1 \mid \theta_2^0, \theta_3^0, \ldots, \theta_k^0, \mathbf{y}\right) \\ \mathrm{p}\left(\theta_2^1 \mid \theta_1^1, \theta_3^0, \ldots, \theta_k^0, \mathbf{y}\right) \\ \vdots \\ \mathrm{p}\left(\theta_k^1 \mid \theta_1^1, \theta_2^1, \ldots, \theta_{k-1}^1, \mathbf{y}\right) \end{gathered} \tag{A.4.2}$$

The stochastic relationship between subsequent draws is described by the first-order Markov transition probabilities

$$\pi(\boldsymbol{\theta}^m, \boldsymbol{\theta}^{m+1}) = \prod_{j=1}^{k} \mathrm{p}\left(\theta_j^{m+1} \mid \theta_h^m \text{ for } h > j, \theta_h^{m+1} \text{ for } h < j, \mathbf{y}\right), \tag{A.4.3}$$

which is the product of the conditional probabilities in (A.4.2). As $m \to \infty$, the vector of outcomes $\boldsymbol{\theta}^m$ converges in distribution to $p(\boldsymbol{\theta} \mid \mathbf{y})$.

Before considering an example, we should comment on some of the practical problems with the Gibbs sampling algorithm. First, we must choose m large enough such that the algorithm converges to a stationary Markov chain. In general, an appropriate value depends on the particular integration problem and the available computing tools, and there are no widely accepted guidelines. Second, early outcomes from the Gibbs sampler are dependent on the starting values $\boldsymbol{\theta}^0$ and are not representative of $p(\boldsymbol{\theta} \mid \mathbf{y})$. To allow the Gibbs sampling algorithm to converge to a stationary Markov chain, the first m^* values of $\boldsymbol{\theta}$ should be discarded. In the MCMC literature, the early iterations are known as the burn-in period. Several authors have studied guidelines for selecting the burn-in length m^*, and numerous diagnostic criteria have been recommended. As a rough rule of thumb, some authors recommend deleting as few as $m^* = 50$ or as many as $m^* = 1000$ parameter vectors generated by the Gibbs sampler. Another simple criterion is to examine the autocorrelation statistics for the outcomes and to set m^* equal to the number of significant lags in the observations.

The dependence in the MCMC algorithm also influences our treatment of estimates based on output from the Gibbs sampler. Given a set of vectors $\boldsymbol{\theta}^m$ generated by the Gibbs sampling algorithm, we use the outcomes to compute functionals of the posterior distribution as in Monte Carlo integration. The Markov character of the Gibbs sampler implies that the draws are not independent, but we may rely on the ergodic (asymptotic independence) properties of the Markov chain to show that sample averages based on these draws are consistent estimators for the underlying expections. More importantly, the Markov dependence character will also bias estimates of the standard errors due to the approximation (i.e., the estimated variation in the sample average due to Monte Carlo sampling error). Other practical issues related to starting values, convergence criteria, and diagnostic tools are discussed by Kass et al. (1998) and by Cowles and Carlin (1996).

In most elementary Bayesian problems, we state our predata beliefs about a parameter $\boldsymbol{\theta}$ through a prior distribution $p(\boldsymbol{\theta} \mid \boldsymbol{\delta})$, which may depend on a set of subjectively selected hyperparameters $\boldsymbol{\delta}$. The Bayesian model may also be extended to account for subjective uncertainty about the hyperparameters, and we can effectively specify a "prior for the prior" in the Bayesian approach. Thus, we can specify probability models with a complex hierarchy of parameter vectors and associated predata beliefs. Although hierarchical models provide a great deal of freedom for model specification, the layers of parameters may increase the potential for computational problems. Accordingly, the Gibbs sampler and other MCMC algorithms are often used to solve inference problems in Bayesian hierarchical models.

More formally, let $p(\boldsymbol{\delta})$ represent the prior distribution for the hyperparameters $\boldsymbol{\delta}$ in the prior distribution $p(\boldsymbol{\theta} \mid \boldsymbol{\delta})$. Then, the joint posterior distribution for the full set of model parameters is

$$p(\boldsymbol{\theta}, \boldsymbol{\delta} \mid \mathbf{y}) \propto L(\mathbf{y} \mid \boldsymbol{\theta}) p(\boldsymbol{\theta} \mid \boldsymbol{\delta}) p(\boldsymbol{\delta}). \qquad \text{(A.4.4)}$$

To derive the marginal posterior distribution of interest $p(\boldsymbol{\theta} \mid \mathbf{y})$, we can simply integrate $\boldsymbol{\delta}$ out of the joint posterior (A.4.4). In hierarchical models, the derivation of marginal posterior distributions from the joint posterior distribution may require the solution to a multiple integration problem in several dimensions. In such cases, the Gibbs sampler is often used to reduce the computational burden.

► **Example A.4.1:** Suppose we have a sample of n iid Poisson(λ) observations, ($y_1, \ldots, y_n$). Let $p(\lambda \mid \alpha, \beta)$ be a Gamma(α, β) prior distribution used to describe our predata beliefs about λ. If we are willing to specify a value for α but are still uncertain about β, we may use a Gamma(γ, δ) prior distribution to describe our prior beliefs about β. For this hierarchical model, the joint posterior distribution takes the form

$$p(\lambda, \beta \mid \alpha, \gamma, \delta, \mathbf{y}) \propto \lambda^{\alpha+n\bar{y}-1}\exp(-n\lambda)\beta^{\alpha+\gamma-1}\exp(-\beta\delta)\exp(-\beta\lambda). \tag{A.4.5}$$

Although the first four terms on the right-hand side are kernels for separate gamma distributions for λ and β, the joint posterior distribution (A.4.5) is complicated by the final term, $\exp(-\beta\lambda)$. However, we can form the pair of univariate conditional distributions

$$\begin{aligned} p(\lambda \mid \beta, \alpha, \mathbf{y}) &= \text{Gamma}(\alpha + n\bar{y}_n, \beta + n) \\ p(\beta \mid \lambda, \alpha, \gamma, \delta, \mathbf{y}) &= \text{Gamma}(\alpha + \gamma, \lambda + \delta) \end{aligned} \tag{A.4.6}$$

To simulate the posterior distribution by the Gibbs sampling algorithm, we select starting values λ^0 and β^0 and iterate through the Markov chain (A.4.6).

The GAUSS program AppGibbs.gss (provided in the examples manual) demonstrates an application of the Gibbs sampling algorithm for this problem. First, GAUSS generates a sample of Poisson(λ) observations (n and λ selected by the user). Then, the user is asked to select the known hyperparameters (α, γ, δ), and GAUSS uses the rndgam() procedure to generate simulated outcomes from the joint posterior distribution according the Gibbs sampling algorithm (A.4.6). Finally, GAUSS computes and plots kernel density estimates of the marginal posterior distributions for λ and β as well as a 90% credible region for λ.

A.4.2. The Metropolis–Hastings Algorithm

If the full set of conditional posterior distributions (A.4.6) are not available, the Gibbs sampling algorithm is not feasible. In such cases, we may be able to employ another MCMC technique known as the Metropolis–Hastings algorithm. The idea was first introduced by Metropolis and Ulam (1949), and the generalized version commonly employed in modern applications originated with Hastings (1970). For our purposes, we will only sketch the key elements of the algorithm, and interested readers should refer to the valuable tutorial provided by Chib and Greenberg (1996) and the advanced treatment provided in the article by Tierney (1991) as well as the associated discussion and cited references.

As in the Gibbs sampling algorithm, the basic idea underlying the Metropolis–Hastings algorithm is to construct a stationary Markov chain that converges to $p(\boldsymbol{\theta} \mid \mathbf{y})$. The key component of the algorithm is the candidate-generating distribution $\pi(\boldsymbol{\theta}^{m+1} \mid \boldsymbol{\theta}^m)$ from which we generate an outcome of $\boldsymbol{\theta}^{m+1}$ conditional on $\boldsymbol{\theta}^m$. For practical purposes, we should select a candidate-generating distribution from which we can conveniently generate multivariate pseudorandom numbers, and Chib and Greenberg (1996) describe five alternatives.

To ensure that the algorithm converges to $p(\boldsymbol{\theta} \mid \mathbf{y})$, the Markov chain must satisfy the reversibility condition

$$p(\boldsymbol{\theta}^m \mid \mathbf{y})\pi(\boldsymbol{\theta}^{m+1} \mid \boldsymbol{\theta}^m) = p(\boldsymbol{\theta}^{m+1} \mid \mathbf{y})\pi(\boldsymbol{\theta}^m \mid \boldsymbol{\theta}^{m+1}), \tag{A.4.7}$$

where the left-hand side is the unconditional probability of generating $\boldsymbol{\theta}^{m+1}$ given $\boldsymbol{\theta}^m$, and the right-hand side is the unconditional probability of generating $\boldsymbol{\theta}^m$ given $\boldsymbol{\theta}^{m+1}$. The reversibility condition can be imposed on (A.4.7) by introducing a balancing weight

$$\mathrm{p}(\boldsymbol{\theta}^m \mid \mathbf{y})\pi(\boldsymbol{\theta}^{m+1} \mid \boldsymbol{\theta}^m)\alpha(\boldsymbol{\theta}^m, \boldsymbol{\theta}^{m+1}) = \mathrm{p}(\boldsymbol{\theta}^{m+1} \mid \mathbf{y})\pi(\boldsymbol{\theta}^m \mid \boldsymbol{\theta}^{m+1}), \tag{A.4.8}$$

where $\alpha(\boldsymbol{\theta}^m, \boldsymbol{\theta}^{m+1})$ is known as the probability of move and is defined as

$$\alpha(\boldsymbol{\theta}^m, \boldsymbol{\theta}^{m+1}) = \min\left[\frac{\mathrm{p}(\boldsymbol{\theta}^{m+1} \mid \mathbf{y})\pi(\boldsymbol{\theta}^m \mid \boldsymbol{\theta}^{m+1})}{\mathrm{p}(\boldsymbol{\theta}^m \mid \mathbf{y})\pi(\boldsymbol{\theta}^{m+1} \mid \boldsymbol{\theta}^m)}, 1\right] \quad \text{if} \quad \mathrm{p}(\boldsymbol{\theta}^m \mid \mathbf{y})\pi(\boldsymbol{\theta}^{m+1} \mid \boldsymbol{\theta}^m) > 0 \tag{A.4.9}$$

and $\alpha(\boldsymbol{\theta}^m, \boldsymbol{\theta}^{m+1}) = 1$ otherwise. If the left-hand side of (A.4.8) is greater than the right-hand side, then $\alpha(\boldsymbol{\theta}^m, \boldsymbol{\theta}^{m+1}) < 1$ balances the unconditional probabilities and the reversibility condition is met. By construction, $\alpha(\boldsymbol{\theta}^m, \boldsymbol{\theta}^{m+1})$ only requires $\pi(\boldsymbol{\theta}^{m+1} \mid \boldsymbol{\theta}^m)$ and the kernel of $\mathrm{p}(\boldsymbol{\theta} \mid \mathbf{y})$, and therefore the Metropolis–Hastings algorithm may be used if the conditional distributions in the Gibbs sampling algorithm (A.4.1) are unavailable.

Chib and Greenberg (1996) outline the following steps for implementing the Metropolis–Hastings procedure:

1. Given the starting value $\boldsymbol{\theta}^0$, draw pseudorandom candidate $\mathbf{z}$ from $\pi(\boldsymbol{\theta}^1 \mid \boldsymbol{\theta}^0)$ and u from U(0,1).

2a. If $u \le \alpha(\boldsymbol{\theta}^0, \boldsymbol{\theta}^1)$, set $\boldsymbol{\theta}^1 = \mathbf{z}$.

2b. Otherwise, set $\boldsymbol{\theta}^1 = \boldsymbol{\theta}^0$.

3. Return to Step 1 and use $\boldsymbol{\theta}^1$ to generate $\boldsymbol{\theta}^2$.

As in the Gibbs sampling algorithm, the process is repeated m times, and the initial outcomes (from the burn-in period) are discarded. The decision to use the current outcome from the Markov chain is designed to simulate the probability of move. This feature of the Metropolis–Hastings algorithm is adapted from the class of acceptance–rejection methods introduced in Section A.1.

Additional background information about Bayesian simulation methods is provided in the article by Evans and Swartz (1995) and the chapter by Geweke (1997). For more detailed information, readers should consult the references cited by these authors.

A.5. Concluding Remarks

Our goal in this chapter has been to provide a brief introduction to computer simulation and resampling methods. A comprehensive review of the core literature on computational economics and statistics would fill at least one volume by itself, and thus we have only focused on fundamental concepts and methods. A large number of articles and books have already been written on the subject, and we have tried to point the reader to the most useful and important references wherever possible. We also hope that our use of these procedures throughout the book will assist the reader in learning how to use and benefit from numerical tools in his or her work. The low cost, speed, and relative ease of using modern computing tools have opened many doors in econometric research. However, we also note that the analytical work must precede the computational effort to avoid the many pitfalls in computer-based research. To paraphrase an old saying, "one good analytical result is generally worth *more* than 1000 simulations."

A.6. Exercises

A.6.1. Idea Checklist

---

1. Why are computer generated random numbers known as pseudorandom numbers?
2. Why are computer simulation methods becoming more widely used in economic research?
3. In Example A.2.1, why may the simulated properties of the expected value differ from the actual properties even if m is very large?
4. In what way does the bootstrap sampling process mimic the actual DSP?

A.6.2. Problems

1–1 Suppose you generate n iid. outcomes $y_1, \ldots, y_n$ from the U(0,1) distribution. Prove that $x = (\sum_{i=1}^{n} y_i - n/2)/\sqrt{n/12}$ may be used as a pseudorandom N(0,1) outcome for large n.

1–2 Under the normal linear regression model with nonstochastic $\mathbf{x}$, prove that the actual bootstrap estimator (not the Monte Carlo approximation) of $\mathrm{E}[\hat{\boldsymbol{\beta}}]$ is unbiased.

1–3 Derive the kernel of the posterior distribution stated in (A.4.5) and verify the conditional posterior distributions stated in (A.4.6).

A.6.3. Computer Problems

1–1 Write a GAUSS procedure that generates pseudorandom U(0,1) outcomes by the linear congruential rule. Then, generate samples of size n using your procedure and the rndu() procedure provided by GAUSS. Use the GAUSS program AppLog.gss provided for Example A.1.1 to compare the sample moments and the empirical distribution function to the moments and CDF of the U(0,1) distribution. Hint: To form the remainder, use the GAUSS procedure fmod().

1–2 Write GAUSS procedures that generate vectors of n iid N(0,1) pseudorandom variables by the Box–Muller and modified polar methods. As in Problem 1, compare the performance of your procedures against the rndn() procedure provided by GAUSS. How well does the Box–Muller procedure compare with the modified polar algorithm? How well do your procedures perform when compared with the GAUSS rndn() procedure?

1–3 Design a linear regression model and write a GAUSS program that compares the properties of the residual resampling, paired resampling, and external bootstrap procedures. In particular, how well do the bootstrap estimators of $\mathrm{E}[\hat{\boldsymbol{\beta}}]$ and $\mathbf{cov}[\hat{\boldsymbol{\beta}}]$ perform if you allow $\mathbf{X}$ to be stochastic? If the model is misspecified? If the errors are heteroscedastic?

1–4 Under the normal linear regression model, derive the expected value $\mathrm{E}[\hat{\boldsymbol{\beta}}'\hat{\boldsymbol{\beta}}]$. Write a GAUSS program that generates a pseudorandom sample of size n from this model. Using the LS–ML estimates of the model parameters, compute the parametric bootstrap estimate of $\mathrm{E}[\hat{\boldsymbol{\beta}}'\hat{\boldsymbol{\beta}}]$ by Monte Carlo approximation.

A.7. References

Beran, R. (1987), "Prepivoting to Reduce Level Error in Confidence Sets," *Biometrika*, Vol. 74, pp. 457–68.

Beran, R. (1988), "Prepivoting Test Statistics: A Bootstrap View of Asymptotic Refinements," *Journal of the American Statistical Association*, Vol. 83, pp. 687–97.

Beran, R., and G. R. Ducharme (1991), *Asymptotic Theory for Bootstrap Methods in Statistics*, Montreal: Centre de Recherches Mathematiques.

Box, G. E. P., and M. E. Muller (1958), "A Note on the Generation of Random Normal Deviates," *Annals of Mathematical Statistics*, Vol. 29, pp. 610–11.

Casella, G., and E. I. George (1992), "Explaining the Gibbs Sampler," *American Statistician*, Vol. 3, pp. 167–74.

Chernick, M. R. (1999), *Bootstrap Methods*, New York: John Wiley and Sons.

Chib, S., and E. Greenberg (1996), "Markov Chain Monte Carlo Simulation Methods in Econometrics," *Econometric Theory*, Vol. 12, pp. 409–31.

Cowles, M. K., and B. P. Carlin (1996), "Markov Chain Monte Carlo Convergence Diagnostics: A Comparative Review," *Journal of the American Statistical Association*, Vol. 91, pp. 883–904.

Davis, P., and P. Rabinowitz (1975), *Methods of Numerical Integration*, New York: Academic Press.

Devroye, L. P. (1986), *Non-Uniform Random Variate Generation*, New York: Springer–Verlag.

Efron, B. (1979), "Bootstrap Methods: Another Look at the Jackknife," *Annals of Statistics*, Vol. 7, pp. 1–26.

Efron, B. (1982), *The Jackknife, the Bootstrap, and other Resampling Plans*, Vol. 38 of CBMS–NSF Regional Conference Series in Applied Mathematics, Philadelphia: SIAM.

Efron, B., and R. J. Tibshirani (1993), *An Introduction to the Bootstrap*, New York: Chapman and Hall.

Evans, M., and T. Swartz (1995), "Methods for Approximating Integrals in Statistics with Special Emphasis on Bayesian Integration Problems," *Statistical Science*, Vol. 10, pp. 254–72.

Gelfand, A. E., and A. F. M. Smith (1990), "Sampling Based Approaches to Calculating Marginal Densities," *Journal of the American Statistical Association*, Vol. 85, pp. 398–409.

Geman, S., and D. Geman (1984), "Stochastic Relaxation, Gibbs Distributions, and the Bayesian Restoration of Images," *IEEE Transactions on Pattern Analysis and Machine Intelligence*, Vol. 6, pp. 721–41.

Geweke, J. (1996), "Monte Carlo Simulation and Numerical Integration," Chapter 15 in H. Amman, D. Kendrick, and J. Rust (Eds.), *Handbook of Computational Economics, Volume 1*, Amsterdam: Elsevier.

Geweke, J. (1997), "Posterior Simulators in Econometrics," Chapter 5 in D. M. Kreps and K. F. Wallis (Eds.), *Advances in Economics and Econometrics: Theory and Applications, Volume 3*. Proceedings of the Seventh World Congress of the Econometric Society, New York: Cambridge University Press.

Hall, P. (1992), *The Bootstrap and Edgeworth Expansion*, New York: Springer–Verlag.

Hall, P. (1994), "Methodology and Theory for the Bootstrap," Chapter 39 in R. F. Engle and D. McFadden (Eds.), *Handbook of Econometrics, Volume 4*, Amsterdam: Elsevier.

Hammersley, J. M., and D. C. Handscomb (1964), *Monte Carlo Methods*, London: Methuen.

Hastings, W. K. (1970), "Monte Carlo Sampling Methods Using Markov Chains and Their Applications," *Biometrika*, Vol. 57, pp. 97–109.

Hendry, D. (1984), "Monte Carlo Experiments in Econometrics," Chapter 16 in *Handbook of Econometrics*, Vol. II, Z. Griliches and M. Intrilligator (Eds.), New York: North–Holland.

Horowitz, J. L. (1997), "Bootstrap Performance in Econometrics: Theory and Numerical Performance." Chapter 7 in D. M. Kreps and K. F. Wallis (Eds.), *Advances in Economics and Econometrics: Theory and Applications, Volume 3*. Proceedings of the Seventh World Congress of the Econometric Society, New York: Cambridge University Press.

Kass, R. E., B. P. Carlin, A. Gelman, and R. M. Neal (1998), "Markov Chain Monte Carlo in Practice: A Roundtable Discussion," *American Statistician*, Vol. 52, pp. 93–100.

Marsaglia, G., and T. A. Bray (1964), "A Convenient Method for Generating Normal Variables," *SIAM Review*, Vol. 6, pp. 260–4.

McCullough, B. D., and H. D. Vinod (1998), "Implementing the Double Bootstrap," *Computational Economics*, Vol. 12, pp. 79–95.

Metropolis, N., and S. Ulam (1949), "The Monte Carlo Method," *Journal of the American Statistical Association*, Vol. 44, pp. 335–41.

Metropolis, N., A. Rosenbluth, W. Rosenbluth, M. Teller, and E. Teller (1953), "Equations of State Calculations by Fast Computing Machines," *The Journal of Chemical Physics*, Vol. 21, pp. 1087–91.

Mittelhammer, R. C. (1996), *Mathematical Statistics for Economics and Business*, New York: Springer–Verlag.

Niederreiter, H. (1992), *Random Number Generation and Quasi-Monte Carlo Methods*. Vol. 63 of CBMS–NSF Regional Conference Series in Applied Mathematics, Philadelphia: SIAM.

Press, W. H., S. A. Teukolsky, W. T. Vetterling, and B. P. Flannery (1992), *Numerical Recipes in C: The Art of Scientific Computing*. New York: Cambridge University Press.

Shao, J., and D. Tu (1995), *The Jackknife and Bootstrap*, New York: Springer–Verlag.

Sobol, I. M. (1994), *A Primer for the Monte Carlo Method*. Boca Raton, FL: CRC Press.

Tierney, L. (1991), "Markov Chains for Exploring Posterior Distributions" (with discussion and rejoinder), *Annals of Statistics*, Vol. 22, pp. 1701–62.

Tintner, G. (1952), *Econometrics*, New York: John Wiley and Sons.

Wu, C.-F. J. (1986), "Jackknife, Bootstrap, and Other Resampling Methods in Regression Analysis," *Annals of Statistics*, Vol. 14, pp. 1261–350.

Author Index

Subject Index

costs of a diskette, tape, or other back-up media), but Publisher shall have sole discretion to elect which remedy to provide. There shall be no other remedies, whether in law or equity.

5. *GAUSS Light™ Software License.* Installation and use of this software is subject to and governed by the License Agreement displayed in the Media. By installing and using the GAUSS Light™ Software, Recipient indicates his or her acceptance of, and Recipient is subject to, all such terms and conditions of the License Agreement. Violation of the License Agreement is also a violation of the copyright laws.

GAUSS Light™ Software is furnished by:

Aptech Systems, Inc. ("Aptech")
28304 SE Kent-Kangley Road
Maple Valley, WA 98038
Phone: 425-432-7855
FAX: 425-432-7832
E-mail: info@aptech.com
www.aptech.com

GAUSS Light™ Software is published by:

Cambridge University Press ("Publisher")
The Edinburgh Building
Cambridge CB2 2RU, UK
40 West 20th Street
New York, NY 10011-4211, USA
10 Stamford Road, Oakleigh
Victoria 3166, Australia
www.cup.org

ELECTRONIC MEDIA TRANSMITTAL AND GAUSS Light^{TM} SOFTWARE:
Terms and Conditions of Use for the CD ROM Accompanying
Econometric Foundations

Notice: Do not unseal the envelope enclosing the CD ROM (Media) or use the Media or its Contents before reading these terms and conditions of use. Publisher authorizes use of the Media and Contents only under these terms and conditions of use. If Recipient does not wish to be bound by these terms and conditions of use, Recipient is prohibited from using the Media and Contents, and Recipient shall return the Media and Contents to Publisher. Recipient's unsealing of the envelope and/or use of the Media or Contents signifies Recipient's agreement to these terms and conditions of use.

1. *Acceptance of Terms.* Recipient's unsealing of the envelope enclosing the Media and Contents or use of the Media or Contents subjects Recipient to all terms and conditions of use described in this document and also all terms and conditions of the GAUSS Light^{TM} License displayed in the Media. Publisher and Aptech authorize use of the Media and Contents only as set forth herein and within the GAUSS Light^{TM} License.

2. *No Warranties.* Publisher and Aptech do not warrant the accuracy of the Contents as contained in the Media against data corruption, computer viruses, errors in file transfer data, unauthorized revisions to the files, or any other alterations or data destruction to the file(s). The Media and its Contents are transmitted as is. Publisher and Aptech shall not have any liability for Recipient's use of the Media or its Contents, including without limitation, any transmittal of bugs, viruses, or other destructive or harmful programs, scripts, aplets, or files to the computers or networks of the Recipient. Recipient acknowledges and agrees that Recipient is fully informed of the possibility of the Media or its Contents being harmful to Recipient's computers or networks and the possibility that the Contents may not be an exact and virus-free copy of masters by Publisher or Aptech. Recipient also acknowledges, agrees, and warrants that Recipient shall be solely responsible for inspection and testing of the Media and the Contents for bugs, viruses, or other destructive or harmful programs, scripts, aplets, or files, before accessing or using the Media or Contents.

3. *No Implied Warranties. There are no implied warranties, including warranties of merchantability or fitness for a particular purpose, with respect either to the Media or the Contents.*

4. *Limitations on Liability and Remedies.* Publisher and Aptech shall have no liability for any general damages, direct or indirect damages, special damages, exemplary damages, statutory damages, punitive damages, or consequential damages, including without limitation, lost profits, interruption of business, for any use of the Media or Contents. Recipient's sole and exclusive remedy for any claim based on Recipient's use of the Media or Contents shall be either (a) the delivery of another copy of the Contents on replacement Media, or (b) the costs of a physical replacement Media (for example, the

(*continued on reverse*)